PEARSON

ALWAYS LEARNING

BENTLEY UNIVERSITY

GB112 Tools and Concepts in Accounting and Finance

GB212 Practice and Applications in Accounting and Finance

Second Edition
Bentley University

Taken from:

Financial Accounting, Seventh Edition
by Walter T. Harrison Jr. and Charles T. Horngren

Managerial Accounting, First Edition
by Linda Smith Bamber, Karen Wilken Braun, and Walter T. Harrison Jr.

Fundamentals of Corporate Finance, First Edition
by Jonathan Berk, Peter DeMarzo, and Jarrad Harford

Business Essentials, Seventh Edition
by Ronald J. Ebert and Ricky W. Griffin

Cover Art: Courtesy of PhotoDisc/Getty Images.

Taken from:

Financial Accounting, Seventh Edition
by Walter T. Harrison, Jr. and Charles T. Horngren
Copyright © 2008, 2006, 2004, 2001, 1998 by Pearson Education, Inc.
Published by Prentice Hall
Upper Saddle River, New Jersey 07458

Managerial Accounting, First Edition
by Linda Smith Bamber, Karen Wilken Braun, and Walter T. Harrison, Jr.
Copyright © 2008, 2007 by Pearson Education, Inc.
Published by Prentice Hall

Fundamentals of Corporate Finance, First Edition
by Jonathan Berk, Peter DeMarzo, and Jarrad Harford
Copyright © 2009 by Pearson Education, Inc.
Published by Prentice Hall

Business Essentials, Seventh Edition
by Ronald J. Ebert and Ricky W. Griffin
Copyright © 2009, 2007, 2005, 2003, 2000 by Pearson Education, Inc.
Published by Prentice Hall

Copyright © 2011, 2009 by Pearson Learning Solutions
All rights reserved.

This copyright covers material written expressly for this volume by the editor/s as well as the compilation itself. It does not cover the individual selections herein that first appeared elsewhere. Permission to reprint these has been obtained by Pearson Learning Solutions for this edition only. Further reproduction by any means, electronic or mechanical, including photocopying and recording, or by any information storage or retrieval system, must be arranged with the individual copyright holders noted.

Grateful acknowledgment is made to the following sources for permission to reprint material copyrighted or controlled by them:

"Case 1.1 Waste Management: The Matching Principle," "Case 1.3 Qwest: The Full Disclosure Principle," "Case 1.4 Sunbeam: The Revenue Recognition Principle," "Case 1.5 Waste Management: The Definition of an Asset," "Case 1.7 WorldCom: The Matching Principle," "Case 1.9 Qwest: The Revenue Recognition Principle," "Case 1.10 The Baptist Foundation of Arizona: The Conservatism Constraint," "Case 2.1 Enron: Independence," "Case 4.1 Enron: The Control Environment," by Dr. Jay C. Thibodeau and Deborah Freier, reprinted from *Auditing After Sarbanes-Oxley: Illustrative Cases*, Second Edition (2009), McGraw-Hill Companies, by permission of the authors.

All trademarks, service marks, registered trademarks, and registered service marks are the property of their respective owners and are used herein for identification purposes only.

Pearson Learning Solutions, 501 Boylston Street, Suite 900, Boston, MA 02116
A Pearson Education Company
www.pearsoned.com

Printed in the United States of America

1 2 3 4 5 6 7 8 9 10 VOCR 16 15 14 13 12 11

000200010270781564

RG/LP

ISBN 10: 1-256-31729-2
ISBN 13: 978-1-256-31729-6

We gratefully acknowledge the generous financial support of the Ernst & Young Foundation for the development of the GB112/212 course sequence at Bentley University.

Unit Contents

BRIEF CONTENTS

Unit One

Taken from *Business Essentials*, Seventh Edition, by Ronald J. Ebert and Ricky W. Griffin

Unit Two

Taken from *Fundamentals of Corporate Finance*, First Edition, by Jonathan Berk, Peter DeMarzo, and Jarrad Harford

PART 3   Valuation and the Firm

PART 4   Risk and Return

PART 5   Long-Term Financing

PART 7   Financial Planning and Forecasting

Unit Three

Taken from *Financial Accounting*, Seventh Edition, by Walter T. Harrison, Jr. and Charles T. Horngren

Unit Four

Unit Five

DETAILED CONTENTS

Unit One

Unit Two

Taken from *Fundamentals of Corporate Finance*,
First Edition, by Jonathan Berk, Peter DeMarzo, and
Jarrad Harford

PART 2   Interest Rates and Valuing Cash Flows

Unit Three

Taken from *Financial Accounting,* Seventh Edition, by
Walter T. Harrison Jr. and Charles T. Horngren

Chapter 4

Internal Control & Cash   213

Chapter 5

Short-Term Investment & Receivables   269

Chapter 6

Inventory & Cost of Goods Sold   315

Chapter 12

The Statement of Cash Flows   619

Unit Four

Taken from *Managerial Accounting*, First Edition, by Linda Smith Bamber, Karen Wilken Braun, and Walter T. Harrison, Jr.

1 Introduction to Managerial Accounting   1

Managerial Accounting: Information for Managers   2
Managers' Four Primary Responsibilities   3
A Road Map: How Does Management Accounting Fit In?   4
Managerial Accounting Versus Financial Accounting   5

The Managerial Accountant Within the Organization   7
Organizational Structure   7
The Changing Roles of Management Accountants   8
The Skills Required of Management Accountants   9
Average Salaries of Management Accountants   10
Professional Association   11
Ethics   11
Examples of Ethical Dilemmas   12

Unit Five

Taken from *Auditing After Sarbanes-Oxley: Illustrative Cases,* Second Edition,
by Dr. Jay C. Thibodeau and Deborah Freier

Taken from *Business Essentials*,
Seventh Edition, by Ronald J. Ebert
and Ricky W. Griffin

chapter 1

part 1 The Contemporary Business World

The U.S. Business Environment

After reading this chapter, you should be able to:

1 Define the nature of U.S. business and identify its main goals and functions.

2 Describe the external environments of business and discuss how these environments affect the success or failure of any organization.

3 Describe the different types of global economic systems according to the means by which they control the factors of production.

4 Show how markets, demand, and supply affect resource distribution in the United States.

5 Identify the elements of private enterprise and explain the various degrees of competition in the U.S. economic system.

6 Explain the importance of the economic environment to business and identify the factors used to evaluate the performance of an economic system.

What Goes Up . . . Can Go Even Higher!

The sign in front of a Texas Mobil gasoline station summed it up nicely: The "prices" for the three grades of gasoline sold at the station were listed as "an arm," "a leg," and "your first born." While the sign no doubt led to a few smiles from motorists, its sentiments were far from a laughing matter. The stark reality was that in mid-2008, retail gasoline prices in the United States were at an all-time high, hovering around $4.00 per gallon. The upward price spiral that began in mid-2004 has left consumers, government officials, and business leaders struggling to find answers.

What made this gas crisis unusual was that it began with an unusual mix of supply, demand, and global forces. In the past, gas prices generally increased only when the supply was reduced. But the circumstances underlying the increases that started in 2004 and continued through 2008 were much more complex. First, global supplies of gasoline have been increasing at a rate that has more than offset the steady decline in U.S. domestic production of gasoline since 1972. As a result, the United States has been relying more on foreign producers and is, therefore, subject to whatever prices those producers want to charge. Second, demand for gasoline in the United States has continued to rise as a result of a growing population, the continued popularity of large gas-guzzling vehicles, and a strong demand for other petroleum-based products.

Another major piece of the puzzle has been a surging global economy that has caused a higher demand for oil and gasoline. More people are buying cars, and petroleum refiners work around the clock to help meet the unprecedented demand for gasoline. China, in particular, has become a major consumer of petroleum, passing Japan in 2005 to trail only the United States in total consumption.

The price increases led to a wide array of consequences. Automobile manufacturers stepped up their commitment to making more fuel-efficient cars. Refiners posted record profits (indeed, some critics charged that the energy companies were guilty of price gouging). And even local police officers were kept busy combating a surge in gasoline theft, yet another indication that gas was becoming an increasingly valuable commodity![1]

What's in It for Me?

The gas crisis is an example of how external environments, a global economy, and supply and demand affect business and distribution in the United States. In addition to these factors, this chapter will discuss the nature and purpose of a business and the elements of private enterprise and competition. It will also prepare you to analyze how different factors affect a business's success or failure and to evaluate the performance of an economic system in the context of business.

BUSINESS organization that provides goods or services to earn profits

PROFIT difference between a business's revenues and its expenses

EXTERNAL ENVIRONMENT everything outside an organization's boundaries that might affect it

DOMESTIC BUSINESS ENVIRONMENT the environment in which a firm conducts its operations and derives its revenues

GLOBAL BUSINESS ENVIRONMENT the international forces that affect a business

TECHNOLOGICAL ENVIRONMENT all the ways by which firms create value for their constituents

The Concept of Business and the Concept of Profit

What do you think of when you hear the word *business*? Does it conjure up images of successful corporations, such as General Electric? Or are you reminded of smaller firms, such as your local supermarket, or family-owned operations, such as your neighborhood pizzeria?

All these organizations are **businesses**—organizations that provide goods or services that are then sold to earn profits. Indeed, the prospect of earning **profits**— the difference between a business's revenues and its expenses—is what encourages people to open and expand businesses. After all, profits are the rewards owners get for risking their money and time. The right to pursue profits distinguishes a business from those organizations—such as most universities, hospitals, and government agencies—that run in much the same way but that generally don't seek profits.[2]

Consumer Choice and Demand In a capitalistic system, such as that in the United States, businesses exist to earn profits for owners; an owner is free to set up a new business, grow that business, sell it, or even shut it down. But consumers also have freedom of choice. In choosing how to pursue profits, businesses must take into account what consumers want and/or need. No matter how efficient, a business won't survive without a demand for its goods or services. Neither a snow-blower shop in Florida nor a beach-umbrella store in Alaska is likely to do well.

Opportunity and Enterprise If enterprising businesspeople can spot a promising opportunity and then develop a good plan for capitalizing on it, they can succeed. The opportunity always involves goods or services that consumers need and/or want—especially if no one else is supplying them or if existing businesses are doing so inefficiently or incompletely.

The Benefits of Business Businesses produce most of the goods and services we consume, and they employ most working people. They create most new innovations and provide a vast range of opportunities for new businesses, which serve as their suppliers. A healthy business climate also contributes to the quality of life and standard of living of people in a society. Business profits enhance the personal incomes of millions of owners and stockholders, and business taxes help to support governments at all levels. Many businesses support charities and provide community leadership. However, some businesses also harm the environment, and their decision makers sometimes resort to unacceptable practices for their own personal benefit.

The External Environments of Business

All businesses, regardless of their size, location, or mission, operate within a larger external environment. This **external environment** consists of everything outside an organization's boundaries that might affect it. (Businesses also have an *internal environment*, more commonly called *corporate culture*.) Managers must have a complete and accurate understanding of the external environment and strive to operate and compete within it or their organizations will not survive. Table 1.1 describes the external environment for the clothing retailer Urban Outfitters.

Domestic Business Environment

The **domestic business environment** refers to the environment in which a firm conducts its operations and derives its revenues. In general, businesses seek to be close to their customers, to establish strong relationships with their suppliers, and to distinguish themselves from their competitors.

Global Business Environment

The **global business environment** refers to the international forces that affect a business. Factors affecting the global environment at a general level include international trade agreements, international economic conditions, political unrest, and so forth. At a more immediate level, any given business is likely to be affected by international market opportunities, suppliers, cultures, competitors, and currency values.

Technological Environment

The **technological environment** generally includes all the ways by which firms create value for their constituents. Technology includes human knowledge, work methods, physical equipment, electronics and telecommunications, and various processing systems that are used to perform business activities.

Political-Legal Environment

The **political-legal environment**, which reflects the relationship between business and government, is important for several reasons. The legal system defines and regulates many aspects of what an organization can and can't do, including advertising practices, safety and health considerations, and acceptable standards of business conduct. Pro- or anti-business sentiment in government and political stability are also important considerations, especially for international firms.

Sociocultural Environment

The **sociocultural environment** includes the customs, mores, values, and demographic characteristics of the society in which an organization functions. Sociocultural processes also determine the goods and services, as well as the standards of business conduct, that a society is likely to value and accept.

Economic Environment

The **economic environment** refers to relevant conditions that exist in the economic system in which a company operates. For example, if an economy is doing well enough that most people have jobs, a growing company may find it necessary to pay higher wages and offer more benefits in order to attract workers from other companies. But if many people in an economy are looking for jobs, a firm may be able to pay less and offer fewer benefits.

Economic Systems

• • • • • • • • • • • • • •

The economic system of a firm's *home country*—the nation in which it does most of its business—is a key factor is determining how a firm operates. An **economic system** is a nation's system for allocating its resources among its citizens, both individuals and organizations.

Factors of Production

A basic difference between economic systems is the way in which a system manages its **factors of production**—the resources that a country's businesses use to produce goods and services. Economists focus on five factors of production. Note that the concept of factors of production can also be applied to the resources that an individual organization *manages* to produce goods and services.

Labor Sometimes called **human resources**, **labor** includes the physical and intellectual contributions people make to a business while engaged in economic

POLITICAL-LEGAL ENVIRONMENT the relationship between business and government

SOCIOCULTURAL ENVIRONMENT the customs, mores, values, and demographic characteristics of the society in which an organization functions

ECONOMIC ENVIRONMENT relevant conditions that exist in the economic system in which a company operates

ECONOMIC SYSTEM a nation's system for allocating its resources among its citizens

FACTORS OF PRODUCTION resources used in the production of goods and services—labor, capital, entrepreneurs, physical resources, and information resources

LABOR (HUMAN RESOURCES) physical and mental capabilities of people as they contribute to economic production

Table 1.1   **The External Environments of Business: Urban Outfitters**

Domestic Business Environment	Global Business Environment	Technological Environment	Political-Legal Environment	Sociocultural Environment	Economic Environment
• Initially located stores near urban college campuses; now has locations in more upscale neighborhoods as well • Strong network of suppliers • Wholesale supplier to other retailers through its Free People division • Competing with Gap and Abercrombie & Fitch for customers and market share	• Global presence with stores in Belgium, Canada, Denmark, Ireland, Sweden, and United Kingdom as well as an online presence in Japan • Many suppliers are foreign companies	• Sophisticated information system that tracks sales and inventory levels, allowing for quick response to customers • Successful e-commerce Web sites	• Subject to a variety of political and legal forces, including product identification and local zoning requirements • Actively protects assets by monitoring copyright infringement by competition	• Pulled items after unfavorable publicity in 2003 for Monopoly-like game called Ghettopoly that was criticized for making light of poverty and social problems • Discontinued sale of Jesus Dress Up magnets in 2004 after pressure from family activist groups	• Employee opportunities are desirable, with competitive salaries and a strong benefits package

CAPITAL funds needed to create and operate a business enterprise

ENTREPRENEUR individual who accepts the risks and opportunities involved in creating and operating a new business venture

PHYSICAL RESOURCES tangible items that organizations use in the conduct of their businesses

INFORMATION RESOURCES data and other information that businesses use

PLANNED ECONOMY economy that relies on a centralized government to control all or most factors of production and to make all or most production and allocation decisions

production. Starbucks, for example, employs over 194,000 people,[3] including baristas who prepare coffees for customers, store managers, regional managers, coffee tasters, quality-control experts, coffee buyers, marketing experts, financial specialists, and other specialized workers and managers.

Capital Obtaining and using labor and other resources requires **capital**—the financial resources needed to start a business, operate it, and keep it growing. For example, Howard Schultz used personal savings and a loan to finance his acquisition of the fledgling Starbucks coffee outfit back in 1987. As Starbucks grew, he came to rely more on its profits and eventually sold stock to other investors to raise even more money. Today, Starbucks continues to rely on a blend of current earnings and both short- and long-term debt to finance its operations and fuel its growth.

Entrepreneurs An **entrepreneur** is a person who accepts the risks and opportunities entailed in creating and operating a new business. Howard Schultz was willing to accept the risks associated with retail growth and, after buying Starbucks, he capitalized on the market opportunities for rapid growth. Had his original venture failed, Schultz would have lost most of his savings. Most economic systems encourage entrepreneurs, both to start new businesses and to make the decisions that allow them to create new jobs and make more profits for their owners.

Physical Resources **Physical resources** are the tangible things that organizations use to conduct their business. They include natural resources and raw materials, offices, storage and production facilities, parts and supplies, computers and peripherals, and a variety of other equipment. For example, Starbucks relies on coffee beans and other food products, the equipment it uses to make its coffee drinks, paper products for packaging, and other retail equipment, as well as office equipment and storage facilities for running its business at the corporate level.

Information Resources The production of tangible goods once dominated most economic systems. Today, **information resources**—data and other information used by businesses—play a major role. Information resources that businesses rely on include market forecasts, the specialized knowledge of people, and economic data. In turn, much of what they do results either in the creation of new information or the repackaging of existing information for new users. For example, Starbucks uses various economic statistics to decide where to open new outlets. It also uses sophisticated forecasting models to predict the future prices of coffee beans. And consumer taste tests help the firm decide when to introduce new products.

Types of Economic Systems

The various types of economic systems differ in how they manage these factors of production and make decisions about production and allocation. In some systems, all ownership is private; in others, all factors of production are owned or controlled by the government. Most systems, however, fall between these extremes.

Planned Economies A **planned economy** relies on a centralized government to control all or most factors of production and to

Starbucks uses various factors of production, including labor such as these baristas.

COMMUNISM political system in which the government owns and operates all factors of production

MARKET ECONOMY economy in which individuals control production and allocation decisions through supply and demand

MARKET mechanism for exchange between buyers and sellers of a particular good or service

Say What You Mean

The Culture of Risk

Risk taking has been a defining feature of U.S. business culture for a long time. From the early pioneers and prospectors heading west to the would-be dot-com billionaires of the 1990s, Americans are known not only for their readiness to try out new ideas, but also for their willingness to risk everything for the chance to make it big. Risk taking has become an important part of California's business culture, especially in the entertainment and high-tech industries, and New York is home to high rollers in the world of finance. Risk taking in the United States differs by industry and size of company. Small companies are more likely to make risky decisions than large companies, where elaborate approval processes may slow things down. Likewise, publicly traded companies whose stockholders usually keep a close eye on investments are less likely to take big risks than privately held firms.

In contrast, many foreign cultures inhibit risk taking by businesses. In Japan, for example, business failure carries with it significant social stigma—a loss of "face." As a result, entrepreneurs there are slow to expand their businesses until they are certain they will succeed. Likewise, in countries like Russia and Poland, where up until a few years ago most businesses were government-owned, many managers today remain cautious and are reluctant to go too far out on a limb for a new opportunity.

---

make all or most production and allocation decisions. There are two basic forms of planned economies: *communism* (discussed here) and *socialism* (discussed as a mixed market economy).

As envisioned by nineteenth-century German economist Karl Marx, **communism** is a system in which the government owns and operates all factors of production. Under such a system, the government would assign people to jobs, own all business, and control all business decisions—what to make, how much to charge, and so forth. Marx proposed that individuals would contribute according to their abilities and receive benefits according to their needs. He also expected government ownership of production factors to be temporary: Once society had matured, government would wither away, and workers would take direct ownership of the factors of production.

The former Soviet Union and many Eastern European countries embraced communism until the end of the twentieth century. In the early 1990s, one country after another renounced communism as both an economic and a

Free Enterprise in China?

Once strictly synonymous with the Maoist communist regime, China is slowly demonstrating internal change. Fundamental events, such as the 2008 Olympics in Beijing, gradually alter the way domestic commerce is conducted as the demand for goods and services drastically increases. The changes will still not affect much of the population, but free enterprise is fragmentarily affecting certain businesses. Although not always the rule, as a country becomes richer, its economy is likely to become less rigid.

political system. Today, North Korea, Vietnam, and the People's Republic of China are among the few nations with openly communist systems. Even in these countries, however, planned economic systems are making room for features of the free enterprise system.

Market Economies In a **market economy**, individual producers and consumers control production and allocation by creating combinations of supply and demand. A **market** is a mechanism for exchange between the buyers and sellers of a particular good or service. (Like *capital*, the term *market* can have multiple meanings.) Market economies rely on capitalism and free enterprise to create an environment in which producers and consumers are free to sell and buy what they choose (within certain limits). As a result, items produced and prices paid are largely determined by supply and demand.

To understand how a market economy works, consider what happens when you go to a fruit market to buy apples. While one vendor is selling apples for $1 per pound, another is charging $1.50. Both vendors are free to charge what they want, and you are free to buy what

CAPITALISM system that sanctions the private ownership of the factors of production and encourages entrepreneurship by offering profits as an incentive

MIXED MARKET ECONOMY economic system featuring characteristics of both planned and market economies

PRIVATIZATION process of converting government enterprises into privately owned companies

SOCIALISM planned economic system in which the government owns and operates only selected major sources of production

Despite becoming a territory of the communist People's Republic of China in 1997, Hong Kong remains one of the world's freest economies. In Hong Kong's Lan Kwai Fong district, for example, traditional Chinese businesses operate next door to standard U.S. chains.

you choose. If both vendors' apples are of the same quality, you will buy the cheaper ones. If the $1.50 apples are fresher, you may buy them instead. In short, both buyers and sellers enjoy freedom of choice.

Individuals in a market system are free to not only buy what they want but also to work where they want and to invest, save, or spend their money in whatever manner they choose. Likewise, businesses are free to decide what products to make, where to sell them, and what prices to charge. This process contrasts markedly with that of a planned economy, in which individuals may be told where they can and cannot work, companies may be told what they can and cannot make, and consumers may have little or no choice in what they purchase or how much they pay. The political basis of market processes is called **capitalism**, which allows the private ownership of the factors of production and encourages entrepreneurship by offering profits as an incentive.

Mixed Market Economies In reality, there are no "pure" planned or "pure" market economies. Most countries rely on some form of **mixed market economy** that features characteristics of both planned and market economies. Even a market economy that strives to be as free and open as possible, such as the U.S. economy, restricts certain activities. Some products can't be sold legally, others can be sold only to people of a certain age, advertising must be truthful, and so forth. And the People's Republic of China, the world's most important planned economy, is increasingly allowing and overseeing certain forms of private ownership and entrepreneurship.

When a government is making a change from a planned economy to a market economy, it usually begins to adopt market mechanisms through **privatization**—the process of converting government enterprises into privately owned companies. The Netherlands, for example, has privatized its TNT Post Group N.V., transforming it into one of the world's most efficient post-office operations. Generally speaking, privatizing enterprises can reduce payroll expenses and boost efficiency, productivity, and profits.

In the partially planned system called **socialism**, the government owns and operates selected major industries. In such mixed market economies, the government may control banking, transportation, or industries producing such basic goods as oil and steel. Smaller businesses, such as clothing stores and restaurants, are privately owned. Many Western European countries, including England and France, allow free market operations in most economic areas but keep government control of others, such as health care.

The Economics of Market Systems

Understanding the complex nature of the U.S. economic system is essential to understanding the environment in which U.S. businesses operate.

Demand and Supply in a Market Economy

A market economy consists of many different markets that function within that economy. As a consumer, for instance, the choices you have and the prices you pay for goods and services are all governed by different sets of market forces. Businesses also have many different choices about buying and selling their products. Managers make decisions about inventory levels, prices, and distribution. Literally billions of exchanges take place every day between businesses and individuals; between businesses; and among individuals, businesses, and governments. Moreover, exchanges conducted in one area often affect exchanges elsewhere. For instance, the high cost of gas may also lead to prices going up for other items, ranging from food to clothing to delivery services, because of the reliance on gas for transportation.

The Laws of Demand and Supply   On all economic levels, decisions about what to buy and what to sell are determined primarily by the forces of demand and supply.[4] **Demand** is the willingness and ability of buyers to purchase a product (a good or a service). **Supply** is the willingness and ability of producers to offer a good or service for sale. Generally speaking, demand and supply follow basic laws:

■ The **law of demand**: Buyers will purchase (demand) *more* of a product as its price *drops* and *less* of a product as its price *increases*.

■ The **law of supply**: Producers will offer (supply) *more* of a product for sale as its price *rises* and *less* of a product as its price *drops*.

The Demand and Supply Schedule   To appreciate these laws in action, consider the market for pizza in your town. If everyone is willing to pay $25 for a pizza (a relatively high price), the town's only pizzeria will produce a large supply. But if everyone is willing to pay only $5 (a relatively low price), it will make fewer pizzas. Through careful analysis, we can determine how many pizzas will be sold at different prices. These results, called a **demand and supply schedule**, are obtained from marketing research, historical data, and other studies of the market. Properly applied, they reveal the relationships among different levels of demand and supply at different price levels.

Demand and Supply Curves   The demand and supply schedule can be used to construct demand and supply curves for pizza in your town. A **demand curve** shows how many products—in this case, pizzas—will be demanded (bought) at different prices. A **supply curve** shows how many pizzas will be supplied (baked or offered for sale) at different prices.

Figure 1.1 shows demand and supply curves for pizzas. As you can see, demand increases as price decreases; supply increases as price increases. When demand and supply curves are plotted on the same graph, the point at which they intersect is the **market price** (also called the **equilibrium price**)—the price at which the quantity of goods demanded and the quantity of goods supplied are equal. In Figure 1.1, the equilibrium price for pizzas in our example is $10. At this point, the quantity of pizzas demanded and the quantity of pizzas supplied are the same: 1,000 pizzas per week.

Surpluses and Shortages
What if the pizzeria decides to make some other number of pizzas—if the owner tried to increase profits by making *more* pizzas to sell or if the owner *reduced* the number of pizzas offered for sale to lower overhead and cut back on store hours? In either case, the result would be an inefficient use of resources and lower profits. For instance, if the pizzeria supplies 1,200 pizzas and tries to sell them for $10 each, 200 pizzas will not be bought. Our demand schedule shows that only 1,000 pizzas will be demanded at this price. The pizzeria will therefore have a **surplus**—a situation in which the quantity supplied exceeds the quantity demanded. It will lose the money that it spent making those extra 200 pizzas.

Conversely, if the pizzeria supplies only 800 pizzas, a **shortage** will result. The quantity demanded will be greater than the quantity supplied. The pizzeria will "lose" the extra profit that it could have made by producing 200 more pizzas. Even though consumers may pay more for pizzas because of the shortage, the pizzeria will still earn lower total profits than if it had made 1,000 pizzas. It will also risk angering customers who cannot buy pizzas and encourage other entrepreneurs to set up competing pizzerias to satisfy unmet demand. Businesses should seek the ideal combination of price charged and quantity supplied so as to maximize profits, maintain goodwill among

DEMAND the willingness and ability of buyers to purchase a good or service

SUPPLY the willingness and ability of producers to offer a good or service for sale

LAW OF DEMAND principle that buyers will purchase (demand) more of a product as its price drops and less as its price increases

LAW OF SUPPLY principle that producers will offer (supply) more of a product for sale as its price rises and less as its price drops

DEMAND AND SUPPLY SCHEDULE assessment of the relationships among different levels of demand and supply at different price levels

DEMAND CURVE graph showing how many units of a product will be demanded (bought) at different prices

SUPPLY CURVE graph showing how many units of a product will be supplied (offered for sale) at different prices

MARKET PRICE (EQUILIBRIUM PRICE) profit-maximizing price at which the quantity of goods demanded and the quantity of goods supplied are equal

SURPLUS situation in which quantity supplied exceeds quantity demanded

SHORTAGE situation in which quantity demanded exceeds quantity supplied

PRIVATE ENTERPRISE economic system that allows individuals to pursue their own interests without undue governmental restriction

COMPETITION vying among businesses for the same resources or customers

Figure 1.1
Demand and Supply[5]

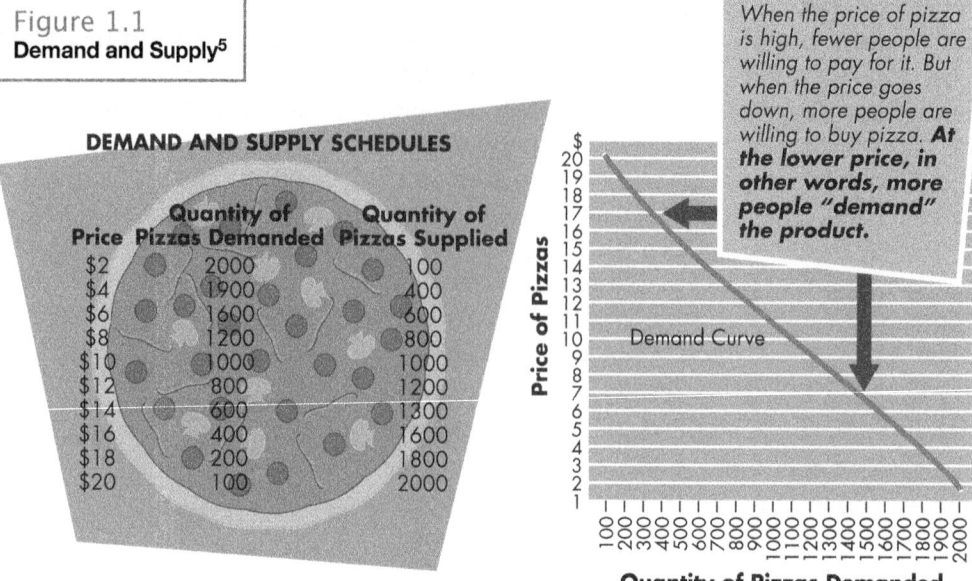

DEMAND AND SUPPLY SCHEDULES

Price	Quantity of Pizzas Demanded	Quantity of Pizzas Supplied
$2	2000	100
$4	1900	400
$6	1600	600
$8	1200	800
$10	1000	1000
$12	800	1200
$14	600	1300
$16	400	1600
$18	200	1800
$20	100	2000

When the price of pizza is high, fewer people are willing to pay for it. But when the price goes down, more people are willing to buy pizza. **At the lower price, in other words, more people "demand" the product.**

customers, and discourage competition. This ideal combination is found at the equilibrium point.

Our example involves only one company, one product, and a few buyers. The U.S. economy—indeed, any market economy—is far more complex. Thousands of companies sell hundreds of thousands of products to millions of buyers every day. In the end, however, the result is much the same: Companies try to supply the quantity and selection of goods that will earn them the largest profits.

When the price of pizza is low, more people are willing to buy pizza. Pizza makers, however, do not have the money to invest in making pizzas and so they make fewer. Supply, therefore, is limited, and **only when the price goes up will pizza makers be willing and able to increase supply.**

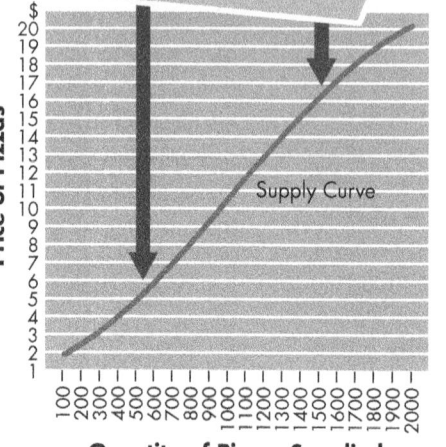

Private Enterprise and Competition in a Market Economy

Market economies rely on a **private enterprise** system— one that allows individuals to pursue their own interests with minimal government restriction. In turn, private enterprise requires the presence of four elements:

1 *Private property rights.* Ownership of the resources used to create wealth is in the hands of individuals.

2 *Freedom of choice.* Individuals can choose which employers to sell their labor to and which products to buy, and producers can choose whom to hire and what to produce.

3 *Profits.* The lure of profits (and freedom) leads some people to abandon the security of working for someone else and to assume the risks of entrepreneurship. Anticipated profits also influence individuals' choices of which goods or services to produce.

When the pizza makers increase supply in order to satisfy demand, there will be **a point at which the price that suppliers can charge is the same as the price that a maximum number of customers is willing to pay.** *That point is the market price, or* **equilibrium** *price.*

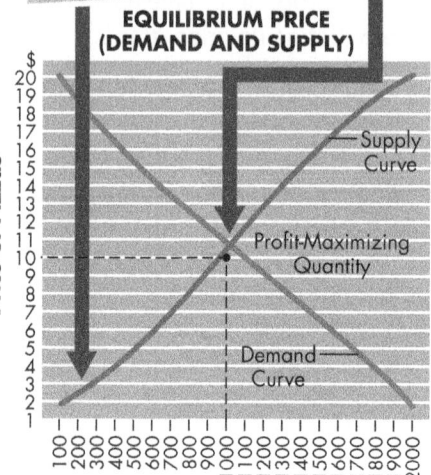

EQUILIBRIUM PRICE (DEMAND AND SUPPLY)

4 *Competition.* If profits motivate individuals to start businesses, competition motivates them to operate those businesses efficiently. **Competition** occurs when two or more businesses vie for the same resources or customers. To gain an advantage over competitors, a business must produce its goods or services efficiently and be able to sell at a reasonable profit by convincing customers that its products are either better or less expensive than those of its competitors. Competition, therefore, forces all businesses to make products better or cheaper. A company that produces inferior, expensive products is likely to fail.

Table 1.2 Degrees of Competition

Characteristic	Perfect Competition	Monopolistic Competition	Oligopoly	Monopoly
Example	Local Farmer	Stationery Store	Steel Industry	Public Utility
Number of Competitors	Many	Many, but fewer than in perfect competition	Few	None
Ease of Entry into the Industry	Relatively easy	Fairly easy	Difficult	Regulated by government
Similarity of Goods/Services Offered by Competing Firms	Identical	Similar	Can be similar or different	No directly competing goods or services
Level of Control over Price by Individual Firms	None	Some	Some	Considerable

Degrees of Competition Even in a free enterprise system, not all industries are equally competitive. Economists have identified four degrees of competition in a private enterprise system: *perfect competition*, *monopolistic competition*, *oligopoly*, and *monopoly*. Note that these are not always truly distinct categories but actually tend to fall along a continuum; perfect competition and monopoly anchor the ends of the continuum, with monopolistic competition and oligopoly falling in between. Table 1.2 summarizes the features of these four degrees of competition.

Perfect Competition For **perfect competition** to exist, two conditions must prevail: (1) all firms in an industry must be small, and (2) the number of firms in the industry must be large. Under these conditions, no single firm is powerful enough to influence the price of its product. Prices are, therefore, determined by such market forces as supply and demand.

In addition, these two conditions also reflect four principles:

1️⃣ The products of each firm are so similar that buyers view them as identical to those of other firms.

2️⃣ Both buyers and sellers know the prices that others are paying and receiving in the marketplace.

3️⃣ Because each firm is small, firms can easily enter or leave the market.

4️⃣ Going prices are set exclusively by supply and demand and accepted by both sellers and buyers.

U.S. agriculture is a good example of perfect competition. The wheat produced on one farm is the same as that from another. Both producers and buyers are aware of prevailing market prices. It is relatively easy to start producing wheat and relatively easy to stop when it's no longer profitable.

Monopolistic Competition In **monopolistic competition**, there are numerous sellers trying to make their products at least seem to be different from those of competitors. While there are many sellers involved in monopolistic competition, there tend to be fewer than in pure competition. Differentiating strategies include brand names, design or styling, and advertising.

Product differentiation also gives sellers some control over prices. For instance, even though Target shirts may have similar styling and other features, Ralph Lauren polo shirts can be priced with little regard for lower Target prices. But the large number of buyers relative to sellers applies potential limits to prices: Although Ralph Lauren might be able to sell shirts for $20 more than a comparable Target shirt, it could not sell as many shirts if they were priced at $200 more. Monopolistically competitive businesses may be large or small, but they can still enter or leave the market easily. For example, many small clothing stores compete successfully with larger apparel retailers, such as Abercrombie & Fitch and Banana Republic. A good case in point is bebe stores. The small clothing chain controls its own manufacturing facilities and can respond just as quickly as firms like the Gap to changes in fashion tastes.

Oligopoly When an industry has only a handful of sellers, an **oligopoly** exists. As a general rule, these sellers are quite large. The entry of new competitors is hard because large capital investment is needed. Thus, oligopolistic industries tend to stay that way—for example, only Boeing and Airbus make large commercial aircraft. Furthermore, as the trend toward globalization continues, most experts believe that oligopolies will become increasingly prevalent.

Oligopolists have more control over their strategies than monopolistically competitive firms, but the actions of one firm can significantly affect the sales of every other firm in the industry. When an airline announces new fare discounts, others adopt the same strategy almost immediately. Just as quickly, when discounts end for one

PERFECT COMPETITION market or industry characterized by numerous small firms producing an identical product

MONOPOLISTIC COMPETITION market or industry characterized by numerous buyers and relatively numerous sellers trying to differentiate their products from those of competitors

OLIGOPOLY market or industry characterized by a handful of (generally large) sellers with the power to influence the prices of their products

EG CHAPTER 1

MONOPOLY market or industry in which there is only one producer that can therefore set the prices of its products

NATURAL MONOPOLY industry in which one company can most efficiently supply all needed goods or services

ECONOMIC INDICATOR a statistic that helps assess the performance of an economy

airline, they usually end for everyone else. Therefore, the prices of comparable products are usually similar.

Monopoly A **monopoly** exists when an industry or market has only one producer (or else is so dominated by one producer that other firms cannot compete with it). A sole supplier enjoys nearly complete control over the prices of its products. Its only constraint is a decrease in consumer demand due to increased prices or government regulation. In the United States, laws, such as the Sherman Antitrust Act (1890) and the Clayton Act (1914), forbid many monopolies and regulate prices charged by **natural monopolies**—industries in which one company can most efficiently supply all needed goods or services.[6] Many electric companies are natural monopolies because they can supply all the power needed in a local area. Duplicate facilities—such as two power plants and two sets of powerlines—would be inefficient.

Economic Indicators

Because economic forces are so volatile and can be affected by so many things, the performance of a country's economic system varies over time. Sometimes it gains strength and brings new prosperity to its members; other times it weakens and damages their fortunes. But knowing how an economy is performing is useful for both business owners and investors alike. Most experts look to various **economic indicators**—statistics that show whether an economic system is strengthening, weakening, or remaining stable—to help assess the performance of an economy.

Economic Growth, Aggregate Output, and Standard of Living

At one time, about half the population of this country was involved in producing the food that we needed. Today, less than 2.5 percent of the U.S. population works in agriculture, and this number is expected to decrease slightly over the next decade.[7] But agricultural efficiency has improved because better ways of producing products have been devised, and better technology has been

---

Entrepreneurship and New Ventures

Business...and Pleasure

Americans are multitaskers. We sip lattes while driving, we walk the dog while checking stock quotes, and we pay our bills online while watching TV; it is no surprise that this trend has taken on bigger dimensions. Business and entertainment are no longer considered two separate entities. Entertainment used to be defined as amusement parks, miniature golf, baseball games, and movies. Business was business: work, dine, shop, etc. But now, in a slowing market economy, industries feel even more pressure to mix business with entertainment. The brightly colored play structures in McDonald's and the first mall roller coaster paved the way for this upsurge of integration that is now almost impossible to avoid.

In September of 2007, Apple and Starbucks announced a partnership that allows customers to preview millions of Apple iTunes while waiting in line. The customers also have the option to buy or download music onto their iPod touch, iPhone, PC, or Mac. JetBlue partnered with XM Radio to offer passengers a sample of the new wave of satellite radio. Select Wal-Mart stores host live broadcasts of concerts enticing shoppers to linger just a little longer. This

growing trend is not likely to change anytime soon. But businesses should be wary of new business cycles created in the entertainment realm. Entertainment-driven corporations are always at a high risk of deflation when the economy falters. Those businesses that rely on partnerships with these high-risk firms may not be as grounded as they seem.

Table 1.3 **U.S. GDP and GDP Per Capita**[8]

Gross Domestic Product (GDP) ($ Trillion)	GDP: Real Growth Rate (%)	GDP per Capita: Purchasing Power Parity
$13.86	2.2	$46,000

invented for getting the job done. We can say that agricultural productivity has increased because we have been able to increase total output in the agricultural sector.

We can apply the same concepts to a nation's economic system, although the computations are more complex. Fundamentally, how do we know whether an economic system is growing or not? Experts call the pattern of short-term ups and downs (or, better, expansions and contractions) in an economy the **business cycle**. The primary measure of growth in the business cycle is **aggregate output**—the total quantity of goods and services produced by an economic system during a given period.[9]

To put it simply, an increase in aggregate output is growth (or economic growth). When output grows more quickly than the population, two things usually follow:

■ Output per capita—the quantity of goods and services per person—goes up.

■ The system provides more of the goods and services that people want.

When these two things occur, people living in an economic system benefit from a higher **standard of living**, which refers to the total quantity and quality of goods and services that they can purchase with the currency used in their economic system. To know how much your standard of living is improving, you need to know how much your nation's economic system is growing (see Table 1.3).

Gross Domestic Product The first number, **gross domestic product (GDP)**, refers to the total value of all goods and services produced within a given period by a national economy through domestic factors of production. GDP is a measure of aggregate output. Generally speaking, if GDP is going up, aggregate output is going up; if aggregate output is going up, the nation is experiencing *economic growth*.

Sometimes, economists also use the term **gross national product (GNP)**, which refers to the total value of all goods and services produced by a national economy within a given period regardless of where the factors of production are located. What, precisely, is the difference between GDP and GNP? Consider a General Motors automobile plant in Brazil. The profits earned by the factory are included in U.S. GNP—but not in GDP—because its output is not produced domestically (that is, in the United States). Conversely, those profits are included in Brazil's GDP—but not GNP—because they are produced domestically (that is, in Brazil). Calculations quickly

become complex because of different factors of production. The labor, for example, will be mostly Brazilian but the capital mostly American. Thus, wages paid to Brazilian workers are part of Brazil's GNP even though profits are not.

Real Growth Rate GDP and GNP usually differ by less than 1 percent, but economists argue that GDP is a more accurate indicator of domestic economic performance because it focuses only on domestic factors of production. With that in mind, let's look at the middle column in Table 1.3. Here we find that the real growth rate of U.S. GDP—the growth rate of GDP *adjusted for inflation and changes in the value of the country's currency*—is 2.2 percent. How good is that rate? Remember that *growth depends on output increasing at a faster rate than population*. The U.S. population is growing at a rate of 0.90 percent per year.[10] The *real growth rate* of the U.S. economic system, therefore, seems quite healthy, and the U.S. standard of living should be improving.

GDP per Capita The number in the third column of Table 1.3 is a reflection of the standard of living: *GDP per capita* means GDP per person. We get this figure by dividing total GDP ($13.86 trillion) by total population, which happens to be about 301 million.[11] In a given period (usually calculated on an annual basis), the United States produces goods and services equal in value to $46,000 for every person in the country. Figure 1.2 shows both GDP and GDP per capita in the United States between 1950 and 2004. GDP per capita is a better measure than GDP itself of the economic well-being of the average person.

Real GDP Real GDP means that GDP has been adjusted to account for changes in currency values and price changes. To understand why adjustments are

BUSINESS CYCLE short-term pattern of economic expansions and contractions

AGGREGATE OUTPUT the total quantity of goods and services produced by an economic system during a given period

STANDARD OF LIVING the total quantity and quality of goods and services people can purchase with the currency used in their economic system

GROSS DOMESTIC PRODUCT (GDP) total value of all goods and services produced within a given period by a national economy through domestic factors of production

GROSS NATIONAL PRODUCT (GNP) total value of all goods and services produced by a national economy within a given period regardless of where the factors of production are located

REAL GDP gross domestic product (GDP) adjusted to account for changes in currency values and price changes

EG CHAPTER 1

NOMINAL GDP gross domestic product (GDP) measured in current dollars or with all components valued at current prices

PURCHASING POWER PARITY the principle that exchange rates are set so that the prices of similar products in different countries are about the same

PRODUCTIVITY a measure of economic growth that compares how much a system produces with the resources needed to produce it

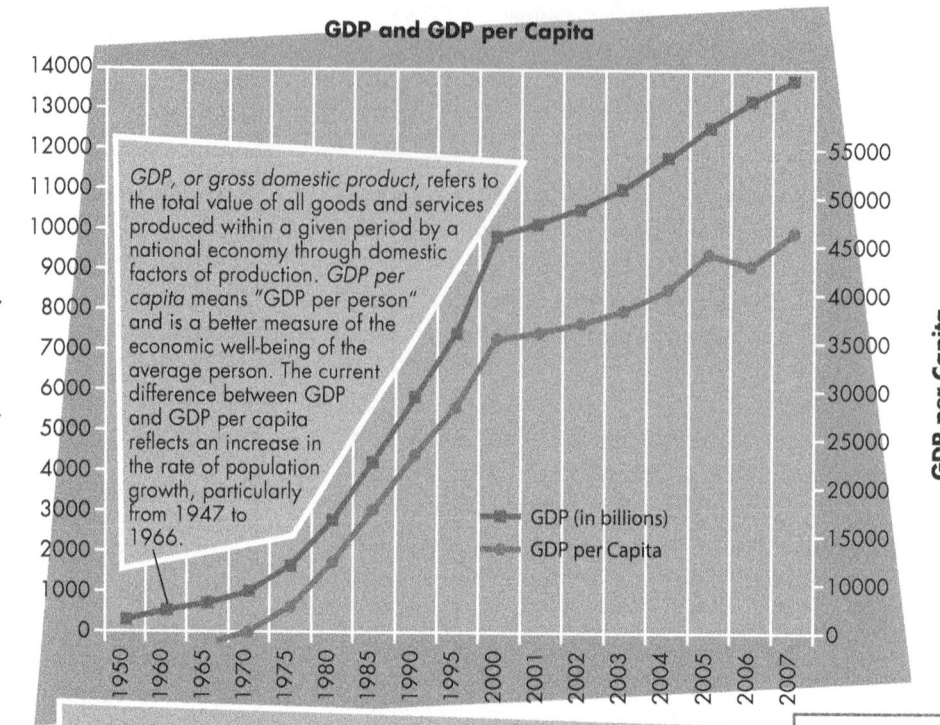

Note: This graph is shown in five-year increments until the year 2000, after which it is shown in one-year increments so as to provide more detail for recent periods. Hence, the curve artificially "flattens" after 2000.

Figure 1.2
GDP and GDP Per Capita[12]

necessary, assume that pizza is the only product in a hypothetical economy. In 2005, a pizza cost $10; in 2006, a pizza cost $11. In both years, exactly 1,000 pizzas were produced. In 2005, the local GDP was $10,000 ($10 × 1,000); in 2006, the local GDP was $11,000 ($11 × 1,000). Has the economy grown? No. Because 1,000 pizzas were produced in both years, *aggregate output* remained the same. The point is to not be misled into believing that an economy is doing better than it is. If it is not adjusted, local GDP for 2006 is **nominal GDP**—GDP measured in current dollars or with all components valued at current prices.[13]

Purchasing Power Parity In the example, *current prices* would be 2006 prices. On the other hand, we calculate real GDP when we adjust GDP to account for changes in *currency values and price changes*. When we make this adjustment, we account for both GDP and **purchasing power parity**—the principle that exchange rates are set so that the prices of similar products in

Figure 1.3
The Big Mac Index[14]
One interesting method for comparing purchasing power in different countries is the Big Mac Index—a comparison of the costs of a McDonald's hamburger in different countries.

different countries are about the same. Purchasing power parity gives us a much better idea of *what people can actually buy with the financial resources allocated to them by their respective economic systems*. In other words, it gives us a better sense of standards of living across the globe. Figure 1.3 illustrates a popular approach to see how purchasing power parity works in relation to a Big Mac. For instance, the figure pegs the price of a Big Mac in the United States at $3.22. Based on currency exchange rates, a Big Mac would cost $3.90 in Britain and $5.05 in Switzerland. But the same burger would cost only $1.54 in Hong Kong and $1.78 in Thailand.

Productivity A major factor in the growth of an economic system is **productivity**, which is a measure of economic growth that compares how much a system produces with the resources needed to produce it. Let's say that it takes 1 U.S. worker and 1 U.S. dollar to make 10 soccer balls in an 8-hour workday. Let's also say that it takes 1.2 Saudi workers and the

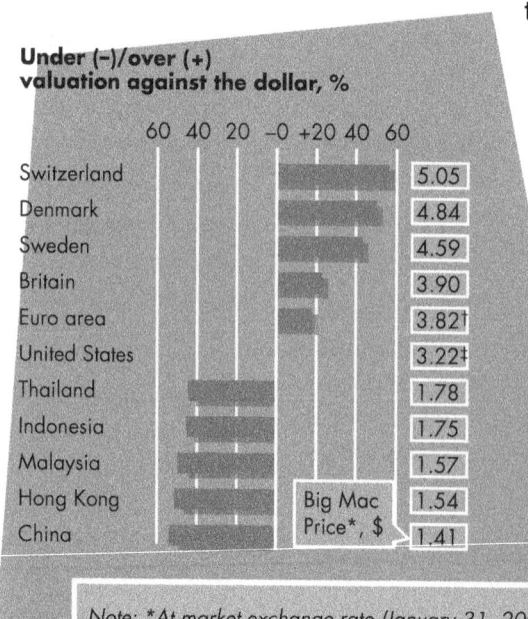

Under (−)/over (+) valuation against the dollar, %

	Big Mac Price*, $
Switzerland	5.05
Denmark	4.84
Sweden	4.59
Britain	3.90
Euro area	3.82†
United States	3.22‡
Thailand	1.78
Indonesia	1.75
Malaysia	1.57
Hong Kong	1.54
China	1.41

Note: *At market exchange rate (January 31, 2007)
† Weighted average of member countries
‡ Average of four cities

equivalent of 1.2 riyals, the currency of Saudi Arabia, to make 10 soccer balls in the same 8-hour workday. We can say that the U.S. soccer-ball industry is more productive than the Saudi soccer-ball industry. The two factors of production in this extremely simple case are labor and capital.

If more products are being produced with fewer factors of production, the prices of these products go down. As a consumer, therefore, you would need less of your currency to purchase the same quantity of these products. In short, your standard of living—at least with regard to these products—has improved. If your entire economic system increases its productivity, then your overall standard of living improves. In fact, *standard of living improves only through increases in productivity*.[15] Real growth in GDP reflects growth in productivity.

Productivity in the United States is increasing, and as a result, so are GDP and GDP per capita. Ultimately, increases in these measures of growth mean an improvement in the standard of living. However, things don't always proceed so smoothly. Several factors can inhibit the growth of an economic system, including *balance of trade* and the *national debt*.

Balance of Trade A country's **balance of trade** is the economic value of all the products that it exports minus the economic value of its imported products. The principle here is quite simple:

◼ A *positive* balance of trade results when a country exports (sells to other countries) more than it imports (buys from other countries).

◼ A *negative* balance of trade results when a country imports more than it exports.

A negative balance of trade is commonly called a *trade deficit*. In 2007, the U.S. trade deficit exceeded $700 billion for the third year in a row. The United States is a *debtor nation* rather than a *creditor nation*. Recent trends in the U.S. balance of trade are shown in Figure 1.4.

Trade deficit affects economic growth because the amount of money spent on foreign products has not been paid in full. Therefore, it is, in effect, borrowed money, and borrowed money costs more in the form of interest. The money that flows out of the country to pay off the deficit can't be used to invest in productive enterprises, either at home or overseas.

National Debt Its **national debt** is the amount of money that the government owes its creditors. As of this writing, the U.S. national debt is over $9.4 trillion. You can find out the

national debt on any given day by going to any one of several Internet sources, including the U.S. National Debt Clock at **www.brillig.com/debt_clock**.

How does the national debt affect economic growth? While taxes are the most obvious way the government raises money, it also sells *bonds*—securities through which it promises to pay buyers certain amounts of money by specified future dates. (In a sense, a bond is an IOU with interest.)[17] These bonds are attractive investments because they are extremely safe: The U.S. government is not going to default on them (that is, fail to make payments when due). Even so, they must also offer a decent return on the buyer's investment, and they do this by paying interest at a competitive rate. By selling bonds, therefore, the U.S. government competes with every other potential borrower for the available supply of loanable money. The more money the government borrows, the less money is available for the private borrowing and investment that increase productivity.

Economic Stability

Stability is a condition in which the amount of money available in an economic system and the quantity of goods and services produced in it are growing at about the same rate. A chief goal of an economic system, stability can be threatened by certain factors.

BALANCE OF TRADE the economic value of all the products that a country exports minus the economic value of all the products it imports

NATIONAL DEBT the amount of money the government owes its creditors

STABILITY condition in which the amount of money available in an economic system and the quantity of goods and services produced in it are growing at about the same rate

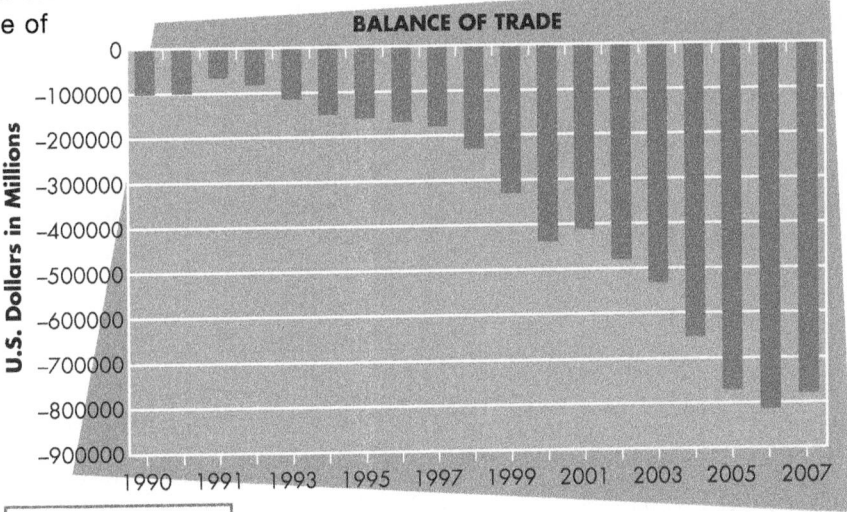

BALANCE OF TRADE

U.S. Dollars in Millions

0
−100000
−200000
−300000
−400000
−500000
−600000
−700000
−800000
−900000

1990 1991 1993 1995 1997 1999 2001 2003 2005 2007

Figure 1.4
Balance of Trade[16]

EG CHAPTER 1

INFLATION occurs when widespread price increases occur throughout an economic system

CONSUMER PRICE INDEX (CPI) a measure of the prices of typical products purchased by consumers living in urban areas

UNEMPLOYMENT the level of joblessness among people actively seeking work in an economic system

RECESSION a period during which aggregate output, as measured by GDP, declines

DEPRESSION a prolonged and deep recession

FISCAL POLICIES policies that a government uses to direct how it collects and spends revenue

MONETARY POLICIES policies that a government uses to control the size of its money supply

STABILIZATION POLICY government economic policy intended to smooth out fluctuations in output and unemployment and to stabilize prices

Inflation **Inflation** occurs when an economic system experiences widespread price increases. Instability results when the amount of money injected into an economy exceeds the increase in actual output, so people have more money to spend but the same quantity of products available to buy. As supply and demand principles tell us, as people compete with one another to buy available products, prices go up. These high prices will eventually bring the amount of money in the economy back down. However, these processes are imperfect—the additional money will not be distributed proportionately to all people, and price increases often continue beyond what is really necessary. As a result, purchasing power for many people declines.

Keeping in mind that our definition of inflation is the occurrence of widespread price increases throughout an economic system, it stands to reason that we can measure inflation by measuring price increases. Price indexes such as the **consumer price index (CPI)** measure the prices of typical products purchased by consumers living in urban areas.[18]

Unemployment Finally, we need to consider the effect of unemployment on economic stability. **Unemployment** is the level of joblessness among people actively seeking work in an economic system. When unemployment is low, there is a shortage of

MCCAIN'S WAR PLAN DEATH IN PAKISTAN NERD GIRLS

Newsweek

A New Kind Of **RECESSION**

DANIEL GROSS AND FAREED ZAKARIA

Rising unemployment and gas prices, combined with slumping housing prices and sluggish GDP growth, led many analysts to fear a recession in 2008.

labor available for businesses to hire. As businesses compete with one another for the available supply of labor, they raise the wages they are willing to pay. Then, because higher labor costs eat into profit margins, they raise the prices of their products. Although consumers have more money to inject into the economy, this increase is soon undone by higher prices, so purchasing power declines.

There are at least two related problems:

- If wage rates get too high, businesses will respond by hiring fewer workers and unemployment will go up.

- Businesses could raise prices to counter increased labor costs, but they won't be able to sell as many of their products at higher prices. Because of reduced sales, they will cut back on hiring and, once again, unemployment will go up.

What if the government tries to correct this situation by injecting more money into the economic system—say by cutting taxes or spending more money? Prices in general may go up because of increased consumer demand. Again, purchasing power declines and inflation may set in.[19]

The U.S. government uses the Federal Reserve System to implement its monetary policies. The chairman of "the Fed" is Ben Bernanke. He is shown here listening to opening remarks before the U.S. Senate Banking Committee in Washington, D.C.

Recessions and Depressions Unemployment is sometimes a symptom of a system-wide disorder in the economy. During a downturn in the business cycle, people in different sectors may lose their jobs at the same time. As a result, overall income and spending may drop. Feeling the pinch of reduced revenues, businesses may cut spending on the factors of production—including labor. Yet more people will be put out of work, and unemployment will only increase further. Unemployment that results from this vicious cycle is called *cyclical unemployment*.

If we look at the relationship between unemployment and economic stability, we are reminded that when prices get high enough, consumer demand for goods and services goes down. We are also reminded that when demand for products goes down, producers cut back on hiring and, not surprisingly, eventually start producing less. Consequently, aggregate output decreases. When we go through a period during which aggregate output declines, we have a recession. During a *recession*, producers need fewer employees—less labor—to produce products. Unemployment, therefore, goes up.

To determine whether an economy is going through a recession, we start by measuring aggregate output. Recall that this is the function of real GDP, which we find by making necessary adjustments to the total value of all goods and services produced within a given period by a national economy through domestic factors of production. A **recession** is more precisely defined as a period during which aggregate output, as measured by real GDP, declines. A prolonged and deep recession is a **depression**.

Managing the U.S. Economy

The government acts to manage the U.S. economic system through two sets of policies: fiscal and monetary. It manages the collection and spending of its revenues through **fiscal policies**. Tax rates, for example, can play an important role in fiscal policies helping to manage the economy.

Monetary policies focus on controlling the size of the nation's money supply. Working primarily through the Federal Reserve System (the nation's central bank, often referred to simply as "the Fed"), the government can influence the ability and willingness of banks throughout the country to lend money.[20]

Taken together, fiscal policy and monetary policy make up **stabilization policy**—government economic policy whose goal is to smooth out fluctuations in output and unemployment and to stabilize prices.

Questions for Review

1. What are the factors of production? Is one factor more important than the others? If so, which one? Why?

2. What is a demand curve? A supply curve? What is the term for the point at which they intersect?

3. What is GDP? Real GDP? What does each measure?

4. Why is inflation both good and bad? How does the government try to control it?

Questions for Analysis

5. In recent years, many countries that previously used planned economies have moved to market economies. Why do you think this has occurred? Can you envision a situation that would cause a resurgence of planned economies?

6. Cite an instance in which a surplus of a product led to decreased prices. Cite an instance in which a shortage led to increased prices. What eventually happened in each case? Why?

7. Explain how current economic indicators, such as inflation and unemployment, affect you personally. Explain how they may affect you as a manager.

8. At first glance, it might seem as though the goals of economic growth and stability are inconsistent with one another. How can you reconcile this apparent inconsistency?

Application Exercises

9. Visit a local shopping mall or shopping area. List each store that you see and determine what degree of competition it faces in its immediate environment. For example, if there is only one store in the mall that sells shoes, that store represents a monopoly. Note those businesses with direct competitors (two jewelry stores) and show how they compete with one another.

10. Interview a business owner or senior manager. Ask this individual to describe for you the following: (1) how demand and supply affect the business, (2) what essential factors of production are most central to the firm's operations, and (3) how fluctuations in economic indicators affect his or her business.

chapter 2

part The Contemporary Business World

Business Ethics and Social Responsibility

After reading this chapter, you should be able to:

1 Explain how individuals develop their personal codes of ethics and why ethics are important in the workplace.

2 Distinguish social responsibility from ethics, identify organizational stakeholders, and characterize social consciousness today.

3 Show how the concept of social responsibility applies both to environmental issues and to a firm's relationships with customers, employees, and investors.

4 Identify four general approaches to social responsibility, and describe the four steps that a firm must take to implement a social responsibility program.

5 Explain how issues of social responsibility and ethics affect small business.

Under the Guise of Green

Oil companies aren't usually known for their environmentally responsible reputations. Global energy giant BP, however, has made an effort to market an environmentally friendly image. For the most part, this strategy has worked—leading many to overlook the facts suggesting that BP is not entirely the environmentally responsible exception it claims to be.

For the past several years, BP has committed environmental offenses almost annually. In 2000, the company was convicted of an environmental felony for failing to report that its subcontractor was dumping hazardous waste in Alaska. In 2005, BP allegedly ignored knowledge that its Texas City refinery was unsafe in a cost-cutting effort that led to an explosion, 15 deaths, and even more injuries. The following year, BP's negligence at its Prudhoe Bay oil field caused a 200,000-gallon oil spill and misdemeanor violation of the Clean Water Act. Then, in 2007, BP lobbied Indiana regulators for an exemption allowing it to increase its daily release of ammonia and sludge into Lake Michigan.

Despite these misdeeds, BP maintains its image as a "green" company. The Natural Resource Defense Council has even praised it for being a leader in the industry's move toward renewable energy. Indeed, true to the tag line, "Beyond Petroleum," that accompanies its green logo, BP's 2007 Sustainability Report projects spending $8 billion over the next ten years on renewable energy products. Its Web site even offers a carbon footprint calculator that lets visitors see how their own choices affect the environment.

BP risks compromising its green image by engaging in what Greenpeace calls the "greatest climate crime" in history—extracting oil from the tar sands of Alberta, Canada. The project is energy- and water-intensive, produces excessive amounts of greenhouse gases, destroys acres of forest, and harms indigenous communities, but it comes at a time when oil prices are high and western consumers are dependent on Middle Eastern oil. It remains to be seen whether BP's seemingly socially responsible ends can justify their environmentally damaging means.[1]

What's in It for Me?

• • • • • • • • • • • •

To make an informed judgment about a company's social responsibility, it's important to understand how individual codes of ethics develop and play a role in the workplace, to distinguish between ethics and social responsibility, and to understand social consciousness. In addition to these elements, this chapter will explore the ethical and social responsibility issues that businesses face in terms of their customers, employees, investors, and immediate and global communities. In addition, it will look at general approaches to social responsibility, the steps businesses must take to implement social responsibility programs, and issues of social responsibility and ethics in small businesses.

ETHICS beliefs about what is right or wrong and good or bad in actions that affect others

ETHICAL BEHAVIOR behavior conforming to generally accepted social norms concerning beneficial and harmful actions

UNETHICAL BEHAVIOR behavior that does not conform to generally accepted social norms concerning beneficial and harmful actions

BUSINESS ETHICS ethical or unethical behaviors by employees in the context of their jobs

MANAGERIAL ETHICS standards of behavior that guide individual managers in their work

Ethics in the Workplace

Ethics are beliefs about what's right or wrong and good or bad based on an individual's values and morals, plus a behavior's social context. In other words, **ethical behavior** conforms to individual beliefs and social norms about what's right and good. **Unethical behavior** conforms to individual beliefs and social norms about what's wrong or bad. **Business ethics** refers to ethical or unethical behaviors by employees in the context of their jobs.

Individual Ethics

Because ethics are based on both individual beliefs and social concepts, they vary among individuals, situations, and cultures. People may develop personal

Tax Revenues Disappear into Bermuda Triangle

The epidemic of scandals that dominated business news over the past decade shows how willing people can be to take advantage of potentially ambiguous situations—indeed, to create them. For example, in 1997, Tyco sold itself to the smaller ADT Ltd. Because its new parent company was based in the tax haven of Bermuda, Tyco no longer had to pay U.S. taxes on its non-U.S. income. In 2000 and 2001, Tyco's subsidiaries in such tax-friendly nations doubled, and the company slashed its 2001 U.S. tax bill by $600 million. "Tyco," complained a U.S. congressman, "has raised tax avoidance to an art," but one tax expert replies that Tyco's schemes "are very consistent with the [U.S.] tax code."[2] Even in the face of blistering criticism and the indictment of its former CEO, Tyco retains its offshore ownership structure.[3]

codes of ethics reflecting a wide range of attitudes and beliefs without violating general standards. Thus, some ethical and unethical behaviors are widely agreed upon, while others fall into gray areas.

Ambiguity, the Law, and the Real World Societies generally adopt formal laws that reflect prevailing ethical standards or social norms. We try to make unambiguous laws, but interpreting and applying them can still lead to ethical ambiguities. It isn't always easy to apply statutory standards to real-life behavior. For instance, during the aftermath of Hurricane Katrina in 2005, desperate survivors in New Orleans looted grocery stores for food and other essentials. While few people criticized this behavior, such actions were technically illegal.

Individual Values and Codes The ethics of business start with the ethics of individuals—managers, employees, and other legal representatives. Each person's personal code of ethics is determined by a combination of factors that are formed and refined throughout our lives.

Business and Managerial Ethics

Managerial ethics are the standards of behavior that guide individual managers in their work.[5] Although managerial ethics can affect business in any number of ways, it's helpful to classify them into three broad categories.

Behavior Toward Employees This category covers such matters as hiring and firing, wages and working conditions, and privacy and respect. Ethical and legal guidelines suggest that hiring and firing decisions should be based solely on the ability to perform a job.

Wages and working conditions, while regulated by law, are also controversial. Consider a manager who pays a worker less than he deserves because the manager knows that the employee can't afford to quit or

Former Volkswagen personnel director Klaus Volkert was given a two-year jail sentence for his involvement in the bribery scandal that financed prostitutes and exotic holidays for union officials in exchange for their support of management plans.[4]

Say What You Mean

The Ethical Soft-Shoe

To bribe or not to bribe? That is the question. Although the textbook answer is a nonnegotiable "no" regardless of the business environment, culture, or country you're in, the real-world answer is much less clear. To varying degrees, complicated business dealings that ignore the strict letter of the law—offering or accepting incentives to get things done, extracting a personal favor or two, using the power and influence of people we know—happen all the time.

In fact, in some cultures ethically ambiguous practices are hallmarks of business culture. Brazilians, for example, apply the philosophy of *jeitinho*—"to find a way"—in which there's always another way to get something done—using personal connections, bending the rules, making a "contribution," or simply approaching the problem from a different angle. If you need an official document, for instance, you might set out determined to take all the proper bureaucratic steps to get it. However, when you find yourself in a maze of rules and regulations, you're likely to resort to *jeitinho*. *Jeitinho* almost never involves butting heads with authority, but is rather a complex dance that enables individuals to go around problems instead of having to go through them.

Even if you're operating in a country like Brazil, in which sidestepping the rules is business as usual, you don't *have* to do an ethical soft-shoe. Many global companies have strict ethical guidelines for doing business: International

U.S. business practices, for example, are regulated by the Foreign Corrupt Practices Act. The key to dancing with a foreign partner is understanding the culture—observing the way business is conducted and preparing yourself for any challenges—before you get out on the dance floor.

In Brazil, someone pressed for time might invoke the philosophy of *jeitinho* when facing a long wait in line. The philosophy allows for rule-bending like cutting in line if fairness and practicality are overriding factors.

---

risk his job by complaining. While some see the behavior as unethical, others see it as a smart business move.

Behavior Toward the Organization Employee behavior toward employers involves ethical issues in such areas as conflict of interest, confidentiality, and honesty. A *conflict of interest* occurs when an activity may benefit the individual to the detriment of his or her employer. To avoid even the appearance of bribery or favoritism, most companies have policies that forbid buyers from accepting gifts from suppliers. Businesses in highly competitive industries—software and fashion apparel, for example—have safeguards, such as nondisclosure agreements, against designers selling company secrets to competitors. Relatively common problems in the general area of honesty include stealing supplies and padding expense accounts.

Behavior Toward Other Economic Agents Advertising, bargaining and negotiation, financial disclosure, ordering and purchasing—ethical ambiguity is possible in just about every activity businesses conduct with *primary agents of interest*—mainly customers, competitors, stockholders, suppliers, dealers, and unions.

Global variations can complicate ethical business practices. For example, while U.S. law forbids bribes, many countries incorporate them into normal business

practices. A U.S. power-generating company recently lost a $320 million contract in the Middle East because it refused to pay bribes that a Japanese firm was willing to pay to get the job. Chapter 4 discusses more ways that social, cultural, and legal differences affect international business.

"From a purely business viewpoint, taking what doesn't belong to you is usually the cheapest way to go."

Assessing Ethical Behavior

The following steps set a simplified course for applying ethical judgments to ethically subjective and ambiguous business situations:

1 Gather the relevant factual information.

2 Analyze the facts to determine the most appropriate moral values.

3 Make an ethical judgment based on the rightness or wrongness of the proposed activity or policy.

The process may not work this smoothly, though; facts may not be clear-cut, and moral values may not be agreed upon. Nevertheless, a judgment and a decision must be made in order to maintain trust, an indispensable element in any business transaction.

Consider a complex dilemma faced by managers with expense accounts to cover work-related expenses when they're traveling for business or entertaining clients for business purposes. If a manager takes a client to a $150 dinner, submitting a $150 reimbursement receipt for that dinner is accurate and appropriate. But suppose that this manager has a $150 dinner the next night with a friend for purely social purposes. Submitting that receipt for reimbursement would be unethical. But some employees would disagree, rationalizing that they're underpaid, so submitting this receipt as well is just a means of "recovering" income due to them.

Consider the following ethical *norms*, which Figure 2.1 incorporates into a model of ethical judgment making that can be applied in cases like this:[6]

1 *Utility*. Does a particular act optimize the benefits to those who are affected by it? (That is, do all relevant parties receive equally useful benefits?)

2 *Rights*. Does it respect the rights of all individuals involved?

3 *Justice*. Is it fair?

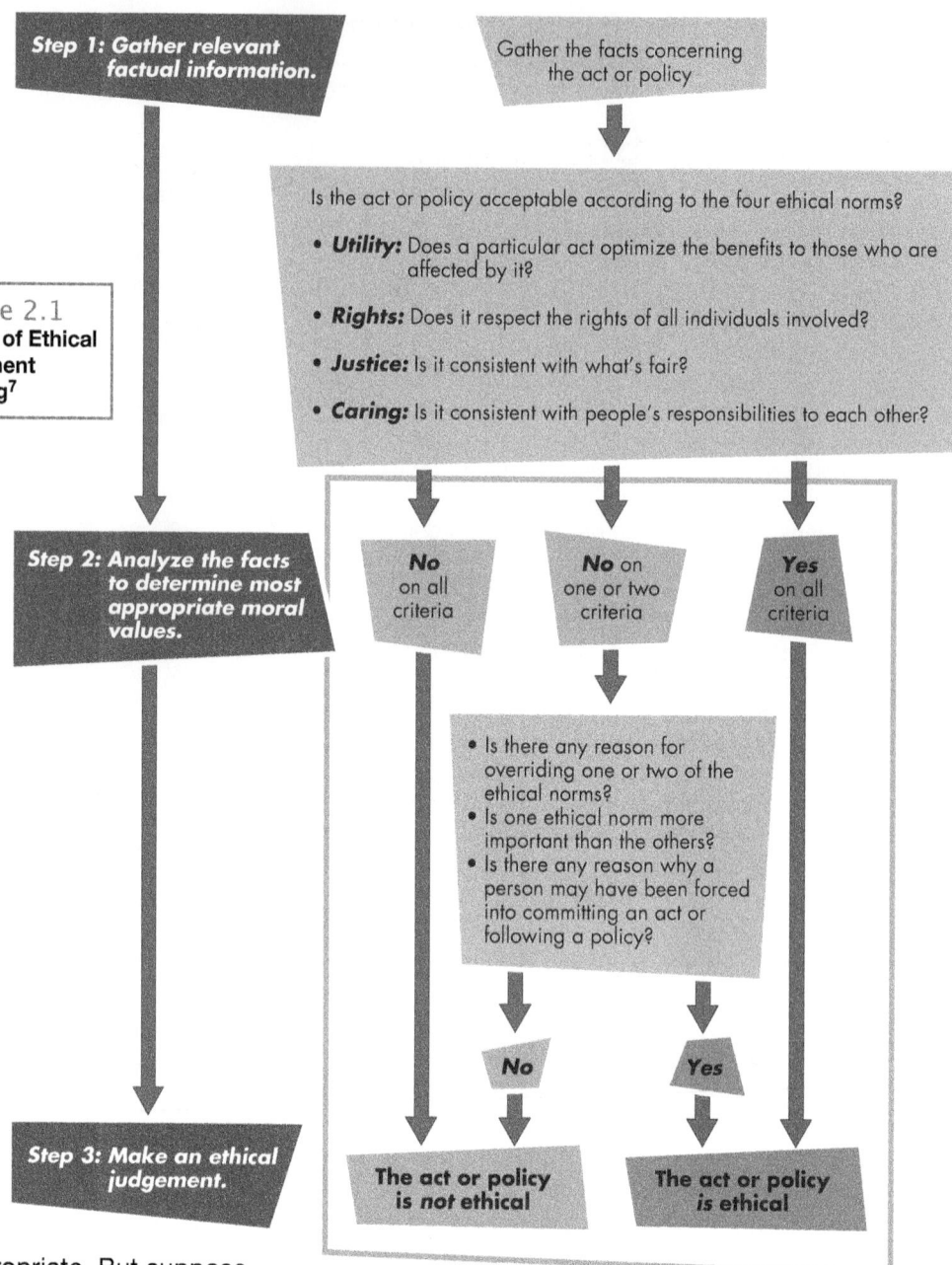

Figure 2.1
Model of Ethical Judgment Making[7]

Step 1: Gather relevant factual information.

Gather the facts concerning the act or policy

Is the act or policy acceptable according to the four ethical norms?

- **Utility:** Does a particular act optimize the benefits to those who are affected by it?
- **Rights:** Does it respect the rights of all individuals involved?
- **Justice:** Is it consistent with what's fair?
- **Caring:** Is it consistent with people's responsibilities to each other?

Step 2: Analyze the facts to determine most appropriate moral values.

No on all criteria

No on one or two criteria

Yes on all criteria

- Is there any reason for overriding one or two of the ethical norms?
- Is one ethical norm more important than the others?
- Is there any reason why a person may have been forced into committing an act or following a policy?

No

Yes

Step 3: Make an ethical judgement.

The act or policy is *not* ethical

The act or policy *is* ethical

4 *Caring*. Is it consistent with people's responsibilities to one another?

While the utility norm acknowledges that the manager benefits from a padded account, others, such as coworkers and owners, don't. Most would also agree that the act doesn't respect the rights of others (such as investors, who have to foot the bill). Moreover, it's clearly unfair and compromises the manager's responsibilities to others. This particular act, then, appears to be clearly unethical.

Figure 2.1, however, also provides mechanisms for dealing with unique circumstances that make ethical issues more or less clear-cut. Suppose, for example, that our manager loses the receipt for the legitimate dinner but retains the receipt for the social dinner. Some will now argue that it's okay to submit the illegitimate receipt because the manager is only doing so to get proper reimbursement. Others, however, will reply that submitting the alternative receipt is wrong under any circumstances.

Company Practices and Business Ethics

To discourage unethical and illegal activities, companies have taken formal steps, such as setting up codes of conduct, developing clear ethical positions, and perhaps most effectively, demonstrating upper-management support of ethical standards. These policies contribute to a corporate culture that values ethical standards and announce that the firm is equally concerned with good citizenship and profits.

Two of the most common approaches to formalizing top management commitment to ethical business practices are *adopting written codes* and *instituting ethics programs*.

Adopting Written Codes   Many companies have written codes that formally announce intent to do business ethically. The number of such companies has risen dramatically in the last three decades, and today almost all major corporations have written codes of ethics. Even Enron had a code of ethics, but managers must follow the code if it's going to work. On one occasion, Enron's board of directors voted to set aside the code in order to complete a deal that would violate it; after the deal was completed, they then voted to reinstate the code!

Instituting Ethics Programs   Many examples suggest that ethical responses can be learned through experience. In the classic 1982 case of a corporate saboteur who poisoned Tylenol capsules and caused the deaths of several consumers, employees at Johnson & Johnson, the maker of Tylenol, didn't wait for instructions or a company directive before informing retailers and pulling the product from shelves. In retrospect, they reported simply knowing that this was what the company would want them to do. Business schools are important players in ethics education, but most analysts agree that companies must take the chief responsibility for educating employees.

More and more firms, like ExxonMobil and Boeing, require managers to go through periodic ethics training

Do No Evil

Although strategies, practices, and objectives can change, an organization's core principles and values should remain steadfast. For example, Google must be flexible enough to adapt its strategies and practices to meet the challenges posed by the rapidly evolving technology industry. Google's core principle is simple: "Don't be evil." Google's code of conduct is built around this idea—ethical responsibility is central to Google's identity, which is especially important for a company that has access to vast amounts of private and sensitive information.

to remind them of the importance of ethical decision making and to update them on current laws and regulations. Others, such as Texas Instruments, have ethics hotlines that employees may call to discuss the ethics of a particular problem or situation or to report unethical behavior or activities by others.

Social Responsibility

While ethics affect individual behavior in the workplace, **social responsibility** refers to the overall way in which a business attempts to balance its commitments to relevant groups and individuals in its social environment. These groups and individuals who are directly affected by the practices of an organization and have a stake in its performance are **organizational stakeholders**.[8]

The Stakeholder Model of Responsibility

Most companies that strive to be responsible to their stakeholders concentrate first and foremost on *customers*, *employees*, *investors*, *suppliers*, and *local communities*. They may then select other stakeholders who are particularly relevant or important to the organization and try to address their needs and expectations as well.

SOCIAL RESPONSIBILITY the attempt of a business to balance its commitments to groups and individuals in its environment, including customers, other businesses, employees, investors, and local communities

ORGANIZATIONAL STAKEHOLDERS those groups, individuals, and organizations that are directly affected by the practices of an organization and who therefore have a stake in its performance

Apple has maintained a strong customer service reputation with features like the Apple Store's "Genius Bar," where Mac specialists answer questions for Mac users.

Entrepreneurship and New Ventures

The Electronic Equivalent of Paper Shredding

In virtually every major corporate scandal of the last few years, the best-laid plans of managerial miscreants have come unraveled, at least in part, when e-mail surfaced as key evidence. For example, Citigroup analyst Jack Grubman changed stock recommendations in exchange for favors from CEO Sandy Weill and confirmed the arrangement via e-mail. Investigators found that David Duncan, Arthur Andersen's head Enron auditor, had deleted incriminating e-mails shortly after the start of the Justice Department's investigation. After Tim Newington, an analyst for Credit Suisse First Boston, refused to give in to pressure to change a client's credit rating, an e-mail circulated on the problem of Newington's troublesome integrity: "Bigger issue," warned an upper manager, "is what to do about Newington in general. I'm not sure he's salvageable at this point."

Many corporations are nervous about the potential liability that employee e-mails may incur. Software developer Omniva Policy Systems saw this concern as an opportunity. Their e-mail software allows users to send encrypted messages, specify an expiration date after which they can no longer be decrypted, and prevent resending or printing. In the event of a lawsuit or investigation, administrators can hit a "red button" that prevents any e-mail from being deleted.

"Our goal," says Omniva CEO Kumar Sreekanti, "is to keep the honest people honest . . . We help organizations comply with regulations automatically so they don't have to rely on people to do it."

E-mails like Jack Grubman's often provide investigators with a smoking gun.

Customers Businesses that are responsible to their customers treat them fairly and honestly, charge fair prices, honor warranties, meet delivery commitments, and stand behind product quality. Apple, Wegmans Food Markets, UPS, and Lexus are among those companies with excellent reputations in this area.[9]

Employees Businesses that are socially responsible in their dealings with employees treat workers fairly, make them part of the team, and respect their dignity and basic human needs. Many of these firms are also committed to hiring and promoting qualified minorities.

Investors A socially responsible stance toward investors means following proper accounting procedures, providing appropriate information about financial performance, and protecting shareholder rights and investments. Accurate and candid assessments of future growth and profitability are also important, as is avoiding even the appearance of impropriety in such sensitive areas as insider trading, stock-price manipulation, and the withholding of financial data.

Suppliers Relations with suppliers should also be managed with care, and firms should recognize the importance of mutually beneficial partnerships.

A large corporation might easily take advantage of suppliers by imposing unrealistic delivery schedules and pushing for lower prices. Instead, it should keep suppliers informed about future plans, negotiate mutually agreeable delivery schedules and prices, and so forth.

Local and International Communities Most businesses try to be socially responsible to local communities by contributing to local programs, getting involved in charities, and minimizing negative impact on communities. Target stores, for example, give over $2 million each week to local neighborhoods, programs, and schools.[10]

Starbucks helps local farmers gain access to credit, works to develop and maintain sustainability of the coffee crop, and is building farmer support centers in Costa Rica, Ethiopia, and Rwanda to provide local farmers with agricultural and technical education and support.[11]

An organization should also recognize international stakeholders. The actions of international businesses affect their suppliers, employees, and customers in multiple countries. International businesses must also address their responsibilities in areas such as wages, working conditions, and environmental protection across different countries with varying regulatory laws and norms.

Contemporary Social Consciousness

Social consciousness and views toward social responsibility have been evolving since entrepreneurs such as John D. Rockefeller, J.P. Morgan, and Cornelius Vanderbilt raised concerns about abuses of power and led to the nation's first laws regulating basic business practices. In the 1930s, many blamed the Great Depression on a climate of business greed and lack of restraint. Out of this economic turmoil emerged new laws that dictated an expanded role for business in protecting and enhancing the general welfare of society, formalizing the concept of *accountability*.

In the 1960s and 1970s, business was again characterized negatively. Some charged that defense contractors had helped promote the Vietnam War to spur their own profits. Eventually, increased social activism prompted increased government regulation that led to changes such as health warnings on cigarette packaging and stricter environmental protection laws.

The general economic prosperity of the 1980s and 1990s led to another period of laissez-faire attitudes toward business. For the most part, business was viewed as a positive force. Many businesses continue to operate in enlightened and socially responsible ways: Wal-Mart and Target have policies against selling weapons, GameStop refuses to sell Mature-rated games to minors, and Anheuser-Busch promotes the concept of responsible drinking in its advertising.

Unfortunately, the recent spate of corporate scandals may revive negative attitudes toward business and result in increased control and constraint of business practices by the government.[12] As just a single illustration, widespread moral

outrage erupted when some of former Tyco CEO Dennis Kozlowski's extravagant perquisites were made public. In addition to the almost $300 million he made between 1998 and 2001 in salary, bonuses, and stock proceeds, his perks included a $50 million Florida mansion, an $18 million New York apartment, $11 million for antiques and furnishings, and a $2.1 million birthday party in Italy for his wife. In 2005, Kozlowski was sentenced to 25 years in prison for misappropriating Tyco funds.[13]

Areas of Social Responsibility

When defining its sense of social responsibility, a firm typically confronts four areas of concern: responsibilities toward the *environment*, *customers*, *employees*, and *investors*.

Responsibility Toward the Environment

The devastating effects of increasing carbon dioxide (Figure 2.2) and other greenhouse gas emissions have begun to reveal themselves in the shrinking Arctic ice cap and the increase in severe weather incidents. With

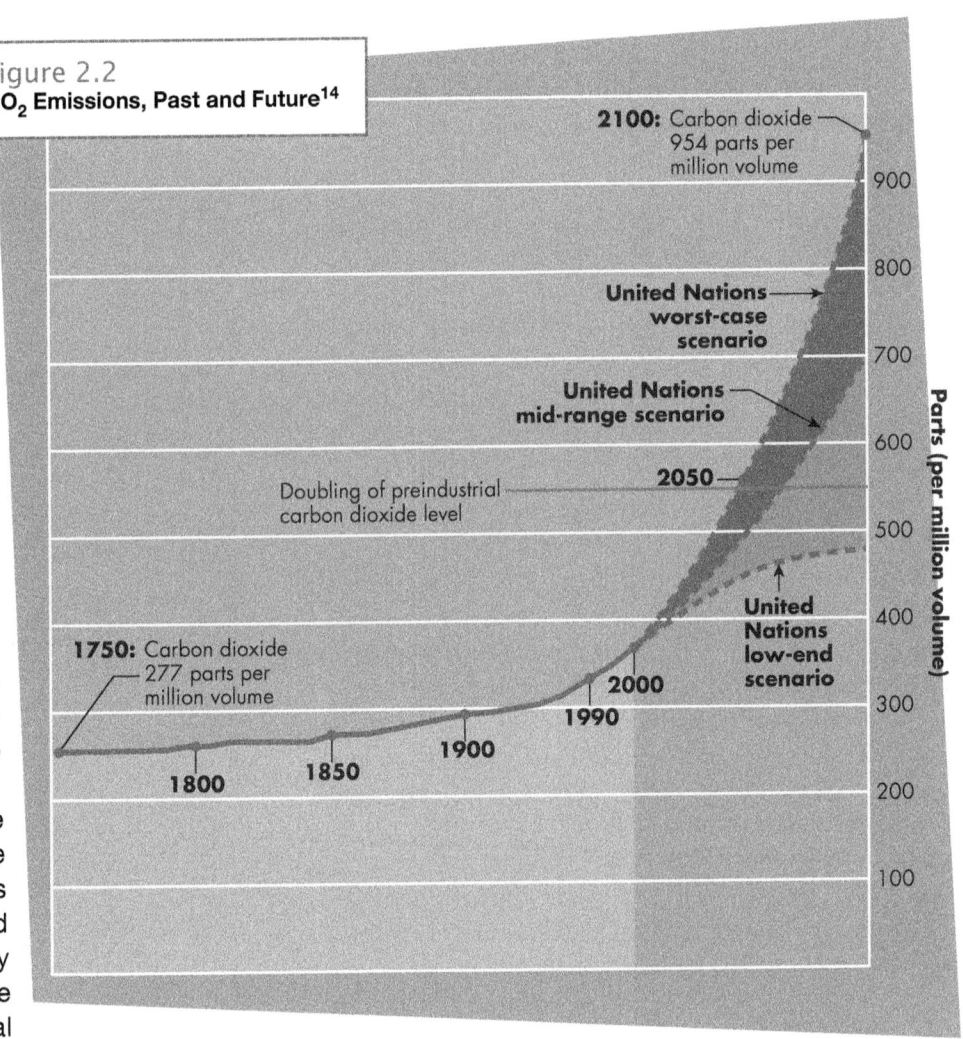

Figure 2.2
CO_2 Emissions, Past and Future[14]

2100: Carbon dioxide 954 parts per million volume

United Nations worst-case scenario

United Nations mid-range scenario

Doubling of preindustrial carbon dioxide level

2050

2000

1990

United Nations low-end scenario

1750: Carbon dioxide 277 parts per million volume

1800 1850 1900

900 800 700 600 500 400 300 200 100

Parts (per million volume)

GREENWASHING using advertising to project a green image without adopting substantive environmentally friendly changes

CONSUMERISM form of social activism dedicated to protecting the rights of consumers in their dealings with businesses

increased attention to global climate change comes pressure on business, both from governments and consumers, to control negative environmental impact.

Many socially responsible companies go beyond what government regulations require. For example, in addition to developing hydrogen fuel technologies, Honda reduced its own CO_2 emissions by five percent between 2000 and 2005 and has pledged to reduce them another five percent by 2010.[15] Although cost concerns have created reluctance to "go green," the opportunity to make money by marketing green products to environmentally conscious consumers is becoming increasingly apparent.

Not all businesses make a sincere effort to adopt green policies and procedures. Some are guilty of **greenwashing**—using advertising to project a green image without adopting substantive environmentally friendly changes. In January 2008, the U.S. Federal Trade Commission (FTC) began a series of hearings to determine the veracity of many green marketing claims. No companies have been censured for false advertising as a result of these hearings, but increased regulation will likely result as the FTC catches up to new trends.[16]

Responsibility Toward Customers

A company that does not act responsibly toward its customers will ultimately lose their trust and their business. To encourage responsibility, the FTC regulates advertising and pricing practices, and the FDA enforces labeling guidelines for food products. These government regulating bodies can impose penalties against violators, who may also face civil litigation. For example, in 2006, the FTC fined the social networking site Xanga $1 million for allowing children under the age of 13 to create accounts in clear violation of the Children's Online Privacy Protection Act.[17]

Consumer Rights Current interest in business responsibility toward customers can be traced to the rise of **consumerism**—social activism dedicated to protecting the rights of consumers in their dealings with businesses. The first formal declaration of consumer rights protection came in the early 1960s when President John F. Kennedy identified four basic consumer rights. Since then, general agreement on two additional rights has emerged; these rights are described in Figure 2.3. The Consumer Bill of Rights is backed by numerous federal and state laws.

Merck provides an instructive example of what can happen to a firm that violates one or more of these

Green marketing (also environmental or ecological marketing)—the marketing of environmentally friendly goods—encompasses a wide variety of business strategies and practices.

- **Production Processes** Businesses, like Ford Motors and General Electric, modify their production processes to limit the consumption of valuable resources like fossil fuels by increasing energy efficiency and reduce their output of waste and pollution by cutting greenhouse gas emissions.

- **Product Modification** Products can be modified to use more environmentally friendly materials, a practice S.C. Johnson encourages with its Greenlist of raw materials classified according to their impact on health and the environment. Committed to only using the safest materials on this list, S.C. Johnson eliminated 1.8 million pounds of volatile organic compounds from its glass cleaner Windex.[18]

- **Carbon Offsets** Many companies are committed to offsetting the CO_2 produced by their products and manufacturing processes. In 2007, Volkswagen began a program of planting trees (which consume CO_2 during photosynthesis) in the so-called VW Forest in the lower Mississippi alluvial valley to offset the CO_2 emissions of every car they sell.[19]

- **Packaging Reduction** Reducing and reusing materials used in packaging products is another important strategy of green marketing, which Starbucks has pioneered. In 2004 the U.S. Food and Drug Administration gave the coffee retailer the first-ever approval to use recycled materials in its food and beverage packaging. Starbucks estimates that using cups composed of 10 percent recycled fibers reduces its packaging waste by more than five million pounds per year.[20]

- **Sustainability** Using renewable resources and managing limited resources responsibly and efficiently are important goals for any business pursuing a green policy. For example, Whole Foods Market is committed to buying food from farmers who use sustainable agriculture practices that protect the environment and agricultural resources, like land and water.

consumer rights. For several years the firm aggressively marketed the painkiller Vioxx, which it was forced to recall in 2004 after clinical trials linked it to an increased risk of heart attacks and strokes. After the recall was announced, it was revealed that Merck had known about

The U.S.-based environmental group Nature Conservancy has recently teamed up with Indonesian logging company Sumalindo Lestari Jaya to help local villagers log a forest in a remote area of Indonesia. Why? The group believes that by working together with the company, it can better enforce sustainable practices.

COLLUSION illegal agreement between two or more companies to commit a wrongful act

GREEN MARKETING the marketing of environmentally friendly goods

these risks as early as 2000 and downplayed them so that they could continue selling it. In 2007, Merck agreed to pay $4.85 billion to individuals or families of those who were injured or died as a result of taking the drug.[21]

Unfair Pricing Interfering with competition can take the form of illegal pricing practices. **Collusion** occurs when two or more firms collaborate on such wrongful acts as price fixing. In 2007, the European airlines Virgin and Lufthansa admitted to colluding with rivals to raise the prices of fuel surcharges on passenger flights as much as 12 times the regular price between August 2004 and January 2006. British Airways and Korean Air Lines were heavily fined, but in exchange for turning them in, Virgin and Lufthansa were not penalized.[22]

Firms can also come under attack for *price gouging*—responding to increased demand with overly steep (and often unwarranted) price increases. For example, during threats of severe weather, people often stock up on bottled water and batteries. Unfortunately, some retailers take advantage of this pattern by marking up prices. Reports were widespread of gasoline retailers doubling or even tripling prices immediately after the events of September 11, 2001, and following the U.S. invasion of Iraq in 2003. Similar problems arose after hurricanes Katrina and Rita damaged oil refineries along the Gulf Coast in late 2005.

Ethics in Advertising In recent years, increased attention has been given to ethics in advertising and product information. Controversy arose when *Newsweek* magazine reported that Sony had literally created a movie critic who happened to be particularly fond of movies released by Sony's Columbia Pictures. When advertising its newest theatrical releases, the studio had been routinely using glowing quotes from a fictitious critic. After the story broke, Sony hastily stopped the practice and apologized.

Another issue concerns advertising that some consumers consider morally objectionable—for products such as underwear, condoms, alcohol, tobacco products, and firearms. Laws regulate some of this advertising (for instance, tobacco can no longer be promoted in television commercials, but can be featured in print ads in magazines), and many advertisers use common sense and discretion in their promotions. But some companies, such as Calvin Klein and Victoria's Secret, have come under fire for being overly explicit in their advertising.

Responsibility Toward Employees

Recruiting, hiring, training, promoting, and compensating are essential human resource

Figure 2.3
Consumer
Bill of Rights

Consumer Bill of Rights

1 Consumers have a right to safe products.

2 Consumers have a right to be informed about all relevant aspects of a product.

3 Consumers have a right to be heard.

4 Consumers have a right to choose what they buy.

5 Consumers have a right to be educated about purchases.

6 Consumers have a right to courteous service.

WHISTLE-BLOWER
employee who detects and tries to put an end to a company's unethical, illegal, or socially irresponsible actions by publicizing them

Because of controversies surrounding the potential misinterpretation of words and phrases, such as *light, reduced calorie, diet*, and *low fat*, food producers are now required to use a standardized format for listing ingredients on product packages.

management activities that provide the basis for social responsibility toward employees.

Legal and Social Commitments   By law, businesses cannot discriminate against people in any facet of the employment relationship. For example, a company cannot refuse to hire someone because of ethnicity or pay someone a lower salary than someone else on the basis of gender. A company that provides its employees with equal opportunities without regard to race, sex, or other irrelevant factors is meeting both its legal and its social responsibilities. Firms that ignore these responsibilities risk losing good employees and leave themselves open to lawsuits.

Most would also agree that an organization should strive to ensure that the workplace is physically and socially safe. Companies with a heightened awareness of social responsibility also recognize an obligation to provide opportunities to balance work and life pressures and preferences, help employees maintain job skills, and, when terminations or layoffs are necessary, treat them with respect and compassion.

Ethical Commitments: The Special Case of Whistle-Blowers
Respecting employees as people also means respecting their behavior as ethical individuals. Ideally, an employee who discovers that a business has been engaging in illegal, unethical, or socially irresponsible practices should be able to report the problem to higher-level management and feel confident that managers will stop the questionable practices. However, if no one in the organization will take action, the employee might elect to drop the matter, or he or she may inform a regulatory agency or the media and become what is known as a **whistle-blower**—an employee who discovers and tries to put an end to a company's unethical, illegal, or socially irresponsible actions by publicizing them.[23]

Enron's Sherron Watkins (right) reported concerns about the company's accounting practices well before the company's problems were made public, warning top management that Enron would "implode in a wave of accounting scandals." CEO Kenneth Lay commissioned a legal review of the firm's finances, but told his investigators not to "second-guess" decisions by Enron's auditor, accounting firm Arthur Andersen.[24]

Unfortunately, whistle-blowers may be demoted, fired, or, if they remain in their jobs, treated with mistrust, resentment, or hostility by coworkers. One recent study suggests that about half of all whistle-blowers eventually get fired, and about half of those who get fired subsequently lose their homes and/or families.[25] The law offers some recourse to employees who take action. The current whistle-blower law stems from the False Claims Act of 1863, which was designed to prevent contractors from selling defective supplies to the Union Army during the Civil War. With 1986 revisions to the law, the government can recover triple damages from fraudulent contractors. If the Justice Department does not intervene, a whistle-blower can proceed with a civil suit. In that case, the whistle-blower receives 25 to 30 percent of any money recovered.[26] Unfortunately, however, the prospect of large cash awards has generated a spate of false or questionable accusations.[27]

Responsibility Toward Investors

Managers can abuse their responsibilities to investors in several ways. As a rule, irresponsible behavior toward shareholders means abuse of a firm's financial resources so that shareholder-owners do not receive their due earnings or dividends. Companies can also act irresponsibly toward shareholder-owners by misrepresenting company resources.

Improper Financial Management
Blatant financial mismanagement—such as paying excessive salaries to senior managers, sending them on extravagant "retreats" to exotic

resorts, and providing frivolous perks—are unethical, but not necessarily illegal. In such situations, creditors and stockholders have few options for recourse. Forcing a management changeover is a difficult process that can drive down stock prices—a penalty that shareholders are usually unwilling to impose on themselves.

Insider Trading   **Insider trading** is using confidential information to gain from the purchase or sale of stocks. Suppose, for example, that a small firm's stock is currently trading at $50 a share. If a larger firm is going to buy the smaller one, it might have to pay as much as $75 a share for a controlling interest. Individuals aware of the impending acquisition before it is publicly announced, such as managers of the two firms or the financial institution making the arrangements, could gain by buying the stock at $50 in anticipation of selling it for $75 after the proposed acquisition is announced.

Informed executives can also avoid financial loss by selling stock that's about to drop in value. Legally, stock can only be sold on the basis of public information available to all investors. Potential violations of this regulation were at the heart of the Martha Stewart scandal. Sam Waksal, president of ImClone, learned that the company's stock was going to drop in value and hastily tried to sell his own stock in 2001. He allegedly tipped off close friend Martha Stewart, who subsequently sold her stock as well. Stewart, who argued that she never received Waksal's call and sold her stock only because she wanted to use the funds elsewhere, eventually pled guilty to other charges (lying to investigators) and served time in prison. Waksal, meanwhile, received a much stiffer sentence because his own attempts to dump his stock were well documented.

Misrepresentation of Finances   In maintaining and reporting its financial status, every corporation must conform to generally accepted accounting principles (GAAP; see Chapter 14). Unethical managers might project profits in excess of what they actually expect to earn, hide losses and/or expenses in order to boost paper profits, or slant financial reports to make the firm seem stronger than is really the case. In 2002, the U.S. Congress passed the *Sarbanes-Oxley Act*, which requires an organization's chief financial officer to personally guarantee the accuracy of all financial reporting (see Chapter 14).

Implementing Social Responsibility Programs

Opinions differ dramatically concerning social responsibility as a business goal. While some oppose any business activity that threatens profits, others argue that social responsibility must take precedence. Some skeptics fear that businesses will gain too much control over the ways social projects are addressed by society as a whole, or that they lack the expertise needed to address social issues. Still, many believe that corporations should help improve the lives of citizens because they are citizens themselves, often control vast resources, and may contribute to the very problems that social programs address.

INSIDER TRADING illegal practice of using special knowledge about a firm for profit or gain

OBSTRUCTIONIST STANCE approach to social responsibility that involves doing as little as possible and may involve attempts to deny or cover up violations

DEFENSIVE STANCE approach to social responsibility by which a company meets only minimum legal requirements in its commitments to groups and individuals in its social environment

Approaches to Social Responsibility

Given these differences of opinion, it is little wonder that corporations have adopted a variety of approaches to social responsibility. As Figure 2.4 illustrates, the four stances that an organization can take concerning its obligations to society fall along a continuum ranging from the lowest to the highest degree of socially responsible practices.

Obstructionist Stance   The few organizations that take an **obstructionist stance** to social responsibility usually do as little as possible to solve social or environmental problems, have little regard for ethical conduct, and will go to great lengths to deny or cover up wrongdoing. For example, IBP, a leading meat-processing firm, has a long record of breaking environmental protection, labor, and food processing laws and then trying to cover up its offenses.

Defensive Stance   Organizations who take a **defensive stance** will do everything that is legally required, including admitting to mistakes and taking corrective actions, but nothing more. Defensive stance managers insist that their job is to generate profits and might, for example, install pollution-control equipment dictated by law but not higher-quality equipment to further limit pollution.

Tobacco companies generally take this position in their marketing efforts. In the United States, they are legally required to include product warnings and to limit advertising to prescribed media. Domestically, they follow these rules to the letter of the law, but in many Asian and African countries, which don't have these rules, cigarettes are heavily promoted, contain higher levels of tar and nicotine, and carry few or no health warning labels.

ACCOMMODATIVE STANCE approach to social responsibility by which a company, if specifically asked to do so, exceeds legal minimums in its commitments to groups and individuals in its social environment

PROACTIVE STANCE approach to social responsibility by which a company actively seeks opportunities to contribute to the well-being of groups and individuals in its social environment

SOCIAL AUDIT systematic analysis of a firm's success in using funds earmarked for meeting its social responsibility goals

Figure 2.4
Spectrum of Approaches to Corporate Social Responsibility

| Obstructionist Stance | Defensive Stance | Accommodative Stance | Proactive Stance |

LOWEST LEVEL OF SOCIAL RESPONSIBILITY

HIGHEST LEVEL OF SOCIAL RESPONSIBILITY

Accommodative Stance A firm that adopts an **accommodative stance** meets and, in certain cases exceeds, its legal and ethical requirements. Such firms will agree to participate in social programs if solicitors convince them that given programs are worthy of their support. Both Shell and IBM, for example, will match contributions made by their employees to selected charitable causes.

Proactive Stance Firms with the highest degree of social responsibility exhibit the **proactive stance**; they take to heart the arguments in favor of social responsibility, view themselves as citizens in a society, indicate sincere commitment to improve the general social welfare, and surpass the accommodative stance by proactively seeking opportunities to contribute. The most common—and direct—way to implement this stance is to set up a foundation for providing direct financial support for various social programs. An excellent example of a proactive stance is the McDonald's Corporation's Ronald McDonald House program. These houses, located close to major medical centers, can be used for minimal cost

by families while their sick children are receiving medical treatment nearby.

However, these categories are not sharply distinct: Organizations do not always fit neatly into one category or another. The Ronald McDonald House program has been widely applauded, but McDonald's has also been accused of misleading consumers about the nutritional value of its food products.

Managing Social Responsibility Programs

A full commitment to social responsibility requires a carefully organized and managed program and managers who take steps to foster a companywide sense of social responsibility:[29]

1 *Social responsibility must start at the top and be considered a factor in strategic planning.* No program can succeed without the support of top management, who must embrace a strong stand on social responsibility and develop a policy statement outlining that commitment.

2 *A committee of top managers must develop a plan detailing the level of management support.* Companies may set aside percentages of profits for social programs or set specific priorities, such as supporting the arts.

Table 2.1 **Top 10 Corporate Foundations**[28]

Foundation	State	Total Giving (In U.S. Dollars)	Fiscal Date
1 Aventis Pharmaceuticals Health Care Foundation	NJ	217,845,821	12/31/05
2 Wal-Mart Foundation	AR	155,073,614	1/31/06
3 The Bank of America Charitable Foundation, Inc.	NC	123,287,819	12/31/05
4 The JPMorgan Chase Foundation	MI	85,458,083	12/31/05
5 Citigroup Foundation	CA	80,764,000	12/31/05
6 Ford Motor Company Fund	TX	79,881,090	12/31/05
7 GE Foundation	NY	70,635,496	12/31/05
8 The Wells Fargo Foundation	NJ	65,007,124	12/31/05
9 ExxonMobil Foundation	NY	63,660,965	12/31/05
10 Verizon Foundation	CT	61,834,820	12/31/05

3 *One executive must be put in charge of the firm's agenda.* Whether a separate job or part of an existing one, the selected individual must monitor the program and ensure implementation consistent with the firm's policy statement and strategic plan.

4 *The organization must conduct occasional* **social audits**—*systematic analyses of its success in using funds earmarked for its social responsibility goals.* Consider the case of a company whose strategic plan calls for spending $200,000 to train 300 unemployed people and to place 275 of them in jobs. If, at the end of a year, the firm has spent $198,000, trained 305 people, and filled 270 jobs, a social audit will confirm the program's success. But if the program has cost $350,000, trained only 190 people, and placed only 40 of them, the audit will reveal the program's failure. Such failure should prompt a rethinking of the program's implementation and its priorities.

Social Responsibility and the Small Business

Small-businesses owners are faced with similar ethical questions, although they may largely be a question of individual ethics. As the owner of a garden supply store, how would you respond to a building inspector's suggestion that a cash payment will speed your building permit application? As a liquor store manager, would you sell alcohol to a customer whose identification card looks forged? As the owner of a small laboratory, would you verify the license of your medical waste disposal company? Who will really be harmed if you pad your small firm's income statement to get a much-needed bank loan?

What about questions of social responsibility? Can your small business afford a social agenda? Should you sponsor Little League teams and donate to the United Way? Do joining the chamber of commerce and supporting the Better Business Bureau cost too much? Clearly, all managers in all organizations have to make decisions about ethics and social responsibility. One key to business success is to decide in advance how to respond to the issues that underlie all questions of ethical and social responsibility.

Questions for Review

1 What basic factors should be considered in any ethical decision?

2 Who are an organization's stakeholders? Who are the major stakeholders with which most businesses must be concerned?

3 What are the major areas of social responsibility with which businesses should be concerned?

4 What are the four basic approaches to social responsibility?

5 In what ways do you think your personal code of ethics might clash with the operations of some companies? How might you try to resolve these differences?

Questions for Analysis

6 What kind of wrongdoing would most likely prompt you to be a whistle-blower? What kind of wrongdoing would least likely cause you to blow the whistle? Why?

7 In your opinion, which area of social responsibility is most important? Why? Are there areas other than those noted in the chapter that you consider important?

8 Identify some specific ethical or social responsibility issues that might be faced by small-business managers and employees in each of the following areas: environment, customers, employees, and investors.

Application Exercises

9 Develop a list of the major stakeholders of your college or university. How do you think the school prioritizes these stakeholders? Do you agree or disagree with this prioritization?

10 Using newspapers, magazines, and other business references, identify and describe at least three companies that take a defensive stance to social responsibility, three that take an accommodative stance, and three that take a proactive stance.

3

chapter

Entrepreneurship, New Ventures, and Business Ownership

After reading this chapter, you should be able to:

1 Define *small business*, discuss its importance to the U.S. economy, and explain popular areas of small business.

2 Explain entrepreneurship and describe some key characteristics of entrepreneurial personalities and activities.

3 Describe the business plan and the start-up decisions made by small businesses and identify sources of financial aid available to such enterprises.

4 Discuss the trends in small business start-ups and identify the main reasons for success and failure among small businesses.

5 Explain sole proprietorships, partnerships, and cooperatives and discuss the advantages and disadvantages of each.

6 Describe corporations, discuss their advantages and disadvantages, and identify different kinds of corporations.

7 Explain the basic issues involved in managing a corporation and discuss special issues related to corporate ownership.

Harvard Dropout Turned Billionaire

In 2004, Mark Zuckerberg created the Web site Facebook for his Harvard classmates. Just a few years later, the social networking site had not only expanded beyond the Harvard campus, it had close to 40 million active users. By 2008, Zuckerberg was widely thought to be the richest person in the world under the age of 25, with a net worth of over $1.5 billion, all due to Facebook's success.

Zuckerberg's vision goes beyond a simple student directory. Facebook, which was made available to anyone with a valid e-mail address in 2006, allows users to re-create their network of social relationships online and facilitates their streamlined communication by, for example, sending newsfeed-style bulletins to everyone in a person's network whenever they make a change to their page, such as adding a friend or uploading a photograph. This feature caused privacy concerns and wasn't very popular when first introduced. But Zuckerberg listened to users, admitted he could have handled the launch better, and provided opt-out options. Now News Feed is one of Facebook's most popular features, and the service's ability to create instant word-of-mouth buzz among networks of friends has attracted software developers and advertisers. In fact, the site has done so well that it's attracted the attention of big-name corporations. Viacom and Yahoo have both expressed interest in buying Facebook, offering as much as $1 billion. But at this point, Zuckerberg isn't selling.

It takes more than a good idea to become the richest 24-year-old in the world, however. Zuckerberg worked long hours and even dropped out of Harvard to make his vision for Facebook a reality. Flexibility has also been important in allowing him to tailor the site to suit its always-expanding audience. Zuckerberg has also had to learn managerial skills on the job, but his willingness to make and learn from mistakes has served him well and helped Zuckerberg make Facebook the second-most popular social networking site in the world.[1]

What's in It for Me?

Zuckerberg displayed many of the characteristics key to entrepreneurial success. This chapter will discuss these and additional elements important for starting and owning a business, including the business plan, reasons for success and failure, and the advantages and disadvantages of different kinds of ownership. First, we'll start by defining a small business and identifying its importance in the U.S. economy.

SMALL BUSINESS ADMINISTRATION (SBA) government agency charged with assisting small businesses

SMALL BUSINESS independently owned business that has relatively little influence in its market

What Is a "Small" Business?

Locally owned and operated restaurants, dry cleaners, and hair salons are obviously small businesses, and giant corporations, such as Dell, Starbucks, and Best Buy, are clearly big businesses. But between these extremes fall thousands of companies that cannot be easily categorized.

The U.S. Department of Commerce and the **Small Business Administration (SBA)**, a government agency that assists small businesses, define the size of a business based on its industry and number of employees. According to SBA standards, a small business can have as many as 1,500 employees. Because strict numerical terms sometimes lead to contradictory classifications, we will consider a **small business** to be an independent (that is, not part of a larger business) business with relatively little influence in its market. A neighborhood grocer would be small, assuming it is not part of a chain and that the prices it pays to wholesalers and charges its customers are largely set by market forces. Dell was a small business when founded by Michael Dell in 1984, but today it's number one in the personal computer market and by no means small. Hence, it can negotiate from a position of strength with its suppliers and can set its prices with less consideration for what others are charging.

Dell-ivering Innovation

Innovations are not always new products. Michael Dell didn't invent the PC; he developed an innovative way to build it (buy finished components and then assemble them) and an innovative way to sell it (directly to consumers, first by telephone and now via the Internet). Today, small businesses produce 13 times as many patents per employee as large patenting firms.[2]

The Importance of Small Business in the U.S. Economy

As Figure 3.1 shows, most U.S. businesses employ fewer than 100 people, and most U.S. workers are employed by small firms. The contribution of small business can be measured in terms of *job creation*, *innovation*, and *contributions to big business*.

Job Creation Small businesses are an important source of new (and often well-paid) jobs. In recent years, small businesses have accounted for 40 percent of all new jobs in high-technology sectors.[3] Small firms often hire at a faster rate than big firms and are generally the first to hire in times of economic recovery. However, they also tend to cut jobs at a higher rate than big firms, which are generally the last to lay off workers during downswings.

Innovation Major innovations are as likely to come from small businesses (or individuals) as from big ones. Small firms and individuals invented the personal

More than 89 percent of all U.S. businesses have **no more than 20 employees**. The total number of people employed by these businesses is approximately one-fourth of the entire U.S. workforce. Another 29 percent work for companies with **fewer than 100 employees**.

(a) Percentage of All U.S. Businesses by Total Employees: Under 20: 89.02; 20–99: 9.16; 100–499: 1.50; 500–999: .15; 1000 or more: .22

(b) Percentage of All U.S. Workers by Total Employees: Under 20: 25.60; 20–99: 29.10; 100–499: 25.50; 500–999: 7.10; 1000 or more: 12.70

Figure 3.1
The Importance of Small Business in the United States[4]

computer, the stainless-steel razor blade, the photocopier, the jet engine, and the self-developing photograph.

Contributions to Big Business Most of the products made by big businesses are sold to consumers by small businesses. For example, most dealerships that sell Fords, Toyotas, and Volvos are independently operated. Even as more shoppers turn to the Internet, many larger online retailers outsource the creation of their Web sites and the distribution of their products to small or regional firms. Smaller businesses also provide data-storage services, as well as other services and raw materials, for larger businesses. Microsoft, for instance, relies on hundreds of small firms to write most of its code.

Popular Areas of Small-Business Enterprise

Small businesses play a major role in services, retailing, construction, wholesaling, finance and insurance, manufacturing, and transportation. Generally, the more resources required, the harder a business is to start and the less likely an industry is dominated by small firms. Remember, too, that small is a relative term. The criteria (number of employees and total annual sales) differ among industries and are often meaningful only when compared with truly large businesses. Figure 3.2 shows the distribution of all U.S. businesses employing fewer than 20 people across industry groups.

Services About 50 percent of businesses with fewer than 20 employees are involved in the service industry, which ranges from marriage counseling to computer software, from management consulting to professional dog walking. Partly because they require few

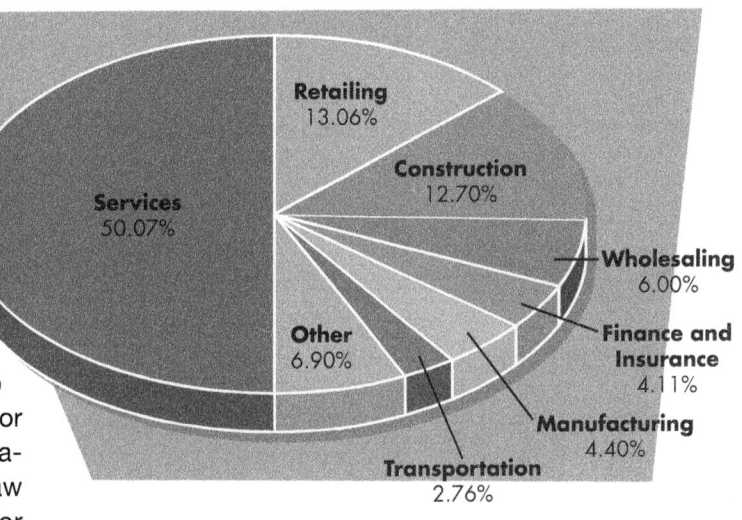

Figure 3.2
Small Business by Industry[5]

Services 50.07%
Retailing 13.06%
Construction 12.70%
Wholesaling 6.00%
Finance and Insurance 4.11%
Manufacturing 4.40%
Transportation 2.76%
Other 6.90%

resources, service providers are the fastest-growing segment of small business.

Retailing Retailers, which sell products made by other firms directly to consumers, account for about 13 percent of these firms. Usually, people who start small retail businesses favor specialty shops—big men's clothing or gourmet coffees—that let them focus limited resources on narrow market segments.

Construction About 13 percent are involved in construction. Because many construction jobs are small local projects, like a homeowner adding a garage or remodeling a room, local contractors are often best suited to handle them.

Wholesaling Small-business owners often do well in wholesaling, which accounts for about 6 percent of businesses with fewer than 20 employees. Wholesalers buy products in bulk from manufacturers or other producers and store them in quantities and locations convenient for selling them to retailers.

Finance and Insurance Financial and insurance firms account for about 4 percent. Most of these businesses, such as local State Farm Insurance offices, are affiliates of or agents for larger national firms.

Manufacturing More than any other industry, manufacturing lends itself to big business, but it still accounts for about 4 percent of firms with fewer than 20 employees. Indeed, small manufacturers sometimes outperform big ones in such innovation-driven industries as electronics, toys, and computer software.

There are many areas in which small businesses excel. This enterprising entrepreneur, for example, has a lucrative business as a dog walker. A small business is much more likely than a large business to succeed in such a venture.

ENTREPRENEUR businessperson who accepts both the risks and the opportunities involved in creating and operating a new business venture

ENTREPRENEURSHIP the process of seeking business opportunities under conditions of risk

Transportation About 3 percent of these small companies are in transportation and related businesses, including many taxi and limousine companies, charter airplane services, and tour operators.

Other The remaining 7 percent or so are in other industries, such as small research-and-development laboratories and independent media companies, like small-town newspapers and radio broadcasters.

Entrepreneurship

Entrepreneurs are people who assume the risk of business ownership. **Entrepreneurship** is the process of seeking business opportunities under conditions of risk. However, not all entrepreneurs have the same goals.

Many entrepreneurs are driven to launch new businesses by the goal of gaining independence from working for someone else and securing a financial future for themselves, but they may not aspire to grow their businesses beyond their capacities to run them. Consider Jack Matz, who opened a photocopy and print service business after losing his job as a corporate executive when his firm merged with another. His goal is to earn enough money to lead a comfortable life until he retires. The term *small business* is most closely associated with these kinds of enterprises.

Others strive to grow and expand their ventures into large businesses. Terms such as *new ventures* and *start-ups* are often used to refer to these kinds of businesses.

In some cases, an entrepreneur's goals may not always be clear in the early stages of business development. For instance, the founders of Google had no idea that their firm would grow to its present size. Others might start out with ambitious growth plans, but find that expected opportunities cannot be realized.

Entrepreneurial Characteristics

Many successful entrepreneurs share certain characteristics: resourcefulness, a concern for good customer relations, the ability to deal with uncertainty and risk, a desire to be their own bosses, to have greater control over their lives, and to build for their families.

Yesterday's entrepreneur was often stereotyped as "the boss"—self-reliant, male, and able to make quick,

---

Say What You Mean

The Wide World of Risk

Globalization and the expanded reach and power of multinational companies require corporations to innovate, grow, and adapt to new markets and economic circumstances. In a highly interconnected world, it's often hard to figure out the complex ownership and organizational structures of many global corporations. Branding strategies and management structures may lead people to think that companies are local when, in fact, the real source of corporate power may lie thousands of miles away. One thing's for sure: if you're going to be dealing with a company overseas, you'd better have a good idea of where and how decisions are made, and who has the real power to make them.

Remember, too, that different cultures have different attitudes when it comes to entrepreneurship. Some countries and cultures, like that of the United States, promote a lively entrepreneurial spirit. Businesspeople are open to taking risks, and if they fail, they tend to pick themselves up and move on to something else. In some Asian countries, the entrepreneurial spirit is often tempered by the need for consensus. This approach requires a lot of patience and the ability to compromise. Knowing the cultural forces that shape both a business organization and people's attitudes toward risk, success, and failure is an elementary but important component of international business.

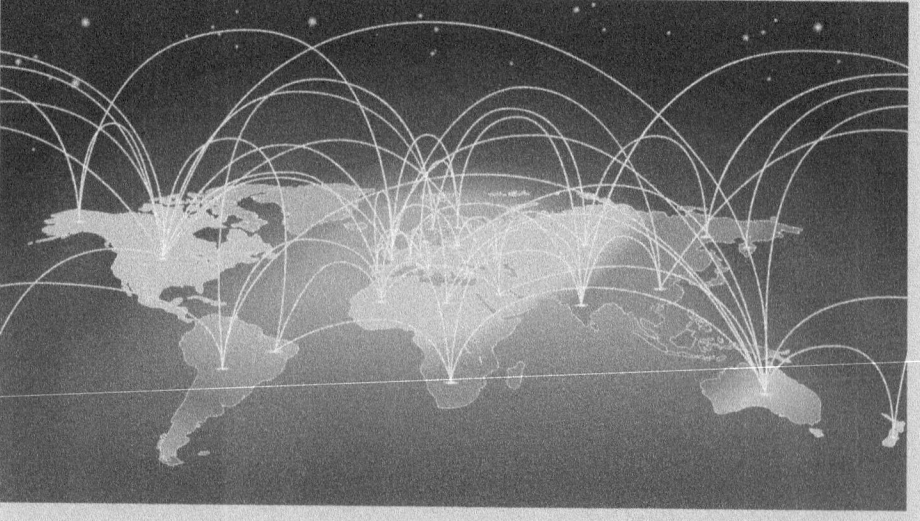

firm decisions. Today's entrepreneur is seen more often as an open-minded leader, just as likely to be male or female, who relies on networks, business plans, and consensus. Past and present entrepreneurs also have different views on such topics as how to succeed, how to automate business, and when to rely on experience in the trade or on basic business acumen.[6]

Consider Yoshiko Shinohara, who had lost her father by the age of 8, was divorced by the age of 28, and never received a college education. At the age of 70, she is president of Tempstaff, a Japanese temp agency that she started out of her one-room apartment more than 30 years ago. Fueled by Japan's need for temps during a period of stagnation in the 1990s and Shinohara's ambition, Tempstaff is now a $1.5 billion company with a high-rise headquarters in Tokyo.[7]

Among other things, Shinohara's story illustrates what is almost always a key element in entrepreneurship: risk. Interestingly, most successful entrepreneurs seldom see what they do as risky. Whereas others may focus on possibilities for failure and balk at gambling everything on a new venture, most entrepreneurs are so passionate about their ideas and plans that they see little or no likelihood of failure. For example, when Shinohara started Tempstaff, few Japanese businesses understood or had even heard of the temporary-worker concept. But Shinohara felt that she "had nothing to lose anyway" and preferred taking that risk to ending up "serving tea or just being a clerical assistant."[8]

Starting and Operating a New Business

Now more than ever, the Internet has made setting up a small business easier and faster, has created more potential opportunities, and has heightened the ability to gather and assess information. Would-be entrepreneurs must still decide whether to buy an existing business or build from the ground up and must know when to seek expert advice and where to find financing.

Crafting a Business Plan

Before investing time and money, the starting point for virtually every new entrepreneur is a **business plan** in which the entrepreneur thoroughly develops and describes her or his business strategy and demonstrates how it will be implemented.[9]

Setting Goals and Objectives   A business plan describes the match between the entrepreneur's abilities and experiences and the requirements for producing and/or marketing a particular product. It defines strategies for production and marketing, legal elements and organization, and accounting and finance. It should specifically answer three questions: (1) What are the entrepreneur's goals and objectives? (2) What strategies will be used to obtain them? (3) How will these strategies be implemented?

> **BUSINESS PLAN** document in which an entrepreneur summarizes her or his business strategy for a proposed new venture and how that strategy will be implemented

Sales Forecasting   Sales forecasts must be based on sound logic and research and demonstrate an understanding of the current market, the strengths and weaknesses of existing firms, and the means by which the new venture will compete. For example, simply asserting that the new venture will sell 100,000 units per month is not credible.

Financial Planning   Financial planning refers to the entrepreneur's plan for turning all other activities into dollars. It generally includes an income statement, balance sheets, a breakeven chart, and a cash budget, which shows how much money is needed before the business opens and how much is needed to keep the business going before it starts earning a profit.[10]

Starting a Small Business
The first step to starting a new business is the individual's commitment to becoming a business owner. In preparing their business plans, entrepreneurs must come to understand the nature of the enterprises in which they are engaged.

"Eventually I'd like to have a business where the money rolls in and I wouldn't have to be there much."

FRANCHISE arrangement in which a buyer (franchisee) purchases the right to sell the good or service of the seller (franchiser)

Buying an Existing Business
Next, the entrepreneur must decide whether to buy an existing business or start from scratch. Because the odds are better, many experts recommend the first approach. If successful, an existing business has already proven its ability to attract customers and generate profit and has established relationships with lenders, suppliers, and other stakeholders. Moreover, potential buyers will have a much clearer picture of what to expect than any estimate of a start-up's prospects. For example, Ray Kroc bought McDonald's as an existing business, added entrepreneurial vision and business insight, and produced a multinational giant.

Franchising   Most Subway, 7-Eleven, RE/MAX, and Blockbuster outlets are franchises operating under licenses issued by parent companies to local owners. A **franchise** agreement involves two parties, a *franchisee* (the local owner) and a *franchiser* (the parent company).

Franchisees benefit from the parent corporation's experience and expertise. The franchiser may pick the store location, negotiate the lease, purchase equipment, and supply financing. Franchises offer the benefit of brand recognition, which can make it easier to attract customers and reduce the costs of advertising as well as increase the likelihood of success.

Perhaps the most significant disadvantage in owning a franchise is the start-up cost, which varies widely. The fee for a Curves fitness center is between $31,400 and $53,500, but a McDonald's franchise costs $506,000 to $1.6 million,[11] and professional sports teams cost an average of $957 million dollars.[12] Franchisees may also be obligated to contribute a percentage of sales to parent corporations. From the perspective of the parent company, some firms, such as Starbucks, choose not to franchise in order to retain more control over quality and earn more profits for themselves.

Starting from Scratch   Despite the odds, some people seek the satisfaction that comes from planting an idea and growing it into a healthy business. A new business

Entrepreneurs must study markets and answer the following questions:
- Who and where are my customers?
- How much will those customers pay for my product?
- How much of my product can I expect to sell?
- Who are my competitors?
- Why will customers buy my product rather than the product of my competitors?

The ability of an entrepreneur to obtain adequate financing is a critical component in the potential success of a new venture. Many entrepreneurs rely on SBA financial programs, venture capital companies, or small-business investment companies to launch their businesses.

doesn't suffer the ill effects of a prior owner's errors, and the start-up owner is free to make all the choices. Of all new businesses begun in the past decade, 64 percent were started from scratch. Dell, Wal-Mart, and Microsoft are among today's most successful businesses that were started from scratch by entrepreneurs.

However, new-business founders can only make projections about their prospects. Success or failure depends on identifying a genuine opportunity, such as a product for which many customers will pay well but which is currently unavailable.

Financing a Small Business

Although the choice of how to start a business is obviously important, it's meaningless without money. According to the National Federation of Independent Business, personal resources, including savings and money borrowed from friends and relatives, account for over two-thirds of all money invested in new small businesses, and one-half of that is used to purchase existing businesses. Getting money from banks, independent investors, and government agencies requires extra effort, like formulating business plans and meeting eligibility requirements. Moreover, lending institutions are more likely to help finance the purchase of an existing established business than a brand-new one.

Other Sources of Investment **Venture capital companies** are groups of small investors seeking to make profits on companies with rapid growth potential. Most of these firms do not lend money to start new businesses; they supply capital to fuel expansion of an existing firm in return for partial ownership, representation on boards of directors, and final approval of major decisions.

Small-business investment companies (SBICs) are federally licensed to borrow money from the SBA and to invest in or lend to small businesses with potential for rapid growth. Past beneficiaries of SBIC capital include Apple Computer, Intel, and FedEx. The government also sponsors *minority enterprise small-business investment companies (MESBICs)*, which target minority-owned businesses.

SBA Financial Programs Since its founding in 1953, the SBA has sponsored financing programs for small businesses that meet standards of size and independence and are unable to get private financing at reasonable terms. The most common form of SBA financing, its *7(a) loans programs*, allows small businesses to borrow from commercial lenders and guarantees to repay a maximum of 75 percent. The SBA's *special purpose loans* target businesses with specific needs, such as meeting international demands or implementing pollution-control measures. For loans under $35,000, the SBA offers the *micro-loan program*. The *Certified Development Company (504) program* offers fixed interest rates on loans from nonprofit community-based lenders to boost local economies.[13]

Other SBA Programs The SBA also helps entrepreneurs improve their management skills. The Service Corps of Retired Executives (SCORE) is made up of retired executives who volunteer to help entrepreneurs start new businesses. The **Small Business Development Center (SBDC)** program consolidates information from various disciplines and institutions for use by new and existing small businesses.

Trends, Successes, and Failures in New Ventures

• •

For every Sam Walton, Russell Simmons, Donald Trump, or Steve Jobs—entrepreneurs who transformed small businesses into big ones—there are many who fail. Each year, between 600,000 and 650,000 new businesses are launched in the United States, and between 500,000 and 600,000 fail.[14] In this section, we will

look at a few key trends in small-business start-ups and examine some of the reasons for their success and failure.

Trends in Small-Business Start-Ups

As noted previously, thousands of new businesses are started in the United States every year. Several factors account for this trend, and in this section, we focus on five of them.

Emergence of E-Commerce The most significant recent trend is the rapid emergence of electronic commerce. Because the Internet provides fundamentally new ways of doing business, savvy entrepreneurs have created and expanded new businesses faster and easier than ever before. Figure 3.3 underscores this point by summarizing the growth in online retail spending from 2003 through 2007.

Crossovers from Big Business More businesses are being started by people who have opted to leave big corporations and put their experience to work for themselves.[16] John Chambers spent several years working at IBM and Wang Laboratories/Wang Global before he signed on to help Cisco, then a small and struggling firm. Under his leadership and entrepreneurial guidance, Cisco has become one of the largest and most important technology companies in the world.

Opportunities for Minorities and Women More small businesses are also being started by minorities and women.[17] The number of businesses owned by African Americans increased by 48 percent during the most recent five-year period for which data are available and now totals about 1.2 million. The number of Hispanic-owned businesses has grown 31 percent and now totals about 1.6 million. Ownership among Asians has increased 24 percent and among Pacific Islanders 64 percent.[18]

Nearly 11 million businesses are now owned by women. Together, they generate a combined $2.5 trillion in revenue a year and employ 19 million workers.[19] Figure 3.4 shows some of the reasons women cite for starting their own businesses.

VENTURE CAPITAL COMPANY group of small investors who invest money in companies with rapid growth potential

SMALL-BUSINESS INVESTMENT COMPANY (SBIC) government-regulated investment company that borrows money from the SBA to invest in or lend to a small business

SMALL BUSINESS DEVELOPMENT CENTER (SBDC) SBA program designed to consolidate information from various disciplines and make it available to small businesses

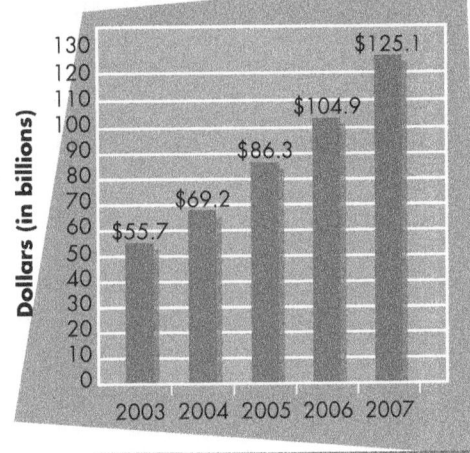

Figure 3.3
Growth of Online Retail Spending[15]

$55.7 $69.2 $86.3 $104.9 $125.1
2003 2004 2005 2006 2007
Dollars (in billions)

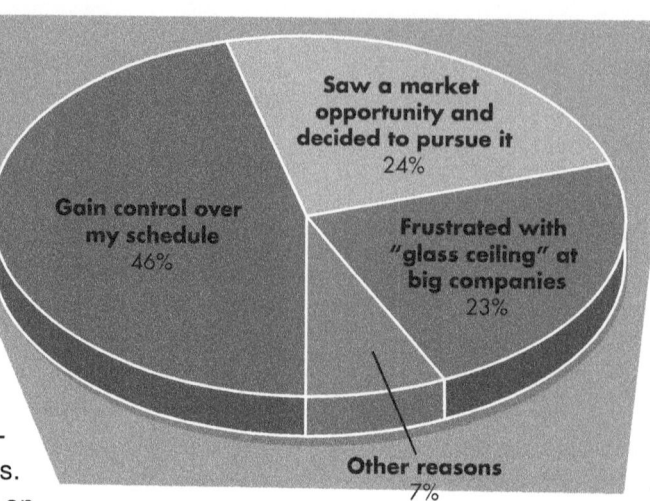

Figure 3.4
Reasons Women Give for Starting Businesses[20]

- Gain control over my schedule — 46%
- Saw a market opportunity and decided to pursue it — 24%
- Frustrated with "glass ceiling" at big companies — 23%
- Other reasons — 7%

Global Opportunities

Many entrepreneurs are also finding new opportunities in foreign markets. Doug Mellinger, founder and CEO of PRT Group, a software development company, had trouble finding trained programmers in the United States. So Mellinger set up shop on Barbados, where the government helps him attract foreign programmers. Today, PRT has customers and suppliers from dozens of nations.

Better Survival Rates

More people are encouraged to test their skills as entrepreneurs because the small-business failure rate has declined. During the 1960s and 1970s, fewer than half of all new start-ups survived more than 18 months; only one in five lasted 10 years. Now, however, 44 percent can expect to survive for at least four years.[21]

Reasons for Failure

Unfortunately, over half of all new businesses will not enjoy long-term success. Although no set pattern is a reliable predictor, four general factors contribute to failure:

1 *Managerial incompetence or inexperience.* Some entrepreneurs put too much faith in common sense, overestimate their own managerial skills, or believe that hard work alone ensures success. Success will likely elude managers who don't know how to make basic business decisions or understand basic management principles.

2 *Neglect.* Starting a small business demands an overwhelming commitment of time and effort. Owners aren't likely to see success if they try to launch ventures in their spare time or devote only limited time to new businesses.

3 *Weak control systems.* Effective control systems keep a business on track and alert managers to potential problems before they become serious. For instance, some businesses fail because they do a poor job of managing their credit-collection policies—anxious to grow, they may be too liberal in extending credit to their customers and then end up not being able to collect all the money that is owed to them.

4 *Insufficient capital.* Some entrepreneurs are overly optimistic about how soon they'll start earning profits. In most cases, it takes months or even years. Amazon.com didn't earn a profit for 10 years but obviously still required capital to pay employees and to cover other expenses. Experts say you need

---

Entrepreneurship and New Ventures

The Road to Recovery

A homeless heroin addict at 24, Bob Williamson never would have expected a car accident to be the luckiest thing that ever happened to him. While recovering, he decided it was time to turn his life around. Although he may not have seemed the ideal hire, Williamson already had a work ethic that would carry him to his current position as CEO of Horizon Software International: "First one in, last to leave."

He lived by this code even when his job was just putting labels on paint cans in the basement at Glidden, which ended up promoting him eight times in two years. After working for two other paint companies, Williamson had the know-how to create a new formula for his

airbrushing hobby. His formula was a hit, and he started his own company, which he spun out into several others. Williamson overcame hard times again when he nearly faced bankruptcy after discovering his accountant was embezzling money.

But luck wasn't far behind him. Williamson started Horizon using the software that he just so happened to be writing as the software industry was about to boom. Once Williamson realized the value of his software, he rode that opportunity wherever it took him, and soon the company was selling the software to colleges, military bases, and hospitals. Now a 61-year-old CEO, Williamson is still "first one in, last to leave."[22]

---

enough capital to operate at least six months to a year without earning a profit.[23]

Reasons for Success

Four basic factors are also typically cited to explain small-business success:

1 *Hard work, drive, and dedication.* Small-business owners must be committed to succeeding and willing to spend the time and effort to make it happen. When Gladys Edmunds, a single mother in Pittsburgh, wanted to open a travel agency, she washed laundry, made chicken dinners to sell to cab drivers, and sold fire extinguishers door to door to earn start-up money. Today, Edmunds Travel Consultants earns about $6 million a year.[24]

2 *Market demand for the products or services being provided.* Careful analysis of market conditions can help small-business owners assess the probable reception of their products. Attempts to expand restaurants specializing in baked potatoes, muffins, and gelato have largely failed, but hamburger and pizza chains continue to expand.

3 *Managerial competence.* Successful owners may acquire competence through training or experience or by drawing on the expertise of others. Most spend time in successful companies or partner with others to bring expertise to a new business.[25]

4 *Luck.* After Alan McKim started Clean Harbors, an environmental cleanup firm in New England, he struggled to keep his business afloat. Then the U.S. government committed $1.6 billion to toxic-waste cleanup—McKim's specialty. Had the government fund not been created at just the right time, McKim might well have failed. Instead, he landed several government contracts.

Noncorporate Business Ownership

All entrepreneurs must decide which form of legal ownership best suits their goals: *sole proprietorship*, *partnership*, or *corporation*. Table 3.1 compares the most important differences among the three major ownership forms.

Sole Proprietorships

A **sole proprietorship** is owned and usually operated by one person. They account for about 72 percent of all U.S. businesses but only about 5 percent of total revenues.

Advantages of Sole Proprietorships
Sole proprietors answer to no one but themselves and can sometimes open up shop just by putting a sign on the door. Low start-up costs, the simplicity of legal setup procedures, and tax benefits make this form appealing.

Disadvantages of Sole Proprietorships
A major drawback is **unlimited liability**: a sole proprietor is personally liable for all debts incurred by the business. Another disadvantage is lack of continuity: a sole proprietorship legally dissolves when the owner dies. Additionally, sole proprietors often find it hard to borrow money to start up or expand what many bankers see as risky businesses.

Partnerships

The most common type of partnership, the **general partnership**, is a sole proprietorship multiplied by the number of partner-owners. Partners may invest equal or unequal sums of money and may earn profits that bear no relation to their financial investments if, for instance, someone contributes a well-known name or special expertise.

Advantages of Partnerships
The most striking advantage of general partnerships is the ability to grow by adding new talent and money. Because banks prefer to make loans to enterprises that are not dependent on single individuals, partnerships find it relatively easy to borrow and can invite new partners to invest.

Partnerships must begin with some kind of agreement that details who invested what sums and who will

SOLE PROPRIETORSHIP business owned and usually operated by one person who is responsible for all of its debts

UNLIMITED LIABILITY legal principle holding owners responsible for paying off all debts of a business

GENERAL PARTNERSHIP business with two or more owners who share in both the operation of the firm and the financial responsibility for its debts

Table 3.1 **Comparative Summary: Three Forms of Business**

Business Form	Liability	Continuity	Management	Sources of Investment
Proprietorship	Personal, unlimited	Ends with death or decision of owner	Personal, unrestricted	Personal
General Partnership	Personal, unlimited	Ends with death or decision of any partner	Unrestricted or depends on partnership agreement	Personal by partner(s)
Corporation	Capital invested	As stated in charter, perpetual or for specified period of years	Under control of board of directors, which is selected by stockholders	Purchase of stock

LIMITED PARTNERSHIP type of partnership consisting of limited partners and a general (or active) partner

LIMITED PARTNER partner who does not share in a firm's management and is liable for its debts only to the limits of said partner's investment

GENERAL (OR ACTIVE) PARTNER partner who actively manages a firm and who has unlimited liability for its debts

MASTER LIMITED PARTNERSHIP form of ownership that sells shares to investors who receive profits and that pays taxes on income from profits

COOPERATIVE form of ownership in which a group of sole proprietorships and/or partnerships agree to work together for common benefits

CORPORATION business that is legally considered an entity separate from its owners and is liable for its own debts; owners' liabilities extend to the limits of their investments

receive profit shares, how responsibilities are assigned, how the partnership may be dissolved and assets distributed, and how surviving partners will be protected from claims of a deceased partner's heirs. In all but two states, the Revised Uniform Limited Partnership Act requires the filing of specific information about the business and its partners. Partners may also agree to bind themselves in ways not specified by law. However, partners are still taxed as individuals.

Disadvantages of Partnerships Unlimited liability is the greatest drawback. Each partner may be liable for all business debts incurred by any of the partners. Partnerships also share with sole proprietorships the potential lack of continuity. When one partner dies or leaves, the original partnership dissolves, even if one or more of the others want it to continue. A related disadvantage

is difficulty in transferring ownership. No partner may sell out, retire, or transfer interest without the others' consent.

Alternatives to General Partnerships Because of these disadvantages, general partnerships are among the least popular forms of business. To resolve some of the problems inherent in general partnerships, some have tried alternative agreements. A **limited partnership** allows for **limited partners** who cannot take active roles in operations but invest money and are liable for debts only to the extent of their investments. For liability purposes, a limited partnership must have at least one **general (or active) partner** who runs the business and is responsible for its survival and growth.

Under a **master limited partnership**, an organization sells shares (partnership interests) to investors on public markets. Investors are paid back from profits. The master partner retains at least 50 percent ownership, runs the business, and provides detailed operating and financial reports to minority partners, who have no management voice.

Cooperatives

Groups of sole proprietorships or partnerships may agree to work together for their common benefit by forming **cooperatives**, which combine the freedom of sole proprietorships with the financial power of corporations. Although cooperatives make up only a minor segment of the U.S. economy, their role is still important in agriculture. Ocean Spray, the Florida Citrus Growers, and Cabot Creamery are among the best-known cooperatives.

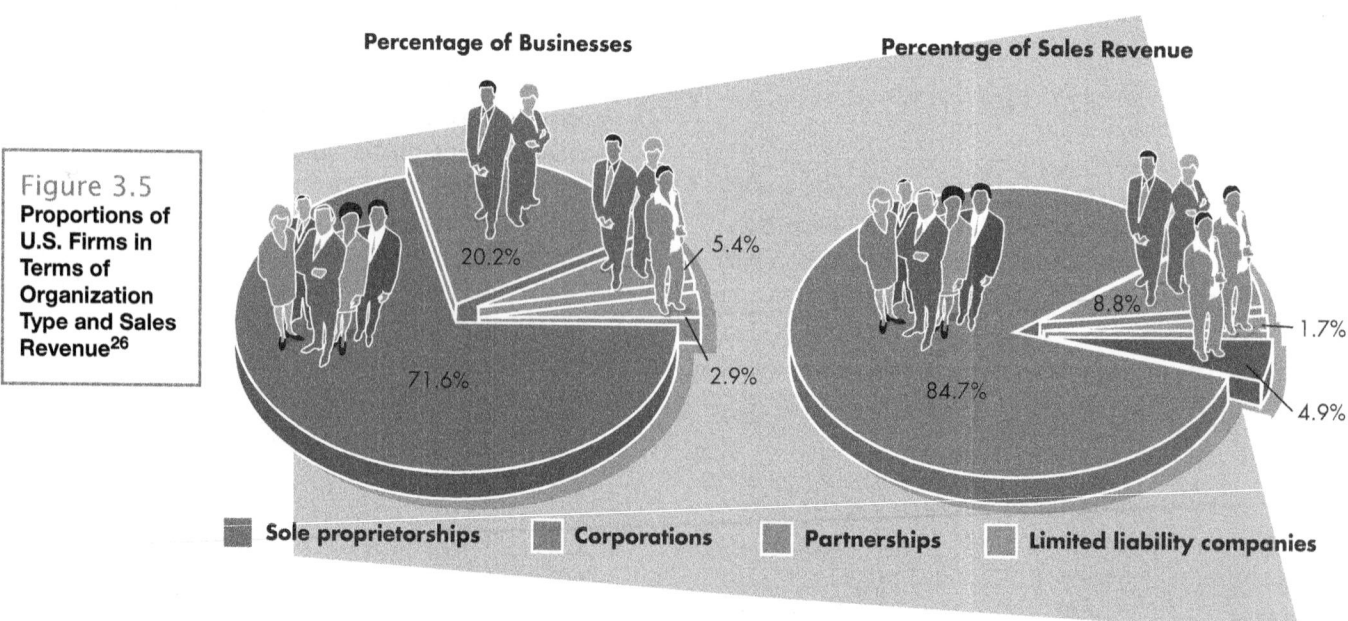

Figure 3.5 Proportions of U.S. Firms in Terms of Organization Type and Sales Revenue[26]

Percentage of Businesses

20.2%   5.4%
71.6%   2.9%

Percentage of Sales Revenue

8.8%   1.7%
84.7%   4.9%

■ Sole proprietorships   ■ Corporations   ■ Partnerships   □ Limited liability companies

Corporations

The 4.93 million corporations in the United States account for about 20 percent of all U.S. businesses but generate about 85 percent of all sales revenues.[27]

The Corporate Entity

The very word *corporation* inspires images of size and power. In reality, however, your corner newsstand has as much right to incorporate as a giant automaker, and they would share the characteristics of all **corporations**: legal status as separate entities, property rights and obligations, and indefinite life spans. As legal entities, like individuals, corporations can sue and be sued; buy, hold, and sell property; make and sell products; and commit crimes and be tried and punished for them.

Advantages of Incorporation The biggest advantage of corporations is **limited liability**: investor liability is limited to personal investment in the corporation. If, for example, you invest $1,000 in stock in a corporation that ends up failing, you may lose your $1,000, but no more.

Another advantage is continuity. Shares of stock may be sold or passed on to heirs, and most corporations also benefit from the continuity provided by professional management. Finally, corporations have advantages in raising money. By selling stock, they expand the number of investors and the amount of available funds, and lenders are more willing to grant loans.

Disadvantages of Incorporation Although a chief attraction is ease of transferring ownership, this same feature can create complications. For example, using a legal process called a **tender offer**—an offer to buy shares made by a prospective buyer directly to a corporation's shareholders—a corporation can be taken over against the will of its managers. Other disadvantages include heavy regulations, high start-up costs, and complex legal requirements.

The biggest disadvantage is **double taxation**. First, a corporation pays income taxes on company profits. Then, stockholders pay taxes on income returned by their investments. Thus, the profits earned by corporations are taxed twice—at both the corporate and ownership levels.

The advantages and disadvantages of corporate ownership have inspired laws establishing different kinds of corporations intended to take advantage of the benefits of the corporate model without assuming all the disadvantages.

Types of Corporations

Within the broad categories of *public* or *private* are several specific types of corporations, some of which are summarized in Table 3.2.

- Most smaller firms are **closely held (or private) corporations**. Stock is held by only a few people and isn't available for public sale. The controlling group of stockholders may be a family, a management group, or even the firm's employees.[28]

- Most large firms are **publicly held (or public) corporations**, in which shares are publicly issued.

- An **S corporation** (*Subchapter S corporation*) is organized and operates like a corporation but treated like a partnership for tax purposes. S corporations must meet stringent eligibility requirements.

- With a **limited liability corporation (LLC)**, owners are taxed like partners but also enjoy the benefits of limited liability. LLCs have grown in popularity in recent years, partially because of IRS rulings that allow corporations, partnerships, and foreign investors to be partial owners.

- **Professional corporations** are most likely composed of doctors, lawyers, accountants, or other professionals. While the corporate structure protects from unlimited financial liability, members are not immune from unlimited liability. Professional negligence by a member can entail personal liability on the individual's part.

- In a **multinational (or transnational) corporation**, stock may be traded on the exchanges of several countries, and managers are likely to be of different nationalities.

LIMITED LIABILITY legal principle holding investors liable for a firm's debts only to the limits of their personal investments in it

TENDER OFFER offer to buy shares made by a prospective buyer directly to a target corporation's shareholders, who then make individual decisions about whether to sell

DOUBLE TAXATION situation in which taxes may be payable both by a corporation on its profits and by shareholders on dividend incomes

CLOSELY HELD (OR PRIVATE) CORPORATION corporation whose stock is held by only a few people and is not available for sale to the general public

PUBLICLY HELD (OR PUBLIC) CORPORATION corporation whose stock is widely held and available for sale to the general public

S CORPORATION hybrid of a closely held corporation and a partnership, organized and operated like a corporation but treated as a partnership for tax purposes

LIMITED LIABILITY CORPORATION (LLC) hybrid of a publicly held corporation and a partnership in which owners are taxed as partners but enjoy the benefits of limited liability

PROFESSIONAL CORPORATION form of ownership allowing professionals to take advantage of corporate benefits while granting them limited business liability and unlimited professional liability

MULTINATIONAL (OR TRANSNATIONAL) CORPORATION form of corporation spanning national boundaries

CORPORATE GOVERNANCE roles of shareholders, directors, and other managers in corporate decision making and accountability

STOCKHOLDER (OR SHAREHOLDER) owner of shares of stock in a corporation

BOARD OF DIRECTORS governing body of a corporation that reports to its shareholders and delegates power to run its day-to-day operations while remaining responsible for sustaining its assets

OFFICERS top management team of a corporation

CHIEF EXECUTIVE OFFICER (CEO) top manager who is responsible for the overall performance of a corporation

STRATEGIC ALLIANCE strategy in which two or more organizations collaborate on a project for mutual gain

JOINT VENTURE strategic alliance in which the collaboration involves joint ownership of the new venture

MERGER the union of two corporations to form a new corporation

ACQUISITION the purchase of one company by another

DIVESTITURE strategy whereby a firm sells one or more of its business units

SPIN-OFF strategy of setting up one or more corporate units as new, independent corporations

Table 3.2 Types of Corporations

Type	Distinguishing Features	Examples
Closely Held	Stock held by only a few people	Blue Cross/Blue Shield
	Subject to corporate taxation	MasterCard
Publicly Held	Stock widely held among many investors	Dell Computer
	Subject to corporate taxation	Starbucks
		Texas Instruments
Subchapter S	Organized much like a closely held corporation	Minglewood Associates
	Subject to additional regulation	Entech Pest Systems
	Subject to partnership taxation	Frontier Bank
Limited Liability	Organized much like a publicly held corporation	Pacific Northwest Associates
	Subject to additional regulation	Global Ground Support
	Subject to partnership taxation	Ritz Ritz-Carlton
Professional	Subject to partnership taxation	Norman Hui, DDS & Associates
	Limited business liability	B & H Engineering
	Unlimited professional liability	Anderson, McCoy & Ortia
Multinational	Spans national boundaries	Toyota
	Subject to regulation in multiple countries	Nestlé
		General Electric

Managing a Corporation

A corporation must be managed on the principles of **corporate governance**—the roles of shareholders, directors, and other managers in corporate decision making and accountability. In this section, we discuss the principles of *stock ownership* and *stockholders' rights*, describe the role of *boards of directors*, and examine some special issues related to corporate ownership.

Corporate Governance Corporate governance is established by a firm's bylaws and usually involves three distinct bodies: **stockholders (or shareholders)**, the *board of directors*, and *officers*.

Stock Ownership and Stockholders' Rights Corporations sell shares, called *stock*, to investors who then become stockholders, or shareholders. Profits are distributed among stockholders in the form of *dividends*, and corporate managers serve at stockholders' discretion.

Boards of Directors The governing body of a corporation is its **board of directors**, which reports to stockholders and other stakeholders and sets policy on dividends, major spending, and executive compensation. Boards of directors are legally responsible and accountable for corporate actions and are increasingly being held personally liable for them.

Presidents of four leading Japanese robot firms pose together to announce their joint venture to accelerate the market development of next generation robots.

Officers Although board members oversee operations, most do not participate in day-to-day management. Rather, they hire a team of **officers**, usually headed by the firm's **chief executive officer (CEO)**, who is responsible for overall performance. Other officers typically include a *president*, who is responsible for internal management, and *vice presidents*, who oversee various functional areas such as marketing and operations.

Special Issues in Corporate Ownership

In recent years, several issues have grown in importance in the area of corporate ownership, including *joint ventures* and *strategic alliances*, *mergers* and *acquisitions*, and *divestitures* and *spin-offs*.

Joint Ventures and Strategic Alliances

In a **strategic alliance**, two or more organizations collaborate on a project for mutual gain. When partners share ownership of what is essentially a new enterprise, it is called a **joint venture**. The number of strategic alliances has increased rapidly in recent years on both domestic and international fronts.

Mergers and Acquisitions (M&As)

A **merger** occurs when two firms combine to create a new company. In an **acquisition**, one firm buys another outright. In general, when the two firms are roughly the same size, the combination is usually called a merger even if one firm is taking control of the other. When the acquiring firm is substantially larger than the acquired firm, the deal is really an acquisition. So-called M&As are an important form of corporate strategy for increasing product lines, expanding operations, going international, and creating new enterprises.

Divestitures and Spin-offs

Sometimes a corporation decides to sell a part of its existing business operations or set it up as a new and independent corporation. If a firm sells off an unrelated and/or underperforming businesses to focus more specifically on its core businesses, the sale is called a **divestiture**. When a firm sells part of itself to raise capital or because it deems a business unit more valuable as a separate company, the strategy is known as a **spin-off**. For example, in 2007, Morgan Stanley spun off its Discover Card division into a standalone company called Discover Financial Services. For every two shares of Morgan Stanley stock, shareholders received one share of Discover Financial Services. In effect, Morgan Stanley still owns Discover, but both companies are free to pursue separate and (hopefully) more profitable business strategies.[29]

Questions for Review

1. Why are small businesses important to the U.S. economy?

2. Which industries are easiest for start-ups to enter? Which are hardest? Why?

3. Describe the key components of a business plan. Why is it important for a new start-up to create a business plan?

4. What are the primary reasons for new business failure and success?

5. What are the basic forms of noncorporate business ownership? What are the key advantages and disadvantages of each?

6. What are the types of corporations? What are the key advantages and disadvantages of incorporation?

Questions for Analysis

7. Why might a closely held corporation choose to remain private? Why might it choose to be publicly traded?

8. If you were going to open a new business, what type would it be? Why?

9. Would you prefer to buy an existing business or franchise, or start from scratch? Why?

10. Under what circumstances might it be wise for an entrepreneur to reject venture capital? Under what circumstances might it be advisable to take more venture capital than he or she actually needs?

Application Exercises

11. Interview the owner/manager of a sole proprietorship or a general partnership. What characteristics of that business form led the owner to choose it? Does he or she ever contemplate changing the form of the business? If yes, what form would the owner choose, and why would he or she change it?

12. Identify two or three of the fastest growing businesses in the United States during the last year. What role has entrepreneurship played in the growth of these firms?

14

chapter

The Role of Accountants and Accounting Information

part V Managing Information

After reading this chapter, you should be able to:

1 Explain the role of accountants and distinguish between the kinds of work done by public accountants, private accountants, management accountants, and forensic accountants.

2 Explain how the accounting equation is used.

3 Describe the three basic financial statements and show how they reflect the activity and financial condition of a business.

4 Explain the key standards and principles for reporting financial statements.

5 Describe how computing financial ratios can help users get more information from financial statements to determine the financial strengths of a business.

6 Discuss the role of ethics in accounting.

CSI: Wall Street

In the aftermath of major accounting scandals such as the Enron case of 2001, many companies are showing an increased interest in the field of forensic accounting: the use of accounting for legal purposes. The expansion of the forensic accounting field—the Association of Certified Fraud Examiners has experienced a 50 percent increase in membership since 2003—is due to increased vigilance as a result of recent scandals, as well as a strong desire on the part of companies to protect themselves from accounting fraud.

Fraud examiners typically begin an investigation of a company by interviewing high-level executives. Team members then comb through e-mails, searching for suspicious words and phrases. The combination of interviews and e-mails may lead investigators to specific accounting files or ledger entries. According to Al Vondra, a Certified Fraud Examiner at PricewaterhouseCoopers, some of the most common fraudulent practices involve hiding revenues and expenses under phony categories such as "Total Noncurrent Assets" or "Other Current Liabilities."

Although major accounting scandals have declined since the early 2000s, recently approved, laxer standards of accounting may soon lead investigators such as Vondra in new directions. Regulations passed by the Financial Accounting Standards Board (FASB) in 2006 allow companies to classify certain stock earnings as Level 3 gains. Under the new FASB standards, Level 3 assets, which are traded infrequently and have no reliable market price, may be counted as earnings according to the judgment of the company based on "unobservable inputs"—or, as journalist Jonathan Weil of Bloomberg News characterizes it, these earnings are "pretty much whatever the companies want them to be." In 2007, Level 3 earnings comprised 35 percent of Wells Fargo Bank's record-breaking third-quarter pretax income of $3.44 billion. Without the Level 3 earnings, Wells Fargo would have posted a loss.[1]

What's in It for Me?

For most of us, the words and ideas in accounting can seem like a foreign language. As we have seen, the specialized terminology can be used to mask fraud and corruption. However, it's also a necessary tool that allows professionals in every industry to analyze growth, understand risk, and communicate complex ideas about a firm's financial health. This chapter will cover the fundamental concepts of accounting and apply them to familiar business situations. By grasping the basic accounting vocabulary you will be able to participate when the conversation turns to the financial matters that constitute so great a part of a firm's daily operations.

ACCOUNTING comprehensive system for collecting, analyzing, and communicating financial information

BOOKKEEPING recording of accounting transactions

ACCOUNTING INFORMATION SYSTEM (AIS) organized procedure for identifying, measuring, recording, and retaining financial information for use in accounting statements and management reports

CONTROLLER person who manages all of a firm's accounting activities (chief accounting officer)

FINANCIAL ACCOUNTING field of accounting concerned with external users of a company's financial information

MANAGERIAL (MANAGEMENT) ACCOUNTING field of accounting that serves internal users of a company's financial information

CERTIFIED PUBLIC ACCOUNTANT (CPA) accountant licensed by the state and offering services to the public

What Is Accounting and Who Uses Accounting Information?

Accounting is a comprehensive system for collecting, analyzing, and communicating financial information to a firm's owners and employees, to the public, and to various regulatory agencies. To perform these functions, accountants keep records of taxes paid, income received, and expenses incurred—a process called **bookkeeping**—and they assess the effects of these transactions on business activities.

Because businesses engage in thousands of transactions, ensuring consistent, dependable financial information is mandatory. This is the job of the **accounting information system (AIS)**—an organized procedure for identifying, measuring, recording, and retaining financial information so that it can be used in accounting statements and management reports. The system includes all of the people, reports, computers, procedures, and resources that are needed to compile financial transactions.[2]

Users of accounting information are numerous:

- *Business managers* use it to develop goals and plans, set budgets, and evaluate future prospects.

- *Employees and unions* use it to plan for and receive compensation and such benefits as health care, vacation time, and retirement pay.

- *Investors and creditors* use it to estimate returns to stockholders, determine growth prospects, and decide whether a firm is a good credit risk.

- *Tax authorities* use it to plan for tax inflows, determine the tax liabilities of individuals and businesses, and ensure that correct amounts are paid on time.

- *Government regulatory agencies* rely on it to fulfill their duties toward the public. The Securities and Exchange Commission (SEC), for example, requires firms to file financial disclosures so that potential investors have valid information about their financial status.

Who Are Accountants and What Do They Do?

The **controller**, or chief accounting officer, manages a firm's accounting activities by ensuring that the AIS provides the reports and statements needed for planning, decision making, and other management activities. This range of activities requires different types of accounting specialists. In this section, we begin by distinguishing between the two main fields of accounting: *financial* and *managerial*. Then, we discuss the different functions and activities of *certified public accountants*, *private accountants*, *management accountants*, and *forensic accountants*.

Financial Versus Managerial Accounting

In any company, the two fields of accounting—financial and managerial—can be distinguished by the users they serve: those outside the company and those within.[3]

Financial Accounting A firm's **financial accounting** system is concerned with external information users: consumer groups, unions, stockholders, suppliers, creditors, and government agencies. It prepares reports such as income statements and balance sheets that focus on the activities of the company as a whole rather than on individual departments or divisions.[4]

Managerial Accounting **Managerial (management) accounting** serves internal users. Managers at all levels need information to make departmental decisions, monitor projects, and plan future activities. Other employees also need accounting information. To set performance goals, for example, salespeople need past sales data organized by geographic region.

Certified Public Accountants

Certified public accountants (CPAs) offer accounting services to the public. They are licensed by a state after passing an exam prepared by the American Institute of Certified Public Accountants (AICPA), which also provides technical support and discipline in matters of ethics. Whereas some CPAs work as individual

Sometimes, companies ignore GAAP and accountants fail to disclose violations. Jamie Olis (left) was a mid-level executive at Texas-based energy producer Dynegy. To cover up the company's financial difficulties and dodge $79 million in federal taxes, Olis helped devise an accounting scheme to disguise a $300 million loan as cash flow. He was sentenced to 24 years in jail, though the judge later reduced it to six years.

AUDIT systematic examination of a company's accounting system to determine whether its financial reports reliably represent its operations

GENERALLY ACCEPTED ACCOUNTING PRINCIPLES (GAAP) accounting guidelines that govern the content and form of financial reports

TAX SERVICES assistance provided by CPAs for tax preparation and tax planning

MANAGEMENT ADVISORY SERVICES assistance provided by CPA firms in areas such as financial planning, information systems design, and other areas of concern for client firms

practitioners, many form or join existing partnerships or professional corporations.

CPA Services Virtually all CPA firms, whether large or small, provide auditing, tax, and management services. Larger firms such as Deloitte Touche Tohmatsu and Ernst & Young earn much of their revenue from auditing services, though consulting (management advisory) services constitute a major growth area. Smaller firms earn most of their income from tax and management services.

Auditing An **audit** examines a company's AIS to determine whether financial reports reliably represent its operations.[5] Organizations must provide audit reports when applying for loans, selling stock, or when going through a major restructuring. Independent auditors who do not work for the company must ensure that clients' accounting systems follow **generally accepted accounting principles (GAAP)**, which are formulated by the Financial Accounting Standards Board (FASB) of the AICPA and govern the content and form of financial reports.[6] The Securities and Exchange Commission (SEC) is the U.S. government agency that legally enforces accounting and auditing rules and procedures.

Tax Services **Tax services** include assistance not only with tax-return preparation but also with tax planning. A CPA's advice can help a business structure (or

restructure) operations and investments and perhaps save millions of dollars in taxes. Staying abreast of tax-law changes is no simple matter. Some critics charge that tax changes have become a full-time vocation among some state and federal legislators who add increasingly complicated laws and technical corrections on taxation each year.

Management Advisory Services As consultants, accounting firms provide **management advisory services** ranging from personal financial planning to planning corporate mergers. Other services include production scheduling, computer-feasibility studies, AIS design, and even executive recruitment. The staffs of the largest CPA firms include engineers, architects, mathematicians, and psychologists, all of whom are available for consulting.

Noncertified Public Accountants Many accountants don't take the CPA exam; others work in the field while getting ready for it or while meeting requirements for state certification. Many small businesses, individuals, and even larger firms rely on these noncertified public accountants for income-tax preparation, payroll accounting, and financial-planning services.

The CPA Vision Project The recent talent shortage in accounting has led the profession to rethink its culture and lifestyle.[7] With grassroots participation from CPAs, educators, and industry leaders, the AICPA, through its

CORE COMPETENCIES FOR ACCOUNTING the combination of skills, technology, and knowledge that will be necessary for the future CPA

PRIVATE ACCOUNTANT salaried accountant hired by a business to carry out its day-to-day financial activities

MANAGEMENT ACCOUNTANT private accountant who provides financial services to support managers in various business activities within a firm

CERTIFIED MANAGEMENT ACCOUNTANT (CMA) professional designation awarded by the Institute of Management Accountants in recognition of management accounting qualifications

FORENSIC ACCOUNTING the practice of accounting for legal purposes

Table 14.1 **Core Competencies for Accounting[8]**

Strategic and Critical Thinking Skills	The accountant can provide competent advice for strategic action by combining data, knowledge, and insight.
Communications and Leadership Skills	The accountant can exchange information meaningfully in a variety of business situations with effective delivery and interpersonal skills.
Focus on the Customer, Client, and Market	The accountant can meet the changing needs of clients, customers, and employers better than the competition and can anticipate those needs better than competitors.
Skills in Interpreting Converging Information	The accountant can interpret new meaning by combining financial and nonfinancial information into a broader understanding that adds more business value.
Technology Skills	The accountant can use technology to add value to activities performed for employers, customers, and clients.

CPA Vision Project, is redefining the role of the accountant for today's world economy. The Vision Project identifies a unique combination of skills, technology, and knowledge—called **core competencies for accounting**—that will be necessary for the future CPA. As Table 14.1 shows, those skills—which include communication, critical thinking, and leadership—go far beyond the ability to "crunch numbers." They include certain communications skills, along with skills in critical thinking and leadership. Indeed, the CPA Vision Project foresees CPAs who combine specialty skills with a broad-based orientation in order to communicate more effectively with people in a wide range of business activities.

Private Accountants and Management Accountants

To ensure integrity in reporting, CPAs are always independent of the firms they audit. However, many businesses also hire their own salaried employees—**private accountants**—to perform day-to-day activities.

Private accountants perform numerous jobs. An internal auditor at ConocoPhillips might fly to the North Sea to confirm the accuracy of oil-flow meters on offshore petroleum drilling platforms. A supervisor responsible for $2 billion in monthly payouts to vendors and employees may never leave the executive suite, with duties such as hiring and training, assigning projects, and evaluating performance of accounting personnel. Large businesses employ specialized accountants in such areas as budgeting, financial planning, internal auditing, payroll, and taxation. In small businesses, a single person may handle all accounting tasks.

Most private accountants are **management accountants** who provide services to support managers in various activities (marketing, production, engineering, and so forth). Many hold the **certified management accountant (CMA)** designation, awarded by the Institute of Management Accountants (IMA), recognizing qualifications of professionals who have passed IMA's experience and examination requirements.

Forensic Accountants

The fastest growing area in accounting is **forensic accounting**—the use of accounting for legal purposes.[9] Forensic accountants may be called upon—by law enforcement agencies, insurance companies, law firms, and business firms—for both investigative accounting and litigation support in crimes against companies, crimes by companies, and civil disagreements. Civil cases often require investigating and quantifying claims of personal injury loss due to negligence and analyzing financial issues in matrimonial disputes. Forensic accountants also assist business firms in tracing and recovering lost assets from employee business fraud or theft.

Investigative Accounting A forensic accountant may be asked to investigate a trail of financial transactions behind a suspected crime, as in a money-laundering scheme or an investment swindle. Try your hand, for example, at "Catch Me If You Can," the popular interactive forensic accounting game sponsored by the AICPA (at **www.startheregoplaces.com**). The forensic accountant, being familiar with the legal concepts and procedures of the case, identifies and analyzes pertinent financial evidence—documents, bank accounts, phone calls, computer records, and people—and presents accounting conclusions and their legal implications.

Litigation Support Forensic accountants assist in the application of accounting evidence for judicial proceedings by preparing and preserving evidence for these proceedings. They also assist by presenting visual aids

Table 14.2 Selected Provisions of the Sarbanes-Oxley Act[10]

- Creates a national Accounting Oversight Board that, among other activities, must establish the ethics standards used by CPA firms in preparing audits.
- Requires that auditors retain audit working papers for specified periods of time.
- Requires auditor rotation by prohibiting the same person from being the lead auditor for more than five consecutive years.
- Requires that the CEO and CFO certify that the company's financial statements are true, fair, and accurate.
- Prohibits corporations from extending personal loans to executives and directors.
- Requires that the audited company disclose whether it has adopted a code of ethics for its senior financial officers.
- Requires that the SEC regularly review each corporation's financial statements.
- Prevents employers from retaliating against research analysts that write negative reports.
- Imposes criminal penalties on auditors and clients for falsifying, destroying, altering, or concealing records (10 years in prison).
- Imposes a fine or imprisonment (up to 25 years) on any person that defrauds shareholders.
- Increases penalties for mail and wire fraud from 5 to 20 years in prison.
- Establishes criminal liability for failure of corporate officers to certify financial reports.

CERTIFIED FRAUD EXAMINER (CFE) professional designation administered by the Association of Certified Fraud Examiners in recognition of qualifications for a specialty area within forensic accounting

SARBANES-OXLEY ACT OF 2002 (SARBOX) enactment of federal regulations to restore public trust in accounting practices by imposing new requirements on financial activities in publicly traded corporations

ACCOUNTING EQUATION Assets = Liabilities + Owners' Equity; used by accountants to balance data for the firm's financial transactions at various points in the year

to support trial evidence, by testifying as expert witnesses, and, especially, in determining economic damages in any case before the court.

Certified Fraud Examiners The **Certified Fraud Examiner (CFE)** designation, administered by the Association of Certified Fraud Examiners, is awarded to those with expertise in fraud-related issues and investigations. Many CFEs, like Al Vondra from our opening story, find employment in corporations seeking to prevent fraud from within. The CFE examination covers four areas:

1. *Criminology and ethics.* Includes theories of fraud prevention and ethical situations

2. *Financial transactions.* Examines types of fraudulent financial transactions incurred in accounting records

3. *Fraud investigation.* Pertains to tracing illicit transactions, evaluating deception, and interviewing and taking statements

4. *Legal elements of fraud.* Includes rules of evidence, criminal and civil law, and rights of the accused and accuser

Federal Restrictions on CPA Services and Financial Reporting: Sarbox

The financial wrongdoings associated with firms such as ImClone Systems, Tyco, WorldCom, Enron, Arthur Andersen, and others have not gone unnoticed in legislative circles. Federal regulations, in particular the **Sarbanes-Oxley Act of 2002 (Sarbox** or **SOX)**, have been enacted to restore public trust in corporate accounting practices.

Sarbox restricts the kinds of nonaudit services that CPAs can provide. Under the new law, for example, a CPA firm cannot help design a client's financial information system if it also does the client's auditing. By prohibiting CPAs from providing auditing and nonauditing services to the same client, Sarbox encourages audits that are independent and unbiased.

Sarbox Compliance Requirements Sarbox imposes new requirements on virtually every financial activity in publicly traded corporations, as well as severe criminal penalties for persons committing or concealing fraud or destroying financial records. Table 14.2 provides brief descriptions of several of Sarbox's many provisions.

The Accounting Equation

All accountants rely on record keeping to enter and track transactions. Underlying all record-keeping procedures is the most basic tool of accounting—the **accounting equation**:

$$\text{Assets} = \text{Liabilities} + \text{Owners' Equity}$$

After each financial transaction (e.g., payments to suppliers, sales to customers, wages to employees), the accounting equation must be in balance. If it isn't, then an accounting error has occurred. To better understand the importance of this equation, we must understand

ASSET any economic resource expected to benefit a firm or an individual who owns it

LIABILITY debt owed by a firm to an outside organization or individual

OWNERS' EQUITY amount of money that owners would receive if they sold all of a firm's assets and paid all of its liabilities

FINANCIAL STATEMENT any of several types of reports summarizing a company's financial status to stakeholders and to aid in managerial decision making

the terms *assets*, *liabilities*, and *owners' equity*.

Assets and Liabilities An **asset** is any economic resource that is expected to benefit a firm or an individual who owns it. Assets include land, buildings, equipment, inventories, and payments due the company (accounts receivable). Google, the Internet search and information provider, for example, held assets amounting to $25.336 billion at year-end 2007.[11]

A **liability** is a debt that a firm owes to an outside party. The total of Google's liabilities—all the debt owed to others—was $2.646 billion at the end of 2007.

Owners' Equity **Owners' equity** is the amount of money that owners would receive if they sold all of a company's assets and paid all of its liabilities. Google's financial reports for 2007 declared shareholders' equity of $22.690 billion. For the Google example, we see that the accounting equation is in balance, as it should be.

> Assets = Liabilities + Owners' Equity
> $25.336 = $2.646 + $22.690 billion

We can rewrite the equation to highlight how owners' equity relates to assets and liabilities.

> Assets − Liabilities = Owners' Equity

Another term for this is *net worth*: the difference between what a firm owns (assets) minus what it owes (liabilities) is its net worth, or owners' equity. If a company's assets exceed its liabilities, owners' equity is *positive*. If the company goes out of business, the owners will receive some cash (a gain) after selling assets and paying off liabilities. If liabilities outweigh assets, owners' equity is *negative*; assets are insufficient to pay off all debts, and the firm is bankrupt. If the company goes out of business, the owners will get no cash, and some creditors won't be paid.

Owners' equity is meaningful for both investors and lenders. Before lending money to owners, for example,

The inventory at this Toyota dealership is among the company's assets: The cars constitute an economic resource because the firm will benefit financially as it sells them.

lenders want to know the amount of owners' equity in a business. A larger owners' equity indicates greater security for lenders. Owners' equity consists of two sources of capital:

1 The amount that the owners originally invested

2 Profits (also owned by the owners) earned by and reinvested in the company

Financial Statements

As noted previously, accountants summarize the results of a firm's transactions and issue reports to help managers make informed decisions. Among the most important reports are **financial statements**, which fall into three broad categories: *balance sheets*, *income statements*, and *statements of cash flows*.

Balance Sheets

Balance sheets supply detailed information about the accounting equation factors: *assets*, *liabilities*, and *owners' equity*. Because they also show a firm's financial condition at one point in time, they are sometimes called *statements of financial position*. Figure 14.1 is a simplified presentation of the balance sheet for Google, Inc.

Assets   From an accounting standpoint, most companies have three types of assets: *current*, *fixed*, and *intangible*.

Current Assets   Current assets include cash and assets that can be converted into cash within a year. The act of converting something into cash is called *liquidating*. Assets are normally listed in order of **liquidity**—the ease of converting them into cash. Debts, for example, are usually paid in cash. A company that needs but cannot generate cash—a company that's not "liquid"—may be forced to sell assets at reduced prices or even to go out of business.

By definition, cash is completely liquid. *Marketable securities* purchased as short-term investments are slightly less liquid but can be sold quickly. These include stocks or bonds of other companies, government securities, and money market certificates. Many companies hold other nonliquid assets such as *merchandise inventory*—the cost of merchandise that's been acquired for sale to customers and is still on hand.

Fixed Assets   Fixed assets (such as land, buildings, and equipment) have long-term use or value, but as buildings and equipment wear out or become obsolete, their value decreases. Accountants use **depreciation** to spread the cost of an asset over the years of its useful life. To reflect decreasing value, accountants calculate an asset's useful life in years, divide its worth by that many years, and subtract the resulting amount each year. Every year, therefore, the remaining value (or net value) decreases on the books.

Intangible Assets   Although their worth is hard to set, intangible assets have monetary value in the form of expected benefits, which may include fees paid by others for obtaining rights or privileges—including patents, trademarks, copyrights,

BALANCE SHEET financial statement that supplies detailed information about a firm's assets, liabilities, and owners' equity

CURRENT ASSET asset that can or will be converted into cash within a year

LIQUIDITY ease with which an asset can be converted into cash

FIXED ASSET asset with long-term use or value, such as land, buildings, and equipment

DEPRECIATION accounting method for distributing the cost of an asset over its useful life

INTANGIBLE ASSET nonphysical asset, such as a patent or trademark, that has economic value in the form of expected benefit

EG CHAPTER 14

Figure 14.1
Google's Balance Sheet[12]

Google, Inc.
Summary of Balance Sheet (condensed)
as of December 31, 2007
(in millions)

Assets		Liabilities and Shareholders' Equity	
Current assets:		Current liabilities:	
Cash	$6,081.59	Accounts payable	$282.11
Marketable securities	8,137.02	Other	1,753.49
Other	3,070.52	**Total current liabilities**	**$2,035.60**
Total current assets	**$17,289.13**		
		Long-term liabilities:	
Fixed assets:		All long-term debts	0.00
Property and equipment, net	$4,039.26	Other	610.52
Other	1,261.44	**Total long-term liabilities**	**$610.52**
Total fixed assets	**$5,300.70**		
		Total liabilities	**$2,646.12**
Intangible assets:			
Intangible assets	446.60	Shareholders' equity:	
Goodwill	2,299.37	Paid-in capital	$13,241.22
Total intangible assets	**$2,745.97**	Retained earnings	9,448.46
		Total shareholders' equity	**$22,689.68**
Total assets	**$25,335.80**		
		Total liabilities and shareholders' equity	**$25,335.80**

Google's balance sheet for year ended December 31, 2007. The balance sheet shows clearly that the firm's total assets are equal to its total liabilities and owners' equity.

GOODWILL amount paid for an existing business above the value of its other assets

CURRENT LIABILITY debt that must be paid within one year

ACCOUNTS PAYABLE (PAYABLES) current liability consisting of bills owed to suppliers, plus wages and taxes due within the coming year

LONG-TERM LIABILITY debt that is not due for at least one year

PAID-IN CAPITAL money that is invested in a company by its owners

RETAINED EARNINGS earnings retained by a firm for its use rather than paid out as dividends

INCOME STATEMENT (PROFIT-AND-LOSS STATEMENT) financial statement listing a firm's annual revenues and expenses so that a bottom line shows annual profit or loss

REVENUES funds that flow into a business from the sale of goods or services

Figure 14.2
Google's Income Statement[13]

Google, Inc.
Summary of Income Statement (condensed)
as of December 31, 2007
(in millions)

Revenues (gross sales)		$16,593.99
Cost of revenues	6,649.09	
Gross profit		9,944.90
Operating expenses:		
Sales and marketing	2,740.51	
Administrative and general	2,119.99	
Total operating expenses		$4,860.50
Operating income (before taxes)		5,084.40
Income taxes*		880.68
Net income		**$4,203.72**

*approximated

Google's income statement for year ended December 31, 2007. The final entry on the income statement, the bottom line, reports the firm's profit or loss.

and franchises—to your products. **Goodwill** is the amount paid for an existing business beyond the value of its other assets. A purchased firm, for example, may have a particularly good reputation or location.

Liabilities Like assets, liabilities are often separated into different categories. **Current liabilities** are debts that must be paid within one year. These include **accounts payable (payables)**—unpaid bills to suppliers for materials as well as wages and taxes that must be paid in the coming year. **Long-term liabilities** are debts that are not due for at least a year. These normally represent borrowed funds on which the company must pay interest.

Owners' Equity The final section of the balance sheet in Figure 14.1 shows owners' equity broken down into *paid-in capital* and *retained earnings*. **Paid-in capital** is money invested by owners, such as purchases of Google's initial public offering of stock in 2004. **Retained earnings** are net profits kept by a firm rather than paid out as dividend payments to stockholders.

The balance sheet for any company, then, is a barometer for its financial condition at one point in time. By comparing the current balance sheet with those of previous years, creditors and owners can better interpret the firm's financial progress and future

prospects in terms of changes in its assets, liabilities, and owners' equity.

Income Statements

The **income statement** is sometimes called a **profit-and-loss statement** because its description of revenues and expenses results in a figure showing the firm's annual profit or loss. In other words,

$$\text{Revenues} - \text{Expenses} = \text{Profit}_1 \text{or Loss}_2$$

Popularly known as the *bottom line*, profit or loss is probably the most important figure in any business enterprise. Figure 14.2 shows the 2007 income statement for Google, whose bottom line was $4.20 (rounded) billion. The income statement is divided into four major categories: *revenues, cost of revenues, operating expenses,* and *net income.* Unlike a balance sheet, which shows the financial condition at a specific *point in time,* an income statement shows the financial results that occurred during a *period of time,* such as a month, quarter, or year.

Revenues When a law firm receives $250 for preparing a will or a supermarket collects $65 from a grocery shopper, both are receiving **revenues**—the funds that flow into a business from the sale of goods or services. In 2007, Google reported revenues of $16.59 (rounded) billion from the sale of advertising and Web-search services to Google Network members, such as AOL.

Cost of Revenues (Cost of Goods Sold) In the Google income statement, the **cost of revenues** section shows the costs of obtaining the revenues from other companies during the year. These are fees Google must pay its network members—revenue sharing from advertising income—and also include expenses arising from the operation of Google's data centers, including labor, energy, and costs of processing customer transactions.

While cost of revenues is a relevant income statement category for service providers like Google, goods producers do not use it. Instead, income statements for manufacturing firms such as Procter & Gamble use the corresponding category, **cost of goods sold**: costs of obtaining materials to make products sold during the year.

Gross Profit Managers are often interested in **gross profit**, a preliminary, quick-to-calculate profit figure that considers just two pieces of data—revenues and cost of revenues (the direct costs of getting those revenues)—from the income statement. To calculate gross profit, subtract cost of revenues from revenues obtained by selling the firm's products.

Operating Expenses In addition to costs directly related to generating revenues, every company has general expenses ranging from erasers to the CEO's salary. Like cost of revenues and cost of goods sold, **operating expenses** are resources that must flow out of a company if it is to earn revenues.

Sales and marketing expenses result from activities related to selling goods or services, such as sales-force salaries and advertising expenses. *Administrative and general expenses*, such as management salaries and maintenance costs, are related to the general management of the company.

Operating and Net Income
Operating income compares the gross profit from operations against operating expenses. This calculation for Google ($9.94 billion – $4.86 billion) reveals an operating income, or income before taxes, of $5.08 billion. Subtracting income taxes from operating income ($5.08 billion – $0.88 billion)

reveals **net income (net profit or net earnings)**. Google's net income for the year was $4.20 billion (rounded).

The step-by-step information in an income statement shows how a company obtained its net income for the period, making it easier for shareholders and other stakeholders to evaluate the firm's financial health.

Statements of Cash Flows

Some companies prepare only balance sheets and income statements. However, the SEC requires all firms whose stock is publicly traded to issue a third report, the **statement of cash flows**, which shows the effects on cash of three aspects of a business: *operating activities*, *investing activities*, and *financing activities*. Google's 2007 statement of cash flows is reproduced in Figure 14.3.

COST OF REVENUES costs that a company incurs to obtain revenues from other companies

COST OF GOODS SOLD costs of obtaining materials for making the products sold by a firm during the year

GROSS PROFIT a preliminary, quick-to-calculate profit figure calculated from the firm's revenues minus its cost of revenues (the direct costs of getting the revenues)

OPERATING EXPENSES costs, other than the cost of revenues, incurred in producing a good or service

OPERATING INCOME gross profit minus operating expenses

NET INCOME (NET PROFIT, NET EARNINGS) gross profit minus operating expenses and income taxes

STATEMENT OF CASH FLOWS financial statement describing a firm's yearly cash receipts and cash payments

Google, Inc. Summary of Statement of Cash Flows (condensed) as of December 31, 2007 Increase (Decrease) in Cash (in millions)			**Figure 14.3** Google's Statement of Cash Flows[14]
Net cash provided by operating activities			$5,775.41
Cash flows from investment activities:			
Payment for purchase of property, equipment, and securities		(3,681.59)	
Net cash used in investing activities			(3,681.59)
Cash flows from financing activities:			
Proceeds from sale of stock (IPO)		23.86	
Other		419.24	
Net cash provided by financing activities			443.10
Net increase in cash			2,536.92
Cash at beginning of year			3,544.67
Cash at end of year			$6,081.59

Google's statement of cash flows for year ended December 31, 2007. The final entry shows year-end cash position resulting from operating activities, investing activities, and financing activities.

BUDGET detailed statement of estimated receipts and expenditures for a future period of time

Figure 14.4
Perfect Posters' Sales Budget

■ **Cash Flows from Operations.** This first section of the statement concerns main operating activities: cash transactions involved in buying and selling goods and services. For the Google example, it reveals how much of the year's cash balance results from the firm's main line of business—sales of advertising and Web-search services.

Perfect Posters, Inc.
555 RIVERVIEW, CHICAGO, IL 60606

Perfect Posters, Inc.
Sales Budget
First Quarter, 2009

	January	February	March	Quarter
Budgeted sales (units)	7,500	6,000	6,500	20,000
Budgeted selling price per unit	$3.50	$3.50	$3.50	$3.50
Budgeted sales revenue	**$26,250**	**$21,000**	**$22,750**	**$70,000**
Expected cash receipts:				
From December sales	$26,210			$26,210
From January sales	17,500	$8,750		26,250
From February sales		14,000	$7,000	21,000
From March sales			15,200	15,200
Total cash receipts:	**$43,710**	**$22,750**	**$22,200**	**$88,660**

■ **Cash Flows from Investing.** The second section reports net cash used in or provided by investing. It includes cash receipts and payments from buying and selling stocks, bonds, property, equipment, and other productive assets. These sources of cash are not the company's main line of business. A cash outflow is shown in parentheses.

■ **Cash Flows from Financing.** The third section reports net cash from all financing activities. It includes cash inflows from borrowing or issuing stock, as well as outflows for payment of dividends and repayment of borrowed money.

The overall change in cash from these three sources is added to or subtracted from the beginning cash (year-end cash from the 2006 balance sheet) to arrive at the end-of-year cash position. When creditors and stockholders know how a firm obtained and used funds during the course of a year, it's easier for them to interpret year-to-year changes in the balance sheet and income statement.

The Budget: An Internal Financial Statement

For planning, controlling, and decision making, the most important internal financial statement is the **budget**—a detailed report on estimated receipts and expenditures for a future period of time. Although that period is usually one year, some companies also prepare three- or five-year budgets, especially when

considering major capital expenditures. The budget differs from the other statements we have discussed in that budgets are not shared outside the company; hence the "internal financial statement" title.

Although the accounting staff coordinates the budget process, it needs input from many areas regarding proposed activities and required resources. Figure 14.4 is a sales budget for a hypothetical wholesaler, Perfect Posters. In preparing the budget, accounting must obtain from the sales group projections for units to be sold and expected expenses for the coming year. Then, accounting draws up the final budget and, throughout the year, compares the budget to actual expenditures and revenues. Discrepancies signal potential problems and spur action to improve financial performance.

Reporting Standards and Practices

Accountants follow standard reporting practices and principles when they prepare external reports. The common language dictated by standard practices and spelled out in GAAP is designed to give external users confidence in the accuracy and meaning of financial information. Forensic accountants such as PricewaterhouseCoopers's Al Vondra watch for deviations from GAAP as indicators of possible fraudulent practices.

Revenue Recognition and Activity Timing The reporting of revenue inflows, and the timing of other transactions, must abide by accounting principles that govern financial statements. **Revenue recognition**, for example, is the formal recording and reporting of revenues at the appropriate time. Although a firm earns revenues continuously as it makes sales, earnings are not reported until the *earnings cycle* is completed. This cycle is complete under two conditions:

1. The sale is complete and the product delivered.

2. The sale price has been collected or is collectible (accounts receivable).

The end of the earnings cycle determines the timing for revenue recognition in a firm's financial statements. Suppose a toy company in January signs a sales contract to supply $1,000 of toys to a retail store, with delivery scheduled in February. Although the sale is completed in January, the $1,000 revenue should not then be recognized because the toys have not been delivered and the sale price is not yet collectible, so the earnings cycle is incomplete. Revenues are recorded in the accounting period—February—in which the product is delivered and collectible (or collected).

Full Disclosure To help users better understand the numbers in a firm's financial statements, GAAP requires that financial statements also include management's interpretations and explanations of those numbers. This is known as the **full disclosure** principle. Because they know about events inside the company, managers prepare additional information to explain certain events or transactions or to disclose the circumstances behind certain results.

REVENUE RECOGNITION formal recording and reporting of revenues at the appropriate time

FULL DISCLOSURE guideline that financial statements should not include just numbers but should also furnish management's interpretations and explanations of those numbers

Entrepreneurship and New Ventures

Reaping the Rewards of Innovation

What do Entrepreneurial Advisory Services, the PKF Academy, and FromGregsHead.com have in common? They are three of the initiatives developed by Pannell Kerr Forster of Texas, P.C. (PKF Texas) that have helped the Houston-based accounting firm capture seven consecutive Practice Innovation Awards. These awards are given by *Practical Accountant* magazine "to public accounting firms that take the lead in developing a new service area, improving services to their clients, or promoting efficiency in the practice of public accounting."

PKF Texas's most recent win, in 2007, was for The Entrepreneur's Playbook, a series of business tips that air weekly on a Houston-area radio station and are posted on a blog run by the company's director of consulting solutions, Gregory Price. (The blog, FromGregsHead.com, won a Practice Innovation Award in 2006.) The tips cover such fundamental accounting matters as preparing a budget and cost analysis, as well as more topical concerns such as "going green" and competing in a global marketplace. Readers and listeners are invited to respond and share their own tips with the community.

According to Kenneth Guidry, president of PKF Texas and himself a certified public accountant, "The Entrepreneur's Playbook has proven to be an effective tool for business owners. We're excited by the feedback from the marketplace that these tips are greatly appreciated." This appreciation has come in forms other than awards. For its continuous efforts to innovate and improve, PKF Texas has grown to be the fourth-largest accounting firm in the Southwest, with revenues in 2007 approaching $20 million.[15]

SOLVENCY RATIO financial ratio, either short- or long-term, for estimating the borrower's ability to repay debt

PROFITABILITY RATIO financial ratio for measuring a firm's potential earnings

ACTIVITY RATIO financial ratio for evaluating management's efficiency in using a firm's assets

SHORT-TERM SOLVENCY RATIO financial ratio for measuring a company's ability to pay immediate debts

CURRENT RATIO financial ratio for measuring a company's ability to pay current debts out of current assets

DEBT a company's total liabilities

LEVERAGE ability to finance an investment through borrowed funds

Analyzing Financial Statements

• • • • • • • • • • • • • •

Financial statements present a lot of information in the form of data. This data, when applied to various *ratios* (comparative numbers), reveals trends that can be used to evaluate a firm's financial health, its progress, and its prospects for the future.

Ratios are normally grouped into three major classifications:

1 **Solvency ratios** for estimating short-term and long-term risk

2 **Profitability ratios** for measuring potential earnings

3 **Activity ratios** for evaluating management's use of assets

Depending on the decisions to be made, a user may apply none, some, or all of these ratios.

Solvency Ratios: Borrower's Ability to Repay Debt

What are the chances that a borrower will be able to repay a loan and the interest due? Solvency ratios provide measures of a firm's ability to meet its debt obligations.

The Current Ratio and Short-Term Solvency **Short-term solvency ratios** measure a company's liquidity and its ability to pay immediate debts. The most commonly used of these is the **current ratio**, or "banker's ratio." This measures a firm's ability to generate cash to meet current obligations through the normal, orderly process of selling inventories and collecting revenues from customers. It is calculated by dividing current assets by current liabilities. The higher a firm's current ratio, the lower the risk to investors.

As a rule, a current ratio is satisfactory at 2:1 or higher—that is, if current assets more than double current liabilities. A smaller ratio may indicate that a firm will have trouble paying its bills.

How does Google measure up? Look again at the balance sheet in Figure 14.1. Judging from current assets and current liabilities at the end of 2007, we see that

$$\frac{\text{Current assets}}{\text{Current liabilities}} = \frac{\$17.29 \text{ billion}}{\$2.04 \text{ billion}} = 8.5$$

The industry average for companies that provide business services is 1.4. Google's current ratio of 8.5 indicates the firm is a good short-run credit risk.

Long-Term Solvency A firm that can't meet its long-term debt obligations is in danger of collapse or takeover—a risk that makes creditors and investors quite cautious. To evaluate a company's risk of running into this problem, creditors turn to the balance sheet to see the extent to which a firm is financed through borrowed money. Long-term solvency is calculated by dividing **debt**—total liabilities—by owners' equity. The lower a firm's debt, the lower the risk to investors and creditors. Companies with more debt may find themselves owing so much that they lack the income needed to meet interest payments or to repay borrowed money.

Leverage Sometimes, high debt can be not only acceptable, but also desirable. Borrowing funds gives a firm **leverage**—the ability to make otherwise unaffordable investments. In *leveraged buyouts*, firms have willingly taken on sometimes huge debts to buy out other

"It's up to you now, Miller. The only thing that can save us is an accounting breakthrough."

companies. If owning the purchased company generates profits above the cost of borrowing the purchase price, leveraging often makes sense. Unfortunately, many buyouts have caused problems because profits fell short of expected levels or because rising interest rates increased payments on the buyer's debt.

Profitability Ratios: Earnings Power for Owners

It's important to know whether a company is solvent in both the long and the short term, but risk alone is not an adequate basis for investment decisions. Investors also want some indication of the returns they can expect. Evidence of earnings power is available from profitability ratios, such as *earnings per share*.

Earnings per Share Defined as net income divided by the number of shares of common stock outstanding, **earnings per share** determines the size of the dividend that a firm can pay shareholders. As the ratio goes up, stock value increases because investors know that the firm can better afford to pay dividends. Naturally, stock loses market value if financial statements report a decline in earnings per share. For Google, we can use the net income total from the income statement in Figure 14.2, together with the number of outstanding shares of stock, to calculate earnings per share as follows:

EARNINGS PER SHARE
profitability ratio measuring the net profit that the company earns for each share of outstanding stock

EG CHAPTER 14

$$\frac{\text{Net income}}{\substack{\text{Number of} \\ \text{common shares} \\ \text{outstanding}}} = \frac{\$4,203.7 \text{ million}}{313.3 \text{ million} \atop \text{shares of stock}} = \frac{\$13.42}{\text{per share}}$$

This means that Google had net earnings of $13.42 (rounded) for each share of stock during 2007. In

Say What You Mean

Technically Speaking

The general manager began the meeting by asking for a report on the budget. The head of accounting replied: "On a static-budget basis, unfavorable variances were realized for variable expenses and total expenses. Favorable budget variances were realized for units sold, sales revenues, and operating income. However, on a flexible-budget basis, unfavorable variances were realized on variable expenses, fixed expenses, total expenses, and operating income."

At this point, you might find yourself wishing that the head of accounting would speak "in plain English." The key obstacle to your comprehending the report is specialization. Accountants and other specialists tend to develop their own languages to communicate with each other efficiently and clearly. These "languages" contain technical terms and jargon that may be confusing to those outside the field, a problem that led the U.S. Securities and Exchange Commission (SEC) to develop *A Plain English Handbook*. The SEC

strongly encourages companies to follow the handbook's guidelines when composing disclosure documents and other financial reports intended for investors. As former SEC Chairman Arthur Levitt argues in the handbook's introduction, "Companies that communicate successfully with their investors form stronger relationships with them."

The situation may be more complicated, however. In a 2006 paper, Feng Li of the University of Michigan's Stephen M. Ross School of Business analyzed the relationship between a company's earnings and the readability of its financial reports. He discovered that poorly performing firms were more likely to issue reports that are difficult to read. This led him to conclude that "managers may be opportunistically choosing the readability of annual reports to hide adverse information from investors." All of which serves to underscore Levitt's words about successful communication—we are more likely to trust what we understand.[16]

Table 14.3 **Overview of the Code of Ethics for CPAs**[17]

Membership in the American Institute of Certified Public Accountants is voluntary. By accepting membership, a certified public accountant assumes an obligation of self-discipline above and beyond the requirements of laws and regulations.	
Responsibilities	In carrying out their responsibilities as professionals, members should exercise sensitive professional and moral judgments in all their activities.
The Public Interest	Members should accept the obligation to act in a way that will serve the public interest, honor the public trust, and demonstrate commitment to professionalism.
Integrity	To maintain and broaden public confidence, members should perform all professional responsibilities with the highest sense of integrity.
Objectivity and Independence	A member should maintain objectivity and be free of conflicts of interest in discharging professional responsibilities. A member in public practice should be independent in fact and appearance when providing auditing and other attestation services.
Due Care	A member should observe the profession's technical and ethical standards, strive continually to improve competence and the quality of services, and discharge professional responsibility to the best of the member's ability.
Scope and Nature of Services	A member in public practice should observe the Principles of the Code of Professional Conduct in determining the scope and nature of services to be provided.

contrast, Time Warner's recent earnings were $1.08 per share, while Microsoft earned $1.70.

Activity Ratios: How Efficiently Is the Firm Using Its Resources?

The efficiency with which a firm uses resources is linked to profitability. As a potential investor, you want to know which company gets more mileage from its resources. Information obtained from the income statement can be used for *activity ratios* to measure this efficiency. For example, two firms use the same amount of resources or assets to perform a particular activity, such as advertising or inventory management. If Firm A generates greater profits or sales, it has used its resources more efficiently and so enjoys a better activity ratio. It means that Firm A is getting more bang for the buck.

Bringing Ethics into the Accounting Equation

The purpose of ethics in accounting is to maintain public confidence in business institutions, financial markets, and the products and services of the accounting profession. Without ethics, all of accounting's tools and methods would be meaningless because their usefulness depends, ultimately, on veracity in their application.

Why Accounting Ethics?

Amidst a flurry of unscrupulous activity, ethics remains an area where one person who is willing to "do the right thing" can make a difference—and people do, every day. Refusing to turn a blind eye to unethical accounting around her at Enron, Lynn Brewer tried to alert people inside about misstatements of the company's assets. When that failed, she, along with colleagues Sherron Watkins and Margaret Ceconi, talked with the U.S. Committee on Energy and Commerce to voice concerns about Enron's condition. To Brewer, maintaining personal and professional integrity was an overriding concern, and she acted accordingly.

AICPA's Code of Professional Conduct The **code of professional conduct** for public accountants in the United States is maintained and enforced by the AICPA.

Table 14.4 **Examples of Unethical and Illegal Accounting Actions**[18]

Corporation	Accounting Violation
AOL Time Warner	America Online (AOL) inflated ad revenues to keep stock prices high before and after merging with Time Warner.
Cendant	Inflated income in financial statements by $500 million through fraud and errors.
HCA, Columbia/HCA	Defrauded Medicare, Medicaid, and TRICARE through false cost claims and unlawful billings (must pay $1.7 billion in civil penalties, damages, criminal fines, and penalties).
Tyco	CEO Dennis Kozlowski illegally used company funds to buy expensive art for personal possession (he received an 8- to 25-year prison sentence).
Waste Management	Overstated income in financial statements (false and misleading reports) by improperly calculating depreciation and salvage value for equipment.
WorldCom	Hid $3.8 billion in expenses to show an inflated (false) profit instead of loss in an annual income statement.

The institute identifies six ethics-related areas—listed in Table 14.3—with which accountants must comply to maintain certification. Comprehensive details for compliance in each area are spelled out in the AICPA Code of Professional Conduct. The IMA maintains a similar code to provide ethical guidelines for the management accounting profession.

In reading the AICPA's Code, you can see that it forbids misrepresentation and fraud in financial statements. Deception certainly violates the call for exercising moral judgments (in "Responsibilities"), is contrary to the public interest (by deceiving investors) and does not honor the public trust (in "The Public Interest"). Misleading statements destroy the public's confidence in the accounting profession and in business in general. While the Code prohibits such abuses, its success depends, ultimately, on its acceptance and use by the professionals it governs.

Violations of Accounting Ethics and GAAP
Unethical and illegal accounting violations have dominated the popular press in recent years. Some of the more notorious cases, listed in Table 14.4, violated the public's trust, ruined retirement plans for thousands of employees, and caused shutdowns and lost jobs. As you read each case, you should be able to see how its violation relates to the presentation of balance sheets and income statements in this chapter. In each case, adversity would have been prevented if employees had followed the code of professional conduct. In each case, nearly all of the code's six ethics-related areas were violated. And in every case, "professionals" willingly participated in unethical behavior. Such was the impetus for Sarbox.

Questions for Review

1. Who are the users of accounting information, and for what purposes do they use it?
2. Identify the three types of services performed by CPAs.
3. Explain the ways in which financial accounting differs from managerial (management) accounting.
4. Discuss the activities and services performed by forensic accountants.
5. What are the three basic financial statements, and what major information does each contain?
6. Explain how financial ratios allow managers to gain additional information from financial statements.

Questions for Analysis

7. If you were planning to invest in a company, which of the three types of financial statements would you most want to see? Why?
8. Suppose that you, as the manager of a company, are making changes to fully comply with provisions of the Sarbanes-Oxley Act. Your company traditionally has relied on CPA firms for auditing, tax services, and management services. What major changes will your company need to make?

Application Exercises

9. Interview an accountant at a local firm. How does the firm use budgets? How does budgeting help managers plan business activities? How does budgeting help them control activities? Give examples.
10. Interview the manager of a local retailer, wholesale business, or manufacturing firm about the role of ethics in that company's accounting practices. Is ethics in accounting an important issue to the manager? If the firm has its own private accountants, what measures are taken for ensuring ethical practices internally? What steps, if any, does the company take to maintain ethical relationships in its dealings with CPA firms?

Managing Finances

After reading this chapter, you should be able to:

1 Explain the concept of the time value of money and the principle of compound growth.

2 Identify the investment opportunities offered by mutual funds and exchange-traded funds.

3 Describe the role of securities markets, and identify the major stock exchanges and stock markets.

4 Explain how securities markets are regulated and tracked.

5 Describe the risk-return relationship, and discuss the use of diversification and asset allocation for investments.

6 Describe the various ways that firms raise capital and identify the pros and cons of each method.

7 Identify the reasons a company might make an initial public offering of its stock, and explain how stock value is determined.

Investing In Green

Traders are accustomed to using financial markets for investing in just about everything, ranging from pig bellies to movie production, in hopes of gaining a profit. New financial markets for commodities known as carbon credits, however, are driven, not just by profit motive, but by a sense of social responsibility. The economic incentives of emissions trading (ET) bring together both environmental polluters and green investors in an effort to both turn a profit and save the planet.

Here's how it works—regulators in various countries are setting limits on the amounts of industrial pollutants that can be released, including carbon dioxide (CO_2), sulfur dioxide, and mercury. A leading example, the European Union's Emissions Trading Scheme (ETS), was started by the European Commission in 2005 to meet the EU's obligations for carbon reductions in accordance with the Kyoto Protocol on Climate Change. The ETS annually sets a cap for the total amount of CO_2 emissions allowed for each EU member state and company. The state totals and the EU total cannot exceed the caps.

Companies are issued a permit containing a number of "credits" (or certificates) representing the right to emit a certain amount of CO_2. Any company producing below its CO_2 cap can sell its surplus credits to other, more pollution-prone companies that need more credits to keep operating. That's where trading comes into play—it's like a stock exchange that quickly matches up buyers and sellers of emissions credits.

With emissions trading, environmentally oriented companies (so-called green companies) sell unneeded emissions allowances and gain a financial return on past investments for reducing pollution. Such companies view environmental cleanup not as an expense, but as a responsible investment. Other companies, finding it cheaper to avoid such investments, are facing higher costs as they bid for others' unused carbon credits. The trading scheme is adding a new financial incentive for cleaner industries that reduce carbon emissions and other greenhouse gases.[1]

What's in It for Me?

Emissions trading is just one of countless activities drawing investors of every kind to the world's financial markets. Businesses from all over the world, representing every industry, converge there each day, seeking funds that can be used to finance their endeavors and pay off their debts. Individual investors gather as well, in person or—increasingly—online, looking to make their money "work" for them. This chapter will help you understand the various ways this is possible, whether your goals are short- or long-term, whether you are motivated by the desire for profit or security, or simply because you enjoy the challenges inherent in the successful raising and investing of capital.

TIME VALUE OF MONEY principle that invested money grows, over time, by earning interest or some other form of return

COMPOUND GROWTH the compounding of interest over time—with each additional time period, interest returns accumulate

STOCK a portion of ownership of a corporation

COMMON STOCK the most basic form of ownership, including voting rights on major issues, in a company

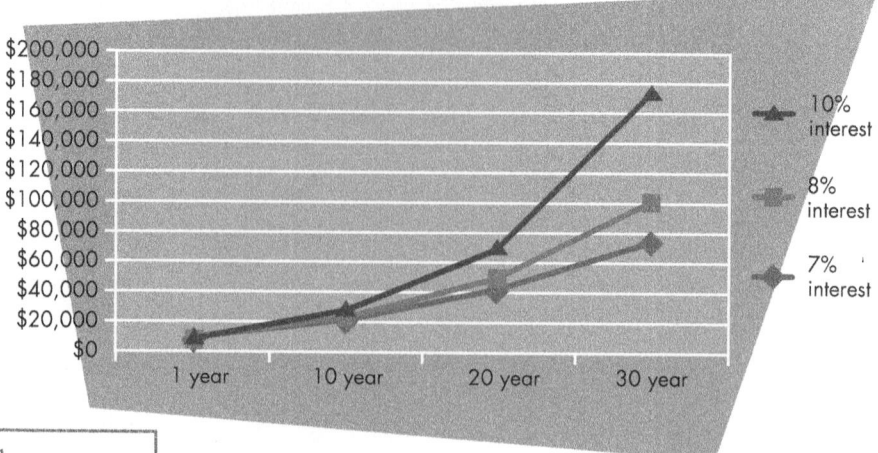

Figure 16.1
Amount to Which an Initial $10,000 Investment Grows

Maximizing Capital Growth

Wise investments are the key to growing your money, especially if you are seeking to build capital to start your own business. In searching for investment opportunities, a number of concepts come into play for evaluating alternative investments and sorting out the good from the bad.

The Time Value of Money

The **time value of money**, perhaps the single most important concept in business finance, recognizes the basic fact that, while it's invested, money grows by earning interest or yielding some other form of return. Time value stems from the principle of **compound growth**—the compounding of interest paid to the investor over given time periods. With each additional time period, interest payments accumulate and earn more interest, thus multiplying the earning capacity of the investment.

Making Better Use of Your Time Value What if you invested $10,000 at seven percent interest for one year? You would earn $700 on your $10,000 investment. If you re-invested the principal amount plus the interest you earned during the first year for another 4 years, you'd end up with $14,025. Now, if you were planning for retirement and reinvested that money at the same interest rate for another 25 years, you could

retire with $76,122—almost eight times the amount you started with!

Figure 16.1 illustrates how the returns from an initial investment of $10,000 accumulate substantially over longer periods of time. Notice that the gains for the last 10 years are much greater than for the first 10 years, illustrating the power of compound growth. Each year, the interest rate is applied to a larger sum. Notice also the larger gains from higher interest rates. Even a seemingly small change in interest rates, from 7% to 8%, results in much larger accumulations.

Common Stock

As you can see from Figure 16.1, the best way to take advantage of the time value of money is to obtain a high rate of return on your investment. One way to achieve a high rate of return is to invest in the stock market. A **stock** is a portion of the ownership of a corporation. The company's total ownership is divided into small parts, called *shares*, that can be bought and sold to determine how much of the company (how many shares of stock) is owned by each shareholder.

While several types of stock exist, common stock is the most prominent. A share of **common stock** is the most basic form of ownership in a company. Individuals and other companies purchase a firm's common stock in the hope that it will increase in value and provide dividend income; in addition, each common share has a vote on major issues that are brought before the shareholders.

The Rule of 72

How long does it take to double an investment? A handy rule of thumb is called the "Rule of 72." You can find the number of years needed to double your money by dividing the annual interest rate (in percent) into 72. If, for example, you re-invest annually at 8 percent, you'll double your money in about 9 years:

$$\frac{72}{8} = 9 \text{ years to double the money}$$

The Rule of 72 can also calculate how much interest you must get if you want to double your money in a given number of years: Simply divide 72 by the desired number of years. If you want to double your money in 10 years, you need to get 7.2 percent:

$$\frac{72}{10} = 7.2 \text{ percent interest needed to double the money}$$

The lesson for the investor is clear: seek *higher* interest rates because money will double more frequently.

Stock values are usually expressed in two different ways: as market value and book value.

1 A stock's real value is its **market value**—the current price of a share in the stock market. Market value reflects the amount that buyers are willing to pay for a share of the company's stock.

2 The **book value** for a share of common stock is determined as the firm's owners' equity (from the balance sheet) divided by the number of common shares owned by all shareholders. Book value is used as a comparison indicator because the market value for successful companies is usually greater than its book value. Thus, when market price falls to near book value, some profit-seeking investors buy the stock on the principle that it is underpriced and will increase in the future.

Investment Traits of Common Stock Common stocks are among the riskiest of all investments. Uncertainties about the stock market itself can quickly change a given stock's value. Furthermore, when companies have unprofitable years, or when economic conditions go sour, potential investors become wary of future stock values, so share price drops. On the upside, however, common stocks offer high growth potential; when a company's performance brightens, because of public acceptance of a hot new product, for example, share price can sharply increase.

Dividends A **dividend** is a payment to shareholders, on a per-share basis, from the company's earnings. Dividend payments are optional and variable—the corporation's board of directors decides whether and when a dividend will be paid, as well as the amount that is best for the future of the company and its shareholders. Many companies distribute between 30 and 70 percent of their profits to shareholders. However, some firms, especially fast-growing companies, do not pay dividends; instead, they use cash earnings for expanding the company so that future earnings can grow even faster. What's more, any company can have a bad year and decide to reduce or omit dividend payments to stockholders.

Mutual Funds and Exchange-Traded Funds

As an alternative to buying stock, mutual funds and exchange-traded funds are popular because they offer attractive investment opportunities for various financial objectives and often do not require large sums of money for entry. In addition, the simple and easy transaction process makes them accessible to the public.

Mutual funds are created by companies such as T. Rowe Price and Vanguard that pool cash investments from individuals and organizations to purchase a portfolio of stocks, bonds, and other securities. The portfolio is expected to appreciate in market value and otherwise produce income for the mutual fund and its investors.

Reasons for Investing It's relatively easy to open a mutual fund account by e-mail or phone. There are numerous funds that meet any chosen financial objective. Three of the most common objectives are financial stability, conservative growth, and aggressive growth.

■ **Stability and Safety**
Funds stressing safety seek only modest growth with little fluctuation in principal value regardless of economic conditions. They include *money market mutual funds* and other funds that preserve the fund holders' capital and reliably pay current income. Typical assets of these funds include lower-risk

MARKET VALUE current price of a share of stock in the stock market

BOOK VALUE value of a common stock expressed as the firm's owners' equity divided by the number of common shares

DIVIDEND payment to shareholders, on a per-share basis, out of the company's earnings

MUTUAL FUND company that pools cash investments from individuals and organizations to purchase a portfolio of stocks, bonds, and other securities

PROSPECTUS registration statement filed with the SEC, containing information for prospective investors about a security to be offered and the issuing company

INSIDER TRADING illegal practice of using special knowledge about a firm for profit or gain

The Securities and Exchange Commission

The U.S. Securities and Exchange Commission (SEC) is the regulation and enforcement agency that oversees the markets' activities, including the ways securities are issued. The SEC was created in 1934 to prevent the kinds of abuses that led to the stock market crash of 1929. The SEC regulates the public offering of new securities by requiring that all companies file prospectuses before proposed offerings commence. To protect investors from fraudulent issues, a **prospectus** contains pertinent information about both the offered security and the issuing company. False statements are subject to criminal penalties.

The SEC also enforces laws against **insider trading**—the use of special knowledge about a firm for profit or gain. It is illegal, for example, for an employee of a firm to tell others about an anticipated event that may affect the value of that firm's stock, such as an acquisition or a merger, before news of that event is made public. Those in possession of such insider knowledge would have an unfair advantage over other investors.

EXCHANGE-TRADED FUND a bundle of stocks or bonds that are in an index that tracks the overall movement of a market but, unlike a mutual fund, can be traded like a stock

SECURITIES stocks, bonds, and mutual funds representing secured, or asset-based, claims by investors against issuers

SECURITIES MARKETS markets in which stocks and bonds are sold

U.S. corporate bonds, U.S. government bonds, and other safe short-term securities that provide stable income from interest and dividends.

■ **Conservative Capital Growth** Mutual funds that stress preservation of capital and current income, but also seek some capital appreciation, are called *balanced funds*. Typically, these funds hold long-term municipal bonds, corporate bonds, and common stocks with good dividend-paying records and potential for market appreciation (higher market value), though there is always the risk of price declines if the general stock market falls.

Founded in 1792 and located at the corner of Wall and Broad Streets in New York City, the New York Stock Exchange sees billions of shares change hands each day.

■ **Aggressive Growth** *Aggressive growth funds* seek maximum long-term capital growth. They sacrifice current income and safety by investing in stocks of new (and even troubled) companies, firms developing new products and technologies, and other high-risk securities. They are designed for investors who can accept the risk of loss inherent in common stock investing with severe price fluctuations, but also the potential for superior returns over time.

Most Mutual Funds Don't Match the Market Many, but not all, mutual funds are managed by "experts" who select the fund's stocks and other securities that provide the fund's income. Unfortunately, some estimates indicate that up to 80% of these managed funds do not perform as well as the average return of the overall stock market, due to costly management expenses and underperforming stocks.[2] This underperformance disadvantage has resulted in the emergence of passively managed mutual funds such as index funds, which nearly match the performance of a particular market. The selection of which stocks to purchase in an index fund is relatively automatic—it holds many of the same stocks as the market it tracks—and requires little human input, thus reducing management expenses.

Exchange-Traded Funds As with an index mutual fund, an **exchange-traded fund (ETF)** is a bundle of stocks (or bonds) that are in an index that tracks the overall movement of a market; unlike a mutual fund, however, an ETF can be traded like a stock. Each share of an ETF rises and falls as market prices change continuously for the market being tracked.

Advantages of ETFs ETFs offer three areas of advantage over mutual funds: They can be traded throughout the day like a stock, they have low operating expenses, and they do not require high initial investments. Because they are traded on stock exchanges (hence, "exchange traded"), ETFs can be bought and sold—priced continuously—any time throughout the day. This *intraday trading* means you can time your transaction during the day to buy or sell when (or if) the market reaches a desired price. Mutual fund shares, in contrast, are priced once daily, at the end of the day. Thus, when you buy or sell during the day, you don't find out the share price until after the day has ended.

Whereas many mutual funds pass the costs of expensive active management onto shareholders, an ETF is bound by a rule that specifies what stocks will be purchased and when; once the rule is established, little or no active human decisions are involved. The *lower annual operating expenses* mean that, for the buy-and-hold investor, annual fees for ETFs are as low as 0.09 percent of assets; annual fees for mutual funds average 1.4 percent.[3]

Finally, unlike mutual funds, ETFs require no minimum investment, meaning they offer *ease of entry* for investors getting started without much money.[4] On the other hand, because ETFs must be bought and sold through a broker, they require payment of a brokerage commission (transaction fees). Traders who buy and sell frequently can end up paying more in transactions fees, even surpassing a mutual fund's high management expenses.[5]

The Business of Trading Securities

Stocks, bonds, and mutual funds are known as **securities** because they represent *secured*, or financially valuable claims on the part of investors. The markets in which stocks and bonds are sold are called **securities markets**. Mutual funds, on the other hand, are not bought and sold on securities markets, but are managed by financial professionals in the investment companies that create, buy, and sell the funds.

Primary and Secondary Securities Markets In **primary securities markets**, new stocks and bonds are bought and sold by firms and governments. Sometimes, new securities are sold to single buyers or small groups of buyers. These so-called *private placements* are desirable because they allow issuers to keep their plans confidential.

Most new stocks and some bonds are sold on the wider public market. To bring a new security to market, the issuing firm must get approval from the U.S. **Securities and Exchange Commission (SEC)**—the government agency that regulates U.S. securities markets. The firm also needs the services of an **investment bank**—a financial institution such as Merrill Lynch or Goldman Sachs that specializes in issuing and reselling new securities. Such investment banking firms provide three important services:

1 They advise companies on the timing and financial terms of new issues.

2 They *underwrite*—that is, assume liability for—new securities, thus providing the issuing firms with 100% of the money (less commission). The inability to resell the securities is a risk that the banks must bear.

3 They create distribution networks for moving new securities through groups of other banks and brokers into the hands of individual investors.

New securities, however, represent only a small portion of traded securities. *Existing* stocks and bonds are sold in the much larger **secondary securities market**, which is handled by such familiar bodies as the New York Stock Exchange and, more recently, by online trading with electronic communication networks.

Stock Exchanges

Most of the buying and selling of stocks, historically, has been handled by organized stock exchanges. A **stock exchange** is an organization of individuals coordinated to provide an institutional auction setting in which stocks can be bought and sold.

The Trading Floor Each exchange regulates the places and times at which trading may occur. The most important difference between traditional exchanges and the electronic market is the geographic location of the trading activity. Brokers at an exchange trade face-to-face on the *trading floor* (also referred to as an *outcry market*). The electronic market, on the other hand, conducts trades electronically among thousands of dealers in remote locations around the world.

Trading floors today are equipped with vast arrays of electronic communications equipment for displaying buy and sell orders or confirming completed trades. A variety of news services furnish up-to-the-minute information about world events and business developments. Any change in these factors, then, may be swiftly reflected in share prices.

The Major Stock Exchanges Among the stock exchanges that operate on trading floors in the United States, the New York Stock Exchange is the largest. Today it faces stiff competition from both the electronic market in the United States—NASDAQ—and large foreign exchanges, such as those in London and Tokyo.

The New York Stock Exchange For many people, "the stock market" means the *New York Stock Exchange (NYSE)*. Founded in 1792, the NYSE is the model for exchanges worldwide. Only firms meeting certain minimum requirements—earning power, total value of outstanding stock, and number of shareholders—are eligible for listing on the NYSE.[6]

Today's NYSE is a *hybrid market* that utilizes both floor and electronic trading. When a client places an order through a brokerage house or online, it is transmitted to a broker on the NYSE floor. Floor brokers who want to trade that stock meet together to agree upon a trading price based on supply and demand, and the order is executed. Alternatively, buyers can use the NYSE's Direct+ service to automatically execute trades electronically.

Other, smaller, U.S. exchanges include the American Stock Exchange (AMEX), also located in New York City, and several regional stock exchanges organized over a century ago to serve investors in places other than New York—including Chicago, Los Angeles, San Francisco, Cincinnati, and Spokane.

Global Stock Exchanges As recently as 1980, the U.S. market accounted for more than half the value of the world market in traded stocks. Market activities, however, have shifted as the value of shares listed on foreign exchanges continues to grow. Table 16.1 identifies several stock exchanges and the volume of shares traded each day. Relatively new exchanges are also flourishing in cities from Shanghai to Warsaw.

PRIMARY SECURITIES MARKET market in which new stocks and bonds are bought and sold by firms and governments

SECURITIES AND EXCHANGE COMMISSION (SEC) government agency that regulates U.S. securities markets

INVESTMENT BANK financial institution that specializes in issuing and reselling new securities

SECONDARY SECURITIES MARKET market in which existing (not new) stocks and bonds are sold to the public

STOCK EXCHANGE an organization of individuals to provide an institutional auction setting in which stocks can be bought and sold

NATIONAL ASSOCIATION OF SECURITIES DEALERS AUTOMATED QUOTATION (NASDAQ) SYSTEM world's oldest electronic stock market consisting of dealers who buy and sell securities over a network of electronic communications

ELECTRONIC COMMUNICATION NETWORK (ECN) electronic trading system that brings buyers and sellers together outside traditional stock exchanges

STOCK BROKER individual or organization that receives and executes buy and sell orders on behalf of outside customers in return for commissions

The NASDAQ Market The **National Association of Securities Dealers Automated Quotation (NASDAQ) system**, the world's oldest electronic stock market, was established in 1971. Whereas buy and sell orders to the NYSE are gathered on the trading floor, NASDAQ orders are gathered and executed on a computer network connecting 350,000 terminals worldwide. Currently, NASDAQ is working with officials in an increasing number of countries in replacing the trading floors of traditional exchanges with electronic networks like NASDAQ's.

The stocks of some 3,300 companies, both emerging and well known, are traded by NASDAQ. Although the volume of shares traded surpasses that of the New York Stock Exchange, the total market value of NASDAQ's U.S. stocks is less than that of the NYSE.

International Consolidation and Cross-Border Ownership A wave of technological advances, along with regulatory and competitive factors, is propelling the consolidation of stock exchanges and the changeover from physical to electronic trading floors across international borders. Electronic communication networks have opened the door to around-the-clock and around-the-globe trading. Every major European stock exchange had gone electronic by the close of the twentieth century, and the United States is catching up. Stock exchanges that don't have enough savvy with electronic technologies to stay competitive are merging or partnering with those having more advanced trading systems. The intensified competition among stock exchanges is resulting in speedier transactions and lower transaction fees for investors.[8]

Non-Exchange Trading: Electronic Communication Networks

The SEC in 1998 authorized the creation of **electronic communication networks (ECNs)**—electronic trading systems that bring buyers and sellers together outside of traditional stock exchanges by automatically matching buy and sell orders at specified prices. ECNs have gained rapid popularity because the trading procedures are fast and efficient, often lowering transactions costs per share to mere pennies. They also allow after-hours

Table 16.1   **Selected Global Stock Exchanges and Markets**[7]

Country	Stock Exchange	Average Daily Trading Volume (millions of shares)
Australia	Australian Stock Exchange	1,200
Brazil	Sao Paulo Bovespa	18,000
Canada	Toronto Stock Exchange	272
France	Paris Bourse Stock Market	55
Hong Kong	Hong Kong Stock Exchange	7,000
Japan	Tokyo Stock Exchange	1,400
United Kingdom	London Stock Exchange	370
United States	New York Stock Exchange	1,400

trading (after traditional markets have closed for the day) and protect traders' anonymity.[9]

ECNs must register with the SEC as broker-dealers. The ECN then provides service to subscribers, that is, other broker-dealers and institutional investors. Subscribers can view all orders at any time on the system's Web site to see information on what trades have taken place and at what times.[10] Individual investors must open an account with a subscriber (a broker-dealer) before they can send buy or sell orders to the ECN system.

Individual Investor Trading

Some of the many individual investors who buy and sell securities are novices who seek the advice of experienced professionals, or brokers. Investors who are well informed and experienced, however, often prefer to invest independently without outside guidance.

Stock Brokers   **Stock brokers** earn commissions by executing buy and sell orders for outside customers. Although they match buyers with sellers, brokers do not own the securities. They earn commissions from the individuals and organizations for whom they place orders.

Discount Brokers Like many products, brokerage assistance can be purchased at either discount or at full-service prices. Discount brokers offer well-informed individual investors who know what they want to buy or sell a fast, low-cost way to participate in the market. Sales personnel receive fees or salaries, not commissions. Unlike many full-service brokers, they do not offer in-depth investment advice or person-to-person sales consultations. They do, however, offer automated online services, such as stock research, industry analysis, and screening for specific types of stocks.

Full-Service Brokers Despite the growth in online investing, full-service brokers remain an important resource, both for new, uninformed investors and for experienced investors who don't have time to keep up with all the latest developments. Full-service firms such as Merrill Lynch offer clients consulting advice in personal financial planning, estate planning, and tax strategies, along with a wider range of investment products. In addition to delivering and interpreting information, financial advisors can point clients toward investments that might otherwise be lost in an avalanche of online financial data.

Online Investing The popularity of online trading stems from convenient access to the Internet, fast, no-nonsense transactions, and the opportunity for self-directed investors to manage their own investments while paying low fees for trading.

Online investors buy into and sell out of the stocks of thousands of companies daily. Consequently, keeping track of who owns what at any given time has become a monumental burden. Relief has come from **book-entry ownership**. Historically, shares of stock have been issued as physical paper certificates; now they are simply recorded in the companies' books, thereby eliminating the costs of storing, exchanging, and replacing certificates.

Tracking the Market Using Stock Indexes

For decades investors have used stock indexes to measure market performance and to predict future movements of stock markets. Although not indicative of the status of individual securities, **market indexes** provide useful summaries of overall price trends, both in specific industries and in the stock market as a whole. Market indexes, for example, reveal bull and bear market trends. **Bull markets** are periods of rising stock prices, generally lasting 12 months or longer; investors are motivated to buy, confident they will realize capital gains. Periods of falling stock prices, usually 20% off peak prices, are called **bear markets**; investors are motivated to sell, anticipating further falling prices.

As Figure 16.2 shows, the past three decades have been characterized primarily by bull markets, including the longest in history, from 1981 to the beginning of 2000. In contrast, the period 2000 to 2003 was characterized by a bear market, as was 2008. The data that characterize such periods are drawn from three leading market indexes: the Dow Jones, Standard & Poor's, and NASDAQ Composite.

BOOK-ENTRY OWNERSHIP procedure that holds investors' shares in book-entry form, rather than issuing a physical paper certificate of ownership

MARKET INDEX statistical indicator designed to measure the performance of a large group of stocks or track the price changes of a stock market

BULL MARKET period of rising stock prices, lasting 12 months or longer, featuring investor confidence for future gains and motivation to buy

BEAR MARKET period of falling stock prices marked by negative investor sentiments with motivation to sell ahead of anticipated losses

---

Say What You Mean

An Insider on Trial

In July 2007, Joseph P. Nacchio, the former CEO of Qwest Communications, was sentenced to serve 6 years in prison following his conviction on 19 counts of insider trading. He was also ordered to pay a fine of $19 million—$1 million per count, the maximum financial penalty allowed by law—and turn over the $52 million from gains he had earned from the illegal trading.

Nacchio had steered Qwest to the top of the telecommunications industry, riding the Internet bubble of the late-1990s. By 2001, however, the bubble had burst, and Qwest seemed increasingly unlikely to hit its aggressive earnings targets. Nacchio chose not to inform investors of these concerns, instead publicly pronouncing favorable growth prospects for the company. At the same time, he accelerated his sale of more than $100 million worth of

Qwest common stock, ultimately making $52 million in violation of insider trading laws.

Nearly a year after Nacchio's conviction, however, an appeals court overturned the guilty verdict, ruling that the trial judge had erred in refusing to allow an expert witness to testify on Nacchio's behalf. The appeals court did, however, find sufficient evidence of insider trading to warrant retrying the case, and the lead prosecutor has vowed to keep fighting, an indication of the seriousness with which insider trading is viewed in the wake of the corporate scandals that marked the early 2000s. Furthermore, this case illustrates the dangers of using insider information to mislead the public.[11]

DOW JONES INDUSTRIAL AVERAGE (DJIA) oldest and most widely cited market index based on the prices of 30 blue-chip, large-cap industrial firms on the NYSE

S&P 500 market index of U.S. equities based on the performance of 500 large-cap stocks representing various sectors of the overall equities market

NASDAQ COMPOSITE INDEX market index that includes all NASDAQ-listed companies, both domestic and foreign, with a high proportion of technology companies and small-cap stocks

RUSSELL 2000 INDEX specialty index that uses 2000 stocks to measure the performance of the smallest U.S. companies

Figure 16.2
Bull and Bear Markets

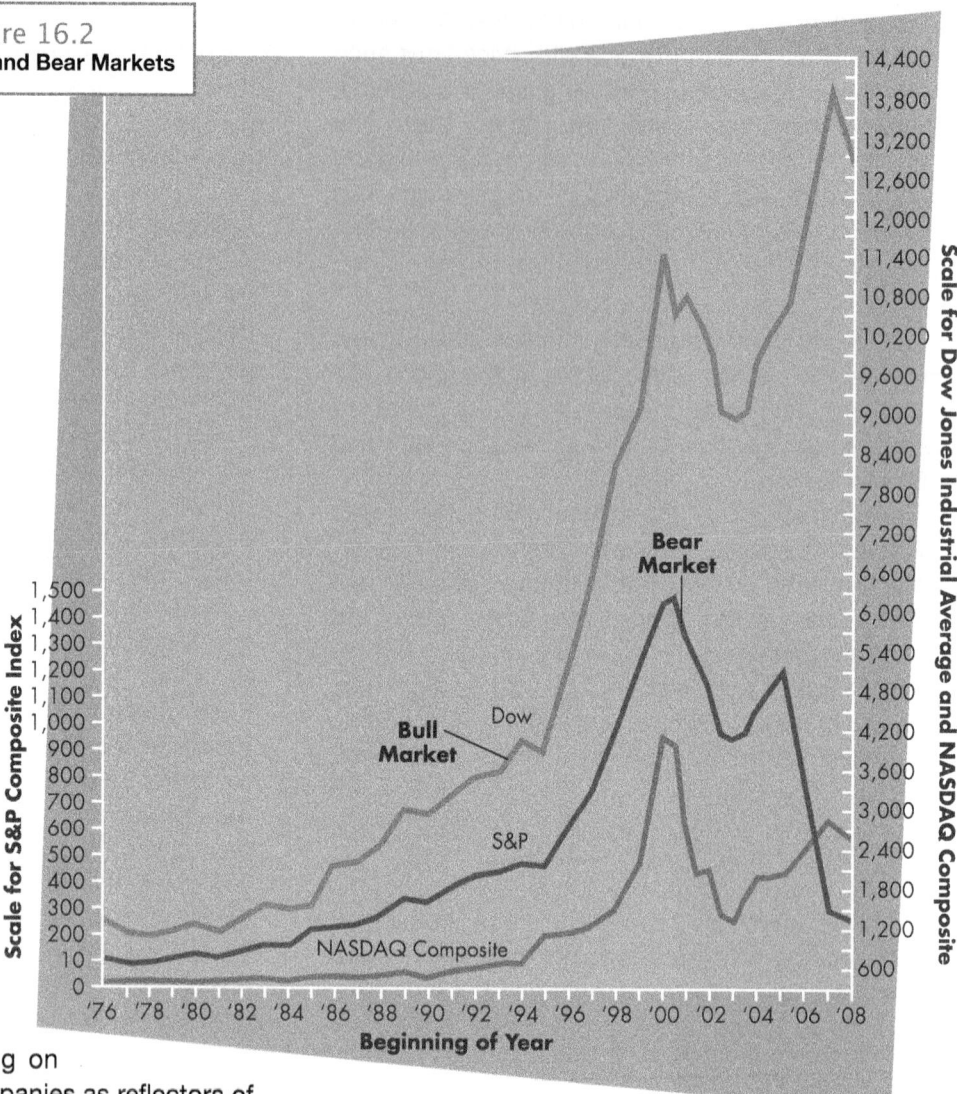

The Dow The **Dow Jones Industrial Average (DJIA)** is the oldest and most widely cited U.S. market index. It measures the performance of the industrial sector of the U.S. stock markets by focusing on just 30 blue-chip, large-cap companies as reflectors of the economic health of the many similar U.S. firms. The Dow is an average of the stock prices for these 30 large firms, and traders and investors use it as a traditional barometer of the market's overall movement.

Over the decades, the Dow has been revised and updated to reflect the changing composition of U.S. companies and industries. The most recent modification occurred in 2004, when three companies were added—insurance giant American International Group, pharmaceuticals goliath Pfizer, telecom titan Verizon—replacing AT&T, Eastman Kodak, and International Paper. These changes better reflect today's information-based economy and the increasing prominence of financial services and pharmaceuticals.

The S&P 500 Because it considers very few firms, the Dow is a limited gauge of the overall U.S. stock market. The **S&P 500** is a broader report, considered by many to be the best single indicator of the U.S. equities market. It consists of 500 large-cap stocks, including companies from various sectors—such as information

technology, energy, industrials, financials, health care, consumer staples, and telecommunications—for a balanced representation of the overall large-cap equities market.

The NASDAQ Composite Because it considers more stocks, some Wall Street observers regard the **NASDAQ Composite Index** as one of the most useful of all market indexes. Unlike the Dow and the S&P 500, all NASDAQ-listed companies, not just a selected few, are included in the index for a total of some 3,200 firms (mostly domestic, and about 300 foreign). However, it includes a high proportion of technology companies, including small-company stocks, and a smaller representation of other sectors—financial, consumer products, and industrials.

The Russell 2000 Investors in the U.S. small-cap market are interested in the **Russell 2000 Index**—a specialty index that measures the performance of the smallest U.S. companies based on market capitalization. As the most quoted index focusing on the small-cap portion of the U.S. economy, its stocks represent a range of sectors such as financials, consumer discretionary, health care, technology, materials, and utilities.

Index-Matching ETFs Countless other specialty indexes exist for specific industries, countries, and economic sectors to meet investors' diverse needs. Additionally, many exchange-traded funds are available to investors for duplicating (or nearly duplicating) the market performance of popular stock-market indexes. For example, one ETF, Standard & Poor's Depository Receipts (SPDRS, known as *Spiders*), owns a portfolio of stocks that matches the composition of the S&P 500 index. Similarly the Fidelity® NASDAQ Composite Index® Tracking Stock holds a portfolio of equities for tracking the NASDAQ Composite Index.

The Risk-Return Relationship

Each type of investment has a **risk–return (risk-reward) relationship**: Whereas safer investments tend to offer lower returns, riskier investments tend to offer higher returns (rewards).

Figure 16.3 shows the general risk–return relationship for various financial instruments, along with the types of investors they attract. Thus, conservative investors, who have a low tolerance for risk, will opt for no-risk U.S. Treasury Bills, or even intermediate-term high-grade corporate bonds that rate low in terms of risk on future returns, but also low on the size of expected returns. The reverse is true of aggressive investors who prefer the higher risks and potential returns from long-term junk bonds and common stocks.

Investment Dividends (or Interest), Appreciation, and Total Return

In evaluating potential investments, investors look at returns from dividends (or from interest),

returns from price appreciation, and total return.

Dividends The returns from stock dividends are commonly referred to as the **current dividend yield** (or, in the case of interest from a loan, the **interest dividend yield**), and are figured by dividing the yearly dollar amount of dividend income by the investment's current market value. In 2008, for example, each share of GE stock was receiving annual dividends payments of $1.24. If, on a particular day, the share price was $33.82, the current yield would be 3.66% ($1.24/$33.82 × 100). This dividend can then be compared against current yields from other investments. Larger dividend yields, of course, are preferred to smaller returns.

Price Appreciation Another source of returns depends on whether the investment is increasing or decreasing in dollar value. **Price appreciation** is an increase in the dollar value of an investment. Suppose, for example, you purchased a share of GE stock for $33.82, then sold it one year later for $36.50. The price appreciation

EG CHAPTER 16

RISK-RETURN (RISK-REWARD) RELATIONSHIP principle that safer investments tend to offer lower returns whereas riskier investments tend to offer higher returns (rewards)

CURRENT/INTEREST DIVIDEND YIELD yearly dollar amount of income divided by the investment's current market value, expressed as a percentage

PRICE APPRECIATION increase in the dollar value of an investment at two points in time (the amount by which the price of a security increases)

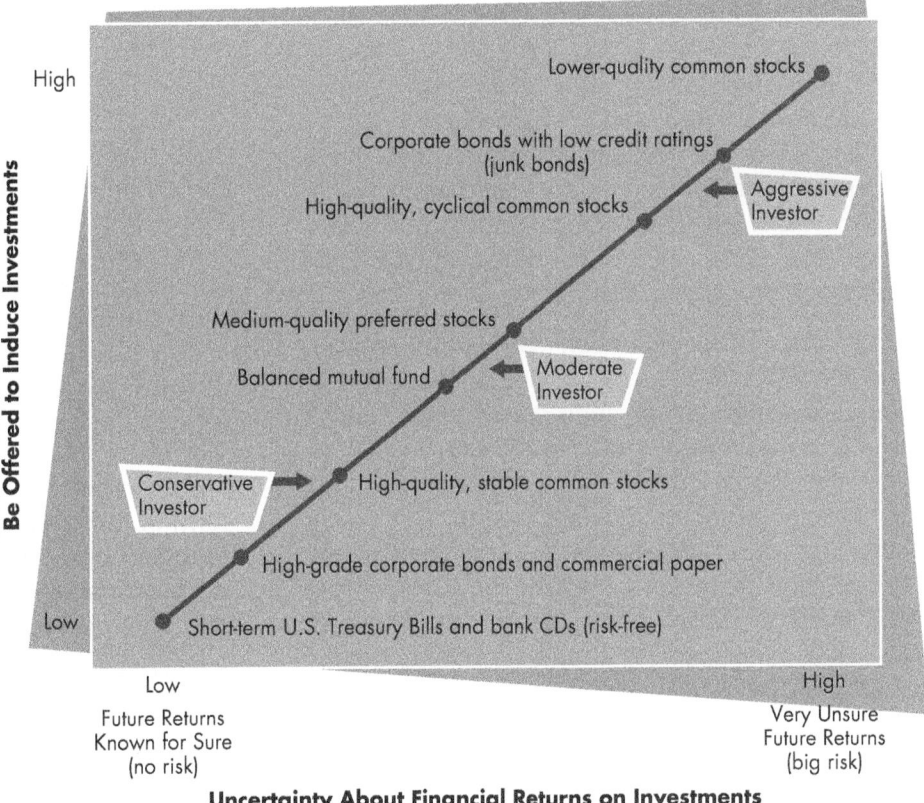

Figure 16.3
Uncertainty About Financial Returns on Investments[12]

Uncertainty About Financial Returns on Investments

CAPITAL GAIN the profit realized from the increased value of an investment

DIVERSIFICATION purchase of several different kinds of investments rather than just one

ASSET ALLOCATION relative amount of funds invested in (or allocated to) each of several investment alternatives

PORTFOLIO combined holdings of all the financial investments of any company or individual

SECURED LOAN (ASSET-BACKED LOAN) a loan to finance an asset, backed by the borrower pledging the asset as collateral to the lender

COLLATERAL an asset pledged for the fulfillment of repaying a loan

LOAN PRINCIPAL the amount of money that is loaned and must be repaid

is $2.68 ($36.50 – 33.82). This profit, realized from the increased value of an investment, is known as a **capital gain**.

Total Return The sum of an investment's current dividend (interest) yield and capital gain is referred to as its total return. Total return cannot be accurately evaluated until it's compared to the investment that was required to get that return. Total return as a percentage of investment is calculated as follows:

Total return (%) = (Current dividend payment + Capital gain)/Original investment × 100.

To complete our GE example, the total return as a percentage of our one-year investment would be 11.59% [($1.24 + $2.68)/$33.82 × 100]. Note that larger total returns are preferred to smaller ones.

Reducing Risk with Diversification and Asset Allocation

Investors seldom take an extreme approach—total risk or total risk avoidance—in selecting their investments. Extreme positions attract extreme results; instead, most investors select a mixed portfolio of investments—some riskier and some more conservative—that, collectively, provides the overall level of risk and financial returns that feel comfortable. After determining the desired *risk-return* balance, they then achieve it in two ways: through *diversification* and *asset allocation*.

Diversification   **Diversification** means buying several different kinds of investments rather than just one. For example, diversification as applied to common stocks means that you invest in stocks of several different companies. The risk of loss is reduced by spreading the total investment across different stocks because although any one stock may tumble, the chances are less that all of them will fall at the same time. More diversification is gained when assets are spread across a variety of investment alternatives—stocks, bonds, mutual funds, real estate, and so on.

Asset allocation   **Asset allocation** is the proportion—the relative amounts—of funds invested in (or allocated to) each of the investment alternatives. You may decide for

example, to allocate 50% of your funds to common stocks, 25% to a money market mutual fund, and 25% to a U.S. Treasury bond mutual fund. Ten years later, with more concern for financial safety, you may decide on a less risky asset allocation of 20%, 40%, and 40% in the same investment categories, respectively.

Performance Differences for Different Portfolios Once an investment objective with acceptable risk level is chosen, the tools of diversification and asset allocation are put to use in the investor's portfolio. A **portfolio** is the combined holdings of all the financial investments—stocks, bonds, mutual funds, real estate—of any company or individual.

Just like investors, investment funds have different investment objectives—ranging from aggressive growth/high risk to stable income/low volatility—and their holdings are diversified accordingly among hundreds of company stocks, corporate bonds, or government bonds that provide the desired orientation. The money in a diversified portfolio is allocated in different proportions among a variety of funds; if all goes according to plan, most of these funds will meet their desired investment objectives and the overall portfolio will increase in value.

Financing the Business Firm

If you invest wisely, you may earn enough money to start your own firm—but that's only the first step in the complicated process of financing a business. Every company needs cash to function. Although a business owner's savings may be enough to get a firm up and running, businesses depend on sales revenues to survive. When current sales revenues are insufficient to pay for expenses, firms tap into various other sources of funds, typically starting with the owners' savings—as discussed in Chapter 14, owners contribute funds, or paid-in capital, from their own pockets. If a firm needs more money, they can turn to borrowing from banks, soliciting cash from private outside investors, or selling bonds to the public.

Secured Loans for Equipment

Money to purchase new equipment often comes in the form of loans from commercial banks. In a **secured loan** the borrower guarantees repayment of the loan by pledging the asset as **collateral** to the lender. That is, if the borrower defaults, or fails to repay the loan, the bank can take possession of his or her assets and sell them to recover the outstanding debt.

Principal and Interest Rates The amount of money that is loaned and must be repaid is called the **loan principal**. However, borrowers also pay the lender an additional fee, called **interest**, for the use of the borrowed funds. The amount of interest owed depends on an **annual percentage rate (APR)** that is agreed upon between the lender and borrower. The interest amount is found by multiplying the APR by the loan principal.

Working Capital and Unsecured Loans from Banks

Firms need more than just fixed assets for daily operations; they need current, liquid assets available to meet short-term operating expenses such as employee wages and marketing expenses. The firm's ability to meet these expenses is measured by its working capital:

Working capital = Current assets – Current liabilities

Positive working capital means the firm's current assets are large enough to pay off current liabilities (see Chapter 14). Negative working capital means the firm's current liabilities are greater than current assets, so it may need to borrow money from a commercial bank. With an **unsecured loan**, the borrower does not have to put up collateral. In many cases, however, the bank requires the borrower to maintain a *compensating balance*—the borrower must keep a portion of the loan amount on deposit with the bank in a non–interest-bearing account.

Firms with bad credit scores typically cannot get unsecured loans. Because access to such loans requires a good credit history, many firms establish a relationship with a commercial bank and, over time, build a good credit record by repaying loan principal and interest on time.

Angel Investors and Venture Capital

Once a business has been successfully launched it needs additional capital for growth. Outside individuals who provide such capital are called **angel investors**. In return for their investment, angel investors typically expect a sizable piece of ownership in the company (up to 50 percent of its equity). They may also want a formal say in how the company is run. If the firm is bought by a larger company or if it sells its stock in a public offering, the angel may receive additional payments.

Angel investors help many firms grow rapidly by providing what is known as **venture capital**—private funds from wealthy individuals or companies (see Chapter 3) that seek investment opportunities in new

INTEREST fee paid to a lender for the use of borrowed funds; like a rental fee

ANNUAL PERCENTAGE RATE (APR) one-year rate that is charged for borrowing, expressed as a percentage of the borrowed principal

UNSECURED LOAN a loan for which collateral is not required

ANGEL INVESTORS outside investors who provide new capital for firms in return for a share of equity ownership

VENTURE CAPITAL private funds by wealthy individuals seeking investment opportunities in new growth companies

---

Entrepreneurship and New Ventures

An Online Community for People 50 and Older

The social networking site Facebook began specifically for college students, and over 90 percent of its users remain under the age of 35. That's one reason Kelly and Jeff Lantz founded *55-Alive!*, a social networking site for users over 50 years old. Launched in 2005, the company's revenues for 2006 were a meager $5,000. The following year they jumped to $30,000, as the site's activities expanded into instant messaging, blogging, and chat rooms for member-created groups. Among its livelier activities is the *55-Alive! Battle of the Boomer Bands*, an online competition for musicians born before 1964.

So what's next? Financed to date with their own money, and with just one part-time employee, Kelly and Jeff project a need for at least $250,000 of outside funding to expand the site's content and to hire someone to help with sales ads. Despite its early success, *55-Alive!* still only receives 100,000 visits per month, just a small fraction of Facebook's 115 million monthly users.[13]

CORPORATE BOND a formal pledge obligating the issuer (the company) to pay interest periodically and repay the principal at maturity

BOND INDENTURE legal document containing complete details of a bond issue

MATURITY DATE (DUE DATE) future date when repayment of the bond is due from the bond issuer (borrower)

FACE VALUE (PAR VALUE) amount of money that the bond buyer (lender) lent the issuer, and that the lender will receive upon repayment

DEFAULT failure of the borrower to make payment when due to lenders

BONDHOLDERS' CLAIM request for court enforcement of a bond's terms of payment

BANKRUPTCY court-granted permission for a company to not pay some or all debts

INITIAL PUBLIC OFFERING (IPO) first sale of a company's stock to the general public

Table 16.2 **Bond Rating Systems**

Rating System	High Grades	Medium Grades (Investment Grades)	Speculative	Poor Grades
Moody's	Aaa, Aa	A, Baa	Ba, B	Caa to C
Standard & Poor's	AAA, AA	A, BBB	BB, B	CCC to D

growth companies. In most cases, the growth firm turns to venture capital sources because they have not yet built enough credit history to get a loan from commercial banks or other lending institutions.

Sale of Corporate Bonds

Corporations can raise capital by issuing bonds. A **corporate bond** is a formal pledge (an IOU) obligating the issuer to pay interest periodically and repay the principal at maturity (a preset future date) to the lender. The federal government also issues bonds to finance projects and meet obligations, as do state and local governments (called *municipal bonds*).

Characteristics of Corporate Bonds The bondholder (the lender) has no claim to ownership of the company and does not receive dividends. However, interest payments and repayment of principal are financial obligations; payments to bondholders have priority over dividend payments to stockholders in cases of financial distress.

Each new bond issue has specific terms and conditions spelled out in a **bond indenture**—a legal document identifying the borrower's obligations and the financial returns to lenders. One of the most important details is the **maturity date** (or **due date**), when the firm must repay the bond's **face value** (also called **par value**, or the amount purchased) to the lender.

Corporate bonds have been traditionally issued to fund outstanding debts and major projects for various lengths of time. Short-term bonds mature in less than five years after they are issued. Bonds with 5- to 10-year lives are considered intermediate term, while anything over 10 years is considered long term. Longer-term corporate bonds are somewhat riskier than shorter-term bonds because they are exposed to greater unforeseen economic conditions that may lead to default.

Default and Bondholders' Claim A bond is said to be in **default** if the borrower fails to make payment when due to lenders. Bondholders may then file a **bondholders' claim**—a request for court enforcement of the bond's terms of payment. When a financially distressed company cannot pay bondholders, it may seek relief by filing for **bankruptcy**—the court-granted permission not to pay some or all debts.

Risk Ratings To aid investors in making purchase decisions, several services measure the default risk of bonds. Table 16.2, for example, shows the rating systems of two well-known services, Moody's and Standard & Poor's. The highest grades are AAA and Aaa, and the lowest are C and D. Low-grade bonds are usually called *junk bonds*. Negative ratings do not necessarily keep issues from being successful. Rather, they raise the interest rates that issuers must offer to attract lenders.

Becoming a Public Corporation

Initial public offerings (IPOs)—the first sale of a company's stock to the general public—are a major source of funds that fuel continued growth for many firms, as well as introduce numerous considerations and complexities inherent in running a public company.

Going Public Means Selling off Part of the Company

Private owners lose some control of the company when shares are sold to the public. Common shareholders usually have voting rights in corporate governance, so they elect the board of directors and vote on major issues put forth at the company's annual shareholders' meeting. Anyone owning a large proportion of the company's shares gains a powerful position in determining who runs the corporation and how.

With an initial public offering in 2004, Google began selling its stock to the public, thus creating additional funds that were needed for expansion. The IPO raised proceeds of $1.9 billion from selling 22.5 million shares at $85 per share.

At an extreme, a **corporate raider**—an investor conducting a type of hostile (unwanted) takeover—buys shares on the open market, attempting to seize control of the company and its assets. The raider then sells off those assets at a profit, resulting in the company's disappearance.

A company is ripe for raiding when its stock price falls so shares can be cheaply bought, although its assets still have high value.

Stock Valuation

There are many factors that affect a stock's value, which in turn affect the value of the business. In addition, different investors measure value differently, and their measurements may change according to circumstance. Because of the uncertainties involved in stock prices, investment professionals believe day-to-day prices to be a generally poor indicator of any stock's real value. Instead, a long-run perspective considers the company's financial health, past history of results and future forecasts, its record for managerial performance, and overall prospects for competing successfully in the coming years. Accordingly, any stock's value today looks beyond the current price and is based on expectations of the financial returns it will provide to shareholders during the long run.

Why Shares Are Different Prices In June 2008 the price of Google Inc. was about $570 per share on the New York Stock Exchange, while GE shares traded at about $29, and Delta Airlines shares were priced at about $5.30. Berkshire Hathaway shares traded for $127,000.[14]

CORPORATE RAIDER an investor conducting a type of hostile corporate takeover against the wishes of the company

STOCK SPLIT stock dividend paid in additional shares to shareholders, thus increasing the number of outstanding shares

MARKET CAPITALIZATION (MARKET CAP) the total dollar value of all the company's outstanding shares

Why such differences? One reason is supply and demand for each company's shares; another is because some corporations want the shares to sell within a particular price range, say between $20 and $80, believing it will attract a larger pool of investors. If the price gets too high, the company can restore it to the desired range by a **stock split**—a stock dividend paid in additional shares to shareholders. Here's how it works. Suppose company *X* has 100,000 common shares outstanding that are trading at $100 per share, but the company wants it priced in the $20 to $80 range. *X* can declare a 2-for-1 stock split, meaning the company gives shareholders one additional share for each share they own. Now *X* has 200,000 shares outstanding but its financial performance has not changed, so the stock price immediately falls to $50 per share. Every shareholder's investment value, however, is unchanged: they previously owned one share at $100, and now they own two shares at $50 each.

Market Capitalization

A widely used measure of corporate size and value is known as **market capitalization (market cap)**—the total dollar value of all the company's outstanding

"Our stock just went up ten points on the rumor that I was replacing you all with burlap sacks stuffed with straw."

DEBT FINANCING long-term borrowing from sources outside a company

EQUITY FINANCING using the owners' funds from inside the company as the source for long-term funding

shares, calculated as the current stock price multiplied by the number of shares outstanding. As indicated in Table 16.4, the investment industry categorizes firms according to size of capitalization.

Investors typically regard larger market caps as less risky, and firms with small market caps (small-cap firms) as being particularly risky investments.

In early 2008 Exxon Mobil's share price was $86.10, and there were 5,454 million common shares outstanding. Its market cap was over $469 billion, making it the largest company in the world.

Choosing Equity versus Debt Capital

Firms can meet their capital needs through two sources: debt financing (from outside the firm) or equity financing (putting the owners' capital to work).

Pros and Cons for Debt Financing

Long-term borrowing from sources outside the company—**debt financing**—via loans or the sale of corporate bonds is a major component in most U.S. firms' financial planning.

Long-Term Loans Long-term loans are attractive for several reasons:

- Because the number of parties involved is limited, loans can often be arranged very quickly.

- The firm need not make public disclosure of its business plans or the purpose for which it is acquiring the loan. (In contrast, the issuance of corporate bonds requires such disclosure.)

Long-term loans also have some disadvantages. Borrowers, for example, may have trouble finding lenders to supply large sums. Long-term borrowers may also face restrictions as conditions of the loan. For example, they may have to pledge long-term assets as collateral or agree to take on no more debt until the loan is paid.

Corporate Bonds Bonds are attractive when firms need large amounts for long periods of time. The issuing company gains access to large numbers of lenders through nationwide bond markets. On the other hand, bonds entail high administrative and selling costs. They may also require stiff interest payments, especially if the issuing company has a poor credit rating. Bonds

Comparing Prices of Different Stocks

Consider a recent day when PepsiCo's share price was $70, while Coca-Cola was $58 per share. Does the price difference mean that PepsiCo is a better company than Coca-Cola, because its shares are more expensive? Or does it mean that Coke shares are a better value because they can be bought at a lower price than PepsiCo's? In fact, neither of these two reasons is correct. Share prices alone do not provide enough information to determine which is the better investment. Table 16.3 can help us make a better comparison.

First, earnings per share (EPS) are greater for PepsiCo. Even though you pay more to own a PepsiCo share, earnings per dollar of investment are greater as well ($3.42 earnings/$70 investment = $0.049; versus $2.16 earnings/$58 investment = $0.037): PepsiCo's earnings were nearly 5 cents for each dollar of its share price, whereas Coca-Cola earned less than 4 cents. PepsiCo generated more earnings power for each dollar of shareholder investment.

Now consider annual dividends paid to shareholders. The dividend yield from Coca-Cola was 2.32%. That is, the dividend payment amounted to a 2.32% return on the shareholder's $58 investment, or $1.35 ($58 × 2.32%). PepsiCo's dividend payment was about $1.50 ($70 × 2.14%), though this represents a somewhat smaller return (yield) on shareholder investment than Coca-Cola.

Based on this limited information, it's not clear which of the two companies is the better investment. A more complete evaluation would compare historical performance consistency over a period of several years, along with indicators of each firm's prospects for the future.

Table 16.3 **Financial Comparison: Coca-Cola and PepsiCo[15]**

	Coca-Cola	PepsiCo
Recent price	$58	$70
EPS	$2.16	$3.42
Dividend yield	2.32%	2.14%

Table 16.4 Corporation Sizes Based on Capitalization

Capitalization Category	Range of Capitalization
Micro-Cap	below $250 million
Small-Cap	$250–$2 billion
Mid-Cap	$2 billion–$10 billion
Large-Cap	over $10 billion

also impose binding obligations on the firm, in many cases for up to 30 years, to pay bondholders a stipulated sum of annual or semiannual interest, even in times of financial distress. If the company fails to make a bond payment, it goes into default.

Pros and Cons for Equity Financing

Although debt financing often has strong appeal, **equity financing**—looking inside the company for long-term funding—is sometimes preferable. Equity financing includes either issuing common stock or retaining the firm's earnings.

The Expense of Common Stock The use of equity financing by means of common stock can be expensive because paying dividends is more expensive than paying bond interest. Interest paid to bondholders is a business expense and therefore a tax deduction for the firm. Payments of cash dividends to shareholders are not tax deductible.

Retained Earnings as a Source of Capital As presented in Chapter 14, *retained earnings* are net profits retained for the firm's use rather than paid out in dividends to stockholders. If a company uses retained earnings as capital, it will not have to borrow money and pay interest. If a firm has a history of reaping profits by reinvesting retained earnings, it may be very attractive to some investors. Retained earnings, however, mean smaller dividends for shareholders. This practice may decrease the demand for—and the price of—the company's stock.

Questions for Review

1. Explain the concept of the *time value of money*.

2. What do mutual funds and exchange-traded funds offer, and how do they work?

3. Identify the various characteristics of corporate bonds.

4. How does the market value of a stock differ from the book value of a stock?

5. How do firms meet their needs through debt financing and equity financing?

Questions for Analysis

6. After researching several stocks online, you notice that they have continually fluctuated in price. What might be the reason for this? Is a higher-priced stock a better investment than a lower-priced stock? What factors would you consider in purchasing stocks?

7. Which type of fund do you think you would invest in, a mutual fund or an exchange traded fund? What is the difference, and why would you favor one over the other?

8. Suppose that you are a business owner and you need new equipment and immediate funds to meet short-term operating expenses. From what sources could you gain the capital you need, and what are some of the characteristics of these sources?

Application Exercises

9. Go to http://www.sec.gov to research how a new security is approved by the Securities and Exchange Commission. What is the process involved and how long would it take? Next, contact a financial institution such as Merrill Lynch and request information about their procedures for issuing or reselling new securities. Share this information with your classmates.

10. If you are not currently involved in investing, imagine that you are analyzing potential investments to build your portfolio. Create a mock portfolio with the investments you would obtain. How would you apply diversification and asset allocation to assure that your risk-return balance is at a point at which you are comfortable?

RISK uncertainty about future events

SPECULATIVE RISK risk involving the possibility of gain or loss

PURE RISK risk involving only the possibility of loss or no loss

RISK MANAGEMENT the process of conserving the firm's earning power and assets by reducing the threat of losses due to uncontrollable events

RISK AVOIDANCE the practice of avoiding risk by declining or ceasing to participate in an activity

RISK CONTROL the practice of minimizing the frequency or severity of losses from risky activities

RISK RETENTION the practice of covering a firm's losses with its own funds

RISK TRANSFER the practice of transferring a firm's risk to another firm

Risk Management

In this appendix, we describe other types of risks that businesses face, and analyze some of the ways in which they typically manage them.

Coping With Risk

Businesses constantly face two basic types of **risk**—uncertainty about future events. **Speculative risks**, such as financial investments, involve the possibility of gain or loss. **Pure risks** involve only the possibility of loss or no loss. Designing and distributing a new product, for example, is a speculative risk—the product may fail, or it may succeed and earn high profits. In contrast, the chance of a warehouse fire is a pure risk.

For a company to survive and prosper, it must manage both types of risk in a cost-effective manner. We can define the process of **risk management** as conserving the firm's earning power and assets by reducing the threat of losses due to uncontrollable events. In every company, each manager must be alert for risks to the firm and their impact on profits.

The risk-management process usually involves five steps:

Step 1: Identify Risks and Potential Losses Managers analyze a firm's risks to identify potential losses.

Step 2: Measure the Frequency and Severity of Losses and Their Impact To measure the frequency and severity of losses, managers must consider both history and current activities. How often can the firm expect the loss to occur? What is the likely size of the loss in dollars?

Step 3: Evaluate Alternatives and Choose the Techniques That Will Best Handle the Losses Having identified and measured potential losses, managers are in a better position to decide how to handle them. They generally have four choices:

- A firm opts for **risk avoidance** by declining to enter or by ceasing to participate in a risky activity.

- When avoidance is not practical or desirable, firms can practice **risk control**—the use of loss-prevention techniques to minimize the frequency or severity of losses.

- When losses cannot be avoided or controlled, firms must cope with the consequences. When such losses are manageable and predictable, the firm may decide to cover them out of company funds. The firm is said to assume or retain the financial consequences of the loss; hence, the practice is known as **risk retention**.

- When the potential for large risks cannot be avoided or controlled, managers often opt for **risk transfer** to another firm—namely, an insurance company—to protect itself.

Step 4: Implement the Risk-Management Program The means of implementing risk-management decisions depend on both the technique chosen and the activity being managed.

- Risk avoidance for certain activities can be implemented by purchasing those activities from outside providers.

- Risk control might be implemented by training employees and designing new work methods and equipment for on-the-job safety.

- For situations in which risk retention is preferred, reserve funds can be set aside from revenues.

- When risk transfer is needed, implementation means selecting an insurance company and buying the appropriate policies.

Step 5: Monitor Results New types of risks emerge with changes in customers, facilities, employees, and products. Insurance regulations change, and new types of insurance become available. Consequently, managers must continuously monitor a company's risks, reevaluate the methods used for handling them, and revise them as necessary.

Insurance as Risk Management

To deal with some risks, both businesses and individuals may choose to purchase insurance. Insurance is purchased by paying **insurance premiums**—payments to an insurance company to buy a policy and keep it active. In return, the insurance company issues an **insurance policy**—a formal agreement to pay the policyholder a specified amount in the event of certain losses. In some cases, the insured party must also pay a **deductible**, an agreed-upon amount of the loss that the insured must absorb prior to reimbursement. Buyers find insurance appealing because they are protected against large, potentially devastating losses in return for a relatively small sum of money.

With insurance, individuals and businesses share risks by contributing to a fund from which those who suffer losses are paid. Insurance companies are willing to accept these risks because they make profits by taking in more premiums than they pay out to cover policyholders' losses. Although many policyholders are paying for protection against the same type of loss, by no means will all of them suffer such a loss.

Insurable Versus Uninsurable Risks Like every business, insurance companies must avoid certain risks. Insurers divide potential sources of loss into *insurable risks* and *uninsurable risks.* They issue policies only for insurable risks. Although there are some exceptions, an insurable risk must meet the following four criteria:

1. *Predictability:* The insurer must be able to use statistical tools to forecast the likelihood of a loss. This forecast also helps insurers determine premiums charged to policyholders.

2. *Casualty:* A loss must result from an *accident,* not from an intentional act by the policyholder. To avoid paying in cases of fraud, insurers may refuse to cover losses when they cannot determine whether policyholders' actions contributed to them.

3. *Unconnectedness:* Potential losses must be random and must occur independently of other losses. No insurer can afford to write insurance when a large percentage of those who are exposed to a particular kind of loss are likely to suffer such a loss. By carefully choosing the risks that it will insure, an insurance company can reduce its chances of a large loss or insolvency.

4. *Verifiability:* Insured losses must be verifiable as to cause, time, place, and amount.

Special Forms of Insurance for Business Businesses have special insurable concerns—*liability, property, business interruption, key person insurance,* and *business continuation agreements.*

Liability Insurance Liability means responsibility for damages in case of accidental or deliberate harm to individuals or property. **Liability insurance** covers losses resulting from damage to people or property when the insured party is judged liable.

A business is liable for any injury to an employee when the injury arises from activities related to the occupation. When workers are permanently or temporarily disabled by job-related accidents or disease, employers are required by law to provide **workers' compensation coverage** for medical expenses, loss of wages, and rehabilitation services.

Property Insurance A firm purchases **property insurance** to cover injuries to itself resulting from physical damage to or loss of real estate or personal property. Property losses may result from fire, lightning, wind, hail, explosion, theft, vandalism, or other destructive forces.

Business Interruption Insurance In some cases, loss to property is minimal in comparison to loss of income. If a firm is forced to close down for an extended time, it will not be able to generate income. During this time, however, certain expenses—such as taxes, insurance premiums, and salaries for key personnel—may

INSURANCE PREMIUM fee paid to an insurance company by a policyholder for insurance coverage

INSURANCE POLICY a formal agreement to pay the policyholder a specified amount in the event of certain losses

DEDUCTIBLE an amount of the loss that the insured must absorb prior to reimbursement

LIABILITY INSURANCE insurance covering losses resulting from damage to people or property when the insured party is judged liable

WORKERS' COMPENSATION COVERAGE coverage provided by a firm to employees for medical expenses, loss of wages, and rehabilitation costs resulting from job-related injuries or disease

PROPERTY INSURANCE insurance covering losses resulting from physical damage to or loss of the insured's real estate or personal property

BUSINESS INTERRUPTION INSURANCE insurance covering income lost during times when a company is unable to conduct business

KEY PERSON INSURANCE special form of business insurance designed to offset expenses entailed by the loss of key employees

BUSINESS CONTINUATION AGREEMENT special form of business insurance whereby owners arrange to buy the interests of deceased associates from their heirs

continue. To cover such losses, a firm may buy **business interruption insurance**.

Key Person Insurance

Many businesses choose to protect themselves against loss of the talents and skills of key employees, as well as the recruitment costs to find a replacement and training expenses once a replacement is hired. **Key person insurance** is designed to offset both lost income and additional expenses.

Business Continuation Agreements

Who takes control of a business when a partner or associate dies? Surviving partners are often faced with the possibility of having to accept an inexperienced heir as a management partner. This contingency can be handled in **business continuation agreements**, whereby owners make plans to buy the ownership interest of a deceased associate from his or her heirs. The value of the ownership interest is determined when the agreement is made. Special policies can also provide survivors with the funds needed to make the purchase.

Taken from *Fundamentals of Corporate Finance*, First Edition, by Jonathan Berk, Peter DeMarzo, and Jarrad Harford

This page intentionally left blank

Introduction to Financial Statement Analysis

LEARNING OBJECTIVES

▶ Know why the disclosure of financial information through financial statements is critical to investors

▶ Understand the function of the balance sheet

▶ Use the balance sheet to analyze a firm

▶ Understand how the income statement is used

▶ Analyze a firm through its income statement, including using the DuPont Identity

▶ Interpret a statement of cash flows

▶ Know what management's discussion and analysis and the statement of stockholders equity are

▶ Analyze the role of accounting manipulation in the Enron and WorldCom bankruptcies

INTERVIEW WITH   Hiral Tolia, CBIZ Valuation Group, LLC

University of Texas, Arlington, 2006

"I use financial statement analysis extensively to understand a company's performance and how it compares to its industry peers."

As a senior consultant for CBIZ Valuation Group, LLC, in Dallas, Texas, Hiral Tolia works on client projects that focus on determining a company's value. For example, a privately held company wishing to issue stock to its employees may hire CBIZ to determine its value before setting a stock price. In mergers and acquisitions, a company may need CBIZ to value certain assets owned by the acquired company, as required for financial reporting purposes.

Hiral, who received a Bachelor of Engineering in Computer Science in 2003 from the University of Mumbai and an MBA in 2006 from the University of Texas, Arlington, uses the concepts she learned in her various finance classes on a daily basis. "Because we have clients from various industry sectors, we need an in-depth knowledge of each of those market segments. I use financial statement analysis extensively to understand a company's performance and how it compares to its industry peers."

Analyzing financial statements gives Hiral insight into a company's current financial position and its performance over time. "This information is useful in making economic decisions, such as to determine a company's future cash flows, the effect of cyclical trends in the industry on operations over a period of time and in the future, and whether to invest in the company's securities or recommend them to other investors," she explains. "Thus, it is important to understand financial statements whether you are an owner of the company, an employee, an investor, or an analyst."

The first step in valuing a company is assessing past performance and determining its current financial position using information contained in the publicly available financial statements. "We use income statements to analyze revenue and expenses and the balance sheets and statement of cash flows to analyze short term cash flow needs and determine capital expenditures."

One of CBIZ's valuation methods involves the review of pricing and performance information for public companies in a generally similar industry to the subject company. "Ratio analysis helps to compare the subject company to market participants, so we can apply our valuation models and determine a fair value for the company."

As we discussed in Chapter 1, anyone with money to invest is a potential investor who can own shares in a corporation. As a result, corporations are often widely held, with investors ranging from individuals who hold one share to large financial institutions that own millions of shares. For example, in 2007 International Business Machines Corporation (IBM) had over 1.3 billion shares outstanding held by over 613,000 stockholders. Although the corporate organizational structure greatly facilitates the firm's access to investment capital, it also means that stock ownership is most investors' sole tie to the company. How, then, do investors learn enough about a company to know whether or not they should invest in it? One way firms evaluate their performance and communicate this information to investors is through their *financial statements.* Financial statements also enable financial managers to assess the success of their own firm and compare it to competitors.

Firms regularly issue financial statements to communicate financial information to the investment community. A detailed description of the preparation and analysis of these statements is sufficiently complicated that to do it justice would require an entire book. In this chapter, we briefly review the subject, emphasizing only the material that investors and corporate financial managers need in order to make the corporate finance decisions we discuss in the text.

We review the four main types of financial statements, present examples of these statements for a firm, and discuss where an investor or manager might find various types of information about the company. We also discuss some of the financial ratios used to assess a firm's performance and value. We close the chapter with a look at highly publicized financial reporting abuses at Enron and WorldCom.

BDeH   CHAPTER 2

2.1 Firms' Disclosure of Financial Information

financial statements Usually quarterly or annual accounting reports issued by a firm that present past performance information and a snapshot of the firm's assets and the financing of those assets.

Financial statements are accounting reports issued by a firm periodically (usually quarterly and annually) that present past performance information and a snapshot of the firm's assets and the financing of those assets. Public companies in the United States are required to file their financial statements with the U.S. Securities and Exchange Commission (SEC) on a quarterly basis on form *10-Q* and annually on form *10-K*.[1] They must also send an **annual report** with their financial statements to their shareholders each year. Often, private companies also prepare financial statements, but they usually do not have to disclose these reports to the public. Financial statements are important tools with which investors, financial analysts, and other interested outside parties (such as creditors) obtain information about a corporation. They are also useful for managers within the firm as a source of information for the corporate financial decisions we discussed in the previous chapter. In this section, we examine the guidelines for preparing financial statements and introduce the different types of financial statements.

annual report The yearly summary of business sent by U.S. public companies to their shareholders that accompanies or includes the financial statement.

---

[1]The Securities and Exchange Commission was established by Congress in 1934 to regulate securities (for example, stocks and bonds) issued to the public and the financial markets (exchanges) on which those securities trade.

BDeH CHAPTER 2

International Financial Reporting Standards

Generally Accepted Accounting Principles (GAAP) differ among countries. As a result, companies face tremendous accounting complexities when they operate internationally. Investors also face difficulty interpreting financial statements of foreign companies, which discourages them from investing abroad. As companies and capital markets become more global, however, interest in harmonization of accounting standards across countries has increased.

The most important harmonization project began in 1973 when representatives of ten countries (including the United States) established the International Accounting Standards Committee. This effort led to the creation of the International Accounting Standards Board

(IASB) in 2001, with headquarters in London. Now the IASB has issued a set of International Financial Reporting Standards (IFRS).

The IFRS are taking root throughout the world. The European Union (EU) approved an accounting regulation in 2002 requiring all publicly traded EU companies to follow IFRS in their consolidated financial statements starting in 2005. Many other countries have adopted IFRS for all listed companies, including Australia and several countries in Latin America and Africa. In fact, all major stock exchanges around the world accept IFRS except the United States and Japan, which maintain their local GAAP.

Preparation of Financial Statements

Generally Accepted Accounting Principles (GAAP) A common set of rules and a standard format for public companies to use when they prepare their financial reports.

Reports about a company's performance must be understandable and accurate. In the United States, the Financial Accounting Standards Board (FASB) establishes **Generally Accepted Accounting Principles (GAAP)** to provide a common set of rules and a standard format for public companies to use when they prepare their reports. This standardization also makes it easier to compare the financial results of different firms.

Investors also need some assurance that the financial statements are prepared accurately. Corporations are required to hire a neutral third party, known as an **auditor**, to check the annual financial statements, ensure they are prepared according to GAAP, and provide evidence to support the reliability of the information.

auditor A neutral third party, which corporations are required to hire, that checks a firm's annual financial statements to ensure they are prepared according to GAAP, and provide evidence to support the reliability of the information.

Types of Financial Statements

Every public company is required to produce four financial statements: the *balance sheet,* the *income statement,* the *statement of cash flows,* and the *statement of stockholders' equity.* These financial statements provide investors and creditors with an overview of the firm's financial performance. In the sections that follow, we take a close look at the content of these financial statements.

Concept Check

1. What is the role of an auditor?
2. What are the four financial statements that all public companies must produce?

balance sheet A list of a firm's assets and liabilities that provides a snapshot of the firm's financial position at a given point in time.

2.2 The Balance Sheet

The **balance sheet** lists the firm's *assets* and *liabilities,* providing a snapshot of the firm's financial position at a given point in time. Table 2.1 shows the balance sheet for a fictitious company, Global Corporation. Notice that the balance sheet is divided into two parts ("sides") with the assets on the left side and the liabilities on the right side:

TABLE 2.1	Global Corporation Balance Sheet for 2007 and 2006

GLOBAL CORPORATION
Balance Sheet
Year ended December 31 (in $ millions)

Assets	2007	2006	Liabilities and Stockholders' Equity	2007	2006
Current Assets			Current Liabilities		
Cash	23.2	20.5	Accounts payable	29.2	26.5
Accounts receivable	18.5	13.2	Notes payable/short-term debt	5.5	3.2
Inventories	15.3	14.3			
Total current assets	57.0	48.0	Total current liabilities	34.7	29.7
Long-Term Assets			Long-Term Liabilities		
Net property, plant, and equipment	113.1	80.9	Long-term debt	113.2	78.0
Total long-term assets	113.1	80.9	Total long-term liabilities	113.2	78.0
			Total Liabilities	147.9	107.7
			Stockholders' Equity	22.2	21.2
Total Assets	170.1	128.9	Total Liabilities and Stockholders' Equity	170.1	128.9

assets The cash, inventory, property, plant and equipment, and other investments a company has made.

liabilities A firm's obligations to its creditors.

shareholders' equity, stockholders' equity An accounting measure of a firm's net worth that represents the difference between the firm's assets and its liabilities.

1. The **assets** list the firm's cash, inventory, property, plant and equipment, and any other investments the company has made.

2. The **liabilities** show the firm's obligations to its creditors.

3. Also shown with liabilities on the right side of the balance sheet is the *stockholders' equity*. **Stockholders' equity**, the difference between the firm's assets and liabilities, is an accounting measure of the firm's net worth.

The assets on the left side show how the firm uses its capital (its investments), and the information on the right side summarizes the sources of capital, or how the firm raises the money it needs. Because of the way stockholders' equity is calculated, the left and right sides must balance:

The Balance Sheet Identity

$$\text{Assets} = \text{Liabilities} + \text{Stockholders' Equity} \qquad (2.1)$$

In Table 2.1, total assets for 2007 ($170.1 million) are equal to total liabilities ($147.9 million) plus stockholders' equity ($22.2 million).

We now examine the firm's assets, liabilities, and stockholders' equity in more detail. Finally, we evaluate the firm's financial standing by analyzing the information contained in the balance sheet.

Assets

current assets Cash or assets that could be converted into cash within one year.

marketable securities Short-term, low-risk investments that can be easily sold and converted to cash.

In Table 2.1, Global's assets are divided into current and long-term assets. We discuss each in turn.

Current Assets. **Current assets** are either cash or assets that could be converted into cash within one year. This category includes:

1. Cash and other **marketable securities**, which are short-term, low-risk investments that can be easily sold and converted to cash (such as money market investments, like government debt, that mature within a year);

accounts receivable
Amounts owed to a firm by customers who have purchased goods or services on credit.

inventories A firm's raw materials as well as its work-in-progress and finished goods.

long-term assets Assets that produce tangible benefits for more than one year.

depreciation A yearly deduction a firm makes from the value of its fixed assets (other than land) over time, according to a depreciation schedule that depends on an asset's life span.

book value The acquisition cost of an asset less its accumulated depreciation.

current liabilities Liabilities that will be satisfied within one year.

accounts payable The amounts owed to creditors for products or services purchased with credit.

notes payable, short-term debt Loans that must be repaid in the next year.

net working capital The difference between a firm's current assets and current liabilities that represents the capital available in the short term to run the business.

2. **Accounts receivable**, which are amounts owed to the firm by customers who have purchased goods or services on credit;

3. **Inventories**, which are composed of raw materials as well as work-in-progress and finished goods; and

4. Other current assets, which is a catch-all category that includes items such as prepaid expenses (expenses that have been paid in advance, such as rent or insurance).

Long-Term Assets. Assets such as real estate or machinery that produce tangible benefits for more than one year are called **long-term assets**. If Global spends $2 million on new equipment, this $2 million will be included with net property, plant, and equipment under long-term assets on the balance sheet. Because equipment tends to wear out or become obsolete over time, Global will reduce the value recorded for this equipment through a yearly deduction called **depreciation** according to a depreciation schedule that depends on an asset's life span. Depreciation is not an actual cash expense that the firm pays; it is a way of recognizing that buildings and equipment wear out and thus become less valuable the older they get. The **book value** of an asset is equal to its acquisition cost less accumulated depreciation. The figures for net property, plant, and equipment show the total book value of these assets.

Other long-term assets can include such items as property not used in business operations, start-up costs in connection with a new business, trademarks and patents, and property held for sale. The sum of all the firms' assets is the total assets at the bottom of the left side of the balance sheet in Table 2.1.

Liabilities

We now examine the liabilities shown on the right side of the balance sheet, which are divided into *current* and *long-term liabilities*.

Current Liabilities. Liabilities that will be satisfied within one year are known as **current liabilities**. They include:

1. **Accounts payable**, the amounts owed to suppliers for products or services purchased with credit.

2. **Notes payable** and **short-term debt**, loans that must be repaid in the next year. Any repayment of long-term debt that will occur within the next year would also be listed here as current maturities of long-term debt.

3. Accrual items, such as salary or taxes, that are owed but have not yet been paid, and deferred or unearned revenue, which is revenue that has been received for products that have not yet been delivered.

The difference between current assets and current liabilities is the firm's **net working capital**, the capital available in the short term to run the business.

$$\text{Net Working Capital} = \text{Current Assets} - \text{Current Liabilities} \qquad (2.2)$$

For example, in 2007 Global's net working capital totaled $22.3 million ($57.0 million in current assets − $34.7 million in current liabilities). Firms with low (or negative) net working capital may face a shortage of funds. In such cases, the liabilities due in the short term exceed the company's cash and expected payments on receivables.

Long-term Liabilities. Long-term liabilities are liabilities that extend beyond one year. When a firm needs to raise funds to purchase an asset or make an investment, it may borrow those funds through a long-term loan. That loan would appear on the balance

BDeH CHAPTER 2

long-term debt Any loan or debt obligation with a maturity of more than a year.

sheet as **long-term debt**, which is any loan or debt obligation with a maturity of more than a year.

Stockholders' Equity

book value of equity The difference between the book value of a firm's assets and its liabilities; also called stockholders' equity, it represents the net worth of a firm from an accounting perspective.

The sum of the current liabilities and long-term liabilities is total liabilities. The difference between the firm's assets and liabilities is the stockholders' equity; it is also called the **book value of equity**. As we stated earlier, it represents the net worth of the firm from an accounting perspective.

Ideally, the balance sheet would provide us with an accurate assessment of the true value of the firm's equity. Unfortunately, this is unlikely to be the case. First, many of the assets listed on the balance sheet are valued based on their historical cost rather than their true value today. For example, an office building is listed on the balance sheet according to its historical cost less its accumulated depreciation. But the actual value of the office building today may be very different than this amount; in fact, it may be much *more* than the amount the firm paid for it years ago. The same is true for other property, plant, and equipment: The true value today of an asset may be very different from, and even exceed, its book value. A second, and probably more important, problem is that *many of the firm's valuable assets are not captured on the balance sheet*. Consider, for example, the expertise of the firm's employees, the firm's reputation in the marketplace, the relationships with customers and suppliers, and the quality of the management team. All these assets add to the value of the firm but do not appear on the balance sheet.

market capitalization The total market value of equity; equals the market price per share times the number of shares.

For these reasons, the book value of equity is an inaccurate assessment of the actual value of the firm's equity. Thus, it is not surprising that it will often differ substantially from the amount investors are willing to pay for the equity. The total market value of a firm's equity equals the market price per share times the number of shares, referred to as the company's **market capitalization**. The market value of a stock does not depend on the historical cost of the firm's assets; instead, it depends on what investors expect those assets to produce in the future.

EXAMPLE 2.1

Market versus Book Value

Problem

If Global has 3.6 million shares outstanding, and these shares are trading for a price of $10.00 per share, what is Global's market capitalization? How does the market capitalization compare to Global's book value of equity?

Solution

▶ **Plan**

Market capitalization is equal to price per share times shares outstanding. We can find Global's book value of equity at the bottom of the right side of its balance sheet.

▶ **Execute**

Global's market capitalization is (3.6 million shares) × ($10.00/share) = $36 million. This market capitalization is significantly higher than Global's book value of equity of $22.2 million.

▶ **Evaluate**

Global must have sources of value that do not appear on the balance sheet. These include potential opportunities for growth, the quality of the management team, relationships with suppliers and customers, etc.

Finally, we note that the book value of equity can be negative (liabilities exceed assets), and that a negative book value of equity is not necessarily an indication of poor performance. Successful firms are often able to borrow in excess of the book value of their assets because creditors recognize that the market value of the assets is far higher. For example, in June 2005 Amazon.com had total liabilities of $2.6 billion and a book value of equity of −$64 million. At the same time, the market value of its equity was over $15 billion. Clearly, investors recognized that Amazon's assets were worth far more than their book value.

Concept Check

3. What is depreciation designed to capture?

4. The book value of a company's assets usually does not equal the market value of those assets. What are some reasons for this difference?

Balance Sheet Analysis

What can we learn from analyzing a firm's balance sheet? Although the book value of a firm's equity is not a good estimate of its true value as an ongoing firm, it is sometimes used as an estimate of the **liquidation value** of the firm, the value that would be left after its assets were sold and liabilities paid. We can also learn a great deal of useful information from a firm's balance sheet that goes beyond the book value of the firm's equity. We now discuss analyzing the balance sheet to assess the firm's value, its leverage, and its short-term cash needs.

liquidation value
The value of a firm after its assets are sold and liabilities paid.

Market-to-Book Ratio

market-to-book ratio (price-to-book [P/B] ratio) The ratio of a firm's market (equity) capitalization to the book value of its stockholders' equity.

In Example 2.1, we compared the market and book values of Global's equity. A common way to make this comparison is to compute the **market-to-book ratio** (also called the **price-to-book [P/B] ratio**), which is the ratio of a firm's market capitalization to the book value of stockholders' equity.

$$\text{Market-to-Book Ratio} = \frac{\text{Market Value of Equity}}{\text{Book Value of Equity}} \qquad (2.3)$$

It is one of many financial ratios used to evaluate a firm. The market-to-book ratio for most successful firms substantially exceeds 1, indicating that the value of the firm's assets when put to use exceeds their historical cost (or liquidation value). The ratio will vary across firms due to differences in fundamental firm characteristics as well as the value added by management. Thus, this ratio is one way a company's stock price provides feedback to its managers on the market's assessment of their decisions.

value stocks Firms with low market-to-book ratios.

growth stocks Firms with high market-to-book ratios.

In early 2006, General Motors Corporation (GM) had a market-to-book ratio of 0.5, a reflection of investors' assessment that many of GM's plants and other assets were unlikely to be profitable and were worth less than their book value. Figure 2.1 shows that at the same time, the average market-to-book ratio for the auto industry was about 1.5, and for large U.S. firms it was close to 4.0. In contrast, consider that Google (GOOG) had a market-to-book ratio of over 15, and the average for technology firms was about 6.0. Analysts often classify firms with low market-to-book ratios as **value stocks**, and those with high market-to-book ratios as **growth stocks**.

leverage A measure of the extent to which a firm relies on debt as a source of financing.

debt-equity ratio It is the ratio of a firm's total amount of short- and long-term debt (including current maturities) to the value of its equity, which may be calculated based on market or book values.

Debt-Equity Ratio

Another important piece of information that we can learn from a firm's balance sheet is the firm's **leverage**, or the extent to which it relies on debt as a source of financing. The **debt-equity ratio** is a common ratio used to assess a firm's leverage that we calculate by

BDeH CHAPTER 2

FIGURE 2.1

Market-to-Book Ratios in 2006

This figure presents market-to-book ratios of different firms and types of firms in 2006. Firms that might be classified as value stocks (low market-to-book ratios) are in blue and those that might be classified as growth stocks (high market-to-book ratios) are in green.

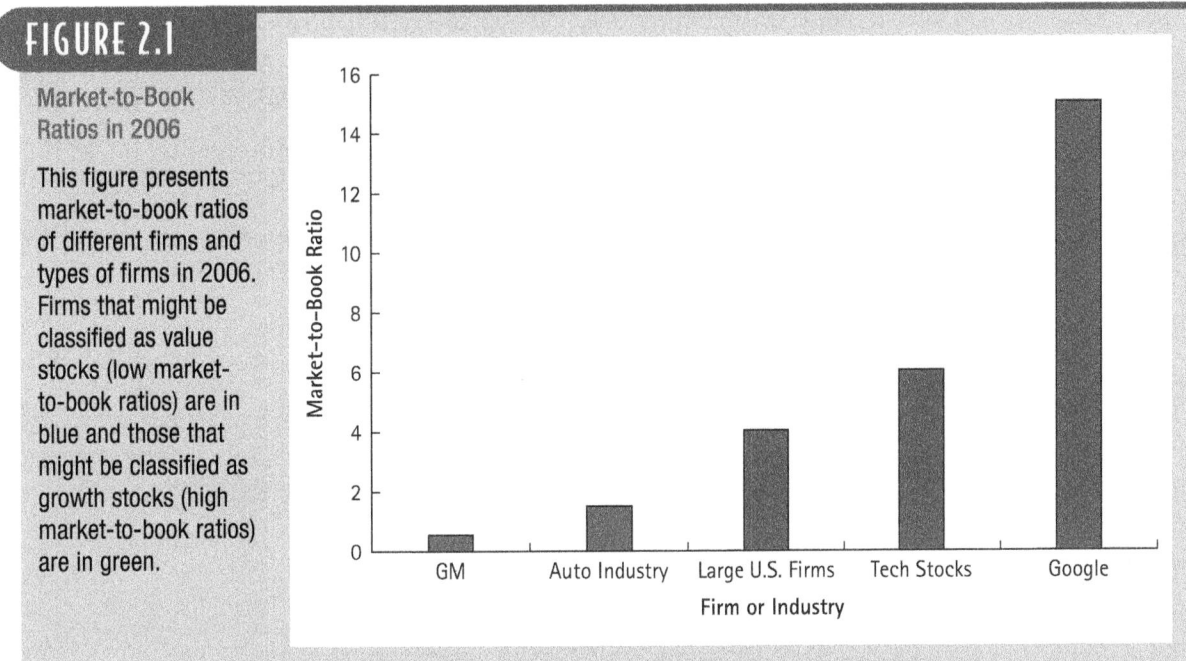

dividing the total amount of short- and long-term debt (including current maturities) by the total stockholders' equity:

$$\text{Debt-Equity Ratio} = \frac{\text{Total Debt}}{\text{Total Equity}} \qquad (2.4)$$

We can calculate this ratio using either book or market values for equity and debt. From Table 2.1, note Global's debt in 2007 includes notes payable ($5.5 million) and long-term debt ($113.2 million), for a total of $118.7 million. Therefore, using the book value of equity, its *book* debt-equity ratio is $118.7/22.2 = 5.3$. Note the large increase from 2006, when the book debt-equity ratio was only $(3.2 + 78)/21.2 = 3.8$.

Because of the difficulty interpreting the book value of equity, the book debt-equity ratio is not especially useful. It is more informative to compare the firm's debt to the market value of its equity. Global's debt-equity ratio in 2007, using the market value of equity (from Example 2.1), is $118.7/36 = 3.3$, which means Global's debt is a bit more than triple the market value of its equity.[2] As we will see later in the text, a firm's *market* debt-equity ratio has important consequences for the risk and return of its stock.

enterprise value The total market value of a firm's equity and debt, less the value of its cash and marketable securities. It measures the value of the firm's underlying business.

Enterprise Value

A firm's market capitalization measures the market value of the firm's equity, or the value that remains after the firm has paid its debts. But what is the value of the business itself? The **enterprise value** of a firm assesses the value of the underlying business assets,

BDeH   CHAPTER 2

---

[2]In this calculation, we have compared the market value of equity to the book value of debt. Strictly speaking, it would be best to use the market value of debt. But because the market value of debt is generally not very different from its book value, this distinction is often ignored in practice.

unencumbered by debt and separate from any cash and marketable securities. We compute it as follows:

$$\text{Enterprise Value} = \text{Market Value of Equity} + \text{Debt} - \text{Cash} \qquad (2.5)$$

For example, given its market capitalization from Example 2.1, Global's enterprise value in 2007 is $36 + 118.7 - 23.2 = \$131.5$ million. We can interpret the enterprise value as the cost to take over the business. That is, it would cost $36 + 118.7 = \$154.7$ million to buy all of Global's equity and pay off its debts. Because we would acquire Global's $23.2 million in cash, the net cost is only $154.7 - 23.2 = \$131.5$ million.

EXAMPLE 2.2

Computing Enterprise Value

Problem

In October 2007, H.J. Heinz Co. (HNZ) had a share price of $46.78, 319.1 million shares outstanding, a market-to-book ratio of 8.00, a book debt-equity ratio of 2.62, and cash of $576 million. What was Heinz's market capitalization? What was its enterprise value?

Solution

▶ **Plan**

Share Price	$46.78
Shares Outstanding	319.1 million
Market-to-Book	8.00
Cash	$576 million
Debt-to-Equity (Book)	2.62

We will solve the problem using Eq. 2.5: Enterprise value = Market capitalization + Debt − Cash. We can compute the market capitalization by multiplying the share price by the shares outstanding. We are given the amount of cash. We are not given the debt directly, but we are given the book debt-to-equity ratio. If we knew the book value of equity, we could use the ratio to infer the value of the debt. Since we can compute the market value of equity (market capitalization) and we have the market-to-book ratio, we can compute the book value of equity, so that is the last piece of information we will need.

▶ **Execute**

Heinz had a market capitalization of $46.78 × 319.1 million shares = $14.93 billion. Since Heinz's market-to-book = 8.00 = $14.93 billion / book equity, then book equity = $14.93 billion / 8.00 = $1.87 billion. Given that the book equity is $1.87 billion and a book debt-to-equity ratio of 2.62, the total value of Heinz's debt is $1.87 billion × 2.62 = $4.90 billion.

▶ **Evaluate**

Thus, Heinz's enterprise value was 14.93 + 4.90 − 0.576 = $19.254 billion.

---

current ratio The ratio of current assets to current liabilities.

quick ratio The ratio of current assets other than inventory to current liabilities.

Other Balance Sheet Information

Creditors often compare a firm's current assets and current liabilities to assess whether the firm has sufficient working capital to meet its short-term needs. This comparison is sometimes summarized in the firm's **current ratio**, the ratio of current assets to current liabilities, or its **quick ratio ("acid-test" ratio)**, the ratio of current assets other than

TABLE 2.2	Ratio	Formula	Manufacturing	Retail	Service	S&P 500
Balance Sheet Ratios	Market-to-Book Ratio	$\dfrac{\text{Market Value of Equity}}{\text{Book Value of Equity}}$	2.27	2.27	2.23	2.68
	Book Debt-to-Equity Ratio	$\dfrac{\text{Total Debt}}{\text{Book Value of Total Equity}}$	11.3%	25.7%	0.6%	49.4%
	Market Debt-to-Equity Ratio	$\dfrac{\text{Total Debt}}{\text{Market Value of Total Equity}}$	8.4%	12.1%	4.6%	18.1%
	Current Ratio	$\dfrac{\text{Current Assets}}{\text{Current Liabilities}}$	2.31	1.51	1.52	1.47
	Quick Ratio	$\dfrac{\text{Current Assets} - \text{Inventory}}{\text{Current Liabilities}}$	1.59	0.73	1.43	1.14

Source: Standard and Poors' Compustat

inventory to current liabilities. A higher current or quick ratio implies less risk of the firm experiencing a cash shortfall in the near future.

$$\text{Current Ratio} = \frac{\text{Current Assets}}{\text{Current Liabilities}} \qquad (2.6)$$

$$\text{Quick Ratio} = \frac{\text{Current Assets} - \text{Inventory}}{\text{Current Liabilities}} \qquad (2.7)$$

Analysts also use the information on the balance sheet to watch for trends that could provide information regarding the firm's future performance. For example, an unusual increase in inventory could be an indicator that the firm is having difficulty selling its products.

Table 2.2 summarizes balance sheet ratios and provides typical values in 2006 of those ratios in the manufacturing, retail, and service sectors along with the S&P 500. The market-to-book ratio is an indicator of potential growth and of managers' ability to generate value from the firm's assets above their historical cost. The other ratios measure the financial health of the firm by assessing its leverage (debt-to-equity and equity multiplier) or liquidity (current and quick ratios).

Concept Check

5. What does a high debt-to-equity ratio tell you?

6. What is a firm's enterprise value?

income statement A list of a firm's revenues and expenses over a period of time.

2.4 The Income Statement

When you want someone to get to the point, you might ask them for the "bottom line." This expression comes from the *income statement*. The **income statement** lists the firm's revenues and expenses over a period of time. The last or "bottom" line of the

TABLE 2.3			
	GLOBAL CORPORATION **Income Statement** **Year ended December 31 (in $ millions)**		

Global Corporation
Income Statement
Sheet for 2007
and 2006

	2007	2006
Total sales	186.7	176.1
Cost of sales	−153.4	−147.3
Gross Profit	33.3	28.8
Selling, general, and administrative expenses	−13.5	−13
Research and development	−8.2	−7.6
Depreciation and amortization	−1.2	−1.1
Operating Income	10.4	7.1
Other income	—	—
Earnings Before Interest and Taxes (EBIT)	10.4	7.1
Interest income (expense)	−7.7	−4.6
Pretax Income	2.7	2.5
Taxes	−0.7	−0.6
Net Income	2.0	1.9
Earnings per share:	$0.56	$0.53
Diluted earnings per share:	$0.53	$0.50

BDeH   CHAPTER 2

net income or earnings
The last or "bottom line"
of a firm's income state-
ment that is a measure of
the firm's income over a
given period of time.

income statement shows the firm's **net income**, which is a measure of its profitability during the period. The income statement is sometimes called a profit and loss, or "P&L," statement, and the net income is also referred to as the firm's **earnings**. In this section, we examine the components of the income statement in detail and introduce ratios we can use to analyze this data.

Earnings Calculations

Whereas the balance sheet shows the firm's assets and liabilities at a given point in time, the income statement shows the flow of revenues and expenses generated by those assets and liabilities between two dates. Table 2.3 shows Global's income statement for 2007 and 2006. We examine each category on the statement.

gross profit The third line
of an income statement
that represents the difference between a firm's
sales revenues and its
costs.

Gross Profit.   The first two lines of the income statement list the revenues from sales of products and the costs incurred to make and sell the products. The third line is **gross profit**, the difference between sales revenues and the costs.

Operating Expenses.   The next group of items is operating expenses. These are expenses from the ordinary course of running the business that are not directly related to producing the goods or services being sold. They include administrative expenses and overhead, salaries, marketing costs, and research and development expenses. The third type of operating expense, depreciation and amortization (a charge that captures the change in value of acquired assets), is not an actual cash expense but represents an estimate of the costs that arise from wear and tear or obsolescence of the firm's assets.[3] The firm's gross profit net of operating expenses is called **operating income**.

operating income A
firm's gross profit less its
operating expenses.

---

[3]Only certain types of amortization are deductible as a pretax expense (e.g., amortization of the cost of an acquired patent). Amortization of goodwill is not a pretax expense and is generally included as an extraordinary item after taxes are deducted.

EBIT A firm's earnings before interest and taxes are deducted.

earnings per share (EPS) A firm's net income divided by the total number of shares outstanding.

stock options Right to buy a certain number of shares of stock by a specific date at a specific price.

convertible bonds Corporate bonds with a provision that gives the bondholder an option to convert each bond owned into a fixed number of shares of common stock.

dilution An increase in the total number of shares that will divide a fixed amount of earnings.

diluted EPS A firm's disclosure of its potential for dilution from options it has awarded.

Earnings Before Interest and Taxes. We next include other sources of income or expenses that arise from activities that are not the central part of a company's business. Cash flows from the firm's financial investments are one example of other income that would be listed here. After we have adjusted for other sources of income or expenses, we have the firm's earnings before interest and taxes, or **EBIT**.

Pretax and Net Income. From EBIT, we deduct the interest paid on outstanding debt to compute Global's pretax income, and then we deduct corporate taxes to determine the firm's net income.

Net income represents the total earnings of the firm's equity holders. It is often reported on a per-share basis as the firm's **earnings per share (EPS)**, which we compute by dividing net income by the total number of shares outstanding:

$$\text{EPS} = \frac{\text{Net Income}}{\text{Shares Outstanding}} = \frac{\$2.0 \text{ million}}{3.6 \text{ million shares}} = \$0.56 \text{ per share} \qquad (2.8)$$

Although Global has only 3.6 million shares outstanding as of the end of 2007, the number of shares outstanding may grow if Global has made commitments that would cause it to issue more shares. Consider these two examples:

1. Suppose Global compensates its employees or executives with **stock options** that give the holder the right to buy a certain number of shares by a specific date at a specific price. If employees "exercise" these options, the company issues new stock and the number of shares outstanding will grow.

2. The number of shares may also grow if the firm issues **convertible bonds**, a form of debt that can be converted to shares of common stock.

In the cases of stock options and convertible bonds, because there will be more total shares to divide the same earnings, this growth in the number of shares is referred to as **dilution**. Firms disclose the potential for dilution from options they have awarded by reporting **diluted EPS**, which shows the earnings per share the company would have if the stock options were exercised. For example, if Global has awarded options for 200,000 shares of stock to its key executives, its diluted EPS is $2.0 million/3.8 million shares = $0.53.

Concept Check

7. What do a firm's earnings measure?
8. What is meant by dilution?

2.5 Income Statement Analysis

The income statement provides very useful information regarding the profitability of a firm's business and how it relates to the value of the firm's shares. We now discuss several ratios that are often used to evaluate a firm's performance and value.

Profitability Ratios

gross margin The ratio of gross profit to revenues (sales), it reflects the ability of the company to sell a product for more than the sum of the direct costs of making it.

We introduce three profitability ratios: *gross margin, operating margin,* and *net profit margin.*

Gross Margin. The **gross margin** of a firm is the ratio of gross profit to revenues (sales):

$$\text{Gross Margin} = \frac{\text{Gross Profit}}{\text{Sales}} \qquad (2.9)$$

The gross margin simply reflects the ability of the company to sell a product for more than the sum of the direct costs of making it. All of the firm's other expenses of doing business (those not directly related to producing the goods sold) must be covered by this margin. In 2007 Global's gross profit was $33.3 million and its sales were $186.7 million, for a gross margin of 33.3/186.7 = 17.84%.

operating margin The ratio of operating income to revenues, it reveals how much a company has earned from each dollar of sales before interest and taxes are deducted.

Operating Margin. Because operating income reflects all of the expenses of doing business, another important profitability ratio is the **operating margin**, the ratio of operating income to revenues:

$$\text{Operating Margin} = \frac{\text{Operating Income}}{\text{Total Sales}} \qquad (2.10)$$

The operating margin reveals how much a company earns before interest and taxes from each dollar of sales. Global's operating margin in 2007 was 10.4/186.7 = 5.57%, an increase from its 2006 operating margin of 7.1/176.1 = 4.03%. By comparing operating margins across firms within an industry, we can assess the relative efficiency of firms' operations. For example, in 2006 American Airlines (AMR) had an operating margin of 1.02% (i.e., they gained 1 cent for each dollar in revenues). However, competitor Southwest Airlines (LUV) had an operating margin of 8.70%.

Differences in operating margins can also result from differences in strategy. For example, in 2006, Wal-Mart Stores had an operating margin of 5.5% while high-end retailer Nordstrom had an operating margin of 12.9%. In this case, Wal-Mart's lower operating margin is not a result of its inefficiency but is part of its strategy of offering lower prices to sell common products in high volume. Indeed, Wal-Mart's sales were more than 40 times higher than those of Nordstrom.

net profit margin The ratio of net income to revenues, it shows the fraction of each dollar in revenues that is available to equity holders after the firm pays its expenses, plus interest and taxes.

Net Profit Margin. A firm's **net profit margin** is the ratio of net income to revenues:

$$\text{Net Profit Margin} = \frac{\text{Net Income}}{\text{Total Sales}} \qquad (2.11)$$

The net profit margin shows the fraction of each dollar in revenues that is available to equity holders after the firm pays its expenses, plus interest and taxes. Global's net profit margin in 2007 was 2.0/186.7 = 1.07%. Differences in net profit margins can be due to differences in efficiency, but they can also result from differences in leverage (the firm's reliance on debt financing), which determines the amount of interest payments.

Asset Efficiency

A financial manager can use the combined information in the firm's income statement and balance sheet to gauge how efficiently his or her firm is utilizing its assets. A first broad measure of efficiency is asset turnover, the ratio of sales to total assets:

$$\text{Asset Turnover} = \frac{\text{Sales}}{\text{Total Assets}} \qquad (2.12)$$

Low values of asset turnover indicate that the firm is not generating much revenue (sales) per dollar of assets. In 2007 Global's $170.1 million in assets generated $186.7 million in sales, for an asset turnover ratio of 1.1. Since total assets includes assets, such as cash, that are not directly involved in generating sales, Global's manager might also look at Global's fixed asset turnover, which is equal to sales divided by fixed assets:

$$\text{Fixed Asset Turnover} = \frac{\text{Sales}}{\text{Fixed Assets}} \qquad (2.13)$$

Global's fixed assets in 2007 were $113.1 million worth of property, plant, and equipment, yielding a fixed asset turnover of 1.7 (= $186.7 / $113.1). Low asset turnover ratios indicate that the firm is generating relatively few sales given the amount of assets it employs.

Working Capital Ratios

accounts receivable days (average collection period or days sales outstanding) An expression of a firm's accounts receivable in terms of the number of days' worth of sales that the accounts receivable represents.

Global's managers might be further interested in how efficiently they are managing their net working capital. We can express the firm's accounts receivable in terms of the number of days' worth of sales that it represents, called the **accounts receivable days, average collection period**, or **days sales outstanding**:[4]

$$\text{Accounts Receivable Days} = \frac{\text{Accounts Receivable}}{\text{Average Daily Sales}} \tag{2.14}$$

accounts payable days An expression of a firm's accounts payable in terms of the number of days' worth of cost of goods sold that the accounts payable represents.

Given average daily sales of $186.7 million/365 = $0.51 million in 2007, Global's receivables of $18.5 million represent 18.5/0.51 = 36 days' worth of sales. In other words, Global takes a little over one month to collect payment from its customers, on average. In 2006, Global's accounts receivable represented only 27 days worth of sales. Although the number of receivable days can fluctuate seasonally, a significant unexplained increase could be a cause for concern (perhaps indicating the firm is doing a poor job collecting from its customers or is trying to boost sales by offering generous credit terms). Similar ratios exist for accounts payable and inventory. Those ratios are called **accounts payable days** (accounts payable divided by average daily cost of goods sold) and **inventory days** (inventory divided by average daily cost of goods sold).

inventory days An expression of a firm's inventory in terms of the number of days' worth or cost of goods sold that the inventory represents.

inventory turnover ratio Sales divided by either the latest cost of inventory or the average inventory over the year, it shows how efficiently companies turn their inventory into sales.

Just as we can analyze how efficiently we are using our total or fixed assets to generate sales, we can also compute how efficiently we turn our inventory into sales. The **inventory turnover ratio** is equal to sales divided by either the latest cost of inventory or the average inventory over the year:

$$\text{Inventory Turnover} = \frac{\text{Sales}}{\text{Inventory}} \tag{2.15}$$

A normal level for this ratio, similar to the others in this section, can vary substantially for different industries, although a higher level (more dollars of sales per dollar of inventory) is generally better.

EBITDA

EBITDA A computation of a firm's earnings before interest, taxes, depreciation, and amortization are deducted.

Financial analysts often compute a firm's earnings before interest, taxes, depreciation, and amortization, or **EBITDA**. Because depreciation and amortization are not cash expenses for the firm, EBITDA reflects the cash a firm has earned from its operations. Global's EBITDA in 2007 was 10.4 + 1.2 = $11.6 million.

Leverage Ratios

interest coverage ratio or times interest earned (TIE) ratio An assessment by lenders of a firm's leverage, it is equal to a measure of earnings divided by interest.

Lenders often assess a firm's leverage by computing an **interest coverage ratio**, also known as a **times interest earned (TIE) ratio**, which, as its name suggests, is equal to a measure of earnings divided by interest. Financial managers watch these ratios carefully because they assess how easily the firm will be able to cover its interest payments. There is no one accepted measure of earnings for these ratios; it is common to consider operating income,

---

[4]Accounts receivable days can also be calculated based on the average accounts receivable at the end of the current and prior years.

EBIT, or EBITDA as a multiple of the firm's interest expenses. When this ratio is high, it indicates that the firm is earning much more than is necessary to meet its required interest payments.

Investment Returns

return on equity (ROE)
The ratio of a firm's net income to the book value of its equity.

Analysts and financial managers often evaluate the firm's return on investment by comparing its income to its investment using ratios such as the firm's **return on equity (ROE)**:[5]

$$\text{Return on Equity} = \frac{\text{Net Income}}{\text{Book Value of Equity}} \qquad (2.16)$$

Global's ROE in 2007 was 2.0/22.2 = 9.0%. The ROE provides a measure of the return that the firm has earned on its past investments. A high ROE may indicate the firm is able to find investment opportunities that are very profitable. Of course, one weakness of this measure is the difficulty in interpreting the book value of equity.

return on assets (ROA)
The ratio of net income to the total book value of the firm's assets.

Another common measure is the **return on assets (ROA)**, which is net income divided by the total assets. A firm must earn both a positive ROE and ROA to grow.

The DuPont Identity

Global's financial manager will need to know that its ROE is 9%, but that financial manager would also need to understand the drivers of his or her firm's return on equity. High margins, efficient use of assets, or even simply high leverage could all lead to a higher return on equity. By delving deeper into the sources of return on equity, the financial manager can gain a clear sense of the firm's financial picture. One common tool for doing so is the **DuPont Identity**, named for the company that popularized it, which expresses return on equity as the product of profit margin, asset turnover, and a measure of leverage.

DuPont Identity
Expresses return on equity as the product of profit margin, asset turnover, and a measure of leverage.

To understand the DuPont Identity, we start with ROE and decompose it in steps into the drivers identified in the identity. First, we simply multiply ROE by (sales/sales), which is just 1, and rearranging terms:

$$\text{ROE} = \left(\frac{\text{Net Income}}{\text{Total Equity}}\right)\left(\frac{\text{Sales}}{\text{Sales}}\right) = \left(\frac{\text{Net Income}}{\text{Sales}}\right)\left(\frac{\text{Sales}}{\text{Total Equity}}\right) \qquad (2.17)$$

This expression says that ROE can be thought of as net income per dollar of sales (profit margin) times the amount of sales per dollar of equity. For example, Global's ROE comes from its profit margin of 1.1% multiplied by its sales per dollar of equity of (186.7/22.2 = 8.41): 1.1% × 8.41 = 9%.[6] While this can be a useful insight into ROE, we can take the

---

[5]Because net income is measured over the year, the ROE can also be calculated based on the average book value of equity at the end of the current and prior years.

[6]The calculations for Global will not exactly match the ROE we computed due to rounding in the financial statements and our calculations.

BDeH CHAPTER 2

decomposition further by multiplying Eq. 2.17 by assets/assets, which again is just 1, and rearranging the terms:

$$\begin{aligned} \text{ROE} &= \left(\frac{\text{Net Income}}{\text{Sales}}\right)\left(\frac{\text{Sales}}{\text{Total Equity}}\right)\left(\frac{\text{Total Assets}}{\text{Total Assets}}\right) \\ &= \left(\frac{\text{Net Income}}{\text{Sales}}\right)\left(\frac{\text{Sales}}{\text{Total Assets}}\right)\left(\frac{\text{Total Assets}}{\text{Total Equity}}\right) \end{aligned} \qquad (2.18)$$

equity multiplier A measure of leverage equal to total assets divided by total equity.

This final expression says that ROE is equal to net income per dollar of sales (profit margin) times sales per dollar of assets (asset turnover) times assets per dollar of equity (a measure of leverage called the **equity multiplier**). Equation 2.18 is the DuPont Identity, expressing return on equity as the product of profit margin, asset turnover, and the equity multiplier. Turning to Global, its equity multiplier is 7.7 (= 170.1/22.2). A financial manager at Global looking for ways to increase ROE could turn to the DuPont Identity to assess the drivers behind its current ROE. With a profit margin of 1.1%, asset turnover of 1.1, and an equity multiplier of 7.7, we have:

$$\text{ROE} \;=\; 9\% \;=\; (1.1\%)(1.1)(7.7)$$

This decomposition of ROE shows that leverage is already high (confirmed by the fact that the book debt-to-equity ratio shows that Global's debt is more than five times its equity). However, Global is operating with only 1% profit margins and relatively low asset turnover. Thus, Global's manager could pursue lowering costs to increase profit margin and utilizing the firm's existing assets more efficiently.[7]

BDeH CHAPTER 2

EXAMPLE 2.3

DuPont Analysis

Problem

The following table contains information about Wal-Mart (WMT) and Nordstrom (JWN). Compute their respective ROEs and then determine how much Wal-Mart would need to increase its profit margin in order to match Nordstrom's ROE.

	Profit Margin	Asset Turnover	Equity Multiplier
Wal-Mart	3.6%	2.4	2.6
Nordstrom	7.7%	1.7	2.4

Solution

▶ **Plan and Organize**

The table contains all the relevant information to use the DuPont Identity to compute the ROE. We can compute the ROE of each company by multiplying together its profit margin, asset turnover, and equity multiplier. In order to determine how much Wal-Mart would need to increase its margin to match Nordstrom's ROE, we can set Wal-Mart's ROE equal to Nordstrom's, keep its turnover and equity multiplier fixed, and solve for the profit margin.

▶ **Execute**

Using the DuPont Identity, we have:

$$\text{ROE}_{\text{WMT}} = 3.6\% \times 2.4 \times 2.6 = 22.5\%$$
$$\text{ROE}_{\text{JWN}} = 7.7\% \times 1.7 \times 2.4 = 31.4\%$$

---

[7]Although the DuPont identity makes it look like you can increase ROE just by increasing leverage, it is not quite that simple. An increase in leverage will increase your interest expense, decreasing your profit margin.

> Now, using Nordstrom's ROE, but Wal-Mart's asset turnover and equity multiplier, we can solve for the margin that Wal-Mart needs to achieve Nordstrom's ROE:
>
> $$31.4\% = \text{Margin} \times 2.4 \times 2.6$$
> $$\text{Margin} = 31.4\%/6.24 = 5.0\%$$
>
> ▶ **Evaluate**
> Wal-Mart would have to increase its profit margin from 3.6% to 5% in order to match Nordstrom's ROE. It would be able to achieve Nordstrom's ROE even with a lower margin than Nordstrom (5.0% vs. 7.7%) because of its higher turnover and slightly higher leverage.

Valuation Ratios

price-earnings ratio (P/E) The ratio of the market value of equity to the firm's earnings, or its share price to its earnings per share.

Analysts and investors use a number of ratios to gauge the market value of the firm. The most important is the firm's **price-earnings ratio (P/E)**:

$$\text{P/E Ratio} = \frac{\text{Market Capitalization}}{\text{Net Income}} = \frac{\text{Share Price}}{\text{Earnings per Share}} \qquad (2.19)$$

That is, the P/E ratio is the ratio of the value of equity to the firm's earnings, either on a total basis or on a per-share basis. For example, Global's P/E ratio in 2007 was 36/2.0 = 10/0.56 = 18. The P/E ratio is a simple measure that is used to assess whether a stock is over- or under-valued, based on the idea that the value of a stock should be proportional to the level of earnings it can generate for its shareholders. P/E ratios can vary widely across industries and tend to be higher for industries with high growth rates. For example, in 2007 the average large U.S. firm had a P/E ratio of about 18. But biotechnology firms, which have low current earnings but the promise of high future earnings if they develop successful drugs, had an average P/E ratio of 30. One way to capture the idea that a higher P/E ratio can be justified by a higher growth rate is to compare it to the company's expected earnings growth rate. For example, if Global's expected growth rate is 18%, then it would have a P/E to Growth, or **PEG ratio**, of 1. Some investors consider PEG ratios of 1 or below as indicating the stock is fairly priced, but would question whether the company is potentially overvalued if the PEG is higher than 1.

PEG ratio The ratio of a firm's P/E to its expected earnings growth rate.

The P/E ratio considers the value of the firm's equity and so depends on its leverage. Recall that the amount of assets controlled by the equity holders can be increased

Common Mistake   **Mismatched Ratios**

When considering valuation (and other) ratios, be sure that the items you are comparing both represent amounts related to the entire firm or that both represent amounts related solely to equity holders. For example, a firm's share price and market capitalization are values associated with the firm's equity. Thus, it makes sense to compare them to the firm's earnings per share or net income, which are amounts to equity holders after interest has been paid to debt holders. We must be careful, however, if we compare a firm's market capitalization to its revenues, operating income, or EBITDA. These amounts are related to the whole firm, and both debt and equity holders have a claim to them. Therefore, it is better to compare revenues, operating income, or EBITDA to the enterprise value of the firm, which includes both debt and equity.

through the use of leverage. To assess the market value of the underlying business, it is common to consider valuation ratios based on the firm's enterprise value. Typical ratios include the ratio of enterprise value to revenue, or enterprise value to operating income or EBITDA. These ratios compare the value of the business to its sales, operating profits, or cash flow. Similar to the P/E ratio, these ratios are used to make intra-industry comparisons of how firms are priced in the market.

The P/E ratio is not useful when the firm's earnings are negative. In this case, it is common to look at the firm's enterprise value relative to sales. The risk in doing so, however, is that earnings might be negative because the firm's underlying business model is fundamentally flawed, as was the case for many Internet firms in the late 1990s.

EXAMPLE 2.4

Computing
Profitability and
Valuation Ratios

Problem

Consider the following data from 2006 for Wal-Mart Stores and Target Corporation ($ billions):

	Wal-Mart Stores (WMT)	Target Corporation (TGT)
Sales	345	60
Operating Income	19	5
Net Income	11	3
Market Capitalization	190	49
Cash	7	1
Debt	36	10

Compare Wal-Mart and Target's operating margin, net profit margin, P/E ratio, and the ratio of enterprise value to operating income and sales.

Solution

▶ **Plan**

The table contains all of the raw data, but we need to compute the ratios using the inputs in the table.

Operating Margin = Operating Income / Sales
Net Profit Margin = Net Income / Sales
P/E ratio = Price / Earnings
Enterprise value to operating income = Enterprise Value / Operating Income
Enterprise value to sales = Enterprise Value / Sales

▶ **Execute**

Wal-Mart had an operating margin of 19/345 = 5.5%, a net profit margin of 11/345 = 3.2%, and a P/E ratio of 190/11 = 17.3. Its enterprise value was 190 + 36 − 7 = $219 billion, which has a ratio of 219/19 = 11.5 to operating income and 219/345 = 0.64 to sales.

Target had an operating margin of 5/60 = 8.3%, a net profit margin of 3/60 = 5.0%, and a P/E ratio of 49/3 = 16.3. Its enterprise value was 49 + 10 − 1 = $58 billion, which has a ratio of 58/5 = 11.6 to operating income and 58/60 = 0.97 to sales.

▶ **Evaluate**

Note that despite their large difference in size, Target and Wal-Mart's P/E and enterprise value to operating income ratios were very similar. Target's profitability was somewhat higher than Wal-Mart's, however, explaining the difference in the ratio of enterprise value to sales.

TABLE 2.4

Income Statement Ratios

Ratio	Formula	Manufacturing	Retail	Service	S&P 500
Profitability Ratios					
Gross margin	$\dfrac{\text{Gross Profit}}{\text{Sales}}$	34.3%	30.8%	50.4%	38.4%
Operating margin	$\dfrac{\text{Operating Income}}{\text{Total Sales}}$	8.4%	7.4%	8.7%	19.7%
Net Profit margin	$\dfrac{\text{Net Income}}{\text{Total Sales}}$	2.0%	2.3%	2.1%	8.7%
Leverage Ratio					
Interest coverage ratio (TIE)	$\dfrac{\text{Operating Income}}{\text{Interest Expense}}$	4.78	7.16	3.58	12.13
Investment Return Ratios					
Return on equity	$\dfrac{\text{Net Income}}{\text{Book Value of Equity}}$	7.9%	10.6%	7.9%	15.8%
Return on assets	$\dfrac{\text{Net Income}}{\text{Total Assets}}$	1.6%	4.3%	1.1%	5.4%
Valuation Ratio					
Price-to-earnings ratio	$\dfrac{\text{Share Price}}{\text{Earnings per Share}}$	10.0	15.2	9.3	18.0
Efficiency and Working Capital Ratios					
Accounts receivable days	$\dfrac{\text{Accounts Receivable}}{\text{Average Daily Sales}}$	56.8	6.7	62.5	57.5
Fixed asset turnover	$\dfrac{\text{Sales}}{\text{Fixed Assets}}$	5.6	6.3	11.8	5.2
Total asset turnover	$\dfrac{\text{Sales}}{\text{Total Assets}}$	0.9	1.8	0.8	0.7
Inventory turnover	$\dfrac{\text{Sales}}{\text{Inventory}}$	7.4	10.0	44.0	10.8

Source: Standard and Poors' Compustat

Table 2.4 summarizes income statement ratios and provides typical values of those ratios in 2006 in the manufacturing, retail, and service sectors along with the 500 firms in the S&P 500 index.

Concept Check

9. How can a financial manager use the DuPont Identity to assess the firm's ROE?

10. How do you use the price-earnings (P/E) ratio to gauge the market value of a firm?

2.6 The Statement of Cash Flows

The income statement provides a measure of the firm's profit over a given time period. However, it does not indicate the amount of *cash* the firm has earned. There are two reasons that net income does not correspond to cash earned. First, there are non-cash entries on the income statement, such as depreciation and amortization. Second, certain uses, such as the purchase of a building or expenditures on inventory, and sources of cash, such as the collection of accounts receivable, are not reported on the income statement. The firm's **statement of cash flows** utilizes the information from the income statement and balance sheet to determine how much cash the firm has generated, and how that cash has been allocated, during a set period. Cash is important because it is needed to pay bills and maintain operations and is the source of any return of investment for investors. Thus, from the perspective of an investor attempting to value the firm or a financial manager concerned about cash flows (vs. earnings), the statement of cash flows provides what may be the most important information of the four financial statements.

statement of cash flows
An accounting statement that shows how a firm has used the cash it earned during a set period.

The statement of cash flows is divided into three sections: operating activities, investment activities, and financing activities. These sections roughly correspond to the three major jobs of the financial manager. The first section, operating activities, starts with net income from the income statement. It then adjusts this number by adding back all non-cash entries related to the firm's operating activities. The next section, investment activities, lists the cash used for investment. The third section, financing activities, shows the flow of cash between the firm and its investors. Global's statement of cash flows is shown in Table 2.5. In this section, we take a close look at each component of the statement of cash flows.

TABLE 2.5	GLOBAL CORPORATION Statement of Cash Flows Year ended December 31 (in $ millions)		
Global Corporation's Statement of Cash Flows for 2007 and 2006		**2007**	**2006**
	Operating activities		
	Net income	2.0	1.9
	Depreciation and amortization	1.2	1.1
	Cash effect of changes in		
	Accounts receivable	−5.3	−0.3
	Accounts payable	2.7	−0.5
	Inventory	−1.0	−1.0
	Cash from operating activities	**−0.4**	**1.2**
	Investment activities		
	Capital expenditures	−33.4	−4.0
	Acquisitions and other investing activity		
	Cash from investing activities	**−33.4**	**−4.0**
	Financing activities		
	Dividends paid	−1.0	−1.0
	Sale or purchase of stock	—	—
	Increase in short-term borrowing	2.3	3.0
	Increase in long-term borrowing	35.2	2.5
	Cash from financing activities	**36.5**	**4.5**
	Change in cash and cash equivalents	**2.7**	**1.7**

BDeH CHAPTER 2

Operating Activity

The first section of Global's statement of cash flows adjusts net income by all non-cash items related to operating activity. For instance, depreciation is deducted when computing net income, but it is not an actual cash expense. Thus, we add it back to net income when determining the amount of cash the firm has generated. Similarly, we add back any other non-cash expenses (for example, deferred taxes).

Next, we adjust for changes to net working capital that arise from changes to accounts receivable, accounts payable, or inventory. When a firm sells a product, it records the revenue as income even though it may not receive the cash from that sale immediately. Instead, it may grant the customer credit and let the customer pay in the future. The customer's obligation adds to the firm's accounts receivable. We use the following guidelines to adjust for changes in working capital:

1. Accounts receivable: When a sale is recorded as part of net income, but the cash has not yet been received from the customer, we must adjust the cash flows by *deducting* the increases in accounts receivable. This increase represents additional lending by the firm to its customers and it reduces the cash available to the firm.

2. Accounts payable: Similarly, we *add* increases in accounts payable. Accounts payable represents borrowing by the firm from its suppliers. This borrowing increases the cash available to the firm.

3. Inventory: Finally, we *deduct* increases in inventory. Increases in inventory are not recorded as an expense and do not contribute to net income (the cost of the goods are only included in net income when the goods are actually sold). However, the cost of increasing inventory is a cash expense for the firm and must be deducted.

We can identify the changes in these working capital items on the balance sheet. For example, from Table 2.1, Global's accounts receivable increased from $13.2 million in 2006 to $18.5 million in 2007. We deduct the increase of $18.5 - 13.2 = \$5.3$ million on the statement of cash flows. Note that although Global showed positive net income on the income statement, it actually had a negative $0.4 million cash flow from operating activity, in large part because of the increase in accounts receivable.

Investment Activity

capital expenditures
Purchases of new property, plant, and equipment.

The next section of the statement of cash flows shows the cash required for investment activities. Purchases of new property, plant, and equipment are referred to as **capital expenditures**. Recall that capital expenditures do not appear immediately as expenses on the income statement. Instead, the firm depreciates these assets and deducts depreciation expenses over time. To determine the firm's cash flow, we already added back depreciation because it is not an actual cash expense. Now, we subtract the actual capital expenditure that the firm made. Similarly, we also deduct other assets purchased or investments made by the firm, such as acquisitions. In Table 2.5, we see that in 2007, Global spent $33.4 million in cash on investing activities.

Financing Activity

retained earnings The difference between a firm's net income and the amount it spends on dividends.

The last section of the statement of cash flows shows the cash flows from financing activities. Dividends paid to shareholders are a cash outflow. Global paid $1 million to its shareholders as dividends in 2007.

The difference between a firm's net income and the amount it spends on dividends is referred to as the firm's **retained earnings** for that year:

$$\text{Retained Earnings} = \text{Net Income} - \text{Dividends} \qquad (2.20)$$

payout ratio The ratio of a firm's dividends to its net income.

Global retained $2 million − $1 million = $1 million, or 50% of its earnings in 2007. This makes its *payout ratio* for 2007 equal to 50%. A firm's **payout ratio** is the ratio of its dividends to its net income:

$$\text{Payout Ratio} = \frac{\text{Dividends}}{\text{Net Income}} \qquad (2.21)$$

Also listed under financing activity is any cash the company received from the sale of its own stock, or cash spent buying (repurchasing) its own stock. Global did not issue or repurchase stock during this period.

The last items to include in this section result from changes to Global's short-term and long-term borrowing. Global raised money by issuing debt, so the increases in short-term and long-term borrowing represent cash inflows. The last line of the statement of cash flows combines the cash flows from these three activities to calculate the overall change in the firm's cash balance over the period of the statement. In this case, Global had cash inflows of $2.7 million. By looking at the statement in Table 2.5 as a whole, we can determine that Global chose to borrow (mainly in the form of long-term debt) to cover the cost of its investment and operating activities. Although the firm's cash balance has increased, Global's negative operating cash flows and relatively high expenditures on investment activities might give investors some reasons for concern. If that pattern continues, Global will need to continue to borrow to remain in business.

EXAMPLE 2.5

The Impact of Depreciation on Cash Flow

Problem
Suppose Global had an additional $1 million depreciation expense in 2007. If Global's tax rate on pretax income is 26%, what would be the impact of this expense on Global's earnings? How would it impact Global's cash at the end of the year?

Solution

▶ **Plan**
Depreciation is an operating expense, so Global's operating income, EBIT, and pretax income would be affected. With a tax rate of 26%, Global's tax bill will decrease by 26 cents for every dollar that pretax income is reduced. In order to determine how Global's cash would be impacted, we have to determine the effect of the additional depreciation on cash flows. Recall that depreciation is not an actual cash outflow, even though it is treated as an expense, so the only effect on cash flow is through the reduction in taxes.

▶ **Execute**
Global's operating income, EBIT, and pretax income would fall by $1 million because of the $1 million in additional operating expense due to depreciation.

This $1 million decrease in pretax income would reduce Global's tax bill by 26% × $1 million = $0.26 million. Therefore, net income would fall by 1 − 0.26 = $0.74 million.

On the statement of cash flows, net income would fall by $0.74 million, but we would add back the additional depreciation of $1 million because it is not a cash expense. Thus, cash from operating activities would rise by −0.74 + 1 = $0.26 million. Therefore, Global's cash balance at the end of the year would increase by $0.26 million, the amount of the tax savings that resulted from the additional depreciation deduction.

▶ **Evaluate**
The increase in cash balance comes completely from the reduction in taxes. Because Global pays $0.26 million less in taxes even though its cash expenses have not increased, it has $0.26 million more in cash at the end of the year.

11. Why does a firm's net income not correspond to cash earned?

12. What are the components of the statement of cash flows?

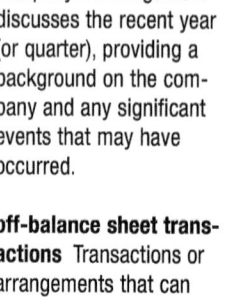

2.7 Other Financial Statement Information

The most important elements of a firm's financial statements are the balance sheet, income statement, and the statement of cash flows, which we have already discussed. Several other pieces of information contained in the financial statements warrant brief mention: the management discussion and analysis, the statement of stockholders' equity, and notes to the financial statement.

Management Discussion and Analysis

management discussion and analysis (MD&A) A preface to the financial statements in which a company's management discusses the recent year (or quarter), providing a background on the company and any significant events that may have occurred.

The **management discussion and analysis (MD&A)** is a preface to the financial statements in which the company's management discusses the recent year (or quarter), providing a background on the company and any significant events that may have occurred. Management may also discuss the coming year, and outline goals and new projects.

Management must also discuss any important risks that the firm faces or issues that may affect the firm's liquidity or resources. Management is also required to disclose any **off-balance sheet transactions**, which are transactions or arrangements that can have a material impact on the firm's future performance yet do not appear on the balance sheet. For example, if a firm has made guarantees that it will compensate a buyer for losses related to an asset purchased from the firm, these guarantees represent a potential future liability for the firm that must be disclosed as part of the MD&A.

off-balance sheet transactions Transactions or arrangements that can have a material impact on a firm's future performance yet do not appear on the balance sheet.

Statement of Stockholders' Equity

statement of stockholders' equity An accounting statement that breaks down the stockholders' equity computed on the balance sheet into the amount that came from issuing new shares versus retained earnings.

The **statement of stockholders' equity** breaks down the stockholders' equity computed on the balance sheet into the amount that came from issuing new shares versus retained earnings. Because the book value of stockholders' equity is not a useful assessment of value for financial purposes, the information contained in the statement of stockholders' equity is also not particularly insightful, so we do not spend time on the statement here.

Notes to the Financial Statements

In addition to the four financial statements, companies provide extensive notes with additional details on the information provided in the statements. For example, the notes document important accounting assumptions that were used in preparing the statements. They often provide information specific to a firm's subsidiaries or its separate product lines. They show the details of the firm's stock-based compensation plans for employees and the different types of debt the firm has outstanding. Details of acquisitions, spin-offs, leases, taxes, and risk management activities are also given. The information provided in the notes is often very important to a full interpretation of the firm's financial statements.

13. Where do off-balance sheet transactions appear in a firm's financial statements?

14. What information do the notes to financial statements provide?

2.8 Financial Reporting in Practice

The various financial statements we have examined are of critical importance to investors and financial managers alike. Even with safeguards such as GAAP and auditors, financial reporting abuses unfortunately do take place. We now review two of the most infamous recent examples and offer some concluding thoughts to guide financial managers through the complexities of financial statements.

Enron

Enron is the most well-known of the accounting scandals of the early 2000s. Enron started as an operator of natural gas pipelines but evolved into a global trader dealing in a range of products including gas, oil, electricity, and even broadband Internet capacity. A series of events unfolded that led Enron to file the largest bankruptcy filing in U.S. history in December 2001. By the end of 2001, the market value of Enron's shares had fallen by over $60 billion.

"We're in good shape.
Nobody understands our financial statement."

Interestingly, throughout the 1990s and up to late 2001, Enron was touted as one of the most successful and profitable companies in America. *Fortune* rated Enron "The Most Innovative Company in America" for six straight years, from 1995 to 2000. But while many aspects of Enron's business were successful, subsequent investigations suggest that Enron executives had been manipulating Enron's financial statements to mislead investors and artificially inflate the price of Enron's stock and to maintain its credit rating. In 2000, for example, 96% of Enron's reported earnings were the result of accounting manipulation.[8]

Although the accounting manipulations that Enron used were quite sophisticated, the essence of most of the deceptive transactions was surprisingly simple. Enron sold assets at inflated prices to other firms (or, in many cases, business entities that Enron's CFO Andrew Fastow had created), together with a promise to buy back those assets at an even higher future price. Thus, Enron was effectively borrowing money, receiving cash today in exchange for a promise to pay more cash in the future. But Enron recorded the incoming cash as revenue and then hid the promises to buy the assets back in a variety of ways.[9] In the end, much of their revenue growth and profits in the late 1990s were the result of this type of manipulation.

WorldCom

On July 21, 2002, WorldCom entered the largest bankruptcy of all time. At its peak, WorldCom had a market capitalization of $120 billion. Again, a series of accounting manipulations beginning in 1998 hid the firm's financial problems from investors.

---

[8]John R. Kroger, "Enron, Fraud and Securities Reform: An Enron Prosecutor's Perspective," *University of Colorado Law Review*, December, 2005, pp. 57–138.

[9]In some cases, these promises were called "price risk management liabilities" and hidden with other trading activities; in other cases they were off-balance sheet transactions that were not fully disclosed.

In WorldCom's case, the fraud was to reclassify $3.85 billion in operating expenses as long-term investment. The immediate impact of this change was to boost WorldCom's reported earnings: Operating expenses are deducted from earnings immediately, whereas long-term investments are depreciated slowly over time. Of course, this manipulation would not boost WorldCom's cash flows, because long-term investments must be deducted on the cash flow statement at the time they are made.

Some investors were concerned by WorldCom's excessive investment compared to the rest of the industry. As one investment advisor commented, "Red flags [were] things like big deviations between reported earnings and excess cash flow . . . [and] excessive capital expenditures for a long period of time. That was what got us out of WorldCom in 1999."[10]

The Sarbanes-Oxley Act

Enron and WorldCom highlight the importance to investors of accurate and up-to-date financial statements for firms they choose to invest in. In 2002, Congress passed the **Sarbanes-Oxley Act (SOX)**. While SOX contains many provisions, the overall intent of the legislation was to improve the accuracy of information given to both boards and to shareholders. SOX attempted to achieve this goal in three ways: (1) by overhauling incentives and independence in the auditing process, (2) by stiffening penalties for providing false information, and (3) by forcing companies to validate their internal financial control processes.

Sarbanes-Oxley Act (SOX) Legislation passed by Congress in 2002, intended to improve the accuracy of financial information given to both boards and to shareholders.

Many of the problems at Enron, WorldCom, and elsewhere were kept hidden from boards and shareholders until it was too late. In the wake of these scandals, many people felt that the accounting statements of these companies, while often remaining true to the letter of GAAP, did not present an accurate picture of the financial health of a company.

Auditing firms are supposed to ensure that a company's financial statements accurately reflect the financial state of the firm. In reality, most auditors have a long-standing relationship with their audit clients; this extended relationship and the auditors' desire to keep the lucrative auditing fees make auditors less willing to challenge management. More importantly perhaps, most accounting firms have developed large and extremely profitable consulting divisions. Obviously, if an audit team refuses to accommodate a request by a client's management, that client will be less likely to choose the accounting firm's consulting division for its next consulting contract. SOX addressed this concern by putting strict limits on the amount of non-audit fees (consulting or otherwise) that an accounting firm can earn from the same firm that it audits. It also required that audit partners rotate every five years to limit the likelihood that auditing relationships become too cozy over long periods of time. Finally, SOX called on the SEC to force companies to have audit committees that are dominated by outside directors, and required that at least one outside director have a financial background.

SOX also stiffened the criminal penalties for providing false information to shareholders. It required both the CEO and the CFO to personally attest to the accuracy of the financial statements presented to shareholders and to sign a statement to that effect. Penalties for providing false or misleading financial statements were increased under SOX—fines of as much as $5 million and imprisonment of a maximum of 20 years are permitted. Further, CEOs and CFOs must return bonuses or profits from the sale of stock or the exercise of options during any period covered by statements that are later restated.

---

[10]Robert Olstein, as reported in the *Wall Street Journal*, August 23, 2002.

BDeH CHAPTER 2

INTERVIEW WITH
Sue Frieden

Sue Frieden is Ernst & Young's Global Managing Partner, Quality & Risk Management. A member of the Global Executive board, she is responsible for every aspect of quality and risk management—employees, services, procedures, and clients. Here, she discusses how financial statements are used, the challenges in defining a common set of accounting rules across countries, the role of auditing in financial markets, and the importance of ethics in auditing.

QUESTION: *Do today's financial statements give the investing public what they need?*

ANSWER: Globally, we are seeing an effort to provide more forward-looking information to investors. But fundamental questions remain, such as how fully do investors understand financial statements and how fully do they read them? Research shows that most individual investors don't rely on financial statements much at all. We need to determine how the financial statements can be improved. To do that we will need a dialogue involving investors, regulators, analysts, auditors, stock exchanges, academics, and others to ensure that financial statements are as relevant as they can be.

QUESTION: *Ernst & Young is a global organization. How do accounting standards in the U.S. compare to those elsewhere?*

answer: In January of 2005, 100 countries outside the United States began the process of adopting new accounting standards (International Financial Reporting Standards) that would in large measure be based on principles rather than rules. As global markets become more complex, it is clear that we all need to be playing by the same set of rules, but as a first step we need to have consistency from country to country. There are definite challenges to overcome in reconciling principle-based and rules-based systems, but we are optimistic that these challenges will inevitably get resolved. At the same time, there are efforts underway to ensure that auditing standards are globally consistent. Ultimately, financial statements prepared under global standards and audited under consistent global auditing standards will better serve investors.

QUESTION: *What role does the audit firm play in our financial markets, and how has that changed since the collapse of Arthur Andersen?*

ANSWER: All of us—the entire business community—have gone through a pivotal, historic moment. And certainly the accounting profession has seen unprecedented change in the past few years as well. The passage of Sarbanes-Oxley and other changes are helping to restore public trust. Things are certainly very different from what we've known before. We're now engaging on a regular basis with a wider range of stakeholders—companies, boards, policymakers, opinion leaders, investors, and academia. And we've had the chance to step back and ask ourselves why we do what we do as accounting professionals, and why it matters. In terms of the services we offer, much of what we do helps companies comply with regulations, guard against undue risks, and implement sound transactions. And part of the value in what we do is providing the basis to all stakeholders to understand whether companies are playing by the rules—whether it is accounting rules, financial reporting rules, or tax rules. We help create confidence in financial data. The public may not fully understand precisely what auditors do or how we do it, but they care that we exist because it provides them the confidence they so badly need and want.

QUESTION: *How does a global accounting firm such as Ernst & Young ensure that each of its partners adheres to the appropriate standards?*

ANSWER: People often tell me, as the global leader for quality and risk management, how hard my job is and how much is on my shoulders. The truth is, doing the right thing—adhering and often exceeding the standards expected of us as independent public auditors—rests on the shoulders of everyone in the organization. All of our more than 107,000 people around the world know it is their responsibility to make this happen. What's more, they know it is their responsibility to raise questions when they have concerns. Perhaps most importantly, all of our people know that no client is too big to walk away from if we sense the company's management is not committed to doing the right thing.

Discussion Questions

Ms. Frieden outlines her view of the role of audit firms and states that it may not be important that the public fully understand what audit firms do.

1. What role do you see for audit firms and how critical do you think it is that the public understand what auditors do?

2. How important is ethics in accounting and what kind of difficult situations between auditors and managers and within audit firms do you think might arise?

Finally, Section 404 of SOX requires senior management and the boards of public companies to be comfortable enough with the process through which funds are allocated and controlled, and outcomes monitored throughout the firm, to be willing to attest to their effectiveness and validity. Section 404 has arguably garnered more attention than any other section in SOX because of the potentially enormous burden it places on every firm to validate its entire financial control system. When the SEC estimated the cost of implementing Section 404, its staff economists put the total cost at $1.24 billion. Recent estimates based on surveys by Financial Executives International and the American Electronics Association predict that the actual cost will be between $20 billion and $35 billion.[11] The burden of complying with this provision is greater, as a fraction of revenue, for smaller companies. The surveys cited earlier found that multibillion-dollar companies will pay less than 0.05% of their revenues to comply, whereas small companies with less than $20 million in revenues will pay more than 3% of their revenues to comply.

The Financial Statements: A Useful Starting Point

In this chapter, we have highlighted the role of the financial statements in informing outside analysts, investors, and the financial managers themselves about the performance, position, and financial condition of the firm. However, especially from the financial manager's perspective, financial statements are only a starting point. For example, we have emphasized the importance of market values over book values. We have also shown that while much can be learned through ratio analysis, these ratios are only markers that point the financial manager toward areas where the firm is doing well or where he or she needs to focus effort for improvement. No single ratio tells the whole story. However, by studying all of the financial statements and considering ratios that assess profitability, leverage, and efficiency, you should be able to develop a clear sense of the health and performance of the firm. Finally, using the cases of Enron and WorldCom, we emphasize that the usefulness of the financial statements to investors relies on the ethics of those constructing them. However, even in these cases of deception, an informed reader of the financial statements could have spotted the warning signs by focusing on the statement of cash flows and carefully reading the notes to the financial statements.

15. Describe the transactions Enron used to increase its reported earnings.

16. What is the Sarbanes-Oxley Act?

---

[11]American Electronics Association, "Sarbanes-Oxley Section 404: The 'Section' of Unintended Consequences and Its Impact on Small Business" (2005).

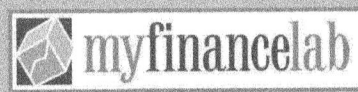

Here is what you should know after reading this chapter. MyFinanceLab will help you identify what you know, and where to go when you need to practice.

Key Points and Equations	Terms	Online Practice Opportunities

2.1 Firms' Disclosure of Financial Information
▶ Financial statements are accounting reports that a firm issues periodically to describe its past performance.
▶ Investors, financial analysts, managers, and other interested parties, such as creditors, rely on financial statements to obtain reliable information about a corporation.
▶ The main types of financial statements are the balance sheet, the income statement, and the statement of cash flows.
	annual report, p. 25
	auditor, p. 26
	balance sheet, p. 26
	financial statements, p. 25
	Generally Accepted
	    Accounting Principles
	    (GAAP), p. 26
		MyFinanceLab
		Study Plan 2.1

2.2 The Balance Sheet ▶ The balance sheet shows the current financial position (assets, liabilities, and stockholders' equity) of the firm at a single point in time. ▶ The two sides of the balance sheet must balance: Assets = Liabilities + Stockholders' Equity (2.1) ▶ Stockholders' equity is the book value of the firm's equity. It differs from the market value of the firm's equity, its market capitalization, because of the way assets and liabilities are recorded for accounting purposes.	accounts payable, p. 28 accounts receivable, p. 28 assets, p. 27 book value, p. 28 book value of equity, p. 29 current assets, p. 27 current liabilities, p. 28 depreciation, p. 28 inventories, p. 28 liabilities, p. 27 long-term assets, p. 28 long-term debt, p. 29 net working capital, p. 28 notes payable, p. 28 short-term debt, p. 28 stockholders' equity, p. 27	MyFinanceLab Study Plan 2.2

2.3 Balance Sheet Analysis
▶ A successful firm's market-to-book ratio typically exceeds 1.
▶ A common ratio used to assess a firm's leverage is:
 	
$$\text{Debt-Equity Ratio} = \frac{\text{Total Debt}}{\text{Total Equity}} \quad (2.4)$$
 	
▶ This ratio is most informative when computed using the market value of equity. It indicates the degree of leverage of the firm.
▶ The enterprise value of a firm is the total value of its underlying business operations:
 	
Enterprise Value = Market Capitalization
                + Debt − Cash   (2.5)
	current ratio, p. 32
	debt-equity ratio, p. 30
	enterprise value, p. 31
	growth stocks, p. 30
	leverage, p. 30
	liquidation value, p. 30
	market capitalization,
	    p. 29
	market-to-book ratio
	    (price- to-book [P/B]
	    ratio), p. 30
	quick ratio, p. 32
	value stocks, p. 30
		MyFinanceLab
		Study Plan 2.3

BDeH CHAPTER 2

2.4 The Income Statement

▶ The income statement reports the firm's revenues and expenses, and it computes the firm's bottom line of net income, or earnings.

▶ Net income is often reported on a per-share basis as the firms earnings per share:

Earnings per Share (EPS)
= Net Income/Shares Outstanding   (2.8)

▶ We compute diluted EPS by adding to the number of shares outstanding the possible increase in the number of shares from the exercise of stock options the firm has awarded.

MyFinanceLab
Study Plan 2.4

2.5 Income Statement Analysis

▶ Profitability ratios show the firm's operating or net income as a fraction of sales, and they are an indication of a firm's efficiency and its pricing strategy.

▶ Asset efficiency ratios assess how efficiently the firm is using its assets by showing how many dollars of revenues the firm produces per dollar of assets.

▶ Working capital ratios express the firm's working capital as a number of days of sales (for receivables) or cost of sales (for inventory or payables).

▶ Interest coverage ratios indicate the ratio of the firm's income or cash flows to its interest expenses, and they are a measure of financial strength.

▶ Return on investment ratios, such as ROE or ROA, express the firm's net income as a return on the book value of its equity or total assets.

▶ Valuation ratios compute market capitalization or enterprise value of the firm relative to its earnings or operating income.

▶ The P/E ratio computes the value of a share of stock relative to the firm's EPS. P/E ratios tend to be high for fast-growing firms.

▶ When comparing valuation ratios, it is important to be sure both numerator and denominator match in terms of whether they include debt.

MyFinanceLab
Study Plan 2.5

2.6 The Statement of Cash Flows

▶ The statement of cash flows reports the sources and uses of the firm's cash. It shows the adjustments to net income for non-cash expenses and changes to net working capital, as well as the cash used (or provided) from investing and financing activities.

MyFinanceLab
Study Plan 2.6

BDeH CHAPTER 2

2.7 Other Financial Statement Information		
▶ The management discussion and analysis section of the financial statement contains management's overview of the firm's performance, as well as disclosure of risks the firm faces, including those from off-balance sheet transactions.	management discussion and analysis (MD&A), p. 46 off-balance sheet transactions, p. 46 statement of stockholders' equity, p. 46	MyFinanceLab Study Plan 2.7
▶ The statement of stockholders' equity breaks down the stockholders' equity computed on the balance sheet into the amount that came from issuing new shares versus retained earnings. It is not particularly useful for financial valuation purposes.		
▶ The notes to a firm's financial statements generally contain important details regarding the numbers used in the main statements.		
2.8 Financial Reporting in Practice		
▶ Recent accounting scandals have drawn attention to the importance of financial statements. New legislation has increased the penalties for fraud, and tightened the procedures firms must use to assure that statements are accurate.	Sarbanes-Oxley Act (SOX), p. 48	MyFinanceLab Study Plan 2.8

Review Questions

1. Why do firms disclose financial information?

2. Who reads financial statements? List at least three different categories of people. For each category, provide an example of the type of information they might be interested in and discuss why.

3. What four financial statements can be found in a firm's 10-K filing? What checks are there on the accuracy of these statements?

4. What is the purpose of the balance sheet?

5. How can you use the balance sheet to assess the health of the firm?

6. What is the purpose of the income statement?

7. How are the balance sheet and the income statement related?

8. What is the DuPont Identity and how can a financial manager use it?

9. How does the statement of cash flows differ from the income statement?

10. Can a firm with positive net income run out of cash? Explain.

11. What can you learn from management's discussion or the notes to the financial statements?

12. How did accounting fraud contribute to the collapse of Enron and WorldCom?

Problems

A blue box (■) indicates problems available in MyFinanceLab. An asterisk (*) indicates problems with a higher level of difficulty.

The Disclosure of Financial Information

1. Find the most recent financial statements for Starbuck's corporation (SBUX) using the following sources:
   a. From the company's Web page www.starbucks.com (*Hint:* Search for "investor relations").
   b. From the SEC Web site www.sec.gov (*Hint:* Search for company filings in the EDGAR database).
   c. From the Yahoo finance Web site finance.yahoo.com.
   d. From at least one other source (*Hint:* Enter "SBUX 10K" at www.google.com).

The Balance Sheet

2. Consider the following potential events that might have occurred to Global on December 30, 2007. For each one, indicate which line items in Global's balance sheet would be affected and by how much. Also indicate the change to Global's book value of equity.
   a. Global used $20 million of its available cash to repay $20 million of its long-term debt.
   b. A warehouse fire destroyed $5 million worth of uninsured inventory.
   c. Global used $5 million in cash and $5 million in new long-term debt to purchase a $10 million building.
   d. A large customer owing $3 million for products it already received declared bankruptcy, leaving no possibility that Global would ever receive payment.
   e. Global's engineers discover a new manufacturing process that will cut the cost of its flagship product by over 50%.
   f. A key competitor announces a radical new pricing policy that will drastically undercut Global's prices.

3. What was the change in Global's book value of equity from 2006 to 2007 according to Table 2.1? Does this imply that the market price of Global's shares increased in 2007? Explain.

4. Find the annual 10-K report for Peet's Coffee and Tea (PEET) online, filed in March 2007. Answer the following questions from its balance sheet:
   a. How much cash did Peet's have at the start of 2007?
   b. What were Peet's total assets?
   c. What were Peet's total liabilities? How much debt did Peet's have?
   d. What was the book value of Peet's equity?

Balance Sheet Analysis

 5. In June 2007, General Electric (GE) had a book value of equity of $117 billion, 10.3 billion shares outstanding, and a market price of $38.00 per share. GE also had cash of $16 billion, and total debt of $467 billion.
   a. What was GE's market capitalization? What was GE's market-to-book ratio?
   b. What was GE's book debt-equity ratio? What was GE's market debt-equity ratio?
   c. What was GE's enterprise value?

6. In July 2007, Apple had cash of $7.12 billion, current assets of $18.75 billion, and current liabilities of $6.99 billion. It also had inventories of $0.25 billion.
a. What was Apple's current ratio?
b. What was Apple's quick ratio?

7. In July 2007, Dell had a quick ratio of 1.25 and a current ratio of 1.30. What can you say about the asset liquidity of Apple relative to Dell?

8. In November 2007, the following information was true about Abercrombie and Fitch (ANF) and The Gap (GPS), both clothing retailers. Values (except price per share) are in millions of dollars.

	Book Equity	Price Per Share	Number of Shares
ANF	1,458	75.01	86.67
GPS	5,194	20.09	798.22

a. What is the market-to-book ratio of each company?
b. What conclusions do you draw from comparing the two ratios?

The Income Statement and Income Statement Analysis

 9. Find the annual 10-K report for Peet's Coffee and Tea (PEET) online, filed in April 2007. Answer the following questions from the income statement:
a. What were Peet's revenues for 2006? By what percentage did revenues grow from 2005?
b. What were Peet's operating and net profit margins in 2006? How do they compare with its margins in 2005?
c. What were Peet's diluted earnings per share in 2006? What number of shares is this EPS based on?

 *10. Suppose that in 2007, Global launched an aggressive marketing campaign that boosted sales by 15%. However, their operating margin fell from 5.57% to 4.50%. Suppose that they had no other income, interest expenses were unchanged, and taxes were the same percentage of pretax income as in 2006.
a. What was Global's EBIT in 2007?
b. What was Global's income in 2007?
c. If Global's P/E ratio and number of shares outstanding remained unchanged, what was Global's share price in 2007?

 11. Suppose a firm's tax rate is 35%.
a. What effect would a $10 million operating expense have on this year's earnings? What effect would it have on next year's earnings?
b. What effect would a $10 million capital expense have on this year's earnings, if the capital is depreciated at a rate of $2 million per year for 5 years? What effect would it have on next year's earnings?

12. You are analyzing the leverage of two firms and you note the following (all values in millions of dollars):

	Debt	Book Equity	Market Equity	Operating Income	Interest Expense
Firm A	500	300	400	100	50
Firm B	80	35	40	8	7

a. What is the market debt-to-equity ratio of each firm?

b. What is the book debt-to-equity ratio of each firm?

c. What is the interest coverage ratio of each firm?

d. Which firm will have more difficulty meeting its debt obligations?

13. For 2007, Wal-Mart and Target had the following information (all values are in millions of dollars):

	Sales (Income Statement)	Accounts Receivable (Balance Sheet)	Inventory (Balance Sheet)
Wal-Mart	348,650	2,767	34,184
Target	59,490	6,397	6,645

a. What is each company's accounts receivable days?

b. What is each company's inventory turnover?

c. Which company is managing its accounts receivable and inventory more efficiently?

*14. Quisco Systems has 6.5 billion shares outstanding and a share price of $18.00. Quisco is considering developing a new networking product in house at a cost of $500 million. Alternatively, Quisco can acquire a firm that already has the technology for $900 million worth (at the current price) of Quisco stock. Suppose that absent the expense of the new technology, Quisco will have EPS of $0.80.

a. Suppose Quisco develops the product in house. What impact would the development cost have on Quisco's EPS? Assume all costs are incurred this year and are treated as an R&D expense, Quisco's tax rate is 35%, and the number of shares outstanding is unchanged.

b. Suppose Quisco does not develop the product in house but instead acquires the technology. What effect would the acquisition have on Quisco's EPS this year? (Note that acquisition expenses do not appear directly on the income statement. Assume the acquired firm has no revenues or expenses of its own, so that the only effect on EPS is due to the change in the number of shares outstanding.)

c. Which method of acquiring the technology has a smaller impact on earnings? Is this method cheaper? Explain.

 15. In December 2006, American Airlines (AMR) had a market capitalization of $6.7 billion, debt of $13.4 billion, and cash of $0.12 billion. American Airlines had revenues of $22.6 billion. British Airways (BAB) had a market capitalization of $11.7 billion, debt of $6.9 billion, cash of $3.0 billion, and revenues of $14.3 billion.

a. Compare the market capitalization-to-revenue ratio (also called the price-to-sales ratio) for American Airlines and British Airways.

b. Compare the enterprise value-to-revenue ratio for American Airlines and British Airways.

c. Which of these comparisons is more meaningful? Explain.

 *16. Find the annual 10-K report for Peet's Coffee and Tea (PEET) online, filed in April 2007.

a. Compute Peet's net profit margin, total asset turnover, and equity multiplier.

b. Verify the DuPont Identity for Peet's ROE.

c. If Peet's managers wanted to increase its ROE by 1 percentage point, how much higher would their asset turnover need to be?

17. Repeat the analysis from parts a and b of the previous problem for Starbucks Coffee (SBUX). Based on the DuPont Identity, what explains the difference between the two firms' ROEs?

BDeH CHAPTER 2

The Statement of Cash Flows

18. Find the annual 10-K report for Peet's Coffee and Tea (PEET) online, filed in April 2007. Answer the following questions from its cash flow statement:
    a. How much cash did Peet's generate from operating activities in 2006?
    b. What was Peet's depreciation expense in 2006?
    c. How much cash was invested in new property and equipment (net of any sales) in 2006?
    d. Did Peet's raise cash through financing activities or spend cash on net in financing activities?

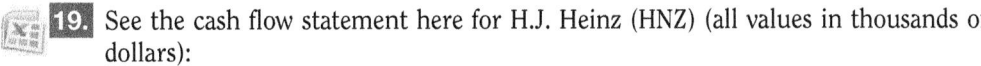 **19.** See the cash flow statement here for H.J. Heinz (HNZ) (all values in thousands of dollars):

Statement of Cash Flows:	1-Aug-07	2-May-07	31-Jan-07	1-Nov-06
Net Income	205,294	181,032	219,038	191,575
Operating Activities, Cash Flows Provided by or Used In				
Depreciation	69,625	71,525	68,712	60,564
Adjustments to net income	−3,789	80,721	19,999	2,732
Changes in accounts receivables	−23,332	80,237	−11,739	−64,366
Changes in liabilities	−134,348	160,089	−187,589	176,491
Changes in inventories	−73,282	98,856	15,325	−194,113
Changes in other operating activities	−31,052	163	1,391	47,010
Total Cash Flow From Operating Activities	9,116	672,623	125,137	219,893
Investing Activities, Cash Flows Provided by or Used In				
Capital expenditures	−58,212	−94,046	−60,974	−50,615
Investments	—	—	—	—
Other cash flows from investing activities	−43,004	-5,307	−36,947	−64,733
Total Cash Flows From Investing Activities	−101,216	−99,353	−97,921	−115,348
Financing Activities, Cash Flows Provided by or Used In				
Dividends paid	−123,204	−113,440	−115,339	−116,084
Sale purchase of stock	−127,332	−196,370	−207,674	−95,575
Net borrowings	14,980	−73,157	324,790	113,396
Other cash flows from financing activities	11,209	−1,535	−2,635	5,057
Total Cash Flows From Financing Activities	−224,347	−384,502	−858	−93,206
Effect of exchange rate changes	15,564	45,118	12,957	289
Change in Cash and Cash Equivalents	−300,883	$233,886	$39,315	$11,628

a. What were Heinz's cumulative earnings over these four quarters? What were its cumulative cash flows from operating activities?
b. What fraction of the cash from operating activities was used for investment over the four quarters?
c. What fraction of the cash from operating activities was used for financing activities over the four quarters?

20. Suppose your firm receives a $5 million order on the last day of the year. You fill the order with $2 million worth of inventory. The customer picks up the entire order the same day and pays $1 million up front in cash; you also issue a bill for the customer to pay the remaining balance of $4 million within 40 days. Suppose your firm's tax rate is 0% (i.e., ignore taxes). Determine the consequences of this transaction for each of the following:

a. Revenues
b. Earnings
c. Receivables
d. Inventory
e. Cash

 21. Nokela Industries purchases a $40 million cyclo-converter. The cyclo-converter will be depreciated by $10 million per year over four years, starting this year. Suppose Nokela's tax rate is 40%.

a. What impact will the cost of the purchase have on earnings for each of the next four years?
b. What impact will the cost of the purchase have on the firm's cash flow for the next four years?

Other Financial Statement Information

 22. The balance sheet information for Clorox Co. (CLX) in 2004–2005 is shown here (all values in thousands of dollars):

Balance Sheet:	31-Mar-05	31-Dec-04	30-Sep-04	30-Jun-04
Assets				
Current Assets				
Cash and cash equivalents	293,000	300,000	255,000	232,000
Net receivables	401,000	362,000	385,000	460,000
Inventory	374,000	342,000	437,000	306,000
Other current assets	60,000	43,000	53,000	45,000
Total Current Assets	1,128,000	1,047,000	1,130,000	1,043,000
Long-term investments	128,000	97,000	—	200,000
Property, plant, and equipment	979,000	991,000	995,000	1,052,000
Goodwill	744,000	748,000	736,000	742,000
Other assets	777,000	827,000	911,000	797,000
Total Assets	3,756,000	3,710,000	3,772,000	3,834,000
Liabilities				
Current Liabilities				
Accounts payable	876,000	1,467,000	922,000	980,000
Short/current long-term debt	410,000	2,000	173,000	288,000
Other current liabilities	—	—	—	—
Total Current Liabilities	1,286,000	1,469,000	1,095,000	1,268,000
Long-term debt	2,381,000	2,124,000	474,000	475,000
Other liabilities	435,000	574,000	559,000	551,000
Total Liabilities	4,102,000	4,167,000	2,128,000	2,294,000
Total Stockholder Equity	−346,000	−457,000	1,644,000	1,540,000
Total Liabilities and Stockholder Equity	$3,756,000	$3,710,000	$3,772,000	$3,834,000

BDeH CHAPTER 2

a. What change in the book value of Clorox's equity took place at the end of 2004?

b. Is Clorox's market-to-book ratio meaningful? Is its book debt-equity ratio meaningful? Explain.

c. Find Clorox's other financial statements from that time online. What was the cause of the change to Clorox's book value of equity at the end of 2004?

d. Does Clorox's book value of equity in 2005 imply that the firm is unprofitable? Explain.

Accounting Manipulation

23. Find the annual 10-K report for Peet's Coffee and Tea (PEET) online, filed in March 2007.

a. Which auditing firm certified these financial statements?

b. Which officers of Peet's certified the financial statements?

24. WorldCom reclassified $3.85 billion of operating expenses as capital expenditures. Explain the effect this reclassification would have on WorldCom's cash flows. (*Hint:* Consider taxes.) WorldCom's actions were illegal and clearly designed to deceive investors. But if a firm could legitimately choose how to classify an expense for tax purposes, which choice is truly better for the firm's investors?

Data Case

This is your second interview with a prestigious brokerage firm for a job as an equity analyst. You survived the morning interviews with the department manager and the vice president of Equity. Everything has gone so well that they want to test your ability as an analyst. You are seated in a room with a computer and a list with the names of two companies—Ford (F) and Microsoft (MSFT). You have 90 minutes to complete the following tasks:

1. Download the annual income statements, balance sheets, and cash flow statements for the last four fiscal years from MarketWatch (www.marketwatch.com). Enter each company's stock symbol and then go to "Financials." Export the statements to Microsoft ® Excel by right-clicking while the cursor is inside each statement.

2. Find historical stock prices for each firm from Yahoo! Finance (http://finance.yahoo.com). Enter your stock symbol, click on "Historical Prices" in the left column, and enter the proper date range to cover the last day of the month corresponding to the date of each financial statement. Use the closing stock prices (not the adjusted close). To calculate the firms' market capitalization at each date, we multiply the firms' historic stock prices by the number of shares outstanding (see "Basic Weighted Shares Outstanding" on the income statement you downloaded in step 1).

3. For each of the four years of statements, compute the following ratios for each firm:

Valuation Ratios

Price-earnings ratio (for EPS use diluted EPS total)

Market-to-book ratio

Enterprise value-to-EBITDA

(For debt, include long-term and short-term debt; for cash, include marketable securities.)

Profitability Ratios

Operating margin (use operating income after depreciation)

Net profit margin

Return on equity

Financial Strength Ratios

Current ratio

Book debt–equity ratio

Market debt–equity ratio

Interest coverage ratio (EBIT ÷ interest expense)

4. Obtain industry averages for each firm from Microsoft at http://moneycentral .msn.com/investor/home.asp). Enter the stock symbol on top of the homepage and then click on "Financial Results" and then "Key Ratios" in the left column.
   a. Compare each firm's ratios to the available industry ratios for the most recent year. The ratios are organized by categories that can be selected at the top of the page. (Ignore the "Company" column as your calculations will be different.)
   b. Analyze the performance of each firm versus the industry and comment on any trends in each individual firm's performance. Identify any strengths or weaknesses you find in each firm.
5. Examine the market-to-book ratios you calculated for each firm. Which, if either, of the two firms can be considered "growth firms" and which, if either, can be considered "value firms"?
6. Compare the valuation ratios across the two firms. How do you interpret the difference between them?
7. Consider the enterprise value of each firm for each of the four years. How have the values of each firm changed over the time period?

This page intentionally left blank

The Valuation Principle: The Foundation of Financial Decision Making

notation

r	interest rate	PV	present value
NPV	net present value		

What do mothballs and finance have in common? Both are important to entrepreneur Matt Herriot, executive vice president of Oxford & Hill Home Products. The company's innovative products, such as Moth Avoid, protect clothing, linens, collectibles and other natural fiber valuables from damage caused by moths, moisture, and mildew. "My finance courses at the University of Georgia's Terry School of Business provided the background I need for my responsibilities, including pricing and sales forecasting. They also help me to communicate with partners and investors in the language of business."

Matt received his MBA in 2005 and immediately put his finance background to work at the newly launched Oxford & Hill. Based on his experience at other clothing care companies, he saw an untapped opportunity in the moth-prevention market. A major hurdle for companies making chemically based products is the Environmental Protection Agency (EPA) regulatory process. "We weighed the high cost of getting EPA registration now against its future benefits—entrance to a big market with significant barriers to entry and a slower moving competitor—and decided the revenues and earnings potential made it a good investment and the basis for a good business." He worked with prospective investors to find the right financing options for the company and with his management team to allocate resources effectively, to increase the value of the business.

Prior to joining Oxford & Hill and before his formal course work in finance, Matt had a successful career in sales management. However, his limited knowledge of finance was a major disadvantage. When the sales brokerage and importing company he started ran out of cash to service its substantial debt, Matt closed the business and worked in sales management for a consumer products company. "Not having a formal business education kept me from advancing, so I decided to get my MBA while continuing to work full time. The analytical course work was fascinating to me, and I could apply what I learned to the real world." The cost of Matt's decision to return to school has certainly been outweighed by the benefits of his experience at Oxford & Hill.

Terry School of Business, University of Georgia, 2005

"We weighed the high cost of getting EPA registration now against its future benefits and decided the revenues and earnings potential made it a good investment."

BDeH CHAPTER 3

In mid 2007, Microsoft decided to enter a bidding war with competitors Google and Yahoo! for a stake in the fast-growing social networking site, Facebook. How did Microsoft's managers decide that this was a good decision?

Every decision has future consequences that will affect the value of the firm. These consequences will generally include both benefits and costs. For example, after raising its offer, Microsoft ultimately succeeded in buying a 1.6% stake in Facebook, along with the exclusive right to place ads on the Facebook Web site, for $240 million. In addition to the upfront cost of $240 million for the deal, Microsoft will also incur ongoing costs associated with software development for the platform, network infrastructure, and international marketing efforts to attract advertisers. The benefits of the deal to Microsoft include the revenues associated with the advertising sales, together with the potential appreciation of its 1.6% stake in Facebook should it be sold or it sells shares to the public. This decision will increase Microsoft's value if these benefits outweigh the costs.

More generally, a decision is good for the firm's investors if it increases the firm's value by providing benefits whose value exceeds the costs. But comparing costs and benefits is often complicated because they occur at different points in time, or are in different currencies, or have different risks associated with them. To make a valid comparison, we must use the tools of finance to express all costs and benefits in common terms. In this chapter, we introduce the central concept of finance, and the unifying theme of this book, the *Valuation Principle*. The Valuation Principle states that we can use current market prices to determine the value today of the different costs and benefits associated with a decision. The Valuation Principle allows us to apply the concept of *net present value (NPV)* to compare the costs and benefits of a project in terms of a common unit—namely, dollars today. We will then be able to evaluate a decision by answering this question: *Does the cash value today of its benefits exceed the cash value today of its costs?* In addition, we will see that the difference between the cash values of the benefits and costs indicates the net amount by which the decision will increase the value of the firm and therefore the wealth of its investors. The Valuation Principle also leads to the important concept of the *Law of One Price*, which will prove to be a key tool in understanding the value of stocks, bonds, and other securities that are traded in the market.

 Managerial Decision Making

A financial manager's job is to make decisions on behalf of the firm's investors. For example, a manager of a manufacturing company has to decide how much to produce. By increasing production more units can be sold, but the price per unit will likely be lower. Does it make sense to increase production? A manager of another company might expect an increase in demand for her products. Should she raise prices or increase production? If the decision is to increase production and a new facility is required, is it better to rent or purchase the facility? When should managers give their workers a pay increase? These are a few examples of the kinds of choices managers face every day.

BDeH CHAPTER 3

BDeH CHAPTER 3

Your Personal Financial Decisions

While the focus of this text is on the decisions a financial manager makes in a business setting, you will soon see that concepts and skills you will learn here apply to personal decisions as well. As a normal part of life we all make decisions that tradeoff benefits and costs across time. Going to college, purchasing this book, saving for a new car or house down payment, taking-out a car loan or home loan, buying shares of stock, and deciding between jobs are just a few examples of such decisions that you have faced or could face in the not-too-distant future. In this chapter we develop the *Valuation Principle* as the foundation of all financial decision making—whether in a business or in a personal context—and begin to show how it is a unifying theme applicable to all the financial concepts you will learn.

Our objective in this book is to explain how to make decisions that increase the value of the firm to its investors. In principal, the idea is simple and intuitive: For good decisions, the benefits exceed the costs. Of course, real-world opportunities are usually complex and so the costs and benefits are often difficult to quantify. Quantifying them often involves using skills from other management disciplines, as in the following examples:

Marketing: to determine the increase in revenues resulting from an advertising campaign

Economics: to determine the increase in demand from lowering the price of a product

Organizational Behavior: to determine the effect of changes in management structure on productivity

Strategy: to determine a competitor's response to a price increase

Operations: to determine production costs after the modernization of a manufacturing plant

For the remainder of this text, we will assume that we can rely on experts in these different areas to provide this information so that the costs and benefits associated with a decision have already been identified. With that task done, the financial manager's job is to compare the costs and benefits and determine the best decision to make for the value of the firm.

Concept Check

1. What defines a good decision?
2. What is the financial manager's role in decision making for the firm?

3.2 Cost-Benefit Analysis

As we have already seen, the first step in decision making is to identify the costs and benefits of a decision. The next step is quantifying the costs and benefits. Any decision in which the value of the benefits exceeds the costs will increase the value of the firm. To evaluate the costs and benefits of a decision, we must value the options in the same terms—cash today. Let's make this concrete with a simple example.

Suppose a jewelry manufacturer has the opportunity to trade 200 ounces of silver for 10 ounces of gold today. An ounce of silver differs in value from an ounce of gold. Consequently, it is incorrect to compare 200 ounces to 10 ounces and conclude that the larger quantity is better. Instead, to compare the costs of the silver and benefit of the gold, we first need to quantify their values in equivalent terms—cash today.

Consider the silver. What is its cash value today? Suppose silver can be bought and sold for a current market price of $10 per ounce. Then the 200 ounces of silver we give up has a cash value of:[1]

$$(200 \text{ ounces of silver}) \times (\$10/\text{ounce of silver}) = \$2000$$

If the current market price for gold is $500 per ounce, then the 10 ounces of gold we receive has a cash value of

$$(10 \text{ ounces of gold}) \times (\$500/\text{ounce of gold}) = \$5000$$

We have now quantified the decision. The jeweler's opportunity has a benefit of $5000 and a cost of $2000. The net benefit of the decision is $5000 − $2000 = $3000 today. The net value of the decision is positive, so by accepting the trade, the jewelry firm will be richer by $3000.

BDeH CHAPTER 3

EXAMPLE 3.1
Comparing Costs and Benefits

Problem

Suppose you work as a customer account manager for an importer of frozen seafood. A customer is willing to purchase 300 pounds of frozen shrimp today for a total price of $1500, including delivery. You can buy frozen shrimp on the wholesale market for $3 per pound today, and arrange for delivery at a cost of $100 today. Will taking this opportunity increase the value of the firm?

Solution

▶ Plan

To determine whether this opportunity will increase the value of the firm, we need to value the benefits and the costs using market prices. We have market prices for our costs:

Wholesale price of shrimp: $3/pound   Delivery cost: $100

We have a customer offering the following market price for 300 pounds of shrimp delivered: $1500. All that is left is to compare them.

▶ Execute

The benefit of the transaction is $1500 today. The costs are (300 lbs.) × $3/lbs. = $900 today for the shrimp, and $100 today for delivery, for a total cost of $1000 today. If you are certain about these costs and benefits, the right decision is obvious: You should seize this opportunity because the firm will gain $1500 − $1000 = $500.

▶ Evaluate

Thus, taking this opportunity contributes $500 to the value of the firm, in the form of cash that can be paid out immediately to the firm's investors.

Concept Check

3. How do we determine whether a decision increases the value of the firm?

4. When costs and benefits are in different units or goods, how can we compare them?

---

[1]You might worry about commissions or other transactions costs that are incurred when buying or selling silver, in addition to the market price. For now, we will ignore transactions costs, and discuss their effect later.

 ## Valuation Principle

In the previous examples, the right decisions for the firms were clear because the costs and benefits were easy to evaluate and compare. They were easy to evaluate because we were able to use current market prices to convert them into equivalent cash values. Once we can express costs and benefits in terms of "cash today," it is a straightforward process to compare them and determine whether the decision will increase the firm's value.

Note that in both the examples, we used market prices to assess the values of the different commodities involved. What about the firm's other possible uses for those commodities? For example, consider the jewelry manufacturer with the opportunity to trade silver for gold. When evaluating the trade, we did not concern ourselves with whether the jeweler thought that the price was fair or whether the jeweler would actually have a use for the silver or gold. Suppose, for example, that the jeweler thinks the current price of silver is too high. Does this matter—would he value the silver at less than $2000? The answer is no—he can always sell the silver at the current market price and receive $2000 right now, so he would never place a lower value on the silver. Similarly, he also will not pay more than $2000 for the silver. Even if he really needs silver or for some reason thinks the price of silver is too low, he can always buy 200 ounces of silver for $2000 and so would not pay more than that amount. Thus, independent of his own views or preferences, the value of the silver to the jeweler is $2000.

competitive market A market in which the good can be bought *and* sold at the same price.

Note that the jeweler can both buy and sell silver at its current market price. His personal preferences or use for the silver and his opinion of the fair price are therefore irrelevant in evaluating the value of this opportunity. This observation highlights an important general principle related to goods trading in a **competitive market**, a market in which a good can be bought *and* sold at the same price. Whenever a good trades in a competitive market, that price determines the value of the good. This point is one of the central and most powerful ideas in finance. It will underlie almost every concept that we develop throughout the text.

BDeH CHAPTER 3

EXAMPLE 3.2

Competitive Market Prices Determine Value

Problem
You have just won a radio contest and are disappointed to find out that the prize is four tickets to the Def Leppard reunion tour (face value $40 each). Not being a fan of 1980s power rock, you have no intention of going to the show. However, it turns out that there is a second choice: two tickets to your favorite band's sold-out show (face value $45 each). You notice that on eBay, tickets to the Def Leppard show are being bought and sold for $30 apiece and tickets to your favorite band's show are being bought and sold at $50 each. What should you do?

Solution

▶ **Plan**
Market prices, not your personal preferences (nor the face value of the tickets), are relevant here:

    4 Def Leppard tickets at $30 apiece
    2 of your favorite band's tickets at $50 apiece

You need to compare the market value of each option and choose the one with the highest market value.

BDeH CHAPTER 3

> ▶ **Execute**
> The Def Leppard tickets have a total value of $120 (4 × $30) versus the $100 total value of the other 2 tickets (2 × $50). Instead of taking the tickets to your favorite band, you should accept the Def Leppard tickets, sell them on eBay, and use the proceeds to buy 2 tickets to your favorite band's show. You'll even have $20 left over to buy a T-shirt.

> ▶ **Evaluate**
> Even though you prefer your favorite band, you should still take the opportunity to get the Def Leppard tickets instead. As we emphasized earlier, whether this opportunity is attractive depends on its net value using market prices. Because the value of Def Leppard tickets is $20 more than the value of your favorite band's tickets, the opportunity is appealing.

Once we use market prices to evaluate the costs and benefits of a decision in terms of cash today, it is then a simple matter to determine the best decision for the firm. The best decision makes the firm and its investors wealthier, because the value of its benefits exceeds the value of its costs. We call this idea the Valuation Principle:

The Valuation Principle:

The value of a commodity or an asset to the firm or its investors is determined by its competitive market price. The benefits and costs of a decision should be evaluated using those market prices. When the value of the benefits exceeds the value of the costs, the decision will increase the market value of the firm.

The Valuation Principle provides the basis for decision making throughout this text. In the remainder of this chapter, we first apply it to decisions whose costs and benefits occur at different points in time and develop the main tool of project evaluation, the *Net Present Value Rule*. We then consider its consequences for the prices of assets in the market and develop the concept of the *Law of One Price*.

When Competitive Market Prices Are Not Available

Competitive market prices allow us to calculate the value of a decision without worrying about the tastes or opinions of the decision maker. When competitive prices are not available, we can no longer do this. Prices at retail stores, for example, are one-sided: You can buy at the posted price, but you cannot sell the good to the store at that same price. We cannot use these one-sided prices to determine an exact cash value. They determine the maximum value of the good (since it can always be purchased at that price), but an individual may value it for much less depending on his or her preferences for the good.

Let's consider an example. It has long been common for banks to try to entice people to open accounts by offering them something for free in exchange (it used to be a toaster). In 2007 Key Bank offered college students a free iPod nano if they would open a new check-

ing account and make two deposits. At the time, the retail price of that model of nano was $199. Because there is no competitive market to trade iPods, the value of the nano depends on whether you were going to buy one or not.

If you planned to buy a nano anyway, then the value to you of the nano is $199, the price you would otherwise pay for it. In this case, the value of the bank's offer is $199. But suppose you do not want or need a nano. If you were to get it from the bank and then sell it, the value of taking the deal would be whatever price you could get for the nano. For example, if you could sell the nano for $150 to your friend, then the bank's offer is worth $150 to you. Thus, depending on your desire to own a new nano, the bank's offer is worth somewhere between $150 (you don't want a nano) and $199 (you definitely want one).

EXAMPLE 3.3

Applying the
Valuation Principle

Problem

You are the operations manager at your firm. Due to a pre-existing contract, you have the opportunity to acquire 200 barrels of oil and 3000 pounds of copper for a total of $25,000. The current market price of oil is $90 per barrel and for copper is $3.50 per pound. You are not sure that you need all of the oil and copper, so you are wondering if you should take this opportunity. How valuable is it? Would your decision change if you believed the value of oil or copper would plummet over the next month?

Solution

▶ **Plan**

We need to quantify the costs and benefits using market prices. We are comparing $25,000 with:

    200 barrels of oil at $90 per barrel
    3000 pounds of copper at $3.50 per pound

▶ **Execute**

Using the competitive market prices we have:

$$(200 \text{ barrels}) \times (\$90/\text{barrel today}) = \$18,000 \text{ today}$$
$$(3000 \text{ pounds of copper}) \times (\$3.50/\text{pound today}) = \$10,500 \text{ today}$$

The value of the opportunity is the value of the oil plus the value of the copper less the cost of the opportunity, or $18,000 + $10,500 − $25,000 = $3500 today. Because the value is positive, we should take it. This value depends only on the *current* market prices for oil and copper. If we do not need all of the oil and copper, we can sell the excess at current market prices. Even if we thought the value of oil or copper was about to plummet, the value of this investment would be unchanged. (We can always exchange them for dollars immediately at the current market prices.)

▶ **Evaluate**

Since we are transacting today, only the current prices in a competitive market matter. Our own use for or opinion about the future prospects of oil or copper do not alter the value of the decision today. This decision is good for the firm, and will increase its value by $3500.

Concept Check

5. How should we determine the value of a good?
6. If crude oil trades in a competitive market, would an oil refiner that has a use for the oil value it differently than another investor would?

3.4 The Time Value of Money and Interest Rates

For most financial decisions, unlike in the examples presented so far, costs and benefits occur at different points in time. For example, typical investment projects incur costs upfront and provide benefits in the future. In this section, we show how to account for this time difference when using the Valuation Principle to make a decision.

The Time Value of Money

Consider a firm's investment opportunity with the following cash flows:

    Cost: $100,000 today
    Benefit: $105,000 in one year

Because both are expressed in dollar terms, are the cost and benefit directly comparable? Calculating the project's net value as $105,000 − $100,000 = $5000 is incorrect because it ignores the *timing* of the costs and benefits. That is, it treats money today as equivalent to money in one year. In general, a dollar today is worth *more* than a dollar in one year. To see why, note that if you have $1 today, you can invest it. For example, if you deposit it in a bank account paying 7% interest, you will have $1.07 at the end of one year. We call the difference in value between money today and money in the future the **time value of money** The difference in value between money today and money in the **time value of money**. We now develop the tools needed to value our $100,000 investment opportunity correctly.

time value of money The difference in value between money today and money in the future; also, the observation that two cash flows at two different points in time have different values.

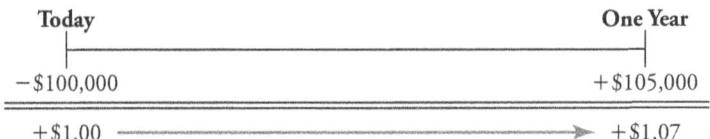

The Interest Rate: Converting Cash Across Time

By depositing money into a savings account, we can convert money today into money in the future with no risk. Similarly, by borrowing money from the bank, we can exchange money in the future for money today. The rate at which we can exchange money today for money in the future is determined by the current interest rate. In the same way that an exchange rate allows us to convert money from one currency to another, the interest rate allows us to convert money from one point in time to another. In essence, an interest rate is like an exchange rate across time. It tells us the market price today of money in the future.

Suppose the current annual interest rate is 7%. By investing $1 today we can convert this $1 into $1.07 in one year. Similarly, by borrowing at this rate, we can exchange **interest rate** The rate $1.07 in one year for $1 today. More generally, we define the **interest rate**, r, for a given period as the interest rate at which money can be borrowed or lent over that period. In our example, the interest rate is 7% and we can exchange 1 dollar today for $(1 + .07)$ dollars in the future. In general, we can exchange 1 dollar today for $(1 + r)$ dollars in the future, and vice versa. We refer to $(1 + r)$ as the **interest rate factor** for cash flows; it defines how we convert cash flows across time, and has units of "$ in one year/$ today."

interest rate The rate at which money can be borrowed or lent over a given period.

interest rate factor One plus the interest rate, it is the rate of exchange between dollars today and dollars in the future. It has units of "$ in one year/$ today."

As with other market prices, the interest rate ultimately depends on supply and demand. In particular, at the interest rate the supply of savings equals the demand for borrowing. But regardless of how it is determined, once we know the interest rate, we can apply the Valuation Principle and use it to evaluate other decisions in which costs and benefits are separated in time.

Value of $100,000 Investment in One Year. Let's reevaluate the investment we considered earlier, this time taking into account the time value of money. If the interest rate is 7%, then we can express the cost of the investment as:

$$\text{Cost} = (\$100,000 \text{ today}) \times (1.07 \text{ } \$ \text{ in one year}/\$ \text{ today})$$
$$= \$107,000 \text{ in one year}$$

Think of this amount as the opportunity cost of spending $100,000 today: The firm gives up the $107,000 it would have had in one year if it had left the money in the bank.

BDeH CHAPTER 3

Alternatively, by borrowing the $100,000 from the same bank, the firm would owe $107,000 in one year.

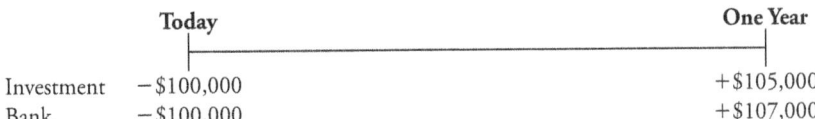

	Today	One Year
Investment	−$100,000	+$105,000
Bank	−$100,000	+$107,000

We have used a market price, the interest rate, to put both the costs and benefits in terms of "dollars in one year," so now we can use the Valuation Principle to compare them and compute the investment's net value by subtracting the cost of the investment from the benefit in one year:

$$\$105,000 - \$107,000 = -\$2000 \text{ in one year}$$

In other words, the firm could earn $2000 more in one year by putting the $100,000 in the bank rather than making this investment. Because the net value is negative, we should reject the investment: If we took it, the firm would be $2000 poorer in one year than if we didn't.

Value of $100,000 Investment Today. The previous calculation expressed the value of the costs and benefits in terms of dollars in one year. Alternatively, we can use the interest rate factor to convert to dollars today. Consider the benefit of $105,000 in one year. What is the equivalent amount in terms of dollars today? That is, how much would we need to have in the bank today so that we would end up with $105,000 in the bank in one year? We find this amount by dividing by the interest rate factor:

$$\text{Benefit} = (\$105,000 \text{ in one year}) \div (1.07 \text{ \$ in one year/\$ today})$$
$$= \$98,130.84 \text{ today}$$

This is also the amount the bank would lend to us today if we promised to repay $105,000 in one year.[2] Thus, it is the competitive market price at which we can "buy" or "sell" $105,000 in one year.

	Today	One Year
Value of Cost Today	−$100,000	+$105,000
Value of Benefit Today	+$ 98,130.84 $\longleftarrow \dfrac{105,000}{1.07} \longleftarrow$	

Now we are ready to compute the net value of the investment by subtracting the cost from the benefit:

$$\$98,130.84 - \$100,000 = -\$1869.16 \text{ today}$$

Once again, the negative result indicates that we should reject the investment. Taking the investment would make the firm $1869.16 poorer today because it gave up $100,000 for something worth only $98,130.84.

---

[2]We are assuming the bank is willing to lend at the same 7% interest rate, which would be the case if there were no risk associated with the cash flow.

BDeH   CHAPTER 3

present value (PV) The value of a cost or benefit computed in terms of cash today.

future value The value of a cash flow that is moved forward in time.

discount factor The value today of a dollar received in the future.

discount rate The appropriate rate to discount a stream of cash flows to determine their value at an earlier time.

Present Versus Future Value.   This calculation demonstrates that our decision is the same whether we express the value of the investment in terms of dollars in one year or dollars today: We should reject the investment. Indeed, if we convert from dollars today to dollars in one year,

$$(-\$1869.16 \text{ today}) \times (1.07 \text{ \$ in one year/\$ today}) = -\$2000 \text{ in one year}$$

we see that the two results are equivalent, but expressed as values at different points in time. When we express the value in terms of dollars today, we call it the **present value** **(PV)** of the investment. If we express it in terms of dollars in the future, we call it the **future value** of the investment.

Discount Factors and Rates.   In the preceding calculation, we can interpret

$$\frac{1}{1 + r} = \frac{1}{1.07} = 0.93458$$

as the *price* today of $1 in one year. In other words, for just under 93.5 cents, you can "buy" $1 to be delivered in one year. Note that the value is less than $1—money in the future is worth less today, and so its price reflects a discount. Because it provides the discount at which we can purchase money in the future, the amount $\frac{1}{1+r}$ is called the one-year **discount factor**. The interest rate is also referred to as the **discount rate** for an investment.

EXAMPLE 3.4

Comparing Revenues at Different Points in Time

Problem

The launch of Sony's PlayStation 3 was delayed until November 2006, giving Microsoft's Xbox 360 a full year on the market without competition. Imagine that it is November 2005 and you are the marketing manager for the PlayStation. You estimate that if PlayStation 3 were ready to be launched immediately, you could sell $2 billion worth of the console in its first year. However, if your launch is delayed a year, you believe that Microsoft's head start will reduce your first-year sales by 20%. If the interest rate is 8%, what is the cost of a delay of the first year's revenues in terms of dollars in 2005?

Solution

▶ **Plan**

Revenues if released today: $2 billion   Revenue decrease if delayed: 20%   Interest rate: 8%

We need to compute the revenues if the launch is delayed and compare them to the revenues from launching today. However, in order to make a fair comparison, we need to convert the future revenues of the PlayStation if they are delayed into an equivalent present value of those revenues today.

▶ **Execute**

If the launch is delayed to 2006, revenues will drop by 20% of $2 billion, or $400 million, to $1.6 billion. To compare this amount to revenues of $2 billion if launched in 2005, we must convert it using the interest rate of 8%:

$$\$1.6 \text{ billion in 2006} \div (\$1.08 \text{ in 2006/\$1 in 2005}) = \$1.481 \text{ billion in 2005}$$

Therefore, the cost of a delay of one year is

$$\$2 \text{ billion} - \$1.481 \text{ billion} = \$0.519 \text{ billion (\$519 million)}.$$

▶ **Evaluate**

Delaying the project for one year was equivalent to giving up $519 million in cash. In this example, we focused only on the effect on the first year's revenues. However, delaying the launch delays the entire revenue stream by one year, so the total cost would be calculated in the same way by summing the cost of delay for each year of revenues.

We can use the interest rate to determine values in the same way we used competitive market prices. Figure 3.1 illustrates how we use competitive market prices and interest rates to convert between dollars today and other goods, or dollars in the future. Once we quantify all the costs and benefits of an investment in terms of dollars today, we can rely on the Valuation Principle to determine whether the investment will increase the firm's value.

FIGURE 3.1

Converting Between Dollars Today and Gold or Dollars in the Future

We can convert dollars today to different goods or points in time by using the competitive market price or interest rate. Once values are in equivalent terms, we can use the Valuation Principle to make a decision.

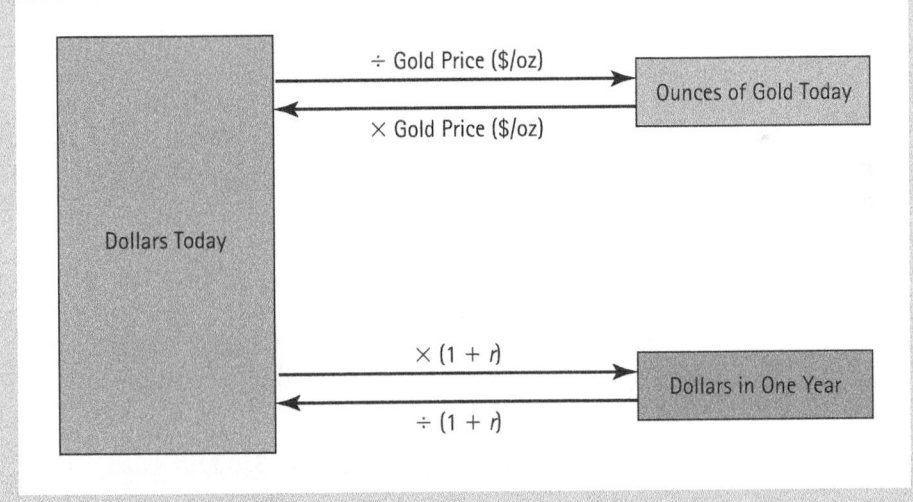

Concept Check

7. How do you compare costs at different points in time?

8. Is the value today of money to be received in one year higher when interest rates are high or when interest rates are low?

3.5 The NPV Decision Rule

In Section 3.4, we converted between cash today and cash in the future using the interest rate. As long as we convert costs and benefits to the same point in time, we can use the Valuation Principle to make a decision. In practice, however, most corporations prefer to measure values in terms of their present value—that is, in terms of cash today. In this section, we apply the Valuation Principle to derive the concept of the *net present value* or *NPV*, which we can use to define the "golden rule" of financial decision making, the *NPV Rule*.

Net Present Value

net present value (NPV)
The difference between the present value of a project or investment's benefits and the present value of its costs.

When the value of a cost or benefit is computed in terms of cash today, we refer to it as the present value (PV). Similarly, we define the **net present value (NPV)** of a project or investment as the difference between the present value of its benefits and the present value of its costs:

Net Present Value
$$NPV = PV(\text{Benefits}) - PV(\text{Costs}) \qquad (3.1)$$

Let's consider a simple example. Suppose your firm is offered the following investment opportunity: In exchange for $500 today, you will receive $550 in one year. If the interest rate is 8% per year then:

$$PV(\text{Benefit}) = (\$550 \text{ in one year}) \div (1.08 \text{ \$ in one year/\$ today})$$
$$= \$509.26 \text{ today}$$

This PV is the amount you would need to put in the bank today to generate $550 in one year ($509.26 $\times$ 1.08 = $550). In other words, *the present value is the amount you need to invest at the current interest rate to recreate the cash flow.* We can think of this as the cash cost today of generating the cash flow ourselves.

Once the costs and benefits are in present value terms, we can compute the investment's NPV:

$$NPV = \$509.26 - \$500 = \$9.26 \text{ today}$$

But what if you don't have the $500 needed to cover the initial cost of the project? Does the project still have the same value? Because we computed the value using competitive market prices, it should not depend on your tastes or the amount of cash you have in the bank. If you don't have the $500, suppose you borrow $509.26 from the bank at the 8% interest rate and then take the project. What are your cash flows in this case?

Today: $509.26 (loan) − $500 (invested in the project) = $9.26

In one year: $550 (from project) − $509.26 $\times$ 1.08 (loan balance) = $0

This transaction leaves you with exactly $9.26 extra cash in your pocket today and no future net obligations. So taking the project is similar to having an extra $9.26 in cash up front. Thus, the NPV expresses the value of an investment decision as an amount of cash received today. *As long as the NPV is positive, the decision increases the value of the firm and is a good decision regardless of your current cash needs or preferences regarding when to spend the money.*

The NPV Decision Rule

As shown in the last example, the Valuation Principle implies that we should undertake projects with a positive NPV. That is, good projects are those for which the present value of the benefits exceeds the present value of the costs. As a result, the value of the firm

BDeH CHAPTER 3

increases and investors are wealthier. Projects with negative NPVs have costs that exceed their benefits. Accepting them is equivalent to losing money today.

We capture this logic in the **NPV Decision Rule**:

When making an investment decision, take the alternative with the highest NPV. Choosing this alternative is equivalent to receiving its NPV in cash today.

NPV Decision Rule When choosing among investment alternatives, take the alternative with the highest NPV. Choosing this alternative is equivalent to receiving its NPV in cash today.

Because NPV is expressed in terms of cash today, using the NPV decision rule is a simple way to apply the Valuation Principle. Decisions that increase wealth are superior to those that decrease wealth. We don't need to know anything about the investor's preferences to reach this conclusion. As long as we have correctly captured all of the cash flows of a project, being wealthier increases our options and makes us better off, whatever our preferences are.

We now look at some common ways the NPV rule is applied in practice.

Accepting or Rejecting a Project. A common financial decision is whether to accept or reject a project. Because rejecting the project generally has *NPV* = 0 (there are no new costs or benefits from not doing the project), the NPV decision rule implies that we should

▶ Accept positive-NPV projects; accepting them is equivalent to receiving their NPV in cash today, and

▶ Reject negative-NPV projects; accepting them would reduce the value of the firm, whereas rejecting them has no cost (NPV = 0).

If the NPV is exactly zero, then you will neither gain nor lose by accepting the project instead of rejecting it, which also has an NPV of zero. It is not a bad project because it does not reduce the firm's value, but it does not add value to the firm either.

EXAMPLE 3.5

The NPV Is Equivalent to Cash Today

Problem

After saving $1500 waiting tables, you are about to buy a 42-inch plasma TV. You notice that the store is offering a "one-year same as cash" deal. You can take the TV home today and pay nothing until one year from now, when you will owe the store the $1500 purchase price. If your savings account earns 5% per year, what is the NPV of this offer? Show that its NPV represents cash in your pocket.

Solution

▶ **Plan**

You are getting something (the TV) worth $1500 today and in exchange will need to pay $1500 in one year. Think of it as getting back the $1500 you thought you would have to spend today to get the TV. We treat it as a positive cash flow.

Cash flows:

Today	In one year
+$1500	−$1500

The discount rate for calculating the present value of the payment in one year is your interest rate of 5%. You need to compare the present value of the cost ($1500 in one year) to the benefit today (a $1500 TV).

▶ **Execute**

$$NPV = +1500 - \frac{1500}{(1.05)} = 1500 - 1{,}428.57 = \$71.43$$

You could take $1428.57 of the $1500 you had saved for the TV and put it in your savings account. With interest, in one year it would grow to $1428.57 × (1.05) = $1500, enough to pay the store. The extra $71.43 is money in your pocket to spend as you like (or put toward the speaker system for your new media room).

▶ **Evaluate**

By taking the delayed payment offer, we have extra net cash flows of $71.43 today. If we put $1428.57 in the bank, it will be just enough to offset our $1500 obligation in the future. Therefore, this offer is equivalent to receiving $71.43 today, without any future net obligations.

Choosing Among Alternatives. Managers also use the NPV decision rule to choose among projects. Suppose you own a coffee stand across from campus and you hire someone to operate it for you. You will be graduating next year and have started to consider selling it. An investor has offered to buy the business from you for $20,000 whenever you are ready. Your interest rate is 10% and you are considering three alternatives:

1. Sell the business now.

2. Operate normally for one more year and then sell the business (requiring you to spend $5000 on supplies and labor now, but earn $10,000 at the end of the year).

3. Be open only in the mornings for one more year and then sell the business (requiring you to spend $3000 on supplies and labor now, but earn $6000 at the end of the year).

The cash flows and NPVs are given in Table 3.1.

TABLE 3.1		Now	One Year	NPV	
Cash Flows and NPVs for Coffee Stand Alternatives	Sell	+$20,000	0	$20,000	
	Operate Normally	−$5,000	+$10,000 +$20,000	$-\$5{,}000 + \dfrac{\$30{,}000}{1.10}$	$= \$22{,}273$
	Mornings Only	−$3,000	+$6,000 +$20,000	$-\$3{,}000 + \dfrac{\$26{,}000}{1.10}$	$= \$20{,}636$

Among these three alternatives, you would choose the one with the highest NPV: operate normally for one year and then sell.

NPV and Cash Needs

When we compare projects with different patterns of present and future cash flows, we may have preferences regarding when to receive the cash. Some may need cash today; others may prefer to save for the future. In our coffee stand example, operating normally for one more year and then selling has the highest NPV. However, this option does require an initial outlay for supplies (as opposed to selling the coffee stand and receiving

TABLE 3.2		Cash Flow Today	Cash Flow in One Year
Cash Flows from Combining One More Year of Operating with Borrowing	Operate Normally	−$5,000	$30,000
	Borrow	$25,000	−$25,000 × (1.10) = −$27,500
	Total	$20,000	$2,500
	Sell Today	$20,000	0

$20,000 today). Suppose we would prefer to avoid the negative cash flow today. Would selling the business be a better choice in that case?

As was true for the jeweler considering trading silver for gold in Section 3.2, the answer is again no. As long as we are able to borrow and lend at the interest rate, operating for one more year is superior, whatever our preferences regarding the timing of the cash flows. To see why, suppose we borrow $25,000 at the rate of 10% (in one year, we will owe $25,000 × (1.10) = $27,500) and operate the stand normally for one more year. Our total cash flows are shown in Table 3.2. Compare these cash flows to those for selling. The combination of borrowing and operating for a year generates the same initial cash flow as selling. Notice, however, that there is a higher final cash flow ($2500 versus $0). Thus, we are better off operating for a year and borrowing $25,000 today than we would be selling immediately.

This example illustrates the following general principle:

Regardless of our preferences for cash today versus cash in the future, we should always maximize NPV first. We can then borrow or lend to shift cash flows through time and find our most preferred pattern of cash flows.

Concept Check

9. What is the NPV decision rule? How is it related to the Valuation Principle?

10. Why doesn't the NPV decision rule depend on the investor's preferences?

3.6 The Law of One Price

Up to this point, we have emphasized the importance of using competitive market prices to compute the NPV. But is there always only one such price? What if the same good trades for different prices in different markets? Consider gold. Gold trades in many different markets, with the largest markets in New York and London. Gold can trade easily in many markets because investors are not literally transacting in the gold bars themselves (which are quite heavy!), but are trading ownership rights to gold that is stored securely elsewhere. To value an ounce of gold, we could look up the competitive price in either of these markets. But suppose gold is trading for $850 per ounce in New York and $900 per ounce in London. Which price should we use?

In fact, situations such as this one, where the same asset is trading with different prices, should not occur in a competitive market. Let's see why. Recall that these are competitive market prices, at which you can both buy *and* sell. Thus, you can make money in this situation simply by buying gold for $850 per ounce in New York and then immediately selling it for $900 per ounce in London. You will make $900 − $850 = $50 per ounce for each ounce you buy and sell. Trading 1 million ounces at these prices, you would make $50 million with no risk or investment! This is a case where that old adage, "Buy low, sell high," can be followed perfectly.

Of course, you will not be the only one making these trades. Everyone who sees these prices will want to trade as many ounces as possible. Within seconds, the market in New York would be flooded with buy orders, and the market in London would be flooded with sell orders. Although a few ounces (traded by the lucky individuals who spotted this opportunity first) might be exchanged at these prices, the price of gold in New York would quickly rise in response to all the orders, and the price in London would rapidly fall. Prices would continue to change until they were equalized somewhere in the middle, such as $875 per ounce. This example illustrates an *arbitrage opportunity*, the focus of this section.

Arbitrage

arbitrage The practice of buying and selling equivalent goods or portfolios to take advantage of a price difference.

The practice of buying and selling equivalent goods in different markets to take advantage of a price difference is known as **arbitrage**. More generally, we refer to any situation in which it is possible to make a profit without taking any risk or making any investment as an **arbitrage opportunity**. Because an arbitrage opportunity has positive NPV, whenever an arbitrage opportunity appears in financial markets, the Valuation Principle indicates that investors will race to take advantage of it. Those investors who spot the opportunity first and who can trade quickly will have the ability to exploit it. Once they place their trades, prices will respond, causing the arbitrage opportunity to evaporate.

arbitrage opportunity Any situation in which it is possible to make a profit without taking any risk or making any investment.

Arbitrage

Retail Prices From Around the World

CITY	CURRENCY	US$
Tokyo	9,800 yen	$80
Hong Kong	HK$4,695	83
NY		85
Frankfurt	€79	102
Rome	€79	102
London	£55	108
Brussels	€89	115
Paris	€89	115

iPod shuffle 1GB

Prices, including taxes, as provided by retailers in each city, averaged and converted to U.S. dollars

The *Wall Street Journal* occasionally reports on "arbitrage opportunities" by noting price differences for the same item in different countries. In this installment from January 2007, the *Journal* compares prices for the iPod shuffle. The price in the local currency and converted to U.S. dollars is listed. If shipping were free, you would buy as many shuffles as you could get your hands on in Tokyo and sell them in Paris and Brussels. If you could buy and sell at retail prices, you would have a profit of $115 − $80 = $35 on each shuffle!

Source: Wall Street Journal, Jan 31, 2007.

Arbitrage opportunities are like money lying in the street; once spotted, they will quickly disappear. Thus, the normal state of affairs in markets should be that no arbitrage opportunities exist.

Law of One Price

Law of One Price In competitive markets, securities or portfolios with the same cash flows must have the same price.

In a competitive market, the price of gold at any point in time will be the same in London and New York. The same logic applies more generally whenever equivalent investment opportunities trade in two different competitive markets. If the prices in the two markets differ, investors will profit immediately by buying in the market where it is cheap and selling in the market where it is expensive. In doing so, they will equalize the prices. As a result, prices will not differ (at least not for long). This important property is the **Law of One Price**:

BDeH CHAPTER 3

An Old Joke

There is an old joke that many finance professors enjoy telling their students. It goes like this:

> A finance professor and a student are walking down a street. The student notices a $100 bill lying on the pavement and leans down to pick it up. The finance professor immediately intervenes and says, "Don't bother; there is no free lunch. If that were a real $100 bill lying there, somebody would already have picked it up!"

This joke makes fun of the principle of no arbitrage in competitive markets. But have you ever *actually* found a real $100 bill lying on the pavement? Herein lies the real lesson behind the joke.

This joke sums up the point of focusing on markets in which no arbitrage opportunities exist. Free $100 bills lying on the pavement, like arbitrage opportunities, are extremely rare for two reasons: (1) Because $100 is a large amount of money, people are especially careful not to lose it, and (2) in the rare event when someone does inadvertently drop $100, the likelihood of your finding it before someone else does is extremely small.

If equivalent investment opportunities trade simultaneously in different competitive markets, then they must trade for the same price in both markets.

The Law of One Price will prove to be a powerful tool later in the text when we value securities such as stocks or bonds. We will show that any financial security can be thought of as a claim to future cash flows. The Law of One Price implies that if there is another way to recreate the future cash flows of the financial security, then the price of the financial security and the cost of recreating it must be the same. Recall that earlier we defined the present value of a cash flow to be the cost of recreating it in a competitive market. Thus, we have the following key implication of the Law of One Price for financial securities:

The price of a security should equal the present value of the future cash flows obtained from owning that security.

EXAMPLE 3.6

Pricing a Security using the Law of One Price

Problem

You are considering purchasing a security, a "bond," that pays $1000 without risk in one year, and has no other cash flows. If the interest rate is 5%, what should its price be?

Solution

▶ **Plan**

The security produces a single cash flow in one-year:

```
0                    1
|_____|
                +$1000
```

The Law of One Price tells you that the value of a security that pays $1000 in one year is the present value of that $1000 cash flow, calculated as the cash flow discounted at the interest rate. The 5% interest rate implies that $1.05 in one year is worth $1 today.

▶ **Execute**

The present value of the $1000 cash flow is

$$\$1000 \text{ in one year} \div \frac{1.05 \ \$ \text{ in one year}}{\$ \text{ today}} = \$952.38 \text{ today}$$

So the price must be $952.38.

transactions costs
Expenses such as broker commission and the bid-ask spread investors must pay in most markets in order to trade securities.

▶ **Evaluate**

Because we can receive $1000 in one year for a "price" of $952.38 by simply investing at the interest rate (i.e., $952.38 × 1.05 = $1000), the Law of One Price tells you that the price of the security must equal this "do it yourself" price, which is the present value of its cash flow evaluated using market interest rates. To see why this must be so, consider what would happen if the price were different. If the price were $950, you could borrow $950 at 5% interest and buy the bond. In one year, you would collect the $1000 from the bond and pay off your loan ($950 × 1.05 = $997.50), pocketing the difference. In fact, you would try to do the same thing for as many bonds as possible. But everyone else would also want to take advantage of this arbitrage by buying the bond, and so its price would quickly rise. Similarly, if the price were above $952.38, everyone would sell the bond, invest the proceeds at 5%, and in one year would have more than the $1000 needed to pay the buyer of the security. The selling would cause the price of the bond to drop until this arbitrage was no longer possible—when it reaches $952.38. This powerful application of the Law of One Price shows that the price you pay for a security's cash flows cannot be different from their present value.

Transactions Costs

In our examples up to this point, we have ignored the costs of buying and selling goods or securities. In most markets, there are additional costs that you will incur when trading assets, called **transactions costs**. As discussed in Chapter 1, when you trade securities in markets such as the NYSE and NASDAQ, you must pay two types of transactions costs. First, you must pay your broker a commission on the trade. Second, because you will generally pay a slightly higher price when you buy a security (the ask price) than you will receive when you sell (the bid price) it, you will also pay the bid-ask spread. For example, a share of Dell Inc. stock (ticker symbol DELL) might be quoted as follows:

Bid: $40.50   Ask: $40.70

We can interpret these quotes as if the competitive price for DELL is $40.60, but there is a transaction cost of $0.10 per share when buying or selling.

What consequence do these transaction costs have for no-arbitrage prices and the Law of One Price? Earlier we stated that the price of gold in New York and London must be identical in competitive markets. Suppose, however, that total transactions costs of $5 per ounce are associated with buying gold in one market and selling it in the other. Then, if the price of gold is $850 per ounce in New York and $852 per ounce in London, the "Buy low, sell high" strategy no longer works:

Cost: $850 per ounce (buy gold in New York) + $5 (transactions costs)

Benefit: $852 per ounce (sell gold in London)

NPV: $852 − $850 − $5 = −$3 per ounce

Indeed, there is no arbitrage opportunity in this case until the prices diverge by more than $5, the amount of the transactions costs.

In general, we need to modify our previous conclusions about prices and values by appending the phrase "up to transactions costs." In this example, there is only one competitive price for gold—up to a discrepancy of the $5 transactions cost.

Fortunately, for most financial markets, these costs are small. For example, in 2007 typical bid-ask spreads for large NYSE stocks were between 2 and 5 cents per share. As a first approximation, we can ignore these spreads in our analysis. Only in situations in which the NPV is small (relative to the transactions costs) will any discrepancy matter. In that case, we will need to carefully account for all transaction costs to decide whether the NPV is positive or negative.

To summarize, when there are transactions costs, arbitrage keeps prices of equivalent goods and securities close to each other. Prices can deviate, but not by more than the amount of the transactions costs.

In the rest of the text, we will explore the details of implementing the Law of One Price to value securities. Specifically, we will determine the cash flows associated with stocks, bonds and other securities, and learn how to compute the present value of these cash flows by taking into account their timing and risk.

Concept Check

11. If the Law of One Price were violated, how could investors profit?

12. What implication does the Law of One Price have for the price of a financial security?

---

myfinancelab

Here is what you should know after reading this chapter. MyFinanceLab will help you identify what you know, and where to go when you need to practice.

BDeH CHAPTER 3

Key Points and Equations	Terms	Online Practice Opportunities
3.1 Managerial Decision Making ▶ To evaluate a decision, we must value the incremental costs and benefits associated with that decision. A good decision is one for which the value of the benefits exceeds the value of the costs.		MyFinanceLab Study Plan 3.1
3.2 Cost-Benefit Analysis ▶ To compare costs and benefits that occur at different points in time we must put all costs and benefits in common terms. Typically, we convert costs and benefits into cash today.		MyFinanceLab Study Plan 3.2
3.3 Valuation Principle ▶ A competitive market is one in which a good can be bought and sold at the same price. We use prices from competitive markets to determine the cash value of a good. ▶ The Valuation Principle states that the value of a commodity or an asset to the firm or its investors is determined by its competitive market price. The benefits and costs of a decision should be evaluated using those market prices. When the value of the benefits exceeds the value of the costs, the decision will increase the market value of the firm	competitive market, p. 67 Valuation Principle, p. 68	MyFinanceLab Study Plan 3.3
3.4 The Time Value of Money ▶ The time value of money is the difference in value between money today and money in the future.	discount factor, p. 72 discount rate, p. 72	MyFinanceLab Study Plan 3.4

▶ The rate at which we can exchange money today for money in the future by borrowing or investing is the current market interest rate.	future value, p. 72 interest rate, p. 70 interest rate factor, p. 70 present value (PV), p. 72 time value of money, p. 70	
▶ The present value (PV) of a cash flow is its value in terms of cash today.		

3.5 The NPV Decision Rule

▶ The net present value (NPV) of a project is $PV(\text{Benefits}) - PV(\text{Costs})$	Net Present Value (NPV), p. 74 NPV Decision Rule, p. 75	MyFinanceLab Study Plan 3.5
▶ A good project is one with a positive net present value.		
▶ The NPV Decision Rule states that when choosing from among a set of alternatives, choose the one with the highest NPV. The NPV of a project is equivalent to the cash value today of the project.		
▶ Regardless of our preferences for cash today versus cash in the future, we should always first maximize NPV. We can then borrow or lend to shift cash flows through time and find our most preferred pattern of cash flows.		

3.6 The Law of One Price

▶ Arbitrage is the process of trading to take advantage of equivalent goods that have different prices in different competitive markets.	arbitrage, p. 78 arbitrage opportunity, p. 78 Law of One Price, p. 78 transactions costs, p. 80	MyFinanceLab Study Plan 3.6
▶ The Law of One Price states that if equivalent goods or securities trade simultaneously in different competitive markets, they will trade for the same price in each market. This law is equivalent to saying that no arbitrage opportunities should exist.		
▶ The price of a security should equal the present value of the expected future cash flows obtained from owning that security.		

Review Questions

1. What makes an investment decision a good one?

2. How important are our personal preferences in valuing an investment decision?

3. Why are market prices useful to a financial manager?

4. How does the Valuation Principle help a financial manager make decisions?

5. Can we directly compare dollar amounts received at different points in time?

6. How is the Net Present Value Rule related to cost-benefit analysis?

7. If there is more than one project to take, how should the financial manager choose among them?

8. What is the relation between arbitrage and the Law of One Price?

Problems

A blue box (■) indicates problems available in MyFinanceLab. An asterisk (*) indicates problems with a higher level of difficulty.

Cost-Benefit Analysis

1. Honda Motor Company is considering offering a $2000 rebate on its minivan, lowering the vehicle's price from $30,000 to $28,000. The marketing group estimates that this rebate will increase sales over the next year from 40,000 to 55,000 vehicles. Suppose Honda's profit margin with the rebate is $6000 per vehicle. If the change in sales is the only consequence of this decision, what are its costs and benefits? Is it a good idea?

2. You are an international shrimp trader. A food producer in the Czech Republic offers to pay you 2 million Czech koruna today in exchange for a year's supply of frozen shrimp. Your Thai supplier will provide you with the same supply for 3 million Thai baht today. If the current competitive market exchange rates are 25.50 koruna per dollar and 41.25 baht per dollar, what is the value of this deal?

3. Suppose your employer offers you a choice between a $5000 bonus and 100 shares of the company's stock. Whichever one you choose will be awarded today. The stock is currently trading for $63 per share.
a. Suppose that if you receive the stock bonus, you are free to trade it. Which form of the bonus should you choose? What is its value?
b. Suppose that if you receive the stock bonus, you are required to hold it for at least one year. What can you say about the value of the stock bonus now? What will your decision depend on?

Valuation Principle

4. Bubba is a shrimp farmer. In an ironic twist, Bubba is allergic to shellfish, so he cannot eat any shrimp. Each day he has a one-ton supply of shrimp. The market price of shrimp is $10,000 per ton.
a. What is the value of a ton of shrimp to him?
b. Would this value change if he were not allergic to shrimp? Why or why not?

5. Brett has almond orchards, but he is sick of almonds and prefers to eat walnuts instead. The owner of the walnut orchard next door has offered to swap this year's crop with him in an even exchange. Assume he produces 1000 tons of almonds and his neighbor produces 800 tons of walnuts. If the market price of almonds is $100 per ton and the market price of walnuts is $1.10 per ton:
a. Should he make the exchange?
b. Does it matter whether he prefers almonds or walnuts? Why or why not?

Interest Rates and the Time Value of Money

6. You have $100 and a bank is offering 5% interest on deposits. If you deposit the money in the bank, how much will you have in one year?

7. You expect to have $1000 in one year. A bank is offering loans at 6% interest per year. How much can you borrow today?

 8. A friend asks to borrow $55 from you and in return will pay you $58 in one year. If your bank is offering a 6% interest rate on deposits and loans:
  a. How much would you have in one year if you deposited the $55 instead?
  b. How much money could you borrow today if you pay the bank $58 in one year?
  c. Should you loan the money to your friend or deposit it in the bank?

 9. Suppose the interest rate is 4%.
  a. Having $200 today is equivalent to having what amount in one year?
  b. Having $200 in one year is equivalent to having what amount today?
  c. Which would you prefer, $200 today or $200 in one year? Does your answer depend on when you need the money? Why or why not?

The NPV Decision Rule

10. Your storage firm has been offered $100,000 in one year to store some goods for one year. Assume your costs are $95,000, payable immediately, and the interest rate is 8%. Should you take the contract?

 11. You run a construction firm. You have just won a contract to build a government office building. Building it will require an investment of $10 million today and $5 million in one year. The government will pay you $20 million in one year upon the building's completion. Suppose the interest rate is 10%.
  a. What is the NPV of this opportunity?
  b. How can your firm turn this NPV into cash today?

 12. Your firm has identified three potential investment projects. The projects and their cash flows are shown here:

Project	Cash Flow Today ($)	Cash Flow in One Year ($)
A	−10.00	20.00
B	5.00	5.00
C	20.00	−10.00

Suppose all cash flows are certain and the interest rate is 10%.
  a. What is the NPV of each project?
  b. If the firm can choose only one of these projects, which should it choose?
  c. If the firm can choose any two of these projects, which should it choose?

 13. Your computer manufacturing firm must purchase 10,000 keyboards from a supplier. One supplier demands a payment of $100,000 today plus $10 per keyboard payable in one year. Another supplier will charge $21 per keyboard, also payable in one year. The interest rate is 6%.
  a. What is the difference in their offers in terms of dollars today? Which offer should your firm take?
  b. Suppose your firm does not want to spend cash today. How can it take the first offer and not spend $100,000 of its own cash today?

BDeH CHAPTER 3

The Law of One Price

14. Suppose Bank One offers an interest rate of 5.5% on both savings and loans, and Bank Enn offers an interest rate of 6% on both savings and loans.
   a. What arbitrage opportunity is available?
   b. Which bank would experience a surge in the demand for loans? Which bank would receive a surge in deposits?
   c. What would you expect to happen to the interest rates the two banks are offering?

15. If the cost of buying a CD and ripping the tracks to your iPod (including your time) is $25, what is the most Apple could charge on iTunes for a whole 15-track CD?

16. Some companies cross-list their shares, meaning that their stock trades on more than one stock exchange. For example, Research in Motion, the maker of Blackberry mobile devices, trades on both the Toronto Stock Exchange and NASDAQ. If its price in Toronto is 100 Canadian dollars per share and anyone can exchange Canadian dollars for U.S. dollars at the rate of US$0.95 per C$1.00, what must RIM's price be on NASDAQ?

*17. Use the concept of arbitrage and the fact that interest rates are positive to prove that time travel will never be possible.

BDeH CHAPTER 3

NPV and the Time Value of Money

LEARNING OBJECTIVES

▶ Construct a cash flow timeline as the first step in solving problems

▶ Calculate the value of distant cash flows in the present and of current cash flows in the future

▶ Value a series of many cash flows

▶ Understand how to compute the net present value of any set of cash flows

▶ Apply shortcuts to value special sets of regular cash flows called *perpetuities* and *annuities*

▶ Compute the number of periods, cash flow, or rate of return in a loan or investment

notation

C	cash flow
C_n	cash flow at date n
FV	future value
FV_n	future value on date n
g	growth rate
IRR	internal rate of return
N	date of the last cash flow in a stream of cash flows

NPV	net present value
P	initial principal or deposit, or equivalent present value
PV	present value
PV_n	present value on date n
r	interest rate

Jonathan Jagolinzer, Ameriprise Financial Services

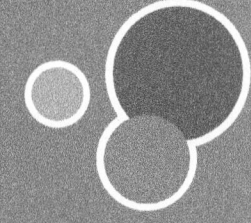

Jonathan Jagolinzer is a financial advisor for Ameriprise Financial Services (formerly American Express Financial), a Fortune 500 financial planning, asset management, and insurance company. A 2005 graduate of George Washington University in Washington, DC, Jon majored in economics and minored in finance.

Jon, who works in Ameriprise's Vienna, Virginia, office, views himself as personal financial trainer for his clients. "Much like a personal trainer, I help them set goals, provide guidance to reach their objectives, and track progress over time," he says. "Working together, we develop sound financial planning strategies for investments, funding children's education, retirement, and estate planning."

Jon's specialty is retirement planning, and he has earned his Chartered Retirement Planning Counselor (CRPC) credential. "My knowledge of time value of money concepts allows me to advise my clients, many of whom are young and just beginning to accumulate personal assets. Some want to spend extravagantly, to buy a new television now, and say they will make up the difference later." He uses a simple example to illustrate how their dollars can grow over time. "Take just $25 each month—money you'd otherwise spend on movies, new clothes, or fancy coffee drinks—and put that into an account earning 6% interest a year. At the end of 15 years, your $4500 investment will have grown to $7270! That $25 may not seem like much today, but the long-term benefits are quite significant."

Jon also encourages his clients to invest in tax-deferred retirement funds. "If you contribute $100 a month to a tax-deferred retirement account that earns 10% a year, at the end of 20 years you will have over $75,000. If it went into a taxable account and you are in the 28% bracket, it would grow to less than $54,000 over the same period. Time value and other financial concepts are, therefore, tools you can use not just on the job but also to make smarter personal financial decisions today that will bring substantial benefits in the future."

George Washington University, 2005

"Time value and other financial concepts are, therefore, tools you can use . . . to make smarter personal financial decisions today that will bring substantial benefits in the future."

BDeH   CHAPTER 4

As we discussed in Chapter 3, to evaluate a project a financial manager must compare its costs and benefits. In most cases, the cash flows in financial investments involve more than one future period. Thus, the financial manager is faced with the task of trading off a known upfront cost against a series of uncertain future benefits. As we learned, calculating the net present value does just that, such that if the NPV of an investment is positive, we should take it.

Calculating the NPV requires tools to evaluate cash flows lasting several periods. We develop these tools in this chapter. The first tool is a visual method for representing a series of cash flows: the *timeline*. After constructing a timeline, we establish three important rules for moving cash flows to different points in time. Using these rules, we show how to compute the present and future values of the costs and benefits of a general stream of cash flows, and how to compute the NPV. Although we can use these techniques to value any type of asset, certain types of assets have cash flows that follow a regular pattern. We develop shortcuts for *annuities*, *perpetuities*, and other special cases of assets with cash flows that follow regular patterns.

 # The Timeline

stream of cash flows A series of cash flows lasting several periods.

timeline A linear representation of the timing of (potential) cash flows.

We begin our discussion of valuing cash flows lasting several periods with some basic vocabulary and tools. We refer to a series of cash flows lasting several periods as a **stream of cash flows**. We can represent a stream of cash flows on a **timeline**, a linear representation of the timing of the expected cash flows. Timelines are an important first step in organizing and then solving a financial problem. We use them throughout this text.

Constructing a Timeline

To illustrate how to construct a timeline, assume that a friend owes you money. He has agreed to repay the loan by making two payments of $10,000 at the end of each of the next two years. We represent this information on a timeline as follows:

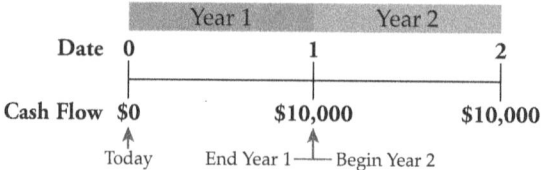

Date 0 represents the present. Date 1 is one year later and represents the end of the first year. The $10,000 cash flow below date 1 is the payment you will receive at the end of the first year. Date 2 is two years from now; it represents the end of the second year. The $10,000 cash flow below date 2 is the payment you will receive at the end of the second year.

Identifying Dates on a Timeline

To track cash flows, we interpret each point on the timeline as a specific date. The space between date 0 and date 1 then represents the time period between these dates—in this case, the first year of the loan. Date 0 is the beginning of the first year, and date 1 is the end of the first year. Similarly, date 1 is the beginning of the second year, and date 2 is the end of the second year. By denoting time in this way, date 1 signifies *both* the end of year 1 and the beginning of year 2, which makes sense since those dates are effectively the same point in time.[1]

Distinguishing Cash Inflows from Outflows

In this example, both cash flows are inflows. In many cases, however, a financial decision will involve both inflows and outflows. To differentiate between the two types of cash flows, we assign a different sign to each: Inflows (cash flows received) are positive cash flows, whereas outflows (cash flows paid out) are negative cash flows.

To illustrate, suppose you're still feeling generous and have agreed to lend your brother $10,000 today. Your brother has agreed to repay this loan in two installments of $6000 at the end of each of the next two years. The timeline is:

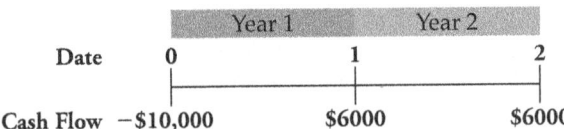

Notice that the first cash flow at date 0 (today) is represented as −$10,000 because it is an outflow. The subsequent cash flows of $6000 are positive because they are inflows.

Representing Various Time Periods

So far, we have used timelines to show the cash flows that occur at the end of each year. Actually, timelines can represent cash flows that take place at any point in time. For example, if you pay rent each month, you could use a timeline such as the one in our first example to represent two rental payments, but you would replace the "year" label with "month."

Many of the timelines included in this chapter are very simple. Consequently, you may feel that it is not worth the time or trouble to construct them. As you progress to more difficult problems, however, you will find that timelines identify events in a transaction or investment that are easy to overlook. If you fail to recognize these cash flows, you will make flawed financial decisions. Therefore, approach *every* problem by drawing the timeline as we do in this chapter.

---

[1]That is, there is no real time difference between a cash flow paid at 11:59 P.M. on December 31 and one paid at 12:01 A.M. on January 1, although there may be some other differences such as taxation that we will overlook for now.

EXAMPLE 4.1

Constructing a Timeline

Problem

Suppose you must pay tuition of $10,000 per year for the next 4 years. Your tuition payments must be made in equal installments of $5000 each every 6 months. What is the timeline of your tuition payments?

Solution

Assuming today is the start of the first semester, your first payment occurs at date 0 (today). The remaining payments occur at 6-month intervals. Using one-half year (6 months) as the period length, we can construct a timeline as follows:

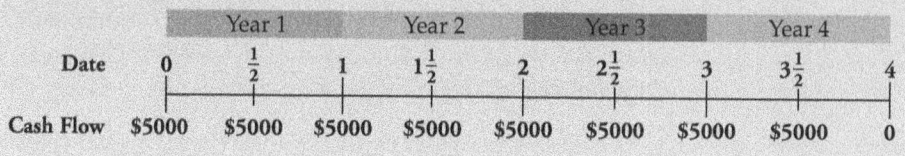

		Year 1		Year 2		Year 3		Year 4	
Date	0	$\frac{1}{2}$	1	$1\frac{1}{2}$	2	$2\frac{1}{2}$	3	$3\frac{1}{2}$	4
Cash Flow	$5000	$5000	$5000	$5000	$5000	$5000	$5000	$5000	0

Concept Check

1. What are the key elements of a timeline?
2. How can you distinguish cash inflows from outflows on a timeline?

4.2 Valuing Cash Flows at Different Points in Time

Financial decisions often require comparing or combining cash flows that occur at different points in time. In this section, we introduce three important rules central to financial decision making that allow us to compare or combine values.

Rule 1: Comparing and Combining Values

Our first rule is that it is only possible to compare or combine values at the same point in time. This rule restates a conclusion introduced in Chapter 3: Only cash flows in the same units can be compared or combined. A dollar today and a dollar in one year are not

Common Mistake   Summing Cash Flows Across Time

Once you understand the Time Value of Money, our first rule may seem straightforward. However, it is very common, especially for those who have not studied finance, to violate this rule, simply treating all cash flows as comparable, regardless of when they are received. One example of this is in sports contracts. In 2007, Alex Rodriguez and the New York Yankees were negotiating what was repeatedly referred to as a "$275 million" contract. The $275 million comes from simply adding up all of the payments that he would receive over the ten years of the contract and an additional ten years of deferred payments—treating dollars received in 20 years the same as dollars received today. The same thing occurred when David Beckham signed a "$250 million" contract with the LA Galaxy soccer team.

BDeH CHAPTER 4

equivalent. Having money now is more valuable than having money in the future; if you have the money today you can earn interest on it.

To compare or combine cash flows that occur at different points in time, you first need to convert the cash flows into the same units by moving them to the same point in time. The next two rules show how to move the cash flows on the timeline.

Rule 2: Compounding

Suppose we have $1000 today, and we wish to determine the equivalent amount in one year's time. If the current market interest rate is 10%, we can use that rate as an exchange rate, meaning the rate at which we exchange money today for money in one year, to move the cash flow forward in time. That is:

($1000 today) $\times$ (1.10 $ in one year / $ today) = $1100 in one year

In general, if the market interest rate for the year is r, then we multiply by the interest rate factor, $(1 + r)$, to move the cash flow from the beginning to the end of the year. We multiply by $(1 + r)$ because at the end of the year you will have (1 $\times$ your original investment) plus interest in the amount of ($r \times$ your original investment). This process of moving forward along the timeline to determine a cash flow's value in the future (its **future value**) is known as **compounding**. *Our second rule stipulates that to calculate a cash flow's future value, you must compound it.*

future value The value of a cash flow that is moved forward in time.

compounding Computing the return on an investment over a long horizon by multiplying the return factors associated with each intervening period.

We can apply this rule repeatedly. Suppose we want to know how much the $1000 is worth in two years' time. If the interest rate for year 2 is also 10%, then we convert as we just did:

($1100 in one year) $\times$ (1.10 $ in two years / $ in one year) = $1210 in two years

Let's represent this calculation on a timeline:

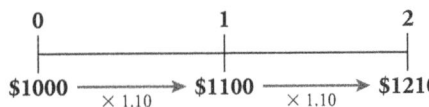

Given a 10% interest rate, all of the cash flows—$1000 at date 0, $1100 at date 1, and $1210 at date 2—are equivalent. They have the same value but are expressed in different units (different points in time). An arrow that points to the right indicates that the value is being moved forward in time—that is, compounded.

In the preceding example, $1210 is the future value of $1000 two years from today. Note that the value grows as we move the cash flow further in the future. In Chapter 3, we defined the time value of money as the difference in value between money today and money in the future. Here, we can say that $1210 in two years is the equivalent amount to $1000 today. The reason money is more valuable to you today is that you have opportunities to invest it. As in this example, by having money sooner, you can invest it (here at a 10% return) so that it will grow to a larger amount of money in the future. Note also that the equivalent amount grows by $100 the first year, but by $110 the second year. In the second year, we earn interest on our original $1000, plus we earn interest on the $100 interest we received in the first year. This effect of earning interest on both the original principal plus the accumulated interest, so that you are earning "interest on interest," is known as **compound interest**. Figure 4.1 shows how over time the amount of money you earn from interest on interest grows so that it

compound interest The effect of earning "interest on interest."

BDeH CHAPTER 4

FIGURE 4.1

The Composition of Interest over Time

This bar graph shows how the account balance and the composition of the interest changes over time when an investor starts with an original deposit of $1000, represented by the red area, in an account earning 10% interest over a 20-year period. Note that the turquoise area representing interest on interest grows, and by year 15 has become larger than the interest on the original deposit, shown in green. In year 20, the interest on interest the investor earned is $3727.50, while the interest earned on the original $1000 is $2000.

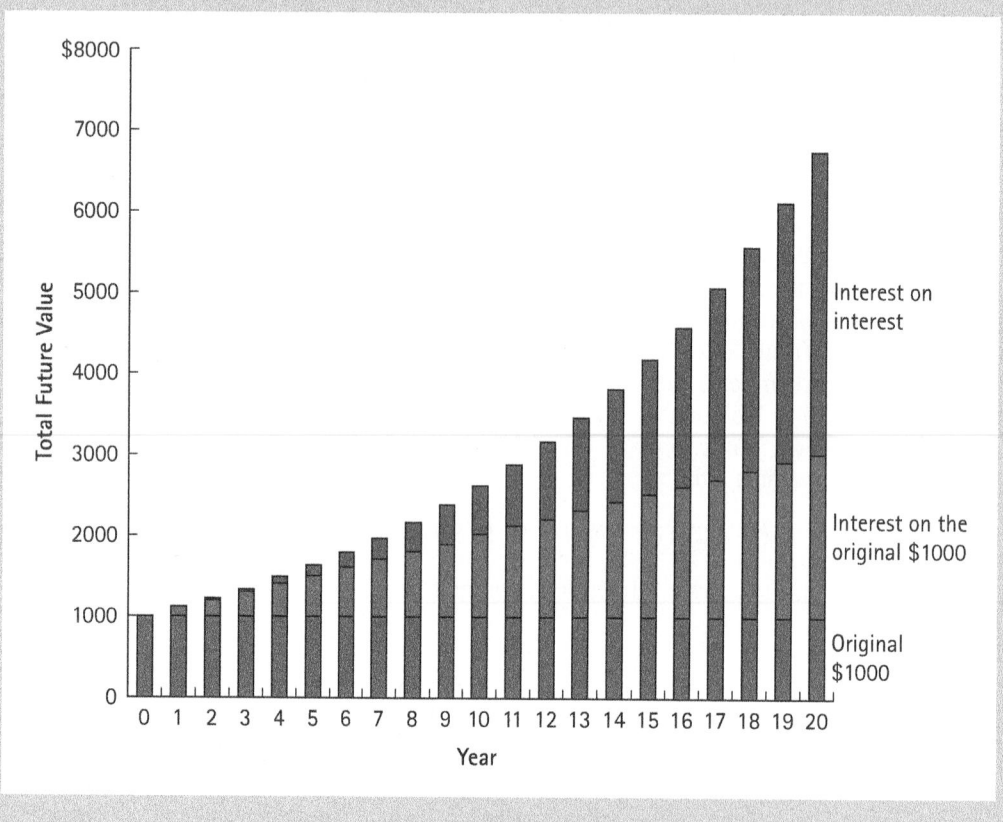

will eventually exceed the amount of money that you earn as interest on your original deposit.

How does the future value change in the third year? Continuing to use the same approach, we compound the cash flow a third time. Assuming the competitive market interest rate is fixed at 10%, we get:

$$\$1000 \times (1.10) \times (1.10) \times (1.10) = \$1000 \times (1.10)^3 = \$1331$$

In general, to compute a cash flow C's value n periods into the future, we must compound it by the n intervening interest rate factors. If the interest rate r is constant, this calculation yields:

Future Value of a Cash Flow

$$FV_n = C \times \underbrace{(1 + r) \times (1 + r) \times \cdots \times (1 + r)}_{n \text{ times}} = C \times (1 + r)^n \qquad (4.1)$$

Rule of 72

Another way to think about the effect of compounding is to consider how long it will take your money to double given different interest rates. Suppose you want to know how many years it will take for $1 to grow to a future value of $2. You want the number of years, N, to solve:

$$FV = \$1 \times (1 + r)^N = \$2$$

If you solve this formula for different interest rates, you will find the following approximation:

Years to double $\approx 72 \div$ (interest rate in percent)

This simple "Rule of 72" is fairly accurate (i.e., within one year of the exact doubling time) for interest rates higher than 2%. For example, if the interest rate is 9%, the doubling time should be about $72 \div 9 = 8$ years. Indeed, $1.09^8 = 1.99$! So, given a 9% interest rate, your money will approximately double every 8 years.

Rule 3: Discounting

The third rule describes how to put a value today on a cash flow that comes in the future. Suppose you would like to compute the value today of $1000 that you anticipate receiving in one year. If the current market interest rate is 10%, you can compute this value by converting units as we did in Chapter 3:

($1000 in one year) $\div$ (1.10 $ in one year / $ today) = $909.09 today

That is, to move the cash flow back along the timeline, we divide it by the interest rate factor, $(1 + r)$, where r is the interest rate. This process of finding the equivalent value today of a future cash flow is known as **discounting**. *Our third rule stipulates that to calculate the value of a future cash flow at an earlier point in time, we must discount it.*

discounting Finding the equivalent value today of a future cash flow by multiplying by a discount factor, or equivalently, dividing by 1 plus the discount rate.

Suppose that you anticipate receiving the $1000 two years from today rather than in one year. If the interest rate for both years is 10%, you can prepare the following timeline:

```
        0              1              2
        |              |              |
   $826.45  ◄────  $909.09  ◄────  $1000
            ÷ 1.10           ÷ 1.10
```

When the interest rate is 10%, all of the cash flows—$826.45 at date 0, $909.09 at date 1, and $1000 at date 2—are equivalent. They represent the same value in different units (different points in time). The arrow points to the left to indicate that the value is being moved backward in time or discounted. Note that the value decreases the further in the future is the original cash flow.

The value of a future cash flow at an earlier point on the timeline is its present value at the earlier point in time. That is, $826.45 is the present value at date 0 of $1000 in two years. Recall from Chapter 3 that the present value is the "do-it-yourself" price to produce a future cash flow. Thus, if we invested $826.45 today for two years at 10% interest, we would have a future value of $1000, using the second rule of valuing cash flows:

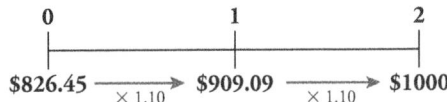

```
        0              1              2
        |              |              |
   $826.45  ────►  $909.09  ────►  $1000
            × 1.10           × 1.10
```

Suppose the $1000 were three years away and you wanted to compute the present value. Again, if the interest rate is 10%, we have:

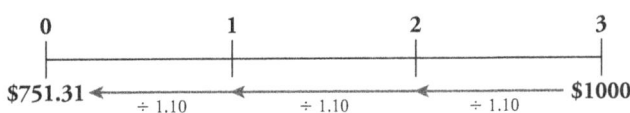

```
        0          1          2          3
        |          |          |          |
   $751.31 ◄──── ◄──── ◄──── $1000
           ÷ 1.10   ÷ 1.10   ÷ 1.10
```

That is, the present value today of a cash flow of $1000 in three years is given by:

$$\$1000 \div (1.10) \div (1.10) \div (1.10) = \$1000 \div (1.10)^3 = \$751.31$$

In general, to compute the present value of a cash flow C that comes n periods from now, we must discount it by the n intervening interest rate factors. If the interest rate r is constant, this yields:

Present Value of a Cash Flow

$$PV = C \div (1 + r)^n = \frac{C}{(1 + r)^n} \qquad (4.2)$$

EXAMPLE 4.2

Personal Finance
Present Value of
a Single Future
Cash Flow

Problem

You are considering investing in a savings bond that will pay $15,000 in ten years. If the competitive market interest rate is fixed at 6% per year, what is the bond worth today?

Solution

▶ **Plan**

First setup your timeline. The cash flows for this bond are represented by the following timeline:

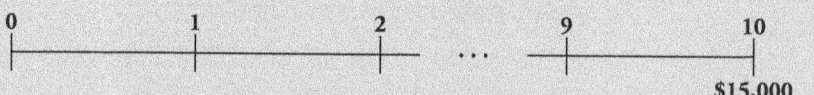

Thus, the bond is worth $15,000 in ten years. To determine the value today, we compute the present value using Equation 4.2 and our interest rate of 6%.

▶ **Execute**

$$PV = \frac{15,000}{1.06^{10}} = \$8375.92 \text{ today}$$

Using a financial calculator or Excel (see the appendix for step-by-step instructions):

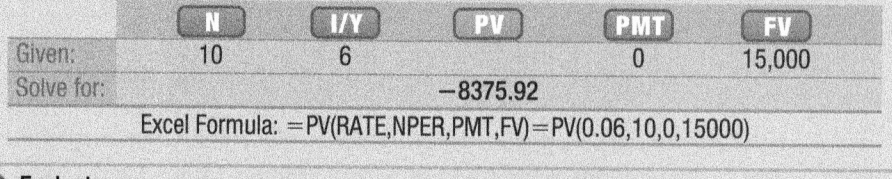

	N	I/Y	PV	PMT	FV
Given:	10	6		0	15,000
Solve for:			−8375.92		
	Excel Formula: =PV(RATE,NPER,PMT,FV)=PV(0.06,10,0,15000)				

▶ **Evaluate**

The bond is worth much less today than its final payoff because of the time value of money.

Applying the Rules of Valuing Cash Flows

The rules of cash flow valuation allow us to compare and combine cash flows that occur at different points in time. Suppose we plan to save $1000 today and $1000 at the end of each of the next two years. If we earn a fixed 10% interest rate on our savings, how much will we have three years from today?

Again, we start with a timeline:

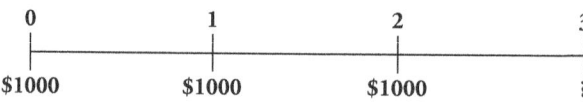

The timeline shows the three deposits we plan to make. We need to compute their value at the end of three years.

Using a Financial Calculator: Solving for Present and Future Values

So far, we have used formulas to compute present values and future values. Both financial calculators and spreadsheets have these formulas pre-programmed to quicken the process. In this box, we focus on financial calculators, but spreadsheets such as Excel have very similar shortcut functions.

Financial calculators have a set of functions that perform the calculations that finance professionals do most often. The functions are all based on the following timeline, which among other things can handle most types of loans:

$$
\begin{array}{ccccc}
0 & 1 & 2 & & NPER \\
\vdash & \vdash & \vdash & \cdots & \vdash \\
PV & PMT & PMT & & PMT + FV
\end{array}
$$

There are a total of five variables: N, PV, PMT, FV, and the interest rate, denoted I/Y. Each function takes four of these variables as inputs and returns the value of the fifth one that ensures that the NPV of the cash flows is zero.

By setting the intermediate payments equal to 0, you could compute present and future values of single cash flows such as we have done above using Equations 4.1 and 4.2. In the examples in Section 4.5, we will calculate cash flows using the PMT button. The best way to learn to use a financial calculator is by practicing. We present one example below. We will also show the calculator buttons for any additional examples in this chapter that can be solved with financial calculator functions. Finally, the appendix to this chapter contains step-by-step instructions for using the two most popular financial calculators.

Example 1

Suppose you plan to invest $20,000 in an account paying 8% interest. How much will you have in the account in 15 years? We represent this problem with the following timeline:

$$
\begin{array}{ccccc}
0 & 1 & 2 & & NPER = 15 \\
\vdash & \vdash & \vdash & \cdots & \vdash \\
PV = -\$20,000 & PMT = \$0 & \$0 & & FV = ?
\end{array}
$$

To compute the solution, we enter the four variables we know, $N = 15$, $I/Y = 8$, $PV = -20,000$, PMT = 0, and solve for the one we want to determine: FV. Specifically, for the HP-10BII or TI-BAII Plus calculators:

1. Enter 15 and press the N key.
2. Enter 8 and press the I/Y key (I/YR for the HP calculator).
3. Enter −20,000 and press the PV key.
4. Enter 0 and press the PMT key.
5. Press the FV key (for the Texas Instruments calculator, press "CPT" and then "FV").

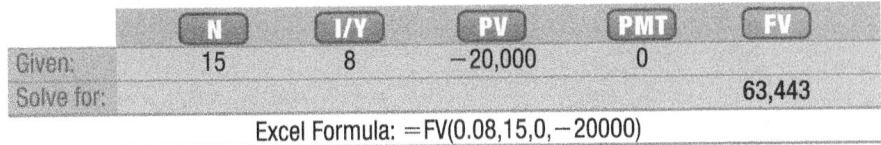

	N	I/Y	PV	PMT	FV
Given:	15	8	−20,000	0	
Solve for:					63,443

Excel Formula: =FV(0.08,15,0,−20000)

The calculator then shows a future value of $63,443.

Note that we entered PV as a negative number (the amount we are putting *into* the bank), and FV is shown as a positive number (the amount we can take *out* of the bank). It is important to use signs correctly to indicate the direction in which the money is flowing when using the calculator functions. You will see more examples of getting the sign of the cash flows correct throughout the chapter.

Excel has the same functions, but it calls "N," "NPER" and "I/Y," "RATE". **Also, it is important to note that you enter an interest rate of 8% as "8" in a financial calculator, but as 0.08 in Excel.**

BDeH CHAPTER 4

We can use the cash flow valuation rules in a number of ways to solve this problem. First, we can take the deposit at date 0 and move it forward to date 1. Because it is then in the same time period as the date 1 deposit, we can combine the two amounts to find out the total in the bank on date 1:

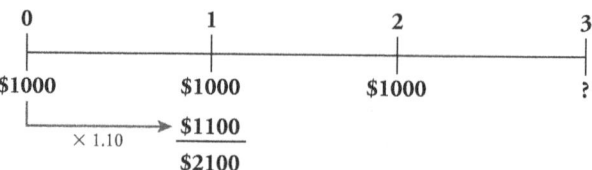

Using the first two rules, we find that our total savings on date 1 will be $2100. Continuing in this fashion, we can solve the problem as follows:

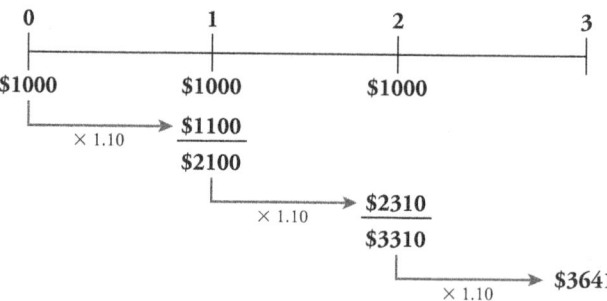

The total amount we will have in the bank at the end of three years is $3641. This amount is the future value of our $1000 savings deposits.

Another approach to the problem is to compute the future value in year 3 of each cash flow separately. Once all three amounts are in year 3 dollars, we can then combine them.

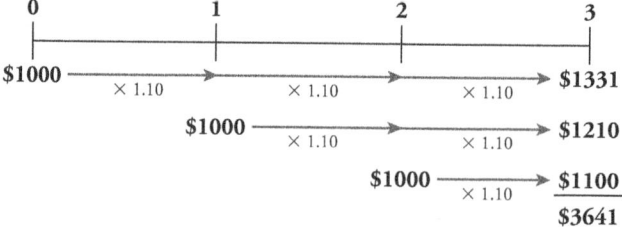

Both calculations give the same future value of $3641. As long as we follow the rules, we get the same result. The order in which we apply the rules does not matter. The calculation we choose depends on which is more convenient for the problem at hand. Table 4.1 summarizes the three rules of valuing cash flows and their associated formulas.

TABLE 4.1	Rule	Formula
The Three Rules of Valuing Cash Flows	1: Only values at the same point in time can be compared or combined.	None
	2: To calculate a cash flow's future value, we must compound it.	Future value of a cash flow: $FV_n = C \times (1 + r)^n$
	3: To calculate the present value of a future cash flow, we must discount it.	Present value of a cash flow: $PV = C \div (1 + r)^n = \dfrac{C}{(1 + r)^n}$

EXAMPLE 4.3

Personal Finance
Computing the
Future Value

Problem

Let's revisit the savings plan we considered earlier: We plan to save $1000 today and at the end of each of the next two years. At a fixed 10% interest rate, how much will we have in the bank three years from today?

Solution

▶ **Plan**

We'll start with the timeline for this savings plan:

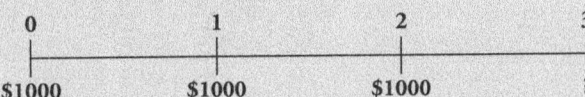

Let's solve this problem in a different way than we did in the text, while still following the rules we established. First we'll compute the present value of the cash flows. Then we'll compute its value three years later (its future value).

▶ **Execute**

There are several ways to calculate the present value of the cash flows. Here, we treat each cash flow separately and then combine the present values.

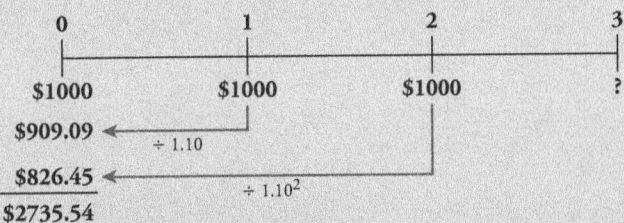

Saving $2735.54 today is equivalent to saving $1000 per year for three years. Now let's compute future value in year 3 of that $2735.54:

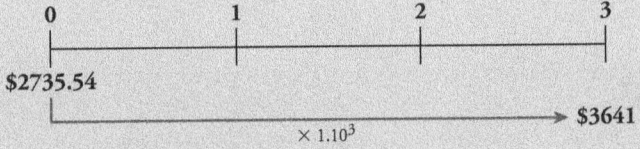

▶ **Evaluate**

This answer of $3641 is precisely the same result we found earlier. As long as we apply the three rules of valuing cash flows, we will always get the correct answer.

Concept Check

3. Can you compare or combine cash flows at different times?

4. What do you need to know to compute a cash flow's present or future value?

4.3 Valuing a Stream of Cash Flows

Most investment opportunities have multiple cash flows that occur at different points in time. In Section 4.2, we learned the rules to value such cash flows. Now we formalize this approach by deriving a general formula for valuing a stream of cash flows.

Consider a stream of cash flows: C_0 at date 0, C_1 at date 1, and so on, up to C_N at date N. We represent this cash flow stream on a timeline as follows:

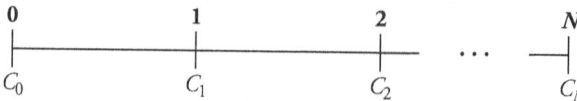

Using the rules of cash flow valuation, we compute the present value of this cash flow stream in two steps. First, we compute the present value of each individual cash flow. Then, once the cash flows are in common units of dollars today, we can combine them. For a given interest rate r, we represent this process on the timeline as follows:

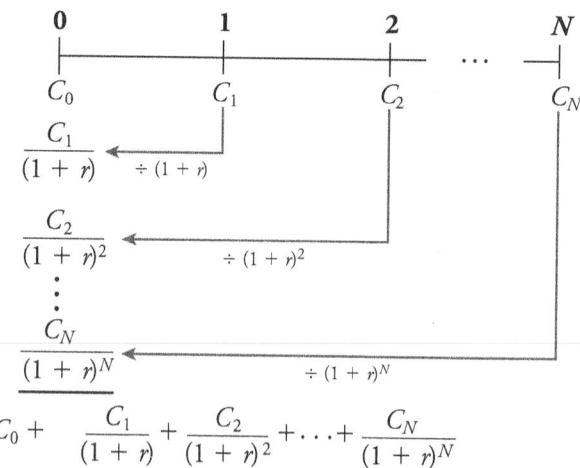

This timeline provides the general formula for the present value of a cash flow stream:

$$PV = C_0 + \frac{C_1}{(1 + r)} + \frac{C_2}{(1 + r)^2} + \cdots + \frac{C_N}{(1 + r)^N} \qquad (4.3)$$

That is, the present value of the cash flow stream is the sum of the present values of each cash flow. Recall from Chapter 3 that we defined the present value as the dollar amount you would need to invest today to produce the single cash flow in the future. The same idea holds in this context. The present value is the amount you need to invest today to generate the cash flows stream $C_0, C_1, \ldots, C_N$. That is, receiving those cash flows is equivalent to having their present value in the bank today.

EXAMPLE 4.4

Personal Finance
Present Value of
a Stream of Cash
Flows

Problem
You have just graduated and need money to buy a new car. Your rich Uncle Henry will lend you the money so long as you agree to pay him back within four years, and you offer to pay him the rate of interest that he would otherwise get by putting his money in a savings account. Based on your earnings and living expenses, you think you will be able to pay him $5000 in one year, and then $8000 each year for the next three years. If Uncle Henry would otherwise earn 6% per year on his savings, how much can you borrow from him?

BDeH CHAPTER 4

Solution

▶ **Plan**

The cash flows you can promise Uncle Henry are as follows:

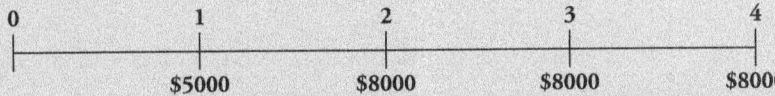

0	1	2	3	4
	$5000	$8000	$8000	$8000

How much money should Uncle Henry be willing to give you today in return for your promise of these payments? He should be willing to give you an amount that is equivalent to these payments in present value terms. This is the amount of money that it would take him to produce these same cash flows. We will (1) solve the problem using Equation 4.3 and then (2) verify our answer by calculating the future value of this amount.

▶ **Execute**

1. We can calculate the PV as follows:

$$PV = \frac{5000}{1.06} + \frac{8000}{1.06^2} + \frac{8000}{1.06^3} + \frac{8000}{1.06^4}$$

$$= 4716.98 + 7119.97 + 6716.95 + 6336.75$$

$$= \$24{,}890.65$$

Now suppose that Uncle Henry gives you the money, and then deposits your payments to him in the bank each year. How much will he have four years from now?

We need to compute the future value of the annual deposits. One way to do so is to compute the bank balance each year:

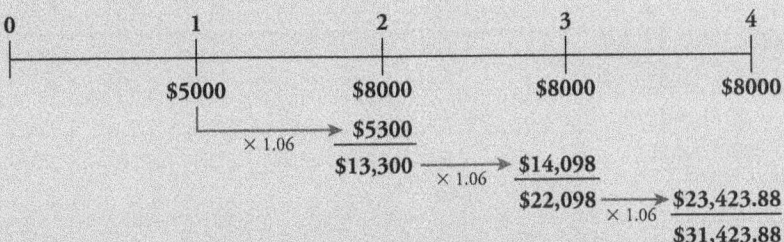

2. To verify our answer, suppose your uncle kept his $24,890.65 in the bank today earning 6% interest. In four years he would have:

$$FV = \$24{,}890.65 \times (1.06)^4 = \$31{,}423.87 \text{ in 4 years}$$

We get the same answer both ways (within a penny, which is because of rounding).

▶ **Evaluate**

Thus, Uncle Henry should be willing to lend you $24,890.65 in exchange for your promised payments. This amount is less than the total you will pay him ($5000 + $8000 + $8000 + $8000 = $29,000) due to the time value of money.

Example 4.4 illustrates that if you want to compute the future value of a stream of cash flows, you can do it directly (the first approach used in Example 4.4), or you can first compute the present value and then move it to the future (the second approach). As always, we use Eq. 4.1 to calculate the future value of any present value. Because we obey the rules of valuing cash flows in both cases, we get the same result.

Concept Check

5. How do you calculate the present value of a cash flow stream?
6. How do you calculate the future value of a cash flow stream?

4.4 The Net Present Value of a Stream of Cash Flows

Now that we have established how to compute present and future values, we are ready to address our central goal: calculating the NPV of future cash flows to evaluate an investment decision. The Valuation Principle tells us that the value of a decision is the value of its benefits minus the value of its costs. NPV values those benefits and costs in today's dollars. Recall from Chapter 3 that we defined the net present value (NPV) of an investment decision as follows:

$$NPV = PV(\text{benefits}) - PV(\text{costs})$$

In this context, the benefits are the cash inflows and the costs are the cash outflows. We can represent any investment decision on a timeline as a cash flow stream, where the cash outflows (investments) are negative cash flows and the inflows are positive cash flows. Thus, the NPV of an investment opportunity is also the *present value* of the stream of cash flows of the opportunity:

$$NPV = PV(\text{benefits}) - PV(\text{costs}) = PV(\text{benefits} - \text{costs})$$

EXAMPLE 4.5

Personal Finance
Net Present Value of
an Investment
Opportunity

Problem

You have been offered the following investment opportunity: If you invest $1000 today, you will receive $500 at the end of each of the next two years, followed by $550 at the end of the third year. If you could otherwise earn 10% per year on your money, should you undertake the investment opportunity?

Solution

▶ **Plan**

As always, start with a timeline. We denote the upfront investment as a negative cash flow (because it is money you need to spend) and the money you receive as a positive cash flow.

To decide whether you should accept this opportunity, you'll need to compute the NPV by computing the present value of the stream.

▶ **Execute**

The NPV is:

$$NPV = -1000 + \frac{500}{1.10} + \frac{500}{1.10^2} + \frac{550}{1.10^3} = \$280.99$$

▶ **Evaluate**

Because the NPV is positive, the benefits exceed the costs and you should make the investment. Indeed, the NPV tells us that taking this opportunity is equivalent to getting an extra

$280.99 that you can spend today. To illustrate, suppose you borrow $1000 to invest in the opportunity and an extra $280.99 to spend today. How much would you owe on the $1280.99 loan in three years? At 10% interest, the amount you would owe would be:

$$FV = (\$1000 + \$280.99) \times (1.10)^3 = \$1705 \text{ in 3 years}$$

At the same time, the investment opportunity generates cash flows. If you put these cash flows into a bank account, how much will you have saved three years from now? The future value of the savings is:

$$FV = (\$500 \times 1.10^2) + (\$500 \times 1.10) + \$550 = \$1705 \text{ in 3 years}$$

As you see, you can use your bank savings to repay the loan. Taking the opportunity therefore allows you to spend $280.99 today at no extra cost.

In principle, we have met the goal we set at the beginning of the chapter: How should financial managers evaluate a project. We have developed the tools to evaluate the cash flows of a project. We have shown how to compute the NPV of an investment opportunity that lasts more than one period. In practice, when the number of cash flows exceeds four or five (as it most likely will), the calculations can become tedious. Fortunately, a number of special cases do not require us to discount each cash flow separately. We derive these shortcuts in the next section.

Concept Check

7. What benefit does a firm receive when it accepts a project with a positive NPV?

8. How do you calculate the net present value of a cash flow stream?

Perpetuities, Annuities, and Other Special Cases

The formulas we have developed so far allow us to compute the present or future value of any cash flow stream. In this section, we consider two types of cash flow streams, *perpetuities* and *annuities*, and learn shortcuts for valuing them. These shortcuts are possible because the cash flows follow a regular pattern.

Perpetuities

perpetuity A stream of equal cash flows that occurs at regular intervals and lasts forever.

consol A bond that promises its owner a fixed cash flow every year, forever.

A **perpetuity** is a stream of equal cash flows that occur at regular intervals and last forever. One example is the British government bond called a **consol** (or perpetual bond). Consol bonds promise the owner a fixed cash flow every year, forever.

Here is the timeline for a perpetuity:

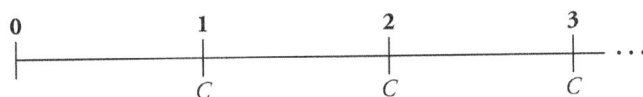

Note from the timeline that the first cash flow does not occur immediately; *it arrives at the end of the first period.* This timing is sometimes referred to as payment *in arrears* and is a standard convention in loan payment calculations and elsewhere, so we adopt it throughout this text.

Using the formula for the present value, the present value of a perpetuity with payment C and interest rate r is given by:

$$PV = \frac{C}{(1 + r)} + \frac{C}{(1 + r)^2} + \frac{C}{(1 + r)^3} + \cdots$$

Notice that all of the cash flows (C in the formula) are the same because the cash flow for a perpetuity is constant. Also, because the first cash flow is in one period, there is no cash flow at time 0 ($C_0 = 0$).

To find the value of a perpetuity by discounting one cash flow at a time would take forever—literally! You might wonder how, even with a shortcut, the sum of an infinite number of positive terms could be finite. The answer is that the cash flows in the future are discounted for an ever increasing number of periods, so their contribution to the sum eventually becomes negligible.

To derive the shortcut, we calculate the value of a perpetuity by creating our own perpetuity. The Valuation Principle tells us that the value of a perpetuity must be the same as the cost we incurred to create our own identical perpetuity. To illustrate, suppose you could invest $100 in a bank account paying 5% interest per year forever. At the end of one year, you will have $105 in the bank—your original $100 plus $5 in interest. Suppose you withdraw the $5 interest and reinvest the $100 for a second year. Again, you will have $105 after one year, and you can withdraw $5 and reinvest $100 for another year. By doing this year after year, you can withdraw $5 every year in perpetuity:

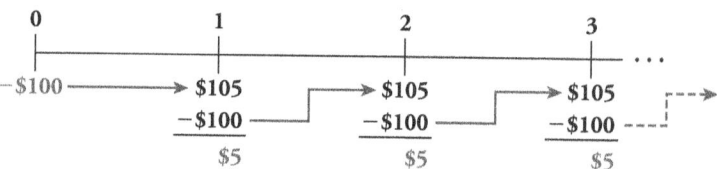

By investing $100 in the bank today, you can, in effect, create a perpetuity paying $5 per year. Recall from Chapter 3 that the Law of One Price tells us that equivalent cash flows must have the same price in every market. Because the bank will "sell" us (allow us to create) the perpetuity for $100, the present value of the $5 per year in perpetuity is this "do-it-yourself" cost of $100.

Now let's generalize this argument. Suppose we invest an amount P in a bank account with an interest rate r. Every year we can withdraw the interest we have earned, $C = r \times P$, leaving the principal, P, in the bank. Because our cost for creating the perpetuity is only the initial investment of principal (P), the value of receiving C in perpetuity is therefore the upfront cost P. Rearranging $C = r \times P$ to solve for P we have $P = C/r$. Therefore:

Present Value of a Perpetuity

$$PV(C \text{ in perpetuity}) = \frac{C}{r} \tag{4.4}$$

By depositing the amount $\frac{C}{r}$ today, we can withdraw interest of $\frac{C}{r} \times r = C$ each period in perpetuity.

Note the logic of our argument. To determine the present value of a cash flow stream, we computed the "do-it-yourself" cost of creating those same cash flows at the bank. This is an extremely useful and powerful approach—and is much simpler and faster than summing those infinite terms!

BDeH CHAPTER 4

Historical Examples of Perpetuities

Companies sometimes issue bonds that they call perpetuities, but in fact are not really perpetuities. For example, according to *Dow Jones International News* (February 26, 2004), in 2004 Korea First Bank sold $300 million of debt in "the form of a so-called 'perpetual bond' that has no fixed maturity date." Although the bond has no fixed maturity date, Korea First Bank has the right to pay it back after ten years, in 2014. Korea First Bank also has the right to extend the maturity of the bond for another 30 years after 2014. Thus, although the bond does not have a fixed maturity date, it will eventually mature—in either 10 or 40 years. The bond is not really a perpetuity because it does not pay interest forever.

Perpetual bonds were some of the first bonds ever issued. The oldest perpetuities that are still making interest payments were issued by the *Hoogheemraadschap Lekdijk Bovendams,* a seventeenth-century Dutch water board responsible for upkeep of the local dikes. The oldest

bond dates from 1624. Two finance professors at Yale University, William Goetzmann and Geert Rouwenhorst, personally verified that these bonds continue to pay interest. On behalf of Yale, they purchased one of these bonds on July 1, 2003, and collected 26 years of back interest. On its issue date in 1648, this bond originally paid interest in Carolus guilders. Over the next 355 years, the currency of payment changed to Flemish pounds, Dutch guilders, and most recently euros. Currently, the bond pays interest of €11.34 annually.

Although the Dutch bonds are the oldest perpetuities still in existence, the first perpetuities date from much earlier times. For example, *cencus agreements* and *rentes,* which were forms of perpetuities and annuities, were issued in the twelfth century in Italy, France, and Spain. They were initially designed to circumvent the usury laws of the Catholic Church: Because they did not require the repayment of principal, in the eyes of the church they were not considered loans.

EXAMPLE 4.6

Personal Finance
Endowing a Perpetuity

Problem
You want to endow an annual graduation party at your alma mater. You want the event to be a memorable one, so you budget $30,000 per year forever for the party. If the university earns 8% per year on its investments, and if the first party is in one year's time, how much will you need to donate to endow the party?

Solution

▶ **Plan**
The timeline of the cash flows you want to provide is:

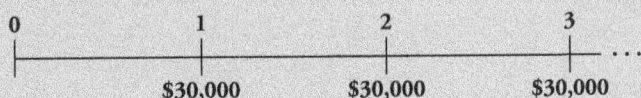

This is a standard perpetuity of $30,000 per year. The funding you would need to give the university in perpetuity is the present value of this cash flow stream.

▶ **Execute**
Use the formula for a perpetuity:

$$PV = C/r = \$30,000/0.08 = \$375,000 \text{ today}$$

▶ **Evaluate**
If you donate $375,000 today, and if the university invests it at 8% per year forever, then the graduates will have $30,000 every year for their graduation party.

BDeH CHAPTER 4

BDeH CHAPTER 4

Common Mistake — Discounting One Too Many Times

The perpetuity formula assumes that the first payment occurs at the end of the first period (at date 1). Sometimes perpetuities have cash flows that start later in the future. In this case, we can adapt the perpetuity formula to compute the present value, but we need to do so carefully to avoid a common mistake.

To illustrate, consider the graduation party described in Example 4.6. Rather than starting in one year, suppose that the first party will be held two years from today. How would this delay change the amount of the donation required?

Now the timeline looks like this:

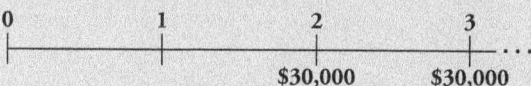

We need to determine the present value of these cash flows, as it tells us the amount of money in the bank needed today to finance the future parties. We cannot apply the perpetuity formula directly, however, because these cash flows are not *exactly* a perpetuity as we defined it. Specifically, the cash flow in the first period is "missing." But consider the situation on date 1—at that point, the first party is one period away and then

the cash flows occur regularly. From the perspective of date 1, this *is* a perpetuity, and we can apply the formula. From the preceding calculation, we know we need $375,000 on date 1 to have enough to start the parties on date 2. We rewrite the timeline as follows:

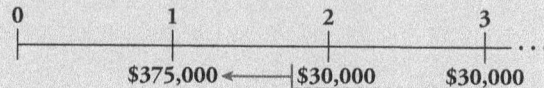

Our goal can now be restated more simply: How much do we need to invest today to have $375,000 in one year? This is a simple present value calculation:

$$PV = \$375{,}000/1.08 = \$347{,}222 \text{ today}$$

A common mistake is to discount the $375,000 twice because the first party is in two periods. *Remember—the present value formula for the perpetuity already discounts the cash flows to one period prior to the first cash flow.* Keep in mind that this common mistake may be made with perpetuities, annuities, and all of the other special cases discussed in this section. All of these formulas discount the cash flows to one period prior to the first cash flow.

Annuities

annuity A stream of equal cash flows arriving at a regular interval over a specified time period.

An **annuity** is a stream of N equal cash flows paid at regular intervals. The difference between an annuity and a perpetuity is that an annuity ends after some fixed number of payments. Most car loans, mortgages, and some bonds are annuities. We represent the cash flows of an annuity on a timeline as follows:

Note that just as with the perpetuity, we adopt the convention that the first payment takes place at date 1, one period from today. The present value of an N-period annuity with payment C and interest rate r is:

$$PV = \frac{C}{(1 + r)} + \frac{C}{(1 + r)^2} + \frac{C}{(1 + r)^3} + \cdots + \frac{C}{(1 + r)^N}$$

Present Value of an Annuity. To find a simpler formula, we use the same approach we followed with the perpetuity: find a way to create your own annuity. To illustrate, suppose you invest $100 in a bank account paying 5% interest. At the end of one year, you will have $105 in the bank—your original $100 plus $5 in interest. Using the same strategy as you did for calculating the value of a perpetuity, suppose you withdraw the $5 interest and reinvest the $100 for a second year. Once again you will have $105 after one year. You can repeat the process, withdrawing $5 and reinvesting $100, every year. For a perpetuity, you left the principal in the bank forever. Alternatively, you might decide after 20 years to close the account and withdraw the principal. In that case, your cash flows will look like this:

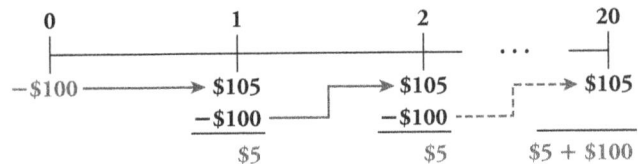

With your initial $100 investment, you have created a 20-year annuity of $5 per year, plus you will receive an extra $100 at the end of 20 years. Again, the Valuation Principle's Law of One Price tells us that because it only took an initial investment of $100 to create the cash flows on the timeline, the present value of these cash flows is $100, or:

$$\$100 = PV(\text{20-year annuity of \$5 per year}) + PV(\$100 \text{ in 20 years})$$

So if we invest $100 now, we can receive $5 per year for 20 years as well as $100 in the 20th year, representing the following cash flows:

0	1	2	20
−$100	$5	$5	$5 + $100

Rearranging the equation above shows that the cost of a 20-year annuity of $5 per year is $100 minus the present value of $100 in 20 years.

$$PV(\text{20-year annuity of \$5 per year}) = \$100 - PV(\$100 \text{ in 20 years})$$
$$= \$100 - \frac{\$100}{(1.05)^{20}} = \$100 - \$37.69 = \$62.31$$

0	1	2	20
−$100	$5	$5	$5 + $100

Removing the $100 in 20 years and its present value leaves the following cash flows:

−$62.31	$5	$5	...	$5

So the present value of $5 for 20 years is $62.31. Intuitively, the value of the annuity is the initial investment in the bank account minus the present value of the principal that will be left in the account after 20 years.

The $5 we receive every year is the interest on the $100 and can be written as $100(.05) = $5. Rearranging, we have $100 = $5/.05. If we substitute $5/.05 into our formula above, we can represent the PV of the annuity as a function of its cash flow ($5), the discount rate (5%) and the number of years (20):

$$PV(\text{20-year annuity of \$5 per year}) = \frac{\$5}{.05} - \frac{\frac{\$5}{.05}}{(1.05)^{20}} = \frac{\$5}{.05}\left(1 - \frac{1}{(1.05)^{20}}\right)$$

$$= \$5 \times \frac{1}{.05}\left(1 - \frac{1}{(1.05)^{20}}\right)$$

BDeH CHAPTER 4

This method is very useful because we will most often want to know the PV of the annuity given its cash flow, discount rate and number of years. We can write this as a general formula for the present value of an annuity of C for N periods:

Present Value of an Annuity

$$PV(\text{annuity of } C \text{ for } N \text{ periods with interest rate } r) = C \times \frac{1}{r}\left(1 - \frac{1}{(1 + r)^N}\right) \quad (4.5)$$

EXAMPLE 4.7

Personal Finance
Present Value of a
Lottery Prize Annuity

Problem

You are the lucky winner of the $30 million state lottery. You can take your prize money either as (a) 30 payments of $1 million per year (starting today), or (b) $15 million paid today. If the interest rate is 8%, which option should you take?

Solution

▶ **Plan**

Option (a) provides $30 million in prize money but paid over time. To evaluate it correctly, we must convert it to a present value. Here is the timeline:

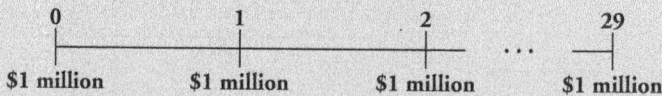

Because the first payment starts today, the last payment will occur in 29 years (for a total of 30 payments).[2] The $1 million at date 0 is already stated in present value terms, but we need to compute the present value of the remaining payments. Fortunately, this case looks like a 29-year annuity of $1 million per year, so we can use the annuity formula.

▶ **Execute**

We use the annuity formula:

$$PV(\text{29-year annuity of \$1 million}) = \$1 \text{ million} \times \frac{1}{0.08}\left(1 - \frac{1}{1.08^{29}}\right)$$

$$= \$1 \text{ million} \times 11.16$$

$$= \$11.16 \text{ million today}$$

Thus, the total present value of the cash flows is $1 million + $11.16 million = $12.16 million. In timeline form:

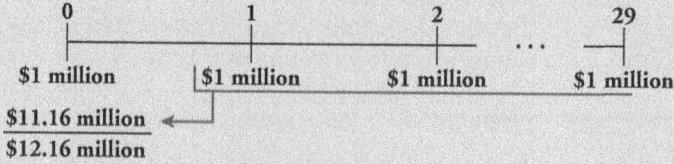

Option (b), $15 million upfront, is more valuable—even though the total amount of money paid is half that of option (a).

---

[2]An annuity in which the first payment occurs immediately is sometimes called an *annuity due*. Throughout this text, we always use the term "annuity" to mean one that is paid in arrears.

Financial calculators or Excel can handle annuities easily—just enter the cash flow in the annuity as the *PMT*:

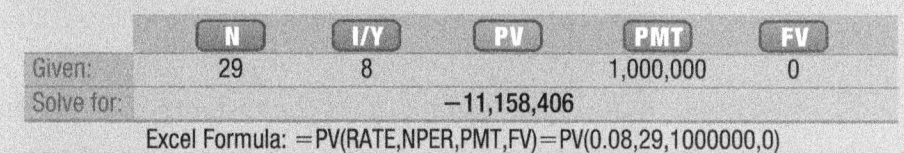

	N	I/Y	PV	PMT	FV
Given:	29	8		1,000,000	0
Solve for:			−11,158,406		
		Excel Formula: =PV(RATE,NPER,PMT,FV)=PV(0.08,29,1000000,0)			

Both the financial calculator and Excel will give you the PV of the 29 payments ($11.16 million) to which you must add the first payment of $1 million just as above.

▶ **Evaluate**
The reason for the difference is the time value of money. If you have the $15 million today, you can use $1 million immediately and invest the remaining $14 million at an 8% interest rate. This strategy will give you $14 million × 8% = $1.12 million per year in perpetuity! Alternatively, you can spend $15 million − $11.16 million = $3.84 million today, and invest the remaining $11.16 million, which will still allow you to withdraw $1 million each year for the next 29 years before your account is depleted.

Future Value of an Annuity. Now that we have derived a simple formula for the present value of an annuity, it is easy to find a simple formula for the future value. If we want to know the value N years in the future, we move the present value N periods forward on the timeline.

$$
\begin{array}{ccccccc}
0 & & 1 & & 2 & & 20 \\
\vdash & & \vdash & & \vdash & \cdots & \dashv \\
& & C & & C & & C
\end{array}
$$

$$PV = \frac{C}{r}\left(1 - \frac{1}{(1+r)^N}\right)$$

$$FV = \frac{C}{r}\left(1 - \frac{1}{(1+r)^N}\right) \times (1 + r)^N$$

As the timeline shows, we compound the present value for N periods at interest rate r:

Future Value of an Annuity

$$FV(\text{annuity}) = PV \times (1 + r)^N$$

$$= \frac{C}{r}\left(1 - \frac{1}{(1 + r)^N}\right) \times (1 + r)^N$$

$$= C \times \frac{1}{r}((1 + r)^N - 1) \tag{4.6}$$

This formula is useful if we want to know how a savings account will grow over time and the investor deposits the same amount every period.

EXAMPLE 4.8

Personal Finance
Retirement Savings
Plan Annuity

Problem
Ellen is 35 years old and she has decided it is time to plan seriously for her retirement. At the end of each year until she is 65, she will save $10,000 in a retirement account. If the account earns 10% per year, how much will Ellen have saved at age 65?

BDeH CHAPTER 4

Solution

▶ **Plan**

As always, we begin with a timeline. In this case, it is helpful to keep track of both the dates and Ellen's age:

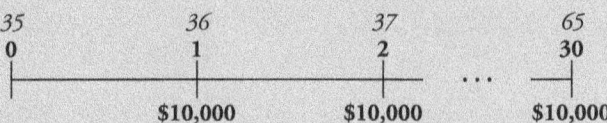

Ellen's savings plan looks like an annuity of $10,000 per year for 30 years. (*Hint:* It is easy to become confused when you just look at age, rather than at both dates and age. A common error is to think there are only $65 - 36 = 29$ payments. Writing down both dates and age avoids this problem.)

   To determine the amount Ellen will have in the bank at age 65, we'll need to compute the future value of this annuity.

▶ **Execute**

$$FV = \$10,000 \times \frac{1}{0.10}(1.10^{30} - 1)$$
$$= \$10,000 \times 164.49$$
$$= \$1.645 \text{ million at age 65}$$

Using a financial calculator or Excel:

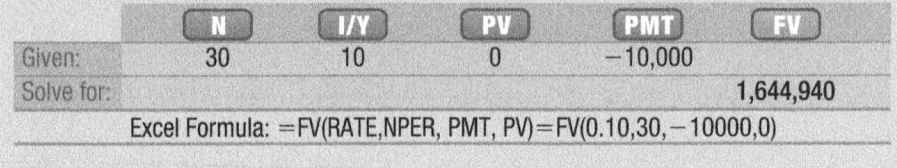

	N	I/Y	PV	PMT	FV
Given:	30	10	0	−10,000	
Solve for:					1,644,940

Excel Formula: =FV(RATE,NPER, PMT, PV)=FV(0.10,30,−10000,0)

▶ **Evaluate**

By investing $10,000 per year for 30 years (a total of $300,000) and earning interest on those investments, the compounding will allow her to retire with $1.645 million.

Growing Cash Flows

So far, we have considered only cash flow streams that have the same cash flow every period. If, instead, the cash flows are expected to grow at a constant rate in each period, we can also derive a simple formula for the present value of the future stream.

growing perpetuity A stream of cash flows that occurs at regular intervals and grows at a constant rate forever.

Growing Perpetuity. A **growing perpetuity** is a stream of cash flows that occur at regular intervals and grow at a constant rate forever. For example, a growing perpetuity with a first payment of $100 that grows at a rate of 3% has the following timeline:

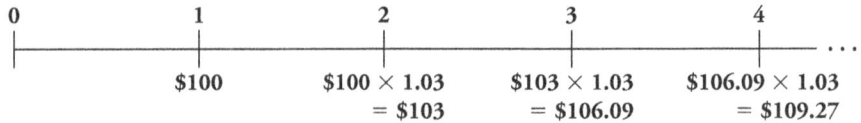

   To derive the formula for the present value of a growing perpetuity, we follow the same logic used for a regular perpetuity: Compute the amount you would need to deposit today to create the perpetuity yourself. In the case of a regular perpetuity, we created a constant payment forever by withdrawing the interest earned each year and reinvesting

BDeH CHAPTER 4

out a loan, you may know the amount you would like to borrow, but may not know the loan payments that will be required to repay it. Or, if you make a deposit into a bank account, you may want to calculate how long it will take before your balance reaches a certain level. In such situations, we use the present and/or future values as inputs, and solve for the variable we are interested in. We examine several special cases in this section.

Solving for the Cash Flows

Let's consider an example where we know the present value of an investment, but do not know the cash flows. The best example is a loan—you know how much you want to borrow (the present value) and you know the interest rate, but you do not know how much you need to repay each year. Suppose you are opening a business that requires an initial investment of $100,000. Your bank manager has agreed to lend you this money. The terms of the loan state that you will make equal annual payments for the next ten years and will pay an interest rate of 8% with the first payment due one year from today. What is your annual payment?

From the bank's perspective, the timeline looks like this:

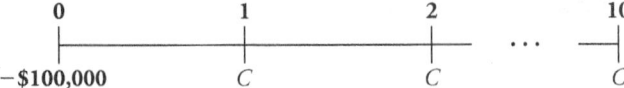

The bank will give you $100,000 today in exchange for ten equal payments over the next decade. You need to determine the size of the payment C that the bank will require. For the bank to be willing to lend you $100,000, the loan cash flows must have a present value of $100,000 when evaluated at the bank's interest rate of 8%. That is:

$100,000 = PV$(10-year annuity of C per year, evaluated at the loan rate)

Using the formula for the present value of an annuity,

$$100,000 = C \times \frac{1}{0.08}\left(1 - \frac{1}{1.08^{10}}\right) = C \times 6.71$$

solving this equation for C gives:

$$C = \frac{100,000}{6.71} = \$14,903$$

You will be required to make ten annual payments of $14,903 in exchange for $100,000 today.

We can also solve this problem with a financial calculator or Excel:

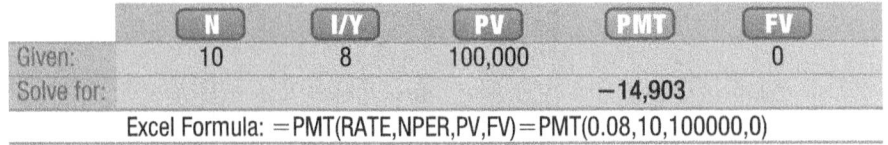

	N	I/Y	PV	PMT	FV
Given:	10	8	100,000		0
Solve for:				−14,903	
Excel Formula: =PMT(RATE,NPER,PV,FV)=PMT(0.08,10,100000,0)					

In general, when solving for a loan payment, think of the amount borrowed (the loan principal) as the present value of the payments. If the payments of the loan are an annuity, we can solve for the payment of the loan by inverting the annuity formula.

Writing the equation for the payments formally for a loan with principal P, requiring N periodic payments of C and interest rate r, we have:

Loan Payment

$$C = \frac{P}{\frac{1}{r}\left(1 - \frac{1}{(1+r)^N}\right)} \tag{4.8}$$

EXAMPLE 4.10

Computing a Loan Payment

Problem

Your firm plans to buy a warehouse for $100,000. The bank offers you a 30-year loan with equal annual payments and an interest rate of 8% per year. The bank requires that your firm pay 20% of the purchase price as a down payment, so you can borrow only $80,000. What is the annual loan payment?

Solution

▶ **Plan**

We start with the timeline (from the bank's perspective):

Using Eq. 4.8, we can solve for the loan payment, C, given $N = 30$, $r = 8\%$ (0.08) and $P = \$80,000$.

▶ **Execute**

Eq. 4.8 gives the following payment (cash flow):

$$C = \frac{P}{\frac{1}{r}\left(1 - \frac{1}{(1+r)^N}\right)} = \frac{80{,}000}{\frac{1}{0.08}\left(1 - \frac{1}{(1.08)^{30}}\right)}$$

$$= \$7106.19$$

Using a financial calculator or Excel:

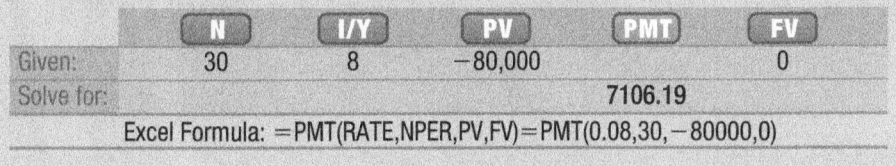

	N	I/Y	PV	PMT	FV
Given:	30	8	−80,000		0
Solve for:				7106.19	

Excel Formula: =PMT(RATE,NPER,PV,FV)=PMT(0.08,30,−80000,0)

▶ **Evaluate**

Your firm will need to pay $7106.19 each year to repay the loan. The bank is willing to accept these payments because the PV of 30 annual payments of $7106.19 at 8% interest rate per year is exactly equal to the $80,000 it is giving you today.

We can use this same idea to solve for the cash flows when we know the future value rather than the present value. As an example, suppose you have just graduated from college and you decide to be prudent and start saving for a down payment on a house. You would like to have $60,000 saved 10 years from now. If you can earn 7% per year on your savings, how much do you need to save each year to meet your goal?

The timeline for this example is:

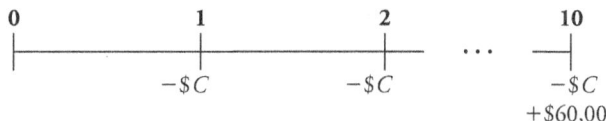

That is, you plan to save some amount C per year, and then withdraw $60,000 from the bank in ten years. Therefore, we need to find the annuity payment that has a future value of $60,000 in ten years. Use the formula for the future value of an annuity from Eq. 4.6:

$$60{,}000 = FV(\text{annuity}) = C \times \frac{1}{0.07}(1.07^{10} - 1) = C \times 13.816$$

Therefore, $C = \frac{60{,}000}{13.816} = \$4{,}343$. Thus, you need to save $4,343 per year. If you do, then at a 7% interest rate your savings will grow to $60,000 in 10 years when you are ready to buy a house.

Now let's solve this problem using a financial calculator or Excel:

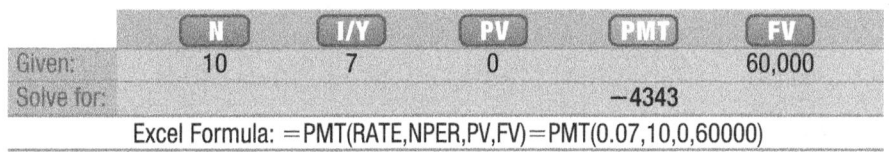

	N	I/Y	PV	PMT	FV
Given:	10	7	0		60,000
Solve for:				−4343	
Excel Formula: =PMT(RATE,NPER,PV,FV)=PMT(0.07,10,0,60000)					

Once again, we find that you need to save $4343 for 10 years to accumulate $60,000.

Internal Rate of Return

In some situations, you know the present value and cash flows of an investment opportunity but you do not know the interest rate that equates them. This interest rate is called the **internal rate of return (IRR)**, defined as the interest rate that sets the net present value of the cash flows equal to zero.

For example, suppose that you have an investment opportunity that requires a $1000 investment today and will have a $2000 payoff in six years. This would appear on a timeline as:

One way to analyze this investment is to ask the question: What interest rate, r, would you need so that the NPV of this investment is zero?

$$NPV = -1000 + \frac{2000}{(1 + r)^6} = 0$$

Rearranging this calculation gives the following:

$$1000 \times (1 + r)^6 = 2000$$

That is, r is the interest rate you would need to earn on your $1000 to have a future value of $2000 in six years. We can solve for r as follows:

$$1 + r = \left(\frac{2000}{1000}\right)^{\frac{1}{6}} = 1.1225$$

internal rate of return (IRR) The interest rate that sets the net present value of the cash flows equal to zero.

Or, $r = 12.25\%$. This rate is the IRR of this investment opportunity. Making this investment is like earning 12.25% per year on your money for six years.

When there are just two cash flows, as in the preceding example, it is easy to compute the IRR. Consider the general case in which you invest an amount P today, and receive FV in N years:

$$P \times (1 + IRR)^N = FV$$
$$1 + IRR = (FV/P)^{1/N}$$

That is, we take the total return of the investment over N years, FV/P, and convert it to an equivalent one-year rate by raising it to the power $1/N$.

Now let's consider a more sophisticated example. Suppose your firm needs to purchase a new forklift. The dealer gives you two options: (1) a price for the forklift if you pay cash and (2) the annual payments if you take out a loan from the dealer. To evaluate the loan that the dealer is offering you, you will want to compare the rate on the loan with the rate that your bank is willing to offer you. Given the loan payment that the dealer quotes, how do you compute the interest rate charged by the dealer?

In this case, we need to compute the IRR of the dealer's loan. Suppose the cash price of the forklift is $40,000, and the dealer offers financing with no down payment and four annual payments of $15,000. This loan has the following timeline:

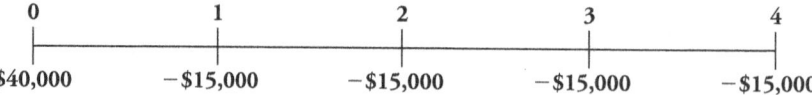

From the timeline, it is clear that the loan is a four-year annuity with a payment of $15,000 per year and a present value of $40,000. Setting the NPV of the cash flows equal to zero requires that the present value of the payments equals the purchase price:

$$40,000 = 15,000 \times \frac{1}{r}\left(1 - \frac{1}{(1 + r)^4}\right)$$

The value of r that solves this equation, the IRR, is the interest rate charged on the loan. Unfortunately, in this case there is no simple way to solve for the interest rate r.[4] The only way to solve this equation is to guess at values of r until you find the right one.

Start by guessing $r = 10\%$. In this case, the value of the annuity is:

$$15,000 \times \frac{1}{0.10}\left(1 - \frac{1}{(1.10)^4}\right) = 47,548$$

The present value of the payments is too large. To lower it, we need to use a higher interest rate. We guess 20% this time:

$$15,000 \times \frac{1}{0.20}\left(1 - \frac{1}{(1.20)^4}\right) = 38,831$$

Now the present value of the payments is too low, so we must pick a rate between 10% and 20%. We continue to guess until we find the right rate. Let's try 18.45%:

$$15,000 \times \frac{1}{0.1845}\left(1 - \frac{1}{(1.1845)^4}\right) = 40,000$$

The interest rate charged by the dealer is 18.45%.

---

[4]With five or more periods and general cash flows, there is *no* general formula to solve for r; trial and error (by hand or computer) is the *only* way to compute the IRR.

USING EXCEL

Computing NPV and IRR

Here we discuss how to use Microsoft ® Excel to solve for NPV and IRR. We also identify some pitfalls to avoid when using Excel.

NPV Function: Leaving Out Date 0

Excel's NPV function has the format, NPV (rate, value1, value2, . . .) where "rate" is the interest rate per period used to discount the cash flows, and "value1", "value2", etc., are the cash flows (or ranges of cash flows). The NPV function computes the present value of the cash flows *assuming the first cash flow occurs at date 1.* Therefore, if a project's first cash flow occurs at date 0, we cannot use the NPV function by itself to compute the NPV. We can use the NPV function to compute the present value of the cash flows from date 1 onwards, and then we must add the date 0 cash flow to that result to calculate the NPV. The screenshot below shows the difference. The first NPV calculation (outlined in blue) is correct: we used the NPV function for all of the cash flows occurring at time 1 and later and then added on the first cash flow occurring at time 0 since it is already in present value. The second (outlined in green) is incorrect: we used the NPV function for all of the cash flows, but the function assumed that the first cash flow occurs in period 1 instead of immediately.

NPV Function: Ignoring Blank Cells

Another pitfall with the NPV function is that cash flows that are left blank are treated differently from cash flows that are equal to zero. If the cash flow is left blank, *both the cash flow and the period are ignored.* For example, the second set of cash flows below is equivalent to the first—we have simply left the cash flow for date 2 blank instead of entering a "0." However, the NPV function ignores the blank cell at date 2 and assumes the cash flow is 10 at date 1 and 110 at date 2, which is clearly not what is intended and produces an incorrect answer (outlined in red).

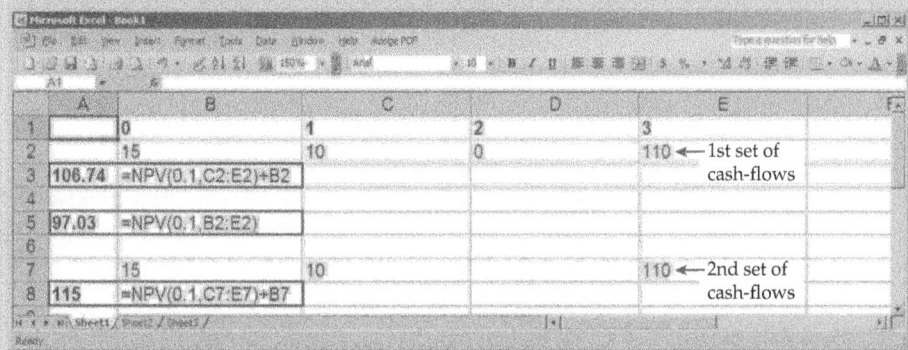

Because of these idiosyncrasies, we avoid using Excel's NPV function. It is more reliable to compute the present value of each cash flow separately in Excel, and then sum them to determine the NPV.

IRR Function

Excel's IRR function has the format IRR (values, guess), where "values" is the range containing the cash flows, and "guess" is an optional starting guess where Excel begins its search for an IRR. Two things to note about the IRR function:

1. The values given to the IRR function should include all of the cash flows of the project, including the one at date 0. In this sense, the IRR and NPV functions in Excel are inconsistent.

2. Like the NPV function, the IRR ignores the period associated with any blank cells.

An easier solution than guessing the IRR and manually calculating values is to use a spreadsheet or calculator to automate the guessing process. When the cash flows are an annuity, as in this example, we can use a financial calculator or Excel to compute the IRR. Both solve (with slightly varying notation) the following equation:

$$NPV = PV + PMT \times \frac{1}{I/Y}\left(1 - \frac{1}{(1 + I/Y)^N}\right) + \frac{FV}{(1 + I/Y)^N} = 0$$

The equation ensures that the NPV of investing in the annuity is zero. When the unknown variable is the interest rate, it will solve for the interest rate that sets the NPV equal to zero—that is, the IRR. For this case, you could use a financial calculator or Excel, as follows:

	N	I/Y	PV	PMT	FV
Given:	4		40,000	−15,000	0
Solve for:		18.45			

Excel Formula: =RATE(NPER,PMT,PV,FV)=RATE(4,−15000,40000,0)

Both the financial calculator and Excel correctly compute an IRR of 18.45%.

EXAMPLE 4.11

Personal Finance

Computing the Internal Rate of Return with a Financial Calculator

Problem

Let's return to the lottery prize in Example 4.7. How high of a rate of return do you need to earn investing on your own in order to prefer the $15 million payout?

Solution

▶ **Plan**

Recall that the lottery offers you the following deal: take either (a) $15 million lump sum payment immediately, or (b) 30 payments of $1 million per year starting immediately. This second option is an annuity of 29 payments of $1 million plus an initial $1 million payment.

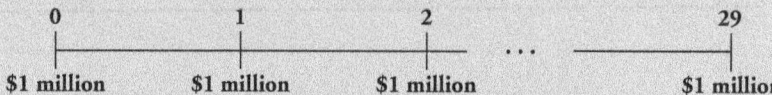

We need to solve for the internal rate of return that makes the two offers equivalent. Anything above that rate of return would make the present value of the annuity lower than the $15 million lump sum payment, and anything below that rate of return would make it greater than the $15 million.

▶ **Execute**

First, we set the present value of option (b) equal to option (a), which is already in present value since it is an immediate payment of $15 million:

$$\$15 \text{ million} = \$1 \text{ million} + \$1 \text{ million} \times \frac{1}{r}\left(1 - \frac{1}{(1 + r)^{29}}\right)$$

$$\$14 \text{ million} = \$1 \text{ million} \times \frac{1}{r}\left(1 - \frac{1}{(1 + r)^{29}}\right)$$

Using a financial calculator to solve for r:

	N	I/Y	PV	PMT	FV
Given:	29		−14,000,000	1,000,000	0
Solve for:		5.72			

Excel Formula: =RATE(NPER,PMT,PV,FV)=RATE(29,1000000,−14000000,0)

The IRR equating the two options is 5.72%.

> **Evaluate**
> 5.72% is the rate of return that makes giving up the $15 million payment and taking the 30 installments of $1 million exactly a zero NPV action. If you could earn more than 5.72% investing on your own, then you could take the $15 million, invest it and generate 30 installments that are each more than $1 million. If you could not earn at least 5.72% on your investments, you would be unable to replicate the $1 million installments on your own and would be better off taking the installment plan.

Solving for the Number of Periods

In addition to solving for cash flows or the interest rate, we can solve for the amount of time it will take a sum of money to grow to a known value. In this case, the interest rate, present value, and future value are all known. We need to compute how long it will take for the present value to grow to the future value.

Suppose we invest $10,000 in an account paying 10% interest, and we want to know how long it will take for the amount to grow to $20,000.

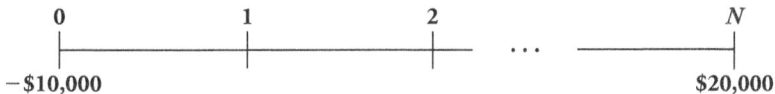

We want to determine N.

In terms of our formulas, we need to find N so that the future value of our investment equals $20,000:

$$FV = \$10{,}000 \times 1.10^{N} = \$20{,}000 \qquad (4.9)$$

One approach is to use trial and error to find N, as with the IRR. For example, with $N = 7$ years, $FV = \$19{,}487$, so it will take longer than 7 years. With $N = 8$ years, $FV = \$21{,}436$, so it will take between 7 and 8 years.

Alternatively, this problem can be solved on a financial calculator or Excel. In this case, we solve for N:

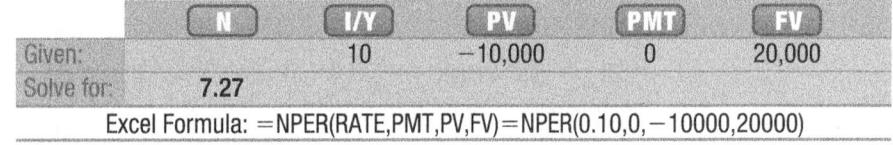

It will take about 7.3 years for our savings to grow to $20,000.

> ### Solving for N Using Logarithms
>
> The problem of solving for the number of periods can be solved mathematically as well. Dividing both sides of Eq. 4.9 by $10,000, we have:
>
> $$1.10^{N} = 20{,}000 / 10{,}000 = 2$$
>
> To solve for an exponent, we take the logarithm of both sides, and use the fact that $\ln(x^{y}) = y\ln(x)$:
>
> $$N\ln(1.10) = \ln(2)$$
> $$N = \ln(2)/\ln(1.10) = 0.6931/0.0953 \approx 7.3 \text{ years}$$

EXAMPLE 4.12

Personal Finance
Solving for the
Number of Periods
in a Savings Plan

Problem

Let's return to your savings for a down payment on a house. Imagine that some time has passed and you have $10,050 saved already, and you can now afford to save $5000 per year at the end of each year. Also, interest rates have increased so that you now earn 7.25% per year on your savings. How long will it take you to get to your goal of $60,000?

Solution

▶ **Plan**

The timeline for this problem is:

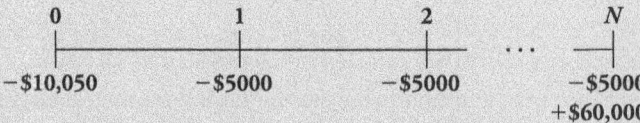

We need to find N so that the future value of your current savings plus the future value of your planned additional savings (which is an annuity) equals your desired amount. There are two contributors to the future value: the initial lump sum of $10,050 that will continue to earn interest, and the annuity contributions of $5,000 per year that will earn interest as they are contributed. Thus, we need to find the future value of the lump sum plus the future value of the annuity.

▶ **Execute**

We can solve this problem using a financial calculator or Excel:

	N	I/Y	PV	PMT	FV
Given:		7.25	−10,050	−5000	60,000
Solve for:	7.00				

Excel Formula: =NPER(RATE,PMT,PV,FV)=NPER(0.0725,−5000,−10050,60000)

There is also a mathematical solution. We can calculate the future value of the initial cash flow by using Eq. 4.1 and the future value of the annuity using Eq. 4.6:

$$10{,}050 \times 1.0725^N + 5000 \times \frac{1}{0.0725}(1.0725^N - 1) = 60{,}000$$

Rearranging the equation to solve for N,

$$1.0725^N = \frac{60{,}000 \times 0.0725 + 5000}{10{,}050 \times 0.0725 + 5000} = 1.632$$

we can then solve for N:

$$N = \frac{\ln(1.632)}{\ln(1.0725)} = 7 \text{ years}$$

▶ **Evaluate**

It will take seven years to save the down payment.

We began this chapter with the goal of developing the tools a financial manager needs to be able to apply the Valuation Principle by computing the net present value of a decision. Starting from the fundamental concept of the time value of money—a dollar today is worth more than a dollar tomorrow—we learned how to calculate the equivalent value of future cash flows today and today's cash flows in the future. We then learned some

BDeH CHAPTER 4

shortcuts for handling common sets of regular cash flows such as those found in perpetuities and loans. As we have seen, the discount rate is a critical input to any of our present value or future value calculations. Throughout this chapter, we have taken the discount rate as given.

What determines these discount rates? The Valuation Principle shows us that we must rely on market information to assess the value of cash flows across time. In the next chapter, we will learn the drivers of market interest rates as well as how they are quoted. Understanding interest rate quoting conventions will also allow us to extend the tools we developed in this chapter to situations where the interest rate is compounded more frequently than once per year.

Concept Check

11. How do you calculate the cash flow of an annuity?

12. What is the internal rate of return, and how do you calculate it?

13. How do you solve for the number of periods to pay off an annuity?

Here is what you should know after reading this chapter. MyFinanceLab will help you identify what you know, and where to go when you need to practice.

Key Points and Equations	Terms	Online Practice Opportunities
4.1 The Timeline ▸ Timelines are a critical first step in organizing the cash flows in a financial problem.	stream of cash flows, p. 88 timeline, p. 88	MyFinanceLab Study Plan 4.1

4.2 Valuing Cash Flows at Different Points in Time
▸ There are three rules of valuing cash flows:
  a. Only cash flows that occur at the same point in time can be compared or combined.
  b. To calculate a cash flow's future value, you must compound it.
  c. To calculate a cash flow's present value, you must discount it.
▸ The future value in n years of a cash flow C today is:
$$C \times (1 + r)^n \qquad (4.1)$$
▸ The present value today of a cash flow C received in n years is:
$$C \div (1 + r)^n \qquad (4.2)$$
	compounding, p. 91
	compound interest, p. 91
	discounting, p. 93
	future value, p. 91
		MyFinanceLab Study Plan 4.2

BDeH   CHAPTER 4

4.3 Valuing a Stream of Cash Flows

▶ The present value of a cash flow stream is:

$$PV = C_0 + \frac{C_1}{(1 + r)} + \frac{C_2}{(1 + r)^2} + \cdots + \frac{C_N}{(1 + r)^N} \quad (4.3)$$

MyFinanceLab
Study Plan 4.3

4.4 The Net Present Value of a Stream of Cash Flows

▶ The NPV of an investment opportunity is $PV(\text{benefits} - \text{costs})$.

MyFinanceLab
Study Plan 4.4

4.5 Perpetuities, Annuities, and Other Special Cases

▶ A perpetuity is a constant cash flow C paid every period, forever. The present value of a perpetuity is:

$$PV \text{ (C in perpetuity)} = \frac{C}{r} \quad (4.4)$$

▶ An annuity is a constant cash flow C paid every period for N periods. The present value of an annuity is:

$$C \times \frac{1}{r}\left(1 - \frac{1}{(1 + r)^N}\right) \quad (4.5)$$

▶ The future value of an annuity at the end of the annuity is:

$$C \times \frac{1}{r}((1 + r)^N - 1) \quad (4.6)$$

▶ In a growing perpetuity, the cash flows grow at a constant rate g each period. The present value of a growing perpetuity is:

$$\frac{C}{r - g} \quad (4.7)$$

annuity, p. 104
consol, p. 101
growing perpetuity,
p. 108
perpetuity, p. 101

MyFinanceLab
Study Plan 4.5
Interactive Annuity
Calculator

4.6 Solving for Variables Other Than Present Value or Future Value

▶ The annuity and perpetuity formulas can be used to solve for the annuity payments when either the present value or the future value is known.
▶ The periodic payment on an N-period loan with principal P and interest rate r is:

$$C = \frac{P}{\frac{1}{r}\left(1 - \frac{1}{(1 + r)^N}\right)} \quad (4.8)$$

▶ The internal rate of return (IRR) of an investment opportunity is the interest rate that sets the NPV of the investment opportunity equal to zero.
▶ The annuity formulas can be used to solve for the number of periods it takes to save a fixed amount of money.

internal rate of return
(IRR), p. 113

MyFinanceLab
Study Plan 4.6
Using Excel:
Computing NPV
and IRR

Review Questions

1. Why is a cash flow in the future worth less than the same amount today?

2. What is compound interest?

3. What is the intuition behind the geometric growth in interest?

4. What is a discount rate?

5. What is the intuition behind the fact that the present value of a stream of cash flows is just the sum of the present values of each individual cash flow?

6. What must be true about the cash flow stream in order for us to be able to use the shortcut formulas?

7. What is the difference between an annuity and a perpetuity?

8. What is an internal rate of return?

Problems

All problems in this chapter are available in MyFinanceLab. An asterisk (*) indicates problems with a higher level of difficulty.

The Timeline

1. You have just taken out a five-year loan from a bank to buy an engagement ring. The ring costs $5000. You plan to put down $1000 and borrow $4000. You will need to make annual payments of $1000 at the end of each year. Show the timeline of the loan from your perspective. How would the timeline differ if you created it from the bank's perspective?

2. You currently have a one-year-old loan outstanding on your car. You make monthly payments of $300. You have just made a payment. The loan has four years to go (i.e., it had an original term of five years). Show the timeline from your perspective. How would the timeline differ if you created it from the bank's perspective?

Valuing Cash Flows

3. Calculate the future value of $2000 in
   a. 5 years at an interest rate of 5% per year.
   b. 10 years at an interest rate of 5% per year.
   c. 5 years at an interest rate of 10% per year.
   d. Why is the amount of interest earned in part (a) less than half the amount of interest earned in part (b)?

4. What is the present value of $10,000 received
   a. 12 years from today when the interest rate is 4% per year?
   b. 20 years from today when the interest rate is 8% per year?
   c. 6 years from today when the interest rate is 2% per year?

5. Your brother has offered to give you either $5000 today or $10,000 in 10 years. If the interest rate is 7% per year, which option is preferable?

6. Your cousin is currently 12 years old. She will be going to college in six years. Your aunt and uncle would like to have $100,000 in a savings account to fund her education at that time. If the account promises to pay a fixed interest rate of 4% per

year, how much money do they need to put into the account today to ensure that they will have $100,000 in six years?

7. Your mom is thinking of retiring. Her retirement plan will pay her either $250,000 immediately on retirement or $350,000 five years after the date of her retirement. Which alternative should she choose if the interest rate is
a. 0% per year?
b. 8% per year?
c. 20% per year?

8. Your grandfather put some money in an account for you on the day you were born. You are now 18 years old and are allowed to withdraw the money for the first time. The account currently has $3996 in it and pays an 8% interest rate.
a. How much money would be in the account if you left the money there until your twenty-fifth birthday?
b. What if you left the money until your sixty-fifth birthday?
c. How much money did your grandfather originally put in the account?

Valuing a Stream of Cash Flows

9. You have just received a windfall from an investment you made in a friend's business. She will be paying you $10,000 at the end of this year, $20,000 at the end of the following year, and $30,000 at the end of the year after that (three years from today). The interest rate is 3.5% per year.
a. What is the present value of your windfall?
b. What is the future value of your windfall in three years (on the date of the last payment)?

10. You have a loan outstanding. It requires making three annual payments of $1000 each at the end of the next three years. Your bank has offered to allow you to skip making the next two payments in lieu of making one large payment at the end of the loan's term in three years. If the interest rate on the loan is 5%, what final payment will the bank require you to make so that it is indifferent to the two forms of payment?

11. You are wondering whether it is worth it to go to college. You figure that the total cost of going to college for four years, including lost wages, is $40,000 per year. However, you feel that if you get a college degree, the present value of your lifetime wages from graduation onward will be $300,000 greater than if you did not go to college. If your discount rate is 9%, what is the NPV of going to college?

The Net Present Value of a Stream of Cash Flows

12. You have been offered a unique investment opportunity. If you invest $10,000 today, you will receive $500 one year from now, $1500 two years from now, and $10,000 ten years from now.
a. What is the NPV of the opportunity if the interest rate is 6% per year? Should you take the opportunity?
b. What is the NPV of the opportunity if the interest rate is 2% per year? Should you take it now?

13. Marian Plunket owns her own business and is considering an investment. If she undertakes the investment, it will pay $4000 at the end of each of the next three years. The opportunity requires an initial investment of $1000 plus an additional investment at the end of the second year of $5000. What is the NPV of this opportunity if the interest rate is 2% per year? Should Marian take it?

BDeH CHAPTER 4

Perpetuities, Annuities, and Other Special Cases

14. Your friend majoring in mechanical engineering has invented a money machine. The main drawback of the machine is that it is slow. It takes one year to manufacture $100. However, once built, the machine will last forever and will require no maintenance. The machine can be built immediately, but it will cost $1000 to build. Your friend wants to know if she should invest the money to construct it. If the interest rate is 9.5% per year, what should your friend do?

15. How would your answer to Problem 14 change if the machine takes one year to build?

16. The British government has a consol bond outstanding paying £100 per year forever. Assume the current interest rate is 4% per year.
    a. What is the value of the bond immediately after a payment is made?
    b. What is the value of the bond immediately before a payment is made?

17. What is the present value of $1000 paid at the end of each of the next 100 years if the interest rate is 7% per year?

*18. When you purchased your car, you took out a five-year annual-payment loan with an interest rate of 6% per year. The annual payment on the car is $5000. You have just made a payment and have now decided to pay the loan off by repaying the outstanding balance. What is the payoff amount if
    a. you have owned the car for one year (so there are four years left on the loan)?
    b. you have owned the car for four years (so there is one year left on the loan)?

19. Your grandmother has been putting $1000 into a savings account on every birthday since your first (that is, when you turned one). The account pays an interest rate of 3%. How much money will be in the account on your eighteenth birthday immediately after your grandmother makes the deposit on that birthday?

20. Assume that your parents wanted to have $160,000 saved for college by your eighteenth birthday and they started saving on your first birthday. If they saved the same amount each year on your birthday and earned 8% per year on their investments,
    a. how much would they have to save each year to reach their goal?
    b. if they think you will take five years instead of four to graduate and decide to have $200,000 saved just in case, how much more would they have to save each year to reach their new goal?

21. A rich relative has bequeathed you a growing perpetuity. The first payment will occur in a year and will be $1000. Each year after that, you will receive a payment on the anniversary of the last payment that is 8% larger than the last payment. This pattern of payments will go on forever. If the interest rate is 12% per year,
    a. what is today's value of the bequest?
    b. what is the value of the bequest immediately after the first payment is made?

*22. You are thinking of building a new machine that will save you $1000 in the first year. The machine will then begin to wear out so that the savings decline at a rate of 2% per year forever. What is the present value of the savings if the interest rate is 5% per year?

23. You work for a pharmaceutical company that has developed a new drug. The patent on the drug will last 17 years. You expect that the drug's profits will be $2 million in its first year and that this amount will grow at a rate of 5% per year for the next 17 years. Once the patent expires, other pharmaceutical companies will be able to produce the same drug and competition will likely drive profits to zero. What is the present value of the new drug if the interest rate is 10% per year?

24. A rich aunt has promised you $5000 one year from today. In addition, each year after that, she has promised you a payment (on the anniversary of the last payment) that is 5% larger than the last payment. She will continue to show this generosity for 20 years, giving a total of 20 payments. If the interest rate is 5%, what is her promise worth today?

 *25. You are running a hot Internet company. Analysts predict that its earnings will grow at 30% per year for the next five years. After that, as competition increases, earnings growth is expected to slow to 2% per year and continue at that level forever. Your company has just announced earnings of $1 million. What is the present value of all future earnings if the interest rate is 8%? (Assume all cash flows occur at the end of the year.)

 *26. When Alex Rodriguez moved to the Texas Rangers, he received a lot of attention for his "$252 million" contract (the total of the payments promised was $252 million). Assume the following:

Rodriguez earns $16 million in the first year, $17 million in years 2 through 4, $19 million in years 5 and 6, $23 million in year 7, and $27 million in years 8 through 10. He would also receive his $10 million signing bonus spread equally over the first 5 years ($2 million per year). His deferred payments will begin in 2011. The deferred payment amounts total $33 million and are $5 million, then $4 million, then 8 amounts of $3 million (ending in 2020). However, the actual payouts will be different. All of the deferred payments will earn 3% per year until they are paid. For example, the $5 million is deferred from 2001 to 2011, or 10 years, meaning that it will actually be $6.7196 million when paid. Assume that the $4 million payment deferred to 2012 is deferred from 2002 (each payment is deferred 10 years).

The contract is a 10-year contract, but each year has a deferred component so that cash flows are paid out over a total of 20 years. The contractual payments, signing bonus, and deferred components are given below. Note that, by contract, the deferred components are not paid in the year they are earned, but instead are paid (plus interest) 10 years later.

2001	2002	2003	2004	2005	2006	2007	2008	2009	2010
$16M	$17M	$17M	$17M	$19M	$19M	$23M	$27M	$27M	$27M
$2M	$2M	$2M	$2M	$2M					
Deferred									
$5M	$4M	$3M	$3M	$3M	$3M	$3M	$3M	$3M	$3M

Assume that an appropriate discount rate for A-Rod to apply to the contract payments is 7% per year.
a. Calculate the true promised payments under this contract, including the deferred payments with interest.
b. Draw a timeline of all of the payments.
c. Calculate the present value of the contract.
d. Compare the present value of the contract to the quoted value of $252 million. What explains the difference?

 *27. You are trying to decide how much to save for retirement. Assume you plan to save $5000 per year with the first investment made 1 year from now. You think you can earn 10% per year on your investments and you plan to retire in 43 years, immediately after making your last $5000 investment.

a. How much will you have in your retirement account on the day you retire?

b. If, instead of investing $5000 per year, you wanted to make one lump-sum investment today for your retirement, how much would that lump sum need to be?

c. If you hope to live for 20 years in retirement, how much can you withdraw every year in retirement (starting one year after retirement) so that you will just exhaust your savings with the twentieth withdrawal (assume your savings will continue to earn 10% in retirement)?

d. If, instead, you decide to withdraw $300,000 per year in retirement (again with the first withdrawal one year after retiring), how many years will it take until you exhaust your savings?

 e. Assuming the most you can afford to save is $5000 per year, but you want to retire with $1 million in your investment account, how high of a return do you need to earn on your investments?

Solving for Variables Other Than Present Value or Future Value

28. You have decided to buy a perpetuity. The bond makes one payment at the end of every year forever and has an interest rate of 5%. If you initially put $1000 into the bond, what is the payment every year?

29. You are thinking of purchasing a house. The house costs $350,000. You have $50,000 in cash that you can use as a down payment on the house, but you need to borrow the rest of the purchase price. The bank is offering a 30-year mortgage that requires annual payments and has an interest rate of 7% per year. What will your annual payment be if you sign up for this mortgage?

*30. You are thinking about buying a piece of art that costs $50,000. The art dealer is proposing the following deal: He will lend you the money, and you will repay the loan by making the same payment every two years for the next 20 years (i.e., a total of 10 payments). If the interest rate is 4% per year, how much will you have to pay every two years?

*31. You would like to buy the house and take the mortgage described in Problem 29. You can afford to pay only $23,500 per year. The bank agrees to allow you to pay this amount each year, yet still borrow $300,000. At the end of the mortgage (in 30 years), you must make a balloon payment; that is, you must repay the remaining balance on the mortgage. How much will this balloon payment be?

32. You are saving for retirement. To live comfortably, you decide you will need to save $2 million by the time you are 65. Today is your twenty-second birthday, and you decide, starting today and continuing on every birthday up to and including your 65th birthday, that you will put the same amount into a savings account. If the interest rate is 5%, how much must you set aside each year to make sure that you will have $2 million in the account on your 65th birthday?

*33. You realize that the plan in Problem 32 has a flaw. Because your income will increase over your lifetime, it would be more realistic to save less now and more later. Instead of putting the same amount aside each year, you decide to let the amount that you set aside grow by 7% per year. Under this plan, how much will you put into the account today? (Recall that you are planning to make the first contribution to the account today.)

34. You have an investment opportunity that requires an initial investment of $5000 today and will pay $6000 in one year. What is the IRR of this opportunity?

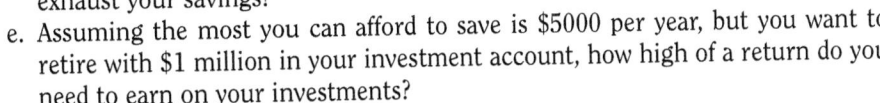

35. You are shopping for a car and read the following advertisement in the newspaper: "Own a new Spitfire! No money down. Four annual payments of just $10,000." You have shopped around and know that you can buy a Spitfire for cash for $32,500. What is the interest rate the dealer is advertising (what is the IRR of the loan in the advertisement)? Assume that you must make the annual payments at the end of each year.

36. A local bank is running the following advertisement in the newspaper: "For just $1000 we will pay you $100 forever!" The fine print in the ad says that for a $1000 deposit, the bank will pay $100 every year in perpetuity, starting one year after the deposit is made. What interest rate is the bank advertising (what is the IRR of this investment)?

*37. The Tillamook County Creamery Association manufactures Tillamook Cheddar Cheese. It markets this cheese in 4 varieties: aged 2 months, 9 months, 15 months, and 2 years. At the shop in the dairy, 2 pounds of each variety sells for the following prices: $7.95, $9.49, $10.95, and $11.95, respectively. Consider the cheese maker's decision whether to continue to age a particular 2-pound block of cheese. At 2 months, he can either sell the cheese immediately or let it age further. If he sells it now, he will receive $7.95 immediately. If he ages the cheese, he must give up the $7.95 today to receive a higher amount in the future. What is the IRR (expressed in percent per month) of the investment of giving up $79.50 today by choosing to store 20 pounds of cheese that is currently 2 months old and instead selling 10 pounds of this cheese when it has aged 9 months, 6 pounds when it has aged 15 months, and the remaining 4 pounds when it has aged 2 years?

*38. Your grandmother bought an annuity from Rock Solid Life Insurance Company for $200,000 when she retired. In exchange for the $200,000, Rock Solid will pay her $25,000 per year until she dies. The interest rate is 5%. How long must she live after the day she retired to come out ahead (that is, to get more in value than what she paid in)?

*39. You are thinking of making an investment in a new plant. The plant will generate revenues of $1 million per year for as long as you maintain it. You expect that the maintenance costs will start at $50,000 per year and will increase 5% per year thereafter. Assume that all revenue and maintenance costs occur at the end of the year. You intend to run the plant as long as it continues to make a positive cash flow (as long as the cash generated by the plant exceeds the maintenance costs). The plant can be built and become operational immediately. If the plant costs $10 million to build, and the interest rate is 6% per year, should you invest in the plant?

*40. You have just turned 22 years old, have just received your bachelors degree, and have accepted your first job. Now you must decide how much money to put into your retirement plan. The plan works as follows: Every dollar in the plan earns 7% per year. You cannot make withdrawals until you retire on your sixty-fifth birthday. After that point, you can make withdrawals as you see fit. You decide that you will plan to live to 100 and work until you turn 65. You estimate that to live comfortably in retirement, you will need $100,000 per year, starting at the end of the first year of retirement and ending on your one-hundredth birthday. You will contribute the same amount to the plan at the end of every year that you work. How much do you need to contribute each year to fund your retirement?

*41. Problem 39 is not very realistic because most retirement plans do not allow you to specify a fixed amount to contribute every year. Instead, you are required to specify a fixed percentage of your salary that you want to contribute. Assume that your starting salary is $45,000 per year and it will grow 3% per year until you retire. Assuming everything else stays the same as in Problem 39, what percentage of your income do you need to contribute to the plan every year to fund the same retirement income?

Data Case

Assume today is August 1, 2007. Natasha Kingery is 30 years old and has a bachelor of science degree in computer science. She is currently employed as a Tier 2 field service representative for a telephony corporation located in Seattle, Washington, and earns $38,000 a year that she anticipates will grow at 3% per year. Natasha hopes to retire at age 65 and has just begun to think about the future.

Natasha has $75,000 that she recently inherited from her aunt. She invested this money in ten-year Treasury Bonds. She is considering whether she should further her education and would use her inheritance to pay for it.

She has investigated a couple of options and is asking for your help as a financial planning intern to determine the financial consequences associated with each option. Natasha has already been accepted to both of these programs, and could start either one soon.

One alternative that Natasha is considering is attaining a certification in network design. This certification would automatically promote her to a Tier 3 field service representative in her company. The base salary for a Tier 3 representative is $10,000 more than what she currently earns and she anticipates that this salary differential will grow at a rate of 3% a year as long as she keeps working. The certification program requires the completion of 20 Web-based courses and a score of 80% or better on an exam at the end of the course work. She has learned that the average amount of time necessary to finish the program is one year. The total cost of the program is $5,000, due when she enrolls in the program. Because she will do all the work for the certification on her own time, Natasha does not expect to lose any income during the certification.

Another option is going back to school for an MBA degree. With an MBA degree, Natasha expects to be promoted to a managerial position in her current firm. The managerial position pays $20,000 a year more than her current position. She expects that this salary differential will also grow at a rate of 3% per year for as long as she keeps working. The evening program, which will take three years to complete, costs $25,000 per year, due at the beginning of each of her three years in school. Because she will attend classes in the evening, Natasha doesn't expect to lose any income while she is earning her MBA if she chooses to undertake the MBA.

1. Determine the interest rate Natasha is currently earning on her inheritance by going to Yahoo! Finance (http://finance.yahoo.com) and clicking on the 10 YR Bond link in the Market Summary section. Then go to the Historical Prices link and enter the appropriate date, August 1, 2007, to obtain the closing yield or interest rate that she is earning. Use this interest rate as the discount rate for the remainder of this problem.

2. Create a timeline in Excel for her current situation, as well as the certification program and MBA degree options, using the following assumptions:
   a. Salaries for the year are paid only once, at the end of the year.
   b. The salary increase becomes effective immediately upon graduating from the MBA program or being certified. That is, because the increases become effective immediately but salaries are paid at the end of the year, the first salary increase will be paid exactly one year after graduation or certification.

3. Calculate the present value of the salary differential for completing the certification program. Subtract the cost of the program to get the NPV of undertaking the certification program.

4. Calculate the present value of the salary differential for completing the MBA degree. Calculate the present value of the cost of the MBA program. Based on your calculations, determine the NPV of undertaking the MBA.

5. Based on your answers to Questions 3 and 4, what advice would you give to Natasha? What if the two programs are mutually exclusive? If Natasha undertakes one of the programs, there is no further benefit to undertaking the other program. Would your advice change?

Chapter 4 APPENDIX   Using a Financial Calculator

Specifying Decimal Places

Make sure you have plenty of decimal places displayed!

HP-10BII

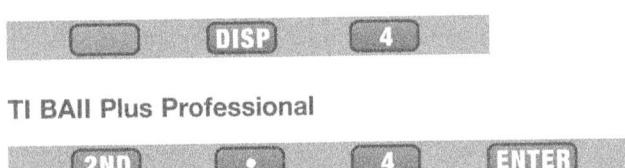

TI BAII Plus Professional

Toggling Between the Beginning and End of a Period

You should always make sure that your calculator is in *end-of-period* mode.

HP-10BII

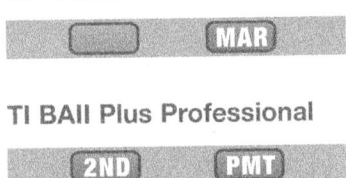

TI BAII Plus Professional

Set the Number of Periods per Year

You will avoid a lot of confusion later if you always set your periods per year "P/Y" to 1:

HP-10BII

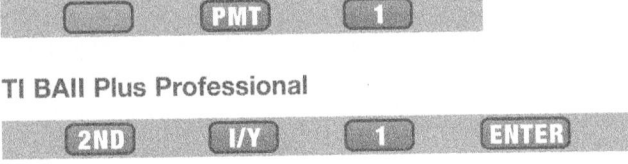

TI BAII Plus Professional

General TVM Buttons

HP-10BII

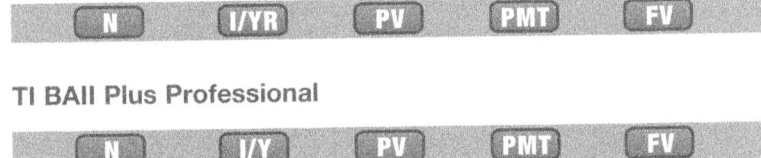

TI BAII Plus Professional

BDeH CHAPTER 4

Solving for the Present Value of a Single Future Cash Flow (Example 4.2)

You are considering investing in a savings bond that will pay $15,000 in ten years. If the competitive market interest rate is fixed at 6% per year, what is the bond worth today? [Answer: 8375.92]

HP-10BII

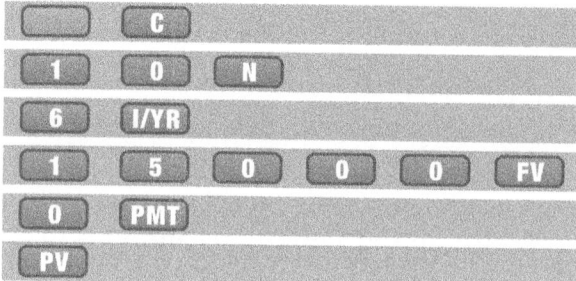

Press [Orange Shift] and then the [C] button to clear all previous entries.

Enter the Number of periods.

Enter the market annual interest rate.

Enter the Value you will recieve in 10 periods.

Indicate that there are no payments.

Solve for the Present Value.

TI-BAII Plus Professional

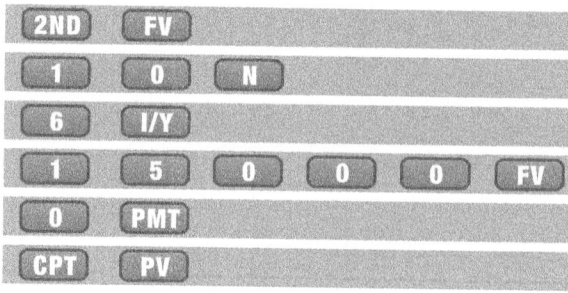

Press [2ND] and then the [FV] button to clear all previous entries.

Enter the Number of periods.

Enter the market annual interest rate.

Enter the Value you will recieve in 10 periods.

Indicate that there are no payments.

Solve for the Present Value.

Solving for the Future Value of an Annuity (Example 4.8)

Ellen is 35 years old, and she has decided it is time to plan seriously for her retirement. At the end of each year until she is 65, she will save $10,000 in a retirement account. If the account earns 10% per year, how much will Ellen have saved at age 65? [Answer: 1,644,940]

HP-10BII

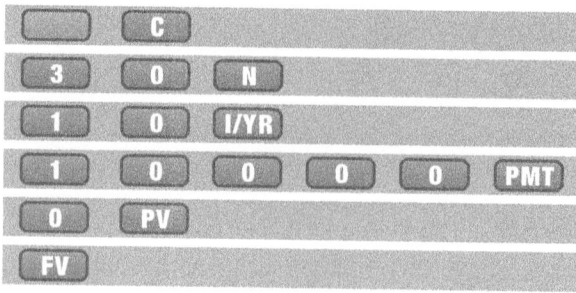

Press [Orange Shift] and then the [C] button to clear all previous entries.

Enter the Number of periods.

Enter the market annual interest rate.

Enter the Payment amount per period.

Indicate that there is no initial amount in the retirement account.

Solve for the Future Value.

TI-BAII Plus Professional

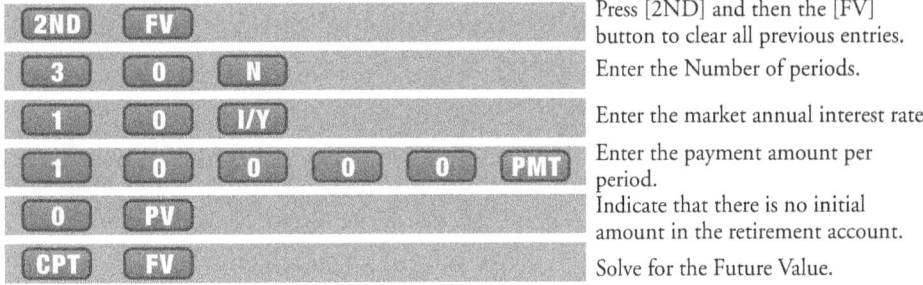

		Press [2ND] and then the [FV] button to clear all previous entries.
3	0	N	Enter the Number of periods.
1	0	I/Y	Enter the market annual interest rate.
1	0	0	0	0	PMT	Enter the payment amount per period.
0	PV	Indicate that there is no initial amount in the retirement account.
CPT	FV	Solve for the Future Value.

Solving for the Internal Rate of Return

If you have an initial cash outflow of $2000 and one cash inflow per year for the following four years of $1000, $400, $400, and $800, what is the internal rate of return on the project per year? [Answer: 12.12%]

HP-10BII

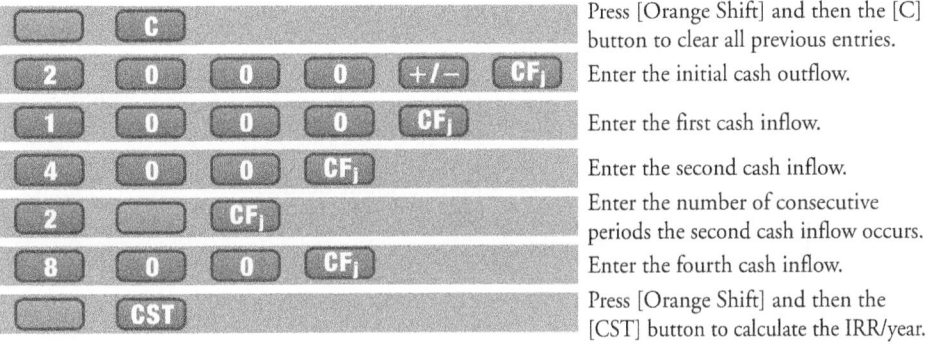

Press [Orange Shift] and then the [C] button to clear all previous entries.

2 0 0 0 +/− CF$_j$ Enter the initial cash outflow.

1 0 0 0 CF$_j$ Enter the first cash inflow.

4 0 0 CF$_j$ Enter the second cash inflow.

2 CF$_j$ Enter the number of consecutive periods the second cash inflow occurs.

8 0 0 CF$_j$ Enter the fourth cash inflow.

CST   Press [Orange Shift] and then the [CST] button to calculate the IRR/year.

TI-BAII Plus Professional

CF	Access Cash Flow Worksheet.
2ND CE|C	Press [2ND] and then the [CE|C] button to clear all previous entries.
2 0 0 0 +/− ENTER	Enter the initial cash outflow.
↓ 1 0 0 0 ENTER	Enter the first cash inflow.
↓	Leave the frequency of the initial cash inflow at 1 (Default Setting).
↓ 4 0 0 ENTER	Enter the second cash inflow.
↓ 2 ENTER	Enter the frequency of the second cash inflow as 2.
↓ 8 0 0 ENTER	Enter the fourth cash inflow.
↓	Leave the frequency of the fourth cash inflow at 1 (Default Setting).
IRR CPT	Solve for the IRR.

BDeH CHAPTER 4

Interest Rates

LEARNING OBJECTIVES

▶ Understand the different ways interest rates are quoted

▶ Use quoted rates to calculate loan payments and balances

▶ Know how inflation, expectations, and risk combine to determine interest rates

▶ See the link between interest rates in the market and a firm's opportunity cost of capital

notation

APR	annual percentage rate		*n*	number of periods
APY	annual percentage yield		*NPV*	net present value
C	cash flow		*PV*	present value
C_n	cash flow that arrives in period *n*		*r*	interest rate or discount rate
EAR	effective annual rate		r_n	interest rate or discount rate for an *n*-year term
FV	future value			

Jason Moore graduated in 2004 from the California State University, Long Beach, with a major in Business Finance. As a fixed-income analyst at Bradford & Marzec, LLC, a Los Angeles-based institutional fixed-income manager with over $4 billion in assets, he pays close attention to interest rate movements. "I perform corporate credit research for basic industries such as metals, mining, chemicals, and forest products, following industry and company news and trends," Jason explains. Then he formulates an opinion and communicates purchase and sell recommendations to the portfolio managers.

California State University, Long Beach, 2004

"As a consumer currently seeking a loan for education expenses, a car, or a house, your perceived risk of default—not being able to repay the loan—is more important now than it was just a few years ago."

One of the trends he watches is inflation, which affects the purchasing power of a given amount of money. When prices increase due to inflation, the value of a given amount of currency declines. Inflation therefore influences the interest rate a lender charges a borrower. "The interest rate charged is often fixed for a long period of time," says Jason. "Any unexpected change in inflation over that time period affects the purchasing power of those fixed future payments, so all interest rates include an inflation expectation. If inflation increases, the purchasing power of those fixed future payments decreases, and vice versa." This means that investors' inflation expectations influence the return they expect to receive when lending money. If they think inflation will rise, they will want a higher interest rate.

In addition, investors' interest rate expectations should be reflected in the length of time an investor is willing to lend funds. "If investors believe that interest rates will rise, they should choose a short-term investment, rather than tie up their money at the current lower interest rate," he says. "If investors believe interest rates will fall, they should choose a longer-term investment, locking in the current higher interest rate."

When economic activity slows and the financial climate is uncertain, as it was in 2008, investors seek lower-risk investment opportunities. "Lenders evaluate borrowers more closely," says Jason. "As a consumer currently seeking a loan for education expenses, a car, or a house, your perceived risk of default—not being able to repay the loan—is more important now than it was just a few years ago."

In Chapter 4, we explored the mechanics of computing present values and future values given a market interest rate. Recall that an interest rate allows us to convert money at one point in time to another. But how do we determine that interest rate? In this chapter, we consider the factors that affect interest rates and discuss how to determine the appropriate discount rate for a set of cash flows. We begin by looking at the way interest is paid and interest rates are quoted, and we show how to calculate the effective interest paid in one year given different quoting conventions. We then consider some of the main determinants of interest rates—namely, inflation and economic growth. Because interest rates tend to change over time, investors will demand different interest rates for different investment horizons, based on their expectations and the risk involved in longer time horizons.

5.1 Interest Rate Quotes and Adjustments

If you spend some time looking through a newspaper, you will find literally dozens of interest rates discussed and advertised, from savings deposit rates to auto loan rates to interest rates being paid on the government's debt. Interest rates are clearly central to the functioning of any financial system. To understand interest rates, it's important to think of interest rates as a price—the price of using money. When you borrow money to buy a car, you are using the bank's money now to get the car and paying the money back over time. The interest rate on your loan is the price you pay to be able to convert your future loan payments into a car today. Similarly, when you deposit money into a savings account, you are letting the bank use your money until you withdraw it later. The interest the bank pays you on your deposit is the price it pays to have the use of your money (for things like making car loans).

Just like any other price, interest rates are set by market forces, in particular the supply of and demand for funds. When the supply (savings) is high and the demand (borrowing) is low, interest rates are low, other things being equal. Additionally, as we discuss later in the chapter, interest rates are also influenced by expected inflation and risk.

In order to be able to study and use interest rates, we have to understand how they are quoted. In practice, interest is paid, and interest rates are quoted, in different ways. For example, in mid-2006 ING Direct, an Internet bank, offered savings accounts with an interest rate of 5.25% paid at the end of one year, while New Century Bank offered an interest rate of 5.12%, but with the interest paid on a daily basis. Interest rates can also differ depending on the investment horizon. In January 2004, investors earned only about 1% on one-year risk-free investments, but could earn more than 5% on 15-year risk-free investments. Interest rates can also vary due to risk. For example, the U.S. government is able to borrow at a much lower interest rate than General Motors.

Because interest rates may be quoted for different time intervals, such as monthly, semiannual, or annual, it is often necessary to adjust the interest rate to a time period that matches that of our cash flows. We explore these mechanics of interest rates in this section.

The Effective Annual Rate

effective annual rate (EAR) or annual percentage yield (APY)
The total amount of interest that will be earned at the end of one year.

Interest rates are often reported as an **effective annual rate (EAR)** or **annual percentage yield (APY)**, which indicates the total amount of interest that will be earned at the end of one year.[1] We have used this method of quoting the interest rate thus far in this textbook, and in Chapter 4 we used the EAR as the discount rate r in our time value of money calculations. For example, with an EAR of 5%, a $100 investment grows to

$$\$100 \times (1 + r) = \$100 \times (1.05) = \$105$$

in one year. After two years it will grow to:

$$\$100 \times (1 + r)^2 = \$100 \times (1.05)^2 = \$110.25$$

Month:	0		1		2
Cash flow:	$100	× (1.05)	= $105	× (1.05)	= $110.25
	$100	×	$(1.05)^2$	=	$110.25
	$100	×	(1.1025)	=	$110.25

Adjusting the Discount Rate to Different Time Periods

The preceding example shows that earning an effective annual rate of 5% for two years is equivalent to earning 10.25% in total interest over the entire period:

$$\$100 \times (1.05)^2 = \$100 \times 1.1025 = \$110.25$$

In general, by raising the interest rate factor $(1 + r)$ to the appropriate power, we can compute an equivalent interest rate for a longer time period.

We can use the same method to find the equivalent interest rate for periods shorter than one year. In this case, we raise the interest rate factor $(1 + r)$ to the appropriate fractional power. For example, earning 5% interest in one year is equivalent to receiving

$$(1 + r)^{0.5} = (1.05)^{0.5} = \$1.0247$$

for each $1 invested every six months (0.5 years). That is, a 5% effective annual rate is equivalent to an interest rate of approximately 2.47% earned every six months. We can verify this result by computing the interest we would earn in one year by investing for two six-month periods at this rate:

$$(1 + r)^2 = (1.0247)^2 = \$1.05$$

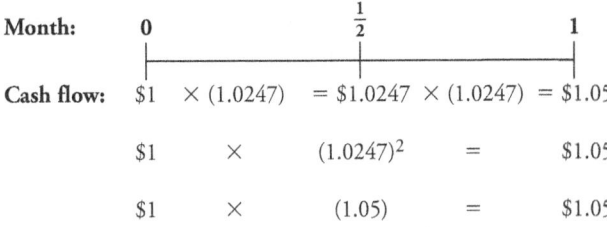

Month:	0		$\frac{1}{2}$		1
Cash flow:	$1	× (1.0247)	= $1.0247	× (1.0247)	= $1.05
	$1	×	$(1.0247)^2$	=	$1.05
	$1	×	(1.05)	=	$1.05

---

[1]The effective annual rate is also referred to as the *effective annual yield* (EAY).

In general, we can convert a discount rate of r for one period to an equivalent discount rate for n periods using the following formula:

$$\text{Equivalent } n\text{-period Discount Rate} = (1 + r)^n - 1 \qquad (5.1)$$

In this formula, n can be larger than 1 (to compute a rate over more than one period) or smaller than 1 (to compute a rate over a fraction of a period).

When computing present or future values, you should adjust the discount rate to match the time period of the cash flows.

This adjustment is necessary to apply the perpetuity or annuity formulas to non-annual cash flows, as in the following example.

BDeH CHAPTER 5

EXAMPLE 5.1

Personal Finance
Valuing Monthly
Cash Flows

Problem

Suppose your bank account pays interest monthly with an effective annual rate of 6%. What amount of interest will you earn each month?

If you have no money in the bank today, how much will you need to save at the end of each month to accumulate $100,000 in 10 years?

Solution

▶ **Plan**

We can use Eq. (5.1) to convert the EAR to a monthly rate, answering the first part of the question. The second part of the question is a future value of an annuity question. It is asking how big a monthly annuity we would have to deposit in order to end up with $100,000 in 10 years. However, in order to do this problem, we need to write the timeline in terms of *monthly* periods because our cash flows (deposits) will be monthly:

Month:	0	1	2		120
Cash flow:		C	C	$\cdots$	C

That is, we can view the savings plan as a monthly annuity with $10 \times 12 = 120$ monthly payments. We have the future value of the annuity ($100,000), the length of time (120 months), and we will have the monthly interest rate from the first part of the question. We can then use the future value of an annuity formula (Eq. 4.6) to solve for the monthly deposit.

▶ **Execute**

From Eq. (5.1), a 6% EAR is equivalent to earning $(1.06)^{1/12} - 1 = 0.4868\%$ per month. The exponent in this equation is 1/12 because the period is 1/12th of a year (a month).

To determine the amount to save each month to reach the goal of $100,000 in 120 months, we must determine the amount C of the monthly payment that will have a future value of $100,000 in 120 months, given an interest rate of 0.4868% per month. Now that we have all of the inputs in terms of months (monthly payment, monthly interest rate, and total number of months), we use the future value of annuity formula from Chapter 4 to solve this problem:

$$FV(\text{annuity}) = C \times \frac{1}{r}[(1 + r)^n - 1]$$

We solve for the payment C using the equivalent monthly interest rate $r = 0.4868\%$, and $n = 120$ months:

$$C = \frac{FV(\text{annuity})}{\frac{1}{r}[(1 + r)^n - 1]} = \frac{\$100,000}{\frac{1}{0.004868}[(1.004868)^{120} - 1]} = \$615.47 \text{ per month}$$

We can also compute this result using a financial calculator:

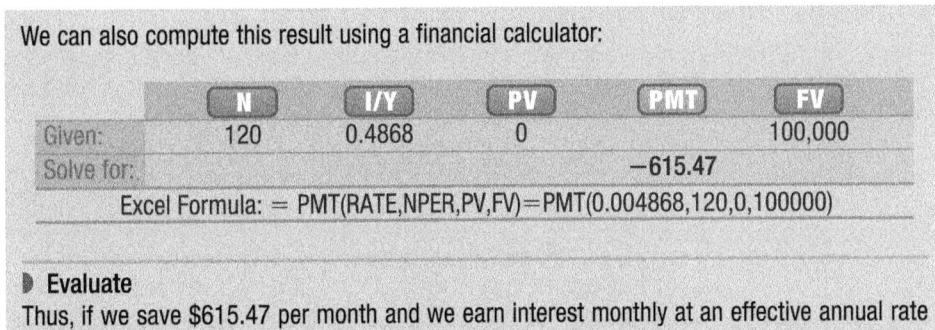

	N	I/Y	PV	PMT	FV
Given:	120	0.4868	0		100,000
Solve for:				−615.47	

Excel Formula: = PMT(RATE,NPER,PV,FV)=PMT(0.004868,120,0,100000)

▶ **Evaluate**

Thus, if we save $615.47 per month and we earn interest monthly at an effective annual rate of 6%, we will have $100,000 in 10 years. Notice that the timing in the annuity formula must be consistent for all of the inputs. In this case, we had a monthly deposit, so we needed to convert our interest rate to a monthly interest rate and then use total number of months (120) instead of years.

Annual Percentage Rates

annual percentage rate (APR) Indicates the amount of interest earned in one year without the effect of compounding.

simple interest Interest earned without the effect of compounding.

The most common way to quote interest rates is in terms of an **annual percentage rate (APR)**, which indicates the amount of **simple interest** earned in one year, that is, the amount of interest earned *without* the effect of compounding. Because it does not include the effect of compounding, the APR quote is typically less than the actual amount of interest that you will earn. To compute the actual amount that you will earn in one year, you must first convert the APR to an effective annual rate.

For example, suppose Granite Bank advertises savings accounts with an interest rate of "6% APR with monthly compounding." When it quotes a rate this way, Granite Bank really means that you will earn 6%/12 = 0.5% every month. That is, an APR with monthly compounding is actually a way of quoting a *monthly* interest rate, rather than an annual interest rate. In this case, the actual rate being quoted is 0.5% *per month*, and by convention, the bank states it as an APR by multiplying by 12 months. Because the interest compounds each month, you will actually have

$$\$1 \times (1.005)^{12} = \$1.061678$$

Common Mistake   Using the EAR in the Annuity Formula

At this point, many students make the mistake of trying to use the EAR in the annuity formula. The interest rate in the annuity formula must match the frequency of the cash flows. That's why in Example 5.1 we first converted the EAR into a monthly rate and then used the annuity formula to compute the monthly loan payments. The common mistake in this case would be to use the EAR in the annuity formula to obtain annual cash flows, and then divide those cash flows by 12 to obtain the monthly payments.

This process will produce the wrong answer. To see why, consider the timing of the first deposit in Example 5.1. With a monthly rate and monthly payments, the annuity formula assumes that the first payment will be made one month from now. It then assumes that you will be making 11 more monthly deposits before the end of the first year. Each of those deposits will start earning interest as soon you make it. In contrast, if you use an EAR and calculate an annual cash flow, the formula assumes that you will make your first deposit one *year* from now, so that you will forgo a whole year of interest before you start earning anything. Thus, you can see that the EAR approach misses the fact that you are making deposits earlier and more often than annually, so you are adding to your interest-earning principal more frequently than once per year.

at the end of one year, for an effective annual rate of 6.1678%. The 6.1678% that you earn on your deposit is higher than the quoted 6% APR due to compounding: In later months, you earn interest on the interest paid in earlier months. To summarize, an actual rate of 0.5% *per month* can be stated in either of the following ways:

▶ 6% APR, compounded monthly

▶ EAR of 6.1678%, which is the actual rate earned *per year*

It is important to remember that because the APR does not reflect the true amount you will earn over one year, *the APR itself cannot be used as a discount rate*. Instead, the APR is a way of quoting the actual interest earned each compounding period:

$$\text{Interest Rate per Compounding Period} = \frac{APR}{m}$$

(m = number of compounding periods per year)

(5.2)

Once we have computed the interest earned per compounding period from Eq. (5.2), we can compute the equivalent interest rate for any other time interval using Eq. (5.1). Thus, the effective annual rate corresponding to an APR is given by the following conversion formula:

Converting an APR to an EAR

$$1 + EAR = \left(1 + \frac{APR}{m}\right)^m$$

(5.3)

(m = number of compounding periods per year)

Table 5.1 shows the effective annual rates that correspond to an APR of 6% with different compounding intervals. The EAR increases with the frequency of compounding because of the ability to earn interest on interest sooner. Investments can compound even more frequently than daily. In principle, the compounding interval could be hourly or every second. As a practical matter, compounding more frequently than daily has a negligible impact on the effective annual rate and is rarely observed.

When working with APRs, we must first convert the APR to a discount rate per compounding interval using Eq. (5.2), or to an EAR using Eq. (5.3), before evaluating the present or future value of a set of cash flows.

TABLE 5.1	Compounding Interval	Effective Annual Rate
Effective Annual Rates for a 6% APR with Different Compounding Periods	Annual	$\left(1 + \dfrac{0.06}{1}\right)^1 - 1 = 6\%$
	Semiannual	$\left(1 + \dfrac{0.06}{2}\right)^2 - 1 = 6.09\%$
	Monthly	$\left(1 + \dfrac{0.06}{12}\right)^{12} - 1 = 6.1678\%$
	Daily	$\left(1 + \dfrac{0.06}{365}\right)^{365} - 1 = 6.1831\%$

EXAMPLE 5.2

Converting the APR to a Discount Rate

Problem

Your firm is purchasing a new telephone system that will last for four years. You can purchase the system for an upfront cost of $150,000, or you can lease the system from the manufacturer for $4000 paid at the end of each month. The lease price is offered for a 48-month lease with no early termination—you cannot end the lease early. Your firm can borrow at an interest rate of 6% APR with monthly compounding. Should you purchase the system outright or pay $4000 per month?

Solution

▶ **Plan**

The cost of leasing the system is a 48-month annuity of $4000 per month:

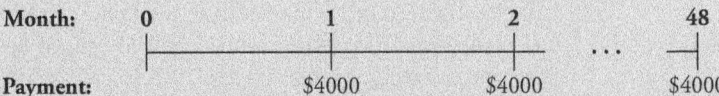

Month:	0	1	2	48
Payment:		$4000	$4000	$4000

We can compute the present value of the lease cash flows using the annuity formula, but first we need to compute the discount rate that corresponds to a period length of one month. To do so, we convert the borrowing cost of 6% APR with monthly compounding to a monthly discount rate using Eq. (5.2). Once we have a monthly rate, we can use the present value of annuity formula (Eq. 4.5) to compute the present value of the monthly payments and compare it to the cost of buying the system.

▶ **Execute**

As Eq. (5.2) shows, the 6% APR with monthly compounding really means 6%/12 = 0.5% every month. The 12 comes from the fact that there are 12 monthly compounding periods per year. Now that we have the true rate corresponding to the stated APR, we can use that discount rate in the annuity formula (Eq. 4.5) to compute the present value of the monthly payments:

$$PV = 4000 \times \frac{1}{0.005}\left(1 - \frac{1}{1.005^{48}}\right) = \$170,321.27$$

Using a financial calculator or Excel:

	N	I/Y	PV	PMT	FV
Given:	48	0.5		−4000	0
Solve for:			170,321.27		

Excel Formula: =PV(RATE,NPER,PMT,FV)=PV(0.005,48,−4000,0)

▶ **Evaluate**

Thus, paying $4000 per month for 48 months is equivalent to paying a present value of $170,321.27 today. This cost is $170,321.27 − $150,000 = $20,321.27 higher than the cost of purchasing the system, so it is better to pay $150,000 for the system rather than lease it. One way to interpret this result is as follows: At a 6% APR with monthly compounding, by promising to repay $4000 per month your firm can borrow $170,321 today. With this loan it could purchase the phone system and have an additional $20,321 to use for other purposes.

Concept Check

1. What is the difference between an EAR and an APR quote?

2. Why can't the APR be used as a discount rate?

 **Application: Discount Rates and Loans**

Now that we have explained how to compute the discount rate from an interest rate quote, let's apply the concept to solve two common financial problems: calculating a loan payment and calculating the remaining balance on a loan.

amortizing loan A loan on which the borrower makes monthly payments that include interest on the loan plus some part of the loan balance.

Computing Loan Payments

Many loans, such as mortgages and car loans, have monthly payments and are quoted in terms of an APR with monthly compounding. These types of loans are **amortizing loans**, which means that each month you pay interest on the loan plus some part of the loan balance. Each monthly payment is the same, and the loan is fully repaid with the final payment. Typical terms for a new car loan might be "6.75% APR for 60 months." When the compounding interval for the APR is not stated explicitly, it is equal to the interval between the payments, or one month in this case. Thus, this quote means that the loan will be repaid with 60 equal monthly payments, computed using a 6.75% APR with monthly compounding. It sometimes helps to look at the loan from the bank's point of view: the bank will give you $30,000 in cash today to use to buy the car. In return, you will give the bank 60 equal payments each month for 60 months, starting one month from now. In order for the bank to be willing to accept this exchange, it must be true that the present value of what you will give the bank, discounted at the loan's interest rate, is equal to the amount of cash the bank is giving you now. Consider the timeline for a $30,000 car loan with these terms:

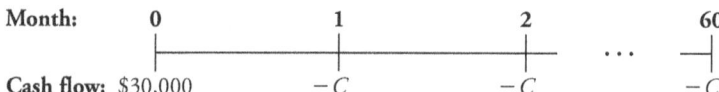

The payment, C, is set so that the present value of the cash flows, evaluated using the loan interest rate, equals the original principal amount of $30,000. In this case, the 6.75% APR with monthly compounding corresponds to a one-month discount rate of 6.75%/12 = 0.5625%. It is important that the discount rate match the frequency of the cash flows—here we have a monthly discount rate and a monthly loan payment, so we can proceed. Because the loan payments are an annuity, we can use Eq. 4.8 to find C:

$$C = \frac{P}{\frac{1}{r}\left(1 - \frac{1}{(1+r)^N}\right)} = \frac{30,000}{\frac{1}{0.005625}\left(1 - \frac{1}{(1+0.005625)^{60}}\right)} = \$590.50$$

Alternatively, we can solve for the payment C using a financial calculator or a spreadsheet:

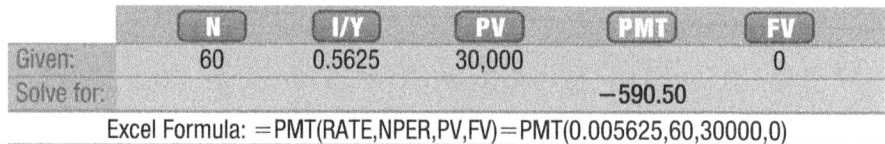

	N	I/Y	PV	PMT	FV
Given:	60	0.5625	30,000		0
Solve for:				−590.50	

Excel Formula: =PMT(RATE,NPER,PV,FV)=PMT(0.005625,60,30000,0)

Your loan payment each month includes interest and repayment of part of the principal, reducing the amount you still owe. Because the loan balance (amount you still owe) is decreasing each month, the interest that accrues on that balance is decreasing. As a result, even though your payment stays the same over the entire 60-month life of the loan, the part of that payment needed to cover interest each month is constantly decreas-

BDeH CHAPTER 5

FIGURE 5.1

Amortizing Loan

Panel (a) shows how the interest (red) and principal portions (turquoise) of the monthly payment on the $30,000 car loan change over the life of the loan. Panel (b) illustrates the effect on the outstanding balance (principal) of the loan. Note that as the balance decreases, the amount of the payment needed to cover interest on that balance decreases, allowing more of the payment to be used to reduce the principal.

Panel (a)

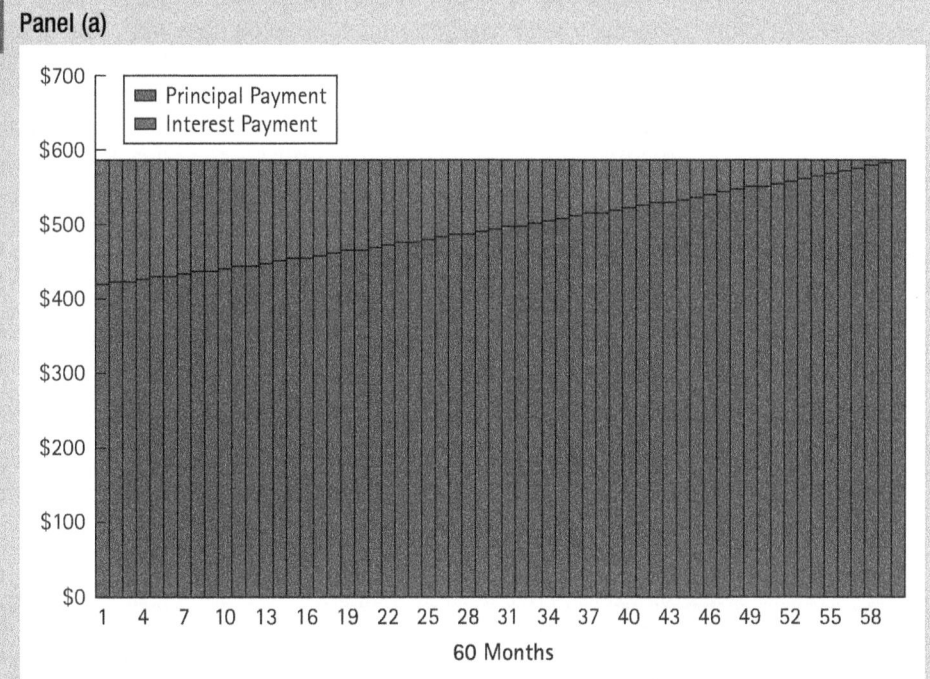

Panel (b)

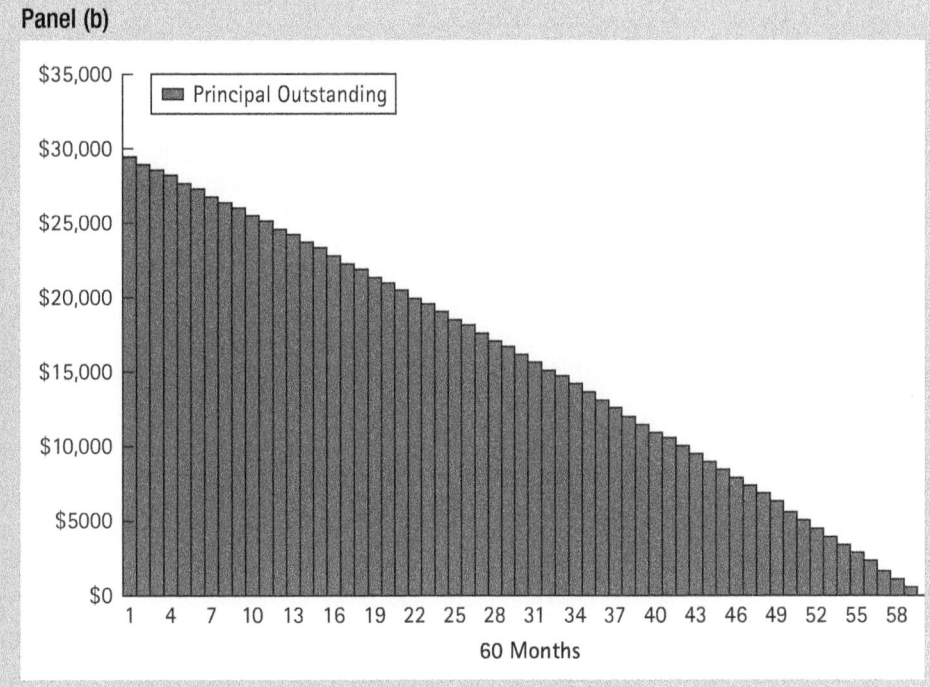

ing and the part left over to reduce the principal further is constantly increasing. We illustrate this effect in panel (a) of Figure 5.1, where we show the proportion of each monthly loan payment that covers interest (red) and the portion left over to reduce the principal (turquoise). As you can see, $168.75 of your first $590.50 payment is needed just to cover interest accrued over the first month ($30,000 \times 0.005625 = 168.75). However, this amount steadily decreases so that by the end of the loan, nearly all of your payment is going toward principal.

Panel (b) of Figure 5.1 shows the effect of your payments on the loan balance. When you make your first payment of $590.50, $168.75 covers interest on the loan, leaving $421.75 to reduce the principal to $30,000 − $421.75 = $29,578.25. The next month, you owe interest only on the $29,578.25 loan balance, which is $166.38, leaving more of your $590.50 payment to reduce the principal further. This effect continues so that each month more of your payment is available to reduce the principal, causing the principal to decrease rapidly toward the end of the loan as you are taking bigger and bigger chunks out of the balance.

Computing the Outstanding Loan Balance

As Figure 5.1 shows, the outstanding balance on an amortizing loan is different each month. The amount you owe at any point in time can be calculated as the present value of your future obligations on the loan. So, the outstanding balance, also called the outstanding principal, is equal to the present value of the remaining future loan payments, again evaluated using the loan interest rate. We calculate the outstanding loan balance by determining the present value of the remaining loan payments using the loan rate as the discount rate.

BDeH   CHAPTER 5

EXAMPLE 5.3

Personal Finance
Computing the Outstanding Loan Balance

Problem

Let's say that you are now 3 years into your $30,000 car loan from the previous section and you decide to sell the car. When you sell the car, you will need to pay whatever the remaining balance is on your car loan. After 36 months of payments, how much do you still owe on your car loan?

Solution

▶ **Plan**

We have already determined that the monthly payments on the loan are $590.50. The remaining balance on the loan is the present value of the remaining 2 years, or 24 months, of payments. Thus, we can just use the annuity formula with the monthly rate of 0.5625%, a monthly payment of $590.50, and 24 months remaining.

▶ **Execute**

$$\text{Balance with 24 months remaining} = \$590.50 \times \frac{1}{0.005625}\left(1 - \frac{1}{1.005625^{24}}\right) = \$13,222.32$$

Thus, after 3 years, you owe $13,222.32 on the loan.

Using a financial calculator or Excel:

	N	I/Y	PV	PMT	FV
Given:	24	0.5625		−590.50	0
Solve for:			13,222.32		

Excel Formula: =PV(RATE,NPER,PMT,FV)=PV(0.005625,24,−590.50,0)

You could also compute this as the FV of the original loan amount after deducting payments:

	N	I/Y	PV	PMT	FV
Given:	36	0.5625	30,000	−590.50	
Solve for:					13,222.41

Excel Formula: =FV(RATE,NPER,PMT,PV)=FV(0.005625,36,−590.50,30000)

The nine-cent difference is due to rounding on the payment amount.

> ▶ **Evaluate**
> At any point in time, including when you first take out the loan, you can calculate the balance of the loan as the present value of your remaining payments. Recall that when the bank gave you the $30,000 in the first place, it was willing to take 60 monthly payments of $590.50 in return only because the present value of those payments was equivalent to the cash it was giving you. Any time that you want to end the loan, the bank will charge you a lump sum equal to the present value of what it would receive if you continued making your payments as planned. As the second approach shows, the amount you owe can also be thought of as the future value of the original amount borrowed after deducting payments made along the way.

Concept Check

3. How is the principal repaid in an amortizing loan?

4. Why does the part of your loan payment covering interest change over time?

5.3 The Determinants of Interest Rates

Now that we understand how interest rates are quoted and used in loans, we turn to a broader question: How are interest rates determined? Fundamentally, interest rates are determined by market forces based on the relative supply and demand of funds. This supply and demand is in turn determined by the willingness of individuals, banks, and firms to borrow, save, and lend. Changes in interest rates affect consumer decisions, such as how much you can borrow for a car loan or mortgage. Because they change the present value of future cash flows, changes in interest rates also have a broad impact on capital budgeting decisions within the firm. In this section, we look at some of the factors that may influence interest rates, such as inflation, current economic activity, and expectations of future growth.

Inflation and Real Versus Nominal Rates

nominal interest rates Interest rates quoted by banks and other financial institutions that indicate the rate at which money will grow if invested for a certain period of time.

Inflation measures how the purchasing power of a given amount of currency declines due to increasing prices. How many times have you heard the expression, "A dollar just doesn't buy what it used to"? We've all witnessed the steady upward climb of prices—for example, your morning coffee probably costs a little more today than it did five years ago. Inflation affects how we evaluate the interest rates being quoted by banks and other financial institutions. Those interest rates, and the ones we have used for discounting cash flows in this book, are **nominal interest rates**, which indicate the rate at which your money will grow if invested for a certain period. Of course, if prices in the economy are also increasing due to inflation, the nominal interest rate does not represent the true increase in purchasing power that will result from investing.

Grand Avenue by Steve Breen, October 20, 2003.

For example, let's say that a cup of coffee costs $1 this year. If you have $100, you could buy 100 coffees. Instead, if you put that $100 in a bank account earning 5.06% per year, you will have $105.06 at the end of the year. But how much better off will you really be? That depends on how much prices have increased over the same year. If inflation was 3% over the year, then that cup of coffee would cost 3% more, or $1.03 at the end of the year. Thus, you could take your $105.06 and buy $105.06/$1.03 = 102 coffees, so you're really only 2% better off.

real interest rate The rate of growth of purchasing power after adjusting for inflation.

That 2% is your **real interest rate**: the rate of growth of your purchasing power, after adjusting for inflation. Just as in the example, we can calculate the rate of growth of purchasing power as follows:

$$\text{Growth in Purchasing Power} = 1 + \text{real rate} = \frac{1 + \text{nominal rate}}{1 + \text{inflation rate}}$$

$$= \frac{\text{Growth of Money}}{\text{Growth of Prices}} \quad (5.4)$$

We can rearrange Eq. (5.4) to find the following formula for the real interest rate, together with a convenient approximation for the real interest rate when inflation rates are low:

The Real Interest Rate

$$\text{real rate} = \frac{\text{nominal rate} - \text{inflation rate}}{1 + \text{inflation rate}} \approx \text{nominal rate} - \text{inflation rate} \quad (5.5)$$

That is, the real interest rate is approximately equal to the nominal interest rate less the rate of inflation.[2]

EXAMPLE 5.4

Calculating the Real Interest Rate

Problem

In the year 2000, short-term U.S. government bond rates were about 5.8% and the rate of inflation was about 3.4%. In 2003, interest rates were about 1% and inflation was about 1.9%. What was the real interest rate in 2000 and 2003?

Solution

▶ **Plan**

The bond rates tell us the nominal rates. Given the nominal rates and inflation for each year, we can use Eq. (5.5) to calculate the real interest rate.

▶ **Execute**

Eq. (5.5) says:

$$\text{real rate} = \frac{\text{nominal rate} - \text{inflation rate}}{1 + \text{inflation rate}}$$

Thus, the real interest rate in 2000 was (5.8% − 3.4%)/(1.034) = 2.32% (which is approximately equal to the difference between the nominal rate and inflation: 5.8% − 3.4% = 2.4%). In 2003, the real interest rate was (1% − 1.9%)/(1.019) = −0.88%.

---

[2]The real interest rate should not be used as a discount rate for future cash flows. It can be used as a discount rate only if the cash flows are not the expected cash flows that will be paid, but are the equivalent cash flows before adjusting them for growth due to inflation (in that case, we say the cash flows are in real terms). This approach is error prone, however, so throughout this book we will always forecast cash flows including any growth due to inflation, and discount using nominal interest rates.

▶ **Evaluate**
Note that the real interest rate was negative in 2003, indicating that interest rates were insufficient to keep up with inflation. As a result, investors in U.S. government bonds were able to buy less at the end of the year than they could have purchased at the start of the year.

Figure 5.2 shows the history of nominal interest rates and inflation rates in the United States since 1955. Note that the nominal interest rate tends to move with inflation. Intuitively, individuals' willingness to save will depend on the growth in purchasing power they can expect (given by the real interest rate). Thus, when the inflation rate is high, a higher nominal interest rate is needed to induce individuals to save. This was evident in the late 1970s and early 1980s when inflation reached double-digits in the United States, and nominal rates increased in response.

Investment and Interest Rate Policy

Interest rates affect not only individuals' propensity to save, but also firms' incentive to raise capital and invest. Consider an opportunity that requires an upfront investment of $10 million and generates a cash flow of $3 million per year for four years. If the interest rate is 5%, this investment has an NPV of:

$$NPV = -10 + \frac{3}{1.05} + \frac{3}{1.05^2} + \frac{3}{1.05^3} + \frac{3}{1.05^4} = \$0.638 \text{ million}$$

If the interest rate is 9%, the NPV falls to

$$NPV = -10 + \frac{3}{1.09} + \frac{3}{1.09^2} + \frac{3}{1.09^3} + \frac{3}{1.09^4} = -\$0.281 \text{ million}$$

FIGURE 5.2

U.S. Interest Rates and Inflation Rates, 1955–2007

The graph shows U.S. nominal interest rates (in blue) and inflation rates (in red) from 1955–2007. Note that interest rates tend to be high when inflation is high. Interest rates are average three-month Treasury bill rates and inflation rates are based on annual increases in the U.S. Bureau of Labor Statistics' consumer price index.

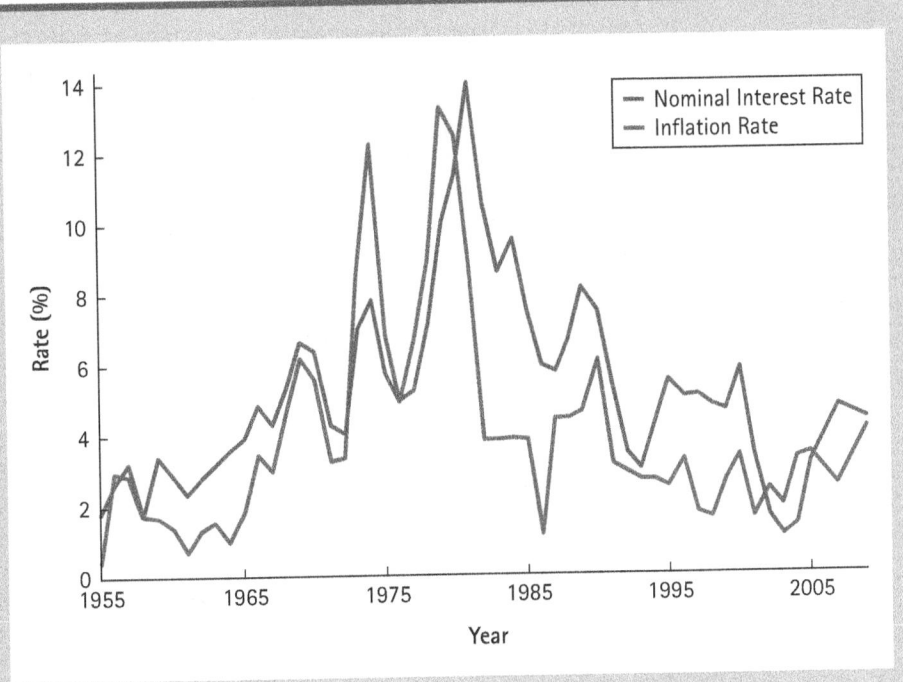

BDeH CHAPTER 5

How Is Inflation Actually Calculated?

Inflation is calculated as the rate of change in the *Consumer Price Index* (CPI). The CPI measures what it costs each month to purchase a standard set of goods that the average consumer would buy. How controversial can price data be?

To gather the price information, data collectors visit stores and gather 80,000 retail price quotes and 5000 housing rent quotes. The data is sent daily to Washington, DC, where analysts at the Bureau of Labor Statistics seek to determine if part of a price change captures a change in quality or inflation. Because this adjustment can be subjective, herein lies the controversy in the CPI calculation. The *Wall Street Journal*, covering the controversy, reported the following examples:

▶ A 57-inch television in which the price dropped from $2238.99 to $1909.97. Going over the checklist, the data gatherer in the field discovered the old version had a built-in high-definition tuner. The new one did not. The analyst estimated that the tuner was valued at $513.69. This turned what appeared to be a 14.7% price decrease into a 10.7% increase.

▶ A 27-inch television where the price appeared to stay the same, but an analyst determined that the price had declined. The latest model had a flat screen, something that consumers value more than the curved screen in the old model. The newer TV also had a ten-watt stereo, compared with the weaker six-watt stereo in the older model.

Critics argue that this quality adjustment most often ends up making a price increase look smaller or even turning it into a decline. Thus, they conclude that the government underestimates the true rate of inflation. Supporters argue that these adjustments are necessary because paying more for a better product is not equivalent to paying more for the same product. This debate is important because many union contracts, for example, have wages linked to inflation, and investors need good inflation data to determine what interest rate to demand.

WSJ Source: Aeppel, T., New and Improved: An Inflation Debate Brews Over Intangibles at the Mall—Critics Say U.S. Plays Down CPI Through Adjustments For Quality, Not Just Price—Value of a TV's Flat Screen, 9 May 2005, A1

and the investment is no longer profitable. The reason, of course, is that we are discounting the positive cash flows at a higher rate, which reduces their present value. The cost of $10 million occurs today, however, so its present value is independent of the discount rate.

More generally, when the costs of an investment precede the benefits, an increase in the interest rate will decrease the investment's NPV. All else being equal, higher interest rates will therefore tend to shrink the set of positive-NPV investments available to firms. The Federal Reserve in the United States and central banks in other countries attempt to use this relationship between interest rates and investment incentives when trying to guide the economy. They will often lower interest rates in attempts to stimulate investment if the economy is slowing, and they will raise interest rates to reduce investment if the economy is "overheating" and inflation is on the rise.

The Yield Curve and Discount Rates

The interest rates that banks offer on investments or charge on loans depend on the horizon, or *term,* of the investment or loan. For example, suppose you are willing to put your money in a CD (certificate of deposit)[3] that matures in two years (meaning that you

---

[3]A certificate of deposit is a short- or medium-term debt instrument offered by banks. You deposit money in the bank for a stated period of time and normally receive a fixed rate of interest. The rate is higher than it would be on a savings account because you cannot withdraw your money early without paying a penalty.

FIGURE 5.3

Term Structure of Risk-Free U.S. Interest Rates, January 2004, 2005, and 2006

The figure shows the interest rate available from investing in risk-free U.S. Treasury securities with different investment terms. In each case, the interest rates differ depending on the horizon. For example, in 2004, the interest rate on a 10-year loan (4.72%) was more than 4 times the rate on a 1-year loan (1.15%). (Data from U.S. Treasury securities.)

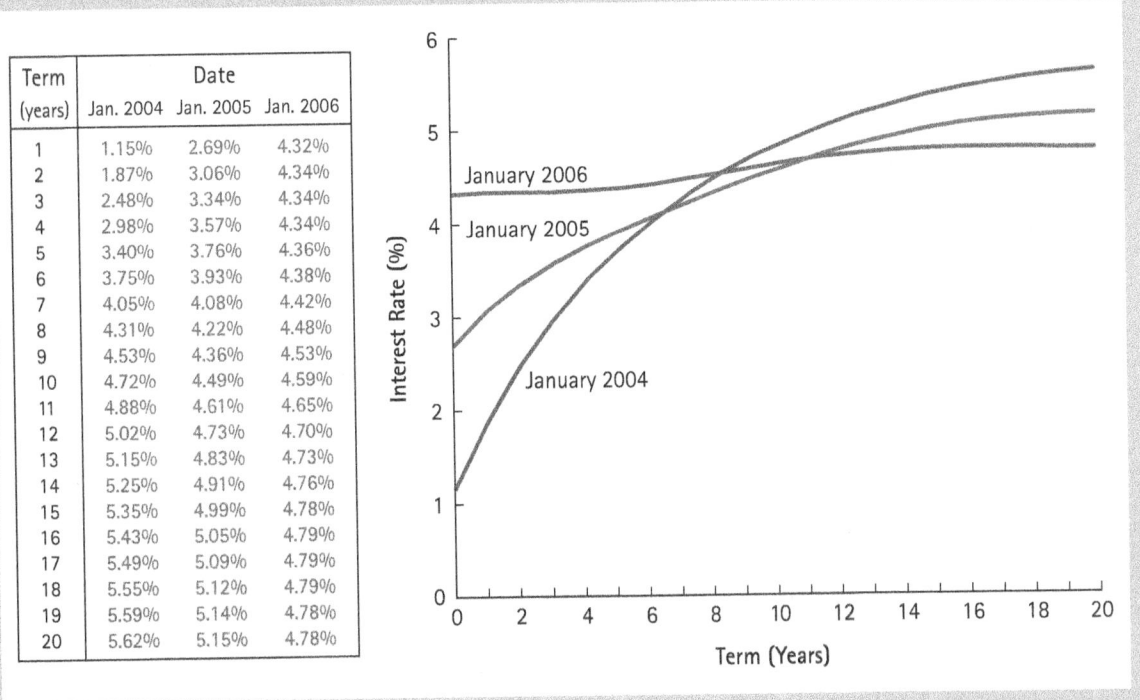

Term	Date		
(years)	Jan. 2004	Jan. 2005	Jan. 2006
1	1.15%	2.69%	4.32%
2	1.87%	3.06%	4.34%
3	2.48%	3.34%	4.34%
4	2.98%	3.57%	4.34%
5	3.40%	3.76%	4.36%
6	3.75%	3.93%	4.38%
7	4.05%	4.08%	4.42%
8	4.31%	4.22%	4.48%
9	4.53%	4.36%	4.53%
10	4.72%	4.49%	4.59%
11	4.88%	4.61%	4.65%
12	5.02%	4.73%	4.70%
13	5.15%	4.83%	4.73%
14	5.25%	4.91%	4.76%
15	5.35%	4.99%	4.78%
16	5.43%	5.05%	4.79%
17	5.49%	5.09%	4.79%
18	5.55%	5.12%	4.79%
19	5.59%	5.14%	4.78%
20	5.62%	5.15%	4.78%

term structure The relationship between the investment term and the interest rate.

yield curve A plot of bond yields as a function of the bonds' maturity date.

risk-free interest rate The interest rate at which money can be borrowed or lent without risk over a given period.

cannot get the money back before then without a penalty). The bank will offer you a higher rate of interest for this CD than if you put your money in a statement savings account, where you can withdraw your funds at any time. The relationship between the investment term and the interest rate is called the **term structure** of interest rates. We can plot this relationship on a graph called the **yield curve**. Figure 5.3 shows the term structure and corresponding yield curve of U.S. interest rates that were available to investors in January of 2004, 2005, and 2006. In each case, note that the interest rate depends on the horizon, and that the difference between short-term and long-term interest rates was especially pronounced in 2004. The rates plotted are interest rates for U.S. Treasury securities, which are considered to be free of any risk of default (the U.S. government will not default on its loans). Thus, each of these rates is a **risk-free interest rate**, which is the interest rate at which money can be borrowed or lent without risk over a given period.

We can use the term structure to compute the present and future values of a risk-free cash flow over different investment horizons. For example, $100 invested for one year at the one-year interest rate in January 2004 would grow to a future value of

$$\$100 \times 1.0115 = \$101.15$$

at the end of one year, and \$100 invested for ten years at the ten-year interest rate in January 2004 would grow to[4]:

$$\$100 \times (1.0472)^{10} = \$158.60$$

We can apply the same logic when computing the present value of cash flows with different maturities. A risk-free cash flow received in two years should be discounted at the two-year interest rate, and a cash flow received in ten years should be discounted at the ten-year interest rate. In general, a risk-free cash flow of C_n received in n years has present value

$$PV = \frac{C_n}{(1 + r_n)^n} \tag{5.6}$$

where r_n is the risk-free interest rate for an n-year term. In other words, when computing a present value we must match the term of the cash flow and term of the discount rate.

Combining Eq. (5.6) for cash flows in different years leads to the general formula for the present value of a cash flow stream:

Present Value of a Cash Flow Stream Using a Term Structure of Discount Rates

$$PV = \frac{C_1}{1 + r_1} + \frac{C_2}{(1 + r_2)^2} + \cdots + \frac{C_N}{(1 + r_N)^N} \tag{5.7}$$

Note the difference between Eq. (5.7) and Eq. (4.3). Here, we use a different discount rate for each cash flow, based on the rate from the yield curve with the same term. When interest rates are very similar across maturities, we say that the yield curve is flat, because it is close to a flat line. When the yield curve is relatively flat, as it was in January 2006, the distinction of using different rates for each cash flow is relatively minor and is often ignored by discounting using a single "average" interest rate r. But when short-term and long-term interest rates vary widely, as they did in January 2004, Eq. (5.7) should be used.

Warning: All of our shortcuts for computing present values (annuity and perpetuity formulas, and financial calculators) are based on discounting all of the cash flows *at the same rate.* They *cannot* be used in situations in which cash flows need to be discounted at different rates.

EXAMPLE 5.5

Using the Term Structure to Compute Present Values

Problem

Compute the present value of a risk-free 5-year annuity of \$1000 per year, given the yield curve for January 2005 in Figure 5.3.

Solution

▶ **Plan**

The timeline of the cash flows of the annuity is:

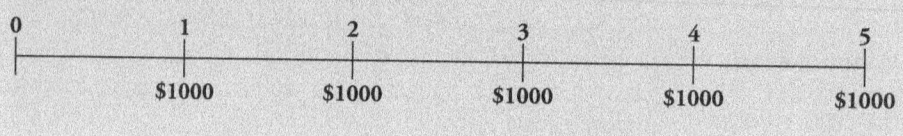

0	1	2	3	4	5
	\$1000	\$1000	\$1000	\$1000	\$1000

---

[4]We could also invest for ten years by investing at the one-year interest rate for ten years in a row. However, because we do not know what future interest rates will be, our ultimate payoff would not be risk free.

BDeH   CHAPTER 5

We can use the table next to the yield curve to identify the interest rate corresponding to each length of time: 1, 2, 3, 4, and 5 years. With the cash flows and those interest rates, we can compute the PV.

▶ **Execute**

From Figure 5.3, we see that the interest rates are: 2.69%, 3.06%, 3.34%, 3.57%, and 3.76%, for terms of 1, 2, 3, 4, and 5 years, respectively.

To compute the present value, we discount each cash flow by the corresponding interest rate:

$$PV = \frac{1000}{1.0269} + \frac{1000}{1.0306^2} + \frac{1000}{1.0334^3} + \frac{1000}{1.0357^4} + \frac{1000}{1.0376^5} = \$4522$$

▶ **Evaluate**

The yield curve tells us the market interest rate per year for each different maturity. In order to correctly calculate the PV of cash flows from five different maturities, we need to use the five different interest rates corresponding to those maturities. Note that we cannot use the annuity formula here because the discount rates differ for each cash flow.

Common Mistake   **Using the Annuity Formula When Discount Rates Vary**

When computing the present value of an annuity, a common mistake is to use the annuity formula with a single interest rate even though interest rates vary with the investment horizon. For example, we *cannot* compute the present value of the five-year annuity in Example 5.5 using the five-year interest rate from January 2005:

$$PV \neq \$1000 \times \frac{1}{0.0376}\left(1 - \frac{1}{1.0376^5}\right) = \$4482$$

If we want to find the single interest rate that we could use to value the annuity, we must first compute the present value of the annuity using Eq. (5.7) and then solve for its IRR. For the annuity in Example 5.5, we use a financial calculator or spreadsheet to find its IRR of 3.45%. The IRR of the annuity is always between the highest and lowest discount rates used to calculate its present value, as is the case in this example.

	N	I/Y	PV	PMT	FV
Given:	5		−4522	1000	0
Solve for:		3.45			
	Excel Formula: =RATE(NPER,PMT,PV,FV)=RATE(5,1000,−4522,0)				

The Yield Curve and the Economy

As Figure 5.4 illustrates, the yield curve changes over time. Sometimes, short-term rates are close to long-term rates, and at other times they may be very different. What accounts for the changing shape of the yield curve?

Interest Rate Determination.   The Federal Reserve determines very short-term interest rates through its influence on the **federal funds rate**, which is the rate at which banks can borrow cash reserves on an overnight basis. All other interest rates on the yield curve are set in the market and are adjusted until the supply of lending matches the demand for borrowing at each loan term. As we shall see in a moment, expectations of future interest rate changes have a major effect on investors' willingness to lend or borrow for longer terms and, therefore, on the shape of the yield curve.

federal funds rate
The overnight loan rate charged by banks with excess reserves at a Federal Reserve bank (called federal funds) to banks that need additional funds to meet reserve requirements.

BDeH CHAPTER 5

FIGURE 5.4

Yield Curve Shapes

The figure shows three different yield curve shapes. The blue line represents a "normal" yield curve. Most of the time the yield curve has this shape—moderately upward sloping. The red line depicts a steep yield curve—note the larger than normal difference between short-term rates (2%) and long-term rates (7%), making the yield curve look steeper than normal. This example of a steep yield curve is from October 1991. Finally, the green line depicts an inverted yield curve, so called because it slopes downward instead of upward. This happens when short-term rates are higher than long-term rates as they were in January 1981. We discuss why the shape of the yield curve changes over time in the rest of this section.

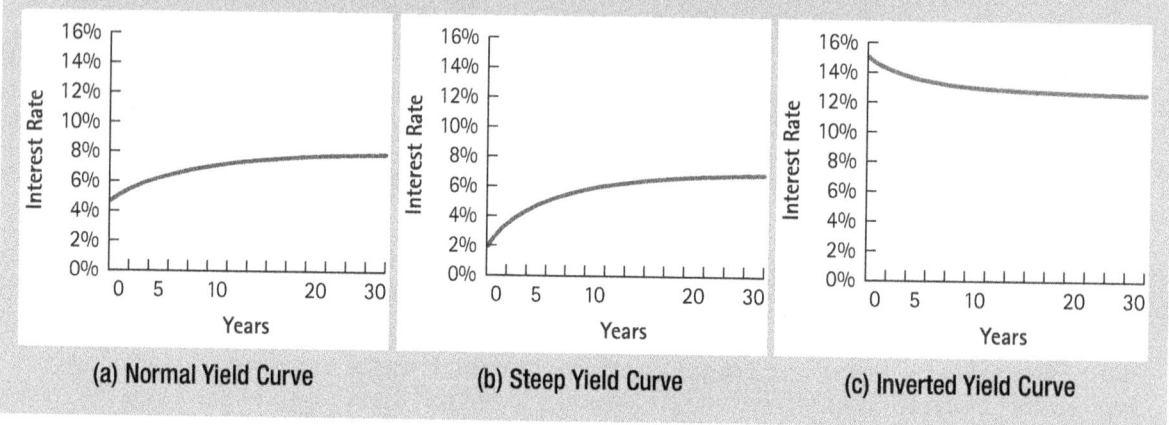

(a) Normal Yield Curve   (b) Steep Yield Curve   (c) Inverted Yield Curve

Suppose short-term interest rates are equal to long-term interest rates. If interest rates are expected to rise in the future, investors would not want to make long-term investments. Instead, they could do better by investing on a short-term basis and then reinvesting after interest rates rose. Thus, if interest rates are expected to rise, long-term interest rates will tend to be higher than short-term rates to attract investors.

Similarly, if interest rates are expected to fall in the future, then borrowers would not wish to borrow at long-term rates that are equal to short-term rates. They would do better by borrowing on a short-term basis, and then taking out a new loan after rates fall. So, if interest rates are expected to fall, long-term rates will tend to be lower than short-term rates to attract borrowers.

Yield Curve Shape. These arguments indicate that the shape of the yield curve will be strongly influenced by interest rate expectations. A sharply increasing (*steep*) yield curve, with long-term rates much higher than short-term rates, generally indicates that interest rates are expected to rise in the future. A decreasing (*inverted*) yield curve, with long-term rates lower than short-term rates, generally signals an expected decline in future interest rates. Because interest rates tend to drop in response to a slowdown in the economy, an inverted yield curve is often interpreted as a negative forecast for economic growth. Indeed, as Figure 5.5 illustrates, each of the last six recessions in the United States was preceded by a period in which the yield curve was inverted (note the red shaded areas before the gray bars indicating a recession). Conversely, the yield curve tends to be steep (and therefore shaded blue) as the economy comes out of a recession and interest rates are expected to rise.

The normal shape of the yield curve is moderately upward sloping. This would be the case if investors almost always believed that interest rates were going to rise in the future. But that is unlikely, so there have to be other forces at work to cause long-term

FIGURE 5.5

Short-Term Versus Long-Term U.S. Interest Rates and Recessions

One-year and ten-year U.S. Treasury rates are plotted, with the spread between them shaded in green if the shape of the yield curve is increasing (the one-year rate is below the ten-year rate) and in red if the yield curve is inverted (the one-year rate exceeds the ten-year rate). Gray bars show the dates of U.S. recessions as determined by the National Bureau of Economic Research. Note that inverted yield curves tend to precede recessions as determined by the National Bureau of Economic Research. In recessions, interest rates tend to fall, with short-term rates dropping further. As a result, the yield curve tends to be steep coming out of a recession.

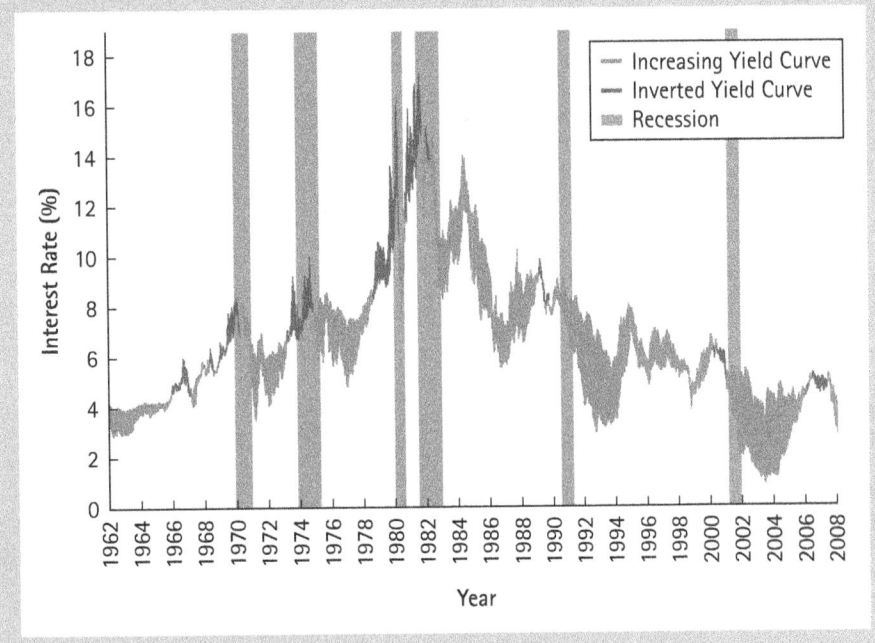

interest rates normally to be higher than short-term rates. The most commonly cited reason is that long-term loans are riskier than short-term loans. If you make a 30-year loan today and lock-in the interest rate, the present value of the payments you receive on the loan is very sensitive to even small changes in market interest rates. This sensitivity is due to the effect of compounding a change in interest rates over a 30-year period. To see this effect, consider the following example.

EXAMPLE 5.6

Long-term Versus
Short-term Loans

Problem

You work for a bank that has just made two loans. In one, you loaned $909.09 today in return for $1000 in one year. In the other, you loaned $909.09 today in return for $15,863.08 in 30 years. The difference between the loan amount and repayment amount is based on an interest rate of 10% per year. Imagine that immediately after you make the loans, news about economic growth is announced that increases inflation expectations, so that the market interest rate for loans like these jumps to 11%. Loans make up a major part of a bank's assets, so you are naturally concerned about the value of these loans. What is the effect of the interest rate change on the value to the bank of the promised repayment of these loans?

BDeH CHAPTER 5

Solution

▶ **Plan**

Each of these loans has only one repayment cash flow at the end of the loan. They differ only by the time to repayment:

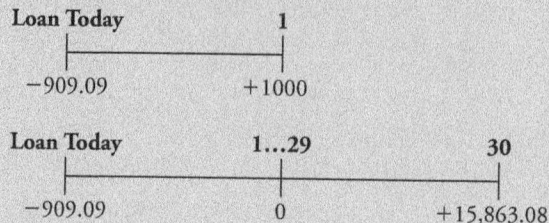

The effect on the value of the future repayment to the bank today is just the PV of the loan repayment, calculated at the new market interest rate.

▶ **Execute**

For the one-year loan:

$$PV = \frac{\$1,000}{(1.11)^1} = \$900.90$$

For the 30-year loan:

$$PV = \frac{\$15,863.08}{(1.11)^{30}} = \$692.94$$

▶ **Evaluate**

The value of the one-year loan decreased by $909.09 − $900.90 = $8.19, or 0.9%, but the value of the 30-year loan decreased by $909.09 − $692.94 = $216.15, or almost 24%! The small change in market interest rates, compounded over a longer period, resulted in a much larger change in the present value of the loan repayment. You can see why investors and banks view longer-term loans as being riskier than short-term loans.

In addition to specifying the discount rates for risk-free cash flows that occur at different horizons, it is also a potential leading indicator of future economic growth. Due to these qualities, the yield curve provides extremely important information for a business manager.

Concept Check

5. What is the difference between a nominal and real interest rate?

6. How are interest rates and the level of investment made by businesses related?

5.4 The Opportunity Cost of Capital

As we have seen in this chapter, the interest rates we observe in the market will vary based on quoting conventions, the term of the investment, and risk. In this chapter, we have developed the tools to account for these differences and gained some insights into how interest rates are determined. This knowledge will provide the foundation for our study of bonds in the next chapter.

In Chapter 3, we argued that the Valuation Principle tells us to use the "market interest rate" to compute present values and evaluate an investment opportunity. But with so many interest rates to choose from, the term "market interest rate" is inherently ambiguous. Therefore, going forward in the textbook, we will base the discount rate that we use to evaluate cash flows on the investor's **opportunity cost of capital** (or more simply, the **cost of capital**), which is *the best available expected return offered in the market on an investment of comparable risk and term to the cash flow being discounted*.

In order to understand the definition of opportunity cost of capital, it helps to think of yourself as a financial manager competing with financial managers at other firms to attract investors' funds (capital). In order to attract investors to invest in your firm or creditors to lend to your firm, you have to be able to offer them an expected return at least as good as what they could get elsewhere in the market for the same risk and length of investment. Now it is easier to see where the term (opportunity) cost of capital comes from—investors in your firm are giving up the opportunity to invest their funds elsewhere. This is an opportunity cost to them and to overcome it you must offer them a return equal to or better than their opportunity cost of capital. Even if you already have the funds internally in the firm to invest, the logic still applies. You could either return the funds to your shareholders to invest elsewhere, or reinvest them in a new project; however, you should only reinvest them if doing so provides a better return than the shareholders' other opportunities.

opportunity cost of capital or **cost of capital** The best available expected return offered in the market on an investment of comparable risk and term to the cash flow being discounted; the return the investor forgoes on an alternative investment of equivalent risk and term when the investor takes on a new investment.

Interest Rates, Discount Rates, and the Cost of Capital

By now, you may have noticed that we are using three terms to refer to rates of return. While many people use these three terms interchangeably, they are distinct. Throughout this book, we will use "interest rate" to mean a quoted rate in the market. A "discount rate" is the appropriate rate for discounting a given cash flow, *matched to the frequency of the cash flow*. Finally, we use "cost of capital" to indicate the rate of return on an investment of similar risk.

The opportunity cost of capital is the return the investor forgoes when the investor takes on a new investment. For a risk-free project, it will typically correspond to the interest rate on U.S. Treasury securities with a similar term. But the cost of capital is a much more general concept that can be applied to risky investments as well.

EXAMPLE 5.7	**Problem**
The Opportunity Cost of Capital	Suppose a friend offers to borrow $100 from you today and in return pay you $110 one year from today. Looking in the market for other options for investing the $100, you find your best alternative option that you view as equally risky as lending it to your friend. That option has an expected return of 8%. What should you do?

Solution

▶ **Plan**

Your decision depends on what the opportunity cost is of lending your money to your friend. If you lend her the $100, then you cannot invest it in the alternative with an 8% expected return. Thus, by making the loan, you are giving up the opportunity to invest for an 8% expected return. You can make your decision by using your 8% opportunity cost of capital to value the $110 in one year.

▶ **Execute**

The value of the $110 in one year is its present value, discounted at 8%:

$$PV = \frac{\$110}{(1.08)^1} = \$101.85$$

The $100 loan is worth $101.85 to you today, so you make the loan.

▶ **Evaluate**

The Valuation Principle tells us that we can determine the value of an investment by using market prices to value the benefits net of the costs. As this example shows, market prices determine what our best alternative opportunities are, so that we can decide whether an investment is worth the cost.

Chapter 3 introduced the Valuation Principle as a unifying theme in finance. In this and the preceding chapter, we have developed the fundamental tools a financial manager needs to value cash flows at different points in time. In this last section, we have reiterated the importance of using market information to determine the opportunity cost of capital, which is your discount rate in valuation calculations. In the next chapter, we will study bonds and how they are priced, which provides us with an immediate application of the knowledge we have built so far.

Concept Check

7. What is the opportunity cost of capital?
8. Can you ignore the cost of capital if you already have the funds inside the firm?

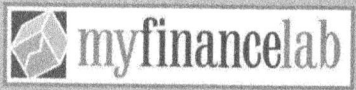

Here is what you should know after reading this chapter. MyFinanceLab will help you identify what you know, and where to go when you need to practice.

Key Points and Equations	Terms	Online Practice Opportunities
5.1 Interest Rate Quotes and Adjustments ▶ Just like any other price, interest rates are set by market forces, in particular the supply and demand of funds. ▶ The effective annual rate (EAR) indicates the actual amount of interest earned in one year. The EAR can be used as a discount rate for annual cash flows.	annual percentage rate (APR) p. 135 effective annual rate (EAR), p. 137 simple interest, p. 137	MyFinanceLab Study Plan 5.1

BDeH CHAPTER 5

▶ Given an EAR r, the equivalent discount rate for an n-year time interval, where n may be more than one year or less than or equal to one year (a fraction), is:

$$\text{Equivalent } n\text{-period Discount Rate} = (1 + r)^n - 1 \tag{5.1}$$

▶ An annual percentage rate (APR) is a common way of quoting interest rates. The actual interest rate per period is the APR/number of compounding periods per year. APRs cannot be used as discount rates.

▶ We need to know the compounding interval of an APR to determine the EAR:

$$1 + EAR = \left(1 + \frac{APR}{m}\right)^m \tag{5.3}$$

m = number of compounding periods per year

▶ For a given APR, the EAR increases with the compounding frequency.

5.2 Application: Discount Rates and Loans

▶ Loan rates are typically stated as APRs. The outstanding balance of a loan is equal to the present value of the loan cash flows, when evaluated using the actual interest rate per payment interval based on the loan rate.

▶ In each loan payment on an amortizing loan, you pay interest on the loan plus some part of the loan balance.

amortizing loans, p. 140

MyFinanceLab
Study Plan 5.2

5.3 The Determinants of Interest Rates

▶ Quoted interest rates are nominal interest rates, which indicate the rate of growth of the money invested. The real interest rate indicates the rate of growth of one's purchasing power after adjusting for inflation.

▶ Given a nominal interest rate and an inflation rate, the real interest rate is:

$$\text{real rate} = \frac{\text{nominal rate} - \text{inflation rate}}{1 + \text{inflation rate}} \tag{5.5}$$

$$\approx \text{real rate} - \text{inflation rate}$$

▶ Nominal interest rates tend to be high when inflation is high and low when inflation is low.

federal funds rate, p. 149
nominal interest rates,
  p. 143
real interest rate, p. 144
risk-free interest rate,
  p. 147
term structure, p. 147
yield curve, p. 147

MyFinanceLab
Study Plan 5.3
Interactive Yield
Curve

BDeH CHAPTER 5

▶ Higher interest rates tend to reduce the NPV of typical investment projects. The U.S. Federal Reserve raises interest rates to moderate investment and combat inflation and lowers interest rates to stimulate investment and economic growth.

▶ Interest rates differ with the investment horizon according to the term structure of interest rates. The graph plotting interest rates as a function of the horizon is called the yield curve.

▶ Cash flows should be discounted using the discount rate that is appropriate for their horizon. Thus, the PV of a cash flow stream is:

$$PV = \frac{C_1}{1 + r_1} + \frac{C_2}{(1 + r_2)^2} + \cdots + \frac{C_N}{(1 + r_N)^N} \quad (5.7)$$

▶ Annuity and perpetuity formulas cannot be applied when discount rates vary with the horizon.

▶ The shape of the yield curve tends to vary with investors' expectations of future economic growth and interest rates. It tends to be inverted prior to recessions and to be steep coming out of a recession. Because investors view long-term loans as riskier, long-term rates are generally higher than short-term rates.

5.4 The Opportunity Cost of Capital

▶ An investor's opportunity cost of capital (or more simply, the cost of capital) is the best available expected return offered in the market on an investment of comparable risk and term to the cash flow being discounted.

(opportunity) cost of capital, p. 153

MyFinanceLab
Study Plan 5.4

Review Questions

1. Explain how an interest rate is just a price.

2. Why is the EAR for 6% APR, with semi-annual compounding, higher than 6%?

3. Why is it so important to match the frequency of the interest rate to the frequency of the cash flows?

4. Why aren't the payments for a 15-year mortgage twice the payments for a 30-year mortgage at the same rate?

5. What mistake do you make when you discount real cash flows with nominal discount rates?

6. How do changes in inflation expectations impact interest rates?

7. Can the nominal interest rate available to an investor be negative? (*Hint:* Consider the interest rate earned from saving cash "under the mattress.") Can the real interest rate be negative?

8. In the early 1980s, inflation was in the double-digits and the yield curve sloped sharply downward. What did the yield curve say about investors' expectations about future inflation rates?

9. What do we mean when we refer to the "opportunity cost" of capital?

Problems

All problems in this chapter are available in MyFinanceLab. An asterisk (*) indicates problems with a higher level of difficulty.

Interest Rate Quotes and Adjustments

1. Your bank is offering you an account that will pay 20% interest in total for a two-year deposit. Determine the equivalent discount rate for a period length of
   a. six months.
   b. one year.
   c. one month.

2. Which do you prefer: a bank account that pays 5% per year (EAR) for three years or
   a. an account that pays 2.5% every six months for three years?
   b. an account that pays 7.5% every 18 months for three years?
   c. an account that pays 0.5% per month for three years?

3. You have been offered a job with an unusual bonus structure. As long as you stay with the firm, you will get an extra $70,000 every seven years, starting seven years from now. What is the present value of this incentive if you plan to work for the company for a total of 42 years and the interest rate is 6% (EAR)?

4. You have found three investment choices for a one-year deposit: 10% APR compounded monthly, 10% APR compounded annually, and 9% APR compounded daily. Compute the EAR for each investment choice. (Assume that there are 365 days in the year.)

5. Your bank account pays interest with an EAR of 5%. What is the APR quote for this account based on semiannual compounding? What is the APR with monthly compounding?

6. Suppose the interest rate is 8% APR with monthly compounding. What is the present value of an annuity that pays $100 every six months for five years?

7. You have been accepted into college. The college guarantees that your tuition will not increase for the four years you attend college. The first $10,000 tuition payment is due in six months. After that, the same payment is due every six months until you have made a total of eight payments. The college offers a bank account that allows you to withdraw money every six months and has a fixed APR of 4% (semiannual) guaranteed to remain the same over the next four years. How much money must you deposit today if you intend to make no further deposits and would like to make all the tuition payments from this account, leaving the account empty when the last payment is made?

Application: Discount Rates and Loans

8. You make monthly payments on your car loan. It has a quoted APR of 5% (monthly compounding). What percentage of the outstanding principal do you pay in interest each month?

9. Suppose Capital One is advertising a 60-month, 5.99% APR motorcycle loan. If you need to borrow $8000 to purchase your dream Harley Davidson, what will your monthly payment be?

10. Suppose Oppenheimer Bank is offering a 30-year mortgage with an EAR of 6.80%. If you plan to borrow $150,000, what will your monthly payment be?

 11. You are buying a house and the mortgage company offers to let you pay a "point" (1% of the total amount of the loan) to reduce your APR from 6.5% to 6.25% on your $400,000, 30-year mortgage with monthly payments. If you plan to be in the house for at least five years, should you do it?

 12. You have decided to refinance your mortgage. You plan to borrow whatever is outstanding on your current mortgage. The current monthly payment is $2356 and you have made every payment on time. The original term of the mortgage was 30 years, and the mortgage is exactly four years and eight months old. You have just made your monthly payment. The mortgage interest rate is 6.375% (APR). How much do you owe on the mortgage today?

 13. You have just sold your house for $1,000,000 in cash. Your mortgage was originally a 30-year mortgage with monthly payments and an initial balance of $800,000. The mortgage is currently exactly 18½ years old, and you have just made a payment. If the interest rate on the mortgage is 5.25% (APR), how much cash will you have from the sale once you pay off the mortgage?

 14. You have just purchased a car and taken out a $50,000 loan. The loan has a five-year term with monthly payments and an APR of 6%.
   a. How much will you pay in interest, and how much will you pay in principal, during the first month, second month, and first year? (*Hint:* Compute the loan balance after one month, two months and one year.)
   b. How much will you pay in interest, and how much will you pay in principal, during the fourth year (i.e., between three and four years from now)?

*15. You have some extra cash this month and you are considering putting it toward your car loan. Your interest rate is 7%, your loan payments are $600 per month and you have 36 months left on your loan. If you pay an additional $1000 with your next regular $600 payment (due in one month), how much will it reduce the amount of time left to pay off your loan?

 *16. You have an outstanding student loan with required payments of $500 per month for the next four years. The interest rate on the loan is 9% APR (monthly). You are considering making an extra payment of $100 today (i.e., you will pay an extra $100 that you are not required to pay). If you are required to continue to make payments of $500 per month until the loan is paid off, what is the amount of your final payment? What effective rate of return (expressed as an APR with monthly compounding) have you earned on the $100?

 *17. Consider again the setting of Problem 16. Now that you realize your best investment is to prepay your student loan, you decide to prepay as much as you can each month. Looking at your budget, you can afford to pay an extra $250 per month in addition to your required monthly payments of $500, or $750 in total each month. How long will it take you to pay off the loan?

*18. If you decide to take the mortgage in Problem 10, Oppenheimer Bank will offer you the following deal: Instead of making the monthly payment you computed in that problem every month, you can make half the payment every two weeks (so that you will make $52 / 2 = 26$ payments per year). How long will it take to pay off the mortgage if the EAR remains the same at 6.80%.

*19. Your friend tells you he has a very simple trick for taking one-third off the time it takes to repay your mortgage: Use your Christmas bonus to make an extra payment on January 1 of each year (that is, pay your monthly payment due on that day twice). If you take out your mortgage on July 1, so your first monthly payment is due August 1, and you make an extra payment every January 1, how long will it take to pay off the mortgage? Assume that the mortgage has an original term of 30 years and an APR of 12%.

20. The mortgage on your house is five years old. It required monthly payments of $1402, had an original term of 30 years, and had an interest rate of 10% (APR). In the intervening five years, interest rates have fallen and so you have decided to refinance—that is, you will roll over the outstanding balance into a new mortgage. The new mortgage has a 30-year term, requires monthly payments, and has an interest rate of $6\frac{5}{8}\%$ (APR).
   a. What monthly repayments will be required with the new loan?
   b. If you still want to pay off the mortgage in 25 years, what monthly payment should you make after you refinance?
   c. Suppose you are willing to continue making monthly payments of $1402. How long will it take you to pay off the mortgage after refinancing?
   d. Suppose you are willing to continue making monthly payments of $1402, and want to pay off the mortgage in 25 years. How much additional cash can you borrow today as part of the refinancing?

21. You have credit card debt of $25,000 that has an APR (monthly compounding) of 15%. Each month you pay a minimum monthly payment only. You are required to pay only the outstanding interest. You have received an offer in the mail for an otherwise identical credit card with an APR of 12%. After considering all your alternatives, you decide to switch cards, roll over the outstanding balance on the old card into the new card, and borrow additional money as well. How much can you borrow today on the new card without changing the minimum monthly payment you will be required to pay?

22. Your firm has taken out a $500,000 loan with 9% APR (compounded monthly) for some commercial property. As is common in commercial real estate, the loan is a 5-year loan based on a 15-year amortization. This means that your loan payments will be calculated as if you will take 15 years to pay off the loan, but you actually must do so in 5 years. To do this, you will make 59 equal payments based on the 15-year amortization schedule and then make a final 60th payment to pay the remaining balance.
   a. What will your monthly payments be?
   b. What will your final payment be?

The Determinants of Interest Rates

23. In 1975, interest rates were 7.85% and the rate of inflation was 12.3% in the United States. What was the real interest rate in 1975? How would the purchasing power of your savings have changed over the year?

24. If the rate of inflation is 5%, what nominal interest rate is necessary for you to earn a 3% real interest rate on your investment?

25. Consider a project that requires an initial investment of $100,000 and will produce a single cash flow of $150,000 in five years.

    a. What is the NPV of this project if the five-year interest rate is 5% (EAR)?

    b. What is the NPV of this project if the five-year interest rate is 10% (EAR)?

    c. What is the highest five-year interest rate such that this project is still profitable?

26. What is the shape of the yield curve given in the following term structure? What expectations are investors likely to have about future interest rates?

Term	1 year	2 years	3 years	5 years	7 years	10 years	20 years
Rate (EAR, %)	1.99	2.41	2.74	3.32	3.76	4.13	4.93

6 Bonds

LEARNING OBJECTIVES

- ▶ Understand bond terminology
- ▶ Compute the price and yield to maturity of a zero-coupon bond
- ▶ Compute the price and yield to maturity of a coupon bond

- ▶ Analyze why bond prices change over time
- ▶ Know how credit risk affects the expected return from holding a corporate bond

notation

CPN	coupon payment on a bond
FV	face value of a bond
n	number of periods
P	initial price of a bond
PV	present value

r_n	interest rate or discount rate for a cash flow that arrives in period n
y	yield to maturity
YTM	yield to maturity
YTM_n	yield to maturity on a zero-coupon bond with n periods to maturity

Marquette University, 2004

"Do not take the information you are learning in your current classes for granted. This valuable information will eventually become the building blocks for a successful career."

"The extraordinary amount of money in the U.S. credit market—about $47 trillion!—creates huge career opportunities for those who understand the dynamics of today's fixed–income markets," says Patrick Brown, Vice President, Investments in Citi's Smith Barney Milwaukee office. A 2004 graduate of Marquette University with majors in finance and information technology, Patrick is also a Chartered Financial Analyst (CFA).

His finance courses gave him the necessary tools to analyze a variety of fixed-income products, including corporate bonds, treasury securities, and other more complex types of debt instruments, and to work with institutional clients. "I use fundamentals such as time value of money and bond valuation techniques every day. Grasping these basics has allowed me to quickly move on to the more complicated analysis techniques and advance my career."

The bond market has seen unprecedented volatility in 2008. "Today's fixed-income markets are extremely volatile and complicated," Patrick says. "Finance professionals should understand how to analyze these securities and the risks and rewards they offer. Sound fundamental analysis is essential to understand returns. Certain fixed-income investments tend to perform well when other asset classes, such as equities, have lower returns, which make them extremely important to investors in the context of a diversified portfolio."

Patrick typically focuses on securities in major aggregate fixed-income indices, such as the Lehman Aggregate Bond Index and Citi Broad Investment Grade Index. "These indices are the fixed-income equivalent of the S&P 500," he says. "We present our best ideas to the appropriate institutional clients, based on their specific risk parameters and needs."

Extracurricular activities such as internships and investment clubs helped Patrick prepare for his career. "Internships bring the theory and textbooks to life and make picking a career path much more efficient," he says. He advises students to challenge themselves to truly understand the material, not simply memorize it. "Do not take the information you are learning in your current classes for granted. This valuable information will eventually become the building blocks for a successful career."

In this chapter, we introduce bonds and apply our tools for valuing cash flows to them. Bonds are simply loans. When an investor buys a bond from an issuer, the investor is lending money to the bond issuer. Who are the issuers of bonds? Federal and local governments issue bonds to finance long-term projects, and many companies issue bonds as part of their debt financing.

Understanding bonds and their pricing is useful for several reasons. First, we can use the prices of risk-free government bonds to determine the risk-free interest rates that produce the yield curve. The yield curve provides important information for valuing risk-free cash flows and assessing expectations of inflation and economic growth. Second, firms often issue bonds to fund their own investments. The return investors receive on those bonds is one factor determining a firm's cost of capital. Finally, bonds provide an opportunity to begin our study of how securities are priced in a competitive market. The bond markets are very large and very liquid; there are more than $45 *trillion* of bonds outstanding[1]. Further, the ideas we develop in this chapter will be helpful when we turn to the topic of valuing stocks in Chapter 9.

Pricing bonds gives us an opportunity to apply what we've learned in the last three chapters about valuing cash flows using competitive market prices. As we explained in Chapter 3, the Valuation Principle implies that the price of a security in a competitive market should be the present value of the cash flows an investor will receive from owning it. Thus, we begin the chapter by evaluating the promised cash flows for different types of bonds. If a bond is risk-free, so that the promised cash flows will be paid with certainty, we can use the Law of One Price to directly relate the return of a bond and its price. We then discuss how and why bond prices change over time. Once we have a firm understanding of the pricing of bonds in the absence of risk, we add the risk of default, where cash flows are not known with certainty. The risk of default and its implications are important considerations for a financial manager who is considering issuing corporate bonds. (In Chapter 14, we will discuss the details of issuing debt financing and cover some additional corporate bond features.)

bond certificate States the terms of a bond as well as the amounts and dates of all payments to be made.

6.1 Bond Terminology

maturity date The final repayment date of a bond.

term The time remaining until the final repayment date of a bond.

Recall from Chapter 3 that a bond is a security sold by governments and corporations to raise money from investors today in exchange for a promised future payment. The terms of the bond are described as part of the **bond certificate**, which indicates the amounts and dates of all payments to be made. A bond certificate is shown in Figure 6.1. Payments on the bond are made until a final repayment date called the **maturity date** of the bond. The time remaining until the repayment date is known as the **term** of the bond.

---

[1]Outstanding U.S. Bond Market Debt, Bond Market Association. November 2006.

BDeH CHAPTER 6

FIGURE 6.1

A Bearer Bond and Its Unclipped Coupons Issued by the Elmira and Williamsport Railroad Company for $500

Source: Courtesy Heritage Auctions, Inc. © 1999–2006.

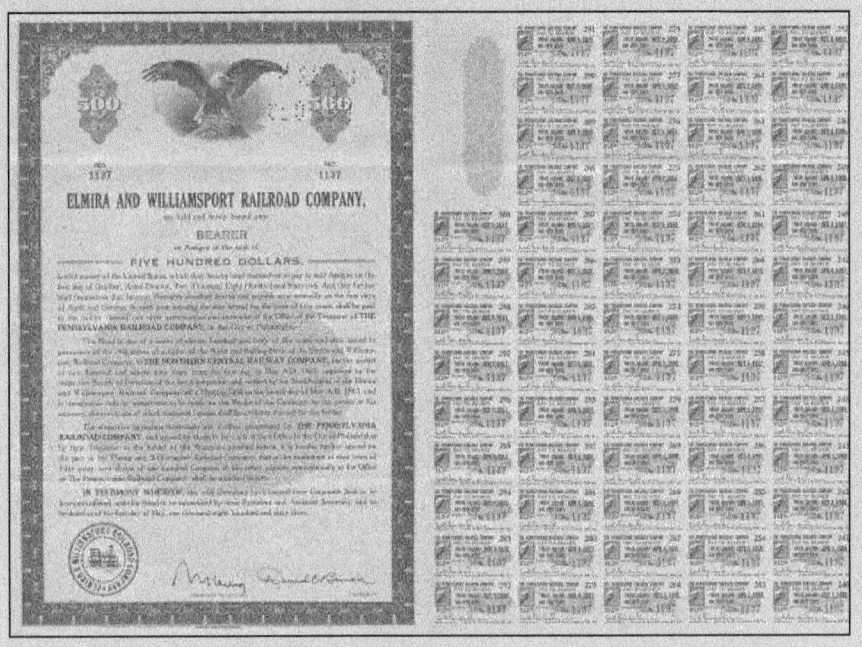

face value The notional amount of a bond used to compute its interest payments. The face value of the bond is generally due at the bond's maturity. Also called par value or principal amount.

coupons The promised interest payments of a bond, paid periodically until the maturity date of the bond.

coupon rate Determines the amount of each coupon payment of a bond. The coupon rate, expressed as an APR, is set by the issuer and stated on the bond certificate.

Bonds typically make two types of payments to their holders. The principal or **face value** (also known as **par value**) of a bond is the notional amount we use to compute the interest payments. Typically, the face value is repaid at maturity. It is generally denominated in standard increments such as $1000. A bond with a $1000 face value, for example, is often referred to as a "$1000 bond."

In addition to the face value, some bonds also promise additional payments called **coupons**. The bond certificate typically specifies that the coupons will be paid periodically (for example, semiannually) until the maturity date of the bond. As you can see from Figure 6.1, historically, on a payment date the holder of the bond would clip off the next coupon for the next payment and present it for payment. It follows that the interest payments on the bond are called coupon payments. Today, the majority of bonds are registered electronically but the term remains.

The amount of each coupon payment is determined by the **coupon rate** of the bond. This coupon rate is set by the issuer and stated on the bond certificate. By convention, the coupon rate is expressed as an APR, so the amount of each coupon payment, *CPN*, is:

Coupon Payment

$$CPN = \frac{\text{Coupon Rate} \times \text{Face Value}}{\text{Number of Coupon Payments per Year}} \qquad (6.1)$$

For example, a "$1000 bond with a 10% coupon rate and semiannual payments" will pay coupon payments of $1000 × 10%/2 = $50 every six months.

Table 6.1 summarizes the bond terminology we have presented thus far.

TABLE 6.1	Maturity Date	Final repayment date of the bond. Payments continue until this date.
Review of Bond Terminology	Term	The time remaining until the repayment date.
	Coupons	The promised interest payments of a bond. Usually paid semi-annually, but the frequency is specified in the bond certificate. The amount paid is equal to: $$\frac{\text{Coupon Rate} \times \text{Face Value}}{\text{Number of Coupon Payments per Year}}$$
	Principal or Face Value	The notional amount used to compute the interest payment. It is usually repaid on the maturity date.

1. What types of cash flows does a bond buyer receive?

2. How are the periodic coupon payments on a bond determined?

 **6.2 Zero-Coupon Bonds**

zero-coupon bond A bond that makes only one payment at maturity.

Treasury bills Zero-coupon bonds, issued by the U.S. government, with a maturity of up to one year.

Not all bonds have coupon payments. Bonds without coupons are called **zero-coupon bonds**. As these are the simplest type of bond, we shall analyze them first. The only cash payment an investor in a zero-coupon bond receives is the face value of the bond on the maturity date. **Treasury bills**, which are U.S. government bonds with a maturity of up to one year, are zero-coupon bonds.

Zero-Coupon Bond Cash Flows

There are only two cash flows if we purchase and hold a zero-coupon bond. First, we pay the bond's current market price at the time we make the purchase. Then, at the maturity date, we receive the bond's face value. For example, suppose that a one-year, risk-free, zero-coupon bond with a $100,000 face value has an initial price of $96,618.36. If you purchased this bond and held it to maturity, you would have the following cash flows:

```
        0              1
        ├──────────────┤
  -$96,618.36      $100,000
```

discount A price at which bonds trade that is less than their face value.

pure discount bonds Zero-coupon bonds.

Note that although the bond pays no "interest" directly, as an investor you are compensated for the time value of your money by purchasing the bond at a discount to its face value. Recall from Chapter 3 that the present value of a future cash flow is less than the cash flow itself. As a result, prior to its maturity date, the price of a zero-coupon bond is always less than its face value. That is, zero-coupon bonds always trade at a **discount** (a price lower than the face value), so they are also called **pure discount bonds**.

Yield to Maturity of a Zero-Coupon Bond

yield to maturity (YTM)
The IRR of an investment in a bond that is held to its maturity date, or the discount rate that sets the present value of the promised bond payments equal to the current market price for the bond.

Now that we understand the cash flows associated with a zero-coupon bond, we can calculate the IRR of buying a bond and holding it until maturity. Recall that the IRR of an investment opportunity is the discount rate at which the NPV of the investment opportunity is equal to zero. So the IRR of an investment in a bond is the discount rate at which the present value of the future bond cash flows equals the price of the bond, that is, the initial investment. The IRR of an investment in a bond is given a special name, the **yield to maturity (YTM)** or just the *yield:*

> *The yield to maturity of a bond is the discount rate that sets the present value of the promised bond payments equal to the current market price of the bond.*

Intuitively, the yield to maturity for a zero-coupon bond is the return you will earn as an investor by buying the bond at is current market price, holding the bond to maturity, and receiving the promised face value payment.

Let's determine the yield to maturity of the one-year zero-coupon bond discussed earlier. According to the definition, the yield to maturity of the one-year bond solves the following equation:

$$96,618.36 = \frac{100,000}{1 + YTM_1}$$

In this case:

$$1 + YTM_1 = \frac{100,000}{96,618.36} = 1.035$$

That is, the yield to maturity for this bond is 3.5%. Because the bond is risk free, investing in this bond and holding it to maturity is like earning 3.5% interest on your initial investment:

$$\$96,618.36 \times 1.035 = \$100,000$$

We can use a similar method to find the yield to maturity for any maturity zero-coupon bond:

Yield to Maturity of an *n*-Year Zero-Coupon Bond

$$1 + YTM_n = \left(\frac{Face\ Value}{Price}\right)^{1/n} \tag{6.2}$$

The yield to maturity (YTM_n) in Eq. 6.2 is the per-period rate of return for holding the bond from today until maturity on date n.

EXAMPLE 6.1
Yields for Different Maturities

Problem

Suppose the following zero-coupon bonds are trading at the prices shown below per $100 face value. Determine the corresponding yield to maturity for each bond.

Maturity	1 year	2 years	3 years	4 years
Price	$96.62	$92.45	$87.63	$83.06

Solution

▶ **Plan**

We can use Eq. 6.2 to solve for the YTM of the bonds. The table gives the prices and number of years to maturity and the face value is $100 per bond.

▶ **Execute**

Using Eq. 6.2, we have

$$YTM_1 = (100/96.62)^{1/1} - 1 = 3.50\%$$

$$YTM_2 = (100/92.45)^{1/2} - 1 = 4.00\%$$

$$YTM_3 = (100/87.63)^{1/3} - 1 = 4.50\%$$

$$YTM_4 = (100/83.06)^{1/4} - 1 = 4.75\%$$

▶ **Evaluate**

Solving for the YTM of a zero-coupon bond is the same process we used to solve for the internal rate of return in Chapter 4. Indeed, the YTM is the internal rate of return of buying the bond.

Risk-Free Interest Rates

Above, we calculated the yield to maturity of the one-year risk-free bond as 3.5%. But recall that the Valuation Principle's Law of One Price implies that all one-year risk-free investments must earn this same return of 3.5%. That is, 3.5% must be *the* competitive market risk-free interest rate.

More generally, in the last chapter we discussed the competitive market interest rate r_n available from today until date n for risk-free cash flows. Recall that we used this interest rate as the cost of capital for a risk-free cash flow that occurs on date n. A default-free zero-coupon bond that matures on date n provides a risk-free return over the same period. So the Law of One Price guarantees that the risk-free interest rate equals the yield to maturity on such a bond. Consequently, we will often refer to the yield to maturity of the appropriate maturity, zero-coupon risk-free bond as *the* risk-free interest rate. Some financial professionals also use the term **spot interest rates** to refer to these default-free, zero-coupon yields because these rates are offered "on the spot" at that point in time.

spot interest rates
Default-free, zero-coupon yields.

Earlier, we introduced the yield curve, which plots the risk-free interest rate for different maturities. These risk-free interest rates correspond to the yields of risk-free zero-coupon bonds. Thus, the yield curve is also referred to as the **zero-coupon yield curve**. Figure 6.2 illustrates the yield curve consistent with the zero-coupon bond prices in Example 6.1.

zero-coupon yield curve
A plot of the yield of risk-free zero-coupon bonds (STRIPS) as a function of the bond's maturity date.

In the previous example, we used the bond's price to compute its yield to maturity. But from the definition of the yield to maturity, we can also use a bond's yield to compute its price. In the case of a zero-coupon bond, the price is simply equal to the present value of the bond's face value, discounted at the bond's yield to maturity.

EXAMPLE 6.2

Computing the Price of a Zero-Coupon Bond

Problem

Given the yield curve shown in Figure 6.2, what is the price of a five-year risk-free zero-coupon bond with a face value of $100?

Solution

▶ **Plan**

We can compute the bond's price as the present value of its face amount, where the discount rate is the bond's yield to maturity. From the yield curve, the yield to maturity for five-year risk-free zero-coupon bonds is 5.0%.

BDeH CHAPTER 6

▶ **Execute**

$$P = 100/(1.05)^5 = 78.35$$

▶ **Evaluate**

We can compute the price of a zero-coupon bond simply by computing the present value of the face amount using the bond's yield to maturity. Note that the price of the five-year zero-coupon bond is even lower than the price of the other zero-coupon bonds in Example 6.1, because the face amount is the same but we must wait longer to receive it.

FIGURE 6.2   Zero-Coupon Yield Curve Consistent with the Bond Prices in Example 6.1

A yield curve simply plots the yield-to-maturity of investments of different maturities. In this figure, we show the yield curve that would be produced by plotting the yield-to-maturities determined by the bond prices in Example 6.1. Note that as in this figure, the longer maturities generally have higher yields.

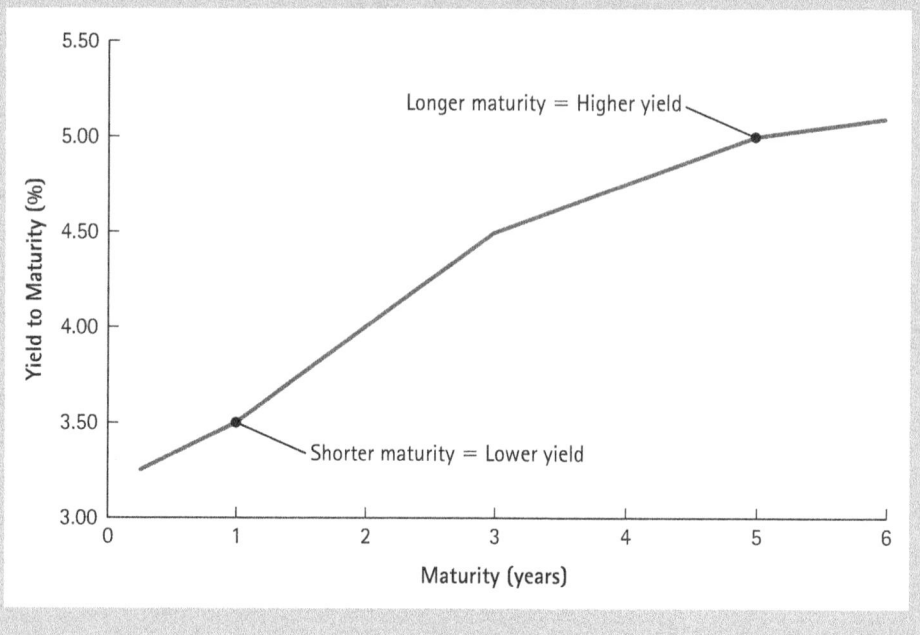

Concept Check

3. Why would you want to know the yield to maturity of a bond?

4. What is the relationship between a bond's price and its yield to maturity?

---

coupon bonds
Bonds that pay regular coupon interest payments up to maturity, when the face value is also paid.

6.3 Coupon Bonds

Similar to zero-coupon bonds, **coupon bonds** pay investors their face value at maturity. In addition, these bonds make regular coupon interest payments. As Table 6.2 indicates, two types of U.S. Treasury coupon securities are currently traded in financial markets:

TABLE 6.2	Treasury Security	Type	Original Maturity
Existing U.S. Treasury Securities	Bills	Discount	4, 13, and 26 weeks
	Notes	Coupon	2, 3, 5, and 10 year
	Bonds	Coupon	20 and 30 year

Treasury notes A type of U.S. Treasury coupon security, currently traded in financial markets, with original maturities from one to ten years.

Treasury bonds A type of U.S. Treasury coupon security, currently traded in financial markets, with original maturities of more than ten years.

Treasury notes, which have original maturities from one to ten years, and **Treasury bonds**, which have original maturities of more than ten years. The original maturity is the term of the bond at the time it was originally issued.

Coupon Bond Cash Flows

While an investor's return on a zero-coupon bond comes from buying it at a discount to its principal value, the return on a coupon bond comes from two sources: (1), any difference between the purchase price and the principal value, and (2), its periodic coupon payments. Before we can compute the yield to maturity of a coupon bond, we need to know all of its cash flows, including the coupon interest payments and when they are paid. In the following example, we take a bond description and translate it into the bond's cash flows.

EXAMPLE 6.3

The Cash Flows of a Coupon Bond or Note

Problem

Assume that it is May 15, 2008 and the U.S. Treasury has just issued securities with a May 2013 maturity, $1000 par value and a 5% coupon rate with semiannual coupons. Since the original maturity is only five years, these would be called "notes" as opposed to "bonds." The first coupon payment will be paid on November 15, 2008. What cash flows will you receive if you hold this note until maturity?

Solution

▶ **Plan**

The description of the note should be sufficient to determine all of its cash flows. The phrase "May 2013 maturity, $1000 par value" tells us that this is a note with a face value of $1000 and five years to maturity. The phrase "5% coupon rate with semiannual coupons" tells us that the note pays a total of 5% of its face value each year in two equal semiannual installments. Finally, we know that the first coupon is paid on November 15, 2008.

▶ **Execute**

The face value of this note is $1000. Because this note pays coupons semiannually, from Eq. 6.1 you will receive a coupon payment every six months of CPN = $1000 × 5%/2 = $25. Here is the timeline based on a six-month period and there are a total of ten cash flows:

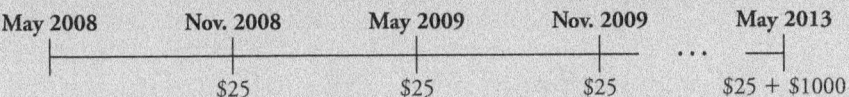

May 2008	Nov. 2008	May 2009	Nov. 2009	May 2013
	$25	$25	$25	$25 + $1000

Note that the last payment occurs five years (ten 6-month periods) from now and is composed of both a coupon payment of $25 and the face value payment of $1000.

▶ **Evaluate**

Since a note is just a package of cash flows, we need to know those cash flows in order to value the note. That's why the description of the note contains all of the information we would need to construct its cash flow timeline.

The U.S. Treasury Market

In most years, the U.S. Federal Government spends more than it takes in through taxes and other revenue sources. To finance this deficit, the U.S. Department of the Treasury issues debt instruments, commonly known as "Treasuries." The market for Treasury securities is huge and extremely liquid. In 2007, the total amount of public debt outstanding was almost $8.85 *trillion*. Treasury securities are held by institutional investors such as insurance companies, pension funds and bond mutual funds, individual investors, and even other governmental agencies (such as the Federal Reserve) as shown in the pie chart below. The figures are in *billions* of dollars (4577 billion is 4.577 trillion).

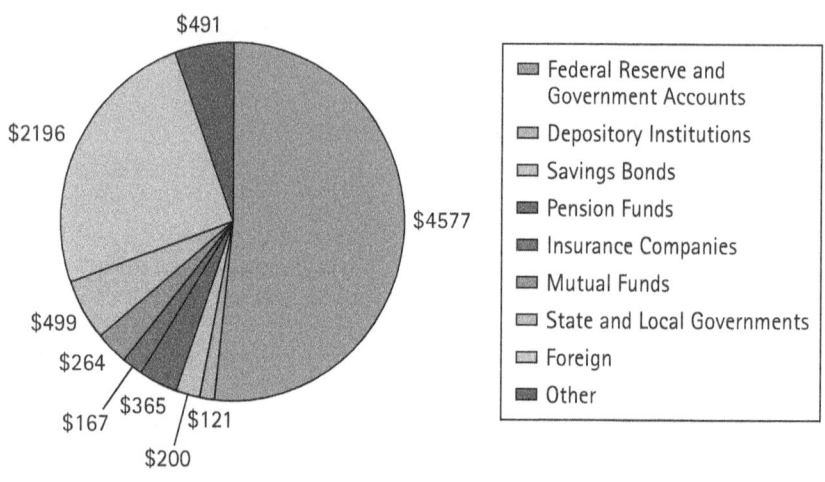

Legend:
- Federal Reserve and Government Accounts
- Depository Institutions
- Savings Bonds
- Pension Funds
- Insurance Companies
- Mutual Funds
- State and Local Governments
- Foreign
- Other

Source: Treasury Bulletin Ownership of Federal Securities, November 2007.

Yield to Maturity of a Coupon Bond

Once we have determined the coupon bond's cash flows, given its market price we can determine its yield to maturity. Recall that the yield to maturity for a bond is the IRR of investing in the bond and holding it to maturity. This investment has the cash flows shown in the timeline below:

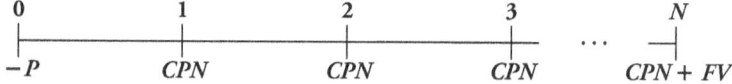

The yield to maturity of the bond is the *single* discount rate that equates the present value of the bond's remaining cash flows to its current price. For zero-coupon bonds, there were only two cash flows. But coupon bonds have many cash flows, complicating the yield to maturity calculation. From the timeline we see that the coupon payments represent an annuity, so the yield to maturity is the interest rate y that solves the following equation:

Yield to Maturity of a Coupon Bond

$$P = CPN \times \underbrace{\frac{1}{y}\left(1 - \frac{1}{(1+y)^N}\right)}_{\substack{\text{Annuity Factor using the YTM } (y) \\ \text{Present Value of all of the periodic coupon payments}}} + \underbrace{\frac{FV}{(1+y)^N}}_{\substack{\text{Present Value of the} \\ \text{Face Value repayment} \\ \text{using the YTM } (y)}} \qquad (6.3)$$

BDeH CHAPTER 6

Unfortunately, unlike zero-coupon bonds, there is no simple formula to solve for the yield to maturity directly. Instead, we need to use either trial and error or, more commonly, a financial calculator or a spreadsheet (using Excel's IRR function) as we introduced in Chapter 4.

When we calculate a bond's yield to maturity by solving Eq. 6.3, the yield we compute will be a rate *per coupon interval*. However, yields are typically quoted as APRs, so we multiply by the number of coupons per year, thereby converting the answer into an APR quote with the same compounding interval as the coupon rate.

EXAMPLE 6.4

Computing the Yield to Maturity of a Coupon Bond

Problem

Consider the five-year, $1000 bond with a 5% coupon rate and semiannual coupons described in Example 6.3. If this bond is currently trading for a price of $957.35, what is the bond's yield to maturity?

Solution

▶ **Plan**

We worked out the bond's cash flows in Example 6.3. From the cash flow timeline, we can see that the bond consists of an annuity of 10 payments of $25, paid every 6 months, and one lump-sum payment of $1000 in 5 years (ten 6-month periods). We can use Eq. 6.3 to solve for the yield to maturity. However, we must use six-month intervals consistently throughout the equation.

▶ **Execute**

Because the bond has ten remaining coupon payments, we compute its yield y by solving Eq. 6.3 for this bond:

$$957.35 = 25 \times \frac{1}{y}\left(1 - \frac{1}{(1 + y)^{10}}\right) + \frac{1000}{(1 + y)^{10}}$$

We can solve it by trial and error, financial calculator, or a spreadsheet. To use a financial calculator, we enter the price we pay as a negative number for the PV (it is a cash outflow), the coupon payments as the PMT, and the bond's par value as its FV. Finally, we enter the number of coupon payments remaining (10) as N.

	N	I/Y	PV	PMT	FV
Given:	10		−957.35	25	1000
Solve for:		3.00			

Excel Formula: =RATE(NPER,PMT,PV,FV)=RATE(10,25,−957.35,1000)

Therefore, $y = 3\%$. Because the bond pays coupons semiannually, this yield is for a six-month period. We convert it to an APR by multiplying by the number of coupon payments per year. Thus, the bond has a yield to maturity equal to a 6% APR with semiannual compounding.

▶ **Evaluate**

As the equation shows, the yield to maturity is the discount rate that equates the present value of the bond's cash flows with its price.

We can also use Eq. 6.3 to compute a bond's price based on its yield to maturity. We simply discount the cash flows using the yield, as in Example 6.5.

Finding Bond Prices on the Web

Unlike the NYSE where many stocks are traded, there is no particular physical location where bonds are traded. Instead, they are traded electronically. Recently, the Financial Industry Regulatory Authority (FINRA) has made an effort to make bond prices more widely available. Their Web site, http://www.finra.org/marketdata, allows anyone to search for the most recent trades and quotes for bonds. Here we show a screen shot from the Web site displaying the pricing information for one of Anheuser Busch's (BUD) bonds.

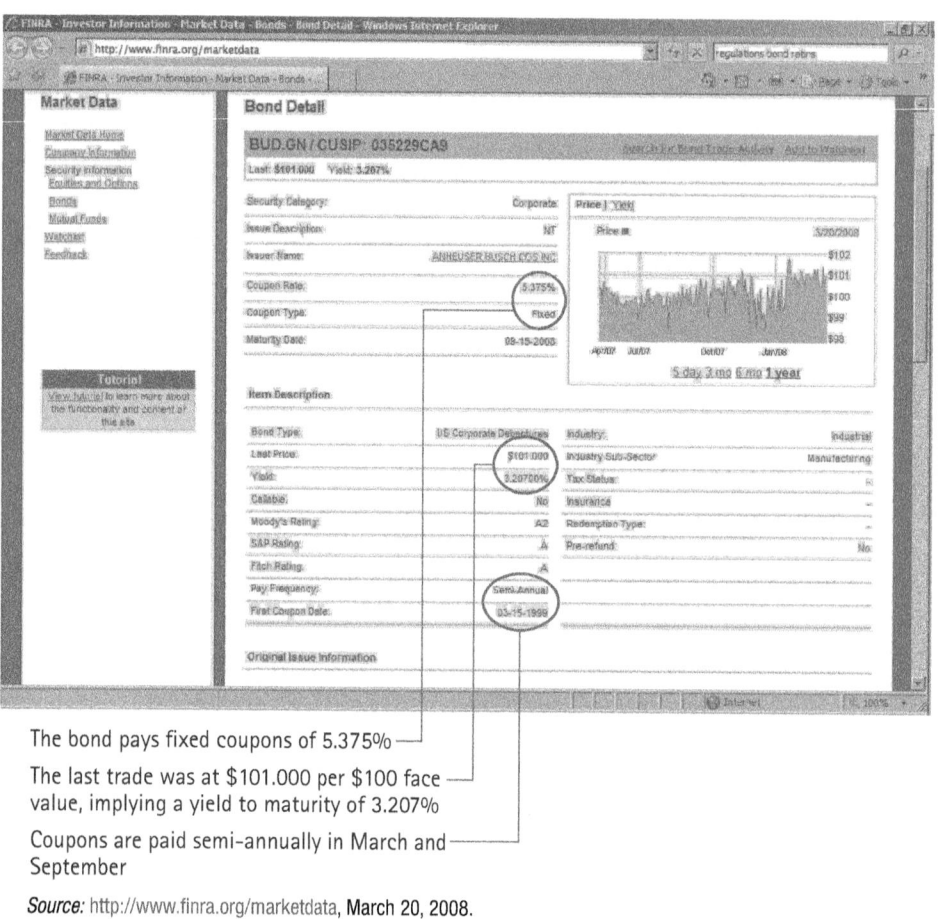

The bond pays fixed coupons of 5.375%

The last trade was at $101.000 per $100 face value, implying a yield to maturity of 3.207%

Coupons are paid semi-annually in March and September

Source: http://www.finra.org/marketdata, March 20, 2008.

EXAMPLE 6.5

Computing a Bond Price from Its Yield to Maturity

Problem

Consider again the five-year, $1000 bond with a 5% coupon rate and semiannual coupons in Example 6.4. Suppose interest rates drop and the bond's yield to maturity decreases to 4.50% (expressed as an APR with semiannual compounding). What price is the bond trading for now?

Solution

▶ **Plan**

Given the yield, we can compute the price using Eq. 6.3. First, note that a 4.50% APR is equivalent to a semiannual rate of 2.25%. Also, recall that the cash flows of this bond are an annuity of 10 payments of $25, paid every 6 months, and one lump-sum cash flow of $1000 (the face value), paid in 5 years (ten 6-month periods).

▶ **Execute**

Using Eq. 6.3 and the 6-month yield of 2.25%, the bond price must be:

$$P = 25 \times \frac{1}{0.0225}\left(1 - \frac{1}{1.0225^{10}}\right) + \frac{1000}{1.0225^{10}} = \$1022.17$$

We can also use a financial calculator:

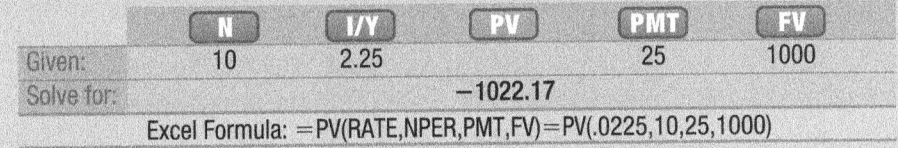

	N	I/Y	PV	PMT	FV
Given:	10	2.25		25	1000
Solve for:			−1022.17		

Excel Formula: =PV(RATE,NPER,PMT,FV)=PV(.0225,10,25,1000)

▶ **Evaluate**

The bond's price has risen to $1022.17, lowering the return from investing in it from 3% to 2.25% per 6-month period. Interest rates have dropped, so the lower return brings the bond's yield into line with the lower competitive rates being offered for similar risk and maturity elsewhere in the market.

Coupon Bond Price Quotes

Because we can convert any price into a yield, and vice versa, prices and yields are often used interchangeably. For example, the bond in Example 6.5 could be quoted as having a yield of 4.50% or a price of $1022.17 per $1000 face value. Indeed, bond traders generally quote bond yields rather than bond prices. One advantage of quoting the yield to maturity rather than the price is that the yield is independent of the face value of the bond. When prices are quoted in the bond market, they are conventionally quoted per $100 face value. Thus, the bond in Example 6.5 would be quoted as having a price of $102.217 (per $100 face value), which would imply an actual price of $1022.17 given the $1000 face value of the bond.

Concept Check

5. What cash flows does a company pay to investors holding its coupon bonds?
6. What do we need in order to value a coupon bond?

6.4 Why Bond Prices Change

As we mentioned earlier, zero-coupon bonds always trade for a discount—that is, prior to maturity, their price is less than their face value. But as shown in Example 6.4 and Example 6.5, coupon bonds may trade at a discount, or at a **premium** (a price greater than their face value). In this section, we identify when a bond will trade at a discount or premium, as well as how the bond's price will change due to the passage of time and fluctuations in interest rates.

> **premium** A price at which coupon bonds trade that is greater than their face value.

Most issuers of coupon bonds choose a coupon rate so that the bonds will *initially* trade at, or very close to, **par** (that is, at the bond's face value). For example, the U.S. Treasury sets the coupon rates on its notes and bonds in this way. After the issue date, the market price of a bond generally changes over time for two reasons. First, as time passes, the bond gets closer to its maturity date. Holding fixed the bond's yield to maturity, the present value of the bond's remaining cash flows changes as the time to maturity

> **par** A price at which coupon bonds trade that is equal to their face value.

BDeH CHAPTER 6

decreases. Second, at any point in time, changes in market interest rates affect the bond's yield to maturity and its price (the present value of the remaining cash flows). We explore these two effects in the remainder of this section.

Interest Rate Changes and Bond Prices

If a bond sells at par (at its face value), the only return investors will earn is from the coupons that the bond pays. Therefore, the bond's coupon rate will exactly equal its yield to maturity. As interest rates in the economy fluctuate, the yields that investors demand to invest in bonds will also change. Imagine that your company issues a bond when market interest rates imply a YTM of 8%, setting the coupon rate to be 8%. Suppose interest rates then rise so that new bonds have a YTM of 9%. These new bonds would have a coupon rate of 9% and sell for $1000. So, for $1000, the investor would get $90 per year until the bond matured. Your existing bond was issued when rates were lower such that its coupon is fixed at 8%, so it offers payments of $80 per year until maturity. Because its cash flows are lower, the 8% bond must have a lower price than the 9% bond.[2] Thus, the price of the 8% bond will fall until the investor is indifferent between buying the 8% bond and buying the 9% bond. Figure 6.3 illustrates the relation between the bond's price and its yield to maturity.

FIGURE 6.3   A Bond's Price vs. Its Yield to Maturity

At a price of $1000, the 8% semi-annual coupon bond offers an 8% YTM. In order for the 8% coupon bond to offer a competitive yield to maturity, its price must fall until its yield to maturity rises to the 9% yield being offered by otherwise similar bonds. In the example depicted here, for a bond with five years left to maturity, its price must fall to $960.44 before investors will be indifferent between buying it and the 9% coupon bond priced at $1000.

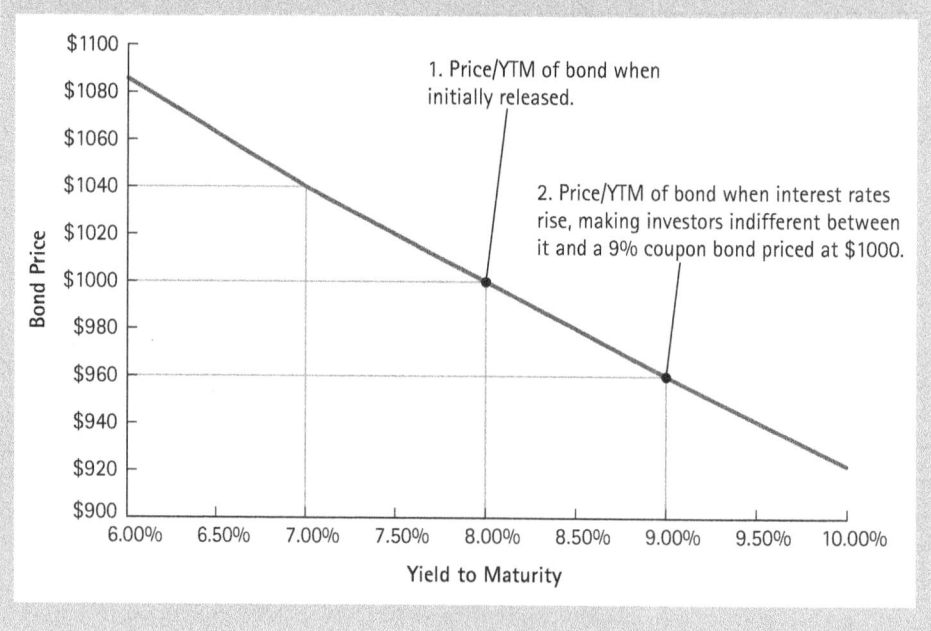

---

[2]Otherwise, if the 8% bond had the same or higher price, there would be an arbitrage opportunity: one could sell the 8% bond and buy the 9% bond, receiving cash today and higher coupons going forward.

	greater than the face value	equal to the face value	less than the face value
When the bond price is . . .			
We say the bond trades . . .	"above par" or "at a premium"	"at par"	"below par" or "at a discount"
This occurs when . . .	Coupon Rate > Yield to Maturity	Coupon Rate = Yield to Maturity	Coupon Rate < Yield to Maturity

TABLE 6.3

Bond Prices Immediately After a Coupon Payment

In our example, the price of the 8% bond will drop to below face value ($1000), so it will be trading at a discount (also called trading *below par*). If the bond trades at a discount, an investor who buys the bond will earn a return both from receiving the coupons *and* from receiving a face value that exceeds the price paid for the bond. As a result, if a bond trades at a discount, its yield to maturity will exceed its coupon rate.

A bond that pays a coupon can also trade at a premium to its face value (trading *above par*). Imagine what would have happened in our example if interest rates had gone down to 7% instead of up to 9%. Then, the holder of the existing 8% bond would not part with it for $1000. Instead, its price would have to rise until the yield to maturity from buying it at that price would be 7%. In this case, an investor's return from the coupons is diminished by receiving a face value less than the price paid for the bond. *Thus, a bond trades at a premium whenever its yield to maturity is less than its coupon rate.*[3]

This example illustrates a general phenomenon. A higher yield to maturity means that investors demand a higher return for investing. They apply a higher discount rate for a bond's remaining cash flows, reducing their present value and hence the bond's price. The reverse holds when interest rates fall. Investors then demand a lower yield to maturity, reducing the discount rate applied to the bond's cash flows and raising the price. Therefore, *as interest rates and bond yields rise, bond prices will fall, and vice versa, so that interest rates and bond prices always move in the opposite direction.*

Table 6.3 summarizes the relationship between interest rates and bond prices.

EXAMPLE 6.6

Determining the Discount or Premium of a Coupon Bond

Problem

Consider three 30-year bonds with annual coupon payments. One bond has a 10% coupon rate, one has a 5% coupon rate, and one has a 3% coupon rate. If the yield to maturity of each bond is 5%, what is the price of each bond per $100 face value? Which bond trades at a premium, which trades at a discount, and which trades at par?

Solution

▶ **Plan**

From the description of the bonds, we can determine their cash flows. Each bond has 30 years to maturity and pays its coupons annually. Therefore, each bond has an annuity of coupon payments, paid annually for 30 years, and then the face value paid as a lump sum in 30 years. They are all priced so that their yield to maturity is 5%, meaning that 5% is the discount rate that equates the present value of the cash flows to the price of the bond. Therefore, we can use Eq. 6.3 to compute the price of each bond as the PV of its cash flows, discounted at 5%.

---

[3]The terms "discount" and "premium" are simply descriptive and are not meant to imply that you should try to buy bonds at a discount and avoid buying bonds at a premium. In a competitive market, the Law of One Price ensures that all similar bonds are priced to earn the same return. That is why buying a bond is a zero NPV proposition: the price exactly equals the present value of the bond's cash flows, so that you earn a fair return, but not an abnormally good (or bad) return.

▶ **Execute**

For the 10% coupon bond, the annuity cash flows are $10 per year (10% of each $100 face value). Similarly, the annuity cash flows for the 5% and 3% bonds are $5 and $3 per year. We use a $100 face value for all of the bonds.

Using Eq. 6.3 and these cash flows, the bond prices are:

$$P(\text{10\% coupon}) = 10 \times \frac{1}{0.05}\left(1 - \frac{1}{1.05^{30}}\right) + \frac{100}{1.05^{30}} = \$176.86 \text{ (trades at a premium)}$$

$$P(\text{5\% coupon}) = 5 \times \frac{1}{0.05}\left(1 - \frac{1}{1.05^{30}}\right) + \frac{100}{1.05^{30}} = \$100.00 \text{ (trades at par)}$$

$$P(\text{3\% coupon}) = 3 \times \frac{1}{0.05}\left(1 - \frac{1}{1.05^{30}}\right) + \frac{100}{1.05^{30}} = \$69.26 \text{ (trades at a discount)}$$

▶ **Evaluate**

The prices reveal that when the coupon rate of the bond is higher than its yield to maturity, it trades at a premium. When its coupon rate equals its yield to maturity, it trades at par. When its coupon rate is lower than its yield to maturity, it trades at a discount.

Time and Bond Prices

Let's consider the effect of time on the price of a bond. As the next payment from a bond grows nearer, the price of the bond increases to reflect the increasing present value of that cash flow. Take a bond paying semi-annual coupons of $50 and imagine tracking the price of the bond starting on the day after the last coupon payment was made. The price would slowly rise over the following six months as the next $50 coupon payment grows closer and closer. It will peak right before the coupon payment is made, when buying the bond still entitles you to receive the $50 payment immediately. If you buy the bond right after the coupon payment is made, you do not have the right to receive that $50 coupon. The price you are willing to pay for the bond will therefore be $50 less than it was right before the coupon was paid. This pattern—the price slowly rising as a coupon payment nears and then dropping abruptly after the payment is made—continues for the life of the bond. Figure 6.4 illustrates this phenomenon.

EXAMPLE 6.7

The Effect of Time on the Price of a Bond

Problem

Suppose you purchase a 30-year, zero-coupon bond with a yield to maturity of 5%. For a face value of $100, the bond will initially trade for:

$$P(\text{30 years to maturity}) = \frac{100}{1.05^{30}} = \$23.14$$

If the bond's yield to maturity remains at 5%, what will its price be five years later? If you purchased the bond at $23.14 and sold it five years later, what would the IRR of your investment be?

Solution

▶ **Plan**

If the bond was originally a 30-year bond and 5 years have passed, then it has 25 years left to maturity. If the yield to maturity does not change, then you can compute the price of the bond with 25 years left exactly as we did for 30 years, but using 25 years of discounting instead of 30.

Once you have the price in five years, you can compute the IRR of your investment just as we did in Chapter 4. The FV is the price in five years, the PV is the initial price ($23.14), and the number of years is 5.

▶ **Execute**

$$P(25 \text{ years to maturity}) = \frac{100}{1.05^{25}} = \$29.53$$

If you purchased the bond for $23.14 and then sold it after five years for $29.53, the IRR of your investment would be

$$\left(\frac{29.53}{23.14}\right)^{1/5} - 1 = 5.0\%$$

That is, your return is the same as the yield to maturity of the bond.

▶ **Evaluate**

Note that the bond price is higher, and hence the discount from its face value is smaller, when there is less time to maturity. The discount shrinks because the yield has not changed, but there is less time until the face value will be received. This example illustrates a more general property for bonds. *If a bond's yield to maturity does not change, then the IRR of an investment in the bond equals its yield to maturity even if you sell the bond early.*

FIGURE 6.4

The Effect of Time on Bond Prices

The graph illustrates the effects of the passage of time on bond prices when the yield remains constant. The price of a zero-coupon bond rises smoothly. The prices of the coupon bonds are indicated by the zigzag lines. Notice that the prices rise between coupon payments, but tumble on the coupon date, reflecting the amount of the coupon payment. For each coupon bond, the gray line shows the trend of the bond price just after each coupon is paid.

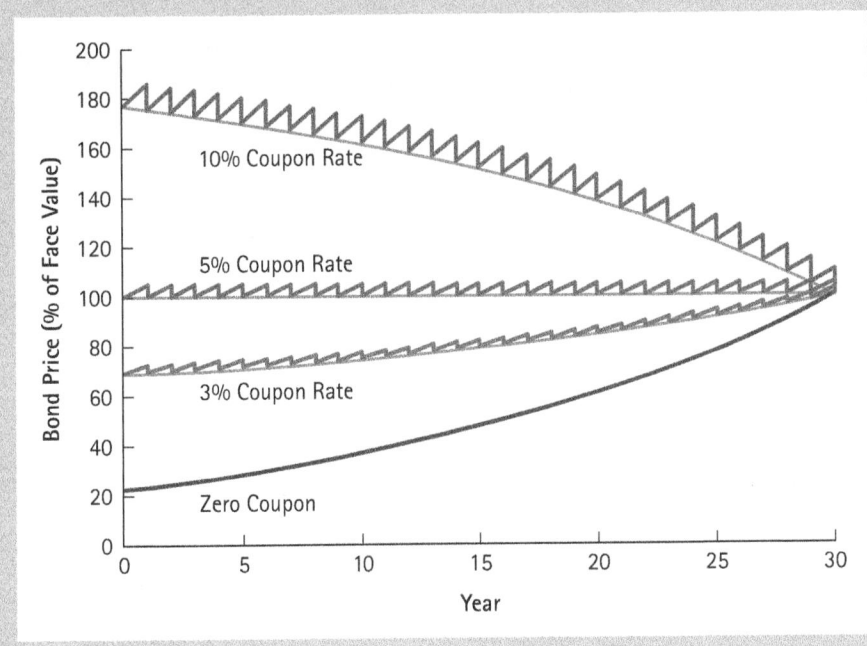

Interest Rate Risk and Bond Prices

While the effect of time on bond prices is predictable, unpredictable changes in interest rates will also affect bond prices. Further, bonds with different characteristics will respond differently to changes in interest rates—some bonds will react more strongly than others. Investors view long-term loans to be riskier than short-term loans. Because bonds are just loans, the same is true of short- versus long-term bonds.

EXAMPLE 6.8

The Interest Rate Sensitivity of Bonds

Problem

Consider a 10-year coupon bond and a 30-year coupon bond, both with 10% annual coupons. By what percentage will the price of each bond change if its yield to maturity increases from 5% to 6%?

Solution

▶ **Plan**

We need to compute the price of each bond for each yield to maturity and then calculate the percentage change in the prices. For both bonds, the cash flows are $10 per year for $100 in face value and then the $100 face value repaid at maturity. The only difference is the maturity: 10 years and 30 years. With those cash flows, we can use Eq. 6.3 to compute the prices.

▶ **Execute**

Yield to Maturity	10-Year, 10% Annual Coupon Bond	30-Year, 10% Annual Coupon Bond
5%	$10 \times \dfrac{1}{0.05}\left(1 - \dfrac{1}{1.05^{10}}\right) + \dfrac{100}{1.05^{10}} = \$138.61$	$10 \times \dfrac{1}{0.05}\left(1 - \dfrac{1}{1.05^{30}}\right) + \dfrac{100}{1.05^{30}} = \$176.86$
6%	$10 \times \dfrac{1}{0.06}\left(1 - \dfrac{1}{1.06^{10}}\right) + \dfrac{100}{1.06^{10}} = \$129.44$	$10 \times \dfrac{1}{0.06}\left(1 - \dfrac{1}{1.06^{30}}\right) + \dfrac{100}{1.06^{30}} = \$155.06$

The price of the 10-year bond changes by $(129.44 - 138.61)/138.61 = -6.6\%$ if its yield to maturity increases from 5% to 6%. For the 30-year bond, the price change is $(155.06 - 176.86)/176.86 = -12.3\%$.

▶ **Evaluate**

The 30-year bond is almost twice as sensitive to a change in the yield than is the 10-year bond. In fact, if we graph the price and yields of the two bonds, we can see that the line for the 30-year bond, shown in blue, is steeper throughout than the green line for the 10-year bond, reflecting its heightened sensitivity to interest rate changes.

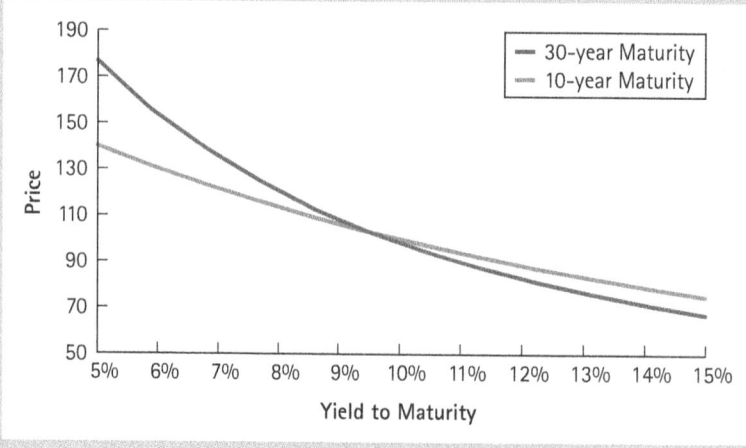

BDeH CHAPTER 6

TABLE 6.4	Bond Characteristic	Effect on Interest Rate Risk
Bond Prices and Interest Rates	Longer term to maturity	Increase
	Higher coupon payments	Decrease

The example illustrates how bonds of different maturity will have different sensitivities to interest rate changes. However, even bonds with the same maturity will differ in interest rate sensitivity if their coupon rates are different. Bonds with higher coupon rates—because they pay higher cash flows upfront—are less sensitive to interest rate changes than otherwise identical bonds with lower coupon rates. Table 6.4 summarizes this conclusion.

EXAMPLE 6.9

Coupons and Interest Rate Sensitivity

Problem

Consider two bonds, each of which pays semi-annual coupons and has five years left until maturity. One has a coupon rate of 5% and the other has a coupon rate of 10%, but both currently have a yield to maturity of 8%. How much will the price of each bond change if its yield to maturity decreases from 8% to 7%?

Solution

▶ **Plan**

As in Example 6.8, we need to compute the price of each bond at 8% and 7% yield to maturities and then compute the percentage change in price. Each bond has ten semi-annual coupon payments remaining along with the repayment of par value at maturity. The cash flows per $100 of face value for the first bond are $2.50 every 6 months and then $100 at maturity. The cash flows per $100 of face value for the second bond are $5 every 6 months and then $100 at maturity. Since the cash flows are semi-annual, the yield to maturity is quoted as a semi-annually compounded APR, so we convert the yields to match the frequency of the cash flows by dividing by 2. With semi-annual rates of 4% and 3.5%, we can use Eq. 6.3 to compute the prices.

▶ **Execute**

Yield to Maturity	5-Year, 5% Coupon Bond	5-Year, 10% Coupon Bond
8%	$2.50 \times \dfrac{1}{0.04}\left(1 - \dfrac{1}{1.04^{10}}\right)$ $+ \dfrac{100}{1.04^{10}} = \$87.83$	$5 \times \dfrac{1}{0.04}\left(1 - \dfrac{1}{1.04^{10}}\right)$ $+ \dfrac{100}{1.04^{10}} = \$108.11$
7%	$2.50 \times \dfrac{1}{0.035}\left(1 - \dfrac{1}{1.035^{10}}\right)$ $+ \dfrac{100}{1.035^{10}} = \$91.68$	$5 \times \dfrac{1}{0.035}\left(1 - \dfrac{1}{1.035^{10}}\right)$ $+ \dfrac{100}{1.035^{10}} = \$112.47$

The 5% coupon bond's price changed from $87.83 to $91.68, or 4.4%, but the 10% coupon bond's price changed from $108.11 to $112.47, or 4.0%. You can calculate the price change very quickly with a financial calculator. Take the 5% coupon bond for example:

	N	I/Y	PV	PMT	FV
Given:	10	4		2.50	100
Solve for:			−87.83		

Excel Formula: =PV(RATE,NPER,PMT,FV)=PV(.04,10,2.5,100)

BDeH   CHAPTER 6

With all of the basic bond information entered, you can simply change the I/Y by entering 3.5 and pressing I/Y and then solve for PV again. So, with just a few keystrokes, you will have the new price of $91.68.

▶ **Evaluate**

The bond with the smaller coupon payments is more sensitive to changes in interest rates. Because its coupons are smaller relative to its par value, a larger fraction of its cash flows are received later. As we learned in Example 6.8, later cash flows are affected more greatly by changes in interest rates, so compared to the 10% coupon bond, the effect of the interest change is greater for the cash flows of the 5% bond.

Bond Prices in Practice

dirty price (invoice price) A bond's actual cash price.

clean price A bond's cash price less an adjustment for accrued interest, the amount of the next coupon payment that has already accrued.

In actuality, bond prices are subject to the effects of both the passage of time and changes in interest rates. Bond prices converge to the bond's face value due to the time effect, but simultaneously move up and down due to unpredictable changes in bond yields. Figure 6.5 illustrates this behavior by demonstrating how the price of the 30-year, zero-coupon bond might change over its life. Note that the bond price tends to converge to the face value as the bond approaches the maturity date, but also moves higher when its yield falls and lower when its yield rises.

As the fluctuating price in Figure 6.5 demonstrates, prior to maturity the bond is exposed to interest rate risk. If an investor chooses to sell and the bond's yield to maturity has decreased, then the investor will receive a high price and earn a high return. If the yield to maturity has increased, the bond price is low at the time of sale and the investor will earn a low return.

BDeH   CHAPTER 6

Clean and Dirty Prices for Coupon Bonds

As Figure 6.4 illustrates, coupon bond prices fluctuate around the time of each coupon payment in a sawtooth pattern: The value of the coupon bond rises as the next coupon payment gets closer and then drops after it has been paid. This fluctuation occurs even if there is no change in the bond's yield to maturity.

Bond traders are more concerned about changes in the bond's price that arise due to changes in the bond's yield, rather than these predictable patterns around coupon payments. As a result, they often do not quote the price of a bond in terms of its actual cash price, which is also called the **dirty price** or **invoice price** of the bond. Instead, bonds are often quoted in terms of a **clean price**, which is the bond's cash price less an adjustment for accrued interest, the amount of the next coupon payment that has already accrued:

$$\text{Clean price} = \text{Cash (dirty) price} - \text{Accrued interest}$$

$$\text{Accrued interest} = \text{Coupon Amount} \times \left(\frac{\text{days since last coupon payment}}{\text{days in current coupon period}} \right)$$

Note that immediately before a coupon payment is made, the accrued interest will equal the full amount of the coupon. Immediately after the coupon payment is made, the accrued interest will be zero. Thus, accrued interest will rise and fall in a sawtooth pattern as each coupon payment passes.

If we subtract accrued interest from the bond's cash price and compute the clean price, the sawtooth pattern is eliminated.

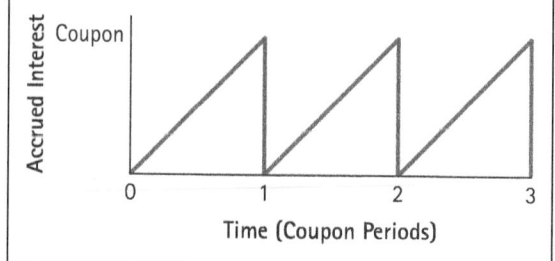

FIGURE 6.5   Yield to Maturity and Bond Price Fluctuations over Time

The graphs illustrate changes in price and yield for a 30-year zero-coupon bond over its life. Panel (a) illustrates the changes in the bond's yield to maturity (YTM) over its life. In Panel (b), the actual bond price is shown in blue. Because the YTM does not remain constant over the bond's life, the bond's price fluctuates as it converges to the face value over time. Also shown is the price if the YTM remained fixed at 4%, 5%, or 6%. Panel (a) shows that the bond's YTM mostly remained between 4% and 6%. The broken lines in Panel (b) show the price of the bond if its YTM had remained constant at those levels. Note that in all cases, the bond's price must eventually converge to $100 on its maturity date.

Panel (a) The Bond's Yield to Maturity over Time

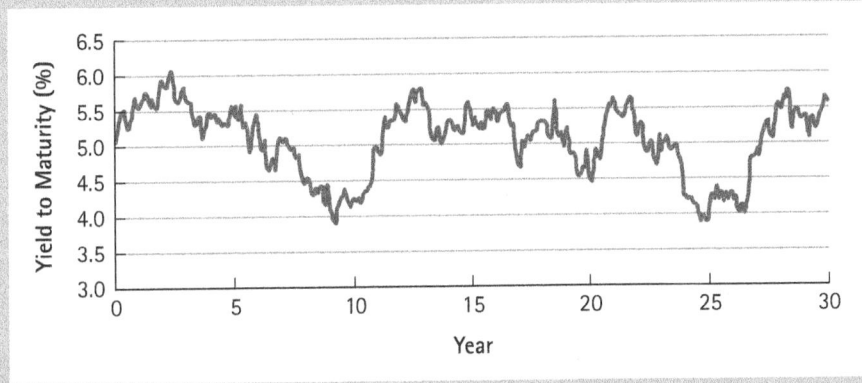

Panel (b) The Bond's Price over Time (Price = $100 on Maturity Date)

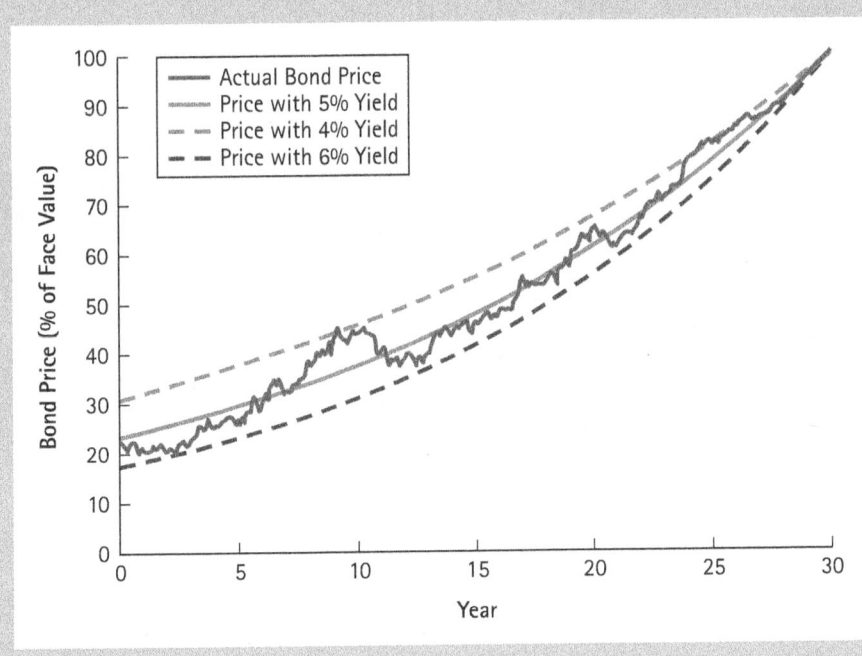

BDeH CHAPTER 6

7. Why do interest rates and bond prices move in opposite directions?

8. If a bond's yield to maturity does not change, how does its cash price change between coupon payments?

6.5 Corporate Bonds

corporate bonds Bonds issued by a corporation.

In the previous sections, we developed the basics of bond pricing in the context of U.S. Treasury bonds, which have no risk of default. In this section, our focus is on **corporate bonds**, which are bonds issued by corporations. We will examine the role of default risk in the price and yield to maturity of corporate bonds. As we will see, corporations with higher default risk will need to pay higher coupons to attract buyers to their bonds.

Credit Risk

Table 6.5 lists the interest rates paid by a number of different borrowers in late 2007 for a five-year bond. Why do these interest rates vary so widely? The lowest interest rate is the 3.70% rate paid on U.S. Treasury notes. United States Treasury securities are widely regarded to be risk-free because there is virtually no chance the government will fail to pay the interest and default on these bonds. Thus, as we noted in Section 6.1, when we refer to the "risk-free interest rate," we mean the rate on U.S. Treasuries.

The remaining bonds are all corporate bonds. With corporate bonds, the bond issuer may default—that is, it might not pay back the full amount promised in the bond prospectus. For example, a company with financial difficulties may be unable to fully repay the loan. This risk of default, which is known as the **credit risk** of the bond, means that the bond's cash flows are not known with certainty. To compensate for the risk that the firm may default, investors demand a higher interest rate than the rate on U.S.

credit risk The risk of default by the issuer of any bond that is not default free; it is an indication that the bond's cash flows are not known with certainty.

Treasuries. The difference between the interest rate of the loan and the Treasury rate will depend on investors' assessment of the likelihood that the firm will default. For example, investors place a higher probability of default on Goodyear Tire than on Abbott Labs, forcing Goodyear to pay a larger credit spread, which is reflected in a higher interest rate.

Borrower	Interest Rate	Credit Spread
U.S. Government (Treasury Notes)	3.70%	
Abbott Laboratories	4.81%	1.11%
Time Warner	5.18%	1.48%
Kraft Foods Inc.	5.41%	1.71%
RadioShack Corp.	6.68%	2.98%
General Motors Acceptance Corp.	7.15%	3.45%
Goodyear Tire and Rubber Co.	7.70%	4.00%

TABLE 6.5 Interest Rates on Five-Year Bonds for Various Borrowers, November 20007

Corporate Bond Yields

How does the credit risk of default affect bond prices and yields? The cash flows promised by the bond are the most that bondholders can hope to receive. Due to credit risk, the cash flows that a purchaser of a corporate bond actually *expects* to receive may be less than that amount. For example, both Ford and GM struggled financially in 2006 and 2007, substantially increasing the chance that they would default on their bonds. Realizing this, investors in GM bonds incorporated an increased probability that the bond payments would not be made as promised and prices of the bonds fell. Because the yield to maturity of GM's bonds is computed by comparing the price to the *promised* cash flows, the yield to maturity *increased* as the probability of being paid as promised decreased. This example highlights the following general truths:

1. Investors pay less for bonds with credit risk than they would for an otherwise identical default-free bond.

2. Because the yield to maturity for a bond is calculated using the promised cash flows instead of the *expected* cash flows, the yield of bonds with credit risk will be higher than that of otherwise identical default-free bonds.

These two points lead us to an important conclusion: *the yield to maturity of a defaultable bond is not equal to the expected return of investing in the bond.* The promised cash flows used to determine the yield to maturity are always higher than the expected cash flows investors use to calculate the expected return. As a result, the yield to maturity will always be higher than the expected return of investing in the bond. *Moreover, a higher yield to maturity does not necessarily imply that a bond's expected return is higher.*

Bond Ratings

The probability of default is clearly important to the price you are willing to pay for a corporate bond. How do you assess a firm's likelihood of default? Several companies rate the creditworthiness of bonds and make this information available to investors. By consulting these ratings, investors can assess the creditworthiness of a particular bond issue. The ratings therefore encourage widespread investor participation and relatively

investment-grade bonds Bonds in the top four categories of creditworthiness with a low risk of default.

speculative bonds (junk bond or high-yield bonds) Bonds in one of the bottom five categories of creditworthiness (below investment grade) that have a high risk of default.

liquid markets. The two best-known bond-rating companies are Standard & Poor's and Moody's. Table 6.6 summarizes the rating classes each company uses. Bonds with the highest rating (Aaa or AAA) are judged to be least likely to default.

Bonds in the top four categories are often referred to as **investment-grade bonds** because of their low default risk. Bonds in the bottom five categories are often called **speculative bonds, junk bonds**, or **high-yield bonds** because their likelihood of default is high and so they promise higher yields. The rating depends on the risk of bankruptcy as well as the bondholders' ability to lay claim to the firm's assets in the event of

"The potato salad maintains its Aa rating this year, but I'm afraid the deviled eggs are downgraded to C."

© Chris Wildt, Reproduction rights obtainable from www.cartoonstock.com

such a bankruptcy. Thus, debt issues with a low-priority claim in bankruptcy will have a lower rating than issues from the same company that have a high priority in bankruptcy or that are backed by a specific asset such as a building or a plant.

TABLE 6.6	Moody's	Standard & Poor's	Number of Public Firms	Description (Moody's)
Bond Ratings and the Number of U.S. Public Firms with Those Ratings at the End of 2006	**Investment**	**Grade Debt**		
	Aaa	AAA	7	Judged to be of the best quality. They carry the smallest degree of investment risk and are generally referred to as "gilt edged."
	Aa	AA	31	Judged to be of high quality by all standards. Together with the Aaa group, they constitute what are generally known as high-grade bonds.
	A	A	213	Possess many favorable investment attributes and are considered as upper-medium-grade obligations. Factors giving security to principal and interest are considered adequate at present, but may not remain that way.
	Baa	BBB	405	Are considered as medium-grade obligations (i.e., they are neither highly protected nor poorly secured).
	Speculative Bonds ("Junk Bonds")			
	Ba	BB	363	Judged to have speculative elements; their future cannot be considered as well assured.
	B	B	264	Generally lack characteristics of the desirable investment. Assurance of interest and principal payments over any long period of time may be small.
	Caa	CCC	22	Are of poor standing. Such issues may be in default or there may be present elements of danger with respect to principal or interest.
	Ca	CC	1	Are speculative to a high degree. Such issues are often in default or have other marked shortcomings.
	C	C, D	5	Lowest-rated class of bonds, and issues so rated can be regarded as having extremely poor prospects of ever attaining any real investment standing.

Source: www.moodys.com and S&P Compustat.

INTERVIEW WITH

Lisa Black

*L*isa Black is Managing Director at Teachers Insurance and Annuity Association, a major financial services company. A Chartered Financial Analyst, she oversees a variety of fixed income funds, including money market, intermediate bond, high-yield, emerging market debt, and inflation-linked bond funds.

QUESTION: *When many people think about the financial markets, they picture the equity markets. How big and how active are the bond markets compared to the equity markets?*

ANSWER: The dollar volume of bonds traded daily is about ten times that of equity markets. For example, a single $15 billion issue of 10-year Treasury bonds will sell in one day. The total amount of just U.S.-dollar denominated debt is almost $10 *trillion*.

QUESTION: *How do the bond markets operate?*

ANSWER: Firms and governments turn to bond markets when they need to borrow money to fund new construction projects, cover budget deficits, and similar reasons. On the other side, you have institutions like TIAA-CREF, endowments, and foundations with funds to invest. Wall Street investment bankers serve as intermediaries between capital raisers and investors, matching up borrowers with creditors in terms of maturity needs and risk appetite. Because we provide annuities for college professors, for example, we invest money for longer periods of time than an insurance company that needs funds to pay claims. In the institutional world, such as the bond funds we manage, we typically trade in blocks of bonds ranging from $5 million to $50 million at a time.

QUESTION: *What drives changes in the values of Treasury bonds?*

ANSWER: The simple answer is that when interest rates rise, bond prices fall. The key is to dig below that reality to see *why* interest rates rise and fall. A major factor is investors' expectation for inflation and economic growth. Right now (July 2006), the Fed Funds (overnight) rate is 5.25%. A 10-year Treasury bond is yielding about 5%, about 0.25% below the overnight rate. This downward-sloping yield curve is saying that inflation is in check and won't erode the value of that 5% yield. Otherwise, investors would require a greater expected return to lend for ten years.

Expectations of future economic growth have an important influence on interest rates—interest rates generally rise when the expectation is that growth will accelerate, because inflation won't be far behind. In 2000, when the bubble burst and there was concern that the economy would go into a recession, interest rates fell because with the expectations of slower growth, the inflation outlook would improve.

QUESTION: *Are there other factors that affect corporate bonds?*

ANSWER: Corporate bonds have asymmetric returns—you expect to get principal and interest back over the life of the bond, but the downside is that if the company files for bankruptcy, you may only get 30 to 50 cents on the dollar. Therefore, another factor that affects the values of corporate bonds is expectations of the likelihood of default. When the economy is very good, a company that is strong financially will need to offer only a very small yield spread over Treasuries. For example, IBM may need to offer just 0.35% more than 10-year Treasuries to attract buyers to their bonds.

On other hand, if an issuer has credit problems, the yield spread of its bonds over Treasuries will widen. GM's yield spreads have widened dramatically since they announced high losses. No longer can they issue debt at 2.5% over the 10-year Treasury rate; now the yields on GM bonds are about 5% higher than Treasuries. Investors demand higher yields to compensate them for the higher risk that GM may default.

Discussion Questions

1. Some financial managers feel that a strong balance sheet (low leverage, plenty of cash, etc.) gives their firm a competitive advantage in the marketplace. Assess that strategy in the context of Ms. Black's discussion of corporate bonds.

2. In what ways might you as a financial manager make use of the information contained in the yield curve?

FIGURE 6.6

Corporate Yield Curves for Various Ratings, March 2008

This figure shows the yield curve for U.S. Treasury securities and yield curves for corporate securities with ratings AAA (in red), BBB (in green), and B (in purple). Note how the yield to maturity is higher for the corporate bonds, which have a higher probability of default than the U.S. Treasury securities.

Source: Reuters.

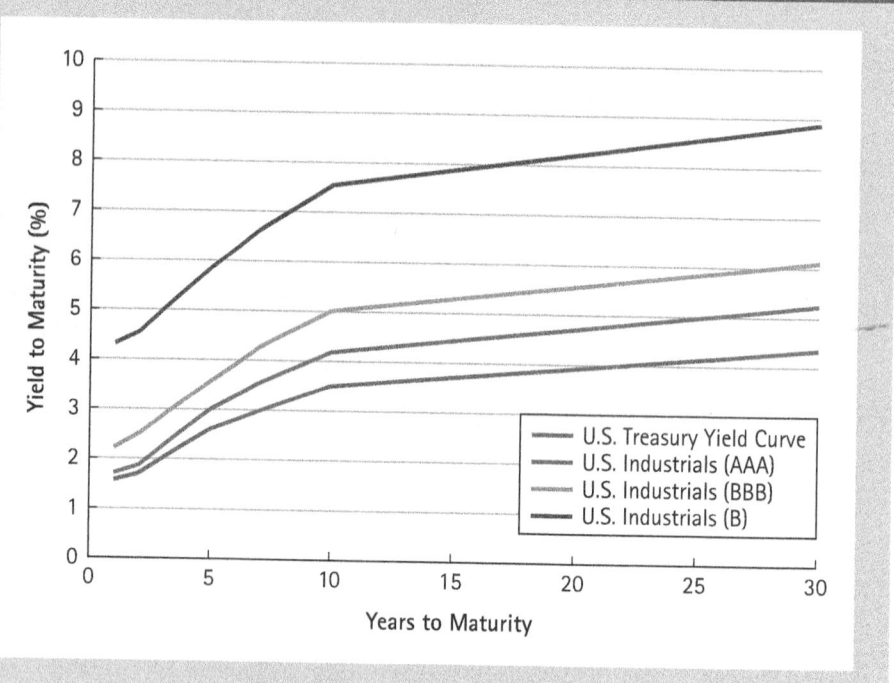

BDeH   CHAPTER 6

default spread (credit spread) The difference between the risk-free interest rate on U.S. Treasury notes and the interest rates on all other loans. The magnitude of the credit spread will depend on investors' assessment of the likelihood that a particular firm will default.

Corporate Yield Curves

Just as we can construct a yield curve from risk-free Treasury securities, we can plot a similar yield curve for corporate bonds. Figure 6.6 shows the average yields of U.S. corporate coupon bonds with three different Standard & Poor's bond ratings: two curves are for investment-grade bonds (AAA and BBB) and one is for junk bonds (B). Figure 6.6 also includes the U.S. (coupon-paying) Treasury yield curve. We refer to the difference between the yields of the corporate bonds and the Treasury yields as the **default spread** or **credit spread**. This difference can be seen in Figure 6.6 as the distance between the bottom blue line for Treasuries and each of the red, green, and purple lines as default probability increases. Credit spreads fluctuate as perceptions regarding the probability of default change. Note that the credit spread is high for bonds with low ratings and therefore a greater likelihood of default.

EXAMPLE 6.10

Credit Spreads and Bond Prices

Problem

Your firm has a credit rating of A. You notice that the credit spread for 10-year maturity debt is 90 basis points (0.90%). Your firm's ten-year debt has a coupon rate of 5%. You see that new 10-year Treasury notes are being issued at par with a coupon rate of 4.5%. What should the price of your outstanding 10-year bonds be?

Solution

▶ **Plan**

If the credit spread is 90 basis points, then the yield to maturity (YTM) on your debt should be the YTM on similar Treasuries plus 0.9%. The fact that new 10-year Treasuries are being issued at par with coupons of 4.5% means that with a coupon rate of 4.5%, these notes are selling for $100 per $100 face value. Thus, their YTM is 4.5% and your debt's YTM should be 4.5% + 0.9% = 5.4%.

The cash flows on your bonds are \$5 per year for every \$100 face value, paid as \$2.50 every 6 months. The 6-month rate corresponding to a 5.4% yield is 5.4%/2 = 2.7%. Armed with this information, you can use Eq. 6.3 to compute the price of your bonds.

▶ **Execute**

$$2.50 \times \frac{1}{0.027}\left(1 - \frac{1}{1.027^{10}}\right) + \frac{100}{1.027^{10}} = \$98.27$$

▶ **Evaluate**

Your bonds offer a higher coupon (5% vs. 4.5%) than Treasuries of the same maturity, but sell for a lower price (\$98.27 vs. \$100). The reason is the credit spread. Your firm's higher probability of default leads investors to demand a higher YTM on your debt. To provide a higher YTM, the purchase price for the debt must be lower. If your debt paid 5.4% coupons, it would sell at \$100, the same as the Treasuries. But to get that price, you would have to offer coupons that are 90 basis points higher than those on the Treasuries—exactly enough to offset the credit spread.

Bond Ratings and the 2007–2008 Subprime Crisis

Over the last 30 years, bond ratings have taken on an increasingly important role as a means to measure and regulate financial risk—even to the extent that the amount of money banks are required to hold in reserve is based partially on the ratings of the bonds they invest in. How do credit rating companies such as Moody's, Standard & Poor's, and Fitch make their profits? That is, who pays them to issue ratings?

Since the 1970s, it is the bond *issuer* that pays for the rating. A corporation will seek to have its bonds rated in order to certify their quality and make the bonds more attractive to investors, and so will pay and cooperate with the rating agencies. At the same time, for their ratings to be valuable, the credit rating companies must maintain their reputation for impartiality. As a result, they will assign a fair credit rating, despite the fact that the firms who pay them would prefer to receive the highest rating possible.

However, during the housing boom that ended in 2007, the credit rating companies came under intense pressure to issue AAA (the highest) ratings to special kinds of bonds backed by home mortgage payments. Issuers naturally wanted high ratings to be able to sell the bonds for high prices. But it seems that many buyers of the bonds also wanted them to receive high ratings. Specifically, many banks wanted to hold these securities, and a AAA-rating would limit the amount of capital the banks would be required to hold to protect against risk.

In the end, many of these mortgage-backed securities did receive AAA ratings, even those that were backed by the riskiest home loans, known as *subprime mortgages*.

The decline in the U.S. housing market that began in 2007 quickly made it apparent that these ratings were suspect. As homeowners began defaulting on mortgage payments in record numbers, these bonds defaulted as well. Thus, they were not nearly as safe as their AAA ratings indicated.

Worse still, the problems with these bonds created a vicious cycle that impacted the entire economy. As the credit rating companies reduced the ratings on the bonds, banks found themselves with losses on their bond portfolios (the prices of the bonds dropped as their ratings dropped and their yields increased). As more and more holders of these bonds moved to sell them, the prices dropped further. These losses reduced banks' capital, while at the same time the lower ratings of the bonds meant that banks were required to hold more capital. This shortage of capital caused many banks to greatly curtail the amount of funds they made available for lending. The end result was a weakened financial system and a severe lack of credit availability, often referred to as a "credit crunch." The crisis made it difficult for many companies to borrow or issue new debt at reasonable rates, which in some cases caused firms to forgo or delay new investment.

As we indicated at the beginning of this chapter, the bond market, while less well-known than the stock markets, is large and important. Because debt is a substantial part of the financing of most corporations, a financial manager needs to understand bonds and how investors price the company's bonds. In this chapter, we have introduced you to the major types of bonds, how bonds repay investors, and how they are priced. In Chapter 14, we will discuss the bond markets further, including the process a firm goes through to issue debt.

Concept Check

9. What is a junk bond?

10. How will the yield to maturity of a bond vary with the bond's risk of default?

Here is what you should know after reading this chapter. MyFinanceLab will help you identify what you know, and where to go when you need to practice.

Key Points and Equations	Terms	Online Practice Opportunities
6.1 Bond Terminology ▶ Bonds pay both coupon and principal or face value payments to investors. By convention, the coupon rate of a bond is expressed as an APR, so the amount of each coupon payment, *CPN*, is: $$CPN = \frac{\text{Coupon Rate} \times \text{Face Value}}{\text{Number of Coupon Payments per Year}} \quad (6.1)$$	bond certificate, p. 163 coupon rate, p. 164 coupons, p. 164 face value, p. 164 maturity date, p. 163 par value, p. 164 term, p. 163	MyFinanceLab Study Plan 6.1
6.2 Zero-Coupon Bonds ▶ Zero-coupon bonds make no coupon payments, so investors receive only the bond's face value. ▶ The internal rate of return of a bond is called its yield to maturity (or yield). The yield to maturity of a bond is the discount rate that sets the present value of the promised bond payments equal to the current market price of the bond. ▶ The yield to maturity for a zero-coupon bond is given by: $$1 + YTM_n = \left(\frac{\text{Face Value}}{\text{Price}}\right)^{1/n} \quad (6.2)$$ ▶ The risk-free interest rate for an investment until date n equals the yield to maturity of a risk-free zero-coupon bond that matures on date n. A plot of these rates against maturity is called the zero-coupon yield curve.	discount, p. 165 pure discount bond, p. 165 spot interest rates, p. 167 Treasury bills, p. 165 yield to maturity (YTM), p. 166 zero-coupon bond, p. 165 zero-coupon yield curve, p. 167	MyFinanceLab Study Plan 6.2

6.3 Coupon Bonds ▶ The yield to maturity for a coupon bond is the discount rate, y, that equates the present value of the bond's future cash flows with its price: $$P = CPN \times \frac{1}{y}\left(1 - \frac{1}{(1+y)^N}\right) + \frac{FV}{(1+y)^N} \quad (6.3)$$	coupon bonds, p. 168 Treasury bonds, p. 169 Treasury notes, p. 169	MyFinanceLab Study Plan 6.3
6.4 Why Bond Prices Change ▶ A bond will trade at a premium if its coupon rate exceeds its yield to maturity. It will trade at a discount if its coupon rate is less than its yield to maturity. If a bond's coupon rate equals its yield to maturity, it trades at par. ▶ As a bond approaches maturity, the price of the bond approaches its face value. ▶ Bond prices change as interest rates change. When interest rates rise, bond prices fall, and vice versa. ▶ Long-term zero-coupon bonds are more sensitive to changes in interest rates than are short-term zero-coupon bonds. ▶ Bonds with low coupon rates are more sensitive to changes in interest rates than similar maturity bonds with high coupon rates.	clean price, p. 180 dirty price, p. 180 invoice price, p. 180 par, p. 173 premium, p. 173	MyFinanceLab Study Plan 6.4 Interactive Interest Rate Sensitivity Analysis

6.5 Corporate Bonds
 	
▶ When a bond issuer does not make a bond payment in full, the issuer has defaulted.
 	
▶ The risk that default can occur is called default or credit risk. United States Treasury securities are free of default risk.
 	
▶ The expected return of a corporate bond, which is the firm's debt cost of capital, equals the risk-free rate of interest plus a risk premium. The expected return is less than the bond's yield to maturity because the yield to maturity of a bond is calculated using the promised cash flows, not the expected cash flows.
 	
▶ Bond ratings summarize the creditworthiness of bonds for investors.
 	
▶ The difference between yields on Treasury securities and yields on corporate bonds is called the credit spread or default spread. The credit spread compensates investors for the difference between promised and expected cash flows and for the risk of default.
	corporate bonds, p. 182
	credit risk, p. 182
	default (credit) spread,
	  p. 186
	high-yield bonds, p. 183
	investment-grade bonds,
	  p. 183
	junk bonds, p. 183
	speculative bonds, p. 183
		MyFinanceLab
		Study Plan 6.5

BDeH CHAPTER 6

Review Questions

1. How is a bond like a loan?

2. How does an investor receive a return from buying a bond?

3. How is yield to maturity related to the concept of internal rate of return?

4. Does a bond's yield to maturity determine its price or does the price determine the yield to maturity?

5. Explain why the yield of a bond that trades at a discount exceeds the bond's coupon rate.

6. Explain the relation between interest rates and bond prices.

7. Why are longer-term bonds more sensitive to changes in interest rates than shorter-term bonds?

8. Explain why the expected return of a corporate bond does not equal its yield to maturity.

Problems

All problems in this chapter are available in MyFinanceLab. An asterisk (*) indicates problems with a higher level of difficulty.

Bond Terminology

1. Consider a 10-year bond with a face value of $1000 that has a coupon rate of 5.5%, with semiannual payments.
   a. What is the coupon payment for this bond?
   b. Draw the cash flows for the bond on a timeline.

2. Assume that a bond will make payments every six months as shown on the following timeline (using six-month periods):

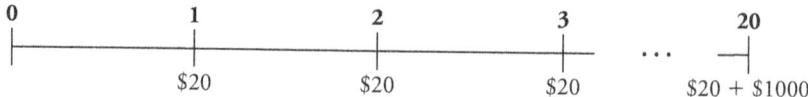

   a. What is the maturity of the bond (in years)?
   b. What is the coupon rate (in percent)?
   c. What is the face value?

Zero-Coupon Bonds

 3. The following table summarizes prices of various default-free zero-coupon bonds (expressed as a percentage of face value):

Maturity (years)	1	2	3	4	5
Price (per $100 face value)	$95.51	$91.05	$86.38	$81.65	$76.51

   a. Compute the yield to maturity for each bond.
   b. Plot the zero-coupon yield curve (for the first five years).
   c. Is the yield curve upward sloping, downward sloping, or flat?

Use the following information for problems 4–6. The current zero-coupon yield curve for risk-free bonds is as follows:

Maturity (years)	1	2	3	4	5
YTM	5.00%	5.50%	5.75%	5.95%	6.05%

4. What is the price per $100 face value of a two-year, zero-coupon, risk-free bond?

5. What is the price per $100 face value of a four-year, zero-coupon, risk-free bond?

6. What is the risk-free interest rate for a five-year maturity?

Coupon Bonds

7. The yield to maturity of a $1000 bond with a 7% coupon rate, semiannual coupons, and two years to maturity is 7.6% APR, compounded semi-annually. What must its price be?

 8. Suppose a ten-year, $1000 bond with an 8% coupon rate and semiannual coupons is trading for a price of $1034.74.
   a. What is the bond's yield to maturity (expressed as an APR with semiannual compounding)?
   b. If the bond's yield to maturity changes to 9% APR, what will the bond's price be?

 9. Suppose a five-year, $1000 bond with annual coupons has a price of $900 and a yield to maturity of 6%. What is the bond's coupon rate?

Why Bond Prices Change

10. The prices of several bonds with face values of $1000 are summarized in the following table:

Bond	A	B	C	D
Price	$972.50	$1040.75	$1150.00	$1000.00

For each bond, state whether it trades at a discount, at par, or at a premium.

11. Suppose a seven-year, $1000 bond with an 8% coupon rate and semiannual coupons is trading with a yield to maturity of 6.75%.
   a. Is this bond currently trading at a discount, at par, or at a premium? Explain.
   b. If the yield to maturity of the bond rises to 7.00% (APR with semiannual compounding), what price will the bond trade for?

Suppose that General Motors Acceptance Corporation issued a bond with ten years until maturity, a face value of $1000, and a coupon rate of 7% (annual payments). The yield to maturity on this bond when it was issued was 6%. Use this information for problems 12–14.

12. What was the price of this bond when it was issued?

13. Assuming the yield to maturity remains constant, what is the price of the bond immediately before it makes its first coupon payment?

14. Assuming the yield to maturity remains constant, what is the price of the bond immediately after it makes its first coupon payment?

15. Suppose you purchase a ten-year bond with 6% annual coupons. You hold the bond for four years, and sell it immediately after receiving the fourth coupon. If the bond's yield to maturity was 5% when you purchased and sold the bond,
    a. What cash flows will you pay and receive from your investment in the bond per $100 face value?
    b. What is the internal rate of return of your investment?

Consider the following bonds for questions 16 and 17:

Bond	Coupon Rate (annual payments)	Maturity (years)
A	0%	15
B	0%	10
C	4%	15
D	8%	10

 16. What is the percentage change in the price of each bond if its yield to maturity falls from 6% to 5%?

 17. Which of the bonds A–D is most sensitive to a 1% drop in interest rates from 6% to 5% and why? Which bond is least sensitive? Provide an intuition explanation for your answer.

 18. Suppose you purchase a 30-year, zero-coupon bond with a yield to maturity of 6%. You hold the bond for five years before selling it.
    a. If the bond's yield to maturity is 6% when you sell it, what is the internal rate of return of your investment?
    b. If the bond's yield to maturity is 7% when you sell it, what is the internal rate of return of your investment?
    c. If the bond's yield to maturity is 5% when you sell it, what is the internal rate of return of your investment?
    d. Even if a bond has no chance of default, is your investment risk free if you plan to sell it before it matures? Explain.

Corporate Bonds

19. The following table summarizes the yields to maturity on several one-year, zero-coupon securities:

Security	Yield (%)
Treasury	3.1
AAA corporate	3.2
BBB corporate	4.2
B corporate	4.9

    a. What is the price (expressed as a percentage of the face value) of a one-year, zero-coupon corporate bond with an AAA rating?
    b. What is the credit spread on AAA-rated corporate bonds?
    c. What is the credit spread on B-rated corporate bonds?
    d. How does the credit spread change with the bond rating? Why?

20. Andrew Industries is contemplating issuing a 30-year bond with a coupon rate of 7% (annual coupon payments) and a face value of $1000. Andrew believes it can get a rating of A from Standard & Poor's. However, due to recent financial difficulties at the company, Standard & Poor's is warning that it may downgrade Andrew Industries bonds to BBB. Yields on A-rated, long-term bonds are currently 6.5%, and yields on BBB-rated bonds are 6.9%.
    a. What is the price of the bond if Andrew maintains the A rating for the bond issue?
    b. What will the price of the bond be if it is downgraded?

 21. HMK Enterprises would like to raise $10 million to invest in capital expenditures. The company plans to issue five-year bonds with a face value of $1000 and a coupon rate of 6.5% (annual payments). The following table summarizes the yield to maturity for five-year (annual-pay) coupon corporate bonds of various ratings:

Rating	AAA	AA	A	BBB	BB
YTM	6.20%	6.30%	6.50%	6.90%	7.50%

    a. Assuming the bonds will be rated AA, what will the price of the bonds be?
    b. How much of the total principal amount of these bonds must HMK issue to raise $10 million today, assuming the bonds are AA rated? (Because HMK cannot issue a fraction of a bond, assume that all fractions are rounded to the nearest whole number.)
    c. What must the rating of the bonds be for them to sell at par?
    d. Suppose that when the bonds are issued, the price of each bond is $959.54. What is the likely rating of the bonds? Are they junk bonds?

22. A BBB-rated corporate bond has a yield to maturity of 8.2%. A U.S. Treasury security has a yield to maturity of 6.5%. These yields are quoted as APRs with semiannual compounding. Both bonds pay semiannual coupons at a rate of 7% and have five years to maturity.
    a. What is the price (expressed as a percentage of the face value) of the Treasury bond?
    b. What is the price (expressed as a percentage of the face value) of the BBB-rated corporate bond?
    c. What is the credit spread on the BBB bonds?

Data Case

You are an intern with Sirius Satellite Radio in its corporate finance division. The firm is planning to issue $50 million of 12% annual coupon bonds with a ten-year maturity. The firm anticipates an increase in its bond rating. Your boss wants you to determine the gain in the proceeds of the new issue if it is rated above the firm's current bond rating. To prepare this information, you will have to determine Sirius' current debt rating and the yield curve for its particular rating. Strangely, no one at Sirius seems to have this information; apparently they are still busy trying to figure out who decided it was a good idea to hire Howard Stern.

1. Begin by finding the current U.S. Treasury yield curve. At the Treasury Web site (www.treas.gov), search using the term "yield curve" and select "US Treasury— Daily Treasury Yield Curve." *Beware:* There will likely be two links with the same title. Look at the description below the link and select the one that does NOT say

"Real Yield? . . ." You want the nominal rates. The correct link is likely to be the first link on the page. Download that table into Excel by right clicking with the cursor in the table and selecting "Export to Microsoft Excel."

2. Find the current yield spreads for the various bond ratings. Unfortunately, the current spreads are available only for a fee, so you will use old ones. Go to BondsOnline (www.bondsonline.com) and click on "Today's Market." Next, click on "Corporate Bond Spreads." Download this table to Excel and copy and paste it to the same file as the Treasury yields.

3. Find the current bond rating for Sirius. Go to Standard & Poor's Web site (www. standardandpoors.com). Select your country. Select "Ratings" from the list at the left of the page, then select "Credit Ratings Search." At this point you will have to register (it's free) or enter the username and password provided by your instructor. Next, you will be able to search by "Organization Name"—enter Sirius and select Sirius Satellite Radio. Use the credit rating for the organization, not the specific issue ratings.

4. Return to Excel and create a timeline with the cash flows and discount rates you will need to value the new bond issue.
   a. To create the required spot rates for Sirius's issue, add the appropriate spread to the Treasury yield of the same maturity.
   b. The yield curve and spread rates you have found do not cover every year that you will need for the new bonds. Specifically, you do not have yields or spreads for four-, six-, eight-, and nine-year maturities. Fill these in by linearly inter-polating the given yields and spreads. For example, the four-year spot rate and spread will be the average of the three- and five-year rates. The six-year rate and spread will be the average of the five- and seven-year rates. For years eight and nine you will have to spread the difference between years seven and ten across the two years.
   c. To compute the spot rates for Sirius' current debt rating, add the yield spread to the Treasury rate for each maturity. However, note that the spread is in basis points, which are 1/100th of a percentage point.
   d. Compute the cash flows that would be paid to bondholders each year and add them to the timeline.

5. Use the spot rates to calculate the present value of each cash flow paid to the bondholders.

6. Compute the issue price of the bond and its initial yield to maturity.

7. Repeat steps 4–6 based on the assumption that Sirius is able to raise its bond rating by one level. Compute the new yield based on the higher rating and the new bond price that would result.

8. Compute the additional cash proceeds that could be raised from the issue if the rating were improved.

Chapter 6 APPENDIX A   Solving for the Yield to Maturity of a Bond Using a Financial Calculator

You are looking to purchase a 3-year, $1000 par, 10% annual coupon bond. Payments begin one year from now in November 2008. The price of the bond is $1074.51 per $1000 par value. What is the yield to maturity of the bond? [answer: 7.15%]?

HP-10BII

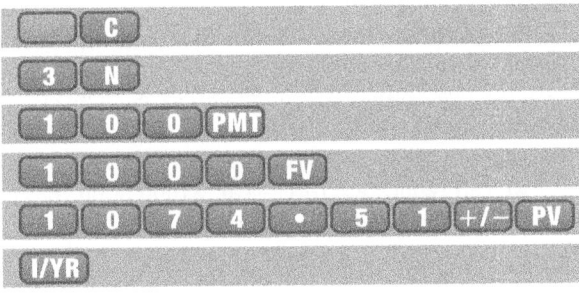

Press [Orange Shift] and then the [C] button to clear all previous entries.

Enter the Number of periods.

Enter the payment amount per period.

Enter the par value of the bond you will receive in year 3.

Enter present value or price of the bond you solved for earlier.

Solves for the yield to maturity.

TI-BAII Plus Professional

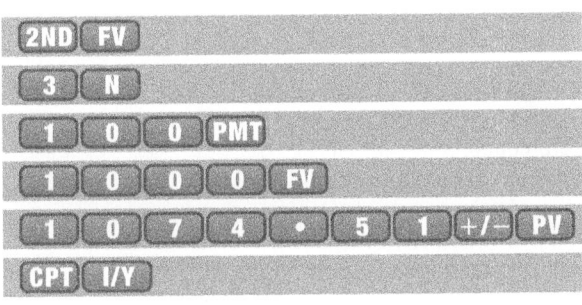

Press [2ND] and then the [FV] button to clear all previous entries.

Enter the Number of periods.

Enter the payment amount per period.

Enter the par value of the bond you will receive in year 3.

Enter present value or price of the bond you solved for earlier.

Solves for the yield to maturity.

Chapter 6 APPENDIX B   # The Yield Curve and the Law of One Price

Thus far, we have focused on the relationship between the price of an individual bond and its yield to maturity. In this section, we explore the relationship between the prices and yields of different bonds. Using the Law of One Price, we show that given the spot interest rates, which are the yields of default-free zero-coupon bonds, we can determine the price and yield of any other default-free bond. As a result, the yield curve provides sufficient information to evaluate all such bonds.

Valuing a Coupon Bond with Zero-Coupon Prices

We begin with the observation that it is possible to replicate the cash flows of a coupon bond using zero-coupon bonds. Therefore, we can use the Valuation Principle's Law of One Price to compute the price of a coupon bond from the prices of zero-coupon bonds. For example, we can replicate a three-year, $1000 bond that pays 10% annual coupons using three zero-coupon bonds as follows:

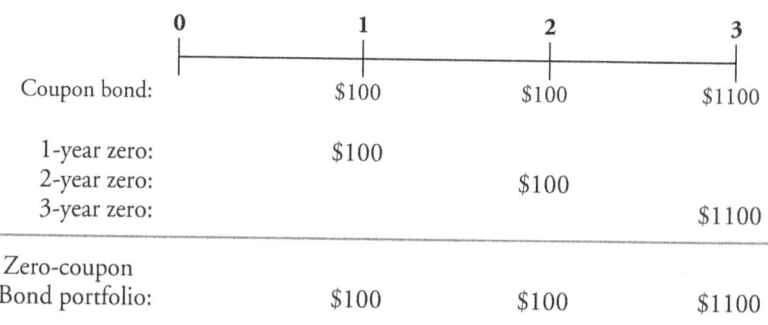

We match each coupon payment to a zero-coupon bond with a face value equal to the coupon payment and a term equal to the time remaining to the coupon date. Similarly, we match the final bond payment (final coupon plus return of face value) in three years to a three-year, zero-coupon bond with a corresponding face value of $1100. Because the coupon bond cash flows are identical to the cash flows of the portfolio of zero-coupon bonds, the Law of One Price states that the price of the portfolio of zero-coupon bonds must be the same as the price of the coupon bond.

To illustrate, assume that current zero-coupon bond yields and prices are as shown in Table 6.7 (they are the same as in Example 6.1).

We can calculate the cost of the zero-coupon bond portfolio that replicates the three-year coupon bond as follows:

Zero-Coupon Bond	Face Value Required	Cost
1 Year	100	96.62
2 Years	100	92.46
3 Years	1100	11 × 87.63 = 963.93
		Total Cost: $1153.00

By the Law of One Price, the three-year coupon bond must trade for a price of $1153. If the price of the coupon bond were higher, you could earn an arbitrage profit by selling

Maturity	1 Year	2 Years	3 Years	4 Years
TABLE 6.7				
YTM	3.50%	4.00%	4.50%	4.75%
Yields and Prices (per $100 Face Value) for Zero-Coupon Bonds — Price	$96.62	$92.46	$87.63	$83.06

the coupon bond and buying the zero-coupon bond portfolio. If the price of the coupon bond were lower, you could earn an arbitrage profit by buying the coupon bond and selling the zero-coupon bonds.

Valuing a Coupon Bond Using Zero-Coupon Yields

To this point, we have used the zero-coupon bond *prices* to derive the price of the coupon bond. Alternatively, we can use the zero-coupon bond *yields*. Recall that the yield to maturity of a zero-coupon bond is the competitive market interest rate for a risk-free investment with a term equal to the term of the zero-coupon bond. Since the cash flows of the bond are its coupon payments and face value repayment, the price of a coupon bond must equal the present value of its coupon payments and face value discounted at the competitive market interest rates (see Eq. 5.7 in Chapter 5):

Price of a Coupon Bond

$$P = PV(\text{Bond Cash Flows})$$
$$= \frac{CPN}{1 + YTM_1} + \frac{CPN}{(1 + YTM_2)^2} + \cdots + \frac{CPN + FV}{(1 + YTM_n)^n} \tag{6.4}$$

where CPN is the bond coupon payment, YTM_n is the yield to maturity of a *zero-coupon* bond that matures at the same time as the nth coupon payment, and FV is the face value of the bond. For the three-year, $1000 bond with 10% annual coupons considered earlier, we can use Eq. 6.4 to calculate its price using the zero-coupon yields in Table 6.7:

$$P = \frac{100}{1.035} + \frac{100}{1.04^2} + \frac{100 + 1000}{1.045^3} = \$1153$$

This price is identical to the price we computed earlier by replicating the bond. Thus, we can determine the no-arbitrage price of a coupon bond by discounting its cash flows using the zero-coupon yields. In other words, the information in the zero-coupon yield curve is sufficient to price all other risk-free bonds.

Coupon Bond Yields

Given the yields for zero-coupon bonds, we can use Eq. 6.4 to price a coupon bond. In Section 6.1, we saw how to compute the yield to maturity of a coupon bond from its price. Combining these results, we can determine the relationship between the yields of zero-coupon bonds and coupon-paying bonds.

Consider again the three-year, $1000 bond with 10% annual coupons. Given the zero-coupon yields in Table 6.7, we calculate a price for this bond of $1153. From Eq. 6.3, the yield to maturity of this bond is the rate y that satisfies:

$$P = 1153 = \frac{100}{(1 + y)} + \frac{100}{(1 + y)^2} + \frac{100 + 1000}{(1 + y)^3}$$

BDeH CHAPTER 6

We can solve for the yield by using a financial calculator:

	N	I/Y	PV	PMT	FV
Given:	3		−1153	100	1000
Solve for:		4.44			

Excel Formula: =RATE(NPER,PMT,PV,FV)=RATE(3,100,−1153,1000)

Therefore, the yield to maturity of the bond is 4.44%. We can check this result directly as follows:

$$P = \frac{100}{1.0444} + \frac{100}{1.0444^2} + \frac{100 + 1000}{1.0444^3} = \$1153$$

Because the coupon bond provides cash flows at different points in time, the yield to maturity of a coupon bond is a weighted average of the yields of the zero-coupon bonds of equal and shorter maturities. The weights depend (in a complex way) on the magnitude of the cash flows each period. In this example, the zero-coupon bonds yields were 3.5%, 4.0%, and 4.5%. For this coupon bond, most of the value in the present value calculation comes from the present value of the third cash flow because it includes the principal, so the yield is closest to the three-year, zero-coupon yield of 4.5%.

EXAMPLE 6.11

Yields on Bonds with the Same Maturity

Problem

Given the following zero-coupon yields, compare the yield to maturity for a three-year, zero-coupon bond; a three-year, coupon bond with 4% annual coupons; and a three-year coupon bond with 10% annual coupons. All of these bonds are default free.

Solution

▶ **Plan**

Maturity	1 Year	2 Years	3 Years	4 Years
Zero-coupon YTM	3.50%	4.00%	4.50%	4.75%

From the information provided, the yield to maturity of the three-year, zero-coupon bond is 4.50%. Also, because the yields match those in Table 6.7, we already calculated the yield to maturity for the 10% coupon bond as 4.44%. To compute the yield for the 4% coupon bond, we first need to calculate its price, which we can do using Eq. 6.4. Since the coupons are 4%, paid annually, they are $40 per year for 3 years. The $1000 face value will be repaid at that time. Once we have the price, we can use Eq. 6.3 to compute the yield to maturity.

▶ **Execute**

Using Eq. 6.4, we have:

$$P = \frac{40}{1.035} + \frac{40}{1.04^2} + \frac{40 + 1000}{1.045^3} = \$986.98$$

The price of the bond with a 4% coupon is $986.98. From Eq. 6.4:

$$\$986.98 = \frac{40}{(1 + y)} + \frac{40}{(1 + y)^2} + \frac{40 + 1000}{(1 + y)^3}$$

We can calculate the yield to maturity using a financial calculator or spreadsheet:

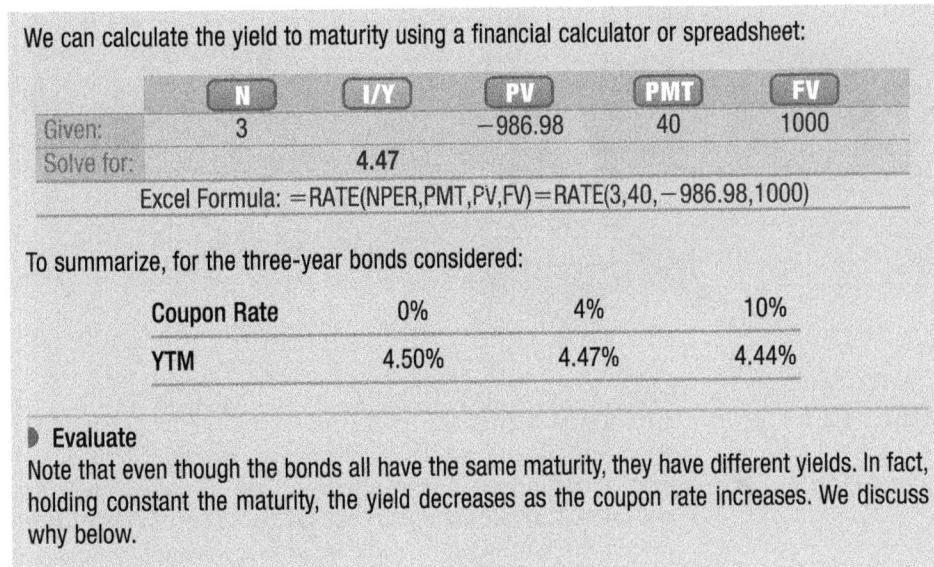

	N	I/Y	PV	PMT	FV
Given:	3		−986.98	40	1000
Solve for:		4.47			

Excel Formula: =RATE(NPER,PMT,PV,FV)=RATE(3,40,−986.98,1000)

To summarize, for the three-year bonds considered:

Coupon Rate	0%	4%	10%
YTM	4.50%	4.47%	4.44%

▶ **Evaluate**
Note that even though the bonds all have the same maturity, they have different yields. In fact, holding constant the maturity, the yield decreases as the coupon rate increases. We discuss why below.

Example 6.11 shows that coupon bonds with the same maturity can have different yields depending on their coupon rates. The yield to maturity of a coupon bond is a weighted average of the yields on the zero-coupon bonds. As the coupon increases, earlier cash flows become relatively more important than later cash flows in the calculation of the present value. The shape of the yield curve keys us in on trends with the yield to maturity:

1. If the yield curve is upward sloping (as it is for the yields in Example 6.11), the resulting yield to maturity decreases with the coupon rate of the bond.
2. When the zero-coupon yield curve is downward sloping, the yield to maturity will increase with the coupon rate.
3. With a flat yield curve, all zero-coupon and coupon-paying bonds will have the same yield, independent of their maturities and coupon rates.

Treasury Yield Curves

As we have shown in this section, we can use the zero-coupon yield curve to determine the price and yield to maturity of other risk-free bonds. The plot of the yields of coupon bonds of different maturities is called the coupon-paying yield curve. When U.S. bond traders refer to "the yield curve," they are often referring to the coupon-paying Treasury yield curve. As we showed in Example 6.11, two coupon-paying bonds with the same maturity may have different yields. By convention, practitioners always plot the yield of the most recently issued bonds, termed the on-the-run bonds. Using similar methods to those employed in this section, we can apply the Law of One Price to determine the zero-coupon bond yields using the coupon-paying yield curve. Thus, either type of yield curve provides enough information to value all other risk-free bonds.

PART 2 Integrative Case

This case draws on material from Chapters 3–6.

Adam Rust looked at his mechanic and sighed. The mechanic had just pronounced a death sentence on his road-weary car. The car had served him well—at a cost of $500 it had lasted through four years of college with minimal repairs. Now, he desperately needs wheels. He has just graduated, and has a good job at a decent starting salary. He hopes to purchase his first new car. The car dealer seems very optimistic about his ability to afford the car payments, another first for him.

The car Adam is considering is $35,000. The dealer has given him three payment options:

1. *Zero percent financing.* Make a $4000 down payment from his savings and finance the remainder with a 0% APR loan for 48 months. Adam has more than enough cash for the down payment, thanks to generous graduation gifts.

2. *Rebate with no money down.* Receive a $4000 rebate, which he would use for the down payment (and leave his savings intact), and finance the rest with a standard 48-month loan, with an 8% APR. He likes this option, as he could think of many other uses for the $4000.

3. *Pay cash.* Get the $4000 rebate and pay the rest with cash. While Adam doesn't have $35,000, he wants to evaluate this option. His parents always paid cash when they bought a family car; Adam wonders if this really was a good idea.

Adam's fellow graduate, Jenna Hawthorne, was lucky. Her parents gave her a car for graduation. Okay, it was a little Hyundai, and definitely not her dream car, but it was serviceable, and Jenna didn't have to worry about buying a new car. In fact, Jenna has been trying to decide how much of her new salary she could save. Adam knows that with a hefty car payment, saving for retirement would be very low on his priority list. Jenna believes she could easily set aside $3000 of her $45,000 salary. She is considering putting her savings in a stock fund. She just turned 22 and has a long way to go until retirement at age 65, and she considers this risk level reasonable. The fund she is looking at has earned an average of 9% over the past 15 years and could be expected to continue earnings this amount, on average. While she has no current retirement savings, five years ago Jenna's grandparents gave her a new 30-year U.S. Treasury bond with a $10,000 face value.

Jenna wants to know her retirement income if she both (1) sells her Treasury bond at its current market value and invests the proceeds in the stock fund, and (2) saves an additional $3000 at the end of each year in the stock fund from now until she turns 65. Once she retires, Jenna wants those savings to last for 25 years until she is 90.

Both Adam and Jenna need to determine their best options.

Case Questions

1. What are the cash flows associated with each of Adam's three car financing options?

2. Suppose that, similar to his parents, Adam had plenty of cash in the bank so that he could easily afford to pay cash for the car without running into debt now or in the foreseeable future. If his cash earns interest at a 5.4% APR (based on monthly compounding) at the bank, what would be his best purchase option for the car?

3. In fact, Adam doesn't have sufficient cash to cover all his debts including his (substantial) student loans. The loans have a 10% APR, and any money spent on the car could not be used to pay down the loans. What is the best option for Adam now? (Hint: Note that having an extra $1 today saves Adam roughly $1.10 next year because he can pay down the student loans. So, 10% is Adam's time value of money in this case.)

4. Suppose instead Adam has a lot of credit card debt, with an 18% APR, and he doubts he will pay off this debt completely before he pays off the car. What is Adam's best option now?

5. Suppose Jenna's Treasury bond has a coupon interest rate of 6.5%, paid semiannually, while current Treasury bonds with the same maturity date have a yield to maturity of 5.4435% (expressed as an APR with semiannual compounding). If she has just received the bond's tenth coupon, for how much can Jenna sell her treasury bond?

6. Suppose Jenna sells the bond, reinvests the proceeds, and then saves as she planned. If, indeed, Jenna earns a 9% annual return on her savings, how much could she withdraw each year in retirement? (Assume she begins withdrawing the money from the account in equal amounts at the end of each year once her retirement begins.)

7. Jenna expects her salary to grow regularly. While there are no guarantees, she believes an increase of 4% a year is reasonable. She plans to save $3000 the first year, and then increase the amount she saves by 4% each year as her salary grows. Unfortunately, prices will also grow due to inflation. Suppose Jenna assumes there will be 3% inflation every year. In retirement, she will need to increase her withdrawals each year to keep up with inflation. In this case, how much can she withdraw at the end of the first month of her retirement? What amount does this correspond to in today's dollars? (Hint: Build a spreadsheet in which you track the amount in her retirement account each month.)

8. Should Jenna sell her Treasury bond and invest the proceeds in the stock fund? Give at least one reason for and against this plan.

This page intentionally left blank

Valuation and the Firm

Valuation Principle Connection. One of the most important decisions facing a financial manager is the choice of which investments the corporation should make. These decisions fundamentally drive value in the corporation. We introduced the NPV rule in Chapter 3 as an application of the Valuation Principle. Now, in Chapter 7, we establish the usefulness of the NPV decision rule for making investment decisions. We also discuss alternative rules found in practice and their drawbacks. The process of allocating the firm's capital for investment is known as *capital budgeting.* In Chapter 8, we outline how to estimate a project's incremental cash flows, which then become the inputs to the NPV decision rule. Chapter 8 also provides a practical demonstration of the power of the discounting tools that were introduced in Chapters 4 and 5. Capital budgeting drives value in the firm, so in Chapter 9, Valuing Stocks, we turn to valuing the ownership claim in the firm—its stock. We show how the Valuation Principle leads to several alternative methods for valuing a firm's equity by considering its future dividends, free cash flows, or how its value compares to that of similar, publicly traded companies.

BDeH CHAPTER 7

Investment Decision Rules

LEARNING OBJECTIVES

▶ Use the NPV rule to make investment decisions

▶ Understand alternative decision rules and their drawbacks

▶ Choose between mutually exclusive alternatives

▶ Rank projects when a company's resources are limited so that it cannot take all positive-NPV projects

notation

C_n	cash flow that arrives at date n
I	initial investment or initial capital committed to the project
IRR	internal rate of return
$MIRR$	modified internal rate of return
NPV	net present value
PV	present value
r	discount rate

As a senior financial analyst at higher education publisher Pearson Education, Katherine Pagelsdorf handles a wide range of financial responsibilities. The 2003 graduate of the University of Wisconsin, Madison, uses the knowledge she acquired as a finance, investments, and banking major to prepare budgets, five-year growth plans for business unit financing, and sales and reporting analysis. Successful new textbook projects are the lifeline of the company; one aspect of her job is to evaluate proposed investments in textbooks like the one you are reading right now.

University of Wisconsin, Madison, 2003

"NPV is beneficial in making both personal and corporate financial decisions."

Chances are that you evaluated options for purchasing a new textbook, used textbook, or online version. Similarly, Katherine uses decision rules to evaluate the profitability of print and multimedia versions of textbooks. "NPV is beneficial in making both personal and corporate financial decisions. Any investment is made to generate a profit. Discounting the expected profit from a point in the future back to today shows us the value of that investment now. It provides a way to compare two projects or investments. The one with the higher NPV is the better choice."

Katherine collaborates with editors contracting with prospective authors for projects. Her financial expertise complements the editors' judgment and market knowledge. "We use net present value (NPV) calculations to determine if the expected outcome of a project makes it a good investment now," she says. She also works with upper-level management to rank projects within limited company resources. In such cases, it is not possible to take all positive-NPV projects.

In addition to NPV, companies also use alternative techniques to assess a project's desirability. As a student, Katherine learned a variety of ways to approach a financial situation. "My mastery of these different techniques allows me to decide for myself which approach gives the most accurate picture of the project and present the results to colleagues compellingly." These alternate investment rules may agree or disagree with NPV at times. "It's important to use these measures together," says Katherine. "If several projects are of equal profitability, then we will choose the project that is most aligned with our organization's strategy."

In 2000, Toshiba and Sony began experimenting with new DVD technology, leading to Sony's decision to develop and produce Blu-ray High-Definition DVD players and Toshiba's decision to develop and produce the HD-DVD player and format. So began an eight-year format war that ended in February 2008 when Toshiba decided to stop producing HD-DVD players and abandon the format. How did Toshiba and Sony managers arrive at the decision to invest in new DVD formats? How did Toshiba managers conclude that the best decision was to stop producing HD-DVD? We focus in this chapter on the decision-making tools managers use to evaluate investment decisions. Examples of these decisions include new products, equipment purchases, or marketing campaigns. Earlier, in Chapter 3, we introduced the NPV rule. Although the NPV investment rule maximizes the value of the firm, some firms nevertheless use other techniques to evaluate investments and decide which projects to pursue. In this chapter, we explain some commonly used techniques—namely, the *payback rule* and the *internal rate of return rule.* In each case, we define the decision rule and compare decisions based on this rule to decisions based on the NPV rule. We also illustrate the circumstances in which each of the alternative rules are likely to lead to bad investment decisions. After establishing these rules in the context of a single, stand-alone project, we broaden our perspective to include evaluating multiple opportunities to select the best one. We conclude with a look at project selection when the firm faces limits on capital or managers' time.

7.1 Using the NPV Rule

We begin our discussion of investment decision rules by considering a take-it-or-leave-it decision involving a single, stand-alone project. By undertaking this project, the firm does not constrain its ability to take other projects. We initiate our analysis with the familiar NPV rule from Chapter 3: *When making an investment decision, take the alternative with the highest NPV. Choosing this alternative is equivalent to receiving its NPV in cash today.* The NPV rule is a direct application of the Valuation Principle and as such, will always lead to the correct decision. In the case of a stand-alone project, the alternatives we are considering are to accept or reject a project. The NPV rule then implies that we should compare the project's NPV to zero (the NPV of rejecting the project and doing nothing). Thus, we should accept the project if its NPV is positive.

Organizing the Cash Flows and Computing the NPV

Researchers at Fredrick's Feed and Farm have made a breakthrough. They believe that they can produce a new, environmentally friendly fertilizer at a substantial cost saving over the company's existing line of fertilizer. The fertilizer will require a new plant that can be built immediately at a cost of $81.6 million. Financial managers estimate that the benefits of the new fertilizer will be $28 million per year, starting at the end of the first year and lasting for four years, as shown by the following timeline:

Month:	0	1	2	3	4
Cash flow:	−$81.60	+$28	+$28	+$28	+$28

Thus, the cash flows are an immediate $81.6 million outflow followed by an annuity inflow of $28 million per year for four years. Therefore, given a discount rate r, the NPV of this project is:

$$NPV = -81.6 + \frac{28}{1 + r} + \frac{28}{(1 + r)^2} + \frac{28}{(1 + r)^3} + \frac{28}{(1 + r)^4} \qquad (7.1)$$

We can also use the annuity formula from Chapter 4 to write the NPV as:

$$NPV = -81.6 + \frac{28}{r}\left(1 - \frac{1}{(1 + r)^4}\right) \qquad (7.2)$$

To apply the NPV rule, we need to know the cost of capital. The financial managers responsible for this project estimate a cost of capital of 10% per year. If we replace r in Eq. 7.1 or 7.2 with the project's cost of capital of 10%, we get an NPV of $7.2 million, which is positive. Recall that a net present value tells us the present value of the benefits (positive cash flows) net of the costs (negative cash flows) of the project. By putting everything into present values, it puts all the costs and benefits on an equal footing for comparison. In this case, the benefits outweigh the costs by $7.2 million in present value. The NPV investment rule indicates that by making the investment, Fredrick's will increase the value of the firm today by $7.2 million, so Fredrick's should undertake this project.

The NPV Profile

NPV profile A graph of a project's NPV over a range of discount rates.

The NPV of the project depends on its appropriate cost of capital. Often, there may be some uncertainty regarding the project's cost of capital. In that case, it is helpful to compute an **NPV profile**, which graphs the project's NPV over a range of discount rates. It is easiest to prepare the NPV profile using a spreadsheet such as Excel. We simply repeat our calculation of the NPV above using a range of different discount rates instead of only 10%. Figure 7.1 presents the NPV profile for Frederick's project by plotting the NPV as a function of the discount rate, r.[1]

Notice that the NPV is positive only for discount rates that are less than 14% (the green shaded area on the graph). Referring to the graph and the accompanying data table, we see that at 14%, the NPV is zero. Recall from Chapter 4 that an investment's internal rate of return (IRR) is the discount rate that sets the net present value of the cash flows equal to zero. Thus, by constructing the NPV profile, we have determined that Fredrick's project has an IRR of 14%. As we showed in Chapter 4, we can also compute the IRR without graphing the NPV by using a financial calculator or a spreadsheet's IRR function (see the appendix to Chapter 4 for detailed calculator instructions).

Measuring Sensitivity with IRR

In our Fredrick's example, the firm's managers provided the cost of capital. If you are unsure of your cost of capital estimate, it is important to determine how sensitive your analysis is to errors in this estimate. The IRR can provide this information. For Fredrick's, if the cost of capital estimate is more than the 14% IRR, the NPV will be negative (see the red shaded area in Figure 7.1). Therefore, as long as our estimate of the cost of capital of 10% is within 4% of the true cost of capital, our decision to accept the project is correct. In general, what the difference between the cost of capital and the IRR tells us is the amount of estimation error in the cost of capital estimate that can exist without altering the original decision.

---

[1]In the appendix to this chapter, we show you how to create an NPV profile in Excel.

BDeH CHAPTER 7

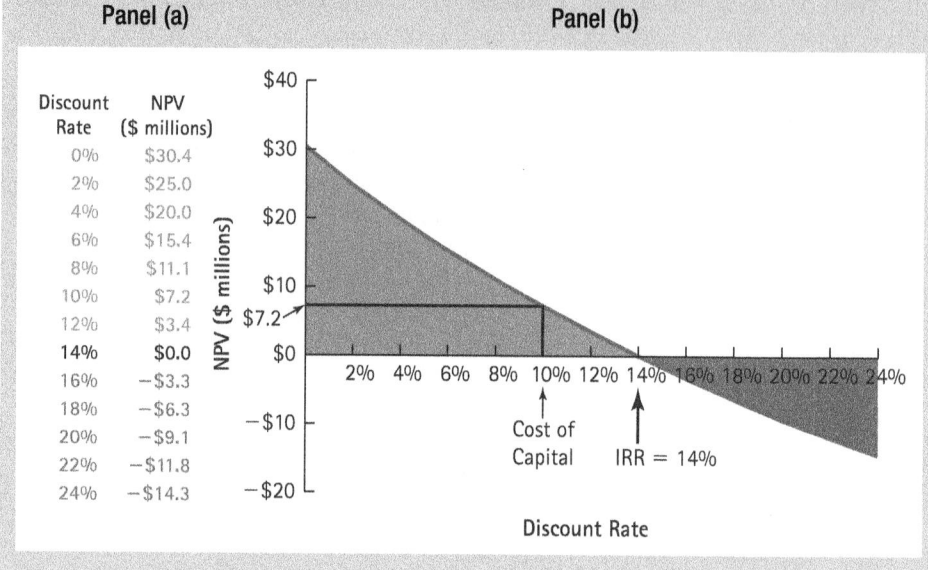

FIGURE 7.1

NPV of Fredrick's New Project

The graph in panel (b) shows the NPV as a function of the discount rate based on the data in panel (a). The NPV is positive, represented by the green-shaded area, only for discount rates that are less than 14%, the internal rate of return (IRR). Given the cost of capital of 10%, the project has a positive NPV of $7.2 million. The red-shaded area indicates discount rates above 14% IRR with negative NPVs.

Alternative Rules Versus the NPV Rule

The NPV rule indicates that Fredrick's should undertake the investment in fertilizer technology. As we evaluate alternative rules for project selection in the subsequent sections, keep in mind that sometimes other investment rules may give the same answer as the NPV rule, but at other times they may disagree. When the rules conflict, always base your decision on the NPV rule, which is the most accurate and reliable decision rule.

Concept Check

1. Explain the NPV rule for stand-alone projects.
2. How can you interpret the difference between the cost of capital and the IRR?

Alternative Decision Rules

Even though the NPV rule is the most accurate and reliable rule, in practice a wide variety of rules are applied, often in tandem with the NPV rule. In a 2001 study, John Graham and Campbell Harvey[2] found that 74.9% of the firms they surveyed used the NPV rule for making investment decisions. This result is substantially different from that found in a

---

[2]John Graham and Campbell Harvey, "The Theory and Practice of Corporate Finance: Evidence from the Field," *Journal of Financial Economics* 60 (2001): 187–243.

similar study in 1977 by L. J. Gitman and J. R. Forrester,[3] who found that only 9.8% of firms used the NPV rule. Business students in recent years have been listening to their finance professors! Even so, Graham and Harvey's study indicates that one-fourth of U.S. corporations do not use the NPV rule. Exactly why other capital budgeting techniques are used in practice is not always clear. Figure 7.2 summarizes the top three decision rules given in the survey. Because you may encounter these techniques in the business world, you should know what they are, how they are used, and how they compare to NPV. In this section, we examine alternative decision rules for single, stand-alone projects within the firm. The focus here is on the *payback rule and the IRR rule.*

payback investment rule Only projects that pay back their initial investment within the payback period are undertaken.

The Payback Rule

The simplest investment rule is the **payback investment rule**, which states that you should only accept a project if its cash flows pay back its initial investment within a pre-specified period. The rule is based on the notion that an opportunity that pays back its initial investment quickly is a good idea. To apply the payback rule,

payback period The amount of time until the cash flows from a project offset the initial investment. The time it takes to pay back the initial investment.

1. Calculate the amount of time it takes to pay back the initial investment, called the **payback period**.

2. Accept the project if the payback period is less than a prespecified length of time—usually a few years.

3. Reject the project if the payback period is greater than that prespecified length of time.

For example, a firm might adopt any project with a payback period of less than two years.

FIGURE 7.2   The Most Popular Decision Rules Used by CFOs

The bar graph shows the most popular decision rules used by CFOs in Professors Graham and Harvey's 2001 survey. Many CFOs used more than one method, but no other methods were mentioned by more than half of CFOs.

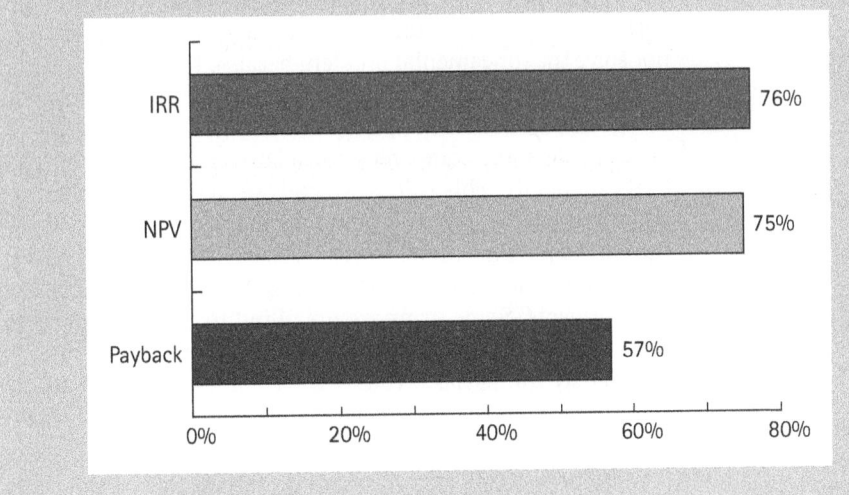

[3]L. J. Gitman and J. R. Forrester, Jr., "A Survey of Capital Budgeting Techniques Used by Major U.S. Firms," *Financial Management* 6 (1977): 66–71.

EXAMPLE 7.1

Using the
Payback Rule

Problem

Assume Fredrick's requires all projects to have a payback period of two years or less. Would the firm undertake the fertilizer project under this rule?

Solution

▶ **Plan**

In order to implement the payback rule, we need to know whether the sum of the inflows from the project will exceed the initial investment before the end of two years. The project has inflows of $28 million per year and an initial investment of $81.6 million.

▶ **Execute**

The sum of the cash flows from year 1 to year 2 is $28 \times 2 = $56 million, which will not cover the initial investment of $81.6 million. In fact, it will not be until year 3 that the cash flows exceed the initial investment ($28 \times 3 = $84 million). Because the payback period for this project exceeds two years, Fredrick's will reject the project.

▶ **Evaluate**

While simple to compute, the payback rule requires us to use an arbitrary cutoff period in summing the cash flows. Further, also note that the payback rule does not discount future cash flows. Instead it simply sums the cash flows and compares them to a cash outflow in the present. In this case, Fredrick's will have rejected a project that would have increased the value of the firm.

Relying on the payback rule analysis in Example 7.1, Fredrick's will reject the project. However, as we saw earlier, with a cost of capital of 10%, the NPV is $7.2 million. Following the payback rule would be a mistake because Frederick's will pass up a project worth $7.2 million.

The payback rule is not as reliable as the NPV rule because it (1) ignores the time value of money, (2) ignores cash-flows after the payback period and (3) lacks a decision criterion grounded in economics (what is the right number of years to require for a payback period?). Some companies have addressed the first failing by computing the payback period using discounted cash flows (called discounted payback). However, this does not solve the fundamental problem because the other two failings remain. Despite these failings, Graham and Harvey found that about 57% of the firms they surveyed reported using the payback rule as part of the decision-making process.

Why do some companies consider the payback rule? The answer probably relates to its simplicity. This rule is typically used for small investment decisions—for example, whether to purchase a new copy machine or to service the old one. In such cases, the cost of making an incorrect decision might not be large enough to justify the time required to calculate the NPV. The appeal of the payback rule is that it favors short-term projects. Some firms are unwilling to commit capital to long-term investments. Also, if the required payback period is short (one to two years), then most projects that satisfy the payback rule will have a positive NPV. So firms might save effort by first applying the payback rule, and only if the rule rejects then take the time to compute NPV.

internal rate of return (IRR) investment rule A decision rule that accepts any investment opportunity where the IRR exceeds the opportunity cost of capital and otherwise rejects the opportunity.

The Internal Rate of Return Rule

Similar to NPV, the **internal rate of return (IRR) investment rule** is based on the concept that if the return on the investment opportunity you are considering is greater than the return on other alternatives in the market with equivalent risk and maturity (i.e., the

TABLE 7.1	NPV at 10%	$7.2 million	Accept ($7.2 million > 0)
Summary of NPV, IRR and Payback for Fredrick's New Project	Payback Period	3 years	Reject (3 years > 2 year required payback)
	IRR	14%	Accept (14% > 10% cost of capital)

project's cost of capital), you should undertake the investment opportunity. We state the rule formally as follows:

> **IRR Investment Rule**: *Take any investment opportunity where IRR exceeds the opportunity cost of capital. Turn down any opportunity whose IRR is less than the opportunity cost of capital.*

The IRR investment rule will give the correct answer (that is, the same answer as the NPV rule) in many—but not all—situations. For instance, it gives the correct answer for Fredrick's fertilizer opportunity. From Figure 7.1, whenever the cost of capital is in the green area below the IRR (14%), the project has a positive NPV and you should undertake the investment. Table 7.1 summarizes our analysis of Fredrick's new project. The NPV and IRR rules agree, but using the payback rule with a required payback period of two years or less would cause Fredrick's to reject the project.

In general, the IRR rule works for a stand-alone project if all of the project's negative cash flows precede its positive cash flows. But in other cases, the IRR rule may disagree with the NPV rule and thus be incorrect. Let's examine several situations in which the IRR fails.

Delayed Investments. Star basketball player Evan Cole is graduating from college with a degree in finance and preparing for the NBA draft. Several companies have already approached him with endorsement contracts. Two competing sports drink companies are trying to sign him. QuenchIt offers him a single upfront payment of $1 million to exclusively endorse their sports drink for three years. PowerUp offers $500,000 per year, payable at the end of each of the next three years, to endorse their product exclusively. Which offer is better? One direct way to compare the two contracts is to realize that signing with QuenchIt causes Evan to forgo the PowerUp contract, or $500,000 per year. Considering the risk of his alternative income sources and available investment opportunities, Evan estimates his opportunity cost of capital to be 10%. The timeline of Evan's investment opportunity is:

```
        0              1              2              3
        |--------------|--------------|--------------|
   $1,000,000     -$500,000      -$500,000      -$500,000
```

The NPV of Evan's investment opportunity is:

$$NPV = 1,000,000 - \frac{500,000}{1 + r} - \frac{500,000}{(1 + r)^2} - \frac{500,000}{(1 + r)^3}$$

By setting the NPV equal to zero and solving for r, we find the IRR. We can use either a financial calculator or a spreadsheet to find the IRR:

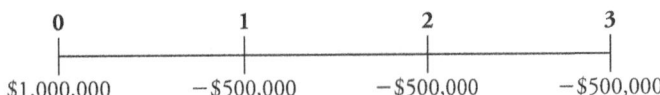

	N	I/Y	PV	PMT	FV
Given:	3		1,000,000	−500,000	0
Solve for:		23.38			

Excel Formula: =RATE(NPER,PMT,PV,FV)=RATE(3,−500000,1000000,0)

FIGURE 7.3

NPV of Cole's $1 Million QuenchIt Deal

When the benefits of an investment occur before the costs, the NPV is an *increasing* function of the discount rate. The NPV is positive in the green-shaded areas and negative in the red-shaded areas. Notice that the NPV is positive when the cost of capital is above 23.38%, the IRR, so the NPV and IRR rules conflict.

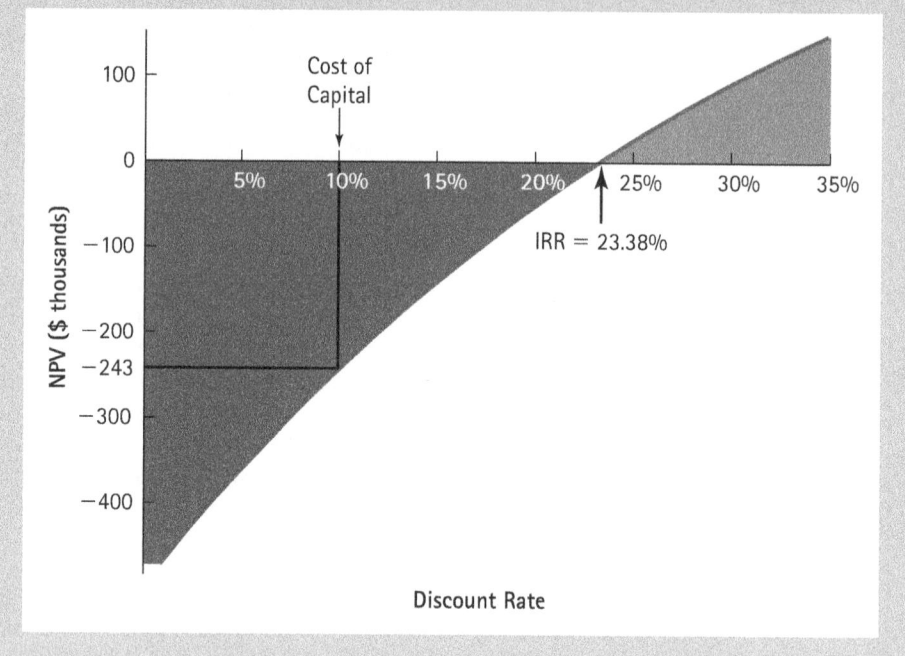

The 23.38% IRR is larger than the 10% opportunity cost of capital. According to the IRR rule, Evan should sign the deal. But what does the NPV rule say?

$$NPV = 1,000,000 - \frac{500,000}{1.1} - \frac{500,000}{1.1^2} - \frac{500,000}{1.1^3} = -\$243,426$$

At a 10% discount rate, the NPV is negative, so signing the deal would reduce Evan's wealth. He should not sign the endorsement deal with QuenchIt, but should sign with PowerUp instead.

To resolve this conflict, we can prepare an NPV profile for the QuenchIt contract. Figure 7.3 plots the NPV of the investment opportunity for a range of discount rates. It shows that, no matter what the cost of capital is, the IRR rule and the NPV rule will give exactly opposite recommendations. That is, the NPV is positive only when the opportunity cost of capital is *above* 23.38% (the IRR). Evan should accept the investment only when the opportunity cost of capital is greater than the IRR, the opposite of what the IRR rule recommends.

Figure 7.3 also illustrates the problem with using the IRR rule in this case. For most investment opportunities, expenses occur initially and cash is received later. In this case, Evan gets cash *upfront* from QuenchIt but the forgone cash flows from PowerUp occurred later. It is as if Evan borrowed money, and when you borrow money you prefer as *low* a rate as possible. Evan's optimal rule is to borrow money so long as the rate at which he borrows is *less* than the cost of capital.

Even though the IRR rule fails to give the correct answer in this case, the IRR itself still provides useful information *in conjunction* with the NPV rule. As mentioned earlier, the IRR provides information on how sensitive the investment decision is to uncertainty in the cost of capital estimate. In this case, the difference between the cost of capital and the IRR is large—10% versus 23.38%. Evan would have to have underestimated the cost of capital by 13.38% to make the NPV positive.

Multiple IRRs.   Evan has informed QuenchIt that it needs to sweeten the deal before he will accept it. In response, the company has agreed to make an additional payment of $600,000 in 10 years as deferred compensation for the long-term increase in sales that even a short-term endorsement by Evan would bring. Should he accept or reject the new offer?

We begin with the new timeline:

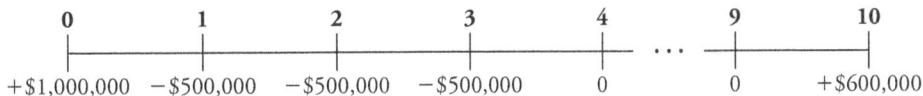

The NPV of Evan's new investment opportunity is:

$$NPV = 1,000,000 - \frac{500,000}{1+r} - \frac{500,000}{(1+r)^2} - \frac{500,000}{(1+r)^3} + \frac{600,000}{(1+r)^{10}}$$

We can find the IRR for this investment opportunity by creating an NPV profile and noting where it crosses zero. Figure 7.4 plots the NPV of the opportunity at different discount rates. In this case, there are *two* IRRs—that is, there are two values of r that set the NPV equal to zero. You can verify this fact by substituting IRRs of 5.79% and 13.80% for

FIGURE 7.4   NPV of Evan's Sports Drink Deal with Additional Deferred Payments

The graph in panel (b) shows the NPV of Evan's deal with additional deferred payment based on the data in panel (a). In this case, there are two IRRs, invalidating the IRR rule. If the opportunity cost of capital is *either* below 5.79% or above 13.80%, Evan should accept the deal because the NPV is then positive, as indicated by the green-shaded areas. At any point between the two IRRs, the NPV is negative (see the red-shaded area).

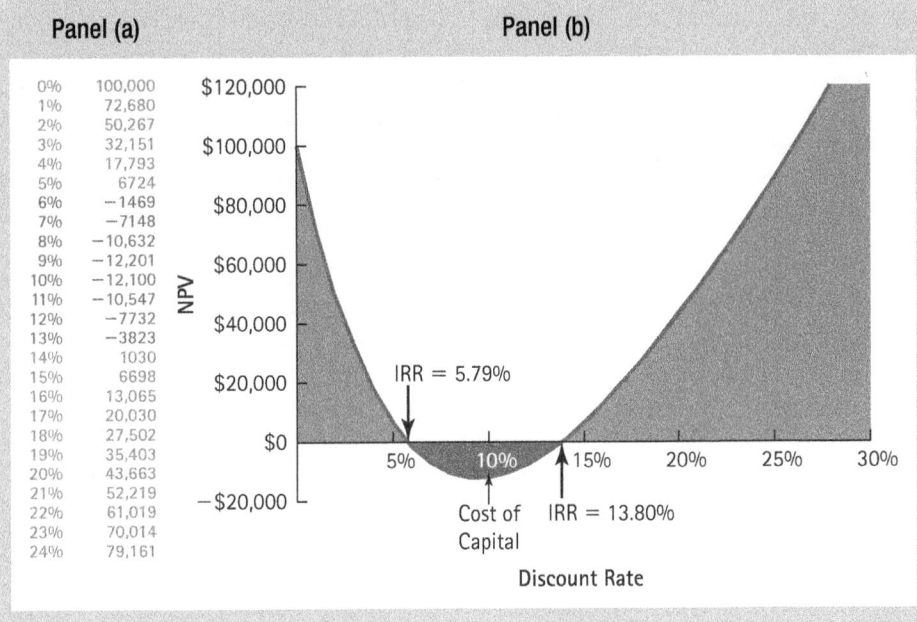

Throughout this subsection, we have distinguished between the IRR itself and the IRR rule. While we have pointed out the shortcomings of using the IRR rule to make investment decisions, *the IRR itself remains a very useful tool.* The IRR measures the average return of the

investment and indicates the sensitivity of the NPV to estimation error in the cost of capital. Thus, knowing the IRR can be very useful, but relying on it to make investment decisions can be hazardous.

r into the equation. Because there is more than one IRR, we cannot apply the IRR rule. It is also worth noting that you should take special care when using a spreadsheet or financial calculator to determine the IRR. Recall that both solve for the IRR through trial and error. In cases where there is more than one IRR, the spreadsheet or calculator will simply produce the first one that it finds, with no mention that there could be others! Thus, it always pays to create the NPV profile.

For guidance, let's turn to the NPV rule. If the cost of capital were *either* below 5.79% or above 13.80%, Evan should undertake the opportunity. But given his cost of capital of 10%, he should still turn it down. Notice that even though the IRR rule fails in this case, the two IRRs are still useful as bounds on the cost of capital estimate. If the cost of capital estimate is wrong, and it is actually smaller than 5.79% or larger than 13.80%, the decision not to pursue the project will change because it will have a positive NPV.

There is no easy fix for the IRR rule when there are multiple IRRs. Although the NPV is negative between the IRRs in this example, the reverse is also possible (see Figure 7.5). In that case, the project would have a positive NPV for discount rates between the IRRs

Why Do Rules Other Than the NPV Rule Persist?

Professors Graham and Harvey found that a sizable minority of firms (25%) in their study do not use the NPV rule at all. In addition, about 50% of firms surveyed used the payback rule. Furthermore, it appears that most firms use *both* the NPV rule and the IRR rule. Why do firms use rules other than NPV if they can lead to erroneous decisions?

One possible explanation for this phenomenon is that Graham and Harvey's survey results might be misleading. CFOs who were using the IRR as a sensitivity measure in conjunction with the NPV rule might have checked both the IRR box and the NPV box on the survey. The question they were asked was, "How frequently does your firm use the following techniques when deciding which projects or acquisitions to pursue?" By computing the IRR and using it in conjunction with the NPV rule to estimate the sensitivity of their results, they might have felt they were using *both* techniques. Nevertheless, a significant minority of managers surveyed replied that they used only the IRR rule, so this explanation cannot be the whole story.

One common reason that managers give for using the IRR rule exclusively is that you do not need to know the opportunity cost of capital to calculate the IRR. On a superficial level, this is true: The IRR does not depend on the cost of capital. You may not need to know the cost of capital to *calculate* the IRR, but you certainly need to know the cost of capital when you *apply* the IRR rule. Consequently, the opportunity cost is as important to the IRR rule as it is to the NPV rule.

In our opinion, some firms use the IRR rule exclusively because the IRR sums up the attractiveness of investment opportunity in a single number without requiring the person running the numbers to make an assumption about the cost of capital. However, if a CFO wants a brief summary of an investment opportunity but does not want her employee to make a cost of capital assumption, she can also request a plot of the NPV as a function of the discount rate. Neither this request nor a request for the IRR requires knowing the cost of capital, but the NPV profile has the distinct advantage of being much more informative and reliable.

rather than for discount rates lower or higher than the IRRs. Furthermore, there are situations in which more than two IRRs exist.[4] In such situations, our only choice is to rely on the NPV rule.

Modified Internal Rate of Return

The fact that there can be multiple IRRs for the cash flows from a project is a clear disadvantage for IRR. To overcome this, some have proposed various ways of modifying the cash flows before computing the IRR. All of these modifications have the common feature that they group the cash flows so that there is only one negative cash flow. With only one negative cash flow, there is only one sign-change for the cash flows as a whole and hence only one IRR. This new IRR, computed as the discount rate that sets the NPV of the modified cash flows of the project equal to zero, is called the **modified internal rate of return (MIRR)**.

modified internal rate of return (MIRR) The discount rate that sets the NPV of modified cash flows of a project equal to zero. Cash flows are modified so there is only one negative cash flow (and one sign change) to ensure that only one IRR exists.

MIRR Technique.   Let's clarify this with an example. You are considering a project that has the following three cash flows:

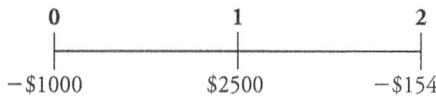

The NPV profile for this project, shown in Figure 7.5, identifies the two IRRs for this project as 10% and 40%.

Assume that your discount rate for this project is 15%. As Figure 7.5 shows, the NPV of the project at 15% is $9.45. We could modify the cash flows of the project to eliminate the multiple IRR problem. By discounting all of the negative cash flows to the present and compounding all of the positive cash flows to the end of the project, we have only

FIGURE 7.5

NPV Profile for a Project with Multiple IRRs

The graph shows the NPV profile for the multiple-IRR project with cash flows of −$1000, $2500 and −$1540 in years 0, 1, and 2, respectively. As the NPV profile shows, the project has two IRRs: 10% and 40%.

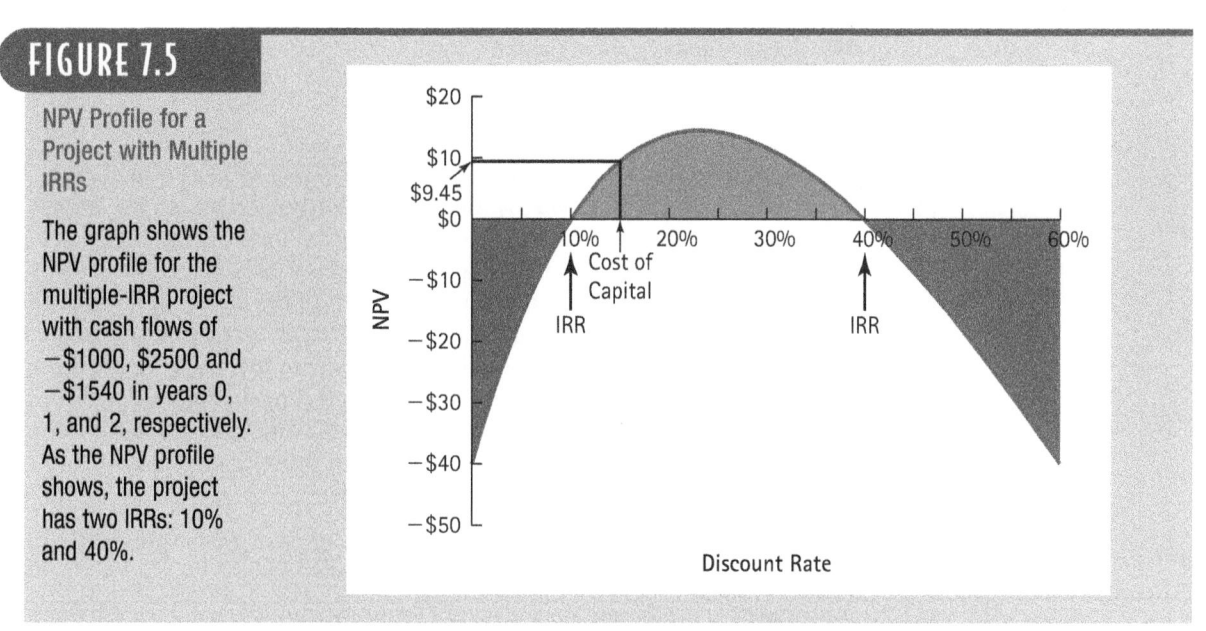

---

[4]In general, there can be as many IRRs as the number of times the project's cash flows change sign over time.

| FIGURE 7.6 | NPV Profile of Modified Cash Flows for the Multiple-IRR Project from Figure 7.5 |

The graph presents the NPV profile for the modified project cash flows of −2164.46 in year 0 and 2875 in year 2. The modified cash flows have only one IRR: 15.25%. Given the 15% cost of capital, the IRR rule confirms that we should accept the project.

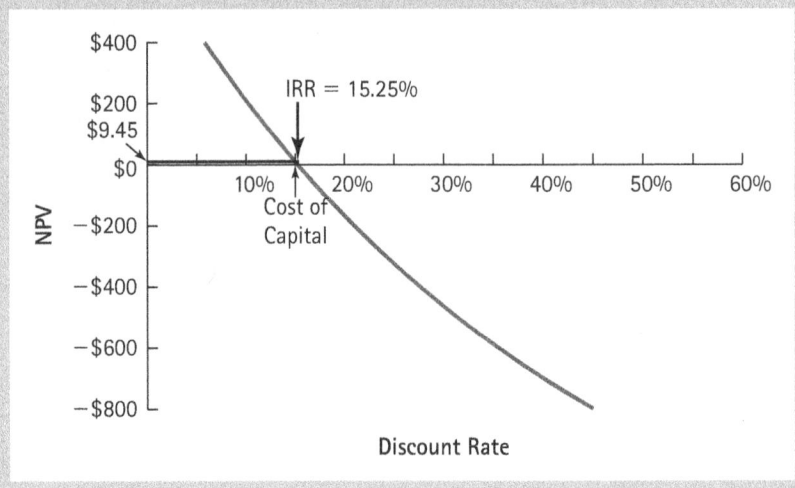

two cash flows, yielding a single IRR. What discount rate and compounding rate should we use? One natural choice is our cost of capital for this project, which is 15%.

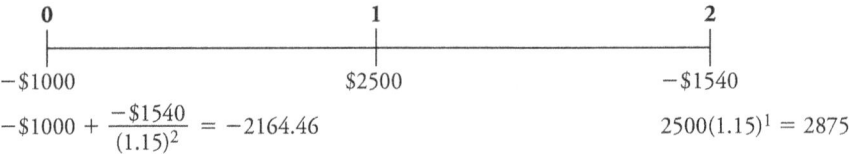

$$-\$1000 + \frac{-\$1540}{(1.15)^2} = -2164.46 \qquad\qquad 2500(1.15)^1 = 2875$$

Figure 7.6 presents the NPV profile for our modified cash flows. As Figure 7.6 shows, there is now only a single IRR, at 15.25%. Because our cost of capital is 15%, we would properly accept the project using the IRR rule. Also note that the advantage of using 15% as our discount and compounding rates when modifying the cash flows is that the NPV of the modified cash flows at 15% is the same as the NPV of the true cash flows at 15%. Figure 7.6 also makes an important point: we are no longer evaluating the true cash flows of the project. Instead, we have modified them to force them to produce a single IRR. The NPV profile of the true cash flows of the project is given in Figure 7.5 above and is clearly different from the one produced by the modified cash flows in Figure 7.6.

There is no set way to modify project cash flows to produce an MIRR. Two other approaches that each solve the multiple IRR problem are:

1. Discount all of the negative cash flows to time 0 and leave the positive cash flows alone.

2. Leave the initial cash flow alone and compound all of the remaining cash flows to the final period of the project. In this approach, you are implicitly reinvesting all of the cash flows from the project at your compound rate until the project is complete.

Again, in either case if you use the project's cost of capital as your discount and compounding rate, you will not alter the NPV of the project at that discount rate. Further, a decision to accept or reject the project based on the modified IRR will be the same as the one based on the NPV decision rule.

MIRR: A Final Word.   There is considerable debate about whether MIRR is truly better than IRR. Most of the argument centers on whether it is advisable to modify the cash flows of the project. The IRR is truly an internal rate of return based solely on the actual cash flows of the project. However, the IRR implicitly assumes that all cash flows generated by the project are reinvested at the project's IRR rather than at the firm's cost of capital until the project ends. For a project with a high IRR, this may be an unrealistic assumption. Further, there may be more than one IRR, which complicates its use. The MIRR avoids these problems, but is based on a set of cash flows modified through the use of a chosen discount and compounding rate. Thus, it is not really an internal rate of return and is no longer based solely on the actual cash flows of the project. Finally, MIRR still does not solve some of the other problems associated with using IRR when choosing among projects.

3. How do you apply the payback rule?

4. Under what conditions will the IRR rule lead to the same decision as the NPV rule?

7.3 Choosing Between Projects

Thus far, we have considered only decisions where the choice is either to accept or to reject a single, stand-alone project. Sometimes, however, a firm must choose just one project from among several possible projects. For example, a manager may be evaluating alternative package designs for a new product. The manager must choose only one of the designs. When choosing any one project excludes us from taking the other projects, we are facing **mutually exclusive projects**.

mutually exclusive projects Projects that compete with one another; by accepting one, you exclude the others.

When projects, such as the package designs, are mutually exclusive, it is not enough to determine which projects have positive NPVs. With mutually exclusive projects, the manager's goal is to rank the projects and choose only the best one. In this situation, the NPV rule provides a straightforward answer: *Pick the project with the highest NPV.*

EXAMPLE 7.2

NPV and Mutually Exclusive Projects

Problem

You own a small piece of commercial land near a university. You are considering what to do with it. You have been approached recently with an offer to buy it for $220,000. You are also considering three alternative uses yourself: a bar, a coffee shop, and an apparel store. You assume that you would operate your choice indefinitely, eventually leaving the business to your children. You have collected the following information about the uses. What should you do?

	Initial Investment	Cash flow in the First Year	Growth rate	Cost of capital
Bar	$400,000	$60,000	3.5%	12%
Coffee shop	$200,000	$40,000	3%	10%
Apparel Store	$500,000	$75,000	3%	13%

BDeH   CHAPTER 7

BDeH CHAPTER 7

Solution

▶ **Plan**

Since you can only do one project (you only have one piece of land), these are mutually exclusive projects. In order to decide which project is most valuable, you need to rank them by NPV. Each of these projects (except for selling the land) has cash flows that can be valued as a growing perpetuity, so from Chapter 4, the present value of the inflows is $CF_1/(r-g)$. The NPV of each investment will be:

$$\frac{CF_1}{r - g} - \text{Initial Investment}$$

▶ **Execute**

The NPVs are:

$$\text{Bar:} \quad \frac{\$60,000}{0.12 - 0.035} - \$400,000 = \$305,882$$

$$\text{Coffee Shop:} \quad \frac{\$40,000}{0.10 - 0.03} - \$200,000 = \$371,429$$

$$\text{Apparel Store:} \quad \frac{\$75,000}{0.13 - 0.03} - \$500,000 = \$250,000$$

So, the ranking is

Alternative	NPV
Coffee Shop	$371,429
Bar	$305,882
Apparel Store	$250,000
Sell the Land	$220,000

and you should choose the coffee shop.

▶ **Evaluate**

All of the alternatives have positive NPVs, but you can only take one of them, so you should choose the one that creates the most value. Even though the coffee shop has the lowest cash flows, its lower start-up cost coupled with its lower cost of capital (it is less risky), make it the best choice.

Because the IRR is a measure of the expected return of investing in the project, you might be tempted to extend the IRR investment rule to the case of mutually exclusive projects by picking the project with the highest IRR. Unfortunately, picking one project over another simply because it has a larger IRR can lead to mistakes. Problems arise when the mutually exclusive investments have differences in scale (require different initial investments) and when they have different cash flow patterns. We discuss each of these situations in turn.

Differences in Scale

Would you prefer a 200% return on $1 or a 10% return on $1 million? The former return certainly sounds impressive and gives you great bragging rights, but at the end of the day you make only $2. The latter opportunity may sound much more mundane, but you make $100,000. This comparison illustrates an important shortcoming of IRR: Because it is a return, you cannot tell how much value has actually been created without knowing the basis for the return—a 10% IRR can have very different value implications for an initial investment of $1 million versus an initial investment of $100 million.

If a project has a positive NPV, then if we can double its size, its NPV will double: By the Valuation Principle, doubling the cash flows of an investment opportunity must make it worth twice as much. However, the IRR rule does not have this property—it is unaffected by the scale of the investment opportunity because the IRR measures the average return of the investment. Hence, the IRR rule cannot be used to compare projects of different scales. Let's illustrate this concept in the context of an example.

Identical Scale.   We begin by considering two mutually exclusive projects with the same scale. Javier is evaluating two investment opportunities. If he went into business with his girlfriend, he would need to invest $10,000 and the business would generate incremental cash flows of $6000 per year for three years. Alternatively, he could start a two-computer Internet café. The computer setup will cost a total of $10,000 and will generate $5000 for three years. The opportunity cost of capital for both opportunities is 12% and both will require all his time, so Javier must choose between them. How valuable is each opportunity, and which one should Javier choose?

Let's consider both the NPV and IRR of each project. The timeline for the investment with Javier's girlfriend is:

0	1	2	3
−10,000	+6000	+6000	+6000

The NPV of the investment opportunity when $r = 12\%$ is:

$$NPV = -10{,}000 + \frac{6000}{1.12} + \frac{6000}{1.12^2} + \frac{6000}{1.12^3} = \$4411$$

We can determine the IRR of this investment by using a financial calculator or spreadsheet:

	N	I/Y	PV	PMT	FV
Given:	3		−10,000	6000	0
Solve for:		36.3			

Excel Formula: =RATE(NPER,PMT,PV,FV)=RATE(3,6000,−10000,0)

Thus, the IRR for Javier's investment in his girlfriend's business is 36.3%.

The timeline for his investment in the Internet café is:

0	1	2	3
−10,000	+5000	+5000	+5000

The NPV of the investment opportunity is:

$$NPV = -10{,}000 + \frac{5000}{1.12} + \frac{5000}{1.12^2} + \frac{5000}{1.12^3} = \$2009$$

The $2009 NPV of the Internet café is lower than the $4411 NPV for his girlfriend's business, so Javier should join his girlfriend in business. Luckily, it appears that Javier does not need to choose between his checkbook and his relationship!

We could also compare IRRs. For the Internet café, we would find that the IRR is 23.4%. The Internet café has a lower IRR than the investment in his girlfriend's business. As Figure 7.7 shows, in this case the project with the higher IRR has the higher NPV.

BDeH CHAPTER 7

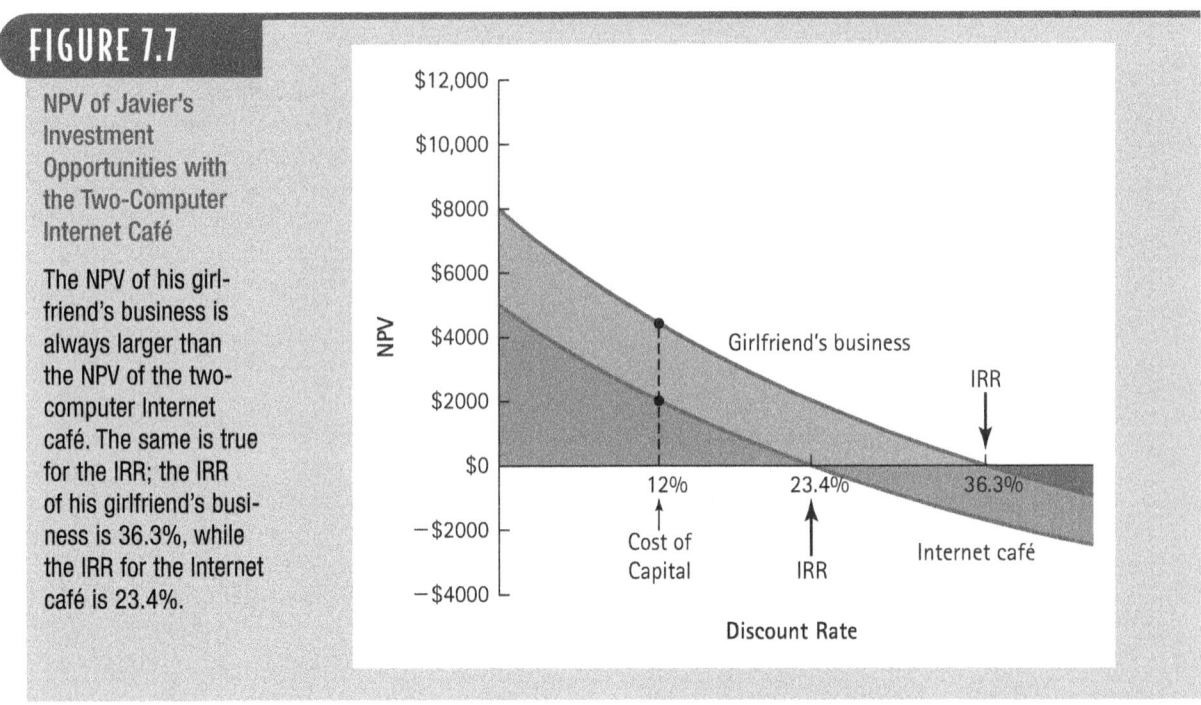

FIGURE 7.7

NPV of Javier's Investment Opportunities with the Two-Computer Internet Café

The NPV of his girl-friend's business is always larger than the NPV of the two-computer Internet café. The same is true for the IRR; the IRR of his girlfriend's business is 36.3%, while the IRR for the Internet café is 23.4%.

Change in Scale.   What happens if we change the scale of one of the projects? Javier's finance professor points out that, given the space available in the facility, he could just as easily install five times as many computers in the Internet café. His setup cost would now be $50,000 and his annual cash flows would be $25,000. What should Javier do now?

Note that the IRR is unaffected by the scale. Because we are scaling all the cash flows up by a factor of 5, a ten-machine Internet café has exactly the same IRR as a two-machine Internet café, so his girlfriend's business still has a higher IRR than the Internet café:

	N	I/Y	PV	PMT	FV
Given:	3		−50,000	25,000	0
Solve for:		36.3			
	Excel Formula: =RATE(NPER,PMT,PV,FV)=RATE(3,25000,−50000,0)				

However, the NPV of the Internet café does grow by the scale: It is five times larger:

$$NPV = -50,000 + \frac{25,000}{1.12} + \frac{25,000}{1.12^2} + \frac{25,000}{1.12^3} = \$10,046$$

Now Javier should invest in the ten-computer Internet café. As Figure 7.8 shows, the NPV of the ten-computer Internet café exceeds the NPV of going into business with his girlfriend whenever the cost of capital is less than 20%. In this case, even though the IRR of going into business with his girlfriend exceeds the IRR of the Internet café, picking the investment opportunity with the higher IRR does not result in taking the opportunity with the higher NPV.

Percentage Return Versus Dollar Impact on Value.   This result might seem counter-intuitive and you can imagine Javier having a difficult time explaining to his girlfriend why he is choosing a lower return over going into business with her. Why would anyone turn down an investment opportunity with a 36.3% return (IRR) in favor of one with

INTERVIEW WITH
Dick Grannis

Dick Grannis is Senior Vice President and Treasurer of Qualcomm Incorporated, a world leader in digital wireless communications technology and semiconductors, headquartered in San Diego. He joined the company in 1991 and oversees the company's $10 billion cash investment portfolio. He works primarily on investment banking, capital structure, and international finance. Here, he talks about project evaluation within Qualcomm and the discount rates Qualcomm uses for the project's forecasted incremental cash flows.

QUESTION: *Qualcomm has a wide variety of products in different business lines. How does your capital budgeting process for new products work?*

ANSWER: Qualcomm evaluates new projects (such as new products, equipment, technologies, research and development, acquisitions, and strategic investments) by using traditional financial measurements including DCF models, IRR levels, the time needed to reach cumulative positive cash flows, the short-term impact of the investment on our reported net earnings, and tracking the maximum amount of funding the project will require. For strategic investments, we consider the possible value of financial, competitive, technology, and/or market value enhancements to our core businesses—even if those benefits cannot be quantified. Overall, we make capital budgeting decisions based on a combination of objective analyses and our own business judgment.

We do not engage in capital budgeting and analysis if the project represents an immediate and necessary requirement for our business operations. One example is new software or production equipment to start a project that has already received approval.

We are also mindful of the opportunity costs of allocating our internal engineering resources on one project versus another project. We view this as a constantly challenging but worthwhile exercise, because we have many attractive opportunities but limited resources to pursue them.

QUESTION: *How often does Qualcomm evaluate its discount rates and what factors does it consider in setting them? How do you allocate capital across areas and regions and assess the risk of non-U.S. investments?*

ANSWER: Qualcomm encourages its financial planners to utilize hurdle (or discount) rates that vary according to the risk of the particular project. We expect a rate of return com-

mensurate with the project's risk. Our finance staff considers a wide range of discount rates and chooses one that fits the project's expected risk profile and time horizon. The range can be from 6% to 8% for relatively safe investments in the domestic market to 50% or more for equity investments in foreign markets that may be illiquid and difficult to predict. We re-evaluate our hurdle rates at least every year.

We analyze key factors including: (1) market adoption risk (whether or not customers will buy the new product or service at the price and volume we expect), (2) technology development risk (whether or not we can develop and patent the new product or service as expected), (3) execution risk (whether we can launch the new product or service cost effectively and on time), and (4) dedicated asset risk (the amount of resources that must be consumed to complete the work).

QUESTION: *How are projects categorized and how are the hurdle rates for new projects determined? What would happen if Qualcomm simply evaluated all new projects against the same hurdle rate?*

ANSWER: We primarily categorize projects by risk level, but we also categorize projects by the expected time horizon. We consider short-term and long-term projects to balance our needs and achieve our objectives. For example, immediate projects and opportunities may demand a great amount of attention, but we also stay focused on long-term projects because they often create greater long-term value for stockholders.

If we were to evaluate all new projects against the same hurdle rate, then our business planners would, by default, consistently choose to invest in the highest risk projects because those projects would appear to have the greatest expected returns in DCF models or IRR analyses. That approach would probably not work well for very long.

Discussion Question

Grannis mentions that Qualcomm does not do analysis if the project is required by an already approved project.

1. Should such potential requirements of a project enter into the investment decision process somewhere? If so, where?

BDeH CHAPTER 7

FIGURE 7.8

NPV of Javier's
Investment
Opportunities with
the Ten-Computer
Internet Café

As in Figure 7.7, the
IRR of his girlfriend's
business is 36.3%,
while the IRR for the
Internet café is 23.4%.
But in this case, the
NPV of his girlfriend's
business is larger
than the NPV of the
10-computer Internet
café only for discount
rates over 20%.

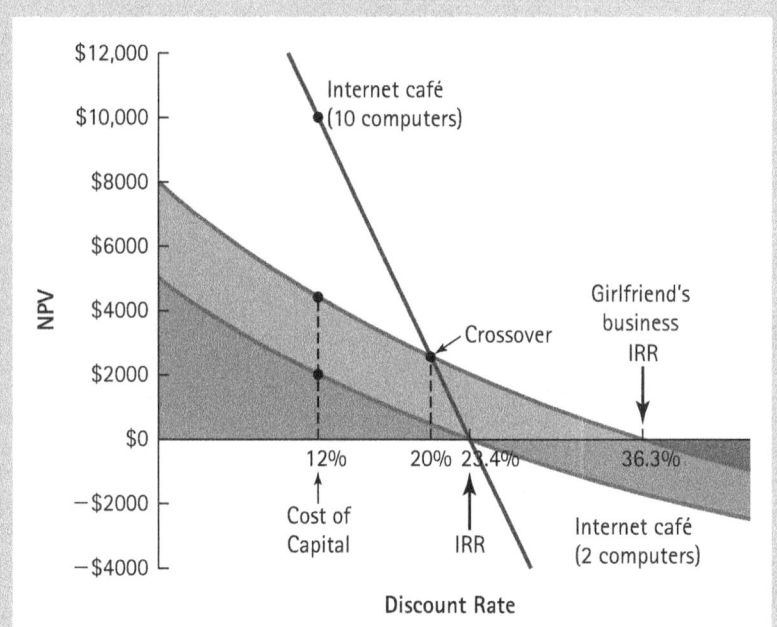

only a 23.4% return? The answer is that the latter opportunity, the Internet café, makes more money. Recall the comparison at the beginning of this section: a 200% return on $1 versus a 10% return on $1 million. We agreed that ranking the returns was not the same as ranking the value created. The IRR is a measure of the average return, which can be valuable information. When you are comparing mutually exclusive projects of different scale, however, you need to know the dollar impact on value—the NPV.

EXAMPLE 7.3

Computing the
Crossover Point

BDeH CHAPTER 7

Problem

Solve for the crossover point for Javier from Figure 7.8.

Solution

▶ **Plan**

The crossover point is the discount rate that makes the NPV of the two alternatives equal. We can find the discount rate by setting the equations for the NPV of each project equal to each other and solving for the discount rate. In general, we can always compute the effect of choosing the Internet café over his girlfriend's business as the difference of the NPVs. At the crossover point the difference is 0.

▶ **Execute**

Setting the difference equal to 0:

$$NPV = -50{,}000 + \frac{25{,}000}{1 + r} + \frac{25{,}000}{(1 + r)^2} + \frac{25{,}000}{(1 + r)^3}$$

$$- \left(-10{,}000 + \frac{6{,}000}{(1 + r)} + \frac{6{,}000}{(1 + r)^2} + \frac{6{,}000}{(1 + r)^3} \right) = 0$$

$$-40{,}000 + \frac{19{,}000}{(1 + r)} + \frac{19{,}000}{(1 + r)^2} + \frac{19{,}000}{(1 + r)^3} = 0$$

As you can see, solving for the crossover point is just like solving for the IRR, so we will need to use a financial calculator or spreadsheet:

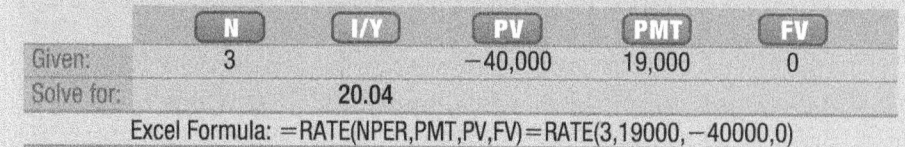

	N	I/Y	PV	PMT	FV
Given:	3		−40,000	19,000	0
Solve for:		20.04			
	Excel Formula: =RATE(NPER,PMT,PV,FV)=RATE(3,19000,−40000,0)				

And we find that the crossover occurs at a discount rate of 20% (20.04% to be exact).

▶ **Evaluate**
Just as the NPV of a project tells us the value impact of taking the project, so the difference of the NPVs of two alternatives tells us the *incremental* impact of choosing one project over another. The crossover point is the discount rate at which we would be indifferent between the two projects because the incremental value of choosing one over the other would be zero.

Timing of the Cash Flows

Even when projects have the same scale, the IRR may lead you to rank them incorrectly due to differences in the timing of the cash flows. The reason for this is that the IRR is expressed as a return, but the dollar value of earning a given return—and therefore the NPV—depends on how long the return is earned. Consider a high-IRR project with cash flows paid back quickly. It may have a lower NPV than a project with a lower IRR whose cash flows are paid back over a longer period. This sensitivity to timing is another reason why you cannot use the IRR to choose between mutually exclusive investments. To see this in the context of an example, let's return to Javier's Internet café.

Javier believes that after starting the Internet café, he may be able to sell his stake in the business at the end of the first year for $40,000 (he will continue to stay on and manage the business after he sells). Thus, counting his first-year profit of $25,000, he would earn a total of $65,000 after one year. In that case, the timeline is:

$$
\begin{array}{cc}
0 & 1 \\
\vdash\!\!\!\!-\!\!\!-\!\!\!-\!\!\!\dashv \\
-\$50,000 & +\$65,000
\end{array}
$$

Figure 7.9 plots the NPV profile for the café with and without selling it after one year. If he sells, the NPV profile crosses the x-axis at 30%, which is its IRR. The IRR for the café if he does not sell is still 23.4%. Therefore, if Javier picks the alternative with the higher IRR, he will sell. However, since the height of each line indicates the NPV of that decision, we can see that his NPV given a 12% cost of capital is higher if he chooses not to sell. (In fact, the NPV is higher as long as the cost of capital is less than 16.3%.) The intuition is as follows: While the 30% IRR from selling is high, this return is only earned in the first year. While the 23.4% IRR from not selling is not as high, it is still attractive relative to the cost of capital, and it is earned over a longer period. Again, only by comparing the NPV can we determine which option is truly more valuable.

The Bottom Line on IRR.   As these examples make clear, picking the investment opportunity with the largest IRR can lead to a mistake. In general, it is dangerous to use the IRR in cases where you are choosing between projects, or anytime when your decision to accept or reject one project would affect your decision on another project. In such a situation, always rely on NPV.

BDeH CHAPTER 7

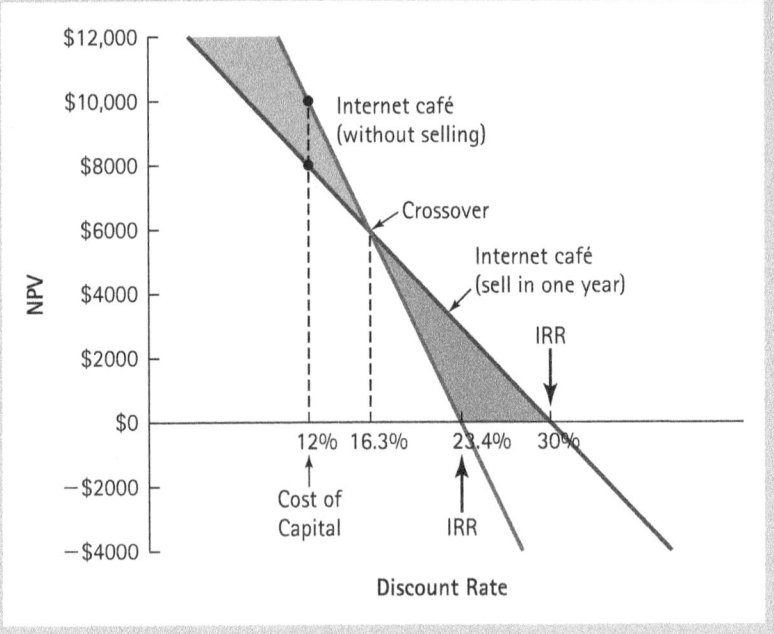

FIGURE 7.9   NPV With and Without Selling

The IRR from selling after one year (30%) is larger than the IRR without selling (23.4%). However, the NPV from selling after one year exceeds the NPV without selling only for discount rates that are in excess of 16.3% (see the yellow-shaded area vs. the blue-shaded area). Thus, given a cost of capital of 12%, it is better not to sell the Internet café after one year, despite the higher IRR.

Concept Check

5. What is the most reliable way to choose between mutually exclusive projects?

6. For mutually exclusive projects, explain why picking one project over another because it has a larger IRR can lead to mistakes.

7.4 Evaluating Projects with Different Lives

Often, a company will need to choose between two solutions to the same problem. A complication arises when those solutions last for different periods of time. For example, a firm could be considering two vendors for its internal network servers. Each vendor offers the same level of service, but they use different equipment. Vendor A offers a more expensive server with lower per-year operating costs that it guarantees to last for three years. Vendor B offers a less expensive server with higher per-year operating costs that it will only guarantee for two years. The costs are shown in Table 7.2 along with the present value of the costs of each option, discounted at the 10% cost of capital for this project.

Note that all of the cash flows are negative, and so is the present value. This is a choice of an internal server, where the project must be taken and the benefits are diffuse (the company could not function effectively without an internal network). Thus, we are

BDeH   CHAPTER 7

TABLE 7.2

Cash Flows ($ Thousands) for Network Server Options

Year	PV at 10%	0	1	2	3
A	−12.49	−10	−1	−1	−1
B	−10.47	−7	−2	−2	

Equivalent Annual Annuity The level annual cash flow that has the same present value as the cash flows of a project. Used to evaluate alternative projects with different lives.

trying to minimize the cost of providing this service for the company. Table 7.2 shows that option A is more expensive on a present value basis (−$12,490 versus −$10,470). However, the comparison is not that simple: option A lasts for three years while option B only lasts for two. The decision comes down to whether it is worth paying $2000 more for option A to get the extra year. One method that is used to evaluate alternatives such as these that have different lives is to compute the **Equivalent Annual Annuity** for each project, which is the level annual cash flow with the same present value as the cash flows of the project. The intuition is that we can think of the cost of each solution as the constant annual cost that gives us the same present value of the lumpy cash flows of buying and operating the server.

When you have a level cash flow at a constant interval, you are dealing with an annuity and that is exactly how to approach this problem. We know the present value (−$12.49), the number of years (3), and the discount rate (10%). We need to solve for the cash flow of an equivalent annuity. Recall from Chapter 4 that the formula (Eq. 4.8) for solving for the cash flow in an annuity is:

$$\text{Cash Flow} = \frac{\text{Present Value}}{\frac{1}{r}\left(1 - \frac{1}{(1+r)^N}\right)} = \frac{-12.49}{\frac{1}{0.10}\left(1 - \frac{1}{(1.10)^3}\right)} = -5.02$$

So, buying and operating server A is equivalent to spending $5020 per year to have a network server. We can repeat the calculation for server B, but for a two-year annuity because server B has only a two-year life (the change in exponent is highlighted):

$$\text{Cash Flow} = \frac{\text{Present Value}}{\frac{1}{r}\left(1 - \frac{1}{(1+r)^N}\right)} = \frac{-10.47}{\frac{1}{0.10}\left(1 - \frac{1}{(1.10)^2}\right)} = -6.03$$

Therefore, we can reinterpret the cost of each alternative as shown in Table 7.3:

TABLE 7.3

Cash Flows ($ Thousands) for Network Server Options, Expressed as Equivalent Annual Annuities

Year	PV at 10%	0	1	2	3
A	−12.49	0	−5.02	−5.02	−5.02
B	−10.47	0	−6.03	−6.03	

Now we are ready to choose between the two servers. Server A is equivalent to spending $5020 per year and server B is equivalent to spending $6030 per year to have a network server. Seen in this light, server A appears to be the less expensive solution.

EXAMPLE 7.4

Computing an Equivalent Annual Annuity

Problem

You are about to sign the contract for server A from Table 7.2 when a third vendor approaches you with another option that lasts for four years. The cash flows for server C are given below. Should you choose the new option or stick with server A?

	0	1	2	3	4
Server C	−14	−1.2	−1.2	−1.2	−1.2

Solution

▶ **Plan**

In order to compare this new option to server A, we need to put server C on an equal footing by computing its annual cost. We can do this by:

1. Computing its NPV at the 10% discount rate we used above.
2. Computing the equivalent four-year annuity with the same present value.

▶ **Execute**

$$PV = -14 - 1.2\left[\frac{1}{.10} - \frac{1}{.10(1.10)^4}\right] = -17.80$$

$$\text{Cash Flow} = \frac{PV}{\left[\dfrac{1}{.10} - \dfrac{1}{.10(1.10)^4}\right]} = \frac{-17.80}{\left[\dfrac{1}{.10} - \dfrac{1}{.10(1.10)^4}\right]} = -5.62$$

Server C's annual cost of 5.62 is greater than the annual cost of server A (5.02), so we should still choose server A.

▶ **Evaluate**

In this case, the additional cost associated with purchasing and maintaining server C is not worth the extra year we get from choosing it. By putting all of these costs into an equivalent annuity, the Equivalent Annual Annuity tool allows us to see that.

Important Considerations When Using the Equivalent Annual Annuity

Although server A appears to be the lowest-cost alternative, there are a number of factors to consider before making our decision.

Required Life. We computed the equivalent annual cost of server A assuming we would use it for three years. But suppose it is likely that we will not need the server in the third year. Then we would be paying for something that we would not use. In that case, it may be cheaper to purchase server B, which provides coverage for the years we will need it at a lower total cost.[5]

Replacement Cost. When we compare servers A and B based on their equivalent annual cost, we are assuming that the cost of servers will not change over time. But suppose we believe a dramatic change in technology will reduce the cost of servers by the third year to an annual cost of $2000 per year. Then server B has the advantage that we can upgrade

---

[5]In this scenario, we should also consider any salvage value that server A might have if we sold it after two years.

to the new technology sooner. The cost of three years of service from either server in this case can be represented as follows:

Year	PV at 10%	0	1	2	3
A	−12.49	0	−5.02	−5.02	−5.02
B	−11.97	0	−6.03	−6.03	−2.00

Therefore, when cost or performance is expected to change significantly over time, it may be cheaper to purchase server B despite its higher equivalent annual cost because it gives us the option to switch to the new technology sooner.

7. Explain why choosing the option with the highest NPV is not always correct when the options have different lives.

8. What issues should you keep in mind when choosing among projects with different lives?

Choosing Among Projects When Resources Are Limited

In the previous sections, we compared projects that had *identical* resource needs. For example, in Javier's case, we assumed that both the Internet café and his girlfriend's business demanded 100% of his time. In this section, we develop an approach for situations where the choices have differing resource needs.

Evaluating Projects with Different Resource Requirements

In some situations, different investment opportunities demand different amounts of a particular resource. If there is a fixed supply of the resource so that you cannot undertake all possible opportunities, simply picking the highest NPV opportunity might not lead to the best decision.

We usually assume that you will be able to finance all positive NPV projects that you have. In reality, managers work within the constraint of a budget that restricts the amount of capital they may invest in a given period. Such a constraint would force a manager to choose among positive NPV projects to maximize the total NPV while staying within her budget. For example, assume you are considering the three projects in Table 7.4, and that you have a budget of $200 million. Table 7.4 shows the NPV of each project and the initial investment that each project requires. Project A has the highest NPV but it uses up the entire budget. Projects B and C can *both* be undertaken (together they use the entire budget), and their combined NPV exceeds the NPV of project A; thus, you should initiate them both. Together, their NPV is $145 million compared to just $100 million for project A alone.

	Project	NPV ($ millions)	Initial Investment ($ millions)	NPV/Initial Investment
TABLE 7.4	A	100	200	0.500
Possible Projects for $200 Million Budget	B	75	120	0.625
	C	70	80	0.875

BDeH CHAPTER 7

profitability index

Measures the NPV per unit of resource consumed.

Profitability Index.   Note that in the last column of Table 7.4 we included the ratio of the project's NPV to its initial investment. We can interpret this as telling us that for every dollar invested in project A, we will generate 50 cents in value (over and above the dollar investment).[6] Both projects B and C generate higher NPVs per dollar invested than project A, consistent with the fact that given our budget of $200 million, the two of them together created a higher NPV than just project A.

In this simple example, identifying the optimal combination of projects to undertake is straightforward. In actual situations replete with many projects and resources, finding the optimal combination can be difficult. Practitioners often use the **profitability index** to help identify the optimal combination of projects to undertake in such situations:

Profitability Index

$$\text{Profitability Index} = \frac{\text{Value Created}}{\text{Resource Consumed}} = \frac{\text{NPV}}{\text{Resource Consumed}} \quad (7.3)$$

The profitability index measures the "bang for your buck"—that is, the value created in terms of NPV per unit of resource consumed. After computing the profitability index, we can rank projects based on it. Starting with the project with the highest index, we move down the ranking, taking all projects until the resource is consumed. In Table 7.4, the ratio in the last column is the profitability index. Note how the profitability index rule would correctly select projects B and C.

EXAMPLE 7.5

Profitability Index with a Human Resource Constraint

Problem

Your division at NetIt, a large networking company, has put together a project proposal to develop a new home networking router. The expected NPV of the project is $17.7 million, and the project will require 50 software engineers. NetIt has a total of 190 engineers available, and is unable to hire additional qualified engineers in the short run. Therefore, the router project must compete with the following other projects for these engineers:

Project	NPV ($ millions)	Engineering Headcount
Router	17.7	50
Project A	22.7	47
Project B	8.1	44
Project C	14.0	40
Project D	11.5	61
Project E	20.6	58
Project F	12.9	32
Total	107.5	332

How should NetIt prioritize these projects?

---

[6]Sometimes, practitioners add 1 to this ratio such that the interpretation would be that every dollar invested returned $1.50. Leaving off the additional 1 allows the ratio to be applied to resources other than budgets as we show in Example 7.5.

Solution

▶ **Plan**

The goal is to maximize the total NPV that we can create with 190 engineers (at most). We can use Eq. 7.3 to determine the profitability index for each project. In this case, since engineers are our limited resource, we will use Engineering Headcount in the denominator. Once we have the profitability index for each project, we can sort them based on the index.

▶ **Execute**

Project	NPV ($ millions)	Engineering Headcount (EHC)	Profitability Index (NPV per EHC)	Cumulative EHC Required
Project A	22.7	47	0.483	47
Project F	12.9	32	0.403	79 (47 + 32)
Project E	20.6	58	0.355	137 (79 + 58)
Router	17.7	50	0.354	187 (137 + 50)
Project C	14.0	40	0.350	
Project D	11.5	61	0.189	
Project B	8.1	44	0.184	

We now assign the resource to the projects in descending order according to the profitability index. The final column shows the cumulative use of the resource as each project is taken on until the resource is used up. To maximize NPV within the constraint of 190 engineers, NetIt should choose the first four projects on the list.

▶ **Evaluate**

By ranking projects in terms of their NPV per engineer, we find the most value we can create, given our 190 engineers. There is no other combination of projects that will create more value without using more engineers than we have. This ranking also shows us exactly what the engineering constraint costs us—this resource constraint forces NetIt to forgo three otherwise valuable projects (C, D, and B) with a total NPV of $33.6 million.

Shortcomings of the Profitability Index.   Although the profitability index is simple to compute and use, in some situations it does not give an accurate answer. For example, suppose in Example 7.5 that NetIt has an additional small project with a NPV of only $100,000 that requires three engineers. The profitability index in this case is 0.1/3 = 0.03, so this project would appear at the bottom of the ranking. However, notice that three of the 190 employees are not being used after the first four projects are selected. As a result, it would make sense to take on this project even though it would be ranked last because it would exactly use up our constraint.

In general, because the profitability index already includes the cost of capital (in computing the NPV), it would be better if the firm could raise additional funding to relieve the constraint. If the constraint is something else (such as engineers or physical capacity), there may be no way to relieve the constraint quickly enough to avoid having to choose among projects. Nonetheless, because all of the projects being ranked are value-increasing positive NPV projects, it is still better to focus on relieving the constraint.

A more serious problem occurs when multiple resource constraints apply. In this case, the profitability index can break down completely. The only surefire way to find the best combination of projects is to search through all of them. Although this process may sound exceedingly time-consuming, there are more advanced techniques that can tackle this specific kind of problem.[7] By using these techniques on a computer, the solution can usually be obtained almost instantaneously.

Concept Check

9. Explain why picking the project with the highest NPV might not be optimal when you evaluate projects with different resource requirements.

10. What does the profitability index tell you?

7.6 Putting It All Together

In Table 7.5, we summarize the decision rules outlined in this chapter. As a financial manager, you are likely to run into many different types of investment decision rules in your career. In fact, in the interview in this chapter, the Treasurer of QUALCOMM mentions five different decision rules used by his company when evaluating investments. We have demonstrated that while alternative decision rules may sometimes (or even often) agree with the NPV decision rule, only the NPV decision rule is always correct. This is because the NPV provides you with a dollar-value measure of the impact of the project on shareholder wealth. Thus, it is the only rule that is directly tied to your goal of maximizing shareholder wealth. Computing the IRR can be a useful supplement to the NPV because knowing the IRR allows you to gauge how sensitive your decision is to errors in your discount rate. And some decision metrics are much simpler to calculate, such as the payback period. However, you should never rely on an alternative rule to make investment decisions.

If you are employed by a firm that uses the IRR rule (or another rule) exclusively, our advice is to always calculate the NPV. If the two rules agree, you can feel comfortable reporting the IRR rule recommendation. If they do not agree, you should investigate why the IRR rule failed by using the concepts in this chapter. Once you have identified the problem, you can alert your superiors to it and perhaps persuade them to adopt the NPV rule.

---

[7]Specifically, there are techniques called integer and linear programming that can be used to find the combination with the highest NPV when there are multiple constraints that must be satisfied. These methods are available, for example, in many spreadsheet programs.

TABLE 7.5	**NPV**	
Summary of Decision Rules	Definition	▶ The difference between the present value of an investment's benefits and the present value of its costs
	Rule	▶ Take any investment opportunity where the NPV is positive; turn down any opportunity where it is negative
	Advantages	▶ Corresponds directly to the impact of the project on the firm's value ▶ Direct application of the Valuation Principle
	Disadvantages	▶ Relies on an accurate estimate of the discount rate ▶ Can be time-consuming to compute
	IRR	
	Definition	▶ The interest rate that sets the net present value of the cash flows equal to zero; the average return of the investment
	Rule	▶ Take any investment opportunity where IRR exceeds the opportunity cost of capital; turn down any opportunity whose IRR is less than the opportunity cost of capital
	Advantages	▶ Related to the NPV rule and usually yields the same (correct) decision
	Disadvantages	▶ Hard to compute ▶ Multiple IRRs lead to ambiguity ▶ Cannot be used to choose among projects ▶ Can be incorrect if project has future liabilities
	Payback Period	
	Definition	▶ The amount of time it takes to pay back the initial investment
	Rule	▶ If the payback period is less than a pre-specified length of time—usually a few years—accept the project; otherwise, turn it down
	Advantages	▶ Simple to compute ▶ Favors liquidity
	Disadvantages	▶ No guidance as to correct payback cutoff ▶ Ignores cash flows after the cutoff completely ▶ Often incorrect
	Profitability Index	
	Definition	▶ NPV/Resource Consumed
	Rule	▶ Rank projects according to their PI based on the constrained resource and move down the list accepting value-creating projects until the resource is exhausted
	Advantages	▶ Uses the NPV to measure the benefit ▶ Allows projects to be ranked on value-created per unit of resource consumed
	Disadvantages	▶ Breaks-down when there is more than one constraint ▶ Requires careful attention to make sure the constrained resource is completely utilized

BDeH   CHAPTER 7

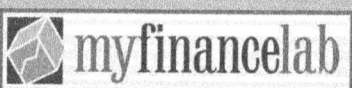

Key Points and Equations	Terms	Online Practice Opportunities
7.1 Using the NPV Rule ▶ If your objective is to maximize wealth, the NPV rule always gives the correct answer. ▶ The difference between the cost of capital and the IRR is the maximum amount of estimation error that can exist in the cost of capital estimate without altering the original decision.	NPV profile, p. 207	MyFinanceLab Study Plan 7.1 Using Excel: Making an NPV Profile
7.2 Alternative Decision Rules ▶ Payback investment rule: Calculate the amount of time it takes to pay back the initial investment (the payback period). If the payback period is less than a prespecified length of time, accept the project. Otherwise, turn it down. ▶ IRR investment rule: Take any investment opportunity whose IRR exceeds the opportunity cost of capital. Turn down any opportunity whose IRR is less than the opportunity cost of capital. ▶ The IRR rule may give the wrong answer if the cash flows have an upfront payment (negative investment). When there are multiple IRRs or the IRR does not exist, the IRR rule cannot be used. ▶ Project cash flows can be modified to eliminate the multiple IRR problem. The Modified IRR is calculated based on these modified cash flows.	internal rate of return (IRR) investment rule, p. 210 modified internal rate of return (MIRR), p. 215 payback investment rule, p. 209 payback period, p. 209	MyFinanceLab Study Plan 7.2 Interactive IRR Analysis
7.3 Choosing Between Projects ▶ When choosing among mutually exclusive investment opportunities, pick the opportunity with the highest NPV. Do not use IRR to choose among mutually exclusive investment opportunities.	mutually exclusive projects, p. 217	MyFinanceLab Study Plan 7.3
7.4 Evaluating Projects with Different Lives ▶ When choosing among projects with different lives, you need a standard basis of comparison. First compute an annuity with an equivalent present value to the NPV of each project. Then the projects can be compared on their cost or value created *per year*.	Equivalent Annual Annuity, p. 225	MyFinanceLab Study Plan 7.4

BDeH CHAPTER 7

7.5 Choosing Among Projects When Resources Are Limited

▶ When choosing among projects competing for the same resource, rank the projects by their profitability indices and pick the set of projects with the highest profitability indices that can still be undertaken given the limited resource.

$$\text{Profitability Index} = \frac{\text{Value Created}}{\text{Resource Consumed}}$$

$$= \frac{\text{NPV}}{\text{Resource Consumed}} \quad (7.3)$$

profitability index, p. 228

MyFinanceLab
Study Plan 7.5

Review Questions

1. How is the NPV rule related to the goal of maximizing shareholder wealth?

2. What is the intuition behind the payback rule? What are some of its drawbacks?

3. What is the intuition behind the IRR rule? What are some of its drawbacks?

4. Under what conditions will the IRR rule and the NPV rule give the same accept/reject decision?

5. When is it possible to have multiple IRR's?

6. How does the MIRR solve the problem of multiple IRRs?

7. Why is it generally a bad idea to use IRR to choose between mutually exclusive projects?

8. When should you use the equivalent annual annuity?

9. What is the intuition behind the profitability index?

Problems

All problems in this chapter are available in MyFinanceLab. An asterisk (*) indicates problems with a higher level of difficulty.

Using the NPV Rule

 1. Your factory has been offered a contract to produce a part for a new printer. The contract would last for three years and your cash flows from the contract would be $5 million per year. Your upfront setup costs to be ready to produce the part would be $8 million. Your discount rate for this contact is 8%.
   a. What does the NPV rule say you should do?
   b. If you take the contract, what will be the change in the value of your firm?

BDeH CHAPTER 7

2. You are considering opening a new plant. The plant will cost $100 million upfront and will take one year to build. After that, it is expected to produce profits of $30 million at the end of every year of production. The cash flows are expected to last forever. Calculate the NPV of this investment opportunity if your cost of capital is 8%. Should you make the investment? Calculate the IRR and use it to determine the maximum deviation allowable in the cost of capital estimate to leave the decision unchanged.

 3. Bill Clinton reportedly was paid $10 million to write his book *My Way*. The book took three years to write. In the time he spent writing, Clinton could have been paid to make speeches. Given his popularity, assume that he could earn $8 million per year (paid at the end of the year) speaking instead of writing. Assume his cost of capital is 10% per year.
   a. What is the NPV of agreeing to write the book (ignoring any royalty payments)?
   b. Assume that, once the book is finished, it is expected to generate royalties of $5 million in the first year (paid at the end of the year) and these royalties are expected to decrease at a rate of 30% per year in perpetuity. What is the NPV of the book with the royalty payments?

 *4. FastTrack Bikes, Inc. is thinking of developing a new composite road bike. Development will take six years and the cost is $200,000 per year. Once in production, the bike is expected to make $300,000 per year for ten years.
   a. Calculate the NPV of this investment opportunity. Should the company make the investment?
   b. Calculate the IRR and use it to determine the maximum deviation allowable in the cost of capital estimate to leave the decision unchanged.
   c. How long must development last to change the decision?

   Assume the cost of capital is 14%.
   d. Calculate the NPV of this investment opportunity. Should the company make the investment?
   e. How much must this cost of capital estimate deviate to change the decision?
   f. How long must development last to change the decision?

 5. OpenSeas, Inc. is evaluating the purchase of a new cruise ship. The ship would cost $500 million, but would operate for 20 years. OpenSeas expects annual cash flows from operating the ship to be $70 million and its cost of capital is 12%.
   a. Prepare an NPV profile of the purchase.
   b. Identify the IRR on the graph.
   c. Should OpenSeas go ahead with the purchase?
   d. How far off could OpenSeas' cost of capital estimate be before your purchase decision would change?

Alternative Decision Rules

6. You are a real estate agent thinking of placing a sign advertising your services at a local bus stop. The sign will cost $5000 and will be posted for one year. You expect that it will generate additional revenue of $500 per month. What is the payback period?

 7. Does the IRR rule agree with the NPV rule in Problem 1?

 8. How many IRRs are there in part (a) of Problem 3? Does the IRR rule give the right answer in this case?

9. How many IRRs are there in part (b) of Problem 3? Does the IRR rule work in this case?

 10. Professor Wendy Smith has been offered the following deal: A law firm would like to retain her for an upfront payment of $50,000. In return, for the next year the firm would have access to 8 hours of her time every month. Smith's rate is $550 per hour and her opportunity cost of capital is 15% per year. What does the IRR rule advise regarding this opportunity? What about the NPV rule?

 11. Innovation Company is thinking about marketing a new software product. Upfront costs to market and develop the product are $5 million. The product is expected to generate profits of $1 million per year for ten years. The company will have to provide product support expected to cost $100,000 per year in perpetuity. Assume all profits and expenses occur at the end of the year.
   a. What is the NPV of this investment if the cost of capital is 6%? Should the firm undertake the project? Repeat the analysis for discount rates of 2% and 11%.
   b. How many IRRs does this investment opportunity have?
   c. What does the IRR rule indicate about this investment?

 12. You own a coal mining company and are considering opening a new mine. The mine itself will cost $120 million to open. If this money is spent immediately, the mine will generate $20 million for the next ten years. After that, the coal will run out and the site must be cleaned and maintained at environmental standards. The cleaning and maintenance are expected to cost $2 million per year in perpetuity. What does the IRR rule say about whether you should accept this opportunity? If the cost of capital is 8%, what does the NPV rule say?

 13. Your firm is considering a project that will cost $4.55 million upfront, generate cash flows of $3,500,000 per year for three years, and then have a cleanup and shutdown cost of $6,000,000 in the fourth year.
   a. How many IRRs does this project have?
   b. Calculate a modified IRR for this project discounting the outflows and leaving the inflows unchanged. Assume a discount and compounding rate of 10%.
   c. Using the MIRR and a cost of capital of 10%, would you take the project?

14. You have just been offered a contract worth $1 million per year for five years. However, to take the contract, you will need to purchase some new equipment. Your discount rate for this project is 12%. You are still negotiating the purchase price of the equipment. What is the most you can pay for the equipment and still have a positive NPV?

*15. You are getting ready to start a new project that will incur some cleanup and shutdown costs when it is completed. The project costs $5.4 million upfront and is expected to generate $1.1 million per year for ten years and then have some shutdown costs in year 11. Use the MIRR approach to find the maximum shutdown costs you could incur and still meet your cost of capital of 15% on this project.

 *16. You are considering investing in a new gold mine in South Africa. Gold in South Africa is buried very deep, so the mine will require an initial investment of $250 million. Once this investment is made, the mine is expected to produce revenues of $30 million per year for the next 20 years. It will cost $10 million per year to operate the mine. After 20 years, the gold will be depleted. The mine must then be stabilized on an ongoing basis, which will cost $5 million per year in perpetuity. Calculate the IRR of this investment. (*Hint:* Plot the NPV as a function of the discount rate.)

17. You are considering making a movie. The movie is expected to cost $10 million upfront and take a year to make. After that, it is expected to make $5 million in the year it is released and $2 million for the following four years. What is the payback period of this investment? If you require a payback period of two years, will you make the movie? Does the movie have positive NPV if the cost of capital is 10%?

Choosing Between Projects

 18. You are choosing between two projects, but can only take one. The cash flows for the projects are given in the following table:

	0	1	2	3	4
A	−$50	25	20	20	15
B	−$100	20	40	50	60

a. What are the IRR's of the two projects?
b. If your discount rate is 5%, what are the NPV's of the two projects?
c. Why do IRR and NPV rank the two projects differently?

19. You are deciding between two mutually exclusive investment opportunities. Both require the same initial investment of $10 million. Investment A will generate $2 million per year (starting at the end of the first year) in perpetuity. Investment B will generate $1.5 million at the end of the first year and its revenues will grow at 2% per year for every year after that.
a. Which investment has the higher IRR?
b. Which investment has the higher NPV when the cost of capital is 7%?
c. In this case, when does picking the higher IRR give the correct answer as to which investment is the best opportunity?

 20. You are considering the following two projects and can only take one. Your cost of capital is 11%.

	0	1	2	3	4
A	−100	25	30	40	50
B	−100	50	40	30	20

a. What is the NPV of each project at your cost of capital?
b. What is the IRR of each project?
c. At what cost of capital are you indifferent between the two projects?
d. What should you do?

21. You need a particular piece of equipment for your production process. An equipment leasing company has offered to lease you the equipment for $10,000 per year if you sign a guaranteed five-year lease. The company would also maintain the equipment for you as part of the lease. Alternatively, you could buy and maintain the equipment yourself. The cash flows (in thousands) from doing so are listed below (the equipment has an economic life of five years). If your discount rate is 7%, what should you do?

0	1	2	3	4	5
−40	−2	−2	−2	−2	−2

Evaluating Projects with Different Lives

22. Gateway Tours is choosing between two bus models. One is more expensive to purchase and maintain, but lasts much longer than the other. Its discount rate is 11%. It plans to continue with one of the two models for the foreseeable future; which one should it choose? Based on the costs of each model shown below, which should it choose?

Model	0	1	2	3	4	5 . . .	7
Old Reliable	−200	−4	−4	−4	−4	−4 . . .	−4
Short and Sweet	−100	−2	−2	−2	−2		

23. Hassle-Free Web is bidding to provide Web-page hosting services for Hotel Lisbon. Hotel Lisbon pays its current provider $10,000 per year for hosting its Web page and handling transactions on it, etc. Hassle-Free figures that it will need to purchase equipment worth $15,000 upfront and then spend $2000 per year on monitoring, updates, and bandwidth to provide the service for three years. If Hassle-Free's cost of capital is 10%, can it bid less than $10,000 per year to provide the service and still increase its value by doing so?

Choosing Among Projects When Resources Are Limited

24. Fabulous Fabricators needs to decide how to allocate space in its production facility this year. It is considering the following contracts:

	NPV	Use of Facility
A	$2 million	100%
B	$1 million	60%
C	$1.5 million	40%

a. What are the profitability indexes of the projects?
b. What should Fabulous Fabricators do?

25. Kartman Corporation is evaluating four real estate investments. Management plans to buy the properties today and sell them three years from today. The annual discount rate for these investments is 15%. The following table summarizes the initial cost and the sale price in three years for each property:

	Cost Today	Sale Price in Year 3
Parkside Acres	$500,000	$ 900,000
Real Property Estates	800,000	1,400,000
Lost Lake Properties	650,000	1,050,000
Overlook	150,000	350,000

Kartman has a total capital budget of $800,000 to invest in properties. Which properties should it choose?

BDeH CHAPTER 7

26. Orchid Biotech Company is evaluating several development projects for experimental drugs. Although the cash flows are difficult to forecast, the company has come up with the following estimates of the initial capital requirements and NPVs for the projects. Given a wide variety of staffing needs, the company has also estimated the number of research scientists required for each development project (all cost values are given in millions of dollars).

Project Number	Initial Capital	Number of Research Scientists	NPV
I	$10	2	$10.1
II	15	3	19.0
III	15	4	22.0
IV	20	3	25.0
V	30	10	60.2

a. Suppose that Orchid has a total capital budget of $60 million. How should it prioritize these projects?
b. Suppose that Orchid currently has 12 research scientists and does not anticipate being able to hire any more in the near future. How should Orchid prioritize these projects?

Data Case

On October 6, 2004 Sirius Satellite Radio announced that it had reached an agreement with Howard Stern to broadcast his radio show exclusively on its system. As a result of this announcement, the Sirius stock price increased dramatically. You are currently working as a stock analyst for a large investment firm and XM Radio, also a satellite radio firm, is one of the firms you track. Your boss wants to be prepared if XM follows Sirius in trying to sign a major personality. Therefore, she wants you to estimate the net cash flows the market had anticipated from the signing of Stern. She advises that you treat the value anticipated by the market as the NPV of the signing, then work backward from the NPV to determine the annual cash flows necessary to generate that value. The potential deal had been rumored for some time prior to the announcement. As a result, the stock price for Sirius increased for several days before the announcement. Thus, your boss advises that the best way to capture all of the value is to take the change in stock price from September 28, 2004 through October 7, 2004. You nod your head in agreement, trying to look like you understand how to proceed. You are relatively new to the job and the term NPV is somewhat familiar to you.

1. To determine the change in stock price over this period, go to Yahoo! Finance (http://finance.yahoo.com) and enter the stock symbol for Sirius (SIRI). Then click on "Historical Prices" and enter the appropriate dates. Use the adjusted closing prices for the two dates.
2. To determine the change in value, multiply the change in stock price by the number of shares outstanding. The number of shares outstanding around those dates can be found by going to finance.google.com and typing "SIRI" into the "Search" window. Next, select the Income Statement link on the left side of the

screen, and then select "Annual Data" in the upper right-hand corner. The "Diluted Weighted Average Shares" can be found for the 12/31/2004 income statement on that page.

Because the change in value represents the "expected" NPV of the project, you will have to find the annual net cash flows that would provide this NPV. For this analysis, you will need to estimate the cost of capital for the project. We show how to calculate the cost of capital in subsequent chapters; for now, use the New York University (NYU) cost of capital Web site (http://pages.stern.nyu.edu/ ~adamodar/New_Home_Page/datafile/wacc.htm). Locate the cost of capital in the far-right column for the "Entertainment Tech" industry.

3. Use the cost of capital from the NYU Web site and the NPV you computed to calculate the constant annual cash flow that provides this NPV. Compute cash flows for 5-, 10-, and 15-year horizons.

4. Your boss mentioned that she believes that the Howard Stern signing by Sirius was actually good for XM because it signaled that the industry has valuable growth potential. To see if she appears to be correct, find the percentage stock price reaction to XM (XMSR) over this same period.

Pages 240–241 intentionally omitted

8

Fundamentals of Capital Budgeting

LEARNING OBJECTIVES

▶ Identify the types of cash flows needed in the capital budgeting process

▶ Forecast incremental earnings in a pro forma earnings statement for a project

▶ Convert forecasted earnings to free cash flows and compute a project's NPV

▶ Recognize common pitfalls that arise in identifying a project's incremental free cash flows

▶ Assess the sensitivity of a project's NPV to changes in your assumptions

▶ Identify the most common options available to managers in projects and understand why these options can be valuable

notation

CapEx	capital expenditures	*NPV*	net present value
EBIT	earnings before interest and taxes	NWC_t	net working capital in year t
FCF_t	free cash flow in year t	*PV*	present value
IRR	internal rate of return	r	projected cost of capital

INTERVIEW WITH James King, Limitless LLC

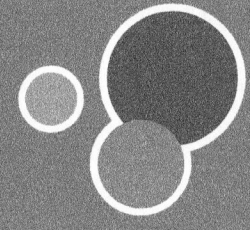

James King is a financial analyst for Limitless LLC, based in Dubai. He received a bachelor of business degree with a concentration in property economics in 2006 from the University of Western Sydney, New South Wales, Australia.

Limitless L.L.C, a business unit of Dubai World, is an integrated global real estate master developer that delivers distinctive and sustainable developments in three specific areas of expertise: master-planning large urban communities; undertaking waterfront development; and implementing large-scale balanced projects. Reflecting on his own education, James remarked that, "In my finance courses I learned the theory before applying it. For example, I studied the theory of discounted cash flow analysis, as well as the technical mathematics behind it. I use these skills day to day, and this same financial theory is what drives the investment decisions of the business." His role at Limitless is to prepare feasibility studies on potential projects across the globe to assess their financial viability.

University of Western Sydney, New South Wales, 2006

"Take advantage of every opportunity that education provides."

Limitless uses traditional financial tools such as the pro forma net profit and profit margin to assess the financial viability of individual projects. However, James notes that due to the extended time frame of real estate development and delayed return on capital outlay, it relies heavily on performance indicators that allow for the time value of money. These include internal rate of return (IRR) and net present value (NPV). "The rate that a project must achieve is based on an equity cost of capital, or the return on the funds Limitless invests. We have a predetermined rate for each market, which we then adjust based on the type of project and other factors."

While each company you work for may choose different capital budgeting methods, it's important that you know and understand them all. James offers you this advice: "Take advantage of every opportunity that education provides. The skill base that you learn from studying will provide a greater range of job opportunities and give you the edge in the ultra-competitive environment of the international work place."

BDeH CHAPTER 8

An important responsibility of corporate financial managers is determining which projects or investments a firm should undertake. *Capital budgeting,* the focus of this chapter, is the process of analyzing investment opportunities and deciding which ones to accept. In doing so, we are allocating the firm's funds to various projects—we are budgeting its capital. Chapter 7 covered the various methods for evaluating projects and proved that NPV will be the most reliable and accurate method for doing so. In retrospect, this may not be surprising as it is the only rule directly tied to the Valuation Principle. To implement the NPV rule, we must compute the NPV of our projects and accept only those projects for which the NPV is positive. We spoke in the last chapter about Sony and Toshiba each using investment decision rules to pursue competing high definition DVD standards (and eventually for Toshiba, to decide to abandon HD-DVD). In order to implement the investment decision rules, financial managers from Toshiba, for example, had to first forecast the incremental cash flows associated with the investments and later to forecast the incremental cash flows associated with the decision to stop investing in HD-DVD. The process of forecasting those cash flows, crucial inputs in the investment decision process, is our focus in this chapter.

We begin by estimating the project's expected cash flows by forecasting the project's revenues and costs. Using these cash flows, we can compute the project's NPV—its contribution to share-holder value. Then, because the cash flow forecasts almost always contain uncertainty, we demonstrate how to compute the sensitivity of the NPV to the uncertainty in the forecasts. Finally, we examine the relationship between a project's flexibility and its NPV.

8.1 The Capital Budgeting Process

capital budget Lists all of the projects that a company plans to undertake during the next period.

capital budgeting The process of analyzing investment opportunities and deciding which ones to accept.

The first step in analyzing various investment opportunities is compiling a list of potential projects. A **capital budget** lists the projects and investments that a company plans to undertake during future years. To create this list, firms analyze alternate projects and decide which ones to accept through a process called **capital budgeting**. This process begins with forecasts of each project's future consequences for the firm. Some of these consequences will affect the firm's revenues; others will affect its costs. Our ultimate goal is to determine the effect of the decision to accept or reject a project on the firm's cash flows, and evaluate the NPV of these cash flows to assess the consequences of the decision for the firm's value. Figure 8.1 depicts the types of cash flows found in a typical project. We will examine each of these as we proceed through our discussion of capital budgeting.

Of course, forecasting these cash flows is frequently challenging. We will often need to rely on different experts within the firm to obtain estimates for many of them. For example, the marketing department may provide sales forecasts, the operations manager may provide information about production costs, and the firm's engineers may estimate the upfront research and development expenses that are required to launch the project. Another important source of information comes from looking at past projects of the firm, or those of other firms in the same industry. In particular, practitioners often base their assessments of a project's revenues and costs using information on revenues and costs that can be learned from the historical financial statements of the firm or its competitors.

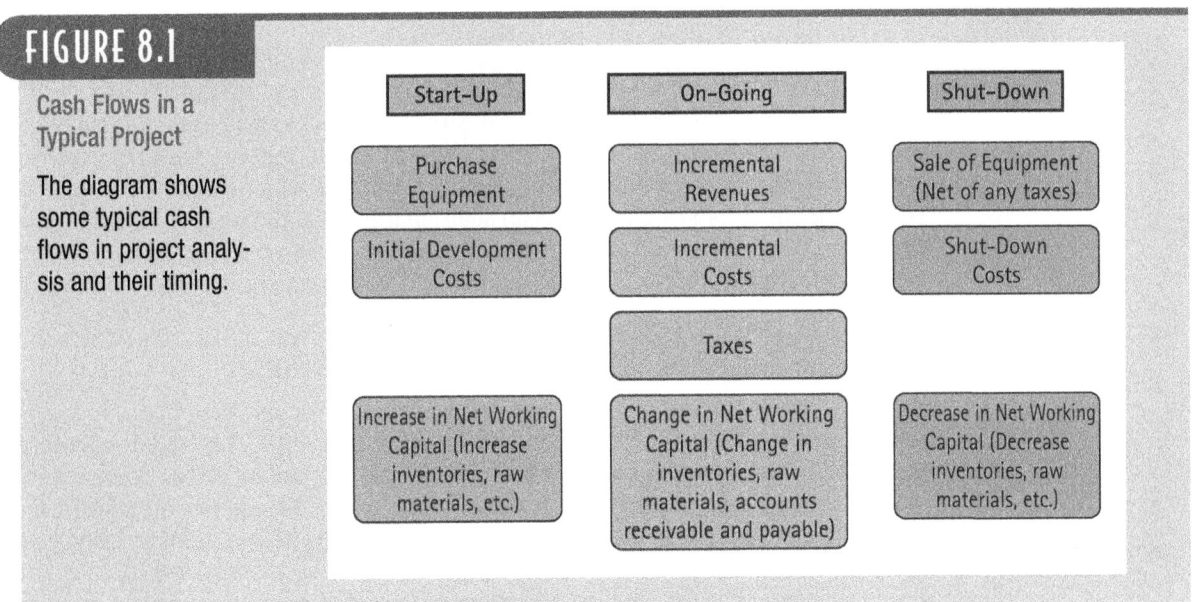

FIGURE 8.1

Cash Flows in a Typical Project

The diagram shows some typical cash flows in project analysis and their timing.

incremental earnings
The amount by which a firm's earnings are expected to change as a result of an investment decision.

Once we have these estimates, how do we organize them? One common starting point is first to consider the consequences of the project for the firm's earnings. Thus, we will *begin* our analysis in Section 8.2 by determining the **incremental earnings** of a project—that is, the amount by which the firm's earnings are expected to change as a result of the investment decision. The incremental earnings forecast tells us how the decision will affect the firm's reported profits from an accounting perspective. However, as we emphasized in Chapter 2, *earnings are not actual cash flows*. We need to estimate the project's cash flows to determine its NPV and decide whether it is a good project for the firm. Therefore, in Section 8.3, we demonstrate how to use the incremental earnings to forecast the actual cash flows of the project. Understanding how to compute the cash flow consequences of an investment based on its earning consequences is important for a number of reasons. First, as a practical matter, financial managers often begin by forecasting earnings. Second, if we are looking at historical data, accounting information is often the only information that is readily available.

Dilbert, May 05, 1994, United Features Syndicate.

Concept Check

1. What is capital budgeting, and what is its goal?
2. Why is computing a project's effect on the firm's earnings insufficient for capital budgeting?

 ## Forecasting Incremental Earnings

Let's begin our discussion of incremental earnings with a simple example that we will examine throughout this section. Suppose you are considering whether to upgrade your manufacturing plant and increase its capacity by purchasing a new piece of equipment. The equipment costs $1 million, plus an additional $20,000 to transport it and install it. You will also spend $50,000 on engineering costs to redesign the plant to accommodate the increased capacity. What are the initial earnings consequences of this decision?

Operating Expenses Versus Capital Expenditures

Most projects require some form of upfront investment—we may need to conduct a marketing survey, develop a prototype, or launch an ad campaign. These types of costs are accounted for as operating expenses in the year that they are incurred. However, many projects also include investments in plant, property, and/or equipment, called capital expenditures. Recall from Chapter 2 that while investments in plant, property, and equipment are a cash expense, they are not directly listed as expenses when calculating *earnings*. Instead, the firm deducts a fraction of the cost of these items each year as depreciation. Financial managers use several different methods to compute depreciation. The simplest method is **straight-line depreciation**, in which the asset's cost is divided equally over its depreciable life (we discuss another common method in Section 8.4).

straight-line depreciation A method of depreciation in which an asset's cost is divided equally over its life.

In our example, the upfront costs associated with the decision to increase capacity have two distinct consequences for the firm's earnings. First, the $50,000 spent on redesigning the plant is an operating expense reported in year 0. For the $1,020,000 spent to buy, ship, and install the machine, accounting principles as well as tax rules require you to depreciate the $1,020,000 over the depreciable life of the equipment. Assuming that the equipment has a five-year depreciable life and that we use the straight-line method, we would expense $1,020,000 / 5 = $204,000 per year for five years. (The motivation for this accounting treatment is to match the cost of acquiring the machine to the timing of the revenues it will generate.)

	Year	0	1	2	3	4	5
1							
2	Operating Expenses (Plant Redesign)	−$50,000					
3	Depreciation (New Equipment)		−$204,000	−$204,000	−$204,000	−$204,000	−$204,000

As the timeline shows, the upfront cash outflow of $1,020,000 to purchase and set-up the machine is not recognized as an expense in year 0. Instead, it appears as depreciation expenses in years 1 through 5. Remember that these *depreciation expenses do not correspond to actual cash outflows*. This accounting and tax treatment of capital expenditures is one of the key reasons why earnings are not an accurate representation of cash flows. We will return to this issue in Section 8.3.

Incremental Revenue and Cost Estimates

Our next step is to estimate the ongoing revenues and costs for the project. Forecasting future revenues and costs is challenging. The most successful practitioners collect as much information as possible before tackling this task—they will talk to members of marketing and sales teams as well as company economists to develop an estimate of sales, and they will talk to engineering and production teams to refine their estimate of costs.

There are several factors to consider when estimating a project's revenues and costs, including the following:

1. A new product typically has lower sales initially, as customers gradually become aware of the product. Sales will then accelerate, plateau, and ultimately decline as the product nears obsolescence or faces increased competition.

2. The average selling price of a product and its cost of production will generally change over time. Prices and costs tend to rise with the general level of inflation in the economy. The prices of technology products, however, often fall over time as newer, superior technologies emerge and production costs decline.

3. For most industries, competition tends to reduce profit margins over time.

Our focus here is on how to get from these forecasts to incremental earnings and then to cash flows; Chapter 17 discusses forecasting methods in more detail.

All our revenue and cost estimates should be *incremental,* meaning that we only account for additional sales and costs generated by the project. For example, if we are evaluating the purchase of a faster manufacturing machine, we are only concerned with how many additional units of the product we will be able to sell (and at what price) and any additional costs created by the new machine. We do not forecast total sales and costs because those include our production using the old machine. *Remember, we are evaluating how the project will* change *the cash flows of the firm. That is why we focus on incremental revenues and costs.*

Let's return to our plant upgrade example. Assume that after we have bought and installed the machine and redesigned the plant, our additional capacity will allow us to generate incremental revenues of $500,000 per year for five years. Those incremental revenues will be associated with $150,000 per year in incremental costs. In that case our revenue, cost, and depreciation estimates for the project are as shown below (in thousands of dollars):

	Year	0	1	2	3	4	5
1							
2	Incremental Revenues		500	500	500	500	500
3	Incremental Costs	−50	−150	−150	−150	−150	−150
4	Depreciation		−204	−204	−204	−204	−204

Now that we have these estimates, we are ready to compute the consequences of our project for the firm's earnings. As we saw in Chapter 2, both depreciation expenses and the actual costs of producing (e.g. cost of goods sold) must be subtracted from revenues, so that:

$$\text{Incremental Earnings Before Interest and Taxes (EBIT)} = \text{Incremental Revenue} - \text{Incremental Costs} - \text{Depreciation} \qquad (8.1)$$

Taxes

marginal corporate tax rate The tax rate a firm will pay on an incremental dollar of pre-tax income.

The final expense we must account for is corporate taxes. The correct tax rate to use is the firm's **marginal corporate tax rate**, which is the tax rate it will pay on an *incremental* dollar of pre-tax income. The incremental income tax expense is calculated as:

$$\text{Income Tax} = \text{EBIT} \times \text{the firm's marginal corporate tax rate} \qquad (8.2)$$

Incremental Earnings Forecast

We're now ready to put the pieces together for an incremental earnings forecast. Assume our firm faces a marginal tax rate of 40%. Then the incremental earnings (or net income) are as follows (in thousands of dollars):[1]

	Year	0	1	2	3	4	5
1	Incremental Revenues		500	500	500	500	500
2	Incremental Costs	−50	−150	−150	−150	−150	−150
3	Depreciation		−204	−204	−204	−204	−204
4	EBIT	−50	146	146	146	146	146
5	Income Tax at 40%	20	−58.4	−58.4	−58.4	−58.4	−58.4
6	**Incremental Earnings**	**−30**	**87.6**	**87.6**	**87.6**	**87.6**	**87.6**

We can also combine Eq. 8.1 and Eq. 8.2 to compute incremental earnings directly. For example, in years 1 through 5 we have:

$$\text{Incremental Earnings} = (\text{Incremental Revenues} - \text{Incremental Cost} - \text{Depreciation}) \times (1 - \text{Tax Rate}) \tag{8.3}$$

$$\text{Incremental Earnings} = (500{,}000 - 150{,}000 - 204{,}000) \times (1 - 0.4) = 87{,}600$$

EXAMPLE 8.1

Incremental Earnings

Problem

Suppose that Linksys is considering the development of a wireless home networking appliance, called HomeNet, that will provide both the hardware and the software necessary to run an entire home from any Internet connection. In addition to connecting PCs and printers, HomeNet will control new Internet-capable stereos, digital video recorders, heating and air-conditioning units, major appliances, telephone and security systems, office equipment, and so on. The major competitor for HomeNet is a product being developed by Brandt-Quigley Corporation.

Based on extensive marketing surveys, the sales forecast for HomeNet is 50,000 units per year. Given the pace of technological change, Linksys expects the product will have a four-year life and an expected wholesale price of $260 (the price Linksys will receive from stores). Actual production will be outsourced at a cost (including packaging) of $110 per unit.

To verify the compatibility of new consumer Internet-ready appliances, as they become available, with the HomeNet system, Linksys must also establish a new lab for testing purposes. It will rent the lab space, but will need to purchase $7.5 million of new equipment. The equipment will be depreciated using the straight-line method over a five-year life.

The lab will be operational at the end of one year. At that time, HomeNet will be ready to ship. Linksys expects to spend $2.8 million per year on rental costs for the lab space, as well as marketing and support for this product. Forecast the incremental earnings from the HomeNet project.

---

[1]While revenues and costs occur throughout the year, the standard convention, which we adopt here, is to list revenues and costs in the year in which they occur. Thus, cash flows that occur at the end of one year will be listed in a different column than those that occur at the start of the next year, even though they may occur only weeks apart. When additional precision is required, cash flows are often estimated on a quarterly or monthly basis.

Solution

▶ **Plan**

We need 4 items to calculate incremental earnings: (1) incremental revenues, (2) incremental costs, (3) depreciation, and (4) the marginal tax rate:

Incremental Revenues are additional units sold × price = 50,000 × \$260 = \$13,000,000

Incremental Costs are: additional units sold × production costs
= 50,000 × \$110 = \$5,500,000

Selling, General, and Administrative = \$2,800,000 for rent, marketing and support

Depreciation is: Depreciable base / Depreciable Life = \$7,500,000 / 5 = \$1,500,000

Marginal Tax Rate: 40%

Note that even though the project lasts for four years, the equipment has a five-year life, so we must account for the final depreciation charge in the fifth year.

▶ **Execute (in \$000s)**

	Year	0	1	2	3	4	5
1							
2	Revenues		13,000	13,000	13,000	13,000	–
3	Cost of Goods Sold		−5,500	−5,500	−5,500	−5,500	–
4	**Gross Profit**		7,500	7,500	7,500	7,500	–
5	Selling, General, and Administrative		−2,800	−2,800	−2,800	−2,800	–
6	Depreciation		−1,500	−1,500	−1,500	−1,500	−1,500
7	**EBIT**		3,200	3,200	3,200	3,200	−1,500
8	Income Tax at 40%		−1,280	−1,280	−1,280	−1,280	600
9	**Incremental Earnings**		**1,920**	**1,920**	**1,920**	**1,920**	**−900**

▶ **Evaluate**

These incremental earnings are an intermediate step on the way to calculating the incremental cash flows that would form the basis of any analysis of the HomeNet project. The cost of the equipment does not affect earnings in the year it is purchased, but does so through the depreciation expense in the following five years. Note that the depreciable life, which is based on accounting rules, does not have to be the same as the economic life of the asset—the period over which it will have value. Here, the firm will use the equipment for four years, but will depreciate it over five years.

Pro Forma Statement. The table calculating incremental earnings that we produced for our plant upgrade, and again in Example 8.1, is often referred to as a **pro forma** statement, because it is not based on actual data but rather depicts the firm's financials under a given set of hypothetical assumptions. In the HomeNet example, the firm's forecasts of revenues and costs were assumptions that allowed Linksys to forecast incremental earnings in a pro forma statement.

pro forma Describes a statement that is not based on actual data but rather depicts a firm's financials under a given set of hypothetical assumptions.

Taxes and Negative EBIT. Notice that in year 0 of our plant upgrade project, and in year 5 of the HomeNet example, EBIT is negative. Why are taxes relevant in this case? Consider the HomeNet example. HomeNet will reduce Linksys's taxable income in year 5 by \$1.5 million. As long as Linksys earns taxable income elsewhere in year 5 against which it can offset HomeNet's losses, Linksys will owe \$1.5 million × 40% = \$600,000 *less* in taxes in year 5 than if it were not undertaking the project. Because the tax savings come from the depreciation expense on equipment for the HomeNet project, the firm should credit this tax savings to the HomeNet project.

BDeH CHAPTER 8

EXAMPLE 8.2

Taxing Losses for Projects in Profitable Companies

Problem

Kellogg Company plans to launch a new line of high-fiber, zero-trans-fat breakfast pastries. The heavy advertising expenses associated with the new product launch will generate operating losses of $15 million next year for the product. Kellogg expects to earn pre-tax income of $460 million from operations other than the new pastries next year. If Kellogg pays a 40% tax rate on its pre-tax income, what will it owe in taxes next year without the new pastry product? What will it owe with the new product?

Solution

▶ Plan

We need Kellogg's pre-tax income with and without the new product losses and its tax rate of 40%. We can then compute the tax without the losses and compare it to the tax with the losses.

▶ Execute

Without the new product, Kellogg will owe $460 million × 40% = $184 million in corporate taxes next year. With the new product, Kellogg's pre-tax income next year will be only $460 million − $15 million = $445 million, and it will owe $445 million × 40% = $178 million in tax.

▶ Evaluate

Thus, launching the new product reduces Kellogg's taxes next year by $184 million − $178 million = $6 million. Because the losses on the new product reduce Kellogg's taxable income dollar for dollar, it is the same as if the new product had a tax bill of *negative* $6 million.

What About Interest Expenses? In Chapter 2, we saw that to compute a firm's net income, we must first deduct interest expenses from EBIT. When evaluating a capital budgeting decision, however, we generally *do not include interest expenses*. Any incremental interest expenses will be related to the firm's decision regarding how to finance the project, which is a separate decision. Here, we wish to evaluate the earnings contributions from the project on its own, separate from the financing decision. Ultimately, managers may also look at the additional earnings consequences associated with different methods of financing the project.

Thus, we evaluate a project *as if* the company will not use any debt to finance it (whether or not that is actually the case), and we postpone the consideration of alternative financing choices until Part V of this book. Because we calculate the net income assuming no debt (no leverage), we refer to the net income we compute using Eq. 8.3, as in the pro forma in Example 8.1, as the **unlevered net income** of the project, to indicate that it does not include any interest expenses associated with debt.

unlevered net income
Net income that does not include interest expenses associated with debt.

Concept Check

3. How are operating expenses and capital expenditures treated differently when calculating incremental earnings?

4. Why do we focus only on *incremental* revenues and costs, rather than all revenues and costs of the firm?

8.3 Determining Incremental Free Cash Flow

As discussed in Chapter 2, earnings are an accounting measure of the firm's performance. They do not represent real profits: The firm cannot use its earnings to buy goods, pay employees, fund new investments, or pay dividends to shareholders. To do those things,

free cash flow The incremental effect of a project on a firm's available cash.

the firm needs cash. Thus, to evaluate a capital budgeting decision, we must determine its consequences for the firm's available cash. The incremental effect of a project on the firm's available cash is the project's incremental **free cash flow**.

Calculating Free Cash Flow from Earnings

As discussed in Chapter 2, there are important differences between earnings and cash flow. Earnings include non-cash charges, such as depreciation, but do not include the cost of capital investment. To determine a project's free cash flow from its incremental earnings, we must adjust for these differences.

Capital Expenditures and Depreciation.   As we have noted, depreciation is not a cash expense that is paid by the firm. Rather, it is a method used for accounting and tax purposes to allocate the original purchase cost of the asset over its life. Because depreciation is not a cash flow, we do not include it in the cash flow forecast. However, that does not mean we can ignore depreciation. The depreciation expense reduces our taxable earnings and in doing so reduces our taxes. Taxes are cash flows, so because depreciation affects our cash flows, it still matters. Our approach for handling depreciation is to add it back to the incremental earnings to recognize the fact that we still have the cash flow associated with it.

For example, a project has incremental gross profit (revenues minus costs) of $1 million and a $200,000 depreciation expense. If the firm's tax rate is 40%, then the incremental earnings will be ($1,000,000 − $200,000) × (1 − 0.40) = $480,000. However, the firm will still have $680,000 because the $200,000 depreciation expense is not an actual cash outflow. Table 8.1 shows the calculation to get the incremental free cash flow in this case. Blue boxes surround all of the actual cash flows in the column labeled "Correct." A good way to check to make sure the incremental free cash flow is correct is to sum the actual cash flows. In this case, the firm generated $1,000,000 in gross profit (a positive cash flow), paid $320,000 in taxes (a negative cash flow), and was left with $1,000,000 − $320,000 = $680,000, which is the amount shown as the incremental free cash flow. In the last column, labeled "Incorrect," we show what would happen if you just ignored depreciation altogether. Because EBIT would be too high, the taxes would be too high as well and consequently, the incremental free cash flow would be too low. (Note that the difference of $80,000 between the two cases is entirely due to the difference in tax payments.)

TABLE 8.1		Correct	Incorrect
Deducting and then Adding Back Depreciation	Incremental Gross Profit	$1,000,000	$1,000,000
	Depreciation	−$200,000	
	EBIT	$800,000	$1,000,000
	Tax at 40%	−$320,000	−$400,000
	Incremental Earnings	$480,000	$600,000
	Add Back depreciation	$200,000	
	Incremental Free Cash Flow	$680,000	$600,000

EXAMPLE 8.3

Incremental Free
Cash Flows

Problem

Let's return to the HomeNet example. In Example 8.1, we computed the incremental earnings for HomeNet, but we need the incremental free cash flows to decide whether Linksys should proceed with the project.

Solution

▶ **Plan**

The difference between the incremental earnings and incremental free cash flows in the HomeNet example will be driven by the equipment purchased for the lab. We need to recognize the $7.5 million cash outflow associated with the purchase in year 0 and add back the $1.5 million depreciation expenses from year 1 to 5 as they are not actually cash outflows.

▶ **Execute** (in $000s)

	Year	0	1	2	3	4	5
1							
2	Revenues		13,000	13,000	13,000	13,000	–
3	Cost of Goods Sold		−5,500	−5,500	−5,500	−5,500	–
4	**Gross Profit**		7,500	7,500	7,500	7,500	–
5	Selling, General, and Administrative		−2,800	−2,800	−2,800	−2,800	–
6	Depreciation		−1,500	−1,500	−1,500	−1,500	−1,500
7	**EBIT**		3,200	3,200	3,200	3,200	−1,500
8	Income Tax at 40%		−1,280	−1,280	−1,280	−1,280	600
9	**Incremental Earnings**		1,920	1,920	1,920	1,920	−900
10	Add Back Depreciation		1,500	1,500	1,500	1,500	1,500
11	Purchase of Equipment	−7,500					
12	**Incremental Free Cash Flows**	−7,500	3,420	3,420	3,420	3,420	600

▶ **Evaluate**

By recognizing the outflow from purchasing the equipment in year 0, we account for the fact that $7.5 million left the firm at that time. By adding back the $1.5 million depreciation expenses in years 1–5, we adjust the incremental earnings to reflect the fact that the depreciation expense is not a cash outflow.

Net Working Capital (NWC).   Another way that incremental earnings and free cash flows can differ is if there are changes in net working capital. We defined net working capital in Chapter 2 as the difference between current assets and current liabilities. The main components of net working capital are cash, inventory, receivables, and payables:

$$\text{Net Working Capital} = \text{Current Assets} - \text{Current Liabilities}$$

$$= \text{Cash} + \text{Inventory} + \text{Receivables} - \text{Payables} \qquad (8.4)$$

Most projects will require the firm to invest in net working capital. Firms may need to maintain a minimum cash balance[2] to meet unexpected expenditures, and inventories of raw materials and finished product to accommodate production uncertainties and demand fluctuations. Also, customers may not pay for the goods they purchase immediately. While sales are immediately counted as part of earnings, the firm does not receive any cash until the customers actually pay. In the interim, the firm includes the amount

---

[2]The cash included in net working capital is cash that is *not* invested to earn a market rate of return. It includes cash held in the firm's checking account, in a company safe or cash box, in cash registers (for retail stores), and other sites.

trade credit The difference between receivables and payables that is the net amount of a firm's capital consumed as a result of those credit transactions; the credit that a firm extends to its customers.

that customers owe in its receivables. Thus, the firm's receivables measure the total credit that the firm has extended to its customers. In the same way, payables measure the credit the firm has received from its suppliers. The difference between receivables and payables is the net amount of the firm's capital that is consumed as a result of these credit transactions, known as **trade credit.**

We care about net working capital because it reflects a short-term investment that ties up cash flow that could be used elsewhere. For example, when a firm holds a lot of unsold inventory or has a lot of outstanding receivables, cash flow is tied up in the form of inventory or in the form of credit extended to customers. It is costly for the firm to tie up that cash flow because it delays the time until the cash flow is available for reinvestment or distribution to shareholders. Since we know that money has time value, we cannot ignore this delay in our forecasts for the project. Thus, whenever net working capital increases, reflecting additional investment in working capital, it represents a reduction in cash flow that year.

It is important to note that only changes in net working capital impact cash flows. For example, consider a three-year project that causes the firm to build up initial inventory by $20,000 and maintain that level of inventory in years 1 and 2, before drawing it down as the project ends and the last product is sold. It is often necessary for the initial increase in inventory to occur prior to the first sale so that the higher level of inventory would be achieved by the end of year 0. The level of the incremental net working capital in each year, the associated change in net working capital and the cash flow implications, would be:

	Year	0	1	2	3
1					
2	Level of Incremental NWC	20,000	20,000	20,000	0
3	*Change* in Incremental NWC	+20,000	0	0	−20,000
4	**Cash Flow from Change in NWC**	**−20,000**	**0**	**0**	**+20,000**

Note that the cash flow effect from a change in net working capital is always equal and opposite in sign to the change in net working capital. For example, an increase in inventory represents an investment or cash outflow, while a reduction in that inventory frees up that investment of capital and represents a cash inflow. Thus in capital budgeting we subtract changes in net working capital to arrive at the cash flows. Also notice that since the level of incremental net working capital did not change in years 1 and 2, there was no new cash flow effect. Intuitively, as the firm is using up inventory and replenishing it, the net new investment in inventory is zero, so no additional cash outflow is required. Finally, note that over the life of the project, the incremental net working capital returns to zero so that the changes (+20,000 in year 0 and −20,000 in year 3) sum to zero. Accounting principles ensure this by requiring the recapture of working capital over the life of the project.

More generally, we define the change in net working capital in year t as:

$$\text{Change in NWC in year } t = NWC_t - NWC_{t-1} \tag{8.5}$$

When a project causes a change in NWC, that change must be subtracted from incremental earnings to arrive at incremental free cash flows.

EXAMPLE 8.4

Incorporating Changes in Net Working Capital

Problem

Suppose that HomeNet will have no incremental cash or inventory requirements (products will be shipped directly from the contract manufacturer to customers). However, receivables related to HomeNet are expected to account for 15% of annual sales, and payables are expected to be 15% of the annual cost of goods sold (COGS). Fifteen percent of $13 million in sales is $1.95 million and 15% of $5.5 million in COGS is $825,000. HomeNet's net working capital requirements are shown in the following table:

	Year	0	1	2	3	4	5
1							
2	**Net Working Capital Forecast ($000s)**						
3	Cash Requirements	0	0	0	0	0	0
4	Inventory	0	0	0	0	0	0
5	Receivables (15% of Sales)	0	1,950	1,950	1,950	1,950	0
6	Payables (15% of COGS)	0	−825	−825	−825	−825	0
7	**Net Working Capital**	**0**	**1,125**	**1,125**	**1,125**	**1,125**	**0**

How does this requirement affect the project's free cash flow?

Solution

▶ Plan

Any increases in net working capital represent an investment that reduces the cash available to the firm and so reduces free cash flow. We can use our forecast of HomeNet's net working capital requirements to complete our estimate of HomeNet's free cash flow. In year 1, net working capital increases by $1.125 million. This increase represents a cost to the firm. This reduction of free cash flow corresponds to the fact that $1.950 million of the firm's sales in year 1, and $0.825 million of its costs, have not yet been paid.

In years 2–4, net working capital does not change, so no further contributions are needed. In year 5, when the project is shut down, net working capital falls by $1.125 million as the payments of the last customers are received and the final bills are paid. We add this $1.125 million to free cash flow in year 5.

▶ Execute (in $000s)

	Year	0	1	2	3	4	5
1							
2	Net Working Capital	0	1,125	1,125	1,125	1,125	0
3	Change in NWC		+1,125	0	0	0	−1,125
4	Cash Flow Effect		−1,125	0	0	0	+1,125

The incremental free cash flows would then be:

	Year	0	1	2	3	4	5
1							
2	Revenues		13,000	13,000	13,000	13,000	0
3	Costs of Goods Sold		−5,500	−5,500	−5,500	−5,500	0
4	**Gross Profit**		7,500	7,500	7,500	7,500	0
5	Selling, General, and Administrative		−2,800	−2,800	−2,800	−2,800	0
6	Depreciation		−1,500	−1,500	−1,500	−1,500	−1,500
7	**EBIT**		3,200	3,200	3,200	3,200	−1,500
8	Income Tax at 40%		−1,280	−1,280	−1,280	−1,280	600
9	**Incremental Earnings**		1,920	1,920	1,920	1,920	−900
10	Add Back Depreciation		1,500	1,500	1,500	1,500	1,500
11	Purchase of Equipment	−7,500					
12	Subtract Changes in NWC		−1,125	0	0	0	1,125
13	**Incremental Free Cash Flows**	**−7,500**	**2,295**	**3,420**	**3,420**	**3,420**	**1,725**

▶ Evaluate

The free cash flows differ from unlevered net income by reflecting the cash flow effects of capital expenditures on equipment, depreciation, and changes in net working capital. Note that in the first two years, free cash flow is lower than unlevered net income, reflecting the upfront investment in equipment and net working capital required by the project. In later years, free cash flow exceeds unlevered net income because depreciation is not a cash expense. In the last year, the firm ultimately recovers the investment in net working capital, further boosting the free cash flow.

Calculating Free Cash Flow Directly

As we noted at the outset of this chapter, because practitioners usually begin the capital budgeting process by first forecasting earnings, we have chosen to do the same. However, we can calculate a project's free cash flow directly by using the following shorthand formula:

Free Cash Flow

$$\text{Free Cash Flow} = \overbrace{(\text{Revenues} - \text{Costs} - \text{Depreciation}) \times (1 - \text{tax rate})}^{\text{Unlevered Net Income}}$$
$$+ \text{ Depreciation} - \text{CapEx} - \text{Change in } NWC \tag{8.6}$$

Note that we first deduct depreciation when computing the project's incremental earnings and then add it back (because it is a non-cash expense) when computing free cash flow. Thus, the only effect of depreciation is to reduce the firm's taxable income. Indeed, we can rewrite Eq. 8.6 as:

$$\text{Free Cash Flow} = (\text{Revenues} - \text{Costs}) \times (1 - \text{tax rate}) - \text{CapEx}$$
$$- \text{ Change in } NWC + \text{tax rate} \times \text{Depreciation} \tag{8.7}$$

depreciation tax shield
The tax savings that result from the ability to deduct depreciation.

The last term in Eq. 8.7, tax rate × Depreciation, is called the **depreciation tax shield**, which is the tax savings that results from the ability to deduct depreciation. As a consequence, depreciation expenses have a *positive* impact on free cash flow. Returning to our example in Table 8.1, if the firm ignored depreciation, its taxes were $400,000 instead of $320,000, leaving it with incremental free cash flow of $600,000 instead of $680,000. Notice that the $80,000 difference is exactly equal to the tax rate (40%) multiplied by the depreciation expense ($200,000). Every dollar of depreciation expense saves the firm 40 cents in taxes, so the $200,000 depreciation expense translates into an $80,000 tax savings.

Firms often report a different depreciation expense for accounting and for tax purposes. Because only the tax consequences of depreciation are relevant for free cash flow, we should use the depreciation expense that the firm will use for tax purposes in our forecast. For tax purposes, many firms use a system called *Modified Accelerated Cost Recovery System*, which we discuss in the next section.

Calculating the NPV

The goal of forecasting the incremental free cash flows is to have the necessary inputs to calculate the project's NPV. To compute a project's NPV, we must discount its free cash flow at the appropriate cost of capital. The cost of capital for a project is the expected return that investors could earn on their best alternative investment with similar risk and maturity. We will develop the techniques needed to estimate the cost of capital later in this text, when we discuss risk and return. For now, we take the cost of capital as given.

We compute the present value of each free cash flow in the future by discounting it at the project's cost of capital. As explained in Chapter 4, using r to represent the cost of capital, the present value of the free cash flow in year t (or FCF_t) is:

$$PV(FCF_t) = \frac{FCF_t}{(1 + r)^t} = FCF_t \times \underbrace{\frac{1}{(1 + r)^t}}_{t\text{-year discount factor}} \tag{8.8}$$

BDeH CHAPTER 8

EXAMPLE 8.5

Calculating the Project's NPV

Problem

Assume that Linksys's managers believe that the HomeNet project has risks similar to its existing projects, for which it has a cost of capital of 12%. Compute the NPV of the HomeNet project.

Solution

▶ **Plan**

From Example 8.4, the incremental free cash flows for the HomeNet project are (in $000s):

	Year	0	1	2	3	4	5
1							
2	Incremental Free Cash Flows	−7,500	2,295	3,420	3,420	3,420	1,725

To compute the NPV, we sum the present values of all of the cash flows, noting that the year 0 cash outflow is already a present value.

▶ **Execute**

Using Eq. 8.8,

$$NPV = -7500 + \frac{2295}{(1.12)^1} + \frac{3420}{(1.12)^2} + \frac{3420}{(1.12)^3} + \frac{3420}{(1.12)^4} + \frac{1725}{(1.12)^5} = 2862$$

▶ **Evaluate**

Based on our estimates, HomeNet's NPV is $2.862 million. While HomeNet's upfront cost is $7.5 million, the present value of the additional free cash flow that Linksys will receive from the project is $10.362 million. Thus, taking the HomeNet project is equivalent to Linksys having an extra $2.862 million in the bank today.

Concept Check

5. If depreciation expense is not a cash flow, why do we have to subtract it and add it back? Why not just ignore it?

6. Why does an increase in net working capital represent a cash outflow?

8.4 Other Effects on Incremental Free Cash Flows

When computing the incremental free cash flows of an investment decision, we should include *all* changes between the firm's free cash flows with the project versus without the project. These include opportunities forgone due to the project and effects of the project on other parts of the firm. In this section, we discuss these other effects, some of the pitfalls and common mistakes to avoid, and finally the complications that can arise when forecasting incremental free cash flows.

Opportunity Costs

opportunity cost The value a resource could have provided in its best alternative use.

Many projects use a resource that the company already owns. Because the firm does not need to pay cash to acquire this resource for a new project, it is tempting to assume that the resource is available for free. However, in many cases the resource could provide value for the firm in another opportunity or project. The **opportunity cost** of using a resource is the value it could have provided in its best alternative use.[3] Because this

---

[3]In Chapter 5, we defined the opportunity cost of capital as the rate you could earn on an alternative investment with equivalent risk. We similarly define the opportunity cost of using an existing asset in a project as the cash flow generated by the next-best alternative use for the asset.

> **Common Mistake** The Opportunity Cost of an Idle Asset
>
> A common mistake is to conclude that if an asset is currently idle, its opportunity cost is zero. For example, the firm might have a warehouse that is currently empty or a machine that is not being used. Often, the asset may have been idled in anticipation of taking on the new project, and would have otherwise been put to use by the firm. Even if the firm has no alternative use for the asset, the firm could choose to sell or rent the asset. The value obtained from the asset's alternative use, sale, or rental represents an opportunity cost that must be included as part of the incremental cash flows.

value is lost when the resource is used by another project, we should include the opportunity cost as an incremental cost of the project. For example, your company may be considering building a retail store on some land that it owns. Even though it already owns the land, it is not free to the store project. If it did not put its store on the land, the company could sell the land, for example. This forgone market price for the land is an opportunity cost of the retail store project.

Project Externalities

project externalities
Indirect effects of a project that may increase or decrease the profits of other business activities of a firm.

Project externalities are indirect effects of a project that may increase or decrease the profits of other business activities of the firm. For instance, some purchasers of Apple's iPhone would otherwise have bought Apple's iPod nano. When sales of a new product displace sales of an existing product, the situation is often referred to as **cannibalization**. The lost sales of the existing project are an incremental cost to the company of going forward with the new product.

cannibalization When sales of a firm's new product displace sales of one of its existing products.

Sunk Costs

sunk cost Any unrecoverable cost for which a firm is already liable.

A **sunk cost** is any unrecoverable cost for which the firm is already liable. Sunk costs have been or will be paid regardless of the decision whether or not to proceed with the project. Therefore, they are not incremental with respect to the current decision and should not be included in its analysis. You may hire a market research firm to do market analysis to determine whether there is demand for a new product you are considering and the analysis may show that there is not enough demand, so you decide not to go forward with the project. Does that mean you do not have to pay the research firm's bill? Of course you still have to pay the bill, emphasizing that the cost was sunk and incurred whether you went forward with the project or not.

A good rule to remember is that *if your decision does not affect a cash flow, then the cash flow should not affect your decision.* If the cash flow is the same regardless of the decision, then it is not relevant to your decision. Following are some common examples of sunk costs you may encounter.

overhead expenses
Those expenses associated with activities that are not directly attributable to a single business activity but instead affect many different areas of a corporation.

Fixed Overhead Expenses. **Overhead expenses** are associated with activities that are not directly attributable to a single business activity but instead affect many different areas of the corporation. Examples include the cost of maintaining the company's headquarters and the salary of the CEO. These expenses are often allocated to the different business activities for accounting purposes. To the extent that these overhead costs are fixed and will be incurred in any case, they are not incremental to the project and should not be included. Only include as incremental expenses the *additional* overhead expenses that arise because of the decision to take on the project.

Common Mistake   **The Sunk Cost Fallacy**

Being influenced by sunk costs is such a widespread mistake that it has a special name: *sunk cost fallacy.* The most common problem is that people "throw good money after bad." That is, people sometimes continue to invest in a project that has a negative NPV because they have already invested a large amount in the project and feel that by not continuing it, the prior investment will be wasted. The sunk cost fallacy is also sometimes called the "Concorde effect," a term that refers to the British and French governments' decision to continue funding the joint development of the Concorde aircraft even after it was clear that sales of the plane would fall far short of what was necessary to justify its continued development. The project was viewed by the British government as a commercial and financial disaster. However, the political implications of halting the project—and thereby publicly admitting that all past expenses on the project would result in nothing—ultimately prevented either government from abandoning the project.

Past Research and Development Expenditures.   A pharmaceutical company may spend tens of millions of dollars developing a new drug, but if it fails to produce an effect in trials (or worse, has only negative effects), should it proceed? The company cannot get its development costs back and the amount of those costs should have no bearing on whether to continue developing a failed drug.

When a firm has already devoted significant resources to develop a new product, there may be a tendency to continue investing in the product even if market conditions have changed and the product is unlikely to be viable. The rationale that is sometimes given is that if the product is abandoned, the money that has already been invested will be "wasted." In other cases, a decision is made to abandon a project because it cannot possibly be successful enough to recoup the investment that has already been made. In fact, neither argument is correct: Any money that has already been spent is a sunk cost and therefore irrelevant. The decision to continue or abandon should be based only on the incremental costs and benefits of the product going forward.

Adjusting Free Cash Flow

Here, we describe a number of complications that can arise when estimating a project's free cash flow.

Timing of Cash Flows.   For simplicity, we have treated the cash flows in our examples as if they occur at annual intervals. In reality, cash flows will be spread throughout the year. While it is common to forecast at the annual level, we can forecast free cash flow on a quarterly or monthly basis when greater accuracy is required. In practice, firms often choose shorter intervals for riskier projects so that they might forecast cash flows at the monthly level for projects that carry considerable risk. For example, cash flows for a new facility in Europe may be forecasted at the quarterly or annual level, but if that same facility were located in a politically unstable country, the forecasts would likely be at the monthly level.

MACRS depreciation The most accelerated cost recovery system allowed by the IRS. Based on the recovery period, MACRS depreciation tables assign a fraction of the purchase price that the firm can depreciate each year.

Accelerated Depreciation.   Because depreciation contributes positively to the firm's cash flow through the depreciation tax shield, it is in the firm's best interest to use the most accelerated method of depreciation that is allowable for tax purposes. By doing so, the firm will accelerate its tax savings and increase their present value. In the United States, the most accelerated depreciation method allowed by the IRS is MACRS (Modified Accelerated Cost Recovery System) depreciation. With **MACRS depreciation**, the firm first categorizes assets according to their recovery period. Based on the recovery period,

MACRS depreciation tables assign a fraction of the purchase price that the firm can recover each year. We provide MACRS tables and recovery periods for common assets in the appendix.

EXAMPLE 8.6

Computing
Accelerated
Depreciation

Problem

What depreciation deduction would be allowed for HomeNet's $7.5 million lab equipment using the MACRS method, assuming the lab equipment is designated to have a five-year recovery period? (See the appendix for information on MACRS depreciation schedules.)

Solution

▶ **Plan**

Table 8.4 in this chapter's Appendix A provides the percentage of the cost that can be depreciated each year. Under MACRS, we take the percentage in the table for each year and multiply it by the original purchase price of the equipment to calculate the depreciation for that year.

▶ **Execute**

Based on the table, the allowable depreciation expense for the lab equipment is shown below (in thousands of dollars):

	Year	0	1	2	3	4	5
1							
2	MACRS Depreciation						
3	Lab Equipment Cost	−7,500					
4	MACRS Depreciation Rate	20.00%	32.00%	19.20%	11.52%	11.52%	5.76%
5	Depreciation Expense	−1,500	−2,400	−1,440	−864	−864	−432

▶ **Evaluate**

Compared with straight-line depreciation, the MACRS method allows for larger depreciation deductions earlier in the asset's life, which increases the present value of the depreciation tax shield and thus will raise the project's NPV. In the case of HomeNet, computing the NPV using MACRS depreciation leads to an NPV of $3.179 million.

Liquidation or Salvage Value.   Assets that are no longer needed often have a resale value, or some salvage value if the parts are sold for scrap. Some assets may have a negative liquidation value. For example, it may cost money to remove and dispose of the used equipment.

In the calculation of free cash flow, we include the liquidation value of any assets that are no longer needed and may be disposed of. When an asset is liquidated, any capital gain is taxed as income. We calculate the capital gain as the difference between the sale price and the book value of the asset:

$$\text{Capital Gain} = \text{Sale Price} - \text{Book Value} \qquad (8.9)$$

The book value is equal to the asset's original cost less the amount it has already been depreciated for tax purposes:

$$\text{Book Value} = \text{Purchase Price} - \text{Accumulated Depreciation} \qquad (8.10)$$

We must adjust the project's free cash flow to account for the after-tax cash flow that would result from an asset sale:

$$\text{After-Tax Cash Flow from Asset Sale} = \text{Sale Price}$$
$$- (\text{Tax Rate} \times \text{Capital Gain}) \qquad (8.11)$$

EXAMPLE 8.7

Computing After-Tax
Cash Flows from an
Asset Sale

Problem

As production manager, you are overseeing the shutdown of a production line for a discontinued product. Some of the equipment can be sold for a total price of $50,000. The equipment was originally purchased four years ago for $500,000 and is being depreciated according to the five-year MACRS schedule. If your marginal tax rate is 35%, what is the after-tax cash flow you can expect from selling the equipment?

Solution

▶ **Plan**

In order to compute the after-tax cash flow, you will need to compute the capital gain, which, as Eq. 8.9 shows requires you to know the book value of the equipment. The book value is given in Eq. 8.10 as the original purchase price of the equipment less accumulated depreciation. Thus, you need to follow these steps:

1. Use the MACRS schedule to determine the accumulated depreciation.
2. Determine the book value as purchase price minus accumulated depreciation.
3. Determine the capital gain as the sale price less the book value.
4. Compute the tax owed on the capital gain and subtract it from the sale price, following Eq. 8.11.

▶ **Execute**

From the chapter appendix, we see that the first five rates of the five-year MACRS schedule (including year 0) are:

	Year	0	1	2	3	4
2	Depreciation Rate	20.00%	32.00%	19.20%	11.52%	11.52%
3	Depreciation Amount	100,000	160,000	96,000	57,600	57,600

Thus, the accumulated depreciation is 100,000 + 160,000 + 96,000 + 57,600 + 57,600 = 471,200, such that the remaining book value is $500,000 − $471,200 = 28,800. (Note we could have also calculated this by summing the rates for years remaining on the MACRS schedule (Year 5 is 5.76%, so .0576 × 500,000 = 28,800).

The capital gain is then $50,000 − $28,800 = $21,200 and the tax owed is 0.35 × $21,200 = $7,420.

Your after-tax cash flow is then found as the sale price minus the tax owed: $50,000 − $7,420 = $42,580.

▶ **Evaluate**

Because you are only taxed on the capital gain portion of the sale price, figuring the after-tax cash flow is not as simple as subtracting the tax rate multiplied by the sale price. Instead, you have to determine the portion of the sale price that represents a gain and compute the tax from there. The same procedure holds for selling equipment at a loss relative to book value—the loss creates a deduction for taxable income elsewhere in the company.

tax loss carryforwards and carrybacks Two features of the U.S. tax code that allow corporations to take losses during a current year and offset them against gains in nearby years. Since 1997, companies can "carry back" losses for two years and "carry forward" losses for 20 years.

Tax Carryforwards.   A firm generally identifies its marginal tax rate by determining the tax bracket that it falls into based on its overall level of pre-tax income. Two additional features of the tax code, called **tax loss carryforwards** and **carrybacks**, allow corporations to take losses during a current year and offset them against gains in nearby years. Since 1997, companies can "carry back" losses for two years and "carry forward" losses for 20 years. This tax rule means that a firm can offset losses during one year against income for the last two years, or save the losses to be offset against income during the next 20 years. When a firm can carry back losses, it receives a refund for back taxes in the current year. Otherwise, the firm must carry forward the loss and use it to offset future taxable income. When a firm has tax loss carryforwards well in excess of its current pre-tax income, then additional income it earns today will simply increase the taxes it owes after it exhausts its carryforwards.

Replacement Decisions

Often the financial manager must decide whether to replace an existing piece of equipment. The new equipment may allow increased production, resulting in incremental revenue, or it may simply be more efficient, lowering costs. The typical incremental effects associated with such a decision are salvage value from the old machine, purchase of the new machine, cost savings and revenue increases, and depreciation effects.

EXAMPLE 8.8

Replacing an Existing Machine

Problem

You are trying to decide whether to replace a machine on your production line. The new machine will cost $1 million, but will be more efficient than the old machine, reducing costs by $500,000 per year. Your old machine is fully depreciated, but you could sell it for $50,000. You would depreciate the new machine over a five-year life using MACRS. The new machine will not change your working capital needs. Your tax rate is 35%.

Solution

▶ **Plan**

Incremental revenues: 0

Incremental costs: − 500,000 (a reduction in costs will appear as a positive number in the costs line of our analysis)

Depreciation schedule (from the appendix):

	Year	0	1	2	3	4	5
2	Depreciation Rate	20.00%	32.00%	19.20%	11.52%	11.52%	5.76%
3	Depreciation Amount	200,000	320,000	192,000	115,200	115,200	57,600

Capital gain on salvage = $50,000 − $0 = $50,000

Cash flow from salvage value: +50,000 − (50,000)(.35) = 32,500

▶ **Execute**

	Year	0	1	2	3	4	5
1							
2	Incremental Revenues						
3	Incremental Costs of Goods Sold		500	500	500	500	500
4	**Incremental Gross Profit**		500	500	500	500	500
5	Depreciation	−200	−320	−192	−115.2	−115.2	−57.6
6	**EBIT**	−200	180	308	384.8	384.8	442.4
7	Income Tax at 35%	70	−63	−107.8	−134.68	−134.68	−154.84
8	**Incremental Earnings**	−130	117	200.2	250.12	250.12	287.56
9	Add Back Depreciation	200	320	192	115.2	115.2	57.6
10	Purchase of Equipment	−1,000					
11	Salvage Cash Flow	32.5					
12	**Incremental Free Cash Flows**	−897.5	437	392.2	365.32	365.32	345.16

▶ **Evaluate**

Even though the decision has no impact on revenues, it still matters for cash flows because it reduces costs. Further, both selling the old machine and buying the new machine involve cash flows with tax implications.

Concept Check

7. Should we include sunk costs in the cash flows of a project? Why or why not?

8. Explain why it is advantageous for a firm to use the most accelerated depreciation schedule possible for tax purposes.

8.5 Analyzing the Project

When evaluating a capital budgeting project, financial managers should make the decision that maximizes NPV. As we have discussed, to compute the NPV for a project you need to estimate the incremental free cash flows and choose a discount rate. Given these inputs, the NPV calculation is relatively straightforward. The most difficult part of capital budgeting is deciding how to estimate the cash flows and cost of capital. These estimates are often subject to significant uncertainty. In this section, we look at methods that assess the importance of this uncertainty and identify the drivers of value in the project.

sensitivity analysis An important capital budgeting tool that determines how the NPV varies as a single underlying assumption is changed.

Sensitivity Analysis

An important capital budgeting tool for assessing the effect of uncertainty in forecasts is sensitivity analysis. **Sensitivity analysis** breaks the NPV calculation into its component assumptions and shows how the NPV varies as the underlying assumptions change. In this way, sensitivity analysis allows us to explore the effects of errors in our NPV estimates for a project. By conducting a sensitivity analysis, we learn which assumptions are the most important; we can then invest further resources and effort to refine these assumptions. Such an analysis also reveals which aspects of a project are most critical when we are actually managing the project.

In fact, we have already performed a type of sensitivity analysis in Chapter 7 when we constructed an NPV profile. By graphing the NPV of a project as a function of the discount rate, we are assessing the sensitivity of our NPV calculation to uncertainty about the correct cost of capital to use as a discount rate. In practice, financial managers explore the sensitivity of their NPV calculation to many more factors than just the discount rate.

To illustrate, consider the assumptions underlying the calculation of HomeNet's NPV in Example 8.5. There is likely to be significant uncertainty surrounding each revenue and cost assumption. In addition to the base case assumptions about units sold, sale price, cost of goods sold, net working capital, and cost of capital, Linksys's managers would also identify best and worst case scenarios for each. For example, assume that they identified the best and worst case assumptions listed in Table 8.2. Note that these are best and worst case scenarios for each parameter rather than representing one worst case scenario and one best case scenario.

To determine the importance of this uncertainty, we recalculate the NPV of the HomeNet project under the best- and worst-case assumptions for each parameter. For example, if the number of units sold is only 35,000 per year, the NPV of the project falls

TABLE 8.2	Parameter	Initial Assumption	Worst Case	Best Case
	Units Sold (thousands)	50	35	65
Best- and Worst-Case	Sale Price ($/unit)	260	240	280
Assumptions for Each	Cost of Goods ($/unit)	110	120	100
Parameter in the	NWC ($ thousands)	1125	1525	725
HomeNet Project	Cost of Capital	12%	15%	10%

FIGURE 8.2

HomeNet's NPV Under Best- and Worst-Case Parameter Assumptions

Bars show the change in NPV going from the best-case assumption to the worst-case assumption for each parameter. For example, the NPV of the project ranges from −$1.24 million if only 35,000 units are sold to $6.96 million if 65,000 units are sold. Under the initial assumptions, HomeNet's NPV is $2.862 million.

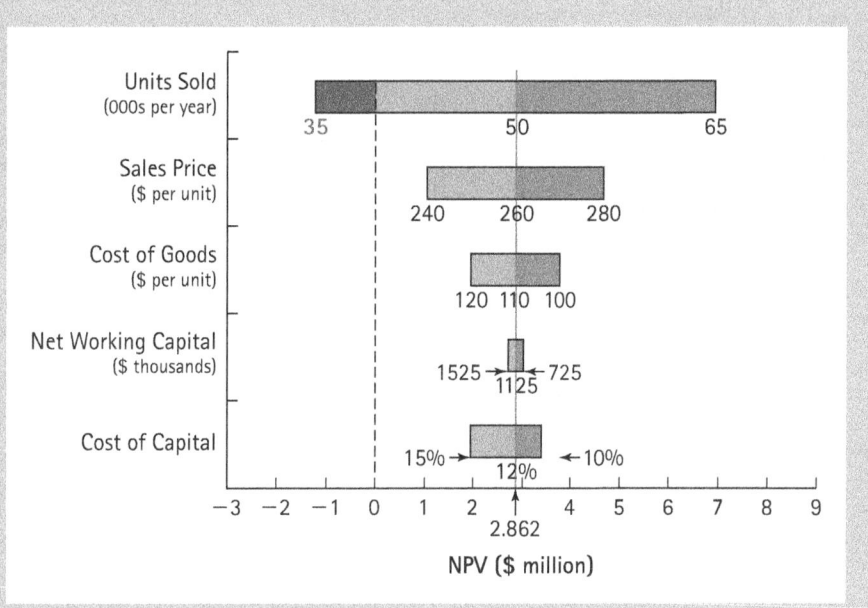

to −$1.24 million. We repeat this calculation for each parameter. The result is shown in Figure 8.2, which reveals that the parameter assumptions with the largest effect on NPV are the number of units sold and the sale price per unit. As a result, these assumptions deserve the greatest scrutiny during the estimation process. In addition, as the most important drivers of the project's value, these factors deserve close attention when managing the project after it starts.

Break-Even Analysis

break-even The level for which an investment has an NPV of zero.

A natural extension of the sensitivity analysis is to ask at what level of each parameter would the project just **break-even**, which is the level for which the investment has an NPV of zero. One example that we have already considered is the calculation of the internal rate of return (IRR). Recall from Chapter 7 that the difference between the IRR of a project and the cost of capital tells you how much error in the cost of capital it would take to change the investment decision. By either graphing the NPV profile or using the Excel function IRR, we would find that the incremental cash flows of HomeNet given in Example 8.5 imply an IRR of 26.6%. Hence, the true cost of capital can be as high as 26.6% and the project will still have a positive NPV.

break-even analysis A calculation of the value of each parameter for which the NPV of the project is zero.

We can determine the uncertainty of other parameters as well. In a **break-even analysis**, for each parameter we calculate the value at which the NPV of the project is zero. This would be tedious to do by hand, so in practice it is always done with a spreadsheet. As with the NPV profile for the discount rate, we can graph the NPV as a function of each of the critical assumptions. In each case, we keep all of the other parameters fixed at their base case values and vary only the parameter in question. Figure 8.3 does this for HomeNet.

EBIT break-even The level of a particular parameter for which a project's EBIT is zero.

Accounting Break-Even. We have examined the break-even levels in terms of the project's NPV, which is the most useful perspective for decision making. Other accounting notions of break-even are sometimes considered, however. For example, we could compute the **EBIT break-even** for sales, which is the level of sales for which the project's EBIT is zero.

FIGURE 8.3

Break-Even Analysis Graphs

The graphs in panels (a) and (b) relate two of the key parameters to the project's NPV to identify the parameters' break-even points. For example, based on the initial assumptions, the HomeNet project will break even with a sales level of just under 40,000 units per year. Similarly, holding sales and the other parameters constant at their initial assumed values, the project will break-even at a cost of goods sold of just over $141 per unit.

Panel (a) Break-Even Based on Units Sold

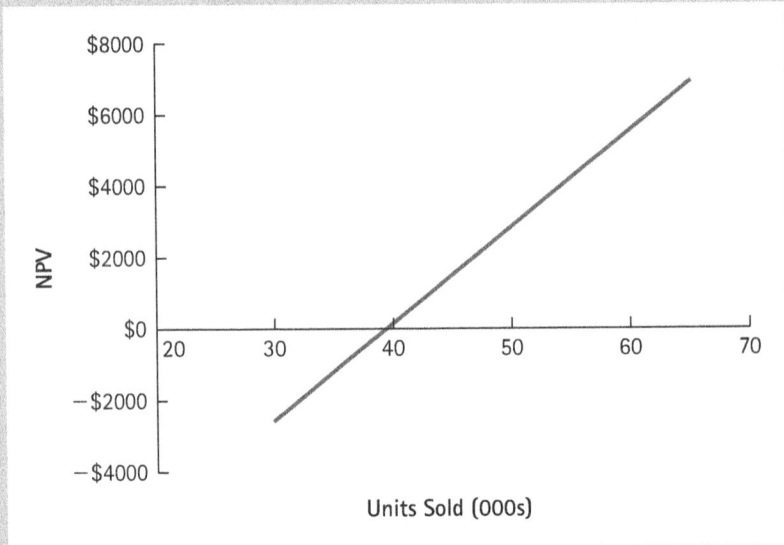

Panel (b) Break-Even Based on Costs of Goods Sold

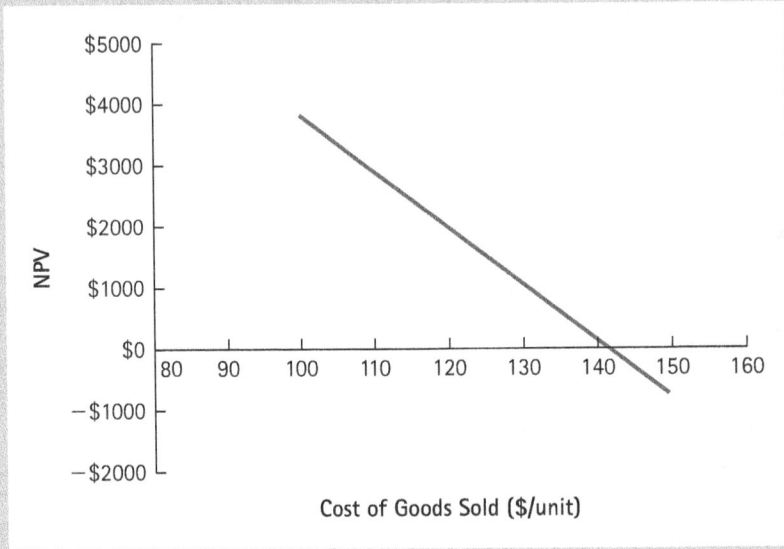

Recall from Eq. 8.1 that the project's EBIT is Revenues − Costs − Depreciation. Costs include cost of goods sold and selling, and general and administrative expense (SG&A). Revenues equal Units Sold × Sale Price, and cost of goods sold equals Units Sold × Cost per Unit, so we have EBIT = (Units Sold × Sale Price) − (Units Sold × Cost per Unit) − SG&A − Depreciation. Setting this equal to zero and solving for units sold:

$$\text{Units Sold} \times (\text{Sale Price} - \text{Cost per unit}) - \text{SG\&A} - \text{Depreciation} = 0$$

$$\text{Units Sold} = \frac{\text{SG\&A} + \text{Depreciation}}{\text{Sales Price} - \text{Cost per unit}} = \frac{2{,}800{,}000 + 1{,}500{,}000}{260 - 110} = 28{,}667$$

		Expected Units	
Strategy	Sale Price ($/unit)	Sold (thousands)	NPV ($ thousands)
Current Strategy	260	50	2862
Price Reduction	245	55	2725
Price Increase	275	45	2725

TABLE 8.3

Scenario Analysis of Alternative Pricing Strategies

However, this EBIT break-even number is misleading. While HomeNet's EBIT break-even level of sales is only 28,667 units per year, given the large upfront investment required in HomeNet, its NPV is −$2.97 million at that sales level.

Scenario Analysis

scenario analysis An important capital budgeting tool that determines how the NPV varies as a number of the underlying assumptions are changed simultaneously.

In the analysis thus far, we have considered the consequences of varying only one parameter at a time. In reality, certain factors may affect more than one parameter. **Scenario analysis** considers the effect on NPV of changing multiple project parameters. For example, lowering HomeNet's price may increase the number of units sold. We can use scenario analysis to evaluate alternative pricing strategies for the HomeNet product in Table 8.3. In this case, the current strategy is optimal. Figure 8.4 shows the combinations of price and volume that lead to the same NPV of $2.862 million for HomeNet as the current strategy. Only strategies with price and volume combinations above the line will lead to a higher NPV.

FIGURE 8.4

Price and Volume Combinations for HomeNet with Equivalent NPV

The graph shows alternative price per unit and annual volume combinations that lead to an NPV of $2.862 million. Pricing strategies with combinations above this line will lead to a higher NPV and are superior. For example, if Linksys managers think they will be able to sell 48,000 units at a price of $275, this strategy would yield a higher NPV ($3,627 million).

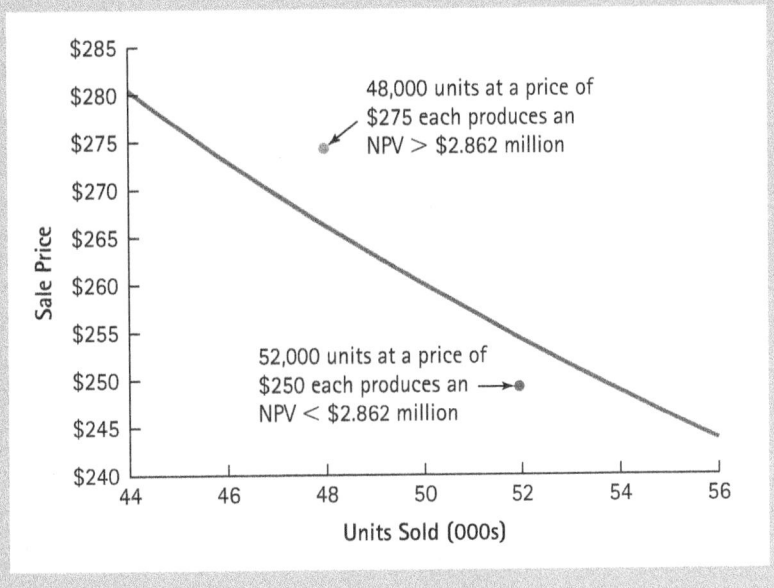

9. What is sensitivity analysis?

10. How does scenario analysis differ from sensitivity analysis?

Real Options in Capital Budgeting

Our approach to capital budgeting thus far has focused on the initial investment decision without explicitly considering future decisions that may need to be made over the life of a project. Rather, we assumed that our forecast of a project's expected future cash flows already incorporated the effect of future decisions that would be made. In truth, most projects contain *real options*. A **real option** is the right, but not the obligation, to make a particular business decision. Because you are not obligated to take the action, you will only do so if it increases the NPV of the project. In particular, because real options allow a decision maker to choose the most attractive alternative after new information has been learned, the presence of real options adds value to an investment opportunity. The tools to estimate the actual value created by real options are beyond the scope of this chapter and are contained later in the book. However, we introduce the concept here to give you a sense of the types of real options you may encounter and establish the intuition that flexibility (more options) is valuable. Let's look at some of the most common real options in the context of Linksys's HomeNet project.

real option The right to make a particular business decision, such as a capital investment.

Option to Delay

option to delay commitment The option to time a particular investment which is almost always present.

The **option to delay commitment** (the option to time the investment) is almost always present. Linksys could wait to commit to the HomeNet project. Waiting could be valuable if Linksys expects prices of the components to decrease substantially, soon-to-be-released new technology that will make the existing components obsolete, or increased sales of Web-ready appliances (heightening the demand for HomeNet). In addition, Linksys may simply want more time to gather information about the potential market for HomeNet. As with any other capital budgeting decision, Linksys would only choose to delay if doing so would increase the NPV of the project by more than the cost of capital over the time of delay.

Option to Expand

option to expand The option to start with limited production and expand only if the project is successful.

In the section on sensitivity analysis, we looked at changes in our assumptions about units sold. All of the analysis was performed, however, under the assumption that Linksys would fully commit to and roll-out the HomeNet product worldwide. We did not consider the **option to expand**, which is the option to start with limited production and expand only if the product is successful. Linksys could, instead, test market the product in limited release before committing to it fully. Doing so would create an option to expand worldwide only if HomeNet were successful in limited release. It is possible that, by reducing its upfront commitment and only choosing to expand if the product is successful, Linksys will increase the NPV of the HomeNet product. However, in this particular case, there are large costs of development that would be paid whether Linksys sells one or one million units, so limiting the initial market does not reduce the financial commitment substantially. Thus, in the case of HomeNet, it is unlikely that Linksys would choose a limited release with an option to expand.

Option to Abandon

abandonment option An option for an investor to cease making investments in a project. Abandonment options can add value to a project because a firm can drop a project if it turns out to be unsuccessful.

An **abandonment option** is the option to walk away. Abandonment options can add value to a project because a firm can drop a project if it turns out to be unsuccessful. Imagine that a competitor developed new technology that allowed it to introduce a competing product priced at $170. At that price, HomeNet would produce negative cash flows every year. But would Linksys continue to sell HomeNet if it had to do so at a loss? Probably not. Linksys has an option to abandon the project. It could stop producing HomeNet and sell the equipment. Depending on how much Linksys believes the equipment would sell for if it abandoned the project, the abandonment option could make HomeNet attractive even if there was a substantial risk of a competing product.

All these options point to the same conclusion: *if you can build greater flexibility into your project, you will increase the NPV of the project.*

Concept Check

11. What are real options?

12. Why do real options increase the NPV of the project?

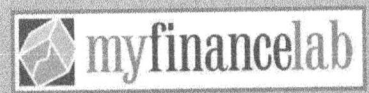

Here is what you should know after reading this chapter. MyFinanceLab will help you identify what you know, and where to go when you need to practice

Key Points and Equations	Terms	Online Practice Opportunities
8.1 The Capital Budgeting Process ▶ Capital budgeting is the process of analyzing investment opportunities and deciding which ones to accept. A capital budget is a list of all projects that a company plans to undertake during the next period. ▶ We use the NPV rule to evaluate capital budgeting decisions, making decisions that maximize NPV. When deciding to accept or reject a project, we accept projects with a positive NPV.	capital budget, p. 244 capital budgeting, p. 244 incremental earnings, p. 245	MyFinanceLab Study Plan 8.1
8.2 Forecasting Incremental Earnings ▶ The incremental earnings of a project comprise the amount by which the project is expected to change the firm's earnings. ▶ Incremental earnings should include all incremental revenues and costs associated with the project. Incremental Earnings = (Incremental Revenues − Incremental Cost − Depreciation) × (1 − Tax Rate) (8.3) ▶ Interest and other financing-related expenses are excluded to determine the project's unlevered net income.	marginal corporate tax rate, p. 247 pro forma, p. 249 straight-line depreciation, p. 246 unlevered net income, p. 250	MyFinanceLab Study Plan 8.2

8.3 Determining Incremental Free Cash Flow

- We compute free cash flow from incremental earnings by eliminating all non-cash expenses and including all capital investment.
- Depreciation is not a cash expense, so it is added back.
- Actual capital expenditures are deducted.
- Increases in net working capital are deducted and decreases are added. Net working capital is defined as:

$$\text{Cash} + \text{Inventory} + \text{Receivables} - \text{Payables} \quad (8.4)$$

- The basic calculation for free cash flow is:

$$\text{Free Cash Flow} = \overbrace{(\text{Revenues} - \text{Costs} - \text{Depreciation})}^{\text{Unlevered Net Income}} \\ \times (1 - \text{tax rate}) + \text{Depreciation} \\ - \text{CapEx} - \text{Change in } NWC \quad (8.6)$$

depreciation tax shield, p. 255
free cash flow, p. 251
trade credit, p. 253

MyFinanceLab
Study Plan 8.3

8.4 Other Effects on Incremental Free Cash Flows

- An opportunity cost is the cost of using an existing asset.
- Project externalities are cash flows that occur when a project affects other areas of the company's business.
- A sunk cost is an unrecoverable cost that has already been incurred.
- Depreciation expenses affect free cash flow only through the depreciation tax shield. The firm should use the most accelerated depreciation schedule possible.
- The discount rate for a project is its cost of capital: the expected return of securities with comparable risk and horizon.
- When you sell an asset, the portion of the proceeds above its book value is taxed:

$$\text{After-Tax Cash Flow from Asset Sale} = \text{Sale Price} \\ - (\text{Tax Rate} \times \text{Capital Gain}) \quad (8.11)$$

cannibalization, p. 257
MACRS depreciation, p. 258
opportunity cost, p. 256
overhead expenses, p. 257
project externalities, p. 257
sunk cost, p. 257
tax loss carryforwards and carrybacks, p. 260

MyFinanceLab
Study Plan 8.4
HomeNet Example
Spreadsheet

8.5 Analyzing the Project

- Sensitivity analysis breaks the NPV calculation down into its component assumptions, showing how the NPV varies as the values of the underlying assumptions change.
- Break-even analysis computes the level of a parameter that makes the project's NPV equal zero.
- Scenario analysis considers the effect of changing multiple parameters simultaneously.

break-even, p. 263
break-even analysis, p. 263
EBIT break-even, p. 263
scenario analysis, p. 265
sensitivity analysis, p. 262

MyFinanceLab
Study Plan 8.5
Interactive Sensitivity Analysis,
Using Excel:
Performing
Sensitivity
Analysis

BDeH CHAPTER 8

8.6 Real Options in Capital Budgeting		
▶ Real options are options to make a business decision, often after gathering more information. The presence of real options in a project increases the project's NPV.	abandonment option, p. 266 option to expand, p. 266 option to delay commitment, p. 266 real option, p. 266	MyFinanceLab Study Plan 8.6

Review Questions

1. What are pro forma incremental earnings?

2. What is the difference between pro forma incremental earnings and pro forma free cash flow?

3. What is the role of net working capital in projects?

4. How does net working capital affect the cash flows of a project?

5. Why is it important to adjust project sales and costs for externalities?

6. Does accelerated depreciation generally increase or decrease NPV relative to straight-line depreciation?

7. How is sensitivity analysis performed and what is its purpose?

Problems

All problems in this chapter are available in MyFinanceLab. An asterisk (*) indicates problems with a higher level of difficulty.

The Capital Budgeting Process

1. Daily Enterprises is purchasing a $10 million machine. It will cost $50,000 to transport and install the machine. The machine has a depreciable life of five years and will have no salvage value. If Daily uses straight-line depreciation, what are the depreciation expenses associated with this machine?

2. The machine in Problem 1 will generate incremental revenues of $4 million per year along with incremental costs of $1.2 million per year. If Daily's marginal tax rate is 35%, what are the incremental earnings associated with the new machine?

3. You are upgrading to better production equipment for your firm's only product. The new equipment will allow you to make more of your product in the same amount of time. Thus, you forecast that total sales will increase next year by 20% over the current amount of 100,000 units. If your sales price is $20 per unit, what are the incremental revenues next year from the upgrade?

4. Pisa Pizza, a seller of frozen pizza, is considering introducing a healthier version of its pizza that will be low in cholesterol and contain no trans fats. The firm expects that sales of the new pizza will be $20 million per year. While many of these sales will be to new customers, Pisa Pizza estimates that 40% will come from customers who switch to the new, healthier pizza instead of buying the original version.

   a. Assume customers will spend the same amount on either version. What level of incremental sales is associated with introducing the new pizza?

   b. Suppose that 50% of the customers who would switch from Pisa Pizza's original pizza to its healthier pizza will switch to another brand if Pisa Pizza does not introduce a healthier pizza. What level of incremental sales is associated with introducing the new pizza in this case?

5. Kokomochi is considering the launch of an advertising campaign for its latest dessert product, the Mini Mochi Munch. Kokomochi plans to spend $5 million on TV, radio, and print advertising this year for the campaign. The ads are expected to boost sales of the Mini Mochi Munch by $9 million this year and by $7 million next year. In addition, the company expects that new consumers who try the Mini Mochi Munch will be more likely to try Kokomochi's other products. As a result, sales of other products are expected to rise by $2 million each year.

   Kokomochi's gross profit margin for the Mini Mochi Munch is 35%, and its gross profit margin averages 25% for all other products. The company's marginal corporate tax rate is 35% both this year and next year. What are the incremental earnings associated with the advertising campaign?

6. Hyperion, Inc. currently sells its latest high-speed color printer, the Hyper 500, for $350. It plans to lower the price to $300 next year. Its cost of goods sold for the Hyper 500 is $200 per unit, and this year's sales are expected to be 20,000 units.

   a. Suppose that if Hyperion drops the price to $300 immediately, it can increase this year's sales by 25% to 25,000 units. What would be the incremental impact on this year's EBIT of such a price drop?

   b. Suppose that for each printer sold, Hyperion expects additional sales of $75 per year on ink cartridges for the next three years, and Hyperion has a gross profit margin of 70% on ink cartridges. What is the incremental impact on EBIT for the next three years of a price drop this year?

Determining Incremental Free Cash Flow

7. You are forecasting incremental free cash flows for Daily Enterprises. Based on the information in Problems 1 and 2, what are the incremental free cash flows associated with the new machine?

 8. Castle View Games would like to invest in a division to develop software for video games. To evaluate this decision, the firm first attempts to project the working capital needs for this operation. Its chief financial officer has developed the following estimates (in millions of dollars):

Year	1	2	3	4	5
Cash	6	12	15	15	15
Accounts Receivable	21	22	24	24	24
Inventory	5	7	10	12	13
Accounts Payable	18	22	24	25	30

Assuming that Castle View currently does not have any working capital invested in this division, calculate the cash flows associated with changes in working capital for the first five years of this investment.

9. In the HomeNet example from the chapter, its receivables are 15% of sales and its payables are 15% of COGS. Forecast the required investment in net working capital for HomeNet assuming that sales and cost of goods sold (COGS) will be:

Year	0	1	2	3	4
Sales		23,500	26,438	23,794	8,566
COGS		9,500	10,688	9,619	3,483

 10. Elmdale Enterprises is deciding whether to expand its production facilities. Although long-term cash flows are difficult to estimate, management has projected the following cash flows for the first two years (in millions of dollars):

Year	1	2
Revenues	125	160
Operating Expenses (other than depreciation)	40	60
Depreciation	25	36
Increase in Net Working Capital	2	8
Capital Expenditures	30	40
Marginal Corporate Tax Rate	35%	35%

    a. What are the incremental earnings for this project for years 1 and 2?

    b. What are the free cash flows for this project for the first two years?

11. Cellular Access, Inc. is a cellular telephone service provider that reported net income of $250 million for the most recent fiscal year. The firm had depreciation expenses of $100 million, capital expenditures of $200 million, and no interest expenses. Net working capital increased by $10 million. Calculate the free cash flow for Cellular Access for the most recent fiscal year.

 12. Recall the HomeNet example from the chapter. Suppose HomeNet's lab will be housed in warehouse space that the company could have otherwise rented out for $200,000 per year during years 1–4. How does this opportunity cost affect HomeNet's incremental earnings?

 *13. One year ago, your company purchased a machine used in manufacturing for $110,000. You have learned that a new machine is available that offers many advantages; you can purchase it for $150,000 today. It will be depreciated on a straight-line basis over ten years and has no salvage value. You expect that the new machine will produce a gross margin (revenues minus operating expenses other than depreciation) of $40,000 per year for the next ten years. The current machine is expected to produce a gross margin of $20,000 per year. The current machine is being depreciated on a straight-line basis over a useful life of 11 years, and has no salvage value, so depreciation expense for the current machine is $10,000 per year. The market value today of the current machine is $50,000. Your company's tax rate is 45%, and the opportunity cost of capital for this type of equipment is 10%. Should your company replace its year-old machine?

 *14. Beryl's Iced Tea currently rents a bottling machine for $50,000 per year, including all maintenance expenses. It is considering purchasing a machine instead and is comparing two options:

    a. Purchase the machine it is currently renting for $150,000. This machine will require $20,000 per year in ongoing maintenance expenses.

    b. Purchase a new, more advanced machine for $250,000. This machine will require $15,000 per year in ongoing maintenance expenses and will lower bottling costs by $10,000 per year. Also, $35,000 will be spent upfront in training the new operators of the machine.

Suppose the appropriate discount rate is 8% per year and the machine is purchased today. Maintenance and bottling costs are paid at the end of each year, as is the rental of the machine. Assume also that the machines will be depreciated via the straight-line method over seven years and that they have a ten-year life with a negligible salvage value. The marginal corporate tax rate is 35%. Should Beryl's Iced Tea continue to rent, purchase its current machine, or purchase the advanced machine?

Other Effects on Incremental Free Cash Flows

 15. The Jones Company has just completed the third year of a five-year MACRS recovery period for a piece of equipment it originally purchased for $300,000.
   a. What is the book value of the equipment?
   b. If Jones sells the equipment today for $180,000 and its tax rate is 35%, what is the after-tax cash flow from selling it?

16. Just before it is about to sell the equipment from Problem 15, Jones receives a new order. It can take the new order if it keeps the old equipment. Is there a cost to taking the order and if so, what is it? Explain.

17. Home Builder Supply, a retailer in the home improvement industry, currently operates seven retail outlets in Georgia and South Carolina. Management is contemplating building an eighth retail store across town from its most successful retail outlet. The company already owns the land for this store, which currently has an abandoned warehouse located on it. Last month, the marketing department spent $10,000 on market research to determine the extent of customer demand for the new store. Now Home Builder Supply must decide whether to build and open the new store.
   Which of the following should be included as part of the incremental earnings for the proposed new retail store?
   a. The original purchase price of the land where the store will be located.
   b. The cost of demolishing the abandoned warehouse and clearing the lot.
   c. The loss of sales in the existing retail outlet, if customers who previously drove across town to shop at the existing outlet become customers of the new store instead.
   d. The $10,000 in market research spent to evaluate customer demand.
   e. Construction costs for the new store.
   f. The value of the land if sold.
   g. Interest expense on the debt borrowed to pay the construction costs.

 18. If Daily Enterprises uses MACRS instead of straight-line depreciation, how would the incremental free cash flows from Problem 7 change?

 19. Markov Manufacturing recently spent $15 million to purchase some equipment used in the manufacture of disk drives. The firm expects that this equipment will have a useful life of five years, and its marginal corporate tax rate is 35%. The company plans to use straight-line depreciation.
   a. What is the annual depreciation expense associated with this equipment?
   b. What is the annual depreciation tax shield?
   c. Rather than straight-line depreciation, suppose Markov will use the MACRS depreciation method for the five-year life of the property. Calculate the depreciation tax shield each year for this equipment under this accelerated depreciation schedule.
   d. If Markov has a choice between straight-line and MACRS depreciation schedules, and its marginal corporate tax rate is expected to remain constant, which schedule should it choose? Why?
   e. How might your answer to part (d) change if Markov anticipates that its marginal corporate tax rate will increase substantially over the next five years?

20. You are a manager at Percolated Fiber, which is considering expanding its operations in synthetic fiber manufacturing. Your boss comes into your office, drops a consultant's report on your desk, and complains, "We owe these consultants $1 million for this report, and I am not sure their analysis makes sense. Before we spend the $25 million on new equipment needed for this project, look it over and give me your opinion." You open the report and find the following estimates (in thousands of dollars):

Year	1	2	...	9	10
Sales Revenue	30,000	30,000		30,000	30,000
Costs of Goods Sold	18,000	18,000		18,000	18,000
Gross Profit	12,000	12,000		12,000	12,000
General, Sales, and Administrative Expenses	2,000	2,000		2,000	2,000
Depreciation	2,500	2,500		2,500	2,500
Net Operating Income	7,500	7,500		7,500	7,500
Income Tax	2,625	2,625		2,625	2,625
Net Income	**4,875**	**4,875**		**4,875**	**4,875**

All of the estimates in the report seem correct. You note that the consultants used straight-line depreciation for the new equipment that will be purchased today (year 0), which is what the accounting department recommended. They also calculated the depreciation assuming no salvage value for the equipment, which is the company's assumption in this case. The report concludes that because the project will increase earnings by $4.875 million per year for ten years, the project is worth $48.75 million. You think back to your halcyon days in finance class and realize there is more work to be done!

First, you note that the consultants have not factored in the fact that the project will require $10 million in working capital upfront (year 0), which will be fully recovered in year 10. Next, you see they have attributed $2 million of selling, general, and administrative expenses to the project, but you know that $1 million of this amount is overhead that will be incurred even if the project is not accepted. Finally, you know that accounting earnings are not the right thing to focus on!

a. Given the available information, what are the free cash flows in years 0 through 10 that should be used to evaluate the proposed project?

b. If the cost of capital for this project is 14%, what is your estimate of the value of the new project?

Analyzing the Projects

21. Bauer Industries is an automobile manufacturer. Management is currently evaluating a proposal to build a plant that will manufacture lightweight trucks. Bauer plans to use a cost of capital of 12% to evaluate this project. Based on extensive research, it has prepared the following incremental free cash flow projections (in millions of dollars):

Year	0	1–9	10
Revenues		100.0	100.0
Manufacturing Expenses (other than depreciation)		−35.0	−35.0
Marketing Expenses		−10.0	−10.0
Depreciation		−15.0	−15.0
EBIT		40.0	40.0
Taxes at 35%		−14.0	−14.0
Unlevered Net Income		26.0	26.0
Depreciation		+15.0	+15.0
Additions to Net Working Capital		−5.0	−5.0
Capital Expenditures	−150.0		
Continuation Value			+12.0
Free Cash Flow	**−150.0**	**36.0**	**48.0**

a. For this base-case scenario, what is the NPV of the plant to manufacture light-weight trucks?

 b. Based on input from the marketing department, Bauer is uncertain about its revenue forecast. In particular, management would like to examine the sensitivity of the NPV to the revenue assumptions. What is the NPV of this project if revenues are 10% higher than forecast? What is the NPV if revenues are 10% lower than forecast?

 c. Rather than assuming that cash flows for this project are constant, management would like to explore the sensitivity of its analysis to possible growth in revenues and operating expenses. Specifically, management would like to assume that revenues, manufacturing expenses, and marketing expenses are as given in the table for year 1 and grow by 2% per year every year starting in year 2. Management also plans to assume that the initial capital expenditures (and therefore depreciation), additions to working capital, and continuation value remain as initially specified in the table. What is the NPV of this project under these alternative assumptions? How does the NPV change if the revenues and operating expenses grow by 5% per year rather than by 2%?

 d. To examine the sensitivity of this project to the discount rate, management would like to compute the NPV for different discount rates. Create a graph, with the discount rate on the *x*-axis and the NPV on the *y*-axis, for discount rates ranging from 5% to 30%. For what ranges of discount rates does the project have a positive NPV?

 *22. Billingham Packaging is considering expanding its production capacity by purchasing a new machine, the XC-750. The cost of the XC-750 is $2.75 million. Unfortunately, installing this machine will take several months and will partially disrupt production. The firm has just completed a $50,000 feasibility study to analyze the decision to buy the XC-750, resulting in the following estimates:

▶ *Marketing:* Once the XC-750 is operational next year, the extra capacity is expected to generate $10 million per year in additional sales, which will continue for the ten-year life of the machine.

▶ *Operations:* The disruption caused by the installation will decrease sales by $5 million this year. As with Billingham's existing products, the cost of goods for the products produced by the XC-750 is expected to be 70% of their sale price. The increased production will also require increased inventory on hand of $1 million during the life of the project, including year 0.

▶ *Human Resources:* The expansion will require additional sales and administrative personnel at a cost of $2 million per year.

▶ *Accounting:* The XC-750 will be depreciated via the straight-line method over the ten-year life of the machine. The firm expects receivables from the new sales to be 15% of revenues and payables to be 10% of the cost of goods sold. Billingham's marginal corporate tax rate is 35%.

a. Determine the incremental earnings from the purchase of the XC-750.

b. Determine the free cash flow from the purchase of the XC-750.

c. If the appropriate cost of capital for the expansion is 10%, compute the NPV of the purchase.

d. While the expected new sales will be $10 million per year from the expansion, estimates range from $8 million to $12 million. What is the NPV in the worst case? In the best case?

e. What is the break-even level of new sales from the expansion? What is the break-even level for the cost of goods sold?

f. Billingham could instead purchase the XC-900, which offers even greater capacity. The cost of the XC-900 is $4 million. The extra capacity would not be useful in the first two years of operation, but would allow for additional sales in years 3–10. What level of additional sales (above the $10 million expected for the XC-750) per year in those years would justify purchasing the larger machine?

Real Options in Capital Budgeting

23. Why is it that real options must have positive value?

24. What kind of real option does the XC-900 machine provide to Billingham in Problem 22?

25. If Billingham knows that it can sell the XC-750 to another firm for $2 million in two years, what kind of real option would that provide?

Data Case

You have just been hired by Dell Computers in its capital budgeting division. Your first assignment is to determine the net cash flows and NPV of a proposed new type of portable computer system similar in size to a Blackberry handheld, but which has the operating power of a high-end desktop system.

Development of the new system will initially require an investment equal to 10% of net property, plant, and equipment (PPE) for the fiscal year ended Feb. 1, 2008. The project will then require an additional investment equal to 10% of the initial investment after the first year of the project, a 5% of initial investment after the second year, and 1% of initial investment after the third, fourth, and fifth years. The product is expected to have a life of five years. First-year revenues for the new product are expected to be 3% of total revenue for Dell's fiscal year ended Feb. 1, 2008. The new product's revenues are expected to grow at 15% for the second year, then 10% for the third, and 5% annually for the final two years of the expected life of the project. Your job is to determine the rest of the cash flows associated with this project. Your boss has indicated that the operating costs and net working capital requirements are similar to the rest of the company's products and that depreciation is straight-line for capital budgeting purposes. Welcome to the "real world." Since your boss hasn't been much help, here are some tips to guide your analysis:

1. Obtain Dell's financial statements. (If you "really" worked for Dell you would already have this data, but at least here you won't get fired if your analysis is off target.) Download the annual income statements, balance sheets, and cash flow statements for the last four fiscal years from MarketWatch (www. marketwatch .com). Enter Dell's ticker symbol (DELL) and then go to "Financials." Export the statements to Excel by right-clicking while the cursor is inside each statement.

2. You are now ready to determine the free cash flow. Compute the free cash flow for each year using Eq. 8.6 from this chapter:

$$\text{Free Cash Flow} = \overbrace{(\text{Revenues} - \text{Costs} - \text{Depreciation}) \times (1 - \text{tax rate})}^{\text{Unlevered Net Income}}$$
$$+ \text{Depreciation} - \text{CapEx} - \text{Change in NWC} \qquad (8.14)$$

Set up the timeline and computation of the free cash flow in separate, contiguous columns for each year of the project life. Be sure to make outflows negative and inflows positive.

a. Assume that the project's profitability will be similar to Dell's existing projects in 2007 and estimate (Revenues − Costs) each year by using the 2007 EBITDA/Sales profit margin.

b. Determine the annual depreciation by assuming Dell depreciates these assets by the straight-line method over a ten-year life.

c. Determine Dell's tax rate by using the income tax rate in 2007.

d. Calculate the net working capital required each year by assuming that the level of NWC will be a constant percentage of the project's sales. Use Dell's 2007 NWC/Sales to estimate the required percentage. (Use only accounts receivable, accounts payable, and inventory to measure working capital. Other components of current assets and liabilities are harder to interpret and not necessarily reflective of the project's required NWC—e.g., Dell's cash holdings.)

e. To determine the free cash flow, calculate the *additional* capital investment and the *change* in net working capital each year.

3. Determine the IRR of the project and the NPV of the project at a cost of capital of 12% using the Excel functions. For the calculation of NPV, include cash flows 1 through 5 in the NPV function and then subtract the initial cost (i.e., $= NPV(\text{rate}, CF_1:CF_5) + CF_0$). For IRR, include cash flows 0 through 5 in the cash flow range.

Chapter 8 APPENDIX A   MACRS Depreciation

The U.S. tax code allows for accelerated depreciation of most assets. The depreciation method that you use for any particular asset is determined by the tax rules in effect at the time you place the asset into service. (Congress has changed the depreciation rules many times over the years, so many firms that have held property for a long time may have to use several depreciation methods simultaneously.)

For most business property placed in service after 1986, the IRS allows firms to depreciate the asset using the MACRS (Modified Accelerated Cost Recovery System) method. Under this method, you categorize each business asset into a recovery class that determines the time period over which you can write off the cost of the asset. The most commonly used items are classified as shown below:

▶ *3-year property:* Tractor units, racehorses over 2 years old, and horses over 12 years old.

▶ *5-year property:* Automobiles, buses, trucks, computers and peripheral equipment, office machinery, and any property used in research and experimentation. Also includes breeding and dairy cattle.

▶ *7-year property:* Office furniture and fixtures, and any property that has not been designated as belonging to another class.

▶ *10-year property:* Water transportation equipment, single-purpose agricultural or horticultural structures, and trees or vines bearing fruit or nuts.

▶ *15-year property:* Depreciable improvements to land such as fences, roads, and bridges.

▶ *20-year property:* Farm buildings that are not agricultural or horticultural structures.

▶ *27.5-year property:* Residential rental property.

▶ *39-year property:* Nonresidential real estate, including home offices. (Note that the value of land may not be depreciated.)

Generally speaking, residential and nonresidential real estate is depreciated via the straight-line method, but other classes can be depreciated more rapidly in early years. Table 8.4 shows the standard depreciation rates for assets in the other recovery classes; refinements of this table can be applied depending on the month that the asset was placed into service (consult IRS guidelines). The table indicates the percentage of the asset's cost that may be depreciated each year, with year 1 indicating the year the asset was first put into use. Generally, year 1 is the acquisition year and the table contains the "half-year" convention, allowing for a half year of depreciation in the acquisition year itself. This is why the first year's depreciation percentage is smaller than the second year's.

Chapter 8 APPENDIX B   Using Excel for Capital Budgeting

In this appendix, we illustrate how to build a pro forma statement and perform a sensitivity analysis in Excel.

Building a Pro Forma Statement

The key to frustration-free capital budgeting is to base your analysis on a spreadsheet containing a flexible model of the project's pro forma free cash flows.

List Assumptions

Start by creating a box in the spreadsheet with all of your assumptions, shown here shaded in gray:

Although this step will take you a little more time upfront, it has two advantages. First, you are forced to present all of your major assumptions clearly, so you can see the drivers of your analysis. Second, setting them apart this way makes it far easier to change your assumptions later and quickly see the impact on the incremental free cash flows.

Base Cell Formulas on Assumptions

Once you have listed all of your assumptions, it is time to build the pro forma statement by dynamically referring back to the cells containing your assumptions. Here, we will show how to build the first year's pro forma cash flows. For example, rather than entering $13,000 into the Sales line of Year 1, you will enter the formula shown in the screen shot.

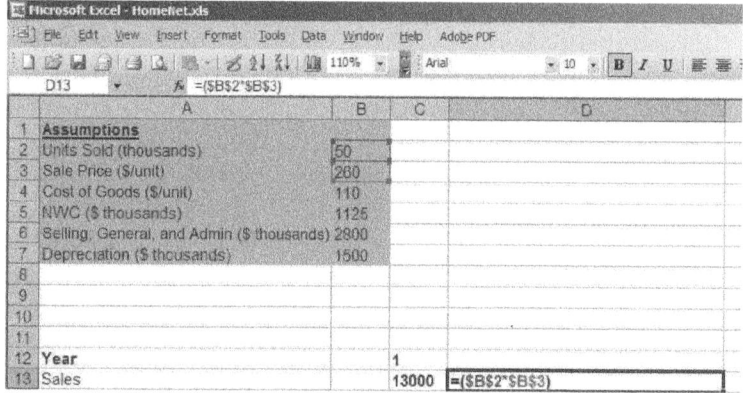

This formula is simply the cell-referenced version of our calculation from Example 8.1: Unit Sold × Price per unit = 50 × $260 = $13,000. As you can see from the screen shot, we have referred back to our Assumptions box for each of these inputs (units sold and price per unit). Later, if we want to change the assumption for price per unit, we can change it in our Assumptions box and it will automatically change the calculation for Sales in Year 1.

To complete the pro forma statement for year 1, we continue down the column. Each time we need to draw on an assumed number, we refer back to our Assumptions box. For calculations such as Gross Profit, we simply refer to the cells in the column: summing Sales and the negative Cost of Goods Sold.

As you can imagine, building a pro forma statement like this greatly eases our analysis of the effects of changes in our assumptions. In the next section, we will show how to use a spreadsheet similar to the one we just constructed to perform sensitivity analysis.

Performing Sensitivity Analysis

Rather than recalculating HomeNet's NPV for each possible number of units sold, we can use Excel's Data Table tool. In Chapter 7, we used the Data Table tool to construct an NPV profile. Recall that a data table shows us how the outcome of a formula (such as the NPV of HomeNet) changes when we change one of the cells in the spreadsheet (such as the number of units sold). In the previous Using Excel box, we showed how to build a pro forma statement of HomeNet that would make it easy to change our assumptions later. That is exactly what we do in sensitivity analysis: change our assumptions and see how the NPV changes. This screen shot shows a completed Excel pro forma statement of the incremental free cash flows of the HomeNet project. It also shows the NPV calculation and a data table (outlined in red) for our assumption on Units Sold:

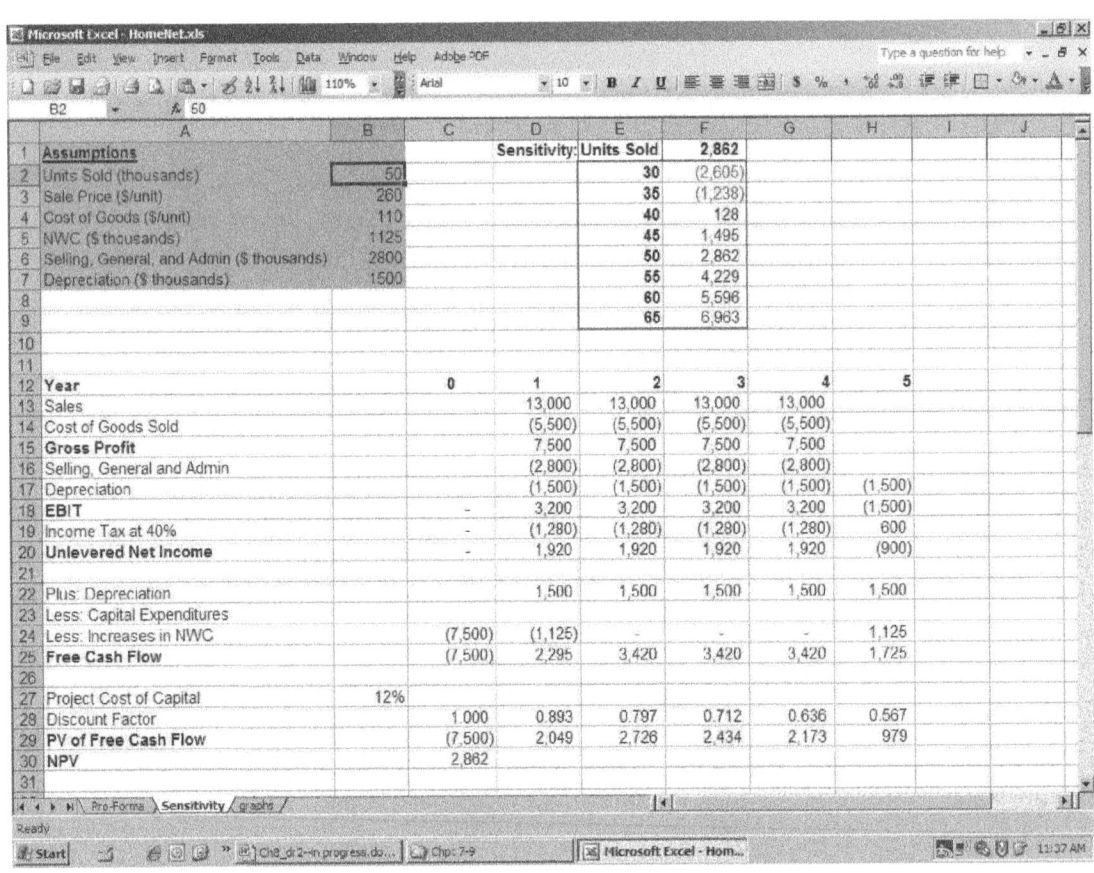

To set up the data table, we first create a cell that simply repeats the NPV. In this case, cell F1 is set to equal cell C30 to create a new NPV column. Next, we create the column that will contain the different assumptions of Units Sold. This column must be directly to the left of the NPV cell (F1). Finally, we highlight the Units Sold and NPV columns, and select Table from the Data menu.

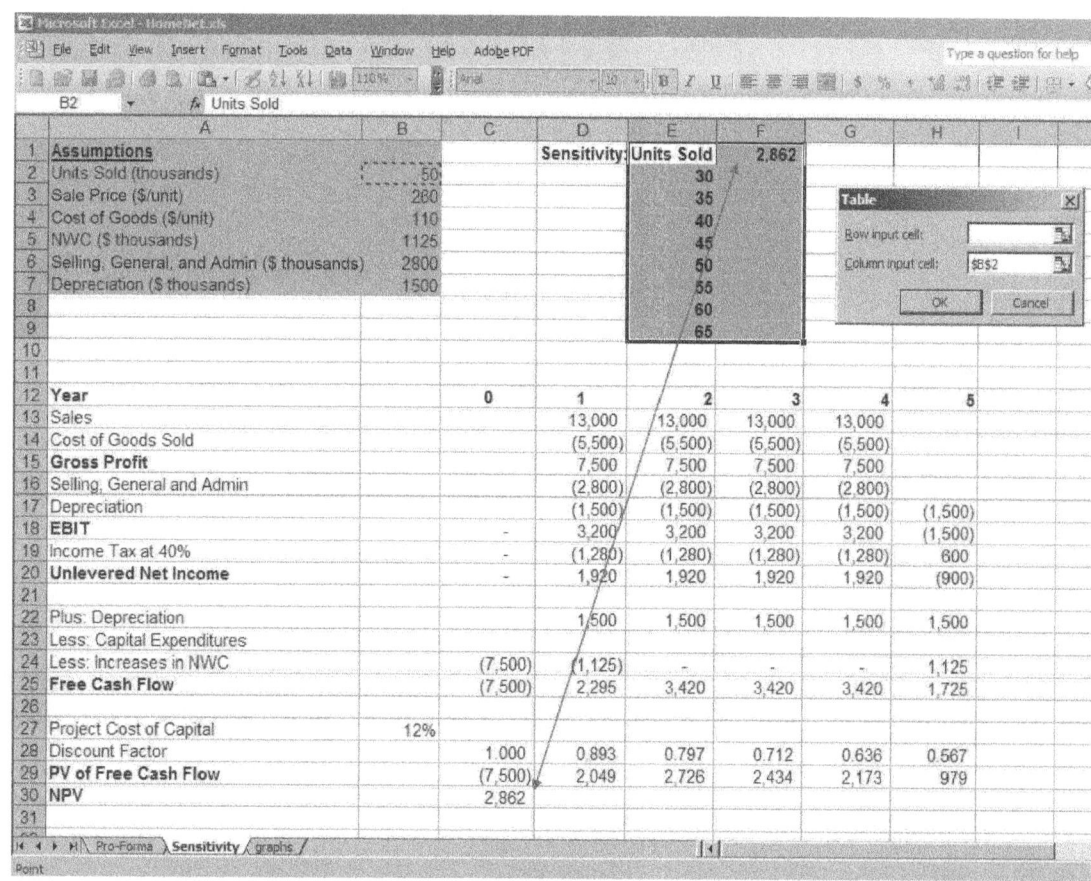

As the screen shot shows, the Table input box will appear. Since our Units Sold assumptions are in a column, we enter, into the column input cell (not the row input cell), the cell in our spreadsheet containing the base case Units Sold assumption (B2). Once we do this and hit Enter, Excel will create the sensitivity table shown in the first screen shot.

9 Valuing Stocks

LEARNING OBJECTIVES

- Read a stock quote
- Value a stock as the present value of its expected future dividends
- Understand the tradeoff between dividends and growth in stock valuation
- Value a stock as the present value of either the company's total payout or its free cash flows

- Value a stock by applying common multiples based on the values of comparable firms
- Compare and contrast different approaches to valuing a stock
- Understand how information is incorporated into stock prices through competition in efficient markets

notation

P_t	stock price at the end of year t	$EBIT$	earnings before interest and taxes
r_E	equity cost of capital	FCF_t	free cash flow on date t
N	terminal date or forecast horizon	V_t	enterprise value on date t
g	expected dividend growth rate	r_{wacc}	weighted average cost of capital
Div_t	dividends paid in year t	g_{FCF}	expected free cash flow growth rate
EPS_t	earnings per share on date t	$EBITDA$	earnings before interest, taxes, depreciation, and amortization
PV	present value		

A 2003 graduate of Michigan State University, finance major Christopher Brigham is an equity research associate at Loomis, Sayles & Company. The Boston-based investment company manages more than $130 billion in equity and fixed-income assets for both institutional investors and mutual funds.

At Loomis Sayles, equity research analysts and portfolio managers work as a team to construct a portfolio of best ideas. "I cover the financial services industry, such as banks, brokerage firms, and insurance companies," says Chris. "To determine a company's valuation—what it is worth—we analyze company fundamentals and apply stock valuation models. Using this information, we work together to determine what companies' stocks to buy, which to avoid, and when to sell current holdings."

Loomis Sayles blends several methods to place a value on common stock. "Every company and every industry is different, so we have no strict rules for valuing a stock," explains Chris. In addition to intrinsic valuation models such as the dividend-discount model, Loomis Sayles uses relative and historic valuation parameters, such as price-to-earnings and price-to-book ratio, and take into account broader economic or sector trends. "Because of the large number of variables, projecting future earnings or growth is always the main challenge in applying earnings and discounted free cash flow models."

Sometimes our valuation analysis reveals a drastically different stock price than the current market price. "When this occurs, we account for all the variables that the model may be missing but the market may be factoring into the price. For example, industry trends and management quality are difficult to quantify, so different analysts can come up with very different assumptions and values for the same stock."

Chris closely follows company and industry news, reads company reports and financial statements, and evaluates industry and economic trends. He also monitors relative valuation metrics and develops detailed up-to-date earnings models. "My finance courses gave me the background I need for this job," Chris says. "The most important educational training was analyzing financial statements and modeling and forecasting earnings and cash flows."

Michigan State University, 2003

"To determine a company's valuation—what it is worth—I analyze company fundamentals and apply stock valuation models."

On January 16, 2006, footwear and apparel maker Kenneth Cole Productions, Inc., announced that its president for the last 15 years, Paul Blum, had resigned to pursue "other opportunities." The price of the company's stock had already dropped more than 16% over the prior two years, and the firm was in the midst of a major undertaking to restructure its brand. The next day, Kenneth Cole Productions' stock price dropped by more than 6% on the New York Stock Exchange to $26.75, with over 300,000 shares being traded—more than twice its average daily volume.

How might an investor decide whether to buy or sell a stock such as Kenneth Cole Productions at this price? Why would the stock suddenly be worth 6% less after the announcement of this news? What actions can Kenneth Cole Productions' managers take to increase the stock price?

To answer these questions, we turn to the valuation principle. As we demonstrated in Chapter 3, the valuation principle indicates that the price of a security should equal the present value of the expected cash flows an investor will receive from owning it. In this chapter, we apply this idea to stocks. Thus, to value a stock, we need to know the expected cash flows an investor will receive and the appropriate cost of capital with which to discount those cash flows. Both of these quantities can be challenging to estimate, and we will develop many of the details needed to do so throughout the remainder of this text. In this chapter, we begin our study of stock valuation by identifying the relevant cash flows and developing the main tools that practitioners use to evaluate them.

Our analysis opens with a consideration of the dividends and capital gains received by investors who hold the stock for different periods, from which we develop the *dividend-discount model* of stock valuation. Next, we apply Chapter 7's tools to value stocks based on the free cash flows generated by the firm. Having developed these stock valuation methods based on discounted cash flows, we then relate them to the practice of using valuation multiples based on comparable firms. We conclude the chapter by discussing the role of competition in the information contained in stock prices and its implications for investors and corporate managers.

 **Stock Basics**

As discussed in Chapter 1, the ownership of a corporation is divided into shares of stock. Figure 9.1 shows a stock quote with basic information about Kenneth Cole Productions' stock from Google Finance.[1] The Web page notes that the company is a public corporation (its shares are widely held and traded in a market) and that its shares trade on the NYSE (New York Stock Exchange) under the ticker symbol KCP. A **ticker symbol** is a unique abbreviation assigned to a publicly traded company used when its trades are reported on the ticker (a real-time electronic display of trading activity). Shares on the NYSE have ticker symbols consisting of three or fewer characters, while shares on the NASDAQ generally have four or more characters in their ticker symbols.

ticker symbol A unique abbreviation assigned to each publicly traded company.

---

[1]There are many places on the Internet to get free stock information, such as Yahoo! Finance, MSN Money, the *Wall Street Journal*'s Web site (wsj.com), and the exchange sites nyse.com and nasdaq.com.

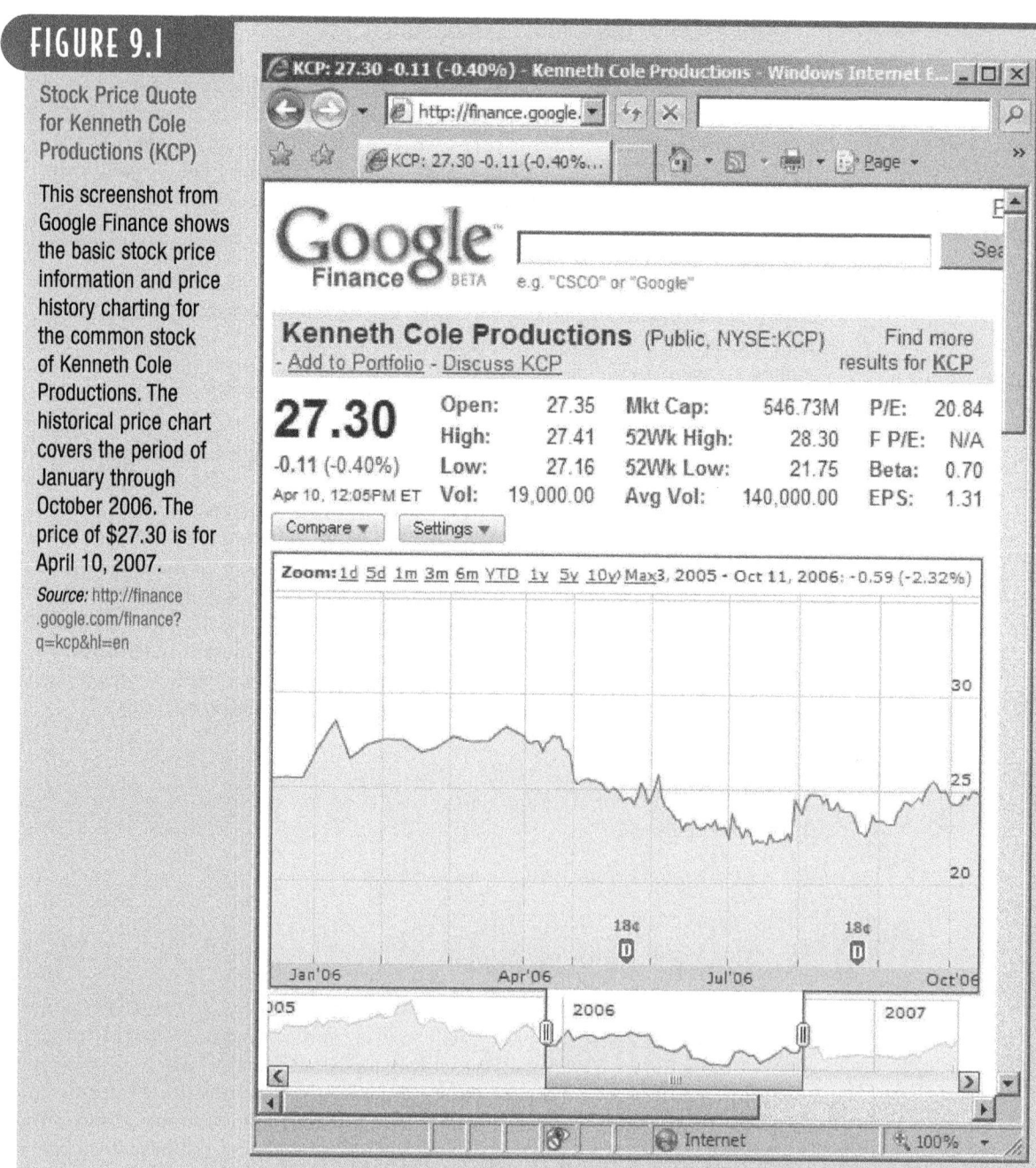

FIGURE 9.1

Stock Price Quote for Kenneth Cole Productions (KCP)

This screenshot from Google Finance shows the basic stock price information and price history charting for the common stock of Kenneth Cole Productions. The historical price chart covers the period of January through October 2006. The price of $27.30 is for April 10, 2007.

Source: http://finance .google.com/finance? q=kcp&hl=en

BDeH CHAPTER 9

common stock A share of ownership in the corporation, which confers rights to any common dividends as well as rights to vote on election of directors, mergers, or other major events.

The information displayed is for the common stock of Kenneth Cole Productions on April 10, 2007. **Common stock** is a share of ownership in the corporation, which gives its owner rights to any common dividends as well as rights to vote on the election of directors, mergers, or other major events. As an ownership claim, common stock carries the right to share in the profits of the corporation through dividend payments. Dividends are periodic payments, usually in the form of cash, that are made to shareholders as a partial return on their investment in the corporation. The board of directors decides the timing and amount of each dividend. Shareholders are paid dividends in proportion to the amount of shares they own.

BDeH CHAPTER 9

Figure 9.1 includes a chart showing the price of the KCP common shares between January and October 2006. During the time period covered by the chart, the company paid two dividends to its common shareholders—one in May 2006 and one in August 2006. The dividends are marked by a "D" and the amount of the dividend. In this case, both the dividends were 18 cents per share. Thus, if you owned 1000 shares of KCP, you would have received $0.18 \times 1000 = $180 on each of the dividend payment dates. The chart also clearly shows the drop in the price of KCP shares in January 2006, as discussed in the introduction to this chapter.

Finally, the Web page displays some basic information about the performance of KCP stock. Notice the price of the last trade of KCP shares in the market ($27.30), the price that shares started at when the market opened that day ($27.35), the high and low prices reached so far during trading that day ($27.41 and $27.16), and the volume of trading for the day (19,000 shares). The total value of all of the equity of KCP is its market capitalization, equal to the price per share multiplied by the number of shares outstanding, here $546.73 million. Over the last 52 weeks, KCP has achieved a high price of $28.30 and a low price of $21.75 and has had average daily volume of shares traded of 140,000 shares. Also, note some basic information about the company: the price-earnings ratio (P/E) and earnings per share (EPS), both of which we discussed in Chapter 2, and the P/E ratio based on an estimate of future earnings (forward P/E), which is not available for KCP. The Web page also notes that KCP's beta is 0.7; beta is a measure of risk.

The current price of KCP is $27.30, but the stock's price has varied over time. In previous chapters, we have learned how financial managers make decisions that affect the value of their company. In this chapter, we explore the different ways investors take information about a company, including information about cash flows from decisions made by financial managers, to arrive at a value for a share of stock.

Concept Check

1. What is a share of stock?

2. What are dividends?

9.2 The Dividend-Discount Model

The valuation principle implies that to value any security, we must determine the expected cash flows that an investor will receive from owning it. We begin our analysis of stock valuation by considering the cash flows for an investor with a one-year investment horizon. We will show how the stock's price and the investor's return from the investment are related. We then consider the perspective of investors with long investment horizons. Finally, we will reach our goal of establishing the first stock valuation method: the *dividend-discount model*.

A One-Year Investor

There are two potential sources of cash flows from owning a stock:

1. The firm might pay out cash to its shareholders in the form of a dividend.

2. The investor might generate cash by selling the shares at some future date.

The total amount received in dividends and from selling the stock will depend on the investor's investment horizon. Let's begin by considering the perspective of a one-year investor.

When an investor buys a stock, she will pay the current market price for a share, P_0. While she continues to hold the stock, she will be entitled to any dividends the stock pays. Let Div_1 be the total dividends paid per share during the year. At the end of the year, the investor will sell her share at the new market price, P_1. Assuming for simplicity that all dividends are paid at the end of the year, we have the following timeline for this investment:

```
0                        1
|------------------------|
-P_0                 Div_1 + P_1
```

Of course, the future dividend payment and stock price in this timeline are not known with certainty. Rather, these values are based on the investor's expectations at the time the stock is purchased. Given these expectations, the investor will be willing to pay a price today up to the point that this transaction has a zero net present value (NPV)— that is, up to the point at which the current price equals the present value of the expected future dividend and sale price.

Because these cash flows are risky, we cannot discount them using the risk-free interest rate, but instead must use the cost of capital for the firm's equity. We have previously defined the cost of capital of any investment to be the expected return that investors could earn on their best alternative investment with similar risk and maturity. Thus we must discount the equity cash flows based on the **equity cost of capital**, r_E, for the stock, which is the expected return of other investments available in the market with equivalent risk to the firm's shares. Doing so leads to the following equation for the stock price:

equity cost of capital The expected rate of return available in the market on other investments that have equivalent risk to the risk associated with the firm's shares.

$$P_0 = \frac{Div_1 + P_1}{1 + r_E} \tag{9.1}$$

If the current stock price were less than this amount, it would be a positive-NPV investment. We would, therefore, expect investors to rush in and buy it, driving up the stock's price. If the stock price exceeded this amount, selling it would produce a positive NPV and the stock price would quickly fall.

Dividend Yields, Capital Gains, and Total Returns

dividend yield The expected annual dividend of a stock divided by its current price; the percentage return an investor expects to earn from the dividend paid by the stock.

A critical part of Eq. 9.1 for determining the stock price is the firm's equity cost of capital, r_E. At the beginning of this section, we pointed out that an investor's return from holding a stock comes from dividends and cash generated from selling the stock. We can rewrite Eq. 9.1 to show these two return components. If we multiply by $(1 + r_E)$, divide by P_0, and subtract 1 from both sides, we have

capital gain The amount by which the selling price of an asset exceeds its initial purchase price.

Total Return

$$r_E = \frac{Div_1 + P_1}{P_0} - 1 = \underbrace{\frac{Div_1}{P_0}}_{\text{Dividend Yield}} + \underbrace{\frac{P_1 - P_0}{P_0}}_{\text{Capital Gain Rate}} \tag{9.2}$$

capital gain rate An expression of capital gain as a percentage of the initial price of the asset.

The first term on the right side of Eq. 9.2 is the stock's **dividend yield**, which is the expected annual dividend of the stock divided by its current price. The dividend yield is the percentage return the investor expects to earn from the dividend paid by the stock. The second term on the right side of Eq. 9.2 reflects the **capital gain** the investor will earn on the stock, which is the difference between the expected sale price and the original purchase price for the stock, $P_1 - P_0$. We divide the capital gain by the current stock price to express the capital gain as a percentage return, called the **capital gain rate**.

total return The sum of a stock's dividend yield and its capital gain rate.

The sum of the dividend yield and the capital gain rate is called the **total return** of the stock. The total return is the expected return that the investor will earn for a one-year investment in the stock. Equation 9.2 states that the stock's total return should equal the equity cost of capital. In other words, *the expected total return of the stock should equal the expected return of other investments available in the market with equivalent risk.*

This result is exactly what we would expect: The firm must pay its shareholders a return commensurate with the return they can earn elsewhere while taking the same risk. If the stock offered a higher return than other securities with the same risk, investors would sell those other investments and buy the stock instead. This activity would then drive up the stock's current price, lowering its dividend yield and capital gain rate until Eq. 9.2 holds true. If the stock offered a lower expected return, investors would sell the stock and drive down its price until Eq. 9.2 was again satisfied.

EXAMPLE 9.1
Stock Prices and Returns

Problem

Suppose you expect Longs Drug Stores to pay an annual dividend of $0.56 per share in the coming year and to trade for $45.50 per share at the end of the year. If investments with equivalent risk to Longs' stock have an expected return of 6.80%, what is the most you would pay today for Longs' stock? What dividend yield and capital gain rate would you expect at this price?

Solution

▶ **Plan**

We can use Eq. 9.1 to solve for the beginning price we would pay now (P_0) given our expectations about dividends ($Div_1 = 0.56$) and future price ($P_1 = \$45.50$) and the return we need to expect to earn to be willing to invest ($r_E = 6.8\%$). We can then use Eq. 9.2 to calculate the dividend yield and capital gain.

▶ **Execute**

Using Eq. 9.1, we have

$$P_0 = \frac{Div_1 + P_1}{1 + r_E} = \frac{0.56 + 45.50}{1.0680} = \$43.13$$

Referring to Eq. 9.2, we see that at this price, Longs' dividend yield is $Div_1/P_0 = 0.56/43.13 = 1.30\%$. The expected capital gain is $\$45.50 - \$43.13 = \$2.37$ per share, for a capital gain rate of $2.37/43.13 = 5.50\%$.

▶ **Evaluate**

At a price of $43.13, Longs' expected total return is $1.30\% + 5.50\% = 6.80\%$, which is equal to its equity cost of capital (the return being paid by investments with equivalent risk to Longs'). This amount is the most we would be willing to pay for Longs' stock. If we paid more, our expected return would be less than 6.8% and we would rather invest elsewhere.

A Multiyear Investor

We now extend the intuition we developed for the one-year investor's return to a multi-year investor. Equation 9.1 depends upon the expected stock price in one year, P_1. But suppose we planned to hold the stock for two years. Then we would receive dividends in both year 1 and year 2 before selling the stock, as shown in the following timeline:

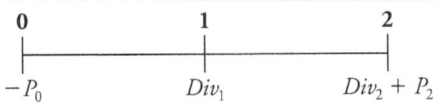

Setting the stock price equal to the present value of the future cash flows in this case implies[2]

$$P_0 = \frac{Div_1}{1 + r_E} + \frac{Div_2 + P_2}{(1 + r_E)^2} \qquad (9.3)$$

Equations 9.1 and 9.3 are different: As a two-year investor we care about the dividend and stock price in year 2, but these terms do not appear in Eq. 9.1. Does this difference imply that a two-year investor will value the stock differently than a one-year investor?

The answer to this question is no. A one-year investor does not care about the dividend and stock price in year 2 directly. She will care about them indirectly, however, because they will affect the price for which she can sell the stock at the end of year 1. For example, suppose the investor sells the stock to another one-year investor with the same expectations. The new investor will expect to receive the dividend and stock price at the end of year 2, so he will be willing to pay

$$P_1 = \frac{Div_2 + P_2}{1 + r_E}$$

for the stock. Substituting this expression for P_1 into Eq. 9.1, we get the same result as in Eq. 9.3:

$$P_0 = \frac{Div_1 + P_1}{1 + r_E} = \frac{Div_1}{1 + r_E} + \frac{1}{1 + r_E}\overbrace{\left(\frac{Div_2 + P_2}{1 + r_E}\right)}^{P_1}$$

$$= \frac{Div_1}{1 + r_E} + \frac{Div_2 + P_2}{(1 + r_E)^2}$$

Thus the formula for the stock price for a two-year investor is the same as that for a sequence of two one-year investors.

Dividend-Discount Model Equation

We can continue this process for any number of years by replacing the final stock price with the value that the next holder of the stock would be willing to pay. Doing so leads to the general **dividend-discount model** for the stock price, where the horizon N is arbitrary:

dividend-discount model A model that values shares of a firm according to the present value of the future dividends the firm will pay.

Dividend-Discount Model

$$P_0 = \frac{Div_1}{1 + r_E} + \frac{Div_2}{(1 + r_E)^2} + \cdots + \frac{Div_N}{(1 + r_E)^N} + \frac{P_N}{(1 + r_E)^N} \qquad (9.4)$$

Equation 9.4 applies to a single N-year investor, who will collect dividends for N years and then sell the stock, or to a series of investors who hold the stock for shorter periods and then resell it. Note that Eq. 9.4 holds for *any* horizon N. As a consequence, all investors (with the same expectations) will attach the same value to the stock, independent of their investment horizons. How long they intend to hold the stock and whether they collect their return in the form of dividends or capital gains is irrelevant. For the special case in which the firm eventually pays dividends and is never acquired or liquidated, it is possible to hold the shares forever. In this scenario,

---

[2]In using the same equity cost of capital for both periods, we are assuming that the equity cost of capital does not depend on the term of the cash flows; that is, r_E is not different for year 2 (or any other year). Otherwise, we would need to adjust for the term structure of the equity cost of capital (as we did with the yield curve for risk-free cash flows). This step would complicate the analysis but would not change its results.

rather than having a stopping point where we sell the shares, we rewrite Eq. 9.4 to show that the dividends go on into the future:

$$P_0 = \frac{Div_1}{1 + r_E} + \frac{Div_2}{(1 + r_E)^2} + \frac{Div_3}{(1 + r_E)^3} + \cdots \tag{9.5}$$

That is, *the price of the stock is equal to the present value of all of the expected future dividends it will pay.*

Concept Check

3. How do you calculate the total return of a stock?

4. What discount rate do you use to discount the future cash flows of a stock?

9.3 Estimating Dividends in the Dividend-Discount Model

Equation 9.5 expresses the value of a stock in terms of the expected future dividends the firm will pay. Of course, estimating these dividends—especially for the distant future—is difficult. A commonly used approximation is to assume that in the long run, dividends will grow at a constant rate. In this section, we consider the implications of this assumption for stock prices and explore the tradeoff between dividends and growth.

Constant Dividend Growth

The simplest forecast for the firm's future dividends states that they will grow at a constant rate, g, forever. That case yields the following timeline for the cash flows for an investor who buys the stock today and holds it:

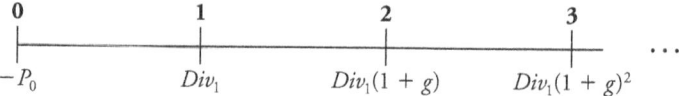

Because the expected dividends are a constant growth perpetuity, we can use Eq. 4.9 to calculate their present value. We then obtain the following simple formula for the stock price:[3]

Constant Dividend Growth Model

constant dividend growth model A model for valuing a stock by viewing its dividends as a constant growth perpetuity.

$$P_0 = \frac{Div_1}{r_E - g} \tag{9.6}$$

According to the **constant dividend growth model**, the value of the firm depends on the dividend level next year, divided by the equity cost of capital adjusted by the growth rate.

EXAMPLE 9.2

Valuing a Firm with Constant Dividend Growth

Problem

Consolidated Edison, Inc. (Con Edison), is a regulated utility company that services the New York City area. Suppose Con Edison plans to pay $2.30 per share in dividends in the coming year. If its equity cost of capital is 7% and dividends are expected to grow by 2% per year in the future, estimate the value of Con Edison's stock.

---

[3]As discussed in Chapter 4, this formula requires that $g < r_E$. Otherwise, the present value of the growing perpetuity is infinite. The implication here is that it is impossible for a stock's dividends to grow at a rate $g > r_E$ *forever*. If the growth rate does exceed r_E, the situation must be temporary, and the constant growth model cannot be applied in such a case.

Solution

▶ **Plan**

Because the dividends are expected to grow perpetually at a constant rate, we can use Eq. 9.6 to value Con Edison. The next dividend (Div_1) is expected to be $2.30, the growth rate ($g$) is 2%, and the equity cost of capital (r_E) is 7%.

▶ **Execute**

$$P_0 = \frac{Div_1}{r_E - g} = \frac{\$2.30}{0.07 - 0.02} = \$46.00$$

▶ **Evaluate**

You would be willing to pay 20 times this year's dividend of $2.30 to own Con Edison stock because you are buying a claim to this year's dividend *and* to an infinite growing series of future dividends.

For another interpretation of Eq. 9.6, note that we can rearrange it as follows:

$$r_E = \frac{Div_1}{P_0} + g \tag{9.7}$$

Comparing Eq. 9.7 with Eq. 9.2, we see that g equals the expected capital gain rate. In other words, with constant expected dividend growth, the expected growth rate of the share price matches the growth rate of the dividends.

Dividends Versus Investment and Growth

In Eq. 9.6, the firm's share price increases with the current dividend level, Div_1, and the expected growth rate, g. To maximize its share price, a firm would like to increase both these quantities. Often, however, the firm faces a tradeoff: Increasing growth may require investment, and money spent on investment cannot be used to pay dividends. The constant dividend growth model provides insight into this tradeoff.

A Simple Model of Growth. What determines the rate of growth of a firm's dividends? If we define a firm's **dividend payout rate** as the fraction of its earnings that the firm pays as dividends each year, then we can write the firm's dividend per share at date t as follows:

dividend payout rate
The fraction of a firm's earnings that the firm pays out as dividends each year.

$$Div_t = \underbrace{\frac{Earnings_t}{Shares\ Outstanding_t}}_{EPS_t} \times Dividend\ Payout\ Rate_t \tag{9.8}$$

That is, the dividend each year is equal to the firm's earnings per share (EPS) multiplied by its dividend payout rate. The firm can, therefore, increase its dividend in three ways:

1. It can increase its earnings (net income).
2. It can increase its dividend payout rate.
3. It can decrease its number of shares outstanding.

Suppose for now that the firm does not issue new shares (or buy back its existing shares), so that the number of shares outstanding remains fixed. We can then explore the tradeoff between options 1 and 2.

A firm can do one of two things with its earnings: It can pay them out to investors, or it can retain and reinvest them. By investing cash today, a firm can increase its future dividends. For simplicity, let's assume that if no investment is made, the firm does not grow, so the current level of earnings generated by the firm remains constant. If all increases in future earnings result exclusively from new investment made with retained earnings, then

$$\text{Change in Earnings} = \text{New Investment} \times \text{Return on New Investment} \quad (9.9)$$

retention rate The fraction of a firm's current earnings that the firm retains.

New investment equals the firm's earnings multiplied by its **retention rate**, or the fraction of current earnings that the firm retains:

$$\text{New Investment} = \text{Earnings} \times \text{Retention Rate} \quad (9.10)$$

Substituting Eq. 9.10 into Eq. 9.9 and dividing by earnings gives an expression for the growth rate of earnings:

$$\text{Earnings Growth Rate} = \frac{\text{Change in Earnings}}{\text{Earnings}}$$

$$= \text{Retention Rate} \times \text{Return on New Investment} \quad (9.11)$$

If the firm chooses to keep its dividend payout rate constant, then the growth in its dividends will equal the growth in its earnings:

$$g = \text{Retention Rate} \times \text{Return on New Investment} \quad (9.12)$$

Profitable Growth. Equation 9.12 shows that a firm can increase its growth rate by retaining more of its earnings. However, if the firm retains more earnings, it will be able to pay out less of those earnings; according to Eq. 9.8, the firm will then have to reduce its dividend. If a firm wants to increase its share price, should it cut its dividend and invest more, or should it cut its investments and increase its dividend? Not surprisingly, the answer to this question will depend on the profitability of the firm's investments. Let's consider an example.

EXAMPLE 9.3

Cutting Dividends for Profitable Growth

Problem

Crane Sporting Goods expects to have earnings per share of $6 in the coming year. Rather than reinvest these earnings and grow, the firm plans to pay out all of its earnings as a dividend. With these expectations of no growth, Crane's current share price is $60.

Suppose Crane could cut its dividend payout rate to 75% for the foreseeable future and use the retained earnings to open new stores. The return on its investment in these stores is expected to be 12%. If we assume that the risk of these new investments is the same as the risk of its existing investments, then the firm's equity cost of capital is unchanged. What effect would this new policy have on Crane's stock price?

Solution

▶ **Plan**

To figure out the effect of this policy on Crane's stock price, we need to know several things. First, we need to compute its equity cost of capital. Next we must determine Crane's dividend and growth rate under the new policy.

Because we know that Crane currently has a growth rate of 0 ($g = 0$), a dividend of $6, and a price of $60, we can use Eq. 9.7 to estimate r_E. Next, the new dividend will simply be 75% of the old dividend of $6. Finally, given a retention rate of 25% and a return on new investment of 12%, we can use Eq. 9.12 to compute the new growth rate (g). Finally, armed with the new dividend, Crane's equity cost of capital, and its new growth rate, we can use Eq. 9.6 to compute the price of Crane's shares if it institutes the new policy.

▶ **Execute**

Using Eq. 9.7 to estimate r_E, we have

$$r_E = \frac{Div_1}{P_0} + g = 10\% + 0\% = 10\%$$

In other words, to justify Crane's stock price under its current policy, the expected return of other stocks in the market with equivalent risk must be 10%.

Next, we consider the consequences of the new policy. If Crane reduces its dividend payout rate to 75%, then from Eq. 9.8 its dividend this coming year will fall to $Div_1 = EPS_1 \times 75\% = \$6 \times 75\% = \$4.50$.

At the same time, because the firm will now retain 25% of its earnings to invest in new stores, from Eq. 9.12 its growth rate will increase to

$$g = \text{Retention Rate} \times \text{Return on New Investment} = 25\% \times 12\% = 3\%$$

Assuming Crane can continue to grow at this rate, we can compute its share price under the new policy using the constant dividend growth model of Eq. 9.6:

$$P_0 = \frac{Div_1}{r_E - g} = \frac{\$4.50}{0.10 - 0.03} = \$64.29$$

▶ **Evaluate**

Crane's share price should rise from $60 to $64.29 if the company cuts its dividend in order to increase its investment and growth, implying that the investment has positive NPV. By using its earnings to invest in projects that offer a rate of return (12%) greater than its equity cost of capital (10%), Crane has created value for its shareholders.

In Example 9.3, cutting the firm's dividend in favor of growth raised the firm's stock price. This is not always the case, however, as Example 9.4 demonstrates.

EXAMPLE 9.4

Unprofitable Growth

Problem

Suppose Crane Sporting Goods decides to cut its dividend payout rate to 75% to invest in new stores, as in Example 9.3. But now suppose that the return on these new investments is 8%, rather than 12%. Given its expected earnings per share this year of $6 and its equity cost of capital of 10% (we again assume that the risk of the new investments is the same as its existing investments), what will happen to Crane's current share price in this case?

Solution

▶ **Plan**

We will follow the steps in Example 9.3, except that in this case, we assume a return on new investments of 8% when computing the new growth rate (g) instead of 12% as in Example 9.3.

▶ **Execute**

Just as in Example 9.3, Crane's dividend will fall to $6 \times 75\% = \$4.50$. Its growth rate under the new policy, given the lower return on new investment, will now be $g = 25\% \times 8\% = 2\%$. The new share price is therefore

$$P_0 = \frac{Div_1}{r_E - g} = \frac{\$4.50}{0.10 - 0.02} = \$56.25$$

▶ **Evaluate**

Even though Crane will grow under the new policy, the new investments have a negative NPV. The company's share price will fall if it cuts its dividend to make new investments with a return of only 8%. By reinvesting its earnings at a rate (8%) that is lower than its equity cost of capital (10%), Crane has reduced shareholder value.

BDeH CHAPTER 9

INTERVIEW WITH
Marilyn Fedak

Marilyn G. Fedak is the Head of Global Value Equities at Alliance-Bernstein, a publicly traded global asset management firm with approximately $618 billion in assets. Here she discusses the methods Alliance-Bernstein uses to identify stocks that may be undervalued in the market.

QUESTION: *What valuation methods do you use to identify buying opportunities?*

ANSWER: Since the early 1980s, we have used the dividend-discount model for U.S. large-cap stocks. At its most basic level, the dividend-discount model provides a way to evaluate how much we need to pay today for a company's future earnings. All things being equal, we are looking to buy as much earnings power as cheaply as we can.

It is a very reliable methodology, *if* you have the right forecasts for companies' future earnings. The key to success in using the dividend-discount model is having deep fundamental research—a large team of analysts who use a consistent process for modeling earnings. We ask our analysts to provide us with 5-year forecasts for the companies they follow.

For non-U.S. stocks and for small caps, we consider companies' current characteristics rather than forecasts. The number of companies in these groups is too large to populate them with quality forecasts, even with our 50-plus research team. We consider a variety of valuation measures, such as P/E and price-to-book ratios and selected success factors—for example, ROE and price momentum. We rank companies and focus on the stocks that rank the highest. Then the investment policy group meets with the analysts who follow these securities to determine whether the quantitative analysis is correctly reflecting the likely financial future of each company.

QUESTION: *Are there drawbacks to the dividend-discount model?*

ANSWER: Two things make the dividend-discount model hard to use in practice. First, you need a huge research depart-ment to generate good forecasts for a large universe of stocks—just looking at the largest companies alone, that means more than 650 companies. Because this is a relative valuation methodology, you need to have as much confidence in the forecast for the stock that ranks 450th as well as the one that ranks 15th. Second, it is very hard to live by the results of the dividend-discount model. At the peak of the bubble in 2000, for example, dividend-discount models found tech stocks to be extremely overvalued. This was hard for most portfolio managers, because the pressure to override the model—to say it isn't working right—was enormous. That situation was extreme, but a dividend-discount model almost always puts you in a position of buying out-of-favor stocks—a difficult position to constantly maintain.

QUESTION: *Why have you focused on value stocks?*

ANSWER: We don't assign labels to companies. Our valuation model is such that we will buy any company if it is selling cheaply relative to our vision of its long-term earnings. In 2006, for example, we owned Microsoft, GE, Time Warner—companies that were considered premier growth stocks just a few years earlier. By using this consistent methodology and investing heavily in research, we have been able to produce strong investment results for our clients over long periods of time. And we believe that this process will continue to be successful in the future because it relies on enduring characteristics of human behavior (such as loss aversion) and the flows of capital in a free economic system.

Discussion Questions

1. Why did the dividend-discount model have trouble matching the valuations assigned to Internet stocks?

2. Do you think this represents a flaw in the model or did the problem lie in how the model was being applied?

Comparing Example 9.3 with Example 9.4, we see that the effect of cutting the firm's dividend to grow crucially depends on the return on new investment. In Example 9.3, the return on new investment of 12% exceeds the firm's equity cost of capital of 10%, so the investment has a positive NPV. In Example 9.4, however, the return on new investment is only 8%, so the new investment has a negative NPV—even though it will lead to earnings growth. Thus *cutting the firm's dividend to increase investment will raise the stock price if, and only if, the new investments have a positive NPV.*

Changing Growth Rates

Successful young firms often have very high initial earnings growth rates. During this period of high growth, firms often retain 100% of their earnings to exploit profitable investment opportunities. As they mature, their growth slows to rates more typical of established companies. At that point, their earnings exceed their investment needs and they begin to pay dividends.

We cannot use the constant dividend growth model to value the stock of such a firm for two reasons:

1. These firms often pay *no* dividends when they are young.
2. Their growth rate continues to change over time until they mature.

However, we can use the general form of the dividend-discount model to value such a firm by applying the constant growth model to calculate the future share price of the stock P_N once the firm matures and its expected growth rate stabilizes:

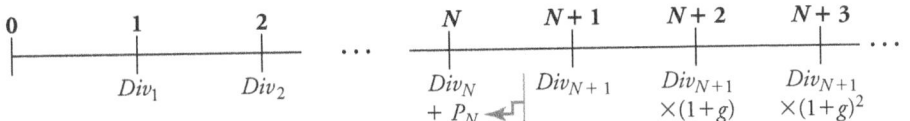

Specifically, if the firm is expected to grow at a long-term rate g after year $N + 1$, then from the constant dividend growth model:

$$P_N = \frac{Div_{N+1}}{r_E - g} \tag{9.13}$$

We can then use this estimate of P_N as a final cash flow in the dividend-discount model. Intuitively, we value the stock as the present value of the dividends we will receive plus the present value of the price we expect to be able to sell the stock for in the future. For example, consider a company with expected dividends of $2.00, $2.50, and $3.00 in each of the next three years. After that point, its dividends are expected to grow at a constant rate of 5%. If its equity cost of capital is 12%, we can combine Eq. 9.4 with Eq. 9.13 to get

$$P_0 = \frac{\$2.00}{1.12} + \frac{\$2.50}{(1.12)^2} + \frac{\$3.00}{(1.12)^3} + \frac{1}{(1.12)^3}\left(\frac{\$3.00(1.05)}{0.12 - 0.05}\right)$$

$$P_0 = \frac{\$2.00}{1.12} + \frac{\$2.50}{(1.12)^2} + \frac{\$3.00}{(1.12)^3} + \frac{\$45.00}{(1.12)^3} = \$37.94$$

EXAMPLE 9.5

Valuing a Firm with Two Different Growth Rates

Problem

Small Fry, Inc., has just invented a potato chip that looks and tastes like a french fry. Given the phenomenal market response to this product, Small Fry is reinvesting all of its earnings to expand its operations. Earnings were $2 per share this past year and are expected to grow at a rate of 20% per year until the end of year 4. At that point, other companies are likely to bring out competing products. Analysts project that at the end of year 4, Small Fry will cut its investment and begin paying 60% of its earnings as dividends. Its growth will also slow to a long-run rate of 4%. If Small Fry's equity cost of capital is 8%, what is the value of a share today?

Solution

▶ Plan

We can use Small Fry's projected earnings growth rate and payout rate to forecast its future earnings and dividends. After year 4, Small Fry's dividends will grow at a constant 4%, so we can use the constant dividend growth model (Eq. 9.13) to value all dividends after that point. Finally, we can pull everything together with the dividend-discount model (Eq. 9.4).

▶ Execute

The following spreadsheet projects Small Fry's earnings and dividends:

	Year	0	1	2	3	4	5	6
1								
2	**Earnings**							
3	EPS Growth Rate (versus prior year)		20%	20%	20%	20%	4%	4%
4	EPS	$2.00	$2.40	$2.88	$3.46	$4.15	$4.31	$4.49
5	**Dividends**							
6	Dividend Payout Rate		0%	0%	0%	60%	60%	60%
7	Div		$ —	$ —	$ —	$2.49	$2.59	$2.69

Starting from $2.00 in year 0, EPS grows by 20% per year until year 4, after which growth slows to 4%. Small Fry's dividend payout rate is zero until year 4, when competition reduces its investment opportunities and its payout rate rises to 60%. Multiplying EPS by the dividend payout ratio, we project Small Fry's future dividends in line 4.

From year 4 onward, Small Fry's dividends will grow at the expected long-run rate of 4% per year. Thus we can use the constant dividend growth model to project Small Fry's share price at the end of year 3. Given its equity cost of capital of 8%,

$$P_3 = \frac{Div_4}{r_E - g} = \frac{\$2.49}{0.08 - 0.04} = \$62.25$$

We then apply the dividend-discount model (Eq. 9.4) with this terminal value:

$$P_0 = \frac{Div_1}{1 + r_E} + \frac{Div_2}{(1 + r_E)^2} + \frac{Div_3}{(1 + r_E)^3} + \frac{P_3}{(1 + r_E)^3} = \frac{\$62.25}{(1.08)^3} = \$49.42$$

▶ Evaluate

The dividend-discount model is flexible enough to handle any forecasted pattern of dividends. Here the dividends were zero for several years and then settled into a constant growth rate, allowing us to use the constant growth rate model as a shortcut.

Limitations of the Dividend-Discount Model

The dividend-discount model values a stock based on a forecast of the future dividends paid to shareholders. But unlike a Treasury bond, whose cash flows are known with virtual certainty, a tremendous amount of uncertainty is associated with any forecast of a firm's future dividends.

Let's reconsider the example of Kenneth Cole Productions (KCP). In early 2006, KCP paid annual dividends of $0.72. With an equity cost of capital of 11% and expected dividend growth of 8%, the constant dividend growth model implies a share price for KCP of

$$P_0 = \frac{Div_1}{r_E - g} = \frac{\$0.72}{0.11 - 0.08} = \$24$$

which is reasonably close to the $26.75 share price that the stock had at the time. With a 10% dividend growth rate, however, this estimate would rise to $72 per share; with a 5%

FIGURE 9.2

KCP Stock Prices for Different Expected Growth Rates

Stock prices are based on the constant dividend growth model, a dividend next year of $0.72, and an equity cost of capital of 11%. The expected dividend growth rate is varied from 0% to 10%. Note how even a small change in the expected growth rate produces a large change in the stock price.

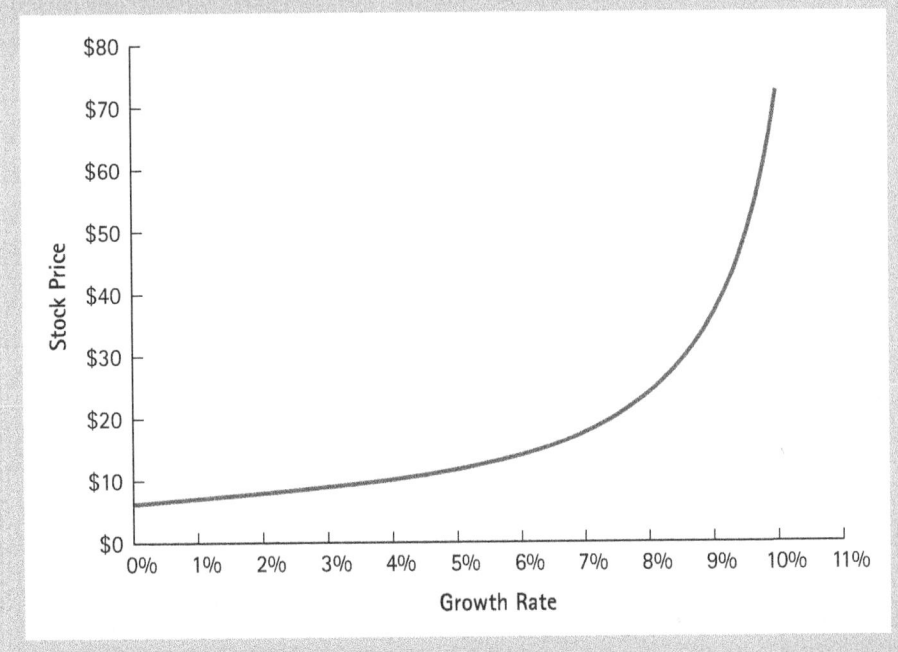

dividend growth rate, the estimate falls to $12 per share. As we see in Figure 9.2, even small changes in the assumed dividend growth rate can lead to large changes in the estimated stock price.

Furthermore, it is difficult to know which estimate of the dividend growth rate is more reasonable. KCP more than doubled its dividend between 2003 and 2005, but its earnings have remained relatively flat over the past few years. Consequently, this rate of increase is not sustainable. From Eq. 9.8, forecasting dividends requires forecasting the firm's earnings, dividend payout rate, and future share count. Future earnings, however, will depend on interest expenses (which, in turn, depend on how much the firm borrows), and the firm's share count and dividend payout rate will depend on whether KCP uses a portion of its earnings to repurchase shares. Because borrowing and repurchase decisions are at management's discretion, they can be more difficult to forecast reliably than other, more fundamental aspects of the firm's cash flows.[4] We look at two alternative methods that avoid some of these difficulties in the next section.

Concept Check

5. What are three ways that a firm can increase the amount of its future dividend per share?
6. Under what circumstances can a firm increase its share price by cutting its dividend and investing more?

---

[4]We discuss management's decision to borrow funds or repurchase shares later in this text.

BDeH CHAPTER 9

9.4 Total Payout and Free Cash Flow Valuation Models

In this section, we outline two alternative approaches to valuing the firm's shares that avoid some of the difficulties of the dividend-discount model. First, we consider the *total payout model,* which allows us to ignore the firm's choice between dividends and share repurchases. Second, we consider the *discounted free cash flow model,* which focuses on the cash flows to all of the firm's investors, both debt and equity holders. This model allows us to avoid the difficulties associated with estimating the impact of the firm's borrowing decisions on earnings.

Share Repurchases and the Total Payout Model

share repurchase A situation in which a firm uses cash to buy back its own stock.

In our discussion of the dividend-discount model, we implicitly assumed that any cash paid out by the firm to shareholders takes the form of a dividend. In recent years, an increasing number of firms have replaced dividend payouts with *share repurchases.* In a **share repurchase**, the firm uses excess cash to buy back its own stock. Share repurchases have two consequences for the dividend-discount model. First, the more cash the firm uses to repurchase shares, the less cash it has available to pay dividends. Second, by repurchasing shares, the firm decreases its share count, which increases its earning and dividends on a per-share basis.

In the dividend-discount model, we valued a share from the perspective of a single shareholder, discounting the dividends the shareholder will receive:

$$P_0 = PV(\text{Future Dividends per Share}) \tag{9.14}$$

total payout model A method that values shares of a firm by discounting the firm's total payouts to equity holders (i.e., all the cash distributed as dividends and stock repurchases) and then dividing by the current number of shares outstanding.

An alternative method that may be more reliable when a firm repurchases shares is the **total payout model**, which values *all* of the firm's equity, rather than a single share. To use this model, we discount the total payouts that the firm makes to shareholders, which is the total amount spent on both dividends *and* share repurchases.[5] This gives the total value of the firm's equity. We then divide by the current number of shares outstanding to determine the share price:

Total Payout Model

$$P_0 = \frac{PV(\text{Future Total Dividends and Repurchases})}{\text{Shares Outstanding}_0} \tag{9.15}$$

We can apply the same simplifications that we obtained by assuming constant growth in Section 9.2 to the total payout method. The only change is that *we discount total dividends and share repurchases and use the growth rate of earnings (rather than earnings per share) when forecasting the growth of the firm's total payouts.* When the firm uses share repurchases, this method can be more reliable and easier to apply than the dividend-discount model.

EXAMPLE 9.6

Valuation with Share Repurchases

Problem
Titan Industries has 217 million shares outstanding and expects earnings at the end of this year of $860 million. Titan plans to pay out 50% of its earnings in total, paying 30% as a dividend and using 20% to repurchase shares. If Titan's earnings are expected to grow by 7.5% per year and these payout rates remain constant, determine Titan's share price assuming an equity cost of capital of 10%.

---

[5]You can think of the total payouts as the amount you would receive if you owned 100% of the firm's shares: You would receive all of the dividends, plus the proceeds from selling shares back to the firm in the share repurchase.

Solution

▶ **Plan**

Based on the equity cost of capital of 10% and an expected earnings growth rate of 7.5%, we can compute the present value of Titan's future payouts as a constant growth perpetuity. The only input missing here is Titan's total payouts this year, which we can calculate as 50% of its earnings. The present value of all of Titan's future payouts is the value of its total equity. To obtain the price of a share, we divide the total value by the number of shares outstanding (217 million).

▶ **Execute**

Titan will have total payouts this year of 50% × $860 million = $430 million. Using the constant growth perpetuity formula, we have

$$PV(\text{Future Total Dividends and Repurchases}) = \frac{\$430 \text{ million}}{0.10 - 0.075} = \$17.2 \text{ billion}$$

This present value represents the total value of Titan's equity (i.e., its market capitalization). To compute the share price, we divide by the current number of shares outstanding:

$$P_0 = \frac{\$17.2 \text{ billion}}{217 \text{ million shares}} = \$79.26 \text{ per share}$$

▶ **Evaluate**

Using the total payout method, we did not need to know the firm's split between dividends and share repurchases. To compare this method with the dividend-discount model, note that Titan will pay a dividend of 30% × $860 million/(217 million shares) = $1.19 per share, for a dividend yield of 1.19/79.26 = 1.50%. From Eq. 9.7, Titan's expected EPS, dividend, and share price growth rate is $g = r_E - Div_1/P_0 = 8.50\%$. This growth rate exceeds the 7.50% growth rate of earnings because Titan's share count will decline over time owing to its share repurchases.[6]

The Discounted Free Cash Flow Model

discounted free cash flow model A method for estimating a firm's enterprise value by discounting its future free cash flow.

In the total payout model, we first value the firm's equity, rather than just a single share. The **discounted free cash flow model** goes one step further and begins by determining the total value of the firm to all investors—both equity holders *and* debt holders. That is, we begin by estimating the firm's enterprise value, which we defined in Chapter 2 as follows:[7]

$$\text{Enterprise Value} = \text{Market Value of Equity} + \text{Debt} - \text{Cash} \tag{9.16}$$

The enterprise value is the value of the firm's underlying business, unencumbered by debt and separate from any cash or marketable securities. We can interpret the enterprise value as the net cost of acquiring the firm's equity, taking its cash, and paying off all debt; in essence, it is equivalent to owning the unlevered business. The advantage of the discounted free cash flow model is that it allows us to value a firm without explicitly forecasting its dividends, share repurchases, or its use of debt.

Valuing the Enterprise. How can we estimate a firm's enterprise value? To estimate the value of the firm's equity, we compute the present value of the firm's total payouts to equity holders. Likewise, to estimate a firm's enterprise value, we compute the present

---

[6]We can check that an 8.5% EPS growth rate is consistent with 7.5% earnings growth and Titan's repurchase plans as follows: Given an expected share price of $79.26 × 1.085 = $86.00 next year, Titan will repurchase 20% × $860 million ÷ ($86.00 per share) = 2 million shares next year. With the decline in the number of shares from 217 million to 215 million, EPS grows by a factor of 1.075 × (217/215) = 1.085 or 8.5%.

[7]To be precise, when we say "cash," we are referring to the firm's cash in excess of its working capital needs, which is the amount of cash it has invested at a competitive market interest rate.

value of the *free cash flow* (FCF) that the firm has available to pay all investors, both debt and equity holders. We saw how to compute the free cash flow for a project in Chapter 8; we now perform the same calculation for the entire firm:

$$\text{Free Cash Flow} = EBIT \times (1 - \text{tax rate}) + \text{Depreciation} \tag{9.17}$$
$$- \text{Capital Expenditures} - \text{Increases in Net Working Capital}$$

Free cash flow measures the cash generated by the firm before any payments to debt or equity holders are considered.

Thus, just as we determine the value of a project by calculating the NPV of the project's free cash flow, so we estimate a firm's current enterprise value, V_0, by computing the present value of the firm's free cash flow:

Discounted Free Cash Flow Model

$$V_0 = PV(\text{Future Free Cash Flow of Firm}) \tag{9.18}$$

Given the enterprise value, we can estimate the share price by using Eq. 9.16 to solve for the value of equity and then divide by the total number of shares outstanding:

$$P_0 = \frac{V_0 + \text{Cash}_0 - \text{Debt}_0}{\text{Shares Outstanding}_0} \tag{9.19}$$

There is an intuitive difference between the discounted free cash flow model and the dividend-discount model. In the dividend-discount model, the firm's cash and debt are included indirectly through the effect of interest income and expenses on earnings. By contrast, in the discounted free cash flow model, we ignore interest income and expenses because free cash flow is based on EBIT (Earnings *Before* Interest and Taxes), but we then adjust for cash and debt directly (in Eq. 9.19).

Implementing the Model. A key difference between the discounted free cash flow model and the earlier models we have considered is the discount rate. In previous calculations, we used the firm's equity cost of capital, r_E, because we were discounting the cash flows to equity holders. Here, we are discounting the free cash flow that will be paid to both debt and equity holders. Thus we should use the firm's **weighted average cost of capital (WACC)**, denoted by r_{wacc}; it is the cost of capital that reflects the risk of the overall business, which is the combined risk of the firm's equity *and* debt. For now, we interpret r_{wacc} as the expected return the firm must pay to investors to compensate them for the risk of holding the firm's debt and equity together. If the firm has no debt, then $r_{wacc} = r_E$. We will develop methods to calculate the WACC explicitly later in this text.[8]

> **weighted average cost of capital (WACC)** The cost of capital that reflects the risk of the overall business, which is the combined risk of the firm's equity and debt.

Given the firm's weighted average cost of capital, we implement the discounted free cash flow model in much the same way as we did the dividend-discount model. That is, we forecast the firm's free cash flow up to some horizon, together with a terminal (continuation) value of the enterprise:

$$V_0 = \frac{FCF_1}{1 + r_{wacc}} + \frac{FCF_2}{(1 + r_{wacc})^2} + \cdots + \frac{FCF_N}{(1 + r_{wacc})^N} + \frac{V_N}{(1 + r_{wacc})^N} \tag{9.20}$$

Often, we estimate the terminal value by assuming a constant long-run growth rate g_{FCF} for free cash flows beyond year N, so that

$$V_N = \frac{FCF_{N+1}}{r_{wacc} - g_{FCF}} = \left(\frac{1 + g_{FCF}}{r_{wacc} - g_{FCF}} \right) \times FCF_N \tag{9.21}$$

---

[8]We can also interpret the firm's weighted average cost of capital as the average cost of capital associated with all of the firm's projects. In that sense, the WACC is the expected return associated with the average risk of the firm's investments.

The long-run growth rate g_{FCF} is typically based on the expected long-run growth rate of the firm's revenues.

<table>
<tr><td>**EXAMPLE 9.7**</td><td>**Problem**</td></tr>
</table>

EXAMPLE 9.7

Valuing Kenneth Cole
Productions Stock
Using Free Cash Flow

Problem

Kenneth Cole Productions (KCP) had sales of $518 million in 2005. Suppose you expect its sales to grow at a rate of 9% in 2006, but then slow by 1% per year to the long-run growth rate that is characteristic of the apparel industry—4%—by 2011. Based on KCP's past profitability and investment needs, you expect EBIT to be 9% of sales, increases in net working capital requirements to be 10% of any increase in sales, and capital expenditures to equal depreciation expenses. If KCP has $100 million in cash, $3 million in debt, 21 million shares outstanding, a tax rate of 37%, and a weighted average cost of capital of 11%, what is your estimate of the value of KCP's stock in early 2006?

Solution

▶ **Plan**

We can estimate KCP's future free cash flow by constructing a pro forma statement as we did for HomeNet in Chapter 8. The only difference is that the pro forma statement is for the whole company, rather than just one project. Further, we need to calculate a terminal (or continuation) value for KCP at the end of our explicit projections. Because we expect KCP's free cash flow to grow at a constant rate after 2011, we can use Eq. 9.21 to compute a terminal enterprise value. The present value of the free cash flows during the years 2006–2011 and the terminal value will be the total enterprise value for KCP. Using that value, we can subtract the debt, add the cash, and divide by the number of shares outstanding to compute the price per share (Eq. 9.19).

▶ **Execute**

The spreadsheet below presents a simplified pro forma for KCP based on the information we have:

	Year	2005	2006	2007	2008	2009	2010	2011
1								
2	**FCF Forecast ($ million)**							
3	Sales	518.0	564.6	609.8	652.5	691.6	726.2	755.3
4	*Growth versus Prior Year*		*9.0%*	*8.0%*	*7.0%*	*6.0%*	*5.0%*	*4.0%*
5	**EBIT** (9% of sales)		50.8	54.9	58.7	62.2	65.4	68.0
6	Less: Income Tax (37%)		−18.8	−20.3	−21.7	−23.0	−24.2	−25.1
7	Plus: Depreciation		—	—	—	—	—	—
8	Less: Capital Expenditures		—	—	—	—	—	—
9	Less: Increase in NWC (10% ΔSales)		−4.7	−4.5	−4.3	−3.9	−3.5	−2.9
10	**Free Cash Flow**		27.4	30.1	32.7	35.3	37.7	39.9

Because capital expenditures are expected to equal depreciation, lines 7 and 8 in the spreadsheet cancel out. We can set them both to zero rather than explicitly forecast them.

Given our assumption of constant 4% growth in free cash flows after 2011 and a weighted average cost of capital of 11%, we can use Eq. 9.21 to compute a terminal enterprise value:

$$V_{2011} = \left(\frac{1 + g_{FCF}}{r_{wacc} - g_{FCF}} \right) \times FCF_{2011} = \left(\frac{1.04}{0.11 - 0.04} \right) \times 39.9 = \$592.8 \text{ million}$$

From Eq. 9.20, KCP's current enterprise value is the present value of its free cash flows plus the firm's terminal value:

$$V_0 = \frac{27.4}{1.11} + \frac{30.1}{1.11^2} + \frac{32.7}{1.11^3} + \frac{35.3}{1.11^4} + \frac{37.7}{1.11^5} + \frac{39.9}{1.11^6} + \frac{592.8}{1.11^6} = \$456.9 \text{ million}$$

We can now estimate the value of a share of KCP's stock using Eq. 9.19:

$$P_0 = \frac{456.9 + 100 - 3}{21} = \$26.38$$

▶ **Evaluate**
The Value Principle tells us that the present value of all future cash flows generated by KCP plus the value of the cash held by the firm today must equal the total value today of all the claims, both debt and equity, on those cash flows and cash. Using that principle, we calculate the total value of all of KCP's claims and then subtract the debt portion to value the equity (stock).

Connection to Capital Budgeting.   There is an important connection between the discounted free cash flow model and the NPV rule for capital budgeting that we developed in Chapter 7. Because the firm's free cash flow is equal to the sum of the free cash flows from the firm's current and future investments, we can interpret the firm's enterprise value as the total NPV that the firm will earn from continuing its existing projects and initiating new ones. Hence, the NPV of any individual project represents its contribution to the firm's enterprise value. To maximize the firm's share price, we should accept those projects that have a positive NPV.

Recall also from Chapter 7 that many forecasts and estimates were necessary to estimate the free cash flows of a project. The same is true for the firm: We must forecast its future sales, operating expenses, taxes, capital requirements, and other factors to obtain its free cash flow. On the one hand, estimating free cash flow in this way gives us flexibility to incorporate many specific details about the future prospects of the firm. On the other hand, some uncertainty inevitably surrounds each assumption. Given this fact, it is important to conduct a sensitivity analysis, as described in Chapter 7, to translate this uncertainty into a range of potential values for the stock.

EXAMPLE 9.8

Sensitivity Analysis for Stock Valuation

Problem
In Example 9.7, KCP's EBIT was assumed to be 9% of sales. If KCP can reduce its operating expenses and raise its EBIT to 10% of sales, how would the estimate of the stock's value change?

Solution

▶ **Plan**
In this scenario, EBIT will increase by 1% of sales compared to Example 9.7. From there, we can use the tax rate (37%) to compute the effect on the free cash flow for each year. Once we have the new free cash flows, we repeat the approach in Example 9.7 to arrive at a new stock price.

▶ **Execute**
In year 1, EBIT will be 1% × \$564.6 million = \$5.6 million higher. After taxes, this increase will raise the firm's free cash flow in year 1 by (1 − 0.37) × \$5.6 million = \$3.5 million, to \$30.9 million. Doing the same calculation for each year, we get the following revised FCF estimates:

Year	2006	2007	2008	2009	2010	2011
FCF	30.9	33.9	36.8	39.7	42.3	44.7

We can now reestimate the stock price as in Example 9.7. The terminal value is $V_{2011} = [1.04/(0.11 − 0.04)] \times 44.7 = \$664.1$ million, so

$$V_0 = \frac{30.9}{1.11} + \frac{33.9}{1.11^2} + \frac{36.8}{1.11^3} + \frac{39.7}{1.11^4} + \frac{42.3}{1.11^5} + \frac{44.7}{1.11^6} + \frac{664.1}{1.11^6} = \$512.5 \text{ million}$$

The new estimate for the value of the stock is $P_0 = (512.5 + 100 − 3)/21 = \$29.02$ per share, a difference of about 10% compared to the result found in Example 9.7.

> ▶ **Evaluate**
> KCP's stock price is fairly sensitive to changes in the assumptions about its profitability. A 1% permanent change in its margins affects the firm's stock price by 10%.

Figure 9.3 summarizes the different valuation methods we have discussed so far. The value of the stock is determined by the present value of its future dividends. We can estimate the total market capitalization of the firm's equity from the present value of the firm's total payouts, which includes dividends and share repurchases. Finally, the present value of the firm's free cash flow, which is the amount of cash the firm has available to make payments to equity or debt holders, determines the firm's enterprise value.

FIGURE 9.3

A Comparison of Discounted Cash Flow Models of Stock Valuation

By computing the present value of the firm's dividends, total payouts, or free cash flows, we can estimate the value of the stock, the total value of the firm's equity, or the firm's enterprise value.

Present Value of ...	Determines the ...
Dividend Payments	Stock Price
Total Payouts (All dividends and repurchases)	Equity Value
Free Cash Flow (Cash available to pay all security holders)	Enterprise Value

Concept Check

7. How does the growth rate used in the total payout model differ from the growth rate used in the dividend-discount model?

8. Why do we ignore interest payments on the firm's debt in the discounted free cash flow model?

9.5　Valuation Based on Comparable Firms

method of comparables
An estimate of the value of a firm based on the value of other, comparable firms or other investments that are expected to generate very similar cash flows in the future.

So far, we have valued a firm or its stock by considering the expected future cash flows it will provide to its owner. The valuation principle then tells us that its value is the present value of its future cash flows, because the present value is the amount we would need to invest elsewhere in the market to replicate the cash flows with the same risk.

Another application of the Law of One Price is the method of comparables. In the **method of comparables** (or "comps"), rather than value the firm's cash flows directly, we estimate the value of the firm based on the value of other, comparable firms or investments that we expect will generate very similar cash flows in the future. For example, consider the case of a new firm that is *identical* to an existing publicly traded company. If these firms will generate identical cash flows, the valuation principle, through the Law of One Price, implies that we can use the value of the existing company to determine the value of the new firm.

Of course, identical companies do not really exist. Even two firms in the same industry selling the same types of products, while similar in many respects, are likely to be of a different size or scale. For example, Gateway and Dell both sell personal computers directly to consumers using the Internet. In 2006, Gateway had sales of only $4 billion, whereas Dell had sales of approximately $56 billion. In this section, we consider ways to adjust for scale differences to use comparables to value firms with similar businesses and then discuss the strengths and weaknesses of this approach.

Valuation Multiples

valuation multiple A ratio of a firm's value to some measure of the firm's scale or cash flow.

We can adjust for differences in scale between firms by expressing their value in terms of a **valuation multiple**, which is a ratio of the value to some measure of the firm's scale. As an analogy, consider valuing an office building. A natural measure to consider would be the price per square foot for other buildings recently sold in the area. Multiplying the size of the office building under consideration by the average price per square foot would typically provide a reasonable estimate of the building's value. We can apply this same idea to stocks, replacing square footage with some more appropriate measure of the firm's scale.

The Price-Earnings Ratio. The most common valuation multiple is the price-earnings ratio, which we introduced in Chapter 2. The P/E ratio is so common that it is almost always part of the basic statistics computed for a stock (as shown in Figure 9.1, the screenshot from Google Finance for KCP). A firm's P/E ratio is equal to the share price divided by its earnings per share. The intuition behind its use is that, when you buy a stock, you are in a sense buying the rights to the firm's future earnings and differences in the scale of firms' earnings are likely to persist. As a consequence, you should be willing to pay proportionally more for a stock with higher current earnings. We can estimate the value of a firm's share by multiplying its current earnings per share by the average P/E ratio of comparable firms.

trailing earnings A firm's earnings over the prior 12 months.

forward earnings A firm's anticipated earnings over the coming 12 months.

trailing P/E The computation of a firm's P/E using its trailing earnings.

forward P/E A firm's price-earnings (P/E) ratio calculated using forward earnings.

We can compute a firm's P/E ratio by using either **trailing earnings** (earnings over the prior 12 months) or **forward earnings** (expected earnings over the coming 12 months), with the resulting ratio being called the **trailing P/E** or the **forward P/E**, respectively. For valuation purposes, the forward P/E is generally preferred, as we are most concerned about future earnings. We can interpret the forward P/E in terms of the dividend-discount model or the total payout model that we introduced earlier. For example, in the case of constant dividend growth, dividing through Eq. 9.6 by EPS_1, we find that

$$\text{Forward P/E} = \frac{P_0}{EPS_1} = \frac{Div_1/EPS_1}{r_E - g} = \frac{\text{Dividend Payout Rate}}{r_E - g} \qquad (9.22)$$

Equation 9.22 implies that if two stocks have the same payout and EPS growth rates, as well as equivalent risk (and, therefore, the same equity cost of capital), then both should have the same P/E ratio. In addition, firms and industries that have high growth rates, and that generate cash well in excess of their investment needs so that they can maintain high payout rates, should have high P/E multiples.

For example, recall Example 9.3 and Example 9.4, where we computed the stock price of Crane Sporting Goods assuming that earnings would grow at rates of 3% per year and 2% per year, respectively. The prices we computed were $64.29 for Example 9.3 and $56.25 for Example 9.4. In each case, Crane started with earnings of $4.50, so the

FIGURE 9.4

Relating the P/E Ratio to Expected Future Growth in the Dividend-Discount Model

The graph shows the expected growth in earnings under the scenarios described in Example 9.3 and Example 9.4. The stock prices we computed in those examples were based on current earnings and expected future growth. Dividing those prices by the current earnings of $4.50 produces P/E ratios of 14.3 (high growth, 3%) and 12.5 (low growth, 2%). The graph shows how higher expected growth translates into a higher P/E.

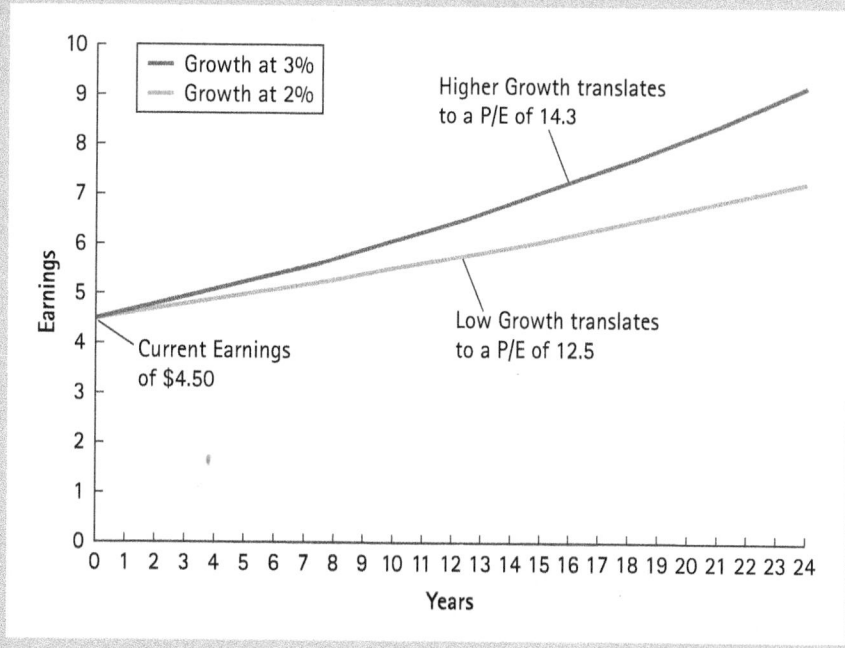

corresponding P/E ratios were 14.3 for the higher growth scenario and 12.5 for the lower growth scenario. Figure 9.4 shows the relationship between expected earnings growth and P/E ratios.

EXAMPLE 9.9

Valuation Using the Price-Earnings Ratio

Problem
Suppose furniture manufacturer Herman Miller, Inc., has earnings per share of $1.38. If the average P/E of comparable furniture stocks is 21.3, estimate a value for Herman Miller's stock using the P/E as a valuation multiple. What are the assumptions underlying this estimate?

Solution

▶ Plan
We estimate a share price for Herman Miller by multiplying its EPS by the P/E of comparable firms:

EPS × P/E = Earnings per Share × (Price per Share ÷ Earnings per Share) = Price per Share

▶ Execute
$P_0 = \$1.38 \times 21.3 = \$29.39$. This estimate assumes that Herman Miller will have similar future risk, payout rates, and growth rates to comparable firms in the industry.

BDeH   CHAPTER 8

> ▶ **Evaluate**
> Although valuation multiples are simple to use, they rely on some very strong assumptions about the similarity of the comparable firms to the firm you are valuing. It is important to consider whether these assumptions are likely to be reasonable—and thus to hold—in each case.

Enterprise Value Multiples. It is also common practice to use valuation multiples based on the firm's enterprise value. As discussed in Section 9.3, because it represents the total value of the firm's underlying business rather than just the value of equity, the enterprise value is advantageous if we want to compare firms with different amounts of leverage.

Because the enterprise value represents the entire value of the firm before the firm pays its debt, to form an appropriate multiple, we divide it by a measure of earnings or cash flows before interest payments are made. Common multiples to consider are enterprise value to EBIT, EBITDA (earnings before interest, taxes, depreciation, and amortization), and free cash flow. However, because capital expenditures can vary substantially from period to period (e.g., a firm may need to add capacity and build a new plant one year, but then may not need to expand further for many years), most practitioners rely on enterprise value to EBITDA multiples. From Eq. 9.21, if expected free cash flow growth is constant, then

$$\frac{V_0}{EBITDA_1} = \frac{\dfrac{FCF_1}{r_{wacc} - g_{FCF}}}{EDITDA_1} = \frac{FCF_1/EBITDA_1}{r_{wacc} - g_{FCF}} \qquad (9.23)$$

As with the P/E multiple, this valuation multiple is higher for firms with high growth rates and low capital requirements (which means that free cash flow is high in proportion to EBITDA).

Other Multiples. Many other valuation multiples are possible. Looking at the enterprise value as a multiple of sales can be useful if it is reasonable to assume that the firm will maintain a similar margin in the future. For firms with substantial tangible assets, the ratio of price to book value of equity per share is sometimes used as a valuation multiple. Some multiples are specific to an industry. In the cable TV industry, for example, it is natural to consider enterprise value per subscriber.

Limitations of Multiples

If comparables were identical, the firms' multiples would match precisely. Of course, firms are not identical, so the usefulness of a valuation multiple will inevitably depend on the nature of the differences between firms and the sensitivity of the multiples to these differences.

Table 9.1 lists several valuation multiples for firms in the footwear industry, as of January 2006. Also shown in the table is the average for each multiple, together with the range around the average (in percentage terms). The bottom rows showing the range make it clear that the footwear industry has a lot of dispersion for all of the multiples (for example, BWS has a P/E of 22.62 while RCKY has a P/E of only 8.66). While the enterprise value to EBITDA multiple shows the smallest variation, even with it we cannot expect to obtain a precise estimate of a firm's value.

The differences in these multiples most likely reflect differences in expected future growth rates, risk (and therefore costs of capital), and, in the case of Puma, differences in accounting conventions between the United States and Germany. Investors in the market understand that these differences exist, so the stocks are priced accordingly. When valu-

TABLE 9.1	Name	Market Capitalization ($ million)	Enterprise Value ($ million)	P/E	Price/ Book	Enterprise Value/Sales	Enterprise Value/ EBITDA
Stock Prices and Multiples for the Footwear Industry, January 2006	Nike	21,830	20,518	16.64	3.59	1.43	8.75
	Puma AG	5,088	4,593	14.99	5.02	2.19	9.02
	Reebok International	3,514	3,451	14.91	2.41	0.90	8.58
	Wolverine World Wide	1,257	1,253	17.42	2.71	1.20	9.53
	Brown Shoe Co.	800	1,019	22.62	1.91	0.47	9.09
	Skechers U.S.A.	683	614	17.63	2.02	0.62	6.88
	Stride Rite Corp.	497	524	20.72	1.87	0.89	9.28
	Deckers Outdoor Corp.	373	367	13.32	2.29	1.48	7.44
	Weyco Group	230	226	11.97	1.75	1.06	6.66
	Rocky Shoes & Boots	106	232	8.66	1.12	0.92	7.55
	R.G. Barry Corp.	68	92	9.20	8.11	0.87	10.75
	LaCrosse Footwear	62	75	12.09	1.28	0.76	8.30
	Average			15.01	2.84	1.06	8.49
	Maximum			+51%	+186%	+106%	+27%
	Minimum			−42%	−61%	−56%	−22%

ing a firm using multiples, however, there is no clear guidance about how to adjust for these differences other than by narrowing the set of comparables used.

Another limitation of comparables is that they provide only information regarding the value of the firm *relative to* the other firms in the comparison set. Using multiples will not help us determine whether an entire industry is overvalued, for example. This issue became especially important during the Internet boom of the late 1990s. Because many of these firms did not have positive cash flows or earnings, new multiples were created to value them (e.g., price to "page views"). While these multiples could justify the value of these firms in relation to one another, it was much more difficult to justify the stock prices of many of these firms using a realistic estimate of cash flows and the discounted free cash flow approach.

Comparison with Discounted Cash Flow Methods

The use of a valuation multiple based on comparables is best viewed as a "shortcut" to the discounted cash flow methods of valuation. Rather than separately estimate the firm's cost of capital and future earnings or free cash flows, we rely on the market's assessment of the value of other firms with similar future prospects. In addition to its simplicity, the multiples approach has the advantage of being based on actual stock prices of real firms, rather than on what may be unrealistic forecasts of future cash flows.

One shortcoming of the comparables approach is that it does not take into account the important differences among firms. For example, we ignore the fact that a firm has an exceptional management team, has developed an efficient manufacturing process, or has just secured a patent on a new technology when we apply a valuation multiple. Discounted cash flows methods have an advantage in this respect, in that they allow us to incorporate specific information about the firm's cost of capital or future growth. Thus, because the true driver of value for any firm is its ability to generate cash flows for its investors, the discounted cash flow methods have the potential to be more accurate than the use of a valuation multiple.

Stock Valuation Techniques: The Final Word

In the end, no single technique provides a final answer regarding a stock's true value. Indeed, all approaches inevitably require assumptions or forecasts that are too uncertain to provide a definitive assessment of the firm's value. Most real-world practitioners use a combination of these approaches and gain confidence in the outcome if the results are consistent across a variety of methods.

Figure 9.5 compares the ranges of values for KCP stock using the different valuation methods discussed in this chapter. The firm's stock price of $26.75 in January 2006 was within the range estimated by all of these methods. Hence, based on this evidence alone, we would not conclude that the stock is obviously under- or over-priced.

We now return to the questions posed at the beginning of the chapter. First, how would an investor decide whether to buy or sell the stock? She would value the stock using her own expectations and as many of valuation methods described in this chapter as possible. Figure 9.5 shows the outcome of such an exercise based on one set of reasonable expectations for KCP stock. If her expectations were substantially different, she might conclude that the stock was over- or under-priced at $26.75. Based on that conclusion, she would buy or sell the stock, and time would reveal whether her expectations were better than the markets.

Second, how could KCP stock suddenly be worth 6% less? The information that the long-time president was resigning caused investors to lower their forecasts of future cash flows enough that the value of a claim on those cash flows was 6% less. As investors digested the news and updated their expectations, they would have determined that the

FIGURE 9.5 Range of Valuations for KCP Stock Using Various Valuation Methods

Valuations from multiples are based on the low, high, and average values of the comparable firms from Table 9.1 (see Problems 20 and 21). The constant dividend growth model is based on an 11% equity cost of capital and 5%, 8%, and 10% dividend growth rates, as discussed at the end of Section 9.2. The discounted free cash flow model is based on Example 9.7 with the range of parameters in Problem 18. Midpoints are based on average multiples or base-case assumptions. Red and blue regions show the variation between the lowest-multiple/worst-case scenario and the highest-multiple/best-case scenario. KCP's actual share price of $26.75 is indicated by the gray line.

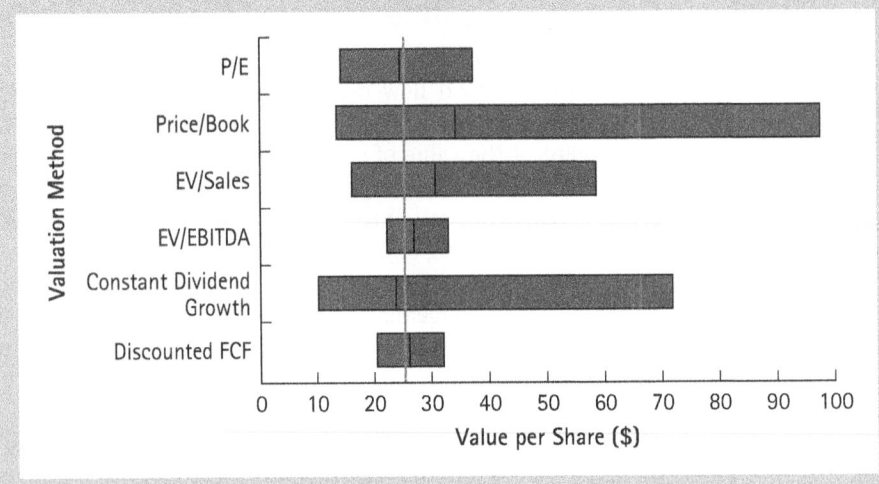

previous day's closing price was too high based on the new information. Selling pressure would then drive the stock price down until the buys and sells came into balance.

Third, what should KCP's managers do to raise the stock price? The only way to raise the stock price is to make value-increasing decisions. As shown in Chapters 7 and 8, through capital budgeting analysis, managers can identify projects that have a positive NPV. The present value of the incremental future free cash flows from such projects is greater than the present value of the costs. As we have seen in this chapter, the value of KCP's stock is the present value of its free cash flows. By increasing that present value through positive-NPV projects, KCP's managers can increase the stock price.

Concept Check

9. What are some common valuation multiples?

10. What implicit assumptions are made when valuing a firm using multiples based on comparable firms?

9.6 Information, Competition, and Stock Prices

As shown in Figure 9.6, the models described in this chapter link the firm's expected future cash flows, its cost of capital (determined by its risk), and the value of its shares. But what conclusions should we draw if the actual market price of a stock does not appear to be consistent with our estimate of its value? Is it more likely that the stock is mispriced or that we are mistaken about its risk and future cash flows? We close this chapter with a consideration of this question and the implications for corporate managers.

Information in Stock Prices

Consider the following situation. You are a new junior analyst assigned to research Kenneth Cole Productions stock and assess its value. You scrutinize the company's recent financial statements, look at the trends in the industry, and forecast the firm's future earnings, dividends, and free cash flows. After you carefully crunch the numbers, you estimate the stock's value to be $30 per share. On your way to present your analysis to your boss, you run into a slightly more experienced colleague in the elevator. It turns

FIGURE 9.6   The Valuation Triad

Valuation models determine the relationship among the firm's future cash flows, its cost of capital, and the value of its shares. The stock's expected cash flows and cost of capital can be used to assess its market price (share value). Conversely, the market price can be used to assess the firm's future cash flows or cost of capital.

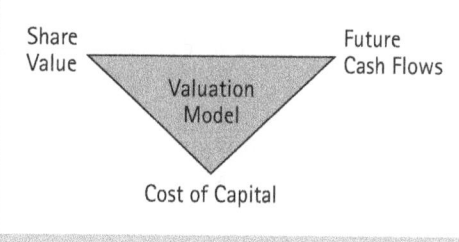

out that your colleague has been researching the same stock. But according to her analysis, the value of KCP stock is only $20 per share. What would you do?

Although you could just assume your colleague is wrong, most of us would reconsider our own analysis. The fact that someone else who has carefully studied the same stock has come to a very different conclusion is powerful evidence that we might be mistaken. In the face of this information from our colleague, we would probably adjust our assessment of the stock's value downward. Of course, our colleague might also revise her opinion upward based on our assessment. After sharing our analyses, we would likely end up with a consensus estimate somewhere between $20 and $30 per share.

This type of encounter happens millions of times every day in the stock market. When a buyer seeks to buy a stock, the willingness of other parties to sell the same stock suggests that they value the stock differently. This information should lead both buyers and sellers to revise their valuations. Ultimately, investors trade until they reach a consensus regarding the value (market price) of the stock. In this way, stock markets aggregate the information and views of many different investors.

Thus, if your valuation model suggests a stock is worth $30 per share when it is trading for $20 per share in the market, the discrepancy is equivalent to knowing that thousands of investors—many of them professionals who have access to the best information about the stock available—disagree with your assessment. This knowledge should make you reconsider your original analysis. You would need a very compelling reason to trust your own estimate in the face of such contrary opinions.

What conclusion can we draw from this discussion? Recall Figure 9.6, in which a valuation model links the firm's future cash flows, its cost of capital, and its share price. In other words, given accurate information about any two of these variables, a valuation model allows us to make inferences about the third variable. Thus the way we use a valuation model will depend on the quality of our information: The model will tell us the most about the variable for which our prior information is the least reliable.

For a publicly traded firm, its market price should already provide very accurate information, aggregated from a multitude of investors, regarding the true value of its shares. In most situations, a valuation model is best applied to tell us something about the firm's future cash flows or cost of capital, based on its current stock price. Only in the relatively rare case in which we have some superior information that other investors lack regarding the firm's cash flows and cost of capital would it make sense to second-guess the stock price.

EXAMPLE 9.10

Using the Information in Market Prices

Problem

Suppose Tecnor Industries will pay a dividend this year of $5 per share. Its equity cost of capital is 10%, and you expect its dividends to grow at a rate of approximately 4% per year, though you are somewhat unsure of the precise growth rate. If Tecnor's stock is currently trading for $76.92 per share, how would you update your beliefs about its dividend growth rate?

Solution

▶ **Plan**

If we apply the constant dividend growth model based on a 4% growth rate, we can estimate a stock price using Eq. 9.6. If the market price is higher than our estimate, it implies that the market expects higher growth in dividends than 4%. Conversely, if the market price is lower than our estimate, the market expects dividend growth to be less than 4%. We can use Eq. 9.7 to solve for the growth rate instead of price, allowing us to estimate the growth rate the market expects.

▶ **Execute**

Using Eq. 9.6, Div_1 of \$5, equity cost of capital (r_E) of 10%, and dividend growth rate of 4%, we get $P_0 = 5/(0.10 - 0.04) = \$83.33$ per share. The market price of \$76.92, however, implies that most investors expect dividends to grow at a somewhat slower rate.

In fact, if we continue to assume a constant growth rate, we can solve for the growth rate consistent with the current market price using Eq. 9.7:

$$g = r_E - Div_1/P_0 = 10\% - 5/76.92 = 3.5\%$$

This 3.5% growth rate is lower than our expected growth rate of 4%.

▶ **Evaluate**

Given the \$76.92 market price for the stock, we should lower our expectations for the dividend growth rate from 4% unless we have very strong reasons to trust our own estimate.

Competition and Efficient Markets

The idea that markets aggregate the information of many investors, and that this information is reflected in security prices, is a natural consequence of investor competition. If information were available that indicated that buying a stock had a positive NPV, investors with that information would choose to buy the stock; their attempts to purchase it would then drive up the stock's price. By a similar logic, investors with information that selling a stock had a positive NPV would sell it, and so the stock's price would fall.

The idea that competition among investors works to eliminate *all* positive-NPV trading opportunities is referred to as the **efficient markets hypothesis**. It implies that securities will be fairly priced, based on their future cash flows, given all information that is available to investors.

efficient markets hypothesis The idea that competition among investors works to eliminate all positive-NPV trading opportunities. It implies that securities will be fairly priced, based on their future cash flows, given all information that is available to investors.

The underlying rationale for the efficient markets hypothesis is the presence of competition. But what if new information becomes available that affects the firm's value? The degree of competition—and, therefore, the accuracy of the efficient markets hypothesis—will depend on the number of investors who possess this information. Next, we consider two important cases.

Public, Easily Interpretable Information. Information that is available to all investors includes information in news reports, financial statements, corporate press releases, or other public data sources. If the effects of this information on the firm's future cash flows can be readily ascertained, then all investors can determine how this information will change the firm's value.

In this situation, we expect competition between investors to be fierce and the stock price to react nearly instantaneously to such news. A few lucky investors might be able to trade a small quantity of shares before the price has fully adjusted. Most investors, however, would find that the stock price already reflected the new information before they were able to trade on it. In other words, the efficient markets hypothesis holds very well with respect to this type of information.[9]

---

[9]This type of market efficiency is often called "semi-strong form" market efficiency, to distinguish it from "strong form" market efficiency, where *all* information (even private information) is already reflected in the stock price. The term "weak form" market efficiency means that only the history of past prices is already reflected in the stock price.

EXAMPLE 9.11

Stock Price Reactions to Public Information

Problem

Myox Labs announces that it is pulling one of its leading drugs from the market, owing to the potential side effects associated with the drug. As a result, its future expected free cash flow will decline by $85 million per year for the next ten years. Myox has 50 million shares outstanding, no debt, and an equity cost of capital of 8%. If this news came as a complete surprise to investors, what should happen to Myox's stock price upon the announcement?

Solution

▶ **Plan**

In this case, we can use the discounted free cash flow method. With no debt, $r_{wacc} = r_E = 8\%$. The effect on the Myox's enterprise value will be the loss of a ten-year annuity of $85 million. We can compute the effect today as the present value of that annuity.

▶ **Execute**

Using the annuity formula, the decline in expected free cash flow will reduce Myox's enterprise value by

$$\$85 \text{ million} \times \frac{1}{0.08}\left(1 - \frac{1}{1.08^{10}}\right) = \$570 \text{ million}$$

Thus the share price should fall by $570/50 = $11.40 per share.

▶ **Evaluate**

Because this news is public and its effect on the firm's expected free cash flow is clear, we would expect the stock price to drop by $11.40 per share nearly instantaneously.

Private or Difficult-to-Interpret Information. Of course, some information is not publicly available. For example, an analyst might spend considerable time and effort gathering information from a firm's employees, competitors, suppliers, or customers that is relevant to the firm's future cash flows. This information is not available to other investors who have not devoted a similar effort to gathering it.

Even when information is publicly available, it may be difficult to interpret. Non-experts in the field may find it difficult to evaluate research reports on new technologies, for example. It may take a great deal of legal and accounting expertise and effort to understand the full consequences of a highly complicated business transaction. Certain consulting experts may have greater insight into consumer tastes and the likelihood of a product's acceptance. In these cases, while the fundamental information may be public, the *interpretation* of how that information will affect the firm's future cash flows is itself private information.

As an example, imagine that Phenyx Pharmaceuticals has just announced the development of a new drug for which the company is seeking approval from the U.S. Food and Drug Administration (FDA). If the drug is approved and subsequently launched in the U.S. market, the future profits from the new drug will increase Phenyx's market value by $750 million, or $15 per share given its 50 million shares outstanding. Assume that the development of this drug comes as a surprise to investors, and that the average likelihood of FDA approval is 10%. In that case, because many investors probably know that the chance of FDA approval is 10%, competition should lead to an immediate jump in Phenyx's stock price of 10% × $15 = $1.50 per share. Over time, however, analysts and experts in the field will likely make their own assessments of the probable efficacy of the drug. If they conclude that the drug looks more promising than average, they will begin to trade on their private information and buy the stock, and the firm's price will tend to drift higher over time. If the experts conclude that the drug looks less

FIGURE 9.7	Possible Stock Price Paths for Phenyx Pharmaceuticals

Phenyx's stock price jumps on the announcement based on the average likelihood of FDA approval. The stock price then drifts up (green path) or down (orange path) as informed traders trade on their more accurate assessment of the drug's likelihood of approval and hence entry into the U.S. market. At the time of the announcement, uninformed investors do not know which way the stock will go.

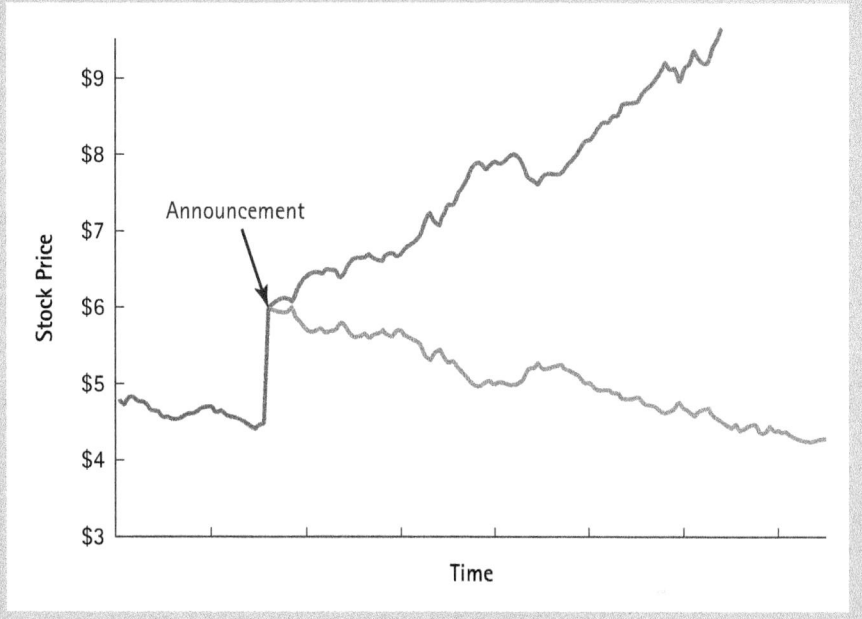

promising than average, however, they will tend to sell the stock, and the firm's price will drift lower over time. Of course, at the time of the announcement, uninformed investors do not know which way it will go. Examples of possible price paths are shown in Figure 9.7.

When private information is only in the hands of a relatively small number of investors, these investors may be able to profit by trading on their information.[10] In this case, the efficient markets hypothesis will not hold in the strict sense. However, as these informed traders begin to trade, their actions will tend to move prices, so over time prices will begin to reflect their information as well.

If the profit opportunities from having this type of information are large, other individuals will attempt to gain the expertise and devote the resources needed to acquire it. As more individuals become better informed, competition to exploit this information will increase. Thus, in the long run, we should expect that the degree of "inefficiency" in the market will be limited by the costs of obtaining the information.

---

[10]Even with private information, informed investors may find it difficult to profit from that information, because they must find others who are willing to trade with them; that is, the market for the stock must be sufficiently *liquid*. A liquid market requires that other investors in the market have alternative motives to trade (e.g., selling shares of a stock to purchase a house) and so be willing to trade even when facing the risk that other traders may be better informed.

Lessons for Investors and Corporate Managers

The effect of competition based on information about stock prices has important consequences for both investors and corporate managers.

Consequences for Investors. As in other markets, investors should be able to identify positive-NPV trading opportunities in securities markets only if some barrier or restriction to free competition exists. An investor's competitive advantage may take several forms. For instance, the investor may have expertise or access to information that is known to only a few people. Alternatively, the investor may have lower trading costs than other market participants and so can exploit opportunities that others would find unprofitable. In all cases, the source of the positive-NPV trading opportunity must be something that is difficult to replicate; otherwise, any gains would be competed away in short order.

While the fact that positive-NPV trading opportunities are hard to come by may be disappointing, there is some good news as well. If stocks are fairly priced according to our valuation models, then investors who buy stocks can expect to receive future cash flows that fairly compensate them for the risk of their investment. In such cases, the average investor can invest with confidence, even if he is not fully informed.

Source: © 2003 by NEA, Inc.

Implications for Corporate Managers. If stocks are fairly valued according to the models we have described, then the value of the firm is determined by the cash flows that it can pay to its investors. This result has several key implications for corporate managers:

- ▶ *Focus on NPV and free cash flow.* A manager seeking to boost the price of her firm's stock should make investments that increase the present value of the firm's free cash flow. Thus the capital budgeting methods outlined in Chapter 7 are fully consistent with the objective of maximizing the firm's share price.

- ▶ *Avoid accounting illusions.* Many managers make the mistake of focusing on accounting earnings as opposed to free cash flows. According to the efficient markets hypothesis, the accounting consequences of a decision do not directly affect the value of the firm and should not drive decision making.

- ▶ *Use financial transactions to support investment.* With efficient markets, the firm can sell its shares at a fair price to new investors. As a consequence, the firm should not be constrained from raising capital to fund positive-NPV investment opportunities.

The Efficient Markets Hypothesis Versus No Arbitrage

An important distinction must be made between the efficient markets hypothesis and the notion of a normal market that we introduced in Chapter 3, which is based on the idea of arbitrage. An arbitrage opportunity is a situation in which two securities (or port-

BDeH CHAPTER 9

folios) with *identical* cash flows have different prices. Because anyone can earn a sure profit in this situation by buying the low-priced security and selling the high-priced one, we expect investors to immediately exploit and eliminate these opportunities. Thus, in a normal market, arbitrage opportunities will not be found.

The efficient markets hypothesis is best expressed in terms of returns, as described in Eq. 9.2. This equation states that securities with *equivalent risk* should have the same *expected return*. The efficient markets hypothesis is, therefore, incomplete without a definition of "equivalent risk." Furthermore, different investors may perceive risks and returns differently (based on their information and preferences). There is no reason to expect the efficient markets hypothesis to hold perfectly; rather, it is best viewed as an idealized approximation for highly competitive markets.

The question of equivalent risk is one that we will ponder later in the text. In the following chapters, we will develop an understanding of the historical tradeoff between risk and return, learn how to measure the relevant risk of a security, and develop a way to estimate a security's expected return given its risk.

Concept Check

11. State the efficient markets hypothesis.

12. What are the implications of the efficient markets hypothesis for corporate managers?

BDeH CHAPTER 9

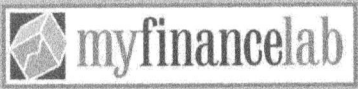

Here is what you should know after reading this chapter. MyFinanceLab will help you identify what you know, and where to go when you need to practice.

Key Points and Equations	Terms	Online Practice Opportunities
9.1 Stock Basics ▶ Ownership in a corporation is divided into shares of stock. These shares carry rights to share in the profits of the firm through future dividend payments.	common stock, p. 285 ticker symbol, p. 284	MyFinanceLab Study Plan 9.1
9.2 The Dividend-Discount Model ▶ The valuation principle states that the value of a stock is equal to the present value of the dividends and future sale price the investor will receive. Because these cash flows are risky, they must be discounted at the equity cost of capital, which is the expected return of other securities available in the market with equivalent risk to the firm's equity. The total return of a stock is equal to the dividend yield plus the capital gain rate. The expected total return of a stock should equal its equity cost of capital: $$r_E = \frac{Div_1 + P_1}{P_0} - 1 = \underbrace{\frac{Div_1}{P_0}}_{\text{Dividend Yield}} + \underbrace{\frac{P_1 - P_0}{P_0}}_{\text{Capital Gain Rate}} \quad (9.2)$$	capital gain, p. 287 capital gain rate, p. 287 dividend-discount model, p. 289 dividend yield, p. 287 equity cost of capital, p. 287 total return, p. 287	MyFinanceLab Study Plan 9.2 Using Excel: Building a Dividend Discount Model

▶ When investors have the same beliefs, the dividend-discount model states that, for any horizon N, the stock price satisfies the following equation:

$$P_0 = \frac{Div_1}{1 + r_E} + \frac{Div_2}{(1 + r_E)^2} + \cdots + \frac{Div_N}{(1 + r_E)^N} + \frac{P_N}{(1 + r_E)^N} \quad (9.4)$$

▶ If the stock eventually pays dividends and is never acquired, the dividend-discount model implies that the stock price equals the present value of all future dividends.

9.3 Estimating Dividends in the Dividend-Discount Model

▶ The constant dividend growth model assumes that dividends grow at a constant expected rate, g. In that case, g is also the expected capital gain rate, and

$$P_0 = \frac{Div_1}{r_E - g} \quad (9.6)$$

▶ Future dividends depend on earnings, shares outstanding, and the dividend payout rate:

$$Div_t = \underbrace{\frac{Earnings_t}{Shares\ Outstanding_t}}_{EPS_t} \times Dividend\ Payout\ Rate_t \quad (9.8)$$

▶ If the dividend payout rate and the number of shares outstanding is constant, and if earnings change only as a result of new investment from retained earnings, then the growth rate of the firm's earnings, dividends, and share price is calculated as follows:

$$g = Retention\ Rate \times Return\ on\ New\ Investment \quad (9.12)$$

▶ Cutting the firm's dividend to increase investment will raise the stock price if, and only if, the new investments have a positive NPV.

▶ If the firm has a long-term growth rate of g after the period $N + 1$, then we can apply the dividend-discount model and use the constant dividend growth formula to estimate the terminal stock value P_N.

▶ The dividend-discount model is sensitive to the dividend growth rate, which is difficult to estimate accurately.

constant dividend growth model, p. 290
dividend payout rate, p. 291
retention rate, p. 292

MyFinanceLab
Study Plan 9.3

9.4 Total Payout and Free Cash Flow Valuation Models

▶ If the firm undertakes share repurchases, it is more reliable to use the total payout model to value the firm. In this model, the value of equity equals the present value of future total dividends and repurchases. To determine the stock price, we divide the equity value by the initial number of shares outstanding of the firm:

$$P_0 = \frac{PV(Future\ Total\ Dividends\ and\ Repurchases)}{Shares\ Outstanding_0} \quad (9.15)$$

discounted free cash flow model, p. 299
share repurchase, p. 298
total payout model, p. 298
weighted average cost of capital (WACC), p. 300

MyFinanceLab
Study Plan 9.4
Interactive
Discounted
Cash Flow
Valuation

▶ The growth rate of the firm's total payout is governed by the growth rate of earnings, not earnings per share.

When a firm has leverage, it is more reliable to use the discounted free cash flow model. In this model, the enterprise value of the firm equals the present value of the firm's future free cash flow:

$$V_0 = PV(\text{Future Free Cash Flow of Firm}) \qquad (9.18)$$

▶ We discount cash flows using the weighted average cost of capital, which is the expected return the firm must pay to investors to compensate them for the risk of holding the firm's debt and equity together.

▶ We can estimate a terminal enterprise value by assuming free cash flow grows at a constant rate (typically equal to the rate of long-run revenue growth).

▶ We determine the stock price by subtracting debt and adding cash to the enterprise value, and then dividing by the initial number of shares outstanding of the firm:

$$P_0 = \frac{V_0 + \text{Cash}_0 - \text{Debt}_0}{\text{Shares Outstanding}_0} \qquad (9.19)$$

9.5 Valuation Based on Comparable Firms

▶ We can also value stocks by using valuation multiples based on comparable firms. Multiples commonly used for this purpose include the P/E ratio and the ratio of enterprise value to EBITDA. When we use multiples, we assume that comparable firms have the same risk and future growth as the firm being valued.

▶ No valuation model provides a definitive value for the stock. It is best to use several methods to identify a reasonable range for the value.

forward earnings, p. 304
forward P/E, p. 304
method of comparables, p. 303
trailing earnings, p. 304
trailing P/E, p. 304
valuation multiple, p. 304

MyFinanceLab Study Plan 9.5

9.6 Information, Competition, and Stock Prices

▶ Stock prices aggregate the information of many investors. Therefore, if our valuation disagrees with the stock's market price, it is most likely an indication that our assumptions about the firm's cash flows are wrong.

Competition between investors tends to eliminate positive-NPV trading opportunities. Competition will be strongest when information is public and easy to interpret. Privately informed traders may be able to profit from their information, which is reflected in prices only gradually.

▶ The efficient markets hypothesis states that competition eliminates all positive-NPV trades, which is equivalent to stating that securities with equivalent risk have the same expected returns.

efficient markets hypothesis, p. 311

MyFinanceLab Study Plan 9.6

BDeH CHAPTER 9

> In an efficient market, investors will not find positive-NPV trading opportunities without some source of competitive advantage. By contrast, the average investor will earn a fair return on his or her investment.

> In an efficient market, to raise the stock price, corporate managers should focus on maximizing the present value of the free cash flow from the firm's investments, rather than accounting consequences or financial policy.

Review Questions

1. What rights come with a share of stock?

2. Which two components make up the total return to an investor in a share of stock?

3. What does the dividend-discount model say about valuing shares of stock?

4. What is the relationship between the NPV of reinvesting cash flows and the change in the price of the stock?

5. How can the dividend-discount model be used with changing growth rates in future dividends?

6. What are share repurchases, and how can they be incorporated into the valuation of a stock?

7. What is the intuition behind valuation by multiples, and what are the limitations of this technique?

8. What is an efficient market?

9. How do interactions in a market lead to information being incorporated into stock prices?

10. Why does market efficiency lead a manager to focus on NPV and free cash flow?

Problems

All problems in this chapter are available in MyFinanceLab. An asterisk (*) indicates problems with a higher level of difficulty.

The Dividend-Discount Model

1. Assume Evco, Inc., has a current stock price of $50 and will pay a $2 dividend in one year; its equity cost of capital is 15%. What price must you expect Evco stock to sell for immediately after the firm pays the dividend in one year to justify its current price?

2. Anle Corporation has a current stock price of $20 and is expected to pay a dividend of $1 in one year. Its expected stock price right after paying that dividend is $22.
   a. What is Anle's equity cost of capital?
   b. How much of Anle's equity cost of capital is expected to be satisfied by dividend yield and how much by capital gain?

3. Suppose Acap Corporation will pay a dividend of $2.80 per share at the end of this year and a dividend of $3.00 per share next year. You expect Acap's stock price to be $52.00 in two years. Assume that Acap's equity cost of capital is 10%.
   a. What price would you be willing to pay for a share of Acap stock today, if you planned to hold the stock for two years?
   b. Suppose instead you plan to hold the stock for one year. For what price would you expect to be able to sell a share of Acap stock in one year?
   c. Given your answer to part (b), what price would you be willing to pay for a share of Acap stock today, if you planned to hold the stock for one year? How does this price compare to your answer in part (a)?

4. Krell Industries has a share price of $22.00 today. If Krell is expected to pay a dividend of $0.88 this year and its stock price is expected to grow to $23.54 at the end of the year, what is Krell's dividend yield and equity cost of capital?

Estimating Dividends in the Dividend-Discount Model

5. NoGrowth Corporation currently pays a dividend of $0.50 per quarter, and it will continue to pay this dividend forever. What is the price per share of NoGrowth stock if the firm's equity cost of capital is 15%?

6. Summit Systems will pay a dividend of $1.50 this year. If you expect Summit's dividend to grow by 6% per year, what is its price per share if the firm's equity cost of capital is 11%?

7. Dorpac Corporation has a dividend yield of 1.5%. Its equity cost of capital is 8%, and its dividends are expected to grow at a constant rate.
   a. What is the expected growth rate of Dorpac's dividends?
   b. What is the expected growth rate of Dorpac's share price?

8. Laurel Enterprises expects earnings next year of $4 per share and has a 70% retention rate, which it plans to keep constant. Its equity cost of capital is 10%, which is also its expected return on new investment. If its earnings are expected to grow forever at a rate of 4% per year, what do you estimate the firm's current stock price to be?

*9. DFB, Inc., expects earnings this year of $5 per share, and it plans to pay a $3 dividend to shareholders. DFB will retain $2 per share of its earnings to reinvest in new projects that have an expected return of 15% per year. Suppose DFB will maintain the same dividend payout rate, retention rate, and return on new investments in the future and will not change its number of outstanding shares.
   a. What growth rate of earnings would you forecast for DFB?
   b. If DFB's equity cost of capital is 12%, what price would you estimate for DFB stock?
   c. Suppose instead that DFB paid a dividend of $4 per share this year and retained only $1 per share in earnings. If DFB maintains this higher payout rate in the future, what stock price would you estimate for the firm now? Should DFB raise its dividend?

10. Cooperton Mining just announced it will cut its dividend from $4 to $2.50 per share and use the extra funds to expand. Prior to the announcement, Cooperton's dividends were expected to grow at a 3% rate, and its share price was $50. With the planned expansion, Cooperton's dividends are expected to grow at a 5% rate. What share price would you expect after the announcement? (Assume that the new expansion does not change Cooperton's risk.) Is the expansion a positive-NPV investment?

11. Gillette Corporation will pay an annual dividend of $0.65 one year from now. Analysts expect this dividend to grow at 12% per year thereafter until the fifth year. After then, growth will level off at 2% per year. According to the dividend-discount model, what is the value of a share of Gillette stock if the firm's equity cost of capital is 8%?

12. Colgate-Palmolive Company has just paid an annual dividend of $0.96. Analysts are predicting an 11% per year growth rate in earnings over the next five years. After then, Colgate's earnings are expected to grow at the current industry average of 5.2% per year. If Colgate's equity cost of capital is 8.5% per year and its dividend payout ratio remains constant, for what price does the dividend-discount model predict Colgate stock should sell?

*13. Halliford Corporation expects to have earnings this coming year of $3 per share. Halliford plans to retain all of its earnings for the next two years. Then, for the subsequent two years, the firm will retain 50% of its earnings. It will retain 20% of its earnings from that point onward. Each year, retained earnings will be invested in new projects with an expected return of 25% per year. Any earnings that are not retained will be paid out as dividends. Assume Halliford's share count remains constant and all earnings growth comes from the investment of retained earnings. If Halliford's equity cost of capital is 10%, what price would you estimate for Halliford stock?

The Total Payout and Free Cash Flow Valuation Models

14. Suppose Cisco Systems pays no dividends but spent $5 billion on share repurchases last year. If Cisco's equity cost of capital is 12%, and if the amount spent on repurchases is expected to grow by 8% per year, estimate Cisco's market capitalization. If Cisco has 6 billion shares outstanding, to what stock price does this correspond?

*15. Maynard Steel plans to pay a dividend of $3 this year. The company has an expected earnings growth rate of 4% per year and an equity cost of capital of 10%.
   a. Assuming that Maynard's dividend payout rate and expected growth rate remain constant, and that the firm does not issue or repurchase shares, estimate Maynard's share price.
   b. Suppose Maynard decides to pay a dividend of $1 this year and to use the remaining $2 per share to repurchase shares. If Maynard's total payout rate remains constant, estimate Maynard's share price.
   c. If Maynard maintains the dividend and total payout rate given in part (b), at what rates are Maynard's dividends and earnings per share expected to grow?

16. Heavy Metal Corporation is expected to generate the following free cash flows over the next five years:

Year	1	2	3	4	5
FCF ($ million)	53	68	78	75	82

After then, the free cash flows are expected to grow at the industry average of 4% per year. Using the discounted free cash flow model and a weighted average cost of capital of 14%:
a. Estimate the enterprise value of Heavy Metal.
b. If Heavy Metal has no excess cash, debt of $300 million, and 40 million shares outstanding, estimate its share price.

 17. Sora Industries has 60 million outstanding shares, $120 million in debt, $40 million in cash, and the following projected free cash flow for the next four years:

	Year	0	1	2	3	4
1						
2	Earnings and FCF Forecast ($ million)					
3	Sales	433.0	468.0	516.0	547.0	574.3
4	Growth versus Prior Year		8.1%	10.3%	6.0%	5.0%
5	Cost of Goods Sold		−313.3	−345.7	−366.5	−384.8
6	Gross Profit		154.4	170.3	180.5	189.5
7	Selling, General, and Administrative		−93.6	−103.2	−109.4	−114.9
8	Depreciation		−7.0	−7.5	−9.0	−9.5
9	EBIT		53.8	59.6	62.1	65.2
10	Less: Income Tax at 40%		−21.5	−23.8	−24.8	−26.1
11	Plus: Depreciation		7.0	7.5	9.0	9.5
12	Less: Capital Expenditures		−7.7	−10.0	−9.9	−10.4
13	Less: Increase in NWC		−6.3	−8.6	−5.6	−4.9
14	Free Cash Flow		25.3	24.6	30.8	33.3

a. Suppose Sora's revenues and free cash flow are expected to grow at a 5% rate beyond year 4. If Sora's weighted average cost of capital is 10%, what is the value of Sora's stock based on this information?
b. Sora's cost of goods sold was assumed to be 67% of sales. If its cost of goods sold is actually 70% of sales, how would the estimate of the stock's value change?
c. Return to the assumptions of part (a) and suppose Sora can maintain its cost of goods sold at 67% of sales. However, the firm reduces its selling, general, and administrative expenses from 20% of sales to 16% of sales. What stock price would you estimate now? (Assume no other expenses, except taxes, are affected.)
*d. Sora's net working capital needs were estimated to be 18% of sales (their current level in year 0). If Sora can reduce this requirement to 12% of sales starting in year 1, but all other assumptions remain as in part (a), what stock price do you estimate for Sora? (*Hint:* This change will have the largest effect on Sora's free cash flow in year 1.)

BDeH CHAPTER 9

18. Consider the valuation of Kenneth Cole Productions given in Example 9.7.

    a. Suppose you believe KCP's initial revenue growth rate will be between 7% and 11% (with growth slowing linearly to 4% by year 2011). What range of prices for KCP stock is consistent with these forecasts?

    b. Suppose you believe KCP's initial revenue EBIT margin will be between 8% and 10% of sales. What range of prices for KCP stock is consistent with these forecasts?

    c. Suppose you believe KCP's weighted average cost of capital is between 10.5% and 12%. What range of prices for KCP stock is consistent with these forecasts?

    d. What range of stock prices is consistent if you vary the estimates as in parts (a), (b), and (c) simultaneously?

Valuation Based on Comparable Firms

19. You notice that Dell Computers has a stock price of $27.85 and EPS of $1.26. Its competitor Hewlett-Packard has EPS of $2.47. What is one estimate of the value of a share of Hewlett-Packard stock?

 20. Suppose that in January 2006, Kenneth Cole Productions had EPS of $1.65 and a book value of equity of $12.05 per share.

    a. Using the average P/E multiple in Table 9.1, estimate KCP's share price.

    b. What range of share prices do you estimate based on the highest and lowest P/E multiples in Table 9.1?

    c. Using the average price to book value multiple in Table 9.1, estimate KCP's share price.

    d. What range of share prices do you estimate based on the highest and lowest price to book value multiples in Table 9.1?

 21. Suppose that in January 2006, Kenneth Cole Productions had sales of $518 million, EBITDA of $55.6 million, excess cash of $100 million, $3 million of debt, and 21 million shares outstanding.

    a. Using the average enterprise value to sales multiple in Table 9.1, estimate KCP's share price.

    b. What range of share prices do you estimate based on the highest and lowest enterprise value to sales multiples in Table 9.1?

    c. Using the average enterprise value to EBITDA multiple in Table 9.1, estimate KCP's share price.

    d. What range of share prices do you estimate based on the highest and lowest enterprise value to EBITDA multiples in Table 9.1?

 22. In addition to footwear, Kenneth Cole Productions designs and sells handbags, apparel, and other accessories. Given this span of operations, you decide to consider comparables for KCP outside the footwear industry.

    a. Suppose that Fossil, Inc., has an enterprise value to EBITDA multiple of 9.73 and a P/E multiple of 18.4. What price would you estimate for KCP stock using each of these multiples, based on the data for KCP given in Problems 19 and 21?

    b. Suppose that Tommy Hilfiger Corporation has an enterprise value to EBITDA multiple of 7.19 and a P/E multiple of 17.2. What price would you estimate for KCP stock using each of these multiples, based on the data for KCP given in Problems 19 and 21?

*23. Suppose Rocky Shoes and Boots has earnings per share of $2.30 and EBITDA of $30.7 million. The firm also has 5.4 million shares outstanding and debt of $125 million (net of cash). You believe Deckers Outdoor Corporation is comparable to

Rocky Shoes and Boots in terms of its underlying business, but Deckers has no debt. If Deckers has a P/E of 13.3 and an enterprise value to EBITDA multiple of 7.4, estimate the value of Rocky Shoes and Boots stock using both multiples. Which estimate is likely to be more accurate?

 24. Consider the following data for the auto industry in mid-2007 (EV = enterprise value, BV = book value, NM = not meaningful because the divisor is negative). Discuss the usefulness of using multiples to value an auto company.

Company Name	Market Cap ($ million)	EV ($ million)	EV/Sales	EV/EBITDA	EV/EBIT	P/E	P/BV
Honda Motor Company Ltd.	62,539.5	92,258.5	1.0	8.9	11.5	12.0	1.6
DaimlerChrysler AG	108,692.8	205,823.76	1.2	9.9	31.8	14.0	2.2
Nissan Motor Company Ltd.	45,072.2	83,307.2	1.2	6.4	11.7	11.1	1.4
Volkswagen AG	101,611.8	129,151.4	0.9	6.9	17.0	20.6	2.5
General Motors Corporation	22,629.2	191,232.4	1.0	9.0	15.7	NM	NM
PSA Peugeot Citroen	19,979.7	53,947.8	0.3	144.1	184.7	109.2	1.0
Ford Motor Company	18,392.4	156,428.4	1.0	18.2	NM	NM	NM
Mitsubishi Motors Corporation	8,730.4	9,970.4	0.4	10.7	52.5	117.3	3.5
Daihatsu Motor Company Ltd.	4,355.93	5440.0	0.1	5.0	11.7	14.8	1.6

Sources: Company financial reports, Reuters, Marketwatch (from Dow Jones), Yahoo Finance.

Information, Competition, and Stock Prices

25. You read in the paper that Summit Systems (from Problem 6) has revised its growth prospects and now expects its dividends to grow at a rate of 3% per year forever.
    a. What is the new value of a share of Summit Systems stock based on this information?
    b. If you tried to sell your Summit Systems stock after reading this news, what price would you be likely to get? Why?

26. Assume that it is mid-2006, when Coca-Cola Company had a share price of $43. The firm paid a dividend of $1.24, and you expect Coca-Cola to raise this dividend by approximately 7% per year in perpetuity.
    a. If Coca-Cola's equity cost of capital is 8%, what share price would you expect based on your estimate of the dividend growth rate?
    b. Given Coca-Cola's share price, what would you conclude about your assessment of Coca-Cola's future dividend growth?

27. Roybus, Inc., a manufacturer of flash memory, just reported that its main production facility in Taiwan was destroyed in a fire. Although the plant was fully insured, the loss of production will decrease Roybus's free cash flow by $180 million at the end of this year and by $60 million at the end of next year.
    a. If Roybus has 35 million shares outstanding and a weighted average cost of capital of 13%, what change in Roybus's stock price would you expect upon this announcement? (Assume the value of Roybus's debt is not affected by the event.)
    b. Would you expect to be able to sell Roybus's stock on hearing this announcement and make a profit? Explain.

BDeH CHAPTER 9

*28. Apnex, Inc., is a biotechnology firm that is about to announce the results of its clinical trials of a potential new cancer drug. If the trials were successful, Apnex stock will be worth $70 per share. If the trials were unsuccessful, Apnex stock will be worth $18 per share. Suppose that the morning before the announcement is scheduled, Apnex shares are trading for $55 per share.

   a. Based on the current share price, what sort of expectations do investors seem to have about the success of the trials?

   b. Suppose hedge fund manager Paul Kliner has hired several prominent research scientists to examine the public data on the drug and make their own assessment of the drug's promise. Would Kliner's fund be likely to profit by trading the stock in the hours prior to the announcement?

   c. Which factors would limit the ability of Kliner's fund to profit on its information?

Data Case

As a new junior analyst for a large brokerage firm, you are anxious to demonstrate the skills you learned in college and prove that you are worth your attractive salary. Your first assignment is to analyze the stock of General Electric Corporation. Your boss recommends determining prices based on both the dividend-discount model and the discounted free cash flow valuation methods. GE has a cost of equity of 10.5% and an after-tax weighted average cost of capital of 7.5%. The expected return on its new investments is 12%. You are a little concerned about your boss's recommendation because your finance professor has told you that these two valuation methods can result in widely differing estimates when applied to real data. You are really hoping that the two methods will reach similar prices. Good luck with that!

1. Go to Yahoo! Finance (http://finance.yahoo.com) and enter the symbol for General Electric (GE). From the main page for GE, gather the following information and enter it onto a spreadsheet:
   a. The current stock price (last trade) at the top of the page.
   b. The current dividend amount, which is in the bottom-right cell in the same box as the stock price.

2. Click on "Key Statistics" at the left side of the page. From the Key Statistics page, gather the following information and enter it on the same spreadsheet:
   a. The number of shares of stock outstanding.
   b. The payout ratio.

3. Click on "Analyst Estimates" at the left side of the page. On the Analyst Estimates page, find the expected growth rate for the next five years and enter it onto your spreadsheet. It will be near the very bottom of the page.

4. Click on "Income Statement" near the bottom of the menu on the left. Place the cursor in the middle of the income statements and right-click. Select "Export to Microsoft Excel." Copy and paste the entire three years' worth of income statements into a new worksheet in your existing Excel file. Repeat this process for both the balance sheet and the cash flow statement for General Electric. Keep all of the different statements in the same Excel worksheet.

5. To determine the stock value based on the dividend-discount model:
   a. Create a timeline in Excel for five years.
   b. Use the dividend obtained from Yahoo! Finance as the current dividend to forecast the next five annual dividends based on the five-year growth rate.

   c. Determine the long-term growth rate based on GE's payout ratio (which is 1 minus the retention ratio) using Eq. 9.12.

   d. Use the long-term growth rate to determine the stock price for year 5 using Eq. 9.13.

   e. Determine the current stock price using the approach from Example 9.5.

6. To determine the stock value based on the discounted free cash flow method:

   a. Forecast the free cash flows using the historic data from the financial statements downloaded from Yahoo! Finance to compute the three-year average of the following ratios:

      i. EBIT/sales

      ii. Tax rate (income tax expense/income before tax)

      iii. Property plant and equipment/sales

      iv. Depreciation/property plant and equipment

      v. Net working capital/sales

   b. Create a timeline for the next seven years.

   c. Forecast future sales based on the most recent year's total revenue growing at the five-year growth rate from Yahoo! Finance for the first five years and then at the long-term growth rate for years 6 and 7.

   d. Use the average ratios computed in part (a) to forecast EBIT, property, plant and equipment, depreciation, and net working capital for the next seven years.

   e. Forecast the free cash flow for the next seven years using Eq. 9.17.

   f. Determine the horizon enterprise value for year 5 using Eq. 9.21.

   g. Determine the enterprise value of the firm as the present value of the free cash flows.

   h. Determine the stock price using Eq. 9.19.

7. Compare the stock prices produced by the two methods to the actual stock price. What recommendations can you make as to whether clients should buy or sell General Electric's stock based on your price estimates?

8. Explain to your boss why the estimates from the two valuation methods differ. Specifically address the assumptions implicit in the models themselves as well as the assumptions you made in preparing your analysis. Why do these estimates differ from the actual stock price of GE?

Chapter 9 APPENDIX

Using Excel to Build a Dividend-Discount Model

In this appendix, we show how to build a flexible model in Excel that computes the current price and year-by-year expected price for a stock based on the dividend-discount model. The model we will build allows you to vary the expected growth rate in earnings and the dividend payout rate year-by-year up until the sixth year. It also gives you the flexibility to see how changes in your assumption about the equity cost of capital change your computed stock prices. The numerical values in the spreadsheet are based on Example 9.5.

Compute Future Earnings

To make the spreadsheet as flexible as possible, we enter the past year's earnings and expected growth rates and let it compute future earnings. That way, we have to change only the past earnings or any of the future growth rates as our assumptions change; the spreadsheet will automatically update the future expected earnings. In the screenshot below, we enter the numbers in blue; the formulas in black instruct Excel how to compute the cell contents. For example, cell F4 is next year's expected EPS and is computed using this past year's EPS ($2, found in cell E4) and the expected growth rate (20%, or 0.2, found in cell F3). We proceed through year 6 in the same way—each year's earnings are computed as the previous year's earnings multiplied by 1 plus the growth rate.

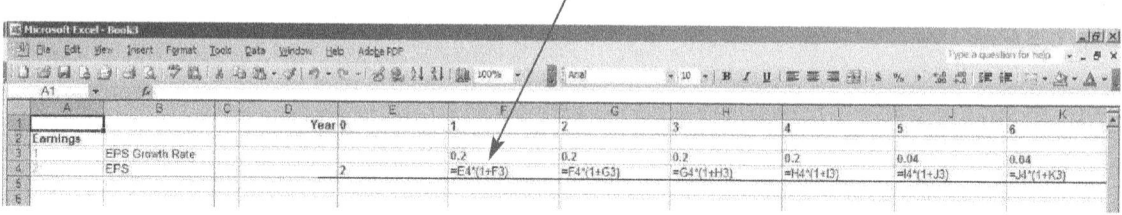

Calculate Expected Dividends

Next, we translate these projected EPS numbers into dividends to apply the dividend-discount model. We do so by adding a line determining the dividend payout ratio each year. Here, we assume that the company will not pay any dividends in years 1–3, and will then pay 60% of its earnings as dividends thereafter. Finally, we compute the expected dividends as the EPS in row 4 multiplied by the dividend payout ratio in row 6.

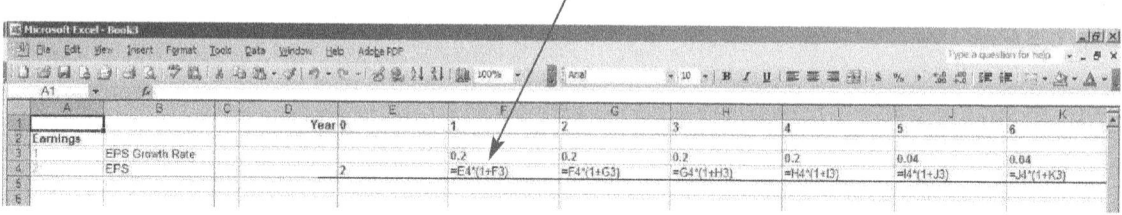

After we complete this step, the entered and calculated values are as follows:

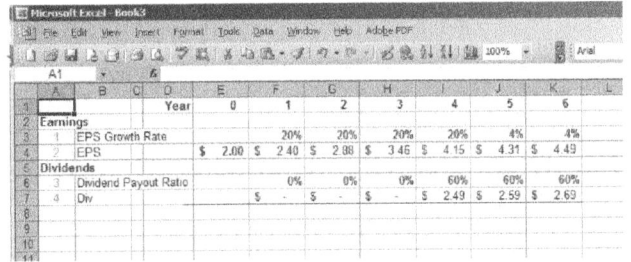

Determine the Stock Price

Now we are ready for the final step, which is to compute the stock price. To do so, we need an equity cost of capital, which we enter into cell F9. We also need to make an assumption about dividends from year 6 onward. We decide to apply the constant growth model, so that the value of the stock in year 5 is equal to the dividend in year 6 divided by the equity cost of capital minus the dividend growth rate, which in this case is equal to the EPS growth rate. Once we have the year 5 price, we can compute the year 4 price as the one-year discounted value of the dividend in year 5 (cell J7) plus the price of the stock in year 5 (cell J10). As a discount rate, we use the equity cost of capital (cell F9). We continue this way until we get to the year 0 (current) price.

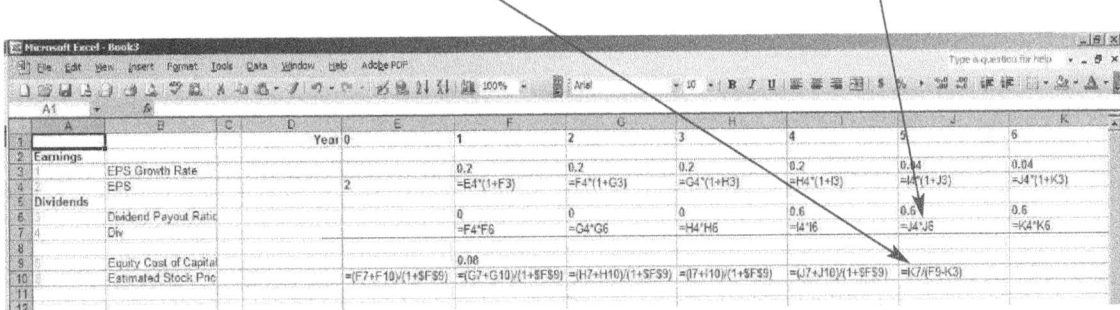

The final spreadsheet will look like the screenshot below. Because we built it with flexibility in mind, we can change any of the numbers in blue and immediately see the effect on the current and future stock prices.

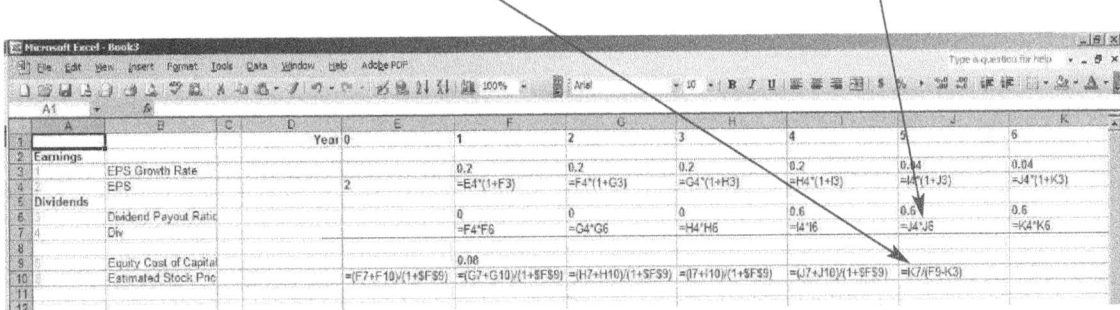

Pages 328–361 intentionally omitted

This page intentionally left blank

11

Systematic Risk and the Equity Risk Premium

LEARNING OBJECTIVES

- Calculate the expected return and volatility (standard deviation) of a portfolio

- Understand the relation between systematic risk and the market portfolio

- Measure systematic risk

- Use the Capital Asset Pricing Model (CAPM) to compute the cost of equity capital for a stock

notation

β_i	beta of security i with respect to the market portfolio
$Corr(R_i, R_j)$	correlation between the returns of security i and security j
$E[R_i]$	expected return of security i
$E[R_{Mkt}]$	expected return of the market portfolio
MV_i	total market value (market capitalization) of security i
N_i	number of shares outstanding of security i
P_i	price per share of security i

r_f	risk-free interest rate
r_i	required return of security i; cost of capital for investing in traded security i
R_i	return of security i
R_P	return of portfolio P
$SD(R_i)$	standard deviation (volatility) of the return of security i
$Var(R_i)$	variance of the return of security i
w_i	fraction of the portfolio invested in security i (its relative *weight* in the portfolio)

Pages 363–374 intentionally omitted

FIGURE 11.4   Volatility of an Equally Weighted Portfolio Versus the Number of Stocks

The graph in panel (b) is based on the data in panel (a). Note that the volatility declines as we increase the number of stocks in the portfolio. Yet even in a very large portfolio, systematic (market) risk remains. Also note that the volatility declines at a decreasing rate (the effect of going from one to two stocks, an 8 percentage point decrease in volatility, is bigger than the effect of going from 4 to 5 stocks, a 1.1 percentage point decrease). The graph is formed based on the assumption that each stock has a volatility of 40% and a correlation with other stocks of 0.28. Both are average for large stocks in the United States.

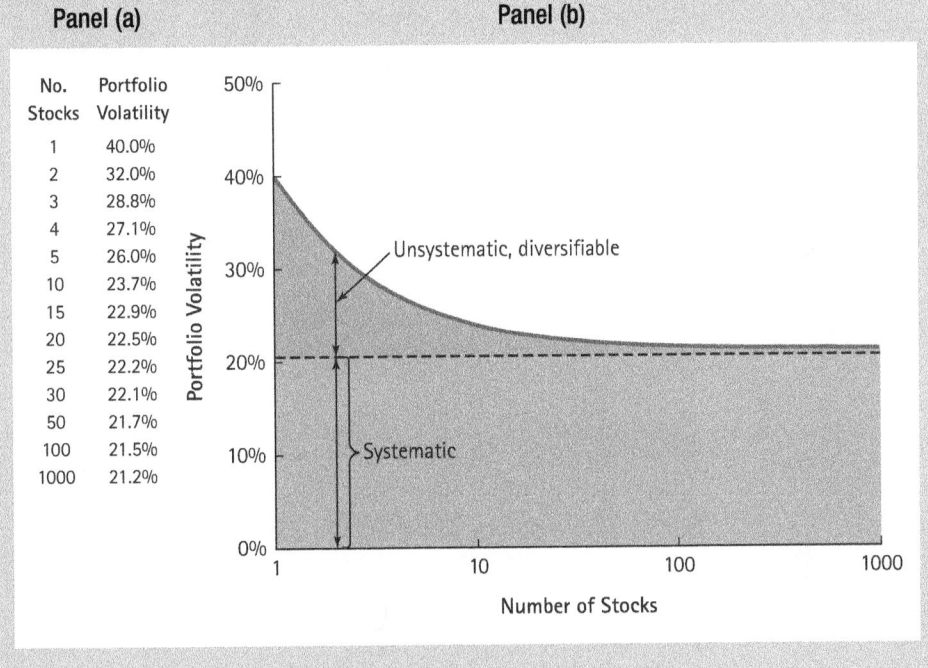

Panel (a)

No. Stocks	Portfolio Volatility
1	40.0%
2	32.0%
3	28.8%
4	27.1%
5	26.0%
10	23.7%
15	22.9%
20	22.5%
25	22.2%
30	22.1%
50	21.7%
100	21.5%
1000	21.2%

Panel (b)

portfolio by diversification. The benefit of diversification is most dramatic initially—the decrease in volatility going from one to two stocks is much larger than the decrease going from 100 to 101 stocks. Even for a very large portfolio, however, we cannot eliminate all of the risk—the systematic risk remains.

Concept Check

3. What determines how much risk will be eliminated by combining stocks in a portfolio?

4. When do stocks have more or less correlation?

11.3   Measuring Systematic Risk

Our goal is to understand the impact of risk on the firm's investors. By understanding how they view risk, we can quantify the relation between risk and required return to produce a discount rate for our present value calculations. In Chapter 10, we established that the only risk that is related to return is systematic risk, but standard deviation measures *total* risk, including the unsystematic part. We need a way to measure just the systematic risk of an investment opportunity. The previous section contains two important insights that we will now build on to determine the sensitivity of individual stocks to risk. To recap:

1. *The amount of a stock's risk that is removed by diversification depends on its correlation with other stocks in the portfolio.* For example, we showed in Example 11.3 that much less of Apple's risk is diversified away in a portfolio with Microsoft than in a portfolio with Starbucks.

2. *If you build a large enough portfolio, you can remove all unsystematic risk by diversification, but you will still be left with systematic risk.* Figure 11.4 shows that as the number of stocks in your portfolio grows, the unsystematic positive and negative events affecting only a few stocks will cancel out, leaving systematic events as the only source of risk for the portfolio.

Role of the Market Portfolio

As we explained in the last chapter, investors should diversify their portfolios in order to reduce their risk. If investors choose their portfolios optimally, they will do so until no further diversifiable risk is present, and only systematic risk remains. Let's assume that all investors behave in this way; that is

Suppose all investors hold portfolios that only contain systematic risk.

market portfolio The portfolio of all risky investments, held in proportion to their value.

If that is the case, then consider the portfolio we obtain by combining the portfolios of every investor. Because each investors' portfolio only contains systematic risk, the same is true for this "aggregate" portfolio. So, the aggregate portfolio held by all investors is a fully-diversified, optimal portfolio. Moreover, we can identify this portfolio: Because all securities are held by someone, the aggregate portfolio contains all shares outstanding of every risky security. We call this portfolio the **market portfolio**.

To illustrate, imagine that there are only two companies in the world, each with 1000 shares outstanding:

	Number of Shares Outstanding	Price Per Share	Market Capitalization
Company A	1,000	$40	$40,000
Company B	1,000	$10	$10,000

market capitalization The total market value of equity; equals the market price per share times the number of shares.

In this simple setting, the market portfolio consists of 1000 shares of each stock and has a total value of $50,000. Stock A's portfolio weight is therefore 80% ($40,000/$50,000) and B's is 20% ($10,000/$50,000). Because all of the shares of A and all of the shares of B must be held by someone, the sum of all investors' portfolios must equal this market portfolio. Note from this example that the portfolio weight of each stock is proportional to the total market value of its outstanding shares, which is called its **market capitalization**:

$$\text{Market Capitalization} = (\text{Number of Shares Outstanding})$$
$$\times (\text{Price per Share}) \qquad (11.5)$$

value-weighted portfolio A portfolio in which each security is held in proportion to its market capitalization.

More generally, the market portfolio will consist of all risky securities in the market, with portfolio weights proportional to their market capitalization. Thus, for example, if Microsoft's market capitalization were equal to 3% of the total market value of all securities, then it would have a 3% weight in the market portfolio. Because stocks are held in proportion to their market capitalization (value), we say that the market portfolio is **value-weighted**.

Because the market portfolio only contains systematic risk, we can use it to measure the amount of systematic risk of other securities in the market. In particular, any risk that is correlated with the market portfolio must be systematic risk. Therefore, by looking at the sensitivity of a stock's return to the overall market, we can calculate the amount of systematic risk the stock has.

Stock Market Indexes as the Market Portfolio

market proxy A portfolio whose return is believed to closely track the true market portfolio.

market index The market value of a broad-based portfolio of securities.

While the market portfolio is easy to identify, actually constructing it is a different matter. Because it should contain all risky securities, we need to include all stocks, bonds, real estate, commodities, etc. both in the United States and around the word. Clearly, it would be impractical if not impossible to collect and update returns on all risky assets everywhere. In practice, we use a **market proxy**—a portfolio whose return should track the underlying, unobservable market portfolio. The most common proxy portfolios are *market indexes,* which are broadly used to represent the performance of the stock market. A **market index** reports the value of a particular portfolio of securities.

Dow Jones Industrial Average. The most familiar stock index in the United States is the Dow Jones Industrial Average, or DJIA. This index consists of a portfolio of 30 large, industrial stocks. While these stocks are chosen to be representative of different sectors of the economy, they clearly do not represent the entire market. Despite being non-representative of the entire market, the DJIA remains widely cited because it is one of the oldest stock market indexes (it was first published in 1884).

S&P 500. A better representation of the entire U.S. stock market is the S&P 500, a value-weighted portfolio of 500 of the largest U.S. stocks.[3] The S&P 500 was the first widely publicized value-weighted index (S&P began publishing its index in 1923), and it is a standard benchmark for professional investors. This index is the most commonly cited index when evaluating the overall performance of the U.S. stock market. It is also the standard portfolio used to represent "the market" in practice. As we show in Figure 11.5, even though the S&P 500 includes only 500 of the over 7000 individual U.S. stocks, because the S&P 500 includes the largest stocks, it represents more than 70% of the U.S. stock market in terms of market capitalization.

Index Funds

One easy way investors can buy (an approximation of) the market portfolio is to invest in an index fund, which in turn invests in stocks and other securities with the goal of matching the performance of a particular market index. The Vanguard Group was the second largest mutual fund company in 2006 and it specializes in index funds. Vanguard was founded in 1975 by John Bogle, who advocates the benefits of index funds for individual investors. Comparing index funds to the strategy of trying to pick hot stocks, Bogle reportedly said: "What's the point of looking for the needle in the haystack? Why not own the haystack?"

In August of 1976, Vanguard created its well-known S&P 500 Index Fund, which tries to match the performance of the S&P 500 index as closely as possible. As of April 2008, this fund had over $100 billion in assets. Vanguard's Total Stock Market Index Fund is designed to track the performance of the MSCI US Broad Market index, an index that measures the performance of all U.S. stocks with available price data.

---

[3]There is no precise formula for determining which stocks will be included in the S&P 500. Standard & Poor's periodically replaces stocks in the index (on average about seven or eight stocks per year). While size is one criterion, Standard & Poor's also tries to maintain appropriate representation of different segments of the economy and chooses firms that are leaders in their industries.

FIGURE 11.5

The S&P 500

The panel (a) pie chart shows the 500 firms in the S&P 500 as a fraction of the approximately 7000 U.S. public firms. Panel (b) shows the S&P 500 firms' importance in terms of market capitalization—these 500 firms represent approximately 70% of the total capitalization of the 7000 public firms.

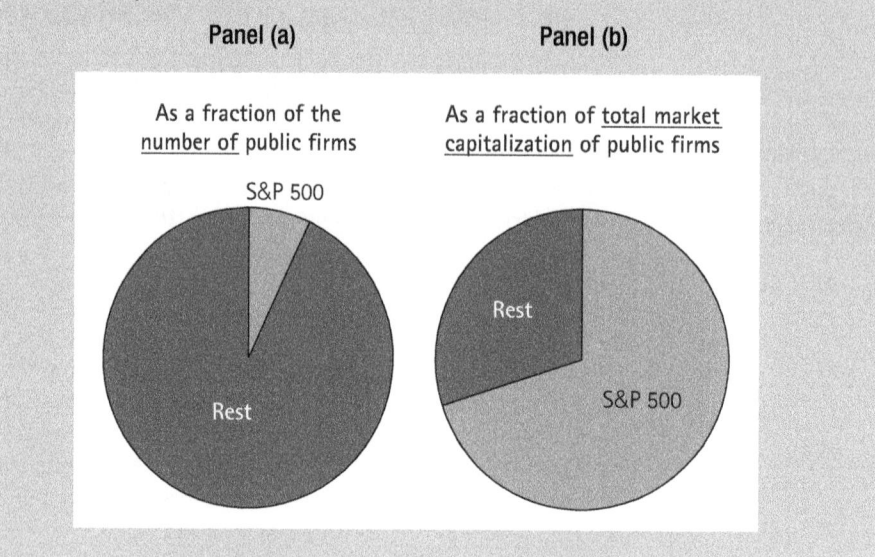

Panel (a)   **Panel (b)**

As a fraction of the <u>number of</u> public firms

As a fraction of <u>total market capitalization</u> of public firms

Market Risk and Beta

Now that we have established that the market portfolio is a good basis for measuring systematic risk, we can use the relation between an individual stock's returns and the market portfolio's returns to measure the amount of systematic risk present in that stock. The intuition is that if a stock's returns are highly sensitive to the market portfolio's returns, then that stock is highly sensitive to systematic risk. That is, events that are systematic and affect the whole market also are strongly reflected in its returns. If a stock's returns do not depend on the market's returns, then it has little systematic risk—when systematic events happen, they are not strongly reflected in its returns. So stocks whose returns are volatile *and* are highly correlated with the market's returns are the riskiest in the sense that they have the most systematic risk.

Specifically, we can measure a stock's systematic risk by estimating the stock's sensitivity to the market portfolio, which we refer to as its **beta** (β):

> *A stock's beta (β) is the percentage change in its return that we expect for each 1% change in the market's return.*

beta (β) The expected percent change in the excess return of a security for a 1% change in the excess return of the market (or other benchmark) portfolio.

There are many data sources that provide estimates of beta based on historical data. Typically, these data sources estimate betas using two to five years of weekly or monthly returns and use the S&P 500 as the market portfolio. Table 11.4 shows estimates of betas for a number of large stocks and their industries. You can find the betas of other companies by going to finance.google.com or finance.yahoo.com (for Yahoo!, click on "Key Statistics").

As we explain below, the beta of the overall market portfolio is 1, so you can think of a beta of 1 as representing average exposure to systematic risk. However, as the table demonstrates, many industries and companies have betas much higher or lower than 1. The differences in betas by industry are related to the sensitivity of each industry's profits

TABLE 11.4

Average Betas for Stocks by Industry (Based on Monthly Data from 2003–2007)

Industry	Average Beta	Ticker	Company	Beta
Personal and Household Prods.	0.4	PG	The Procter & Gamble Company	0.5
Food Processing	0.6	HNZ	H.J. Heinz Company	0.6
Electric Utilities	0.6	EIX	Edison International	0.7
Beverages (Alcoholic)	0.6	BUD	Anheuser-Busch Companies Inc.	0.5
Major Drugs	0.6	PFE	Pfizer Inc.	0.7
Beverages (Nonalcoholic)	0.6	KO	The Coca-Cola Company	0.8
Conglomerates	0.9	GE	General Electric Company	0.8
Retail (Grocery)	1.0	SWY	Safeway Inc.	0.5
Forestry and Wood Products	1.1	WY	Weyerhaeuser Company	1.1
Recreational Products	1.2	HDI	Harley-Davidson Inc.	1.1
Computer Services	1.2	GOOG	Google	1.2
Retail (Home Improvement)	1.2	HD	Home Depot Inc.	1.4
Restaurants	1.3	SBUX	Starbucks Corporation	0.6
Software and Programming	1.3	MSFT	Microsoft Corporation	1.0
Apparel/Accessories	1.3	LIZ	Liz Claiborne	0.8
Computer Hardware	1.6	AAPL	Apple Computer Inc.	1.4
Communications Equipment	1.6	MOT	Motorola	1.2
Auto and Truck Manufacturers	1.8	GM	General Motors Corporation	1.6
Semiconductors	2.2	INTC	Intel Corporation	1.6

Source: Reuters.

to the general health of the economy. For example, Intel and other technology stocks have high betas (near or above 1.5) because demand for their products usually varies with the business cycle (cyclical stocks): Companies tend to expand and upgrade their information technology infrastructure when times are good, but cut back on these expenditures when the economy slows. Thus, systematic events have a greater-than-average impact on these firms and their exposure to systematic risk is greater than average. On the other hand, the demand for personal and household products such as shampoo has very little relation to the state of the economy (stocks of companies providing these types of products are often

Common Mistake   Mixing Standard Deviation and Beta

Volatility (standard deviation) and beta are measured in different units (standard deviation is measured in % and beta is unitless). So even though total risk (volatility) is equal to the sum of systematic risk (measured by beta) and firm-specific risk, our measure of volatility does not have to be a bigger number than our measure for beta. To illustrate, consider Microsoft. It has total risk (volatility), measured as standard deviation, of 38% or 0.38 (see Table 11.3), but Table 11.4 shows that it has systematic risk, measured as a beta, of 1.0, which is greater than 0.38. Volatility (standard deviation) is measured in percentage terms, but beta is not, so 0.38 does not have to be greater than 1.0. For the same reason, it is possible for Starbucks to have a higher standard deviation than Microsoft (41%), but a lower beta (0.6). Figure 11.6 illustrates one possible breakdown of total risk for Microsoft and Starbucks that would be consistent with these data.

FIGURE 11.6

Systematic Versus Firm-Specific Risk in Microsoft and Starbucks

Beta, measuring systematic risk, and standard deviation, measuring total risk, are in different units. Even though Microsoft's total risk (standard deviation) is 0.38 (38%), its beta, measuring only systematic risk, is 1.0. In this case, the beta of 1.0 corresponds to a breakdown in total risk as depicted in the figure. Formally, the portion of Microsoft's total risk that is in common with the market is calculated by multiplying the correlation between Microsoft and the market by the standard deviation (total risk) of Microsoft. We can do a similar breakdown of Starbucks' risk. Note that Starbucks has more total, but less systematic, risk than Microsoft.

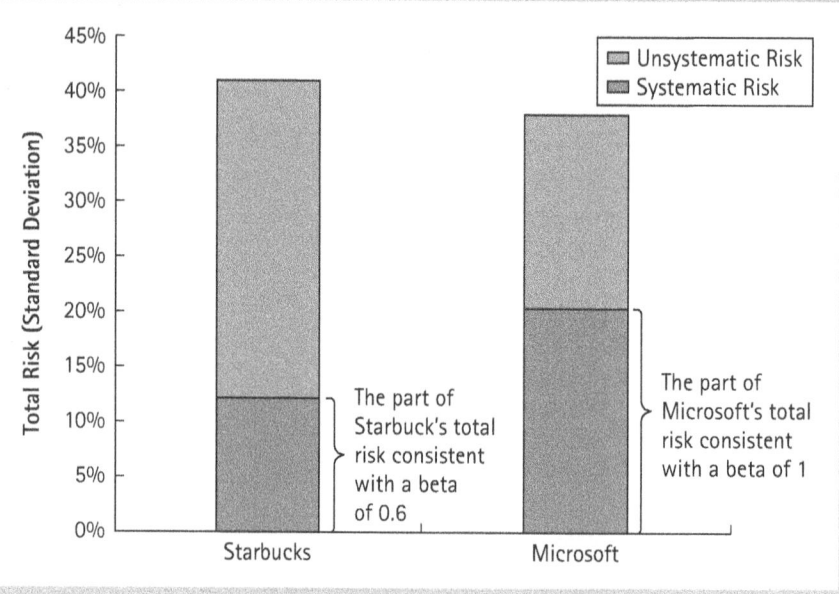

called defensive stocks). Firms producing these types of goods, such as Proctor and Gamble, tend to have low betas (near 0.5). Note also that even within an industry, each company's specific strategy and focus can lead to different exposures to systematic events, so that there is variation in beta even within industries (see, for example Starbucks in the restaurant industry and Liz Claiborne in the apparel industry).

EXAMPLE 11.4

Total Risk Versus Systematic Risk

Problem

Suppose that in the coming year, you expect Target stock to have a standard deviation of 30% and a beta of 1.2, and Starbuck's stock to have a standard deviation of 41% and a beta of 0.6. Which stock carries more total risk? Which has more systematic risk?

Solution

Plan

	Standard Deviation (Total Risk)	Beta (β) (Systematic Risk)
Target	30%	1.2
Starbucks	41%	0.6

Execute

Total risk is measured by standard deviation; therefore, Starbuck's stock has more total risk. Systematic risk is measured by beta. Target has a higher beta, and so has more systematic risk.

Evaluate

As we discuss in the Common Mistake box on p. 379, a stock can have high total risk, but if a lot of it is diversifiable, it can still have low or average systematic risk.

Estimating Beta from Historical Returns

A security's beta is the expected percentage change in the return of the security for a 1% change in the return of the market portfolio. That is, beta represents the amount by which risks that affect the overall market are amplified or dampened in a given stock or investment. As demonstrated in Table 11.4, securities whose returns tend to move one for one with the market on average have a beta of one. Securities that tend to move more than the market have higher betas, while those that move less than the market have lower betas.

Let's look at Apple's stock as an example. Figure 11.7 shows the monthly returns for Apple and the monthly returns for the S&P 500 from the beginning of 2002 to 2006. Note the overall tendency for Apple to have a high return when the market is up and a low return when the market is down. Indeed, Apple tends to move in the same direction as the market, but its movements are larger. The pattern suggests that Apple's beta is greater than one.

BDeH CHAPTER 11

FIGURE 11.7

Monthly Excess Returns for Apple Stock and for the S&P 500, 2002–2006

Note that Apple's returns tend to move in the same direction but farther than those of the S&P 500.

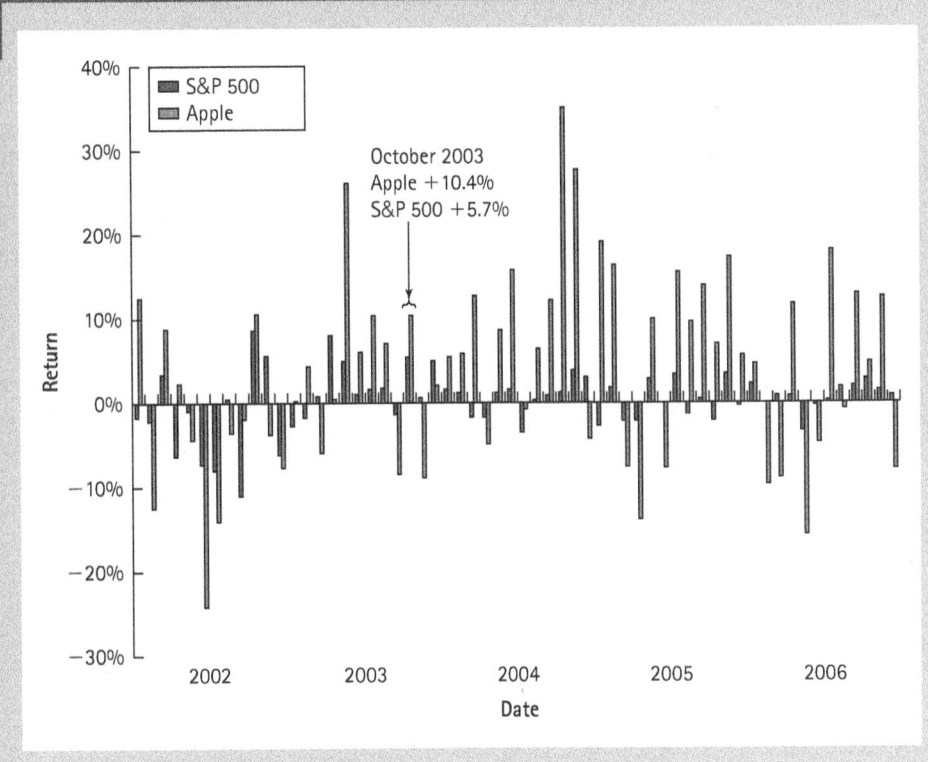

FIGURE 11.8

Scatterplot of Monthly Returns for Apple Versus the S&P 500, 2002-2006

Beta corresponds to the slope of the best-fitting line. Beta measures the expected change in Apple's return per 1% change in the market's return. Deviations from the best-fitting line, such as in July 2002, correspond to diversifiable, unsystematic risk.

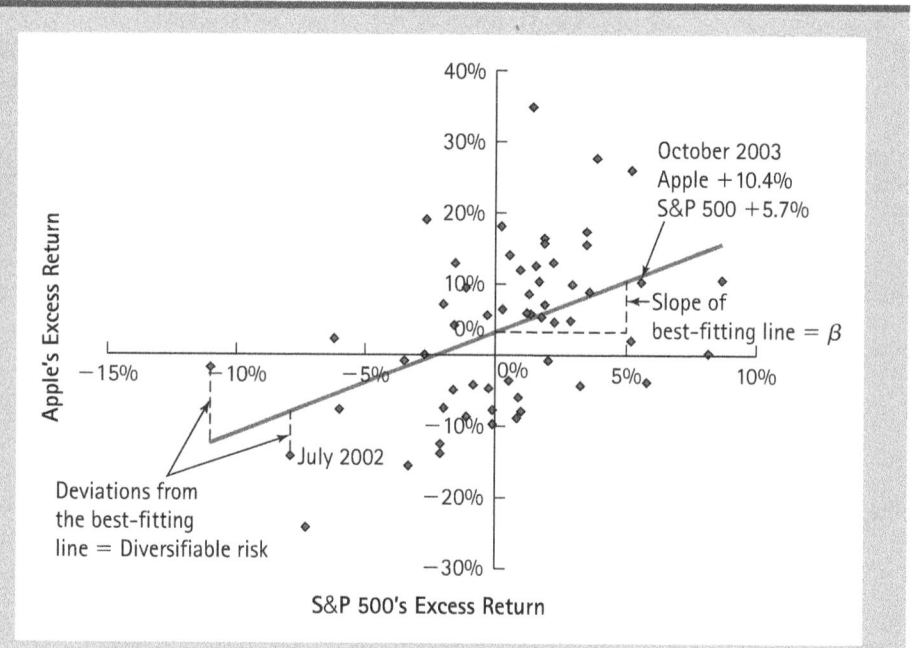

We can see Apple's sensitivity to the market even more clearly by plotting Apple's return as a function of the S&P 500 return, as shown in Figure 11.8. Each point in this figure represents the returns of Apple and the S&P 500 for one of the months in Figure 11.7. For example, in October 2003, Apple's return was 10.4% and the S&P 500's was 5.7%.

As the scatterplot makes clear, Apple's returns have a positive correlation with the market: Apple tends to be up when the market is up, and vice versa. In practice, we use linear regression to estimate the relation between Apple's returns and the market's return. The output of the linear regression analysis is the best-fitting line that represents the historical relation between the stock and the market. The slope of this line is our estimate of its beta. That slope tells us how much, on average, the stock's return changes for a 1% change in the market's return.[4]

For example, in Figure 11.8 the best-fitting line shows that a 5% change in the market's return corresponds to about a 7% change in Apple's return. That is, Apple's return moves about 1.4 times (7/5) the overall market's movement, and so Apple's beta is about 1.4.

To fully understand this result, recall that beta measures the systematic, market risk of a security. The best-fitting line in Figure 11.8 captures the components of a security's returns that can be explained by market-risk factors. In any individual month the security's returns will be higher or lower than the best-fitting line. Such deviations from the best-fitting line result from risk that is not related to the market as a whole. This risk is diversifiable risk that averages out in a large portfolio.

But what is the beta of the market portfolio? Imagine plotting the returns of the S&P 500 against themselves. You would have a line with a slope of one and no deviations from that line. Thus, the beta of the market portfolio is 1. What about a risk-free invest-

---

[4]Formally, the beta of an investment is defined as:

$$\beta_i = \frac{\overbrace{SD(R_i) \times Corr(R_i, R_{Mkt})}^{\text{Volatility of } i \text{ that is Common with the Market}}}{SD(R_{Mkt})} = \frac{Cov(R_i, R_{Mkt})}{Var(R_{Mkt})}$$

USING EXCEL

Calculating a
Stock's Beta

1. Enter or import the historical returns for the stock and the S&P 500 into Excel.
2. Next, from the pull-down menus, choose: **Tools > Data Analysis > Regression.**
3. For the "Input Y Range" Box, **highlight the stock's returns.**
4. For the "Input X Range" Box, **highlight the S&P 500's returns,** as shown in the screen capture.
5. Click OK.

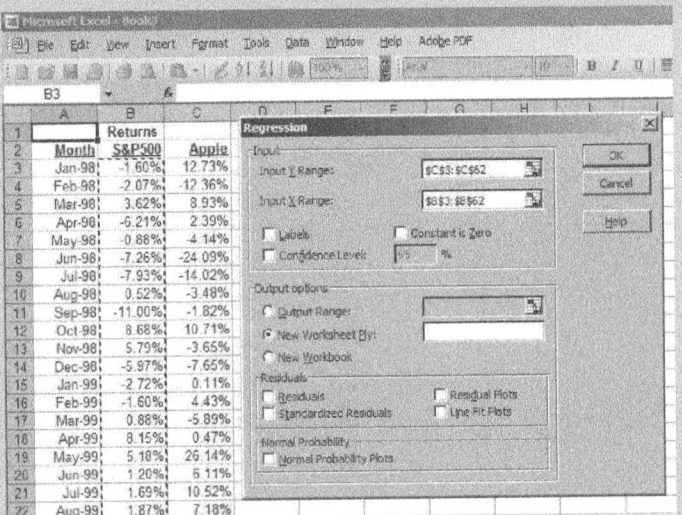

6. The output will appear in a separate sheet. The stock's beta is the coefficient on "X Variable 1." In this case, the beta is 1.424, circled in the screen capture.

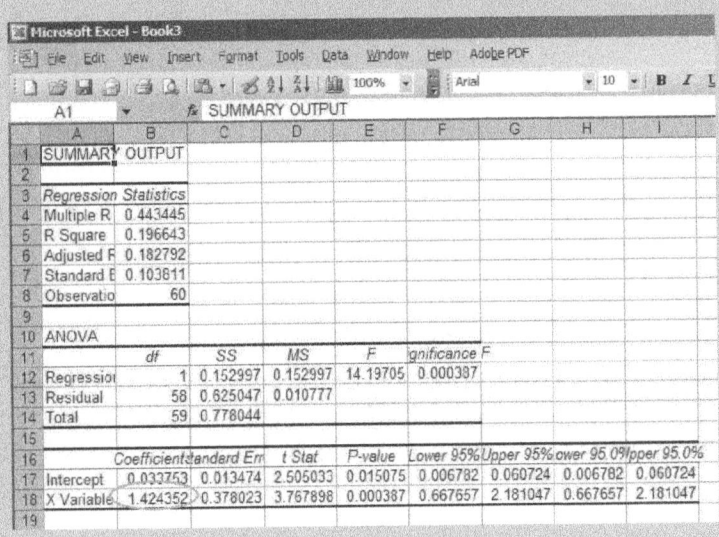

ment? Because the risk-free return is the return earned on a Treasury bond and is therefore known in advance, it has no volatility and hence no correlation with the market. Therefore, the beta of the risk-free investment is 0.

Concept
Check

5. What is the market portfolio?
6. What does beta (β) tell us?

BDeH CHAPTER 11

 ## Putting it All Together: The Capital Asset Pricing Model

One of our goals in this chapter is to compute the cost of equity capital for Apple, which is the best available expected return offered in the market on an investment of comparable risk and term. Thus, in order to compute the cost of capital, we need to know the relation between Apple's risk and its expected return. Over the last three sections, we have laid the foundation for a practical way of measuring this relation. In this section, we put all the pieces together to build a model for determining the expected return of any investment.

The CAPM Equation Relating Risk to Expected Return

As we have learned, only common, systematic risk determines expected returns—firm-specific risk is diversifiable and does not warrant extra return. In the introduction to this chapter, we stated that, intuitively, the expected return on any investment should come from two components:

1. A baseline risk-free rate of return that we would demand to compensate for inflation and the time value of money, even if there were no risk of losing our money.

2. A risk premium that varies with the amount of systematic risk in the investment.

Expected Return = Risk-Free Rate + Risk Premium for Systematic Risk

We devoted the last section to measuring systematic risk. Beta is our measure of the amount of systematic risk in an investment:

Expected Return for Investment i =
Risk-Free Rate + β_i × Risk Premium per Unit of Systematic Risk (per unit of β).

market risk premium (equity risk premium) The historical average excess returns on the market portfolio.

But what is the risk premium per unit of systematic risk? Well, we know that the market portfolio, by definition, has exactly one unit of systematic risk (it has a beta of 1). So, a natural estimate of the risk premium per unit of systematic risk is the historical average excess return on the market portfolio, also known as the **market** or **equity risk premium.** Historically, the average excess return of the S&P500 over the return on U.S.

Why Not Estimate Expected Returns Directly?

If we have to use historical data to estimate beta and determine a security's expected return (or an investment's cost of capital), why not just use the security's historical average return as an estimate for its expected return instead? This method would certainly be simpler and more direct.

The answer is that it is extremely difficult to infer the average return of individual stocks from historical data. Because stock returns are so volatile, with even 100 years of data we would have little confidence in our estimate of the true average. (Imagine drawing 100 numbers from a swimming pool full of widely ranging numbers and being asked to guess the average of all of the numbers in the pool). Worse, few stocks have existed for 100 years, and those that have probably bear little resemblance today to what they were like 100 years ago. If we use less than 10 years of data, we would have very little confidence in our estimate at all. In fact, if the volatility of the stock's return is 20%, it turns out that we would need 1600 years of data to be 95% confident that our estimate of its true average return was within +/−1% of being correct!

On the other hand, the linear regression technique allows us to infer beta from historical data reasonably accurately with just a few years of data. Thus, in theory at least, using beta and the CAPM can provide much more accurate estimates of expected returns for stocks than we could obtain from their historical average return.

Treasury bonds (the risk-free rate) has been 5% to 7%, depending on the period of measurement (we'll discuss this more in the next chapter). With this last piece of the puzzle, we can write down the equation for the expected return of an investment:

Capital Asset Pricing Model (CAPM) An equilibrium model of the relationship between risk and return that characterizes a security's expected return based on its beta with the market portfolio.

Capital Asset Pricing Model

$$E[R_i] = r_f + \underbrace{\beta_i(E[R_{Mkt}] - r_f)}_{\text{Risk Premium for Security } i} \tag{11.6}$$

This equation for the expected return of any investment is the **Capital Asset Pricing Model (CAPM)**. In words, the CAPM simply says that the return we should expect on any investment is equal to the risk-free rate of return plus a risk premium proportional to the amount of systematic risk in the investment. Specifically, the risk premium of an investment is equal to the market risk premium ($E[R_{Mkt}] - r_f$) multiplied by the amount of systematic (market) risk present in the investment, measured by its beta with the market (β_i). Because investors will not invest in this security unless they can expect at least the return given in Eq. 11.6, we also call this return the investment's **required return**.

required return The expected return of an investment that is necessary to compensate for the risk of undertaking the investment.

The CAPM is the main method used by most major corporations to determine the equity cost of capital. In a survey of CFOs, Graham and Harvey find that over 70% rely on the CAPM and Bruner, Eades, Harris, and Higgins report that 85% of a sample of large firms rely on it.[5] It has become the most important model of the relationship between risk and return, and for his contributions to the theory, William Sharpe was awarded the Nobel Prize in Economics in 1990.

EXAMPLE 11.5

Computing the Expected Return for a Stock

Problem

Suppose the risk-free return is 4% and you measure the market risk premium to be 6%. Apple has a beta of 1.4. According to the CAPM, what is its expected return?

Solution

▶ **Plan**

We can use Eq. 11.6 to compute the expected return according to the CAPM. For that equation, we will need the market risk premium, the risk-free return, and the stock's beta. We have all of these inputs, so we are ready to go.

▶ **Execute**

Using Eq. 11.6:

$$E[R_{AAPL}] = r_f + \beta_{AAPL}(E[R_{Mkt}] - r_f) = 4\% + 1.4(6\%)$$
$$= 12.4\%$$

▶ **Evaluate**

Because of Apple's beta of 1.4, investors will require a risk premium of 8.4% over the risk-free rate for investments in its stock to compensate for the systematic risk of Apple stock. This leads to a total expected return of 12.4%.

---

[5] J. Graham and C. Harvey, "The Theory and Practice of Corporate Finance: Evidence from the Field." *Journal of Financial Economics* 60 (2001): 187–243; and F. Bruner, K. Eades, R. Harris, and R. Higgins, "Best Practices in Estimating the Cost of Capital: Survey and Synthesis." *Financial Practice and Education* 8 (1998): 13–28.

Pages 386–388 intentionally omitted

Summary of the Capital Asset Pricing Model

The CAPM is a powerful tool that is widely used to estimate the expected return on stocks and on investments within companies. To summarize the model and its use:

- Investors require a risk premium proportional to the amount of *systematic* risk they are bearing.

- We can measure the systematic risk of an investment by its β, which is the sensitivity of the investment's return to the market's return. For each 1% change in the market portfolio's return, the investment's return is expected to change by β percent due to risks that it has in common with the market.

- The most common way to estimate a stock's beta is to regress its historical returns on the market's historical returns. The stock's beta is the slope of the line that best explains the relation between the market's return and the stock's return.

- The CAPM says that we can compute the expected, or required, return for any investment using the following equation:

$$E[R_i] = r_f + \beta_i(E[R_{Mkt}] - r_f)$$

which when graphed is called the *security market line*.

NOBEL PRIZE — William Sharpe

The CAPM was proposed as a model of risk and return by William Sharpe in a 1964 paper, and in related papers by Jack Treynor (1961), John Lintner (1965), and Jan Mossin (1966).*

Below is an excerpt from a 1998 interview with William Sharpe:

Portfolio Theory focused on the actions of a single investor with an optimal portfolio. I said what if everyone was optimizing? They've all got their copies of Markowitz and they're doing what he says. Then some people decide they want to hold more IBM, but there aren't enough shares to satisfy demand. So they put price pressure on IBM and up it goes, at which point they have to change their estimates of risk and return, because now they're paying more for the stock. That process of upward and downward pressure on prices continues until prices reach an equilibrium and everyone collectively wants to hold what's available. At that point, what can you say about the relationship between risk and return? The answer is that expected return is proportionate to beta relative to the market portfolio.

The CAPM was and is a theory of equilibrium. Why should anyone expect to earn more by investing in one security as opposed to another? You need to

be compensated for doing badly when times are bad. The security that is going to do badly just when you need money when times are bad is a security you have to hate, and there had better be some redeeming virtue or else who will hold it? That redeeming virtue has to be that in normal times you expect to do better. The key insight of the Capital Asset Pricing Model is that higher expected returns go with the greater risk of doing badly in bad times. Beta is a measure of that. Securities or asset classes with high betas tend to do worse in bad times than those with low betas.

Source: Jonathan Burton, "Revisiting the Capital Asset Pricing Model." *Dow Jones Asset Manager* (May/June 1998): 20–28.

*W. F. Sharpe: "Capital Asset Prices: A Theory of Market Equilibrium Under Conditions of Risk." *Journal of Finance* 19 (September 1964): 425–442.
Jack Treynor, "Toward a Theory of the Market Value of Risky Assets." unpublished manuscript (1961).
J. Lintner: "The Valuation of Risk Assets and the Selection of Risky Investments in Stock Portfolios and Capital Budgets." *Review of Economics and Statistics* 47 (February 1965): 13–37.
J. Mossin "Equilibrium in a Capital Asset Market." *Econometrica* 34 (4) (1966): 768–783.

The Big Picture

The CAPM marks the culmination of our examination of how investors in capital markets trade off risk and return. It provides a powerful and widely used tool to quantify the return that should accompany a particular amount of systematic risk. We have already reached our goal (in Example 11.5) of estimating the cost of equity capital for Apple. While our finding that equity investors in Apple should reasonably expect (and therefore require) a return of 12.4% on their investments is an important piece of information to Apple's managers, it is not the whole picture. While some firms, like Apple and Microsoft, have only equity investors, most have bond investors as well. In the next chapter we will apply what we have learned here and in Chapters 6 and 9 on bonds and stocks to develop the overall cost of capital for a company. The Valuation Principle tells us to use this cost of capital to discount the future expected cash flows of the firm to arrive at the value of the firm. Thus, the cost of capital is an essential input to the financial manager's job of analyzing investment opportunities, and so knowing this overall cost of capital is critical to the company's success at creating value for its investors.

Concept Check

7. What does the CAPM say about the required return of a security?
8. What is the security market line?

Page 391 intentionally omitted

Review Questions

1. What information do you need to compute the expected return of a portfolio?

2. What does correlation tell us?

3. Why isn't the total risk of a portfolio simply equal to the weighted average of the risks of the securities in the portfolio?

4. What does beta measure? How do we use beta?

5. What, intuitively, does the CAPM say drives expected return?

6. What relation is described by the security market line?

Problems

All problems in this chapter are available in MyFinanceLab. An asterisk (*) indicates problems with a higher level of difficulty.

The Expected Return of a Portfolio

1. Fremont Enterprises has an expected return of 15% and Laurelhurst News has an expected return of 20%. If you put 70% of your portfolio in Laurelhurst and 30% in Fremont, what is the expected return of your portfolio?

2. You are considering how to invest part of your retirement savings. You have decided to put $200,000 into three stocks: 50% of the money in GoldFinger (currently $25/share), 25% of the money in Moosehead (currently $80/share), and the remainder in Venture Associates (currently $2/share). If GoldFinger stock goes up to $30/share, Moosehead stock drops to $60/share, and Venture Associates stock rises to $3 per share,
   a. What is the new value of the portfolio?
   b. What return did the portfolio earn?
   c. If you don't buy or sell shares after the price change, what are your new portfolio weights?

3. There are two ways to calculate the expected return of a portfolio: either calculate the expected return using the value and dividend stream of the portfolio as a whole, or calculate the weighted average of the expected returns of the individual stocks that make up the portfolio. Which return is higher?

The Volatility of Portfolio

4. If the returns of two stocks have a correlation of 1, what does this imply about the relative movements in the stock prices?

 5. Download the data for Table 11.3 from MyFinanceLab.
   a. Compute the correlation of monthly returns between Dell and Starbucks.
   b. Compute the monthly standard deviation of Dell and Starbucks.
   c. Compute the monthly variance and standard deviation of a portfolio of 30% Dell stock and 70% Starbucks stock.

6. Using the data in the following table, estimate the average return and volatility for each stock.

	Realized Returns	
Year	Stock A	Stock B
1998	−10%	21%
1999	20%	30%
2000	5%	7%
2001	−5%	−3%
2002	2%	−8%
2003	9%	25%

 7. Using your estimates from Problem 6 and the fact that the correlation of A and B is 0.48, calculate the volatility (standard deviation) of a portfolio that is 70% invested in stock A and 30% invested in stock B.

 8. The following spreadsheet contains monthly returns for Coca-Cola (Ticker: KO) and Exxon Mobil (Ticker: XOM) for 1990. Using these data, estimate the average monthly return and volatility for each stock.

Date	KO	XOM
19900131	−10.84%	−6.00%
19900228	2.36%	1.28%
19900330	6.60%	−1.86%
19900430	2.01%	−1.90%
19900531	18.36%	7.40%
19900629	−1.22%	−0.26%
19900731	2.25%	8.36%
19900831	−6.89%	−2.46%
19900928	−6.04%	−2.00%
19901031	13.61%	0.00%
19901130	3.51%	4.68%
19901231	0.54%	2.22%

 9. Using the spreadsheet from Problem 8 and the fact that KO and XOM have a correlation of 0.6083, calculate the volatility (standard deviation) of a portfolio that is 55% invested in Coca-Cola stock and 45% invested in Exxon Mobil stock. Calculate the volatility by
a. Using Eq. 11.4, and
b. Calculating the monthly returns of the portfolio and computing its volatility directly.
c. How do your results compare?

10. Suppose Johnson & Johnson and the Walgreen Company have the expected returns and volatilities shown below, with a correlation of 22%.

	E[R]	SD[R]
Johnson & Johnson	7%	16%
Walgreen Company	10%	20%

For a portfolio that is equally invested in Johnson & Johnson's and Walgreen's stock, calculate:
a. The expected return.
b. The volatility (standard deviation).

11. You have a portfolio with a standard deviation of 30% and an expected return of 18%. You are considering adding one of the two stocks in the table below. If after adding the stock you will have 20% of your money in the new stock and 80% of your money in your existing portfolio, which one should you add?

	Expected Return	Standard Deviation	Correlation with Your Portfolio's Returns
Stock A	15%	25%	0.2
Stock B	15%	20%	0.6

Measuring Systematic Risk

 12. Suppose all possible investment opportunities in the world are limited to the five stocks listed in the table below. What are the market portfolio weights?

Stock	Price/Share ($)	Number of Shares Outstanding (millions)
A	10	10
B	20	12
C	8	3
D	50	1
E	45	20

13. Given $100,000 to invest, construct a value-weighted portfolio of the four stocks listed below.

Stock	Price/Share ($)	Number of Shares Outstanding (millions)
Golden Seas	13	1.00
Jacobs and Jacobs	22	1.25
MAG	43	30
PDJB	5	10

14. If one stock in a value-weighted portfolio goes up in price and all other stock prices remain the same, what trades are necessary to keep the portfolio value weighted?

15. You hear on the news that the S&P 500 was down 2% today relative to the risk-free rate (the market's excess return was −2%). You are thinking about your portfolio and your investments in Apple and Proctor and Gamble.
    a. If Apple's beta is 1.4, what is your best guess as to Apple's excess return today?
    b. If Proctor and Gamble's beta is 0.5, what is your best guess as to P&G's excess return today?

 16. Go to Chapter Resources on MyFinanceLab and use the data in the spreadsheet provided to estimate the beta of Nike stock using linear regression.

 17. The Chapter Resources section of MyFinanceLab has data on Microsoft and the S&P 500 from 1986 to 2005.
    a. Estimate Microsoft's beta using linear regression over the periods 1987–1991, 1992–1996, 1997–2001, and 2002–2006.
    b. Compare the four estimated betas. What do you conclude about how Microsoft's exposure to systematic risk has changed over time? What do you think explains the change?

Putting it All Together: The Capital Asset Pricing Model

18. Suppose the risk-free return is 4% and the market portfolio has an expected return of 10% and a standard deviation of 16%. Johnson and Johnson Corporation stock has a beta of 0.32. What is its expected return?

19. What is the sign of the risk premium of a negative-beta stock? Explain. (Assume the risk premium of the market portfolio is positive.)

20. Suppose Intel stock has a beta of 1.6, whereas Boeing stock has a beta of 1. If the risk-free interest rate is 4% and the expected return of the market portfolio is 10%, according to the CAPM,
    a. What is the expected return of Intel stock?
    b. What is the expected return of Boeing stock?
    c. What is the beta of a portfolio that consists of 60% Intel stock and 40% Boeing stock?
    d. What is the expected return of a portfolio that consists of 60% Intel stock and 40% Boeing stock (show both ways to solve this)?

*21. You are thinking of buying a stock priced at $100 per share. Assume that the risk-free rate is about 4.5% and the market risk premium is 6%. If you think the stock will rise to $117 per share by the end of the year, at which time it will pay a $1 dividend, what beta would it need to have for this expectation to be consistent with the CAPM?

*22. You are analyzing a stock that has a beta of 1.2. The risk-free rate is 5% and you estimate the market risk premium to be 6%. If you expect the stock to have a return of 11% over the next year, should you buy it? Why or why not?

23. You have risen through the ranks of Starbucks, from the lowly green apron barista to the coveted black apron, and all the way to CFO. A quick Internet check shows you that Starbucks' beta is 0.6. The risk free rate is 5% and you believe the market risk premium to be 5.5%. What is your best estimate of investors' expected return on Starbucks' stock (its cost of equity capital)?

24. At the beginning of 2007, Apple's beta was 1.4 and the risk-free rate was about 4.5%. Apple's price was $84.84. Apple's price at the end of 2007 was 198.08. If you estimate the market risk premium to have been 6%, did Apple's managers exceed their investors' required return as given by the CAPM?

Pages 396–398 intentionally omitted

12 Determining the Cost of Capital

LEARNING OBJECTIVES

- Understand the drivers of the firm's overall cost of capital.

- Measure the costs of debt, preferred stock, and common stock.

- Compute a firm's overall, or weighted average, cost of capital.

- Apply the weighted average cost of capital to value projects.

- Adjust the cost of capital for the risk associated with the project.

- Account for the direct costs of raising external capital.

notation

$D\%$	fraction of the firm financed with debt
Div_1	dividend due in one year
Div_{pfd}	dividend on preferred stock
$E\%$	fraction of the firm financed with equity
FCF_t	incremental free cash flow in year t
g	expected growth rate for dividends
$P\%$	fraction of the firm financed with preferred stock
P_E	price of common stock
P_{pfd}	price of preferred stock

r_D	required return (cost of capital) for debt
r_E	required return (cost of capital) of levered equity
r_{pfd}	required return (cost of capital) for preferred stock
r_U	required return (cost of capital) of unlevered equity
r_{wacc}	weighted average cost of capital
T_c	marginal corporate tax rate
V_0^L	initial levered value

Cornell University, 2007

"Whenever you assess a project, whether it's a marketing campaign, an operations initiative, or a new market segment, you must evaluate the benefits and costs of doing the project."

As a staff financial analyst in Qualcomm's Strategic Finance group, Priscilla Srbu is responsible for valuation analysis for mergers and acquisitions, internal business units, and internal strategic initiatives. She received her MBA from Cornell University in 2007 and her BS from New York University in 2000.

Qualcomm, a world leader in digital wireless communications technology products and services, uses the weighted average cost of capital (WACC) as one of several tools to value an investment. When Priscilla analyzes a new line of business or an acquisition candidate, she uses the WACC as the discount rate for future cash flows in calculating the net present value of a potential investment. "The WACC represents the minimum rate of return at which an investment or project produces value for investors," Priscilla explains. "It also serves as a hurdle rate against which Qualcomm assesses return on invested capital and plays a key role in determining economic value added. For example, assume that a project produces a return of 25 percent and a company's WACC is 15 percent. Every $1 the company invests in this project creates 10 cents of value. If the company's return is less than the WACC, however, it is destroying economic value, indicating that the company should invest in other projects."

WACC appears easier to calculate than it really is, Priscilla cautions. "Two individuals may interpret the pieces used to calculate WACC very differently and derive different WACC numbers. Also, the methodologies behind the calculations may differ. Therefore companies like Qualcomm establish guidelines and methodologies for calculating WACC."

WACC has relevance for people in non-financial positions as well. "Whenever you assess a project, whether it's a marketing campaign, an operations initiative, or a new market segment, you must evaluate the benefits and costs of doing the project. The WACC allows you to ascribe a certain level of risk to the future cash flows associated with these projects. If the NPV is positive, the project's benefits cover, at a minimum, its cost and create value for shareholders—the number one concern for management."

Previously, we learned how to determine a firm's equity cost of capital. In reality, most firms are financed with a combination of equity, debt, and other securities such as preferred stock. As a result, financial managers must determine their firm's overall cost of capital based on all sources of financing. This overall cost of capital is a critical input into the capital budgeting process. The Valuation Principle tells us that the value of a project is the present value of its benefits net of the present value of its costs. In capital budgeting, we implement this important concept with net present value (NPV). To calculate a project's NPV, we need a cost of capital to use as a discount rate.

In this chapter, we will learn how to calculate and use the firm's overall cost of capital, which is typically referred to as its weighted average cost of capital (WACC). We will see that the WACC is a weighted average of the costs of capital from each of the firm's different financing sources. After we have learned how to estimate the WACC, we will apply it in capital budgeting. As part of that discussion, we will learn the conditions under which we can use the firm's overall cost of capital as a discount rate and identify those situations in which we will instead need to determine a cost of capital specific to a project or division of the firm.

12.1 A First Look at the Weighted Average Cost of Capital

Most firms draw on some combination of equity, debt, and other securities to raise the funds they need for investment. In this section, we examine the role of financing sources in determining the firm's overall cost of capital. We begin by stepping back to assess these financing sources in the context of the firm's balance sheet.

The Firm's Capital Structure

capital A firm's sources of financing—debt, equity, and other securities that it has outstanding.

A firm's sources of financing, which usually consist of debt and equity, represent its **capital**. The typical firm raises funds to invest by selling shares to stockholders (its equity) and borrowing from lenders (its debt). Recall the most basic form of the balance sheet, as represented in Figure 12.1. The left side of the balance sheet lists the firm's assets, and the right side describes the firm's capital.

FIGURE 12.1   A Basic Balance Sheet

This figure provides a very basic balance sheet for reference. As discussed in Chapter 2, the two sides of the balance sheet must equal each other: Assets = Liabilities + Equity. The right side represents the way the assets are financed. In this chapter, we will focus on the required returns for the different forms of financing found on the right side of the balance sheet.

Assets	Liabilities and Equity
Current Assets Long-Term Assets	Debt Preferred Stock Equity

FIGURE 12.2

Two Capital Structures

This figure shows the capital structures of two real firms. Apple is financed 100% with common equity, shown in blue, while Anheuser Busch is financed 82% with common equity and 18% with debt, shaded in yellow.

Source: Authors' calculations based on publicly available data in 2007.

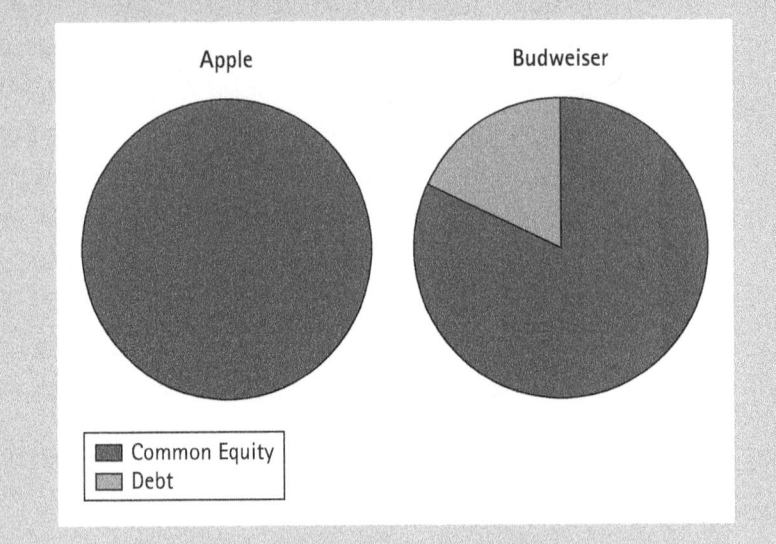

capital structure The relative proportions of debt, equity, and other securities that a firm has outstanding.

The relative proportions of debt, equity, and other securities that a firm has outstanding constitute its **capital structure**. When corporations raise funds from outside investors, they must choose which type of security to issue. The most common choices are financing through equity alone and financing through a combination of debt and equity. Figure 12.2 shows the capital structures of Apple and Anheuser Busch. Capital structures vary widely across firms.

Opportunity Cost and the Overall Cost of Capital

Financial managers take into account each component of the firm's capital structure when determining the firm's overall cost of capital. Throughout the discussion that follows, keep in mind the intuition behind the term "cost of capital." When investors buy the stock or bonds of a company, they forgo the opportunity to invest that money elsewhere. The expected return from those alternative investments constitutes an opportunity cost to them. Thus, to attract their investments as capital to the firm, the firm must offer potential investors an expected return equal to what they could expect to earn elsewhere for assuming the same level of risk. Providing this return is the cost a company bears in exchange for obtaining capital from investors.

weighted average cost of capital (WACC) The average of a firm's equity and debt costs of capital, weighted by the fractions of the firm's value that correspond to equity and debt, respectively.

Weighted Averages and the Overall Cost of Capital

Intuitively, the firm's overall cost of capital should be a blend of the costs of the different sources of capital. In fact, we calculate the firm's overall cost of capital as a weighted average of its equity and debt costs of capital, known as the firm's **weighted average cost of capital (WACC)**

But what should the weights be? Imagine you owned all of the stock and all of the debt of the firm. If that was all you had in your portfolio, the return on your portfolio would be the total return of the firm. A portfolio return is the weighted average of the returns of the securities in the portfolio. In this case, the return on your portfolio—the total return of the firm—is a weighted average of the return you earn holding all the stock of the firm and the return you earn holding all of the debt. Since you hold all of each, your portfolio weights are just the relative amount of debt and equity issued by the firm. Thus the weights we use in the WACC are the proportions of debt and equity used in the firm's capital structure. For example, if the firm is financed 30% by debt and 70% by equity, then the weights used in its WACC would be 30% on the debt cost of capital and 70% on the equity cost of capital.

This example suggests that you can determine the weights by looking at the right side of the firm's balance sheet. That assumption is correct, with one important modification: You must use the *market values* of the debt and equity to determine the proportions, not the accounting-based *book values* listed on the balance sheet. Recall from Chapter 2 that book values reflect historical costs, but market values are forward-looking, based on what the assets are expected to produce in the future. Holders of the firm's financial claims—equity and, if the firm has it, debt—assess the firm based on the market value of its assets, not the book value.

market-value balance sheet Similar to an accounting balance sheet, but all values are current market values rather than historical costs.

In fact, it is useful to think about the **market-value balance sheet**, where the assets, debt, and equity are all listed in terms of their market values, instead of their book values. Of course, the market-value balance sheet must still balance:

$$\text{Market Value of Equity} + \text{Market Value of Debt} = \text{Market Value of Assets} \quad (12.1)$$

Equation 12.1 states that the total market value of all the claims (equity and debt) issued by the firm must be equal to the total market value of all its assets. This equality drives home the point that the equity and debt issued by the firm derive their value from the underlying assets they claim. The risk, and hence the required return, of the debt and equity of the firm are determined by the risk of the firm's assets. This point will be useful as we derive the firm's WACC.

Weighted Average Cost of Capital Calculations

In this section, we will develop the intuition behind the use of market-value weights as well as the link between the risk of the assets and the risk of the debt and equity claims on those assets.

unlevered A firm that does not have debt outstanding.

levered A firm that has debt outstanding.

leverage The relative amount of debt on a firm's balance sheet.

We begin with the straightforward case of the firm that does not issue debt—the **unlevered** firm that pays out all of the free cash flows generated by its assets to its equity holders. When some of a firm's financing comes from debt, we say the firm is **levered**. Just as a lever allows you to lift a heavy object by exerting relatively little force, so borrowing money through debt allows equity holders to control highly valued assets with relatively little investment of their own money. We refer to the relative amount of debt on the balance sheet as the firm's **leverage**.

The Weighted Average Cost of Capital: Unlevered Firm.　If a firm is unlevered, so that it has no debt, all of the free cash flows generated by its assets are ultimately paid out to its equity holders. Because the free cash flows to the equity holders are the same as the free cash flows from the assets, the Valuation Principle tells us that the market value, risk, and cost of capital for the firm's equity are equal to the corresponding amounts for its assets. Given this relationship, we can estimate the firm's equity cost of capital using the Capital Asset Pricing Model (CAPM). The resulting estimate is the cost of capital for the firm as a whole. For example, both Cisco and Apple do not issue debt, so the cost of capital for Cisco's or Apple's assets is the same as the firms' costs of equity.

The Weighted Average Cost of Capital: Levered Firm.　But what if the firm has debt? How should we incorporate the cost of this debt to determine the cost of capital for the firm's assets as a whole? The market-value balance sheet provides the answer. We can interpret the equality in Eq. 12.1 in terms of a portfolio: By holding a portfolio of the firm's equity and debt, we can get the same cash flows as if we held the assets directly. Because the return of a portfolio is equal to the weighted average of the returns of the securities in it, this equality implies the following relationship between the required returns (costs) of equity, debt, and assets:

Weighted Average Cost of Capital (Pre-tax)

$$
\begin{aligned}
r_{wacc} &\equiv \left(\begin{array}{c} \text{Fraction of Firm Value} \\ \text{Financed by Equity} \end{array} \right) \left(\begin{array}{c} \text{Equity} \\ \text{Cost of Capital} \end{array} \right) \\
&+ \left(\begin{array}{c} \text{Fraction of Firm Value} \\ \text{Financed by Debt} \end{array} \right) \left(\begin{array}{c} \text{Debt} \\ \text{Cost of Capital} \end{array} \right) \\
&= \left(\begin{array}{c} \text{Asset} \\ \text{Cost of Capital} \end{array} \right)
\end{aligned}
\tag{12.2}
$$

We now have the justification for our intuition that the overall cost of capital for a firm should be a weighted average of its equity and debt costs of capital. Eq. 12.2 shows that we can calculate the cost of capital of the firm's assets by computing the weighted average of the firm's equity and debt cost of capital. In the next section, we explore how to estimate the firm's costs of equity and debt capital.

EXAMPLE 12.1
Calculating the Weights in the WACC

Problem

Suppose Sony Corporation has debt with a market value of $12 billion outstanding, and common stock with a market value of $49 billion and a book value of $30 billion. Which weights should Sony use in calculating its WACC?

Solution

▶ **Plan**

Equation 12.2 tells us that the weights are the fractions of Sony financed with debt and financed with equity. Furthermore, these weights should be based on market values because the cost of capital is based on investors' current assessment of the value of the firm, not their assessment of accounting-based book values. As a consequence, we can ignore the book value of equity.

▶ **Execute**

Given its $12 billion in debt and $49 billion in equity, the total value of the firm is $61 billion. The weights are

$$
\frac{\$12\,\text{billion}}{\$61\,\text{billion}} = 19.7\% \text{ for debt} \quad \text{and} \quad \frac{\$49\,\text{billion}}{\$61\,\text{billion}} = 80.3\% \text{ for equity.}
$$

▶ **Evaluate**

When calculating its overall cost of capital, Sony will use a weighted average of the cost of its debt capital and the cost of its equity capital, giving a weight of 19.7% to its cost of debt and a weight of 80.3% to its cost of equity.

Concept Check

1. Why does a firm's capital have a cost?

2. Why do we use market value weights in the weighted average cost of capital?

 # The Firm's Costs of Debt and Equity Capital

Section 12.1 made it clear that to measure the firm's overall cost of capital, we need to start by determining the cost of each type of capital a firm might use. We now turn to how a company measures the costs of its debt, preferred stock, and common stock. We will use Alcoa, Inc., a global aluminum producer, as an example.

Cost of Debt Capital

We will start at the top of the right side of the balance sheet with the cost of the firm's debt. A firm's cost of debt is the interest rate it would have to pay to refinance its existing debt, such as through new bond issues. This rate differs from the coupon rate on the firm's existing debt, which reflects the interest rate the firm had to offer at the time the debt was issued.

Yield to Maturity and the Cost of Debt. Existing debt trades in the marketplace, so its price fluctuates to reflect both changes in the overall credit environment and changes in the risk specifically associated with the firm. As we learned in Chapter 6, the market price of the firm's existing debt implies a yield to maturity, which is the return that current purchasers of the debt would earn if they held the debt to maturity and received all of the payments as promised. So, we can use the yield to maturity to estimate the firm's current cost of debt: It is the yield that investors demand to hold the firm's debt (new or existing).[1]

Suppose Alcoa has debt due in 2017 with a coupon rate of 5.55% priced at $961.85 per $1000 face value. Because the market price of the debt is below its face value, investors in debt earn a yield that exceeds the 5.55% coupon rate. In fact, using Eq. 6.3 in Chapter 6, we can calculate that this price implies a yield to maturity of 6.09%, which is Alcoa's current cost of debt. In reality, you would not need to actually compute the yield to maturity yourself because prices and their implied yields to maturity are always quoted together in the bond market.[2]

Taxes and the Cost of Debt. In the case of debt, the return paid to the debt holders is not the same as the cost to the firm. How could this be? The difference arises because interest paid on debt is a tax-deductible expense. When a firm uses debt financing, the cost of the interest it must pay is offset to some extent by the tax savings from the tax deduction.

For example, suppose a firm with a 35% tax rate borrows $100,000 at 10% interest per year. Then its net cost at the end of the year is calculated as follows:

		Year-End
Interest expense	$r_D \times \$100{,}000 =$	10,000
Tax savings	$-\text{Tax Rate} \times r_D \times \$100{,}000 =$	−3,500
Effective after-tax interest expense	$r_D \times (1 - \text{Tax Rate}) \times \$100{,}000 =$	$6,500

---

[1] In fact, the yield to maturity is the *most* the firm will pay because there is some risk the firm may not repay its debt.

[2] Chapter 6 demonstrated how to find current prices and yields to maturity for corporate bonds online using the Web site http://cxa.marketwatch.com/finra/BondCenter/Default.aspx.

BDeH   CHAPTER 12

BDeH CHAPTER 12

Common Mistake Using the Coupon Rate as the Cost of Debt

A common mistake in estimating a company's overall cost of capital is to use the coupon rate on its existing debt as its debt cost of capital. The company's cost of capital is forward-looking and based on current conditions. By contrast, the coupon rate on existing debt is historical and set under potentially very different conditions. A better estimate of the firm's debt cost of capital is the yield to maturity of its existing debt, which is the promised return its lenders currently demand.

Consider Ford Motor Company as an example. Ford has bonds that were originally issued in 1998 and are due in 2018; these bonds have a coupon rate of 6.5%. In recent years, however, Ford's performance has suffered

and the risk that it might not be able to meet all of its debt obligations has increased. By the end of 2007, those 6.5% coupon bonds were trading at a yield to maturity of 10.2%. Thus the market was saying that to be willing to take a creditor position in Ford, investors must be offered a yield to maturity of 10.2%.

So, which is a better estimate of the cost of debt capital for Ford in 2007: the 6.5% coupon or the 10.2% yield to maturity? Ford should use 10.2% as its cost of debt capital. The 6.5% rate, which was set under different circumstances, is not a relevant measure of Ford's debt holders' required return in 2007, so it should not enter into the WACC calculation.

effective cost of the debt
A firm's net cost of interest on its debt after accounting for the interest tax deduction.

The **effective cost of the debt**—the firm's net cost of interest on the debt after taxes—is only $6500/$100,000 = 6.50\%$ of the loan amount, rather than the full 10% interest. Thus the tax deductibility of interest lowers the effective cost of debt financing for the firm. More generally, with tax-deductible interest and denoting the corporate tax rate as T_C, the effective after-tax borrowing rate is

$$r_D(1 - T_C) \tag{12.3}$$

EXAMPLE 12.2

Effective Cost of Debt

Problem

By using the yield to maturity on Alcoa's debt, we found that its pre-tax cost of debt is 6.09%. If Alcoa's tax rate is 35%, what is its effective cost of debt?

Solution

▶ **Plan**

We can use Eq. 12.3 to calculate Alcoa's effective cost of debt: $r_D(1 - T_C)$.

$$r_D = 6.09\% \text{ (pre-tax cost of debt)}$$
$$T_C = 35\% \text{ (corporate tax rate)}$$

▶ **Execute**

Alcoa's effective cost of debt is $0.0609(1 - 0.35) = 0.039585 = 3.9585\%$.

▶ **Evaluate**

For every $1000 it borrows, Alcoa pays its bondholders $0.0609($1000) = 60.90 in interest every year. Because it can deduct that $60.90 in interest from its income, every dollar in interest saves Alcoa 35 cents in taxes, so the interest tax deduction reduces the firm's tax payment to the government by $0.35($60.90) = 21.315. Thus Alcoa's net cost of debt is the $60.90 it pays minus the $21.315 in reduced tax payments, which is $39.9585 per $1000 or 3.9585%.

Cost of Preferred Stock Capital

Firms may also raise capital by issuing preferred stock. Typically, holders of the preferred stock are promised a fixed dividend, which must be paid "in preference to" (i.e., before) any dividends can be paid to common stockholders.

If the preferred dividend is known and fixed, we can estimate the preferred stock's cost of capital using Eq. 9.7 of Chapter 9,

$$r_E = \frac{Div_1}{P_0} + g$$

where the growth rate g = 0. Thus,

$$\text{Cost of Preferred Stock Capital} = \frac{\text{Preferred Dividend}}{\text{Preferred Stock Price}} = \frac{Div_{pfd}}{P_{pfd}} \quad (12.4)$$

For example, Alcoa's preferred stock has a price of $54.50 and an annual dividend of $3.75. Its cost of preferred stock, therefore, is 3.75/54.50 = 6.88%.

Cost of Common Stock Capital

A company cannot directly observe its cost of common stock (equity), but must instead estimate it. We now present and compare the two major methods for doing so.

Capital Asset Pricing Model. The most common approach is to use the CAPM. To summarize that approach:

1. Estimate the firm's beta of equity, typically by regressing 60 months of the company's returns against 60 months of returns for a market proxy such as the S&P 500.
2. Determine the risk-free rate, typically by using the yield on Treasury bills or bonds.
3. Estimate the market risk premium, typically by comparing historical returns on a market proxy to contemporaneous risk-free rates.
4. Apply the CAPM:

Cost of Equity = Risk-Free Rate + Equity Beta × Market Risk Premium

For example, suppose the equity beta of Alcoa is 2.05, the yield on 10-year Treasury notes is 4.5%, and you estimate the market risk premium to be 5%. Alcoa's cost of equity is 4.5% + 2.05 × 5% = 14.75%.

Constant Dividend Growth Model. Another way to estimate a company's cost of equity comes from the Constant Dividend Growth Model (CDGM) introduced in Chapter 9. Equation 9.7 from Chapter 9 shows that

$$\text{Cost of Equity} = \frac{\text{Dividend (in one year)}}{\text{Current Price}} + \text{Dividend Growth Rate} = \frac{Div_1}{P_E} + g \quad (12.5)$$

Thus, to estimate the cost of equity, we need the current price of the stock, the expected dividend in one year, and an estimate of the dividend growth rate. The current price of the stock is easy to obtain online. We may even have a reasonable estimate of next year's dividend. However, as we discussed in Chapter 9, estimating the future dividend growth rate can be very difficult. For example, Alcoa's dividend was 60 cents per share per year from 2001 to 2006 and then increased to 68 cents in 2007. Perhaps it is reasonable to assume that 2008's dividend would be 68 cents per year, but what about the dividend's long-term growth rate? Should we assume that it will increase by about 8/60 (13.3%) every six years?

Rather than looking backward at historical growth, one common approach is to use estimates produced by stock analysts, as these estimates are forward-looking. As discussed in Chapter 9, if Alcoa keeps its dividend payout rate constant, then the long-run growth

TABLE 12.1		Capital Asset Pricing Model	Constant Dividend Growth Model
Estimating the Cost of Equity	Inputs	Equity beta Risk-free rate Market risk premium	Current stock price Expected dividend next year Future dividend growth rate
	Major Assumptions	Estimated beta is correct Market risk premium is accurate CAPM is the correct model	Dividend estimate is correct Growth rate matches market expectations Future dividend growth is constant

in dividends will equal the long-run growth in earnings. In late 2007, the average forecast for Alcoa's long-run earnings growth rate was 11%. Thus, with an expected dividend in one year of $0.68, a price of $39.35, and long-run dividend growth of 11%, the CDGM estimates Alcoa's cost of equity as follows (using Eq. 12.5) as:

$$\text{Cost of Equity} = \frac{Div_1}{P_E} + g = \frac{\$0.68}{\$39.35} + 0.11 = 0.127, \text{ or } 12.7\%$$

We should not be surprised that the two estimates of Alcoa's cost of equity (14.75% and 12.7%) do not match, because each was based on different assumptions. Further, even given an estimate of future growth of dividends, Eq. 12.5 makes an assumption that future dividend growth will continue at a constant rate. This assumption is unlikely to be valid for most firms. Looking again at Alcoa, prior to the six-year run of 60 cents per share per year dividends, the firm paid 50 cents per share for one year. Finally, many young, growing firms do not pay a dividend and have no plans to do so in the near future.

We could use any model relating a firm's stock price to its future cash flows to estimate its cost of equity—the CDGM is just one of the possible models. For example, we could use the discounted free cash flow model from Chapter 9 to solve for the firm's cost of equity.

CAPM and CDGM Comparison. Because of the difficulties with the CDGM, the CAPM is the most popular approach for estimating the cost of equity. Table 12.1 compares the two approaches.

EXAMPLE 12.3

Estimating the Cost of Equity

Problem

The equity beta for Weyerhaeuser (ticker: WY) is 1.2. The yield on 10-year treasuries is 4.5%, and you estimate the market risk premium to be 5%. Further, Weyerhaeuser issues an annual dividend of $2. Its current stock price is $71, and you expect dividends to increase at a constant rate of 4% per year. Estimate Weyerhaeuser's cost of equity in two ways.

Solution

▶ **Plan**

The two ways to estimate Weyerhaeuser's cost of equity are to use the CAPM and the CDGM.

1. The CAPM requires the risk-free rate, an estimate of the equity's beta, and an estimate of the market risk premium. We can use the yield on 10-year Treasury bills as the risk-free rate.

2. The CDGM requires the current stock price, the expected dividend next year, and an estimate of the constant future growth rate for the dividend:

Risk-free rate: 4.5%	Current price: $71
Equity beta: 1.2	Expected dividend: $2
Market risk premium: 5%	Estimated future dividend growth rate: 4%

We can use the CAPM to estimate the cost of equity using the CAPM approach and Eq. 12.5 to estimate it using the CDGM approach.

▶ **Execute**

1. The CAPM says that

Cost of Equity = Risk-Free Rate + Equity Beta × Market Risk Premium

For Weyerhaeuser, this implies that its cost of equity is 4.5% + 1.2 × 5% = 10.5%.

2. The CDGM says

$$\text{Cost of Equity} = \frac{\text{Dividend (in one year)}}{\text{Current Price}} + \text{Dividend Growth Rate} = \frac{\$2}{\$71} + 4\% = 6.8\%$$

▶ **Evaluate**

According to the CAPM, the cost of equity capital is 10.5%; the CDGM produces a result of 6.8%. Because of the different assumptions we make when using each method, the two methods do not have to produce the same answer—in fact, it would be highly unlikely that they would. When the two approaches produce different answers, we must examine the assumptions we made for each approach and decide which set of assumptions is more realistic.

We can also see what assumption about future dividend growth would be necessary to make the answers converge. By rearranging the CDGM and using the cost of equity we estimated from the CAPM, we have

$$\text{Dividend Growth Rate} = \text{Cost of Equity} - \frac{\text{Dividend (in one year)}}{\text{Current Price}} = 10.5\% - 2.8\% = 7.7\%$$

Thus, if we believe that Weyerhaeuser's dividends will grow at a rate of 7.7% per year, the two approaches would produce the same cost of equity estimate.

Concept Check

3. How can you measure a firm's cost of debt ?

4. What are the major tradeoffs in using the CAPM versus the CDGM to estimate the cost of equity?

12.3 A Second Look at the Weighted Average Cost of Capital

Now that we have estimated the costs of Alcoa's different sources of capital, we are ready to calculate the firm's overall WACC. The weights are the percentage of firm value financed by equity, preferred stock, and debt. We can represent these as $E\%$, $P\%$, and $D\%$, respectively, and note that they must sum to 100% (i.e., we must account for all the sources of financing).

WACC Equation

Formally, denoting the cost of equity, preferred and debt capital as r_E, r_{pfd}, and r_D, and the corporate tax rate as T_C, the WACC is

Weighted Average Cost of Capital

$$r_{wacc} = r_E E\% + r_{pfd} P\% + r_D (1 - T_C) D\% \tag{12.6}$$

For a company that does not have preferred stock, the WACC condenses to

$$r_{wacc} = r_E E\% + r_D (1 - T_C) D\% \tag{12.7}$$

For example, in late 2007, the market values of Alcoa's common stock, preferred stock, and debt were $31,420 million, $40 million, and $7397 million, respectively. Its total value was, therefore, $31,420 million + $40 million + $7397 million = $38,857 million. Given the costs of common stock, preferred stock, and debt we have already computed, Alcoa's WACC in late 2007 was

$$WACC = r_E E\% + r_{pfd}P\% + (1 - T_C)r_D D\%$$

$$WACC = 14.75\%\left(\frac{31{,}420}{38{,}857}\right) + 6.88\%\left(\frac{40}{38{,}857}\right) + (1 - 0.35)6.09\%\left(\frac{7397}{38{,}857}\right)$$

$$WACC = 12.69\%$$

EXAMPLE 12.4

Computing the WACC

Problem

The expected return on Target's equity is 11.5%, and the firm has a yield to maturity on its debt of 6%. Debt accounts for 18% and equity for 82% of Target's total market value. If its tax rate is 35%, what is this firm's WACC?

Solution

▶ **Plan**

We can compute the WACC using Eq. 12.7. To do so, we need to know the costs of equity and debt, their proportions in Target's capital structure, and the firm's tax rate. We have all that information, so we are ready to proceed.

▶ **Execute**

$$r_{wacc} = r_E E\% + r_D(1 - T_C)D\% = (0.115)(0.82) + (0.06)(1 - 0.35)(0.18) = 0.101, \text{ or } 10.1\%$$

▶ **Evaluate**

Even though we cannot observe the expected return of Target's investments directly, we can use the expected return on its equity and debt and the WACC formula to estimate it, adjusting for the tax advantage of debt. Target needs to earn at least a 10.1% return on its investment in current and new stores to satisfy both its debt and equity holders.

Weighted Average Cost of Capital in Practice

The WACC is driven by the risk of a company's line of business and, because of the tax effect of interest, its leverage. As a result, WACCs vary widely across industries and companies. Figure 12.3 presents the WACC for several real companies to provide a sense of the degree to which the cost of capital can vary. Some lines of business are clearly riskier than others. For example, selling beer is a fairly low-risk proposition, but selling high-end electronics (as Apple and TiVo do) is much riskier.

Methods in Practice

We now turn to some issues that arise for financial managers when they are estimating the WACC in practice.

net debt Total debt outstanding minus any cash balances.

Net Debt.   When calculating the weights for the WACC, it is increasingly common practice to make an adjustment to the debt. Many practitioners now use **net debt**, the total debt outstanding minus any cash balances:

$$\text{Net Debt} = \text{Debt} - \text{Cash and Risk-Free Securities} \tag{12.8}$$

Why subtract a company's cash from its debt? The assets on a firm's balance sheet include any holdings of cash or risk-free securities. If a firm holds $1 in cash and has $1 of risk-free debt, then the interest earned on the cash will equal the interest paid on the debt. The cash flows from each source cancel each other, just as if the firm held no cash and no debt. In fact, we can view cash as being equivalent to negative debt. Significant

FIGURE 12.3

WACCs for Real Companies

The cost of equity is computed using the company's equity beta, a risk-free rate of 4.5%, and a market risk premium of 5%. The cost of debt is taken from the company's debt. The percent equity and percent debt are determined from the company's market capitalization and balance sheet. The WACC is computed using Eq. 12.7 with a 35% tax rate and is shown in the accompanying bar graph. "N/A" means that the cost of debt is not applicable and refers to companies that have no debt.

Source: Authors' calculations based on publicly available information in 2007.

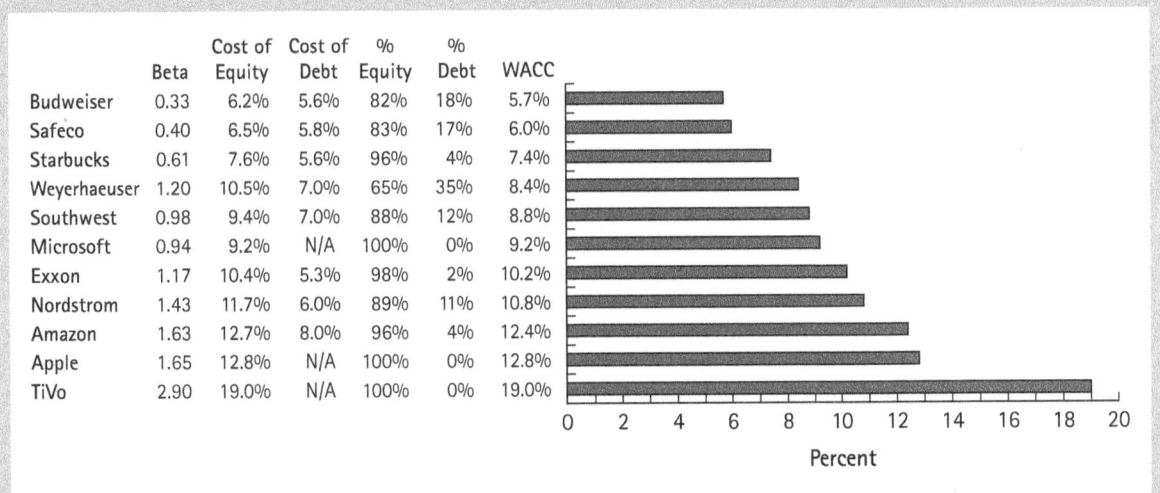

	Beta	Cost of Equity	Cost of Debt	% Equity	% Debt	WACC
Budweiser	0.33	6.2%	5.6%	82%	18%	5.7%
Safeco	0.40	6.5%	5.8%	83%	17%	6.0%
Starbucks	0.61	7.6%	5.6%	96%	4%	7.4%
Weyerhaeuser	1.20	10.5%	7.0%	65%	35%	8.4%
Southwest	0.98	9.4%	7.0%	88%	12%	8.8%
Microsoft	0.94	9.2%	N/A	100%	0%	9.2%
Exxon	1.17	10.4%	5.3%	98%	2%	10.2%
Nordstrom	1.43	11.7%	6.0%	89%	11%	10.8%
Amazon	1.63	12.7%	8.0%	96%	4%	12.4%
Apple	1.65	12.8%	N/A	100%	0%	12.8%
TiVo	2.90	19.0%	N/A	100%	0%	19.0%

excess cash on a firm's balance sheet can complicate the assessment of the risk (and hence the cost of capital) of the assets the firm actually uses in the course of business. Thus, when trying to evaluate a firm's business assets separate from any cash holdings, practitioners often measure the leverage of the firm in terms of its net debt and measure the market value of a firm's business assets using its enterprise value. Recall Chapter 2's definition of the enterprise value as the market value of its equity plus its net debt.

Using this approach, the weights in the WACC would then be

$$\left(\frac{\text{Market Value of Equity}}{\text{Enterprise Value}}\right) \quad \text{and} \quad \left(\frac{\text{Net Debt}}{\text{Enterprise Value}}\right)$$

For firms with substantial excess cash reserves, this adjustment could be important. For firms with relatively low levels of cash, it will not have a large effect on the overall WACC estimate.

The Risk-Free Interest Rate. Estimating the equity cost of capital using the CAPM requires the risk-free interest rate. The risk-free interest rate is generally determined using the yields of U.S. Treasury securities, which are free from default risk. But which horizon should we choose? The CAPM states that we should use the risk-free interest corresponding to the investment horizon of the firm's investors. When surveyed, the vast majority of large firms and financial analysts report using the yields of long-term (10- to 30-year) bonds to determine the risk-free rate.[3]

---

[3]See Robert Bruner, et al., "Best Practices in Estimating the Cost of Capital: Survey and Synthesis," *Financial Practice and Education* 8 (1998): 13–28.

TABLE 12.2	Risk-Free Security	Period	S&P 500 Excess Return
	One-year Treasury security	1926–2005	8.0%
		1955–2005	5.7%
	Ten-year Treasury security*	1955–2005	4.5%

Historical Excess Returns of the S&P 500 Compared to One-Year Treasury Bills and Ten-Year Treasury Notes

*Based on a comparison of compounded returns over a ten-year holding period.

The Market Risk Premium.   Using the CAPM also requires an estimate of the market risk premium. One way to estimate the market risk premium is to look at historical data. Because we are interested in the *future* market risk premium, we face a tradeoff in terms of the amount of data we use. It takes many years of data to produce even moderately accurate estimates of expected returns—yet data that are very old may have little relevance for investors' expectations of the market risk premium today.

Table 12.2 reports excess returns of the S&P 500 versus one-year and ten-year Treasury rates. Since 1926, the S&P 500 has produced an average return of 8.0% above the rate for one-year Treasury securities. However, some evidence indicates that the market risk premium has declined over time. Since 1955, the S&P 500 has shown an excess return of only 5.7% over the rate for one-year Treasury securities. Compared with ten-year Treasury securities, the S&P 500 had an average excess return of only 4.5% (due primarily to the fact that ten-year Treasury bond rates tend to be higher than one-year rates).

How can we explain this decline? One reason may be that as more investors have begun to participate in the stock market and the costs of constructing a diversified portfolio have declined, investors have tended to hold less risky portfolios. As a result, the return they require as compensation for taking on that risk has diminished. In addition, the overall volatility of the market has declined over time. Some researchers believe that the future expected returns for the market are likely to be even lower than these historical numbers, in a range of 3% to 5% over Treasury bills.[4] Consequently, many financial managers currently use market risk premiums closer to 5%, rather than 8%.

Concept Check

5. Why do different companies have different WACCs?

6. What are the tradeoffs in estimating the market risk premium?

 ## Using the WACC to Value a Project

A project's cost of capital depends on its risk. When the market risk of the project is similar to the average market risk of the firm's investments, then its cost of capital is equivalent to the cost of capital for a portfolio of all the firm's securities. In other words, the project's cost of capital is equal to the firm's WACC. As shown in Eq. 12.6, the WACC incorporates the benefit of the interest tax deduction by using the firm's *after-tax* cost of capital for debt.

Because the WACC incorporates the tax savings from debt, we can compute the value of an investment including the benefit of the interest tax deduction given the

---

[4]See Ivo Welch, "The Equity Premium Consensus Forecast Revisited," Cowles Foundation Discussion Paper 1325 (2001), and John Graham and Campbell Harvey, "The Long-Run Equity Risk Premium," SSRN working paper (2005).

levered value The value of an investment, including the benefit of the interest tax deduction, given the firm's leverage policy.

firm's leverage policy, sometimes called the investment's **levered value**. To do so, we discount the firm's future incremental free cash flow using the WACC, a process we refer to as the **WACC method**. Specifically, if FCF_t is the expected incremental free cash flow of an investment at the end of year t, then the Valuation Principle tells us that the investment's levered value, V_0^L, is

$$V_0^L = \frac{FCF_1}{1 + r_{wacc}} + \frac{FCF_2}{(1 + r_{wacc})^2} + \frac{FCF_3}{(1 + r_{wacc})^3} + \cdots \qquad (12.9)$$

WACC method
Discounting future incremental free cash flows using the firm's WACC. This method produces the levered value of a project.

The intuition for the WACC method is that the firm's WACC represents the average return the firm must pay to its investors (both debt and equity holders) on an after-tax basis. Thus, to have a positive NPV, a project with the same risk as the average risk for the firm's projects should generate an expected return of at least the firm's WACC.

EXAMPLE 12.5

The WACC Method

Problem
Suppose Anheuser Busch is considering introducing a new ultra-light beer with zero calories to be called BudZero. The firm believes that the beer's flavor and appeal to calorie-conscious drinkers will make it a success. The cost of bringing the beer to market is $200 million, but Anheuser Busch expects first-year incremental free cash flows from BudZero to be $100 million and to grow at 3% per year thereafter. Should Anheuser Busch go ahead with the project?

Solution

▶ **Plan**
We can use the WACC method shown in Eq. 12.9 to value BudZero and then subtract the upfront cost of $200 million. We will need Anheuser Busch's WACC, which was estimated in Figure 12.3 as 5.7%.

▶ **Execute**
The cash flows for BudZero are a growing perpetuity. Applying the growing perpetuity formula with the WACC method, we have

$$V_0^L = FCF_0 + \frac{FCF_1}{r_{wacc} - g} = -200 + \frac{\$100 \text{ million}}{0.057 - 0.03} = \$3{,}503.7 \text{ million } (\$3.5 \text{ billion})$$

▶ **Evaluate**
The BudZero project has a positive NPV because it is expected to generate a return on the $200 million far in excess of Anheuser Busch's WACC of 5.7%. As discussed in Chapter 3, taking positive-NPV projects adds value to the firm. Here, we can see that the value is created by exceeding the required return of the firm's investors.

Key Assumptions

While it is common practice to use the WACC as the discount rate in capital budgeting, it is important to be aware of the underlying assumptions. We examine the critical assumptions here and then explore these assumptions further in the context of an application.

Assumption 1: Average Risk.   We assume initially that the market risk of the project is equivalent to the average market risk of the firm's investments. In that case, we assess the project's cost of capital based on the risk of the firm.

Assumption 2: Constant Debt-Equity Ratio.   We assume that the firm adjusts its leverage continuously to maintain a constant ratio of the market value of debt to the market

debt-equity ratio A ratio of the market value of debt to the market value of equity.

value of equity—a relationship referred to as the **debt-equity ratio**. This policy determines the amount of debt the firm will take on when it accepts a new project. It also implies that the risk of the firm's equity and debt, and therefore its WACC, will not fluctuate owing to leverage changes.

Assumption 3: Limited Leverage Effects.   We assume initially that the main effect of leverage on valuation follows from the interest tax deduction. We assume that any other factors (such as possible financial distress) are not significant at the level of debt chosen.

Assumptions in Practice.   These assumptions are reasonable for many projects and firms. The first assumption is likely to fit typical projects of firms with investments concentrated in a single industry. In that case, the market risk of both the project and the firm will primarily depend on the sensitivity of the industry to the overall economy. The second assumption, while unlikely to hold exactly, reflects the fact that firms tend to increase their levels of debt as they grow larger; some may even have an explicit target for their debt-equity ratio. Finally, for firms without very high levels of debt, the interest tax deduction is likely to be the most important factor affecting the capital budgeting decision. Hence, the third assumption is a reasonable starting point to begin our analysis.

Of course, while these three assumptions may be a reasonable approximation in many situations, there are certainly projects and firms for which they do not apply. In the following section, we apply the WACC method under all three assumptions. Next, we relax the first assumption, which states that the project has average risk. (We will relax the other two assumptions in later chapters.)

WACC Method Application: Extending the Life of an Alcoa Mine

Let's apply the WACC method to value a project. Suppose Alcoa is considering an investment that would extend the life of one of its aluminum mines for four years. The project would require upfront costs of $6.67 million plus a $24 million investment in equipment. The equipment will be obsolete in four years and will be depreciated via the straight-line method over that period. During the next four years, however, Alcoa expects annual sales of $60 million per year from this mine. Mining costs and operating expenses are expected to total $25 million and $9 million, respectively, per year. Finally, Alcoa expects no net working capital requirements for the project, and it pays a corporate tax rate of 35%.

Using this information, the spreadsheet in Table 12.3 forecasts the project's expected free cash flow. The market risk of the project of extending the life of the mine is the same as that for the Alcoa's business of aluminum mining. As a consequence, we can use Alcoa's WACC to compute the NPV of the project.

We can determine the value of the project, including the present value of the interest tax deduction from the debt, by calculating the present value of its future free cash flows, V_0^L, using the WACC method and Alcoa's WACC of 12.69%, which we computed in Section 12.3:

$$V_0^L = \frac{19}{1.1269} + \frac{19}{1.1269^2} + \frac{19}{1.1269^3} + \frac{19}{1.1269^4} = \$56.88 \text{ million}$$

Because the upfront cost of launching the product line is only $28 million, this project is a good idea. Taking the project results in an NPV of $56.88 million – $28.34 million = $28.54 million for the firm.

TABLE 12.3

Expected Free Cash Flow from Alcoa's Mining Project

	Year	0	1	2	3	4
1						
2	**Incremental Earnings Forecast ($million)**					
3	Sales	—	60.00	60.00	60.00	60.00
4	Cost of Goods Sold	—	−25.00	−25.00	−25.00	−25.00
5	**Gross Profit**	—	35.00	35.00	35.00	35.00
6	Operating Expenses	−6.67	−9.00	−9.00	−9.00	−9.00
7	Depreciation	—	−6.00	−6.00	−6.00	−6.00
8	**EBIT**	−6.67	20.00	20.00	20.00	20.00
9	Income Tax at 35%	2.33	−7.00	−7.00	−7.00	−7.00
10	**Unlevered Net Income**	−4.43	13.00	13.00	13.00	13.00
11	**Incremental Free Cash Flow ($ million)**					
12	Plus: Depreciation	—	6.00	6.00	6.00	6.00
13	Less: Capital Expenditures	−24.00	—	—	—	—
14	Less: Increases in NWC	—	—	—	—	—
15	**Incremental Free Cash Flow**	−28.34	19.00	19.00	19.00	19.00

Summary of the WACC Method

To summarize, the key steps in the WACC valuation method are as follows:

1. Determine the incremental free cash flow of the investment.
2. Compute the weighted average cost of capital using Eq. 12.6.
3. Compute the value of the investment, including the tax benefit of leverage, by discounting the incremental free cash flow of the investment using the WACC.

In many firms, the corporate treasurer performs the second step, calculating the firm's WACC. This rate can then be used throughout the firm as the companywide cost of capital for new investments *that are of comparable risk to the rest of the firm and that will not alter the firm's debt-equity ratio*. Employing the WACC method in this way is very simple and straightforward. As a result, this method is the most commonly used in practice for capital budgeting purposes.

Concept Check

7. What are the main assumptions you make when you use the WACC method?
8. What inputs do you need to be ready to apply the WACC method?

12.5 Project-Based Costs of Capital

Up to this point we have assumed that both the risk and the leverage of the project under consideration matched those characteristics for the firm as a whole. This assumption allowed us, in turn, to assume that the cost of capital for a project matched the firm's cost of capital.

In reality, specific projects often differ from the average investment made by the firm. Consider General Electric Company, a large firm with many divisions that operate in completely different lines of business. Projects in GE's health care division are likely to have different market risk than projects in its air transportation equipment division or at NBC Universal. Projects may also vary in terms of the amount of leverage they will support—for example, acquisitions of real estate or capital equipment are often highly levered, while investments in intellectual property are not. We will study the effect of leverage on the cost of capital when we cover the leverage decision elsewhere. In this section, we show how to calculate the cost of capital for the project's cash flows when a project's risk differs from the firm's overall risk.

Cost of Capital for a New Acquisition

We begin by explaining how to calculate the cost of capital of a project with market risk that is different from the risk for the rest of the firm. Suppose Alcoa wants to enter the forest products business. To do so, it is considering acquiring Weyerhaeuser, a company that is focused on timber, paper, and other forest products. Weyerhaeuser faces different market risks than Alcoa does in its mining business. What cost of capital should Alcoa use to value a possible acquisition of Weyerhaeuser?

Because the risks are different, Alcoa's WACC would be inappropriate for valuing Weyerhaeuser. Instead, Alcoa should calculate and use Weyerhaeuser's WACC when assessing the acquisition. In Figure 12.3, we find the following information for Weyerhaeuser:

	Beta	Cost of Equity	Cost of Cost	% Equity	% Debt	WACC
Weyerhaeuser	1.20	10.5%	7.0%	65%	35%	8.4%

Assuming that Alcoa will find it appropriate to continue to finance Weyerhaeuser with the same mix of debt and equity after it buys Weyerhaeuser, we can use Weyerhaeuser's WACC as the cost of capital for acquiring it. Thus Alcoa would use a cost of capital of 8.4% to value Weyerhaeuser for purchase.

Divisional Costs of Capital

Now assume Alcoa makes a different decision: It decides to create a forest products division internally, rather than buying Weyerhaeuser. What should the cost of capital for the new division be? If Alcoa plans to finance the division with the same proportion of debt as is used by Weyerhaeuser, then Alcoa would use Weyerhaeuser's WACC as the WACC for its new division. Because Weyerhaeuser's WACC is the right cost of capital given the risks of forest products and 35% debt financing, it has to be the right cost of capital for an internally created forest products division that is financed 35% with debt.

In reality, firms with more than one division rarely use a single companywide WACC to evaluate projects. More typically, they perform analyses similar to Alcoa's analysis of Weyerhaeuser. Multidivisional firms benchmark their own divisions off of companies that compete with their division and are focused in that single line of business. By performing the same analysis as we did in Figure 12.3, the multidivisional firm can estimate the WACCs of its divisions' competitors—adjusting for different financing if necessary—to estimate the cost of capital for each division.

EXAMPLE 12.6

A Project in a New Line of Business

Problem

You are working for Cisco evaluating the possibility of selling digital video recorders (DVRs). Cisco's WACC is 13.3%. DVRs would be a new line of business for Cisco, however, so the systematic risk of this business would likely differ from the systematic risk of Cisco's current business. As a result, the assets of this new business should have a different cost of capital. You need to find the cost of capital for the DVR business. Assuming that the risk-free rate is 4.5% and the market risk premium is 5%, how would you estimate the cost of capital for this type of investment?

Solution

▶ **Plan**

The first step is to identify a company operating in Cisco's targeted line of business. TiVo, Inc., is a well-known marketer of DVRs. In fact, that is all TiVo does. Thus the cost of capital for TiVo would be a good estimate of the cost of capital for Cisco's proposed DVR business. Many Web sites are available that provide betas for traded stocks, including http://finance.yahoo.com. Suppose you visit that site and find that the beta of TiVo stock is 2.9. With this beta, the risk-free rate, and the market risk premium, you can use the CAPM to estimate the cost of equity for TiVo. Fortunately for us, TiVo has no debt, so its cost of equity is the same as its cost of capital for its assets.

▶ **Execute**

Using the CAPM, we have

TiVo's Cost of Equity = Risk-Free Rate + TiVo's Equity Beta × Market Risk Premium
$$= 4.5\% + 2.9 \times 5\% = 19\%$$

Because TiVo has no debt, its WACC is equivalent to its cost of equity.

▶ **Evaluate**

The correct cost of capital for evaluating a DVR investment opportunity is 19%. If we had used the 13.3% cost of capital that is associated with Cisco's *existing* business, we would have mistakenly used too low of a cost of capital. That could lead us to go ahead with the investment, even though it truly had a negative NPV.

9. When evaluating a project in a new line of business, which assumption about the WACC method are most likely to be violated?

10. How can you estimate the WACC to be used in a new line of business?

 # When Raising External Capital Is Costly

So far, we have assumed that there are no important factors to consider in seeking capital other than taxes. Among other things, this implies that we can raise external capital without any extra costs associated with the capital-raising transaction. As a consequence, we have no reason to treat a project financed with new external funds any differently than a project financed with internal funds (retained earnings).

In reality, issuing new equity or bonds carries a number of costs. These costs include the costs of filing and registering with the Securities and Exchange Commission and the fees charged by investment bankers to place the securities. We will discuss the process for issuing equity and bonds in detail in the next two chapters. Here, we mention it briefly in the context of the cost of capital.

Because of these issuing costs, a project that can be financed from internal funds will be less costly overall than the same project if it were financed with external funds. One approach would be to adjust the costs of equity and debt capital in the WACC to incorporate the issuing costs. A better and far more direct route is to simply treat the issuing costs as what they are—cash outflows that are necessary to the project. We can then incorporate this additional cost as a negative cash flow in the NPV analysis.

EXAMPLE 12.7

Evaluating an Acquisition with Costly External Financing

Problem

You are analyzing Alcoa's potential acquisition of Weyerhaeuser. Alcoa plans to offer $23 billion as the purchase price for Weyerhaeuser, and it will need to issue additional debt and equity to finance such a large acquisition. You estimate that the issuance costs will be $800 million and will be paid as soon as the transaction closes. You estimate the incremental free cash flows from the acquisition will be $1.4 billion in the first year and will grow at 3% per year thereafter. What is the NPV of the proposed acquisition?

Solution

▶ **Plan**

We know from Section 12.5 that the correct cost of capital for this acquisition is Weyerhaeuser's WACC. We can value the incremental free cash flows as a growing perpetuity:

$$PV = FCF_1/(r - g)$$

where

FCF_1 = $1.4 billion
r = Weyerhaeuser's WACC = 8.4%
g = 3%

The NPV of the transaction, including the costly external financing, is the present value of this growing perpetuity net of both the purchase cost and the transaction costs of using external financing.

▶ **Execute**

Noting that $800 million is $0.8 billion,

$$NPV = -\$23 - 0.8 + \frac{1.4}{0.084 - 0.03} = \$2.126 \text{ billion}$$

▶ **Evaluate**

It is not necessary to try to adjust Weyerhaeuser's WACC for the issuance costs of debt and equity. Instead, we can subtract the issuance costs from the NPV of the acquisition to confirm that the acquisition remains a positive-NPV project even if it must be financed externally.

In this chapter, we learned what a firm's cost of capital is, where it comes from, and how it is used in capital budgeting. The role of capital budgeting is to identify positive-NPV projects that allow a firm to cover the costs of its various types of capital. Now we turn to another aspect of capital financing—where the firm gets that capital. In the following chapters, we explore how a firm raises equity and debt capital and how it decides the proportion of each to have in its capital structure.

Concept Check

11. What types of additional costs does a firm incur when accessing external capital?

12. What is the best way to incorporate these additional costs into capital budgeting?

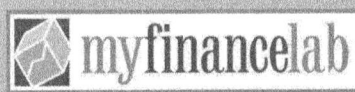

Key Points and Equations	Terms	Online Practice Opportunities

12.1 A First Look at the Weighted Average Cost of Capital
▶ A firm's debt and equity represent its capital. The relative proportions of debt, equity, and other securities that a firm has outstanding constitute its capital structure.
▶ Investors of each type of capital have a required return. Providing this return is the cost a company bears to obtain capital from investors.
▶ We calculate the firm's overall cost of capital as a weighted average of its equity and debt costs of capital, referred to as the firm's weighted average cost of capital.
▶ The weights in the WACC must be based on the market values of each of the firm's debt and equity, not the book values.
	capital, p. 401
	capital structure, p. 402
	leverage, p. 403
	levered, p. 403
	market-value
	    balance sheet, p. 403
	unlevered, p. 403
	weighted average
	    cost of capital (WACC),
	    p. 402
		MyFinanceLab
		Study Plan 12.1

12.2 The Firm's Costs of Debt and Equity Capital
▶ To estimate the cost of capital for a company as a whole, we usually start by estimating the cost of each of the company's sources of capital.
▶ The cost of debt is the interest a firm would need to pay on *new* debt. It will generally differ from the coupon rate on existing debt, but can be estimated from the yield to maturity on existing debt.
▶ The cost of preferred stock is straightforward to estimate because of its constant and known dividend:
 	
Cost of Preferred Stock Capital $= \dfrac{Div_{pfd}}{P_{pfd}}$ (12.4)
 	
▶ The Capital Asset Pricing Model (CAPM) is the most common approach for estimating the cost of equity capital. To apply the CAPM, we need an estimate of the firm's equity beta, the market risk premium, and the risk-free rate:
 	
Cost of Equity = Risk-Free Rate + Equity Beta
        × Market Risk Premium
	effective cost
	    of debt, p. 406
		MyFinanceLab
		Study Plan 12.2

BDeH CHAPTER 12

▶ Another approach to estimating the cost of equity is to use the Constant Dividend Growth Model (CDGM). To apply this model, we need the current stock price, the expected future dividend, and an estimate of the dividend's constant growth rate:

$$\text{Cost of Equity} = \frac{Div_1}{P_E} + g \qquad (12.5)$$

12.3 A Second Look at the Weighted Average Cost of Capital

▶ The WACC equation is

$$r_{wacc} = r_E E\% + r_{pfd}P\% + r_D(1 - T_C)D\% \quad (12.6)$$

net debt, p. 410

MyFinanceLab
Study Plan 12.3

▶ For a company that does not have preferred stock, the WACC equation condenses to

$$r_{wacc} = r_E E\% + r_D(1 - T_C)D\% \qquad (12.7)$$

▶ The WACC is driven by the risk of a company's line of business and, because of the tax effect of interest, its leverage. As a result, WACCs vary widely across industries and companies.

12.4 Using the WACC to Value a Project

▶ Assuming a project has average risk for the firm, that the firm will maintain its current leverage ratio, and that a firm's leverage affects its value only through taxes, the WACC can be used to value the cash flows from a new project.

debt-equity ratio, p. 414
levered value, p. 413
WACC method, p. 413

MyFinanceLab
Study Plan 12.4

Spreadsheet
Table 12.3

12.5 Project-Based Costs of Capital

▶ If the project's risk differs from the average risk for the firm, the WACC will not be the appropriate discount rate for the project. Instead, you must estimate the WACC from the WACC of other firms operating in the same line of business as the new project.

MyFinanceLab
Study Plan 12.5

12.6 When Raising External Capital Is Costly

▶ The WACC is calculated without accounting for the direct costs of raising external financing. Rather than adjusting the WACC, the correct way to account for these costs is to subtract their present value from the NPV of the project.

MyFinanceLab
Study Plan 12.6

Review Questions

1. What does the WACC measure?

2. Why are market-based weights important?

3. Why is the coupon rate of existing debt irrelevant for finding the cost of debt capital?

4. Why is it easier to determine the costs of preferred stock and of debt than it is to determine the cost of common equity?

5. Describe the steps involved in the CAPM approach to estimating the cost of equity.

6. Under what assumptions can the WACC be used to value a project?

7. What are some possible problems that might be associated with the assumptions used in applying the WACC method?

8. How should you value a project in a line of business with risk that is different than the average risk of your firm's projects?

9. What is the right way to adjust for the costs of raising external financing?

Problems

All problems in this chapter are available in MyFinanceLab.

A First Look at the Weighted Average Cost of Capital

1. MV Corporation has debt with market value of $100 million, common equity with a book value of $100 million, and preferred stock worth $20 million outstanding. Its common equity trades at $50 per share, and the firm has 6 million shares outstanding. What weights should MV Corporation use in its WACC?

2. Andyco, Inc., has the following balance sheet and an equity market-to-book ratio of 1.5. Assuming the market value of debt equals its book value, what weights should it use for its WACC calculation?

Assets	Liabilities and Equity	
1000	Debt	400
	Equity	600

3. Consider a simple firm that has the following market-value balance sheet:

Assets	Liabilities and Equity	
1000	Debt	400
	Equity	600

Next year, there are two possible values for its assets, each equally likely: $1200 and $960. Its debt will be due with 5% interest. Because all of the cash flows from the assets must go to either the debt or the equity, if you hold a portfolio of the debt and equity in the same proportions as the firm's capital structure, your portfolio should earn exactly the expected return on the firm's assets. Show that a portfolio invested 40% in the firm's debt and 60% in its equity will have the same expected return as the assets of the firm. That is, show that the firm's pre-tax WACC is the same as the expected return on its assets.

The Firm's Costs of Debt and Equity Capital

4. Avicorp has a $10 million debt issue outstanding, with a 6% coupon rate. The debt has semi-annual coupons, the next coupon is due in six months, and the debt matures in five years. It is currently priced at 95% of par value.
   a. What is Avicorp's pre-tax cost of debt?
   b. If Avicorp faces a 40% tax rate, what is its after-tax cost of debt?

5. Laurel, Inc., has debt outstanding with a coupon rate of 6% and a yield to maturity of 7%. Its tax rate is 35%. What is Laurel's effective (after-tax) cost of debt?

6. Dewyco has preferred stock trading at $50 per share. The next preferred dividend of $4 is due in one year. What is Dewyco's cost of capital for preferred stock?

7. Steady Company's stock has a beta of 0.20. If the risk-free rate is 6% and the market risk premium is 7%, what is an estimate of Steady Company's cost of equity?

8. Wild Swings, Inc.'s stock has a beta of 2.5. Given the information in Problem 7, what is an estimate of Wild Swings' cost of equity?

9. HighGrowth Company has a stock price of $20. The firm will pay a dividend next year of $1, and its dividend is expected to grow at a rate of 4% per year thereafter. What is your estimate of HighGrowth's cost of equity capital?

10. Slow 'n Steady, Inc., has a stock price of $30, will pay a dividend next year of $3, and has expected dividend growth of 1% per year. What is your estimate of Slow 'n Steady's cost of equity capital?

11. Mackenzie Company has a price of $36 and will issue a dividend of $2 next year. It has a beta of 1.2, the risk-free rate is 5.5% and it estimates the market risk premium to be 5%.
    a. Estimate the equity cost of capital for Mackenzie.
    b. Under the CGDM, at what rate do you need to expect Mackenzie's dividends to grow to get the same equity cost of capital as in part (a)?

A Second Look at the Weighted Average Cost of Capital

12. CoffeeCarts has a cost of equity of 15%, has an effective cost of debt of 4%, and is financed 70% with equity and 30% with debt. What is this firm's WACC?

13. Pfd Company has debt with a yield to maturity of 7%, a cost of equity of 13%, and a cost of preferred stock of 9%. The market values of its debt, preferred stock, and equity are $10 million, $3 million and $15 million, respectively, and its tax rate is 40%. What is this firm's WACC?

14. Growth Company's current share price is $20 and it is expected to pay a $1 dividend per share next year. After that, the firm's dividends are expected to grow at a rate of 4% per year.
    a. What is an estimate of Growth Company's cost of equity?
    b. Growth Company also has preferred stock outstanding that pays a $2 per share fixed dividend. If this stock is currently priced at $28, what is Growth Company's cost of preferred stock?

c. Growth Company has existing debt issued 3 years ago with a coupon rate of 6%. The firm just issued new debt at par with a coupon rate of 6.5%. What is Growth Company's pre-tax cost of debt?

d. Growth Company has 5 million common shares outstanding and 1 million preferred shares outstanding, and its equity has a total book value of $50 million. Its liabilities have a market value of $20 million. If Growth Company's common and preferred shares are priced as in parts (a) and (b), what is the market value of Growth Company's assets?

e. Growth Company faces a 35% tax rate. Given the information in parts (a)–(d), and your answers to those problems, what is Growth Company's WACC?

Using the WACC to Value a Project

15. RiverRocks, Inc., is considering a project with the following projected free cash flows:

0	1	2	3	4
−50	10	20	20	15

The firm believes that, given the risk of this project, the WACC method is the appropriate approach to valuing the project. RiverRocks' WACC is 12%. Should it take on this project? Why or why not?

Project-Based Costs of Capital

16. RiverRocks (whose WACC is 12%) is considering an acquisition of Raft Adventures (whose WACC is 15%0). What is the appropriate discount rate for RiverRocks to use to evaluate the acquisition? Why?

17. RiverRocks' purchase of Raft Adventures (from Problem 16) will cost $100 million, but will generate cash flows that start at $15 million in one year and then grow at 4% per year forever. What is the NPV of the acquisition?

18. Starbucks primarily sells coffee. It recently introduced a premium coffee-flavored liquor. Suppose the firm faces a tax rate of 35% and collects the following information. If it plans to finance 11% of the new liquor-focused division with debt and the rest with equity, what WACC should it use for its liquor division? Assume a risk-free rate of 55% and a risk premium of 5%.

	Beta	% Equity	% Debt
Starbucks	0.61	96%	4%
Brown-Forman Liquors	0.26	89%	11%

19. Your company has two divisions: One division sells software and the other division sells computers through a direct sales channel, primarily taking orders over the Internet. You have decided that Dell Computer is very similar to your computer division, in terms of both risk and financing. You go online and find the following information: Dell's beta is 1.21, the risk-free rate is 4.5%, its market value of equity is $67 billion, and it has $700 million worth of debt with a yield to maturity of 6%. Your tax rate is 35% and you use a market risk premium of 5% in your WACC estimates.

a. What is an estimate of the WACC for your computer sales division?

b. If your overall company WACC is 12% and the computer sales division represents 40% of the value of your firm, what is an estimate of the WACC for your software division?

When Raising External Capital Is Costly

20. RiverRocks realizes that it will have to raise the financing for the acquisition of Raft Adventures (described in Problem 17) by issuing new debt and equity. The firm estimates that the direct issuing costs will come to $7 million. How should it account for these costs in evaluating the project? Should RiverRocks go ahead with the project?

● Data Case

You work in Walt Disney Company's corporate finance and treasury department and have just been assigned to the team estimating Disney's WACC. You must estimate this WACC in preparation for a team meeting later today. You quickly realize that the information you need is readily available online.

1. Go to http://finance.yahoo.com. Under "Market Summary," you will find the yield to maturity for ten-year Treasury bonds listed as "10 Yr Bond(%)." Collect this number as your risk-free rate.

2. In the box next to the "Get Quotes" button, type Walt Disney's ticker symbol (DIS) and press enter. Once you see the basic information for Disney, find and click "Key Statistics" on the left side of the screen. From the key statistics, collect Disney's market capitalization (its market value of equity), enterprise value (market-value equity + net debt), cash, and beta.

3. To get Disney's cost of debt and the market value of its long-term debt, you will need the price and yield to maturity on the firm's existing long-term bonds. Go to http://cxa.marketwatch.com/finra/BondCenter/Default.aspx. Under "Quick Bond Search," click "Corporate" and type Disney's ticker symbol. A list of Disney's outstanding bond issues will appear. Assume that Disney's policy is to use the yield to maturity on non-callable ten-year obligations as its cost of debt. Find the non-callable bond issue that is as close to ten years from maturity as possible. (*Hint:* You will see a column titled "Callable"; make sure the issue you choose has "No" in this column.) Find the yield to maturity for your chosen bond issue (it is in the column titled "Yield"). Hold the mouse over the table of Disney's bonds and right-click. Select "Export to Microsoft Excel." An Excel spreadsheet with all of the data in the table will appear.

4. You now have the price for each bond issue, but you need to know the size of the issue. Returning to the Web page, click "Walt Disney Company" in the first row. This brings up a Web page with all of the information about the bond issue. Scroll down until you find "Amount Outstanding" on the right side. Noting that this amount is quoted in thousands of dollars (e.g., $60,000 means $60 million = $60,000,000), record the issue amount in the appropriate row of your spreadsheet. Repeat this step for all of the bond issues.

5. The price for each bond issue in your spreadsheet is reported as a percentage of the bond's par value. For example, 104.50 means that the bond issue is trading at 104.5% of its par value. You can calculate the market value of each bond issue by multiplying the amount outstanding by (Price ÷ 100). Do so for each issue and then calculate the total of all the bond issues. This is the market value of Disney's debt.

6. Compute the weights for Disney's equity and debt based on the market value of equity and Disney's market value of debt, computed in step 6.

BDeH CHAPTER 12

7. Calculate Disney's cost of equity capital using the CAPM, the risk-free rate you collected in step 1, and a market risk premium of 5%.

8. Assuming that Disney has a tax rate of 35%, calculate its effective cost of debt capital.

9. Calculate Disney's WACC.

10. Calculate Disney's net debt by subtracting its cash (collected in step 2) from its debt. Recalculate the weights for the WACC using the market value of equity, net debt, and enterprise value. Recalculate Disney's WACC using the weights based on the net debt. How much does it change?

11. How confident are you of your estimate? Which implicit assumptions did you make during your data collection efforts?

PART 4 Integrative Case

This case draws on material from Chapters 10–12.

You work for HydroTech, a large manufacturer of high-pressure industrial water pumps. The firm specializes in natural disaster services, ranging from pumps that draw water from lakes, ponds, and streams in drought-stricken areas to pumps that remove high water volumes in flooded areas. You report directly to the CFO. Your boss has asked you to calculate HydroTech's WACC in preparation for an executive retreat. Too bad you're not invited, as water pumps and skiing are on the agenda in Sun Valley, Idaho. At least you have an analyst on hand to gather the following required information:

1. The risk-free rate of interest, in this case, the yield of the ten-year government bond, which is 6%.

2. HydroTech's:
   a. Market capitalization (its market value of equity), $100 million.
   b. CAPM beta, 1.2.
   c. Total book value of debt outstanding, $50 million.
   d. Cash, $10 million.

3. The cost of debt (using the quoted yields on HydroTech's outstanding bond issues), which is 7%.

With this information in hand, you are now prepared to undertake the analysis.

Case Questions

1. Calculate HydroTech's net debt.

2. Compute HydroTech's equity and (net) debt weights based on the market value of equity and the book value of net debt.

3. Calculate the cost of equity capital using the CAPM, assuming a market risk premium of 5%.

4. Using a tax rate of 35%, calculate HydroTech's effective cost of debt capital.

5. Calculate HydroTech's WACC.

6. When is it appropriate to use this WACC to evaluate a new project?

PART 5

Long-Term Financing

Valuation Principle Connection. How should a firm raise the funds it needs to undertake its investments? In this part of the book, we explain the mechanics of raising equity and issuing debt. Chapter 13 describes the process a company goes through when it raises equity capital. In Chapter 14, we review firms' use of debt markets to raise capital. Later, in the capital structure section of the text, we will discuss the financial manager's choice between these two major categories of financing. A firm's ability to raise capital depends on the value the market applies to its securities. The Valuation Principle tells us that the price of any securities issued by the firm will be the present value of the cash flows accruing to them. Thus, while we discuss the process for raising capital in the following two chapters, it is important to remember that the price investors are willing to pay for a firm's securities depends on the financial manager making investment decisions that maximize the value of the firm.

Chapter 13
Raising Equity Capital

Chapter 14
Debt Financing

13

Raising Equity Capital

LEARNING OBJECTIVES

▶ Contrast the different ways to raise equity capital for a private company

▶ Understand the process of taking a company public

▶ Gain insight into puzzles associated with initial public offerings

▶ Explain how to raise additional equity capital once the company is public

Working on the Markets Desk in Goldman Sachs' Equity Capital Markets group, Sandra Pfeiler and her colleagues coordinate between the firm's equity sales force and the corporations who are issuing equity. "It is our job to convey compelling details about the company issuing equity to the sales force, who then provide that information to their investing clients and attract demand for new offerings," she explains. "Once a new deal launches, we handle a variety of tasks, from determining which investors the company should meet to collecting investor feedback to help gauge market sentiment as we make pricing judgments."

University of Iowa, 2004

Sandy, who received her BBA degree in Finance and Marketing from the University of Iowa in 2004, comments that her corporate finance courses provided the background in capital structure and valuation her job requires. "By understanding how clients apply valuation models, I can help them determine whether equity or debt is the better option for them now, which one is less expensive in terms of cost of capital, which one is the easiest to execute if they need to finance quickly, and what the pros and cons are of taking a company public."

"By understanding how clients apply valuation models, I can help them determine whether equity or debt is the better option for them."

Before going public, a company must determine if it is ready to take this step. "We help our client ask itself tough questions," says Sandy. "Does it have a solid story that investors will want to buy? Can the management team handle being a public company from a financial reporting and governance standpoint? Does it meet the listing requirements of the exchange on which they plan to list?"

Sandy advises on share prices for initial public offerings. Pricing a company's first public equity offering requires managing competing interests of issuers and investors. "Obviously the investor wants the lowest price, the issuer wants the highest price, and both parties want the stock to trade well in the aftermarket," Sandy says. "At the end of the day, both parties have to give a bit. A deal that is priced too low will be vastly oversubscribed; many investors will not get the amount of stock they requested. If the deal is priced too high, there will not be enough demand to support the offering."

BDeH CHAPTER 13

As we pointed out in Chapter 1, most U.S. businesses are small sole proprietorships and partnerships. That said, these firms as a whole generate less than 15% of total U.S. sales. Sole proprietorships are not allowed to access outside equity capital, so these businesses have relatively little capacity for growth. Sole proprietors are also forced to hold a large fraction of their wealth in a single asset—the company—and therefore are likely to be undiversified. By incorporating, businesses can gain access to capital and founders can reduce the risk of their portfolios by selling some of their equity and diversifying. Consequently, even though corporations make up only about 20% of U.S. businesses, they account for 85% of sales in the U.S. economy.

In this chapter, we discuss how companies raise equity capital. To illustrate this concept, we follow the case of an actual company, RealNetworks, Inc. (ticker: RNWK). RealNetworks is a leading creator of digital media services and software. Customers use RealNetworks products to find, play, purchase, and manage digital music, videos, and games. RealNetworks was founded in 1993 and incorporated in 1994. Using the example of RealNetworks, we first discuss the alternative ways new companies can raise capital and then examine the impact of these funding alternatives on current and new investors.

13.1 Equity Financing for Private Companies

The initial capital that is required to start a business is usually provided by the entrepreneur herself and her immediate family. Few families, however, have the resources to finance a growing business, so growth almost always requires outside capital. In this section, we examine the sources that can provide a private company this capital and the effect of the infusion of outside capital on the control of the company.

Sources of Funding

When a private company decides to raise outside equity capital, it can seek funding from several potential sources: *angel investors, venture capital firms, institutional investors,* and *corporate investors*.

Angel Investors. Individual investors who buy equity in small private firms are called **angel investors**. For many start-ups, the first round of outside private equity financing is often obtained from angels. The term originated a hundred years ago in New York when wealthy investors came to the rescue of new Broadway productions by providing critical funding. These investors are frequently friends or acquaintances of the entrepreneur. Because their capital investment is often large relative to the amount of capital already in place at the firm, they typically receive a sizeable equity share in the business in return for their funds. As a result, these investors may have substantial influence in the business decisions of the firm. Angels may also bring expertise to the firm that the entrepreneur lacks.

In most cases, firms need more capital than what a few angels can provide. Finding angels is difficult—often it is a function of how well connected the entrepreneur is in the local community. Most entrepreneurs, especially those launching their first start-up company, have few relationships with people who have substantial capital to invest. At some point, many firms that require equity capital for growth must turn to the *venture capital* industry.

angel investors
Individual investors who buy equity in small private firms.

FIGURE 13.1

Most Active U.S. Venture Capital Firms in 2006 (by Number of Deals Completed)

Source: MoneyTree Report, PriceWaterhouseCoopers, 2007.

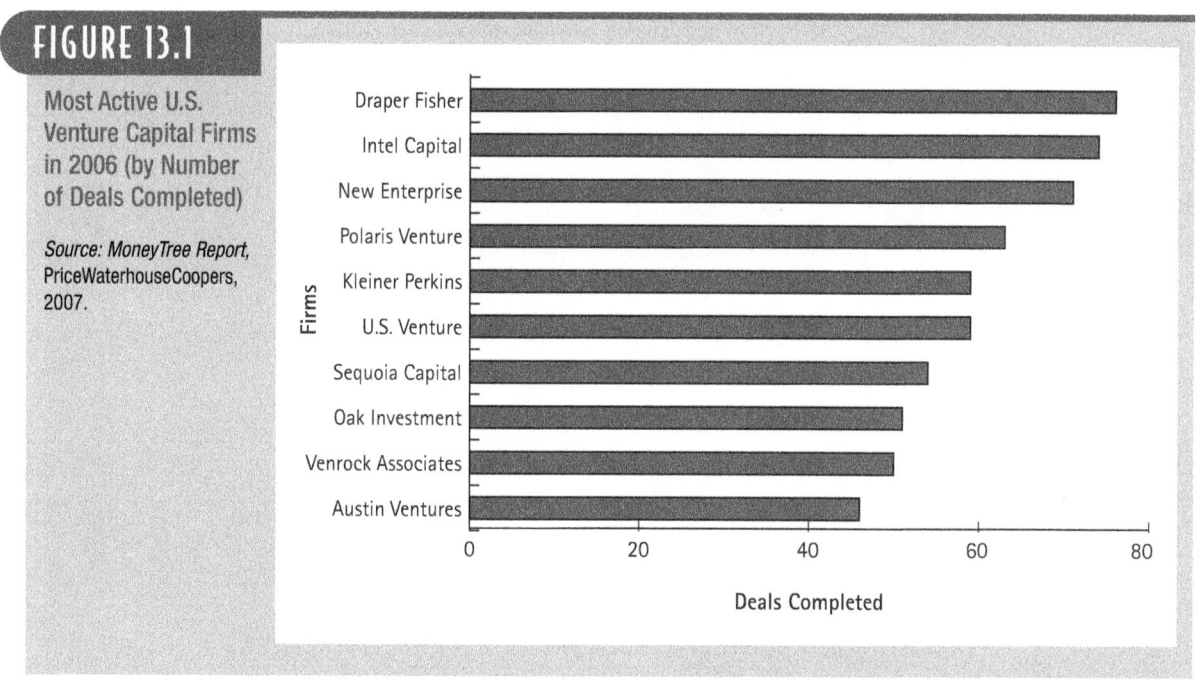

Venture Capital Firms. A **venture capital firm** is a limited partnership that specializes in raising money to invest in the private equity of young firms. Figure 13.1 lists the ten most active U.S. venture capital firms in 2006, based on the number of deals completed.

venture capital firm A limited partnership that specializes in raising money to invest in the private equity of young firms.

venture capitalists The general partners who work for and run a venture capital firm.

Typically, institutional investors, such as pension funds, are the limited partners in the venture capital firm. The general partners are known as **venture capitalists** and they work for and run the venture capital firm. Venture capital firms offer limited partners a number of advantages over investing directly in start-ups themselves as angel investors. Because these firms invest in many start-ups, limited partners are more diversified than if they invested on their own. They also benefit from the expertise of the general partners. However, these advantages come at a cost. General partners usually charge substantial fees, taken mainly as a percentage of the positive returns they generate. Most firms charge 20% of any positive returns they make, but the successful firms may charge more than 30%. They also generally charge an annual management fee of about 2% of the fund's committed capital.

Venture capital firms can provide substantial capital for young companies. For example, during 2007 venture capital firms invested $29.4 billion in 3811 venture capital deals, for an average investment of about $7.7 million per deal.[1] In return, venture capitalists often demand a great deal of control. Paul Gompers and Josh Lerner[2] report that venture capitalists typically control about one-third of the seats on a start-up's board of directors, and often represent the single largest voting block on the board. Although entrepreneurs generally view this control as a necessary cost of obtaining venture capital, it can actually be an important benefit of accepting venture financing. Venture capitalists use their control to protect their investments, so they may therefore perform a key nurturing and monitoring role for the firm.

---

[1]"MoneyTree Report," PriceWaterhouseCoopers. Data provided by Thomson Financial.

[2]Paul A. Gompers and Josh Lerner, *The Venture Capital Cycle* (Cambridge, MA: MIT Press, 1999).

FIGURE 13.2

Venture Capital Funding in the United States

Panel (a) indicates the total number of venture capital deals by year. Panel (b) shows the total dollar amount of venture capital investment.

Source: Venture Economics, 2008.

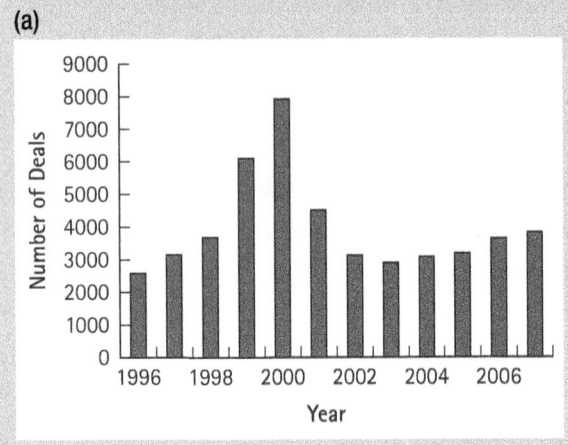

(a)

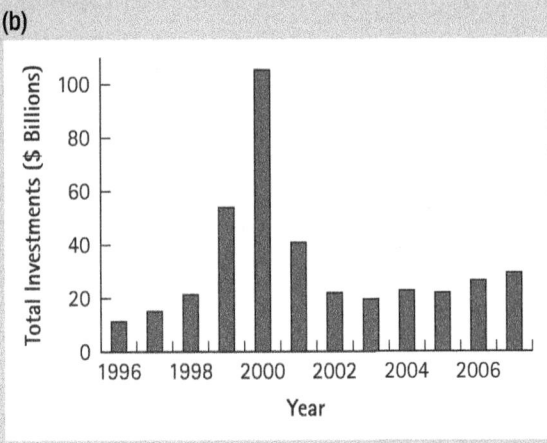

(b)

The importance of the venture capital sector has grown enormously in the last 50 years. As Figure 13.2 shows, growth in the sector increased in the 1990s and peaked at the height of the Internet boom. Although the size of the industry has decreased substantially since then, it remains larger than it was in 1998.

Institutional Investors. Institutional investors such as pension funds, insurance companies, endowments, and foundations manage large quantities of money. They are major investors in many different types of assets, so, not surprisingly, they are also active investors in private companies. Institutional investors may invest directly in private firms, or they may invest indirectly by becoming limited partners in venture capital firms. Institutional interest in private equity has grown dramatically in recent years. For example, *The Wall Street Journal* reported that universities, endowments, and pension funds invested $17.6 billion in venture capital during 2004, up 67% from 2003.

Source: Mick Stevens, *The New Yorker,* June 29, 2001, I.D. No. 45038.

corporate investor, corporate partner, strategic partner, strategic investor
A corporation that invests in private companies.

Corporate Investors.   Many established corporations purchase equity in younger, private companies. A corporation that invests in private companies is referred to by many different names, including **corporate investor**, **corporate partner**, **strategic partner**, and **strategic investor**. Most of the other types of investors in private firms that we have considered so far are primarily interested in the financial return that they will earn on their investments. Corporate investors, by contrast, might invest for corporate strategic objectives in addition to the desire for investment returns. For example, in 2007 Microsoft

Corporation, as part of a strategic partnership, invested $240 million in Facebook. The deal gave Microsoft a 1.6% stake in Facebook and control over its banner ad placement outside the United States.

Securities and Valuation

preferred stock
Preferred stock issued by mature companies such as banks usually has a preferential dividend and seniority in any liquidation and sometimes special voting rights. Preferred stock issued by young companies has seniority in any liquidation but typically does not pay cash dividends and contains a right to convert to common stock.

convertible preferred stock A preferred stock that gives the owner an option to convert it into common stock on some future date.

When a company founder decides to sell equity to outside investors for the first time, it is common practice for private companies to issue preferred stock rather than common stock to raise capital. **Preferred stock** issued by mature companies such as banks usually has a preferential dividend and seniority in any liquidation, and sometimes special voting rights. Conversely, while retaining its seniority, the preferred stock issued by young companies typically does not pay regular cash dividends. However, this preferred stock usually gives the owner an option to convert it into common stock on some future date, so it is often called **convertible preferred stock**. In short, it will have all of the future rights and benefits of common stock if things go well. On the other hand, if the company runs into financial difficulties, the preferred stockholders have a senior claim on the assets of the firm relative to any common stockholders (who are often the employees of the firm).

To illustrate, let's consider RealNetworks, which was founded by Robert Glaser in 1993, and was initially funded with an investment of approximately $1 million by Glaser. As of April 1995, Glaser's $1 million initial investment in RealNetworks represented 13,713,439 shares of Series A preferred stock, implying an initial purchase price of about $0.07 per share. RealNetworks needed more capital, and management decided to raise this money by selling equity in the form of convertible preferred stock.

The company's first round of outside equity funding was Series B preferred stock. RealNetworks sold 2,686,567 shares of Series B preferred stock at $0.67 per share in April 1995.[3] It is important to understand that RealNetworks remained a private company after this transaction. Simply selling equity to outside investors does not cause a company to be public. Companies may remain private, meaning their shares are not listed on an exchange and they are not required to file their financial statements with the SEC, as long as the number of shareholders remains small. Later in this chapter we discuss the process of offering shares to the general public and thereby transitioning to public status. After this funding round the distribution of ownership was:

	Number of Shares	Price per Share ($)	Total Value ($ million)	Percentage Ownership
Series A	13,713,439	0.67	9.2	83.6%
Series B	2,686,567	0.67	1.8	16.4%
	16,400,006		11.0	100.0%

pre-money valuation The value of a firm's prior shares outstanding at the price in the funding round.

post-money valuation The value of the whole firm (old plus new shares) at the price at which the new equity is sold.

The Series B preferred shares were new shares of stock being sold by RealNetworks. At the price the new shares were sold for, Glaser's shares were worth $9.2 million and represented 83.6% of the outstanding shares. It is important to note that the increase in the value of Glaser's shares was very uncertain when he founded the company. The value of the prior shares outstanding at the price in the funding round ($9.2 million in this example) is called the **pre-money valuation**. The value of the whole firm (old plus new shares) at the funding round price ($11.0 million) is known as the **post-money valuation**.

---

[3]The number of shares of RealNetworks preferred stock given here for this and subsequent funding comes from the IPO prospectus (available on EDGAR at http://www.sec.gov/edgar/searchedgar/webusers .htm). For simplicity, we have ignored warrants to purchase additional shares that were also issued and a small amount of employee common stock that existed.

EXAMPLE 13.1

Funding and Ownership

Problem

You founded your own firm two years ago. You initially contributed $100,000 of your money and, in return received 1.5 million shares of stock. Since then, you have sold an additional 500,000 shares to angel investors. You are now considering raising even more capital from a venture capitalist (VC). This VC would invest $6 million and would receive 3 million newly issued shares. What is the post-money valuation? Assuming that this is the VC's first investment in your company, what percentage of the firm will she end up owning? What percentage will you own? What is the value of your shares?

Solution

▶ **Plan**

After this funding round, there will be a total of 5 million shares outstanding:

Your shares	1,500,000
Angel investors' shares	500,000
Newly issued shares	3,000,000
Total	5,000,000

The VC would be paying $6,000,000 / 3,000,000 = $2 per share. The post-money valuation will be the total number of shares multiplied by the price paid by the VC. The percentage of the firm owned by the VC is the number of her shares divided by the total number of shares. Your percentage will be the number of your shares divided by the total number of shares and the value of your shares will be the number of shares you own multiplied by the price the VC paid.

▶ **Execute**

There are 5 million shares and the VC paid $2 per share. Therefore, the post-money valuation would be 5,000,000 × $2 = $10 million.

Because she is buying 3 million shares, and there will be 5 million total shares outstanding after the funding round, the VC will end up owning 3,000,000 / 5,000,000 = 60% of the firm.

You will own 1,500,000 / 5,000,000 = 30% of the firm, and the post-money valuation of your shares is 1,500,000 × $2 = $3,000,000.

▶ **Evaluate**

Funding your firm with new equity capital, whether it is from an angel or a venture capitalist, involves a tradeoff—you must give up part of the ownership of the firm in return for the money you need to grow. If you can negotiate a higher price per share, the percentage of your firm that you will have to give up for a specified amount of capital will be smaller.

Over the next few years, RealNetworks raised three more rounds of outside equity in addition to the Series B funding round:

Series	Date	Number of Shares	Share Price ($)	Capital Raised ($ million)
B	April 1995	2,686,567	0.67	1.8
C	Oct. 1995	2,904,305	1.96	5.7
D	Nov. 1996	2,381,010	7.53	17.9
E	July 1997	3,338,374	8.99	30.0

In each case, investors bought preferred stock in the private company. These investors were very similar to the profile of typical investors in private firms that we described earlier. Angel investors purchased the Series B stock. The investors in Series C and D stock were primarily venture capital funds. Microsoft purchased the Series E stock as a corporate investor.

Exiting an Investment in a Private Company

exit strategy An important consideration for investors in private companies, it details how they will eventually realize the return from their investment.

Similar to any relationship, the one between a firm and its investors is subject to change as needs and resources develop. An important consideration for investors in private companies is their **exit strategy**—how they will eventually realize the return from their investment. Investors exit in two main ways: through an acquisition or through a public offering. Often, large corporations purchase successful start-up companies. In such a case, the acquiring company purchases the outstanding stock of the private company, allowing all investors to cash out. From 2001–2005, roughly 85% of venture capital exits occurred through mergers or acquisitions.[4] The alternative way for the company to allow its investors to liquidate their investment is to become a publicly traded company.

Over time, the value of a share of RealNetworks' stock and the size of its funding rounds increased. Because investors in Series E were willing to pay $8.99 for a share of preferred stock with equivalent rights in July 1997, the post-money valuation of existing preferred stock was $8.99 per share. Because RealNetworks was still a private company, however, investors could not liquidate their investment by selling their stock in the public stock markets. In the next section, we discuss the process a firm goes through to sell shares to the public and have its shares traded on a public market.

1. What are the main sources of funding for private companies to raise outside equity capital?

2. What is a venture capital firm?

Taking Your Firm Public: The Initial Public Offering

initial public offering (IPO) The process of selling stock to the public for the first time.

The process of selling stock to the public for the first time is called an **initial public offering (IPO)**. In this section, we look at the mechanics of IPOs in two cases—the traditional set-up and recent innovations.

Advantages and Disadvantages of Going Public

Going public provides companies with greater liquidity and better access to capital. By going public, companies give their private equity investors the ability to diversify. In addition, public companies typically have access to much larger amounts of capital through the public markets, both in the initial public offering and in subsequent offerings. For example, during 2007 the ten largest equity issues in the world each raised $6 billion or more, as shown in Table 13.1. In RealNetworks' case, its last round of private equity funding raised about $30 million in July 1997. The firm raised $43 million when it went public in November of the same year; less than two years later, it raised an additional $267 million by selling more stock to the public. As a public company, RealNetworks was able to raise substantially more money.

---

[4]The National Venture Capital Association.

BDeH CHAPTER 13

TABLE 13.1	Issuer	Date	Amount ($ billion)
Largest Global Equity Issues, 2007	Fortis Group NV	Oct. 11	19.3
	PetroChina Co., Ltd.	Oct. 29	8.9
	China Shenhua Energy Co., Ltd.	Sep. 26	8.9
	Sberbank	Feb. 21	8.8
	OAO VTB Bank	May 10	8.0
	China Construction Bank Corp	Sep. 11	7.7
	Pol-Aqua SA	Nov. 29	7.7
	Marfin Investment Group	Jul. 6	7.1
	Imperial Tobacco Group PLC	Aug. 14	6.0
	Iberdrola Renovables SA	Dec. 11	6.0

Source: Thomson Financial.

The major advantage of undertaking an IPO is also one of the major disadvantages of an IPO: When investors sell their stake and thereby diversify their holdings, the equity holders of the corporation become more widely dispersed. This undermines investors' ability to monitor the company's management and thus represents a loss of control. Furthermore, once a company goes public, it must satisfy all of the requirements of public companies. Several high-profile corporate scandals during the early part of the twenty-first century prompted tougher regulations designed to address corporate abuses. Organizations such as the Securities and Exchange Commission (SEC), the securities exchanges (including the New York Stock Exchange and the NASDAQ), and Congress (through the Sarbanes-Oxley Act of 2002) adopted new standards that focused on more thorough financial disclosure, greater accountability, and more stringent requirements for the makeup and responsibilities of the board of directors. In general, these standards were designed to provide better protection for investors. However, compliance with the new standards is costly and time-consuming for public companies.

Primary and Secondary IPO Offerings

underwriter An investment banking firm that manages a security issuance and designs its structure.

After deciding to go public, managers of the company work with an **underwriter**, an investment banking firm that manages the security issuance and designs its structure. In this case, the underwriter is managing the company's offering of securities to the public. Choices for the offering's structure include the type of shares to be sold and the mechanism the underwriter will use to sell the stock.

primary offering New shares available in a public offering that raise new capital.

At an IPO, a firm offers a large block of shares for sale to the public for the first time. The shares that are sold in the IPO may either be new shares that raise new capital, known as a **primary offering**, or existing shares that are sold by current shareholders (as part of their exit strategy), known as a **secondary offering**.

secondary offering An equity offering of shares sold by existing shareholders (as part of their exit strategy).

The traditional IPO process follows a standardized form. We will explore the steps that underwriters go though during an IPO.

lead underwriter The primary banking firm responsible for managing a security issuance.

Underwriters and the Syndicate.   Many IPOs, especially the larger offerings, are managed by a group of underwriters. The **lead underwriter** is the primary banking firm responsible for managing the security issuance. The lead underwriter provides most of the advice on the sale and arranges for a group of other underwriters, called the **syndicate**, to help market and sell the issue. Table 13.2 shows the lead underwriters who were responsible for the largest number of IPOs in the United States during 2007. As you can see, the major U.S. investment and commercial banks dominate the underwriting business.

syndicate A group of underwriters who jointly underwrite and distribute a security issuance.

BDeH CHAPTER 13

TABLE 13.2	Rank	Lead Underwriter	Number of Issues	Total Net Proceeds ($ million)
	1	Morgan Stanley	33	10,323
International IPO	2	Citigroup	20	8,225
Underwriter Ranking	3	Goldman Sachs	29	7,273
Report for 2007	4	CS First Boston	27	6,379
	5	Merrill Lynch	18	4,075
	6	Lehman Brothers	13	3,880
	7	J.P. Morgan	19	3,154
	8	Deutsch Bank	9	1,872
	9	WR Hambrecht	2	1,320
	10	Bear Sterns	3	1,268

Source: IPO Home by Renaissance Capital (rankings are based on data collected by Renaissance Capital from January 8, 2007, to January 8, 2008, for lead underwriters only), http://www.ipohome.com/marketwatch/urankings.asp?list=proceeds&nav=f.

Underwriters market the IPO, and they help the company with all the necessary filings. More importantly, as we discuss below, they actively participate in determining the offer price. In many cases, the underwriter will also commit to making a market in the stock by matching buyers and sellers after the issue, thereby guaranteeing that the stock will be liquid.

registration statement
A legal document that provides financial and other information about a company to investors prior to a security issuance.

preliminary prospectus (red herring) Part of the registration statement prepared by a company prior to an IPO that is circulated to investors before the stock is offered.

final prospectus Part of the final registration statement prepared by a company prior to an IPO that contains all the details of the offering, including the number of shares offered and the offer price.

SEC Filings.   The SEC requires that companies prepare a **registration statement**, a legal document that provides financial and other information about the company to investors prior to a security issuance. Company managers work closely with the underwriters to prepare this registration statement and submit it to the SEC. Part of the registration statement, called the **preliminary prospectus** or **red herring**, circulates to investors before the stock is offered. The term "red herring" derives from the warning in red ink on the front of the prospectus stating that it is preliminary and is not an offer to sell the shares. (Interestingly, the term red herring originates from the sport of fox hunting, where traditionally a red (smoked) herring was used to distract the dogs and throw them off the scent of their prey.)

The SEC reviews the registration statement to make sure that the company has disclosed all of the information necessary for investors to decide whether to purchase the stock. Once the company has satisfied the SEC's disclosure requirements, the SEC approves the stock for sale to the general public. Prior to the IPO, the company prepares the final registration statement, which includes the **final prospectus** that contains all the details of the IPO, including the number of shares offered and the offer price.[5]

To illustrate this process, let's return to RealNetworks. Figure 13.3 shows the cover page for the final prospectus for RealNetworks' IPO. This cover page includes the name of the company, the list of lead underwriters, and summary information about the pricing of the deal. This was a primary offering of 3 million shares.

Valuation.   Before the offer price is set, the underwriters work closely with the company to come up with a price range that they believe provides a reasonable valuation for the firm using the techniques described in Chapter 9. As we pointed out in that chapter, there are two ways to value a company: estimate the future cash flows and compute the

---

[5]Registration statements may be found at EDGAR, the SEC Web site providing registration information to investors: http://www.sec.gov/edgar/searchedgar/webusers.htm.

FIGURE 13.3

The Cover Page of RealNetworks' IPO Prospectus

The cover page includes the name of the company, a list of lead underwriters, and summary information about the pricing of the offering.

Source: Courtesy of RealNetworks, Inc.

BDeH   CHAPTER 13

3,000,000 Shares

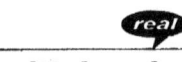

RealNetworks, Inc.

(formerly "Progressive Networks, Inc.")

Common Stock
(par value $.001 per share)

All of the 3,000,000 shares of Common Stock offered hereby are being sold by RealNetworks, Inc. Prior to the offering, there has been no public market for the Common Stock. For factors considered in determining the initial public offering price, see "Underwriting".

The Common Stock offered hereby involves a high degree of risk. See "Risk Factors" beginning on page 6.

The Common Stock has been approved for quotation on the Nasdaq National Market under the symbol "RNWK," subject to notice of issuance.

THESE SECURITIES HAVE NOT BEEN APPROVED OR DISAPPROVED BY THE SECURITIES AND EXCHANGE COMMISSION OR ANY STATE SECURITIES COMMISSION NOR HAS THE SECURITIES AND EXCHANGE COMMISSION OR ANY STATE SECURITIES COMMISSION PASSED UPON THE ACCURACY OR ADEQUACY OF THIS PROSPECTUS. ANY REPRESENTATION TO THE CONTRARY IS A CRIMINAL OFFENSE.

	Initial Public Offering Price(1)	Underwriting Discount(2)	Proceeds to Company(3)
Per Share	$12.50	$0.875	$11.625
Total(4)	$37,500,000	$2,625,000	$34,875,000

---

(1) In connection with the offering, the Underwriters have reserved up to 300,000 shares of Common Stock for sale at the initial public offering price to employees and friends of the Company.

(2) The Company has agreed to indemnify the Underwriters against certain liabilities, including liabilities under the Securities Act of 1933, as amended. See "Underwriting".

(3) Before deducting estimated expenses of $950,000 payable by the Company.

(4) The Company has granted the Underwriters an option for 30 days to purchase up to an additional 450,000 shares at the initial public offering price per share, less the underwriting discount, solely to cover over-allotments. If such option is exercised in full, the total initial public offering price, underwriting discount and proceeds to Company will be $43,125,000, $3,018,750 and $40,106,250, respectively. See "Underwriting".

The shares offered hereby are offered severally by the Underwriters, as specified herein, subject to receipt and acceptance by them and subject to their right to reject any order in whole or in part. It is expected that certificates for the shares will be ready for delivery in New York, New York on or about November 26, 1997, against payment therefor in immediately available funds.

Goldman, Sachs & Co.
BancAmerica Robertson Stephens
NationsBanc Montgomery Securities, Inc.

The date of this Prospectus is November 21, 1997.

road show During an IPO, when a company's senior management and its lead underwriters travel to promote the company and explain their rationale for an offer price to institutional investors such as mutual funds and pension funds.

present value, or estimate the value by examining comparable companies. Most underwriters use both techniques. However, when these techniques give substantially different answers, underwriters often rely on comparables based on recent IPOs.

Once an initial price range is established, the underwriters try to determine what the market thinks of the valuation. They begin by arranging a **road show**, in which senior management and the lead underwriters travel around the country (and sometimes around the world) promoting the company and explaining their rationale for the offer price to the underwriters' largest customers—mainly institutional investors such as mutual funds and pension funds.

EXAMPLE 13.2

Valuing an IPO Using Comparables

Problem

Wagner, Inc., is a private company that designs, manufactures, and distributes branded consumer products. During its most recent fiscal year, Wagner had revenues of $325 million and earnings of $15 million. Wagner has filed a registration statement with the SEC for its IPO. Before the stock is offered, Wagner's investment bankers would like to estimate the value of the company using comparable companies. The investment bankers have assembled the following information based on data for other companies in the same industry that have recently gone public. In each case, the ratios are based on the IPO price.

Company	Price/Earnings	Price/Revenues
Ray Products Corp.	18.8×	1.2×
Byce-Frasier Inc.	19.5×	0.9×
Fashion Industries Group	24.1×	0.8×
Recreation International	22.4×	0.7×
Average	21.2×	0.9×

After the IPO, Wagner will have 20 million shares outstanding. Estimate the IPO price for Wagner using the price/earnings ratio and the price/revenues ratio.

Solution

▶ **Plan**

If the IPO price of Wagner is based on a price/earnings ratio that is similar to those for recent IPOs, then this ratio will equal the average of recent deals. Thus, to compute the IPO price based on the P/E ratio, we will first take the average P/E ratio from the comparison group and multiply it by Wagner's total earnings. This will give us a total value of equity for Wagner. To get the per share IPO price, we need to divide the total equity value by the number of shares outstanding after the IPO (20 million). The approach will be the same for the price/revenues ratio.

▶ **Execute**

The average P/E ratio for recent deals is 21.2. Given earnings of $15 million, the total market value of Wagner's stock will be $15 million × 21.2 = $318 million. With 20 million shares outstanding, the price per share should be $318 million / 20 million = $15.90.

Similarly, if Wagner's IPO price implies a price/revenues ratio equal to the recent average of 0.9, then using its revenues of $325 million, the total market value of Wagner will be $325 million × 0.9 = $292.5 million, or $14.63 per share ($292.5/20).

▶ **Evaluate**

As we found in Chapter 9, using multiples for valuation always produces a range of estimates—you should not expect to get the same value from different ratios. Based on these estimates, the underwriters will probably establish an initial price range for Wagner stock of $13 to $17 per share to take on the road show.

BDeH CHAPTER 13

book building A process used by underwriters for coming up with an offer price based on customers' expressions of interest.

At the end of the road show, customers inform the underwriters of their interest by telling the underwriters how many shares they may want to purchase. Although these commitments are nonbinding, the underwriters' customers value their long-term relationships with the underwriters, so they rarely go back on their word. The underwriters then add up the total demand and adjust the price until it is unlikely that the issue will fail. This process for coming up with the offer price based on customers' expressions of interest is called **book building**.

firm commitment An agreement between an underwriter and an issuing firm in which the underwriter guarantees that it will sell all of the stock at the offer price.

Pricing the Deal and Managing Risk. In the most common arrangement, an underwriter and an issuing firm agree to a **firm commitment** IPO, in which the underwriter guarantees that it will sell all of the stock at the offer price. The underwriter purchases the entire issue (at a slightly lower price than the offer price) and then resells it at the offer price. If the entire issue does not sell out, the underwriter is on the hook: The remaining shares must be sold at a lower price and the underwriter must take the loss. The most notorious loss in the industry happened when the British government privatized British Petroleum. In a highly unusual deal, the company was taken public gradually. The British government sold its final stake in British Petroleum at the time of the October 1987 stock market crash. The offer price was set just before the crash, but the offering occurred after the crash.[6] At the end of the first day's trading, the underwriters were facing a loss of $1.29 billion. The price then fell even further, until the Kuwaiti Investment Office stepped in and started purchasing a large stake in the company.

spread The fee a company pays to its underwriters that is a percentage of the issue price of a share of stock.

In the RealNetworks' IPO, the final offer price was $12.50 per share.[7] The company agreed to pay the underwriters a fee, called a **spread**, which is a percentage of the issue price of a share of stock, in this case $0.875 per share—exactly 7% of the issue price. Because this was a firm commitment deal, the underwriters bought the stock from RealNetworks for $12.50 − $0.875 = $11.625 per share and then resold it to their customers for $12.50 per share.

Recall that when an underwriter provides a firm commitment, it is potentially exposing itself to the risk that the banking firm might have to sell the shares at less than the offer price and take a loss. However, according to Tim Loughran and Jay Ritter, between 1990 and 1998, just 9% of U.S. IPOs experienced a fall in share price on the first day.[8] For another 16% of firms, the price at the end of the first day was the same as the offer price. Therefore, the vast majority of IPOs experienced a price increase on the first day of trading, indicating that the initial offer price was generally lower than the price that stock market investors were willing to pay.

over-allotment allocation (greenshoe provision) In an IPO, an option that allows the underwriter to issue more stock, usually amounting to 15% of the original offer size, at the IPO offer price.

Underwriters appear to use the information they acquire during the book-building stage to intentionally underprice the IPO, thereby reducing their exposure to losses. Furthermore, once the issue price (or offer price) is set, underwriters may invoke another mechanism that allows them to sell extra shares of more successful offerings—the **over-allotment allocation**, or **greenshoe provision**.[9] This option allows the underwriter to issue more stock, amounting to 15% of the original offer size, at the IPO offer price. Look at footnote 4 on the front page of the RealNetworks prospectus in Figure 13.3. This footnote is a greenshoe provision.

---

[6]This deal was exceptional in that the offer price was determined more than a week before the issue date. In the United States, the underwriter usually sets the final offer price within a day of the IPO date.

[7]Stock prices for RealNetworks throughout this chapter have not been adjusted for two subsequent stock splits.

[8]"Why Don't Issuers Get Upset About Leaving Money on the Table in IPOs?" *Review of Financial Studies* 15 (2) (2002): 413–443.

[9]The name derives from the Green Shoe Company, the first issuer to have an over-allotment option in its IPO.

Once the IPO process is complete, the company's shares trade publicly on an exchange. The lead underwriter usually makes a market in the stock by matching buyers and sellers and assigns an analyst to cover it. By doing so, the underwriter increases the liquidity of the stock in the secondary market. This service is of value to both the issuing company and the underwriter's customers. A liquid market ensures that investors who purchased shares via the IPO are able to trade those shares easily. If the stock is actively traded, the issuer will have continued access to the equity markets in the event that the company decides to issue more shares in a new offering. In most cases, the existing shareholders are subject to a **lockup**, a restriction that prevents them from selling their shares for some period (usually 180 days) after the IPO. Once the lockup period expires, they are free to sell their shares.

lockup A restriction that prevents existing shareholders from selling their shares for some period (usually 180 days) after an IPO.

Other IPO Types

Now that we have established the traditional method for IPOs, we will discuss three other ways shares may be sold during an IPO.

best-efforts For smaller initial public offerings (IPOs), a situation in which the underwriter does not guarantee that the stock will be sold, but instead tries to sell the stock for the best possible price.

Best-Efforts Basis.   For smaller IPOs, the underwriter commonly accepts the deal on a **best-efforts** basis. In this case, the underwriter does not guarantee that the stock will be sold, but instead tries to sell the stock for the best possible price. Often such deals have an all-or-none clause: either all of the shares are sold in the IPO, or the deal is called off.

auction IPO An online method for selling new issues directly to the public that lets the market determine the price through bids from potential investors.

Auction IPO.   In recent years, the investment banking firm of W.R. Hambrecht and Company has attempted to change the IPO process by selling new issues directly to the public using an online **auction IPO** mechanism called OpenIPO. Rather than setting the price itself in the traditional way, Hambrecht lets the market determine the price of the stock by auctioning off the company.[10] Investors place bids over a set period of time. An auction IPO then sets the highest price such that the number of bids at or above that price equals the number of offered shares. All winning bidders pay this price, even if their bids were higher. The first OpenIPO was the $11.55 million IPO for Ravenswood Winery, completed in 1999.

It's easier to understand how an auction IPO works by considering an example. Your firm is planning an auction IPO for 3 million shares. Potential buyers submit bids at various prices and their bids are then aggregated. Table 13.2 summarizes those bids. The column "Shares sought at this price" shows the total number of shares from investors' bids at each price. The last column contains the total number of shares bid at or above each price. Because investors are willing to buy at prices lower than the amount they bid, this total represents the number of shares that can be sold at each price. For example, while investors were only willing to buy a total of 75,000 shares at a price of $19.50, at a price of $19.00 a total of 225,000 (150,000 + 75,000) can be sold.

TABLE 13.3	Price	Shares Sought at this Price	Total Shares Sought at or above this Price
Bids Received to Purchase Shares in a Hypothetical Auction IPO (in '000)	$16.50	3,200	11,800
	$17.00	2,900	8,600
	$17.50	2,700	5,700
	$18.00	1,925	3,000
	$18.50	850	1,075
	$19.00	150	225
	$19.50	75	75

[10]You can find details about Hambrecht's auction IPO process at http://www.openipo.com/ind/index.html.

FIGURE 13.4

Aggregating the Shares Sought in the Hypothetical Auction IPO
The figure graphs the last column in Table 13.3, which indicates the total number of shares that can be sold at each price. In this case, investors are willing to buy a total of 3 million shares at or above a price of $18. So, you would set your IPO price at $18 to give you the highest price at which you could place 3 million shares.

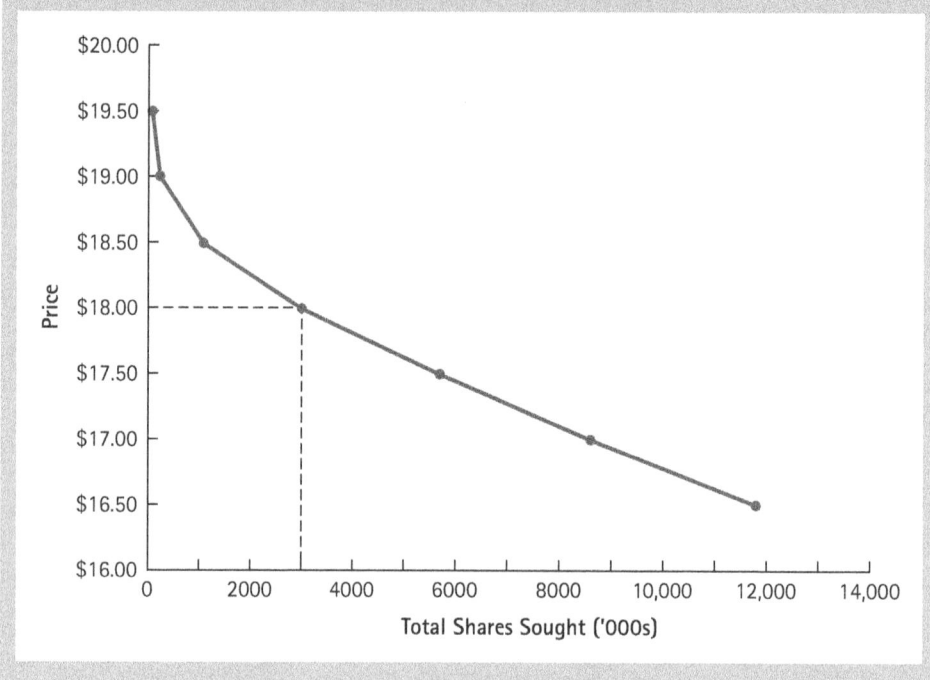

You are interested in selling a total of 3 million shares at the highest price possible. This suggests that you should look in the left column of Table 13.3 to find the highest price at which the total demand is at least 3 million shares. In this case, the highest price at which we can sell 3 million shares is $18. Figure 13.4 shows this graphically.

EXAMPLE 13.3

Auction IPO Pricing

Problem
Fleming Educational Software, Inc., is selling 500,000 shares of stock in an auction IPO. At the end of the bidding period, Fleming's investment bank has received the following bids:

Price ($)	Number of Shares Bid
8.00	25,000
7.75	100,000
7.50	75,000
7.25	150,000
7.00	150,000
6.75	275,000
6.50	125,000

What will the offer price of the shares be?

Solution

▶ **Plan**

First, we must compute the total number of shares demanded at or above any given price. Then, we pick the highest price that will allow us to sell the full issue (500,000 shares).

▶ **Execute**

Converting the table of bids into a table of cumulative demand produces we have:

Price ($)	Cumulative Demand
8.00	25,000
7.75	125,000
7.50	200,000
7.25	350,000
7.00	500,000
6.75	775,000
6.50	900,000

For example, the company has received bids for a total of 125,000 shares at $7.75 per share or higher (25,000 + 100,000 = 125,000).

Fleming is offering a total of 500,000 shares. The winning auction price would be $7 per share, because investors have placed orders for a total of 500,000 shares at a price of $7 or higher. All investors who placed bids of at least this price will be able to buy the stock for $7 per share, even if their initial bid was higher.

In this example, the cumulative demand at the winning price exactly equals the supply. If the total demand at this price were greater than the supply, all auction participants who bid prices higher than the winning price would receive their full bid (at the winning price). Shares would be awarded on a pro rata basis to bidders who bid exactly the winning price.

▶ **Evaluate**

Although the auction IPO does not provide the certainty of the firm commitment, it has the advantage of using the market to determine the offer price. It also reduces the underwriter's role and, consequently, fees.

Although the auction IPO mechanism seems to represent an attractive alternative to traditional IPO procedures, it has not been widely adopted either in the United States or abroad. Between 1999 and 2004, Hambrecht completed less than a dozen auction IPOs. However, in 2004 Google went public using the auction mechanism (see the box describing Google's IPO), which generated renewed interest in this alternative. In May 2007, Interactive Brokers Group raised $1.2 billion in its IPO using a Hambrecht OpenIPO auction.

Because no offer price is set in an auction IPO, book building is not as important in that venue as it is in traditional IPOs. In a recent paper, Professors Ravi Jagannathan and Ann Sherman examine why auctions have failed to become a popular IPO method and why they have been plagued by inaccurate pricing and poor performance following the issue. They suggest that because auctions do not use the book-building process, which aids in collecting large investors' valuations of the stock, investors are discouraged from participating in auctions.[11] Table 13.4 summarizes the methods a firm can use for an initial public offering of its stock.

---

[11]"Why Do IPO Auctions Fail?" NBER working paper 12151, March 2006.

TABLE 13.4	Firm Commitment	Best Efforts	Auction IPO
Summary of IPO Methods	Underwriter purchases the entire issue at an agreed price and sells it to investors at a higher price.	Underwriter makes its "best effort" to sell the issue to investors at an agreed price.	Firm or underwriter solicits bids (price and quantity) from investors, and chooses the highest price at which there is sufficient demand to sell the entire issue.

BDeH CHAPTER 13

Google's IPO

On April 29, 2004, Google, Inc., announced plans to go public. Breaking with tradition, Google startled Wall Street by declaring its intention to rely heavily on the auction IPO mechanism for distributing its shares. Google had been profitable since 2001, so according to Google executives, access to capital was not the only motive to go public. The company also wanted to provide employees and private equity investors with liquidity.

One of the major attractions of the auction mechanism was the possibility of allocating shares to more individual investors. Google also hoped to set an accurate offer price by letting market bidders set the IPO price. After the Internet stock market boom, there were many lawsuits related to the way underwriters allocated shares. Google hoped to avoid the allocation scandals by letting the auction allocate shares.

Investors who wanted to bid opened a brokerage account with one of the deal's underwriters and then placed their bids with the brokerage house. Google and its underwriters identified the highest bid that allowed the company to sell all of the shares being offered. They also had the flexibility to choose to offer shares at a lower price.

On August 18, 2004, Google sold 19.6 million shares at $85 per share. The $1.67 billion raised was easily the largest auction IPO ever. Google stock (ticker: GOOG) opened trading on the NASDAQ market the next day at $100 per share. Although the Google IPO sometimes stumbled along the way, it represents the most significant example of the use of the auction mechanism as an alternative to the traditional IPO mechanism.

Sources: Kevin Delaney and Robin Sidel, "Google IPO Aims to Change the Rules," *The Wall Street Journal*, April 30, 2004, p. C1; Ruth Simon and Elizabeth Weinstein, "Investors Eagerly Anticipate Google's IPO," *The Wall Street Journal*, April 30, 2004, p. C1; Gregory Zuckerman, "Google Shares Prove Big Winners—for a Day," *The Wall Street Journal*, August 20, 2004, p. C1.

Concept Check

3. What services does the underwriter provide in a traditional IPO?

4. Explain the mechanics of an auction IPO.

13.3 IPO Puzzles

Four characteristics of IPOs puzzle financial economists, and all are relevant to the financial manager:

1. On average, IPOs appear to be underpriced: The price at the end of trading on the first day is often substantially higher than the IPO price.

2. The number of IPOs is highly cyclical. When times are good, the market is flooded with IPOs; when times are bad, the number of IPOs dries up.

3. The transaction costs of the IPO are very high, and it is unclear why firms willingly incur such high costs.

4. The long-run performance of a newly public company (three to five years from the date of issue) is poor. That is, on average, a three- to five-year buy-and-hold strategy appears to be a bad investment.

We will now examine each of these puzzles that financial economists seek to understand.

Underpriced IPOs

Generally, underwriters set the issue price so that the average first-day return is positive. For RealNetworks, the underwriters offered the stock at an IPO price of $12.50 per share on November 21, 1997. RealNetworks stock opened trading on the NASDAQ market at a price of $19.375 per share, and it closed at the end of its first trading day at $17.875. So at the end of the first day of trading, its shares were priced $5.375 higher than the IPO price. Such performance is not atypical. On average, between 1960 and 2003, the price in the U.S. aftermarket was 18.3% higher than the IPO price at the end of the first day of trading.[12] As is evident in Figure 13.5, the one-day average return for IPOs has historically been very large around the world. Note that although underpricing is a persistent and global phenomenon, it is generally smaller in more developed capital markets.

Who benefits from the offer price being set below the market price at the end of the first day of trading (underpricing)? We have already explained how the underwriters benefit by controlling their risk—it is much easier to sell the firm's shares if the price is set low. Of course, investors who are able to buy stock from underwriters at the IPO price also gain from the first-day underpricing. Who bears the cost? The pre-IPO shareholders of the issuing firms do. In effect, these owners are selling stock in their firm for less than they could get in the aftermarket.

"Hot" and "Cold" IPO Markets

Figure 13.6 shows the number of IPOs by year from 1975 to 2006. As the figure makes clear, the dollar volume of IPOs has grown significantly, reaching a peak in 1996. An even more important feature of the data is that the trends related to the number of issues are cyclical. Sometimes, as in 1996, the volume of IPOs is unprecedented by historical standards, yet within a year or two the volume of IPOs may decrease significantly. This cyclicality by itself is not particularly surprising. We would expect there to be a greater need for capital in times with more growth opportunities than in times with fewer growth opportunities. What is surprising is the magnitude of the swings. For example, it is difficult to explain the almost seven-fold increase in IPO's from the early to mid-1990s, and the nearly 75% drop from 2000 to 2001. It appears that the number of IPOs is not solely driven by the demand for capital. Sometimes firms and investors seem to favor IPOs; at other times firms appear to rely on alternative sources of capital.

---

[12]See Tim Loughran, Jay R. Ritter, and Kristian Rydqvist, "Initial Public Offerings: International Insights," *Pacific-Basin Finance Journal* 2 (2004): 165–199.

FIGURE 13.5

International Comparison of First-Day IPO Returns

The bars show the average initial returns from the offer price to the first closing market price. For China, the bar shows the average initial return on A share IPOs, available only to residents of China. The date in parentheses indicates the sample period for each country.

Source: Adapted courtesy of Jay Ritter (http://bear.cba.ufl.edu/ritter).

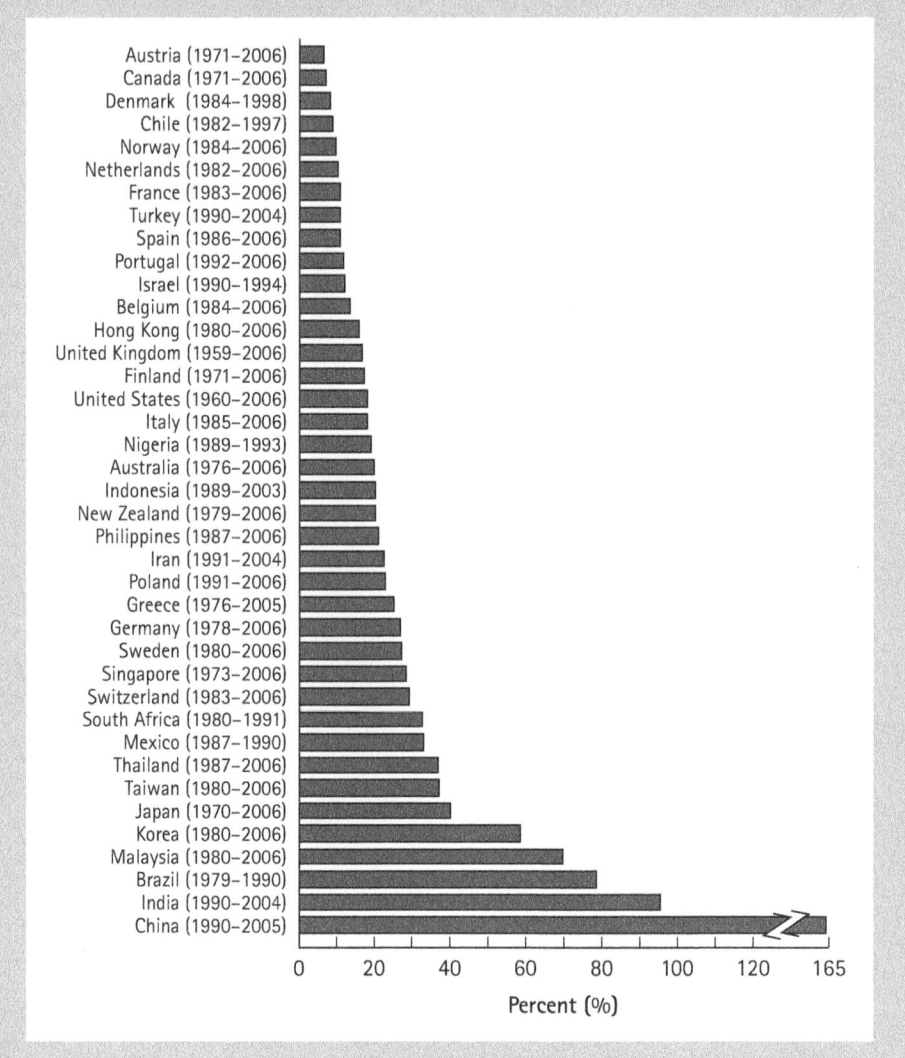

High Cost of Issuing an IPO

In the United States, a typical spread—that is, the discount below the issue price at which the underwriter purchases the shares from the issuing firm—is 7% of the issue price. For an issue size of $50 million, this amounts to $3.5 million. This fee covers the cost to the underwriter of managing the syndicate and helping the company prepare for the IPO, as well as providing it with a return on the capital employed to purchase and market the issue. By most standards, however, this fee is large, especially considering the additional cost to the firm associated with underpricing. Internationally, spreads are generally about half this amount. As Figure 13.7 shows, compared to other security issues, the total cost of issuing stock for the first time is substantially larger than the costs for other securities.

FIGURE 13.6

Cyclicality of Initial Public Offerings in the United States, (1975–2006)

The graph shows the number of IPOs by year. The number of IPOs reached a peak in 1996 demonstrating that trends related to the number of issues are highly cyclical.

Source: Adapted courtesy of Jay R. Ritter (http://bear.cba.ufl.edu/ritter).

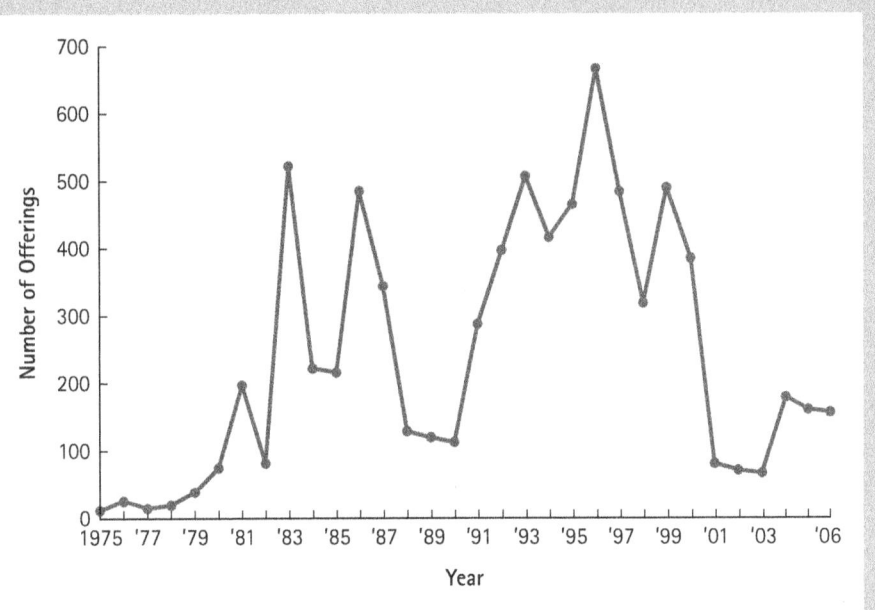

FIGURE 13.7

Relative Costs of Issuing Securities

This figure shows the total direct costs (all underwriting, legal, and auditing costs) of issuing securities as a percentage of the amount of money raised. The figure reports results for IPOs, seasoned equity offerings (subsequent equity offerings), convertible bonds, and standard bonds for issues of different sizes from 1990–1994.

Source: Adapted from I. Lee, S. Lochhead, J. Ritter, and Q. Zhao, "The Costs of Raising Capital," *Journal of Financial Research* 19 (1) (1996): 59–74.

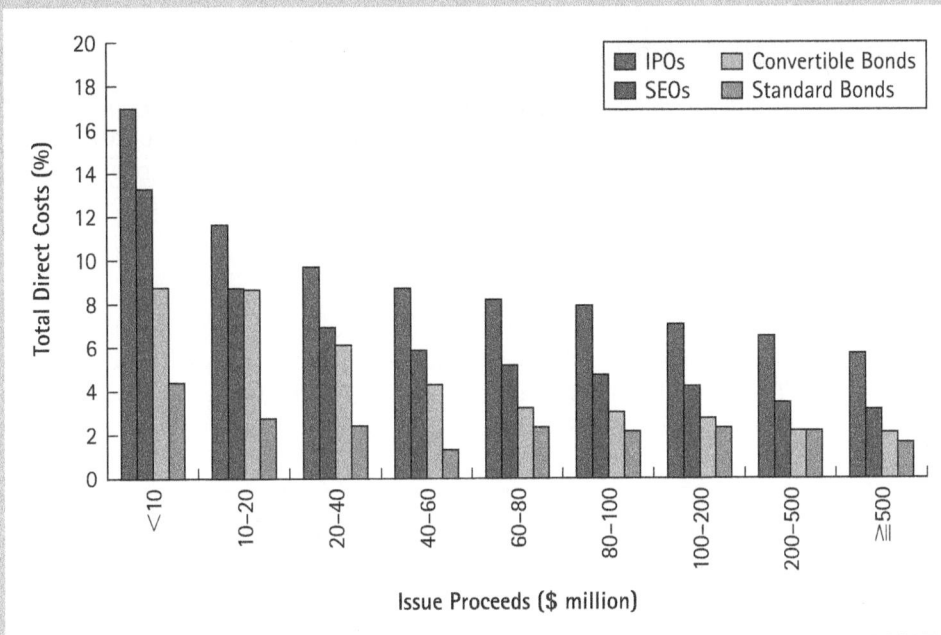

BDeH CHAPTER 13

Even more puzzling is the seeming lack of sensitivity of fees to issue size. Although a large issue requires some additional effort, one would not expect the increased effort to be rewarded as lucratively. For example, Hsuan-Chi Chen and Jay Ritter found that almost all issues ranging in size from $20 million to $80 million paid underwriting fees of about 7% (in addition to other direct costs).[13] It is difficult to understand how a $20 million issue can be profitably done for "only" $1.4 million, while an $80 million issue requires paying fees of $5.6 million. Some have argued that these fees are kept artificially high by the small number of "top" underwriters in the United States who often work together, though others view the 7% as an "insurance premium" that may reflect the greater risk underwriters face in larger deals.

Poor Post-IPO Long-Run Stock Performance

We know that the shares of IPOs generally perform very well immediately following the public offering. It's perhaps surprising, then, that Jay Ritter found that newly listed firms subsequently appear to perform relatively poorly over the following three to five years after their IPOs.[14] This creates a puzzle as to why investors are willing to pay as much as they do for the shares when they begin trading after the IPO.

As we will see in the next section, underperformance is not unique to an initial public issuance of equity: It is associated with subsequent issuances as well. Recently, researchers have begun to explore the possibility that underperformance might not result from the issue of equity itself, but rather from the conditions that motivated the equity issuance in the first place. We will explain this idea in more detail in the next section after we explain how a public company issues additional equity.

Concept Check

5. List and discuss four characteristics about IPOs that are puzzling.

6. For each of the characteristics, identify its relevance to financial managers.

13.4 Raising Additional Capital: The Seasoned Equity Offering

seasoned equity offering (SEO) When a public company returns to the equity markets and offers new shares for sale.

A firm's need for outside capital rarely ends at the IPO. Usually, profitable growth opportunities occur throughout the life of the firm, and in some cases it is not feasible to finance these opportunities out of retained earnings. Thus, a public company more often than not returns to the equity markets and offers new shares for sale in a type of offering called a **seasoned equity offering (SEO)**.

SEO Process

When a firm issues stock using an SEO, it follows many of the same steps as for an IPO. The main difference is that a market price for the stock already exists, so the price-setting process is not necessary.

---

[13]Hsuan-Chi Chen and Jay R. Ritter, "The Seven Percent Solution," *Journal of Finance* 55 (3) (2000): 1105–1131.

[14]Jay R. Ritter, "The Long-Run Performance of Initial Public Offerings," *Journal of Finance* 46 (1) (1991): 3–27.

primary shares New shares issued by a company in an equity offering.

secondary shares Shares sold by existing shareholders in an equity offering.

tombstone Newspaper advertisements in which underwriters advertise a security issuance.

RealNetworks has conducted several SEOs since its IPO in 1997. On June 17, 1999, the firm offered 4 million shares in an SEO at a price of $58 per share. Of these shares, 3,525,000 were **primary shares**—new shares issued by the company. The remaining 475,000 shares were **secondary shares**—shares sold by existing shareholders, including the company's founder, Robert Glaser, who sold 310,000 of his shares. Most of the rest of RealNetworks' SEOs occurred between 1999 and 2004 and included secondary shares sold by existing shareholders rather than directly by RealNetworks.

Historically, underwriters would advertise the sale of stock (both IPOs and SEOs) by taking out newspaper advertisements called **tombstones**. Through these ads, investors would know who to call to buy stock. Today, investors become informed about the impending sale of stock by the news media, via a road show, or through the book-building process, so these tombstones are purely ceremonial. Figure 13.8 shows the tombstone advertisement for one RealNetworks SEO.

FIGURE 13.8

Tombstone Advertisement for a RealNetworks SEO

This tombstone appeared in *The Wall Street Journal* and advertised the underwriters' participation in this RealNetworks SEO.

Source: Courtesy RealNetworks, Inc.

4,600,000 Shares

RealNetworks, Inc.

Common Stock

———

Price $58 Per Share

———

Upon request, a copy of the Prospectus describing these securities and the business of the Company may be obtained within any State from any Underwriter who may legally distribute it within such State. The securities are offered only by means of the Prospectus, and this announcement is neither an offer to sell nor a solicitation of an offer to buy.

Goldman, Sachs & Co.

BancBoston Robertson Stephens

Donaldson, Lufkin & Jenrette

Lehman Brothers

Thomas Weisel Partners LLC

Bear, Stearns & Co. Inc.	**Credit Suisse First Boston**	**Ragen MacKenzie** Incorporated
Warburg Dillon Read LLC		**Wasserstein Perella Securities, Inc.**
Friedman Billings Ramsey		**Pacific Crest Securities Inc.**

July 7, 1999

BDeH CHAPTER 13

cash offer A type of seasoned equity offering (SEO) in which a firm offers the new shares to investors at large.

rights offer A type of seasoned equity offering (SEO) in which a firm offers the new shares only to existing shareholders.

Two types of seasoned equity offerings exist: a cash offer and a rights offer. In a **cash offer**, the firm offers the new shares to investors at large. In a **rights offer**, the firm offers the new shares only to existing shareholders. In the United States, most offers are cash offers, but the same is not true internationally. For example, in the United Kingdom, most seasoned offerings of new shares are rights offers.

Rights offers protect existing shareholders from underpricing. To illustrate, suppose a company holds $100 in cash as its sole asset and has 50 shares outstanding. Each share is worth $2. The company announces a cash offer for 50 shares at $1 per share. Once this offer is complete, the company will have $150 in cash and 100 shares outstanding. The price per share is now $1.50 to reflect the fact that the new shares were sold at a discount. The new shareholders therefore receive a $0.50 per share windfall at the expense of the old shareholders.

The old shareholders would be protected if, instead of a cash offer, the company did a rights offer. In this case, rather than offer the new shares for general sale, every shareholder would have the right to purchase an additional share for $1 per share. If all shareholders chose to exercise their rights, then after the sale the value of the company would be the same as with a cash offer: It would be worth $150 with 100 shares outstanding and a price of $1.50 per share. In this case, however, the $0.50 windfall accrues to existing shareholders, which exactly offsets the drop in the stock price. Thus, if a firm's management is concerned that its equity may be underpriced in the market, by using a rights offer the firm can continue to issue equity without imposing a loss on its current shareholders.

EXAMPLE 13.4

Raising Money with Rights Offers

Problem

You are the CFO of a company that has a market capitalization of $1 billion. The firm has 100 million shares outstanding, so the shares are trading at $10 per share. You need to raise $200 million and have announced a rights issue. Each existing shareholder is sent one right for every share he or she owns. You have not decided how many rights you will require to purchase a share of new stock. You will require either four rights to purchase one share at a price of $8 per share, or five rights to purchase two new shares at a price of $5 per share. Which approach will raise more money?

Solution

▶ **Plan**

In order to know how much money will be raised, we need to compute how many total shares would be purchased if everyone exercises their rights. Then we can multiply it by the price per share to calculate the total amount of capital raised.

▶ **Execute**

There are 100 million shares, each with one right attached. In the first case, four rights will be needed to purchase a new share, so 100 million / 4 = 25 million new shares will be purchased. At a price of $8 per share, that would raise $8 × 25 million = $200 million.

In the second case, for every five rights, two new shares can be purchased, so there will be 2 × (100 million / 5) = 40 million new shares. At a price of $5 per share, that would also raise $200 million. If all shareholders exercise their rights, both approaches will raise the same amount of money.

▶ **Evaluate**

In both cases, the value of the firm after the issue is $1.2 billion. In the first case, there are 125 million shares outstanding after the issue, so the price per share after the issue is $1.2 billion/

125 million = $9.60. This price exceeds the issue price of $8, so the shareholders will exercise their rights. Because exercising will yield a profit of ($9.60 − $8.00) / 4 = $0.40 per right, the total value per share to each shareholder is $9.60 + 0.40 = $10.00. In the second case, the number of shares outstanding will grow to 140 million, resulting in a post-issue stock price of $1.2 billion / 140 million shares = $8.57 per share (also higher than the issue price). Again, the shareholders will exercise their rights, and receive a total value per share of $8.57 + 2($8.57 − $5.00) / 5 = $10.00. Thus, in both cases the same amount of money is raised and shareholders are equally well off.

SEO Price Reaction

Researchers have found that, on average, the market greets the news of an SEO with a price decline. Often, the value lost due to the price decline can be a significant fraction of the new money raised. Figure 13.9 shows the typical stock price reaction when an SEO is announced. To see why the market price of the stock drops when an SEO is announced, consider the following situation: Suppose a used-car dealer tells you he is willing to sell you a nice-looking sports car for $5000 less than its typical price. Rather than feel lucky, perhaps your first thought is that there must be something wrong with the car—it is probably a "lemon." Buyers will be skeptical of a seller's

FIGURE 13.9

Price Reaction to an SEO Announcement

The figure shows the typical stock price reaction to the announcement of an SEO. The days are relative to the announcement day, so that day 0 is the announcement day. Notice that the stock price is typically increasing prior to the announcement—managers do not like to issue stock when its price has been dropping. Also note that the stock drops by about 1.5% when the SEO is announced and remains relatively flat afterward. The data include all SEOs from 2004 to 2007.

Source: CRSP and authors' calculations.

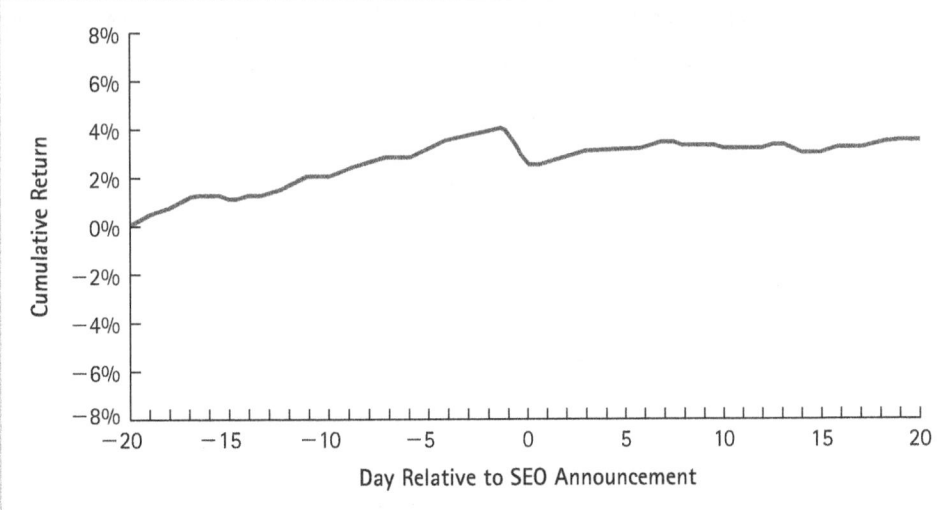

BDeH CHAPTER 13

motivation for selling because the seller has private information about the quality of the car. Thus, his *desire to sell* reveals the car is probably of low quality. Buyers are therefore reluctant to buy except at heavily discounted prices. Owners of high-quality cars are reluctant to sell because they know buyers will think they are selling a lemon and offer only a low price. Consequently, the quality and prices of cars sold in the used-car market are both low. This lemons principle—that when quality is hard to judge, the average quality of goods being offered for sale will be low—is referred to as **adverse selection**.

adverse selection
Reflects the lemons principle or the idea that when quality is hard to judge, the average quality of goods being offered for sale will be low.

The lemons problem is very real for financial managers contemplating selling new equity. Because managers concerned about protecting their existing shareholders will tend to sell only at a price that correctly values or overvalues the firm, investors infer from the decision to sell that the company is likely to be overvalued. As a result, the price drops with the announcement of the SEO.

As with IPOs, there are several puzzles surrounding SEOs. First, by offering a rights issue a company can mitigate the problem leading to the price decline (because it is offering the shares directly to its existing shareholders, the firm will not benefit its shareholders by issuing shares that are overvalued). It is not clear, at least in the United States, why companies do not initiate more rights issues. Second, as with IPOs, evidence suggests that companies underperform following a seasoned offering. This underperformance appears to suggest that the stock price decrease is not large enough, because underperformance implies that the price following the issue was too high.

SEO Costs

Although not as costly as IPOs, seasoned offerings are still expensive as Figure 13.7 shows. In addition to the price drop when the SEO is announced, the firm must pay direct costs as well. Underwriting fees amount to 5% of the proceeds of the issue and, as with IPOs, the variation across issues of different sizes is relatively small. Furthermore, rights offers have lower costs than cash offers.[15] Given the other advantages of a rights offer, it is a puzzle why the majority of offers in the United States are cash offers. The one advantage of a cash offer is that the underwriter takes on a larger role and, therefore, can credibly attest to the issue's quality.

Concept Check

7. What is the difference between a cash offer and a rights offer for a seasoned equity offering?

8. What is the typical stock price reaction to an SEO?

---

[15]In the United Kingdom, Myron Slovin, Marie Sushka, and Kam Wah Lai [*Journal of Financial Economics* 57 (2) (2000)] found that the average fee for a cash offer is 6.1% versus 4.6% for an underwritten rights offer.

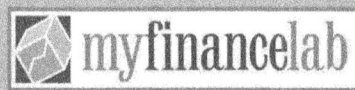

Here is what you should know after reading this chapter. MyFinanceLab will help you identify what you know, and where to go when you need to practice.

Key Points and Equations	Key Terms	Online Practice Opportunities
13.1 Equity Financing for Private Companies ▶ Private companies can raise outside equity capital from angel investors, venture capital firms, institutional investors, or corporate investors. ▶ When a company founder sells stock to an outsider to raise capital, the founder's ownership share and control over the company are reduced. ▶ Equity investors in private companies plan to sell their stock eventually through one of two main exit strategies: an acquisition or a public offering.	angel investors, p. 430 convertible preferred stock, p. 433 corporate investor, corporate partner, strategic partner, strategic investor, p. 432 exit strategy, p. 435 post-money valuation, p. 433 preferred stock, p. 433 pre-money valuation, p. 433 venture capital firm, p. 431 venture capitalist, p. 431	MyFinanceLab Study Plan 13.1
13.2 Taking Your Firm Public: The Initial Public Offering ▶ An initial public offering (IPO) is the first time a company sells its stock to the public. ▶ The main advantages of going public are greater liquidity and better access to capital. Disadvantages include regulatory and financial reporting requirements and the undermining of the investors' ability to monitor the company's management. ▶ During an IPO, the shares sold may represent either a primary offering (if the shares are being sold to raise new capital) or a secondary offering (if the shares are sold by earlier investors). ▶ An underwriter is an investment bank that manages the IPO process and helps the company sell its stock. ▶ The lead underwriter is responsible for managing the IPO. ▶ The lead underwriter forms a group of underwriters, called the syndicate, to help sell the stock.	auction IPO, p. 441 best-efforts, p. 441 book building, p. 440 final prospectus, p. 437 firm commitment, p. 440 initial public offering (IPO), p. 435 lead underwriter, p. 436 lockup, p. 441 over-allotment allocation (greenshoe provision), p. 440 preliminary prospectus (red herring), p. 437 primary offering, p. 436 registration statement, p. 437 road show, p. 439 secondary offering, p. 436 spread, p. 440	MyFinanceLab Study Plan 13.2

BDeH CHAPTER 13

▶ The SEC requires that a company file a registration statement prior to an IPO. The preliminary prospectus is part of the registration statement that circulates to investors before the stock is offered. After the deal is completed, the company files a final prospectus.

▶ Underwriters value a company before an IPO using valuation techniques and by book building.

▶ Stock may be sold during an IPO on a best-efforts basis, as a firm commitment IPO or using an auction IPO. The firm commitment process is the most common practice in the United States.

syndicate, p. 436
underwriter, p. 436

13.3 IPO Puzzles

▶ Several puzzles are associated with IPOs.
1. IPOs are underpriced on average.
2. New issues are highly cyclical.
3. The transaction costs of an IPO are very high.
4. Long-run performance (three to five years) after an IPO is poor on average.

MyFinanceLab
Study Plan 13.3

13.4 Raising Additional Capital: The Seasoned Equity Offering

▶ A seasoned equity offering (SEO) is the sale of stock by a company that is already publicly traded.

▶ Two kinds of SEOs exist: a cash offer (when new shares are sold to investors at large) and a rights offer (when new shares are offered only to existing shareholders).

▶ The stock price reaction to an SEO is negative on average.

adverse selection, p. 452
cash offer, p. 450
primary shares, p. 449
rights offer, p. 450
seasoned equity offering (SEO), p. 448
secondary shares, p. 449
tombstone, p. 449

MyFinanceLab
Study Plan 13.4

Review Questions

1. What are some of the alternative sources from which private companies can raise equity capital?

2. What are the advantages and the disadvantages to a private company of raising money from a corporate investor?

3. What are the main advantages and disadvantages of going public?

4. What are the main differences between a firm commitment IPO and an auction IPO?

5. Do underwriters face the most risk from a best-efforts IPO, a firm commitment IPO, or an auction IPO?

6. How is the price set in an auction IPO?

7. Why should a financial manager be concerned about underpricing?

8. IPOs are very cyclical. In some years, there are large numbers of IPOs; in other years, there are very few. Why is this cyclicality a puzzle?

9. What are the advantages of a rights offer?

10. What are the advantages to a company of selling stock in an SEO using a cash offer?

Problems

A blue box (■) indicates problems available in MyFinanceLab. An asterisk (*) indicates problems with a higher level of difficulty.

Equity Financing for Private Companies

1. Starware Software was founded last year to develop software for gaming applications. The founder initially invested $800,000 and received 8 million shares of stock. Starware now needs to raise a second round of capital, and it has identified a venture capitalist who is interested in investing. This venture capitalist will invest $1 million and wants to own 20% of the company after the investment is completed.
   a. How many shares must the venture capitalist receive to end up with 20% of the company? What is the implied price per share of this funding round?
   b. What will the value of the whole firm be after this investment (the post-money valuation)?

 2. Three years ago, you founded your own company. You invested $100,000 of your money and received 5 million shares of Series A preferred stock. Your company has since been through three additional rounds of financing.

Round	Price ($)	Number of Shares
Series B	0.50	1,000,000
Series C	2.00	500,000
Series D	4.00	500,000

   a. What is the pre-money valuation for the Series D funding round?
   b. What is the post-money valuation for the Series D funding round?

 3. Based on the information in Problem 2 (and that each share of all series of preferred stock is convertible into one share of common stock), what fractions of the firm do the Series B, C, and D investors each own in the your firm?

 4. Assuming that you own only the Series A preferred stock in Problem 2 (and that each share of all series of preferred stock is convertible into one share of common stock), what percentage of the firm do you own after the last funding round?

BDeH CHAPTER 13

Taking Your Firm Public: The Initial Public Offering

5. Roundtree Software is going public using an auction IPO. The firm has received the following bids:

Price ($)	Number of Shares
14.00	100,000
13.80	200,000
13.60	500,000
13.40	1,000,000
13.20	1,200,000
13.00	800,000
12.80	400,000

Assuming Roundtree would like to sell 1.8 million shares in its IPO, what will be the winning auction offer price?

6. If Roundtree from Problem 5 decides to issue an extra 500,000 shares (for a total of 2.3 million shares), how much total money will it raise?

7. Three years ago, you founded Outdoor Recreation, Inc., a retailer specializing in the sale of equipment and clothing for recreational activities such as camping, skiing, and hiking. So far, your company has gone through three funding rounds:

Round	Date	Investor	Shares	Share Price ($)
Series A	Feb. 2005	You	500,000	1.00
Series B	Aug. 2006	Angels	1,000,000	2.00
Series C	Sept. 2007	Venture capital	2,000,000	3.50

It is now 2008 and you need to raise additional capital to expand your business. You have decided to take your firm public through an IPO. You would like to issue an additional 6.5 million new shares through this IPO. Assuming that your firm successfully completes its IPO, you forecast that 2008 net income will be $7.5 million.

a. Your investment banker advises you that the prices of other recent IPOs have been set such that the P/E ratios based on 2008 forecasted earnings average 20.0. Assuming that your IPO is set at a price that implies a similar multiple, what will your IPO price per share be?

b. What percentage of the firm will you own after the IPO?

8. Margoles Publishing recently completed its IPO. The stock was offered at a price of $14 per share. On the first day of trading, the stock closed at $19 per share.

a. What was the initial return on Margoles?

b. Who benefited from this underpricing? Who lost, and why?

9. If Margoles Publishing from Problem 8 paid an underwriting spread of 7% for its IPO and sold 10 million shares, what was the total cost (exclusive of underpricing) to it of going public?

10. Chen Brothers, Inc., sold 4 million shares in its IPO, at a price of $18.50 per share. Management negotiated a fee (the underwriting spread) of 7% on this transaction. What was the dollar cost of this fee?

BDeH   CHAPTER 13

11. Your firm is selling 3 million shares in an IPO. You are targeting an offer price of $17.25 per share. Your underwriters have proposed a spread of 7%, but you would like to lower it to 5%. However, you are concerned that if you do so, they will argue for a lower offer price. Given the potential savings from a lower spread, how much lower can the offer price go before you would have preferred to pay 7% to get $17.25 per share?

Use the following information for Problems 12 through 14: The firm you founded currently has 12 million shares, of which you own 7 million. You are considering an IPO where you would sell 2 million shares for $20 each.

12. If all of the shares sold are primary shares, how much will the firm raise? What will your percentage ownership of the firm be after the IPO?

13. If all of the shares sold are from your holdings, how much will the firm raise? What will your percentage ownership of the firm be after the IPO?

14. What is the maximum number of secondary shares you could sell and still retain more than 50% ownership of the firm? How much would the firm raise in that case?

Raising Additional Capital: The Seasoned Equity Offering

15. On January 20, Metropolitan, Inc., sold 8 million shares of stock in an SEO. The market price of Metropolitan at the time was $42.50 per share. Of the 8 million shares sold, 5 million shares were primary shares being sold by the company, and the remaining 3 million shares were being sold by the venture capital investors. Assume the underwriter charges 5% of the gross proceeds as an underwriting fee.
    a. How much money did Metropolitan raise?
    b. How much money did the venture capitalists receive?
    c. If the stock price dropped 3% on announcement of the SEO and the new shares were sold at that price, how much money would Metropolitan receive?

*16. Foster Enterprises' stock is trading for $50 per share and there are currently 10 million shares outstanding. It would like to raise $100 million. If its underwriter charges 5% of gross proceeds,
    a. How many shares must it sell?
    b. If it expects the stock price to drop by 2% upon announcement of the SEO, how many shares should it plan to sell?
    c. If all of the shares are primary shares and are sold to new investors, what percentage reduction in ownership will all of the existing shareholders experience?

17. MacKenzie Corporation currently has 10 million shares of stock outstanding at a price of $40 per share. The company would like to raise money and has announced a rights issue. Every existing shareholder will be sent one right per share of stock that he or she owns. The company plans to require ten rights to purchase one share at a price of $40 per share. How much money will it raise if all rights are exercised?

14

Debt Financing

LEARNING OBJECTIVES

▶ Identify different types of debt financing available to a firm

▶ Understand limits within bond contracts that protect the interests of bondholders

▶ Describe the various options available to firms for the early repayment of debt

notation

YTC	yield to call on a callable bond	*PV*	present value
YTM	yield to maturity on a bond		

Southern Methodist University, 2004

"My finance studies helped me develop a disciplined approach to financial analysis and problem solving."

"Firms have many borrowing sources," says Bryan Milner, an Assistant Vice President at Wells Fargo Foothill in Dallas. His primary responsibility is finding new lending opportunities for Wells Fargo Foothill, which provides secured short-and long-term financing ranging from $10 million to $1 billion to companies in a wide range of industries.

Bryan received his BBA in finance from the University of North Texas in 2000 and his MBA from Southern Methodist University in 2004. "My finance studies helped me develop a disciplined approach to financial analysis and problem solving, and provided me with the theoretical foundations to make good decisions," he says. "The technical skills I learned help me evaluate a company's financial statements and pro forma cash flows to assess risk of the issuer defaulting."

Choosing the most suitable loan depends on the firm's current situation, what it will do with the loan proceeds, and how it plans to repay the loan. "When structuring debt transactions, lenders typically try to match the term of the financing to the borrowing need," Bryan says. "A company buying a new plant that they plan to use for 20 years would seek long-term financing. If the same company needed to finance inventory that they expected to sell during the summer, they would seek short-term financing."

Many of Wells Fargo Foothill's loans are short-term loans to help a company manage working capital shortfalls when liabilities due in the short term exceed the company's cash and expected payments on receivables. "This type of credit facility is backed by a pledge of company assets such as accounts receivable and inventory," Bryan explains. "It is particularly attractive to companies operating in a seasonal business, such as toy manufacturers, who require cash to build inventory all year but don't sell the majority of it until December."

A number of factors come into play when setting interest rates on these and other loans. "In theory, the interest rate on a loan is determined by its risk: the greater the risk of the company not repaying the loan, the higher the interest rate," says Bryan. "In practice, competition, opportunities to sell other banking services, and personal relationships also influence pricing."

In Chapter 13, we discussed the process a firm uses to raise equity capital, starting with angel investors for a young private firm and continuing through to seasoned equity offerings for an established public firm. We noted that each round of new equity financing dilutes the founder's ownership of the firm. An alternative financing source is to borrow the money—debt financing. In fact, debt is the most important source of financing; American businesses had over $10.1 *trillion* dollars in debt outstanding at the end of 2007, borrowing over $1 trillion in 2007 alone. While debt financing does not dilute the ownership of the firm, the disadvantage is that loans must be repaid. That is, the firm is legally obligated to make interest and principal payments on its debt. If it fails to do so, it is in default and can be forced into bankruptcy. We discuss the relative advantages and disadvantages of debt versus equity financing in the next chapter, "Capital Structure." Here, we focus on the process for financing part of the firm with debt and on the features of corporate debt.

In mid-2005, Ford Motor Company decided to put one of its subsidiaries, Hertz Corporation, up for competitive bid. On September 13, 2005, *The Wall Street Journal* reported that a group of private investors led by Clayton, Dubilier & Rice (CDR), a private equity firm, had reached a deal with Ford to purchase Hertz's outstanding equity for $5.6 billion. In addition, Hertz had $9.1 billion in existing debt that it needed to refinance as part of the deal. CDR planned to finance the transaction in part by raising over $11 billion in new debt. We will examine the details of this transaction throughout this chapter to illustrate debt financing.

When companies raise capital by issuing debt, they have several potential sources from which to seek funds. To complete the Hertz purchase, the group led by CDR relied on at least four different kinds of debt: domestic- and foreign-denominated high-yield bonds, bank loans, and *asset-backed securities*. In addition, each debt issue has its own specific terms determined at the time of issue. Building on the discussion of bond valuation in Chapter 6, we begin our exploration of debt financing by explaining the process of issuing debt and the types of debt available to companies. We continue by discussing restrictions on company actions in the debt agreement. Finally, we discuss some of the more advanced features of bonds such as the call provision.

14.1 Corporate Debt

Corporate debt can be private debt, which is negotiated directly with a bank or a small group of investors, or public debt, which trades in a public market. As we will see, the Hertz example described in the introduction included both.

Private Debt

private debt Debt that is not publicly traded.

The first debt financing many young firms undertake is a bank loan. However, even very large, established firms use bank loans as part of their debt financing. Bank loans are an example of **private debt**, debt that is not publicly traded. The private debt market is larger

---

Debt Financing at Hertz: Bank Loans

As part of the transaction with CDR, Hertz took out more than $2 billion in bank loans. Hertz negotiated a $1.7 billion syndicated term loan with a seven-year term. Deutsche Bank AG negotiated the loan and then sold portions of it off to other banks—mostly smaller regional banks that had excess cash but lacked the resources to negotiate a loan of this magnitude by themselves. In addition to the term loan, Hertz negotiated an asset-backed revolving line of credit (for five years and $1.6 billion), which it could use as needed. Hertz's initial draw on the line of credit was $400 million.

---

term loan A bank loan that lasts for a specific term.

syndicated bank loan A single loan that is funded by a group of banks rather than just a single bank.

revolving line of credit A credit commitment for a specific time period, typically two to three years, which a company can use as needed.

asset-backed line of credit A type of credit commitment, where the borrower secures a line of credit by pledging an asset as collateral.

private placement A bond issue that does not trade on a public market but rather is sold to a small group of investors.

than the public debt market. Private debt has the advantage that it avoids the cost and delay of registration with the U.S. Securities and Exchange Commission (SEC). The disadvantage is that because it is not publicly traded, it is illiquid, meaning that it is hard for a holder of the firm's private debt to sell it in a timely manner.

There are several segments of the private debt market: *Bank loans* (*term loans and lines of credit*), and *private placements*.

Bank Loans.   A **term loan** is a bank loan that lasts for a specific term. When a single loan is funded by a group of banks rather than just a single bank, it is called a **syndicated bank loan**. Usually, one member of the syndicate (the lead bank) negotiates the terms of the bank loan. Many companies establish a **revolving line of credit**, a credit commitment for a specific time period up to some limit, typically two to three years, which a company can use as needed. A company may be able to get a larger line of credit or a lower interest rate if it secures the line of credit by pledging an asset as collateral. Such a line of credit is referred to as an **asset-backed line of credit**

Private Placements.   Recall from Chapter 6 that corporate bonds are securities issued by corporations. They account for a significant amount of invested capital. At the end of 2006, the value of outstanding U.S. corporate bonds was about $5.5 trillion. Bonds can be issued publicly or placed privately. A **private placement** is a bond issue that does not trade on a public market but rather is sold to a small group of investors. Because a private placement does not need to be registered with the SEC, it is less costly to issue and often a simple promissory note is sufficient. Privately placed debt also need not conform to the same standards as public debt; as a consequence, it can be tailored to the particular situation.

In 1990, the SEC issued Rule 144A, which significantly increased the liquidity of certain privately placed debt. Private debt issued under this rule can be traded by large financial institutions among themselves. The rule was motivated by a desire to increase the access of foreign corporations to U.S. debt markets. Bonds that are issued under

BDeH CHAPTER 14

Debt Financing at Hertz: Private Placements

Hertz privately placed an additional $4.2 billion of U.S. asset-backed securities and $2.1 billion of international asset-backed securities. In this case, the assets backing the debt were the fleet of rental cars Hertz owned; hence, this debt was termed "fleet debt."

Hertz had an additional $2.7 billion bond issue that it issued under Rule 144A. As part of the offering, it agreed to publicly register the bonds within 390 days.* Because the debt was marketed and sold with the understanding that it would become public debt, we classified that issue as public debt.

---

*If Hertz failed to fulfill this commitment, the interest rate on all the outstanding bonds would increase by 0.5%.

indenture Included in a prospectus, it is a formal contract between a bond issuer and a trust company, which represents the bondholders' interests.

original issue discount (OID) bond A coupon bond issued at a discount.

unsecured debt A type of corporate debt that, in the event of a bankruptcy, gives bondholders a claim to only the assets of the firm that are not already pledged as collateral on other debt.

notes A type of unsecured corporate debt with maturities shorter than ten years.

debentures A type of unsecured corporate debt with maturities of ten years or longer.

secured debt A type of corporate loan or debt security in which specific assets are pledged as a firm's collateral that bondholders have a direct claim to in the event of a bankruptcy.

mortgage bonds A type of secured corporate debt in which real property is pledged as collateral.

asset-backed bonds A type of secured corporate debt in which specific assets are pledged as collateral.

this rule are nominally private debt, but because they are tradable between financial institutions they are only slightly less liquid than public debt. Many firms issue debt under Rule 144A with the explicit promise to publicly register the debt within a certain time frame. The advantage of this approach to debt financing is that companies can raise the capital quickly and then spend the time it takes to comply with all of the filing requirements.

Public Debt

The Prospectus.   A public bond issue is similar to a stock issue. A prospectus or offering memorandum must be produced that describes the details of the offering. Figure 14.1 shows the front page of the Hertz offering memorandum. In addition, the prospectus for a public offering must include an **indenture**, a formal contract that specifies the firm's obligations to the bondholders. This contract is actually written between the bond issuer and a trust company that represents the bondholders and makes sure that the terms of the indenture are enforced. In the case of default, the trust company represents the bondholders' interests.

While corporate bonds almost always pay coupons semiannually, a few corporations (for instance, Coca-Cola) have issued zero-coupon bonds. Corporate bonds have historically been issued with a wide range of maturities. Most corporate bonds have maturities of 30 years or less, although in the past there have been original maturities of up to 999 years. In July 1993, for example, Walt Disney Company issued $150 million in bonds with a maturity of 100 years that soon became known as the "Sleeping Beauty" bonds.

The face value or principal amount of the bond is denominated in standard increments, usually $1000. The face value does not always correspond to the actual money raised because of underwriting fees and the possibility that the bond might not actually sell for its face value when it is offered for sale initially. If a coupon bond is issued at a discount, it is called an **original issue discount (OID) bond**.

Secured and Unsecured Corporate Debt.   Four types of corporate debt are typically issued: *notes, debentures, mortgage bonds*, and *asset-backed bonds* (see Table 14.1). These types of debt fall into two categories: *unsecured* and *secured debt*. With **unsecured debt**, in the event of a bankruptcy bondholders have a claim to only the assets of the firm that are not already pledged as collateral on other debt. **Notes** are a type of unsecured debt, typically with maturities of less than ten years, and **debentures** are a type of unsecured debt with maturities of ten years or longer. With **secured debt**, specific assets are pledged as collateral that bondholders have a direct claim to in the event of a bankruptcy. **Mortgage bonds** are secured by real property, but **asset-backed bonds** can be secured by any kind of asset. Although the word "bond" is commonly used to mean any kind of debt security, technically a corporate bond must be secured.

TABLE 14.1	Secured	Unsecured
Types of Corporate Debt	Mortgage bonds (secured with real property)	Notes (original maturity less than ten years)
	Asset-backed bonds (secured with any asset)	Debentures

FIGURE 14.1

Front Cover of the Offering Memorandum for the Hertz Junk Bond Issue

Source: Courtesy of Hertz Corporation.

OFFERING MEMORANDUM   CONFIDENTIAL

CCMG Acquisition Corporation
to be merged with and into The Hertz Corporation
$1,800,000,000 8.875% Senior Notes due 2014
$600,000,000 10.5% Senior Subordinated Notes due 2016
€225,000,000 7.875% Senior Notes due 2014

The Company is offering $1,800,000,000 aggregate principal amount of its 8.875% Senior Notes due 2014 (the "Senior Dollar Notes"), $600,000,000 aggregate principal amount of its 10.5% Senior Subordinated Notes due 2016 (the "Senior Subordinated Notes" and, together with the Senior Dollar Notes, the "Dollar Notes"), and €225,000,000 aggregate principal amount of its 7.875% Senior Notes due 2014 (the "Senior Euro Notes"). The Senior Dollar Notes and the Senior Euro Notes are collectively referred to as the "Senior Notes," and the Dollar Notes and the Senior Euro Notes are collectively referred to as the "Notes."

The Senior Notes will mature on January 1, 2014 and the Senior Subordinated Notes will mature on January 1, 2016. Interest on the Notes will accrue from December 21, 2005. We will pay interest on the Notes on January 1 and July 1 of each year, commencing July 1, 2006.

We have the option to redeem all or a portion of the Senior Notes and the Senior Subordinated Notes at any time (1) before January 1, 2010 and January 1, 2011, respectively, at a redemption price equal to 100% of their principal amount plus the applicable make-whole premium set forth in this offering memorandum and (2) on or after January 1, 2010 and January 1, 2011, respectively, at the redemption prices set forth in this offering memorandum. In addition, on or before January 1, 2009, we may, on one or more occasions, apply funds equal to the proceeds from one or more equity offerings to redeem up to 35% of each series of Notes at the redemption prices set forth in this offering memorandum. If we undergo a change of control or sell certain of our assets, we may be required to offer to purchase Notes from holders.

The Senior Notes will be senior unsecured obligations and will rank equally with all of our senior unsecured indebtedness. The Senior Subordinated Notes will be unsecured obligations and subordinated in right of payment to all of our existing and future senior indebtedness. Each of our domestic subsidiaries that guarantees specified bank indebtedness will guarantee the Senior Notes with guarantees that will rank equally with all of the senior unsecured indebtedness of such subsidiaries and the Senior Subordinated Notes with guarantees that will be unsecured and subordinated in right of payment to all existing and future senior indebtedness of such subsidiaries.

We have agreed to make an offer to exchange the Notes for registered, publicly tradable notes that have substantially identical terms as the Notes. The Dollar Notes are expected to be eligible for trading in the Private Offering, Resale and Trading Automated Linkages (PORTAL℠) market. This offering memorandum includes additional information on the terms of the Notes, including redemption and repurchase prices, covenants and transfer restrictions.

Investing in the Notes involves a high degree of risk. See "Risk Factors" beginning on page 23.

We have not registered the Notes under the federal securities laws of the United States or the securities laws of any other jurisdiction. The Initial Purchasers named below are offering the Notes only to qualified institutional buyers under Rule 144A and to persons outside the United States under Regulation S. See "Notice to Investors" for additional information about eligible offerees and transfer restrictions.

Price for each series of Notes: 100%

We expect that (i) delivery of the Dollar Notes will be made to investors in book-entry form through the facilities of The Depository Trust Company on or about December 21, 2005 and (ii) delivery of the Senior Euro Notes will be made to investors in book-entry form through the facilities of the Euroclear System and Clearstream Banking, S.A. on or about December 21, 2005.

Joint Book-Running Managers

Deutsche Bank Securities   **Lehman Brothers**

Merrill Lynch & Co.   **Goldman, Sachs & Co.**   **JPMorgan**

Co-Lead Managers

BNP PARIBAS   **RBS Greenwich Capital**   **Calyon**

The date of this offering memorandum is December 15, 2005.

BDeH CHAPTER 14

Debt Financing at Hertz: Public Debt

As part of the transaction's financing, Hertz planned to issue $2.7 billion worth of unsecured debt—in this case, high-yield notes known as junk bonds. Recall from Chapter 6 that bonds rated below investment grade are called junk bonds. Further, remember that companies such as Standard & Poor's and Moody's rate the credit-worthiness of bonds and make this information available to investors (see Table 6.6 for the specific ratings). The high-yield issue for the Hertz transaction was divided into three kinds of debt or **tranches**, different classes of securities comprising a single bond issue and paid from the same cash flow source (see Table 14.2), all of which made semiannual coupon payments and were issued at par. The largest tranche was a $1.8 billion face-value note maturing in eight years. It paid a coupon of 8.875%, which at the time represented a 4.45% spread over Treasuries.

tranches Different classes of securities that comprise a single bond issuance.

seniority A bondholder's priority, in the event of a default, in claiming assets not already securing other debt.

subordinated debenture A debenture issue that has a lower priority claim to the firm's assets than other outstanding debt.

domestic bonds Bonds issued by a local entity, denominated in the local currency, and traded in a local market, but purchased by foreigners.

Seniority. Debentures and notes are unsecured. Because more than one debenture might be outstanding, the bondholder's priority in claiming assets in the event of default, known as the bond's **seniority**, is important. As a result, most debenture issues contain clauses restricting the company from issuing new debt with equal or higher priority than existing debt.

When a firm conducts a subsequent debenture issue that has lower priority than its outstanding debt, the new debt is known as a **subordinated debenture**. In the event of default, the assets not pledged as collateral for outstanding bonds cannot be used to pay off the holders of subordinated debentures until all more senior debt has been paid off. In Hertz's case, one tranche of the junk bond issue is a note that is subordinated to the other two tranches. In the event of bankruptcy, this note has a lower-priority claim on the firm's assets. Because holders of this tranche are likely to receive less in the event Hertz defaults, the yield on this debt is higher than that of the other tranches—10.5% compared to 8.875% for the first tranche.

International Bond Markets. The second tranche of Hertz's junk bond issue is a note that is denominated in euros rather than U.S. dollars—it is an international bond. International bonds are classified into four broadly defined categories.

1. **Domestic bonds** are bonds issued by a local entity and traded in a local market, but purchased by foreigners. They are denominated in the local currency of the country in which they are issued.

TABLE 14.2		Tranche 1: Senior Dollar-Denominated Note	Tranche 2: Senior Euro-Denominated Note	Tranche 3: Senior Subordinated Dollar-Denominated Note
Hertz's December 2005 Junk Bond Issues	Face value	$1.8 billion	€225 million	$600 million
	Maturity	December 1, 2014	December 1, 2014	December 1, 2016
	Coupon	8.875%	7.875%	10.5%
	Issue price	Par	Par	Par
	Yield	8.875%	7.875%	10.5%
	Rating Standard and Poor's	B	B	B
	Moody's	B1	B1	B3
	Fitch	BB−	BB−	BB+

foreign bonds Bonds issued by a foreign company in a local market and are intended for local investors. They are also denominated in the local currency.

Eurobonds International bonds that are not denominated in the local currency of the country in which they are issued.

global bonds Bonds that are offered for sale in several different markets simultaneously.

2. **Foreign bonds** are bonds issued by a foreign company in a local market and are intended for local investors. They are also denominated in the local currency. Foreign bonds in the United States are known as Yankee bonds. In other countries, foreign bonds also have special names; for example, in Japan they are called Samurai bonds; in the United Kingdom, they are known as Bulldogs.

3. **Eurobonds** are international bonds that are not denominated in the local currency of the country in which they are issued. Consequently, there is no connection between the physical location of the market on which they trade and the location of the issuing entity. They can be denominated in any number of currencies that might or might not be connected to the location of the issuer. The trading of these bonds is not subject to any particular nation's regulations.

4. **Global bonds** combine the features of domestic, foreign, and Eurobonds, and are offered for sale in several different markets simultaneously. Unlike Eurobonds, global bonds can be offered for sale in the same currency as the country of issuance. The Hertz junk bond issue is an example of a global bond issue: It was simultaneously offered for sale in the United States and Europe.

A bond that makes its payments in a foreign currency contains the risk of holding that currency and, therefore, is priced off the yields of similar bonds in that currency. Hence, the euro-denominated note of the Hertz junk bond issue has a different yield from the dollar-denominated note, even though both bonds have the same seniority and maturity. While they have the same default risk, they differ in their exchange rate risk—the risk that the foreign currency will depreciate in value relative to the local currency.

Table 14.3 summarizes Hertz's debt after the LBO transaction. About $2.7 billion of the $11.1 billion total was public debt and the rest was private debt consisting of a term loan, a revolving line of credit, and fleet debt. Both the fleet debt and the line of credit were backed by specific assets of the firm.

TABLE 14.3	Type of Debt	Amount ($ million)
Summary of New Debt Issued as Part of the Hertz LBO	Public Debt	
	Senior dollar-denominated	1,800.0
	Senior Euro-denominated (€225 million)	268.9
	Subordinated dollar-denominated	600.0
	Private Debt	
	Term loan	1,707.0
	Asset-backed revolving line of credit	400.0
	Asset-backed "fleet debt"	6,348.0
	Total	$11,123.9

Concept Check

1. List the four types of corporate public debt that are typically issued.
2. What are the four categories of international bonds?

Bond Covenants

covenants Restrictive clauses in a bond contract that limit the issuer from taking actions that may undercut its ability to repay the bonds.

Now that we have established the main types of debt, we are prepared to take a closer look at the bond contract provisions. **Covenants** are restrictive clauses in a bond contract that limit the issuer from taking actions that may undercut its ability to repay the bonds. Why are such covenants necessary? After all, why would managers voluntarily take actions that increase the firm's default risk? Remember—managers work for the equity holders and sometimes there are actions they can take that benefit the equity holders at the expense of debt holders. Covenants are there to protect debt holders in such cases.

Types of Covenants

Once bonds are issued, equity holders have an incentive to increase dividends at the expense of debt holders. Think of an extreme case in which a company issues a bond, and then immediately liquidates its assets, pays out the proceeds (including those from the bond issue) in the form of a dividend to equity holders, and declares bankruptcy. In this case, the equity holders receive the value of the firm's assets plus the proceeds from the bond, while bondholders are left with nothing. Consequently, bond agreements often contain covenants that restrict the ability of management to pay dividends. Other covenants may restrict how much more debt the firm can issue or they may specify that the firm must maintain a minimum amount of working capital. If the firm fails to live up to any covenant, the bond goes into technical default and the bondholder can demand immediate repayment or force the company to renegotiate the terms of the bond. Table 14.4 summarizes typical bond covenants. All of the covenants are designed to limit the company's (the borrower's) ability to increase the risk of the bond. For example, without restric-

TABLE 14.4 Typical Bond Covenants	Restrictions on:	Typical Restrictions
	Issuing new debt	New debt must be subordinate to existing debt No new debt unless firm maintains specific leverage or interest coverage ratios
	Dividends and share repurchases	Payouts can be made only from earnings generated after the bond issue Payouts can be made only if earnings exceed some threshold
	Mergers and acquisitions	Mergers are allowed only if the combined firm has a minimum ratio of net tangible assets to debt
	Asset disposition	Maximum amount of assets that can be sold, and/or minimum amount of assets that must be maintained Restrictions on making loans or any other provision of credit
	Requiring Maintenance of:	
	Accounting Measures	Minimum retained earnings, working capital, and/or net assets Maximum leverage ratios

Source: Adapted from the American Bar Association's *Commentaries on Debentures.*

tions on the issuance of new debt, the company could issue new debt of equal or greater seniority than the existing bonds, thus increasing the risk that it will not repay the existing bonds.

Advantages of Covenants

You might expect that equity holders would try to include as few covenants as possible in a bond agreement. In fact, this is not necessarily the case. The stronger the covenants in the bond contract, the less likely the firm will default on the bond, and thus the lower the interest rate investors will require to buy the bond. That is, by including more covenants, firms can reduce their costs of borrowing. The reduction in the firm's borrowing costs can more than outweigh the cost of the loss of flexibility associated with covenants.

Application: Hertz's Covenants

Covenants in the Hertz junk bond issue limited Hertz's ability to incur more debt, make dividend payments, redeem stock, make investments, transfer or sell assets, and merge or consolidate. They also included a requirement that Hertz offer to repurchase the bonds at 101% of face value if the corporation experiences a change in control.

3. What happens if an issuer fails to live up to a bond covenant?

4. Why can bond covenants reduce a firm's borrowing costs?

14.3 Repayment Provisions

A firm repays its bonds by making coupon and principal payments as specified in the bond contract. However, this is not the only way a firm can repay bonds. For example, the firm can repurchase a fraction of the outstanding bonds in the market, or it can make a tender offer for the entire issue, as Hertz did on its existing bonds. In this section, we explain the three main bonds features affecting the repayment of the bond: *call provisions, sinking funds,* and *convertible provisions.*

Call Provisions

callable bonds Bonds containing a call provision that allows the issuer to repurchase the bonds at a predetermined price.

call date The date in the call provision on or after which the bond issuer has the right to retire the bond.

call price A price specified at the issuance of a bond for which the issuer can redeem the bond.

Firms can repay bonds by exercising a *call* provision. **Callable bonds** allow the issuer of the bond to repurchase the bonds at a predetermined price. A call feature also allows the issuer the right (but not the obligation) to retire all outstanding bonds on (or after) a specific date known as the **call date**, for the **call price** that is specified at the issuance of the bond. The call price is expressed as a percentage of the bond's face value and is generally set at or above the face value.

Hertz's Callable Bonds. Hertz's junk bonds are examples of callable bonds. Table 14.5 lists the call features in each tranche. In Hertz's case, the call dates of the two senior tranches are at the end of the fourth year. For the duration of 2010, the first tranche has a call price of 104.438% of the bond's face value. In the following years, the call price is gradually reduced until in 2012 the bond becomes callable at par (100% of face value). The euro-denominated bond has similar terms at slightly different call prices. The subordinated tranche's call date is a year later and has a different call-price structure.

TABLE 14.5 Call Features of Hertz's Bonds	Call Features	Tranche 1: Senior Dollar-Denominated Note	Tranche 2: Senior Euro-Denominated Note	Tranche 3: Senior Subordinated Dollar-Denominated Note
	Call Features	Up to 35% of the outstanding principal callable at 108.875% in the first three years. After four years, fully callable at: • 104.438% in 2010. • 102.219% in 2011. • Par thereafter.	Up to 35% of the outstanding principal callable at 107.875% in the first three years. After four years, fully callable at: • 103.938% in 2010. • 101.969% in 2011. • Par thereafter.	Up to 35% of the outstanding principal callable at 110.5% in the first three years. After five years, fully callable at: • 105.25% in 2011. • 103.50% in 2012. • 101.75% in 2013.

The Hertz bonds are also partially callable in the first three years. Hertz has the option to retire up to 35% of the outstanding principal at the call prices listed in Table 14.5, as long as the funds needed to repurchase the bonds are derived from the proceeds of an equity issuance.

Call Provisions and Bond Prices.   When would a financial manager choose to exercise the firm's right to call the bond? A firm can always retire one of its bonds early by repurchasing the bond in the open market. If the call provision offers a cheaper way to retire the bond, however, the firm will forgo the option of purchasing the bond in the open market and call the bond instead. Thus, when the market price of the bond exceeds the call price, the firm will call the bond.

We know from Chapter 6 that bond prices rise when market interest rates fall. If market interest rates have decreased since the bond was issued and are now less than the bond's coupon rate, the bond will be trading at a premium. If the firm has the option to call the bond at less than the premium, it could do so and refinance its debt at the new, lower market interest rates.

Given the flexibility a call provision provides to a financial manager, you might expect all bonds to be callable. However, that is not the case and to see why, we must consider how the investor views the call provision. The financial manager will choose to call the bonds only when the coupon rate the investor is receiving exceeds the market interest rate. By calling the bond, the firm is forcing the investor to relinquish the bond at a price below the value it would have were it to remain outstanding. Naturally, investors view this possibility negatively and pay less for callable bonds than for otherwise identical non-callable bonds. That means that a firm raising capital by issuing callable bonds instead of non-callable bonds will either have to pay a higher coupon rate or accept lower proceeds. A firm will choose to issue callable bonds despite their higher yield if they find the option to refinance the debt in the future particularly valuable.

Yield to Call.   A financial manager needs to understand how investors are evaluating the firm's callable bonds. For callable bonds, the **yield to call (YTC)**, the annual yield of a callable bond calculated under the assumption that the bond is called on the earliest call date, is most often quoted. In Chapter 6, we learned how investors evaluate a firm's bonds by computing their yield to maturity. The yield to maturity is always calculated on the assumption that the bond will remain outstanding until maturity and make all of its promised payments. In the case of a callable bond, that assumption is not realistic. Thus,

yield to call (YTC) The yield of a callable bond calculated under the assumption that the bond will be called on the earliest call date.

TABLE 14.6	Bond coupons relative to market yields	Bond price is . . .	Likelihood of call is . . .	Yield to Worst is . . .
Bond Calls and Yields	Coupons are higher	At a premium	High	Yield to call
	Coupons are lower	At a discount	Low	Yield to maturity

yield to worst Quoted by bond traders as the lower of the yield to call or yield to maturity.

the yield to maturity of a callable bond is the interest rate the bondholder receives if the bond is not called and repaid in full. When the bond's coupon rate is above the yield for similar securities, the, the yield to call is less than the yield to maturity. However, when the bond's coupon rate is below the yield for similar securities, the bond is unlikely to be called (the firm would not call a bond when it is paying a below-market interest rate). In that case, calling would actually be good for the bondholders and the yield to call would be above the yield to maturity. To keep all this straight, most bond traders quote **yield to worst**, which is the lower of the yield to call or yield to maturity. Table 14.6 summarizes the yield to call and yield to worst.

EXAMPLE 14.1
Calculating the Yield to Call

Problem

IBM has just issued a callable (at par) five-year, 8% coupon bond with annual coupon payments. The bond can be called at par in one year or anytime thereafter on a coupon payment date. It has a price of $103 per $100 face value, implying a yield to maturity of 7.26%. What is the bond's yield to call?

Solution

▶ **Plan**

The timeline of the promised payments for this bond (if it is not called) is:

	0	1	2	5
Cash flow		$8	$8	$108

If IBM calls the bond at the first available opportunity, it will call the bond at year 1. At that time, it will have to pay the coupon payment for year 1 ($8 per $100 of face value) and the face value ($100). The timeline of the payments if the bond is called at the first available opportunity (at year 1) is:

Period	0	1
Cash flow		$108

To solve for the yield to call, we use these cash flows and proceed as shown in Chapter 6, setting the price equal to the discounted cash flows and solving for the discount rate.

▶ **Execute**

For the yield to call, setting the present value of these payments equal to the current price gives:

$$103 = \frac{108}{(1 + YTC)}$$

Solving for the yield to call gives:

$$YTC = \frac{108}{103} - 1 = 4.85\%$$

We can use a financial calculator to derive the same result:

	N	I/Y	PV	PMT	FV
Given:	1		−103	8	100
Solve for:		4.85			

Excel Formula: =RATE(NPER,PMT,PV,FV)=RATE(1,8,−103,100)

▶ **Evaluate**

The yield to maturity is higher than the yield to call because it assumes that you will continue receiving your coupon payments for five years, even though interest rates have dropped below 8%. Under the yield to call assumptions, since you are repaid the face value sooner, you are deprived of the extra four years of coupon payments resulting in a lower total return.

Sinking Funds

Some bonds are repaid through a **sinking fund**, a provision that allows the company to make regular payments into a fund administered by a trustee over the life of the bond instead of repaying the entire principal balance on the maturity date. These payments are then used to repurchase bonds, usually at par. In this way, the company can reduce the amount of outstanding debt without affecting the cash flows of the remaining bonds.

Sinking fund provisions usually specify a minimum rate at which the issuer must contribute to the fund. In some cases, the issuer has the option to accelerate these payments. Because the sinking fund allows the issuer to repurchase the bonds at par, the option to accelerate the payments is another form of a call provision. As with all call provisions, this option is not free—including this provision lowers the price the company would get for the bonds initially.

The manner in which an outstanding balance is paid off using a sinking fund depends on the issue. Some issues specify equal payments over the life of the bond, ultimately retiring the issue on the maturity date of the bond. In other cases, the sinking fund payments are not sufficient to retire the entire issue and the company must make a large payment on the maturity date, known as a **balloon payment**. Sinking fund payments often start only a few years after the bond issue. Bonds can be issued with both a sinking fund and a call provision.

Convertible Provisions

Another way to retire bonds is by converting them into equity. **Convertible bonds** are corporate bonds with a provision that gives the bondholder an option to convert each bond owned into a fixed number of shares of common stock at a ratio called the **conversion ratio**. The provision usually gives bondholders the right to convert the bond into stock at any time up to the maturity date for the bond.[1] The conversion ratio is usually stated per $1000 of face value.

Convertible Bond Pricing.   Consider a convertible bond with a $1000 face value and a conversion ratio of 20. If you converted the bond into stock on its maturity date, you would receive 20 shares. If you did not convert, you would receive $1000. Hence, by converting the bond you essentially "paid" $1000 for 20 shares, implying a price per share of 1000/20 = $50. This implied price per share equal to the face value of the bond

sinking fund A method for repaying a bond in which a company makes regular payments into a fund administered by a trustee over the life of the bond. These payments are then used to repurchase bonds, usually at par.

balloon payment A large payment that must be made on the maturity date of a bond when the sinking fund payments are not sufficient to retire the entire bond issue.

convertible bonds Corporate bonds with a provision that gives the bondholder an option to convert each bond owned into a fixed number of shares of common stock.

conversion ratio The number of shares received upon conversion of a convertible bond, usually stated per $1000 face value.

BDeH CHAPTER 14

---

[1]Some convertible bonds do not allow conversion for a specified amount of time after the issue date.

FIGURE 14.2	Convertible Bond Value

At maturity, the value of a convertible bond is the maximum of the value of a $1000 straight bond (a non-convertible, non-callable bond) and 20 shares of stock, and it will be converted if the stock is above the conversion price. Prior to maturity, the value of the convertible bond will depend upon the likelihood of conversion, and will be above that of a straight bond or 20 shares of stock.

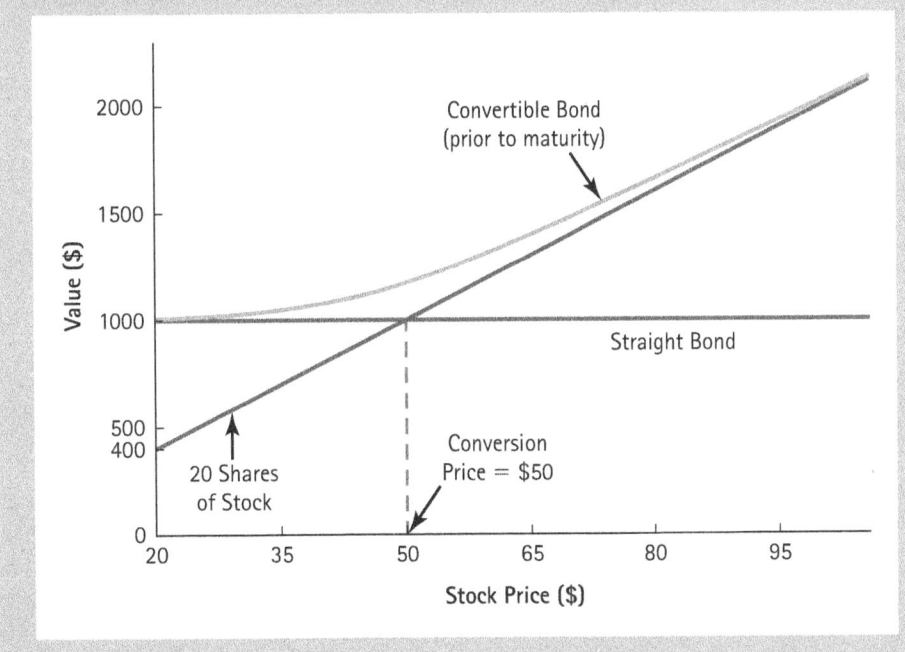

conversion price The face value of a convertible bond divided by the number of shares received if the bond is converted.

divided by the number of shares received in conversion is called the **conversion price**. If the price of the stock exceeds $50, you would choose to convert; otherwise, you would take the cash. Thus, as shown in Figure 14.2, the value of the bond on its maturity date is the maximum of its face value ($1000) and the value of 20 shares of stock.

Often companies issue convertible bonds that are callable. With these bonds, if the issuer calls them, the holder can choose to convert rather than let the bonds be called. When the bonds are called, the holder faces exactly the same decision as he or she would face on the maturity date of the bonds: He or she will choose to convert if the stock price exceeds the conversion price and let the bonds be called otherwise. Thus, by calling the bonds a company can force bondholders to make their decision to convert earlier than they would otherwise have preferred.

straight bond A non-callable, non-convertible bond (also called a plain-vanilla bond).

The option (which is not an obligation) to convert the bonds into equity is worth something to a bondholder. Thus, prior to the bond maturity date a convertible bond is worth more than an otherwise identical **straight bond**, a non-callable, non-convertible bond (also called a plain-vanilla bond). Consequently, if both bonds are issued at par the straight bond must offer a higher interest rate. Similarly, the option to receive the bond's face value means the convertible bond is also worth more than 20 shares of stock. This relationship is illustrated in Figure 14.2, where the convertible bond's value prior to maturity (the yellow curve) exceeds the value of both the straight bond and the stock (red and blue lines). The company (meaning its existing shareholders) must weigh the benefit of the lower interest rate on the convertible bond against the cost of giving those bondholders the option to buy new shares of stock at a fixed price.

BDeH CHAPTER 14

TABLE 14.7	Convertible Subordinated Notes	
RealNetworks' 2003 Convertible Debt Issue	Issued under Rule 144A	
	Aggregate principal amount:	$100 million
	Proceeds net of offering costs:	$97.0 million
	Coupon:	0%
	Conversion ratio:	107.5650 shares per $1000 principal amount
	Call date:	July 1, 2008
	Call price	100%
	Maturity	July 1, 2010

Convertible Bonds and Stock Prices. Note that the likelihood of eventually converting a convertible bond depends upon the current stock price. When the stock price is low, conversion is unlikely, and the value of the convertible bond is close to that of a straight bond. When the stock price is much higher than the conversion price, conversion is very likely and the convertible bond's price is close to the price of the converted shares. Finally, when the stock price is in the middle range, near the conversion price, there is the greatest uncertainty about whether it will be optimal to convert or not. In this case, the bondholder's option to decide later whether to convert is most valuable, and the value of the convertible bond exceeds the value of straight debt or equity by the greatest amount.

Combining Features. Companies have flexibility in setting the features of the bonds they issue. As we mentioned above, companies will often add a call provision to convertible bonds or bonds with sinking funds. Another example of flexibility is to add convertibility to subordinated bonds. Subordinated bonds typically have a higher yield because of their riskier position relative to senior bonds. But if the subordinated bond contains a convertibility feature that the senior bonds do not have, the yield on the subordinated bond could be lower than the senior bonds. In Chapter 13, we studied RealNetworks' equity financing. In 2003, RealNetworks issued $100 million in subordinated convertible debt as described in Table 14.7. The debt also contained a provision allowing the company to call the debt at par anytime after July 1, 2008.

Leveraged Buyouts. Recall from Chapter 13 our discussion of how private companies become public companies. The deal in which CDR bought Hertz is an example of the opposite transition—a public company becoming private, in this case through a *leveraged buyout*. In a **leveraged buyout (LBO)**, a group of private investors purchases all the equity of a public corporation and finances the purchase primarily with debt.[2] With a total value of $15.2 billion,[3] the leveraged buyout of Hertz was the second largest transaction of its kind at the time of its announcement. This left Hertz with a substantial amount of debt on its balance sheet. As with most LBOs, Hertz's long-term plan was to reduce its leverage through continued profitability. In November 2006, Hertz went pub-

leveraged buyout (LBO)
When a group of private investors purchases all the equity of a public corporation and finances the purchase primarily with debt.

---

[2]At the time of the deal, Hertz was a wholly owned subsidiary of Ford Motor Company, which itself is a public company. Prior to Ford's acquisition of Hertz's outstanding shares in 2001, Hertz was publicly traded.

[3]The total value includes $14.7 billion for Hertz, and $0.5 billion in fees and expenses. In addition to $11.1 billion in new debt, the transaction was financed using $1.8 billion of Hertz's own cash and securities (including a $1.2 billion obligation from Ford, which was forgiven as part of the payment to Ford). The remaining $2.3 billion in private equity was contributed by Clayton, Dubilier & Rice, The Carlyle Group, and Merrill Lynch Global Private Equity.

lic again by selling new stock through an IPO. As of 2007, Hertz was still able to meet its debt obligations, but had not significantly reduced the debt burden from the transaction.

Concept Check

5. Do callable bonds have a higher or lower yield than otherwise identical bonds without a call feature? Why?

6. What is a sinking fund?

7. Why does a convertible bond have a lower yield than an otherwise identical bond without the option to convert?

Here is what you should know after reading this chapter. MyFinanceLab will help you identify what you know, and where to go when you need to practice.

Key Points and Equations	Key Terms	Online Practice Opportunities
14.1 Corporate Debt		
▶ Companies can raise debt using different sources. Typical kinds of debt are public debt, which trades in a public market, and private debt, which is negotiated directly with a bank or a small group of investors. The securities that companies issue when raising debt are called corporate bonds.	asset-backed bonds, p. 462 asset-backed line of credit, p. 461 debentures, p. 462 domestic bonds, p. 464	MyFinanceLab Study Plan 14.1
▶ Private debt can be in the form of term loans or private placements. A term loan is a bank loan that lasts for a specific term. A private placement is a bond issue that is sold to a small group of investors.	Eurobonds, p. 465 foreign bonds, p. 465	
▶ For public offerings, the bond agreement takes the form of an indenture, a formal contract between the bond issuer and a trust company. The indenture lays out the terms of the bond issue.	global bonds, p. 465 indenture, p. 462 mortgage bonds, p. 462	
▶ Four types of corporate bonds are typically issued: notes, debentures, mortgage bonds, and asset-backed bonds. Notes and debentures are unsecured. Mortgage bonds and asset-backed bonds are secured.	notes, p. 462 original issue discount (OID) bond, p. 462 private debt, p. 460 private placement, p. 461	
▶ Corporate bonds differ in their level of seniority. In case of bankruptcy, senior debt is paid in full before subordinated debt is paid.	revolving line of credit, p. 461 secured debt, p. 462 seniority, p. 464	

BDeH CHAPTER 14

| International bonds are classified into four broadly defined categories: domestic bonds that trade in foreign markets; foreign bonds that are issued in a local market by a foreign entity; Eurobonds that are not denominated in the local currency of the country in which they are issued; and global bonds that trade in several markets simultaneously. | subordinated debenture, p. 464
syndicated bank loan, p. 461
term loan, p. 461
tranches, p. 464
unsecured debt, p. 462 | |

14.2 Bond Covenants

| ▶ Covenants are restrictive clauses in the bond contract that help investors by limiting the issuer's ability to take actions that will increase its default risk and reduce the value of the bonds. | covenants, p. 466 | MyFinanceLab Study Plan 14.2 |

14.3 Repayment Provisions

| ▶ A call provision gives the issuer of the bond the right (but not the obligation) to retire the bond after a specific date (but before maturity).
▶ A callable bond will generally trade at a lower price than an otherwise equivalent non-callable bond.
▶ The yield to call is the yield of a callable bond assuming that the bond is called at the earliest opportunity.
▶ Another way in which a bond is repaid before maturity is by periodically repurchasing part of the debt through a sinking fund.
▶ Some corporate bonds, known as convertible bonds, have a provision that allows the holder to convert them into equity.
▶ Convertible debt carries a lower interest rate than other comparable non-convertible debt. | balloon payment, p. 470
call date, p. 467
call price, p. 467
callable bonds, p. 467
conversion price, p. 471
conversion ratio, p. 470
convertible bonds, p. 470
leveraged buyout (LBO), p. 472
sinking fund, p. 470
straight bond, p. 471
yield to call (YTC), p. 468
yield to worst, p. 469 | MyFinanceLab Study Plan 14.3 |

BDeH CHAPTER 14

Review Questions

1. What are the different types of corporate debt and how do they differ?

2. Explain some of the differences between a public debt offering and a private debt offering.

3. Explain the difference between a secured corporate bond and an unsecured corporate bond.

4. Why do bonds with lower seniority have higher yields than equivalent bonds with higher seniority?

5. What is the difference between a foreign bond and a Eurobond?

6. Why would companies voluntarily choose to put restrictive covenants into a new bond issue?

7. Why would a call feature be valuable to a company issuing bonds?

8. What is the effect of including a call feature on the price a company can receive for its bonds?

9. When will the yield to maturity be higher than the yield to call for a callable bond?

10. How does a sinking fund provision affect the cash flows associated with a bond issue from the company's perspective? From a single bondholder's perspective?

11. Why is the yield on a convertible bond lower than the yield on an otherwise identical bond without a conversion feature?

Problems

All problems in this chapter are available in MyFinanceLab.

Corporate Debt

1. You are finalizing a bank loan for $200,000 for your small business and the closing fees payable to the bank are 2% of the loan. After paying the fees, what will be the net amount of funds from the loan available to your business?

2. Your firm is issuing $100 million in straight bonds at par with a coupon rate of 6% and paying total fees of 3%. What is the net amount of funds that the debt issue will provide for your firm?

Repayment Provisions

3. General Electric has just issued a callable (at par) ten-year, 6% coupon bond with annual coupon payments. The bond can be called at par in one year or anytime thereafter on a coupon payment date. It has a price of $102.
   a. What is the bond's yield to maturity?
   b. What is its yield to call?
   c. What is its yield to worst?

 4. Boeing Corporation has just issued a callable (at par) three-year, 5% coupon bond with semiannual coupon payments. The bond can be called at par in two years or anytime thereafter on a coupon payment date. It has a price of $99.
   a. What is the bond's yield to maturity?
   b. What is its yield to call?
   c. What is its yield to worst?

 5. You own a bond with a face value of $10,000 and a conversion ratio of 450. What is the conversion price?

6. You are the CFO of RealNetworks on July 1, 2008. The company's stock price is $9.70 and its convertible debt (as shown in Table 14.7) is now callable.
   a. What is the value of the shares the bondholders would receive per $1000 bond if they convert?
   b. What is the value per $1000 bond they would receive under the call?
   c. If you call the bonds, will the bondholders convert into shares or accept the call price?

Chapter 14 APPENDIX   ## Using a Financial Calculator to Calculate Yield to Call

Calculate the yield to call of the bond from Example 14.1. In the example, the bond is called at year one; however, this can be generalized and solved for longer periods than one year.

HP-10BII

[ ] [C]		Press [Orange Shift] and then the [C] button to clear all previous entries.
[1] [N]		Enter the Number of periods.
[8] [PMT]		Enter the Payment amount per period.
[1] [0] [0] [FV]		Enter the price you would receive when it is called.
[1] [0] [3] [+/−] [PV]		Enter the present value or price of the bond.
[I/YR]		Solve for yield to call.

TI-BAII Plus Professional

[2ND] [FV]		Press [2nd] and then the [FV] button to clear all previous entries.
[1] [N]		Enter the Number of periods.
[8] [PMT]		Enter the Payment amount per period.
[1] [0] [0] [FV]		Enter the price you would receive when it is called.
[1] [0] [3] [+/−] [PV]		Enter the present value or price of the bond.
[CPT] [I/Y]		Solve for yield to call.

If the bond was called after two years, you would simply use 2 instead of 1 for the number of periods.

Pages 477–559 intentionally omitted

Financial Modeling and Pro Forma Analysis

LEARNING OBJECTIVES

▶ Understand the goals of long-term financial planning

▶ Create pro forma income statements and balance sheets using the *percent of sales method*

▶ Develop financial models of the firm by directly forecasting capital expenditures, working capital needs, and financing events

▶ Distinguish between the concepts of sustainable growth and value-increasing growth

INTERVIEW WITH David Hollon, Goldman Sachs

Texas A&M University, 2005

"What differentiates an average analyst from an exceptional analyst is attention to detail and understanding what goes into the key assumptions."

Financial models are central to David Hollon's job as an analyst in Goldman Sachs' Houston-based energy investing group. "We invest in oil and gas companies, providing both debt and equity financing," says the 2005 graduate of Texas A&M University. "I screen potential investments, performing company due diligence and industry research to develop and refine my financial model. I then draft an investment memorandum and work with internal business units to present the investment for approval. This position requires a high level of proficiency in Excel analysis, along with financial statement analysis, accounting knowledge, and the ability to apply many investment decision rules, including NPV."

After meeting with senior management of the proposed investment company, David creates a financial model based on the company's projections and incorporates the proposed investment structure. "Then I run various scenarios that change the assumptions of key variables, which in the oil and gas industry include commodity prices, drilling success, capital and operating costs, and production volumes. We sensitize these key investment variables to determine how to maximize both the company's value and Goldman Sachs' potential return on investment over time."

Coming up with realistic assumptions is the biggest challenge to creating accurate models. "The mechanics and fundamentals of financial modeling are pretty straightforward. What differentiates an average analyst from an exceptional analyst is attention to detail and understanding what goes into the key assumptions. Making good assumptions requires thorough due diligence and lots of research. You have to step back and ask yourself what is realistic for this company with regard to capital expenditures, operating margins, cost of financing, and more. The goal is to build clean, accurate, and simple spreadsheets that are easy for the user to understand."

Financial modeling and NPV analysis affords an investor a way to compare competing projects with varying return and risk profiles. "Suppose we have to choose between two energy investment projects: a high-risk investment with a return of 30% or a relatively low-risk investment with a 20% return. We calculate the NPV of the first at a higher discount rate to compensate for the incremental risk. If its NPV is larger than the second, we'd likely choose to pursue it."

Most decisions a financial manager makes have long-term consequences. For example, in the late 1990s, Airbus managers decided to bet the future of the company on the market for mega-jets, giving the green light to development of the 555-seat A380. Shortly thereafter, Boeing managers bet that airlines would favor improvements in fuel efficiency and gave the go-ahead to the all-composite, technologically advanced 787. The outcomes of these decisions are still playing out today. In this chapter, we will learn how to build a financial model to analyze the consequences of our financial decisions well into the future. In particular, we will use these models to forecast when the firm will need to secure additional external funding and to determine how the decision will affect the value of the firm.

We will start by explaining the goals of forecasting through financial modeling and pro forma analysis, and how this analysis relates to the overall goal of maximizing firm value. Then, we will move to a basic forecasting technique based on projections of the firm's future sales. Next, we will develop an improved approach to forecasting that produces a more realistic financial model of the firm. Finally, we will use our financial model to value the firm under the new business plan and discuss value-increasing versus value-decreasing growth. In doing so, we will see the connection between the role of forecasting, NPV analysis, and the Valuation Principle that underlies all of finance.

17.1 Goals of Long-Term Financial Planning

The goal of the financial manager is to maximize the value of the stockholders' stake in the firm. One tool to help with this goal is long-term financial planning and modeling. In the following sections, we will develop specific methods to forecast the financial statements and cash flows for the firm as a whole. For context, in this section we discuss the objectives of long-term planning.

Identify Important Linkages

As you will see in Sections 17.2 and 17.3, when you build a model of the future course of the firm, by necessity you will uncover important linkages between—for example, sales, costs, capital investment, and financing. A well-designed spreadsheet model will allow you to examine how a change in your cost structure will impact your future free cash flows, financing needs, etc. Some links may be obvious, but others are much more difficult to determine without building a forecast of the entire firm's financial statements years into the future. For example, technological improvements leading to reduced costs could allow the firm to reduce prices and sell more product. However, increased production will require more equipment and facilities, and the associated capital expenditures will require financing and create additional depreciation tax shields. None of these links would be easy to see without a careful forecasting model. This is an important outcome of long-term planning because it allows the financial manager to understand the business and, through that understanding, to increase its value.

Analyze the Impact of Potential Business Plans

Perhaps your firm is planning a big expansion or considering changes in how it manages its inventory. By building a long-term model of your firm's financials, you can examine exactly how such business plans will impact the firm's free cash flows and hence value. In

Chapter 8, we developed the tools of capital budgeting with the goal of deciding whether to invest in a new project. To consider a fundamental change in the firm's business plan, the financial manager models the firm as a whole, rather than just a single project. In Section 17.3, we will analyze the impact of a firm-wide expansion plan, including necessary capital investment, debt financing, changes in free cash flows, and changes in value.

Plan for Future Funding Needs

Building a model for long-term forecasting reveals points in the future where the firm will need additional external financing—for example, where its retained earnings will not be enough to fund planned capital investment. Identifying the firm's funding needs in advance gives financial managers enough time to plan for them and line up the source of financing that is most advantageous for the firm. In a perfect capital market, this would be unnecessary—you would be able to secure financing instantaneously for any positive-NPV project and the source of financing would have no effect on the firm's value. However, in reality market frictions mean that you need time to issue debt or new equity and financing decisions impact firm value. Thus, identifying and planning for these financing decisions far in advance is a valuable exercise.

Concept Check

1. How does long-term financial planning fit into the goal of the financial manager?

2. What are the three main things that the financial manager can accomplish by building a long-term financial model of the firm?

17.2 Forecasting Financial Statements: The Percent of Sales Method

We will illustrate our discussion of forecasting financial statements via an application: the firm KMS Designs. KMS Designs is a boutique women's fashion house, specializing in affordable fashion-forward separates, with its own production facility. KMS Designs is a growing firm and its financial managers predict that it will need external financing to fuel its growth. In order to predict when KMS will need this financing and the amount the managers will need to secure, we need to prepare a financial model in Excel for KMS that will allow us to produce pro forma income statements and balance sheets. After developing a technique for forecasting, we will turn to the steps involved in preparing the pro forma income statement and balance sheet.

Percent of Sales Method

percent of sales method
A forecasting method that assumes that as sales grow, many income statement and balance sheet items will grow, remaining the same percent of sales.

A common starting point for forecasting is the *percent of sales method*. The **percent of sales method** assumes that as sales grow, many income statement and balance sheet items will grow, remaining the same percent of sales. For example, Table 17.1 shows that KMS's costs excluding depreciation were 78% of sales in 2007. There were sales of $74,889. If KMS forecasts that sales will grow by 18% in 2008, then:

- Sales will grow to $74,889 × 1.18 = $88,369.
- Costs excluding depreciation will remain 78% of sales, so that costs will be $88,369 × 0.78 = $68,928 in 2008.[1]

---

[1]For ease of exposition, we will base our forecast on a single year, 2007. Companies often take into account averages and trends over several years in forecasting for the future.

TABLE 17.1

KMS Designs 2007
Income Statement
and Balance Sheet

	Year	2007	% of Sales
1			
2	**Income Statement ($000s)**		
3	**Sales**	74,889	100%
4	Costs Except Depreciation	−58,413	78%
5	**EBITDA**	16,476	22%
6	Depreciation	−5,492	7.333%
7	**EBIT**	10,984	15%
8	Interest Expense (net)	−306	NM*
9	**Pretax Income**	10,678	14%
10	Income Tax (35%)	−3,737	NM
11	**Net Income**	6,941	9%

*NM indicates representing the item as a percent of sales is not meaningful.

	Year	2007	% of Sales
1			
2	**Balance Sheet ($000s)**		
3	**Assets**		
4	Cash and Equivalents	11,982	16%
5	Accounts Receivable	14,229	19%
6	Inventories	14,978	20%
7	**Total Current Assets**	41,189	55%
8	Property, Plant, and Equipment	49,427	66%
9	**Total Assets**	90,616	121%
10	**Liabilities and Stockholders' Equity**		
11	Accounts Payable	11,982	16%
12	Debt	4,500	NM
13	**Total Liabilities**	16,482	NM
14	**Stockholders' Equity**	74,134	NM
15	**Total Liabilities and Equity**	90,616	121%

We are essentially assuming that KMS will maintain its profit margins as its sales revenues grow. We proceed by making similar assumptions about working capital items on the balance sheet such as cash, accounts receivable, inventory, and accounts payable. The far-right column of Table 17.1 shows what percent of sales each of these items was in 2007. We can use those percentages to forecast part of the balance sheet in 2008. For example, if sales grow to $88,369 as we predict, then our inventory will need to grow to $88,369 × 0.20 = $17,674 to support those sales.

Some of the items are marked "NM" for "Not Meaningful" in the percent of sales column. For example, our assets and accounts payables might reasonably be expected to grow in line with sales, our long-term debt and equity will not naturally grow in line with sales. Instead, the change in equity and debt will reflect choices we make about dividends and net new financing.

Pro Forma Income Statement

Table 17.2 shows KMS's pro forma income statement for 2008 along with how each line was determined. KMS is forecasting 18% growth in sales from 2007 to 2008. In addition to the sales forecast, we require three other details to prepare the pro forma income statement: costs excluding depreciation in 2007 as a percent of sales, depreciation as a percent of sales, and the tax rate. KMS's info from Table 17.1 is as follows:

▸ Costs excluding depreciation were 78% of sales.

▸ Depreciation was 7% of sales in 2007.

▸ KMS pays a 35% tax rate.

TABLE 17.2

KMS Designs Pro
Forma Income
Statement for 2008

	Year	2007	2008	Calculation
1				
2	**Income Statement ($000s)**			
3	**Sales**	74,889	88,369	74,889 × 1.18
4	Costs Except Depreciation	−58,413	−68,928	78% of Sales
5	**EBITDA**	16,476	19,441	Lines 3 + 4
6	Depreciation	−5,492	−6,480	7.333% of Sales
7	**EBIT**	10,984	12,961	Lines 5 + 6
8	Interest Expense (net)	−306	−306	Remains the same
9	**Pretax Income**	10,678	12,655	Lines 7 + 8
10	Income Tax (35%)	−3,737	−4,429	35% of Line 9
11	**Net Income**	**6,941**	**8,226**	Lines 9 + 10

The one final assumption we need to make is about our interest expense.[2] We assume for now that it will remain the same as in 2007 because we will determine if our debt needs will change as part of the forecasting process.

Based on our pro forma balance sheet, we are forecasting an increase in net income of $8226 − $6941 = $1285, which represents an 18.5% increase over 2007 net income.[3] We now turn to forecasting the balance sheet to determine whether we will need any new financing in 2008 to pay for our growth. The net income we forecast in Table 17.2 will be one of the inputs to the pro forma balance sheet. The part of that net income not distributed as dividends will add to stockholders' equity on the balance sheet.

EXAMPLE 17.1

Percent of Sales

Problem
KMS has just revised its sales forecast downward. If KMS expects sales to grow by only 10% next year, what are its costs, except for depreciation, projected to be?

Solution

▶ **Plan**
Forecasted 2008 sales will now be: $74,889 × (1.10) = $82,378. With this figure in hand and the information from Table 17.1, we can use the percent of sales method to calculate KMS's forecasted costs.

▶ **Execute**
From Table 17.1, we see that costs are 78% of sales. With forecasted sales of $82,378, that leads to forecasted costs except depreciation of $82,378 × (0.78) = $64,255.

Pro Forma Balance Sheet

Forecasting the balance sheet using the percent of sales method requires a few iterating steps. In any balance sheet analysis, we know that assets and liabilities/equity must be equal. The assets and liabilities/equity sides of the pro forma balance sheet will not

---

[2]The interest expense should be interest paid on debt, net of interest earned on any invested cash—just as interest paid is tax deductible, interest earned is taxable—so KMS's tax shield comes from its net interest expense. In order to focus on forecasting, we will assume that all cash held by KMS is a necessary part of its working capital needed for transactions. Thus, we assume that KMS holds all of its cash in a non-interest-bearing account. In Chapter 18, we will discuss alternative ways to invest cash.

[3]This is higher than the sales growth of 18% because we assumed that interest expenses would not increase.

TABLE 17.3

First-Pass Pro Forma Balance Sheet for 2008

	Year	2007	2008	Calculation
1				
2	**Balance Sheet ($000s)**			
3	**Assets**			
4	Cash and Cash Equivalents	11,982	14,139	16% of Sales
5	Accounts Receivable	14,229	16,790	19% of Sales
6	Inventories	14,978	17,674	20% of Sales
7	**Total Current Assets**	41,189	48,603	Lines 4 + 5 + 6
8	Property, Plant, and Equipment	49,427	58,324	66% of Sales
9	**Total Assets**	90,616	106,927	Lines 7 + 8
10	**Liabilities**			
11	Accounts Payable	11,982	14,139	16% of Sales
12	Debt	4,500	4,500	Remains the same
13	**Total Liabilities**	16,482	18,639	Lines 11 + 12
14	**Stockholders' Equity**	74,134	79,892	74,134 + 70% of 8,226
15	**Total Liabilities and Equity**	90,616	98,531	Lines 13 + 14
16	**Net New Financing**		8,396	Line 9 − Line 15

net new financing The amount of additional external financing a firm needs to secure to pay for the planned increase in assets.

balance, however, until we make assumptions about how our equity and debt will grow with sales. We see this point in Table 17.3, where we have taken a first stab at the pro forma balance sheet (we will explain the details of the calculation below). Our assets are projected to be $8396 more than our liabilities and equity. The imbalance indicates that we will need $8396 in *net new financing* to fund our growth. **Net new financing** is the amount of additional external financing we will need to secure to pay for the planned increase in assets. It can be computed as:

Net New Financing = Projected Assets − Projected Liabilities and Equity

Let's take a closer look at how we arrived at the $8396 figure. Because we are using the percent of sales method, we assume that assets increase in line with sales. Thus, total assets have increased by 18%, the same as sales. The liabilities side of the balance sheet is more complicated. The amount of dividends a company pays will affect the retained earnings it has to finance growth. Further, any increases in debt or equity reflect capital structure decisions and require managers to actively raise capital, as discussed in Chapters 13 and 14. The bottom line is that we cannot simply assume that debt and equity increase in line with sales.

In KMS's case, it has a policy of paying out 30% of its net income as dividends. Thus, $2468 of its forecasted $8226 net income will be distributed to stockholders as dividends:

2008 Net Income:	$8,226
− 2008 Dividends (30% of NI)	−$2,468
= 2008 Retained Earnings	=$5,758

The $5758 in retained earnings (the remaining 70% of net income after dividends are paid) adds to stockholders' equity on the balance sheet. As a result, stockholders' equity is forecast to increase from $74,134 to $79,892 in Table 17.3.

2007 Stockholders' Equity:	$74,134
+ 2008 Retained Earnings	+$5,758
= 2008 Stockholders' Equity	=$79,892

We also assume that accounts payable will grow along with sales, remaining at 16% of sales as they were in 2007, so they are forecast to grow to $14,139. However, our initial assumption is that debt will remain the same, so our forecasted growth in liabilities and equity falls short of our forecasted growth in assets by $8396.

Common Mistake   **Confusing Stockholders' Equity with Retained Earnings**

It is easy to confuse new retained earnings, total retained earnings, and stockholders' equity. As in the example above, new retained earnings are the amount of net income left over after paying dividends. These new retained earnings are then added to the *total* accumu-

lated retained earnings from the life of the firm. Total retained earnings makes up one part of stockholders' equity, which also includes the par value of the stock and any paid-in capital.

The Plug: Net New Financing

How do we address this $8396 difference between assets and liabilities? The projected difference between KMS's assets and liabilities in the pro forma balance sheet indicates that KMS will need to obtain new financing from its investors. The net new financing of $8396 in this case is sometimes referred to as **the plug**—the amount we have to add to (plug into) the liabilities and equity side of the pro forma balance sheet to make it balance.

the plug *The amount of net new financing that needs to be added to the liabilities and equity side of the pro forma balance sheet to make it balance.*

While KMS definitely has to secure $8396 in new financing, it could come from new debt or new equity. We discussed the issues involved in the equity versus debt decision. It is a complex decision weighing many factors. Rather than complicating our analysis here, we assume that KMS's financial managers have evaluated these factors and decided that the best way to finance the growth is through additional debt. Table 17.4 shows our second-pass pro forma balance sheet including the $8396 in additional debt financing that brings the sheet into balance.

We should note that the decision to take on additional debt in 2008 makes our initial assumption that our interest expense would remain constant in 2008 potentially incorrect. If KMS takes on the debt before the end of the year, then there will be a partial-year interest expense from the debt. We would need to adjust the pro forma income statement and iterate with the pro forma balance sheet to get the exact amount of new debt needed. However, we have achieved our primary objective: to identify a future funding need and determine approximately how much we will need and how we will fund it. This will give KMS's managers enough time to begin the debt-issuance process with its bankers. We also note that debt has more than doubled, which justifies our original decision not to assume that it will increase in proportion to sales.

TABLE 17.4

Second-Pass Pro Forma Balance Sheet for KMS

	Year	2007	2008	Calculation
1	Year	2007	2008	Calculation
2	**Balance Sheet ($000s)**			
3	**Assets**			
4	Cash and Cash Equivalents	11,982	14,139	16% of Sales
5	Accounts Receivable	14,229	16,790	19% of Sales
6	Inventories	14,978	17,674	20% of Sales
7	**Total Current Assets**	41,189	48,603	Lines 4 + 5 + 6
8	Property, Plant, and Equipment	49,427	58,324	66% of Sales
9	**Total Assets**	90,616	106,927	Lines 7 + 8
10	**Liabilities**			
11	Accounts Payable	11,982	14,139	16% of Sales
12	Debt	4,500	**12,896**	4,500 + 8,396
13	**Total Liabilities**	16,482	27,035	Lines 11 + 12
14	**Stockholders' Equity**	74,134	79,892	74,134 + 70% of 8,226
15	**Total Liabilities and Equity**	90,616	106,927	Lines 13 + 14

EXAMPLE 17.2

Net New Financing

Problem

If instead of paying out 30% of earnings as dividends, KMS decides not to pay any dividend and instead retains all of its 2007 earnings, how would its net new financing change?

Solution

▶ **Plan**

KMS currently pays out 30% of its net income as dividends, so rather than retaining only $5758, it will retain the entire $8226. This will increase stockholders' equity, reducing the net new financing.

▶ **Execute**

The additional retained earnings are $8226 − $5758 = $2468. Compared to Table 17.3, stockholders' equity will be $79,892 + $2468 = $82,360 and total liabilities and equity will also be $2468 higher, rising to $100,999. Net new financing, the imbalance between KMS's assets and liabilities and equity, will decrease to $8396 − $2468 = $5928.

1	Year	2007	2008
2	Balance Sheet ($000s)		
3	Liabilities		
4	Accounts Payable	11,982	14,139
5	Debt	4,500	4,500
6	**Total Liabilities**	16,482	18,639
7	**Stockholders' Equity**	74,134	82,360
8	**Total Liabilities and Equity**	90,616	100,999
9	**Net New Financing**		5,928

▶ **Evaluate**

When a company is growing faster than it can finance internally, any distributions to shareholders will cause it to seek greater additional financing. It is important not to confuse the need for external financing with poor performance. Most growing firms need additional financing to fuel that growth as their expenditures for growth naturally precede their income from that growth. We will revisit the issue of growth and firm value in Section 17.5.

Concept Check

3. What is the basic idea behind the percent of sales method for forecasting?

4. How does the pro forma balance sheet help the financial manager forecast net new financing?

17.3 Forecasting a Planned Expansion

The percent of sales method is a useful starting point and may even be sufficient for mature companies with relatively stable but slow growth. Its shortcoming is handling the realities of fast growth requiring "lumpy" investments in new capacity. The typical firm cannot smoothly add capacity in line with expected sales. Instead, it must occasionally make a large investment in new capacity that it expects to be sufficient for several years. This kind of capacity expansion also implies that new funding will happen in large, infrequent financing rounds, rather than small increments each year as sales grow. However, we can address these realities in our long-term forecasting by modeling our capacity needs and capital expenditures directly. In this section, we consider a planned expansion by KMS and generate pro forma statements that allow us to decide whether the expansion will increase the value of KMS. First, we identify capacity needs and how to finance that capacity. Next, we construct pro forma income statements and forecast future free cash flows. Finally, we use those forecasted free cash flows to assess the impact of the expansion on firm value.

TABLE 17.5

KMS Forecasted
Production Capacity
Requirements

Year	2007	2008	2009	2010	2011	2012
Production Volume (000s units)						
Market Size	10,000	10,500	11,025	11,576	12,155	12,763
Market Share	10.0%	11.0%	12.0%	13.0%	14.0%	15.0%
Production Volume (1 × 2)	1,000	1,155	1,323	1,505	1,702	1,914
Additional Market Information						
Average Sales Price	$ 74.89	$ 76.51	$ 78.04	$ 79.60	$ 81.19	$ 82.82

KMS's managers have constructed a detailed sales forecast by first forecasting the size of the market and what market share KMS can expect to capture. While the size of the market is generally based on demographics and the overall economy, KMS's market share will depend on the appeal of its product and its price, which KMS has forecast as well. KMS currently has the capacity to produce a maximum of 1.1 million units (i.e., 1100 thousand units). However, as detailed in Table 17.5, KMS expects both the total market size and its share of the market to grow to the point where the company will quickly exceed that capacity. Thus, KMS is considering an expansion that will increase its capacity to 2 million units—enough to handle its projected requirements through 2012.

KMS Design's Expansion: Financing Needs

The first step in our analysis is estimating KMS's financing needs based on the capital expenditures required for the expansion.

Capital Expenditures for the Expansion. The new equipment to increase KMS's capacity will cost $20 million and will need to be purchased in 2008 to meet the company's production needs. Table 17.6 details KMS's forecasted capital expenditures and depreciation over the next five years. Based on the estimates for capital expenditures and depreciation, this spreadsheet tracks the book value of KMS's plant, property, and equipment starting from the book value's level at the beginning of 2007.[4] The depreciation entries in Table 17.6 are based on the appropriate depreciation schedule for each type of property. Those calculations are quite specific to the nature of the property and are not detailed here. The depreciation shown will be used for tax purposes.[5] KMS has ongoing capital investment requirements to cover the replacement of existing equipment—these were expected to be $5 million per year without the new equipment. The additional

TABLE 17.6

KMS Forecasted
Capital Expenditures

Year	2007	2008	2009	2010	2011	2012
Fixed Assets and Capital Investment ($000s)						
Opening Book Value	49,919	49,427	66,984	67,486	67,937	68,344
Capital Investment	5,000	25,000	8,000	8,000	8,000	8,000
Depreciation	−5,492	−7,443	−7,498	−7,549	−7,594	−7,634
Closing Book Value	49,427	66,984	67,486	67,937	68,344	68,709

[4]In this table, and elsewhere in the chapter, we display rounded numbers. Calculations such as Closing Book Value are based on the actual numbers in the spreadsheet with all significant digits. As a result, there will occasionally be a small discrepancy between the Excel-calculated value shown and the hand-calculated value using the rounded numbers displayed.

[5]Firms often maintain separate books for accounting and tax purposes, and they may use different depreciation assumptions for each. Because depreciation affects cash flows through its tax consequences, tax depreciation is more relevant for valuation.

TABLE 17.7

KMS Planned Debt
and Interest
Payments

Year		2007	2008	2009	2010	2011	2012
Debt and Interest Table ($000s)							
Outstanding Debt		4,500	24,500	24,500	24,500	24,500	24,500
Net New Borrowing		—	20,000	—	—	—	—
Interest on Debt	6.80%	306	306	1,666	1,666	1,666	1,666

$20 million is reflected in 2008, bringing the total to $25 million for 2008 and increasing expected recurring investment to $8 million per year in years 2009–2012.

Financing the Expansion.   While KMS believes it can fund recurring investment from its operating cash flows, as shown in Table 17.7, it will have to seek external financing for the $20 million in new equipment. KMS plans to finance the new equipment by issuing ten-year coupon bonds with a coupon rate of 6.8%. Thus, KMS will pay only interest on the bonds until the repayment of principal in ten years. The principal on its outstanding debt of $4500 is also not due before 2012.

Given KMS's outstanding debt, its interest expense each year is computed as:[6]

$$\text{Interest in Year } t = \text{Interest Rate} \times \text{Ending Balance in Year } (t-1) \quad (17.1)$$

The interest on the debt will provide a valuable tax shield to offset KMS's taxable income.

KMS Design's Expansion: Pro Forma Income Statement

The value of any investment opportunity arises from the future cash flows it will generate. To estimate the cash flows resulting from the expansion, we begin by projecting KMS's future earnings. We then consider KMS's working capital and investment needs and estimate its free cash flows. With its free cash flows and projected interest tax shields, we can compute the value of KMS with and without the expansion to decide whether the benefit of the new equipment is worth the cost.

Forecasting Earnings.   To build the pro forma income statement, we begin with KMS's sales. We calculate sales for each year from the estimates in Table 17.5 as follows:

$$\text{Sales} = \text{Market Size} \times \text{Market Share} \times \text{Average Sales Price} \quad (17.2)$$

For example, in 2008, KMS has projected sales of 10.5 million units × 11% market share × $76.51 average sales price = $88.369 million. We will assume that costs except depreciation will continue to be 78% of sales, so that our projected costs, except depreciation in 2008, will be 78% × $88,369 = $68,928. To arrive at forecasted earnings, we take the following steps:

▸ Deducting these operating expenses from KMS's sales, we can project EBITDA over the next five years as shown in Table 17.8.

▸ Subtracting the depreciation expenses we estimated in Table 17.6, we arrive at KMS's earnings before interest and taxes.

▸ We next deduct interest expenses according to the schedule given in Table 17.7.

▸ The final expense is the corporate income tax. KMS pays a 35% tax rate, and the income tax is computed as:

$$\text{Income Tax} = \text{Pretax Income} \times \text{Tax Rate} \quad (17.3)$$

---

[6]Equation 17.1 assumes that changes in debt occur at the end of the year. If debt changes during the year, it is more accurate to compute interest expenses based on the average level of debt during the year.

TABLE 17.8

Pro Forma Income Statement for KMS Expansion

Year	2007	2008	2009	2010	2011	2012
Income Statement ($000s)						
Sales	74,889	88,369	103,247	119,793	138,167	158,546
Costs Except Depreciation	−58,413	−68,928	−80,533	−93,438	−107,770	−123,666
EBITDA	16,476	19,441	22,714	26,354	30,397	34,880
Depreciation	−5,492	−7,443	−7,498	−7,549	−7,594	−7,634
EBIT	10,984	11,998	15,216	18,806	22,803	27,246
Interest Expense (net)	−306	−306	−1,666	−1,666	−1,666	−1,666
Pretax Income	10,678	11,692	13,550	17,140	21,137	25,580
Income Tax	−3,737	−4,092	−4,742	−5,999	−7,398	−8,953
Net Income	**6,941**	**7,600**	**8,807**	**11,141**	**13,739**	**16,627**

After subtracting the income tax from the pretax income, we arrive at the forecasted net income as the bottom line in Table 17.8.

Working Capital Requirements. We have one more step before we are ready to forecast the free cash flows for KMS. Recall that increases in working capital reduce free cash flows. Thus, we still need to forecast KMS's working capital needs. The spreadsheet in Table 17.9 lists KMS's current working capital requirements and forecasts the firm's future working capital needs. (See Chapter 18 for a further discussion of working capital requirements and their determinants.) We have forecast that the minimum required cash will be 16% of sales, accounts receivable will be 19% of sales, inventory will be 20% of sales, and accounts payable will be 16% of sales, all as they were in 2007.

The minimum required cash represents the minimum level of cash needed to keep the business running smoothly, allowing for the daily variations in the timing of income and expenses. Firms generally earn little or no interest on these balances, which are held in cash or in a checking or short-term savings account. As a consequence, we account for this opportunity cost by including the cash balance as part of the firm's working capital. We will make the assumption that KMS distributes all cash in excess of the minimum required cash as dividends. If our forecast shows that KMS's cash flows will be insufficient to fund the minimum required cash, then we know that we need to plan to finance those cash needs. Again, identifying these future funding needs is one of the advantages of forecasting.

If KMS instead retained some cash above the amount needed for transactions, the company would likely invest it in some short-term securities that earn interest. Most companies choose to do this to provide funds for future investment so that they do not need to raise as much capital externally. In this case, the excess amount of cash would not be included in working capital. We discuss cash management in Chapter 18.

TABLE 17.9

KMS Projected Working Capital Needs

Year	2007	2008	2009	2010	2011	2012
Working Capital ($000s)						
Assets						
Cash	11,982	14,139	16,520	19,167	22,107	25,367
Accounts Recivable	14,229	16,790	19,617	22,761	26,252	30,124
Inventory	14,978	17,674	20,649	23,959	27,633	31,709
Total Current Assets	41,189	48,603	56,786	65,886	75,992	87,201
Liabilities						
Accounts Payable	11,982	14,139	16,520	19,167	22,107	25,367
Total Current Liabilities	11,982	14,139	16,520	19,167	22,107	25,367
Net Working Capital						
Net Working Capital (7 − 10)	29,207	34,464	40,266	46,719	53,885	61,833
Increase in Net Working Capital		5,257	5,802	6,453	7,166	7,948

TABLE 17.10

Pro Forma Balance
Sheet for KMS, 2008

	Year	2007	2008	Source for 2008 Data	2008 (Revised)
1	Year	2007	2008	Source for 2008 Data	2008 (Revised)
2	**Balance Sheet ($000s)**				
3	**Assets**				
4	Cash and Cash Equivalents	11,982	14,139	Table 17.9	14,139
5	Accounts Receivable	14,229	16,790	Table 17.9	16,790
6	Inventories	14,978	17,674	Table 17.9	17,674
7	**Total Current Assets**	41,189	48,603	Lines 4 + 5 + 6	48,603
8	Property, Plant, and Equipment	49,427	66,984	Table 17.6	66,984
9	**Total Assets**	90,616	115,587	Lines 7 + 8	115,587
10	**Liabilities**				
11	Accounts Payable	11,982	14,139	Table 17.9	14,139
12	Debt	4,500	24,500	Table 17.7	24,500
13	**Total Liabilities**	16,482	38,639	Lines 11 + 12	38,639
14	**Stockholders' Equity**				
15	Starting Stockholders' Equity	69,275	74,134	2007 Line 18	74,134
16	Net Income	6,941	7,600	Table 17.8	7,600
17	Dividends	−2,082	0	**Assumed**	−4,786
18	**Stockholders' Equity**	74,134	81,734	Lines 15 + 16 + 17	76,948
19	**Total Liabilities and Equity**	90,616	120,373	Lines 13 + 18	115,587

Forecasting the Balance Sheet

We have enough data now to forecast the balance sheet for our planned expansion. Recall from Section 17.2 with the percent of sales method that forecasting the balance sheet helps us identify any future funding needs because the balance sheet must balance. Here, we have explicitly planned for the funding of the expansion in 2008. Nonetheless, we can check to make sure that our debt issue will be enough and then forecast past the expansion to see if we will need any future financing. Table 17.10 shows the balance sheet for 2007 and 2008 filled in with the information we have so far. The only piece of information we are missing is the dividend amount, so we assume for now that we will not pay any dividends in 2008.

As we can see from the column for 2008 in the pro forma balance sheet, KMS's balance sheet does not initially balance: the liabilities and equity are greater than the assets. In Section 17.2, KMS faced the opposite situation—its assets were greater than its liabilities and equity—and this told KMS's managers that they needed external financing. When liabilities and equity are greater than the assets, we have generated more cash than we had planned to consume and we need to decide what to do with it. KMS's options are:

▶ Build-up extra cash reserves (which would increase the cash account to bring assets in line with liabilities and equity).

▶ Pay-down (retire) some of its debt.

▶ Distribute the excess as dividends.

▶ Repurchase shares.

Let's assume that KMS's managers choose to distribute the excess as dividends. The excess is the amount by which liabilities and equity exceeds assets: $120,373 − $115,587 = $4786. The final column of Table 17.10, labeled "2008 (Revised)," shows the new pro forma balance sheet, including KMS's planned dividend. The balance sheet now balances! We can do this for the full forecast horizon (2008–2012). The completed pro forma balance sheet is shown in the chapter appendix.

The general lesson from the example in Section 17.2, as well as in this section, is summarized in Table 17.11.

TABLE 17.11

Pro Forma Balance
Sheets and Financing

Liabilities and equity are ...	less than assets	greater than assets
	New financing needed—the firm must borrow or issue new equity to fund the shortfall.	Excess cash available—the firm can retain it as extra cash reserves (thus increasing assets), pay dividends, or reduce external financing by retiring debt or repurchasing shares.

Concept Check

5. What is the advantage of forecasting capital expenditures, working capital, and financing events directly?

6. What role does minimum required cash play in working capital?

17.4 Valuing the Planned Expansion

Now that we have the implications of the planned expansion for the debt, net income, and working capital of KMS, we are ready to determine whether the expansion is a good idea. The Valuation Principle guides us here—we need to forecast the cash flows and compute their present value.

Forecasting Free Cash Flows

We now have the data needed to forecast KMS's free cash flows over the next five years. KMS's earnings are available from the income statement (Table 17.8), as are its depreciation and interest expenses. Capital expenditures are available from Table 17.6, and changes in net working capital can be found in Table 17.9. We combine these items to estimate the free cash flows in the spreadsheet shown in Table 17.12.

To compute KMS's free cash flows, which exclude cash flows associated with leverage, we first adjust net income by adding back the after-tax interest payments associated with the net debt in its capital structure:[7]

$$\text{After-Tax Interest Expense} = (1 - \text{Tax Rate})$$
$$\times (\text{Interest Earned on Debt} - \text{Interest Paid on Excess Cash}) \qquad (17.4)$$

TABLE 17.12

KMS Forecasted Free
Cash Flows

	Year	2008	2009	2010	2011	2012
1	Year	2008	2009	2010	2011	2012
2	Free Cash Flow ($000s)					
3	Net Income	7,600	8,807	11,141	13,739	16,627
4	Plus: After-Tax Interest Expense	199	1,083	1,083	1,083	1,083
5	Unlevered Net Income	7,799	9,890	12,224	14,822	17,710
6	Plus: Depreciation	7,443	7,498	7,549	7,594	7,634
7	Less: Increases in NWC	−5,257	−5,802	−6,453	−7,166	−7,948
8	Less: Capital Expenditures	−25,000	−8,000	−8,000	−8,000	−8,000
9	Free Cash Flow of Firm	−15,015	3,586	5,320	7,250	9,396

---

[7]If KMS had some interest income or expenses from working capital, we would *not* include that interest here. We adjust only for interest that is related to the firm's *financing*—that is, interest associated with debt and excess cash (cash not included as part of working capital).

Because KMS has no excess cash, its after-tax interest expense in 2008 is $(1 - 35\%) \times \$306 = \$199$ (thousand), providing unlevered net income of $\$7600 + 199 = \$7799$. We could also compute the unlevered net income in Table 17.12 by starting with EBIT and deducting taxes. For example, in 2008 EBIT is forecasted as $11.998 million (Table 17.8), which amounts to:

$$\$11.998 \times (1 - 35\%) = \$7.799 \text{ million after taxes}$$

To compute KMS's free cash flows from its unlevered net income, we add back depreciation (which is not a cash expense), and deduct KMS's increases in net working capital and capital expenditures. The free cash flows on line 9 of Table 17.12 show the cash the firm will generate for its investors, both debt and equity holders.[8] While KMS will generate substantial free cash flows over the next five years, the level of free cash flows varies substantially from year to year. They are even forecasted to be negative in 2008 (when the expansion takes place).

As we noted, free cash flows compute the total cash available to all investors (debt and equity holders). To determine the amount that can be paid out to equity holders, we can adjust the free cash flows to account for all (after-tax) payments to or from debt holders. For example, in 2008 KMS will pay after-tax interest of $199,000 and receive $20 million by issuing new debt as follows:

	2008
Free Cash Flows	−15,015
Less: After-tax Interest Expense	−199
Plus: Increase in Debt	20,000
Free Cash Flows to Equity	4,786

Note that the free cash flows that are available to equity holders in 2008, $4.786 million, are exactly the amount of dividends we forecast at the end of Section 17.3. This is no coincidence—we chose in that section to pay out all excess available cash flows as a dividend. This is exactly what the free cash flows to equity tell us—the total amount of excess cash flows that belongs to the equity holders for them to use to pay dividends, repurchase shares, retain in the firm as cash, or retire debt. (See the appendix to this chapter for a forecast of free cash flows to equity and dividends through 2012.)

BDeH CHAPTER 17

Common Mistake   Confusing Total and Incremental Net Working Capital

When calculating free cash flows from earnings, students often make the mistake of subtracting the firm's *total* net working capital each year rather than only the incremental change in net working capital. Remember that only a change in net working capital results in a new cash inflow or outflow for the firm. Subtracting the entire *level* of net working capital will reduce the free cash flows, often even making them negative, and lead the student to understate the NPV of the decision.

---

[8] While we are maintaining the assumption that after paying the interest on its debt, KMS will distribute any excess funds to shareholders as dividends, this payout decision has no impact on the amount of free cash flows the firm generates in the first place, and hence has no impact on the value we will compute for KMS.

KMS Design's Expansion: Effect on Firm Value

We've accomplished a lot by carefully forecasting the impact of the planned expansion on KMS's net income, capital expenditures, and working capital needs. First, we identified future financing needs, allowing us ample time to plan to secure the necessary funding. Next, in order to construct our pro forma statements, we built an Excel model of the interactions between sales growth, costs, capital investment, working capital needs, and financing choices. This model allows us to study how changes in any of these factors will affect the others and our expansion plans.[9] Finally, we can now use these forecasts to determine whether the expansion plan is a good idea—does it increase the value of KMS?

Absent distress costs, the value of a firm with debt is equal to the value of the firm without debt plus the present value of its interest tax shields. Our careful forecast of the financing of KMS's expansion allows us to apply the same approach to valuing the expansion: we compute the present value of the *unlevered* free cash flows of KMS and add to it the present value of the tax shields created by our planned interest payments.[10] However, we have only forecast cash flows out to 2012, so we will need to account for the remaining value of KMS at that point. We do so using the tools developed in Chapter 9 for valuing common stock.

Multiples Approach to Continuation Value.   Practitioners generally estimate a firm's continuation value (also called the terminal value) at the end of the forecast horizon using a valuation multiple. Explicitly forecasting cash flows is useful in capturing those specific aspects of a company that distinguish the firm from its competitors in the short run. However, because of competition between firms, the long-term expected growth rates, profitability, and risk of firms in the same industry should move toward one another. As a consequence, long-term expectations of multiples are likely to be relatively homogeneous across firms. Thus, a realistic assumption is that a firm's multiple will eventually move toward the industry average. Because distant cash flows are difficult to forecast accurately, estimating the firm's continuation or terminal value based on a long-term estimate of the valuation multiple for the industry is a common (and, generally, reasonably reliable) approach.

Of the different valuation multiples available, the EBITDA (earnings before interest, taxes, depreciation, and amortization) multiple is most often used in practice. In most settings, the EBITDA multiple is more reliable than sales or earnings multiples because it accounts for the firm's operating efficiency and is not affected by leverage differences between firms. We discussed the use of multiples in valuation in Chapter 9. As in that context, here we estimate the continuation value using an EBITDA multiple as follows:

$$\text{Continuation Enterprise Value at Forecast Horizon}$$
$$= \text{EBITDA at Horizon} \times \text{EBITDA Multiple at Horizon} \qquad (17.5)$$

From the income statement in Table 17.8, KMS's EBITDA in 2012 is forecast to be $34.880 million. Firms in KMS's industry are valued at an average EBITDA multiple of 9. If we assume that the appropriate EBITDA multiple in 2012 is unchanged from the current value of 9, then KMS's continuation value in 2012 is $34.880 \times 9 = \$313.920$ million.

---

[9]You can download a copy of the forecasting model in Excel from the book's Web site and experiment with changes in these factors yourself.

[10]This approach is called the adjusted present value because it adjusts the present value of the unlevered free cash flows for the effect of the interest tax shields.

This assumption is important—the EBITDA multiple at horizon will have a large impact on our value calculation. A careful analysis of the prospects for industry growth (which tends to be related to higher multiples) at the horizon is important. Here, we assume that the design and apparel industry is mature and will remain relatively stable, but this assumption can be probed, especially in sensitivity analysis.

KMS Design's Value with the Expansion. Assume that KMS's financial managers have estimated KMS's unlevered cost of capital to be 10% (specifically, 10% is their pretax WACC; see the details regarding the estimation of the cost of capital in Chapter 12). Now we have all the inputs we need to value KMS with the expansion. Table 17.13 presents the calculation. First, we compute the present value of the forecasted free cash flows of the firm over the next five years. These are the cash flows available to both bondholders and equity holders, so they are free of any effects of leverage. Because they represent cash flows to both debt and equity holders, and because we will account for the benefits of the interest tax shield separately, we discount KMS's free cash flows at the firm's pretax WACC of 10%. Using the free cash flows we forecasted for 2008–2012 in Table 17.12, we get a present value of $4096:

$$PV(FCF) = \frac{-15{,}015}{(1.10)^1} + \frac{3586}{(1.10)^2} + \frac{5320}{(1.10)^3} + \frac{7250}{(1.10)^4} + \frac{9396}{(1.10)^5} = 4096 \quad (17.6)$$

TABLE 17.13

Calculation of KMS Firm Value with the Expansion

	Year	2007	2008	2009	2010	2011	2012
1							
2	Free Cash Flow of Firm		−15,015	3,586	5,320	7,250	9,396
3	PV Free Cash Flow (at 10%)	4,096					
4	Continuation Value						313,920
5	PV Continuation Value (at 10%)	194,920					
6	Net Interest Expense		−306	−1,666	−1,666	−1,666	−1,666
7	Interest Tax Shield		107	583	583	583	583
8	PV Interest Tax Shield (at 6.8%)	1,958					
9	Firm Value (3+5+8)	200,974					

Even though the PV of the cash flows over the next five years is small, the expansion pays off in the long run by providing higher free cash flows from 2012 onward. This growth results in a higher EBITDA in 2012 than would otherwise be possible, and thus a higher continuation value once that EBIDTA is multiplied by the continuation multiple of 9. The $313,920 continuation value in 2012 that we calculated is included in Table 17.13. However, because it is a 2012 value, we need to discount it to the present:

$$PV\ Continuation\ Value = \frac{313{,}920}{(1.10)^5} = 194{,}920 \quad (17.7)$$

Finally, because we are financing the expansion with debt, we will have additional interest tax shields. The total net interest expense is included in the table and the interest tax shield in the table is calculated by multiplying the interest expense by the tax rate (35% for KMS):

$$Interest\ Tax\ Shield = Net\ Interest\ Expense \times Tax\ Rate \quad (17.8)$$

We calculate the present value of the interest tax shield using the interest rate on debt as the discount rate, *not* using the WACC. Recall that the reason for doing so is that the tax shield is only as risky as the debt that creates it, so that the proper discount rate is the debt's interest rate, here at 6.8%:[11]

$$\text{PV Interest Tax Shield} = \frac{107}{(1.068)^1} + \frac{583}{(1.068)^2} + \frac{583}{(1.068)^3} + \frac{583}{(1.068)^4}$$

$$+ \frac{583}{(1.068)^5} = 1,958 \tag{17.9}$$

The total value of KMS with the expansion is the sum of the present values of the forecasted unlevered free cash flows, the continuation value of the firm, and the interest tax shields. As shown in Table 17.13, the total firm value is $200.974 million.

KMS Design's Value Without the Expansion.   But how do we know if the expansion is a good idea? We can compare KMS's value with the expansion to its value without the expansion. If KMS does not invest in the new equipment, it will be stuck with a maximum capacity of 1100 units. While its sales revenue will grow due to price increases, its main source of growth will be cut off. Table 17.14 shows the sales revenue without the expansion. By 2008, KMS reaches maximum production capacity and can no longer expand. Comparing the sales revenue in the table to the sales revenue with the expansion given in Table 17.8, we see how much higher sales are forecasted to be with the expansion.

TABLE 17.14

Sales Forecast Without Expansion

	Year	2007	2008	2009	2010	2011	2012
1							
2	Production Volume	1,000	1,100	1,100	1,100	1,100	1,100
3	Sales Price	$ 74.89	$ 76.51	$ 78.04	$ 79.60	$ 81.19	$ 82.82
4	Sales Revenue	$74,889	$84,161	$85,844	$87,561	$89,312	$91,099

We can complete the same process for forecasting the free cash flows of the firm without the expansion as we did for the firm with the expansion. In this case, we would find that the 2012 EBITDA would only be $20,042, so that the continuation value would drop to $20,042 × 9 = $180,378. Also, KMS will not be taking on any additional debt, so the interest expense will remain constant at $306 per year. The final result of the valuation is presented in Table 17.15.

While the PV of the free cash flows over the next five years is higher because we don't have to spend $20 million for the new equipment, the lower growth substantially

TABLE 17.15

KMS'S Value Without the Expansion

	Year	2007	2008	2009	2010	2011	2012
1							
2	Free Cash Flow of Firm		5,324	8,509	8,727	8,952	9,182
3	**PV Free Cash Flow** (at 10%)	30,244					
4	Continuation Value						180,378
5	**PV Continuation Value** (at 10%)	112,001					
6	Net Interest Expense		−306	−306	−306	−306	−306
7	Interest Tax Shield		107	107	107	107	107
8	**PV Interest Tax Shield** (at 6.8%)	441					
9	**Firm Value (3+5+8)**	142,686					

---

[11]We have not ignored the rest of the interest tax shields from the new debt. The value of those shields is subsumed in the continuation value of the firm. When we say that the firm will be worth 9 times EBITDA, we are saying that the total value at that point, including all unused tax shields, will be 9 times EBITDA.

reduces our continuation value and the reduced debt (because we do not need to borrow to fund the equipment) produces a much lower present value of interest tax shields as well. The resulting firm value is almost $60 million lower without the expansion than it is with the expansion. Thus, the expansion is certainly a good idea for KMS.

Optimal Timing and the Option to Delay

We just showed that if the alternative is not to expand at all, KMS should definitely expand in 2008. However, what if it also has the option to simply delay expansion to 2009 or later, rather than not to expand at all? If we repeat the valuation analysis above for expansion in each year from 2008 to 2012, we get the following firm values in 2007:[12]

Expand in . . .	2008	2009	2010	2011	2012
KMS's Firm Value in 2007:	200,974	203,553	204,728	204,604	203,277

KMS's firm value is maximized by delaying the expansion to 2010. The reason is that while delaying expansion means that KMS cannot produce enough units to meet demand, the shortfall is not too great until 2010. The value gained from putting off such a large financial outlay is greater than the value lost from forgone sales.

The timing analysis recalls an important point from Chapter 8: Managers often have real options embedded in capital budgeting decisions. In this case, it is important for KMS's managers to realize that the alternative is not: expand or do nothing. Rather, it is expand or delay expansion for another year (or more). As we see here, this option is valuable, allowing KMS's managers to add almost $4 million in additional value to the firm.

Concept Check

7. What is the multiples approach to continuation value?

8. How does forecasting help the financial manager decide whether to implement a new business plan?

17.5 Growth and Firm Value

While the expansion we just analyzed for KMS turned out to represent very valuable growth, not all growth is worth the price. It is possible to pay so much to enable growth that the firm, on net, is worth less. Even if the cost of the growth is not an issue, other aspects of growth can leave the firm less valuable. For example, expansion may strain managers' capacity to monitor and handle the firm's operations. It may surpass the firm's distribution capabilities or quality control or even change customers' perceptions of the firm and its brand.

For example, in Starbucks's 2005 annual report, Chairman Howard Schultz and CEO Jim Donald wrote to shareholders that Starbucks planned to continue opening new stores—1800 in 2006 alone—and planned revenue growth of approximately 20% for the next 5 years. Around the time that Starbucks's shareholders were reading this (early 2006), the price of the company's stock was about $36. By the end of 2007, Starbucks's

---

[12]Interested students may perform this analysis for themselves using the spreadsheet that accompanies this chapter on the textbook's Web site.

stock price had fallen to $21, Jim Donald had been fired as CEO, and chairman and founder Howard Schultz had written a memo to employees that Starbucks's recent expansion had caused it to "lose its soul," meaning that the Starbucks experience that was the key to its success and loyalty of its customers had been watered down. To distinguish between growth that adds to or detracts from the value of the firm, we will discuss two growth rates that factor in financing needs and revisit our top decision rule: NPV analysis.

Sustainable Growth Rate and External Financing

internal growth rate The maximum growth rate a firm can achieve without resorting to external financing.

The Starbucks example makes the point that not all growth is valuable growth. The distinction between value-enhancing and value-destroying growth can only be made through careful NPV analysis such as we performed earlier in this chapter. However, this distinction is often confused with the concept of a firm's **internal growth rate**—the maximum growth rate a firm can achieve without resorting to external financing. Intuitively, this is the growth the firm can support by reinvesting its earnings. A closely related and more commonly used measure is the firm's **sustainable growth rate**—the maximum growth rate the firm can sustain without issuing new equity or increasing its debt-to-equity ratio. Let's discuss each of these in turn.

sustainable growth rate The maximum growth rate a firm can achieve without issuing new equity or increasing its debt-to-equity ratio.

Internal Growth Rate Formula. Both of these benchmark growth rates are aimed at identifying how much growth a firm can support based on its existing net income. For a firm that does not pay any dividends, its internal growth rate is its return on assets because that tells us how fast it could grow its assets using only its net income. If the firm pays some of its net income out as a dividend, then its internal growth rate is reduced to only the growth supported by its retained earnings. This reasoning suggests a more general formula for the internal growth rate:

$$\text{Internal Growth Rate} = \left(\frac{\text{Net Income}}{\text{Beginning Assets}}\right) \times (1 - \text{payout ratio})$$

$$= \text{ROA} \times \text{retention rate} \qquad (17.10)$$

plowback ratio One minus the payout ratio of the firm, also called the retention ratio.

Recall from Chapter 9 that the fraction of net income retained for reinvestment in the firm is called the retention rate. In the context of internal and sustainable growth rates, the retention rate is often called the **plowback ratio**. The internal growth rate is simply the ROA multiplied by the retention rate (plowback ratio).

Sustainable Growth Rate Formula. The sustainable growth rate allows for some external financing. It assumes that no new equity will be issued and that the firm's managers want to maintain the same debt-to-equity ratio. Thus, it tells us how fast the firm can grow by reinvesting its retained earnings and issuing only as much new debt as can be supported by those retained earnings. The formula for the sustainable growth rate is:

$$\text{Sustainable Growth Rate} = \left(\frac{\text{Net Income}}{\text{Beginning Equity}}\right) \times (1 - \text{payout ratio})$$

$$= \text{ROE} \times \text{retention rate} \qquad (17.11)$$

Sustainable Growth Rate Versus Internal Growth Rate. Because your ROE will be larger than your ROA anytime you have debt, the sustainable growth rate will be greater than the internal growth rate. While the internal growth rate assumes no external financing, the sustainable growth rate assumes that you will make use of some outside financing equal to the amount of new debt that will keep your debt-to-equity ratio constant as your equity grows through reinvested net income.

EXAMPLE 17.3

Internal and Sustainable Growth Rates and Payout Policy

Problem

Your firm has $70 million in equity and $30 million in debt and forecasts $14 million in net income for the year. It currently pays dividends equal to 20% of its net income. You are analyzing a potential change in payout policy—an increase in dividends to 30% of net income. How would this change affect your internal and sustainable growth rates?

Solution

▶ **Plan**

We can use Eqs. 17.10 and 17.11 to compute your firm's internal and sustainable growth rates under the old and new policy. To do so, we'll need to compute its ROA, ROE, and retention rate (plowback ratio). The company has $100 million (= $70 million in equity + $30 million in debt) in total assets.

$$\text{ROA} = \frac{\text{Net Income}}{\text{Beginning Assets}} = \frac{14}{100} = 14\% \quad \text{ROE} = \frac{\text{Net Income}}{\text{Beginning Equity}} = \frac{14}{70} = 20\%$$

$$\text{Old Retention Rate} = (1 - \text{payout ratio}) = (1 - 0.20) = 0.80$$
$$\text{New Retention Rate} = (1 - 0.30) = 0.70$$

▶ **Execute**

Using Eq. 17.10 to compute the internal growth rate before and after the change, we have:

$$\text{Old Internal Growth Rate} = \text{ROA} \times \text{retention rate} = 14\% \times 0.80 = 11.2\%$$
$$\text{New Internal Growth Rate} = 14\% \times 0.70 = 9.8\%$$

Similarly, we can use Eq. 17.11 to compute the sustainable growth rate before and after:

$$\text{Old Sustainable Growth Rate} = \text{ROE} \times \text{retention rate} = 20\% \times 0.80 = 16\%$$
$$\text{New Sustainable Growth Rate} = 20\% \times 0.70 = 14\%$$

▶ **Evaluate**

By reducing the amount of retained earnings available to fund growth, an increase in the payout ratio necessarily reduces your firm's internal and sustainable growth rates.

Whenever you forecast growth greater than the internal growth rate, you will have to either reduce your payout ratio (increase your plowback ratio), plan to raise additional external financing, or both. If your forecasted growth is greater than your sustainable growth rate, you will have to increase your plowback ratio, raise additional equity financing, or increase your leverage (increase your debt faster than keeping your debt-to-equity ratio constant would allow). Table 17.16 compares internal and sustainable growth rates.

TABLE 17.16

Summary of Internal Growth Rate Versus Sustainable Growth Rate

	Internal Growth Rate	Sustainable Growth Rate
Formula:	ROA × retention rate	ROE × retention rate
Maximum growth financed only by:	Retained earnings	Retained earnings and new debt that keeps D/E ratio constant
To grow faster, a firm must:	Reduce payout or raise external capital	Reduce payout, or raise new equity, or increase leverage

BDeH CHAPTER 17

While the internal and sustainable growth rates are useful in alerting you to the need to plan for external financing, they cannot tell you whether your planned growth increases or decreases the firm's value. The growth rates do not evaluate the future costs and benefits of the growth and the Valuation Principle tells us that the value implications of the growth can only be assessed by doing so. There is nothing inherently bad or unsustainable about growth greater than your sustainable growth rate as long as that growth is value increasing. Your firm will simply need to raise additional capital to finance the growth.

For example, in the 1990s Starbucks's average revenue growth was above 50% even though its average ROE was 12%. Starbucks has never paid dividends, so its retention rate is 1, making its sustainable growth rate at the time also 12%.

$$\text{SGR} = \text{ROE} \times \text{retention rate} = 12\% \times 1 = 12\%$$

Despite expanding at four times its sustainable growth rate, Starbucks's value increased almost ten times (1000%), as shown in Figure 17.1.

Conversely, Starbucks's recent experience illustrates that sustainable growth need not be value-increasing growth. We noted at the beginning of this section that starting

FIGURE 17.1

Starbucks's Stock Price During Periods of Growth at and above Its SGR

The figure graphs Starbucks's stock price since its initial public offering. During most of its early years, Starbucks grew at well above its sustainable growth rate (SGR) and its value increased substantially. In 2006, it planned growth at its SGR but suffered a share decrease in value. The figure demonstrates that there is no necessary relationship between a firm's growth relative to its SGR and whether that growth is valuable.

Source: http://finance.google.com and authors' calculations.

in 2006, Starbucks was aiming for annual growth of 20%. How does this compare to its sustainable growth rate at the time? When Schultz and Donald wrote their letter to shareholders, Starbucks ROE was 20% (based on its 2005 annual report). Again, Starbucks has never paid dividends, so its retention rate is 1, making its sustainable growth rate also 20%. Thus, 20% growth was sustainable—it just wasn't value increasing.[13]

As we discussed in Chapters 13 and 14, there are costs to seeking external financing—the flotation and issuance costs associated with issuing new equity or new bonds. Thus, the internal growth rate indicates the fastest growth possible without incurring any of these costs. The sustainable growth rate still assumes some new debt will be sought, so the company reduces, but does not eliminate entirely, its costs of external financing when growing at the sustainable growth rate. Thus, managers, especially those at small firms, concerned with these costs might track these growth rates. However, these costs are generally small relative to the NPV of, for example, an expansion plan.

While these costs are usually small relative to the NPV of expanding the business, it would be wrong to ignore them completely. The proper way to incorporate them is to calculate the cash outflow associated with these costs and subtract it from the NPV of the expansion. The point remains that growth above a firm's internal or sustainable growth rates is not necessarily bad, but will require external financing and the costs associated with that financing.

Concept Check

9. What is the difference between internal growth rate and sustainable growth rate?

10. If a firm grows faster than its sustainable growth rate, is that growth value decreasing?

---

[13]The book's Web site contains a spreadsheet with a proposed further expansion of KMS Designs that allows you to explore further the differences between sustainable growth, internal growth rate, and value-increasing growth.

Here is what you should know after reading this chapter. MyFinanceLab will help you identify what you know, and where to go when you need to practice.

Key Points and Equations	Key Terms	Online Practice Opportunities
17.1 Goals of Long-Term Financial Planning Building a financial model to forecast the financial statements and free cash flows of a firm allows the financial manager to: ▶ Identify important linkages. ▶ Analyze the impact of potential business plans. ▶ Plan for future funding needs.		MyFinanceLab Study Plan 17.1

17.2 Forecasting Financial Statements: The Percent of Sales Method

▶ One common approach to forecasting is the percent of sales approach where you assume that costs, working capital, and total assets will remain a fixed percent of sales as sales grow.

▶ A pro forma income statement projects the firm's earnings under a given set of hypothetical assumptions.

▶ A pro forma balance sheet projects the firm's assets, liabilities and equity under the same assumptions used to construct the pro form income statement.

▶ Forecasting the balance sheet with the percent of sales method requires two passes.

▶ The first pass reveals by how much equity and liabilities would fall short of the amount needed to finance the expected growth in assets.

▶ The amount by which the financing falls short is called the plug, and indicates the total net new financing needed from external sources.

▶ In the second pass, the pro forma balance sheet shows the necessary financing from the planned sources and is in balance.

net new financing, p. 566
percent of sales method, p. 563
the plug, p. 567

MyFinanceLab
Study Plan 17.2
Spreadsheet Tables
17.1–17.4

17.3 Forecasting a Planned Expansion

▶ An improvement over the percent of sales method is to forecast the firm's working capital and capital investment, along with planned financing of those investments directly.

▶ Such a financial model will have the correct timing of external financing and capital investment so that we can estimate the firm's future free cash flows.

MyFinanceLab
Study Plan 17.3
Spreadsheet Tables
17.5–17.10

17.4 Valuing the Planned Expansion

▶ In addition to forecasting cash flows for a few years, we need to estimate the firm's continuation value at the end of the forecast horizon.

▶ We discussed continuation values in depth in Chapter 9. One method is to use a valuation multiple based on comparable firms.

▶ Given the forecasted cash flows and an estimate of the cost of capital, the final step is to combine these inputs to estimate the value of the firm based on the business plan. We can compare this to the value of the firm without the new plan to determine whether to implement the plan.

MyFinanceLab
Study Plan 17.4
Interactive Financial
Statement Model
Spreadsheet Tables
17.12–17.15

BDeH CHAPTER 17

17.5 Growth and Firm Value

▶ Two common concepts are internal growth rate and sustainable growth rate.

▶ The internal growth rate identifies the maximum rate at which the firm can grow without external financing:

Internal Growth Rate = ROA
$$\times \text{ retention rate} \qquad (17.10)$$

▶ The sustainable growth rate identifies the maximum rate at which the firm can grow if it wants to keep its D/E ratio constant without any new equity financing:

Sustainable Growth Rate = ROA
$$\times \text{ retention rate} \qquad (17.11)$$

▶ Neither the internal growth rate nor the sustainable growth rate indicates whether planned growth is good or bad. Only an NPV analysis can tell us whether the contemplated growth will increase or decrease the value of the firm.

internal growth rate, p. 579
plowback ratio, p. 579
sustainable growth rate, p. 579

MyFinanceLab
Study Plan 17.5

Review Questions

1. What is the purpose of long-term forecasting?

2. What are the advantages and disadvantages of the percent of sales method?

3. What is gained by forecasting capital expenditures and external financing specifically?

4. How can the financial manager use the long-term forecast to decide on adopting a new business plan?

5. What can the sustainable growth rate tell a financial manager and what can it not tell?

Problems

A blue box (■) indicates problems available in MyFinanceLab.

Forecasting Financial Statements: The Percent of Sales Method

1. Your company has sales of $100,000 this year and cost of goods sold of $72,000. You forecast sales to increase to $110,000 next year. Using the percent of sales method, forecast next year's cost of goods sold.

2. For the next fiscal year, you forecast net income of $50,000 and ending assets of $500,000. Your firm's payout ratio is 10%. Your beginning stockholders' equity is $300,000 and your beginning total liabilities are $120,000. Your non-debt liabilities such as accounts payable are forecasted to increase by $10,000. What is your net new financing needed for next year?

 3. Assume your beginning debt in Problem 2 is $100,000. What amount of equity and what amount of debt would you need to issue to cover the net new financing in order to keep your debt equity ratio constant?

For Problems 4–6, use the following income statement and balance sheet for Jim's Espresso:

Income Statement

Sales	200,000
Costs Except Depreciation	(100,000)
EBITDA	100,000
Depreciation	(6,000)
EBIT	94,000
Interest Expense (net)	(400)
Pretax Income	93,600
Income Tax	(32,760)
Net Income	60,840

Balance Sheet

Assets	
Cash and Equivalents	15,000
Accounts Receivable	2,000
Inventories	4,000
Total Current Assets	21,000
Property, Plant, and Equipment	10,000
Total Assets	31,000
Liabilities and Equity	
Accounts Payable	1,500
Debt	4,000
Total Liabilities	5,500
Stockholders' Equity	25,500
Total Liabilities and Equity	31,000

 4. Jim's expects sales to grow by 10% next year. Using the percent of sales method, forecast:
a. Costs
b. Depreciation
c. Net Income
d. Cash
e. Accounts receivable
f. Inventory
g. Property, plant, and equipment

 5. Assume that Jim's pays out 90% of its net income. Use the percent of sales method to forecast:
a. Stockholders' equity
b. Accounts payable

 6. What is the amount of net new financing needed for Jim's?

 7. Download the data for Dell Computers from the textbook's Web site. Using the financial statements from 2006, use the percent of sales method and the actual sales growth from 2006 to 2007 to forecast Dell's 2007 statements. How accurate were your forecasts and what caused them to vary the most from the true outcome?

Forecasting a Planned Expansion

For problems in this section, you should download the KMS spreadsheets available on the textbook's Web site.

 8. Assume that KMS's market share will increase by 0.25% per year rather than the 1% used in the chapter (see Table 17.5) and that its prices remain as in the chapter. What production capacity will KMS require each year? When will an expansion become necessary (that is, when will production volume exceed 1100)?

9. Under the assumption that KMS's market share will increase by 0.25% per year, you determine that the plant will require an expansion in 2009. The expansion will cost $20 million. Assuming that the financing of the expansion will be delayed accordingly, calculate the projected interest payments and the amount of the projected interest tax shields (assuming that KMS still uses a ten-year bond and interest rates remain the same as in the chapter) through 2012.

10. Under the assumption that KMS's market share will increase by 0.25% per year (and the investment and financing will be adjusted as described in Problem 9), you project the following depreciation:

Year	2007	2008	2009	2010	2011	2012
Depreciation	5,492	5,443	7,398	7,459	7,513	7,561

Using this information, project net income through 2012 (that is, reproduce Table 17.8 under the new assumptions).

11. Assuming that KMS's market share will increase by 0.25% per year (implying that the investment, financing, and depreciation will be adjusted as described in Problems 9 and 10), and that the working capital assumptions used in the chapter still hold, calculate KMS's working capital requirements though 2012 (that is, reproduce Table 17.9 under the new assumptions).

12. Forecast KMS's free cash flows (reproduce Table 17.12), assuming KMS's market share will increase by 0.25% per year; investment, financing, and depreciation will be adjusted accordingly; and working capital will be as you projected in Problem 11).

13. Calculate the continuation value of KMS using your reproduction of Table 17.8 from Problem 10, and assuming an EBITDA multiple of 8.5.

14. Assuming a cost of capital of 10%, compute the value of KMS under the 0.25% growth scenario.

Growth and Firm Value

15. Using the information in the table below, calculate this company's:

Net Income	50,000
Beginning Total Assets	400,000
Beginning Stockholders' Equity	250,000
Payout Ratio	0%

a. Internal growth rate.
b. Sustainable growth rate.
c. Sustainable growth rate if it pays out 40% of its net income as a dividend.

BDeH CHAPTER 17

16. Did KMS's expansion plan call for it to grow slower or faster than its sustainable growth rate?

17. Your firm has an ROE of 12%, a payout ratio of 25%, $600,000 of stockholders' equity, and $400,000 of debt. If you grow at your sustainable growth rate this year, how much additional debt will you need to issue?

18. IZAX, Co. has the following items on its balance sheet:

Assets		Liabilities and Equity	
Cash	50,000	Debt	100,000
PPE	350,000	Equity	300,000

Its net income this year is $20,000 and it pays dividends of $5,000. If it grows at its internal growth rate, what will its D/E ratio be next year?

 19. Using data available on the textbook's Web site, compute the sustainable and internal growth rates for Boeing, Coca-Cola, and Google at the start of 2007. Next, compute their actual growth rates in 2007 and the change in their stock prices over the same period. Is there a relation between their growth relative to SGR or IGR and the change in their value?

Chapter 17 APPENDIX **The Balance Sheet and Statement of Cash Flows**

The information we have calculated so far can be used to project KMS's balance sheet and statement of cash flows through 2012. While these statements are not critical for our valuation of the expansion, they often prove helpful in providing a more complete picture of how a firm will grow during the forecast period. These statements for KMS are shown in the spreadsheets in Table 17.17 and Table 17.18.

The balance sheet (Table 17.17) continues the work we started in Table 17.10. Current assets and liabilities come from the net working capital spreadsheet (Table 17.9). The inventory entry on the balance sheet includes both raw materials and finished goods. Property, plant, and equipment information comes from the forecasted capital expenditure spreadsheet (Table 17.6), and the debt comes from Table 17.7.

TABLE 17.17

Pro Forma Balance
Sheet for KMS,
2007–2012

	Year	2007	2008	2009	2010	2011	2012
1	Year	2007	2008	2009	2010	2011	2012
2	**Balance Sheets ($000s)**						
3	**Assets**						
4	Cash and Cash Equivalents	11,982	14,139	16,520	19,167	22,107	25,367
5	Accounts Receivable	14,229	16,790	19,617	22,761	26,252	30,124
6	Inventories	14,978	17,674	20,649	23,959	27,633	31,709
7	**Total Current Assets**	41,189	48,603	56,786	65,886	75,992	87,201
8	Property, Plant, and Equipment	49,427	66,984	67,486	67,937	68,344	68,709
9	**Total Assets**	90,616	115,587	124,272	133,823	144,335	155,910
10							
11	**Liabilities**						
12	Accounts Payable	11,982	14,139	16,520	19,167	22,107	25,367
13	Debt	4,500	24,500	24,500	24,500	24,500	24,500
14	**Total Liabilities**	16,482	38,639	41,020	43,667	46,607	49,867
15							
16	**Stockholders' Equity**						
17	Starting Stockholders' Equity	69,275	74,134	76,948	83,252	90,156	97,729
18	Net Income	6,940	7,600	8,807	11,141	13,739	16,627
19	Dividends	−2,082	−4,786	−2,503	−4,237	−6,167	−8,313
20	**Stockholders' Equity**	74,134	76,948	83,252	90,156	97,729	106,042
21	**Total Liabilities and Equity**	90,616	115,587	124,272	133,823	144,335	155,910

TABLE 17.18

Pro Forma Statement
of Cash Flows for
KMS, 2008–2012

	Year	2007	2008	2009	2010	2011	2012
1	Year	2007	2008	2009	2010	2011	2012
2	**Statement of Cash Flows ($000s)**						
3	**Net Income**		7,600	8,807	11,141	13,739	16,627
4	Depreciation		7,443	7,498	7,549	7,594	7,634
5	**Changes in Working Capital**						
6	Accounts Receivable		−2,561	−2,827	−3,144	−3,491	−3,872
7	Inventory		−2,696	−2,976	−3,309	−3,675	−4,076
8	Accounts Payable		2,157	2,381	2,647	2,940	3,261
9	**Cash from Operating Activities**		11,942	12,884	14,884	17,107	19,574
10	Capital Expenditures		−25,000	−8,000	−8,000	−8,000	−8,000
11	Other Investment		—	—	—	—	—
12	**Cash from Investing Activities**		−25,000	−8,000	−8,000	−8,000	−8,000
13	Net Borrowing		20,000	—	—	—	—
14	Dividends		−4,786	−2,503	−4,237	−6,167	−8,313
15	**Cash from Financing Activities**		15,214	−2,503	−4,237	−6,167	−8,313
16							
17	**Change in Cash (9+12+15)**		2,157	2,381	2,647	2,940	3,261

KMS's book value of equity will steadily grow as it expands and remains profitable, only paying out a portion of its net income each year. Its debt will jump from $4500 to $24,500 in 2008 when it finances its expansion. KMS's other liabilities—accounts payable—will grow steadily with sales. KMS's book debt-equity ratio will jump from $4500/74,134 = 6\%$ in 2007 to $24,500/76,948 = 32\%$ in 2008, and then will steadily decline to 23% by 2012.

The statement of cash flows in Table 17.18 starts with net income. Cash from operating activities includes depreciation as well as *changes* to working capital items (other than cash) from Table 17.9. Cash from investing activities includes the capital expenditures in Table 17.6. Cash from financing activities includes net borrowing from Table 17.7, and dividends are equal to free cash flows to equity because we assume KMS pays out all excess cash. We can compute FCF to equity from Table 17.12 using the following equation:

$$\text{FCF to Equity} = \text{FCF of the Firm} + \text{Net Borrowing}$$
$$- \text{After-tax Interest Expense} \qquad (17.12)$$

KMS is not planning to raise any additional equity financing, so there are no capital contributions on the cash flow statement. As a final check on the calculations, note that the change in the minimum cash balance shown on the balance sheet (Table 17.17). For example, in 2008, the change in cash and cash equivalents is 2157, which is the amount by which 2008 cash exceeds 2007 cash on the balance sheet.

Taken from *Financial Accounting*,
Seventh Edition, by Walter T. Harrison, Jr.
and Charles T. Horngren

1 The Financial Statements

SPOTLIGHT

YUM! BRANDS

What's your favorite fast food? If it's not a hamburger, it may be a pizza, a taco, or fried chicken. **YUM! Brands** operates **Pizza Hut**, **Taco Bell**, **KFC**, **A&W**, and **Long John Silver's** restaurants.

As you can see, YUM! Brands sells lots of pizza, tacos, and drumsticks—$9,561 million in 2006 (lines 1–3 of YUM! Brands' income statement). On these revenues YUM! Brands earned net income of $824 million in 2006.

These terms—revenues and net income—may be foreign to you now. But after you read this chapter, you'll be able to use these and other business terms. Welcome to the world of accounting!

YUM! Brands, Inc.
Statement of Income (Adapted)
Years Ended December 31, 2006, and 2005

(In millions)	2006	2005
Revenues		
1 Company sales..	$8,365	$8,225
2 Franchise and license fees....................................	1,196	1,124
3 Total revenues..	9,561	9,349
Expenses		
Company restaurants		
4 Food and paper (Cost of goods sold)....................	2,549	2,584
5 Payroll and employee benefits expense..................	2,142	2,171
6 Occupancy and other operating expenses..............	2,403	2,315
	7,094	7,070
7 General and administrative expenses........................	1,187	1,158
8 Other operating expenses (income)...........................	18	(32)
9 Total expenses	8,299	8,196
10 Operating profit...	1,262	1,153
11 Interest expense	154	127
12 Income before income taxes....................................	1,108	1,026
13 Income tax expense...	284	264
14 Net income	$ 824	$ 762

Each chapter of this book begins with an actual financial statement.
In this chapter, it's the income statement of YUM! Brands, Inc. The core of financial accounting revolves around the basic financial statements:

- Income statement (the statement of operations)
- Statement of retained earnings
- Balance sheet (the statement of financial position)
- Statement of cash flows

Financial statements are the business documents that companies use to represent their finances to the public. In this chapter we explain all the items that appear in each statement. To learn accounting, focus on decisions. Decisions require information, and accounting provides much of the information for people's decisions, as illustrated in the following diagram:

You take actions every day that require accounting information. For example, the decision to go off for spring break depends on whether you can afford it. The same is true for big companies like **Google** and YUM! Brands. They must weigh what they want to accomplish against what they can afford.

We begin with an overview of how accounting is practiced.

LEARNING OBJECTIVES

1 **Use** accounting vocabulary

2 **Learn** accounting concepts and principles

3 **Apply** the accounting equation to business organizations

4 **Evaluate** business operations

5 **Use** financial statements

For more practice and review of accounting cycle concepts, use ACT, the Accounting Cycle Tutorial, online at www.prenhall.com/harrison. Margin logos like this one, directing you to the appropriate ACT section and material, appear throughout Chapters 1, 2, and 3. When you enter the tutorial, you'll find 3 buttons on the opening page of each chapter module. Here's what the buttons mean: **Tutorial** gives you a review of the major concepts, **Application** gives you practice exercises, and **Glossary** reviews important terms.

BUSINESS DECISIONS

YUM! Brands managers make lots of decisions. Which is selling faster—pizza, fried chicken, or tacos? Is pizza bringing in profits? Should YUM! Brands expand into Asia? Accounting helps companies make these decisions.

Take a look at YUM! Brands' income statement on page 2. Focus on net income (line 14). Net income is profit, the excess of revenues over expenses. You can see that YUM! Brands earned an $824 million profit in 2006. That's good news because it means that YUM had $824 million more revenue (income) than expenses for the year.

YUM's income statement conveys more good news. Net income for 2006 exceeded the net income for 2005. YUM is growing, and investors buy the stocks of growing companies.

Suppose you have $5,000 to invest. What information would you need before investing in YUM! Brands? Let's see how accounting works.

ACCOUNTING IS THE LANGUAGE OF BUSINESS

Accounting is an information system. It measures business activities, processes data into reports, and communicates results to people. Accounting is "the language of business." The better you understand the language, the better you can manage your finances.

Accounting produces **financial statements**, which report information about a business entity. The financial statements measure performance and tell where a business stands in financial terms. In this chapter we focus on YUM! Brands. After completing this chapter, you'll understand financial statements.

OBJECTIVE

1 **Use** accounting vocabulary

Don't confuse bookkeeping and accounting. Bookkeeping is a mechanical part of accounting, just as arithmetic is a part of mathematics. Exhibit 1-1 illustrates accounting's role in business. The process starts and ends with people making decisions.

EXHIBIT 1-1 The Flow of Accounting Information

Who Uses Accounting Information?

Decision makers need information. A banker decides who gets a loan. YUM! Brands decides where to locate a new Pizza Hut. Let's see how some others use accounting information.

- *Individuals.* People like you manage bank accounts and decide whether to rent an apartment or buy a house. Accounting provides the information you need.
- *Investors and Creditors.* Investors and creditors provide the money to finance YUM! Brands. People want to know how much income they can expect to earn on an investment. This requires accounting data.
- *Taxing Authorities.* There are all kinds of taxes. Pizza Hut pays property tax on its assets and income tax on its profits. Taco Bell collects sales tax from you. Taxes are based on accounting data.
- *Nonprofit Organizations.* Nonprofit organizations—churches, hospitals, and charities such as Habitat for Humanity and the Red Cross—base their decisions on accounting data.

Two Kinds of Accounting: Financial Accounting and Management Accounting

There are both *external users* and *internal users* of accounting information. We can therefore classify accounting into 2 branches.

Financial accounting provides information for people outside the firm, such as investors, bankers, government agencies, and the public. This information must meet standards of relevance and reliability.

Management accounting generates inside information for the managers of YUM! Brands. Management information doesn't have to meet external standards of reliability because only company employees use these data.

Ethics in Accounting: Standards of Professional Conduct

Ethical considerations are important to accounting. Companies need money to operate. To attract investors, companies must provide information to the public. Without that information, people won't invest. The United States has laws that require companies to report relevant and reliable information to outsiders. Relevant means "able to affect a decision." Reliable means "verifiable and free of error and bias." The infographic that follows diagrams this process.

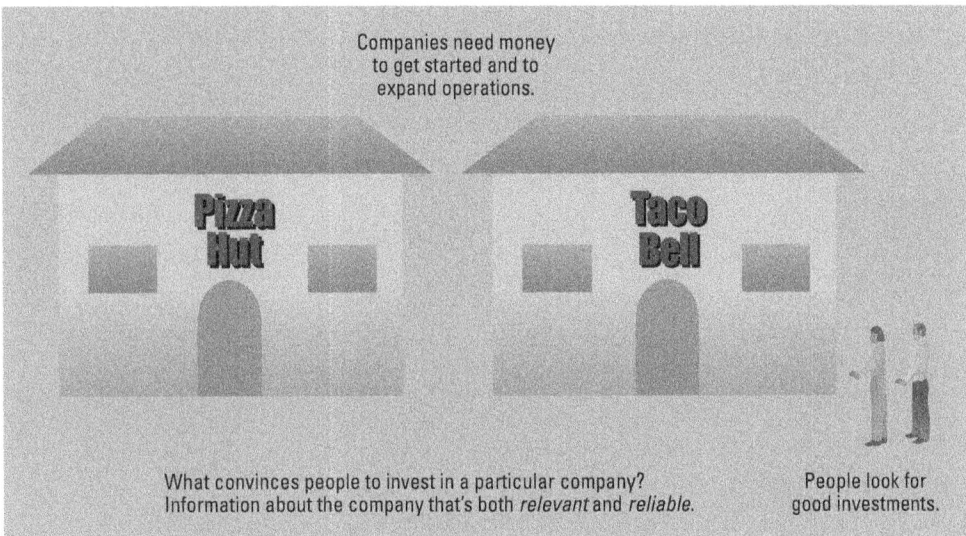

Occasionally, a company will report biased information. It may overstate profits or understate the company's debts. In recent years, several well-known companies reported misleading information. Enron Corporation, once one of the largest companies in the United States, admitted understating its debts. Tyco, WorldCom, and Qwest were accused of overstating profits. These companies' data were unreliable, and their information failed the test of reliability. The results? People invested in them, lost money, and filed lawsuits to recover their losses. Reporting relevant and reliable information to the public is the only ethical course of action.

What are the criteria for ethical judgments in accounting? The *American Institute of Certified Public Accountants (AICPA)*, other professional organizations, and most companies have codes of conduct that require ethical conduct. The AICPA is the country's largest organization of accountants, similar to the American Medical Association for physicians and the American Bar Association for attorneys.

We Need an Audit to Validate the Financial Statements

Each chapter of this book begins with an actual financial statement—Chapter 1 opens with the income statement of YUM! Brands, Inc. YUM! Brands reports that it's profitable. But did the company really sell that many pizzas, tacos, and drumsticks? Were profits really $824 million? Who reports these figures?

YUM's top management is responsible both for (a) company operations and (b) the information YUM *reports* to the public. Can you see the conflict of interest here? A company's *real* performance may differ from what gets *reported* to the public.

How does society deal with this conflict of interest? U.S. law requires all companies that sell their stock to the public to have an annual audit by independent accountants. Audits are intended to protect the public by ensuring that accounting data are relevant and reliable.

Organizing a Business

A business can take 1 of several forms:

- proprietorship
- partnership
- limited-liability company (LLC)
- corporation

Exhibit 1-2 compares ways to organize a business.

EXHIBIT 1-2   The Various Forms of Business Organization

	Proprietorship	Partnership	Corporation	LLC
1. *Owner(s)*	Proprietor—one owner	Partners—2 or more owners	Stockholders—generally many owners	Members
2. *Personal liability of owner(s) for business debts*	Proprietor is personally liable	Partners are personally liable	Stockholders are *not* personally liable	Members are *not* personally liable

Proprietorship. A **proprietorship** has a single owner, called the proprietor. Dell Computer started out in the dorm room of Michael Dell, the owner. Proprietorships tend to be small retail stores or a professional service—a physician, an attorney, or an accountant. Legally, the business *is* the proprietor, and the proprietor is personally liable for all the business's debts. But for accounting, a proprietorship is distinct from its proprietor. Thus, the business records do not include the proprietor's personal finances.

Partnership. A **partnership** has 2 or more persons as co-owners, and each owner is a partner. Many retail establishments and some professional organizations are partnerships. Most partnerships are small or medium-sized, but some are gigantic, with 2,000 or more partners. Like proprietorships, the law views a partnership as the partners. The business is its partners. For this reason, each partner is personally liable for all the partnership's debts. Partnerships are therefore quite risky. This unlimited liability of partners has spawned the creation of limited-liability partnerships (LLPs).

A *limited-liability partnership* is one in which a wayward partner cannot create a large liability for the other partners. Therefore, each partner is liable ony for his or her own actions and those under his or her control.

HH CHAPTER 1

Limited-Liability Company (LLC). A **limited-liability company** is one in which the business (and not the owner) is liable for the company's debts. An LLC may have 1 owner or many owners, called *members*. Unlike a proprietorship or a basic partnership, the members do *not* have personal liability for the business's debts. Therefore, we say that the members have limited liability—limited to the amount they've invested in the business. Also, an LLC pays no business income tax. Instead, the LLC's income flows through to the members, and they pay personal income tax at their own individual tax rates. Today most proprietorships and partnerships are organized as LLCs or LLPs.

Corporation. A **corporation** is a business owned by the **stockholders**, or **shareholders**. These people own **stock**, which represents shares of ownership in a corporation. Even though proprietorships and partnerships are more numerous, corporations transact much more business and are larger in terms of assets, income, and number of employees. Most well-known companies, such as YUM! Brands, Yahoo!, and Dell Computer, are corporations. Their full names include *Corporation* or *Incorporated* (abbreviated *Corp.* and *Inc.*) to indicate that they are corporations—for example, YUM! Brands, Inc., and Starbucks Corporation. Some bear the name *Company*, such as Ford Motor Company.

A corporation is formed under state law. Unlike proprietorships and partnerships, a corporation is legally distinct from its owners. The corporation is like an artificial person and possesses many of the rights that a person has. The stockholders have no personal obligation for the corporation's debts. So we say the stockholders have limited liability, as do the partners of an LLP and the members of an LLC. Also unlike the other forms of organization, a corporation pays a business income tax.

Ultimate control of a corporation rests with the stockholders, who get 1 vote for each share of stock they own. Stockholders elect the **board of directors**, which sets policy and appoints officers. The board elects a chairperson, who holds the most power in the corporation and often carries the title chief executive officer (CEO). The board also appoints the president as Chief Operating Officer (COO). Corporations have vice presidents in charge of sales, accounting and finance, and other key areas.

ACCOUNTING PRINCIPLES AND CONCEPTS

Accountants follow professional guidelines called **GAAP**, which stands for **generally accepted accounting principles**. In the United States, the *Financial Accounting Standards Board (FASB)* formulates GAAP. GAAP is designed to meet the primary objective of financial reporting, which is to provide information useful for making investment and credit decisions.

Exhibit 1-3 gives an overview of the conceptual framework of accounting. GAAP, at the bottom, follows the conceptual framework. To be useful, information must be relevant, reliable, comparable, and consistent. This course will expose you to generally accepted accounting. We summarize GAAP in Appendix E. We begin with the basic concepts that form accounting practice.

OBJECTIVE

2 **Learn** accounting concepts and principles

HH CHAPTER 1

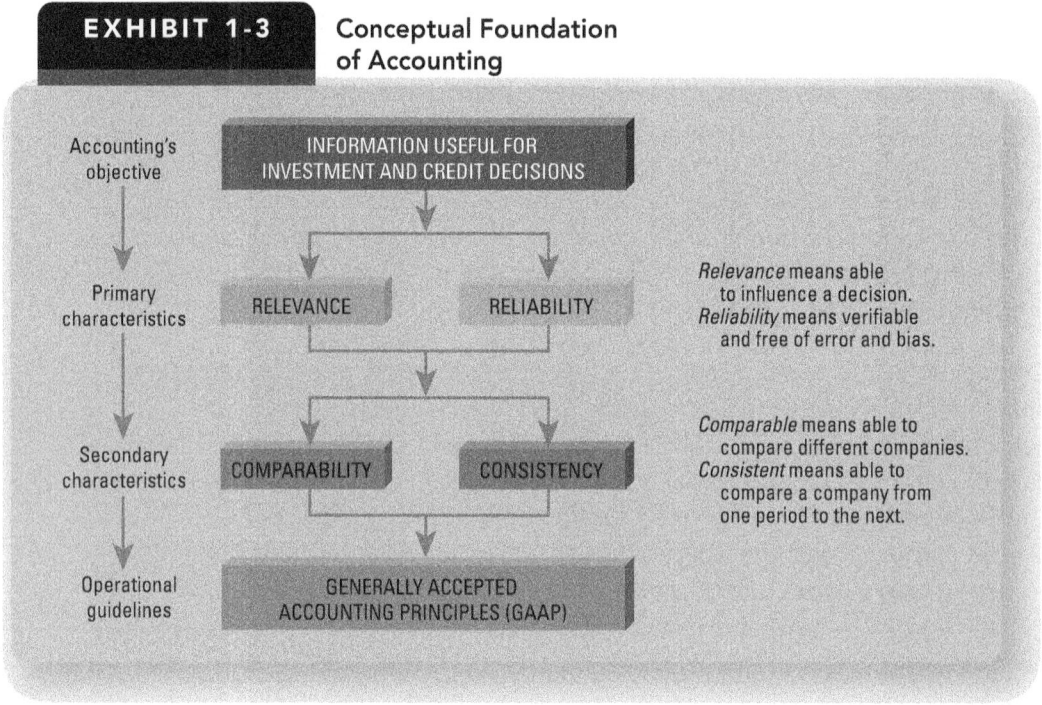

EXHIBIT 1-3 Conceptual Foundation of Accounting

The Entity Concept

The most basic accounting concept is the **entity**, which is any organization that stands apart as a separate economic unit. Sharp boundaries are drawn around each entity so as not to confuse its affairs with those of others.

Consider David C. Novak, Chairman of the Board of YUM! Brands, Inc. Mr. Novak owns a home and several automobiles. He may owe money on some personal loans. All these assets and liabilities belong to David Novak and have nothing to do with YUM! Brands. Likewise, YUM's cash, computers, and food inventories belong to the company and not to Novak. Why? Because the entity concept draws a sharp boundary around each entity; in this case YUM! Brands is 1 entity, and David Novak is a separate entity.

Let's consider the various restaurant chains that make up YUM! Brands. Top managers evaluate Pizza Hut separately from Taco Bell and KFC. If pizza sales are dropping, YUM can identify the reason. But if sales figures from all the restaurant chains are combined in a single total, managers can't tell how many pizzas and how many tacos the company is selling. To correct the problem, managers need data for each division of the company. Each restaurant chain keeps its own records in order to be evaluated separately.

The Reliability Principle

To ensure relevance and reliability, accounting records are based on the most objective data available. This is the **reliability principle**, also called the **objectivity principle**. Ideally, accounting records are based on information supported by objective evidence. For example, your purchase of a pizza is supported by a paid receipt, which gives objective evidence of the cost of the pizza, say $10. Without the reliability principle, accounting records would be based on opinions and subject to dispute.

Suppose YUM! Brands opens a Taco Bell/Pizza Hut store, and YUM is buying a building. YUM believes the building is worth $185,000. Two real estate professionals appraise the building at $210,000. The owner of the building demands $200,000. Suppose YUM pays $190,000. Beliefs about the building's value and the real-estate appraisals are merely opinions. The accounting value of the building is $190,000 because that amount is supported by a completed transaction. YUM! Brands should, therefore, record the building at its cost of $190,000.

The Cost Principle

The **cost principle** states that assets and services should be recorded at their actual *historical cost.*[1] Suppose a Pizza Hut store purchases kitchen equipment from Domino's Pizza. Assume that YUM gets a good deal on this purchase and pays only $50,000 for equipment that would have cost $70,000 elsewhere. The cost principle requires YUM to record this equipment at its actual cost of $50,000, not the $70,000 that YUM believes it's worth.

The cost principle also holds that accounting records should maintain historical costs for as long as the business holds the asset. Why? Because cost is a reliable measure. Suppose the Taco Bell store holds the equipment for 6 months. Prices increase and the equipment can be sold for $60,000. Should its accounting value be the actual cost of $50,000 or the current market value of $60,000? According to the cost principle, the equipment remains on YUM! Brands' books at a cost of $50,000.

The Going-Concern Concept

The **going-concern concept** assumes that the entity will remain in operation long enough to use existing assets—land, buildings, supplies—for their intended purpose. Consider the alternative to the going-concern concept: going out of business.

A store that is going out of business sells all its assets. In that case, the relevant measure of the assets is their current market value. But going out of business is the exception rather than the rule, and so accounting lists a going concern's assets at their historical cost.

The Stable-Monetary-Unit Concept

In the United States, we record transactions in dollars because that is our medium of exchange. British accountants record transactions in pounds sterling, Japanese in yen, and Europeans in euros.

Unlike a liter or a mile, the value of a dollar changes over time. A rise in the general price level is called *inflation.* During inflation, a dollar will purchase less food, less toothpaste, and less of other goods and services. When prices are stable—there is little inflation—a dollar's purchasing power is also stable.

---

[1]The cost principle may not be as powerful as it once was. Accounting may be moving in the direction of reporting assets and liabilities at their fair value. **Fair value** is the amount that the business could sell the asset for, or the amount that the business could pay to settle the liability. In 2007, the Financial Accounting Standards Board (FASB) issued a statement that *permits* companies to report many financial assets and liabilities at their fair value. Time will tell whether companies will follow this path and whether the FASB will *require* extensive use of fair-value accounting.

Under the **stable-monetary-unit concept**, accountants assume that the dollar's purchasing power is stable. We ignore inflation, and this allows us to add and subtract dollar amounts as though each dollar has the same purchasing power.

THE ACCOUNTING EQUATION

OBJECTIVE

3 **Apply** the accounting equation to business organizations

YUM! Brands' financial statements tell us how the business is performing and where it stands. But how do we arrive at the financial statements? Let's see their building blocks.

Assets and Liabilities

The financial statements are based on the **accounting equation**. This equation presents the resources of a company and the claims to those resources.

- **Assets** are economic resources that are expected to produce a benefit in the future. YUM! Brands' cash, food inventory, equipment, land, and buildings are examples of assets.

Claims on assets come from 2 sources:

- **Liabilities** are "outsider claims." They are debts that are payable to outsiders, called *creditors*. For example, a creditor who has loaned money to YUM! Brands has a claim—a legal right—to a part of YUM's assets until YUM repays the debt.
- **Owners' equity** (also called **capital**) represents the "insider claims" of a business. Equity means ownership, so YUM's stockholders' equity is the stockholders' interest in the assets of the corporation.

The accounting equation shows the relationship among assets, liabilities, and owners' equity. Assets appear on the left side and liabilities and owners' equity on the right. As Exhibit 1-4 shows, the 2 sides must be equal:

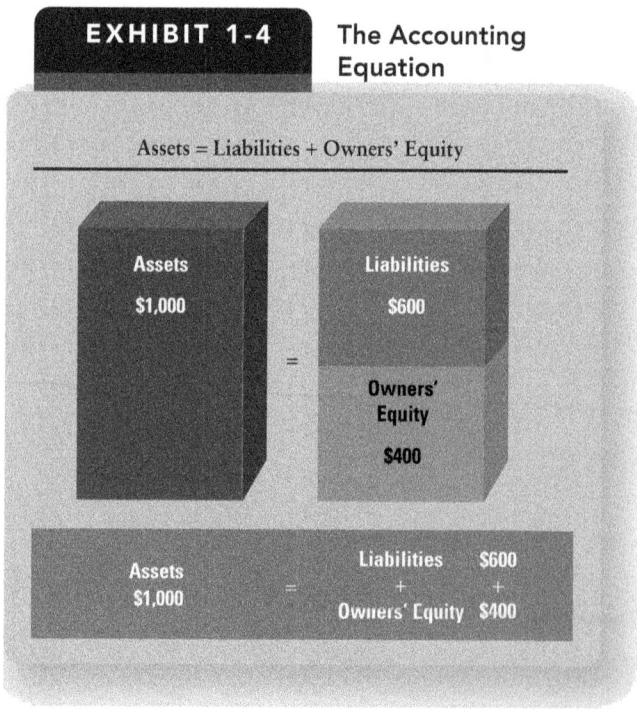

EXHIBIT 1-4 The Accounting Equation

Assets = Liabilities + Owners' Equity

Assets	Liabilities
$1,000	$600
	Owners' Equity
	$400

Assets		Liabilities	$600
$1,000	=	+	+
		Owners' Equity	$400

HH CHAPTER 1

What are some of YUM! Brands' assets? The first asset is **cash**, the liquid asset that's the medium of exchange. Another important asset is **merchandise inventory** (often called inventories)—the food and paper items—that YUM's restaurants sell. YUM also has assets in the form of property, plant, and equipment. These are the long-lived assets the company uses to do business—kitchen equipment, buildings, computers, and so on. Land, buildings, and equipment are called **property, plant, and equipment** (abbreviated as **PPE**), **plant assets**, or **fixed assets**.

YUM! Brands' liabilities include a number of payables, such as accounts payable and notes payable. The word *payable* always signifies a liability. An **account payable** is a liability for goods or services purchased on credit and supported by the credit standing of the purchaser. A **note payable** is a written promise to pay on a certain date. YUM! Brands calls its notes payble "*short-term borrowings.*" **Long-term debt** is a liability that's payable beyond 1 year from the date of the financial statements.

Owners' Equity

The owners' equity of any business is its assets minus its liabilities. We can write the accounting equation to show that owners' equity is what's left over when we subtract liabilities from assets.

$$\text{Assets} - \text{Liabilities} = \text{Owners' Equity}$$

A corporation's equity—called **stockholders' equity**—has 2 main subparts:

■ paid-in capital and
■ retained earnings

The accounting equation can be written as

$$\text{Assets} = \text{Liabilities} + \text{Stockholders' Equity}$$
$$\text{Assets} = \text{Liabilities} + \text{Paid-in Capital} + \text{Retained Earnings}$$

Paid-in capital is the amount the stockholders have invested in the corporation. The basic component of paid-in capital is **common stock**, which the corporation issues to the stockholders as evidence of their ownership. All corporations have common stock.

Retained earnings is the amount earned by income-producing activities and kept for use in the business. Two types of transactions affect retained earnings:

■ **Revenues** increase retained earnings by delivering goods or services to customers. For example, Pizza Hut's sale of a sausage pizza brings in revenue and increases YUM! Brands' retained earnings.
■ **Expenses** decrease retained earnings due to operations. For example, the wages that Pizza Hut pays employees are an expense and decrease retained earnings. Expenses are the cost of doing business; they are the opposite of revenues. Expenses include building rent, salaries, and utility payments. Expenses also include the depreciation of computers and other equipment.

Businesses strive for profits, the excess of revenues over expenses.

■ When total revenues exceed total expenses, the result is called **net income, net earnings**, or **net profit**.

- When expenses exceed revenues, the result is a **net loss.**
- Net income or net loss is the "bottom line" on an income statement. YUM! Brands' bottom line reports 2006 net income of $824 million on page 2 (line 14).

A successful business may pay dividends. **Dividends** are distributions to stockholders of assets (usually cash) generated by net income. Remember: **Dividends are not expenses. Dividends never affect net income.** Exhibit 1-5 shows the relationships among

- Retained earnings
- Revenues − Expenses = Net income (or net loss)
- Dividends

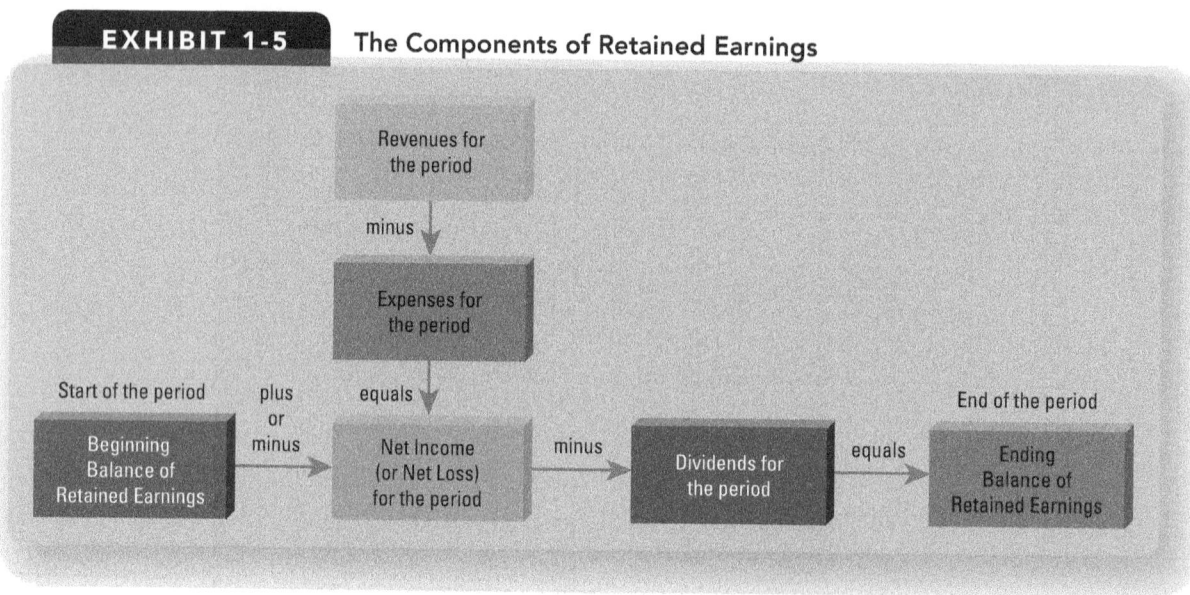

EXHIBIT 1-5   The Components of Retained Earnings

The owners' equity of proprietorships and partnerships is different. Proprietorships and partnerships don't identify paid-in capital and retained earnings. Instead, they use a single heading—Capital—for example, Randall Walker, Capital, for a proprietorship and Pratt, Capital and Salazar, Capital for a partnership.

STOP & think. . .

1. If the assets of a business are $190,000 and the liabilities are $80,000, how much is the owners' equity?
2. If the owners' equity in a business is $60,000 and the liabilities are $30,000, how much are the assets?
3. A company reported monthly revenues of $79,000 and expenses of $81,000. What is the result of operations for the month?

Answers:

1. $110,000 ($190,000 − $80,000)
2. $90,000 ($60,000 + $30,000)
3. Net loss of $2,000 ($79,000 − $81,000); revenues minus expenses

THE FINANCIAL STATEMENTS

The financial statements present a company to the public in financial terms. Each financial statement relates to a specific date or time period. What would investors want to know about YUM! Brands, Inc., at the end of December? Exhibit 1-6 shows 4 questions decision makers may ask. Each answer comes from one of the financial statements.

OBJECTIVE

4 **Evaluate** business operations

EXHIBIT 1-6	Information Reported in the Financial Statements	
Question	**Financial Statement**	**Answer**
1. How well did the company perform during the year?	Income statement (also called the Statement of operations)	Revenues – Expenses Net income (or Net loss)
2. Why did the company's retained earnings change during the year?	Statement of retained earnings	Beginning retained earnings + Net income (or – Net loss) – Dividends Ending retained earnings
3. What is the company's financial position at December 31?	Balance sheet (also called the Statement of financial position)	Assets = Liabilities + Owners' Equity
4. How much cash did the company generate and spend during the year?	Statement of cash flows	Operating cash flows ± Investing cash flows ± Financing cash flows Increase (decrease) in cash

To learn how to use financial statements, let's work through YUM! Brands' statements for the year ended December 31, 2006. The following diagram shows how the data flow from one financial statement to the next. The order is important.

We begin with the income statement in Exhibit 1-7.

The Income Statement Measures Operating Performance

The **income statement**, or **statement of operations**, reports revenues and expenses for the period. The bottom line is net income or net loss *for the period*. At the top of Exhibit 1-7 is the company's name, YUM! Brands, Inc.

HH CHAPTER 1

EXHIBIT 1-7   Income Statement (Adapted)

YUM! Brands, Inc.
Statement of Income (Adapted)
Years Ended December 31, 2006, and 2005

(In millions)	2006	2005
Revenues		
1 Company sales...	$8,365	$8,225
2 Franchise and license fees..	1,196	1,124
3 Total revenues...	9,561	9,349
Expenses		
Company restaurants		
4 Food and paper (Cost of goods sold)......................	2,549	2,584
5 Payroll and employee benefits expense..................	2,142	2,171
6 Occupancy and other operating expenses..............	2,403	2,315
	7,094	7,070
7 General and administrative expenses	1,187	1,158
8 Other operating expenses (income)...........................	18	(32)
9 Total expenses	8,299	8,196
10 Operating profit...	1,262	1,153
11 Interest expense	154	127
12 Income before income taxes.................................	1,108	1,026
13 Income tax expense...	284	264
14 Net income	$ 824	$ 762

The date of YUM's income statement is "Years Ended December 31, 2006, and 2005." YUM uses the calendar period as its accounting year, as do around 60% of large companies.[2] Some use a fiscal year, which ends on a date other than December 31. For example, Pier 1 Imports, Wal-Mart, and most other retailers end their accounting year on or around January 31. FedEx's year end falls on May 31. Companies adopt an accounting year that ends at the low point of their operations.

YUM! Brands' income statement in Exhibit 1-7 reports operating results for 2 years, 2006 and 2005, to show trends for revenues, expenses, and net income. To avoid clutter, YUM reports in millions of dollars. During 2006, YUM increased total revenues (line 3) from $9,349 million to $9,561 million. Net income rose from $762 million to $824 million (line 14). YUM! Brands restaurants sold more pizzas, tacos, and fried chicken in 2006, and that boosted profits. Focus on 2006. We show 2005 only for completeness. An income statement reports 2 main categories:

■ Revenues and gains   ■ Expenses and losses

We measure net income as follows:

Net Income = Total Revenues and Gains – Total Expenses and Losses

10. *d*

11. *d $30,000 + Net income ($15,000) – Dividends = $40,000; Dividends = $5,000*

In accounting, the word *net* refers to an amount after a subtraction. *Net* income is the profit left over after subtracting expenses and losses from revenues and gains. **Net income is the single most important item in the financial statements.**

Revenues. Revenues do not always carry the term *revenue* in their titles. For example, net sales revenue is often abbreviated as *net sales*. *Net* sales means sales revenue after subtracting all the goods customers have returned to the company. Wal-Mart, Best Buy, and Gap get some goods back from customers due to product defects. YUM! Brands and other restauranteurs don't have much in the way of sales returns.

YUM! Brands has 2 sources of revenue: company sales (line 1) and fees that YUM earns by licensing its products to others (line 2).

Expenses. Not all expenses have the word *expense* in their title. For example, YUM! Brands' largest expense is for Food and Paper (line 4). Another title of this expense is Cost of goods sold. *Cost of goods sold* (also called *cost of sales*, line 4) represents the cost to YUM of the food it sold to customers. For example, suppose it costs Pizza Hut $3 to make a sausage pizza. Assume Pizza Hut sells the pizza for $10. Sales revenue is $10, and cost of goods sold is $3. Cost of goods sold is the major expense of merchandising entities such as Yum, Best Buy, Wal-Mart, and Safeway (the grocery store chain).

YUM has some other expenses.

- Payroll and Employee Benefits Expense (line 5) is for the salaries, wages, and benefits paid to company employees.
- Occupancy and Other Operating Expenses (line 6) include building rent, utilities, advertising, and depreciation on computers and kitchen equipment.
- General and Administrative Expenses (line 7) are executive salaries and other home-office expenses.
- Other Operating Expenses (line 8) is a catchall label for expenses that don't fit another category. During 2006, YUM had other operating expenses of $18 million. In 2005, YUM had other operating income. Parentheses around the $32 million mean that this amount's category runs opposite the others in its column.
- Interest Expense (line 11) was $154 million for 2006. This is YUM's cost of borrowing money.
- Income Tax Expense (line 13) is the expense levied on YUM! Brands' income by the government.

YUM! Brands reports both Operating Profit (line 10) and Net Income (line 14). Some investors use operating profit to measure operating performance. Others use the "bottom-line" net income.

Now let's move on to the statement of retained earnings in Exhibit 1-8.

**Accounting Cycle Tutorial
Income Statement Accounts**

The Statement of Retained Earnings Shows What a Company Did with Its Net Income

Retained earnings means exactly what the term implies, that portion of net income the company has kept. Net income flows from the income statement to the **statement of retained earnings** (line 2 in Exhibit 1-8).

Net income increases retained earnings, and dividends decrease retained earnings. Why the decrease? Because the company didn't keep the net income that it gave to its stockholders in the form of dividends.

EXHIBIT 1-8	Statement of Retained Earnings (Adapted)

YUM! Brands, Inc.
Statement of Retained Earnings (Adapted)
Years Ended December 31, 2006, and 2005

(In millions)	2006	2005
Retained earnings:		
1 Balance, beginning of year	$1,619	$1,067
2 Net income	824	762
3 Less: Dividends and other		
distributions to the stockholders..............	(850)	(210)
4 Balance, end of year	$1,593	$1,619

YUM's statement of retained earnings needs explanation. Start with 2005. At the beginning of 2005, YUM! Brands had retained earnings of $1,067 million (line 1). During 2005, YUM earned net income of $762 million (line 2) and gave the stockholders dividends of $210 million (line 3). YUM ended 2005 with retained earnings of $1,619 million (line 4).

YUM began 2006 with the ending balance left over from 2005. Then net income added to retained earnings, and dividends decreased retained earnings, as in 2005.

Which item on the statement of retained earnings comes directly from the income statement? It's net income. Line 2 of the retained earnings statement comes directly from line 14 of the income statement. Trace this amount from one statement to the other.

Give yourself a pat on the back. You're already learning how to analyze financial statements!

After a company earns net income, the board of directors decides whether to pay a dividend to the stockholders. In 2006 and 2005, YUM! Brands declared and paid dividends and other distributions to the stockholders (line 3). The dividends decrease retained earnings (the parentheses indicate a subtraction). YUM ended 2006 with retained earnings of $1,593 million (line 4).

Trace retained earnings to the balance sheet in Exhibit 1-9 (line 29). Ending retained earnings from 2006 carries over and becomes the beginning retained earnings of 2007.

The Balance Sheet Measures Financial Position

A company's **balance sheet**, also called the **statement of financial position**, reports 3 items: assets (line 1), liabilities (line 16), and stockholders' equity, which YUM! Brands calls *shareholders' equity* (line 27). The balance sheet is dated at the *moment in time* when the accounting period ends.

Assets. Assets have 2 main categories, current and long-term. **Current assets** are assets that are expected to be converted to cash, sold, or consumed during the next 12 months or within the business's operating cycle if longer than a year. Current assets consist of Cash, Short-Term Investments, Accounts and Notes Receivable, Merchandise Inventory, and Prepaid Expenses (lines 3 to 7). YUM's current assets at

EXHIBIT 1-9	Balance Sheet (Adapted)

YUM! Brands, Inc.
Balance Sheet (Adapted)
December 31, 2006, and 2005

(In millions)		2006		2005
1 ASSETS				
2 Current Assets				
3 Cash and cash equivalents		$ 319		$ 158
4 Short-term investments		6		43
5 Accounts and notes receivable		220		236
6 Inventories		93		85
7 Prepaid expenses and other current assets		263		333
8 Total Current Assets		901		855
9 Property, plant and equipment, at cost	$6,777		$6,186	
10 Less: Accumulated depreciation	(3,146)		(2,830)	
11 Property, plant and equipment, net		3,631		3,356
12 Intangible assets		1,009		868
13 Investments		138		173
14 Other assets		674		545
15 Total Assets		$6,353		$5,797
16 LIABILITIES				
17 Current Liabilities				
18 Accounts payable		$ 554		$ 473
19 Income taxes payable		37		79
20 Short-term borrowings (Notes payable)		227		211
21 Salaries and wages payable		302		274
22 Other current liabilities		604		586
23 Total Current Liabilities		1,724		1,623
24 Long-term debt		2,045		1,649
25 Other long-term liabilities		1,147		1,076
26 Total Liabilities		4,916		4,348
27 SHAREHOLDERS' EQUITY				
28 Common stock		27		28
29 Retained earnings		1,593		1,619
30 Other equity		(183)		(198)
31 Total Shareholders' Equity		1,437		1,449
32 Total Liabilities and Shareholders' Equity		$6,353		$5,797

December 31, 2006, total $901 million (line 8). Let's examine each asset that YUM! Brands holds.

- All companies have cash. **Cash** is the liquid asset that's the medium of exchange, and cash equivalents include money-market accounts that are the same as cash.
- **Short-term investments** include stocks and bonds of other companies that YUM intends to sell within the next year.
- **Accounts receivable** are amounts the company expects to collect from customers.

- **Notes receivable** are amounts YUM expects to collect from a party who has signed a promissory note to YUM. These notes receivable come from people to whom YUM has lent money.
- **Cash, short-term investments, and current receivables** are the most liquid assets, in that order.
- **Merchandise Inventory** (line 6) is the company's most important asset even though it totals only $93 million. *Inventory* is a common abbreviation for *Merchandise inventory*, and the 2 names are used interchangeably.
- **Prepaid Expenses** represent prepayments for advertisements, rent, insurance, and supplies. Prepaid expenses are assets because YUM Brands will benefit from these expenditures in the future.
- **An asset always represents a future benefit.**

The main categories of *long-term assets* are Property, Plant, and Equipment (lines 9–11), Intangibles, and Investments.

- **Property, plant, and equipment (PPE)** includes YUM! Brands' land, buildings, computers, store fixtures, and kitchen equipment. YUM reports PPE on 3 lines. Line 9 shows the company's cost of PPE, which is $6,777 million through December 31, 2006. Cost means the acquisition price to YUM. It does not mean that YUM could sell its PPE for $6,777 million. After all, the company may have acquired the assets several years ago.
- Line 10 shows how much accumulated depreciation YUM has recorded on its PPE. *Depreciation* allocates an asset's cost to expense. Accumulated depreciation is the total amount of depreciation recorded on PPE from acquisition through the end of the year. Accumulated depreciation represents the used-up portion of the asset. We subtract accumulated depreciation from the cost of PPE to determine its book value ($3,631 million on line 11).
- **Intangibles** are assets with no physical form, such as patents and trademarks.
- **Investments** (line 13), with no other words attached, are *long-term* because YUM does not expect to sell them within the next year.
- **Other assets** (line 14) is a catchall category for items difficult to classify.
- Overall, YUM! Brands reports total assets of $6,353 million at December 31, 2006 (line 15).

Liabilities. Liabilities are also divided into current and long-term categories. **Current liabilities** (lines 17–23) are debts payable within 1 year or within YUM's operating cycle if longer than a year. Chief among the current liabilities are Accounts Payable, Income Taxes Payable, Short-Term Borrowing (same as short-term notes Payable), and Salaries and Wages Payable. *Long-term liabilities* are payable after 1 year.

- **Accounts payable** (line 18) represents amounts owed for food and paper inventory.
- **Income taxes payable** are tax debts owed to the government.
- **Short-term borrowings** (line 20) are notes payable that YUM has promised to pay back within 1 year or less.
- **Salaries and wages payable** (line 21) are amounts owed to employees.
- YUM's last current liability is **Other Current Liabilities**. Included in this catch-all category are interest payable on borrowed money, utility payables, and expenses that YUM has not yet paid.

- At December 31, 2006, YUM's current liabilities total $1,724 million. YUM also owes $2,045 million in long-term debt (line 24). These liabilities include notes payable due after 1 year.
- At the end of 2006, total liabilities are $4,916 million (line 26). This is high relative to total assets (line 15), and that indicates a not-so-strong financial position.

Owners' Equity. The accounting equation states that

$$\text{Assets} - \text{Liabilities} = \text{Owners' Equity}$$

The assets (resources) and the liabilities (debts) of YUM! Brands are fairly easy to understand. Owners' equity is harder to pin down. Owners' equity is simple to calculate, but what does it *mean*?

YUM! Brands calls its owners' equity *shareholders' equity* (line 27), and this title is descriptive. Remember that a company's owners' equity represents the shareholders' ownership of the business's assets. YUM's equity consists of

**Accounting Cycle Tutorial
Balance Sheet Accounts**

- Common Stock, represented by shares issued to stockholders for $27 million through December 31, 2006 (line 28).
- Retained earnings at December 31, 2006, is $1,593 million (line 29). A year earlier YUM! Brands had retained earnings of $1,619 million. We saw these figures on the statement of retained earnings in Exhibit 1-8 (line 4). Retained earnings' final resting place is the balance sheet.
- YUM! Brands' equity holds another item, Other Equity, which is a collection of miscellaneous items. For now, focus on the two main components of stockholders' equity: common stock and retained earnings.
- At December 31, 2006, YUM! Brands has Total Shareholders' Equity of $1,437 million (line 31). We can now prove that YUM's total assets equal total liabilities and equity (amounts in millions):

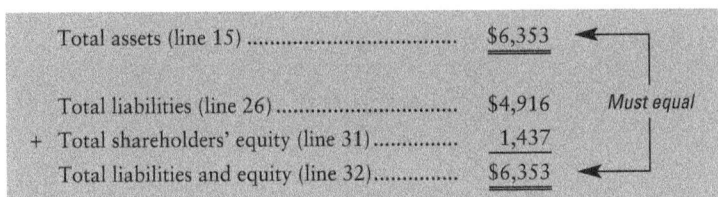

Total assets (line 15)	$6,353	
Total liabilities (line 26)	$4,916	*Must equal*
+ Total shareholders' equity (line 31)	1,437	
Total liabilities and equity (line 32)	$6,353	

The statement of cash flows is the fourth required financial statement.

The Statement of Cash Flows Measures Cash Receipts and Payments

Companies engage in 3 basic types of activities:

1. **Operating activities**   2. **Investing activities**   3. **Financing activities**

The **statement of cash flows** reports cash flows under these 3 categories. Think about the cash flows (receipts and payments) in each category:

- *Companies **operate** by selling goods and services to customers.* Operating activities result in net income or net loss, and they either increase or decrease cash. The income statement tells whether the company is profitable. The cash-flow statement reports whether operations increased cash. Operating activities are most important, and they should be the company's main source of cash. Negative cash flow from operations can lead to bankruptcy.

- **Companies *invest* in long-term assets.** YUM! Brands buys buildings and equipment, and when these assets wear out, the company sells them. Both purchases and sales of long-term assets are investing cash flows. Investing cash flows are next most important after operations.
- **Companies *need money for financing*.** Financing includes both issuing stock and borrowing. YUM issues stock to its shareholders and borrows from banks. These are cash receipts. The company pays off loans. YUM also pays dividends. These payments are financing cash flows.

Overview. Each category of cash flows—operating, investing, and financing—either increases or decreases cash. In Exhibit 1-10, YUM! Brands' operating activities provided cash of $1,302 million in 2006 (line 4). This signals strong cash flow from operations. 2006's investing activities used cash of $476 million (line 9). That signals expansion. Financing activities used $665 million (line 16). YUM paid off some debt and also paid dividends (lines 13 and 14). On a statement of cash flows, cash receipts appear as positive amounts. Cash payments are negative and enclosed by parentheses.

EXHIBIT 1-10	Statement of Cash Flows (Adapted)

YUM! Brands, Inc.
Statement of Cash Flows (Adapted)
Years Ended December 31, 2006, and 2005

(In millions)	2006	2005
1 Cash Flows—Operating Activities:		
2 Net income	$ 824	$ 762
3 Adjustments to reconcile net income to net cash		
provided by operating activities	478	476
4 Net Cash Provided by Operating Activities	1,302	1,238
5 Cash Flows—Investing Activities:		
6 Purchases of property, plant, and equipment	(614)	(609)
7 Sales of property, plant, and equipment	57	81
8 Other	81	183
9 Net Cash Used in Investing Activities	(476)	(345)
10 Cash Flows—Financing Activities:		
11 Issuance of common stock	–	–
12 Issuance of short-term and long-term debt		
(Borrowing)	540	160
13 Repayments of short-term and long-term debt	(288)	(48)
14 Payment of dividends and other distributions		
to stockholders	(850)	(210)
15 Other payments	(67)	(733)
16 Net Cash Used in Financing Activities	(665)	(831)
17 Net Increase in Cash and Cash Equivalents	161	62
18 Cash and Cash Equivalents—Beginning of Year	158	96
19 Cash and Cash Equivalents—End of Year	$ 319	$ 158

Overall, YUM's cash increased by $161 million during 2006 (line 17) and ended the year at $319 million (line 19). Trace ending cash back to the balance sheet in Exhibit 1-9 (line 3). Cash links the statement of cash flows to the balance sheet. You've just performed more financial-statement analysis!

Let's now summarize the relationships that link the financial statements.

RELATIONSHIPS AMONG THE FINANCIAL STATEMENTS

Exhibit 1-11 summarizes the relationships among the financial statements of ABC Company for 2009. Study the exhibit carefully because these relationships apply to all organizations. Specifically, note the following:

OBJECTIVE

5 **Use** financial statements

1. The income statement for the year ended December 31, 2009
   a. Reports revenues and expenses of the year. Revenues and expenses are reported *only* on the income statement.
   b. Reports net income if total revenues exceed total expenses. If expenses exceed revenues, there is a net loss.

2. The statement of retained earnings for the year ended December 31, 2009
   a. Opens with the beginning retained earnings balance.
   b. Adds net income (or subtracts net loss). Net income comes directly from the income statement (arrow ① in Exhibit 1-11).
   c. Subtracts dividends.
   d. Reports the retained earnings balance at the end of the year.

3. The balance sheet at December 31, 2009, end of the accounting year
   a. Reports assets, liabilities, and stockholders' equity at the end of the year. Only the balance sheet reports assets and liabilities.
   b. Reports that assets equal the sum of liabilities plus stockholders' equity. This balancing feature follows the accounting equation and gives the balance sheet its name.
   c. Reports retained earnings, which comes from the statement of retained earnings (arrow ② in Exhibit 1-11).

4. The statement of cash flows for the year ended December 31, 2009
   a. Reports cash flows from operating, investing, and financing activities. Each category results in net cash provided (an increase) or used (a decrease).
   b. Reports whether cash increased (or decreased) during the year. The statement shows the ending cash balance, as reported on the balance sheet (arrow ③ in Exhibit 1-11).

Accounting Cycle Tutorial
Glossary

Accounting Cycle Tutorial
Glossary Quiz

EXHIBIT 1-11 Relationships Among the Financial Statements (these statements are summarized with all amounts assumed for the illustration)

ABC Company
Income Statement
Year Ended December 31, 2009

Revenues..................	$700,000
Expenses	670,000
Net income..............	$ 30,000

①

ABC Company
Statement of Retained Earnings
Year Ended December 31, 2009

Beginning retained earnings..............	$180,000
Net income.......................................	30,000 ◄
Cash dividends..................................	(10,000)
Ending retained earnings..................	$200,000

②

ABC Company
Balance Sheet
December 31, 2009

Assets

Cash	$ 35,000
All other assets...	265,000
Total assets	$300,000

Liabilities

Total liabilities..	$120,000

Stockholders' Equity

Common stock	40,000
Retained earnings	200,000 ◄
Other equity..	(60,000)
Total stockholders' equity...............................	180,000
Total liabilities and stockholders' equity..............	$300,000

③

ABC Company
Statement of Cash Flows
Year Ended December 31, 2009

Net cash provided by operating activities...............	$ 90,000
Net cash used for investing activities.....................	(100,000)
Net cash provided by financing activities	40,000
Net increase in cash..	30,000
Cash balance, December 31, 2008	5,000
Cash balance, December 31, 2009	$ 35,000

Accounting Cycle Tutorial
Applications Cottage Kitchen

Accounting Cycle Tutorial
Applications Marwood Homes

DECISION GUIDELINES

IN EVALUATING A COMPANY, WHAT DO DECISION MAKERS LOOK FOR?

These Decision Guidelines illustrate how people use financial statements. Decision Guidelines appear throughout the book to show how accounting information aids decision making.

Suppose you are considering an investment in YUM! Brands stock. How do you proceed? Where do you get the information you need? What do you look for?

Question/Decision	What to Look For
1. Can the company sell its products?	1. Sales revenue on the income statement. Are sales growing or falling?
2. What are the main income measures to watch for trends?	2. a. Gross profit (Sales − Cost of goods sold) b. Operating income (Gross profit − Operating expenses) c. Net income (bottom line of the income statement) All 3 income measures should be increasing over time.
3. What percentage of sales revenue ends up as profit?	3. Divide net income by sales revenue. Examine the trend of the net income percentage from year to year.
4. Can the company collect its receivables?	4. From the balance sheet, compare the percentage increase in accounts receivable to the percentage increase in sales. If receivables are growing much faster than sales, collections may be too slow, and a cash shortage may result.
5. Can the company pay its a. Current liabilities? b. Current and long-term liabilities?	5. From the balance sheet, compare a. Current assets to current liabilities. Current assets should be somewhat greater than current liabilities. b. Total assets to total liabilities. Total assets must be somewhat greater than total liabilities.
6. Where is the company's cash coming from? How is cash being used?	6. On the cash-flow statement, operating activities should provide the bulk of the company's cash during most years. Otherwise, the business will fail. Examine investing cash flows to see if the company is purchasing long-term assets—property, plant, and equipment and intangibles (this signals growth). Examine financing cash flows for heavy borrowing (a bad sign) or issuance of stock (a good sign).

HH CHAPTER 1

END-OF-CHAPTER SUMMARY PROBLEM

Genie Car Wash, Inc., began operations on April 1, 20X9. During April, the business provided services for customers. It is now April 30, and investors wonder how well Genie performed during its first month. The investors also want to know the company's financial position at the end of April and its cash flows during the month.

The following data are listed in alphabetical order. Prepare the Genie financial statements at the end of April 20X9.

Accounts payable	$ 1,800	Land	$18,000
Accounts receivable	2,000	Payments of cash:	
Adjustments to reconcile net income to net cash provided by operating activities	(3,900)	Acquisition of land	40,000
		Dividends	2,100
		Rent expense	1,100
Cash balance at beginning of April	0	Retained earnings at beginning	
Cash balance at end of April	?	of April	0
Cash receipts:		Retained earnings at end of April	?
Issuance (sale) of stock to owners	50,000	Salary expense	1,200
Sale of land	22,000	Service revenue	10,000
Common stock	50,000	Supplies	3,700
		Utilities expense	400

I Required

1. Prepare the income statement, the statement of retained earnings, and the statement of cash flows for the month ended April 30, 20X9, and the balance sheet at April 30, 20X9. Draw arrows linking the statements.
2. Answer the following questions:
   a. How well did Genie perform during its first month of operations?
   b. Where does Genie stand financially at the end of April?

Answers

I Requirement 1

Financial Statements of Genie Car Wash, Inc.

Genie Car Wash, Inc.
Income Statement
Month Ended April 30, 20X9

Revenue:		
Service revenue		$10,000
Expenses:		
Salary expense	$1,200	
Rent expense	1,100	
Utilities expense	400	
Total expenses		2,700
Net income		$ 7,300

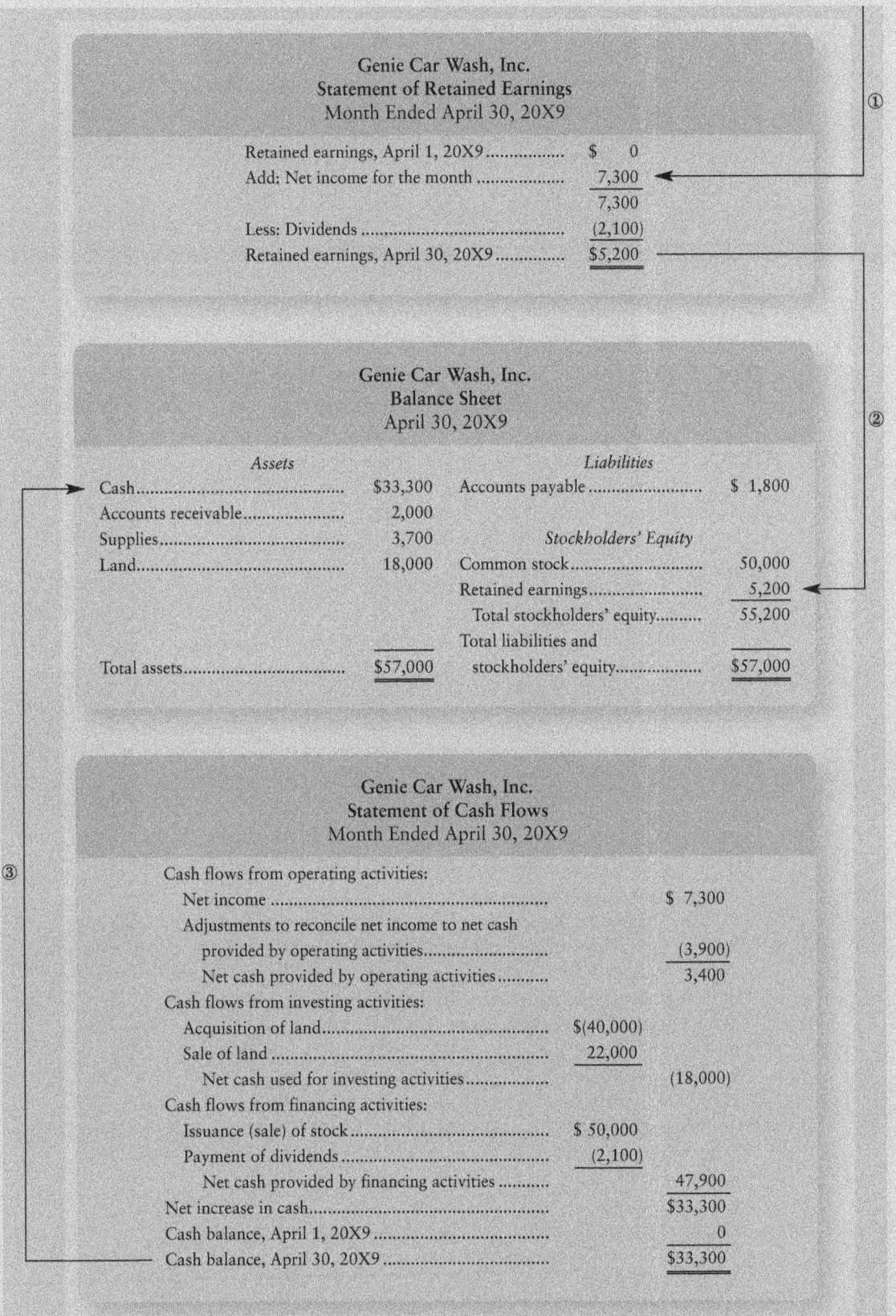

Genie Car Wash, Inc.
Statement of Retained Earnings
Month Ended April 30, 20X9

Retained earnings, April 1, 20X9	$ 0
Add: Net income for the month	7,300
	7,300
Less: Dividends	(2,100)
Retained earnings, April 30, 20X9	$5,200

①

Genie Car Wash, Inc.
Balance Sheet
April 30, 20X9

Assets		Liabilities	
Cash...	$33,300	Accounts payable	$ 1,800
Accounts receivable.....................	2,000		
Supplies.......................................	3,700	*Stockholders' Equity*	
Land...	18,000	Common stock.............................	50,000
		Retained earnings........................	5,200
		Total stockholders' equity..........	55,200
		Total liabilities and	
Total assets..................................	$57,000	stockholders' equity..................	$57,000

②

Genie Car Wash, Inc.
Statement of Cash Flows
Month Ended April 30, 20X9

③

Cash flows from operating activities:		
Net income		$ 7,300
Adjustments to reconcile net income to net cash		
provided by operating activities............................		(3,900)
Net cash provided by operating activities...........		3,400
Cash flows from investing activities:		
Acquisition of land..	$(40,000)	
Sale of land	22,000	
Net cash used for investing activities..................		(18,000)
Cash flows from financing activities:		
Issuance (sale) of stock	$ 50,000	
Payment of dividends..	(2,100)	
Net cash provided by financing activities...........		47,900
Net increase in cash...		$33,300
Cash balance, April 1, 20X9		0
Cash balance, April 30, 20X9		$33,300

HH **CHAPTER 1**

| **Requirement 2**

2. **a.** Genie performed rather well in April. Net income was $7,300—very good in relation to service revenue of $10,000. The company was able to pay cash dividends of $2,100.
   b. Genie ended April with cash of $33,300. Total assets of $57,000 far exceed total liabilities of $1,800. Stockholders' equity of $55,200 provides a good cushion for borrowing. The business's financial position at April 30, 20X9, is strong.

REVIEW THE FINANCIAL STATEMENTS

Quick Check (Answers are given on page 47.)

1. All of the following statements are true except one. Which statement is false?
   a. Bookkeeping is only a part of accounting.
   b. A proprietorship is a business with several owners.
   c. Professional accountants are held to a high standard of ethical conduct.
   d. The organization that formulates generally accepted accounting principles is the Financial Accounting Standards Board.
2. The valuation of assets on the balance sheet is generally based on:
   a. Historical cost
   b. What it would cost to replace the asset
   c. Current fair market value as established by independent appraisers
   d. Selling price
3. The accounting equation can be expressed as:
   a. Assets + Liabilities = Owners' Equity
   b. Owners' Equity - Assets = Liabilities
   c. Assets = Liabilities – Owners' Equity
   d. Assets – Liabilities = Owners' Equity
4. The nature of an asset is best described as:
   a. Something with physical form that's valued at cost in the accounting records.
   b. An economic resource representing cash or the right to receive cash in the future.
   c. An economic resource that's expected to benefit future operations.
   d. Something owned by a business that has a ready market value.
5. Which financial statement covers a period of time?
   a. Balance sheet   **c.** Statement of cash flows
   b. Income statement   **d.** Both B and C
6. How would net income be most likely to affect the accounting equation?
   a. Increase assets and increase stockholders' equity
   b. Increase liabilities and decrease stockholders' equity
   c. Increase assets and increase liabilities
   d. Decrease assets and decrease liabilities
7. During the year, ChemDry, Inc., has $100,000 in revenues, $40,000 in expenses, and $3,000 in dividend payments. Stockholders' equity changed by:
   a. +$27,000   **c.** +$12,000
   b. +$57,000   **d.** –$8,000
8. ChemDry in question 7 had net income (or net loss) of
   a. Net income of $100,000.   **c.** Net income of $60,000.
   b. Net income of $57,000.   **d.** Net loss of $40,000.

9. Prestige Corporation holds cash of $5,000 and owes $25,000 on accounts payable. Prestige has accounts receivable of $30,000, inventory of $20,000, and land that cost $50,000. How much are Prestige's total assets and liabilities?

	Total assets	Liabilities
a.	$100,000	$25,000
b.	$105,000	$80,000
c.	$105,000	$25,000
d.	$25,000	105,000

10. Which item(s) is (are) reported on the balance sheet?
   a. Retained earnings
   b. Accounts payable
   c. Inventory
   d. All of the above

11. During the year, Brooks Company's stockholders' equity increased from $30,000 to $40,000. Brooks earned net income of $15,000. How much in dividends did Brooks declare during the year?
   a. $6,000
   b. $-0-
   c. $8,000
   d. $5,000

12. Stuebs Company had total assets of $300,000 and total stockholders' equity of $100,000 at the beginning of the year. During the year assets increased by $50,000 and liabilities increased by $40,000. Stockholders' equity at the end of the year is:
   a. $90,000
   b. $110,000
   c. $140,000
   d. $150,000

Accounting Vocabulary

account payable (p. 11) A liability backed by the general reputation and credit standing of the debtor.

accounting (p. 3) The information system that measures business activities, processes that information into reports and financial statements, and communicates the results to decision makers.

accounting equation (p. 10) The most basic tool of accounting: Assets = Liabilities + Owners' Equity.

assets (p. 10) An economic resource that is expected to be of benefit in the future.

balance sheet (p. 16) List of an entity's assets, liabilities, and owners' equity as of a specific date. Also called the *statement of financial position*.

board of directors (p. 7) Group elected by the stockholders to set policy for a corporation and to appoint its officers.

capital (p. 10) Another name for the *owners' equity* of a business.

cash (p. 11) Money and any medium of exchange that a bank accepts at face value.

common stock (p. 11) The most basic form of capital stock.

corporation (p. 7) A business owned by stockholders. A corporation is a legal entity, an "artificial person" in the eyes of the law.

cost principle (p. 9) Principle that states that assets and services should be recorded at their actual cost.

current assets (p. 16) An asset that is expected to be converted to cash, sold, or consumed during the next 12 months, or within the business's normal operating cycle if longer than a year.

current liabilities (p. 18) A debt due to be paid within 1 year or within the entity's operating cycle if the cycle is longer than a year.

dividends (p. 12) Distributions (usually cash) by a corporation to its stockholders.

entity (p. 8) An organization or a section of an organization that, for accounting purposes, stands apart from other organizations and individuals as a separate economic unit.

expenses (p. 11) Decrease in retained earnings that results from operations; the cost of doing business; opposite of revenues.

fair value (p. 9) The amount that a business could sell an asset for, or the amount that a business could pay to settle a liability.

financial accounting (p. 4) The branch of accounting that provides information to people outside the firm.

financial statements (p. 2) Business documents that report financial information about a business entity to decision makers.

financing activities (p. 19) Activities that obtain from investors and creditors the cash needed to launch and sustain the business; a section of the statement of cash flows.

HH CHAPTER 1

fixed assets (p. 11) Another name for *property, plant, and equipment*.

generally accepted accounting principles (GAAP) (p. 7) Accounting guidelines, formulated by the Financial Accounting Standards Board, that govern how accounting is practiced.

going-concern concept (p. 9) Holds that the entity will remain in operation for the foreseeable future.

income statement (p. 14) A financial statement listing an entity's revenues, expenses, and net income or net loss for a specific period. Also called the *statement of operations*.

investing activities (p. 19) Activities that increase or decrease the long-term assets available to the business; a section of the statement of cash flows.

liabilities (p. 10) An economic obligation (a debt) payable to an individual or an organization outside the business.

limited liability company (p. 7) A business organization in which the business (not the owner) is liable for the company's debts.

long-term debt (p. 11) A liability that falls due beyond 1 year from the date of the financial statements.

management accounting (p. 4) The branch of accounting that generates information for the internal decision makers of a business, such as top executives.

merchandise inventory (p. 11) The merchandise that a company sells to customers, also called *inventory*.

net earnings (p. 11) Another name for *net income*.

net income (p. 11) Excess of total revenues over total expenses. Also called *net earnings* or *net profit*.

net loss (p. 12) Excess of total expenses over total revenues.

net profit (p. 11) Another name for *net income*.

note payable (p. 11) A liability evidenced by a written promise to make a future payment.

objectivity principle (p. 8) Another name for the *reliability principle*.

operating activities (p. 19) Activities that create revenue or expense in the entity's major line of business; a section of the statement of cash flows. Operating activities affect the income statement.

owners' equity (p. 10) The claim of the owners of a business to the assets of the business. Also called *capital, stockholders' equity,* or *net assets*.

paid-in capital (p. 11) The amount of stockholders' equity that stockholders have contributed to the corporation. Also called *contributed capital*.

partnership (p. 6) An association of 2 or more persons who co-own a business for profit.

plant assets (p. 11) Another name for *property, plant, and equipment*.

property, plant, and equipment (p. 11) Long-lived assets, such as land, buildings, and equipment, used in the operation of the business. Also called *plant assets* or *fixed assets*.

proprietorship (p. 6) A business with a single owner.

reliability principle (p. 8) The accounting principle that ensures that accounting records and statements are based on the most reliable data available. Also called the *objectivity principle*.

retained earnings (p. 11) The amount of stockholders' equity that the corporation has earned through profitable operation and has not given back to stockholders.

revenues (p. 11) Increase in retained earnings from delivering goods or services to customers or clients.

shareholder (p. 7) Another name for *stockholder*.

stable-monetary-unit concept (p. 10) The reason for ignoring the effect of inflation in the accounting records, based on the assumption that the dollar's purchasing power is relatively stable.

statement of cash flows (p. 19) Reports cash receipts and cash payments classified according to the entity's major activities: operating, investing, and financing.

statement of financial position (p. 16) Another name for the *balance sheet*.

statement of operations (p. 14) Another name for the *income statement*.

statement of retained earnings (p. 15) Summary of the changes in the retained earnings of a corporation during a specific period.

stock (p. 7) Shares into which the owners' equity of a corporation is divided.

stockholders (p. 7) A person who owns stock in a corporation. Also called a *shareholder*.

stockholders' equity (p. 11) The stockholders' ownership interest in the assets of a corporation.

ASSESS YOUR PROGRESS

Short Exercises

S1-1 (*Learning Objective 1: Using accounting vocabulary*) Suppose you manage a Pizza Hut restaurant. Identify the missing amount for each situation: (pp. 10–12)

Total Assets	=	Total Liabilities	+	Stockholder's Equity
a. $?		$150,000		$150,000
b. 290,000		90,000		?
c. 220,000		?		120,000

S1-2 (*Learning Objective 1: Making ethical judgments*) Accountants follow ethical guidelines in the conduct of their work. What are these standards of professional conduct designed to produce? Why is this goal important? (p. 5)

S1-3 (*Learning Objective 2: Applying accounting concepts*) David Novak is Chairman of the Board of YUM! Brands, Inc. Suppose Mr. Novak has just founded YUM! Brands, and assume that he treats his home and other personal assets as part of YUM! Brands. Answer these questions about the evaluation of YUM! Brands, Inc. (pp. 8–9)

1. Which accounting concept governs this situation?
2. How can the *proper* application of this accounting concept give Novak and others a realistic view of YUM! Brands, Inc.? Explain in detail.

S1-4 (*Learning Objective 3: Using the accounting equation*)

1. Use the accounting equation to show how to determine the amount of a company's owners' equity. How would your answer change if you were analyzing your own household or a single IHOP restaurant? (pp. 10–12)
2. If you know the assets and the owners' equity of a business, how can you measure its liabilities? Give the equation. (pp. 10–12)

S1-5 (*Learning Objective 1: Defining key accounting terms*) Accounting definitions are precise, and you must understand the vocabulary to properly use accounting. Sharpen your understanding of key terms by answering the following questions. (pp. 10–11)

1. How do the *assets* and *owners' equity* of Intel Corporation differ from each other? Which one (assets or owners' equity) must be at least as large as the other? Which one can be smaller than the other?
2. How are Intel's *liabilities* and *owners' equity* similar? How are they different?

S1-6 (*Learning Objective 1: Classifying assets, liabilities, and owners' equity*) Consider Wal-Mart, the world's largest retailer. Classify the following items as an Asset (A), a Liability (L), or an Owners' Equity (E) for Wal-Mart (pp. 10–11):

____ **a.** Accounts payable   ____ **g.** Accounts receivable

____ **b.** Common stock   ____ **h.** Long-term debt

____ **c.** Supplies   ____ **i.** Merchandise inventory

____ **d.** Retained earnings   ____ **j.** Notes payable

____ **e.** Land   ____ **k.** Expenses payable

____ **f.** Prepaid expenses   ____ **l.** Equipment

S1-7 (*Learning Objective 4: Using the income statement*)

1. Identify the 2 basic categories of items on an income statement. (pp. 13–14)
2. What do we call the bottom line of the income statement? (pp. 13–14)

S1-8 (*Learning Objective 4: Preparing an income statement*) Split Second Wireless, Inc., began 2009 with total assets of $110 million and ended 2009 with assets of $160 million. During 2009 Split Second earned revenues of $90 million and had expenses of $20 million. Split Second paid dividends of $10 million in 2009. Prepare the company's income statement for the year ended December 31, 2009, complete with an appropriate heading. (pp. 13–14).

S1-9 (*Learning Objective 4: Preparing a statement of retained earnings*) Nextel Corp. began 2008 with retained earnings of $200 million. Revenues during the year were $400 million and expenses totaled $300 million. Nextel declared dividends of $40 million. What was the company's ending balance of retained earnings? To answer this question, prepare Nextel's statement of retained earnings for the year ended December 31, 2008, complete with its proper heading. (pp. 15–16)

S1-10 (*Learning Objective 4: Preparing a balance sheet*) At December 31, 2008, Womack Travel Services has cash of $13,000, receivables of $2,000, and ticket inventory of $40,000. The company's equipment totals $85,000. Womack owes accounts payable of $10,000, and long-term notes payable of $80,000. Common stock is $15,000.

Prepare Womack's balance sheet at December 31, 2008, complete with its proper heading. Use the accounting equation to compute retained earnings. (pp. 10–12)

S1-11 (*Learning Objective 4 : Preparing a statement of cash flows*) Brazos Medical, Inc., ended 2009 with cash of $24,000. During 2010, Brazos earned net income of $80,000 and had adjustments to reconcile net income to net cash provided by operations totaling $20,000 (this is a negative amount).

Brazos paid $40,000 to purchase equipment during 2010. During 2010, the company paid dividends of $10,000.

Prepare Brazos's statement of cash flows for the year ended December 31, 2010, complete with its proper heading. Follow the format in the summary problem starting on page 25.

S1-12 (*Learning Objective 5: Identifying items with the appropriate financial statement*) Suppose you are analyzing the financial statements of Martin Audiology, Inc. Identify each item with its appropriate financial statement, using the following abbreviations: Income statement (IS), Statement of retained earnings (SRE), Balance sheet (BS), and Statement of cash flows (SCF). Three items appear on 2 financial statements, and one item shows up on 3 statements. (p. 22)

____ **a.** Dividends

____ **b.** Salary expense

____ **c.** Inventory

____ **d.** Sales revenue

____ **e.** Retained earnings

____ **f.** Net cash provided by operating activities

____ **g.** Net income

____ **h.** Cash

____ **i.** Net cash used for financing activities

____ **j.** Accounts payable

____ **k.** Common stock

____ **l.** Interest revenue

____ **m.** Long-term debt

____ **n.** Increase or decrease in cash

Exercises

writing assignment ■

E1-13 (*Learning Objective 1: Organizing a business*) Quality Environmental, Inc., needs funds, and Martha Beard, the president, has asked you to consider investing in the business. Answer the following questions about the different ways that Beard might organize the business. Explain each answer. (p. 7)

a. What forms of organization will enable the owners of Quality Environmental to limit their risk of loss to the amounts they have invested in the business?

b. What form of business organization will give Beard the most freedom to manage the business as she wishes?

c. What form of organization will give creditors the maximum protection in the event that Quality Environmental fails and cannot pay its debts?

E1-14 (*Learning Objective 2: Applying accounting concepts and principles*) Identify the accounting concept or principle that best applies to each of the following situations. (pp. 8–10)

   a. Wendy's, the restaurant chain, sold a store location to Burger King. How can Wendy's determine the sale price of the store—by a professional appraisal, Wendy's cost, or the amount actually received from the sale?

   b. Inflation has been around 6% for some time. Trammel Crow Realtors is considering measuring its land values in inflation-adjusted amounts.

   c. Toyota wants to determine which division of the company—Toyota or Lexus—is more profitable.

   d. You get an especially good buy on a laptop, paying only $399 for a computer that normally costs $799. What is your accounting value for this computer?

E1-15 (*Learning Objective 3: Accounting equation*) Compute the missing amount in the accounting equation for each company (amounts in billions):

	Assets	Liabilities	Owners' Equity
Apple	$?	$ 7	$10
PepsiCo	32	?	14
FedEx	23	11	?

Which company appears to have the strongest financial position? Explain your reasoning. (pp. 10–12)

E1-16 (*Learning Objective 3, 4: Accounting equation*) Krispy Kreme Doughnuts has current assets of $147 million; property, plant, and equipment of $206 million; and other assets totaling $58 million. Current liabilities are $154 million and long-term liabilities total $148 million. (pp. 10–12)

❘ Requirements

   1. Use these data to write Krispy Kreme Doughnuts' accounting equation.

   2. How much in resources does Krispy Kreme have to work with?

   3. How much does Krispy Kreme owe creditors?

   4. How much of the company's assets do the Krispy Kreme stockholders actually own?

E1-17 (*Learning Objective 3: Accounting equation*) Store Front, Inc.'s, comparative balance sheet at January 31, 2009, and 2008, reports (in millions):

	2009	2008
Total assets	$40	$30
Total liabilities	12	10

❘ Required

Three situations about Store Front's issuance of stock and payment of dividends during the year ended January 31, 2009, follow. For each situation, use the accounting equation and the statement of retained earnings to compute the amount of Store Front's net income or net loss during the year ended January 31, 2009. (pp. 10–12, 15–16)

   1. Store Front issued $1 million of stock and paid no dividends.

   2. Store Front issued no stock but paid dividends of $2 million.

   3. Store Front issued $11 million of stock and paid dividends of $1 million.

HH CHAPTER 1

E1-18 (*Learning Objective 3, 4: Accounting equation*) Answer these questions about 2 companies.

1. Peru, Inc., began the year with total liabilities of $140,000 and total stockholders' equity of $300,000. During the year, total assets increased by 20%. How much are total assets at the end of the year? (pp. 10–12)

2. Social Networking Associates began the year with total assets of $500,000 and total liabilities of $200,000. Net income for the year was $100,000, and dividends were zero. How much is stockholders' equity at the end of the year? (pp. 10–12, 15–16)

E1-19 (*Learning Objective 4: Identifying financial statement information*) Assume MySpace is expanding into Japan. The company must decide where to locate and how to finance the expansion. Identify the financial statement where these decision makers can find the following information about MySpace, Inc. In some cases, more than one statement will report the needed data. (pp. 15–20)

a. Common stock

b. Income tax payable

c. Dividends

d. Income tax expense

e. Ending balance of retained earnings

f. Total assets

g. Long-term debt

h. Revenue

i. Cash spent to acquire the building

j. Selling, general, and administrative expenses

k. Adjustments to reconcile net income to net cash provided by operations

l. Ending cash balance

m. Current liabilities

n. Net income

■ **spreadsheet**

E1-20 (*Learning Objective 2, 5: Business organization, balance sheet*) Amounts of the assets and liabilities of Maxwell Banking Company, as of December 31, 2008, are given as follows. Also included are revenue and expense figures for the year ended on that date (amounts in millions):

Property and equipment, net	$ 4	Total revenue	$ 35
Investment assets	72	Receivables	253
Long-term liabilities	73	Current liabilities	290
Other expenses	14	Common stock	12
Cash	28	Interest expense	3
Retained earnings, beginning	19	Salary and other employee expenses	9
Retained earnings, ending	?	Other assets	43

❙ *Required*

Prepare the balance sheet of Maxwell Banking Company at December 31, 2008. Use the accounting equation to compute ending retained earnings (pp. 10–11, 15–17)

■ **spreadsheet**

E1-21 (*Learning Objective 2, 5: Income statement*) This exercise should be used with Exercise 1-20. Refer to the data of Maxwell Banking Company in Exercise 1-20.

❙ *Required*

1. Prepare the income statement of Maxwell Banking Company, for the year ended December 31, 2008. (pp. 13–14)

2. What amount of dividends did Maxwell declare during the year ended December 31, 2008? Hint: Prepare a statement of retained earnings. (pp. 15–16)

E1-22 (*Learning Objective 2, 4, 5: Statement of cash flows*) Groovy, Inc., began 2008 with $95,000 in cash. During 2008, Groovy earned net income of $300,000, and adjustments to reconcile net income to net cash provided by operations totaled $60,000, a positive amount. Investing activities used cash of $400,000, and financing activities provided cash of $70,000. Groovy ended 2008 with total assets of $250,000 and total liabilities of $110,000.

I Required

Prepare Groovy, Inc.'s, statement of cash flows for the year ended December 31, 2008. Identify the data items given that do not appear on the statement of cash flows. Also identify the financial statement that reports each unused item. (pp. 16–17)

E1-23 (*Learning Objective 5: Preparing an income statement and a statement of retained earnings*) Assume a Ricoh Copy Center ended the month of July 20X9 with these data:

Payments of cash:			Cash balance, June 30, 20X9.....	$ 0
Acquisition of equipment.......	$36,000		Cash balance, July 31, 20X9......	8,100
Dividends..............................	2,000		Cash receipts:	
Retained earnings,			Issuance (sale) of stock	
June 30, 20X9......................	0		to owners..........................	35,000
Retained earnings,			Rent expense............................	700
July 31, 20X9......................	?		Common stock..........................	35,000
Utilities expense	200		Equipment.................................	36,000
Adjustments to reconcile			Office supplies..........................	1,200
net income to cash provided			Accounts payable	3,200
by operations	2,000		Service revenue........................	14,000
Salary expense...........................	4,000			

I Required

Prepare the income statement and the statement of retained earnings of Ricoh Copy Center, Inc., for the month ended July 31, 20X9. (pp. 13–14, 15–16)

E1-24 (*Learning Objective 5: Preparing a balance sheet*) Refer to the data in the preceding exercise. Prepare the balance sheet of Ricoh Copy Center, Inc., at July 31, 20X9. (pp. 16–17)

E1-25 (*Learning Objective 5: Preparing a statement of cash flows*) Refer to the data in Exercise 1-23. Prepare the statement of cash flows of Ricoh Copy Center, Inc., for the month ended July 31, 20X9. Draw arrows linking the statements you prepared for Exercises 1-23 through 1-25. (pp. 19–20)

E1-26 (*Learning Objective 4, 5: Advising a business*) This exercise should be used in conjunction with Exercises 1-23 through 1-25.

writing assignment ■

The owner of Ricoh Copy Center now seeks your advice as to whether he should cease operations or continue the business. Write a report giving him your opinion of net income, dividends, financial position, and cash flows during his first month of operations. Cite specifics from the financial statements to support your opinion. Conclude your memo with advice on whether to stay in business or cease operations. (Challenge)

E1-27 (*Learning Objective 2, 5: Applying accounting concepts to explain business activity*)

writing assignment ■

Apply your understanding of the relationships among the financial statements to answer these questions. (Challenge)

a. How can a business earn large profits but have a small balance of retained earnings?

b. Give 2 reasons why a business can have a steady stream of net income over a 5-year period and still experience a cash shortage.

c. If you could pick a single source of cash for your business, what would it be? Why?

d. How can a business lose money several years in a row and still have plenty of cash?

Quiz

Test your understanding of the financial statements by answering the following questions. Select the best choice from among the possible answers given.

Q1-28 The *primary* objective of financial reporting is to provide information (p. 7)
a. Useful for making investment and credit decisions.
b. About the profitability of the enterprise.
c. On the cash flows of the company.
d. To the federal government.

Q1-29 For a company of a certain size, which type of business organization provides the least amount of protection for bankers and other creditors of the company? (pp. 6–7)
a. Proprietorship
b. Partnership
c. Both a and b
d. Corporation

Q1-30 Assets are usually reported at their (pp. 9–10)
a. Appraised value.
b. Current market value.
c. Historical cost.
d. None of the above (<u>fill in the blank</u>).

Q1-31 During January, assets increased by $20,000 and liabilities increased by $4,000. Stockholders' equity must have (pp. 10–11)
a. Increased by $16,000.
b. Increased by $24,000.
c. Decreased by $16,000.
d. Decreased by $24,000.

Q1-32 The amount a company expects to collect from customers appears on the (pp. 16–17)
a. Income statement in the expenses section.
b. Balance sheet in the current assets section.
c. Balance sheet in the stockholders' equity section.
d. Statement of cash flows.

Q1-33 All of the following are current assets except (pp. 16–17)
a. Cash.
b. Accounts Receivable.
c. Inventory.
d. Sales Revenue.

Q1-34 Revenues are (p. 11)
a. Increases in paid-in capital resulting from the owners investing in the business.
b. Increases in retained earnings resulting from selling products or performing services.
c. Decreases in liabilities resulting from paying off loans.
d. All of the above.

Q1-35 The financial statement that reports revenues and expenses is called the (pp. 13–14)
a. Statement of retained earnings.
b. Income statement.
c. Statement of cash flows.
d. Balance sheet.

Q1-36 Another name for the balance sheet is the (pp. 16–17)
a. Statement of operations.
b. Statement of earnings.
c. Statement of profit and loss.
d. Statement of financial position.

Q1-37 Baldwin Corporation began the year with cash of $35,000 and a computer that cost $20,000. During the year Baldwin earned sales revenue of $140,000 and had the following expenses: salaries, $59,000; rent, $8,000; and utilities, $3,000. At year end Baldwin's cash balance was down to $16,000. How much net income (or net loss) did Baldwin experience for the year? (pp. 13–14)
a. ($19,000)
b. $70,000
c. $107,000
d. $140,000

HH CHAPTER 1

Q1-38 Quartz Instruments had retained earnings of $145,000 at December 31, 20X1. Net income for 20X2 totaled $90,000, and dividends for 20X2 were $30,000. How much retained earnings should Quartz report at December 31, 20X2? (pp. 15–16)
a. $205,000
b. $235,000
c. $140,000
d. $175,000

Q1-39 Net income appears on which financial statement(s)? (pp. 13–14)
a. Income statement
b. Statement of retained earnings
c. Both A and B
d. Balance sheet

Q1-40 Cash paid to purchase a building appears on the statement of cash flows among the (pp. 19–20)
a. Operating activities.
b. Financing activities.
c. Investing activities.
d. Stockholders' equity.

Q1-41 The stockholders' equity of Chernasky Company at the beginning and end of 20X0 totaled $15,000 and $18,000, respectively. Assets at the beginning of 20X0 were $25,000. If the liabilities of Chernasky Company increased by $8,000 in 20X0, how much were total assets at the end of 20X0? Use the accounting equation. (pp. 10–12)
a. $36,000
b. $16,000
c. $2,000
d. Some other amount (fill in the blank)

Q1-42 Drexler Company had the following on the dates indicated:

	12/31/X3	12/31/X2
Total assets	$750,000	$520,000
Total liabilities	300,000	200,000

Drexler had no stock transactions in 20X3 and, thus, the change in stockholders' equity for 20X3 was due to net income and dividends. If dividends were $50,000, how much was Drexler's net income for 20X3? Use the accounting equation and the statements of retained earnings. (pp. 10–12, 15–16)
a. $100,000
b. $130,000
c. $180,000
d. Some other amount (fill in the blank)

Problems
(Group A)

Some of these A problems can be found within My Accounting Lab (MAL), an online homework and practice environment. Your instructor may ask you to complete these exercises using MAL.

MyAccountingLab

P1-43A (*Learning Objective 1, 2, 4, 5: Applying accounting vocabulary, concepts, and principles to the income statement*) Assume that the **Kinko's Division of FedEx Corporation** experienced the following transactions during the year ended December 31, 20X5:

a. Suppose Kinko's provided copy services for Microsoft for the discounted price of $250,000. Under normal conditions Kinko's would have provided these services for $280,000. Other revenues totaled $50,000.

b. Salaries cost Kinko's $20,000 to provide these services. Kinko's had to pay employees overtime. Ordinarily the salary cost for these services would have been $18,000.

c. Other expenses totaled $240,000. Income tax expense was 40% of income before tax.

d. Kinko's has 2 operating subdivisions: basic retail and special contracts. Each subdivision is accounted for separately to indicate how well each is performing. At year end, Kinko's combines the statements of all subdivisions to show results for the Kinko's Division as a whole.

e. Inflation affects the amounts that Kinko's must pay for copy machines. To show the effects of inflation, net income would drop by $3,000.

f. If Kinko's were to go out of business, the sale of its assets would bring in $150,000 in cash.

I Required

1. Prepare the Kinko's Division's income statement for the year ended December 31, 20X5. (pp. 13–14)

2. For items a through f, identify the accounting concept or principle that provides guidance in accounting for the item. State how you have applied the concept or principle in preparing Kinko's income statement.(pp. 8–9)

P1-44A (*Learning Objective 3: Using the accounting equation*) Compute the missing amount (?) for each company—amounts in millions. (pp. 13–17)

	Diamond Corp.	Lance Co.	Berger Inc.
		(In Millions)	
Beginning			
Assets.............................	$78	$30	$?
Liabilities	47	19	2
Common stock..................	6	1	2
Retained earnings..............	?	10	3
Ending			
Assets.............................	$?	$48	$9
Liabilities	48	30	?
Common stock..................	6	?	2
Retained earnings..............	29	?	?
Income statement			
Revenues..........................	$218	$?	$20
Expenses	211	144	?
Net income.......................	?	?	?
Statement of retained earnings			
Beginning RE	$25	$10	$ 3
+ Net income....................	?	9	1
– Dividends.......................	(3)	(2)	(0)
= Ending RE......................	$29	$17	$ 4

Which company has the
- Highest net income?
- Highest percent of net income to revenues?

HH CHAPTER 1

P1-45A (*Learning Objective 2, 5: Balance sheet*) Danielle Stone, the manager of **Image Runner, Inc.**, prepared the company's balance sheet while the accountant was ill. The balance sheet contains some errors. In particular, Stone knew that the balance sheet should balance, so she plugged in the stockholders' equity amount needed to achieve this balance. The stockholders' equity amount is *not* correct. All other amounts are accurate.

Image Runner, Inc.
Balance Sheet
Month Ended October 31, 20X8

Assets		Liabilities	
Cash...............................	$ 9,100	Notes receivable.......................	$ 14,000
Equipment............................	36,700	Interest expense.......................	2,000
Accounts payable	3,000	Office supplies........................	800
Utilities expense	2,100	Accounts receivable................	2,600
Advertising expense.................	300	Note payable.........................	50,000
Land....................................	80,500	Total	69,400
Salary expense........................	3,300	**Stockholders' Equity**	
		Stockholders' equity	65,600
Total assets............................	$135,000	Total liabilities	$135,000

❙ Required

1. Prepare the correct balance sheet and date it properly. Compute total assets, total liabilities, and stockholders' equity. (pp. 16–17)

2. Is Image Runner actually in better (or worse) financial position than the erroneous balance sheet reports? Give the reason for your answer. (Challenge)

3. Identify the accounts listed on the incorrect balance sheet that should not be reported on the balance sheet. State why you excluded them from the correct balance sheet you prepared for Requirement 1. On which financial statement should these accounts appear? (pp. 13–14)

P1-46A (*Learning Objective 2, 5: Balance sheet, entity concept*) Heather Hutchison is a realtor. She organized the business as a corporation on March 10, 2008. The business received $50,000 cash from Hutchison and issued common stock. Consider the following facts as of March 31, 2008:

   a. Hutchison has $9,000 in her personal bank account and $16,000 in the business bank account.
   b. Office supplies on hand at the real estate office total $1,000.
   c. Hutchison's business spent $35,000 for a **Keller Williams** franchise, which entitles her to represent herself as an agent. Keller Williams is a national affiliation of independent real estate agents. This franchise is a business asset.
   d. Hutchison's business owes $33,000 on a note payable for some land acquired for a total price of $100,000.
   e. Hutchison owes $65,000 on a personal mortgage on her personal residence, which she acquired in 2002 for a total price of $190,000.
   f. Hutchison owes $300 on a personal charge account with **Sears**.
   g. Hutchison acquired business furniture for $18,000 on March 26. Of this amount, Hutchison's business owes $6,000 on accounts payable at March 31.

❙ Required

1. Prepare the balance sheet of the real estate business of Heather Hutchison, Realtor, Inc., at March 31, 2008. (pp. 16–17)
2. Does it appear that Hutchison's business can pay its debts? How can you tell? (Challenge)

(continued)

3. Identify the personal items given in the preceding facts that should not be reported on the balance sheet of the business. (pp. 16–17)

■ **spreadsheet**

P1-47A (*Learning Objective 5: Income statement, statement of retained earnings, balance sheet*) The assets and liabilities of Post Oak, Inc., as of December 31, 20X7, and revenues and expenses for the year ended on that date are listed here.

Land	$ 8,000	Equipment	$ 31,000
Note payable	31,000	Interest expense	4,000
Property tax expense	2,000	Interest payable	1,000
Rent expense	14,000	Accounts payable	12,000
Accounts receivable	25,000	Salary expense	34,000
Service revenue	140,000	Building	126,000
Supplies	2,000	Cash	14,000
Utilities expense	3,000	Common stock	10,000

Beginning retained earnings was $111,000, and dividends totaled $42,000 for the year.

❚ Required

1. Prepare the income statement of Post Oak, Inc., for the year ended December 31, 20X7. (pp. 13–14)
2. Prepare the company's statement of retained earnings for the year. (pp. 15–16)
3. Prepare the company's balance sheet at December 31, 20X7. (pp. 16–17)
4. Analyze Post Oak by answering these questions: (Challenge)

   a. Was Post Oak profitable during 20X7? By how much?
   b. Did retained earnings increase or decrease? By how much?
   c. Which is greater, total liabilities or total equity? Who owns more of Post Oak's assets, creditors of the company or the Post Oak stockholders?

P1-48A (*Learning Objective 4: Preparing a statement of cash flows*) The following data come from the financial statements of Kawasaki, Inc., at the end of a recent year (in millions):

Other investing cash payments	$ 200	Purchases of property, plant, and equipment	$ 3,300
Accounts receivable	900	Net income	3,000
Payment of dividends	300	Adjustments to reconcile	
Common stock	5,500	net income to cash	
Issuance of common stock	200	provided by operations	2,900
Sales of property, plant, and equipment	100	Revenues	53,500
		Cash, beginning of year	200
Retained earnings	12,700	end of year	2,600
Cost of goods sold	37,400		

❚ Required

1. Prepare Kawasaki's statement of cash flows for the year ended January 31, 20X3. Follow the format of the summary problem starting on page 25. Not all items given are reported on the statement of cash flows. (pp. 19–20)
2. What was Kawasaki's largest source of cash? Is this a sign of financial strength or weakness? (Challenge)

P1-49A *(Learning Objective 4, 5: Analyzing a company's financial statements)* Summarized versions of Gonzales Company's financial statements are given for 2 recent years.

	20X5	20X4
Income Statement		
Revenues..	$ k	$15,400
Cost of goods sold..	11,000	a
Other expenses...	1,200	1,100
Income before income taxes	900	1,400
Income taxes (40% in 20X5)	l	100
Net income..	$ m	$ b
Statement of Retained Earnings		
Beginning balance	n	$ 2,700
Net income..	o	c
Dividends..	(60)	(50)
Ending balance..	$ p	$ d
Balance Sheet		
Assets:		
Cash..	$ q	$ e
Property, plant, and equipment..................	1,500	1,700
Other assets..	r	10,100
Total assets	$ s	$12,870
Liabilities:		
Current liabilities	$ t	$ 5,400
Notes payable and long-term debt.............	2,500	3,100
Other liabilities	70	70
Total liabilities.......................................	$ 8,300	$ f
Shareholders' Equity:		
Common stock...	$ 100	$ 100
Retained earnings......................................	u	g
Other shareholders' equity	180	250
Total shareholders' equity.......................	v	4,300
Total liabilities and shareholders' equity	$ w	$ h
Statement of Cash Flows		
Net cash provided by operating activities..............	$ x	$ 500
Net cash provided by investing activities...............	60	400
Net cash used for financing activities	(700)	(1,000)
Increase (decrease) in cash..................................	310	i
Cash at beginning of year...............................	y	1,170
Cash at end of year	$ z	$ j

❚ Required

Complete Gonzales' financial statements by determining the missing amounts denoted by the letters. (pp. 13–20)

(Group B)

P1-50B *(Learning Objective 1, 2, 4, 5: Applying accounting vocabulary, concepts, and principles to the income statement)* ABM Corporation experienced the following transactions during the year ended December 31, 20X8:

    a. ABM sold products for $53 billion. Company management believes the value of these products is approximately $80 billion. Other revenues totaled $40 billion.

(continued)

writing assignment ■

    b. It cost ABM $36 billion to manufacture the products ABM sold. If ABM had purchased the products instead of manufacturing them, ABM's cost would have been $42 billion.

    c. All other expenses, excluding income taxes, totaled $27 billion for the year. Income tax expense was 40% of income before tax.

    d. ABM has several operating divisions. Each division is accounted for separately to show how well each division is performing. At year end, ABM combines the statements of all the divisions to report on the company as a whole.

    e. Inflation affects ABM's cost to manufacture goods. To show the effects of inflation, the company's net income would drop by $3 billion.

    f. If ABM were to go out of business, the sale of company assets should bring in $65 billion in cash.

▌ Required

1. Prepare ABM Corporation's income statement for the year ended December 31, 20X8. (pp. 13–14)
2. For items a through f, identify the accounting concept or principle that tells how to account for the item described. State how you have applied the concept or principle in preparing ABM's income statement. (pp. 8–9)

P1-51B (*Learning Objective 3: Using the accounting equation*) Compute the missing amount (?) for each company—amounts in millions. (pp. 13–17)

	Samurai, Inc.	Peking Co.	Osaka Corp.
		(In Millions)	
Beginning			
Assets	$300	$?	$35
Liabilities	200	10	?
Common stock	30	4	8
Retained earnings	?	6	10
Ending			
Assets	$?	$24	$36
Liabilities	210	?	17
Common stock	30	4	?
Retained earnings	100	8	11
Income statement			
Revenues	$220	$19	$?
Expenses	180	?	55
Net income	?	?	?
Statement of retained earnings			
Beginning RE	$ 70	$ 6	$10
+ Net income	?	5	6
– Dividends	(10)	(3)	?
= Ending RE	$100	$ 8	$11

Which company has the
- Highest net income?
- Highest percent of net income to revenues?

P1-52B (*Learning Objective 2, 5: Balance sheet:*) The manager of Upod, Inc., prepared the balance sheet of the company while the accountant was ill. The balance sheet contains numerous errors. In particular, the manager knew that the balance sheet should balance so he plugged in the stockholders' equity amount needed to achieve this balance. The stockholders' equity amount, however, is *not* correct. All other amounts are accurate.

UPod, Inc.
Balance Sheet
Month Ended July 31, 20X7

Assets		Liabilities	
Cash..	$11,000	Accounts receivable................	$12,000
Office furniture......................	10,000	Service revenue........................	50,000
Note payable..........................	16,000	Property tax expense..............	800
Rent expense..........................	4,000	Accounts payable....................	5,000
Office supplies.......................	1,000	Total.......................................	67,800
Land..	44,000	**Stockholders' Equity**	
Advertising expense..............	2,500	Stockholders' equity..............	20,700
Total assets............................	$88,500	Total liabilities......................	$88,500

❙ Required

1. Prepare the correct balance sheet and date it properly. Compute total assets, total liabilities, and stockholders' equity. (pp. 16–17)
2. Is Upod, Inc., actually in better (or worse) financial position than the erroneous balance sheet reports? Give the reason for your answer. (Challenge)
3. Identify the preceding accounts that should *not* be reported on the balance sheet. State why you excluded them from the correct balance sheet you prepared for Requirement 1. Which financial statement should these accounts appear on? (pp. 13–14)

P1-53B (*Learning Objective 2, 5: Balance sheet, entity concept*) Linda Shriber is a realtor. Shriber organized her business as a corporation on November 14, 2009. The business received $50,000 from Shriber and issued common stock. Consider these facts as of November 30, 2009:

   a. Shriber has $10,000 in her personal bank account and $42,000 in the business bank account.
   b. Shriber owes $1,800 on a personal charge account with **Macy's**.
   c. The business bought furniture for $17,000 on November 25. Of this amount, the business owes $6,000 on accounts payable at November 30.
   d. Office supplies on hand at the real estate office total $1,000.
   e. The business owes $40,000 on a note payable for some land acquired for a total price of $120,000.
   f. The business spent $20,000 for a **Coldwell Banker** real estate franchise, which entitles Shriber to represent herself as a Coldwell Banker agent. Coldwell Banker is a national affiliation of independent real estate agents. This franchise is a business asset.
   g. Shriber owes $100,000 on a personal mortgage on her personal residence, which she acquired in 2004 for a total price of $160,000.

❙ Required

1. Prepare the balance sheet of the real estate business of Linda Shriber, Realtor, Inc., at November 30, 2009. (pp. 16–17)
2. Does it appear that Shriber's realty business can pay its debts? How can you tell? (Challenge)
3. Identify the personal items given in the preceding facts that should not be reported on the balance sheet of the business. (pp. 16–17)

P1-54B (*Learning Objective 5: Income statement, statement of retained earnings, balance sheet*) The assets and liabilities of HD Radio Corporation as of December 31, 20X8, and revenues and expenses for the year ended on that date follow.

■ **spreadsheet**

(continued)

Property tax expense......	$ 4,000	Land............................	$ 78,000
Accounts receivable........	12,000	Note payable..................	85,000
Advertising expense........	13,000	Accounts payable...........	19,000
Building.........................	50,000	Rent expense..................	23,000
Salary expense................	63,000	Cash..............................	10,000
Salary payable...............	1,000	Common stock...............	40,000
Service revenue..............	180,000	Furniture.......................	20,000
Supplies........................	3,000	Interest expense.............	9,000

Beginning retained earnings were $10,000, and dividends totaled $50,000 for the year.

I Required

1. Prepare the income statement of HD Radio Corporation for the year ended December 31, 20X8. (pp. 13–14)
2. Prepare HD Radio's statement of retained earnings for the year. (pp. 15–16)
3. Prepare HD Radio's balance sheet at December 31, 20X8. (pp. 16–17)
4. Analyze HD Radio Corporation by answering these questions: (Challenge)

   a. Was HD Radio profitable during 20X8? By how much?
   b. Did retained earnings increase or decrease? By how much?
   c. Which is greater, total liabilities or total equity? Who owns more of HD Radio's assets, creditors of the company or the HD Radio stockholders?

P1-55B (*Learning Objective 4: Preparing a statement of cash flows*) The following data are taken from the financial statements of Armstrong Company at the end of 2008 (in millions).

I Required

Sales of property, plant,		Revenues..............................	$9,100
and equipment..........................	$ 20	Cash, beginning of year........	200
Adjustments to reconcile		end of year.................	300
net income to net cash		Purchases of property	
provided by operating activities....	(400)	plant, and equipment........	500
Cost of goods sold.........................	5,500	Long-term debt....................	200
Other investing cash		Net income..........................	700
receipts.....................................	80	Payment of dividends...........	170
Accounts receivable......................	1,700	Common stock.....................	2,800
Retained earnings.........................	2,900	Issuance of common stock.....	370

1. Prepare Armstrong Company's statement of cash flows for the year ended December 31, 2008. Follow the solution of the summary problem starting on page 25. Not all the items given appear on the statement of cash flows. (pp. 19–20)
2. Which activities provided the largest amount of Armstrong's cash? Is this a sign of financial strength or weakness? (Challenge)

P1-56B (*Learning Objective 4, 5: Analyzing a company's financial statements*) Condensed versions of Mobile Phone Enterprises' financial statements follow for 2 recent years.

	20X6	20X5
Income Statement		
Revenues..	$ k	$88,400
Cost of goods sold....................................	74,500	a
Other expenses...	15,800	13,500
Income before income taxes	4,000	9,200
Income taxes (40% in 20X6)	l	1,500
Net income...	$ m	$ b
Statement of Retained Earnings		
Beginning balance	n	$ 9,900
Net income..	o	c
Dividends..	(500)	(400)
Ending balance...	$ p	$ d
Balance Sheet		
Assets:		
Cash...	$ q	$ e
Property, plant, and equipment..........	23,800	20,800
Other assets...	r	16,500
Total assets	$ s	$37,600
Liabilities:		
Current liabilities	$ t	$ 9,900
Long-term debt and other liabilities ...	11,300	10,100
Total liabilities..............................	22,700	f
Shareholders' Equity:		
Common stock.....................................	$ 200	$ 200
Retained earnings...............................	u	g
Other shareholders' equity	100	200
Total shareholders' equity	v	17,600
Total liabilities and shareholders' equity	$ w	$ h
Statement of Cash Flows		
Net cash provided by operating activities..............	$ x	$ 2,900
Net cash used for investing activities.......................	(3,300)	(3,700)
Net cash provided by financing activities	900	900
Increase (decrease) in cash............................	100	i
Cash at beginning of year.............................	y	200
Cash at end of year	$ z	$ j

HH CHAPTER 1

❚ Required

Complete Mobile Phone Enterprises' financial statements by determining the missing amounts denoted by the letters. (pp. 13–20)

APPLY YOUR KNOWLEDGE

Decision Cases

Case 1. *(Learning Objective 1, 2: Using financial statements to evaluate a loan request)*
Two businesses, Open Skies Corp., and Roadster, Inc., have sought business loans from you. To decide whether to make the loans, you have requested their balance sheets.

(continued)

Open Skies Corp.
Balance Sheet
August 31, 2005

Assets		Liabilities	
Cash......................................	$ 10,000	Accounts payable...............	$100,000
Accounts receivable..............	20,000	Notes payable	160,000
Furniture...............................	30,000	Total liabilities	260,000
Land.......................................	150,000	**Owners' Equity**	
Equipment.............................	90,000	Owners' equity...................	40,000
		Total liabilities and	
Total assets...........................	$300,000	owners' equity.................	$300,000

Roadster, Inc.
Balance Sheet
August 31, 2005

Assets		Liabilities	
Cash..	$ 10,000	Accounts payable....................	$ 12,000
Accounts receivable...................	20,000	Note payable............................	18,000
Merchandise inventory...............	30,000	Total liabilities	30,000
Building....................................	70,000	**Stockholders' Equity**	
		Stockholders' equity................	100,000
		Total liabilities and	
Total assets..............................	$130,000	stockholders' equity..............	$130,000

❙ Required

Using only these balance sheets, to which entity would you be more comfortable lending money? Explain fully, citing specific items and amounts from the respective balance sheets. (Challenge)

Case 2. *(Learning Objective 2, 4, 5: Analyzing a company as an investment)* A year out of college, you have $5,000 to invest. A friend has started Sweepstakes Unlimited, Inc., and she asks you to invest in her company. You obtain the company's financial statements, which are summarized at the end of the first year as follows:

Sweepstakes Unlimited, Inc.
Income Statement
Year Ended Dec. 31, 20X4

Revenues...................	$50,000
Expenses	40,000
Net income................	$10,000

Sweepstakes Unlimited, Inc.
Balance Sheet
Dec. 31, 20X4

Cash........................	$ 3,000	Liabilities	$30,000
Other assets.............	50,000	Equity......................	23,000
		Total liabilities	
Total assets..............	$53,000	and equity	$53,000

Visits with your friend turn up the following facts:
  a. Revenues and receivables of $20,000 were overlooked and omitted.

   b. Software costs of $25,000 were recorded as assets. These costs should have been expenses. Sweepstakes Unlimited paid cash for these expenses and recorded the cash payment correctly.

   c. The company owes an additional $5,000 for accounts payable.

I *Required*

1. Prepare corrected financial statements. (pp. 13–17)

2. Use your corrected statements to evaluate Sweepstakes Unlimited's results of operations and financial position. (Challenge)

3. Will you invest in Sweepstakes Unlimited? Give your reason. (Challenge)

Ethical Issue

During 2002, **Enron Corporation** admitted hiding large liabilities from its balance sheet. **WorldCom** confessed to recording expenses as assets. Both companies needed to improve their appearance as reported in their financial statements.

I *Required*

1. What is the fundamental ethical issue in these situations?

2. Use the accounting equation to show how Enron abused good accounting. Use a separate accounting equation to demonstrate WorldCom's error.

3. What can happen when companies report financial data that are untrue?

Focus on Financials: ■ YUM! Brands

(*Learning Objective 4: Identifying items from a company's financial statements*) This and similar cases in succeeding chapters are based on the financial statements of YUM! Brands, Inc. As you work with YUM! Brands throughout this course, you will develop the ability to use the financial statements of actual companies.

I *Required*

Refer to the YUM! Brands' financial statements in Appendix A at the end of the book.

1. Suppose you own stock in YUM. If you could pick 1 item on the company's income statement to increase year after year, what would it be? Why is this item so important? Did this item increase or decrease during 2006? Is this good news or bad news for the company? (pp. 14–15)

2. What was YUM's largest expense each year? In your own words, explain the meaning of this item. Give specific examples of items that make up this expense. The chapter gives another title for this expense. What is it? (pp. 14–15)

3. Use the balance sheet of YUM in Appendix A to answer these questions: At the end of 2006, how much in total resources did YUM have to work with? How much did the company owe? How much of its assets did the company's stockholders actually own? Use these amounts to write YUM's accounting equation at December 30, 2006. (pp. 14–15)

4. How much cash did YUM have at the beginning of the most recent year? How much cash did YUM have at the end of the year? (pp. 16–17)

Focus on Analysis: ■ Pier 1 Imports

(*Learning Objective 3, 4: Evaluating a leading company*) This and similar cases in each chapter are based on the financial statements of Pier 1 Imports, Inc., given in Appendix B at the end of this book. As you work with Pier 1, you will develop the ability to analyze the financial statements of actual companies.

❙ *Required*

1. Write Pier 1's accounting equation at the end of 2006 (express all items in millions and round to the nearest $1 million). Does Pier 1's financial condition look strong or weak? How can you tell? (pp. 10–11)

2. What was the result of Pier 1's operations during 2006? Identify both the name and the dollar amount of the result of operations for 2006. Does an increase (decrease) signal good news or bad news for the company and its stockholders? (pp. 15–16)

3. Examine retained earnings on the balance sheet and on the statement of stockholders' equity. What caused retained earnings to decrease during 2006? (pp. 15–16)

4. Which statement reports cash as part of Pier 1's financial position? Which statement tells *why* cash increased (or decreased) during the year? What 2 individual items caused Pier 1's cash to increase the most during 2006? (pp. 16–20)

Group Projects

Project 1. As instructed by your professor, obtain the annual report of a well-known company.

❙ *Required*

1. Take the role of a loan committee of Charter Bank, a large banking company headquartered in Charlotte, North Carolina. Assume the company has requested a loan from Charter Bank. Analyze the company's financial statements and any other information you need to reach a decision regarding the largest amount of money you would be willing to lend. Go as deeply into the analysis and the related decision as you can. Specify the following:
   a. The length of the loan period—that is, over what period will you allow the company to pay you back?
   b. The interest rate you will charge on the loan. Will you charge the prevailing interest rate, a lower rate, or a higher rate? Why?
   c. Any restrictions you will impose on the borrower as a condition for making the loan.

   Note: The long-term debt note to the financial statements gives details of the company's existing liabilities.

2. Write your group decision in a report addressed to the bank's board of directors. Limit your report to 2 double-spaced word-processed pages.

3. If your professor directs, present your decision and your analysis to the class. Limit your presentation to 10 to 15 minutes.

Project 2. You are the owner of a company that is about to "go public"—that is, issue its stock to outside investors. You wish to make your company look as attractive as possible to raise $1 million of cash to expand the business. At the same time, you want to give potential investors a realistic picture of your company.

❙ *Required*

1. Design a booklet to portray your company in a way that will enable outsiders to reach an informed decision as to whether to buy some of your stock. The booklet should include the following:
   a. Name and location of your company.
   b. Nature of the company's business (be as detailed as possible).
   c. How you plan to spend the money you raise.
   d. The company's comparative income statement, statement of retained earnings, balance sheet, and statement of cash flows for 2 years: the current year and the preceding year. Make the data as realistic as possible with the intent of receiving $1 million.

2. Word-process your booklet, not to exceed 5 pages.

3. If directed by your professor, make a copy for each member of your class. Distribute copies to the class and present your case with the intent of interesting your classmates in investing in the company. Limit your presentation to 10 to 15 minutes.

For Internet Exercises go to the Web site www.prenhall.com/harrison.

Quick Check Answers

1. *b*
2. *a*
3. *d*
4. *c*
5. *d*
6. *a*
7. *b* ($100,000 − $40,000 − $3,000 = $57,000)
8. *c* ($100,000 − $40,000 = $60,000)
9. *c Total assets = $105,000 ($5,000 + $30,000 + $20,000 + $50,000). Liabilities = $25,000.*
10. *d*
11. *d $30,000 + Net income ($15,000) − Dividends = $40,000; Dividends = $5,000*
12. *b*

	Assets		Liabilities		Equity
Beginning	$300,000	=	$200,000*	+	$100,000
Increase	50,000	=	40,000	+	10,000*
Ending	$350,000*	=	$240,000*	+	$110,000*

*Must solve for these amounts.

Demo Doc

The Accounting Equation and Financial Statement Preparation

Demo Doc: To make sure you understand this material, work through the following demonstration "Demo Doc" with detailed comments to help you see the concept within the framework of a worked-through problem.

Learning Objectives 3, 4, 5

David Richardson is the only shareholder of DR Painting Inc., a painting business near an historical housing district. At March 31, 2009, DR Painting had the following information:

Cash	$27,300
Accounts receivable	1,400
Supplies	1,800
Truck	20,000
Accounts payable	1,000
Common stock	40,000
Retained earnings (March 1)	5,000
Retained earnings (March 31)	?
Dividends	1,500
Service revenue	7,000
Salary expense	1,000

Requirements

1. **Prepare the income statement and statement of retained earnings for the month of March 2009 and the balance sheet of the business at March 31, 2009. Use Exhibits 1-7, 1-8, and 1-9 (pp. 14, 16, and 17) in the text as a guide.**

2. **Write the accounting equation of the business.**

Demo Doc Solutions

Requirement 1

Prepare the income statement, statement of retained earnings, and balance sheet of the business. Use Exhibits 1-7, 1-8, and 1-9 (pp. 14, 16, and 17) in the text as a guide.

Part 1	Part 2	Part 3	Part 4	Demo Doc Complete

Income Statement

The income statement is the first statement to prepare because the other financial statements rely upon the net income number calculated on the income statement.

The income statement reports the profitability of the business. To prepare an income statement, begin with the proper heading. A proper heading includes the name of the company (DR Painting, Inc.), the name of the statement (Income Statement), and the time period covered (Month Ended March 31, 2009). Notice that we are reporting income for a period of time, rather than at a single date.

The income statement lists all revenues and expenses. It uses the following formula to calculate net income:

$$\text{Revenues} - \text{Expenses} = \text{Net income}$$

First, you should list revenues. Second, list the expenses. After you have listed and totaled the revenues and expenses, subtract the total expenses from total revenues to determine net income or net loss. A positive number means you earned net income (revenues exceeded expenses). A negative number indicates that expenses exceeded revenues, and this is a net loss.

DR Painting's total Service Revenue for the month was $7,000. The only expense is Salary Expense of $1,000. On the income statement, these would be reported as follows:

DR PAINTING, INC.
Income Statement
Month Ended March 31, 2009

Revenue:		
Service revenue		$7,000
Expenses:		
Salary expense	$1,000	
Total expenses		1,000
Net income		$6,000

Note that the result is a net income of $6,000 ($7,000 − $1,000 = $6,000). You will also report net income on the statement of retained earnings, which comes next.

Statement of Retained Earnings

Part 1	Part 2	Part 3	Part 4	Demo Doc Complete

The statement of retained earnings shows the changes in Retained Earnings for a period of time. To prepare a statement of retained earnings, begin with the proper heading. A proper heading includes the name of the company (DR Painting, Inc.), the name of the statement (Statement of Retained Earnings), and the time period covered (Month Ended March 31, 2009). As with the income statement, we are reporting the changes in Retained Earnings for a period of time, rather than at a single date.

Net income is used on the statement of retained earnings to calculate the new balance in Retained Earnings. This calculation uses the following formula:

> Beginning Retained Earnings
> + Net Income (or – Net Loss)
> – Dividends
> = Ending Retained Earnings

Start the body of the statement of retained earnings with the Retained Earnings at the beginning of the period (March 1). Then list net income. Observe that the amount of net income comes directly from the income statement. Following net income you will list the dividends declared, which reduce Retained Earnings. Finally, total all amounts and compute the Retained Earnings at the end of the period.

The beginning Retained Earnings of $5,000 was given in the problem. Net income of $6,000 comes from the income statement and is added. Dividends of $1,500 amounts are deducted. On the statement of retained earnings, these amounts are reported as follows:

DR PAINTING, INC.
Statement of Retained Earnings
Month Ended March 31, 2009

Beginning retained earnings	$ 5,000
Add: Net income	6,000
	11,000
Less: Dividends	(1,500)
Retained earnings, March 31, 2009	$ 9,500

Note that Retained Earnings has a balance of $9,500 at March 31, 2009. You will also report Retained Earning's ending balance on the balance sheet, which you prepare last.

Balance Sheet

Part 1	Part 2	Part 3	Part 4	Demo Doc Complete

The balance sheet reports the financial position of the business at a moment in time. To prepare a balance sheet, begin with the proper heading. A proper heading includes the name of the company (DR Painting, Inc.), the name of the statement (Balance Sheet), and the time of the ending balances (March 31, 2009). Unlike the income statement and statement of retained earnings, we are reporting the financial position of the company at a specific date rather than for a period of time.

The balance sheet lists all assets, liabilities, and equity of the business, with the accounting equation verified at the bottom.

To prepare the body of the balance sheet, begin by listing assets. Then list all the liabilities and stockholders' equity. Notice that the balance sheet is organized in the same order as the accounting equation. The amount of Retained Earnings comes directly from the ending balance on your statement of retained earnings. You should then total both sides of the balance sheet to make sure that they are equal. If they are not equal, then you must correct an error.

In this case, assets accounts include cash of $27,300, accounts receivable of $1,400, $1,800 worth of supplies, and the truck, valued at $20,000. The only liability is accounts payable of $1,000. Stockholders' equity consists of common stock of $40,000, and the updated retained earnings of $9,500, from the statement of retained earnings.

DR PAINTING, INC.
Balance Sheet
March 31, 2009

Assets		Liabilities	
Cash	$27,300	Accounts payable	$ 1,000
Accounts receivable	1,400		
Supplies	1,800	**Stockholders' Equity**	
Truck	20,000	Common stock	40,000
		Retained earnings	9,500
		Total stockholders' equity	49,500
		Total liabilities and	
Total assets	$50,500	stockholders' equity	$50,500

Assets = Liabilities + Stockholders' Equity

Requirement 2

Write the accounting equation of the business
In this case, asset accounts total $50,500. Liabilities total $1,000—the balance of Accounts Payable, and stockholder's equity is $49,500. This gives us a total for liabilities and equity of $50,500 ($1,000 + $49,500).

The accounting equation is:

Assets of $50,500 = Liabilities of $1,000 + Stockholders' Equity of $49,500

Part 1	Part 2	Part 3	Part 4	Demo Doc Complete

This page intentionally left blank

2 Transaction Analysis

SPOTLIGHT

APPLE COMPUTER, INC.

How do you manage your music library? You may use **Apple Computer's iTunes®**, which along with the company's iPods® generates lots of income for the company.

How does Apple determine the amount of its revenues, expenses, and net income? Like all other companies, Apple Computer has a comprehensive accounting system. Apple's income statement (statement of operations) is given at the start of this chapter. The income statement shows that during fiscal year 2006, Apple made over $19 billion of sales and earned net income of $2 billion. Where did those figures come from? In this chapter, we'll show you.

Apple Computer, Inc.
Statement of Operations (Adapted)
Fiscal Year Ended September 30, 2006

(In billions)	2006
Net sales..	$19.3
Cost of goods sold..	13.7
Gross profit...	5.6
Operating expenses:	
Research and development expense............................	0.7
Selling, general, and administrative expense..............	2.4
Total operating expenses..	3.1
Operating income (loss)...	2.5
Other income...	0.3
Income before income taxes.....................................	2.8
Income tax expense..	0.8
Net income..	$ 2.0

Chapter 1 introduced the financial statements. Chapter 2 will show you how companies actually record the transactions that eventually become part of the financial statements.

LEARNING OBJECTIVES

1 **Analyze** transactions

2 **Understand** how accounting works

3 **Record** transactions in the journal

4 **Use** a trial balance

5 **Analyze** transactions using only T-accounts

For more practice and review of accounting cycle concepts, use ACT, the Accounting Cycle Tutorial, online at www.prenhall.com/harrison. Margin logos like this one, directing you to the appropriate ACT section and material, appear throughout Chapters 1, 2, and 3. When you enter the tutorial, you'll find three buttons on the opening page of each chapter module. Here's what the buttons mean: **Tutorial** gives you a review of the major concepts, **Application** gives you practice exercises, and **Glossary** reviews important terms.

TRANSACTIONS

Business activity is all about transactions. A **transaction** is any event that has a financial impact on the business and can be measured reliably. For example, Apple Computer pays programmers to create iTunes® software. Apple sells computers, borrows money, and repays the loan—three separate transactions.

But not all events qualify as transactions. iTunes® may be featured in *Showtime Magazine* and motivate you to buy an Apple iPod. The magazine article may create lots of new business for Apple. But no transaction occurs until someone actually buys an Apple product. A transaction must occur before Apple records anything.

Transactions provide objective information about the financial impact on a company. Every transaction has two sides:

- You give something, and
- You receive something

In accounting we always record both sides of a transaction. And we must be able to measure the financial impact of the event on the business before recording it as a transaction.

THE ACCOUNT

As we saw in Chapter 1, the accounting equation expresses the basic relationships of accounting:

$$\text{Assets} = \text{Liabilities} + \text{Stockholders' (Owners') Equity}$$

For each asset, each liability, and each element of stockholders' equity, we use a record called the account. An **account** is the record of all the changes in a particular asset, liability, or stockholders' equity during a period. The account is the basic summary device of accounting. Before launching into transaction analysis, let's review the accounts that a company such as Apple Computer uses.

Assets

Assets are economic resources that provide a future benefit for a business. Most firms use the following asset accounts:

Cash. **Cash** means money and any medium of exchange including bank account balances, paper currency, coins, certificates of deposit, and checks.

Accounts Receivable. Apple Computer, like most other companies, sells its goods and services and receives a promise for future collection of cash. The Accounts Receivable account holds these amounts.

Notes Receivable. Apple may receive a note receivable from a customer, who signed the note promising to pay Apple Computer. A note receivable is similar to an account receivable, but a note receivable is more binding because the customer signed the note. Notes receivable usually specify an interest rate.

Inventory. Apple Computer's most important asset is its inventory—the hardware and software Apple sells to customers. Other titles for this account include *Merchandise* and *Merchandise Inventory*.

Prepaid Expenses. Apple Computer pays certain expenses in advance, such as insurance and rent. A **prepaid expense** is an asset because the payment provides a *future* benefit for the business. Prepaid Rent, Prepaid Insurance, and Supplies are prepaid expenses.

Land. The Land account shows the cost of the land Apple uses in its operations.

Buildings. The costs of Apple's office building, manufacturing plant, and the like appear in the Buildings account.

Equipment, Furniture, and Fixtures. Apple has a separate asset account for each type of equipment, for example, Manufacturing Equipment and Office Equipment. The Furniture and Fixtures account shows the cost of these assets, which are similar to equipment.

Liabilities

Recall that a *liability* is a debt. A payable is always a liability. The most common types of liabilities include:

Accounts Payable. The Accounts Payable account is the direct opposite of Accounts Receivable. Apple's promise to pay a debt arising from a credit purchase of inventory or from a utility bill appears in the Accounts Payable account.

Notes Payable. A note payable is the opposite of a note receivable. The Notes Payable account includes the amounts Apple must *pay* because Apple signed notes promising to pay a future amount. Notes payable, like notes receivable, also carry interest.

Accrued Liabilities. An **accrued liability** is a liability for an expense you have not yet paid. Interest Payable and Salary Payable are accrued liability accounts for most companies. Income Tax Payable is another accrued liability.

Stockholders' (Owners') Equity

The owners' claims to the assets of a corporation are called *stockholders' equity*, *shareholders' equity*, or simply *owners' equity*. A corporation such as Apple Computer uses Common Stock, Retained Earnings, and Dividends accounts to record changes in the company's stockholders' equity. In a proprietorship, there is a single capital account. For a partnership, each partner has a separate owner equity account.

Common Stock. The Common Stock account shows the owners' investment in the corporation. Apple Computer receives cash and issues common stock to its stockholders. A company's common stock is its most basic element of equity. All corporations have common stock.

STOP & think. . .

Name two things that (1) increase Apple Computer's stockholders' equity and (2) decrease Apple's stockholders' equity.

Answer:

(1) Increases in equity: Sale of stock and net income (revenue greater than expenses).

(2) Decreases in equity: Dividends and net loss (expenses greater than revenue).

Retained Earnings. The Retained Earnings account shows the cumulative net income earned by Apple Computer over the company's lifetime, minus its cumulative net losses and dividends.

Dividends. After profitable operations, the board of directors of Apple Computer may (or may not) declare and pay a cash dividend. Dividends are optional; they are decided by the board of directors. The corporation may keep a separate account titled *Dividends*, which indicates a decrease in Retained Earnings.

Revenues. The increase in stockholders' equity from delivering goods or services to customers is called *revenue*. The company uses as many revenue accounts as needed. Apple Computer uses a Sales Revenue account for revenue earned by selling its products. Apple has a Service Revenue account for the revenue it earns by providing services to customers. A lawyer provides legal services for clients and also uses a Service Revenue account. A business that loans money to an outsider needs an Interest Revenue account. If the business rents a building to a tenant, the business needs a Rent Revenue account.

Expenses. The cost of operating a business is called *expense*. Expenses *decrease* stockholders' equity, the opposite effect of revenues. A business needs a separate account for each type of expense, such as Cost of Goods Sold, Salary Expense, Rent Expense, Advertising Expense, Insurance Expense, Utilities Expense, and Income Tax Expense. Businesses strive to minimize expenses and thereby maximize net income.

ACCOUNTING FOR BUSINESS TRANSACTIONS

Example: Genie Car Wash, Inc.

To illustrate the accounting for transactions, let's return to Genie Car Wash, Inc. In Chapter 1's End-of-Chapter Problem, Van Gray opened Genie Car Wash, Inc., in April 20X9.

OBJECTIVE

1 **Analyze** transactions

We consider 11 events and analyze each in terms of its effect on Genie Car Wash. We begin by using the accounting equation. In the second half of the chapter, we record transactions using the journal and ledger of accounting.

Transaction 1. Gray and a few friends invest $50,000 to begin Genie Car Wash and the business issues common stock to the stockholders. The effect of this transaction on the accounting equation of Genie Car Wash, Inc., is a receipt of cash and issuance of common stock, as follows:

Assets		Liabilities	+	Stockholders' Equity	Type of Stockholders' Equity Transaction
Cash	=			Common Stock	
(1) + 50,000				+ 50,000	Issued stock

Every transaction's net amount on the left side of the equation must equal the net amount on the right side. The first transaction increases both the cash and the common stock of the business. To the right of the transaction we write "Issued stock" to show the reason for the increase in stockholders' equity.

Every transaction affects the financial statements of the business, and we can prepare financial statements after 1, 2, or any number of transactions. For example, Genie Car Wash could report the company's balance sheet after its first transaction, shown here.

Genie Car Wash, INC
Balance Sheet
April 1, 20X9

Assets			Liabilities	
Cash..........................	$50,000		None	
			Stockholders' Equity	
			Common stock...............................	$50,000
			Total stockholders' equity............	50,000
			Total liabilities and	
Total assets................	$50,000		stockholders' equity....................	$50,000

This balance sheet shows that the business holds cash of $50,000 and owes no liabilities. The company's equity (ownership) is denoted as *Common Stock* on the balance sheet. A bank would look favorably on this balance sheet because the business has $50,000 cash and no debt—a strong financial position.

As a practical matter, most entities report their financial statements at the end of the accounting period—not after each transaction. But an accounting system can produce statements whenever managers need to know where the business stands.

Transaction 2. Genie purchases land for a new location and pays cash of $40,000. The effect of this transaction on the accounting equation is:

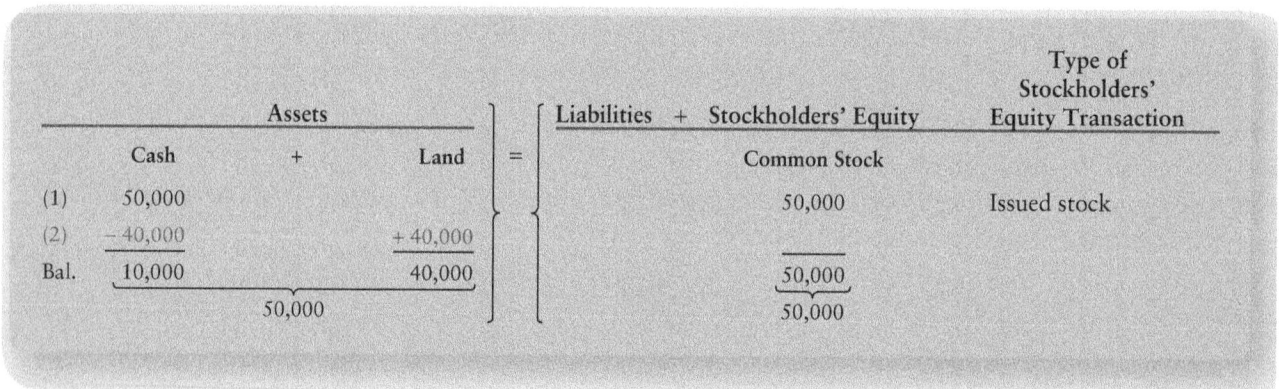

	Assets			=	Liabilities +	Stockholders' Equity	Type of Stockholders' Equity Transaction
	Cash	+	Land	=		Common Stock	
(1)	50,000					50,000	Issued stock
(2)	−40,000		+40,000				
Bal.	10,000		40,000			50,000	
		50,000				50,000	

The purchase increases one asset (Land) and decreases another asset (Cash) by the same amount. After the transaction is completed, Genie has cash of $10,000, land of $40,000 and no liabilities. Stockholders' equity is unchanged at $50,000. Note that total assets must always equal total liabilities plus equity.

Transaction 3. The business buys supplies on account, agreeing to pay $3,700 within 30 days. This transaction increases both the assets and the liabilities of the business. Its effect on the accounting equation follows.

	Assets						Liabilities	+	Stockholders' Equity
	Cash	+	Supplies	+	Land		Accounts Payable	+	Common Stock
Bal.	10,000				40,000				50,000
(3)			+ 3,700			=	+ 3,700		
Bal.	10,000		3,700		40,000		3,700		50,000
			53,700					53,700	

The new asset is Supplies, and the liability is an Account Payable. Genie signs no formal promissory note, so the liability is an account payable, not a note payable.

Transaction 4. Genie earns $7,000 of service revenue by providing services for customers. The business collects the cash. The effect on the accounting equation is an increase in the asset Cash and an increase in Retained Earnings, as follows:

	Assets						Liabilities	+	Stockholders' Equity				Type of Stockholders' Equity Transaction
	Cash	+	Supplies	+	Land		Accounts Payable	+	Common Stock	+	Retained Earnings		
Bal.	10,000		3,700		40,000	=	3,700		50,000				
(4)	+ 7,000										+ 7,000		Service revenue
Bal.	17,000		3,700		40,000		3,700		50,000		7,000		
			60,700					60,700					

To the right we record "Service revenue" to show where the $7,000 of increase in Retained Earnings came from.

Transaction 5. Genie performs service on account, which means that Genie lets some customers pay later. Genie earns revenue but doesn't receive the cash immediately. In transaction 5, Genie cleans a fleet of UPS delivery trucks, and UPS promises to pay Genie $3,000 within 1 month. This promise is an account receivable—an asset—of Genie Car Wash. The transaction record follows.

	Assets							Liabilities	+	Stockholders' Equity				Type of Stockholders' Equity Transaction
	Cash	+	Accounts Receivable	+	Supplies	+	Land	Accounts Payable	+	Common Stock	+	Retained Earnings		
Bal.	17,000		3,000		3,700		40,000	=	3,700		50,000	7,000		
(5)			+ 3,000									+ 3,000		Service revenue
Bal.	17,000		3,000		3,700		40,000		3,700		50,000	10,000		
			63,700							63,700				

It's performing the service that earns the revenue—not collecting the cash. Therefore, Genie records revenue when it performs the service—regardless of whether Genie receives cash now or later.

Transaction 6. During the month, Genie Car Wash pays $2,700 for the following expenses: equipment rent, $1,100; employee salaries, $1,200; and utilities, $400. The effect on the accounting equation is:

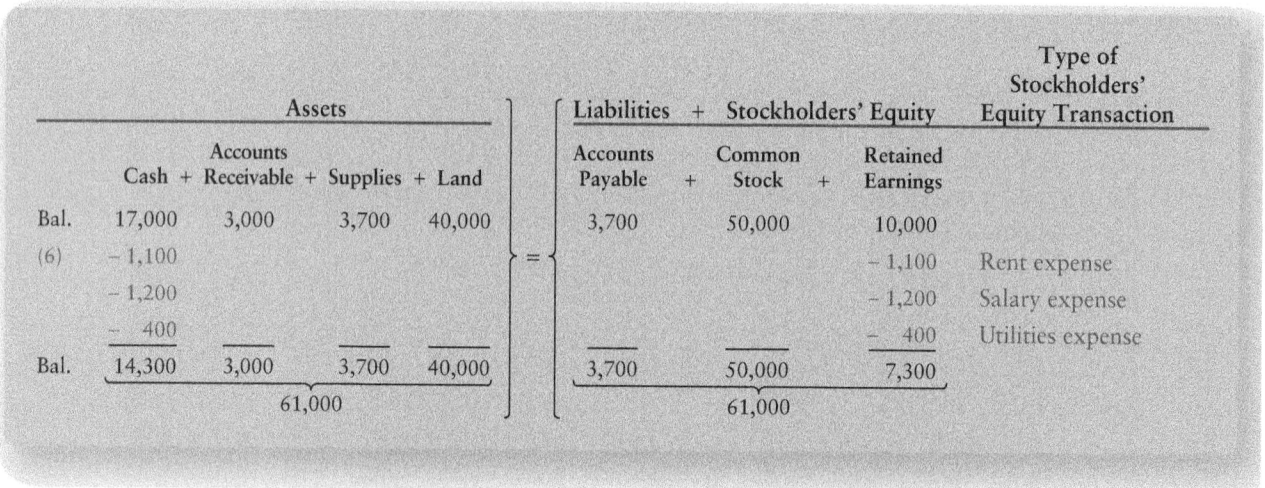

	Assets					Liabilities	+	Stockholders' Equity			Type of Stockholders' Equity Transaction
	Cash	+ Accounts Receivable	+ Supplies	+ Land		Accounts Payable	+	Common Stock	+	Retained Earnings	
Bal.	17,000	3,000	3,700	40,000	=	3,700		50,000		10,000	
(6)	− 1,100									− 1,100	Rent expense
	− 1,200									− 1,200	Salary expense
	− 400									− 400	Utilities expense
Bal.	14,300	3,000	3,700	40,000		3,700		50,000		7,300	
			61,000					61,000			

The expenses decrease Genie's Cash and Retained Earnings. List each expense separately to keep track of its amount.

Transaction 7. Genie pays $1,900 on account, which means to pay off an account payable. In this transaction Genie pays the store from which it purchased supplies in transaction 3. The transaction decreases Cash and also decreases Accounts Payable as follows:

	Assets									Liabilities	+	Stockholders' Equity		
	Cash	+	Accounts Receivable	+	Supplies	+	Land		=	Accounts Payable	+	Common Stock	+	Retained Earnings
Bal.	14,300		3,000		3,700		40,000			3,700		50,000		7,300
(7)	− 1,900									− 1,900				
Bal.	12,400		3,000		3,700		40,000			1,800		50,000		7,300
				59,100								59,100		

Transaction 8. Van Gray, the major stockholder of Genie Car Wash, paid $30,000 to remodel his home. This event is a personal transaction of the Gray family. It is not recorded by the Genie Car Wash business. We focus solely on the business entity, not on its owners. This transaction illustrates the entity concept from Chapter 1.

Transaction 9. In transaction 5, Genie performed services for UPS on account. The business now collects $1,000 from UPS. We say that Genie *collects the cash on* *account*, which means that Genie will record an increase in Cash and a decrease in Accounts Receivable. This is not service revenue because Genie already recorded the revenue in transaction 5. The effect of collecting cash on account is:

	Assets						Liabilities	+	Stockholders' Equity		
	Cash	+	Accounts Receivable	+	Supplies	+	Land	Accounts Payable	+	Common Stock	+	Retained Earnings
Bal.	12,400		3,000		3,700		40,000	=	1,800		50,000		7,300
(9)	+ 1,000		− 1,000									
Bal.	13,400		2,000		3,700		40,000		1,800		50,000		7,300
				59,100						59,100		

Transaction 10. Genie sells some land for $22,000, which is the same amount that Genie paid for the land. Genie receives $22,000 cash, and the effect on the accounting equation is:

	Assets						Liabilities	+	Stockholders' Equity		
	Cash	+	Accounts Receivable	+	Supplies	+	Land	Accounts Payable	+	Common Stock	+	Retained Earnings
Bal.	13,400		2,000		3,700		40,000	=	1,800		50,000		7,300
(10)	+ 22,000						− 22,000					
Bal.	35,400		2,000		3,700		18,000		1,800		50,000		7,300
				59,100						59,100		

Note that the company did not sell all its land; Genie still owns $18,000 worth of land.

Transaction 11. Genie Car Wash declares a dividend and pays the stockholders $2,100 cash. The effect on the accounting equation is:

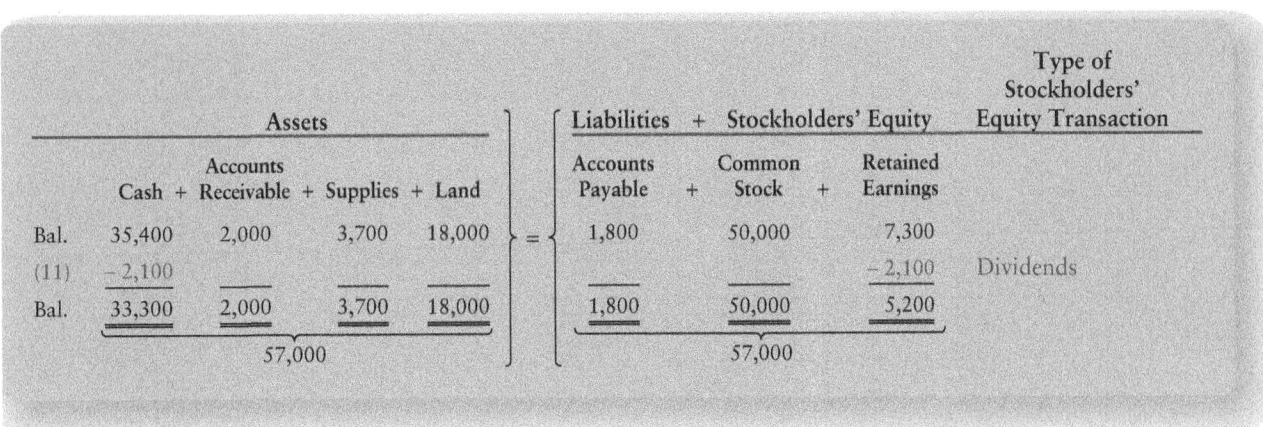

	Assets				Liabilities	+	Stockholders' Equity		Type of Stockholders' Equity Transaction
	Cash +	Accounts Receivable +	Supplies +	Land	Accounts Payable	+	Common Stock +	Retained Earnings	
Bal.	35,400	2,000	3,700	18,000	=	1,800	50,000	7,300	
(11)	− 2,100							− 2,100	Dividends
Bal.	33,300	2,000	3,700	18,000		1,800	50,000	5,200	
			57,000				57,000		

The dividend decreases both the Cash and the Retained Earnings of the business. *But dividends are not an expense.*

Transactions and Financial Statements

Exhibit 2-1 summarizes the 11 preceding transactions. Panel A gives the details of the transactions, and Panel B shows the transaction analysis. As you study the exhibit, note that every transaction maintains the equality:

$$\text{Assets} = \text{Liabilities} + \text{Stockholders' Equity}$$

Exhibit 2-1 provides the data for Genie Car Wash's financial statements:

EXHIBIT 2-1 Transaction Analysis: Genie Car Wash, Inc.

PANEL A—Transaction Details

(1) Received $50,000 cash and issued stock to the owners
(2) Paid $40,000 cash for land
(3) Bought $3,700 of supplies on account
(4) Received $7,000 cash from customers for service revenue earned
(5) Performed services for a customer on account, $3,000
(6) Paid cash expenses: rent, $1,100; employee salary, $1,200; utilities, $400

(7) Paid $1,900 on the account payable created in transaction 3
(8) Major stockholder paid personal funds to remodel home, *not* a transaction of the business
(9) Received $1,000 on account
(10) Sold land for cash at the land's cost of $22,000
(11) Declared and paid a dividend of $2,100 to the stockholders

PANEL B—Transaction Analysis

		Assets			=	Liabilities	+	Stockholders' Equity		Type of Stockholders' Equity Transaction
	Cash	Accounts Receivable	Supplies	Land		Accounts Payable	Common Stock	Retained Earnings		
(1)	50,000						50,000			Issued stock
(2)	− 40,000			+ 40,000						
(3)			+ 3,700			+ 3,700				
(4)	+ 7,000							+7,000		Service revenue
(5)		+ 3,000						+ 3,000		Service revenue
(6)	− 1,100							− 1,100		Rent expense
	− 1,200							− 1,200		Salary expense
	− 400							− 400		Utilities expense
(7)	− 1,900					− 1,900				
(9)	+ 1,000	− 1,000								
(10)	+ 22,000			− 22,000						
(11)	− 2,100							− 2,100		Dividends
Bal.	33,300	2,000	3,700	18,000		1,800	50,000	5,200		
			57,000					57,000		

Statement of Cash Flows Data (left bracket)

Income Statement Data (right bracket for transactions 4–6)

Statement of Retained Earnings Data (right bracket for transaction 11)

Balance Sheet Data

- *Income statement* data appear as revenues and expenses under Retained Earnings. The revenues increase retained earnings; the expenses decrease retained earnings.
- The *balance sheet* data are composed of the ending balances of the assets, liabilities, and stockholders' equities shown at the bottom of the exhibit. The accounting equation shows that total assets ($57,000) equal total liabilities plus stockholders' equity ($57,000).
- The *statement of retained earnings* repeats net income (or net loss) from the income statement. Dividends are subtracted. Ending retained earnings is the final result.
- Data for the *statement of cash flows* are aligned under the Cash account. Cash receipts increase cash, and cash payments decrease cash.

Exhibit 2-2 shows the Genie Car Wash financial statements at the end of April, the company's first month of operations. Follow the flow of data to observe the following:

1. The income statement reports revenues, expenses, and either a net income or a net loss for the period. During April, Genie earned net income of $7,300. Compare Genie's income statement with that of Apple Computer at the beginning of the chapter. The income statement includes only 2 types of accounts: revenues and expenses.

2. The statement of retained earnings starts with the beginning balance of retained earnings, (zero for a new business). Add net income for the period (arrow ①), subtract dividends, and compute the ending balance of retained earnings ($5,200).

3. The balance sheet lists the assets, liabilities, and stockholders' equity of the business at the end of the period. Included in stockholders' equity is retained earnings, which comes from the statement of retained earnings (arrow ②).

HH CHAPTER 2

Let's put into practice what you have learned thus far.

EXHIBIT 2-2   Financial Statements of Genie Car Wash, Inc.

Genie Car Wash, Inc.
Income Statement
Month Ended April 30, 20X9

Revenues		
Service revenue ($7,000 + $3,000)		$10,000
Expenses		
Salary expense...	$1,200	
Rent expense	1,100	
Utilities expense	400	
Total expenses...		2,700
Net income...		$ 7,300

Genie Car Wash, Inc.
Statement of Retained Earnings
Month Ended April 30, 20X9

Retained earnings, April 1, 20X9.................	$ 0	
Add: Net income for the month	7,300	
	7,300	
Less: Dividends	(2,100)	
Retained earnings, April 30, 20X9...............	$5,200	

①

Genie Car Wash, Inc.
Balance Sheet
April 30, 20X9

Assets		Liabilities	
Cash..	$33,300	Accounts payable	$ 1,800
Accounts receivable...............	2,000	**Stockholders' Equity**	
Supplies..................................	3,700	Common stock................................	50,000
Land..	18,000	Retained earnings..........................	5,200
		Total stockholders' equity.............	55,200
Total assets.............................		Total liabilities and	
	$57,000	stockholders' equity.....................	$57,000

②

MID-CHAPTER SUMMARY PROBLEM

Shelly Herzog opens a research service near a college campus. She names the corporation Herzog Researchers, Inc. During the first month of operations, July 20X3, the business engages in the following transactions:

a. Herzog Researchers, Inc., issues its common stock to Shelly Herzog, who invests $25,000 to open the business.
b. The company purchases on account office supplies costing $350.
c. Herzog Researchers pays cash of $20,000 to acquire a lot next to the campus. The company intends to use the land as a building site for a business office.
d. Herzog Researchers performs research for clients and receives cash of $1,900.
e. Herzog Researchers pays $100 on the account payable it created in transaction b.
f. Herzog pays $2,000 of personal funds for a vacation.
g. Herzog Researchers pays cash expenses for office rent ($400) and utilities ($100).
h. The business sells a small parcel of the land for its cost of $5,000.
i. The business declares and pays a cash dividend of $1,200.

I Required

1. Analyze the preceding transactions in terms of their effects on the accounting equation of Herzog Researchers, Inc. Use Exhibit 2-1, Panel B as a guide.
2. Prepare the income statement, statement of retained earnings, and balance sheet of Herzog Researchers, Inc., after recording the transactions. Draw arrows linking the statements.

Solutions
I Requirement 1

PANEL B—Analysis of Transactions

	Assets			=	Liabilities	+	Stockholders' Equity		Type of Stockholders' Equity Transaction
	Cash	+ Office Supplies	+ Land		Accounts Payable	+ Common Stock	+ Retained Earnings		
(a)	+ 25,000					+ 25,000			Issued stock
(b)		+ 350			+ 350				
(c)	− 20,000		+ 20,000						
(d)	+ 1,900						+ 1,900		Service revenue
(e)	− 100				− 100				
(f)	Not a transaction of the business								
(g)	− 400						− 400		Rent expense
	− 100						− 100		Utilities expense
(h)	+ 5,000		− 5,000						
(i)	− 1,200						− 1,200		Dividends
Bal.	10,100	350	15,000		250	25,000	200		
		25,450					25,450		

Herzog Researchers, Inc.
Income Statement
Month Ended July 31, 20X3

Revenues		
Service revenue..................		$1,900
Expenses		
Rent expense....................	$400	
Utilities expense	100	
Total expenses.................		500
Net income.............................		$1,400

Herzog Researchers, Inc.
Statement of Retained Earnings
Month Ended July 31, 20X3

Retained earnings, July 1, 20X3.................	$ 0
Add: Net income for the month	1,400
	1,400
Less: Dividends	(1,200)
Retained earnings, July 31, 20X3..............	$ 200

Herzog Researchers, Inc.
Balance Sheet
July 31, 20X3

Assets		**Liabilities**	
Cash...............................	$10,100	Accounts payable	$ 250
Office supplies...............	350	**Stockholders' Equity**	
Land..............................	15,000	Common stock...............................	25,000
		Retained earnings............................	200
		Total stockholders' equity.............	25,200
		Total liabilities and	
Total assets....................	$25,450	stockholders' equity.....................	$25,450

The analysis in the first half of this chapter can be used, but it is cumbersome. Apple Computer has hundreds of accounts and millions of transactions. The spreadsheet to account for Apple's transactions would be huge! In the second half of this chapter we discuss double-entry accounting as it is actually used in business.

Double-Entry Accounting

All business transactions include 2 parts:

- You give something.
- You receive something.

Accounting is, therefore, based on a double-entry system, which records the *dual effects* on the entity. *Each transaction affects at least two accounts.* For example, Genie Car Wash's receipt of $50,000 cash and issuance of stock increased both Cash and Common Stock. It would be incomplete to record only the increase in Cash or only the increase in Common Stock.

The T-Account

An account can be represented by the letter T. We call them *T-accounts*. The vertical line in the letter divides the account into its two sides: left and right. The account title appears at the top of the T. For example, the Cash account can appear as follows:

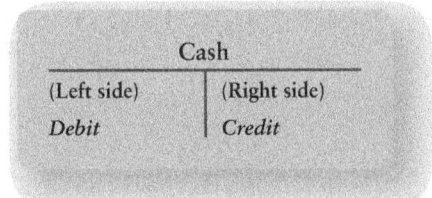

The left side of each account is called the **debit** side, and the right side is called the **credit** side. Often, students are confused by the words *debit* and *credit*. To become comfortable using these terms, remember that for every account

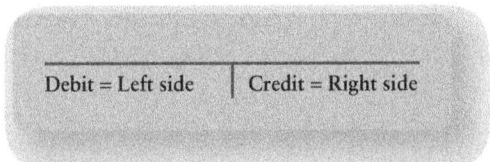

Every business transaction involves both a debit and a credit. The debit side of an account shows what you received. The credit side shows what you gave.

Increases and Decreases in the Accounts: The Rules of Debit and Credit

The type of account determines how we record increases and decreases. *The rules of debit and credit follow* in Exhibit 2-3.

- Increases in *assets* are recorded on the left (debit) side of the account. Decreases in *assets* are recorded on the right (credit) side. You receive cash and debit the Cash account. You pay cash and credit the Cash account.
- Conversely, increases in *liabilities* and *stockholders' equity* are recorded by credits. Decreases in *liabilities* and *stockholders' equity* are recorded by debits.

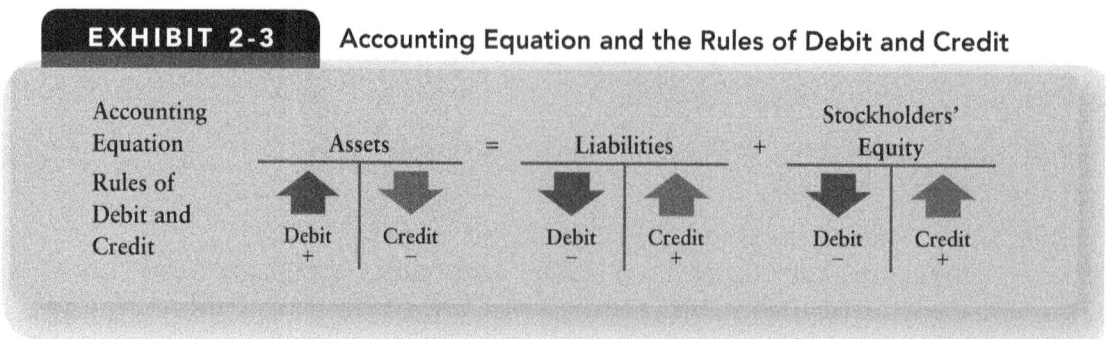

EXHIBIT 2-3 Accounting Equation and the Rules of Debit and Credit

To illustrate the ideas diagrammed in Exhibit 2-3, let's review the first transaction. Genie Car Wash received $50,000 and issued (gave) stock. Which accounts are affected? The Cash account and the Common Stock account will hold these amounts:

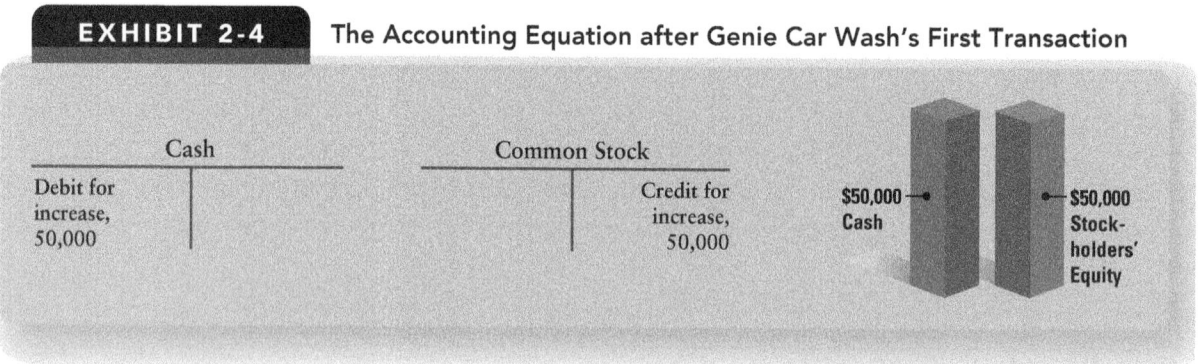

EXHIBIT 2-4 The Accounting Equation after Genie Car Wash's First Transaction

The amount remaining in an account is called its *balance*. This first transaction gives Cash a $50,000 debit balance and Common Stock a $50,000 credit balance. Exhibit 2-4 shows this relationship.

Genie's second transaction is a $40,000 cash purchase of land. This transaction decreases Cash with a credit and increases Land with a debit, as shown in the following T-accounts (focus on Cash and Land):

	Cash				Common Stock	
Bal.	50,000	Credit for decrease, 40,000			Bal.	50,000
Bal.	10,000					

	Land	
Debit for increase, 40,000		
Bal.	40,000	

After this transaction, Cash has a $10,000 debit balance, Land has a debit balance of $40,000, and Common Stock has a $50,000 credit balance, as shown in Exhibit 2-5.

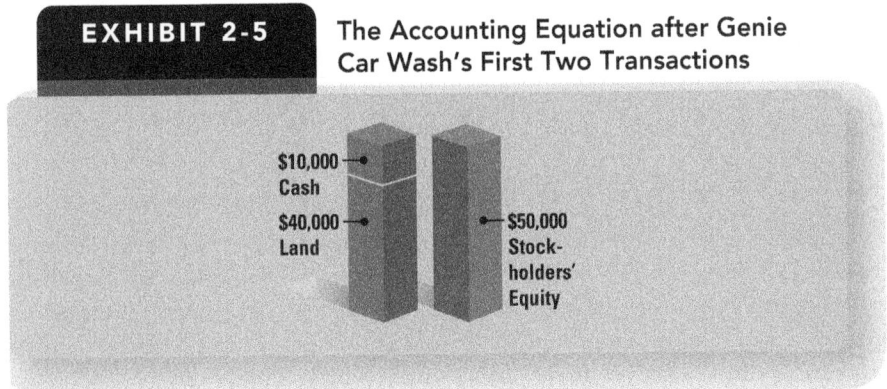

EXHIBIT 2-5 The Accounting Equation after Genie Car Wash's First Two Transactions

Additional Stockholders' Equity Accounts: Revenues and Expenses

Stockholders' equity also includes the two categories of income statement accounts, Revenues and Expenses:

- *Revenues* are increases in stockholders' equity that result from delivering goods or services to customers.
- *Expenses* are decreases in stockholders' equity due to the cost of operating the business.

Therefore, the accounting equation may be expanded as shown in Exhibit 2-6. Revenues and expenses appear in parentheses because their net effect—revenues minus expenses—equals net income, which increases stockholders' equity. If expenses exceed revenues, there is a net loss, which decreases stockholders' equity.

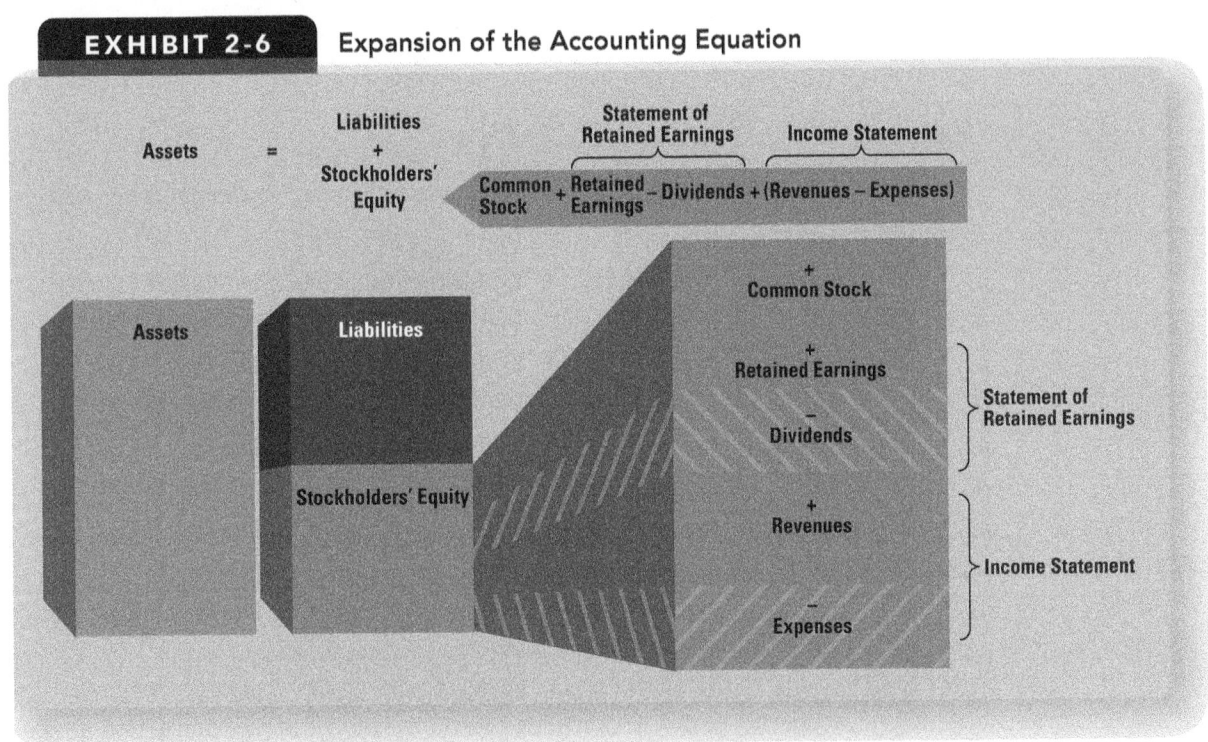

EXHIBIT 2-6 Expansion of the Accounting Equation

We can now express the final form of the rules of debit and credit, as shown in Exhibit 2-7. *You should not proceed until you have learned these rules.* For example, you must remember that

- A debit increases an asset account.
- A credit decreases an asset.

Liabilities and stockholders' equity are the opposite.

- A credit increases a liability account.
- A debit decreases a liability.

Dividends and Expense accounts are exceptions to the rule. Dividends and Expenses are equity accounts that are increased by a debit. Dividends and Expense accounts are negative (or *contra*) equity accounts.

Revenues and Expenses are often treated as separate account categories because they appear on the income statement. Exhibit 2-7 shows Revenues and Expenses below the other equity accounts.

EXHIBIT 2-7   **Final Form of the Rules of Debit and Credit**

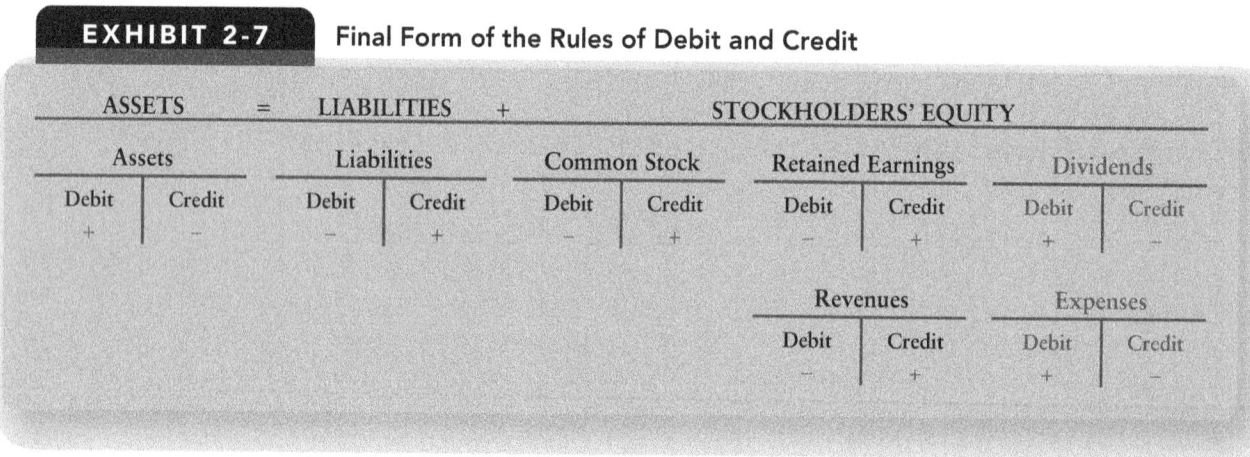

RECORDING TRANSACTIONS

OBJECTIVE

3 **Record** transactions in the journal

Accountants use a chronological record of transactions called a **journal**. The journalizing process follows three steps:

1. Specify each account affected by the transaction and classify each account by type (asset, liability, stockholders' equity, revenue, or expense).

2. Determine whether each account is increased or decreased by the transaction. Use the rules of debit and credit to increase or decrease each account.

3. Record the transaction in the journal, including a brief explanation. The debit side is entered on the left margin, and the credit side is indented to the right.

Step 3 is also called "making the journal entry" or "journalizing the transaction." Let's apply the steps to journalize the first transaction of Genie Car Wash.

    Step 1   The business receives cash and issues stock. Cash and Common Stock are affected. Cash is an asset, and Common Stock is equity.

    Step 2   Both Cash and Common Stock increase. Debit Cash to record an increase in this asset. Credit Common Stock to record an increase in this equity account.

Step 3 Journalize the transaction as follows:

JOURNAL

Date	Accounts and Explanation	Debit	Credit
Apr. 2	Cash	50,000	
	Common Stock		50,000
	Issued common stock.		

When analyzing a transaction, first pinpoint the effects (if any) on cash. Did cash increase or decrease? Typically, it is easiest to identify cash effects. Then identify the effects on the other accounts.

Copying Information (Posting) from the Journal to the Ledger

The journal is a chronological record of all company transactions listed by date. But the journal does not indicate how much cash or accounts receivable the business has.

The **ledger** is a grouping of all the T-accounts, with their balances. For example, the balance of the Cash T-account shows how much cash the business has. The balance of Accounts Receivable shows the amount due from customers. Accounts Payable shows how much the business owes suppliers on open account, and so on.

In the phrase "keeping the books," *books* refers to the accounts in the ledger. In most accounting systems, the ledger is computerized. Exhibit 2-8 shows how the asset, liability, and stockholders' equity accounts are grouped in the ledger.

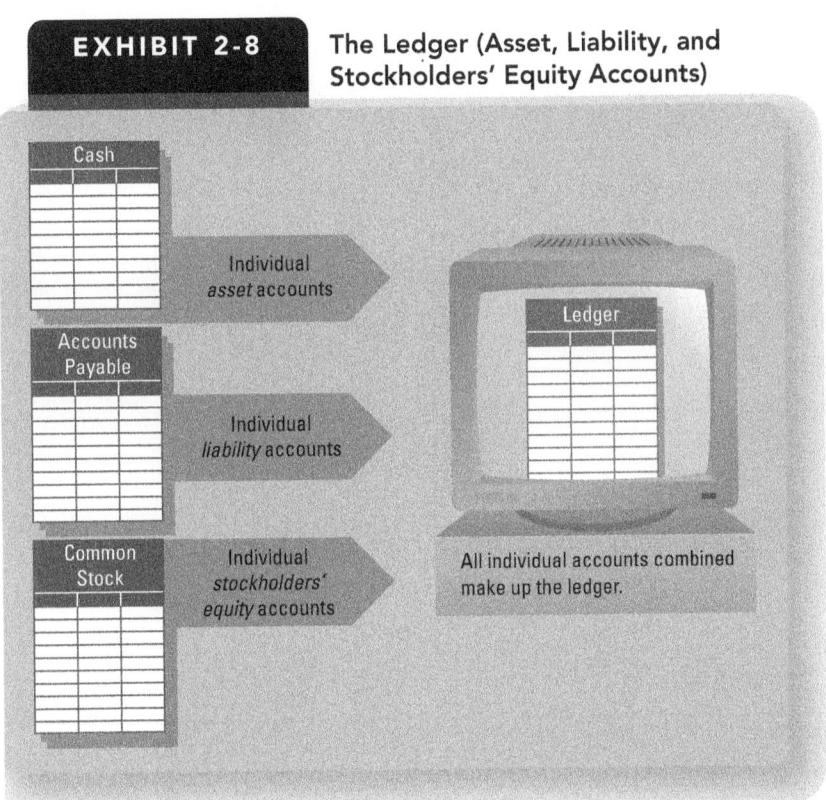

EXHIBIT 2-8 The Ledger (Asset, Liability, and Stockholders' Equity Accounts)

Entering a transaction in the journal does not get the data into the ledger. Data must be copied to the ledger—a process called **posting**. Debits in the journal are always posted as debits in the accounts, and likewise for credits. Exhibit 2-9 shows how Genie Car Wash's stock issuance transaction is posted to the accounts.

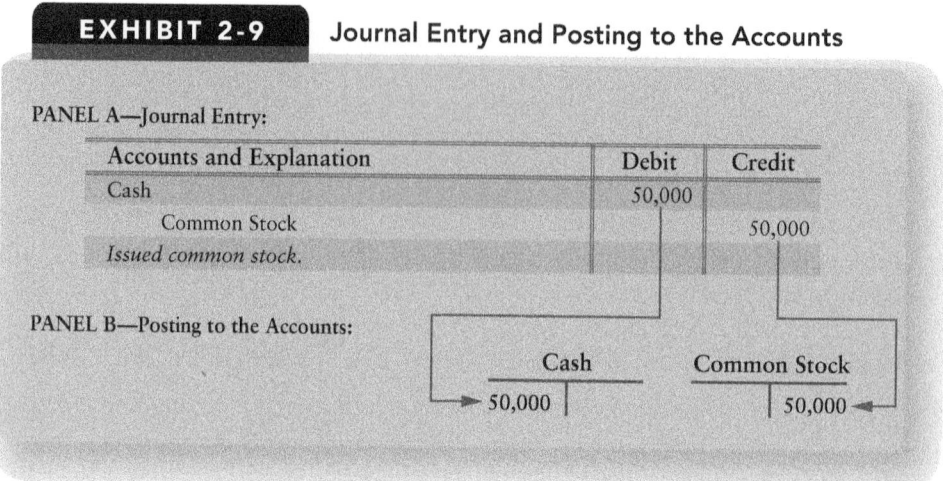

EXHIBIT 2-9 Journal Entry and Posting to the Accounts

PANEL A—Journal Entry:

Accounts and Explanation	Debit	Credit
Cash	50,000	
Common Stock		50,000
Issued common stock.		

PANEL B—Posting to the Accounts:

Cash   Common Stock
50,000 | | 50,000

The Flow of Accounting Data

Exhibit 2-10 summarizes the flow of accounting data from the business transaction to the ledger.

EXHIBIT 2-10 Flow of Accounting Data

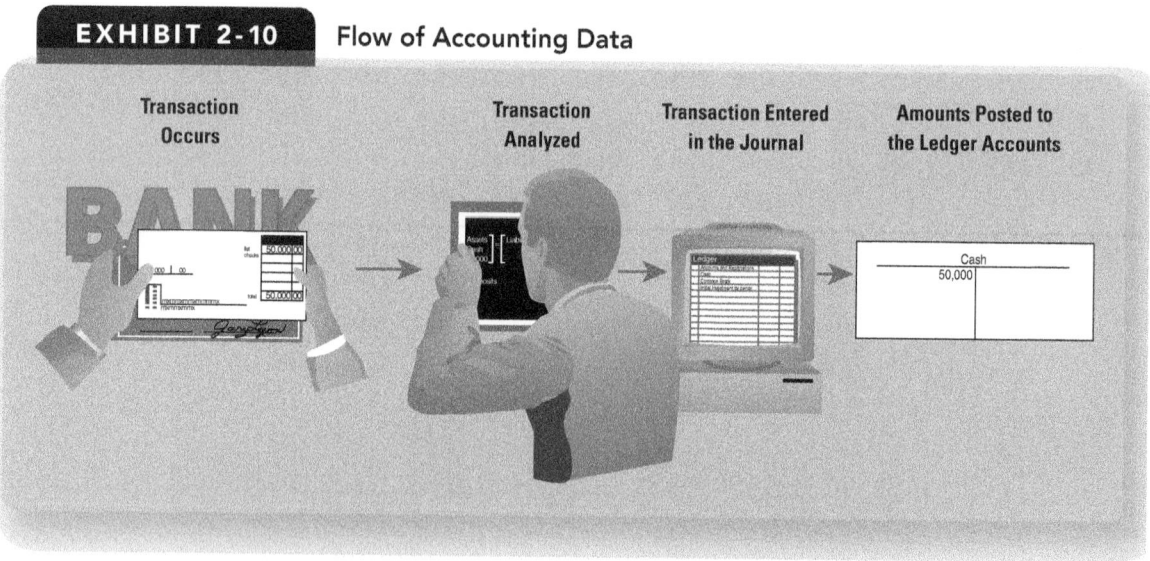

Let's continue the example of Genie Car Wash, Inc., and account for the same 11 transactions we illustrated earlier. Here we use the journal and the accounts. Each journal entry posted to the accounts is keyed by date or by transaction number. This linking allows you to locate any information you may need.

Transaction 1 Analysis. Genie Car Wash, Inc., received $50,000 cash from the stockholders and in turn issued common stock to them. The journal entry, accounting equation, and ledger accounts follow.

Journal entry

Cash	50,000	
Common Stock		50,000
Issued common stock.		

Accounting equation	Assets	=	Liabilities	+	Stockholders' Equity
	50,000	=	0	+	50,000

The ledger accounts

Cash		Common Stock	
(1) 50,000		(1) 50,000	

Transaction 2 Analysis. The business paid $40,000 cash for land. The purchase decreased cash; therefore, credit Cash. The purchase increased the asset land; to record this increase, debit Land.

Journal entry

Land	40,000	
Cash		40,000
Paid cash for land.		

Accounting equation	Assets	=	Liabilities	+	Stockholders' Equity
	+ 50,000	=	0	+	0
	− 40,000				

The ledger accounts

Cash		Land	
(1) 50,000	(2) 40,000	(2) 40,000	

Transaction 3 Analysis. The business purchased supplies for $3,700 on account payable. The purchase increased supplies, an asset, and Accounts Payable, a liability.

Journal entry

Supplies	3,700	
Accounts Payable		3,700
Purchased office supplies on account.		

Accounting equation	Assets	=	Liabilities	+	Stockholders' Equity
	+ 3,700	=	+ 3,700	+	0

The ledger accounts

Supplies		Accounts Payable	
(3) 3,700		(3) 3,700	

Transaction 4 Analysis. The business performed services for clients and received cash of $7,000. The transaction increased cash and service revenue. To record the revenue, credit Service Revenue.

Journal entry

Cash	7,000	
Service Revenue		7,000
Performed services for cash.		

Accounting equation

Assets	=	Liabilities	+	Stockholders' Equity	+	Revenues
+7,000	=	0			+	7,000

The ledger accounts

Cash				Service Revenue	
(1)	50,000	(2)	40,000	(4)	7,000
(4)	7,000				

Transaction 5 Analysis. Genie performed services for UPS on account. UPS did not pay immediately, so Genie billed UPS for $3,000. The transaction increased accounts receivable; therefore, debit Accounts Receivable. Service revenue also increased, so credit the Service Revenue account.

Journal entry

Accounts Receivable	3,000	
Service Revenue		3,000
Performed services on account.		

Accounting equation

Assets	=	Liabilities	+	Stockholders' Equity	+	Revenues
+3,000	=	0			+	3,000

The ledger accounts

Accounts Receivable		Service Revenue	
(5)	3,000	(4)	7,000
		(5)	3,000

Transaction 6 Analysis. The business paid $2,700 for the following expenses: equipment rent, $1,100; employee salary, $1,200; and utilities, $400. Credit Cash for the sum of the expense amounts. The expenses increased, so debit each expense account separately.

Journal entry

Rent Expense	1,100	
Salary Expense	1,200	
Utilities Expense	400	
Cash		2,700
Paid expenses.		

Accounting equation

Assets	=	Liabilities	+	Stockholders' Equity	−	Expenses
− 2,700	=	0			−	2,700

The ledger accounts

Cash				Rent Expense	
(1)	50,000	(2)	40,000	(6)	1,100
(4)	7,000	(6)	2,700		

Salary Expense		Utilities Expense	
(6)	1,200	(6)	400

Transaction 7 Analysis. The business paid $1,900 on the account payable created in transaction 3. Credit Cash for the payment. The payment decreased a liability, so debit Accounts Payable.

Journal entry

Accounts Payable	1,900	
Cash		1,900
Paid cash on account.		

Accounting equation

Assets	=	Liabilities	+	Stockholders' Equity
− 1,900	=	− 1,900	+	0

The ledger accounts

Cash				Accounts Payable			
(1)	50,000	(2)	40,000	(7)	1,900	(3)	3,700
(4)	7,000	(6)	2,700				
		(7)	1,900				

Transaction 8 Analysis. Van Gray, the major stockholder of Genie Car Wash, remodeled his personal residence. This is not a transaction of the car-wash business, so the business does not record the transaction.

Transaction 9 Analysis. The business collected $1,000 cash on account from the clients in transaction 5. Cash increased so debit Cash. The asset accounts receivable decreased; therefore, credit Accounts Receivable.

Journal entry

Cash	1,000	
Accounts Receivable		1,000
Collected cash on account.		

HH CHAPTER 2

	Assets	=	Liabilities	+	Stockholders' Equity
Accounting equation	+ 1,000	=	0	+	0
	− 1,000				

The ledger accounts

	Cash				Accounts Receivable		
(1)	50,000	(2)	40,000	(5)	3,000	(9)	1,000
(4)	7,000	(6)	2,700				
(9)	1,000	(7)	1,900				

Transaction 10 Analysis. The business sold land for its cost of $22,000, receiving cash. The asset cash increased; debit Cash. The asset land decreased; credit Land.

Journal entry

Cash	22,000	
Land		22,000
Sold land.		

	Assets	=	Liabilities	+	Stockholders' Equity
Accounting equation	+ 22,000	=	0	+	0
	− 22,000				

The ledger accounts

	Cash				Land		
(1)	50,000	(2)	40,000	(2)	40,000	(10)	22,000
(4)	7,000	(6)	2,700				
(9)	1,000	(7)	1,900				
(10)	22,000						

Transaction 11 Analysis. Genie Car Wash paid its stockholders cash dividends of $2,100. Credit Cash for the payment. The transaction also decreased stockholders' equity and requires a debit to an equity account. Therefore, debit Dividends.

Journal entry

Dividends	2,100	
Cash		2,100
Declared and paid dividends.		

	Assets	=	Liabilities	+	Stockholders' Equity	−	Dividends
Accounting equation	− 2,100	=	0			−	2,100

		Cash					Dividends	
The ledger accounts	(1)	50,000	(2)	40,000	(11)	2,100		
	(4)	7,000	(6)	2,700				
	(9)	1,000	(7)	1,900				
	(10)	22,000	(11)	2,100				

Accounts After Posting to the Ledger

Exhibit 2-11 shows the accounts after all transactions have been posted to the ledger. Group the accounts under assets, liabilities, and equity.

Each account has a balance, denoted as Bal., which is the difference between the account's total debits and its total credits. For example, the Accounts Payable's balance of $1,800 is the difference between the credit ($3,700) and the debit ($1,900). Cash has a debit balance of $33,300.

A horizontal line separates the transaction amounts from the account balance. If an account's debits exceed its total credits, that account has a debit balance, as for Cash. If the sum of the credits is greater, the account has a credit balance, as for Accounts Payable.

Accounting Cycle Tutorial
Application 1—Xpert Driving School

Accounting Cycle Tutorial
Application 2—Small Business Services

HH CHAPTER 2

EXHIBIT 2-11 Genie Car Wash's Ledger Accounts After Posting

Assets	=	Liabilities	+	Stockholders' Equity

	Cash					Accounts Payable					Common Stock					Dividends	
(1)	50,000	(2)	40,000		(7)	1,900	(3)	3,700				(1)	50,000		(11)	2,100	
(4)	7,000	(6)	2,700				Bal.	1,800				Bal.	50,000		Bal.	2,100	
(9)	1,000	(7)	1,900														
(10)	22,000	(11)	2,100														
Bal.	33,300																

	Revenue				Expenses	
	Service Revenue				Rent Expense	

	Accounts Receivable				(4)	7,000		(6)	1,100	
(5)	3,000	(9)	1,000		(5)	3,000		Bal.	1,100	
Bal.	2,000				Bal.	10,000				

	Salary Expense	
	Supplies	
(3)	3,700				(6)	1,200	
Bal.	3,700				Bal.	1,200	

	Utilities Expense	
	Land	
(2)	40,000	(10)	22,000		(6)	400	
Bal.	18,000				Bal.	400	

THE TRIAL BALANCE

A **trial balance** lists all accounts with their balances—assets first, then liabilities and stockholders' equity. The trial balance summarizes all the account balances for the financial statements and shows whether total debits equal total credits. A trial balance

OBJECTIVE

4 Use a trial balance

may be taken at any time, but the most common time is at the end of the period. Exhibit 2-12 is the trial balance of Genie Car Wash, Inc., after all transactions have been journalized and posted at the end of April.

Accounting Cycle Tutorial Glossary

Accounting Cycle Tutorial Glossary Quiz

EXHIBIT 2-12   **Trial Balance**

Genie Car Wash, Inc.
Trial Balance
April 30, 20X9

Account Title	Balance Debit	Balance Credit
Cash......................................	$33,300	
Accounts receivable................	2,000	
Supplies.................................	3,700	
Land.......................................	18,000	
Accounts payable		$ 1,800
Common stock.......................		50,000
Dividends..............................	2,100	
Service revenue......................		10,000
Rent expense.........................	1,100	
Salary expense.......................	1,200	
Utilities expense	400	
Total	$61,800	$61,800

Analyzing Accounts

You can often tell what a company did by analyzing its accounts. This is a powerful tool for a manager who knows accounting. For example, if you know the beginning and ending balance of Cash, and if you know total cash receipts, you can compute your total cash payments during the period.

In our chapter example, suppose Genie Car Wash began May with cash of $1,000. During May Genie received cash of $8,000 and ended the month with a cash balance of $3,000. You can compute total cash payments by analyzing Genie's Cash account as follows:

Cash			
Beginning balance	1,000		
Cash receipts	8,000	Cash payments	$x = 6,000$
Ending balance	3,000		

Or, if you know Cash's beginning and ending balances and total payments, you can compute cash receipts during the period—for any company!

You can compute either sales on account or cash collections on account by analyzing the Accounts Receivable account as follows (using assumed amounts):

Accounts Receivable			
Beginning balance	6,000		
Sales on account	10,000	Collections on account	11,000
Ending balance	5,000		

Also, you can determine how much you paid on account by analyzing Accounts Payable as follows (using assumed amounts):

Accounts Payable			
		Beginning balance	9,000
Payments on account	4,000	Purchases on account	6,000
		Ending balance	11,000

Please master this powerful technique. It works for any company and for your own personal finances! You will find this tool very helpful when you become a manager.

Correcting Accounting Errors

Accounting errors can occur even in computerized systems. Input data may be wrong, or they may be entered twice or not at all. A debit may be entered as a credit, and vice versa. You can detect the reason or reasons behind many out-of-balance conditions by computing the difference between total debits and total credits. Then perform one or more of the following actions:

1. Search the records for a missing account. Trace each account back and forth from the journal to the ledger. A $200 transaction may have been recorded incorrectly in the journal or posted incorrectly to the ledger. Search the journal for a $200 transaction.

2. Divide the out-of-balance amount by 2. A debit treated as a credit, or vice versa, doubles the amount of error. Suppose Genie Car Wash added $300 to Cash instead of subtracting $300. The out-of-balance amount is $600, and dividing by 2 identifies $300 as the amount of the transaction. Search the journal for the $300 transaction and trace to the account affected.

3. Divide the out-of-balance amount by 9. If the result is an integer (no decimals), the error may be a

   ■ *slide* (writing $400 as $40). The accounts would be out of balance by $360 ($400 – $40 = $360). Dividing $360 by 9 yields $40. Scan the trial balance in Exhibit 2-12 for an amount similar to $40. Utilities Expense (balance of $400) is the misstated account.

■ *transposition* (writing $2,100 as $1,200). The accounts would be out of balance by $900 ($2,100 − $1,200 = $900). Dividing $900 by 9 yields $100. Trace all amounts on the trial balance back to the T-accounts. Dividends (balance of $2,100) is the misstated account.

Chart of Accounts

As you know, the ledger contains the accounts grouped under these headings:

1. **Balance sheet accounts: Assets, Liabilities, and Stockholders' Equity**
2. **Income statement accounts: Revenues and Expenses**

Organizations use a **chart of accounts** to list all their accounts and account numbers. Account numbers usually have 2 or more digits. Asset account numbers may begin with 1, liabilities with 2, stockholders' equity with 3, revenues with 4, and expenses with 5. The second, third, and higher digits in an account number indicate the position of the individual account within the category. For example, Cash may be account number 101, which is the first asset account. Accounts Payable may be number 201, the first liability. All accounts are numbered by using this system.

Organizations with many accounts use lengthy account numbers. For example, the chart of accounts of Apple Computer may use 5-digit account numbers. The chart of accounts for Genie Car Wash appears in Exhibit 2-13. The gap between account numbers 111 and 141 leaves room to add another category of receivables, for example, Notes Receivable, which may be numbered 121.

EXHIBIT 2-13 Chart of Accounts—Genie Car Wash, Inc.

Balance Sheet Accounts

Assets		Liabilities		Stockholders' Equity	
101	Cash	201	Accounts Payable	301	Common Stock
111	Accounts Receivable	231	Notes Payable	311	Dividends
141	Office Supplies			312	Retained Earnings
151	Office Furniture				
191	Land				

Income Statement Accounts (Part of Stockholders' Equity)

	Revenues		Expenses	
401	Service Revenue	501	Rent Expense	
		502	Salary Expense	
		503	Utilities Expense	

The Normal Balance of an Account

An account's *normal balance* falls on the side of the account—debit or credit—where increases are recorded. The normal balance of assets is on the debit side, so assets are *debit-balance accounts*. Conversely, liabilities and stockholders' equity usually have a credit balance, so these are *credit-balance accounts*. Exhibit 2-14 illustrates the normal balances of all the assets, liabilities, and stockholders' equities, including revenues and expenses.

EXHIBIT 2-14	Normal Balances of the Accounts

Assets	Debit	
Liabilities		Credit
Stockholders' Equity—overall		Credit
Common stock.................................		Credit
Retained earnings............................		Credit
Dividends..	Debit	
Revenues...		Credit
Expenses	Debit	

As explained earlier, stockholders' equity usually contains several accounts. Dividends and expenses carry debit balances because they represent decreases in stockholders' equity. In total, the equity accounts show a normal credit balance.

Account Formats

So far we have illustrated accounts in a 2-column T-account format, with the debit column on the left and the credit column on the right. Another format has 4 *amount* columns, as illustrated for the Cash account in Exhibit 2-15. The first pair of amount columns are for the debit and credit amounts of individual transactions. The last two columns are for the account balance. This 4-column format keeps a running balance in the 2 right columns.

Accounting Cycle Tutorial
The Journal, the Ledger, and the Trial Balance

EXHIBIT 2-15	Account in Four-Column Format

Account: Cash					Account No. 101
				Balance	
Date	Item	Debit	Credit	Debit	Credit
20X9 Apr. 2		50,000		50,000	
3			40,000	10,000	

Analyzing Transactions Using Only T-Accounts

OBJECTIVE

5 **Analyze** transactions using only T-accounts

Businesspeople must often make decisions without the benefit of a complete accounting system. For example, the managers of Apple Computer may consider borrowing $100,000 to buy equipment. To see how the two transactions [(a) borrowing cash and (b) buying equipment] affect Apple, the manager can go directly to T-accounts, as follows:

T-accounts:

	Cash				Note Payable	
(a)	100,000			(a)	100,000	

T-accounts:

	Cash				Equipment				Note Payable	
(a)	100,000	(b)	100,000	(b)	100,000			(a)	100,000	

This informal analysis shows immediately that Apple will add $100,000 of equipment and a $100,000 note payable. Assuming that Apple began with zero balances, the equipment and note payable transactions would result in the following balance sheet (date assumed for illustration only):

Apple Computer, Inc.
Balance Sheet
September 12, 20X8

Assets			Liabilities		
Cash............................	$ 0		Note payable...........................	$100,000	
Equipment.....................	100,000				
			Stockholders' Equity	0	
			Total liabilities and		
Total assets....................	$100,000		stockholders' equity...............	$100,000	

Accounting Cycle Tutorial
Application Constanza Architect

Companies don't actually keep records in this shortcut fashion. But a decision maker who needs information quickly may not have time to journalize, post to the accounts, take a trial balance, and prepare the financial statements. A manager who knows accounting can analyze the transaction and make the decision quickly.

Now apply what you've learned. Study the Decision Guidelines, which summarize the chapter.

DECISION GUIDELINES

HOW TO MEASURE RESULTS OF OPERATIONS AND FINANCIAL POSITION

Any entrepreneur must determine whether the venture is profitable. To do this, he or she needs to know its results of operations and financial position. If Steve Jobs, who founded Apple Computer, Inc., wants to know whether the business is making money, the Guidelines that follow will help him.

Decision	Guidelines
Has a transaction occurred?	If the event affects the entity's financial position and can be reliably recorded—Yes. If either condition is absent—No.
Where to record the transaction?	In the *journal*, the chronological record of transactions
How to record an increase or decrease in the following accounts?	Rules of *debit* and *credit*:

	Increase	Decrease
Assets	Debit	Credit
Liabilities	Credit	Debit
Stockholders' equity	Credit	Debit
Revenues	Credit	Debit
Expenses	Debit	Credit

Decision	Guidelines
Where to store all the information for each account?	In the *ledger*, the book of accounts
Where to list all the accounts and their balances?	In the *trial* balance
Where to report the:	
Results of operations?	In the *income* statement (Revenues – Expenses = Net income or net loss)
Financial position?	In the balance sheet (Assets = Liabilities + Stockholders' equity)

END-OF-CHAPTER SUMMARY PROBLEM

The trial balance of Calderon Service Center, Inc., on March 1, 20X3, lists the entity's assets, liabilities, and stockholders' equity on that date.

	Balance	
Account Title	Debit	Credit
Cash......................................	$26,000	
Accounts receivable...............	4,500	
Accounts payable..................		$ 2,000
Common stock.......................		10,000
Retained earnings...................		18,500
Total	$30,500	$30,500

During March, the business completed the following transactions:
a. Borrowed $45,000 from the bank, with Calderon signing a note payable in the name of the business.
b. Paid cash of $40,000 to a real estate company to acquire land.
c. Performed service for a customer and received cash of $5,000.
d. Purchased supplies on credit, $300.
e. Performed customer service and earned revenue on account, $2,600.
f. Paid $1,200 on account.
g. Paid the following cash expenses: salaries, $3,000; rent, $1,500; and interest, $400.
h. Received $3,100 on account.
i. Received a $200 utility bill that will be paid next week.
j. Declared and paid dividend of $1,800.

▌Required

1. Open the following accounts, with the balances indicated, in the ledger of Calderon Service Center, Inc. Use the T-account format.
   - Assets—Cash, $26,000; Accounts Receivable, $4,500; Supplies, no balance; Land, no balance
   - Liabilities—Accounts Payable, $2,000; Note Payable, no balance
   - Stockholders' Equity—Common Stock, $10,000; Retained Earnings, $18,500; Dividends, no balance
   - Revenues—Service Revenue, no balance
   - Expenses—(none have balances) Salary Expense, Rent Expense, Interest Expense, Utilities Expense
2. Journalize the preceding transactions. Key journal entries by transaction letter.
3. Post to the ledger and show the balance in each account after all the transactions have been posted.
4. Prepare the trial balance of Calderon Service Center, Inc., at March 31, 20X3.
5. To determine the net income or net loss of the entity during the month of March, prepare the income statement for the month ended March 31, 20X3. List expenses in order from the largest to the smallest.

Answers

Requirement 1

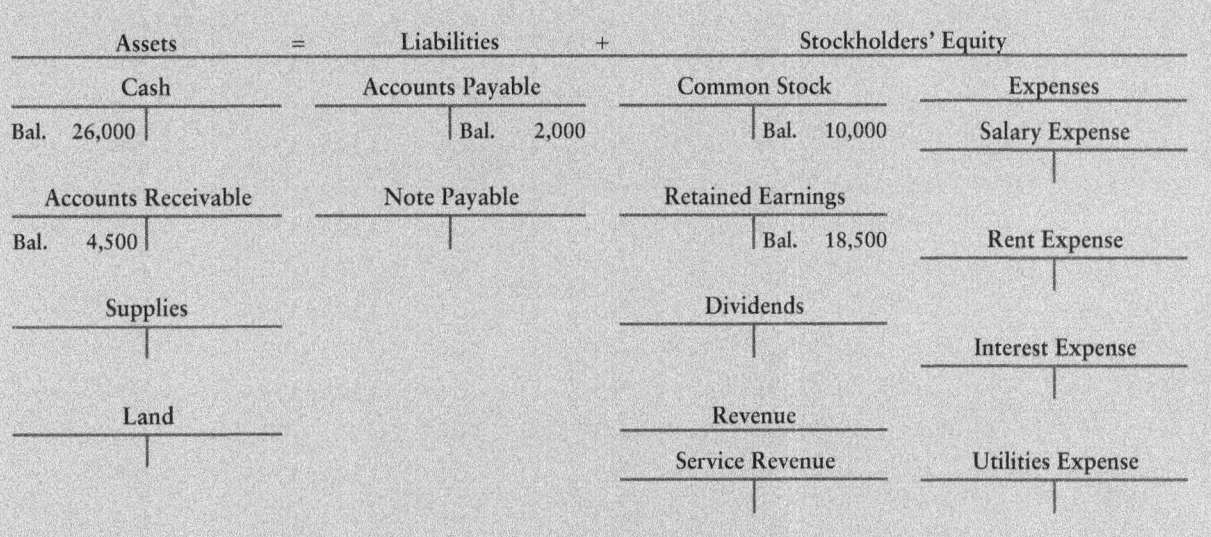

		Assets	=	Liabilities	+	Stockholders' Equity	
		Cash		Accounts Payable		Common Stock	Expenses
Bal.	26,000			Bal. 2,000		Bal. 10,000	Salary Expense
		Accounts Receivable		Note Payable		Retained Earnings	
Bal.	4,500					Bal. 18,500	Rent Expense
		Supplies				Dividends	Interest Expense
		Land				Revenue	
						Service Revenue	Utilities Expense

Requirement 2

Accounts and Explanation	Debit	Credit	Accounts and Explanation	Debit	Credit
a. Cash..	45,000		g. Salary Expense	3,000	
Note Payable		45,000	Rent Expense	1,500	
Borrowed cash on note payable.			Interest Expense	400	
b. Land...	40,000		Cash		4,900
Cash		40,000	Paid cash expenses.		
Purchased land for cash.			h. Cash...	3,100	
c. Cash...	5,000		Accounts Receivable		3,100
Service Revenue		5,000	Received on account.		
Performed service and received cash.			i. Utilities Expense..........................	200	
d. Supplies.....................................	300		Accounts Payable...................		200
Accounts Payable...............		300	Received utility bill.		
Purchased supplies on account.			j. Dividends....................................	1,800	
e. Accounts Receivable.................	2,600		Cash		1,800
Service Revenue		2,600	Declared and paid dividends.		
Performed service on account.					
f. Accounts Payable	1,200				
Cash		1,200			
Paid on account.					

HH CHAPTER 2

I *Requirement 3*

| Assets | = | Liabilities | + | Stockholders' Equity |

Cash

Bal.	26,000	(b)	40,000
(a)	45,000	(f)	1,200
(c)	5,000	(g)	4,900
(h)	3,100	(j)	1,800
Bal.	31,200		

Accounts Receivable

Bal.	4,500	(h)	3,100
(e)	2,600		
Bal.	4,000		

Supplies

(d)	300	
Bal.	300	

Land

(b)	40,000	
Bal.	40,000	

Accounts Payable

(f)	1,200	Bal.	2,000
		(d)	300
		(i)	200
		Bal.	1,300

Note Payable

	(a)	45,000
	Bal.	45,000

Common Stock

Bal.	10,000

Retained Earnings

Bal.	18,500

Dividends

(j)	1,800	
Bal.	1,800	

Revenue

Service Revenue

	(c)	5,000
	(e)	2,600
	Bal.	7,600

Expenses

Salary Expense

(g)	3,000	
Bal.	3,000	

Rent Expense

(g)	1,500	
Bal.	1,500	

Interest Expense

(g)	400	
Bal.	400	

Utilities Expense

(i)	200	
Bal.	200	

I *Requirement 4*

Calderon Service Center, Inc.
Trial Balance
March 31, 20X3

Account Title	Balance Debit	Balance Credit
Cash..	$31,200	
Accounts receivable...............	4,000	
Supplies..................................	300	
Land..	40,000	
Accounts payable...................		$ 1,300
Note payable..........................		45,000
Common stock.......................		10,000
Retained earnings..................		18,500
Dividends...............................	1,800	
Service revenue......................		7,600
Salary expense........................	3,000	
Rent expense..........................	1,500	
Interest expense.....................	400	
Utilities expense....................	200	
Total	$82,400	$82,400

I Requirement 5

Calderon Service Center, Inc.
Income Statement
Month Ended March 31, 20X3

Revenue

Service revenue..................		$7,600

Expenses

Salary expense..................	$3,000	
Rent expense....................	1,500	
Interest expense...............	400	
Utilities expense	200	
Total expenses.....................		5,100
Net income..........................		$2,500

REVIEW TRANSACTION ANALYSIS

Quick Check (Answers are given on page 110.)

1. A debit entry to an account:
   - **a.** increases liabilities
   - **b.** increases stockholders' equity
   - **c.** increases assets
   - **d.** both a and c

2. Which account types normally have a credit balance?
   - **a.** liabilities
   - **b.** revenues
   - **c.** expenses
   - **d.** both a and b

3. An attorney performs services of $800 for a client and receives $200 cash with the remainder on account. The journal entry for this transaction would:
   - **a.** debit Cash, credit Accounts Receivable, credit Service Revenue
   - **b.** debit Cash, debit Accounts Receivable, credit Service Revenue
   - **c.** debit Cash, credit Service Revenue
   - **d.** debit Cash, debit Service Revenue, credit Accounts Receivable

4. Accounts Payable had a normal beginning balance of $1,000. During the period, there were debit postings of $400 and credit postings of $600. What was the ending balance?
   - **a.** $800 debit
   - **b.** $800 credit
   - **c.** $1,200 debit
   - **d.** $1,200 credit

5. The list of all accounts with their balances is the:
   - **a.** trial balance
   - **b.** chart of accounts
   - **c.** journal
   - **d.** balance sheet

6. The basic summary device of accounting is the:
   - **a.** ledger
   - **b.** account
   - **c.** journal
   - **d.** trial balance

7. The beginning Cash balance was $5,000. At the end of the period, the balance was $6,000. If total cash paid out during the period was $24,000, the amount of cash receipts was:
   - **a.** $23,000
   - **b.** $13,000
   - **c.** $25,000
   - **d.** $35,000

8. In a double-entry accounting system
   - **a.** a debit entry is recorded on the left side of a T-account.
   - **b.** half of all the accounts have a normal credit balance.
   - **c.** liabilities, owners' equity, and revenue accounts all have normal debit balances.
   - **d.** both a and c are correct.

9. Which accounts appear on which financial statement?

Balance sheet	Income statement
a. Cash, revenues, land	Expenses, payables
b. Receivables, land, payables	Revenues, supplies
c. Expenses, payables, cash	Revenues, receivables, land
d. Cash, receivables, payables	Revenues, expenses

10. A doctor purchases medical supplies of $670 and pays $200 cash with the remainder on account. The journal entry for this transaction would be:
   - **a.** Supplies
     - Accounts Payable
     - Cash
   - **b.** Supplies
     - Cash
       - Accounts Payable
   - **c.** Supplies
     - Accounts Receivable
       - Cash
   - **d.** Supplies
     - Accounts Payable
     - Cash

11. Which is the correct sequence for recording transactions and preparing financial statements?
   - **a.** Journal, ledger, trial balance, financial statements
   - **b.** Ledger, trial balance, journal, financial statements
   - **c.** Financial statements, trial balance, ledger, journal
   - **d.** Ledger, journal, trial balance, financial statements

12. The error of posting $100 as $10 can be detected by
   - **a.** Dividing the out-of-balance amount by 2.
   - **b.** Totalling each account's balance in the ledger.
   - **c.** Dividing the out-of-balance amount by 9.
   - **d.** Examining the chart of accounts.

Accounting Vocabulary

account (p. 55) The record of the changes that have occurred in a particular asset, liability, or stockholders' equity during a period. The basic summary device of accounting.

accrued liability (p. 56) A liability for an expense that has not yet been paid by the company.

cash (p. 55) Money and any medium of exchange that a bank accepts at face value.

chart of accounts (p. 80) List of a company's accounts and their account numbers.

credit (p. 67) The right side of an account.

debit (p. 67) The left side of an account.

journal (p. 70) The chronological accounting record of an entity's transactions.

ledger (p. 71) The book of accounts and their balances.

posting (p. 71) Copying amounts from the journal to the ledger.

prepaid expense (p. 55) A category of miscellaneous assets that typically expire or get used up in the near future. Examples include Prepaid Rent, Prepaid Insurance, and Supplies.

transaction (p. 54) Any event that has a financial impact on the business and can be measured reliably.

trial balance (p. 77) A list of all the ledger accounts with their balances.

ASSESS YOUR PROGRESS

Short Exercises

S2-1 *(Learning Objective 1: Explaining an asset versus an expense)* Lou Ann Staas opened a software consulting firm that immediately paid $9,000 for a computer. Was Staas's payment an expense of the business? Explain your answer. (pp. 55–56)

S2-2 *(Learning Objective 1: Analyzing the effects of transactions)* Hourglass Software began with cash of $10,000. Hourglass then bought supplies for $2,000 on account. Separately, Hourglass paid $5,000 for a computer. Answer these questions.

a. How much in total assets does Hourglass have? (pp. 58–59)
b. How much in liabilities does Hourglass owe? (pp. 58–59)

S2-3 *(Learning Objective 1: Analyzing transactions)* Sandy Lyle, MD, opened a medical practice. The business completed the following transactions:

June 1	Lyle invested $25,000 cash to start her medical practice. The business issued common stock to Lyle.
1	Purchased medical supplies on account totaling $9,000.
2	Paid monthly office rent of $4,000.
3	Recorded $8,000 revenue for service rendered to patients, received cash of $2,000, and sent bills to patients for the remainder.

After these transactions, how much cash does the business have to work with? Use a T-account to show your answer. (pp. 57–60)

S2-4 *(Learning Objective 1: Analyzing transactions)* Refer to Short Exercise S2-3. Which of the transactions of Sandy Lyle, MD, increased the total assets of the business? For each transaction, identify the asset that was increased.

S2-5 *(Learning Objective 2, 3: Recording transactions)* After operating for several months, architect Paul Marciano completed the following transactions during the latter part of October:

October 15	Borrowed $25,000 from the bank, signing a note payable.
22	Performed service for clients on account totaling $9,000.
28	Received $6,000 cash on account from clients.
29	Received a utility bill of $600, an account payable that will be paid during May.
31	Paid monthly salary of $3,000 to employee.

Journalize the transactions of Paul Marciano, Architect. Include an explanation with each journal entry. (pp. 72–76)

S2-6 *(Learning Objective 2, 3: Journalizing transactions; posting)* Adam Lowry, Inc., purchased supplies on account for $5,000. Later Lowry paid $3,000 on account.

1. Journalize the two transactions on the books of Adam Lowry, Inc. Include an explanation for each transaction. (pp. 73–76)

2. Open a T-account for Accounts Payable and post to Accounts Payable. Compute the balance and denote it as Bal. (pp. 73–76)

3. How much does the Lowry business owe after both transactions? In which account does this amount appear? (pp. 73–76)

S2-7 (*Learning Objective 2, 3: Journalizing transactions; posting*) Motion Unlimited performed service for a client who could not pay immediately. Motion expected to collect the $4,000 the following month. A month later, Motion received $2,500 cash from the client.

1. Record the two transactions on the books of Motion Unlimited. Include an explanation for each transaction. (pp. 73–76)

2. Open these T-accounts: Cash, Accounts Receivable, and Service Revenue. Post to all three accounts. Compute each account balance and denote as Bal. (pp. 73–76)

S2-8 (*Learning Objective 4: Preparing and using a trial balance*) Assume that **Old Navy**, reported the following summarized data at December 31, 20X8. Accounts appear in no particular order; dollar amounts are in millions.

Other liabilities	$ 2	Revenues	$36
Cash	8	Other assets	9
Expenses	24	Accounts payable	1
Stockholders' equity	2		

Prepare the trial balance of Old Navy at December 31, 20X8. List the accounts in their proper order, as on page 71. How much was Old Navy's net income or net loss? (pp. 77–78)

S2-9 (*Learning Objective 4: Using a trial balance*) Blackberry's trial balance follows.

Blackberry, Inc.
Trial Balance
June 30, 20X6

	Debit	Credit
Cash	$ 6,000	
Accounts receivable	13,000	
Supplies	4,000	
Equipment	22,000	
Land	50,000	
Accounts payable		$ 19,000
Note payable		20,000
Common stock		10,000
Retained earnings		8,000
Service revenue		70,000
Salary expense	21,000	
Rent expense	10,000	
Utilities expense	1,000	
Total	$127,000	$127,000

Compute these amounts for Blackberry: (pp. 77–78)

1. Total assets

2. Total liabilities

3. Net income or net loss during June

S2-10 (*Learning Objective 4: Using a trial balance*) Refer to Blackberry's trial balance in Short Exercise S2-9. The purpose of this exercise is to help you learn how to correct three common accounting errors. (pp. 79–80)

Error 1. Slide. Suppose the trial balance lists Land as $5,000 instead of $50,000. Recompute column totals, take the difference, and divide by 9. The result is an integer (no decimals), which suggests that the error is either a transposition or a slide.

Error 2. Transposition. Assume the trial balance lists Accounts Receivable as $31,000 instead of $13,000. Recompute column totals, take the difference, and divide by 9. The result is an integer (no decimals), which suggests that the error is either a transposition or a slide.

Error 3. Mislabelling an item. Assume that Blackberry accidentally listed Accounts Receivable as a credit balance instead of a debit. Recompute the trial balance totals for debits and credits. Then take the difference between total debits and total credits, and divide the difference by 2. You get back to the original amount of Accounts Receivable.

S2-11 (*Learning Objective 2: Using key accounting terms*) Accounting has its own vocabulary and basic relationships. Match the accounting terms at left with the corresponding definition or meaning at right. (pp. 55–80)

____ **1.** Debit	**A.**	The cost of operating a business; a decrease in stockholders' equity
____ **2.** Expense		
____ **3.** Net income	**B.**	Always a liability
____ **4.** Ledger	**C.**	Revenues – Expenses
____ **5.** Posting	**D.**	Grouping of accounts
____ **6.** Normal balance	**E.**	Assets – Liabilities
____ **7.** Payable	**F.**	Record of transactions
____ **8.** Journal	**G.**	Always an asset
____ **9.** Receivable	**H.**	Left side of an account
____ **10.** Owners' equity	**I.**	Side of an account where increases are recorded
	J.	Copying data from the journal to the ledger

S2-12 (*Learning Objective 5: Analyzing transactions without a journal*) Singapore Investments, Inc., began by issuing common stock for cash of $100,000. The company immediately purchased computer equipment on account for $60,000.

1. Set up the following T-accounts of Singapore Investments, Inc.: Cash, Computer Equipment, Accounts Payable, Common Stock. (pp. 81–82)
2. Record the first two transactions of the business directly in the T-accounts without using a journal. (pp. 81–82)
3. Show that total debits equal total credits.

Exercises

E2-13 (*Learning Objective 1: Reporting on business activities*) Assume **J. Crew** opened a store in St. Louis, starting with cash and common stock of $100,000. Monique Farris, the store manager, then signed a note payable to purchase land for $90,000 and a building for $120,000. Farris also paid $60,000 for equipment and $10,000 for supplies to use in the business.

Suppose the home office of J. Crew requires a weekly report from store managers. Write Farris's memo to the home office to report on her purchases. Include the store's balance sheet as the final part of your memo. Prepare a T-account to compute the balance for Cash. (pp. 58–59, 63–64)

E2-14 (*Learning Objective 1: Business transactions and the accounting equation*) **Advanced Design** specializes in imported clothing. During April, Advanced completed a series of transactions. For each of the following items, give an example of a transaction that has the described effect on the accounting equation of Advanced Design. (pp. 57–62)

a. Increase one asset and decrease another asset.
b. Decrease an asset and decrease owners' equity.
c. Decrease an asset and decrease a liability.
d. Increase an asset and increase owners' equity.
e. Increase an asset and increase a liability.

E2-15 *(Learning Objective 1: Transaction analysis)* The following selected events were experienced by either Problem Solvers, Inc., a corporation, or Peter Fleming, the major stockholder. State whether each event (1) increased, (2) decreased, or (3) had no effect on the total assets of the business. Identify any specific asset affected. (pp. 57–62)

a. Received $9,000 cash from customers on account.
b. Fleming used personal funds to purchase a swimming pool for his home.
c. Sold land and received cash of $60,000 (the land was carried on the company's books at $60,000).
d. Borrowed $50,000 from the bank.
e. Made cash purchase of land for a building site, $85,000.
f. Received $20,000 cash and issued stock to a stockholder.
g. Paid $60,000 cash on accounts payable.
h. Purchased equipment and signed a $100,000 promissory note in payment.
i. Purchased merchandise inventory on account for $15,000.
j. The business paid Fleming a cash dividend of $4,000.

E2-16 *(Learning Objective 1: Transaction analysis; accounting equation)* Randolph Noble opened a medical practice specializing in surgery. During the first month of operation (August), the business, titled Randolph Noble, Professional Corporation (P.C.), experienced the following events:

August	6	Noble invested $50,000 in the business, which in turn issued its common stock to him.
	9	The business paid cash for land costing $30,000. Noble plans to build an office building on the land.
	12	The business purchased medical supplies for $2,000 on account.
	15	Randolph Noble, P.C., officially opened for business.
	15–31	During the rest of the month, Noble treated patients and earned service revenue of $8,000, receiving cash for half the revenue earned.
	15–31	The business paid cash expenses: employee salaries, $1,400; office rent, $1,000; utilities, $300.
	31	The business sold supplies to another physician for the supplies' cost of $500.
	31	The business borrowed $10,000, signing a note payable to the bank.
	31	The business paid $1,000 on account.

❙ *Required*

1. Analyze the effects of these events on the accounting equation of the medical practice of Randolph Noble, P.C. Use a format similar to that of Exhibit 2-1, Panel B, with headings for Cash, Accounts Receivable, Medical Supplies, Land, Accounts Payable, Note Payable, Common Stock, and Retained Earnings. (pp. 57–62)

2. After completing the analysis, answer these questions about the business.
   a. How much are total assets? (pp. 61–62)
   b. How much does the business expect to collect from patients? (pp. 61–62)
   c. How much does the business owe in total? (pp. 61–62)
   d. How much of the business's assets does Noble really own?
   e. How much net income or net loss did the business experience during its first month of operations? (pp. 63–64)

E2-17 *(Learning Objective 2, 3: Journalizing transactions)* Refer to Exercise 2-16. Record the transactions in the journal of Randolph Noble, P.C. List the transactions by date and give an explanation for each transaction. (pp. 72–77)

E2-18 (*Learning Objective 2, 3: Journalizing transactions*) Double Tree Cellular, Inc., completed the following transactions during April 20X6, its first month of operations:

■ **general ledger**

Apr.	1	Received $25,000 and issued common stock.
	2	Purchased $800 of office supplies on account.
	4	Paid $20,000 cash for land to use as a building site.
	6	Performed service for customers and received cash of $2,000.
	9	Paid $100 on accounts payable.
	17	Performed service for FedEx on account totaling $1,200.
	23	Collected $900 from FedEx on account.
	30	Paid the following expenses: salary, $1,000; rent, $500.

I *Required*

Record the transactions in the journal of Double Tree Cellular, Inc. Key transactions by date and include an explanation for each entry, as illustrated in the chapter. (pp. 72–77)

E2-19 (*Learning Objective 3, 4: Posting to the ledger and preparing and using a trial balance*) Refer to Exercise 2-18.

■ **general ledger**

I *Required*

1. After journalizing the transactions of Exercise 2-18, post the entries to the ledger, using T-accounts. Key transactions by date. Date the ending balance of each account April 30. (pp. 72–77)

2. Prepare the trial balance of Double Tree Cellular, Inc., at April 30, 20X6. (pp. 77–78)

3. How much are total assets, total liabilities, and total stockholders' equity on April 30? Use the accounting equation. (pp. 62–63)

E2-20 (*Learning Objective 2, 3: Journalizing transactions*) The first 7 transactions of Yellow Pages Advertising, Inc., have been posted to the company's accounts as follows:

	Cash				Supplies				Equipment			Land	
(1)	20,000	(3)	8,000	(4)	1,000	(5)	100	(6)	8,000		(3)	31,000	
(2)	7,000	(6)	8,000										
(5)	100	(7)	400										

	Accounts Payable				Note Payable			Common Stock	
(7)	400	(4)	1,000		(2)	7,000		(1)	20,000
					(3)	23,000			

I *Required*

Prepare the journal entries that served as the sources for the 7 transactions. Include an explanation for each entry. (pp. 72–77) As Yellow Pages moves into the next period, how much cash does the business have? (pp. 77–78) How much does Yellow Pages owe in total liabilities? (pp. 77–78)

HH CHAPTER 2

▪ **spreadsheet**

E2-21 (*Learning Objective 4: Preparing and using a trial balance*) The accounts of Custom Pool Service, Inc., follow with their normal balances at June 30, 20X6. The accounts are listed in no particular order.

Account	Balance	Account	Balance
Dividends.........................	$ 6,000	Common stock...................	$ 8,500
Utilities expense	1,400	Accounts payable	4,300
Accounts receivable...........	15,500	Service revenue.................	22,000
Delivery expense	300	Land.................................	29,000
Retained earnings.............	21,400	Note payable....................	13,000
Salary expense..................	8,000	Cash...............................	9,000

▌ Required

1. Prepare the company's trial balance at June 30, 20X6, listing accounts in proper sequence, as illustrated in the chapter. For example, Supplies comes before Land. List the expense with the largest balance first, the expense with the next largest balance second, and so on. (pp. 77–78)

2. Prepare the financial statement for the month ended June 30, 20X6, that will tell the company the results of operations for the month. (pp. 63–64)

E2-22 (*Learning Objective 4: Correcting errors in a trial balance*) The trial balance of Haigood, Inc., at September 30, 20X3, does not balance:

Cash...	$ 4,200	
Accounts receivable.................	13,000	
Inventory................................	17,000	
Supplies...................................	600	
Land...	55,000	
Accounts payable.....................		$12,000
Common stock........................		47,900
Service revenue.......................		32,100
Salary expense.........................	1,700	
Rent expense...........................	800	
Utilities expense	700	
Total.......................................	$93,000	$92,000

The accounting records hold the following errors:
   a. Recorded a $1,000 cash revenue transaction by debiting Accounts Receivable. The credit entry was correct.
   b. Posted a $1,000 credit to Accounts Payable as $100.
   c. Did not record utilities expense or the related account payable in the amount of $200.
   d. Understated Common Stock by $1,100.
   e. Omitted Insurance Expense of $1,000, from the trial balance.

▌ Required

Prepare the correct trial balance at September 30, 20X3, complete with a heading. Journal entries are not required. (pp. 77–78)

E2-23 (*Learning Objective 5: Recording transactions without a journal*) Set up the following T-accounts: Cash, Accounts Receivable, Office Supplies, Office Furniture, Accounts Payable, Common Stock, Dividends, Service Revenue, Salary Expense, and Rent Expense.

Record the following transactions directly in the T-accounts without using a journal. Use the letters to identify the transactions. (pp. 81–82)

a. Linda English opened a law firm by investing $10,000 cash and office furniture valued at $5,000. Organized as a professional corporation, the business issued common stock to English.

b. Paid monthly rent of $1,500.

c. Purchased office supplies on account, $800.

d. Paid employees' salaries of $1,800.

e. Paid $400 of the account payable created in transaction c.

f. Performed legal service on account, $8,300.

g. Declared and paid dividends of $2,000.

E2-24 *(Learning Objective 4: Preparing and using a trial balance)* Refer to Exercise 2-23.

1. After recording the transactions in Exercise 2-23, prepare the trial balance of Linda English, Attorney, at May 31, 20X9. (pp. 77–78)

2. How well did the business perform during its first month? Compute net income (or net loss) for the month. (pp. 63–64)

Serial Exercise

Exercise 2-25 begins an accounting cycle that is completed in Chapter 3.

E2-25 *(Learning Objective 2, 3, 4: Recording transactions and preparing a trial balance)* Lance Sedberry, Certified Public Accountant, operates as a professional corporation (P.C.). The business completed these transactions during the first part of January:

Jan.	2	Received $5,000 cash from Sedberry, and issued common stock to him.
	2	Paid monthly office rent, $500.
	3	Paid cash for a Dell computer, $3,000, with the computer expected to remain in service for 5 years.
	4	Purchased office furniture on account, $6,000, with the furniture projected to last for 5 years.
	5	Purchased supplies on account, $900.
	9	Performed tax service for a client and received cash for the full amount of $800.
	12	Paid utility expenses, $200.
	18	Performed consulting service for a client on account, $1,700.

▌ *Required*

1. Set up T-accounts for Cash, Accounts Receivable, Supplies, Equipment, Furniture, Accounts Payable, Common Stock, Dividends, Service Revenue, Rent Expense, Utilities Expense, and Salary Expense. (pp. 67–77)

2. Journalize the transactions. Explanations are not required. (pp. 72–77)

3. Post to the T-accounts. Key all items by date and denote an account balance on January 18 as Bal. (pp. 72–77)

4. Prepare a trial balance at January 18. In the Serial Exercise of Chapter 3, we add transactions for the remainder of January and will require a trial balance at January 31. (pp. 77–78)

Challenge Exercises

E2-26 *(Learning Objective 5: Computing financial statement amounts)* The manager of Dubois Furniture needs to compute the following amounts.

a. Total cash paid during March. (pp. 77–78)

b. Cash collections from customers during March. Analyze Accounts Receivable. (pp. 77–78)

c. Cash paid on a note payable during March. Analyze Notes Payable. (pp. 77–78)

(continued)

writing assignment ■

■ general ledger

Here are the additional data you need to analyze the accounts:

		Balance		
Account		Feb. 28	Mar. 31	Additional Information for the Month of March
1. Cash............................		$10,000	$ 5,000	Cash receipts, $80,000
2. Accounts Receivable.......		26,000	24,000	Sales on account, $50,000
3. Notes Payable		13,000	21,000	New borrowing, $25,000

Prepare a T-account to compute each amount *a* through *c*.

E2-27 (*Learning Objective 1, 4: Analyzing transactions; using a trial balance*) The trial balance of Loop 340, Inc., at December 31, 20X5, does not balance.

Cash..............................	$ 3,900	Common stock...................	$20,000
Accounts receivable.............	7,200	Retained earnings...............	7,300
Land..............................	34,000	Service revenue..................	9,100
Accounts payable...............	5,800	Salary expense..................	3,400
Note payable....................	5,000	Advertising expense............	900

▌ Required

1. How much out of balance is the trial balance? Determine the out-of-balance amount. The error lies in the Accounts Receivable account. Add the out-of-balance amount to, or subtract it from, Accounts Receivable to determine the correct balance of Accounts Receivable.

2. After correcting Accounts Receivable, advise the top management of Loop 340, Inc., on the company's
   a. Total assets
   b. Total liabilities
   c. Net income or net loss for December. (pp. 63–64)

E2-28 (*Learning Objective 1: Analyzing transactions*) This question concerns the items and the amounts that 2 entities, Rogers Co., and Providence Hospital, should report in their financial statements.

During June, Providence provided Rogers with medical exams for Rogers employees and sent a bill for $20,000. On July 7 Rogers sent a check to Providence for $15,000. Rogers began June with a cash balance of $25,000; Providence began with cash of $0.

▌ Required

For this situation, show everything that both Rogers and Providence will report on their June and July income statements and on their balance sheets at June 30 and July 31. Use the following format for your answer: (pp. 72–74, 63–64)

Rogers:		
Income statement	June	July
Balance sheet	June 30	July 31
Providence:		
Income statement	June	July
Balance sheet	June 30	July 31

After showing what each company should report, briefly explain how Rogers and the Providence data relate to each other. Be specific. (Challenge)

Quiz

Test your understanding of transaction analysis by answering the following questions. Select the best choice from among the possible answers.

Q2-29 An investment of cash into the business will (pp. 57–58)

a. Decrease total assets.
b. Decrease total liabilities.
c. Increase stockholders' equity.
d. Have no effect on total assets.

Q2-30 Purchasing a computer on account will (pp. 58–59)

a. Increase total assets.
b. Increase total liabilities.
c. Have no effect on stockholders' equity.
d. All of the above.

Q2-31 Performing a service on account will (pp. 59–60)

a. Increase total assets.
b. Increase stockholders' equity.
c. Both a and b.
d. Increase total liabilities.

Q2-32 Receiving cash from a customer on account will (pp. 60–61)

a. Have no effect on total assets.
b. Increase total assets.
c. Decrease liabilities.
d. Increase stockholders equity.

Q2-33 Purchasing computer equipment for cash will (pp. 58–59)

a. Increase both total assets and total liabilities.
b. Decrease both total assets and stockholders' equity.
c. Decrease both total liabilities and stockholders' equity.
d. Have no effect on total assets, total liabilities, or stockholders' equity.

Q2-34 Purchasing a building for $100,000 by paying cash of $20,000 and signing a note payable for $80,000 will (pp. 58–59)

a. Increase both total assets and total liabilities by $100,000.
b. Increase both total assets and total liabilities by $80,000.
c. Decrease total assets and increase total liabilities by $20,000.
d. Decrease both total assets and total liabilities by $20,000.

Q2-35 What is the effect on total assets and stockholders' equity of paying the electric bill as soon as it is received each month? (pp. 59–60)

	Total assets	Stockholders' equity
a.	Decrease	No effect
b.	No effect	No effect
c.	Decrease	Decrease
d.	No effect	Decrease

Q2-36 Which of the following transactions will increase an asset and increase a liability? (pp. 58–59)

a. Buying equipment on account.
b. Purchasing office equipment for cash.
c. Issuing stock.
d. Payment of an account payable.

Q2-37 Which of the following transactions will increase an asset and increase stockholders' equity? (pp. 59–60)

a. Collecting cash from a customer on an account receivable.
b. Performing a service on account for a customer.
c. Borrowing money from a bank.
d. Purchasing supplies on account.

Q2-38 Where do we first record a transaction? (pp. 70–71)

a. Ledger

b. Trial balance

c. Account

d. Journal

Q2-39 Which of the following is not an asset account? (pp. 55–56, 63–64)

a. Common Stock

b. Salary Expense

c. Service Revenue

d. None of the above accounts is an asset.

Q2-40 Which statement is false? (pp. 70–71)

a. Revenues are increased by credits.

b. Assets are increased by debits.

c. Dividends are increased by credits.

d. Liabilities are decreased by debits.

Q2-41 The journal entry to record the receipt of land and a building and issuance of common stock (pp. 72–73)

a. Debits Land and Building and credits Common Stock.

b. Debits Land and credits Common Stock.

c. Debits Common Stock and credits Land and Building.

d. Debits Land, Building, and Common Stock.

Q2-42 The journal entry to record the purchase of supplies on account (pp. 73–74)

a. Credits Supplies and debits Cash.

b. Debits Supplies and credits Accounts Payable.

c. Debits Supplies Expense and credits Supplies.

d. Credits Supplies and debits Accounts Payable.

Q2-43 If the credit to record the purchase of supplies on account is not posted, (pp. 73–74)

a. Liabilities will be understated.

b. Expenses will be overstated.

c. Assets will be understated.

d. Stockholders' equity will be understated.

Q2-44 The journal entry to record a payment on account will (pp. 74–76)

a. Debit Accounts Payable and credit Retained Earnings.

b. Debit Cash and credit Expenses.

c. Debit Expenses and credit Cash.

d. Debit Accounts Payable and credit Cash.

Q2-45 If the credit to record the payment of an account payable is not posted, (pp. 74–76)

a. Liabilities will be understated.

b. Expenses will be understated.

c. Cash will be overstated.

d. Cash will be understated.

Q2-46 Which statement is false? (pp. 77–78)

a. A trial balance lists all the accounts with their current balances.

b. A trial balance is the same as a balance sheet.

c. A trial balance can verify the equality of debits and credits.

d. A trial balance can be taken at any time.

Q2-47 A business's purchase of a $100,000 building with an $85,000 mortgage payable and issuance of $15,000 of common stock will (pp. 62–63)

a. Increase stockholders' equity by $15,000.

b. Increase assets by $15,000.

c. Increase assets by $85,000.

d. Increase stockholders' equity by $100,000.

Q2-48 Martex, Inc., a new company, completed these transactions. What will Martex's total assets equal? (pp. 62–63)

(1) Stockholders invested $50,000 cash and inventory worth $25,000.

(2) Sales on account, $12,000.

a. $75,000

b. $87,000

c. $63,000

d. $62,000

Problems
(Group A)

> Some of these A problems can be found within My Accounting Lab (MAL), an online homework and practice environment. Your instructor may ask you to complete these exercises using MAL.

P2-49A (*Learning Objective 1: Analyzing a trial balance*) The trial balance of Amusement Specialties, Inc., follows.

Amusement Specialties, Inc. Trial Balance December 31, 20X6		
Cash..	$ 14,000	
Accounts receivable...............	11,000	
Prepaid expenses	4,000	
Equipment.............................	171,000	
Building..................................	100,000	
Accounts payable		$ 30,000
Note payable...........................		120,000
Common stock........................		102,000
Retained earnings....................		40,000
Dividends................................	22,000	
Service revenue.......................		86,000
Rent expense...........................	14,000	
Advertising expense................	3,000	
Wage expense..........................	32,000	
Supplies expense.....................	7,000	
Total	$378,000	$378,000

Rhonda Ray, your best friend, is considering investing in Amusement Specialties. Rhonda seeks your advice in interpreting this information. Specifically, she asks how to use this trial balance to compute the company's total assets, total liabilities, and net income or net loss for the year.

I Required

Write a short note to answer Rhonda's questions. In your note, state the amounts of Amusement Specialties' total assets, total liabilities, and net income or net loss for the year. Also show how you computed each amount. (pp. 77–78, 63–64)

P2-50A (*Learning Objective 1: Analyzing transactions with the accounting equation and preparing the financial statements*) The following amounts summarize the financial position of Ready Resources, Inc., on May 31, 20X8:

			Assets					=	Liabilities	+	Stockholders' Equity		
	Cash	+	Accounts Receivable	+	Supplies	+	Land	=	Accounts Payable	+	Common Stock	+	Retained Earnings
Bal.	1,200		1,500				12,000		8,000		4,000		2,700

During June 20X8, Ready Resources completed these transactions:

a. The business received cash of $5,000 and issued common stock.
b. Performed services for a customer and received cash of $6,700.
c. Paid $5,000 on accounts payable.
d. Purchased supplies on account, $1,000.
e. Collected cash from a customer on account, $500.
f. Consulted on the design of a computer system and billed the customer for services rendered, $2,400.
g. Recorded the following business expenses for the month: (1) paid office rent—$900; (2) paid advertising—$300.
h. Declared and paid a cash dividend of $1,800.

❙ Required

1. Analyze the effects of the preceding transactions on the accounting equation of Ready Resources, Inc. Adapt the format of Exhibit 2-1, Panel B. (pp. 62, 63)
2. Prepare the income statement of Ready Resources, Inc., for the month ended June 30, 20X8. List expenses in decreasing order by amount. (pp. 63–64).
3. Prepare the entity's statement of retained earnings for the month ended June 30, 20X8. (pp. 63–64)
4. Prepare the balance sheet of Ready Resources, Inc., at June 30, 20X8. (pp. 63–64)

■ **general ledger**

P2-51A (*Learning Objective 2, 3: Recording transactions, posting*) This problem can be used in conjunction with Problem 2-50A. Refer to Problem 2-50A.

❙ Required

1. Journalize the transactions of Ready Resources, Inc. Explanations are not required. (pp. 72–77)
2. Set up the following T-accounts: Cash, Accounts Receivable, Supplies, Land, Accounts Payable, Common Stock, Retained Earnings, Dividends, Service Revenue, Rent Expense, and Advertising Expense. Insert in each account its balance as given (example: Cash $1,200). Post the transactions to the accounts. (pp. 72–77)
3. Compute the balance in each account. For each asset account, each liability account, and for Common Stock, compare its balance to the ending balance you obtained in Problem 2-50A. Are the amounts the same or different? (In Chapter 3, we complete the accounting process. There you will learn how the Retained Earnings, Dividends, Revenue, and Expense accounts work together in the processing of accounting information.) (pp. 72–77)

P2-52A (*Learning Objective 1, 2: Analyzing transactions with the accounting equation*) Perry Real Estate Co. experienced the following events during the organizing phase and its first month of operations. Some of the events were personal for the stockholders and did not affect the business. Others were transactions of the business.

Nov.	4	Gaylord Perry, the major stockholder of real estate company, received $50,000 cash from an inheritance.
	5	Perry deposited $50,000 cash in a new business bank account titled Perry Real Estate Co. The business issued common stock to Perry.
	6	The business paid $300 cash for letterhead stationery for the new office.
	7	The business purchased office equipment. The company paid cash of $30,000 and agreed to pay the account payable for the remainder, $7,000, within 3 months.
	10	Perry sold Dell stock, which he had owned for several years, receiving $75,000 cash from his personal stockbroker.
	11	Perry deposited the $75,000 cash from sale of the Dell stock in his personal bank account.
	12	A representative of a large company telephoned Perry and told him of the company's intention to transfer $10,000 of business to Perry.
	18	Perry finished a real estate deal for a client and submitted his bill for services, $10,000. Perry expects to collect from this client within 2 weeks.
	21	The business paid half its account payable for the equipment purchased on November 7.
	25	The business paid office rent of $4,000.
	30	The business declared and paid a cash dividend of $2,000.

❙ *Required*

1. Classify each of the preceding events as one of the following: (pp. 57–63)
   a. A business-related event but not a transaction to be recorded by Perry Real Estate Co.
   b. A personal transaction for a stockholder, not to be recorded by Perry Real Estate Co.
   c. A business transaction to be recorded by Perry Real Estate Co.

2. Analyze the effects of the preceding events on the accounting equation of Perry Real Estate Co. Use a format similar to that in Exhibit 2-1, Panel B. (pp. 62–63)

3. Record the transactions of the business in its journal. Include an explanation for each entry. (pp. 72–77)

P2-53A (*Learning Objective 2, 3: Analyzing and recording transactions*) During December, Barnett Auction Co. completed the following transactions:

■ **general ledger**

Dec.	1	Barnett received $10,000 cash and issued common stock to the stockholders.
	5	Paid monthly rent, $1,000.
	9	Paid $5,000 cash and signed a $25,000 note payable to purchase land for an office site.
	10	Purchased supplies on account, $1,200.
	19	Paid $600 on account.
	22	Borrowed $15,000 from the bank for business use. Barnett signed a note payable to the bank in the name of the business.
	31	Service revenues earned during the month included $6,000 cash and $5,000 on account.
	31	Paid employees' salaries ($2,000), advertising expense ($1,500), and utilities expense ($1,100).
	31	Declared and paid a cash dividend of $4,000.

(*continued*)

Barnett's business uses the following accounts: Cash, Accounts Receivable, Supplies, Land, Accounts Payable, Notes Payable, Common Stock, Dividends, Service Revenue, Salary Expense, Advertising Expense, and Utilities Expense.

❙ Required

1. Journalize each transaction of Barnett Auction Co. Explanations are not required. (pp. 72–77)

2. Prepare T-accounts for Cash, Accounts Payable, and Notes Payable. Post to these three accounts. (pp. 76)

3. After these transactions, how much cash does the business have? How much in total liabilities does it owe? (pp. 62–64)

■ **general ledger**

P2-54A (*Learning Objective 2, 3, 4: Journalizing transactions, posting, and preparing and using a trial balance*) During the first month of operations, Double R Heating and Air Conditioning, Inc., completed the following transactions:

Jan.	2	Double R received $30,000 cash and issued common stock to the stockholders.
	3	Purchased supplies, $1,000, and equipment, $2,600, on account.
	4	Performed service for a customer and received cash, $1,500.
	7	Paid cash to acquire land, $22,000.
	11	Performed service for a customer and billed the customer, $800. We expect to collect within 1 month.
	16	Paid for the equipment purchased January 3 on account.
	17	Paid the telephone bill, $100.
	18	Received partial payment from customer on account, $500.
	22	Paid the water and electricity bills, $400.
	29	Received $1,800 cash for servicing the heating unit of a customer.
	31	Paid employee salary, $1,300.
	31	Declared and paid dividends of $2,200.

❙ Required

Set up the following T-accounts: Cash, Accounts Receivable, Supplies, Equipment, Land, Accounts Payable, Common Stock, Dividends, Service Revenue, Salary Expense, and Utilities Expense.

1. Record each transaction in the journal, using the account titles given. Key each transaction by date. Explanations are not required. (pp. 72–77)

2. Post the transactions to the T-accounts, using transaction dates as posting references. Label the ending balance of each account *Bal.*, as shown in the chapter. (pp. 72–77)

3. Prepare the trial balance of Double R Heating and Air Conditioning, Inc., at January 31 of the current year.

4. The manager asks you how much in total resources the business has to work with, how much it owes, and whether January was profitable (and by how much). (pp. 63–64)

■ **general ledger**

P2-55A (*Learning Objective 3, 4: Recording transactions directly in T-accounts; preparing and using a trial balance*) During the first month of operations (April 20X1), Music Services Corporation completed the following selected transactions:

a. The business received cash of $25,000 and a building valued at $50,000. The corporation issued common stock to the stockholders.

b. Borrowed $50,000 from the bank; signed a note payable.

c. Paid $60,000 for music equipment.

d. Purchased supplies on account, $1,000.

e. Paid employees' salaries, $1,300.

f. Received $500 for service performed for customers.

g. Performed service for customers on account, $1,800.

h. Paid $600 of the account payable created in Transaction d.

i. Received a $500 bill for utility expense that will be paid in the near future.
j. Received cash on account, $1,100.
k. Paid the following cash expenses: (1) rent, $1,000; (2) advertising, $800.

Required

1. Set up the following T-accounts: Cash, Accounts Receivable, Supplies, Music Equipment, Building, Accounts Payable, Note Payable, Common Stock, Service Revenue, Salary Expense, Rent Expense, Advertising Expense, and Utilities Expense. (pp. 81–82)

2. Record the foregoing transactions directly in the T-accounts without using a journal. Use the letters to identify the transactions. (pp. 81–82)

3. Prepare the trial balance of Music Services Corporation at April 30, 20X1. (p. 73)

(Group B)

P2-56B *(Learning Objective 1: Analyzing a trial balance)* Your best friend is considering making an investment in Photometric Tailoring Co. She seeks your advice in interpreting the company's information. Specifically, she asks whether this trial balance provides the data to prepare a balance sheet and an income statement.

writing assignment ■

Photometric Tailoring Co.
Trial Balance
December 31, 20X9

Cash	$ 12,000	
Accounts receivable	47,000	
Prepaid expenses	4,000	
Equipment	236,000	
Accounts payable		$105,000
Note payable		92,000
Common stock		30,000
Retained earnings		32,000
Service revenue		139,000
Salary expense	63,000	
Rent expense	26,000	
Supplies expense	7,000	
Advertising expense	3,000	
Total	$398,000	$398,000

Required

Write a memo to answer your friend's questions. State which accounts go on the balance sheet and which accounts go on the income statement. In your memo, state the amount of net income that Photometric Tailoring earned in 20X9, and explain your computation. (pp. 77–78, 63–64)

P2-57B *(Learning Objective 1: Analyzing transactions with the accounting equation and preparing the financial statements)* Donald Healey operates and is the major stockholder of an interior design studio called DH Designers, Inc. The following amounts summarize the business on April 30, 20X1:

		Assets					=	Liabilities	+		Stockholders' Equity		
	Cash	+	Accounts Receivable	+	Supplies	+	Land	=	Accounts Payable	+	Common Stock	+	Retained Earnings
Bal.	1,700		2,200				24,100		5,400		10,000		12,600

(continued)

During May 20X1, the business completed these transactions:

a. Healey received $30,000 as a gift and deposited the cash in the business bank account. The business issued common stock to Healey.

b. Paid $1,400 on accounts payable.

c. Performed services for a client and received cash of $4,100.

d. Collected cash from a customer on account, $700.

e. Purchased supplies on account, $800.

f. Consulted on the interior design of a major office building and billed the client for services rendered, $5,000.

g. Received cash of $1,700 and issued common stock to a stockholder.

h. Recorded the following expenses for the month: (1) paid office rent—$1,200; (2) paid advertising—$600.

i. Declared and paid a cash dividend of $2,000.

❙ Required

1. Analyze the effects of the preceding transactions on the accounting equation of DH Designers, Inc. Adapt the format of Exhibit 2-1, Panel B. (pp. 62–63)

2. Prepare the income statement of DH Designers, Inc., for the month ended May 31, 20X1. List expenses in decreasing order by amount. (pp. 63–64)

3. Prepare the statement of retained earnings of DH Designers, Inc., for the month ended May 31, 20X1. (pp. 63–64)

4. Prepare the balance sheet of DH Designers, Inc., at May 31, 20X1. (pp. 63–64)

■ **general ledger**

P2-58B (*Learning Objective 2, 3: Recording transactions, posting*) This problem can be used in conjunction with Problem 2-57B. Refer to Problem 2-57B.

❙ Required

1. Journalize the transactions of DH Designers, Inc. Explanations are not required. (pp. 72–77)

2. Set up the following T-accounts: Cash, Accounts Receivable, Supplies, Land, Accounts Payable, Common Stock, Retained Earnings, Dividends, Service Revenue, Rent Expense, and Advertising Expense. Insert in each account its balance as given (example: Cash $1,700). Post to the accounts. (pp. 72–77)

3. Compute the balance in each account. For each asset account, each liability account, and for Common Stock, compare its balance to the ending balance you obtained in Problem 2-57B. Are the amounts the same or different? (In Chapter 3, we complete the accounting process. There you will learn how the Retained Earnings, Dividends, Revenue, and Expense accounts work together in the processing of accounting information.)(pp. 72–77)

P2-59B (*Learning Objective 1, 2: Analyzing transactions with the accounting equation*) Lane Kohler opened a law office, which he operates as a professional corporation. The name of the new entity is Lane Kohler, Attorney and Counselor, Professional Corporation (P.C.). Kohler experienced the following events during the organizing phase of his new business and its first month of operations. Some of the events were personal transactions of the stockholders and did not affect the law practice. Others were transactions that should be accounted for by the business.

March	1	Kohler sold 1,000 shares of YouTube stock and received $75,000 cash from his stockbroker.
	2	Kohler deposited in his personal bank account the $75,000 cash from sale of the YouTube stock.
	3	Kohler received $100,000 cash from his former partners in the law firm from which he resigned.
	5	Kohler deposited $50,000 cash in a new business bank account titled Lane Kohler, Attorney and Counselor, P.C. The business issued common stock to Kohler.
	6	A representative of a large company telephoned Kohler and told him of the company's intention to transfer $15,000 of legal business to Kohler.
	7	The business paid $500 cash for letterhead stationery for the law office.
	9	The business purchased office furniture. Kohler paid cash of $10,000 and agreed to pay the account payable for the remainder, $9,500, within 3 months.
	23	Kohler finished court hearings on behalf of a client and submitted his bill for legal services, $3,000. He expected to collect from this client within 1 month.
	29	The business paid $5,000 of its account payable on the furniture purchased on March 9.
	30	The business paid office rent of $1,900.
	31	The business declared and paid a cash dividend of $1,000.

❚ Required

1. Classify each of the preceding events as one of the following: (pp. 57–63)
   a. A personal transaction of a stockholder, not to be recorded by the business of Lane Kohler, Attorney and Counselor, P.C.
   b. A business transaction to be recorded by the business of Lane Kohler, Attorney and Counselor, P.C.
   c. A business-related event but not a transaction to be recorded by the business of Lane Kohler, Attorney and Counselor, P.C.

2. Analyze the effects of the preceding events on the accounting equation of the business of Lane Kohler, Attorney and Counselor, P.C. Use a format similar to Exhibit 2-1, Panel B. (pp. 62–63)

3. Record the transactions of the business in its journal. Include an explanation for each entry. (pp. 72–77)

P2-60B (*Learning Objective 2, 3: Analyzing and recording transactions*) Blanton Glass Etching, Inc., owns shops in outlet malls. The business completed the following transactions during June:

■ **general ledger**

June	1	Received cash of $25,000 and issued common stock to the stockholders.
	2	Paid $10,000 cash and signed a $30,000 note payable to purchase land.
	7	Received $15,000 cash from service revenue and deposited that amount in the bank.
	10	Purchased supplies on account, $1,700.
	15	Paid employees' salaries, $2,800, and rent on a shop, $1,800.
	15	Paid advertising expense, $1,200.
	16	Paid $800 on account.
	17	Declared and paid a cash dividend of $3,000.

(*continued*)

Blanton uses the following accounts: Cash, Supplies, Land, Accounts Payable, Notes Payable, Common Stock, Dividends, Service Revenue, Salary Expense, Rent Expense, and Advertising Expense.

❙ Required

1. Journalize each transaction. Explanations are not required. (pp. 72–77)

2. Prepare T-accounts for Cash, Accounts Payable, and Notes Payable. Post to these 3 accounts.

3. After these transactions, how much cash does the business have? How much does it owe in total liabilities? (pp. 62–64)

■ **general ledger**

P2-61B (*Learning Objective 2, 3, 4: Journalizing transactions, posting, and preparing and using a trial balance*) During the first month of operations, Barron Environmental Services, Inc., completed the following transactions:

Sept.	3	Received $20,000 cash and issued common stock.
	4	Purchased supplies, $800, and furniture, $1,800, on account.
	6	Performed services for a client and received $5,000 cash.
	7	Paid $15,000 cash to acquire land for an office site.
	10	Worked for a client, billed the client, and received her promise to pay the $600 within 1 week.
	14	Paid for the furniture purchased September 4 on account.
	16	Paid the telephone bill, $200.
	17	Received partial payment from client on account, $500.
	24	Paid the water and electricity bills, $400.
	28	Received $1,500 cash for helping a client meet environmental standards.
	30	Paid secretary's salary, $1,200.
	30	Declared and paid dividends of $2,000.

❙ Required

Set up the following T-accounts: Cash, Accounts Receivable, Supplies, Furniture, Land, Accounts Payable, Common Stock, Dividends, Service Revenue, Salary Expense, and Utilities Expense.

1. Record each transaction in the journal, using the account titles given. Key each transaction by date. Explanations are not required. (pp. 72–77)

2. Post the transactions to the T-accounts, using transaction dates as posting references. Label the ending balance of each account Bal., as shown in the chapter (pp. 72–77)

3. Prepare the trial balance of Barron Environmental Services, Inc., at September 30 of the current year. (pp. 63–64)

4. Barron asks you how much in total resources the business has to work with, how much it owes, and whether September was profitable (and by how much). (pp. 63–64)

P2-62B (*Learning Objective 3, 4: Recording transactions directly in T-accounts; preparing and using a trial balance*) During the first month of operations (June 20X3), Walker Consulting Company completed the following selected transactions:

a. Began the business with an investment of $20,000 cash and a building valued at $60,000. The corporation issued common stock to the stockholders.

b. Borrowed $90,000 from the bank; signed a note payable.

c. Purchased supplies on account for $1,300.

d. Paid $35,000 for computer equipment.

e. Paid employees' salaries totaling $2,200.

f. Performed consulting service on account for a client, $2,100.

g. Paid $800 of the account payable created in transaction c.
h. Received a $600 bill for advertising expense that will be paid in the near future.
i. Performed service for clients and received $1,100 in cash.
j. Received $1,200 cash on account.
k. Paid the following cash expenses: (1) rent, $700; (2) utilities, $400.

I Required

1. Set up the following T-accounts: Cash, Accounts Receivable, Supplies, Computer Equipment, Building, Accounts Payable, Note Payable, Common Stock, Service Revenue, Salary Expense, Advertising Expense, Rent Expense, and Utilities Expense. (pp. 81–82)

2. Record each transaction directly in the T-accounts without using a journal. Use the letters to identify the transactions. (pp. 81–82)

3. Prepare the trial balance of Walker Consulting Company, at June 30, 20X3. (p. 71)

APPLY YOUR KNOWLEDGE

Decision Cases

Case 1. (*Learning Objective 4, 5: Recording transactions directly in T-accounts, preparing a trial balance, and measuring net income or loss*) A friend named Jay Barlow has asked what effect certain transactions will have on his company. Time is short, so you cannot apply the detailed procedures of journalizing and posting. Instead, you must analyze the transactions without the use of a journal. Barlow will continue the business only if he can expect to earn monthly net income of $10,000. The following transactions occurred this month:

a. Barlow deposited $10,000 cash in a business bank account, and the corporation issued common stock to him.

b. Borrowed $5,000 cash from the bank and signed a note payable due within 1 year.

c. Paid $300 cash for supplies.

d. Purchased advertising in the local newspaper for cash, $800.

e. Purchased office furniture on account, $4,400.

f. Paid the following cash expenses for 1 month: employee salary, $1,700; office rent, $600.

g. Earned revenue on account, $7,000.

h. Earned revenue and received $2,500 cash.

i. Collected cash from customers on account, $1,200.

j. Paid on account, $1,000.

I Required

1. Set up the following T-accounts: Cash, Accounts Receivable, Supplies, Furniture, Accounts Payable, Notes Payable, Common Stock, Service Revenue, Salary Expense, Advertising Expense, and Rent Expense. (pp. 81–82)

2. Record the transactions directly in the accounts without using a journal. Key each transaction by letter. (pp. 81–82)

3. Prepare a trial balance for Barlow Networks, Inc., at the current date. List expenses with the largest amount first, the next largest amount second, and so on. (pp. 77–78)

4. Compute the amount of net income or net loss for this first month of operations. Why or why not would you recommend that Barlow continue in business? (pp. 63–64)

Case 2. *(Learning Objective 2: Correcting financial statements; deciding whether to expand a business)* Sophia Loren opened an Italian restaurant. Business has been good, and Loren is considering expanding the restaurant. Loren, who knows little accounting, produced the following financial statements for Little Italy, Inc., at December 31, 20X1, end of the first month of operations:

Little Italy, Inc. Income Statement Month Ended December 31, 20X1		
Sales revenue		$36,000
Common stock		10,000
Total revenue		46,000
Accounts payable		$ 8,000
Advertising expense		5,000
Rent expense		6,000
Total expenses		19,000
Net income		$27,000

Little Italy, Inc. Balance Sheet December 31, 20X1		
Assets		
Cash		$ 6,000
Cost of goods sold (expense)		22,000
Food inventory		5,000
Furniture		10,000
Total Assets		43,000
Liabilities		
None		
Owners' Equity		$43,000

In these financial statements all *amounts* are correct, except for Owners' Equity. Loren heard that total assets should equal total liabilities plus owners' equity, so she plugged in the amount of owners' equity at $43,000 to make the balance sheet come out even.

❙ Required

Sophia Loren has asked whether she should expand the restaurant. Her banker says Loren may be wise to expand if (a) net income for the first month reached $5,000 and (b) total assets are at least $25,000. It appears that the business has reached these milestones, but Loren doubts whether her financial statements tell the true story. She needs your help in making this decision. Prepare a corrected income statement and balance sheet. (Remember that Retained Earnings, which was omitted from the balance sheet, should equal net income for the first month; there were no dividends.) After preparing the statements, give Sophia Loren your recommendation as to whether she should expand the restaurant. (pp. 63–64)

Ethical Issues

Issue 1. Scruffy Murphy is the president and principal stockholder of Scruffy's Bar & Grill, Inc. To expand, the business is applying for a $250,000 bank loan. To get the loan, Murphy is considering two options for beefing up the owners' equity of the business:

> *Option 1.*   Issue $100,000 of common stock for cash. A friend has been wanting to invest in the company. This may be the right time to extend the offer.
> *Option 2.*   Transfer $100,000 of Murphy's personal land to the business, and issue common stock to Murphy. Then, after obtaining the loan, Murphy can transfer the land back to himself and zero out the common stock.

Journalize the transactions required by each option. Which plan is ethical? Which is unethical and why? (pp.72–74)

Issue 2. Community Charities has a standing agreement with Empire State Bank. The agreement allows Community Charities to overdraw its cash balance at the bank when donations are running low. In the past, Community Charities managed funds wisely and rarely used this privilege. Recently, however, Douglas Byrd has been named president of Community Charities. To expand operations, Byrd is acquiring equipment and spending a lot for fund-raising. During Byrd's presidency, Community Charities has maintained a negative bank balance of about $3,000.

I Required

What is the ethical issue in this situation? Do you approve or disapprove of Byrd's management of Community Charities' and Empire State Bank's funds? Why? (Challenge)

Focus on Financials: ■ YUM! Brands

(Learning Objective 3, 4: Recording transactions and computing net income) Refer to YUM! Brands' financial statements in Appendix A at the end of the book. Assume that YUM completed the following selected transactions during 2006.

  a. Made company sales (revenue) and collected cash of $8,365 million.

  b. Earned franchise and license fee revenue on account, $1,196 million.

  c. Purchased inventories, paying cash of $2,557 million.

  d. Incurred food and paper expense of $2,549 million. Credit the Inventories account.

  e. Paid operating and other expenses of $6,188 million.

  f. Collected cash on accounts and notes receivable, $1,212 million.

  g. Paid cash for other assets, $671 million.

I Required

  1. Set up T-accounts for: Cash (debit balance of $158 million); Accounts and Notes Receivable (debit balance of $236 million); Inventories (debit balance of $85 million); Other Assets ($0 balance); Company Sales (Revenue: $0 balance); Franchise and License Fee Revenue ($0 balance); Food and Paper Expense ($0 balance); Operating and Other Expenses ($0 balance). (pp. 72–77)

  2. Journalize YUM's transactions a–g. Explanations are not required. (pp. 72–77)

  3. Post to the T-accounts, and compute the balance for each account. Key postings by transaction letters a–g. (pp. 72–77)

  4. For each of the following accounts, compare your computed balance to YUM's actual balance as shown on YUM's 2006 income statement or balance sheet in Appendix A. Your amounts should agree to the actual figures. (pp. 77–78)

  a. Cash
  b. Accounts and Notes Receivable
  c. Inventories
  d. Company Sales (Revenue)
  e. Franchise and License Fee Revenue
  f. Food and Paper Expense

  5. Use the relevant accounts from requirement 4 to prepare a summary income statement for YUM! Brands, Inc., for 2006. Compare the net income you computed to YUM's actual net income. The 2 amounts should be equal. (p. 23)

Focus on Analysis: ■ Pier 1 Imports

(Learning Objective 1, 2: Analyzing a leading company's financial statements) Refer to the **Pier 1 Imports** financial statements in Appendix B at the end of the book. Suppose you are an investor considering buying Pier 1 stock. The following questions are important: **Show amounts in millions and round to the nearest $1 million.**

  1. Explain whether Pier 1 had more sales revenue, or collected more cash from customers, during 2006. Combine Pier 1's 2 receivable accounts, and then analyze total receivables to answer this question. (pp. 77–78, Challenge).

  2. A major concern of lenders, such as banks, is the amount of "long-term debt" a company owes. How much long-term debt does Pier 1 owe at the end of 2006? at the end of 2005? What must have happened to Pier 1's long-term debt during 2006? (Challenge)

  3. Investors are vitally interested in a company's sales and profits, and its trends of sales and profits over time. Consider Pier 1's net sales and net income (net loss) during the period from 2004 through 2006. Compute the percentage increase or decrease in net sales and also in net income (net loss) from 2004 to 2006. Which item grew faster during this 2-year period, net sales or net income (net loss)? (Challenge)

Group Projects

Project 1. You are promoting a rock concert in your area. Your purpose is to earn a profit, so you need to establish the formal structure of a business entity. Assume you organize as a corporation.

▌ Required

1. Make a detailed list of 10 factors you must consider as you establish the business.

2. Describe 10 of the items your business must arrange to promote and stage the rock concert.

3. Identify the transactions that your business can undertake to organize, promote, and stage the concert. Journalize the transactions, and post to the relevant T-accounts. Set up the accounts you need for your business ledger. Refer to the appendix at the end of book if needed.

4. Prepare the income statement, statement of retained earnings, and balance sheet immediately after the rock concert, that is, before you have had time to pay all the business bills and to collect all receivables.

5. Assume that you will continue to promote rock concerts if the venture is successful. If it is unsuccessful, you will terminate the business within 3 months after the concert. Discuss how to evaluate the success of your venture and how to decide whether to continue in business.

Project 2. Contact a local business and arrange with the owner to learn what accounts the business uses.

▌ Required

1. Obtain a copy of the business's chart of accounts.

2. Prepare the company's financial statements for the most recent month, quarter, or year. You may use either made-up account balances or balances supplied by the owner.

If the business has a large number of accounts within a category, combine related accounts and report a single amount on the financial statements. For example, the company may have several cash accounts. Combine all cash amounts and report a single Cash amount on the balance sheet.

You will probably encounter numerous accounts that you have not yet learned. Deal with these as best you can. The charts of accounts given in the appendix at the end of the book can be helpful.

For Internet Exercises go to the Web site www.prenhall.com/harrison.

Quick Check Answers

1. *c*   2. *d*   3. *b*   4. *d*   5. *a*   6. *b*   7. *c*   8. *a*   9. *d*   10. *d*   11. *a*   12. *c*

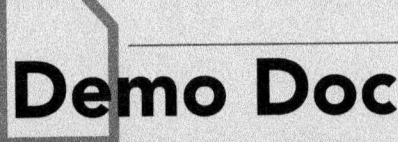

Demo Doc

Debit/Credit Transaction Analysis

Demo Doc: To make sure you understand this material, work through the following demonstration "demo doc" with detailed comments to help you see the concept within the framework of a worked-through problem.

Learning Objectives 1, 2, 3, 4

On September 1, 2008, Michael Moe incorporated Moe's Mowing, Inc., a company that provides mowing and landscaping services. During the month of September, the business incurred the following transactions:

a. To begin operations, Michael deposited $10,000 cash in the business's bank account. The business received the cash and issued common stock to Michael.

b. The business purchased equipment for $3,500 on account.

c. The business purchased office supplies for $800 cash.

d. The business provided $2,600 of services to a customer on account.

e. The business paid $500 cash toward the equipment previously purchased on account in transaction b.

f. The business received $2,000 in cash for services provided to a new customer.

g. The business paid $200 cash to repair equipment.

h. The business paid $900 cash in salary expense.

i. The business received $2,100 cash from a customer on account.

j. The business paid cash dividends of $1,500.

Requirements

1. Create blank T-accounts for the following accounts: Cash, Accounts Receivable, Supplies, Equipment, Accounts Payable, Common Stock, Dividends, Service Revenue, Salary Expense, Repair Expense.

2. Journalize the transactions and then post to the T-accounts. Use the table in Exhibit 2-16 to help with the journal entries.

EXHIBIT 2-16	The Rules of Debit and Credit	
	Increase	Decrease
Assets	debit	credit
Liabilities	credit	debit
Stockholders' Equity	credit	debit
Revenues	credit	debit
Expenses	debit	credit
Dividends	debit	credit

3. Total each T-account to determine its balance at the end of the month.

4. Prepare the trial balance of Moe's Mowing, Inc., at September 30, 2008.

Demo Doc Solutions

Requirement 1

Create blank T-accounts for the following accounts: Cash, Accounts Receivable, Supplies, Equipment, Accounts Payable, Common Stock, Dividends, Service Revenue, Salary Expense, Repair Expense.

| Part 1 | Part 2 | Part 3 | Part 4 | Demo Doc Complete |

Opening a T-account means drawing a blank account that looks like a capital "T" and putting the account title across the top. T-accounts show the additions and subtractions made to each account. For easy reference, the accounts are grouped into assets, liabilities, stockholders' equity, revenue, and expenses (in that order).

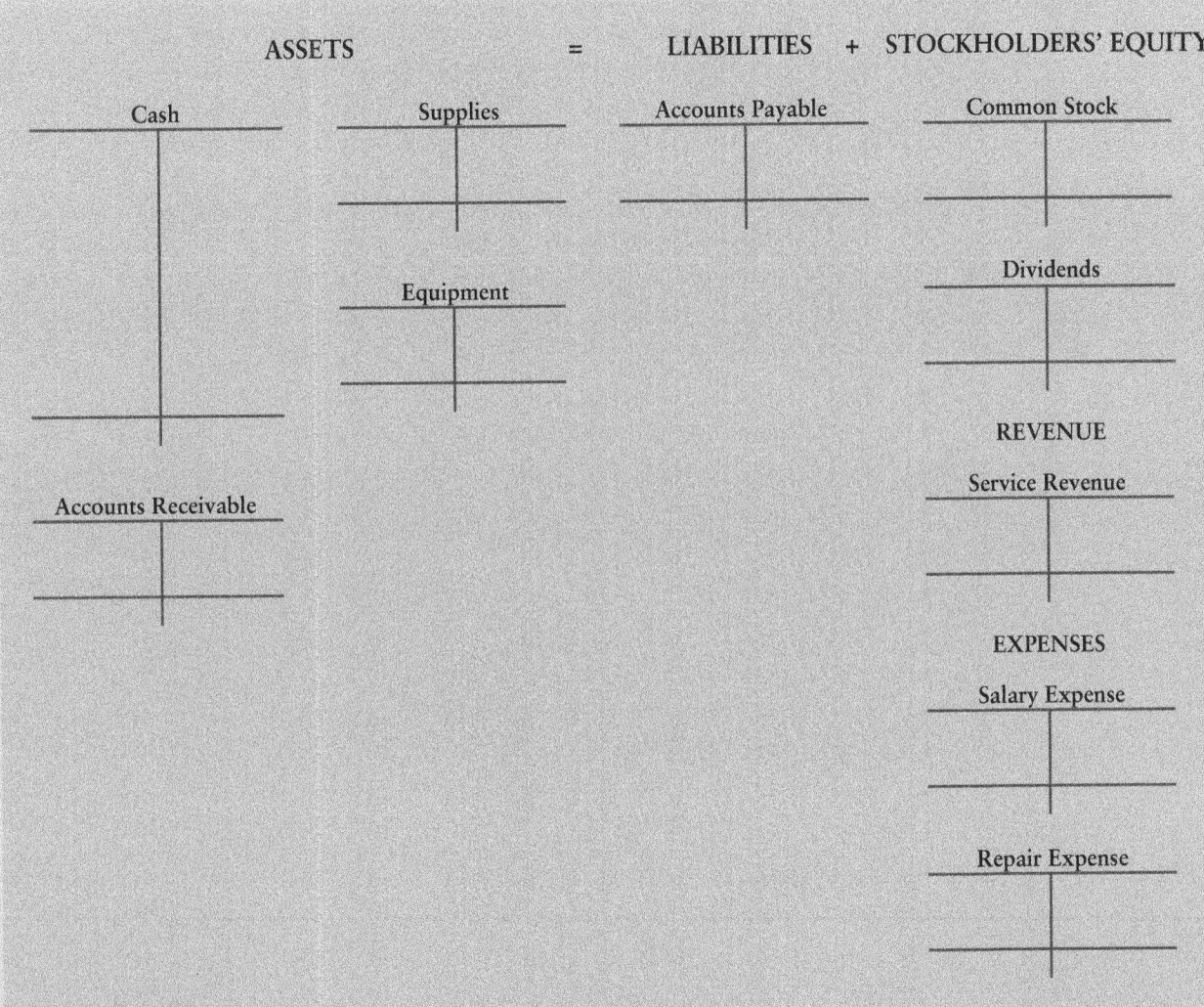

Requirement 2

Journalize the transactions and show how they are recorded in T-accounts.

Part 1	**Part 2**	Part 3	Demo Doc Complete

a. To begin operations, Michael deposited $10,000 cash in the business's bank account. The business received the cash and issued common stock to Michael.

First, we must determine which accounts are affected by the transaction.

The business received $10,000 cash from its principal stockholder (Michael Moe). In exchange, the business issued common stock to Michael. So, the accounts involved are Cash and Common Stock.

Remember that we are recording the transactions of Moe's Mowing, Inc., not the transactions of Michael Moe, the person. Michael and his business are 2 entirely separate accounting entities.

The next step is to determine what type of accounts these are. Cash is an asset, Common Stock is part of equity.

Next, we must determine if these accounts increased or decreased. From the business's point of view, Cash (an asset) has increased. Common Stock (equity) has also increased.

Now we must determine if these accounts should be debited or credited. According to the rules of debit and credit (see Exhibit 2-16 on p. 112), an increase in assets is a debit, while an increase in equity is a credit.

So, Cash (an asset) increases, which requires a debit. Common Stock (equity) also increases, which requires a credit.

The journal entry follows.

a.	Cash (Asset ↑; debit)	10,000	
	Common Stock (Equity ↑; credit)		10,000
	Issued common stock.		

The total dollar amounts of debits must always equal the total dollar amounts of credits.

Remember to use the transaction letters as references. This will help as we post entries to the T-accounts.

Each T-account has 2 sides—one for recording debits and the other for recording credits. To post the transaction to a T-account, simply transfer the amount of each debit to the correct account as a debit (left-side) entry, and transfer the amount of each credit to the correct account as a credit (right-side) entry.

This transaction includes a debit of $10,000 to cash. This means that $10,000 is posted to the left side of the Cash T-account. The transaction also includes a credit of $10,000 to Common Stock. This means that $10,000 is posted to the right side of the Common Stock account, as follows:

Cash		Common Stock	
a. 10,000			a. 10,000

Now the first transaction has been journalized and posted. We repeat this process for every journal entry. Let's proceed to the next transaction.

b. The business purchased equipment for $3,500 on account.

The business received equipment in exchange for a promise to pay for the $3,500 cost at a future date. So the accounts involved in the transaction are Equipment and Accounts Payable.

Equipment is an asset and Accounts Payable is a liability.

The asset Equipment has increased. The liability Accounts Payable has also increased.

Looking at Exhibit 2-16 (p. 112), an increase in assets (in this case, the increase in Equipment) is a debit, while an increase in liabilities (in this case, Accounts Payable) is a credit.

The journal entry follows.

b.	Equipment (Asset ↑; debit)	3,500	
	Accounts Payable (Liability ↑; credit)		3,500
	Purchased equipment on account.		

$3,500 is then posted to the debit (left) side of the Equipment T-account. $3,500 is posted to the credit (right) side of Accounts Payable, as follows:

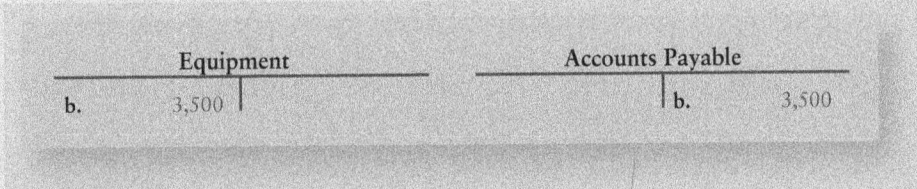

	Equipment			Accounts Payable	
b.	3,500		b.		3,500

c. The business purchased office supplies for $800 cash.

The business purchased supplies, paying cash of $800. So the accounts involved in the transaction are Supplies and Cash.

Supplies and Cash are both assets.

Supplies (an asset) has increased. Cash (an asset) has decreased.

Looking at Exhibit 2-16 (p. 112), an increase in assets is a debit, while a decrease in assets is a credit.

So the increase to Supplies (an asset) is a debit, while the decrease to Cash (an asset) is a credit.

The journal entry follows:

c.	Supplies (Asset ↑; debit)	800	
	Cash (Asset ↓; credit)		800
	Purchased supplies for cash.		

$800 is then posted to the debit (left) side of the Supplies T-account. $800 is posted to the credit (right) side of the Cash account, as follows:

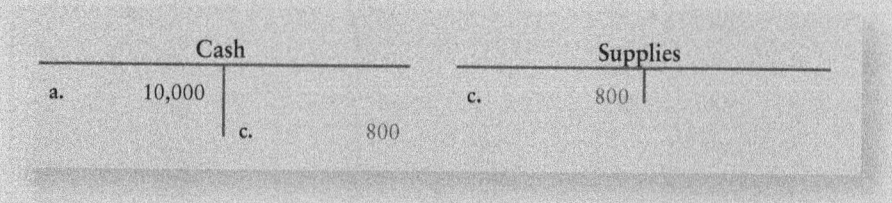

	Cash				Supplies	
a.	10,000			c.	800	
		c.	800			

Notice the $10,000 already on the debit side of the Cash account. This came from transaction a.

d. The business provided $2,600 of services to a customer on account.

The business rendered service for a customer and received a promise from the customer to pay us $2,600 cash next month. So the accounts involved in the transaction are Accounts Receivable and Service Revenue.

Accounts Receivable is an asset and Service Revenue is revenue.

Accounts Receivable (an asset) has increased. Service Revenue (revenue) has also increased.

Looking at Exhibit 2-16 (p. 112), an increase in assets is a debit, while an increase in revenue is a credit.

So the increase to Accounts Receivable (an asset) is a debit, while the increase to Service Revenue (revenue) is a credit.

The journal entry follows.

d.	Accounts Receivable (Asset ↑; debit)	2,600	
	Service Revenue (Revenue ↑; credit)		2,600
	Provided services on account.		

$2,600 is posted to the debit (left) side of the Accounts Receivable T-account. $2,600 is posted to the credit (right) side of the Service Revenue account, as follows:

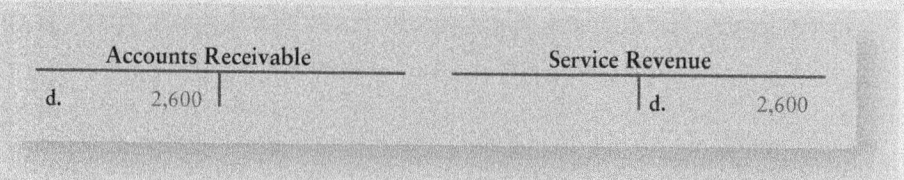

	Accounts Receivable			Service Revenue	
d.	2,600		d.		2,600

e. The business paid $500 cash toward the equipment previously purchased on account in transaction b.

The business paid some of the money that it owed on the purchase of equipment in transaction b. The accounts involved in the transaction are Accounts Payable and Cash.

Accounts Payable is a liability that has decreased. Cash is an asset that has also decreased.

Remember that Accounts Payable shows the amount the business must pay in the future (a liability). When the business pays these creditors, Accounts Payable will decrease because the business will then owe less (in this case, Accounts Payable drops from $3,500—in transaction b—to $3,000).

Looking at Exhibit 2-16 (p. 112), a decrease in liabilities is a debit, while a decrease in assets is a credit.

So Accounts Payable (a liability) decreases, which is a debit. Cash (an asset) decreases, which is a credit.

e.	Accounts Payable (Liability ↓; debit)		500	
	Cash (Asset ↓; credit)			500
	Partial payment on account.			

$500 is posted to the debit (left) side of the Accounts Payable T-account. $500 is posted to the credit (right) side of the Cash account, as follows:

		Cash					Accounts Payable		
a.	10,000							b.	3,500
		c.	800		e.	500			
		e.	500						

Again notice the amounts already in the T-accounts from previous transactions. The reference letters show which transaction caused each amount to appear in the T-account.

f. The business received $2,000 in cash for services provided to a new customer.

The business received $2,000 cash in exchange for mowing and landscaping services rendered to a customer. The accounts involved in the transaction are Cash and Service Revenue.

Cash is an asset that has increased and Service Revenue is revenue, which has also increased.

Looking at Exhibit 2-16 (p. 112), an increase in assets is a debit, while an increase in revenue is a credit.

So the increase to Cash (an asset) is a debit. The increase to Service Revenue (revenue) is a credit.

f.	Cash (Asset ↑; debit)		2,000	
	Service Revenue (Revenue ↑; credit)			2,000
	Provided services for cash.			

$2,000 is then posted to the debit (left) side of the Cash T-account. $2,000 is posted to the credit (right) side of the Service Revenue account, as follows:

		Cash					Service Revenue		
a.	10,000							d.	2,600
		c.	800					f.	2,000
		e.	500						
f.	2,000								

Notice how we keep adding onto the T-accounts. The values from previous transactions remain in their places.

g. The business paid $200 cash to repair equipment.

The business paid $200 cash to have equipment repaired. Because the benefit of the repairs has already been used, the repairs are recorded as Repair Expense. Because the repairs were paid in cash, the Cash account is also involved.

Repair Expense is an expense that has increased and Cash is an asset that has decreased.

Looking at Exhibit 2-16 (p. 112), an increase in expenses calls for a debit, while a decrease in an asset requires a credit.

So Repair Expense (an expense) increases, which is a debit. Cash (an asset) decreases, which is a credit.

g.	Repair Expense (Expense ↑ ; debit)	200	
	Cash (Asset ↓; credit)		200
	Paid for repairs.		

$200 is then posted to the debit (left) side of the Repair Expense T-account. $200 is posted to the credit (right) side of the Cash account, as follows:

	Cash				**Repair Expense**	
a.	10,000			g.	200	
		c.	800			
		e.	500			
f.	2,000					
		g.	200			

h. The business paid $900 cash for salary expense.

The business paid employees $900 in cash. Because the benefit of the employees' work has already been used, their salaries are recorded as Salary Expense. Because the salaries were paid in cash, the Cash account is also involved.

Salary Expense is an expense that has increased and Cash is an asset that has decreased.

Looking at Exhibit 2-16 (p. 112), an increase in expenses is a debit, while a decrease in an asset is a credit.

In this case, Salary Expense (an expense) increases, which is a debit. Cash (an asset) decreases, which is a credit.

h.	Salary Expense (Expense ↑; debit)	900	
	Cash (Asset ↓; credit)		900
	Paid salary.		

$900 is posted to the debit (left) side of the Salary Expense T-account. $900 is posted to the credit (right) side of the Cash account, as follows:

Cash					Salary Expense		
a.	10,000			h.	900	
		c.	800			
		e.	500			
f.	2,000					
		g.	200			
		h.	900			

i. The business received $2,100 cash from a customer on account.

The business received cash of $2,100 from a customer for services previously provided in transaction **d**. The accounts affected by this transaction are Cash and Accounts Receivable.

Cash and Accounts Receivable are both assets.

The asset Cash has increased, and the asset Accounts Receivable has decreased.

Remember, Accounts Receivable shows the amount of cash the business has coming from customers. When the business receives cash from these customers, Accounts Receivable will decrease, because the business will have less to receive in the future (in this case, it reduces from $2,600—in transaction d—to $500).

Looking at Exhibit 2-16 (p. 112), an increase in assets is a debit, while a decrease in assets is a credit.

So Cash (an asset) increases, which is a debit. Accounts Receivable (an asset) decreases, which is a credit.

i.	Cash (Asset ↑; debit)	2,100	
	Accounts Receivable (Asset ↓; credit)		2,100
	Received cash on account.		

$2,100 is posted to the debit (left) side of the Cash T-account. $2,100 is posted to the credit (right) side of the Accounts Receivable account, as follows:

Cash					Accounts Receivable		
a.	10,000			d.	2,600		
		c.	800			i.	2,100
		e.	500				
f.	2,000						
		g.	200				
		h.	900				
i.	2,100						

j. The business declared and paid cash dividends of $1,500.

The business paid Michael dividends from the earnings it had retained on his behalf. This caused Michael's ownership interest (equity) to decrease. The accounts involved in this transaction are Dividends and Cash.

Dividends have increased and Cash is an asset that has decreased.

Looking at Exhibit 2-16 (p. 112), an increase in dividends is a debit, while a decrease in an asset is a credit.

Remember that Dividends are a negative element of stockholders' equity. Therefore, when Dividends increase, stockholders' equity decreases. So in this case, Dividends decrease equity with a debit. Cash (an asset) decreases with a credit.

j.	Dividends (Dividends ↑; debit)	1,500	
	Cash (Asset ↓; credit)		1,500
	Paid dividends.		

$1,500 is posted to the debit (left) side of the Dividends T-account. $1,500 is posted to the credit (right) side of the Cash account, as follows:

	Cash					Dividends	
a.	10,000				j.	1,500	
		c.	800				
		e.	500				
f.	2,000						
		g.	200				
		h.	900				
i.	2,100						
		j.	1,500				

Now we can summarize all of the journal entries during the month:

Requirement 3

Total each T-account to determine its balance at the end of the month.

	Part 1	Part 2	**Part 3**	Demo Doc Complete

Ref.	Accounts and Explanation	Debit	Credit
a.	Cash	10,000	
	Common Stock		10,000
	Issued common stock.		
b.	Equipment	3,500	
	Accounts Payable		3,500
	Purchased equipment on account.		
c.	Supplies	800	
	Cash		800
	Purchased supplies for cash.		
d.	Accounts Receivable	2,600	
	Service Revenue		2,600
	Provided services on account.		
e.	Accounts Payable	500	
	Cash		500
	Partial payment on account.		
f.	Cash	2,000	
	Service Revenue		2,000
	Provided services for cash.		
g.	Repair Expense	200	
	Cash		200
	Paid for repairs.		
h.	Salary Expense	900	
	Cash		900
	Paid salary.		
i.	Cash	2,100	
	Accounts Receivable		2,100
	Received cash on account.		
j.	Dividends	1,500	
	Cash		1,500
	Paid dividends.		

To compute the balance in a T-account (total the T-account), add up the numbers on the debit/left side of the account and (separately) add the credit/right side of the account. The difference between the total debits and the total credits is the account's balance, which is placed on the side that holds the larger total. This gives the balance in the T-account.

For example, for the Cash account, the numbers on the debit/left side total $10,000 + $2,000 + $2,100 = $14,100. The credit/right side = $800 + $500 + $200 + $900 + $1,500 = $3,900. The difference is $14,100 − $3,900 = $10,200. At the end of the period Cash has a debit balance of $10,200. We put the $10,200 at the bottom of the debit side because that was the side that showed the bigger total ($14,100). This is called a debit balance.

An easy way to think of totaling T-accounts is:

> Beginning balance in a T-account
> + Increases to the T-account
> − Decreases to the T-account
> T-account balance (net total)

T-accounts after posting all transactions and totaling each account:

ASSETS		=	LIABILITIES	+	STOCKHOLDERS' EQUITY

Cash

a.	10,000		
		c.	800
		e.	500
f.	2,000		
		g.	200
		h.	900
i.	2,100		
		j.	1,500
Bal.	10,200		

Accounts Receivable

d.	2,600		
		i.	2,100
Bal.	500		

Supplies

c.	800		
Bal.	800		

Equipment

b.	3,500		
Bal.	3,500		

Accounts Payable

		b.	3,500
e.	500		
		Bal.	3,000

Common Stock

		a.	10,000
		Bal.	10,000

Dividends

j.	1,500		
Bal.	1,500		

REVENUE

Service Revenue

		d.	2,600
		f.	2,000
		Bal.	4,600

EXPENSES

Salary Expense

h.	900		
Bal.	900		

Repair Expense

g.	200		
Bal.	200		

Requirement 4

The trial balance lists all the accounts along with their balances. This listing is helpful because it summarizes all the accounts in one place. Otherwise one must plow through all the T-accounts to find the balance of Accounts Payable, Salary Expense, or any other account.

The trial balance is an *internal* accounting document that accountants and managers use to prepare the financial statements. It's not like the income statement and balance sheet, which are presented to the public.

Data for the trial balance come directly from the T-accounts that we prepared in Requirement 3. A debit balance in a T-account remains a debit in the trial balance, and likewise for credits. For example, the T-account for Cash shows a debit balance of $10,200, and the trial balance lists Cash the same way. The Accounts Payable T-account shows a $3,000 credit balance, and the trial balance lists Accounts Payable correctly.

The trial balance or Moe's Mowing at September 30, 2008, appears as follows. Notice that we list the accounts in their proper order—assets, liabilities, stockholder's equity, revenues, and expenses.

Moe's Mowing, Inc.
Trial Balance
September 30, 2008

		Balance	
		Debit	Credit
Assets	Cash	$10,200	
	Accounts receivable	500	
	Supplies	800	
	Equipment	3,500	
Liabilities	Accounts payable		$ 3,000
Equity	Common stock		10,000
	Dividends	1,500	
Revenues	Service revenue		4,600
Expenses	Salary expense	900	
	Repair expense	200	
	Total	$17,600	$17,600

You should trace each account from the T-accounts to the trial balance.

Part 1	Part 2	Part 3	**Demo Doc Complete**

This page intentionally left blank

3 Accrual Accounting & Income

SPOTLIGHT

STARBUCKS CORPORATION

Starbucks has changed coffee from a breakfast drink to an experience. The corporation began in Seattle, Washington, in 1985 and now has over 10,000 locations in the United States alone, with almost 2,000 more abroad.

As you can see from Starbucks' income statement, the company sold almost $8 billion of coffee and related products during the 2006 fiscal year. How does Starbucks know whether these revenues translated into profit? The income statement reports net income of $564 million. That's a lot of coffee!

Starbucks Corporation
Income Statement (Adapted)
Year Ended September 30, 2006

	Millions
Revenues:	
Net operating revenues	$7,787
Other income	89
Total net revenues	7,876
Expenses:	
Cost of sales (cost of goods sold)	3,179
Store operating expenses	2,688
Other operating expenses	260
Depreciation and amortization expenses	387
General and administrative expenses	473
Total operating expenses	6,987
Income before income tax	889
Income tax expense	325
Net income	$ 564

This chapter completes our coverage of the accounting cycle. It gives the basics of what you need before tackling individual topics such as receivables, inventory, and cash flows.

LEARNING OBJECTIVES

1 **Relate** accrual accounting and cash flows

2 **Apply** the revenue and matching principles

3 **Adjust** the accounts

4 **Prepare** the financial statements

5 **Close** the books

6 **Use** 2 new ratios to evaluate a business

> **ac**
> **t**
> For more practice and review of accounting cycle concepts, use ACT, the accounting Cycle Tutorial, online at www.prenhall.com/harrison. Margin logos like this one, directing you to the appropriate ACT section and material, appear throughout Chapters 1, 2, and 3. When you enter the tutorial, you'll find three buttons on the opening page of each chapter module. Here's what the buttons mean: **Tutorial** gives you a review of the major concepts, **Application** gives you practice exercises, and **Glossary** reviews important terms.

ACCRUAL ACCOUNTING VERSUS CASH-BASIS ACCOUNTING

Managers want to earn a profit. Investors search for companies whose stock prices will increase. Banks seek borrowers who'll pay their debts. Accounting provides the information these people use for decision making. Accounting can be based on either the

- accrual basis, or the
- cash basis

Accrual accounting records the impact of a business transaction as it occurs. When the business performs a service, makes a sale, or incurs an expense, the accountant records the transaction even if it receives or pays no cash.

Cash-basis accounting records only cash transactions—cash receipts and cash payments. Cash receipts are treated as revenues, and cash payments are handled as expenses.

Generally accepted accounting principles (GAAP) require accrual accounting. The business records revenues as the revenues are earned and expenses as the expenses are incurred—not necessarily when cash changes hands. Consider a sale on account. Which transaction increases your wealth—making an $800 sale on account, or collecting the $800 cash? Making the sale increases your wealth by $300 because you gave up inventory that cost you $500 and you got a receivable worth $800. Collecting cash later merely swaps your $800 receivable for $800 cash—no gain on this transaction. Making the sale—not collecting the cash—increases your wealth.

The basic defect of cash-basis accounting is that the cash basis ignores important information. That makes the financial statements incomplete. The result? People using the statements make bad decisions.

Suppose your business makes a sale *on account*. The cash basis does not record the sale because you received no cash. You may be thinking, "Let's wait until we collect cash and then record the sale. After all, we pay the bills with cash, so ignore transactions that don't affect cash."

What's wrong with this argument? There are 2 defects—one on the balance sheet and the other on the income statement.

Balance-Sheet Defect. If we fail to record a sale on account, the balance sheet reports no account receivable. Why is this so bad? The receivable is a real asset, and it should appear on the balance sheet. Without this information, your assets are understated as shown on the balance sheet.

Income-Statement Defect. A sale on account provides revenue that increases the company's wealth. Ignoring the sale understates your revenue and net income on the income statement.

The take-away lessons from this discussion are:

- Watch out for companies that use the cash basis of accounting. Their financial statements omit important information.
- All but the smallest businesses use the accrual basis of accounting.

HH CHAPTER 3

Accrual Accounting and Cash Flows

OBJECTIVE

1 **Relate** accrual accounting and cash flows

Accrual accounting is more complex—and more complete—than cash-basis accounting. Accrual accounting records *cash* transactions, such as

- Collecting cash from customers
- Receiving cash from interest earned
- Paying salaries, rent, and other expenses
- Borrowing money
- Paying off loans
- Issuing stock

Accrual accounting also records *noncash* transactions, such as

- Sales on account
- Purchases of inventory on account
- Accrual of expenses incurred but not yet paid
- Depreciation expense
- Usage of prepaid rent, insurance, and supplies
- Earning of revenue when cash was collected in advance

Accrual accounting is based on a framework of concepts and principles. We turn now to the time-period concept, the revenue principle, and the matching principle.

The Time-Period Concept

The only way for a business to know for certain how well it performed is to shut down, sell the assets, pay the liabilities, and return any leftover cash to the owners. This process, called liquidation, means going out of business. Ongoing companies can't wait until they go out of business to measure income! Instead, they need regular progress reports. Accountants, therefore, prepare financial statements for specific periods. The **time-period concept** ensures that accounting information is reported at regular intervals.

The basic accounting period is 1 year, and virtually all businesses prepare annual financial statements. Around 60% of large companies—including Amazon.com, eBay, and YUM! Brands—use the calendar year from January 1 through December 31.

A *fiscal* year ends on a date other than December 31. Most retailers, including Wal-Mart and JCPenney, use a fiscal year that ends on January 31 because the low point in their business activity falls after Christmas. Starbucks Corporation uses a fiscal year that ends on September 30.

Companies also prepare financial statements for interim periods of less than a year, such as a month, a quarter (3 months), or a semiannual period (6 months). Most of the discussions in this text are based on an annual accounting period.

The Revenue Principle

OBJECTIVE

2 **Apply** the revenue and matching principles

The **revenue principle** governs two things:

1. When to record revenue (make a journal entry)
2. The amount of revenue to record

When should you record revenue? After it has been earned—and not before. In most cases, revenue is earned when the business has delivered a good or service to a customer. It has done everything required to earn the revenue by transferring the good or service to the customer.

Exhibit 3-1 shows two situations that provide guidance on when to record revenue for Starbucks Corporation. Situation 1 illustrates when not to record revenue. No transaction has occurred, so Starbucks Corporation records nothing. Situation 2 illustrates when revenue should be recorded—after a transaction has occurred.

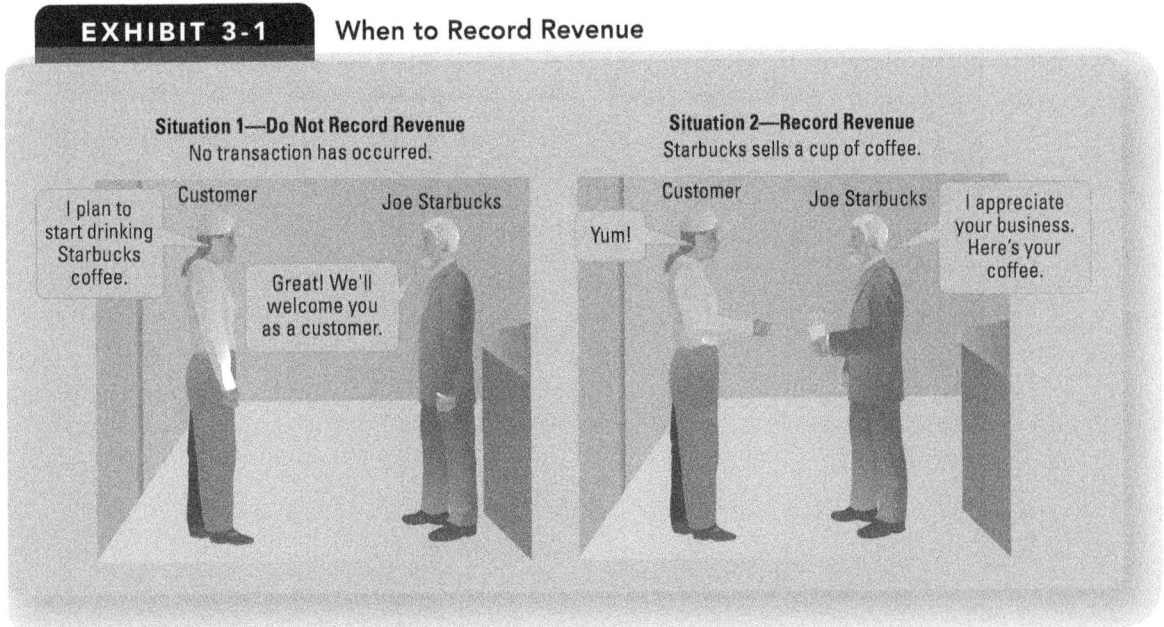

EXHIBIT 3-1 When to Record Revenue

The *amount* of revenue to record is the cash value of the goods or services transferred to the customer. Suppose that in order to promote business, Starbucks runs a promotion and sells coffee for the discount price of $2 per cup. Ordinarily Starbucks would charge $4 for this coffee. How much revenue should Starbucks record? The answer is $2—the cash value of the transaction. The amount of the sale, $2, is the amount of revenue earned—not the regular price of $4.

The Matching Principle

The **matching principle** is the basis for recording expenses. Expenses are the costs of assets used up, and of liabilities created, in the earning of revenue. Expenses have no future benefit to the company. The matching principle includes two steps:

1. Identify all the expenses incurred during the accounting period.
2. Measure the expenses, and match expenses against the revenues earned.

To *match* expenses against revenues means to subtract expenses from revenues to compute net income or net loss. Exhibit 3-2 illustrates the matching principle.

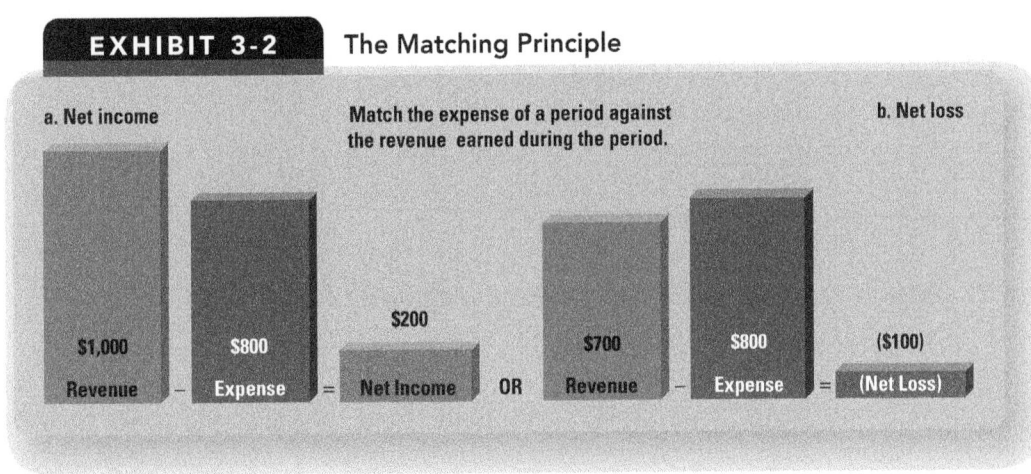

EXHIBIT 3-2 The Matching Principle

Some expenses are paid in cash. Other expenses arise from using up an asset such as supplies. Still other expenses occur when a company creates a liability. For example, Starbucks' salary expense occurs when employees work for the company. Starbucks may pay the salary expense immediately, or Starbucks may record a liability for the salary to be paid later. In either case, Starbucks has salary expense. The critical event for recording an expense is the employees' working for the company, not the payment of cash.

STOP & think. . .

1. A customer pays Starbucks $100 on March 15 for coffee to be served at a party in April. Has Starbucks earned revenue on March 15? When will Starbucks earn the revenue?
2. Starbucks pays $4,500 on July 1 for store rent for the next 3 months. Has Starbucks incurred an expense on July 1?

Answers:

1. No. Starbucks has received the cash but will not deliver the coffee until later. Starbucks earns the revenue when it gives the goods to the customer.
2. No. Starbucks has paid cash for rent in advance. There is no expense. This prepaid rent is an asset because Starbucks has the use of a store location in the future.

Ethical Issues in Accrual Accounting

Accrual accounting provides some ethical challenges that cash accounting avoids. For example, suppose that in 2008, Starbucks Corporation prepays a $3 million advertising campaign to be conducted by a large advertising agency. The advertisements are scheduled to run during December, January, and February. In this case, Starbucks is buying an asset, a prepaid expense.

Suppose Starbucks pays for the advertisements on December 1 and the ads start running immediately. Starbucks should record one-third of the expense ($1 million) during the year ended December 31, 2008, and two-thirds ($2 million) during 2009.

Suppose 2008 is a great year for Starbucks—net income is better than expected. Starbucks' top managers believe that 2009 will not be as profitable. In this case, the company has a strong incentive to expense the full $3 million during 2008 in order to report all the advertising expense in the 2008 income statement. This unethical action would keep $2 million of advertising expense off the 2009 income statement and make 2009's net income look better.

UPDATING THE ACCOUNTS: THE ADJUSTING PROCESS

OBJECTIVE

3 **Adjust** the accounts

At the end of the period, the business reports its financial statements. This process begins with the trial balance introduced in Chapter 2. We refer to this trial balance as unadjusted because the accounts are not yet ready for the financial statements. In most cases the simple label "Trial Balance" means "unadjusted."

Which Accounts Need to Be Updated (Adjusted)?

The stockholders need to know how well Genie Car Wash is performing. The financial statements report this information, and all accounts must be up-to-date. That

HH CHAPTER 3

means some accounts must be adjusted. Exhibit 3-3 gives the trial balance of Genie Car Wash, Inc., at June 30, 20X9.

This trial balance is unadjusted. That means it's not completely up-to-date. It's not quite ready for preparing the financial statements for presentation to the public.

EXHIBIT 3-3 Unadjusted Trial Balance

Genie Car Wash, Inc.
Unadjusted Trial Balance
June 30, 20X9

Cash	$24,800	
Accounts receivable	2,200	
Supplies	700	
Prepaid rent	3,000	
Equipment	24,000	
Accounts payable		$13,100
Unearned service revenue		400
Common stock		20,000
Retained earnings		18,800
Dividends	3,200	
Service revenue		7,000
Salary expense	900	
Utilities expense	500	
Total	$59,300	$59,300

Cash, Equipment, Accounts Payable, Common Stock, and Dividends are up-to-date and need no adjustment at the end of the period. Why? Because the day-to-day transactions provide all the data for these accounts.

Accounts Receivable, Supplies, Prepaid Rent, and the other accounts are another story. These accounts are not yet up-to-date on June 30. Why? Because certain transactions have not yet been recorded. Consider Supplies. During June, Genie Car Wash used cleaning supplies to wash cars. But Genie didn't make a journal entry for supplies used every time it washed a car. That would waste time and money. Instead, Genie waits until the end of the period and then records the supplies used up during the entire month.

The cost of supplies used up is an expense. An adjusting entry at the end of June updates both Supplies (an asset) and Supplies Expense. We must adjust all accounts whose balances are not yet up-to-date.

Categories of Adjusting Entries

Accounting adjustments fall into three basic categories: deferrals, depreciation, and accruals.

Deferrals. A **deferral** is an adjustment for an item that the business paid or received cash in advance. Starbucks purchases supplies for use in its operations. During the period, some supplies (assets) are used up and become expenses. At the end of the period, an adjustment is needed to decrease the Supplies account for the supplies used up. This is Supplies Expense. Prepaid rent, prepaid insurance, and all other prepaid expenses require deferral adjustments.

There are also deferral adjustments for liabilities. Companies such as Starbucks may collect cash from a grocery-store chain in advance of earning the revenue. When Starbucks receives cash up front, Starbucks has a liability to provide coffee for the customer. This liability is called Unearned Sales Revenue. Then, when Starbucks delivers the goods to the customer, it earns Sales Revenue. This earning process requires an adjustment at the end of the period. The adjustment decreases the liability and increases the revenue for the revenue earned. Publishers such as Time, Inc., and your cell-phone company collect cash in advance. They too must make adjusting entries for revenues earned later.

Depreciation. **Depreciation** allocates the cost of a plant asset to expense over the asset's useful life. Depreciation is the most common long-term deferral. Starbucks buys buildings and equipment. As Starbucks uses the assets, it records depreciation for wear-and-tear and obsolescence. The accounting adjustment records Depreciation Expense and decreases the asset's book value over its life. The process is identical to a deferral-type adjustment; the only difference is the type of asset involved.

Accruals. An **accrual** is the opposite of a deferral. For an accrued *expense*, Starbucks records the expense before paying cash. For an accrued *revenue*, Starbucks records the revenue before collecting cash.

Salary Expense can create an accrual adjustment. As employees work for Starbucks Corporation, the company's salary expense accrues with the passage of time. At September 30, 2006, Starbucks owed employees some salaries to be paid after year end. At September 30, Starbucks recorded Salary Expense and Salary Payable for the amount owed. Other examples of expense accruals include interest expense and income tax expense.

An accrued revenue is a revenue that the business has earned and will collect next year. At year end Starbucks must accrue the revenue. The adjustment debits a receivable and credits a revenue. For example, accrual of interest revenue debits Interest Receivable and credits Interest Revenue.

Let's see how the adjusting process actually works for Genie Car Wash at June 30. We start with prepaid expenses.

Prepaid Expenses

A **prepaid expense** is an expense paid in advance. Therefore, prepaid expenses are assets because they provide a future benefit for the owner. Let's do the adjustments for prepaid rent and supplies.

Prepaid Rent. Companies pay rent in advance. This prepayment creates an asset for the renter, who can then use the rented item in the future. Suppose Genie Car Wash prepays 3 months' store rent ($3,000) on June 1. The entry for the prepayment of 3 months' rent debits Prepaid Rent as follows:

June 1	Prepaid Rent ($1,000 × 3)	3,000	
	Cash		3,000
	Paid 3 months' rent in advance.		

The accounting equation shows that one asset increases and another decreases. Total assets are unchanged.

Assets	=	Liabilities	+	Stockholders' Equity
3,000	=	0	+	0
– 3,000				

After posting, the Prepaid Rent account appears as follows:

Prepaid Rent	
June 1 3,000	

Throughout June, the Prepaid Rent account carries this beginning balance, as shown in Exhibit 3-3 (p. 131). The adjustment transfers $1,000 from Prepaid Rent to Rent Expense as follows:*

		Adjusting entry a
June 30	Rent Expense ($3,000 × 1/3)	1,000	
	Prepaid Rent		1,000
	To record rent expense.		

Both assets and stockholders' equity decrease.

Assets	=	Liabilities	+	Stockholders' Equity	–	Expenses
– 1,000	=	0				– 1,000

After posting, Prepaid Rent and Rent Expense appear as follows:

Prepaid Rent			Rent Expense	
June 1 3,000	June 30 1,000 →	June 30 1,000	
Bal. 2,000		Bal. 1,000	

This expense illustrates the matching principle. We record an expense in order to measure net income.

---

*See Exhibit 3-8, page 143, for a summary of adjustments a–g.

Supplies. Supplies are another type of prepaid expense. On June 2, Genie Car Wash paid cash of $700 for cleaning supplies:

June 2	Supplies	700	
	Cash		700
	Paid cash for supplies.		

Assets	=	Liabilities	+	Stockholders' Equity
700	=	0	+	0
– 700				

The cost of the supplies Genie used is supplies expense. To measure June's supplies expense, the business counts the supplies on hand at the end of the month. The count shows that $400 of supplies remain. Subtracting the $400 of supplies on hand from the supplies available ($700) measures supplies expense for the month ($300), as follows:

Asset Available During the Period	–	Asset on Hand at the End of the Period	=	Asset Used (Expense) During the Period
$700	–	$400	=	$300

The June 30 adjusting entry debits the expense and credits the asset, as follows:

Adjusting entry b

June 30	Supplies Expense ($700 – $400)	300	
	Supplies		300
	To record supplies expense.		

Assets	=	Liabilities	+	Stockholders' Equity	–	Expenses
– 300	=	0				– 300

After posting, the Supplies and Supplies Expense accounts appear as follows. The adjustment is highlighted for emphasis.

Supplies				Supplies Expense		
June 2	700	June 30	300 →	June 30	300	
Bal.	400			Bal.	300	

At the start of July, Supplies has this $400 balance, and the adjustment process is repeated each month.

STOP & think. . .

At the beginning of the month, supplies were $5,000. During the month, $7,000 of supplies were purchased. At month's end, $3,000 of supplies are still on hand. What are the

- adjusting entry
- ending balance in the Supplies account?

Answer:

Supplies Expense ($5,000 + $7,000 – $3,000)	9,000	
Supplies		9,000
Ending balance of supplies = $3,000 (the supplies still on hand)		

Depreciation of Plant Assets

Plant assets are long-lived tangible assets, such as land, buildings, furniture, and equipment. All plant assets but land decline in usefulness, and this decline is an expense. Accountants spread the cost of each plant asset, except land, over its useful life. Depreciation is the process of allocating cost to expense for a long-term plant asset.

To illustrate depreciation, consider Genie Car Wash. Suppose that on June 2 Genie purchased car-washing equipment on account for $24,000:

June 3	Equipment	24,000	
	Accounts Payable		24,000
	Purchased equipment on account.		

Assets	=	Liabilities	+	Stockholders' Equity
24,000	=	24,000	+	0

After posting, the Equipment account appears as follows:

Equipment	
June 3 24,000	

Genie records an asset when it purchases equipment. Then, as the asset is used, a portion of the asset's cost is transferred to Depreciation Expense. Accounting matches the expense against revenue—this is the matching principle. Computerized systems program the depreciation for automatic entry each period.

Genie's equipment will remain useful for 5 years and then be worthless. One way to compute the amount of depreciation for each year is to divide the cost of the asset ($24,000 in our example) by its expected useful life (5 years). This procedure—called the straight-line depreciation method—gives annual depreciation of $4,800. The depreciation amount is an estimate.

Annual Depreciation = $24,000/5 years = $4,800 per year

Depreciation for June is $400.

Monthly Depreciation = $4,800/12 months = $400 per month

The Accumulated Depreciation Account. Depreciation expense for June is recorded as follows:

			Adjusting entry c
June 30	Depreciation Expense—Equipment	400	
	Accumulated Depreciation—Equipment		400
	To record depreciation.		

Total assets decrease by the amount of the expense:

Assets	=	Liabilities	+	Stockholders' Equity	−	Expenses
− 400	=	0				− 400

The Accumulated Depreciation account, (not Equipment) is credited to preserve the original cost of the asset in the Equipment account. Managers can then refer to the Equipment account if they ever need to know how much the asset cost.

The **Accumulated Depreciation** account shows the sum of all depreciation expense from using the asset. Therefore, the balance in the Accumulated Depreciation account increases over the asset's life.

Accumulated Depreciation is a contra asset account—an asset account with a normal credit balance. A **contra account** has two distinguishing characteristics:

1. It always has a companion account.

2. Its normal balance is opposite that of the companion account.

In this case, Accumulated Depreciation is the contra account to Equipment, so Accumulated Depreciation appears directly after Equipment on the balance sheet. A business carries an accumulated depreciation account for each depreciable asset, for example, Accumulated Depreciation—Building and Accumulated Depreciation—Equipment.

After posting, the plant asset accounts of Genie Car Wash are as follows—with the adjustment highlighted:

Equipment			Accumulated Depreciation—Equipment			Depreciation Expense—Equipment		
June 3	24,000			June 30	400	June 30	400	
Bal.	24,000			Bal.	400	Bal.	400	

Book Value. The net amount of a plant asset (cost minus accumulated depreciation) is called that asset's **book value**, or carrying amount. Exhibit 3-4 shows how Genie would report the book value of its equipment and building at June 30 (the building data are assumed for this illustration).

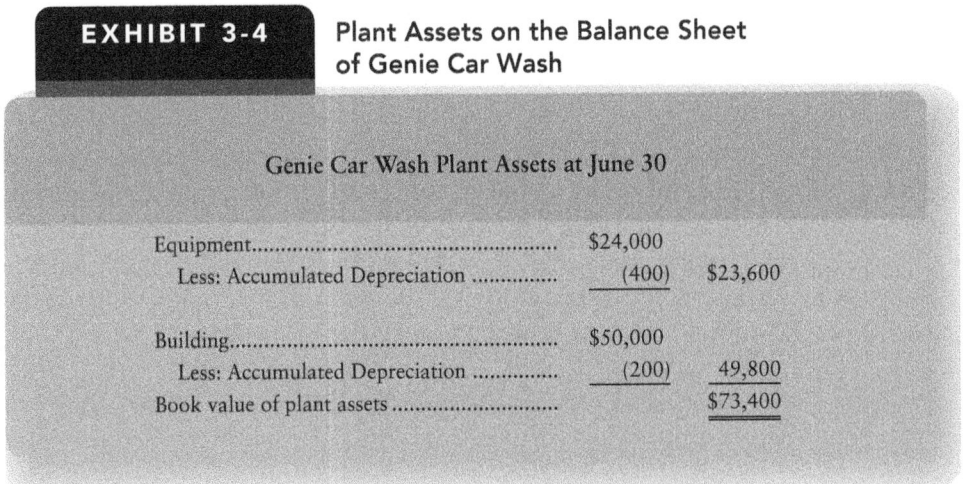

EXHIBIT 3-4 Plant Assets on the Balance Sheet of Genie Car Wash

Genie Car Wash Plant Assets at June 30

Equipment..	$24,000	
Less: Accumulated Depreciation	(400)	$23,600
Building..	$50,000	
Less: Accumulated Depreciation	(200)	49,800
Book value of plant assets		$73,400

At June 30, the book value of equipment is $23,600; the book value of the building is $49,800.

STOP & think. . .

What will be the book value of Genie's equipment at the end of July?

Answer:
$24,000 – $400 – $400 = $23,200.

Exhibit 3-5 shows how Starbucks Corporation reports property, plant, and equipment in its annual report. Lines 1 to 6 list specific assets and their cost. Line 7 shows the cost of all Starbucks plant assets. Line 8 gives the amount of accumulated depreciation, and line 9 shows the assets' book value of $2,288 million.

HH CHAPTER 3

EXHIBIT 3-5	Starbucks Corporation's Reporting of Property, Plant, and Equipment (Adapted, in millions)

1	Land...	$ 32
2	Buildings..	109
3	Leasehold improvements..................................	2,437
4	Store equipment...	785
5	Roasting equipment..	197
6	Furniture, fixtures, and other...........................	698
7	Property, plant, and equipment, at cost..............	4,258
8	Less: Accumulated depreciation	(1,970)
9	Property, plant, and equipment, net...................	$2,288

Accrued Expenses

Businesses incur expenses before they pay cash. Consider an employee's salary. Starbucks' expense and payable grow as the employee works, so the liability is said to accrue. Another example is interest expense on a note payable. Interest accrues as the clock ticks. The term **accrued expense** refers to a liability that arises from an expense that has not yet been paid.

Companies don't record accrued expenses daily or weekly. Instead, they wait until the end of the period and use an adjusting entry to update each expense (and related liability) for the financial statements. Let's look at salary expense.

Most companies pay their employees at set times. Suppose Genie Car Wash pays its employee a monthly salary of $1,800, half on the 15th and half on the last day of the month. The following calendar for June has the paydays circled:

			June			
Sun.	Mon.	Tue.	Wed.	Thur.	Fri.	Sat.
						1
2	3	4	5	6	7	8
9	10	11	12	13	14	(15)
16	17	18	19	20	21	22
23	24	25	26	27	28	29
(30)						

Assume that if a payday falls on a Sunday, Genie pays the employee on the following Monday. During June, Genie paid its employees the first half-month salary of $900 and made the following entry:

June 15	Salary Expense	900	
	Cash		900
	To pay salary.		

Assets	=	Liabilities	+	Stockholders' Equity	–	Expenses
– 900	=	0				– 900

After posting, the Salary Expense account is

Salary Expense	
June 15	900

The trial balance at June 30 (Exhibit 3-3, p. 131) includes Salary Expense with its debit balance of $900. Because June 30, the second payday of the month, falls on a Sunday, the second half-month amount of $900 will be paid on Monday, July 1. At June 30, therefore, Genie adjusts for additional salary expense and salary payable of $900 as follows:

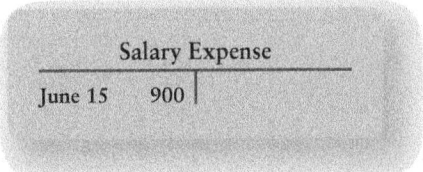

				Adjusting entry d
June 30	Salary Expense		900	
	Salary Payable			900
	To accrue salary expense.			

An accrued expense increases liabilities and decreases stockholders' equity:

Assets	=	Liabilities	+	Stockholders' Equity	–	Expenses
0	=	900				– 900

After posting, the Salary Payable and Salary Expense accounts appear as follows (adjustment highlighted):

Salary Payable		
	June 30	900
	Bal.	900

Salary Expense		
June 15	900	
June 30	900	
Bal.	1,800	

The accounts now hold all of June's salary information. Salary Expense has a full month's salary, and Salary Payable shows the amount owed at June 30. All accrued expenses are recorded this way—debit the expense and credit the liability.

Computerized systems contain a payroll module. Accrued salaries can be automatically journalized and posted at the end of each period.

Accrued Revenues

Businesses often earn revenue before they receive the cash. A revenue that has been earned but not yet collected is called an **accrued revenue**.

Assume that FedEx hires Genie on June 15 to wash FedEx delivery trucks each month. Suppose FedEx will pay Genie $600 monthly, with the first payment on July 15. During June, Genie will earn half a month's fee, $300, for work done June 15 through June 30. On June 30, Genie makes the following adjusting entry:

		Adjusting entry e	
June 30	Accounts Receivable ($600 × 1/2)	300	
	Service Revenue		300
	To accrue service revenue.		

Revenue increases both total assets and stockholders' equity:

Assets	=	Liabilities	+	Stockholders' Equity	+	Revenues
300	=	0				+ 300

Recall that Accounts Receivable has an unadjusted balance of $2,200, and Service Revenue's unadjusted balance is $7,000 (Exhibit 3-3, p. 131). This June 30 adjusting entry has the following effects (adjustment highlighted):

Accounts Receivable		Service Revenue	
	2,200		7,000
June 30	300	June 30	300
Bal.	2,500	Bal.	7,300

All accrued revenues are accounted for similarly—debit a receivable and credit a revenue.

STOP & think...

Suppose Genie Car Wash holds a note receivable as an investment. At the end of June, $100 of interest revenue has been earned. Journalize the accrued revenue adjustment at June 30.

Answer:

June 30	Interest Receivable	100	
	Interest Revenue		100
	To accrue interest revenue.		

Unearned Revenues

Some businesses collect cash from customers before earning the revenue. This creates a liability called **unearned revenue**. Only when the job is completed does the business earn the revenue. Suppose **Home Depot** engages Genie Car Wash to wash Home Depot trucks, agreeing to pay Genie $400 monthly, beginning immediately. If Genie collects the first amount on June 15, then Genie records this transaction as follows:

June 15	Cash	400	
	Unearned Service Revenue		400
	Received cash for revenue in advance.		

Assets	=	Liabilities	+	Stockholders' Equity
400	=	400	+	0

After posting, the liability account appears as follows:

Unearned Service Revenue

	June 15	400

Unearned Service Revenue is a liability because Genie is obligated to perform services for Home Depot. The June 30 unadjusted trial balance (Exhibit 3-3, p. 131) lists Unearned Service Revenue with a $400 credit balance. During the last 15 days of the month, Genie will earn one-half of the $400, or $200. On June 30, Genie makes the following adjustment:

Adjusting entry f

June 30	Unearned Service Revenue ($400 × 1/2)	200	
	Service Revenue		200
	To record unearned service revenue that has been earned.		

Assets	=	Liabilities	+	Stockholders' Equity	+	Revenues
0	=	− 200				+ 200

HH CHAPTER 3

This adjusting entry shifts $200 of the total amount received ($400) from liability to revenue. After posting, Unearned Service Revenue is reduced to $200, and Service Revenue is increased by $200, as follows (adjustment highlighted):

Unearned Service Revenue				Service Revenue		
June 30	200	June 15	400			7,000
		Bal.	200		June 30	300
					June 30	200
					Bal.	7,500

All revenues collected in advance are accounted for this way. An unearned revenue is a liability, not a revenue.

One company's prepaid expense is the other company's unearned revenue. For example, Home Depot's prepaid expense is Genie Car Wash's liability for unearned revenue.

Exhibit 3-6 diagrams the distinctive timing of prepaids and accruals. Study prepaid expenses all the way across. Then study unearned revenues across, and so on.

EXHIBIT 3-6 Prepaid and Accrual Adjustments

PREPAIDS—Cash First

	First		Later	
Prepaid expenses	*Pay cash and record an asset:*		*Record an expense and decrease the asset:*	
	Prepaid Expense...... XXX		Expense............................. XXX	
	Cash..............	XXX	Prepaid Expense.........	XXX
Unearned revenues	*Receive cash and record unearned revenue:*		*Record revenue and decrease unearned revenue:*	
	Cash...................... XXX		Unearned Revenue XXX	
	Unearned Revenue	XXX	Revenue	XXX

ACCRUALS—Cash Later

	First		Later	
Accrued expenses	*Accrue expense and a payable:*		*Pay cash and decrease the payable:*	
	Expense................... XXX		Payable............................. XXX	
	Payable..........	XXX	Cash.........................	XXX
Accrued revenues	*Accrue revenue and a receivable:*		*Receive cash and decrease the receivable:*	
	Receivable.............. XXX		Cash................................ XXX	
	Revenue	XXX	Receivable.................	XXX

The authors thank Professors Darrel Davis and Alfonso Oddo for suggesting this exhibit.

Summary of the Adjusting Process

Two purposes of the adjusting process are to

- Measure income
- Update the balance sheet

Therefore, every adjusting entry affects at least one

- Revenue or expense—to measure income
- Asset or liability—to update the balance sheet

Exhibit 3-7 summarizes the standard adjustments.

EXHIBIT 3-7 Summary of Adjusting Entries

	Type of Account	
Category of Adjusting Entry	Debit	Credit
Prepaid expense..................	Expense	Asset
Depreciation......................	Expense	Contra asset
Accrued expense................	Expense	Liability
Accrued revenue................	Asset	Revenue
Unearned revenue..............	Liability	Revenue

Adapted from material provided by Beverly Terry.

Exhibit 3-8 summarizes the adjustments of Genie Car Wash, Inc., at June 30—the adjusting entries we've examined over the past few pages.

EXHIBIT 3-8 The Adjusting Process of Genie Car Wash, Inc.

PANEL A—Information for Adjustments at June 30, 20X9	PANEL B—Adjusting Entries		
(a) Prepaid rent expired, $1,000.	(a) Rent Expense	1,000	
	Prepaid Rent		1,000
	To record rent expense.		
(b) Supplies used, $300.	(b) Supplies Expense	300	
	Supplies		300
	To record supplies used.		
(c) Depreciation on equipment, $400.	(c) Depreciation Expense—Equipment	400	
	Accumulated Depreciation—Equipment		400
	To record depreciation.		
(d) Accrued salary expense, $900.	(d) Salary Expense	900	
	Salary Payable		900
	To accrue salary expense.		
(e) Accrued service revenue, $300.	(e) Accounts Receivable	300	
	Service Revenue		300
	To accrue service revenue.		
(f) Amount of unearned service revenue that has been earned, $200.	(f) Unearned Service Revenue	200	
	Service Revenue		200
	To record unearned revenue that has been earned.		
(g) Accrued income tax expense, $600.	(g) Income Tax Expense	600	
	Income Tax Payable		600
	To accrue income tax expense.		

PANEL C—Ledger Accounts

Assets	Liabilities	Stockholders' Equity

Assets

Cash

Bal. 24,800	

Accounts Receivable

2,200	
(e) 300	
Bal. 2,500	

Supplies

700	(b)	300
Bal. 400		

Prepaid Rent

3,000	(a)	1,000
Bal. 2,000		

Equipment

Bal. 24,000	

Accumulated Depreciation— Equipment

	(c)	400
	Bal.	400

Liabilities

Accounts Payable

	Bal. 13,100

Salary Payable

	(d)	900
	Bal.	900

Unearned Service Revenue

(f) 200		400
	Bal.	200

Income Tax Payable

	(g)	600
	Bal.	600

Stockholders' Equity

Common Stock

	Bal. 20,000

Retained Earnings

	Bal. 18,800

Dividends

Bal. 3,200	

Revenue

Service Revenue

		7,000
	(e)	300
	(f)	200
	Bal.	7,500

Expenses

Rent Expense

(a)	1,000	
Bal.	1,000	

Salary Expense

	900	
(d)	900	
Bal.	1,800	

Supplies Expense

(b)	300	
Bal.	300	

Depreciation Expense—Equipment

(c)	400	
Bal.	400	

Utilities Expense

Bal.	500	

Income Tax Expense

(g)	600	
Bal.	600	

- Panel A repeats the data for each adjustment.
- Panel B gives the adjusting entries.
- Panel C shows the accounts after posting the adjusting entries. The adjustments are keyed by letter.

Exhibit 3-8 includes an additional adjusting entry that we have not yet discussed—the accrual of income tax expense. Like individual taxpayers, corporations are subject to income tax. They typically accrue income tax expense and the related income tax payable as the final adjusting entry of the period. Genie Car Wash accrues income tax expense with adjusting entry g, as follows:

			Adjusting entry g
June 30	Income Tax Expense	600	
	Income Tax Payable		600
	To accrue income tax expense.		

The income tax accrual follows the pattern for accrued expenses.

The Adjusted Trial Balance

This chapter began with the unadjusted trial balance (see Exhibit 3-3, p. 131). After the adjustments are journalized and posted, the accounts appear as shown in Exhibit 3-8, Panel C. A useful step in preparing the financial statements is to list the accounts, along with their adjusted balances, on an **adjusted trial balance**. This document lists all the accounts and their final balances in a single place. Exhibit 3-9 shows the adjusted trial balance of Genie Car Wash.

EXHIBIT 3-9   Adjusted Trial Balance

Genie Car Wash, Inc.
Preparation of Adjusted Trial Balance
June 30, 20X9

Account Title	Trial Balance Debit	Trial Balance Credit	Adjustments Debit	Adjustments Credit	Adjusted Trial Balance Debit	Adjusted Trial Balance Credit	
Cash	24,800				24,800		⎫
Accounts receivable	2,200		(e) 300		2,500		⎪
Supplies	700			(b) 300	400		⎪
Prepaid rent	3,000			(a) 1,000	2,000		⎪
Equipment	24,000				24,000		⎪
Accumulated depreciation—equipment				(c) 400		400	**Balance Sheet**
Accounts payable		13,100				13,100	(*Exhibit 3-12*)
Salary payable				(d) 900		900	⎪
Unearned service revenue		400	(f) 200			200	⎪
Income tax payable				(g) 600		600	⎪
Common stock		20,000				20,000	⎭
Retained earnings		18,800				18,800	⎫ **Statement of**
Dividends	3,200				3,200		⎬ **Retained Earnings**
Service revenue		7,000		(e) 300		7,500	⎭ (*Exhibit 3-11*)
				(f) 200			⎫
Rent expense			(a) 1,000		1,000		⎪
Salary expense	900		(d) 900		1,800		**Income Statement**
Supplies expense			(b) 300		300		(*Exhibit 3-10*)
Depreciation expense			(c) 400		400		⎪
Utilities expense	500				500		⎪
Income tax expense			(g) 600		600		⎭
	59,300	59,300	3,700	3,700	61,500	61,500	

Note how clearly the adjusted trial balance presents the data. The Account Title and the Trial Balance data come from the trial balance. The two Adjustments columns summarize the adjusting entries. The Adjusted Trial Balance columns then give the final account balances. Each adjusted amount in Exhibit 3-9 is the unadjusted balance plus or minus the adjustments. For example, Accounts Receivable starts with a

Accounting Cycle
Tutorial Glossary

balance of $2,200. Add the $300 debit adjustment to get Accounts Receivable's ending balance of $2,500. Spreadsheets are designed for this type of analysis.

PREPARING THE FINANCIAL STATEMENTS

OBJECTIVE

4 **Prepare** the financial statements

The June financial statements of Genie Car Wash can be prepared from the adjusted trial balance. At the far right, Exhibit 3-9 shows how the accounts are distributed to the financial statements.

- The income statement (Exhibit 3-10) lists the revenue and expense accounts.
- The statement of retained earnings (Exhibit 3-11) shows the changes in retained earnings.
- The balance sheet (Exhibit 3-12) reports assets, liabilities, and stockholders' equity.

The arrows in Exhibits 3-10, 3-11, and 3-12 show the flow of data from one statement to the next.

Why is the income statement prepared first and the balance sheet last?

1. The income statement reports net income or net loss, the result of revenues minus expenses. Revenues and expenses affect stockholders' equity, so net income is then transferred to retained earnings. The first arrow tracks net income.

2. Retained Earnings is the final balancing element of the balance sheet. To solidify your understanding, trace the $18,500 retained earnings figure from Exhibit 3-11 to Exhibit 3-12. Arrow ② tracks retained earnings.

EXHIBIT 3-10   Income Statement

Genie Car Wash, Inc.
Income Statement
Month Ended June 30, 20X9

Revenues:		
Service revenue		$7,500
Expenses:		
Salary expense	$1,800	
Rent expense...........................	1,000	
Utilities expense	500	
Depreciation expense..............	400	
Supplies expense	300	4,000
Income before tax		3,500
Income tax expense		600
Net income..................................		$2,900

①

EXHIBIT 3-11   Statement of Retained Earnings

Genie Car Wash, Inc.
Statement of Retained Earnings
Month Ended June 30, 20X9

Retained earnings, May 31, 20X9...............	$18,800
Add: Net income..	2,900
	21,700
Less: Dividends	(3,200)
Retained earnings, June 30, 20X9..............	$18,500

②

EXHIBIT 3-12   Balance Sheet

Genie Car Wash, Inc.
Balance Sheet
June 30, 20X9

Assets			Liabilities		
Cash.............................		$24,800	Accounts payable		$13,100
Accounts receivable........		2,500	Salary payable..........................		900
Supplies.........................		400	Unearned service revenue		200
Prepaid rent....................		2,000	Income tax payable		600
Equipment......................	$24,000		Total liabilities		14,800
Less: Accumulated					
depreciation	(400)	23,600	**Stockholders' Equity**		
			Common stock..........................		20,000
			Retained earnings.....................		18,500
			Total stockholders' equity		38,500
			Total liabilities and		
Total assets.....................		$53,300	stockholders' equity..............		$53,300

HH CHAPTER 3

MID-CHAPTER SUMMARY PROBLEM

The trial balance of Goldsmith Company shown below pertains to December 31, 20X5, which is the end of its year-long accounting period. Data needed for the adjusting entries include the following:

a. Supplies on hand at year end, $2,000.

b. Depreciation on furniture and fixtures, $20,000.

c. Depreciation on building, $10,000.

d. Salaries owed but not yet paid, $5,000.

e. Accrued service revenue, $12,000.

f. Of the $45,000 balance of unearned service revenue, $32,000 was earned during the year.

g. Accrued income tax expense, $35,000.

I Required

1. Open the ledger accounts with their unadjusted balances. Show dollar amounts in thousands, as shown for Accounts Receivable:

Accounts Receivable	
370	

2. Journalize the Goldsmith Company adjusting entries at December 31, 20X5. Key entries by letter, as in Exhibit 3-8, page 143.
3. Post the adjusting entries.
4. Prepare an adjusted trial balance, as shown in Exhibit 3-9, page 145.
5. Prepare the income statement, the statement of retained earnings, and the balance sheet. (At this stage, it is not necessary to classify assets or liabilities as current or long term.) Draw arrows linking these three financial statements.

Goldsmith Company
Trial Balance
December 31, 20X5

Cash	$ 198,000	
Accounts receivable	370,000	
Supplies	6,000	
Furniture and fixtures	100,000	
Accumulated depreciation— furniture and fixtures		$ 40,000
Building	250,000	
Accumulated depreciation—building		130,000
Accounts payable		380,000
Salary payable		
Unearned service revenue		45,000
Income tax payable		
Common stock		100,000
Retained earnings		193,000
Dividends	65,000	
Service revenue		286,000
Salary expense	172,000	
Supplies expense		
Depreciation expense—furniture and fixtures		
Depreciation expense—building		
Income tax expense		
Miscellaneous expense	13,000	
Total	$1,174,000	$1,174,000

Answers

Requirements 1 and 3

Assets

Cash	
Bal.	198

Accounts Receivable	
	370
(e)	12
Bal.	382

Supplies		
	6	(a) 4
Bal.	2	

Furniture and Fixtures	
Bal.	100

Accumulated Depreciation—Furniture and Fixtures	
	40
(b)	20
Bal.	60

Building	
Bal.	250

Accumulated Depreciation—Building	
	130
(c)	10
Bal.	140

Liabilities

Accounts Payable	
Bal.	380

Salary Payable	
(d)	5
Bal.	5

Unearned Service Revenue		
(f) 32		45
	Bal.	13

Income Tax Payable	
(g)	35
Bal.	35

Stockholders' Equity

Common Stock	
Bal.	100

Retained Earnings	
Bal.	193

Dividends	
Bal.	65

Revenues

Service Revenue	
	286
(e)	12
(f)	32
Bal.	330

Expenses

Salary Expense	
	172
(d)	5
Bal.	177

Supplies Expense	
(a)	4
Bal.	4

Depreciation Expense—Furniture and Fixtures	
(b)	20
Bal.	20

Depreciation Expense—Building	
(c)	10
Bal.	10

Income Tax Expense	
(g)	35
Bal.	35

Miscellaneous Expense	
Bal.	13

Requirements 2

(a)	Dec. 31	Supplies Expense ($6,000 – $2,000)	4,000	
		Supplies		4,000
		To record supplies used.		
(b)	31	Depreciation Expense—Furniture and Fixtures	20,000	
		Accumulated Depreciation—Furniture and Fixtures		20,000
		To record depreciation expense on furniture and fixtures.		
(c)	31	Depreciation Expense—Building	10,000	
		Accumulated Depreciation—Building		10,000
		To record depreciation expense on building.		
(d)	31	Salary Expense	5,000	
		Salary Payable		5,000
		To accrue salary expense.		
(e)	31	Accounts Receivable	12,000	
		Service Revenue		12,000
		To accrue service revenue.		
(f)	31	Unearned Service Revenue	32,000	
		Service Revenue		32,000
		To record unearned service revenue that has been earned.		
(g)	31	Income Tax Expense	35,000	
		Income Tax Payable		35,000
		To accrue income tax expense.		

I *Requirements 4*

Goldsmith Company
Preparation of Adjusted Trial Balance
December 31, 20X5

Account Title	Trial Balance Debit	Trial Balance Credit	Adjustments Debit		Adjustments Credit		Adjusted Trial Balance Debit	Adjusted Trial Balance Credit
Cash	198						198	
Accounts receivable	370		(e)	12			382	
Supplies	6				(a)	4	2	
Furniture and fixtures	100						100	
Accumulated depreciation— furniture and fixtures		40			(b)	20		60
Building	250						250	
Accumulated depreciation—building		130			(c)	10		140
Accounts payable		380						380
Salary payable					(d)	5		5
Unearned service revenue		45	(f)	32				13
Income tax payable					(g)	35		35
Common stock		100						100
Retained earnings		193						193
Dividends	65						65	
Service revenue		286			(e)	12		330
					(f)	32		
Salary expense	172		(d)	5			177	
Supplies expense			(a)	4			4	
Depreciation expense— furniture and fixtures			(b)	20			20	
Depreciation expense—building			(c)	10			10	
Income tax expense			(g)	35			35	
Miscellaneous expense	13						13	
	1,174	1,174	118		118		1,256	1,256

| Requirements 5

Goldsmith Company
Income Statement
Year Ended December 31, 20X5

(Amounts in thousands)

Revenue:		
Service revenue		$330
Expenses:		
Salary expense	$177	
Depreciation expense—furniture and fixtures	20	
Depreciation expense—building	10	
Supplies expense	4	
Miscellaneous expense	13	224
Income before tax		106
Income tax expense		35
Net income		$ 71

①

Goldsmith Company
Statement of Retained Earnings
Year Ended December 31, 20X5

(Amounts in thousands)

Retained earnings, December 31, 20X4	$193
Add: Net income	71
	264
Less: Dividends	(65)
Retained earnings, December 31, 20X5	$199

Goldsmith Company
Balance Sheet
December 31, 20X5

②

(Amounts in thousands)

Assets			Liabilities		
Cash		$198	Accounts payable		$380
Accounts receivable		382	Salary payable		5
Supplies		2	Unearned service revenue		13
Furniture and fixtures	$100		Income tax payable		35
Less: Accumulated			Total liabilities		433
depreciation	(60)	40			
			Stockholders' Equity		
Building	$250		Common stock		100
Less: Accumulated			Retained earnings		199
depreciation	(140)	110	Total stockholders' equity		299
			Total liabilities and		
Total assets		$732	stockholders' equity		$732

HH CHAPTER 3

Which Accounts Need to Be Closed?

OBJECTIVE

5 **Close** the books

It is now June 30, the end of the month. Van Gray, the manager, will continue Genie Car Wash into July, August, and beyond. But wait—the revenue and the expense accounts still hold amounts for June. At the end of each accounting period, it is necessary to close the books.

Closing the books means to prepare the accounts for the next period's transactions. The **closing entries** set the revenue, expense, and dividends balances back to zero at the end of the period. The idea is the same as setting the scoreboard back to zero after a game.

Closing is easily handled by computers. Recall that the income statement reports only one period's income. For example, net income for Starbucks or Genie Car Wash for 2008 relates exclusively to 2008. At each year end, Starbucks accountants close the company's revenues and expenses for that year.

Temporary accounts. Because revenues and expenses relate to a limited period, they are called **temporary accounts**. The Dividends account is also temporary. The closing process applies only to temporary accounts (revenues, expenses, and dividends).

Permanent accounts. Let's contrast the temporary accounts with the **permanent accounts**: assets, liabilities, and stockholders' equity. The permanent accounts are not closed at the end of the period because they carry over to the next period. Consider Cash, Receivables, Equipment, Accounts Payable, Common Stock, and Retained Earnings. Their ending balances at the end of one period become the beginning balances of the next period.

Closing entries transfer the revenue, expense, and dividends balances to Retained Earnings. Here are the steps to close the books of a company such as Starbucks Corporation or Genie Car Wash:

① Debit each revenue account for the amount of its credit balance. Credit Retained Earnings for the sum of the revenues. Now the sum of the revenues is in Retained Earnings.

② Credit each expense account for the amount of its debit balance. Debit Retained Earnings for the sum of the expenses. The sum of the expenses is now in Retained Earnings.

③ Credit the Dividends account for the amount of its debit balance. Debit Retained Earnings. This entry places the dividends amount in the debit side of Retained Earnings. Remember that dividends are not expenses. Dividends never affect net income.

After closing the books, the Retained Earnings account of Genie Car Wash appears as follows (data from page 147):

		Retained Earnings	
		Beginning balance	18,800
Expenses	4,600	Revenues	7,500
Dividends	3,200		
		Ending balance	18,500

Assume that Genie Car Wash closes the books at the end of June. Exhibit 3-13 presents the complete closing process for the business. Panel A gives the closing journal entries, and Panel B shows the accounts after closing.

EXHIBIT 3-13 Journalizing and Posting the Closing Entries

PANEL A—Journalizing the Closing Entries   Page 5

		Closing Entries		
①	June 30	Service Revenue..............................	7,500	
		Retained Earnings		7,500
②	30	Retained Earnings	4,600	
		Rent Expense		1,000
		Salary Expense		1,800
		Supplies Expense.....................		300
		Depreciation Expense..............		400
		Utilities Expense......................		500
		Income Tax Expense		600
③	30	Retained Earnings	3,200	
		Dividends.................................		3,200

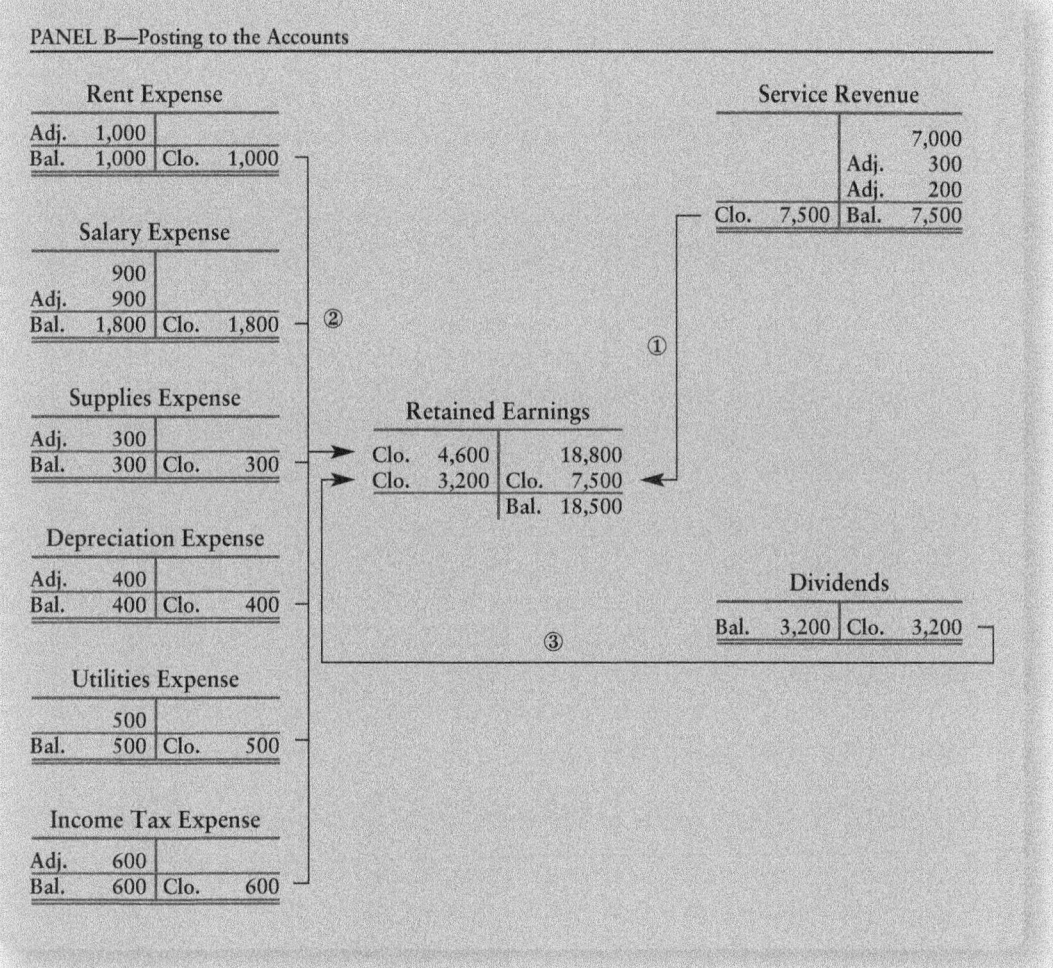

PANEL B—Posting to the Accounts

Adj. = Amount posted from an adjusting entry
Clo. = Amount posted from a closing entry
Bal. = Balance
As arrow ② in Panel B shows, we can make a compound closing entry for all the expenses.

HH CHAPTER 3

Accounting Cycle Tutorial
Adjusting & Closing the Books

Accounting Cycle Tutorial
Application—Cottage Kitchen

Accounting Cycle Tutorial
Application—Cottage
Kitchen 2

Classifying Assets and Liabilities Based on Their Liquidity

On the balance sheet, assets and liabilities are classified as current or long term to indicate their relative liquidity. **Liquidity** measures how quickly an item can be converted to cash. Cash is the most liquid asset. Accounts receivable are relatively liquid because cash collections usually follow quickly. Inventory is less liquid than accounts receivable because the company must first sell the goods. Equipment and buildings are even less liquid because these assets are held for use and not for sale. A balance sheet lists assets and liabilities in the order of relative liquidity.

Current Assets. As we saw in Chapter 1, **current assets** are the most liquid assets. They will be converted to cash, sold, or consumed during the next 12 months or within the business's normal operating cycle if longer than a year. The **operating cycle** is the time span during which cash is paid for goods and services and these goods and services are sold to bring in cash.

For most businesses, the operating cycle is a few months. Cash, Short-Term Investments, Accounts Receivable, Merchandise Inventory, and Prepaid Expenses are the current assets.

Long-Term Assets. **Long-term assets** are all assets not classified as current assets. One category of long-term assets is plant assets, often labeled Property, Plant, and Equipment. Land, Buildings, Furniture and Fixtures, and Equipment are plant assets. Of these, Genie Car Wash has only Equipment. Long-Term Investments, Intangible Assets, and Other Assets (a catchall category for assets that are not classified more precisely) are also long-term.

Current Liabilities. As we saw in Chapter 1, **current liabilities** are debts that must be paid within 1 year or within the entity's operating cycle if longer than a year. Accounts Payable, Notes Payable due within 1 year, Salary Payable, Unearned Revenue, Interest Payable, and Income Tax Payable are current liabilities.

Bankers and other lenders are interested in the due dates of an entity's liabilities. The sooner a liability must be paid, the more pressure it creates. Therefore, the balance sheet lists liabilities in the order in which they must be paid. Balance sheets usually report two liability classifications, current liabilities and long-term liabilities.

Long-Term Liabilities. All liabilities that are not current are classified as **long-term liabilities**. Many notes payable are long term. Some notes payable are paid in installments, with the first installment due within 1 year, the second installment due the second year, and so on. The first installment is a current liability and the remainder is long term.

Let's see how Starbucks Corporation reports these asset and liability categories on its balance sheet.

Reporting Assets and Liabilities: Starbucks Corporation

Exhibit 3-14 shows the actual classified balance sheet of Starbucks Corporation. A **classified balance sheet** separates current assets from long-term assets and current liabilities from long-term liabilities. You should be familiar with most of Starbucks' accounts. Study the Starbucks balance sheet all the way through—line by line.

EXHIBIT 3-14	Classified Balance Sheet of Starbucks Corporation (Adapted, in millions)

Starbucks Corporation
Balance Sheet (Adapted)
September 30, 2006

(millions)

Assets

Current assets:

Cash and cash equivalents	$ 313
Short-term investments	140
Accounts receivable	224
Inventories	636
Prepaid expenses and other current assets	217
Total current assets	1,530
Long-term investments	225
Property, plant, and equipment, net	2,288
Intangible assets	199
Other assets	187
Total assets	$4,429

Liabilities and Shareholders' Equity

Current liabilities:

Accounts payable	$ 341
Accrued expenses payable	661
Short-term notes payable	700
Current portion of long-term	1
Unearned revenue	232
Total current liabilities	1,935
Long-term debt	2
Other long-term liabilities	263
Total liabilities	2,200

Shareholders' equity:

Common stock	40
Retained earnings	2,151
Other equity	38
Total shareholders' equity	2,229
Total liabilities and shareholders' equity	$4,429

FORMATS FOR THE FINANCIAL STATEMENTS

Companies can format their financial statements in different ways. Both the balance sheet and the income statement can be formatted in two basic ways.

Balance Sheet Formats

The **report format** lists the assets at the top, followed by the liabilities and stockholders' equity below. The balance sheet of Starbucks Corporation in Exhibit 3-14 illustrates the report format. The report format is more popular, with approximately 60% of large companies using it.

The **account format** lists the assets on the left and the liabilities and stockholders' equity on the right in the same way that a T-account appears, with assets (debits) on the left and liabilities and equity (credits) on the right. Exhibit 3-12 (p. 147) shows an account-format balance sheet for Genie Car Wash. Either format is acceptable.

Income Statement Formats

A **single-step income statement** lists all the revenues together under a heading such as Revenues, or Revenues and Gains. The expenses are listed together in a single category titled Expenses, or Expenses and Losses. There is only one step, the subtraction of Expenses and Losses from the sum of Revenues and Gains, in arriving at net income. Starbucks' income statement (p.126) appears in single-step format.

A **multi-step income statement** reports a number of subtotals to highlight important relationships between revenues and expenses. Exhibit 3-15 shows Starbucks' income statement in multi-step format. Gross profit, income from operations, income before tax, and net income are highlighted for emphasis.

EXHIBIT 3-15   Starbucks Corporation Income Statement in Multi-Step Format

Starbucks Corporation
Income Statement (Adapted)
Year Ended September 30, 2006

		Millions
Net operating revenues		$7,787
Cost of sales (Cost of goods sold)		3,179
Gross profit		4,608
Store operating expenses	$2,688	
Other operating expenses	260	
Depreciation and amortization expenses	387	
General and administrative expenses	473	
Total operating expenses		3,808
Income from operations		800
Other income		89
Income before income taxes		889
Income tax expense		325
Net income		$ 564

In particular, income from operations ($800 million) is separated from "Other income," which Starbucks did not earn by selling coffee. The other income was mainly interest revenue and other investment income. Most companies consider it important to report their operating income separately from nonoperating income such as interest and dividends.

Most companies' income statements do not conform to either a pure single-step format or a pure multi-step format. Business operations are too complex for all companies to conform to rigid reporting formats.

USING ACCOUNTING RATIOS

OBJECTIVE

6 Use 2 new ratios to evaluate a business

As we've seen, accounting provides information for decision making. A bank considering lending money must predict whether the borrower can repay the loan. If the borrower already has a lot of debt, the probability of repayment may be low. If the borrower owes little, the loan may go through. To analyze a company's financial position, decision makers use ratios computed from various items in the financial statements. Let's see how this process works.

Current Ratio

One of the most widely used financial ratios is the **current ratio**, which divides total current assets by total current liabilities, taken from the balance sheet.

$$\text{Current ratio} = \frac{\text{Total current assets}}{\text{Total current liabilities}}$$

For Starbucks Corporation (amounts in millions on page 155):

$$\text{Current ratio} = \frac{\text{Total current assets}}{\text{Total current liabilities}} = \frac{\$1,530}{\$1,935} = 0.79$$

The current ratio measures the company's ability to pay current liabilities with current assets. A company prefers a high current ratio, which means that the business has plenty of current assets to pay current liabilities. An increasing current ratio from period to period indicates improvement in financial position.

As a rule of thumb, a strong current ratio is 1.50, which indicates that the company has $1.50 in current assets for every $1.00 in current liabilities. A company with a current ratio of 1.50 would probably have little trouble paying its current liabilities. Most successful businesses operate with current ratios between 1.20 and 1.50. A current ratio of 1.00 is considered quite low.

Starbucks' current ratio of 0.79 is very low and indicates a weak current position. How does Starbucks survive with so low a current ratio? The company makes most sales for cash, and it has little debt. That leads us to the next ratio.

Debt Ratio

A second aid to decision making is the **debt ratio**, which is the ratio of total liabilities to total assets:

$$\text{Debt ratio} = \frac{\text{Total liabilities}}{\text{Total assets}}$$

For Starbucks (amounts in millions on page 155),

$$\text{Debt ratio} = \frac{\text{Total liabilities}}{\text{Total assets}} = \frac{\$2,200}{\$4,429} = 0.50$$

HH CHAPTER 3

The debt ratio indicates the proportion of a company's assets that is financed with debt. This ratio measures a business's ability to pay both current and long-term debts (total liabilities).

A low debt ratio is safer than a high debt ratio. Why? Because a company with few liabilities has low required debt payments. This company is unlikely to get into financial difficulty. By contrast, a business with a high debt ratio may have trouble paying its liabilities, especially when sales are low and cash is scarce.

Starbucks' debt ratio of 50% (0.50) is low compared to most companies in the United States. The norm for the debt ratio ranges from 60% to 70%. Starbucks' debt ratio indicates low risk for the company, and that partly offsets Starbucks' risky current ratio.

When a company fails to pay its debts, creditors can take the company away from its owners. Most bankruptcies result from high debt ratios.

How Do Transactions Affect the Ratios?

Companies such as Starbucks are keenly aware of how transactions affect their ratios. Lending agreements often require that a company's current ratio not fall below a certain level. Another loan requirement is that the company's debt ratio may not rise above a threshold, such as 0.70. When a company fails to meet one of these conditions, it is said to violate its lending agreements. The penalty can be severe: The lender can require immediate payment of the loan. Starbucks has so little debt that the company is not in much danger. But many companies are.

Let's use Starbucks Corporation to examine the effects of some transactions on the company's current ratio and debt ratio. As shown in the preceding section, Starbucks' ratios are as follows (dollar amounts in millions):

$$\text{Current ratio} = \frac{\$1,530}{\$1,935} = 0.79 \qquad \text{Debt ratio} = \frac{\$2,200}{\$4,429} = 0.50$$

The managers of any company would be concerned about how inventory purchases, payments on account, expense accruals, and depreciation would affect its ratios. Let's see how Starbucks would be affected by some typical transactions. For each transaction, the journal entry helps identify the effects on the company.

a. Issued stock and received cash of $50 million.

Journal entry:

Cash	50	
Common Stock		50

Cash, a current asset, affects both the current ratio and the debt ratio as follows:

$$\text{Current ratio} = \frac{\$1,530 + \$50}{\$1,935} = 0.82 \qquad \text{Debt ratio} = \frac{\$2,200}{\$4,429 + \$50} = 0.49$$

The issuance of stock improves both ratios.

b. Paid cash to purchase buildings for $20 million.

Journal entry:

| Buildings | 20 | |
| Cash | | 20 |

Cash, a current asset, decreases, but total assets stay the same. Liabilities are unchanged.

$$\text{Current ratio} = \frac{\$1,530 - \$20}{\$1,935} = 0.78$$

$$\text{Debt ratio} = \frac{\$2,200}{\$4,429 + \$20 - \$20} = 0.50; \text{ no change}$$

A cash purchase of a building hurts the current ratio, but doesn't affect the debt ratio.

c. Made a $30 million sale on account to a grocery chain.

Journal entry:

| Accounts Receivable | 30 | |
| Sales Revenue | | 30 |

The increase in Accounts Receivable increases current assets and total assets, as follows:

$$\text{Current ratio} = \frac{\$1,530 + \$30}{\$1,935} = 0.81$$

$$\text{Debt ratio} = \frac{\$2,200}{\$4,429 + \$30} = 0.49$$

A sale on account improves both ratios.

d. Collected the account receivable, $30 million.

Journal entry:

| Cash | 30 | |
| Accounts Receivable | | 30 |

This transaction has no effect on total current assets, total assets, or total liabilities. Both ratios are unaffected.

e. Accrued expenses at year end, $40 million.

Journal entry:

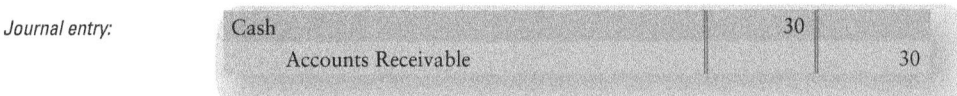

| Expenses | 10 | |
| Expenses Payable | | 10 |

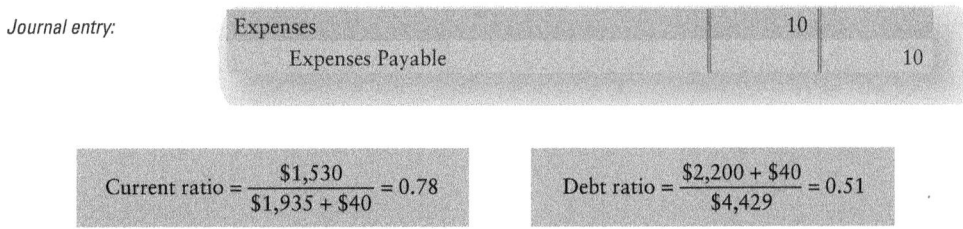

$$\text{Current ratio} = \frac{\$1,530}{\$1,935 + \$40} = 0.78$$

$$\text{Debt ratio} = \frac{\$2,200 + \$40}{\$4,429} = 0.51$$

Most expenses hurt both ratios.

f. Recorded depreciation, $80 million.

Journal entry:

Depreciation Expense	80	
Accumulated Depreciation		80

No current accounts are affected, so only the debt ratio is affected.

$$\text{Current ratio} = \frac{\$1,530}{\$1,935} = 0.79 \qquad \text{Debt ratio} = \frac{\$2,200}{\$4,429 - \$80} = 0.51$$

Depreciation decreases total assets and therefore hurts the debt ratio.

g. Earned interest revenue and collected cash, $40 million.

Journal entry:

Cash	40	
Interest Revenue		40

Cash, a current asset, affects both the current ratio and the debt ratio as follows:

$$\text{Current ratio} = \frac{\$1,530 + \$40}{\$1,935} = 0.81 \qquad \text{Debt ratio} = \frac{\$2,200}{\$4,429 + \$40} = 0.49$$

A revenue improves both ratios.

Now, let's wrap up the chapter by seeing how to use the current ratio and the debt ratio for decision making. The Decision Guidelines feature offers some clues.

DECISION GUIDELINES

USING THE CURRENT RATIO AND THE DEBT RATIO

In general, a *high* current ratio is preferable to a low current ratio. *Increases* in the current ratio improve financial position. By contrast, a *low* debt ratio is preferable to a high debt ratio. Improvement is indicated by a *decrease* in the debt ratio.

No single ratio gives the whole picture about a company. Therefore, lenders and investors use many ratios to evaluate a company. Let's apply what we have learned. Suppose you are a loan officer at Bank One, and Starbucks Corporation has asked you for a $20 million loan to launch a new blend of coffee. How will you make this loan decision? The Decision Guidelines show how bankers and investors use two key ratios.

USING THE CURRENT RATIO

Decision	Guidelines
How can you measure a company's ability to pay current liabilities with current assets?	$$\text{Current ratio} = \frac{\text{Total current assets}}{\text{Total current liabilities}}$$
Who uses the current ratio for decision making?	*Lenders and other creditors*, who must predict whether a borrower can pay its current liabilities. *Stockholders*, who know that a company that cannot pay its debts is not a good investment because it may go bankrupt. *Managers*, who must have enough cash to pay the company's current liabilities.
What is a good value of the current ratio?	Depends on the industry: A company with strong cash flow can operate successfully with a low current ratio of, say, 1.10–1.20. A company with weak cash flow needs a higher current ratio of, say, 1.30–1.50. Traditionally, a current ratio of 2.00 was considered ideal. Recently, acceptable values have decreased as companies have been able to operate more efficiently; today, a current ratio of 1.50 is considered strong. Cash-rich companies like Starbucks and Yum! Brands can operate with a current ratio below 1.0.

USING THE DEBT RATIO

Decision	Guidelines
How can you measure a company's ability to pay total liabilities?	$$\text{Debt ratio} = \frac{\text{Total liabilities}}{\text{Total assets}}$$
Who uses the debt ratio for decision making?	*Lenders and other creditors*, who must predict whether a borrower can pay its debts. *Stockholders*, who know that a company that cannot pay its debts is not a good investment because it may go bankrupt. *Managers*, who must have enough assets to pay the company's debts.
What is a good value of the debt ratio?	Depends on the industry: A company with strong cash flow can operate successfully with a high debt ratio of, say, 0.70–0.80 A company with weak cash flow needs a lower debt ratio of, say, 0.50–0.60. Traditionally, a debt ratio of 0.50 was considered ideal. Recently, values have increased as companies have been able to operate more efficiently; today, a normal value of the debt ratio is around 0.60–0.65.

HH CHAPTER 3

END-OF-CHAPTER SUMMARY PROBLEM

Refer to the mid-chapter summary problem that begins on page 148.

| Required

1. Make Goldsmith Company's closing entries at December 31, 20X5. Explain what the closing entries accomplish and why they are necessary. Show amounts in thousands.
2. Post the closing entries to Retained Earnings and compare Retained Earnings' ending balance with the amount reported on the balance sheet on page 151. The two amounts should be the same.
3. Prepare Goldsmith Company's classified balance sheet to identify the company's current assets and current liabilities. (Goldsmith has no long-term liabilities.) Then compute the company's current ratio and debt ratio at December 31, 20X5.
4. The top management of Goldsmith Company has asked you for a $500,000 loan to expand the business. Goldsmith proposes to pay off the loan over a 10-year period. Recompute Goldsmith's debt ratio assuming you make the loan. Use the company financial statements plus the ratio values to decide whether to grant the loan at an interest rate of 8%, 10%, or 12%. Goldsmith's cash flow is strong. Give the reasoning underlying your decision.

Answers

| Requirement 1

20X5			(In thousands)
Dec. 31	Service Revenue..	330	
	Retained Earnings		330
31	Retained Earnings	259	
	Salary Expense...		177
	Depreciation Expense—		
	Furniture and Fixtures...........................		20
	Depreciation Expense—Building		10
	Supplies Expense.......................................		4
	Income Tax Expense		35
	Miscellaneous Expense.............................		13
31	Retained Earnings	65	
	Dividends..		65

| Explanation of Closing Entries

The closing entries set the balance of each revenue, expense, and Dividends account back to zero for the start of the next accounting period. We must close these accounts because their balances relate only to one accounting period.

| Requirement 2

Retained Earnings

			193
Clo.	259	Clo.	330
Clo.	65		
		Bal.	199

The balance in the Retained Earnings account agrees with the amount reported on the balance sheet, as it should.

Requirement 3

Goldsmith Company
Balance Sheet
December 31, 20X5

(Amounts in thousands)

Assets			Liabilities		
Current assets:			Current liabilities:		
Cash		$198	Accounts payable		$380
Accounts receivable		382	Salary payable		5
Supplies		2	Unearned service revenue		13
Total current assets		582	Income tax payable		35
Furniture and			Total current liabilities		433
fixtures	$100		*Stockholders' Equity*		
Less: Accumulated					
depreciation	(60)	40	Common stock		100
Building	$250		Retained earnings		199
Less: Accumulated			Total stockholders' equity		299
depreciation	(140)	110	Total liabilities and		
Total assets		$732	stockholders' equity		$732

$$\text{Current ratio} = \frac{\$582}{\$433} = 1.34$$

$$\text{Debt ratio} = \frac{\$433}{\$732} = 0.59$$

Requirement 4

$$\frac{\text{Debt ratio assuming}}{\text{the loan is made}} = \frac{\$433 + \$500}{\$732 + \$500} = \frac{\$933}{\$1,232} = .76$$

Decision: Make the loan at 10%.

Reasoning: Prior to the loan, the company's financial position and cash flow are strong. The current ratio is in a middle range, and the debt ratio is not too high. Net income (from the income statement) is high in relation to total revenue. Therefore, the company should be able to repay the loan.

The loan will increase the company's debt ratio from 59% to 76%, which is more risky than the company's financial position at present. On this basis, a midrange interest rate appears reasonable—at least as the starting point for the negotiation between Goldsmith Company and the bank.

REVIEW ACCRUAL ACCOUNTING & INCOME

Quick Check (Answers are given on page 196.)

1. On November 1, Rosewood Apartments received $4,800 from a tenant for three months' rent. The receipt was credited to Unearned Rent Revenue. What adjusting entry is needed on December 31?

a. Unearned Rent Revenue	3,200	
Rent Revenue		3,200
b. Rent Revenue	1,600	
Unearned Rent Revenue		1,600
c. Unearned Rent Revenue	1,600	
Rent Revenue		1,600
d. Cash	1,600	
Rent Revenue		1,600

2. The following normal balances appear on the *adjusted* trial balance of Augusta National Company:

Equipment..	$90,000
Accumulated depreciation, equipment...............	15,000
Depreciation expense, equipment......................	5,000

The book value of the equipment is
   a. $85,000.   c. $75,000.
   b. $70,000.   d. $60,000.

3. Cadillac, Inc., purchased supplies for $900 during 20X3. At year end Cadillac had $600 of supplies left. The adjusting entry should:
   a. debit Supplies $300.   c. credit Supplies $600.
   b. debit Supplies Expense $300.   d. debit Supplies $600.

4. The accountant for Eldorado Corp. failed to make the adjusting entry to record depreciation for the current year. The effect of this error is:
   a. Assets are overstated, stockholders' equity and net income are understated.
   b. Assets and expenses are understated; net income is understated.
   c. Net income is overstated and liabilities are understated.
   d. Assets, net income, and stockholders' equity are all overstated.

5. Interest earned on a note receivable at December 31 equals $125. What adjusting entry is required to accrue this interest?

a. Interest Payable	125	
Interest Expense		125
b. Interest Expense	125	
Cash		125
c. Interest Receivable	125	
Interest Revenue		125
d. Interest Expense	125	
Interest Payable		125

6. If a real estate company fails to accrue commission revenue,
   a. liabilities are overstated and owners' equity is understated.
   b. assets are understated and net income is understated.
   c. revenues are understated and net income is overstated.
   d. net income is understated and stockholders' equity is overstated.

7. All of the following statements are true except one. Which statement is false?
   a. Adjusting entries are required for a business that uses the cash basis.
   b. Accrual accounting produces better information than cash-basis accounting.
   c. The matching principle directs accountants to identify and measure all expenses incurred and deduct them from revenues earned during the same period.
   d. A fiscal year ends on some date other than December 31.

8. The account Unearned Revenue is a(n):
   a. revenue   c. asset
   b. expense   d. liability

9. Adjusting entries:
   a. are needed to measure the period's net income or net loss.
   b. update the accounts.
   c. do not debit or credit cash.
   d. all of the above.

10. An adjusting entry that debits an expense and credits a liability is which type?
   a. accrued expense   c. prepaid expense
   b. depreciation expense   d. cash expense

Use the following data for questions 11 and 12.
Here are key figures from the balance sheet of Seville, Inc., at the end of 20X3 (amounts in thousands):

	December 31, 20X3
Total assets (of which 40% are current)	$4,000
Current liabilities	800
Bonds payable (long-term)	1,200
Common stock	1,500
Retained earnings	500
Total liabilities and stockholders' equity	4,000

11. Seville's current ratio at the end of 20X3 is:
   a. 6.25   c. 3.75
   b. 2.0   d. 2.24

12. Seville's debt ratio at the end of 20X3 is:
   a. 42% (rounded)   c. 60%
   b. 17% (rounded)   d. 50%

13. On a trial balance, which of the following would indicate that an error has been made?
   a. Service Revenue has a debit balance
   b. Salary Expense has a debit balance
   c. Accumulated Depreciation has a credit balance
   d. All of the above indicate errors

14. The entry to close Management Fee Revenue would be:
   a. Management Fee Revenue does not need to be closed out.
   b. Retained Earnings
          Management Fee Revenue
   c. Management Fee Revenue
          Retained Earnings
   d. Management Fee Revenue
          Service Revenue

15. Which of the following accounts is not closed out?
   a. Accumulated Depreciation
   b. Depreciation Expense
   c. Dividends
   d. Interest Revenue

16. FedEx earns service revenue of $500,000. How does this transaction affect FedEx's ratios?
    a. Hurts the current ratio and improves the debt ratio.
    b. Hurts both ratios.
    c. Improves both ratios.
    d. Improves the current ratio and doesn't affect the debit ratio.
17. Suppose Starbucks Corporation borrows $50 million on a 10-year note payable. How does this transaction affect Starbucks' ratios?
    a. Improves both ratios.
    b. Improves the current ratio and hurts the debt ratio.
    c. Hurts both ratios.
    d. Hurts the current ratio and improves the debt ratio.

Accounting Vocabulary

account format (p. 156) A balance-sheet format that lists assets on the left and liabilities and stockholders' equity on the right.

accrual (p. 132) An expense or a revenue that occurs before the business pays or receives cash. An accrual is the opposite of a deferral.

accrual accounting (p. 127) Accounting that records the impact of a business event as it occurs, regardless of whether the transaction affected cash.

accrued expense (p. 138) An expense incurred but not yet paid in cash.

accrued revenue (p. 139) A revenue that has been earned but not yet received in cash.

accumulated depreciation (p. 136) The cumulative sum of all depreciation expense from the date of acquiring a plant asset.

adjusted trial balance (p. 145) A list of all the ledger accounts with their adjusted balances.

book value (of a plant asset) (p. 137) The asset's cost minus accumulated depreciation.

cash-basis accounting (p. 127) Accounting that records only transactions in which cash is received or paid.

classified balance sheet (p. 154) A balance sheet that shows current assets separate from long-term assets, and current liabilities separate from long-term liabilities.

closing the books (p. 152) The process of preparing the accounts to begin recording the next period's transactions. Closing the accounts consists of journalizing and posting the closing entries to set the balances of the revenue, expense, and dividends accounts to zero. Also called closing the accounts.

closing entries (p. 152) Entries that transfer the revenue, expense, and dividends balances from these respective accounts to the Retained Earnings account.

contra account (p. 136) An account that always has a companion account and whose normal balance is opposite that of the companion account.

current assets (p. 154) An asset that is expected to be converted to cash, sold, or consumed during the next 12 months, or within the business's normal operating cycle if longer than a year.

current liabilities (p. 154) A debt due to be paid within one year or within the entity's operating cycle if the cycle is longer than a year.

current ratio (p. 157) Current assets divided by current liabilities. Measures a company's ability to pay current liabilities with current assets.

debt ratio (p. 157) Ratio of total liabilities to total assets. States the proportion of a company's assets that is financed with debt.

deferral (p. 131) An adjustment for which the business paid or received cash in advance. Examples include prepaid rent, prepaid insurance, and supplies.

depreciation (p. 132) the cost of a plant asset over its useful life.

liquidity (p. 154) Measure of how quickly an item can be converted to cash.

long-term assets (p. 154) An asset that is not a current asset.

long-term liabilities (p. 154) A liability that is not a current liability.

matching principle (p. 129) The basis for recording expenses. Directs accountants to identify all expenses incurred during the period, to measure the expenses, and to match them against the revenues earned during that same period.

multi-step income statement (p. 156) An income statement that contains subtotals to highlight important relationships between revenues and expenses.

operating cycle (p. 154) Time span during which cash is paid for goods and services that are sold to customers who pay the business in cash.

permanent accounts (p. 152) Asset, liability, and stockholders' equity accounts that are not closed at the end of the period.

plant assets (p. 135) Long-lived assets, such as land, buildings, and equipment, used in the operation of the business. Also called fixed assets.

prepaid expense (p. 130) A category of miscellaneous assets that typically expire or get used up in the near future. Examples include prepaid rent, prepaid insurance, and supplies.

report format (p. 155) A balance-sheet format that lists assets at the top, followed by liabilities and stockholders' equity below.

revenue principle (p. 128) The basis for recording revenues; tells accountants when to record revenue and the amount of revenue to record.

single-step income statement (p. 156) An income statement that lists all the revenues together under a heading such as Revenues or Revenues and Gains. Expenses appear in a separate category called Expenses or perhaps Expenses and Losses.

temporary accounts (p. 152) The revenue and expense accounts that relate to a limited period and are closed at the end of the period are temporary accounts. For a corporation, the Dividends account is also temporary.

time-period concept (p. 128) Ensures that accounting information is reported at regular intervals.

unearned revenue (p. 141) A liability created when a business collects cash from customers in advance of earning the revenue. The obligation is to provide a product or a service in the future.

HH CHAPTER 3

ASSESS YOUR PROGRESS

Short Exercises

S3-1 (*Learning Objective 1: Linking accrual accounting and cash flows*) Fleetwood Corporation made sales of $700 million during 20X3. Of this amount, Fleetwood collected cash for all but $30 million. The company's cost of goods sold was $300 million, and all other expenses for the year totaled $350 million. Also during 20X3, Fleetwood paid $400 million for its inventory and $280 million for everything else. Beginning cash was $100 million. Fleetwood's top management is interviewing you for a job and they ask two questions:

a. How much was Fleetwood's net income for 20X3? (p. 147)

b. How much was Fleetwood's cash balance at the end of 20X3? (pp. 77–78)

You will get the job only if you answer both questions correctly.

S3-2 (*Learning Objective 1: Linking accrual accounting and cash flows*) Docker Corporation began 20X9 owing notes payable of $4.0 million. During 20X9 Docker borrowed $2.6 million on notes payable and paid off $2.5 million of notes payable from prior years. Interest expense for the year was $1.0 million, including $0.2 million of interest payable accrued at December 31, 20X9.

Show what Docker should report for these facts on the following financial statements:

- Income statement (p. 147)
  Interest expence
- Balance sheet (p.147)
  Notes payable
  Interest payable

S3-3 (*Learning Objective 2: Applying the revenue and the matching principles*) Ford Motor Company sells large fleets of vehicles to auto rental companies, such as Enterprise and Hertz. Suppose Enterprise is negotiating with Ford to purchase 1,000 Explorers. Write a short paragraph to explain to Ford when Ford should, and should not, record this sales revenue and the related expense for cost of goods sold. Mention the accounting principles that provide the basis for your explanation. (p. 128)

writing assignment ■

S3-4 (*Learning Objective 3: Adjusting prepaid expenses*) Answer the following questions about prepaid expenses:

    a. On November 1, Air & Sea Travel prepaid $3,000 for 6 months' rent. Give the adjusting entry to record rent expense at December 31. Include the date of the entry and an explanation. Then post all amounts to the 2 accounts involved, and show their balances at December 31. Air & Sea Travel adjusts the accounts only at December 31. (pp. 132–133)

    b. On Dec. 1, Air & Sea Travel paid $800 for supplies. At December 31, Air & Sea Travel has $500 of supplies on hand. Make the required journal entry at December 31. Then post all amounts to the accounts and show their balances at December 31. (pp. 133–134)

S3-5 (*Learning Objective 1, 3: Recording depreciation; cash flows*) Suppose that on January 1 **Callaway Golf Company** paid cash of $30,000 for computers that are expected to remain useful for 3 years. At the end of 3 years, the computers' values are expected to be zero.

    1. Make journal entries to record (a) purchase of the computers on January 1 and (b) annual depreciation on December 31. Include dates and explanations, and use the following accounts: Computer Equipment; Accumulated Depreciation—Computer Equipment; and Depreciation Expense—Computer Equipment. (pp. 135–136)

    2. Post to the accounts and show their balances at December 31. (pp. 136–137)

    3. What is the computer equipment's book value at December 31? (pp. 136–137)

S3-6 (*Learning Objective 2: Applying the matching principle and the time-period concept*) During 20X8, Jetway Airlines paid salary expense of $40 million. At December 31, 20X8, Jetway accrued salary expense of $2 million. Jetway then paid $1.9 million to its employees on January 3, 20X9, the company's next payday after the end of the 20X8 year. For this sequence of transactions, show what Jetway would report on its 20X8 income statement and on its balance sheet at the end of 20X8. (p. 147)

S3-7 (*Learning Objective 3: Accruing and paying interest expense*) Mizuno Travel borrowed $100,000 on October 1 by signing a note payable to **Texas First Bank**. The interest expense for each month is $500. The loan agreement requires Mizuno to pay interest on December 31.

    1. Make Mizuno's adjusting entry to accrue monthly interest expense at October 31, at November 30, and at December 31. Date each entry and include its explanation. (pp. 138–139)

    2. Post all three entries to the Interest Payable account. You need not take the balance of the account at the end of each month. (pp. 138–139)

    3. Record the payment of three months' interest at December 31. (Challenge)

S3-8 (*Learning Objective 3: Accruing and receiving cash from interest revenue*) Return to the situation in Short Exercise S3-7. Here you are accounting for the same transactions on the books of Texas First Bank, which lent the money to Mizuno Travel. Perform all three steps of Short Exercise S3-7 for Texas First Bank using the bank's own accounts. (pp. 139–140)

<u>**writing assignment** ■</u>   **S3-9** (*Learning Objective 3: Explaining unearned revenues*) Write a paragraph to explain why unearned revenues are liabilities instead of revenues. In your explanation, use the following actual example: **The Wall Street Journal** collects cash from subscribers in advance and later delivers newspapers to subscribers over a 1-year period. Explain what happens to the unearned revenue over the course of a year as *The Wall Street Journal* delivers papers to subscribers. Into what account does the earned subscription revenue go as *The Wall Street Journal* delivers papers? Give the journal entries that *The Wall Street Journal* would make to (a) collect $40,000 of subscription revenue in advance and (b) record earning $40,000 of subscription revenue. Include an explanation for each entry, as illustrated in the chapter. (pp. 139–140)

S3-10 (*Learning Objective 4: Reporting prepaid expenses*) Eagle Golf Co. prepaid 3 years' rent ($6,000) on January 1. At December 31, Eagle prepared a trial balance and then made the necessary adjusting entry at the end of the year. Eagle adjusts its accounts once each year—on December 31.

What amount appears for Prepaid Rent on

    a. Eagle's *unadjusted* trial balance at December 31? (pp. 144–145)

    b. Eagle's *adjusted* trial balance at December 31? (pp. 144–145)

What amount appears for Rent Expense on

    c. Eagle's *unadjusted* trial balance at December 31? (pp. 144–145)

    d. Eagle's *adjusted* trial balance at December 31? (pp. 144–145)

S3-11 (*Learning Objective 3: Updating the accounts*) Bentley, Inc., collects cash from customers two ways:

    a. Accrued revenue. Some customers pay Bentley after Bentley has performed service for the customer. During 20X8, Bentley made sales of $50,000 on account and later received cash of $40,000 on account from these customers.

    b. Unearned revenue. A few customers pay Bentley in advance, and Bentley later performs the service for the customer. During 20X8 Bentley collected $7,000 cash in advance and later earned $6,000 of this amount.

Journalize for Bentley

    a. Earning service revenue of $50,000 on account and then collecting $40,000 on account. (pp. 139–140)

    b. Receiving $7,000 in advance and then earning $6,000 as service revenue. (pp. 141–142)

Explanations are not required.

S3-12 (*Learning Objective 4: Preparing the financial statements*) Falcon Sporting Goods Company reported the following data at March 31, 20X4, with amounts in thousands:

Retained earnings,			Cost of goods sold..............	$126,000
March 31, 20X3	$	1,300	Cash...........................	900
Accounts receivable.......		27,700	Property and equipment,	
Net revenues		174,500	net.......................	7,200
Total current liabilities ..		53,600	Common stock....................	26,000
All other expenses		45,000	Inventories	33,000
Other current assets		4,800	Long-term liabilities	13,500
Other assets..................		24,300	Dividends...........................	0

Use these data to prepare Falcon Sporting Goods Company's income statement for the year ended March 31, 20X4; statement of retained earnings for the year ended March 31, 20X4; and classified balance sheet at March 31, 20X4. Use the report format for the balance sheet. Draw arrows linking the three statements. (pp. 147, 155, 156)

S3-13 (*Learning Objective 5: Making closing entries*) Use the Falcon Sporting Goods data in Short Exercise S3-12 to make the company's closing entries at March 31, 20X4. Then set up a T-account for Retained Earnings and post to that account. Compare Retained Earnings' ending balance to the amount reported on Falcon's statement of retained earnings and balance sheet. What do you find? (pp. 153–154)

S3-14 (*Learning Objective 6: Computing the current ratio and the debt ratio*) Use the Falcon Sporting Goods data in short Exercise S3-12 to compute Falcon's

    1. Current ratio (pp. 157–158)

    2. Debit ratio (pp. 158–159)

Round to 2 decimal places. Do these ratio values look strong, weak or middle-of-the-road?

S3-15 (*Learning Objective 6: Using the current ratio and the debit ratio*) Use the Falcon Sporting Goods data in Short Exercise S3-12 to compute Falcon's (a) current ratio and (b) debt ratio after each of the following transactions (all amounts in thousands, as in the Falcon financial statements):

1. Falcon earned revenue of $10,000 on account (pp. 159–160)

2. Falcon paid off accounts payable of $10,000. (Challenge)

Round ratios to 2 decimal places.

Exercises

Most of the even-numbered exercises can be found within My Accouting Lab (MAL), an online homework and practice environment. Your instructor may ask you to complete these exercises using MAL.

E3-16 (*Learning Objective 1: Linking accrual accounting and cash flows*) During 20X8 Consolidated Foods Corporation made sales of $4,000 (assume all on account) and collected cash of $4,100 from customers. Operating expenses totaled $800, all paid in cash. At year end, 20X8, Consolidated customers owed the company $400. Consolidated owed creditors $700 on account. All amounts are in millions.

1. For these facts, show what Consolidated reported on the following financial statements (p. 147):

- Income statement
- Balance sheet

2. Suppose Consolidated had used the cash basis of accounting. What would Consolidated have reported for these facts? (p. 127)

E3-17 (*Learning Objective 1: Linking accrual accounting and cash flows*) During 2009 Valley Sales, Inc., earned revenues of $500,000 on account. Valley collected $510,000 from customers during the year. Expenses totaled $420,000, and the related cash payments were $400,000. Show what Valley would report on its 2009 income statement under the

a. Cash basis

b. Accrual basis

Compute net income under both bases of accounting. Which basis measures net income better? Explain your answer. (p. 127)

E3-18 (*Learning Objective 1, 2: Accrual basis of accounting, applying accounting principles*) During 20X6, Dish Network, Inc., which designs network servers, earned revenues of $700 million. Expenses totaled $540 million. Dish collected all but $20 million of the revenues and paid $550 million on its expenses. Dish's top managers are evaluating 20X6, and they ask you the following questions:

a. Under accrual accounting, what amount of revenue should Dish Network report for 20X6? Is the revenue the $700 million earned or is it the amount of cash actually collected? How does the revenue principle help to answer these questions? (pp. 127, 128)

b. Under accrual accounting, what amount of total expense should Dish Network report for 20X6—$540 million or $550 million? Which accounting principle helps to answer this question? (pp. 127–129)

c. Which financial statement reports revenues and expenses? Which statement reports cash receipts and cash payments? (p. 147)

writing assignment ■

E3-19 (*Learning Objective 2: Applying accounting concepts and principles*) Write a short paragraph to explain in your own words the concept of depreciation as used in accounting. (pp. 135–136)

E3-20 (*Learning Objective 2: Applying accounting concepts and principles*) Identify the accounting concept or principle that gives the most direction on how to account for each of the following situations: (pp. 128–130)

a. Salary expense of $20,000 is accrued at the end of the period to measure income properly.

b. October has been a particularly slow month, and the business will have a net loss for the third quarter of the year. Management is considering not following its customary practice of reporting quarterly earnings to the public.

c. A physician performs a surgical operation and bills the patient's insurance company. It may take 3 months to collect from the insurance company. Should the physician record revenue now or wait until cash is collected?

d. A construction company is building a highway system, and construction will take 3 years. When should the company record the revenue it earns?

e. A utility bill is received on December 30 and will be paid next year. When should the company record utility expense?

writing assignment ■

E3-21 (*Learning Objective 1, 3: Journalizing adjusting entries and analyzing their effects on net income; accrual versus cash basis*) An accountant made the following adjustments at December 31, the end of the accounting period:

a. Prepaid insurance, beginning, $700. Payments for insurance during the period, $2,100. Prepaid insurance, ending, $800.

b. Interest revenue accrued, $900.

c. Unearned service revenue, beginning, $800. Unearned service revenue, ending, $300.

d. Depreciation, $6,200.

e. Employees' salaries owed for 3 days of a 5-day work week; weekly payroll, $9,000.

f. Income before income tax, $20,000. Income tax rate is 40%.

■ general ledger

I Required

1. Journalize the adjusting entries. (pp. 132–144)

2. Suppose the adjustments were not made. Compute the overall overstatement or understatement of net income as a result of the omission of these adjustments.

E3-22 (*Learning Objective 2, 3: Allocating supplies cost to the asset and the expense*) Bird-Kultgen, Inc., experienced four situations for its supplies. Compute the amounts indicated by question marks for each situation. For situations 1 and 2, journalize the needed transaction. Consider each situation separately. (pp. 133–134)

■ spreadsheet

	Situation			
	1	2	3	4
Beginning supplies....................................	$ 500	$1,000	$300	$ 900
Payments for supplies during the year.......	?	3,100	?	1,100
Total cost to account for..........................	1,300	?	?	2,000
Ending supplies..	400	500	700	?
Supplies expense.....................................	$ 900	$?	$700	$1,400

E3-23 (*Learning Objective 3: Journalizing adjusting entries*) Clark Motor Company faced the following situations. Journalize the adjusting entry needed at December 31, 20X6, for each situation. Consider each fact separately. (pp. 132–144)

■ general ledger

a. The business has interest expense of $9,000 that it must pay early in January 20X7.

b. Interest revenue of $3,000 has been earned but not yet received.

c. On July 1, when we collected $3,000 rent in advance, we debited Cash and credited Unearned Rent Revenue. The tenant was paying us for 2 years' rent.

d. Salary expense is $1,000 per day—Monday through Friday—and the business pays employees each Friday. This year, December 31 falls on a Tuesday.

e. The unadjusted balance of the Supplies account is $3,100. The total cost of supplies on hand is $800.

(continued)

f. Equipment was purchased at the beginning of this year at a cost of $60,000. The equipment's useful life is 5 years. Record depreciation for this year and then determine the equipment's book value.

E3-24 *(Learning Objective 3: Making adjustments in T-accounts)* The accounting records of Belmont Publishing Company include the following unadjusted balances at May 31: Accounts Receivable, $1,300; Supplies, $900; Salary Payable, $0; Unearned Service Revenue, $800; Service Revenue, $14,400; Salary Expense, $4,200; Supplies Expense, $0. Belmont's accountant develops the following data for the May 31 adjusting entries:

a. Supplies on hand, $300.
b. Salary owed to employees, $2,000.
c. Service revenue accrued, $600.
d. Unearned service revenue that has been earned, $700.

Open the foregoing T-accounts with their beginning balances. Then record the adjustments directly in the accounts, keying each adjustment amount by letter. Show each account's adjusted balance. Journal entries are not required. (p. 144)

E3-25 *(Learning Objective 4: preparing the financial statements)* The adjusted trial balance of Honeybee Hams, Inc., follows.

Honeybee Hams, Inc.
Adjusted Trial Balance
December 31, 20X6

(Thousands)	Adjusted Trial Balance	
	Debit	Credit
Cash	$ 3,300	
Accounts receivable	1,800	
Inventories	1,100	
Prepaid expenses	1,900	
Property, plant, equipment	6,600	
Accumulated depreciation		$ 2,400
Other assets	9,900	
Accounts payable		7,700
Income tax payable		600
Other liabilities		2,200
Common stock		4,900
Retained earnings (beginning, December 31, 20X5)		4,500
Dividends	1,700	
Sales revenue		41,000
Cost of goods sold	25,000	
Selling, administrative, and general expense	10,000	
Income tax expense	2,000	
Total	$63,300	$63,300

I *Required*

Prepare Honeybee Hams, Inc.'s, income statement and statement of retained earnings for the year ended December 31, 20X6, and its balance sheet on that date. Draw the arrows linking the three statements. (p. 147)

E3-26 (*Learning Objective 3: Measuring financial statement amounts*) The adjusted trial balances of Triumph Corporation at March 31, 2008, and March 31, 2007, include these amounts (in millions):

	2008	2007
Receivables..	$300	$200
Prepaid insurance..	180	110
Accrued liabilities payable (for other operating expenses).....	700	600

Triumph completed these transactions during the year ended March 31, 2008.

Collections from customers...	$20,800
Payment of prepaid insurance	400
Cash payments for other operating expenses..............	4,100

Compute the amount of sales revenue, insurance expense, and other operating expenses to report on the income statement for the year ended March 31, 2008. (pp. 77–78)

E3-27 (*Learning Objective 4: Reporting on the financial statements*) This question deals with the items and the amounts that two entities, Mother Frances Hospital (Mother Frances) and City of St. Paul (St. Paul) should report in their financial statements. Fill in the blanks.

❙ *Required*

1. On July 1, 20X5, Mother Frances collected $3,000 in advance from St. Paul, a client. Under the contract, Mother Frances is obligated to perform medical exams for City of St. Paul employees evenly during the 12 months ending June 30, 20X6. Assume you are Mother Frances.
    Mother Frances's income statement for the year ended December 31, 20X5, will report ___ of $ ___. (pp. 139–140, 147)
    Mother Frances's balance sheet at December 31, 20X5, will report ___ of $___. (pp. 139–140, 147)

2. Assume now that you are City of St. Paul (St. Paul).
    St. Paul's income statement for the year ended December 31, 20X5, will report ___ of $___. (pp. 132, 147)
    St. Paul's balance sheet at December 31, 20X5, will report ___ of $___. (pp. 132, 147)

E3-28 (*Learning Objective 1, 3: Linking deferrals and cash flows*) This exercise builds from a simple situation to a slightly more complex situation. **Vodafone**, the British wireless phone service provider, collects cash in advance from customers. All amounts are in millions of pounds sterling, (£) the British monetary unit.
    Assume Vodafone collected £500 in advance during 2008 and at year end still owed customers phone service worth £100.

❙ *Required*

1. Show what Vodafone will report for 2008 on its (pp. 139–140, 147)
    *   Income statement
    *   Balance sheet

(continued)

2. Use the same facts for Vodafone as in item 1. Further, assume Vodafone reported unearned service revenue of £70 back at the end of 2007.

Show what Vodafone will report for 2008 on the same financial statements. Explain why your answer here differs from your answer to item 1. (pp. 139–142, 147)

E3-29 (*Learning Objective 5: Closing the accounts*) Prepare the closing entries from the following selected accounts from the records of Ulrich Corporation at December 31, 20X2:

Cost of services sold............	$11,600	Service revenue........................	$23,600
Accumulated depreciation...	17,800	Depreciation expense	4,100
Selling, general, and		Other revenue	600
administrative expense	6,900	Dividends................................	400
Retained earnings,		Income tax expense................	400
December 31, 20X1........	1,900	Income tax payable................	300

How much net income did Ulrich earn during 20X2? (p. 147) Prepare a T-account for Retained Earnings to show the December 31, 20X2, balance of Retained Earnings. (p. 153)

E3-30 (*Learning Objective 3, 5: Identifying and recording adjusting and closing entries*) The unadjusted trial balance and income statement amounts from the December 31 adjusted trial balance of Kopec Production Company follow.

▎*Required*

Journalize the adjusting and closing entries of Kopec Production Company at December 31. There was only one adjustment to Service Revenue. (pp. 144, 153)

Kopec Production Company

Account Title	Unadjusted Trial Balance		From the Adjusted Trial Balance	
Cash..	10,200			
Prepaid rent..................................	1,100			
Equipment....................................	32,100			
Accumulated depreciation...............		3,800		
Accounts payable		4,600		
Salary payable................................				
Unearned service revenue		8,400		
Income tax payable.........................				
Note payable, long-term..................		10,000		
Common stock...............................		8,700		
Retained earnings...........................		1,300		
Dividends......................................	1,000			
Service revenue..............................		12,800		19,500
Salary expense................................	4,000		4,900	
Rent expense..................................	1,200		1,400	
Depreciation expense			300	
Income tax expense.........................			1,600	
Net income....................................	49,600	49,600	8,200	19,500

E3-31 (*Learning Objective 4, 6: Preparing a classified balance sheet and using the ratios*)
Refer to Exercise 3-30.

❚ Required

1. After solving Exercise 3-30, use the data in that exercise to prepare Kopec Production Company's classified balance sheet at December 31 of the current year. Use the report format. First you must compute the adjusted balance for several of the balance-sheet accounts. (pp. 144–145, 155–156).

2. Compute Kopec Production Company's current ratio and debt ratio at December 31. A year ago, the current ratio was 1.55 and the debt ratio was 0.45. Indicate whether the company's ability to pay its debts—both current and total—improved or deteriorated during the current year. (pp. 156–158)

E3-32 (*Learning Objective 6: Measuring the effects of transactions on the ratios*) Ben Williams Company reported these ratios at December 31, 2008 (dollar amounts in millions):

$$\text{Current ratio} = \frac{\$20}{\$10} = 2.00 \qquad \text{Debt ratio} = \frac{\$20}{\$50} = 0.40$$

Ben Williams Company completed these transactions during 2009:
  a. Purchased equipment on account, $4.
  b. Paid long-term debt, $5.
  c. Collected cash from customers in advance, $2.
  d. Accrued interest expense, $1.
  e. Made cash sales, $6.

Determine whether each transaction improved or hurt Williams' current ratio and debt ratio. Round all ratios to 2 decimal places. (pp. 157–160)

Serial Exercise

Exercise 3-33 continues the Lance Sedberry, Certified Public Accountant, P.C., situation begun in Exercise 2-25 of Chapter 2 (p. 95).

■ general ledger

E3-33 (*Learning Objectives 3, 4, 5, 6: Adjusting the accounts, preparing the financial statements, closing the accounts, and evaluating the business*) Refer to Exercise 2-25 of Chapter 2. Start from the trial balance and the posted T-accounts that Lance Sedberry, Certified Public Accountant, Professional Corporation (P.C.), prepared for his accounting practice at January 18. A professional corporation is not subject to income tax. Later in January, the business completed these transactions:

Jan. 21	Received $900 in advance for tax work to be performed over the next 30 days.
21	Hired a secretary to be paid on the 15th day of each month.
26	Paid $900 on account.
28	Collected $600 on account.
31	Declared and paid dividends of $1,000.

❚ Required

1. Open these T-accounts: Accumulated Depreciation—Equipment, Accumulated Depreciation—Furniture, Salary Payable, Unearned Service Revenue, Retained Earnings, Depreciation Expense—Equipment, Depreciation Expense—Furniture, and Supplies Expense. Also, use the T-accounts that you opened for Exercise 2-25. (pp. 77–78).

2. Journalize the transactions of January 21 through 31. (pp. 77–78)

3. Post the January 21 to 31 transactions to the T-accounts, keying all items by date. (pp. 77–78)

(continued)

HH CHAPTER 3

4. Prepare a trial balance at January 31. Also set up columns for the adjustments and for the adjusted trial balance, as illustrated in Exhibit 3-9, page 145.

5. At January 31, Sedberry gathers the following information for the adjusting entries:
   a. Accrued service revenue, $1,000.
   b. Earned $300 of the service revenue collected in advance on January 21.
   c. Supplies on hand, $300.
   d. Depreciation expense—equipment, $100; furniture, $200.
   e. Accrued expense for secretary's salary, $700.
   Make these adjustments directly in the adjustments columns and complete the adjusted trial balance at January 31. (pp. 144–145)

6. Journalize and post the adjusting entries. Denote each adjusting amount as Adj. and an account balance as Bal. (pp. 143–144)

7. Prepare the income statement and statement of retained earnings of Lance Sedberry, Certified Public Accountant, P.C., for the month ended January 31 and the classified balance sheet at that date. Draw arrows to link the financial statements. (p. 147)

8. Journalize and post the closing entries at January 31. Denote each closing amount as Clo. and an account balance as Bal. (p. 153)

9. Compute the current ratio and the debt ratio of Sedberry's accounting practice and evaluate these ratio values as indicative of a strong or weak financial position. (pp. 156–158)

Challenge Exercises

E3-34 (*Learning Objective 6: Evaluating the current ratio*) Valley Forge Corporation reported the following current accounts at December 31, 2008 (amounts in thousands):

Cash	$1,700
Receivables	5,600
Inventory	1,800
Prepaid expenses	800
Accounts payable	2,400
Unearned revenues	1,200
Accrued expenses payable	1,700

During 2009, Valley Forge completed these selected transactions:
- Sold services on account, $8,500.
- Depreciation expense, $400.
- Paid for expenses, $7,100.
- Collected from customers on account, $7,500.
- Accrued expenses, $300.
- Paid on account, $1,000.
- Used up prepaid expenses, $200.

Compute Valley Forge's current ratio at December 31, 2008, and again at December 31, 2009. Did the current ratio improve or deteriorate during 2009? Comment on the level of the company's current ratio. (pp. 157–160)

E3-35 (*Learning Objective 3, 4: Computing financial statement amounts*) The accounts of Gleneagles Company prior to the year-end adjustments follow on the next page.

Adjusting data at the end of the year include:
   a. Unearned service revenue that has been earned, $1,000.
   b. Accrued service revenue, $2,000.
   c. Supplies used in operations, $3,000.
   d. Accrued salary expense, $3,000.
   e. Perpaid insurance expired, $1,000.
   f. Depreciation expense—building, $2,000.

Cash	$ 4,000		Common stock	$ 10,000
Accounts receivable	7,000		Retained earnings	43,000
Supplies	4,000		Dividends	16,000
Prepaid insurance	3,000		Service revenue	155,000
Building	107,000		Salary expense	32,000
Accumulated depreciation—			Depreciation expense—	
building	14,000		building	
Land	51,000		Supplies expense	
Accounts payable	6,000		Insurance expense	
Salary payable			Advertising expense	7,000
Unearned service revenue	5,000		Utilities expense	2,000

Mack Shaughnessy, the principal stockholder, has received an offer to sell Gleneagles Company. He needs to know the following information within 1 hour:

a. Net income for the year covered by these data
b. Total assets
c. Total liabilities
d. Total stockholders' equity
e. Proof that total assets = total liabilities + total stockholders' equity after all items are updated.

I Required

Without opening any accounts, making any journal entries, or using a work sheet, provide Mr. Shaughnessy with the requested information. The business is not subject to income tax. Show all computations. (pp. 143–144, 147)

Practice Quiz

Test your understanding of accrual accounting by answering the following questions. Select the best choice from among the possible answers given.

Questions 36–38 are based on the following facts:

Freddie Handel began a music business in July 20X4. Handel prepares monthly financial statements and uses the accrual basis of accounting. The following transactions are Handel Company's only activities during January through April:

Jan. 14	Bought music on account for $10, with payment to the supplier due in 90 days.	
Feb. 3	Performed a job on account for Joey Bach for $25, collectible from Bach in 30 days. Used up all the music purchased on Jan. 14.	
Mar. 16	Collected the $25 receivable from Bach.	
Apr. 22	Paid the $10 owed to the supplier from the January 14 transaction.	

Q3-36 In which month should Handel record the cost of the music as an expense? (pp. 127–129)

a. January
b. February

c. March
d. April

Q3-37 In which month should Handel report the $25 revenue on its income statement? (pp. 127–128)

a. January
b. February

c. March
d. April

Q3-38 If Handel Company uses the *cash* basis of accounting instead of the accrual basis, in what month will Handel report revenue and in what month will it report expense? (pp. 127–128)

	Revenue	**Expense**
a.	March	April
b.	March	January
c.	February	April
d.	March	February

Q3-39 In which month should revenue be recorded? (p. 129)
a. In the month that goods are ordered by the customer.
b. In the month that goods are shipped to the customer.
c. In the month that the invoice is mailed to the customer.
d. In the month that cash is collected from the customer.

Q3-40 On January 1 of the current year, Aladdin Company paid $600 rent to cover six months (January–June). Aladdin recorded this transactions as follows:

Prepaid Rent	600	
Cash		600

Aladdin adjusts the accounts at the end of each month. Based on these facts, the adjusting entry at the end of January should include (p. 132)
a. a credit to Prepaid Rent for $500.
b. a debit to Prepaid Rent for $500.
c. a debit to Prepaid Rent for $100.
d. a credit to Prepaid Rent for $100.

Q3-41 Assume the same facts as in the previous problem. Aladdin's adjusting entry at the end of February should include a debit to Rent Expense in the amount of (p. 132)
a. $-0-.   c. $200.
b. $500.   d. $100.

Q3-42 What effect does the adjusting entry in question 41 have on Aladdin's net income for February? (p. 132)
a. increase by $100   c. decrease by $100
b. increase by $200   d. decrease by $200

Q3-43 An adjusting entry recorded March salary expense that will be paid in April. Which statement best describes the effect of this adjusting entry on the company's accounting equation at the end of March? (p. 139)
a. Assets are not affected, liabilities are increased, and stockholders' equity is decreased.
b. Assets are decreased, liabilities are increased, and stockholders' equity is decreased.
c. Assets are not affected, liabilities are increased, and stockholders' equity is increased.
d. Assets are decreased, liabilities are not affected, and stockholders' equity is decreased.

Q3-44 On April 1, 20X1, Metro Insurance Company sold a one-year insurance policy covering the year ended April 1, 20X2. Metro collected the full $1,200 on April 1, 20X1. Metro made the following journal entry to record the receipt of cash in advance:

Cash	1,200	
Unearned Revenue		1,200

Nine months have passed, and Metro has made no adjusting entries. Based on these facts, the adjusting entry needed by Metro at December 31, 20X1, is (pp. 141–142)

a.	Unearned Revenue	300	
	Insurance Revenue		300
b.	Insurance Revenue	300	
	Unearned Revenue		300
c.	Unearned Revenue	900	
	Insurance Revenue		900
d.	Insurance Revenue	900	
	Unearned Revenue		900

Q3-45 The Unearned Revenue account of Dean, Incorporated, began 20X5 with a normal balance of $5,000 and ended 20X5 with a normal balance of $12,000. During 20X5, the Unearned Revenue account was credited for $19,000 that Dean will earn later. Based on these facts, how much revenue did Dean earn in 20X5? (pp. 141–142)
a. $5,000
b. $19,000
c. $24,000
d. $12,000

Q3-46 What is the effect on the financial statements of *recording* depreciation on equipment? (pp. 134, 147)
a. Assets are decreased, but net income and stockholders' equity are not affected.
b. Net income, assets, and stockholders' equity are all decreased.
c. Net income and assets are decreased, but stockholders' equity is not affected.
d. Net income is not affected, but assets and stockholders' equity are decreased.

Q3-47 For 20X3, Monterrey Company had revenues in excess of expenses. Which statement describes Monterrey's closing entries at the end of 20X3? (p. 153)
a. Revenues will be debited, expenses will be credited, and retained earnings will be debited.
b. Revenues will be credited, expenses will be debited, and retained earnings will be debited.
c. Revenues will be debited, expenses will be credited, and retained earnings will be credited.
d. Revenues will be credited, expenses will be debited, and retained earnings will be credited.

Q3-48 Which of the following accounts would *not* be included in the closing entries? (p. 153)
a. Accumulated Depreciation
b. Service Revenue
c. Depreciation Expense
d. Retained Earnings

Q3-49 A major purpose of preparing closing entries is to (p. 152)
a. zero out the liability accounts.
b. close out the Supplies account.
c. adjust the asset accounts to their correct current balances.
d. update the Retained Earnings account.

Q3-50 Selected data for Austin Company follow:

Current assets.............	$50,000	Current liabilities	$40,000
Long-term assets	70,000	Long-term liabilities	35,000
Total revenues.............	30,000	Total expenses................	20,000

Based on these facts, what are Austin's current ratio and debt ratio? (pp. 156–158)

Current ratio	Debt ratio
a. 2 to 1	0.5 to 1
b. .83 to 1	0.5 to 1
c. 1.25 to 1	0.625 to 1
d. 2 to 1	0.633 to 1

HH CHAPTER 3

Q3-51 Unadjusted net income equals $5,000. After the following adjustments, net income will be (fill in the blank) $___ (pp. 144, 147, Challenge)
(1) Salaries payable to employees, $500.
(2) Interest due on note payable at the bank, $100.
(3) Unearned revenue that has been earned, $600.
(4) Supplies used, $200.

Q3-52 Salary Payable at the beginning of the month totals $24,000. During the month salaries of $125,000 were accrued as expense. If ending Salary Payable is $10,000, what amount of cash did the company pay for salaries during the month? (Hint: Draw a T-account, as on pp. 77–78.).

a. $129,000
b. $149,000

c. $125,000
d. $139,000

Problems
(Group A)

MyAccountingLab | Some of these A problems can be found within My Accounting Lab (MAL), an online homework and practice environment. Your instructor may ask you to complete these exercises using MAL.

P3-53A (*Learning Objective 1: Linking accrual accounting and cash flows*) Cherokee Corporation earned revenues of $35 million during 20X1 and ended the year with net income of $8 million. During 20X1, Cherokee collected $33 million from customers and paid cash for all of its expenses plus an additional $1 million for amounts payable at December 31, 20X0. Answer these questions about Cherokee's operating results, financial position, and cash flows during 20X1:

I Required

1. How much were Cherokee's total expenses? Show your work. (pp. 127–128)
2. Identify all the items that Cherokee will report on its 20X1 income statement. Show each amount. (p. 147)
3. Cherokee began 20X1 with receivables of $4 million. All sales are on account. What was the company's receivables balance at the end of 20X1? Identify the appropriate financial statement, and show how Cherokee will report ending receivables in the 20X1 annual report. (pp. 77–78)
4. Cherokee began 20X1 owing accounts payable of $9 million. All expenses are increased on account. During 20X1 Cherokee paid $28 million on account. How much in accounts payable did the company owe at the end of the year? Identify the appropriate financial statement and show how Cherokee will report accounts payable in its 20X1 annual report. (pp. 77–78)

P3-54A (*Learning Objective 1: Cash basis versus accrual basis*) Masters Consulting had the following selected transactions in August:

Aug. 1	Prepaid insurance for August through December, $1,000.
4	Purchased software for cash, $800.
5	Performed service and received cash, $900.
8	Paid advertising expense, $300.
11	Performed service on account, $3,000.
19	Purchased computer on account, $1,600.
24	Collected for the August 11 service.
26	Paid account payable from August 19.
29	Paid salary expense, $900.
31	Adjusted for August insurance expense (see Aug. 1).
31	Earned revenue of $800 that was collected in advance back in July.

I *Required*

1. Show how each transaction would be handled using the cash basis and the accrual basis. Under each column, give the amount of revenue or expense for August. Journal entries are not required. Use the following format for your answer, and show your computations: (pp. 127–128)

	Masters Consulting Amount of Revenue (Expense) for August	
Date	Cash Basis	Accrual Basis

2. Compute August income (loss) before tax under each accounting method. (p. 125)

3. Indicate which measure of net income or net loss is preferable. Use the transactions on August 11 and 24 to explain. (p. 127)

P3-55A (*Learning Objective 1, 2: Applying accounting principles*) Write a memo to explain for a new employee the difference between the cash basis of accounting and the accrual basis. Mention the roles of the revenue principle and the matching principle in accrual accounting. (pp. 127–128)

P3-56A (*Learning Objective 3: Making accounting adjustments*) Journalize the adjusting entry needed on December 31, end of the current accounting period, for each of the following independent cases affecting Callaway Corp. Include an explanation for each entry. (pp. 132–144)

writing assignment ■

a. Details of Prepaid Insurance are shown in the account:

Prepaid Insurance	
Jan. 1 Bal.	400
Mar. 31	3,600

Callaway prepays insurance on March 31 each year. At December 31, $600 is still prepaid.

b. Callaway pays employees each Friday. The amount of the weekly payroll is $6,000 for a 5-day work week. The current accounting period ends on Wednesday.

c. Callaway has a note receivable. During the current year, Callaway has earned accrued interest revenue of $500 that it will collect next year.

d. The beginning balance of supplies was $2,600. During the year, Callaway purchased supplies costing $6,100, and at December 31 supplies on hand total $2,100.

e. Callaway is providing services for Manatee Investments, and the owner of Manatee paid Callaway $12,000 as the annual service fee. Callaway recorded this amount as Unearned Service Revenue. Callaway estimates that it has earned one-third of the total fee during the current year.

f. Depreciation for the current year includes Office Furniture, $1,000 and Equipment, $2,700. Make a compound entry.

HH CHAPTER 3

P3-57A (*Learning Objective 3, 4, 6: Preparing an adjusted trial balance and the financial statements; using the current ratio to evaluate the business*) The unadjusted trial balance of Princess, Inc., at January 31, 20X2, and the related month-end adjustment data follow.

Princess, Inc.
Trial Balance
January 31, 20X2

Cash..	$ 8,000	
Accounts receivable..................................	10,000	
Prepaid rent..	3,000	
Supplies...	2,000	
Furniture...	36,000	
Accumulated depreciation........................		$ 3,000
Accounts payable		10,000
Salary payable...		
Common stock...		26,000
Retained earnings (December 31, 20X1)....		13,000
Dividends...	4,000	
Service revenue...		14,000
Salary expense...	2,000	
Rent expense...		
Utilities expense	1,000	
Depreciation expense		
Supplies expense.......................................		
Total	$66,000	$66,000

Adjustment data:

    a. Accrued service revenue at January 31, $2,000.

    b. Prepaid rent expired during the month. The unadjusted prepaid balance of $3,000 relates to the period January through March.

    c. Supplies used during January, $2,000.

    d. Depreciation on furniture for the month. The estimated useful life of the furniture is 3 years.

    e. Accrued salary expense at January 31 for Monday, Tuesday, and Wednesday. The 5-day weekly payroll of $5,000 will be paid on Friday, February 2.

❙ Required

1. Using Exhibit 3-9, page 145, as an example, prepare the adjusted trial balance of Princess, Inc., at January 31, 20X2. Key each adjusting entry by letter.

2. Prepare the monthly income statement, the statement of retained earnings, and the classified balance sheet. Draw arrows linking the three financial statements. (p. 147)

P3-58A (*Learning Objective 3: Analyzing and recording adjustments*) Peppertree Apartments, Inc.'s, unadjusted and adjusted trial balances at April 30, 20X1, is given on the next page.

Peppertree Apartments, Inc.
Adjusted Trial Balance
April 30, 20X1

Account Title	Trial Balance		Adjusted Trial Balance	
	Debit	Credit	Debit	Credit
Cash	8,300		8,300	
Accounts receivable	6,300		6,800	
Interest receivable			300	
Note receivable	4,100		4,100	
Supplies	900		200	
Prepaid insurance	2,400		700	
Building	66,400		66,400	
Accumulated depreciation		16,000		18,200
Accounts payable		6,900		6,900
Wages payable				400
Unearned rental revenue		600		100
Common stock		18,000		18,000
Retained earnings		42,700		42,700
Dividends	3,600		3,600	
Rental revenue		9,900		10,900
Interest revenue				300
Wage expense	1,600		2,000	
Insurance expense			1,700	
Depreciation expense			2,200	
Property tax expense	300		300	
Supplies expense			700	
Utilities expense	200		200	
	94,100	94,100	97,500	97,500

I Required

1. Make the adjusting entries that account for the differences between the two trial balances. (p. 145)

2. Compute Peppertree's total assets, total liabilities, total equity, and net income. (p. 147)

P3-59A (*Learning Objective 4, 6: Preparing the financial statements and using the debt ratio*) The adjusted trial balance of Snead Corporation, at December 31, 20X6, follows on the next page.

I Required

1. Prepare Snead Corporation's 20X6 income statement, statement of retained earnings, and balance sheet. List expenses (except for income tax) in decreasing order on the income statement and show total liabilities on the balance sheet. Draw arrows linking the three financial statements. (p. 147)

■ general ledger

■ spreadsheet

(continued)

2. Snead's lenders require that the company maintain a debt ratio no higher than 0.60. Compute Snead's debt ratio at December 31, 20X6, to determine whether the company is in compliance with this debt restriction. If not, suggest a way that Snead could have avoided this difficult situation. (pp. 157–158)

Snead Corporation Adjusted Trial Balance December 31, 20X6		
Cash	$ 1,400	
Accounts receivable	8,900	
Supplies	2,300	
Prepaid rent	1,600	
Equipment	37,100	
Accumulated depreciation		$ 4,300
Accounts payable		3,700
Interest payable		800
Unearned service revenue		600
Income tax payable		2,100
Note payable		18,600
Common stock		5,000
Retained earnings		1,000
Dividends	24,000	
Service revenue		107,900
Depreciation expense	1,600	
Salary expense	39,900	
Rent expense	10,300	
Interest expense	3,100	
Insurance expense	3,800	
Supplies expense	2,900	
Income tax expense	7,100	
Total	$144,000	$144,000

P3-60A (*Learning Objective 5: Closing the books and evaluating retained earnings*) The accounts of Meadowbrook Services, Inc., at March 31, 20X3, are listed in alphabetical order.

Accounts payable	$14,700	Interest expense	$ 600	
Accounts receivable	16,500	Note payable, long-term...	6,200	
Accumulated depreciation—		Other assets	14,100	
equipment	7,100	Prepaid expenses	5,300	
Advertising expense	10,900	Retained earnings,		
Cash	7,500	March 31, 20X2	20,200	
Common stock	9,100	Salary expense	17,800	
Current portion of note		Salary payable	2,400	
payable	800	Service revenue	94,100	
Depreciation expense	1,900	Supplies	3,800	
Dividends	31,200	Supplies expense	4,600	
Equipment	43,200	Unearned service revenue ...	2,800	

❚ Required

1. All adjustments have been journalized and posted, but the closing entries have not yet been made. Journalize Meadowbrook's closing entries at March 31, 20X3. (p. 153)
2. Set up a T-account for Retained Earnings and post to that account. Compute Meadowbrook's net income for the year ended March 31, 20X3. What is the ending balance of Retained Earnings? (pp. 147–153)
3. Did Retained Earnings increase or decrease during the year? What caused the increase or the decrease? (p. 153).

P3-61A *(Learning Objective 4, 6: Preparing a classified balance sheet and using the ratios to evaluate the business)* Refer back to Problem 3-60A.

1. Use the Meadowbrook Services data in Problem 3-60A to prepare the company's classified balance sheet at March 31, 20X3. Show captions for total assets, total liabilities, and total liabilities and stockholders' equity. (p. 155)
2. Compute Meadowbrook's current ratio and debt ratio at March 31, 20X3, rounding to 2 decimal places. At March 31, 20X2, the current ratio was 1.30 and the debt ratio was 0.30. Did Meadbrook's ability to pay both current and total debts improve or deteriorate during 20X3? Evaluate Meadowbrook's debt position as strong or weak and give your reason. (pp. 158–159)

P3-62A *(Learning Objectives 6: Analyzing financial ratios)* This problem demonstrates the effects of transactions on the current ratio and the debt ratio of Hialeah Company. Hialeah's condensed and adapted balance sheet at December 31, 20X6, is:

	(In millions)
Total current assets	$15.5
Properties, plant, equipment, and other assets	15.8
	$31.3
Total current liabilities	$ 9.2
Total long-term liabilities	5.3
Total stockholders' equity	16.8
	$31.3

Assume that during the first quarter of the following year, 20X7, Hialeah completed the following transactions:

a. Paid half the current liabilities.
b. Borrowed $3 million on long-term debt.
c. Earned revenue, $2.5 million, on account.
d. Paid selling expense of $1 million.
e. Accrued general expense of $0.8 million. Credit General Expense Payable, a current liability.
f. Purchased equipment for $4.2 million, paying cash of $1.4 million and signing a long-term note payable for $2.8 million.
g. Recorded depreciation expense of $0.6 million.

❚ Required

1. Compute Hialeah's current ratio and debt ratio at December 31, 20X6. Round to 2 decimal places. (pp. 159–160)
2. Consider each transaction separately. Compute Hialeah's current ratio and debt ratio after each transaction during 20X7, that is, 7 times. Round ratios to 2 decimal places. (pp. 158–160)

(continued)

3. Based on your analysis, you should be able to readily identify the effects of certain transactions on the current ratio and the debt ratio. Test your understanding by completing these statements with either "increase" or "decrease": (pp. 158–160)

  a. Revenues usually _____ the current ratio.
  b. Revenues usually _____ the debt ratio.
  c. Expenses usually _____ the current ratio. (*Note:* Depreciation is an exception to this rule.)
  d. Expenses usually _____ the debt ratio.
  e. If a company's current ratio is greater than 1.0, as it is for Hialeah, paying off a current liability will always _____ the current ratio.
  f. Borrowing money on long-term debt will always _____ the current ratio and _____ the debt ratio.

(Group B)

P3-63B (*Learning Objective 1: Linking accrual accounting and cash flows*) During 20X1, Schubert, Inc., earned revenues of $19 million from the sale of its products. Schubert ended the year with net income of $4 million. Schubert collected cash of $20 million from customers and paid cash for all 20X1 expenses plus an additional $3 million on account for amounts payable at the end of 20X0. Answer these questions about Schubert's operating results, financial position, and cash flows during 20X1:

1. How much were Schubert's total expenses? Show your work. (pp. 127–128)
2. Identify all the items that Schubert will report on its income statement for 20X1. Show each amount. (p. 147)
3. Schubert began 20X1 with receivables of $6 million. All sales are on account. What was Schubert's receivables balance at the end of 20X1? Identify the appropriate financial statement and show how Schubert will report its ending receivables balance in the company's 20X1 annual report. (pp. 77–78)
4. Schubert began 20X1 owing accounts payable of $9 million. Schubert incurs all expenses on account. During 20X1, Schubert paid $18 million on account. How much in accounts payable did Schubert owe at the end of 20X1? Identify the appropriate financial statement and show how Schubert will report accounts payable in its 20X1 annual report. (pp. 77–72)

P3-64B (*Learning Objective 1: Cash basis versus accrual basis*) Bombay Foods had the following selected transactions during November:

Nov. 1	Received $800 in advance for food to be delivered later.
5	Paid electricity expenses, $700.
9	Received cash for the day's sales, $2,000.
14	Purchased two food warmers, $1,800.
23	Served a banquet, receiving a note receivable, $700.
30	Accrued salary expense, $900.
30	Prepaid building rent for December and January, $3,000.

I *Required*

1. Show how each transaction would be handled using the cash basis and the accrual basis. Under each column, give the amount of revenue or expense for November. Journal entries are not required. Use the following format for your answer, and show your computations: (pp. 127–128)

	Amount of Revenue (Expense) for November	
Date	Cash Basis	Accrual Basis

2. Compute income (loss) before tax for November under the two accounting methods. (p. 147)

3. Which method better measures income and assets? Use the last transaction to explain. (p. 127)

P3-65B (*Learning Objective 1, 2: Applying accounting principles*) As the controller of Avon Systems, you have hired a new employee, whom you must train. He objects to making an adjusting entry for accrued salaries at the end of the period. He reasons, "We will pay the salaries soon. Why not wait until payment to record the expense? In the end, the result will be the same." Write a reply to explain to the employee why the adjusting entry is needed for accrued salary expense. (pp. 127–129)

P3-66B (*Learning Objective 3: Making accounting adjustments*) Journalize the adjusting entry needed on December 31, the end of the current accounting period, for each of the following independent cases affecting Chicago Mercantile Services (CMS). Include an explanation for each entry. (pp. 132–144)

    a. Each Friday, CMS pays employees for the current week's work. The amount of the payroll is $2,000 for a 5-day work week. The current accounting period ends on Tuesday.

    b. CMS has received notes receivable from some clients for professional services. During the current year, CMS has earned accrued interest revenue of $1,100, which will be received next year.

    c. The beginning balance of Supplies was $1,800. During the year, CMS purchased supplies costing $12,500, and at December 31 the inventory of supplies on hand is $2,900.

    d. CMS is conducting market research, and the client paid CMS $20,000 at the start of the project. CMS recorded this amount as Unearned Service Revenue. The research will take several months to complete. CMS executives estimate that the company has earned three-fourths of the revenue during the current year.

    e. Depreciation for the current year includes Equipment, $6,300; and Building, $3,700. Make a compound entry.

    f. Details of Prepaid Insurance are shown in the account:

Prepaid Insurance		
Jan. 1 Bal.	1,800	
Sept. 30	3,600	

    CMS pays the annual insurance premium (the payment for insurance coverage is called a *premium*) on September 30 each year. At December 31, $2,700 is still prepaid.

P3-67B (*Learning Objective 3, 4, 6: Preparing an adjusted trial balance and the financial statements; using the current ratio to evaluate the business*) Consider the unadjusted trial balance of Omega Advertising, Inc., at October 31, 20X2, and the related month-end adjustment data.

(*continued*)

HH CHAPTER 3

Omega Advertising, Inc.
Trial Balance
October 31, 20X2

Cash	$16,300	
Accounts receivable	7,000	
Prepaid rent	4,000	
Supplies	600	
Furniture	36,000	
Accumulated depreciation		$ 3,000
Accounts payable		8,800
Salary payable		
Common stock		15,000
Retained earnings (September 30, 20X2)		21,000
Dividends	4,600	
Advertising revenue		25,400
Salary expense	4,400	
Rent expense		
Utilities expense	300	
Depreciation expense		
Supplies expense		
Total	$73,200	$73,200

Adjustment data:

    a. Accrued advertising revenue at October 31, $2,900.

    b. Prepaid rent expired during the month. The unadjusted prepaid balance of $4,000 relates to the period October 20X2 through January 20X3.

    c. Supplies used during October, $200.

    d. Depreciation on furniture for the month. The furniture's expected useful life is 5 years.

    e. Accrued salary expense at October 31 for Monday through Thursday; the 5-day weekly payroll is $2,000.

❚ Required

1. Using Exhibit 3-9, page 145, as an example, prepare the adjusted trial balance of Omega Advertising at October 31, 20X2. Key each adjusting entry by letter.

2. Prepare the monthly income statement, the statement of retained earnings, and the classified balance sheet. Draw arrows linking the three financial statements. (p. 147)

P3-68B (*Learning Objective 3: Analyzing and recording adjustments*) Valero Sales Company's unadjusted and adjusted trial balances at December 31, 20X7, are given on the next page.

❚ Required

1. Make the adjusting entries that account for the differences between the two trial balances. (p. 145)

2. Compute Valero's total assets, total liabilities, total equity, and net income. (p. 147)

	Valero Sales Company Adjusted Trial Balance December 31, 20X7			
	Trial Balance		Adjusted Trial Balance	
Account Title	Debit	Credit	Debit	Credit
Cash	4,100		4,100	
Accounts receivable	11,200		12,400	
Supplies	1,000		700	
Prepaid insurance	2,600		900	
Office furniture	21,600		21,600	
Accumulated depreciation		8,200		9,300
Accounts payable		6,300		6,300
Salary payable				900
Interest payable				400
Note payable		6,000		6,000
Unearned commission revenue		1,500		1,100
Common stock		5,000		5,000
Retained earnings		3,500		3,500
Dividends	18,300		18,300	
Sales commission revenue		72,800		74,400
Depreciation expense			1,100	
Supplies expense			300	
Utilities expense	4,900		4,900	
Salary expense	26,600		27,500	
Rent expense	12,200		12,200	
Interest expense	800		1,200	
Insurance expense			1,700	
	103,300	103,300	106,900	106,900

P3-69B (*Learning Objective 4, 6: Preparing the financial statements and using the debt ratio*) The adjusted trial balance of Duff & Carson, Inc., at December 31, 20X1, follows on the next page.

⏐ Required

1. Prepare Duff & Carson's 20X1 income statement, statement of retained earnings, and balance sheet. List expenses in decreasing order on the income statement and show total liabilities on the balance sheet. Draw arrows linking the 3 financial statements. (p. 147)
2. Compute Duff & Carson's debt ratio at December 31, 20X1, rounding to 2 decimal places. Evaluate the company's debt ratio as strong or weak. (pp. 157–158)

HH   CHAPTER 3

Duff & Carson, Inc.
Adjusted Trial Balance
December 31, 20X1

Cash	$ 11,600	
Accounts receivable	41,400	
Prepaid rent	1,300	
Equipment	67,600	
Accumulated depreciation		$ 12,900
Accounts payable		3,600
Unearned service revenue		4,500
Interest payable		2,100
Salary payable		900
Income tax payable		8,800
Note payable		26,200
Common stock		12,000
Retained earnings, Dec. 31, 20X0		20,300
Dividends	48,000	
Service revenue		165,900
Depreciation expense	11,300	
Salary expense	44,000	
Rent expense	12,000	
Interest expense	1,200	
Income tax expense	18,800	
Total	$257,200	$257,200

P3-70B (*Learning Objective 5: Making closing entries and evaluating retained earnings*)
The accounts of Cookie Lapp eTravel, Inc., at December 31, 20X5, are listed in alphabetical order.

Accounts payable	$ 5,100		Note payable, long-term	$10,600
Accounts receivable	6,600		Other assets	3,600
Accumulated depreciation—			Retained earnings,	
furniture	11,600		December 31, 20X4	5,300
Advertising expense	2,200		Salary expense	24,600
Cash	7,300		Salary payable	3,900
Common stock	15,000		Service revenue	93,500
Depreciation expense	1,300		Supplies	7,700
Dividends	47,400		Supplies expense	5,700
Furniture	41,400		Unearned service	
Interest expense	800		revenue	3,600

❙ Required

1. All adjustments have been journalized and posted, but the closing entries have not yet been made. Journalize Lapp's closing entries at December 31, 20X5. (p. 153)
2. Set up a T-account for Retained Earnings and post to that account. Then compute Lapp's net income for 20X5. What is the ending balance of Retained Earnings? (p. 159)
3. Did Retained Earnings increase or decrease during the year? What caused the increase or decrease? (p. 153)

P3-71B (*Learning Objective 4, 6: Preparing a classified balance sheet and using the ratios*)
Refer back to Problem 3-70B.

1. Use the Cookie Lapp eTravel data in Problem 3-70B to prepare the company's classified balance sheet in report form at December 31, 20X5. Label total assets, total liabilities, and stockholders' equity. (p. 153)

2. Compute Cookie Lapp's current ratio and debt ratio at December 31, 20X5. At December 31, 20X4, the current ratio was 1.50 and the debt ratio was 0.45. Did Lapp's ability to pay both current and total liabilities improve or deteriorate during 20X5? (p. 159)

P3-72B (*Learning Objective 6: Analyzing financial ratios*) This problem demonstrates the effects of transactions on the current ratio and the debt ratio of Rockwell Company. Rockwell's condensed balance sheet at March 31, 20X1, follows.

	(In millions)
Total current assets	$3.0
Properties, net, and other assets	3.8
	$6.8
Total current liabilities	$2.2
Total long-term liabilities	2.4
Total stockholders' equity	2.2
	$6.8

During the *following* year, ending March 31, 20X2, Rockwell completed the following transactions:

   a. Paid half the current liabilities.
   b. Borrowed $3 million on long-term debt.
   c. Earned revenue of $2.5 million on account.
   d. Paid selling expense of $1 million.
   e. Accrued salary expense of $0.8 million. Credit Salary Payable, a current liability.
   f. Purchased equipment for $4.2 million, paying cash of $1.4 million and signing a long-term note payable for $2.8 million.
   g. Recorded depreciation expense of $0.6 million.

❚ *Required*

1. Compute Rockwell's current ratio and debt ratio at March 31, 20X1. Round to 2 decimal places. (p. 159)

2. Consider each transaction separately. Compute Rockwell's current ratio and debt ratio after each transaction during 20X2, that is, 7 times. Round ratios to 2 decimal places. (pp. 160–161)

3. Based on your analysis, you should be able to readily identify the effects of certain transactions on the current ratio and the debt ratio. Test your understanding by completing these statements with either "increase" or "decrease": (pp. 160–161)

   a. Revenues usually _____ the current ratio.
   b. Revenues usually _____ the debt ratio.
   c. Expenses usually _____ the current ratio. (*Note:* Depreciation is an exception to this rule.)
   d. Expenses usually _____ the debt ratio.
   e. If a company's current ratio is greater than 1.0, as for Rockwell, paying off a current liability will always _____ the current ratio.
   f. Borrowing money on long-term debt will always _____ the current ratio and _____ the debt ratio.

APPLY YOUR KNOWLEDGE

Decision Cases

Case 1. (*Learning Objectives 3, 6: Adjusting and correcting the accounts; computing and evaluating the current ratio*) The unadjusted trial balance of Good Times, Inc., at January 31, 20X6, does not balance. In addition, the trial balance needs to be adjusted before the financial statements at January 31, 20X6 can be prepared. The manager of Good Times needs to know the business's current ratio.

Cash	$ 6,000
Accounts receivable	2,200
Supplies	800
Prepaid rent	1,200
Land	41,000
Accounts payable	10,000
Salary payable	0
Unearned service revenue	700
Note payable, due in 3 years	25,400
Common stock	5,000
Retained earnings	7,300
Service revenue	9,100
Salary expense	3,400
Rent expense	0
Advertising expense	900
Supplies expense	0

❙ Required

1. How much *out of balance* is the trial balance? The error is in the Land account. (pp. 144–145)

2. Good Times needs to make the following adjustments at January 31:
   a. Supplies of $600 were used during January.
   b. The balance of Prepaid Rent was paid on January 1 and covers the whole year 20X6. No adjustment was made on January 31.
   c. At January 31, Good Times owes employees $400.
   d. Unearned service revenue of $200 was earned during January.
   Prepare a corrected, adjusted trial balance. Give Land its correct balance. (pp. 144–145)

3. After the error is corrected and after these adjustments are made, compute the current ratio of Good Times, Inc. If your business had this current ratio, could you sleep at night? (p. 159)

Case 2. (*Learning Objectives 4: Preparing financial statements; continue or shut down the business?*) On October 1, Tiger Woods opened Eagle Restaurant, Inc. Woods is now at a crossroads. The October financial statements paint a glowing picture of the business, and Woods has asked you whether he should expand the business. To expand the business, Woods wants to be earning net income of $10,000 per month and have total assets of $35,000. Woods believes he is meeting both goals.

To start the business, Woods invested $20,000, not the $10,000 amount reported as "Common stock" on the balance sheet. The business issued $20,000 of common stock to Woods. The bookkeeper plugged the $10,000 "Common stock" amount into the balance sheet to make it balance. The bookkeeper made some other errors too. Woods shows you the following financial statements that the bookkeeper prepared.

Required

Prepare corrected financial statements for Eagle Restaurant, Inc.: Income Statement, Statement of Retained Earnings, and Balance Sheet. Then, based on Woods' goals and your corrected statements, recommend to Woods whether he should expand the restaurant. (p. 147)

Eagle Restaurant, Inc.
Income Statement
Month Ended October 31, 20X4

Revenues:		
Investments by owner	$20,000	
Unearned banquet sales revenue	3,000	
		$23,000
Expenses:		
Wages expense	$ 5,000	
Rent expense	4,000	
Dividends	3,000	
Depreciation expense—fixtures	1,000	
		13,000
Net income		$10,000

Eagle Restaurant, Inc.
Balance Sheet
October 31, 20X4

Assets:		Liabilities:	
Cash	$ 6,000	Accounts payable	$ 5,000
Prepaid insurance	1,000	Sales revenue	32,000
Insurance expense	1,000	Accumulated depreciation—	
Food inventory	3,000	fixtures	1,000
Cost of goods sold (expense)	14,000		38,000
Fixtures (tables, chairs, etc.)	19,000	**Owners' equity:**	
Dishes and silverware	4,000	Common stock	10,000
	$48,000		$48,000

Case 3. (*Learning Objective 3, 4: Valuing a business on the basis of its net income*) Sherwin Williams has owned and operated SW Advertising, Inc., since its beginning 10 years ago. Recently, Williams mentioned that he would consider selling the company for the right price.

Assume that you are interested in buying this business. You obtain its most recent monthly trial balance, which follows. Revenues and expenses vary little from month to month, and June is a typical month. Your investigation reveals that the trial balance does not include the effects of monthly revenues of $5,000 and expenses totaling $1,100. If you were to buy SW Advertising, you would hire a manager so you could devote your time to other duties. Assume that your manager would require a monthly salary of $6,000.

SW Advertising, Inc.
Trial Balance
June 30, 20XX

Cash...	$ 10,000	
Accounts receivable.............................	4,900	
Prepaid expenses...............................	3,200	
Plant assets.....................................	115,000	
Accumulated depreciation.......................		$ 76,500
Land...	158,000	
Accounts payable................................		13,800
Salary payable...................................		
Unearned advertising revenue..................		56,700
Common stock...................................		50,000
Retained earnings................................		88,000
Dividends.......................................	9,000	
Advertising revenue.............................		20,000
Rent expense....................................		
Salary expense...................................	4,000	
Utilities expense.................................	900	
Depreciation expense............................		
Supplies expense................................		
Total	$305,000	$305,000

I *Required*

1. Assume that the most you would pay for the business is 20 times the amount of monthly net income *you could expect to earn* from it. Compute this possible price. (p. 147)

2. Williams states that the least he will take for the business is 1.5 times its stockholders' equity on June 30. Compute this amount. (p. 147)

3. Under these conditions, how much should you offer Williams? Give your reason. (Challenge)

Ethical Issues

Issue 1. Cross Timbers Energy Co. is in its third year of operations, and the company has grown. To expand the business, Cross Timbers borrowed $1 million from Bank of Fort Worth. As a condition for making this loan, the bank required that Cross Timbers maintain a current ratio of at least 1.50 and a debt ratio of no more than 0.50.

Business recently has been worse than expected. Expenses have brought the current ratio down to 1.47 and the debt ratio up to 0.51 at December 15. Lane Collins, the general manager, is considering the result of reporting this current ratio to the bank. Collins is considering recording this year some revenue on account that Cross Timbers will earn next year. The contract for this job has been signed, and Cross Timbers will deliver the natural gas during January of next year.

I *Required*

1. Journalize the revenue transaction, and indicate how recording this revenue in December would affect the current ratio and the debt ratio.

2. State whether it is ethical to record the revenue transaction in December. Identify the accounting principle relevant to this situation.

3. Propose for Cross Timbers a course of action that is ethical.

Issue 2. The net income of Accent Photography Company decreased sharply during 2009. Lisa Brown, owner of the company, anticipates the need for a bank loan in 2010. Late in 2009, Brown instructed the accountant to record a $20,000 sale of portraits to the Brown family, even though the photos will not be shot until January 2010. Brown also told the accountant *not* to make the following December 31, 2009, adjusting entries:

Salaries owed to employees $5,000
Prepaid insurance that has expired 1,000

▌Required

1. Compute the overall effect of these transactions on the company's reported income for 2009. Is reported net income overstated or understated?
2. Why did Brown take these actions? Are they ethical? Give your reason, identifying the parties helped and the parties harmed by Brown's action.
3. As a personal friend, what advice would you give the accountant?

Focus on Financials: ■ YUM! Brands

(Learning Objectives 3, 6: Tracing account balances to the financial statements) **YUM! Brands, Inc.**—like all other businesses—adjusts accounts prior to year end to get correct amounts for the financial statements. Examine YUM's balance sheet in Appendix A, and pay particular attention to (a) Prepaid Expenses and Other Current Assets and (b) Income Taxes Payable.

▌Required

1. Why aren't Prepaid Expenses "true" expenses? Why does a company have income taxes payable at year end? (p. 132)
2. Open T-accounts for the two accounts listed above. Insert YUM's balances (in millions) at December 31, 2005. (p. 132)
3. Journalize the following transactions for the year ended December 30, 2006. Key entries by letter, and show amounts in millions. Explanations are not required. (pp. 139–140)

   a. Recorded General Expense for expiration of the beginning balance of Prepaid Expenses.
   b. Paid off the beginning balance of Income Taxes Payable.
   c. Paid the ending balance of Prepaid Expenses.
   d. Recorded Income Tax Expense of $284 million, paying $247 million in cash and accruing the remainder.
4. Post these entries to the 2 accounts and show that the ending balances of Prepaid Expenses and Other Current Assets and of Income Taxes Payable agree with the corresponding amounts reported in YUM's December 30, 2006, balance sheet. (pp. 139–140)
5. Compute the current ratios and debt ratios for YUM! Brands at December 31, 2005, and at December 30, 2006. Did the ratio values improve, deteriorate, or hold steady during 2006? Do YUM's ratio values indicate financial strength or weakness? (pp. 159–160)

Focus on Analysis: ■ Pier 1 Imports

(Learning Objective 3: Explaining accruals and deferrals) During 2006, **Pier 1 Imports** had numerous accruals and deferrals. As a new member of Pier 1's accounting staff, it is your job to explain the effects of accruals and deferrals on Pier 1's net income for 2006. The accrual and deferral data follow, along with questions that Pier 1 stockholders have raised (all amounts in millions):

1. Beginning total receivables for 2006 were $47. Ending receivables for 2006 are $64. Which of these amounts did Pier 1 earn in 2005? Which amount did Pier 1 earn in 2006? Which amount is included in Pier 1's net income for 2006? (pp. 138–139)
2. Accumulated depreciation stood at $383 at the end of 2005 and at $370 at year end 2006. Depreciation expense for 2006 was $56. How can accumulated depreciation decrease during 2006 when the company is adding more depreciation each year? (Challenge) (pp. 134–135)

3. Pier 1 reports an account titled Gift Cards and other Deferred (Unearned) Revenue. This account carried credit balances of $61 at the end of 2005 and $64 at the end of 2006. What type of account is Gift Cards and other Deferred (Unearned) Revenue? Make a single journal entry to show how this account could have increased its balance during 2006. Then explain the event in your own words. (pp. 141–142)

4. Certain income-statement accounts are directly linked to specific balance-sheet accounts other than cash. Examine Pier 1's income statement in Appendix B at the end of this book. For each "Operating cost and expense," each "Nonoperating (income) and expense," and Provision for income taxes, identify the related balance sheet account (other than cash). Use standard account titles, not necessarily the titles Pier 1 uses. (pp. 131–143)

Group Project

Matt Davis formed a lawn service company as a summer job. To start the business on May 1, he deposited $1,000 in a new bank account in the name of the corporation. The $1,000 consisted of an $800 loan from his father and $200 of his own money. The corporation issued 200 shares of common stock to Davis.

Davis rented lawn equipment, purchased supplies, and hired high school students to mow and trim his customers' lawns. At the end of each month, Davis mailed bills to his customers. On August 31, Davis was ready to dissolve the business and return to Duke University for the fall semester. Because he had been so busy, he had kept few records other than his checkbook and a list of amounts owed by customers.

At August 31, Davis's checkbook shows a balance of $1,390, and his customers still owe him $560. During the summer, he collected $5,150 from customers. His checkbook lists payments for supplies totaling $400, and he still has gasoline, weedeater cord, and other supplies that cost a total of $50. He paid his employees wages of $1,900, and he still owes them $200 for the final week of the summer.

Davis rented some equipment from Ludwig Tool Company. On May 1, he signed a 6-month lease on mowers and paid $600 for the full lease period. Ludwig will refund the unused portion of the prepayment if the equipment is in good shape. To get the refund, Davis has kept the mowers in excellent condition. In fact, he had to pay $300 to repair a mower that ran over a hidden tree stump.

To transport employees and equipment to jobs, Davis used a trailer that he bought for $300. He figures that the summer's work used up one-third of the trailer's service potential. The business checkbook lists an expenditure of $460 for dividends paid to Davis during the summer. Also, Davis paid his father back during the summer.

I *Required*

1. Prepare the income statement of Davis Lawn Service, Inc., for the 4 months May through August. The business is not subject to income tax.

2. Prepare the classified balance sheet of Davis Lawn Service, Inc., at August 31.

For Internet Exercises go to the Web site www.prenhall.com/harrison.

Quick Check Answers:

1. *a*	6. *b*	11. *b*	16. *c*
2. *c*	7. *a*	12. *d*	17. *b*
3. *b*	8. *d*	13. *a*	
4. *d*	9. *d*	14. *c*	
5. *c*	10. *a*	15. *a*	

Demo Doc

Preparation of Adjusting Entries, Closing Entries, and Financial Statements

Demo Doc: To make sure you understand this material, work through the following demonstration "Demo Doc" with detailed comments to help you see the concept within the framework of a worked-through problem.

Learning Objectives 2–5

Cloud Break Consulting, Inc., has the following information at June 30, 2008:

CLOUD BREAK CONSULTING, INC.
Unadjusted Trial Balance
June 30, 2008

Account Title	Balance Debit	Balance Credit
Cash	$131,000	
Accounts receivable	104,000	
Supplies	4,000	
Prepaid rent	27,000	
Land	45,000	
Building	300,000	
Accumulated depreciation—building		$155,000
Accounts payable		159,000
Unearned service revenue		40,000
Common stock		50,000
Retained earnings		52,000
Dividends	7,000	
Service revenue		450,000
Salary expense	255,000	
Rent expense	25,000	
Miscellaneous expense	8,000	
Total	$906,000	$906,000

June 30 is Cloud Break's fiscal year end; accordingly, it must make adjusting entries for the following items:

a. **Supplies on hand at year-end, $1,000.**

b. **Nine months of rent totaling $27,000 were paid in advance on April 1, 2008. Cloud Break has recorded no rent expense yet.**

c. **Depreciation expense has not been recorded on the building for the 2008 fiscal year. The building has a useful life of 25 years.**

d. **Employees work Monday through Friday. The weekly payroll is $5,000 and is paid every Friday. June 30, 2008, falls on a Thursday.**

(continued)

e. Service revenue of $15,000 must be accrued.

f. Cloud Break received $40,000 in advance for consulting services to be provided evenly from January 1, 2008 through August 31, 2008. Cloud Break has recorded none of this revenue.

Requirements

1. Open the T-accounts with their unadjusted balances.

2. Journalize Cloud Break's adjusting entries at June 30, 2008, and post the entries to the T-accounts.

3. Total each T-account in the ledger.

4. Journalize and post Cloud Break's closing entries.

5. Prepare Cloud Break's income statement and statement of retained earnings for the year ended June 30, 2008, and the balance sheet at June 30, 2008. Draw arrows linking the 3 financial statements.

Demo Doc Solutions

Requirement 1

Open the T-accounts with their unadjusted balances.

| Part 1 | Part 2 | Part 3 | Part 4 | Part 5 | Part 6 | Part 7 | Demo Doc Complete |

Remember from Chapter 2 that opening a T-account means drawing a blank account that looks like a capital "T" and putting the account title across the top. To help find the accounts later, they are grouped into assets, liabilities, stockholders' equity, revenues, and expenses (in that order). If the account has a starting balance, it *must* appear on the correct side.

Remember that debits are always on the left side of the T-account and credits are always on the right side. This is true for *every* account.

The correct side to enter each account's starting balance is the side of *increase* in the account. This is because we expect all accounts to have a *positive* balance (that is, more increases than decreases).

For assets, an increase is a debit, so we would expect all assets (except contra assets such as Accumulated Depreciation) to have a debit balance. For liabilities and stockholders' equity, an increase is a credit, so we would expect all liabilities and equities (except Dividends) to have a credit balance. By the same reasoning, we expect revenues to have credit balances and expenses and dividends to have debit balances.

The unadjusted balances appearing in the T-accounts are simply the amounts from the starting trial balance.

ASSETS

Cash
Bal. 131,000

Accounts Receivable
Bal. 104,000

Supplies
Bal. 4,000

Prepaid Rent
Bal. 27,000

Land
Bal. 45,000

Building
Bal. 300,000

Accumulated Depreciation—Building
Bal. 155,000

LIABILITIES

Accounts Payable
Bal. 159,000

Unearned Service Revenue
Bal. 40,000

STOCKHOLDERS' EQUITY

Common Stock
Bal. 50,000

Retained Earnings
Bal. 52,000

Dividends
Bal. 7,000

REVENUE

Service Revenue
Bal. 450,000

EXPENSES

Salary Expense
Bal. 255,000

Rent Expense
Bal. 25,000

Miscellaneous Expense
Bal. 8,000

Requirement 2

Journalize Cloud Break's adjusting entries at June 30, 2008, and post the entries to the T-accounts.

Part 1	**Part 2**	Part 3	Part 4	Part 5	Part 6	Part 7	Demo Doc Complete

a. Supplies on hand at year end, $1,000.

On June 30, 2008, the unadjusted balance in the Supplies account was $4,000. However, a count shows that only $1,000 of supplies actually remains on hand. The supplies that are no longer there have been used. When assets/benefits are used, an expense is created.

Cloud Break will need to make an adjusting journal entry in order to report the correct amount of supplies on the balance sheet.

Looking at the Supplies T-account:

Supplies			
	4,000		
		Used up	X
Bal.	1,000		

The supplies have decreased because they have been used up. The amount of the decrease is X. X = $4,000 − $1,000 = $3,000.

$3,000 of supplies expense must be recorded to show the value of supplies that have been used.

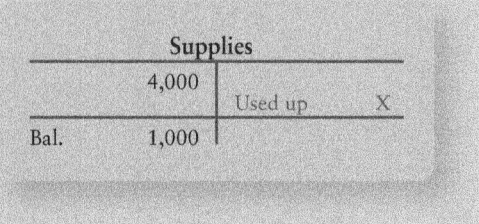

a.	June 30	Supplies Expense ($4,000 − $1,000) (Expense ↑; debit)	3,000	
		Supplies (Asset ↓; credit)		3,000
		To record supplies expense.		

After posting, Supplies and Supplies Expense hold their correct ending balances:

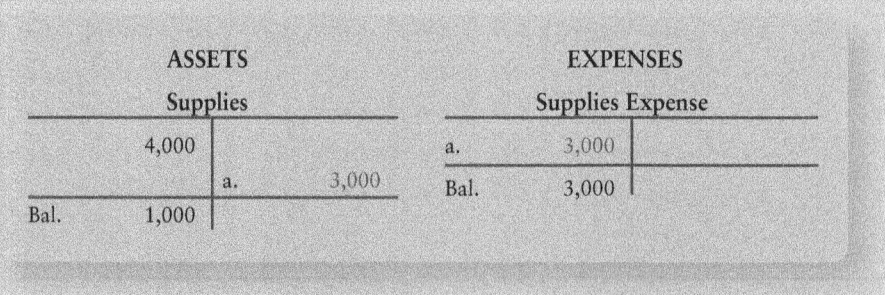

ASSETS				EXPENSES		
Supplies				Supplies Expense		
	4,000			a.	3,000	
		a.	3,000	Bal.	3,000	
Bal.	1,000					

b. Nine months of rent (totalling $27,000) were paid in advance on April 1, 2008. Cloud Break has recorded no rent expense yet.

A prepayment for something, such as for rent or insurance, creates a *future* benefit (an asset) because the business is now entitled to receive the prepaid goods or services. Once those goods or services are received (in this case, once Cloud Break has occupied the building being rented), the benefit expires, and the prepaid cost becomes an expense.

Cloud Break prepaid $27,000 for 9 months of rent on April 1. This means that Cloud Break pays $27,000/9 = $3,000 a month for rent. At June 30, Prepaid Rent is adjusted for the amount of the asset that has been used up. Because Cloud Break has occupied the building being rented for 3 months (April, May, and June), 3 months of the prepayment have been used. The amount of rent used is $3 \times \$3,000 = \$9,000$. Because that portion of the past benefit (asset) has expired, it becomes an expense (in this case, the adjustment transfers $9,000 from Prepaid Rent to Rent Expense).

This means that Rent Expense must be increased (a debit) and Prepaid Rent (an asset) must be decreased (a credit), with the following journal entry:

b.	June 30	Rent Expense (Expense ↑; debit)	9,000	
		Prepaid Rent (Asset ↓; credit)		9,000
		To record rent expense.		

Posting places $9,000 in each account, as follows:

ASSETS			EXPENSES		
Prepaid Rent			Rent Expense		
27,000			25,000		
	b.	9,000	b.	9,000	
Bal.	18,000		Bal.	34,000	

c. Depreciation expense has not been recorded on the building for the 2008 fiscal year. The building has a useful life of 25 years.

Depreciation expense per year is calculated as:

$$\text{Depreciation expense per year} = \frac{\text{Original cost of asset}}{\text{Useful life of asset (in years)}}$$

The cost principle compels us to keep the original cost of a plant asset in that asset account. Because there is $300,000 in the Building account, we know that this is the original cost of the building. We are told in the question that the building's useful life is 25 years.

$$\text{Depreciation expense per year} = \$300,000/25 \text{ years} = \$12,000 \text{ per year}$$

We will record depreciation of $12,000 in an adjusting journal entry. The journal entry for depreciation expense is *always* the same. Only the dollar amount changes. There is always an increase to Depreciation Expense (a debit) and an increase to the contra-asset account of Accumulated Depreciation (a credit).

c.	June 30	Depreciation Expense—Building (Expense ↑; debit)	12,000	
		Accumulated Depreciation—Building		
		(Contra Asset ↑; credit)		12,000
		To record depreciation on building.		

ASSETS

ASSET	CONTRA ASSET
Building	Accumulated Depreciation—Building

300,000				155,000
			c.	12,000
Bal.	300,000		Bal.	167,000

EXPENSES

Depreciation Expense—Building

c.	12,000	
Bal.	12,000	

The book value of the building is its original cost (the amount in the Building T-account) minus the accumulated depreciation on the building.

Book value of plant assets:	
Building	$300,000
Less: Accumulated depreciation	(167,000)
Book value of the building	$133,000

d. Employees work Monday through Friday. The weekly payroll is $5,000 and is paid every Friday. June 30, 2008, falls on a Thursday.

Salary is an accrued expense. That is, it's a liability that comes from an *expense* that hasn't been paid yet. Most employers pay their employees *after* the work has been done, so the work is a past benefit to the employer. This expense (Salary Expense, in this case) grows until payday.

Cloud Break's employees are paid $5,000 for 5 days of work. That means they earn $5,000/5 = $1,000 per day. By the end of the day on Thursday, June 30, they have earned $1,000/day × 4 days = $4,000 of salary.

If the salaries have not been paid, then they are pay*able* (or in other words, they are *owed*) and must be recorded as some kind of payable account. You might be tempted to use Accounts Payable, but this account is usually reserved for *bills* received. But employees don't bill employers for their paychecks. The appropriate payable account for salaries is Salary Payable.

The accrual of salary expense creates an increase to Salary Expense (a debit) and an increase to the liability Salary Payable (a credit) of $4,000.

d.	June 30	Salary Expense (Expense ↑; debit)	4,000	
		Salary Payable (Liability ↑; credit)		4,000
		To accrue salary expense.		

EXPENSES			LIABILITIES		
Salary Expense			**Salary Payable**		
	255,000			d.	4,000
d.	4,000				
Bal.	259,000			Bal.	4,000

e. Service revenue of $15,000 must be accrued.

Accrued revenue is another way of saying "accounts receivable" (or receipt in the future). When *accrued* revenue is recorded, it means that accounts receivable are also recorded (that is, the business gave goods or services to customers, but the business has not yet received the cash). The business is entitled to these receivables because the revenue has been earned.

Service Revenue must be increased by $15,000 (a credit) and the Accounts Receivable asset must be increased by $15,000 (a debit).

e.	June 30	Accounts Receivable (Asset ↑; debit)	15,000	
		Service Revenue (Revenue ↑; credit)		15,000
		To accrue service revenue.		

ASSETS			REVENUES		
Accounts Receivable			**Service Revenue**		
	104,000				450,000
e.	15,000			e.	15,000
Bal.	119,000			Bal.	465,000

f. Cloud Break received $40,000 in advance for consulting services to be provided evenly from January 1, 2008, through August 31, 2008. Cloud Break has recorded none of this revenue.

Cloud Break received cash in advance for work to be performed in the future. By accepting the cash, Cloud Break also accepted the obligation to perform that work (or provide a refund). In accounting, an obligation is a liability. We call this liability "unearned revenue" because it *will* be revenue (after the work is performed) but it is not revenue *yet*.

The $40,000 collected in advance is still in the Unearned Service Revenue account. However, some of the revenue has been earned as of June 30. Six months of the earnings period have passed (January through June), so Cloud Break has earned 6 months of the revenue.

The entire revenue-earning period is 8 months (January through August), so the revenue earned per month is $40,000/8 = $5,000. The 6 months of revenue that Cloud Break has earned through the end of June totals $30,000 (6 × $5,000).

So Unearned Service Revenue, a liability, must be decreased by $30,000 (a debit). Because that portion of the revenue is now earned, Service Revenue is increased by $30,000 (a credit).

f.	June 30	Unearned Service Revenue (Liability ↓; debit)	30,000	
		Service Revenue (Revenue ↑; credit)		30,000
		To record the earning of service revenue that was collected in advance.		

Essentially, the $30,000 has been shifted from "unearned revenue" to "earned" revenue.

LIABILITIES			REVENUES		
Unearned Service Revenue			**Service Revenue**		
		40,000			450,000
f.	30,000			e.	15,000
				f.	30,000
	Bal.	10,000		Bal.	495,000

Now we can summarize all of the adjusting journal entries:

Ref.	Date	Accounts and Explanation	Debit	Credit
	2008			
a.	June 30	Supplies Expense ($4,000 – $1,000)	3,000	
		Supplies		3,000
		To record supplies expense.		
b.	30	Rent Expense	9,000	
		Prepaid Rent		9,000
		To record rent expense.		
c.	30	Depreciation Expense—Building	12,000	
		Accumulated Depreciation—Building		12,000
		To record depreciation on building.		
d.	30	Salary Expense	4,000	
		Salary Payable		4,000
		To accrue salary expense.		
e.	30	Accounts Receivable	15,000	
		Service Revenue		15,000
		To accrue service revenue.		
f.	30	Unearned Service Revenue	30,000	
		Service Revenue		30,000
		To record the earning of service revenue that was collected in advance.		

Requirement 3

Total each T-account in the ledger.

| Part 1 | Part 2 | **Part 3** | Part 4 | Part 5 | Part 6 | Part 7 | Demo Doc Complete |

After posting all of these entries and totaling all of the T-accounts, we have:

ASSETS

Cash

Bal. 131,000	

Accounts Receivable

104,000	
e. 15,000	
Bal. 119,000	

Supplies

4,000	
	a. 3,000
Bal. 1,000	

Prepaid Rent

27,000	
	b. 9,000
Bal. 18,000	

Land

| Bal. 45,000 | |

Building

| Bal. 300,000 | |

Accumulated Depreciation—Building

	155,000
	c. 12,000
	Bal. 167,000

LIABILITIES

Accounts Payable

| | Bal. 159,000 |

Salary Payable

| | d. 4,000 |
| | Bal. 4,000 |

Unearned Service Revenue

	40,000
f. 30,000	
	Bal. 10,000

STOCKHOLDERS' EQUITY

Common Stock

| | Bal. 50,000 |

Retained Earnings

| | Bal. 52,000 |

Dividends

| Bal. 7,000 | |

REVENUE

Service Revenue

	450,000
	e. 15,000
	f. 30,000
	Bal. 495,000

EXPENSES

Salary Expense

255,000	
d. 4,000	
Bal. 259,000	

Supplies Expense

| a. 3,000 | |
| Bal. 3,000 | |

Rent Expense

25,000	
b. 9,000	
Bal. 34,000	

Depreciation Expense— Building

| c. 12,000 | |
| Bal. 12,000 | |

Miscellaneous Expense

| Bal. 8,000 | |

Requirement 4

Journalize and post Cloud Break's closing entries.

| Part 1 | Part 2 | Part 3 | **Part 4** | Part 5 | Part 6 | Part 7 | Demo Doc Complete |

We prepare closing entries to (1) clear out the revenue, expense, and dividends accounts to a zero balance in order to get them ready for the next period. They must begin the next period empty so that we can evaluate each period's income separately from all other periods. We also need to (2) update the Retained Earnings account by transferring all revenues, expenses, and dividends into it.

The Retained Earnings balance is calculated each year using the following formula:

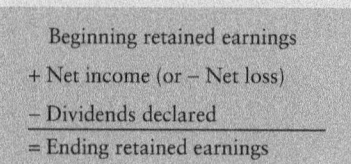

Beginning retained earnings
+ Net income (or − Net loss)
− Dividends declared
= Ending retained earnings

You can see this in the Retained Earnings T-account as well:

Retained Earnings

	Beginning retained earnings
	Net income
Dividends	
	Ending retained earnings

This formula is the key to preparing the closing entries. We will use this formula, but we will do it *inside* the Retained Earnings T-account.

From the trial balance given in the problem, we know that beginning Retained Earnings is $52,000. The first component of the formula is already in the T-account.

The next component is net income, which is *not* yet in the Retained Earnings account. There is no T-account with net income in it, but we can place all the components of net income into the Retained Earnings account and come out with the net income number at the bottom. Remember:

Revenues − Expenses = Net income

This means that we need to get all of the revenues and expenses into the Retained Earnings account.

We start with our revenue T-account:

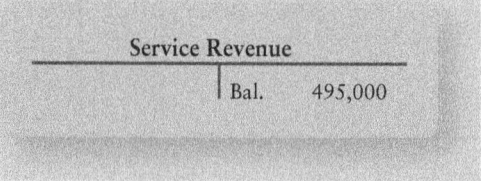

Service Revenue

| | Bal. 495,000 |

In order to clear out all the income statement accounts so that they are empty to begin the next year, the first step is to debit each revenue account for the amount of its credit balance. Service Revenue has a *credit* balance of $495,000, so to bring that to zero, we need to *debit* Service Revenue for $495,000.

This means that we have part of our first closing entry:

1.	Service Revenue	495,000	
	???		495,000

What is the credit side of this entry? The reason we started with Service Revenue was to help calculate net income in the Retained Earnings account. So the other side of the entry must go to Retained Earnings:

1.	Service Revenue	495,000	
	Retained Earnings		495,000

Part 1	Part 2	Part 3	Part 4	**Part 5**	Part 6	Part 7	Demo Doc Complete

The second step is to *credit* each expense account for the amount of its *debit* balance to bring each expense account to zero. In this case, we have 5 different expenses:

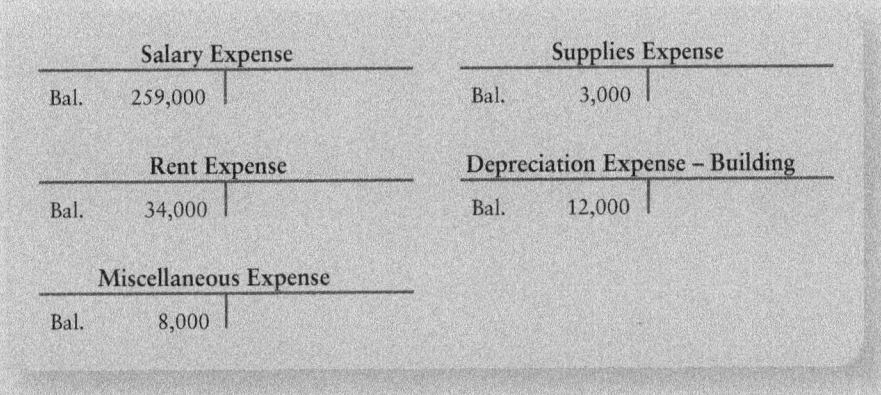

	Salary Expense			Supplies Expense
Bal.	259,000		Bal.	3,000

	Rent Expense			Depreciation Expense – Building
Bal.	34,000		Bal.	12,000

	Miscellaneous Expense
Bal.	8,000

The sum of all the expenses will go to the debit side of the Retained Earnings account:

2.	Retained Earnings	316,000	
	Salary Expense		259,000
	Supplies Expense		3,000
	Rent Expense		34,000
	Depreciation Expense—Building		12,000
	Miscellaneous Expense		8,000

HH CHAPTER 3

The last component of the Retained Earnings formula is dividends. There is a Dividends account:

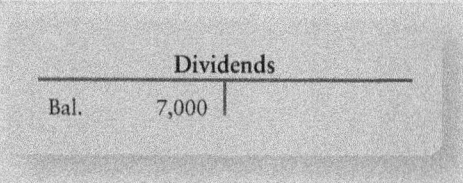

The final step in the closing process is to transfer Dividends to the debit side of the Retained Earnings account. The Dividends account has a *debit* balance of $7,000, so to bring that to zero, we need to *credit* Dividends by $7,000. The balancing debit will go to Retained Earnings:

3.	Retained Earnings	7,000	
	Dividends		7,000

This entry subtracts Dividends from Retained Earnings. Retained Earnings now holds the following data:

		Retained Earnings				
					52,000	**Beginning retained earnings**
Expenses	2.	316,000	1.		495,000	Revenue } Net income
Dividends	3.	7,000				
			Bal.		224,000	**Ending retained earnings**

The formula to update Retained Earnings has now been re-created inside the Retained Earnings T-account.

The following accounts are included in the closing process:

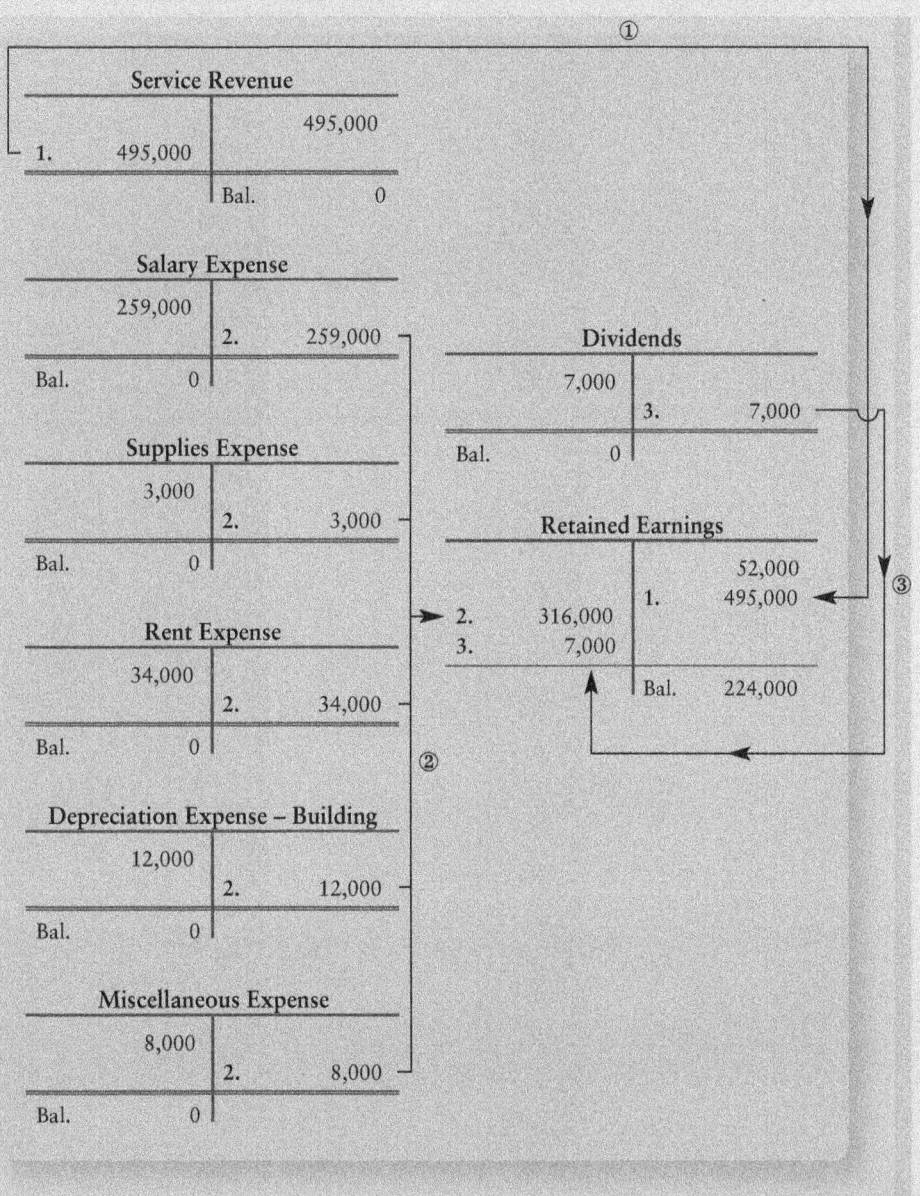

Notice that each temporary account (the revenues, the expenses, and Dividends), now has a zero balance.

Requirement 5

Prepare Cloud Break's income statement and the statement of retained earnings for the year ended June 30, 2008, and the balance sheet at June 30, 2008. Draw arrows linking the 3 financial statements.

| Part 1 | Part 2 | Part 3 | Part 4 | Part 5 | Part 6 | **Part 7** | Demo Doc Complete |

CLOUD BREAK CONSULTING, INC.
Income Statement
Year Ended June 30, 2008

Revenue:		
Service revenue		$495,000
Expenses:		
Salary expense	$259,000	
Rent expense	34,000	
Depreciation expense—building	12,000	
Supplies expense	3,000	
Miscellaneous expense	8,000	
Total expenses		316,000
Net income		$179,000

CLOUD BREAK CONSULTING, INC.
Statement of Retained Earnings
Year Ended June 30, 2008

Retained earnings, June 30, 2007	$ 52,000
Add: Net income	179,000
	231,000
Less: Dividends	(7,000)
Retained earnings, June 30, 2008	$224,000

CLOUD BREAK CONSULTING, INC.
Balance Sheet
June 30, 2008

Assets			Liabilities	
Cash		$131,000	Accounts payable	$159,000
Accounts receivable		119,000	Salary payable	4,000
Supplies		1,000	Unearned service revenue	10,000
Prepaid rent		18,000	Total liabilities	173,000
Land		45,000		
Building	$300,000		**Stockholders' Equity**	
Less: Accumulated			Common stock	50,000
depreciation	(167,000)	133,000	Retained earnings	224,000
			Total stockholders' equity	274,000
			Total liabilities and	
Total assets		$447,000	stockholders' equity	$447,000

RELATIONSHIPS AMONG THE FINANCIAL STATEMENTS

The arrows in these statements show how the financial statements relate to each other. Follow the arrow that takes the ending balance of Retained Earnings to the balance sheet.

1. Net income from the income statements is reported as an increase to Retained Earnings on the statement of retained earnings. A net loss would be reported as a decrease to Retained Earnings.

2. Ending Retained Earnings from the statement of retained earnings is transferred to the balance sheet. The ending Retained Earnings is the final balancing amount for the balance sheet.

Part 1	Part 2	Part 3	Part 4	Part 5	Part 6	Part 7	Demo Doc Complete

This page intentionally left blank

4 Internal Control & Cash

CURRENCY EXCHANGE

SPOTLIGHT

AMEX PRODUCTS TAKES A HIT

"I've never been so shocked in my life!" exclaimed Lee Grant, manager of the AMEX Products office in Palo Alto, California. "This goes to show how important internal controls are."

Grant just returned from the trial of Marty Popplewell, who was convicted of embezzlement. Popplewell had been the cashier of the AMEX Products office in Palo Alto. As cashier, Popplewell received client cash that came in by mail. Unknown to Grant, Popplewell had been "robbing Peter to pay Paul"—that is transferring client collections to Popplewell's own account and then applying the next client cash receipt to cover the missing amount. With access to client accounts, Popplewell could juggle the books to keep anyone from discovering his scheme. This embezzlement had been going on for 3 years, and the trial proved that Popplewell had stolen $622,000 from the company.

What tipped off Grant to the embezzlement? Popplewell was involved in an auto accident and couldn't work for 2 weeks. The employee covering for Popplewell saw too many irregularities in client accounts. The ensuing investigation pointed to Popplewell, and Grant then turned the case over to the police.

Shortly after the trial, Grant revamped the internal controls at AMEX Products. Now Grant rotates employees from job to job. That way there's always someone checking up on someone else. And now the cashier has no access to client accounting records.

Popplewell's scheme is well known to accountants. It is called lapping—similar to laying shingles on a roof. Lapping takes lots of ingenuity and purpose. The thief has to keep the scheme going or it unravels quickly. That's what happened when Popplewell wasn't on the job to juggle the books.

AMEX Products, Inc.
Balance Sheet (Partial, Adapted)

Assets	December 31, 2007
Cash and cash equivalents	$ 6,260
Cash pledged as collateral	2,000
Accounts receivable	8,290
Inventories	36,200
Prepaid expenses	1,400
Investments	10,000
Equipment and facilities (net of accumulated depreciation of ($2,400)	13,170
Other assets	3,930
Total assets	$81,250

This chapter covers the basics of internal control. It also shows how to account for cash. These 2 topics—internal control and cash—go together because cash is the asset that is stolen most often.

The excerpt from the AMEX Products balance sheet reports the company's assets. Focus on the top line, Cash and cash equivalents. At December 31, 2007, AMEX reported cash of $6,260. If Popplewell's scheme hadn't been detected, the reported cash balance would have been overstated. One purpose of internal control is to produce accurate and reliable accounting records.

LEARNING OBJECTIVES

1 **Set up** an internal control system

2 **Prepare** and **use** a bank reconciliation

3 **Apply** internal controls to cash receipts and payments

4 **Use** a budget to manage your cash

5 **Make** ethical business judgments

INTERNAL CONTROL

A key responsibility of a manager is to control the operations of the business. Owners and top executives set company goals, they hire managers to lead the way, and employees carry out the plan. **Internal control** is the organizational plan and all the related measures designed to accomplish 5 objectives:

1. **Safeguard assets.** A company must safeguard its assets; otherwise it's throwing away resources. If you fail to safeguard your cash, it will slip away.

2. **Encourage employees to follow company policy.** Everyone in an organization—managers and employees—needs to work toward the same goal. It's also important for managers to develop policies so that the company treats customers and employees fairly.

3. **Promote operational efficiency.** You cannot afford to waste resources. You work hard to make a sale, and you don't want to waste any of the benefits. If the company can buy something for $30, why pay $35? Eliminate waste, and increase your profits.

4. **Ensure accurate, reliable accounting records.** Good records are essential. Without reliable records, you cannot tell which part of the business is profitable and which part needs improvement. You could be losing money on every product you sell—unless you keep good records for the cost of your products.

5. **Comply with legal requirements**, such as the Sarbanes-Oxley Act. Companies, like people, are subject to the law. When companies disobey the law, they must pay fines, or in extreme cases their top executives go to prison.

How critical are internal controls? They're so important that the U.S. Congress passed a law to require public companies—those that sell their stock to the public—to maintain a system of internal controls. Exhibit 4-1 gives AMEX Products' Management Discussion of Financial Responsibility.

EXHIBIT 4-1   **AMEX Products, Inc., Management Discussion of Financial Responsibility**

Management's Discussion of Financial Responsibility

AMEX Products regularly reviews its framework of internal controls, which includes the company's policies, procedures and organizational structure. Corrective actions are taken to address any control deficiencies, and improvements are implemented as appropriate.

The Sarbanes-Oxley Act (SOX)

The Enron and WorldCom accounting scandals rocked the United States. Enron overstated profits and went out of business almost overnight. WorldCom (now MCI) reported expenses as assets and overstated both profits and assets. The company only recently emerged from bankruptcy. Sadly, the same international accounting firm, Arthur Andersen, had audited both companies' financial statements. Arthur Andersen then closed its doors.

As the scandals unfolded, many people asked, "How can these things happen? Where were the auditors?" To address public concern, Congress passed the Sarbanes-Oxley Act, abbreviated as SOX. SOX revamped corporate governance in the United States and affected the accounting profession. Here are some of the SOX provisions:

1. Public companies must issue an internal control report, and the outside auditor must evaluate the client's internal controls.

2. A new body, the Public Company Accounting Oversight Board, oversees the auditors of public companies.

3. An accounting firm may not both audit a public client and also provide certain consulting services for the same client.

4. Stiff penalties await violators—25 years in prison for securities fraud; 20 years for an executive making false sworn statements.

Recently, the former chief executive of WorldCom was convicted of securities fraud and sentenced to 25 years in prison. The top executives of Enron were also sent to prison. You can see that internal controls and related matters can have serious consequences.

Exhibit 4-2 diagrams the shield that internal controls provide for an organization. Protected by the wall, people do business securely. How does a business achieve good internal control? The next section identifies the components of internal control.

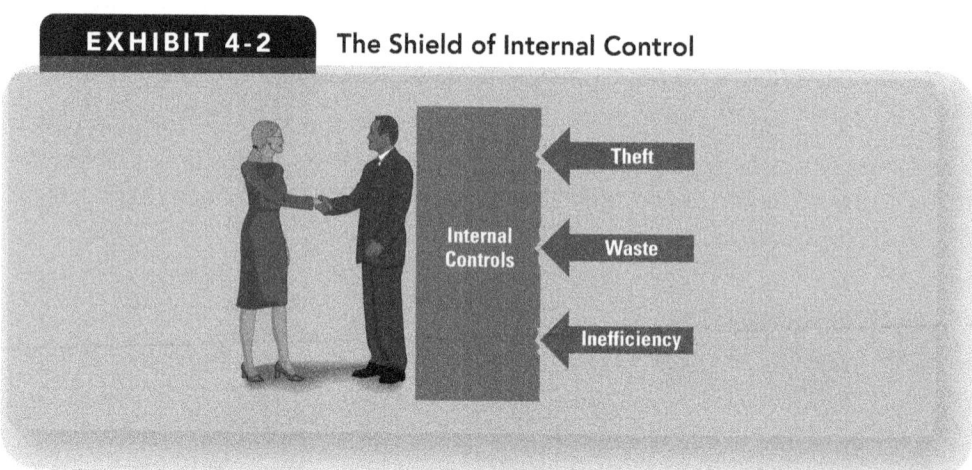

EXHIBIT 4-2   The Shield of Internal Control

The Components of Internal Control

OBJECTIVE

1 Set up an internal control system

Internal control can be broken down into 5 components:

- Control environment
- Risk assessment
- Control procedures
- Monitoring of controls
- Information system

Control Environment. The control environment is the "tone at the top" of the business. It starts with the owner and the top managers. They must behave honorably to set a good example for company employees. The owner must demonstrate the importance of internal controls if he or she expects employees to take the controls seriously. Former executives of Enron, WorldCom, and Tyco failed to establish a good control environment, and they are in prison as a result.

Risk Assessment. A company must identify its risks. For example, Kraft Foods faces the risk that its food products may harm people. American Airlines planes may crash. And all companies face the risk of bankruptcy. Companies facing difficulties are tempted to falsify the financial statements to make themselves look better than they really are.

Control Procedures. These are the procedures designed to ensure that the business's goals are achieved. Examples include assigning responsibilities, separating duties, and using security devices to protect assets from theft. The next section discusses internal control procedures.

Monitoring of Controls. Companies hire auditors to monitor their controls. Internal auditors monitor company controls to safeguard the company's assets, and external auditors monitor the controls to ensure that the accounting records are accurate.

Information System. As we have seen, the information system is critical. The owner of a business needs accurate information to keep track of assets and measure profits and losses.

Exhibit 4-3 diagrams the components of internal control.

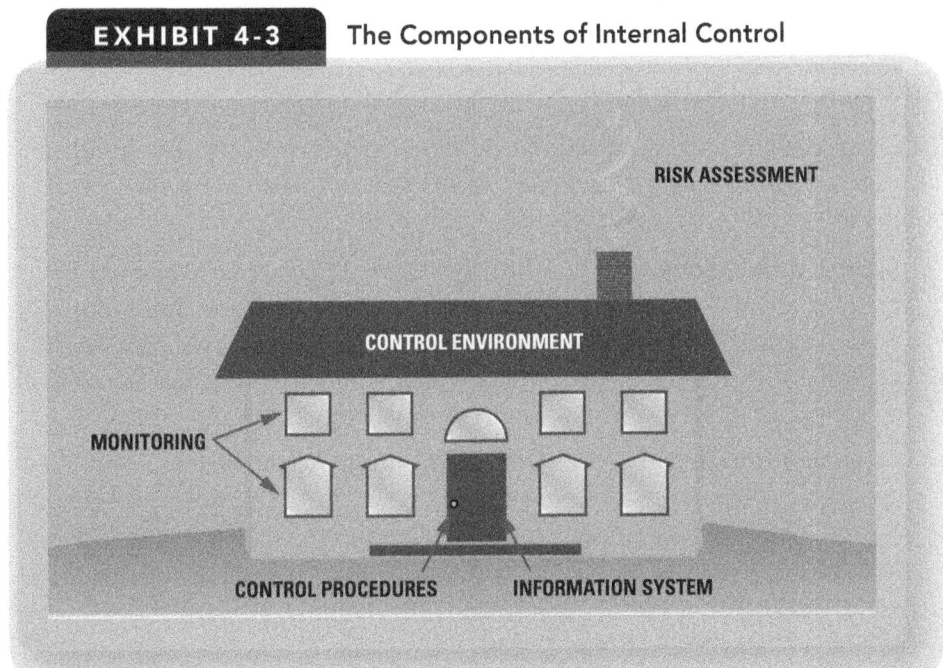

EXHIBIT 4-3   The Components of Internal Control

INTERNAL CONTROL PROCEDURES

Whether the business is AMEX Products, Microsoft, or an Exxon gas station, you need the following internal control procedures.

Competent, Reliable, and Ethical Personnel

Employees should be *competent*, *reliable*, and *ethical*. Paying good salaries will attract high-quality employees. You also must train them to do the job, supervise their work, and reward them fairly. This will build a competent staff.

Assignment of Responsibilities

In a business with good internal controls, no important duty is overlooked. Each employee has certain responsibilities. In a company such as AMEX Products, the person in charge of writing checks is called the treasurer. The chief accounting officer is called the **controller**. With clearly assigned responsibilities, all important jobs get done.

Separation of Duties

Smart management divides related duties between 2 or more people. *Separation of duties* limits fraud and promotes the accuracy of the accounting records. Separation of duties can be divided into 2 parts:

1. **Separate operations from accounting.** Accounting should be completely separate from the operating departments, such as production and sales. What would happen if sales personnel recorded the company's revenue? Sales figures could be inflated, and top managers wouldn't know how much the company actually sold. This is why you should separate accounting and sales duties.

2. **Separate the custody of assets from accounting.** Accountants must not handle cash, and cashiers must not have access to the accounting records. If one employee has both cash-handling and accounting duties, that person can steal cash and conceal the theft. This is what happened at AMEX Products. The **treasurer** of a company should handle cash, and the **controller** should account for the cash. Neither person should have both jobs.

Audits

To validate their accounting records, most companies have an audit. An **audit** is an examination of the company's financial statements and accounting system. To evaluate the system, auditors examine the internal controls.

Audits can be internal or external. *Internal auditors* are employees of the business. They ensure that employees are following company policies and operations are running efficiently. Internal auditors also determine whether the company is following legal requirements.

External auditors are completely independent of the business. They are hired to determine that the company's financial statements agree with generally accepted accounting principles. Auditors examine the client's financial statements and the underlying transactions in order to form a professional opinion of the financial statements.

Documents

Documents provide the details of business transactions. Documents include invoices and fax orders. Documents should be prenumbered to prevent theft and inefficiency. A gap in the numbered sequence draws attention.

In a bowling alley a key document is the score sheet. The manager can compare the number of games scored with the amount of cash received. Multiply the number of games by the charge per game and compare the revenue with cash receipts. You can see whether the business is collecting all the revenue.

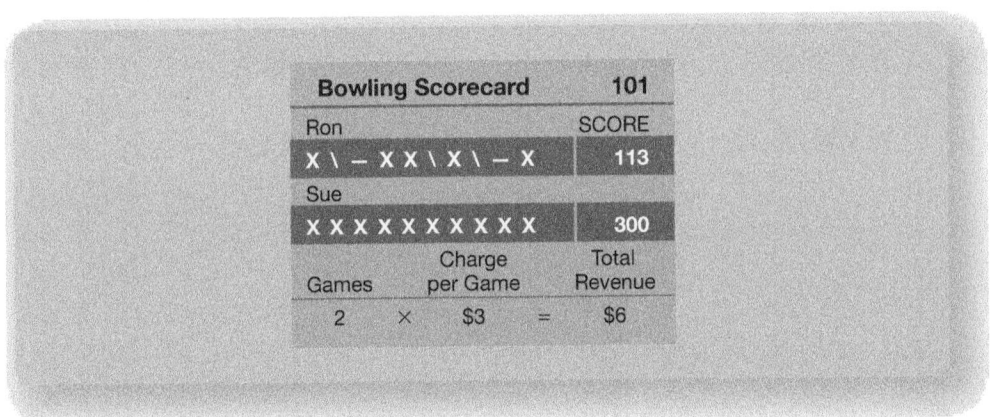

Electronic Devices

Accounting systems are relying less on documents and more on digital storage devices. For example, retailers such as Target Stores and Macy's control inventory by attaching an *electronic sensor* to merchandise. The cashier removes the sensor. If a customer tries to leave the store with the sensor attached, an alarm sounds. According to Checkpoint Systems, these devices reduce theft by as much as 50%.

Bar codes speed checkout at a store, and *surveillance cameras* help identify shoplifters.

Other Controls

Businesses keep important documents in *fireproof vaults*. *Burglar alarms* protect buildings, and *security cameras* protect other property. *Loss-prevention specialists* train employees to spot suspicious activity.

Employees who handle cash are in a tempting position. Many businesses purchase *fidelity bonds* on cashiers. The bond is an insurance policy that reimburses the company for any losses due to employee theft. Before issuing a fidelity bond, the insurance company investigates the employee's background.

Mandatory vacations and *job rotation* improve internal control. Companies move employees from job to job. This improves morale by giving employees a broad view of the business. Also, knowing someone else will do your job next month keeps you honest. AMEX Products didn't rotate employees to different jobs, and it cost the company $622,000.

INTERNAL CONTROLS FOR E-COMMERCE

E-commerce creates its own risks. Hackers may gain access to confidential information such as account numbers and passwords.

Pitfalls

E-commerce pitfalls include:

- Stolen credit-card numbers
- Computer viruses and Trojan Horses
- Phishing expeditions

Stolen Credit-Card Numbers. Suppose you buy CDs from EMusic.com. To make the purchase, your credit-card number must travel through cyberspace. Wireless networks (Wi-Fi) are creating new security hazards.

Amateur hacker Carlos Salgado, Jr., used his home computer to steal 100,000 credit-card numbers with a combined limit exceeding $1 billion. Salgado was caught when he tried to sell the numbers to an undercover FBI agent.

Computer Viruses and Trojan Horses. A **computer virus** is a malicious program that (a) enters program code without consent and (b) performs destructive actions in the victim's computer files or programs. A **Trojan Horse** is a malicious computer program that hides inside a legitimate program and works like a virus. Viruses can destroy or alter data, make bogus calculations, and infect files. Most firms have found a virus in their system.

Suppose the U.S. Department of Defense takes bids for a missile system. Raytheon and Lockheed-Martin are competing for the contract. A hacker infects Raytheon's system and alters Raytheon's design. Then the government labels the Raytheon design as flawed and awards the contract to Lockheed.

Phishing Expeditions. Thieves phish by creating bogus Web sites, such as AOL4Free.com and BankAmerica.com. The neat-sounding Web site attracts lots of visitors, and the thieves obtain account numbers and passwords from unsuspecting people. The thieves then use the data for illicit purposes.

Security Measures

To address the risks posed by e-commerce, companies have devised a number of security measures, including

- Encryption
- Firewalls

Encryption. The server holding confidential information may not be secure. One technique for protecting customer data is encryption. **Encryption** rearranges messages by a mathematical process. The encrypted message can't be read by those who don't know the code. An accounting example uses check-sum digits for account numbers. Each account number has its last digit equal to the sum of the previous digits. For example, consider Customer Number 2237, where $2 + 2 + 3 = 7$. Any account number that fails this test triggers an error message.

Firewalls. **Firewalls** limit access into a local network. Members can access the network but nonmembers can't. Usually several firewalls are built into the system. Think of a fortress with multiple walls protecting the king's chamber in the center. At the point of entry, passwords, PINs (personal identification numbers), and signatures are used. More sophisticated firewalls are used deeper in the network. Start with Firewall 1, and work toward the center.

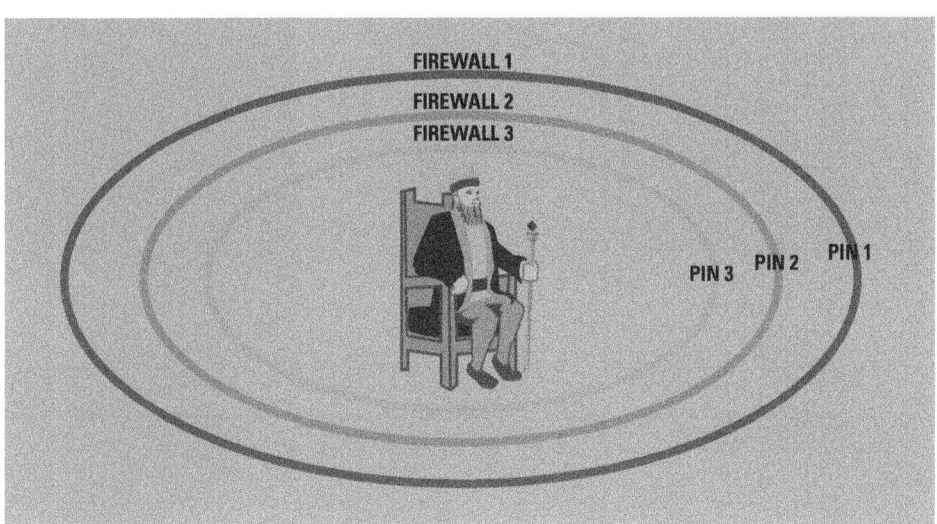

The Limitations of Internal Control—Costs and Benefits

Unfortunately, most internal controls can be overcome. Collusion—2 or more people working together—can beat internal controls. Consider Galaxy Theater. Ralph and Lana can design a scheme in which Ralph sells tickets and pockets the cash from 10 customers. Lana, the ticket taker, admits 10 customers without tickets. Ralph and Lana split the cash. To prevent this situation, the manager must take additional steps, such as matching the number of people in the theater against the number of ticket stubs retained. But that takes time away from other duties.

The stricter the internal control system, the more it costs. A complex system of internal control can strangle the business with red tape. How tight should the controls be? Internal controls must be judged in light of their costs and benefits. An example of a good cost/benefit relationship: A security guard at a **Wal-Mart** store costs about $28,000 a year. On average, each guard prevents about $50,000 of theft. The net savings to Wal-Mart is $22,000.

Pages 223–231 intentionally omitted

OBJECTIVE

3 **Apply** internal controls to cash receipts and payments

INTERNAL CONTROL OVER CASH RECEIPTS

Cash requires some specific internal controls because cash is relatively easy to steal and it's easy to convert to other forms of wealth. Moreover, all transactions ultimately affect cash. That's why cash is called the "eye of the needle." Let's see how to control cash receipts.

All cash receipts should be deposited for safekeeping in the bank—quickly. Companies receive cash over the counter and through the mail. Each source of cash has its own security measures.

Cash Receipts over the Counter

Exhibit 4-9 illustrates a cash receipt over the counter in a department store. The point-of-sale terminal (cash register) provides control over the cash receipts. Consider a Macy's store. For each transaction, Macy's issues a receipt to ensure that each sale is recorded. The cash drawer opens when the clerk enters a transaction, and the machine records it. At the end of the day, a manager proves the cash by comparing the cash in the drawer against the machine's record of sales. This step helps prevent theft by the clerk.

EXHIBIT 4-9 **Cash Receipts over the Counter**

At the end of the day—or several times a day if business is brisk—the cashier deposits the cash in the bank. The machine tape then goes to the accounting department for the journal entry to record sales revenue. These measures, coupled with oversight by a manager, discourage theft.

Cash Receipts by Mail

Many companies receive cash by mail. Exhibit 4-10 shows how companies control cash received by mail. All incoming mail is opened by a mailroom employee. The mailroom then sends all customer checks to the treasurer, who has the cashier deposit the money in the bank. The remittance advices go to the accounting department for journal entries to Cash and customer accounts receivable. As a final step, the controller compares the following records for the day:

- Bank deposit amount from the treasurer
- Debit to Cash from the accounting department

The debit to Cash should equal the amount deposited in the bank. All cash receipts are safe in the bank, and the company books are up-to-date.

Many companies use a lock-box system. Customers send their checks directly to the company's bank account. Internal control is tight because company personnel never touch incoming cash. The lock-box system puts your cash to work immediately.

EXHIBIT 4-10   **Cash Receipts by Mail**

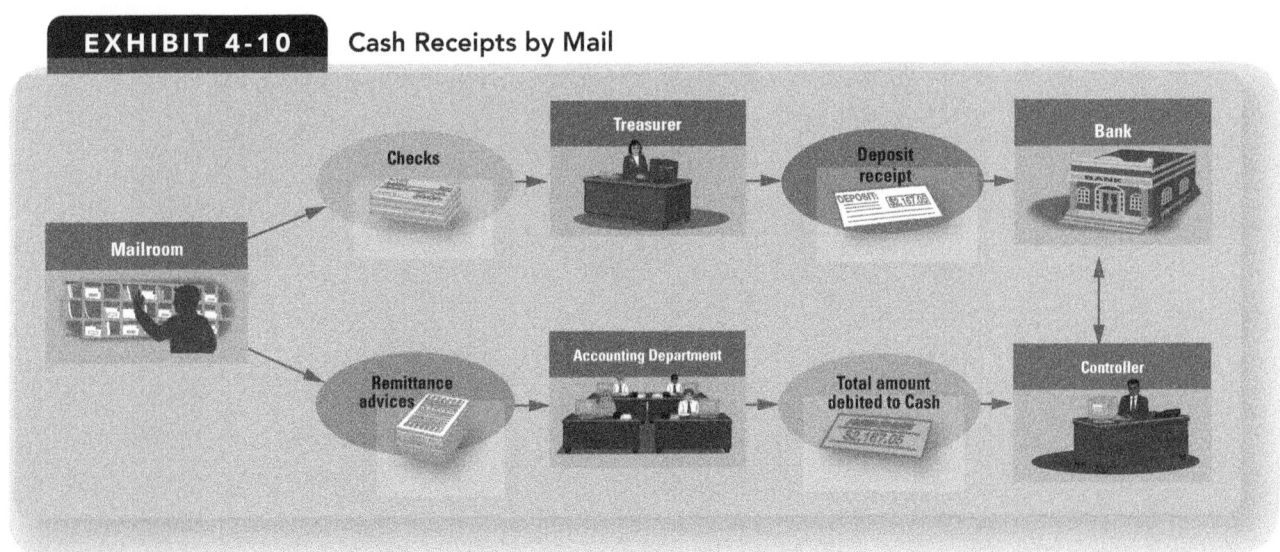

INTERNAL CONTROL OVER CASH PAYMENTS

Companies make most payments by check. Let's see how to control cash payments by check.

Controls over Payment by Check

As we have seen, you need a good separation of duties between (a) operations and (b) writing checks for cash payments. Payment by check is an important internal control, as follows:

- The check provides a record of the payment.
- The check must be signed by an authorized official.
- Before signing the check, the official should study the evidence supporting the payment.

Controls over Purchase and Payment. To illustrate the internal control over cash payments by check, suppose AMEX Products buys some of its inventory from Hanes Textiles. The purchasing and payment process follows these steps, as shown in Exhibit 4-11. Start with the box for AMEX Products on the left side.

1 AMEX faxes a *purchase order* to Hanes Textiles. AMEX says, "Please send us 100 T-shirts."

2 Hanes Textiles ships the goods and faxes an *invoice* back to AMEX. Hanes sent the goods.

3 AMEX receives the *inventory* and prepares a *receiving report* to list the goods received. AMEX got its T-shirts.

4 After approving all documents, AMEX sends a *check* to Hanes. AMEX says, "Okay, we'll pay you."

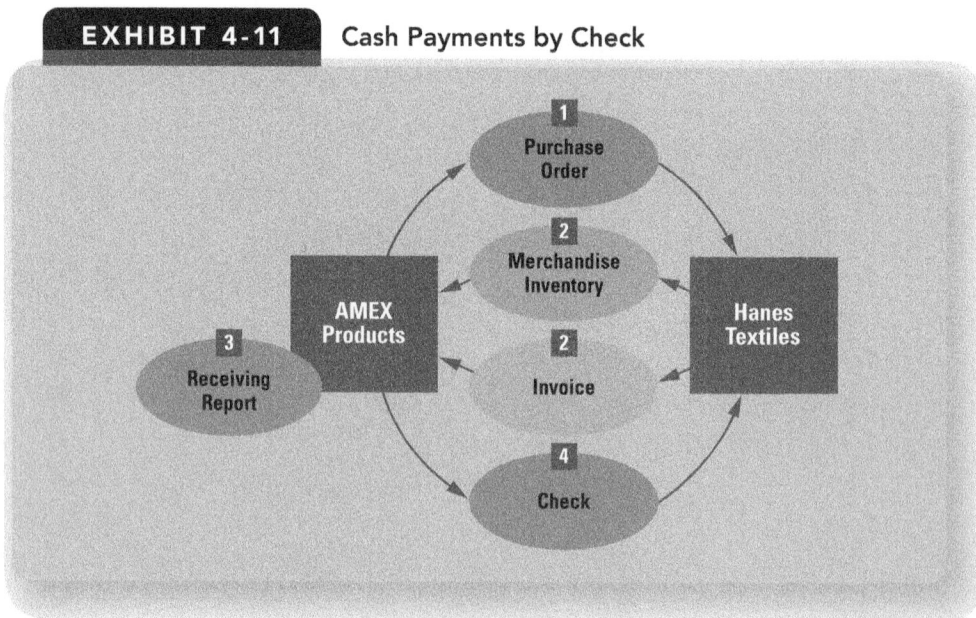

EXHIBIT 4-11   Cash Payments by Check

For good internal control, the purchasing agent should neither receive the goods nor approve the payment. If these duties aren't separated, a purchasing agent can buy goods and have them shipped to his or her home. Or a purchasing agent can spend too much on purchases, approve the payment, and split the excess with the supplier. To avoid these problems, companies split the following duties among different employees:

- purchasing goods
- receiving goods
- approving and paying for goods

Exhibit 4-12 shows AMEX's payment packet of documents. Before signing the check, the controller or the treasurer should examine the packet to prove that all the documents agree. Only then does the company know that:

1. It received the goods ordered.
2. It is paying only for the goods received.

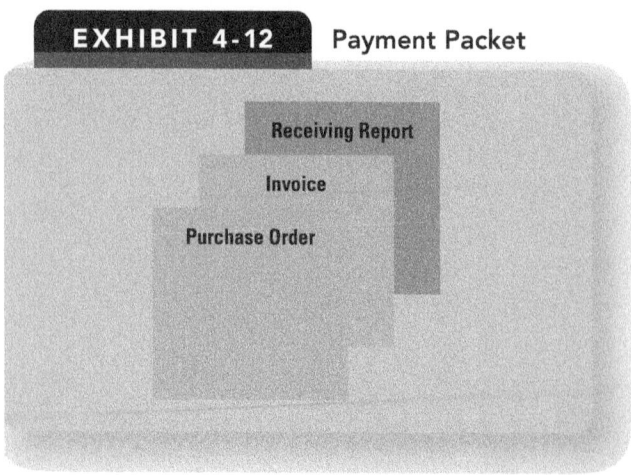

EXHIBIT 4-12   Payment Packet

After payment, the check signer punches a hole through the payment packet. Dishonest people have tried to run a bill through twice for payment. This hole shows that the bill has been paid.

Petty Cash. It would be wasteful to write separate checks for an executive's taxi fare, name tags needed right away, or delivery of a package across town. Therefore, companies keep a **petty cash** fund on hand to pay such minor amounts.

The petty cash fund is opened with a particular amount of cash. A check for that amount is then issued to Petty Cash. Assume that on February 28 **Cisco Systems**, the worldwide leader in networks for the Internet, establishes a petty cash fund of $500 in a sales department. The custodian of the petty cash fund cashes the check and places $500 in the fund, which may be a cash box or other device.

For each petty cash payment, the custodian prepares a petty cash ticket to list the item purchased. The sum of the cash in the petty cash fund plus the total of the ticket amounts should equal the opening balance at all times—in this case, $500. The Petty Cash account keeps its $500 balance at all times. Maintaining the Petty Cash account at this balance, supported by the fund (cash plus tickets), is how an **imprest system** works. The control feature is that it clearly identifies the amount for which the custodian is responsible.

Using a Budget to Manage Cash

OBJECTIVE

4 **Use** a budget to manage your cash

Managers control operations with a budget. A **budget** is a financial plan that helps coordinate business activities. Cash is budgeted most often.

How for example does AMEX Products decide when to invest in new inventory-tracking technology? How will AMEX decide how much to spend? Will borrowing be needed, or can AMEX finance the purchase with internally generated cash? Similarly, by what process do you decide how much to spend on your education? On an automobile? On a house? All these decisions depend to some degree on the information that a cash budget provides.

A *cash budget helps a company or an individual manage cash by planning receipts and payments during a future period.* The company must determine how much cash it will need and then decide whether or not operations will bring in the needed cash. Managers proceed as follows:

1. Start with the entity's cash balance at the beginning of the period. This is the amount left over from the preceding period.

2. Add the budgeted cash receipts and subtract the budgeted cash payments.

3. The beginning balance plus receipts and minus payments equals the expected cash balance at the end of the period.

4. Compare the cash available before new financing to the budgeted cash balance at the end of the period. Managers know the minimum amount of cash they need (the budgeted balance). If the budget shows excess cash, managers can invest the excess. But if the cash available falls below the budgeted balance, the company will need additional financing. The company may need to borrow the shortfall amount. The budget is a valuable tool for helping the company plan for the future.

The budget period can span any length of time—a day, a week, a month, or a year. Exhibit 4-13 shows a cash budget for AMEX Products, Inc., for the year ended December 31, 2008. Study it carefully, because at some point you will use a cash budget.

AMEX Products' cash budget in Exhibit 4-13 begins with $6,260 of cash (line 1). Then add budgeted cash receipts and subtract budgeted payments. In this case, AMEX expects to have $3,900 of cash available at year end (line 10). AMEX managers need to maintain a cash balance of at least $5,000 (line 11). Line 12 shows that AMEX must arrange $1,100 of financing in order to achieve its goals for 2008.

EXHIBIT 4-13   Cash Budget

AMEX Products, Inc.
Cash Budget
For the Year Ended December 31, 2008

(1)	Cash balance, December 31, 2007		$ 6,260
	Budgeted cash receipts:		
(2)	Collections from customers		55,990
(3)	Dividends on investments		1,200
(4)	Sale of store fixtures		5,700
			69,150
	Budgeted cash payments:		
(5)	Purchases of inventory	$33,720	
(6)	Operating expenses	11,530	
(7)	Expansion of store	12,000	
(8)	Payment of long-term debt	5,000	
(9)	Payment of dividends	3,000	65,250
(10)	Cash available (needed) before new financing		$ 3,900
(11)	Budgeted cash balance, December 31, 2008		(5,000)
(12)	Cash available for additional investments, or		
	(New financing needed)		$ (1,100)

Reporting Cash on the Balance Sheet

Most companies have numerous bank accounts, but they usually combine all cash amounts into a single total called "Cash and Cash Equivalents." Cash equivalents include liquid assets such as time deposits and certificates of deposit, which are interest-bearing accounts that can be withdrawn with no penalty. Slightly less liquid than cash, cash equivalents are sufficiently similar to be reported along with cash. The balance sheet of AMEX Products (repeated from page 214) reported the following:

AMEX Products, Inc.
Balance Sheet (Excerpts, adapted)
For the Year Ended December 31, 2007

	(In millions)
Assets	
Cash and cash equivalents	$ 6,260
Cash pledged as collateral	2,000

Compensating Balance Agreements

The Cash account on the balance sheet reports the liquid assets available for day-to-day use. None of the Cash balance is restricted in any way.

Any restricted amount of cash should *not* be reported as Cash on the balance sheet. For example, on the AMEX Products balance sheet, *cash pledged as collateral* (p. 236) is reported separately because that cash is not available for day-to-day use. Instead, AMEX has pledged the cash as security (collateral) for a loan. If AMEX fails to pay the loan, the lender can take the pledged cash. For this reason, the pledged cash is less liquid.

Also, banks often lend money under a compensating balance agreement. The borrower agrees to maintain a minimum balance in a checking account at all times. This minimum balance becomes a long-term asset and is therefore not cash in the normal sense.

Suppose AMEX Products borrowed $10,000 at 8% from First Interstate Bank and agreed to keep 20% ($2,000) on deposit at all times. The net result of the compensating balance agreement is that AMEX actually borrowed only $8,000. And by paying 8% interest on the full $10,000, AMEX's actual interest rate is really 10%, as shown here:

$$\$10,000 \times .08 = \$800 \text{ interest}$$
$$\$800/\$8,000 = .10 \text{ interest rate}$$

ETHICS AND ACCOUNTING

OBJECTIVE

5 **Make** ethical business judgments

Roger Smith, the former chairman of General Motors, said, "Ethical practice is [. . .] good business." Smith knows that unethical behavior doesn't work. Sooner or later it comes back to haunt you. Moreover, ethical behavior wins out in the long run because right triumphs over wrong.

Corporate and Professional Codes of Ethics

Most companies have a code of ethics to encourage employees to behave ethically. But codes of ethics are not enough by themselves. Owners and managers must set a high ethical tone, as we saw in the section on Control Environment. Top managers must make it clear that the company will not tolerate unethical conduct.

As professionals, accountants are expected to maintain higher standards than society in general. Their ability to do business depends entirely on their reputation. Most independent accountants are members of the American Institute of Certified Public Accountants and must abide by the *AICPA Code of Professional Conduct*. Accountants who are members of the Institute of Management Accountants are bound by the *Standards of Ethical Conduct for Management Accountants*.

Ethical Issues in Accounting

In many situations, the ethical choice is easy. For example, stealing cash is both unethical and illegal. In other cases, the choices are more difficult. But in every instance, ethical judgments boil down to a personal decision: What should I do in a given situation? Let's consider 3 ethical issues in accounting.

HH CHAPTER 4

Situation 1. Brian Bivona is preparing the income tax return of a client who has earned more income than expected. On January 2, the client pays for advertising and asks Bivona to backdate the expense to the preceding year. Backdating the deduction would lower the client's immediate tax payments. After all, there is a difference of only 2 days between January 2 and December 31. This client is important to Bivona. What should Bivona do?

> Bivona should refuse the request because the transaction took place in January of the new year.

What control device could prove that Bivona behaved unethically if he backdated the transaction in the accounting records? An IRS audit could prove that the expense occurred in January rather than in December. Falsifying IRS documents is both unethical and illegal.

Situation 2. Marlene Reed Software Company owes $40,000 to Bank of America. The loan agreement requires Reed's company to maintain a current ratio (current assets divided by current liabilities) of 1.50 or higher. At present, the company's current ratio is 1.40. At this level, Reed is in violation of her loan agreement. She can increase the current ratio to 1.53 by paying off some current liabilities right before year end. Is it ethical to do so?

> Yes, because the action is a real business transaction.

Reed should be aware that paying off the liabilities is only a delaying tactic. It will hold off the bank for now, but the business must improve in order to keep from violating the agreement in the future.

Situation 3. David Duncan, the lead Arthur Anderson auditor of Enron Corporation, thinks Enron may be understating the liabilities on its balance sheet. Enron's transactions are very complex, and outsiders may never figure this out. Duncan asks his firm's Standards Committee how he should handle the situation. They reply, "Require Enron to report all its liabilities." Enron is Duncan's most important client, and Enron is pressuring him to certify the liabilities. Duncan can rationalize that Enron's reported amounts are okay. What should Duncan do? To make his decision, Duncan could follow the framework outlined in the following Decision Guidelines feature.

DECISION GUIDELINES

FRAMEWORK FOR MAKING ETHICAL JUDGMENTS

Weighing tough ethical judgments requires a decision framework. Answering these 4 questions will guide you through tough decisions. Let's apply them to David Duncan's situation. (situation 3 on page 238)

Question	Decision Guidelines
1. What is the ethical issue?	1. *Identify the ethical issue.* The root word of ethical is ethics, which Webster's dictionary defines as "the discipline dealing with what is good and bad and with moral duty and obligation." Duncan's ethical dilemma is to decide what he should do with the information he has uncovered.
2. What are Duncan's options?	2. *Specify the alternatives.* For David Duncan, the alternatives include (a) go along with Enron's liabilities as reported or (b) force Enron to report higher amounts of liabilities.
3. What are the possible consequences?	3. *Assess the possible outcomes.* a. If Duncan certifies Enron's present level of liabilities—and if no one ever objects—Duncan will keep this valuable client. But if Enron's actual liabilities turn out to be higher than reported, Enron investors may lose money and take Duncan to court. That would damage his reputation as an auditor and hurt his firm. b. If Duncan follows his company policy, he must force Enron to increase its reported liabilities. That will anger the company, and Enron may fire Duncan as its auditor. In that case, Duncan will save his reputation, but it will cost him dearly in the short run.
4. What should Duncan do?	4. *Make the decision.* In the end Duncan went along with Enron and certified the company's liabilities. He went directly against his firm's policies. Enron later admitted understating its liabilities, Duncan had to retract his audit opinion, and Duncan's worldwide firm, Arthur Andersen, collapsed quickly. Duncan should have followed company policy. Rarely is one person smarter than a team of experts. Duncan got out from under his firm's umbrella of protection, and it cost him and many others dearly.

END-OF-CHAPTER SUMMARY PROBLEM

Assume the following situation for PepsiCo Inc.: PepsiCo ended 20X3 with cash of $200 million. At December 31, 20X3, Bob Detmer, the CFO of PepsiCo, is preparing the budget for 20X4.

During 20X4, Detmer expects PepsiCo to collect $26,400 million from customers and $80 million from interest earned on investments. PepsiCo expects to pay $12,500 million for its inventories and $5,400 million for operating expenses. To remain competitive, PepsiCo plans to spend $2,200 million to upgrade production facilities and an additional $350 million to acquire other companies. PepsiCo also plans to sell older assets for approximately $300 million and to collect $220 million of this amount in cash. PepsiCo is budgeting dividend payments of $550 million during the year. Finally, the company is scheduled to pay off $1,200 million of long-term debt plus the $6,600 million of current liabilities left over from 20X3.

Because of the growth planned for 20X4, Detmer budgets the need for a minimum cash balance of $300 million.

I *Required*

1. How much must PepsiCo borrow during 20X4 to keep its cash balance from falling below $330 million? Prepare the 20X4 cash budget to answer this important question.

Answer

PepsiCo, Inc.
Cash Budget
For the Year Ended December 31, 20X4

(In millions)

Cash balance, December 31, 20X3.................................		$ 200
Estimated cash receipts:		
Collections from customers...		26,400
Receipt of interest		80
Sales of assets..		220
		26,900
Estimated cash payments:		
Purchases of inventory...	$12,500	
Payment of operating expenses	5,400	
Upgrading of production facilities............................	2,200	
Acquisition of other companies................................	350	
Payment of dividends	550	
Payment of long-term debt and other		
liabilities ($1,200 + $6,600)................................	7,800	(28,800)
Cash available (needed) before new financing..............		$ (1,900)
Budgeted cash balance, December 31, 20X4		(300)
Cash available for additional investments, or		
(New financing needed)		$ (2,200)

PepsiCo. must borrow $2,200 million.

REVIEW INTERNAL CONTROL AND CASH

Quick Check (Answers are given on page 260.)

1. Internal control has its own terminology. On the left are some key internal control concepts. On the right are some key terms. Match each internal control concept with its term by writing the appropriate letter in the space provided. Not all letters are used.

___ This procedure limits access to sensitive data.

___ This type of insurance policy covers losses due to employee theft.

___ Trusting your employees can lead you to overlook this procedure.

___ The most basic purpose of internal control.

___ Internal control cannot always safeguard against this problem.

___ Often mentioned as the cornerstone of a good system of internal control.

___ Pay employees enough to require them to do a good job.

    a. Competent personnel
    b. Encryption
    c. Separation of duties
    d. Safeguarding assets
    e. Fidelity bond
    f. Collusion
    g. Firewalls
    h. Supervision
    i. External audits

2. Each of the following is an example of a control procedure, *except*
   a. a sound marketing plan.
   b. sound personnel procedures.
   c. limited access to assets.
   d. separation of duties.

3. Which of the following is an example of poor internal control?
   a. The accounting department compares goods received with the related purchase order
   b. Employees must take vacations
   c. Rotate employees through various jobs
   d. The mailroom clerk records daily cash receipts in the journal

Driver Corporation has asked you to prepare its bank reconciliation at the end of the current month. Answer questions 4–8 using the following code letters to indicate how the item described would be reported on the bank reconciliation.

    a. Deduct from the book balance
    b. Does not belong on the bank reconciliation
    c. Add to the bank balance
    d. Deduct from the bank balance
    e. Add to the book balance

4. A check for $435 written by Driver during the current month was erroneously recorded as a $354 payment.

5. A $250 deposit made on the last day of the current month did not appear on this month's bank statement.

6. The bank statement showed interest earned of $45.

7. The bank statement included a check from a customer that was marked NSF.

8. The bank statement showed the bank had credited Driver's account for a $600 deposit made by Dover Company.

9. Which of the following reconciling items does not require a journal entry?
   a. NSF check
   b. deposit in transit
   c. bank collection of note receivable
   d. bank service charge

10. A check was written for $628 to purchase supplies. The check was recorded in the journal as $682. The entry to correct this error would:
    a. increase Supplies, $54.
    b. decrease Supplies, $54.
    c. decrease Cash, $54.
    d. a. and c.

11. A cash budget helps control cash by
    a. developing a plan for increasing sales.
    b. ensuring accurate cash records.
    c. helping to determine whether additional cash is available for investments or new financing is needed.
    d. All of the above.

Accounting Vocabulary

audit (p. 218) A periodic examination of a company's financial statements and the accounting systems, controls, and records that produce them.

bank collections (p. 225) Collection of money by the bank on behalf of a depositor

bank reconciliation (p. 223) A document explaining the reasons for the difference between a depositor's records and the bank's records about the depositor's cash.

bank statement (p. 222) Document showing the beginning and ending balances of a particular bank account listing the month's transactions that affected the account.

budget (p. 235) A quantitative expression of a plan that helps managers coordinate the entity's activities.

check (p. 222) Document instructing a bank to pay the designated person or business the specified amount of money.

controller (p. 218) The chief accounting officer of a business.

deposits in transit (p. 224) A deposit recorded by the company but not yet by its bank.

electronic fund transfer (EFT) (p. 225) System that transfers cash by electronic communication rather than by paper documents.

imprest system (p. 235) A way to account for petty cash by maintaining a constant balance in the petty cash account, supported by the fund (cash plus payment tickets) totaling the same amount.

internal control (p. 215) Organizational plan and related measures adopted by an entity to safeguard assets, encourage adherence to company policies, promote operational efficiency, and ensure accurate and reliable accounting records.

nonsufficient funds (NSF) check (p. 225) A "hot" check, one for which the payer's bank account has insufficient money to pay the check. NSF checks are cash receipts that turn out to be worthless.

outstanding checks (p. 224) A check issued by the company and recorded on its books but not yet paid by its bank.

petty cash (p. 235) Fund containing a small amount of cash that is used to pay minor amounts.

treasurer (p. 218) In a large company, the person in charge of writing checks.

Page 243 intentionally omitted

Exercises

E4-14 *(Learning Objective 1: Explaining the role of internal control)* Answer the following questions on internal control:

a. Separation of duties is an important internal control procedure. Why is this so? (pp. 215–216)

b. Cash may be a small item on the financial statements. Nevertheless, internal control over cash is very important. Why is this true? (p. 232)

Pages 245–249 intentionally omitted

writing assignment ■   **P4-42A** (*Learning Objective 1, 3: Identifying internal control weakness*) Each of the following situations reveals an internal control weakness.

  a. Accounting firms use paraprofessional employees to perform routine tasks. For example, an accounting paraprofessional might prepare routine tax returns for clients. In the firm of Dunham & Lee, Rodney Lee, one of the partners, turns over a significant portion of his high-level accounting work to his paraprofessional staff. (pp. 217–218)

  c. Charlotte James owns an architecture firm. James's staff consists of 12 professional architects, and James manages the office. Often, James's work requires her to travel to meet with clients. During the past 6 months, James has observed that when she returns from a business trip, the architecture jobs in the office have not progressed satisfactorily. James learns that when she is away, 2 of her senior architects take over office management and neglect their normal duties. One employee could manage the office. (pp. 217–218)

  d. B.J. Tanner has been an employee of the City of Marlin for many years. Because the city is small, Tanner performs all accounting duties, plus opening the mail, preparing the bank deposit, and preparing the bank reconciliation. (pp. 217–218)

  e. Part of an internal auditor's job is to evaluate how efficiently the company is running. For example, is the company purchasing inventory from the least expensive supplier? After a particularly bad year, Long Photographic Products eliminates its internal audit department to reduce expenses. (pp. 218–219)

Pages 251–253 intentionally omitted

writing assignment ■

P4-49B *(Learning Objective 1, 3: Identifying internal control weaknesses)* Each of the following situations has an internal control weakness:

    b. The office supply company from which Martin Audiology Service purchases cash receipt forms recently notified Martin that the last-shipped sales receipts were not prenumbered. Derek Martin, the owner, replied that he did not use the receipt numbers, so the omission is unimportant to him. (pp. 219–220)

    c. Azbell Electronics specializes in programs with musical applications. The company's most popular product prepares musical programs for large gatherings. In the company's early days, the owner and 8 employees wrote the programs, lined up production of the programs, sold the products, and performed the general management of the company. As Azbell has grown, the number of employees has increased dramatically. Recently, the development of a new musical series stopped while the programmers redesigned Azbell's sound system. Azbell could have hired outsiders to do this task. (pp. 217–218)

    d. Paul Allen, who has no known sources of outside income, has been a trusted employee of Chapparall Cosmetics for 20 years. Allen performs all cash-handling and accounting duties, including opening the mail, preparing the bank deposit, accounting for cash and accounts receivable, and preparing the bank reconciliation. Allen has just purchased a new Lexus. Linda Altman, owner of the company, wonders how Allen can afford the new car on his salary. (pp. 217–218)

    e. Monica Wade employs 3 professional interior designers in her design studio. The studio is located in an area with a lot of new construction, and her business is booming. Ordinarily, Wade does all the purchasing of materials needed to complete jobs. During the summer, Wade takes a long vacation, and in her absence she allows each designer to purchase materials. On her return, Wade reviews operations and observes that expenses are higher and net income is lower than in the past. (pp. 217–218)

Pages 255–260 intentionally omitted

5 Short-Term Investments & Receivables

SPOTLIGHT

RECEIVABLES ARE PEPSICO'S LARGEST CURRENT ASSET

What comes to mind when you think of **PepsiCo**? Do you think of a soft drink or a snack chip? PepsiCo's 2 main products are soft drinks and snack foods. PepsiCo also owns Frito Lay, the snack-food company.

Take a look at PepsiCo's balance sheet. Does it surprise you that receivables are PepsiCo's largest current asset? It turns out that receivables are the largest current asset for lots of companies, including **FedEx** and **Yum! Brands**.

Another category of current asset is short-term investments. As you can see from PepsiCo's balance sheet, PepsiCo had over $1 billion of short-term investments at the end of 2006. You'll notice that short-term investments are listed on the balance sheet immediately after cash and before receivables. Let's see why.

Pages 262–270 intentionally omitted

ACCOUNTING FOR UNCOLLECTIBLE RECEIVABLES

A company gets an account receivable only when it sells its product or service on credit (on account). You'll recall that the entry to record the earning of revenue on account is (amount assumed)

Accounts Receivable	1,000	
Sales Revenue (or Service Revenue)		1,000
Earned revenue on account.		

Ideally, the company would collect cash for all of its receivables. But unfortunately the entry to record cash collections on account is for only $950.

Cash	950	
Accounts Receivable		950
Collections on account.		

You can see that companies rarely collect all of their accounts receivables. So companies must account for their uncollectible accounts—$50 in this example. Selling on credit creates both a benefit and a cost:

- *Benefit*: Customers who cannot pay cash immediately can buy on credit, so sales and profits increase.
- *Cost*: The company cannot collect from some customers. Accountants label this cost **uncollectible-account expense**, **doubtful-account expense**, or **bad-debt expense**.

PepsiCo reports receivables as follows on its 2006 balance sheet (in millions):

| Accounts and notes receivable, net of allowance for doubtful accounts of $64 .... | $3,725 |

The allowance ($64) represents the amount that PepsiCo does *not* expect to collect. The net amount of the receivables ($3,725 million) is the amount that PepsiCo *does* expect to collect. This is called the *net realizable value* because it's the amount of cash PepsiCo expects to realize in cash receipts.

Uncollectible-account expense is an operating expense along with salaries, depreciation, rent, and utilities. To measure uncollectible-account expense, accountants use the allowance method or, in certain limited cases, the direct write-off method (p. 277).

Allowance Method

The best way to measure bad debts is by the **allowance method.** This method records collection losses based on estimates developed from the company's collection experience. PepsiCo doesn't wait to see which customers will not pay. Instead, PepsiCo records the estimated amount as Uncollectible-Account Expense and also sets up **Allowance for Uncollectible Accounts.** Other titles for this account are **Allowance for Doubtful Accounts** and **Allowance for Bad Debts.** This is a contra

OBJECTIVE

3 **Use** the allowance method for uncollectible receivables

HH CHAPTER 5

account to Accounts Receivable. The allowance shows the amount of the receivables the business expects *not* to collect.

In Chapter 3 we used the Accumulated Depreciation account to show the amount of a plant asset's cost that has been expensed—the portion of the asset that's no longer a benefit to the company. Allowance for Uncollectible Accounts serves a similar purpose for Accounts Receivable. The allowance shows how much of the receivable has been expensed. You'll find this diagram helpful (amounts are assumed):

Equipment.........................	$100,000	Accounts receivable..................	$10,000
Less: Accumulated		Less: Allowance for	
depreciation	(40,000)	uncollectible accounts	(900)
Equipment, net..................	60,000	Accounts receivable, net............	9,100

Focus on Accounts Receivable. Customers owe this company $10,000, but it expects to collect only $9,100. The *net realizable value* of the receivables is therefore $9,100. Another way to report these receivables is

| Accounts receivable, less allowance of $900................. | $9,100 |

You can work backward to determine the full amount of the receivable, $10,000 (net realizable value of $9,100 plus the allowance of $900).

The income statement reports Uncollectible-Account Expense among the operating expenses, as follows (using assumed figures):

Income statement (partial):

Expenses:

    Uncollectible-account expense:............... $2,000

STOP & think. . .

Refer to the PepsiCo balance sheet on page 262. At December 31, 2006, how much did customers owe PepsiCo? How much did PepsiCo expect *not* to collect? How much did PepsiCo expect to collect? What was the net realizable value of PepsiCo's receivables?

Answer:

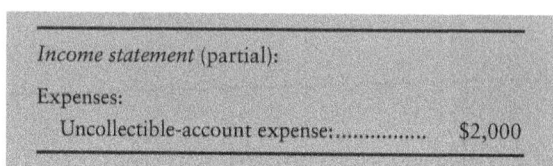

	Millions
Customers owed PepsiCo...	$3,789
PepsiCo expected not to collect the allowance of	(64)
PepsiCo expected to collect—net realizable value........	$3,725

The best way to estimate uncollectibles uses the company's history of collections from customers. There are 2 basic ways to estimate uncollectibles:

- Percent-of-sales method
- Aging-of-receivables method

Percent-of-Sales. The **percent-of-sales method** computes uncollectible-account expense as a percent of revenue. This method takes an *income-statement approach* because it focuses on the amount of expense to be reported on the income statement. Assume it is December 31, 2006, and PepsiCo's accounts have these balances *before the year-end adjustments* (amounts in millions):

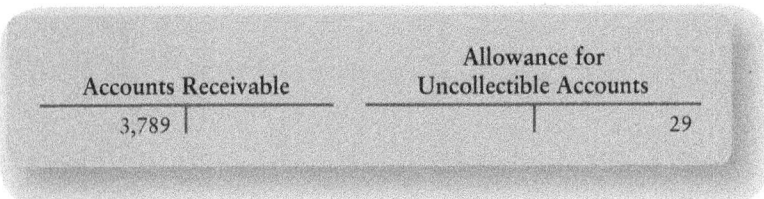

Accounts Receivable		Allowance for Uncollectible Accounts	
3,789			29

Customers owe PepsiCo $3,789, and the Allowance amount on the books is $29. But PepsiCo's top managers know that the company will fail to collect more than $29. Suppose PepsiCo's credit department estimates that uncollectible-account expense is 1/10 of 1% (0.001) of total revenues, which were $35,000. The entry that records uncollectible-account expense for the year also updates the allowance as follows (using PepsiCo figures):

2006			
Dec. 31	Uncollectible-Account Expense		
	($35,000 × .001)	35	
	Allowance for Uncollectible Accounts		35
	Recorded expense for the year.		

The expense decreases PepsiCo's assets, as shown by the accounting equation.

Assets	=	Liabilities	+	Stockholders' Equity	–	Expenses
– 35	=	0			–	35

Now PepsiCo's accounts are ready for reporting in the financial statements.

Accounts Receivable		Allowance for Uncollectible Accounts		Uncollectible-Account Expense	
3,789			29	35	
		Adj.	35		
		End. bal.	64		

Net accounts receivable, $3,725

Compare these amounts to the Stop and Think answer on page 272. They are the same.

Customers owe PepsiCo $3,789, and now the Allowance for Uncollectibles balance is realistic. PepsiCo's balance sheet actually reported accounts receivable at this net realizable value amount of $3,725 ($3,789 – $64).

Aging-of-Receivables. The other popular method for estimating uncollectibles is called **aging-of-receivables.** This method is a *balance-sheet approach* because it focuses on accounts receivable. In the aging method, individual receivables from specific customers are analyzed based on how long they have been outstanding.

Suppose it is December 31, 2006, and PepsiCo's receivables accounts show the following before the year-end adjustment (amounts in millions):

Accounts Receivable		Allowance for Uncollectible Accounts	
3,789			29

These accounts are not yet ready for the financial statements because the allowance balance is not realistic.

PepsiCo's computerized accounting package ages the company's accounts receivable. Exhibit 5-2 shows a representative aging schedule at December 31, 2006. PepsiCo's receivables total $3,789. Of this amount, the aging schedule shows that the company will *not* collect $64 (lower right corner).

EXHIBIT 5-2   Aging the Accounts Receivable of PepsiCo.

	Age of Account (Dollar amounts in millions)				
Customer	1-30 Days	31-60 Days	61-90 Days	Over 90 Days	Total Balance
Taco Bell					
Pizza Hut					
Totals..	$3,300	$ 300	$ 100	$ 89	$3,789
Estimated percent uncollectible..............................	× 1%	× 2%	× 7%	× 20%	
Allowance for Uncollectible Accounts balance should be	$ 33 +	$ 6 +	$ 7 +	$ 18 =	$ 64

The aging method will bring the balance of the allowance account ($29) to the needed amount as determined by the aging schedule ($64). The lower right corner of the aging schedule gives the needed balance in the allowance account. To update the allowance, PepsiCo would make this adjusting entry at year end:

2006			
Dec. 31	Uncollectible-Account Expense	35	
	Allowance for Uncollectible Accounts		
	($64 – $29)		35
	Recorded expense for the year.		

The expense decreases PepsiCo's assets, as shown by the accounting equation.

Assets	=	Liabilities	+	Stockholders' Equity	–	Expenses
– 35	=	0				– 35

Now the balance sheet can report the amount that PepsiCo actually expects to collect from customers: $3,725 ($3,789 – $64). This is the net realizable value of PepsiCo's accounts receivable.

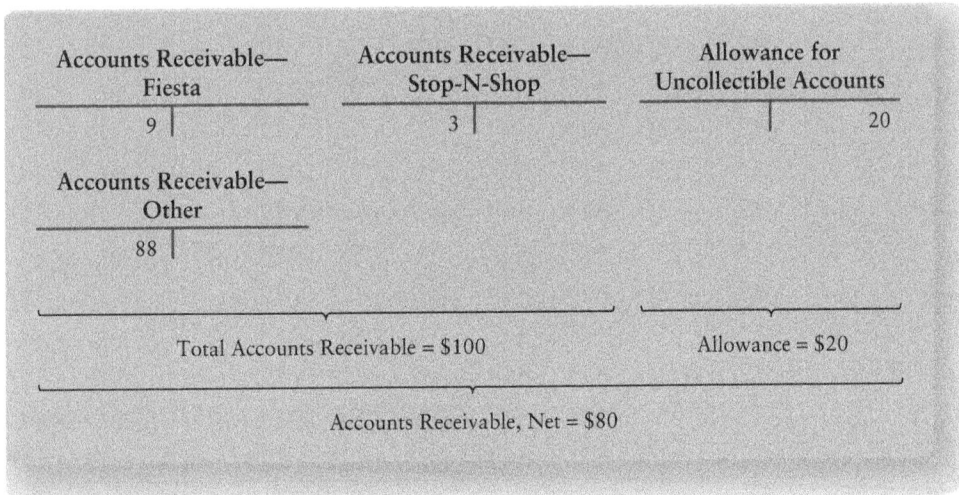

Writing Off Uncollectible Accounts. Assume that at the beginning of 2007 a division of PepsiCo had these accounts receivable (amounts in thousands):

Suppose that early in 2007, PepsiCo's credit department determines that PepsiCo cannot collect from customers Fiesta and Stop–N–Shop. PepsiCo then writes off the receivables from these 2 customers with the following entry:

2007			
Jan. 31	Allowance for Uncollectible Accounts	12	
	Accounts Receivable—Fiesta		9
	Accounts Receivable—Stop-N-Shop		3
	Wrote off uncollectible receivables.		

After the write-off, PepsiCo's accounts show these amounts:

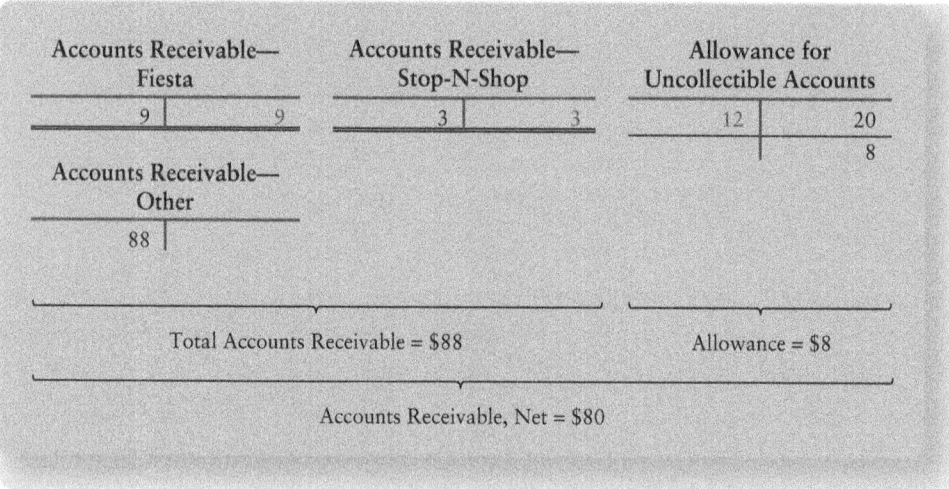

The accounting equation shows that the write-off of uncollectibles has no effect on PepsiCo's total assets. Accounts Receivable, Net is still $80. There is no effect on net income either. Why is there no effect on net income? Net income is unaffected because the write-off of uncollectibles affects no expense account.

Assets	=	Liabilities	+	Stockholders' Equity
+ 12 – 12	=	0	+	0

Combining the Percent-of-Sales and the Aging Methods. Most companies use the percent-of-sales and aging-of-accounts methods together, as follows:

■ For *interim statements* (monthly or quarterly), companies use the percent-of-sales method because it is easier to apply. The percent-of-sales method focuses on the uncollectible-account *expense*, but that is not enough.

■ At the end of the year, companies use the aging method to ensure that Accounts Receivable is reported at *net realizable value* on the balance sheet. The aging method focuses on the amount of the receivables that is uncollectible.

■ Using the two methods together provides good measures of both the *expense* and the *asset*. Exhibit 5-3 compares the two methods.

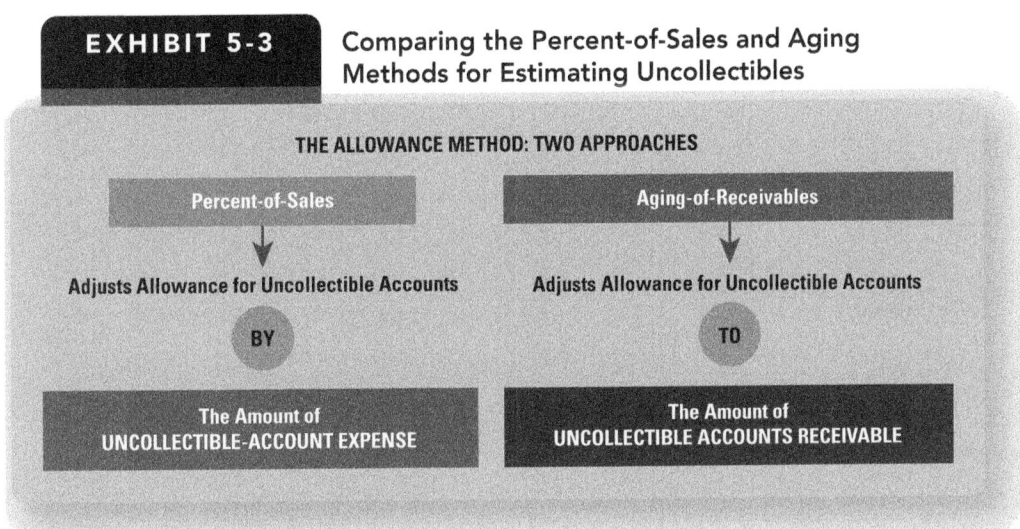

EXHIBIT 5-3 Comparing the Percent-of-Sales and Aging Methods for Estimating Uncollectibles

THE ALLOWANCE METHOD: TWO APPROACHES

Percent-of-Sales

Adjusts Allowance for Uncollectible Accounts

BY

The Amount of
UNCOLLECTIBLE-ACCOUNT EXPENSE

Aging-of-Receivables

Adjusts Allowance for Uncollectible Accounts

TO

The Amount of
UNCOLLECTIBLE ACCOUNTS RECEIVABLE

Direct Write-Off Method

There is another, less preferable, way to account for uncollectible receivables. Under the **direct write-off method**, the company waits until a specific customer's receivable proves uncollectible. Then the accountant writes off the customer's account and records Uncollectible-Account Expense, as follows (using assumed data):

2007			
Jan. 2	Uncollectible-Account Expense	12	
	Accounts Receivable—Fiesta		9
	Accounts Receivable—Stop-N-Shop		3
	Wrote off bad accounts by direct write-off method.		

The direct write-off method is defective for 2 reasons:

1. The direct write-off method uses no allowance for uncollectibles. As a result, receivables are always reported at their full amount, which is more than the business expects to collect. *Assets on the balance sheet are overstated.*

2. The direct write-off method causes a poor matching of uncollectible-account expense against revenue. In this example, PepsiCo made the sales to Fiesta and Stop–N–Shop in 2006 and should have recorded the uncollectible-account expense during 2006, not in 2007 when it wrote off the accounts.

Because of these deficiencies, PepsiCo and virtually all other large companies use the allowance method. The direct write-off method is acceptable only when uncollectibles are so low that there would be no allowance for uncollectible accounts.

Computing Cash Collections from Customers

A company earns revenue and then collects the cash from customers. For PepsiCo and most other companies, there is a time lag between earning the revenue and collecting the cash. Collections from customers are the single most important source of cash for any business. You can compute a company's collections from customers by analyzing its Accounts Receivable account. Receivables typically hold only 5 items, as follows (amounts assumed):

Accounts Receivable			
Beg. balance (left over from last period)	200	Write-offs of uncollectibles	100**
Sales (or service) revenue	1,800*	Collections from customers	X = 1,500†
End. balance (carries over to next period)	400		

*The journal entry that places revenue into the receivable account is

Accounts Receivable	1,800	
Sales (or Service) Revenue		1,800

**The journal entry for write-offs is

Allowance for Uncollectibles	100	
Accounts Receivable		100

†The journal entry that places collections into the receivable account is

Cash	1,500	
Accounts Receivable		1,500

Suppose you know all these amounts expect collections from customers. You can compute collections by solving for X in the T-account.[1] Often write-offs are unknown and must be omitted. Then the computation of collections becomes an approximation.

Pages 279–285 intentionally omitted

REVIEW RECEIVABLES AND INVESTMENTS

Quick Check (Answers are given on page 308.)

1. **Harvey Penick Golf Academy** held trading investments valued at $55,000 at December 31, 2008. These investments cost Penick $50,000. What is the appropriate amount for Penick to report for these investments on the December 31, 2008, balance sheet?

   a. $50,000

   b. $55,000

   c. $5,000 gain

   d. Cannot be determined from the data given

2. Return to Harvey Penick Golf Academy in question 1. What should appear on the Penick income statement for the year ended December 31, 2008, for the trading investments?

   a. $50,000

   b. $55,000

   c. $5,000 unrealized gain

   d. Cannot be determined from the data given

Use the following information to answer questions 3–7.

Neal Company had the following information relating to credit sales in 20X3:

Accounts receivable 12/31/X3	$ 8,000
Allowance for uncollectible accounts 12/31/X3 (before adjustment)	750
Credit sales during 20X3	38,000
Cash sales during 20X3	12,000
Collections from customers on account during 20X3	41,000

3. Uncollectible accounts are determined by the percent-of-sales method to be 2% of credit sales. How much is uncollectible-account expense for 20X3?
   a. $750   c. $750
   b. $1,000   d. $10

4. Using the percent-of-sales method, what is the adjusted balance in the Allowance account at year end 20X3?
   a. $750   c. $1,750
   b. $760   d. $1,510

5. If uncollectible accounts are determined by the aging-of-receivables method to be $1,140, the uncollectible account expense for 20X3 would be:
   a. $390   c. $760
   b. $750   d. $1,140

6. Using the aging-of-receivables method, the balance of the Allowance account after the adjusting entry would be:
   a. $390   c. $760
   b. $750   d. $1,140

7. Assuming the aging-of-receivables method is used, the net realizable value of accounts receivable on the 12/31/X3 balance sheet would be:
   a. $6,110   c. $7,250
   b. $6,860   d. $8,000

8. Accounts Receivable has a debit balance of $2,300, and the Allowance for Uncollectible Accounts has a credit balance of $200. An $80 account receivable is written off. What is the amount of net receivables (net realizable value) after the write-off?
   a. $2,020   c. $2,180
   b. $2,100   d. $2,220

9. Ridgewood Corporation began 20X1 with Accounts Receivable of $500,000. Sales for the year totaled $2,000,000. Ridgewood ended the year with accounts receivable of $600,000. Ridgewood's bad-debt losses are minimal. How much cash did Ridgewood collect from customers in 20X1?
   a. $1,900,000   c. $2,000,000
   b. $1,940,000   d. $2,600,000

10. Saturn Company received a 2-month, 8%, $1,500 note receivable on December 1. The adjusting entry on December 31 will:
    a. debit Interest Receivable $10
    b. credit Interest Revenue $10
    c. Both a and b
    d. credit Interest Revenue $120

11. What is the maturity value of a $30,000, 10%, 6-month note?
    a. $25,000   c. $31,500
    b. $30,000   d. $33,000

12. If the adjusting entry to accrue interest on a note receivable is omitted, then:
    a. assets, net income, and stockholders' equity are overstated.
    b. assets, net income, and stockholders' equity are understated.
    c. liabilities are understated, net income is overstated, and stockholders' equity is overstated.
    d. assets are overstated, net income is understated, and stockholders' equity is understated.

13. Net sales total $730,000. Beginning and ending accounts receivable are $62,000 and $58,000, respectively. Calculate days' sales in receivables.
 a. 32 days   c. 43 days
 b. 23 days   d. 30 days
14. From the following list of accounts, calculate the quick ratio.

Cash	$ 3,000	Accounts payable	$ 8,000
Accounts receivable	6,000	Salary payable	3,000
Inventory	10,000	Notes payable (due in 2 years)	8,000
Prepaid insurance	2,000	Short-term investments	2,000

 a. 2.1   c. 1.0
 b. 1.3   d. 1.4

Accounting Vocabulary

acid-test ratio (p. 284) Ratio of the sum of cash plus short-term investments plus net current receivables to total current liabilities. Tells whether the entity can pay all its current liabilities if they come due immediately. Also called the *quick ratio*.

accounts receivable turnover (p. 284) Net sales divided by average net accounts receivable.

aging-of-accounts receivable (p. 271) A way to estimate bad debts by analyzing individual accounts receivable according to the length of time they have been receivable from the customer.

Allowance for Doubtful Accounts (p. 271) Another name for *Allowance for Uncollectible Accounts*.

Allowance for Uncollectible Accounts (p. 271) A contra account, related to accounts receivable, that holds the estimated amount of collection losses. Another name for *Allowance for Doubtful Accounts*.

allowance method (p. 271) A method of recording collection losses based on estimates of how much money the business will not collect from its customers.

bad-debt expense (p. 271) Another name for *uncollectible-account expense*.

creditor (p. 278) The party to whom money is owed.

days' sales in receivables (p. 283) Ratio of average net accounts receivable to one day's sales. Indicates how many days' sales remain in Accounts Receivable awaiting collection. Also called the *collection period*.

debtor (p. 278) The party who owes money.

direct write-off method (p. 277) A method of accounting for bad debts in which the company waits until a customer's account receivable proves uncollectible and then debits Uncollectible-Account Expense and credits the customer's Account Receivable.

doubtful-account expense (p. 271) Another name for *uncollectible-account expense*.

interest (p. 278) The borrower's cost of renting money from a lender. Interest is revenue for the lender and expense for the borrower.

marketable securities (p. 262) Another name for *short-term investments*.

maturity (p. 278) The date on which a debt instrument must be paid.

percent-of-sales method (p. 273) Computes uncollectible-account expense as a percentage of net sales. Also called the income statement approach because it focuses on the amount of expense to be reported on the income statement.

principal (p. 278) The amount borrowed by a debtor and lent by a creditor.

quick ratio (p. 284) Another name for *acid-test ratio*.

receivables (p. 268) Monetary claims against a business or an individual, acquired mainly by selling goods or services and by lending money.

short-term investments (p. 262) Investments that a company plans to hold for one year or less. Also called *marketable securities*.

term (p. 278) The length of time from inception to maturity.

trading investments (p. 263) Stock investments that are to be sold in the near future with the intent of generating profits on the sale.

uncollectible-account expense (p. 271) Cost to the seller of extending credit. Arises from the failure to collect from credit customers. Also called doubtful-account expense or bad-debt expense.

ASSESS YOUR PROGRESS

S5-5 (*Learning Objective 3: Applying the allowance method (percent-of-sales) to account for uncollectibles*) During its first year of operations, Scottish Products, Inc., had sales of $900,000, all on account. Industry experience suggests that Scottish Products' uncollectibles will amount to 2% of credit sales. At December 31, 20X4, Scottish Products' accounts receivable total $80,000. The company uses the allowance method to account for uncollectibles.

writing assignment ■

1. Make Scottish Products' journal entry for uncollectible-account expense using the percent-of-sales method. (p. 273)

2. Show how Scottish Products should report accounts receivable on its balance sheet at December 31, 20X4. Follow the reporting format illustrated in the middle of page 272.

S5-6 (*Learning Objective 3: Applying the allowance method (percent-of-sales) to account for uncollectibles*) This exercise continues the situation of Short Exercise S5-5, in which Scottish Products ended the year 20X4 with accounts receivable of $80,000 and an allowance for uncollectible accounts of $18,000. During 20X5, Scottish Products completed the following transactions:

1. Credit sales, $1,000,000 (p. 271)

2. Collections on account, $880,000. (p. 271)

3. Write-offs of uncollectibles, $16,000 (p. 275)

4. Uncollectible-account expense, 1.5% of credit sales (p. 273)

Journalize the 20X5 transactions for Scottish Products. Explanations are not required.

Pages 290–292 intentionally omitted

E5-19 (*Learning Objective 2: Controlling cash receipts from customers*) As a recent college graduate, you land your first job in the customer collections department of Backroads Publishing. Shawn Dugan, the manager, asked you to propose a system to ensure that cash received from customers by mail is handled properly. Draft a short memorandum to explain the essential element in your proposed plan. State why this element is important. Refer to Chapter 4 if necessary. (p. 269)

E5-20 (*Learning Objective 3: Reporting bad debts by the allowance method*) At December 31, 20X8, Delaware Valley Nissan has an accounts receivable balance of $101,000. Allowance for Doubtful Accounts has a credit balance of $2,000 before the year-end adjustment. Service revenue for 20X8 was $800,000. Delaware Valley estimates that doubtful-account expense for the year is 1% of sales. Make the December 31 entry to record doubtful-account expense. Show how the accounts receivable and the allowance for doubtful accounts are reported on the balance sheet. Use the reporting format of PepsiCo on page 262.

Pages 294 and 296–308 intentionally omitted

E5-29 *(Learning Objective 5: Analyzing a company's financial statements)* **Best Buy Co., Inc.**, the electronics and appliance chain, reported these figures in millions of dollars:

	2006	2005
Net sales..	$30,848	$27,433
Receivables at end of year	506	375

❙ Required

1. Compute Best Buy's average collection period during 2006. (p. 283)

2. Is Best Buy's collection period long or short? **Hewlett Packard** takes 41 days to collect its average level of receivables. **FedEx**, the overnight shipper, takes 38 days. What causes Best Buy's collection period to be so different? (Challenge)

This page intentionally left blank

6 Inventory & Cost of Goods Sold

SPOTLIGHT

PIER 1 IMPORTS

You've just graduated from college, taken a job, and you're moving into an apartment. The place is unfurnished, so you'll need a sofa, a table, and a few chairs. Where will you find these things? Pier 1 Imports may get some of your business.

Pier 1 is known for featuring stylish home furnishings at popular prices–just about right for a new graduate. The company operates 1,100 stores in the U.S., plus 43 Pier 1 Kids stores that sell children's furniture and accessories.

Pier 1's balance sheet is summarized here. You can see that the merchandise inventory (labeled simply as Inventories) is Pier 1's largest asset. That's not surprising since Pier 1, like other retailers, attracts customers with goods that they can purchase and take home immediately.

Pages 310–316 intentionally omitted

INVENTORY COSTING

Inventory is the first asset for which a manager can decide which accounting method to use. The accounting method selected affects the profits to be reported, the amount of income tax to be paid, and the values of the ratios derived from the balance sheet.

What Goes into Inventory Cost?

The cost of inventory on Pier 1's balance sheet represents all the costs that Pier 1 incurred to bring its inventory to the point of sale. The following cost principle applies to all assets:

> **The cost of any asset, such as inventory, is the sum of all the costs incurred to bring the asset to its intended use, less any discounts.**

As we have seen, inventory's cost includes its basic purchase price, plus freight-in, insurance while in transit, and any fees or taxes paid to get the inventory ready to sell, less returns, allowances, and discounts.

After a Pier 1 chair is sitting in the showroom, other costs, such as advertising and sales commissions, are *not* included as the cost of inventory. Advertising, sales commissions, and delivery costs are expenses.

The Various Inventory Costing Methods

OBJECTIVE

2 Understand the various inventory methods

Determining the cost of inventory is easy when the unit cost remains constant, as in Exhibit 6-2. But the unit cost usually changes. For example, prices often rise. The desk lamp that cost Pier 1 $10 in January may cost $14 in June and $18 in October. Suppose Pier 1 sells 1,000 lamps in November. How many of those lamps cost $10, how many cost $14, and how many cost $18?

To compute cost of goods sold and the cost of ending inventory still on hand, we must assign unit cost to the items. Accounting uses 4 generally accepted inventory methods:

1. **Specific unit cost**
2. **Average cost**
3. **First-in, first-out (FIFO) cost**
4. **Last-in, first-out (LIFO) cost**

A company can use any of these methods. The methods can have very different effects on reported profits, income taxes, and cash flow. Therefore, companies select their inventory method with great care.

Specific Unit Cost. Some businesses deal in unique inventory items, such as automobiles, antique furniture, jewels, and real estate. These businesses cost their inventories at the specific cost of the particular unit. For instance, a Toyota dealer may have 2 vehicles in the showroom—a "stripped-down" model that cost the dealer $19,000 and a "loaded" model that cost the dealer $24,000. If the dealer sells the loaded model, the cost of goods sold is $24,000. The stripped-down auto will be the only unit left in inventory, and so ending inventory is $19,000.

The **specific-unit-cost method** is also called the *specific identification method.* This method is too expensive to use for inventory items that have common characteristics, such as bushels of wheat, gallons of paint, or auto tires.

The other inventory accounting methods—average, FIFO, and LIFO—are fundamentally different. These other methods do not use the specific cost of a particular unit. Instead, they assume different flows of inventory costs. To illustrate average, FIFO, and LIFO costing, we use a common set of data, given in Exhibit 6-6.

EXHIBIT 6-6	Inventory Data Used to Illustrate the Various Inventory Costing Methods

Inventory				
Begin. bal.	(10 units @ $10)	100		
Purchases:			Cost of goods sold	
No. 1	(25 units @ $14)	350	(40 units @ ?)	?
No. 2	(25 units @ $18)	450		
Ending balance	(20 units @ ?)	?		

In Exhibit 6-6, Pier 1 began the period with 10 lamps that cost $10 each; the beginning inventory was therefore $100. During the period Pier 1 bought 50 more lamps, sold 40 lamps, and ended the period with 20 lamps, summarized in the T-account as follows:

Goods Available		Number of Units	Total Cost
Goods available	=	10 + 25 + 25 = 60 units	$100 + $350 + $450 = $900
Cost of goods sold	=	40 units	?
Ending inventory	=	20 units	?

The big accounting questions are

1. What is the cost of goods sold for the income statement?
2. What is the cost of the ending inventory for the balance sheet?

It all depends on which inventory method Pier 1 uses. Pier 1 actually uses the average-cost method, so let's look at average costing first.

Average Cost. The **average-cost method**, sometimes called the *weighted-average method*, is based on the average cost of inventory during the period. Average cost per unit is determined as follows (data from Exhibit 6-6):

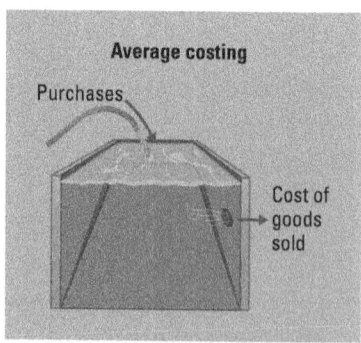

$$\text{Average cost per unit} = \frac{\text{Cost of goods available*}}{\text{Number of units available*}} = \frac{\$900}{60} = \$15$$

*Goods available = Beginning inventory + Purchases

Cost of goods sold =	Number of units sold	× Average cost per unit	
=	40 units	× $15	= $600

Ending inventory =	Number of units on hand	× Average cost per unit	
=	20 units	× $15	= $300

The following T-account shows the effects of average costing:

Inventory (at Average Cost)

Begin. bal.	(10 units @ $10)	100		
Purchases:				
No. 1	(25 units @ $14)	350		
No. 2	(25 units @ $18)	450	Cost of goods sold (40 units	
			@ average cost of $15 per unit)	600
Ending balance	(20 units @ average			
	cost of $15 per unit)	300		

FIFO Cost. Under the FIFO method, the first costs into inventory are the first costs assigned to cost of goods sold—hence, the name *first-in, first-out*. The diagram near the bottom of the page shows the effect of FIFO costing. The following T-account shows how to compute FIFO cost of goods sold and ending inventory for the Pier 1 lamps (data from Exhibit 6-6):

Inventory (at FIFO cost)

Begin. bal.	(10 units @ $10)	100			
Purchases:			Cost of goods sold (40 units):		
No. 1	(25 units @ $14)	350	(10 units @ $10)	100	
No. 2	(25 units @ $18)	450	(25 units @ $14)	350	} 540
			(5 units @ $18)	90	
Ending bal.	(20 units @ $18)	360			

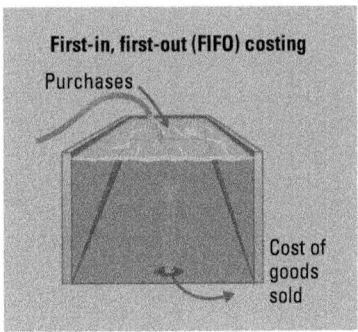

First-in, first-out (FIFO) costing

Purchases

Cost of goods sold

Under FIFO, the cost of ending inventory is always based on the latest costs incurred—in this case $18 per unit.

LIFO Cost. LIFO costing is the opposite of FIFO. Under LIFO, the last costs into inventory go immediately to cost of goods sold, as shown in the diagram. Compare LIFO and FIFO, and you will see a vast difference.

The following T-account shows how to compute the LIFO inventory amounts for the Pier 1 lamps (data from Exhibit 6-6).

Inventory (at LIFO cost)						
Begin. bal.	(10 units @ $10)	100				
Purchases:			Cost of goods sold (40 units):			
No. 1	(25 units @ $14)	350	(25 units @ $18)	450	}	660
No. 2	(25 units @ $18)	450	(15 units @ $14)	210		
Ending bal.	(10 units @ $10)	} 240				
	(10 units @ $14)					

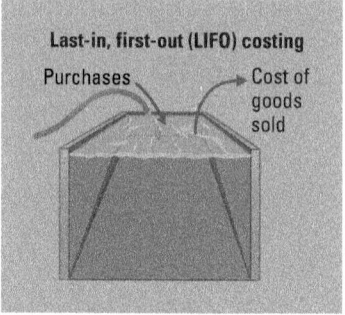

Under LIFO, the cost of ending inventory is always based on the oldest costs—from beginning inventory plus the early purchases of the period—$10 and $14 per unit.

The Effects of FIFO, LIFO and Average Cost on Cost of Goods Sold, Gross Profit, and Ending Inventory

In our Pier 1 example, the cost of inventory rose from $10 to $14 to $18. When inventory unit costs change this way, the various inventory methods produce different cost-of-goods sold figures. Exhibit 6-7 summarizes the income effects (sales – cost of goods sold = gross profit) of the 3 inventory methods (remember that prices are rising). Study Exhibit 6-7 carefully, focusing on cost of goods sold and gross profit.

EXHIBIT 6-7 Income Effects of the FIFO, LIFO, and Average Inventory Methods

	FIFO	LIFO	Average
Sales revenue (assumed)	$1,000	$1,000	$1,000
Cost of goods sold.......................	540 (lowest)	660 (highest)	600
Gross profit.................................	$ 460 (highest)	$ 340 (lowest)	$ 400

Exhibit 6-8 graphs the flow of costs under FIFO and LIFO during both increasing costs (Panel A) and decreasing costs (Panel B). Study this exhibit carefully; it will help you *really* understand FIFO and LIFO.

EXHIBIT 6-8 Cost of Goods Sold and Ending Inventory— FIFO and LIFO; Increasing Costs and Decreasing Costs

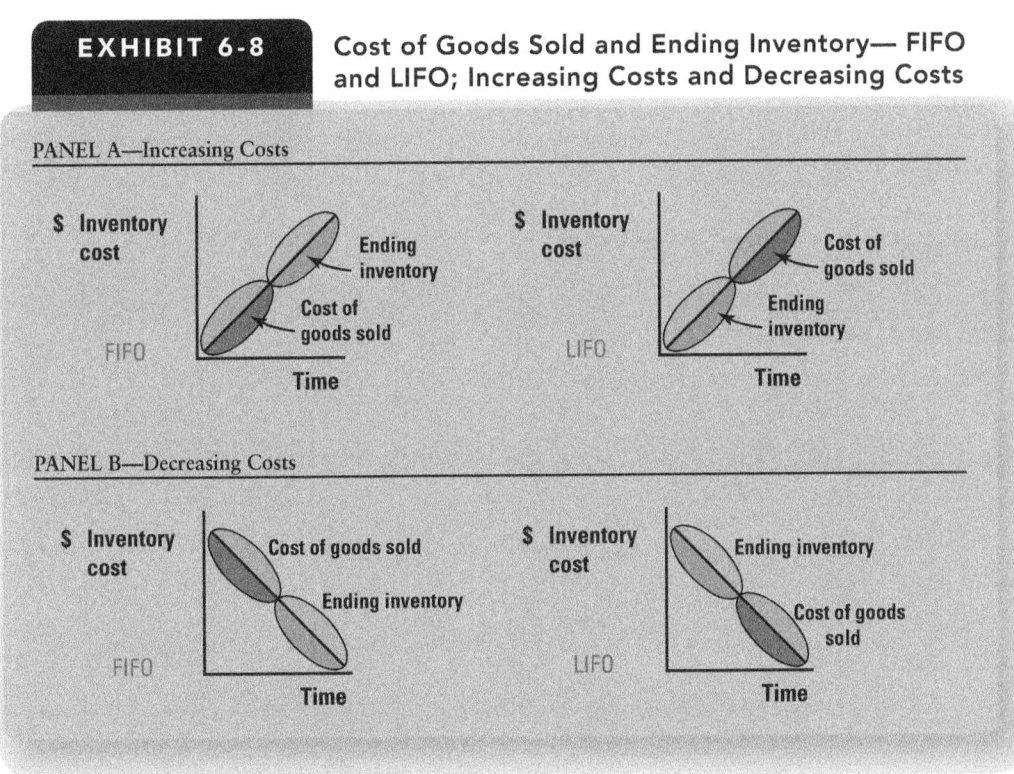

When inventory costs are increasing,

	Cost of Goods Sold (COGS)	Ending Inventory (EI)
FIFO	FIFO COGS is lowest because it's based on the oldest costs, which are low. Gross profit is, therefore, the highest.	FIFO EI is highest because it's based on the most recent costs, which are high.
LIFO	LIFO COGS is highest because it's based on the most recent costs, which are high. Gross profit is, therefore, the lowest.	LIFO EI is lowest because it's based on the oldest costs, which are low.

When inventory costs are decreasing,

	Cost of Goods Sold (COGS)	Ending Inventory (EI)
FIFO	FIFO COGS is highest because it's based on the oldest costs, which are high. Gross profit is, therefore, the lowest.	FIFO EI is lowest because it's based on the most recent costs, which are low.
LIFO	LIFO COGS is lowest because it's based on the most recent costs, which are low. Gross profit is, therefore, the highest.	LIFO EI is highest because it's based on the oldest costs, which are high.

Financial analysts search the stock markets for companies with good prospects for income growth. Analysts sometimes need to compare the net income of a company that uses LIFO with the net income of a company that uses FIFO. Appendix 6B, pages 365–366, shows how to convert a LIFO company's net income to the FIFO basis in order to compare the 2 companies.

The Tax Advantage of LIFO

Inventory methods directly affect income taxes, which must be paid in cash. When prices are rising, LIFO results in the *lowest taxable income* and thus the *lowest income taxes*. Let's use the gross profit data of Exhibit 6-7 to illustrate.

	FIFO	LIFO
Gross profit (from Exhibit 6-7)..............	$460	$340
Operating expenses (assumed)................	260	260
Income before income tax......................	$200	$ 80
Income tax expense (40%)....................	$ 80	$ 32

Income tax expense is lowest under LIFO ($32). **This is the most attractive feature of LIFO—low income tax payments**, which is why about one-third of all companies use LIFO. During periods of inflation, many companies switch to LIFO for its tax and cash-flow advantage. Exhibit 6-9, based on an American Institute of Certified Public Accountants (AICPA) survey of 600 companies, indicates that FIFO remains the most popular inventory method.

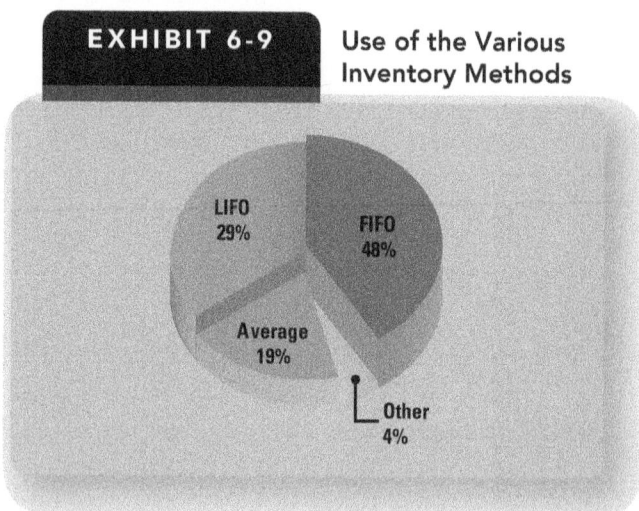

EXHIBIT 6-9   Use of the Various Inventory Methods

LIFO 29%

FIFO 48%

Average 19%

Other 4%

Comparison of the Inventory Methods

Let's compare the average, FIFO, and LIFO inventory methods.

1. Measuring Cost of Goods Sold. How well does each method match inventory expense—cost of goods sold—against revenue? LIFO results in the most realistic net income figure because LIFO assigns the most recent inventory costs to expense. In contrast, FIFO matches old inventory costs against revenue—a poor measure of expense. FIFO income is therefore less realistic than LIFO income.

2. Measuring Ending Inventory. Which method reports the most up-to-date inventory cost on the balance sheet? FIFO. LIFO can value inventory at very old costs because LIFO leaves the oldest prices in ending inventory.

LIFO and Managing Reported Income. LIFO allows managers to manipulate net income by timing their purchases of inventory. When inventory prices are rising rapidly and a company wants to show less income (in order to pay less taxes), managers can buy a large amount of inventory near the end of the year. Under LIFO, these high inventory costs go straight to cost of goods sold. As a result, net income is decreased.

If the business is having a bad year, management may wish to report higher income. The company can delay the purchase of high-cost inventory until next year. This avoids decreasing current-year income. In the process, the company draws down inventory quantities, a practice known as *LIFO inventory liquidation*.

LIFO Liquidation. When LIFO is used and inventory quantities fall below the level of the previous period, the situation is called a *LIFO liquidation*. To compute cost of goods sold, the company must dip into older layers of inventory cost. Under LIFO, and when prices are rising, that action shifts older, lower costs into cost of goods sold. The result is higher net income. Managers try to avoid a LIFO liquidation because it increases income taxes.

International Perspective. Many U.S. companies that use LIFO must use another method in foreign countries. Why? LIFO is not allowed in Australia, the United Kingdom, and some other British commonwealth countries. Virtually all countries permit FIFO and the average cost method.

HH CHAPTER 6

MID-CHAPTER SUMMARY PROBLEM

Suppose a division of **Texas Instruments** that handles computer microchips has these inventory records for January 20X9:

Date	Item	Quantity	Unit Cost	Total cost
Jan. 1	Beginning inventory	100 units	$ 8	$ 800
6	Purchase	60 units	9	540
21	Purchase	150 units	9	1,350
27	Purchase	90 units	10	900

Company accounting records show sales of 310 units for revenue of $6,770. Operating expense for January was $1,900.

I *Required*

1. Prepare the January income statement, showing amounts for FIFO, LIFO, and average cost. Label the bottom line "Operating income." Round average cost per unit to 3 decimal places and all other figures to whole-dollar amounts. Show your computations.

2. Suppose you are the financial vice president of Texas Instruments. Which inventory method will you use if your motive is to
   a. Minimize income taxes?
   b. Report the highest operating income?
   c. Report operating income between the extremes of FIFO and LIFO?
   d. Report inventory on the balance sheet at the most current cost?
   e. Attain the best measure of net income for the income statement?
   State the reason for each of your answers.

Answers

▌Requirement 1

Texas Instruments Incorporated
Income Statement for Microchip
Month Ended January 31, 20X9

	FIFO	LIFO	Average
Sales revenue..........................	$6,770	$6,770	$6,770
Cost of goods sold................	2,870	2,782	2,690
Gross profit..........................	3,900	3,988	4,080
Operating expenses	1,900	1,900	1,900
Operating income.................	$2,000	$2,088	$2,180

Cost of goods sold computations:
FIFO: (100 @ $8) + (60 @ $9) + (150 @ $9) = $2,690
LIFO: (90 @ $10) + (150 @ $9) + (60 @ $9) + (10 @ $8) = $2,870
Average: 310 × $8.975* = $2,782

$$^*\frac{(\$800 + \$540 + \$1,350 + \$900)}{(100 + 60 + 150 + 90)} = \$8.975$$

▌Requirement 2

a. Use LIFO to minimize income taxes. Operating income under LIFO is lowest when inventory unit costs are increasing, as they are in this case (from $8 to $10). (If inventory costs were decreasing, income under FIFO would be lowest.)
b. Use FIFO to report the highest operating income. Income under FIFO is highest when inventory unit costs are increasing, as in this situation.
c. Use the average cost method to report an operating income amount between the FIFO and LIFO extremes. This is true in this situation and in others when inventory unit costs are increasing or decreasing.
d. Use FIFO to report inventory on the balance sheet at the most current cost. The oldest inventory costs are expensed as cost of goods sold, leaving in ending inventory the most recent (most current) costs of the period.
e. Use LIFO to attain the best measure of net income. LIFO produces the best matching of current expense with current revenue. The most recent (most current) inventory costs are expensed as cost of goods sold.

ACCOUNTING PRINCIPLES RELATED TO INVENTORY

Several accounting principles have special relevance to inventories:

- Consistency
- Disclosure
- Conservatism

Consistency Principle

The **consistency principle** states that businesses should use the same accounting methods and procedures from period to period. Consistency enables investors to compare a company's financial statements from one period to the next.

Suppose you are analyzing Interfax Corporation's net income pattern over a 2-year period. Interfax switched from LIFO to FIFO during that time. Its net income increased dramatically but only because of the change in inventory method. If you did not know of the accounting change, you might believe that Interfax's income increased due to improved operations, but that's not the case.

The consistency principle does not mean that a company is not permitted to change its accounting methods. However, a company making an accounting change must disclose the effect of the change on net income. American-Saudi Oil Company, Inc., disclosed the following in a note to its annual report:

> **EXCERPT FROM NOTE 6 OF THE FINANCIAL STATEMENTS**
> . . . American-Saudi changed its method of accounting for the cost of crude oil . . . from the FIFO method to the LIFO method. The company believes that the LIFO method better matches current costs with current revenues. . . . The change decreased the Company's 2007 net income . . . by $3 million. . . .

Disclosure Principle

The **disclosure principle** holds that a company's financial statements should report enough information for outsiders to make informed decisions about the company. The company should report *relevant*, *reliable*, and *comparable* information about itself. That means disclosing inventory accounting methods. Without knowledge of the accounting method, a banker could make an unwise lending decision. Suppose the banker is comparing two companies—one using LIFO and the other, FIFO. The FIFO company reports higher net income but only because it uses FIFO. Without knowing this, the banker could loan money to the wrong business.

Accounting Conservatism

Conservatism in accounting means reporting financial statement amounts that paint the gloomiest immediate picture of the company. What advantage does conservatism give a business? Many accountants regard conservatism as a brake on management's optimistic tendencies. The goal of accounting conservatism is to present reliable data.

Conservatism appears in accounting guidelines such as "anticipate no gains, but provide for all probable losses" and "if in doubt, record an asset at the lowest reasonable amount and report a liability at the highest reasonable amount." Conservatism directs accountants to decrease the accounting value of an asset if it appears unrealistically high. Assume that **Texas Instruments** paid $35,000 for inventory that has become outdated and whose current value is only $12,000. Conservatism dictates that Texas Instruments must record a $23,000 loss immediately and write the inventory down to $12,000.

Lower-of-Cost-or-Market Rule

The **lower-of-cost-or-market rule** (abbreviated as **LCM**) is based on accounting conservatism. LCM requires that inventory be reported in the financial statements at whichever is lower—the inventory's historical cost or its market value. Applied to inventories, *market value* generally means *current replacement cost* (that is, how much the business would have to pay now to replace its inventory). If the replacement cost of inventory falls below its historical cost, the business must write down the value of its goods to market value. **The business reports ending inventory at its LCM value on the balance sheet**. All this can be done automatically by a computerized accounting system. How is the write-down accomplished?

Suppose Pier 1 Imports paid $3,000 for inventory on September 26. By December 31, the inventory can be replaced for $2,000. Pier 1's December 31 balance sheet must report this inventory at LCM value of $2,000. Exhibit 6-10 presents the effects of LCM on the balance sheet and the income statement. Before any LCM effect, cost of goods sold is $9,000. An LCM write-down decreases Inventory and increases Cost of Goods Sold, as follows:

Cost of Goods Sold	1,000	
Inventory		1,000
Wrote inventory down to market value.		

EXHIBIT 6-10   Lower-of-Cost-or-Market (LCM) Effects on Inventory and Cost of Goods Sold

Balance Sheet

Current assets:

Cash	$ XXX
Short-term investments	XXX
Accounts receivable	XXX
Inventories, at market	
(which is lower than $3,000 cost)	2,000
Prepaid expenses	XXX
Total current assets	$X,XXX

Income Statement

Sales revenue	$21,000
Cost of goods sold ($9,000 + $1,000)	10,000
Gross profit	$11,000

If the market value of Pier 1's inventory had been above cost, Pier 1 would have made no adjustment for LCM. In that case, simply report the inventory at cost, which is the lower of cost or market.

Companies disclose LCM in notes to their financial statements, as shown on the following page for Pier 1 Imports:

NOTE 1: ACCOUNTING POLICIES
■ *Inventories.* Inventories are . . . stated at the *lower of average cost* or *market.* [Emphasis added.]

LCM is not optional. It is required by GAAP.

INVENTORY AND THE FINANCIAL STATEMENTS

Detailed Income Statement

Exhibit 6-11 provides an example of a detailed income statement, complete with all the discounts and expenses in their proper places. Study it carefully.

EXHIBIT 6-11 Detailed Income Statment

New Jersey Technology, Inc.
Income Statement
Year Ended December 31, 20X7

Sales revenue	$100,000	
Less: Sales discounts	(2,000)	
Sales returns and allowances	(3,000)	
Net sales		$95,000*
Cost of goods sold		45,000
Gross profit		50,000
Operating expenses:		
Selling:		
Sales commission expense	$ 5,000	
Freight-out (delivery expense)	1,000	
Other expenses (detailed)	6,000	12,000
Administrative:		
Salary expense	$ 2,000	
Depreciation expense	2,000	
Other expenses (detailed)	4,000	8,000
Income before income tax		30,000
Income tax expense (40%)		12,000
Net income		$18,000

*Most companies report only the net sales figure, $95,000.

Analyzing Financial Statements

Owners, managers, and investors use ratios to evaluate a business. Two ratios relate directly to inventory: gross profit percentage and the rate of inventory turnover.

OBJECTIVE

3 **Use** gross profit percentage and inventory turnover to evaluate operations

Gross Profit Percentage. Gross profit—sales minus cost of goods sold—is a key indicator of a company's ability to sell inventory at a profit. Merchandisers strive to increase **gross profit percentage**, also called the *gross margin percentage.* Gross profit percentage is markup stated as a percentage of sales. Gross profit percentage is computed as follows for Pier 1 Imports. Data (in millions) for 2006 are taken from Exhibit 6-3, page 313.

$$\text{Gross profit percentage} = \frac{\text{Gross profit}}{\text{Net sales revenue}} = \frac{\$602}{\$1,777} = 0.339 = 33.9\%$$

The gross profit percentage is watched carefully by managers and investors. A 33.9% gross margin means that each dollar of sales generates about 34 cents of gross profit. On average, cost of goods sold consumes 66 cents of each sales dollar for Pier 1. For most firms, the gross profit percentage changes little from year to year, so a small downturn may signal trouble.[1]

Pier 1's gross profit percentage of 34% is similar to that of Home Depot (33%), but much lower than the gross profit percentage of Federated Department Stores (40.6%). Exhibit 6-12 graphs the gross profit percentages for these 3 companies.

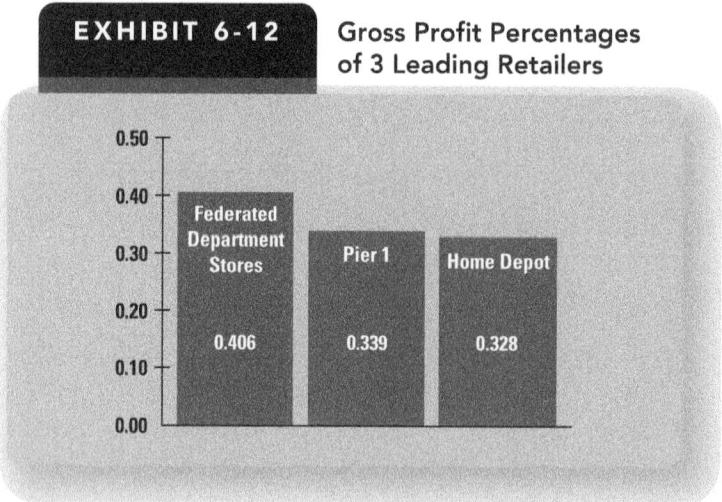

EXHIBIT 6-12 Gross Profit Percentages of 3 Leading Retailers

Inventory Turnover. Pier 1 Imports strives to sell its inventory as quickly as possible because the goods generate no profit until they're sold. The faster the sales, the higher the income, and vice versa for slow-moving goods. Ideally, a business could operate with zero inventory, but most businesses, especially retailers, must keep some goods on hand. **Inventory turnover**, the ratio of cost of goods sold to average inventory, indicates how rapidly inventory is sold. The 2006 computation for Pier 1 Imports follows (data in millions from Exhibit 6-3, page 313):

$$\text{Inventory turnover} = \frac{\text{Cost of goods sold}}{\text{Average inventory}} = \frac{\text{Cost of goods sold}}{\left(\begin{array}{c}\text{Beginning} \\ \text{inventory}\end{array} + \begin{array}{c}\text{Ending} \\ \text{inventory}\end{array}\right) \div 2}$$

$$= \frac{\$1,175}{(\$369 + \$366)/2} = \begin{array}{c}\text{3.2 times per year} \\ \text{(every 114 days)}\end{array}$$

The inventory turnover statistic shows how many times the company sold (or turned over) its average level of inventory during the year. Inventory turnover varies from industry to industry.

Exhibit 6-13 graphs the rates of inventory turnover for the same 3 companies. Let's compare Pier 1 and Home Depot because their gross profit percentages are so similar. You can see that Home Depot turns inventory over much faster than Pier 1. As a

---

[1]Recall from the chapter-opening story that Pier 1 had a net loss in 2006. The loss may have resulted from a declining gross profit percentage. As recently as 2003, Pier 1's gross profit percentage was 43%.

result, Home Depot is much more profitable than Pier 1. Federated Department Stores sells its inventory more slowly because Federated stores (Macy's and Bloomingdale's) sell more expensive goods that take longer to sell.

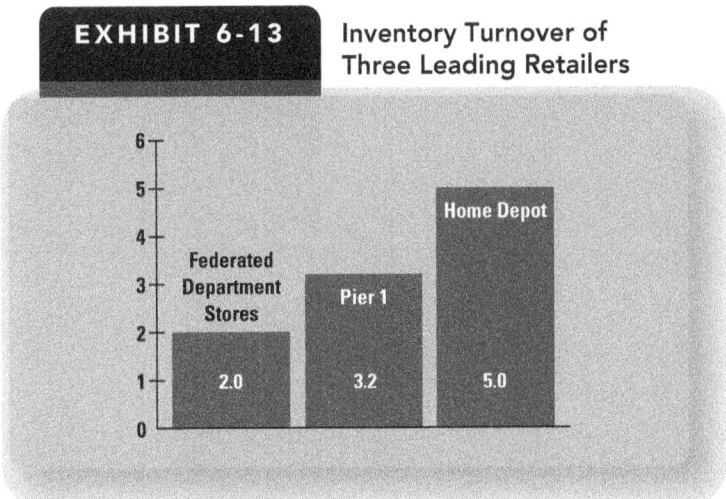

EXHIBIT 6-13 Inventory Turnover of Three Leading Retailers

STOP & think. . .

Examine Exhibits 6-12 and 6-13. What do those ratio values say about the merchandising (pricing) strategies of Federated Department Stores and Home Depot?

Answer:
It's obvious that Federated sells high-end merchandise. Federated's gross profit percentage is much higher than Home Depot's. Home Depot has a much faster rate of inventory turnover. The lower the price, the faster the turnover, and vice versa.

Pages 330–332 intentionally omitted

DECISION GUIDELINES

ACCOUNTING FOR INVENTORY

Suppose a Pier 1 store stocks 2 basic categories of merchandise:

- Furniture pieces, such as tables and chairs
- Small items of low value, near the checkout stations, such as cupholders and breath mints

    Jacob Stiles, the store manager, is considering how accounting will affect the business. Let's examine several decisions Stiles must make to properly account for the store's inventory.

Decision	Guidelines	System or Method
Which inventory system to use?	• Expensive merchandise • Cannot control inventory by visual inspection	→ Perpetual system for the furniture
	• Can control inventory by visual inspection	→ Periodic system for the small, low-value items
Which costing method to use?	• Unique inventory items	→ Specific unit cost for art objects because they are unique
	• Most current cost of ending inventory • Maximizes reported income when costs are rising	→ FIFO
	• Most current measure of cost of goods sold and net income • Minimizes income tax when costs are rising	→ LIFO
	• Middle-of-the-road approach for income tax and reported income	→ Average

HH CHAPTER 6

END-OF-CHAPTER SUMMARY PROBLEM

Town & Country Gift Ideas began 20X6 with 60,000 units of inventory that cost $36,000. During 20X6, Town & Country purchased merchandise on account for $352,500 as follows:

Purchase 1	(100,000 units costing)	$ 65,000
Purchase 2	(270,000 units costing)	175,500
Purchase 3	(160,000 units costing)	112,000

Cash payments on account totaled $326,000 during the year.

Town & Country's sales during 20X6 consisted of 520,000 units of inventory for $660,000, all on account. The company uses the FIFO inventory method.

Cash collections from customers were $630,000. Operating expenses totaled $240,500, of which Town & Country paid $211,000 in cash. Town & Country credited Accrued Liabilities for the remainder. At December 31, Town & Country accrued income tax expense at the rate of 35% of income before tax.

I Required

1. Make summary journal entries to record Town & Country's transactions for the year, assuming the company uses a perpetual inventory system.
2. Determine the FIFO cost of Town & Country's ending inventory at December 31, 20X6 2 ways:
   a. Use a T-account.
   b. Multiply the number of units on hand by the unit cost.
3. Show how Town & Country would compute cost of goods sold for 20X6. Follow the FIFO example on page 319.
4. Prepare Town & Country's income statement for 20X6. Show totals for the gross profit and income before tax.
5. Determine Town & Country's gross profit percentage, rate of inventory turnover, and net income as a percentage of sales for the year. In Town & Country's industry, a gross profit percentage of 40%, an inventory turnover of 6 times per year, and a net income percentage of 7% are considered excellent. How well does Town & Country compare to these industry averages?

Answers

I Requirement 1

Inventory ($65,000 + $175,500 + $112,000)	$352,500	
Accounts Payable		352,500
Accounts Payable	326,000	
Cash		326,000
Accounts Receivable	660,000	
Sales Revenue		660,000
Cost of Goods Sold (see Requirement 3)	339,500	
Inventory		339,500
Cash	630,000	
Accounts Receivable		630,000
Operating Expenses	240,500	
Cash		211,000
Accrued Liabilities		29,500
Income Tax Expense (see Requirement 4)	28,000	
Income Tax Payable		28,000

Requirement 2

Inventory			
Beginning bal.	36,000		
Purchases	352,500	Cost of goods sold	339,500
Ending bal.	49,000		

Number of units in ending inventory (60,000 + 100,000 + 270,000 + 160,000 − 520,000)		70,000
Unit cost of ending inventory at FIFO ($112,000 ÷ 160,000 from Purchase 3).....	×	$ 0.70
FIFO cost of ending inventory.......................		$49,000

Requirement 3

Cost of goods sold (520,000 units):	
60,000 units costing..	$ 36,000
100,000 units costing..	65,000
270,000 units costing..	175,500
90,000 units costing $0.70 each*.................................	63,000
Cost of goods sold..	$339,500

*From Purchase 3: $112,000/160,000 units = $0.70 per unit.

Requirement 4

Town & Country Gift Ideas
Income Statement
Year Ended December 31, 20X6

Sales revenue	$660,000
Cost of goods sold...	339,500
Gross profit...	320,500
Operating expenses	240,500
Income before tax	80,000
Income tax expense (35%)..	28,000
Net income..	$ 52,000

Requirement 5

		Industry Average
Gross profit percentage:	$320,500 ÷ $660,000 = 48.6%	40%
Inventory turnover:	$\dfrac{\$339,500}{(\$36,000 + \$49,000)/2} = 8$ times	6 times
Net income as a percent of sales:	$52,000 ÷ $660,000 = 7.9%	7%

Town & Country's statistics are better than the industry averages.

REVIEW INVENTORY & COST OF GOODS SOLD

Quick Check (Answers are given on page 360.)

1. Which statement is true?
   a. The Sales account is used to record only sales on account.
   b. The invoice is the purchaser's request for collection from the customer.
   c. Gross profit is the excess of sales revenue over cost of goods sold.
   d. A service company purchases products from suppliers and then sells them.

2. Sales discounts should appear in the financial statements:
   a. As an addition to inventory
   b. As an addition to sales
   c. As an operating expense
   d. Among the current liabilities
   e. As a deduction from sales

3. How is inventory classified in the financial statements?
   a. as an asset   d. as a revenue
   b. as a liability   e. as a contra account to Cost of Goods Sold
   c. as an expense

Questions 4–6 use the following data of Manatee, Inc.

	Units	Unit Cost	Total Cost	Units Sold
Beginning inventory	20	$6	$120	
Purchase on May 23	30	7	210	
Purchase on Nov. 5	15	8	120	
Sales	50	?	?	

4. Manatee uses a FIFO inventory system. Cost of goods sold for the period is:
   a. $330   c. $355
   b. $347   d. $365

5. Manatee's LIFO cost of ending inventory would be:
   a. $161   c. $208
   b. $90   d. $225

6. Manatee's average cost of ending inventory is:
   a. $161   c. $104
   b. $90   d. $225

7. When applying lower-of-cost-or-market to inventory, "market" generally means
   a. resale value.   c. replacement cost.
   b. original cost.   d. original cost, less physical deterioration.

8. During a period of rising prices, the inventory method that will yield the highest net income and asset value is:
   a. Specific identification   c. LIFO
   b. Average cost   d. FIFO

9. Which statement is true?
   a. The inventory method that best matches current expense with current revenue is FIFO.
   b. Application of the lower-of-cost-or-market rule often results in a lower inventory value.
   c. An error overstating ending inventory in 20X1 will understate 20X1 net income.
   d. When prices are rising, the inventory method that results in the lowest ending inventory value is FIFO.

10. The ending inventory of Bar Harbor Co. is $44,000. If beginning inventory was $50,000 and goods available totaled $104,000, the cost of goods sold is:
    a. $112,000
    b. $198,000
    c. $60,000
    d. $50,000
    e. none of the above ($ <u>fill in the blank</u>).

11. Bell Company had cost of goods sold of $130,000. The beginning and ending inventories were $10,000 and $20,000, respectively. Purchases for the period must have been:
    a. $82,000
    b. $94,000
    c. $132,000
    d. $140,000
    e. $138,000

Use the following information for questions 12–14.

12. Tee Company had a $20,000 beginning inventory and a $24,000 ending inventory. Net sales were $160,000; purchases, $80,000; purchase returns and allowances, $5,000 and freight-in, $6,000. Cost of goods sold for the period is
    a. $69,000.
    b. $49,000.
    c. $77,000.
    d. $85,000.
    e. none of the above.

13. What is Tee's gross profit percentage (rounded to the nearest percentage)?
    a. 52%
    b. 88%
    c. 47%
    d. none of the above

14. What is Tee's rate of inventory turnover?
    a. 3.4 times
    b. 3.5 times
    c. 6.4 times
    d. 6.2 times

15. Beginning inventory is $60,000, purchases are $180,000 and sales total $300,000. The normal gross profit is 30%. Using the gross profit method, how much is ending inventory?
    a. $120,000
    b. $106,400
    c. $244,000
    d. $30,000
    e. None of the above; $(<u>fill in the blank</u>).

16. An overstatement of ending inventory in one period results in:
    a. no effect on net income of the next period
    b. an understatement of net income of the next period
    c. an overstatement of net income of the next period
    d. an understatement of the beginning inventory of the next period

Accounting Vocabulary

average-cost method (p. 318) Inventory costing method based on the average cost of inventory during the period. Average cost is determined by dividing the cost of goods available by the number of units available. Also called the *weighted-average method*.

conservatism (p. 325) The accounting concept by which the least favorable figures are presented in the financial statements.

consistency principle (p. 325) A business must use the same accounting methods and procedures from period to period.

cost of goods sold (p. 311) Cost of the inventory the business has sold to customers.

cost-of-goods-sold model (p. 329) Formula that brings together all the inventory data for the entire accounting period: Beginning inventory + Purchases = Goods available.

Then, Goods available – Ending inventory = Cost of goods sold.

disclosure principle (p. 325) A business's financial statements must report enough information for outsiders to make knowledgeable decisions about the business. The company should report relevant, reliable, and comparable information about its economic affairs.

first-in, first-out (FIFO) cost (method) (p. 325) Inventory costing method by which the first costs into inventory are the first costs out to cost of goods sold. Ending inventory is based on the costs of the most recent purchases.

gross margin (p. 313) Another name for *gross profit*.

gross margin method (p. 330) Another name for the *gross profit method*.

gross margin percentage (p. 327) Another name for the *gross profit percentage.*

gross profit (p. 313) Sales revenue minus cost of goods sold. Also called *gross margin.*

gross profit method (p. 330) A way to estimate inventory based on a rearrangement of the cost-of-goods-sold model: Beginning inventory + Net purchases = Goods available – Cost of goods sold = Ending inventory. Also called the *gross margin method.*

gross profit percentage (p. 337) Gross profit divided by net sales revenue. Also called the *gross margin percentage.*

inventory (p. 311) The merchandise that a company sells to customers.

inventory turnover (p. 328) Ratio of cost of goods sold to average inventory. Indicates how rapidly inventory is sold.

last-in, first-out (LIFO) cost (method) (p. 328) Inventory costing method by which the last costs into inventory are the first costs out to cost of goods sold. This method leaves the oldest costs—those of beginning inventory and the earliest purchases of the period—in ending inventory.

lower-of-cost-or-market (LCM) rule (p. 326) Requires that an asset be reported in the financial statements at whichever is lower—its historical cost or its market value (current replacement cost for inventory).

periodic inventory system (p. 314) An inventory system in which the business does not keep a continuous record of the inventory on hand. Instead, at the end of the period, the business makes a physical count of the inventory on hand and applies the appropriate unit costs to determine the cost of the ending inventory.

perpetual inventory system (p. 314) An inventory system in which the business keeps a continuous record for each inventory item to show the inventory on hand at all times.

purchase allowance (p. 315) A decrease in the cost of purchases because the seller has granted the buyer a subtraction (an allowance) from the amount owed.

purchase discount (p. 316) A decrease in the cost of purchases earned by making an early payment to the vendor.

purchase return (p. 315) A decrease in the cost of purchases because the buyer returned the goods to the seller.

specific-unit-cost method (p. 317) Inventory cost method based on the specific cost of particular units of inventory.

weighted-average method (p. 318) Another name for the *average-cost method.*

HH CHAPTER 6

Pages 339–357 intentionally omitted

APPLY YOUR KNOWLEDGE

Decision Cases

writing assignment ■

Case 1. *(Learning Objective 1, 2: Assessing the impact of a year-end purchase of inventory)* Duracraft Corporation is nearing the end of its first year of operations. Duracraft made inventory purchases of $745,000 during the year, as follows:

January	1,000 units @	$100.00 =	$100,000
July	4,000	121.25	485,000
November	1,000	160.00	160,000
Totals	6,000		$745,000

Sales for the year are 5,000 units for $1,200,000 of revenue. Expenses other than cost of goods sold and income taxes total $200,000. The president of the company is undecided about whether to adopt the FIFO method or the LIFO method for inventories. The income tax rate is 40%.

❙ Required

1. To aid company decision making, prepare income statements under FIFO and under LIFO. (pp. 310, 324)
2. Compare the net income under FIFO with net income under LIFO. Which method produces the higher net income? What causes this difference? Be specific. (pp. 322, 323)

writing assignment ■

Case 2. (*Learning Objective 2: Assessing the impact of the inventory costing method on the financial statements*) The inventory costing method a company chooses can affect the financial statements and thus the decisions of the people who use those statements.

❙ Required

1. Company A uses the LIFO inventory method and discloses its use of the LIFO method in notes to the financial statements. Company B uses the FIFO method to account for its inventory. Company B does *not* disclose which inventory method it uses. Company B reports a higher net income than Company A. In which company would you prefer to invest? Give your reason. (p. 325)
2. Conservatism is an accepted accounting concept. Would you want management to be conservative in accounting for inventory if you were a shareholder or a creditor of a company? Give your reason. (p. 325)

Ethical Issue

During 20X8, Vanguard, Inc., changed to the LIFO method of accounting for inventory. Suppose that during 20X9, Vanguard changes back to the FIFO method and the following year Vanguard switches back to LIFO again.

❙ Required

1. What would you think of a company's ethics if it changed accounting methods every year?
2. What accounting principle would changing methods every year violate?
3. Who can be harmed when a company changes its accounting methods too often? How?

Focus on Financials: ■ YUM! Brands

(*Learning Objective 2, 3: Analyzing inventories*) The notes are part of the financial statements. They give details that would clutter the statements. This case will help you learn to use a company's inventory notes. Refer to **YUM! Brands'** statements and related notes in Appendix A at the end of the book and answer the following questions:

1. How much was YUM's merchandise inventory at December 30, 2006? At December 30, 2005? (p. 310)
2. How does YUM *value* its inventories? Which *cost* method does the company use? (p. 317)
3. How much were Yum's purchases of food and paper inventory during the year ended December 30, 2006? (p. 330)
4. Did YUM's gross profit percentage on company sales improve or deteriorate in 2006 compared to 2005? (p. 327)
5. Would you rate YUM's rate of inventory turnover as fast or slow in comparison to most other companies? Explain your answer. (pp. 328–329)

Focus on Analysis: ■ Pier 1 Imports

(Learning Objective 1, 2, 3: Measuring critical inventory amounts) Refer to the **Pier 1 Imports** financial statements in Appendix B at the end of this book. Show amounts in millions and round to the nearest $1 million.

1. Three important pieces of inventory information are (a) the cost of inventory on hand, (b) the cost of goods sold, and (c) the cost of inventory purchases. Identify or compute each of these items for Pier 1 at the end of 2006. (p. 330)
2. Which item in requirement 1 is most directly related to cash flow? Why? (Challenge)
3. Assume that all inventory purchases were made on account, and that only inventory purchases increased Accounts Payable. Compute Pier 1's cash payments for inventory during 2006. (p. 646)
4. How does Pier 1 *value* its inventories? Which *costing* method does Pier 1 use? (pp. 317–320)
5. Did Pier 1's gross profit percentage and rate of inventory turnover improve or deteriorate in 2006 (versus 2005)? Consider the overall effect of these 2 ratios. Did Pier 1 improve during 2006? How did these factors affect the net loss for 2006? Pier 1's inventories totaled $374 million at the end of 2004. Round decimals to 3 places. (pp. 327–329)

Group Project

(Learning Objective 3: Comparing companies' inventory turnover ratios) Obtain the annual reports of 10 companies, 2 from each of 5 different industries. Most companies' financial statements can be downloaded from their Web sites.

writing assignment ■

1. Compute each company's gross profit percentage and rate of inventory turnover for the most recent 2 years. If annual reports are unavailable or do not provide enough data for multiple-year computations, you can gather financial statement data from *Moody's Industrial Manual*.
2. For the industries of the companies you are analyzing, obtain the industry averages for gross profit percentage and inventory turnover from Robert Morris Associates, *Annual Statement Studies*; Dun and Bradstreet, *Industry Norms and Key Business Ratios*; or Leo Troy, *Almanac of Business and Industrial Financial Ratios*.
3. How well does each of your companies compare to the other company in its industry? How well do your companies compare to the average for their industry? What insight about your companies can you glean from these ratios?
4. Write a memo to summarize your findings, stating whether your group would invest in each of the companies it has analyzed.

For Internet Exercises go to the Web site www.prenhall.com/harrison.

Quick Check Answers

1. *c*
2. *e*
3. *a*
4. *a* [(20 × $6) + (30 × $7) = $330]
5. *b* (15 × $6 =$90)
6. *c* 15 × [($120 + $210 + $120) ÷ 65] = $103.85
7. *c*
8. *d*
9. *b*
10. *c* ($104,000 – $44,000 = $60,000)

11. *d* ($10,000 + X – $20,000 = $130,000; X = $140,000)
12. *c* ($20,000 + $80,000 – $5,000 + $6,000 – $24,000 = $77,000)
13. *a* ($160,000 – $77,000)/$160,000 = .519
14. *b* [$77,000 ÷ ($20,000 + $24,000)/2 = 3.5]
15. *d* $60,000 + $180,000 – [$300,000 × (1 – .30)] = $30,000
16. *b*

12 The Statement of Cash Flows

SPOTLIGHT

GOOGLE: THE ULTIMATE ANSWER MACHINE

What do you use to find Web sites on the Internet? It's probably Google, the world's largest search engine. Google was created by Larry Page and Sergey Brin when they were students at Stanford University. These guys have done well. Recently the market value of Google stock surpassed that of Wal-Mart, the world's largest retailer.

The beauty of Google is that it's so easy to use. Access the Internet at www.google.com, and you can simply enter what you want to find in the search box. You get a whole list of helpful Web sites. Google may be the ultimate answer machine.

Google Inc.
Consolidated Statement of Cash Flows (Adapted; in millions)
Year Ended December 31, 2006

Cash Flows from Operating Activities		
Net income	$ 3,077	
Adjustments to reconcile net income to net cash provided by operating activities:		
Depreciation and amortization..	572	
Change in assets and liabilities, net of acquired businesses:		
Accounts receivable	(624)	
Other current assets...	(289)	
Accounts payable..	95	
Accrued expenses and other liabilities.........................	292	
Unearned revenue	31	
Income taxes payable...	398	
Other, net...	29	
Net cash provided by operating activities.....................		$ 3,581
Cash Flows from Investing Activities		
Purchases of property and equipment	$ (1,903)	
Purchases of investments...	(27,701)	
Sales of investments	23,107	
Acquisitions of other companies	(402)	
Net cash used in investing activities		(6,899)
Cash Flows from Financing Activities		
Proceeds from issuance of common stock, net..............	$ 2,384	
Other, net...	582	
Net cash provided by financing activities		2,966
Other, net...		20
Net increase (decrease) in cash and cash equivalents		(332)
Cash and cash equivalents at beginning of year............		3,877
Cash and cash equivalents at end of year		$ 3,545

In preceding chapters, we covered cash flows as they related to various topics: receivables, plant assets, and so on. In this chapter, we show you how to prepare and use the statement of cash flows. We begin with the statement format used by the vast majority (98.7%) of companies, called the *indirect approach*. We end with the alternate format of the statement of cash flows, the *direct approach*, used by 1.3% of companies in a recent survey. After working through this chapter, you can analyze the cash flows of actual companies.

This chapter has 3 distinct sections:

- Introduction, beginning on this page
- Preparing the Statement of Cash Flows: Indirect Method, page 624
- Preparing the Statement of Cash Flows: Direct Method, page 638

The introduction applies to all the cash-flow topics. Professors who wish to cover only the indirect method can assign the first 2 parts of the chapter. Those interested only in the direct method can proceed from the introduction, which ends on page 624, to the direct method, on page 638.

LEARNING OBJECTIVES

1 **Identify** the purposes of the statement of cash flows

2 **Distinguish** among operating, investing, and financing cash flows

3 **Prepare** a statement of cash flows by the indirect method

4 **Prepare** a statement of cash flows by the direct method

BASIC CONCEPTS: THE STATEMENT OF CASH FLOWS

The balance sheet reports financial position, and balance sheets from two periods show whether cash increased or decreased. But that doesn't tell *why* the cash balance changed. The income statement reports net income and offers clues about cash, but the income statement doesn't tell *why* cash increased or decreased. We need a third financial statement.

The **statement of cash flows** reports **cash flows**—cash receipts and cash payments—in other words, where cash came from (receipts) and how it was spent (payments). The statement covers a span of time and therefore is dated "Year Ended December 31, 2008" or "Month Ended June 30, 2009." Exhibit 12-1 illustrates the relative timing of the 4 basic statements.

OBJECTIVE

1 **Identify** the purposes of the statement of cash flows

EXHIBIT 12-1   **Timing of the Financial Statements**

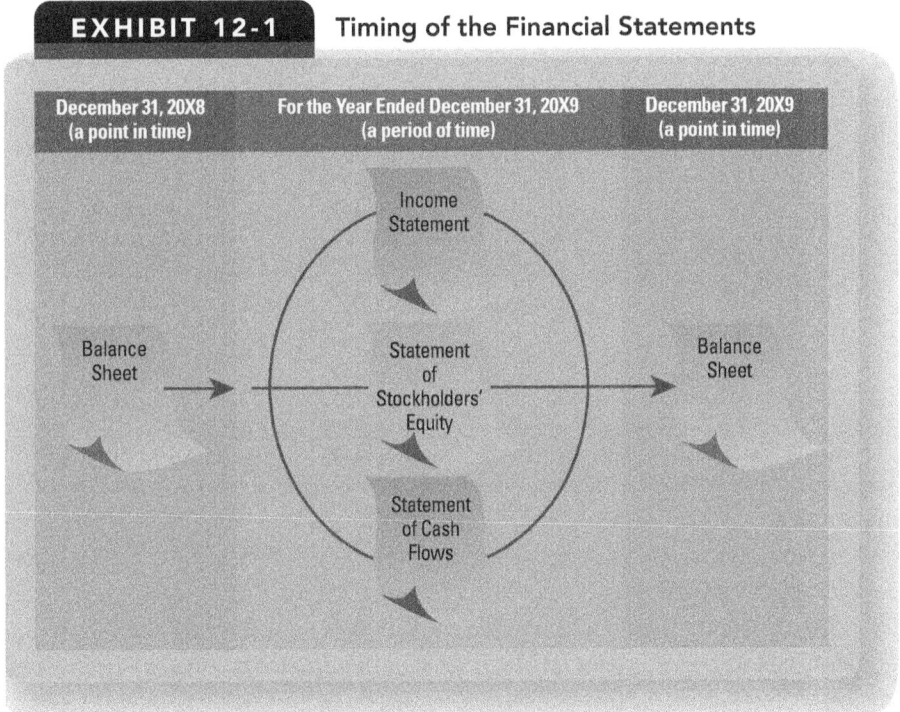

The statement of cash flows serves these purposes:

1. ***Predicts future cash flows.*** Past cash receipts and payments are reasonably good predictors of future cash flows.

2. ***Evaluates management decisions.*** Businesses that make wise decisions prosper, and those that make unwise decisions suffer losses. The statement of cash flows reports how managers got cash and how they used cash to run the business.

3. *Determines ability to pay dividends and interest.* Stockholders want dividends on their investments. Creditors demand interest and principal on their loans. The statement of cash flows reports on the ability to make these payments.

4. *Shows the relationship of net income to cash flows.* Usually, high net income leads to an increase in cash, and vice versa. But cash flow can suffer even when net income is high.

On a statement of cash flows, *cash* means more than just cash in the bank. It includes **cash equivalents,** which are highly liquid short-term investments that can be converted into cash immediately. Examples include money-market accounts and investments in U.S. Government securities. Throughout this chapter, the term cash refers to cash and cash equivalents.

How's Your Cash Flow? Telltale Signs of Financial Difficulty

Companies want to earn net income because profit measures success. Without net income, a business sinks. There will be no dividends, and the stock price suffers. High net income attracts investors, but you can't pay bills with net income. That requires cash.

A company needs both net income and strong cash flow. Income and cash flow usually move together because net income generates cash. Sometimes, however, net income and cash flow take different paths. To illustrate, consider Fastech Company:

Fastech Company Income Statement Year Ended December 31, 20X7	
Sales revenue	$100,000
Cost of goods sold	30,000
Operating expenses	10,000
Net income	$ 60,000

Fastech Company Balance Sheet December 31, 20X7			
Cash	$ 3,000	Total current liabilities	$ 50,000
Receivables	37,000	Long-term liabilities	20,000
Inventory	40,000		
Plant assets, net	60,000	Stockholders' equity	70,000
Total assets	$140,000	Total liabilities and equity	$140,000

What can we glean from Fastech's income statement and balance sheet?

- Fastech is profitable. Net income is 60% of revenue. Fastech's profitability looks outstanding.
- The current ratio is 1.6, and the debt ratio is only 50%. These measures suggest little trouble in paying bills.
- But Fastech is on the verge of bankruptcy. Can you spot the problem? Can you see what is causing the problem? Three trouble spots leap out to a financial analyst.

1. The cash balance is very low. Three thousand dollars isn't enough cash to pay the bills of a company with sales of $100,000.

2. Fastech isn't selling inventory fast enough. Fastech turned over its inventory only 0.75 times during the year. As we saw in Chapter 6, inventory turnover

rates of 3–8 times a year are common. A turnover ratio of 0.75 times means it takes Fastech far too long to sell its inventory, and that delays cash collections.

3. Fastech's days' sales in receivables ratio is 135 days. Very few companies can wait that long to collect from customers.

The takeaway lesson from this discussion is this:

■ You need both net income and strong cash flow to succeed in business.

Let's turn now to the different categories of cash flows.

Operating, Investing, and Financing Activities

A business engages in 3 types of business activities:

   ■ Operating activities   ■ Investing activities   ■ Financing activities

OBJECTIVE

2 **Distinguish** among operating, investing, and financing cash flows

Google's statement of cash flows reports cash flows under these 3 headings, as shown for Google on page 620.

Operating activities create revenues, expenses, gains, and losses—*net income*, which is a product of accrual-basis accounting. The statement of cash flows reports on operating activities. Operating activities are the most important of the 3 categories because they reflect the core of the organization. *A successful business must generate most of its cash from operating activities.*

Investing activities increase and decrease *long-term assets*, such as computers, land, buildings, equipment, and investments in other companies. Purchases and sales of these assets are investing activities. Investing activities are important, but they are less critical than operating activities.

Financing activities obtain cash from investors and creditors. Issuing stock, borrowing money, buying and selling treasury stock, and paying cash dividends are financing activities. Paying off a loan is another example. Financing cash flows relate to *long-term liabilities* and *owners' equity*. They are the least important of the 3 categories of cash flows, and that's why they come last. Exhibit 12-2 shows how operating, investing, and financing activities relate to the various parts of the balance sheet.

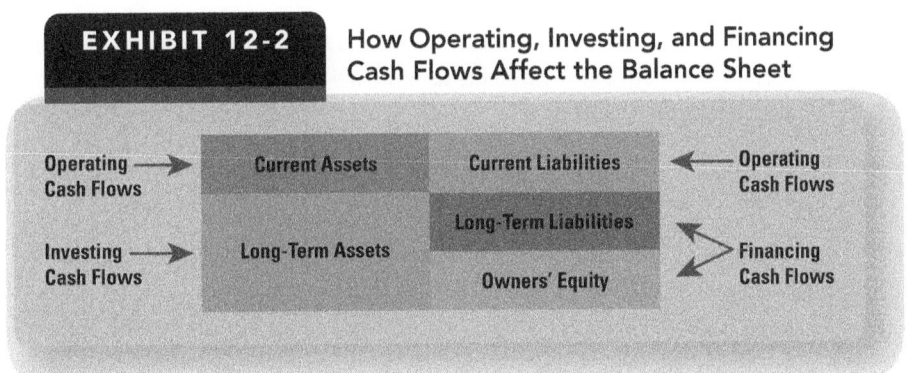

EXHIBIT 12-2   **How Operating, Investing, and Financing Cash Flows Affect the Balance Sheet**

Examine Google's statement of cash flows on page 620. Focus on the final line of each section: Operating, Investing, and Financing. Google has very strong cash flows.

During 2006, Google's operating activities provided $3.6 billion of cash. Google invested almost $7 billion and received $3 billion in financing. These figures show that

- *Operations* are Google's largest source of cash.
- The company is *investing* in the future.
- People are willing to *finance* Google.

Two Formats for Operating Activities

There are 2 ways to format operating activities on the statement of cash flows:

- **Indirect method**, which reconciles from net income to net cash provided by operating activities. (pp. 624–638)
- **Direct method**, which reports all cash receipts and cash payments from operating activities. (pp. 638–649)

The 2 methods use different computations, but they produce the same figure for cash from *operating activities*. The 2 methods do not affect *investing* or *financing activities*. The following table summarizes the differences between the 2 approaches:

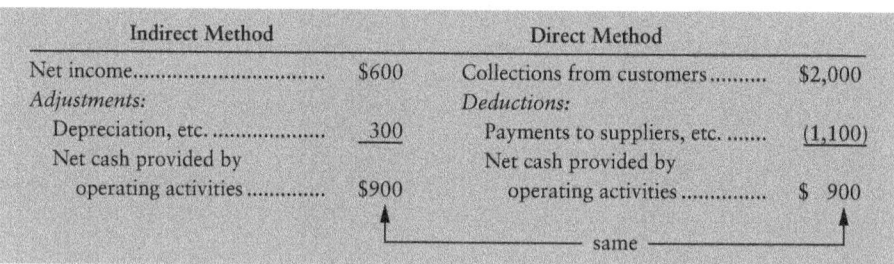

We begin with the indirect method because 98 out of 100 companies use it.

PREPARING THE STATEMENT OF CASH FLOWS: INDIRECT METHOD

OBJECTIVE

3 **Prepare** a statement of cash flows by the indirect method

To illustrate the statement of cash flows, we use **The Roadster Factory, Inc. (TRF)**, a dealer in auto parts for sports cars. Proceed as follows to prepare the statement of cash flows by using the indirect method:

Step 1 Lay out the template as shown in Part 1 of Exhibit 12-3. The exhibit is comprehensive. The diagram in Part 2 (p. 626) gives a visual picture of the statement.

Step 2 Use the balance sheet to determine the increase or decrease in cash during the period. The change in cash is the "check figure" for the statement of cash flows. Exhibit 12-4 (p. 627) gives The Roadster Factory's (TRF's) comparative balance sheet, with cash highlighted. TRF's cash decreased by $8,000 during 20X9. *Why* did cash decrease? The statement of cash flows will provide the answer.

Step 3 From the income statement, take net income, depreciation, depletion, and amortization expense, and any gains or losses on the sale of long-term assets. Print these items on the statement of cash flows. Exhibit 12-5 (p. 627) gives TRF's income statement, with relevant items highlighted.

Step 4 Use the income statement and balance sheet data to prepare the statement of cash flows. The statement of cash flows is complete only after you have explained the year-to-year changes in all the balance sheet accounts.

EXHIBIT 12-3	Part 1: Template of the Statement of Cash Flows: Indirect Method

The Roadster Factory, Inc. (TRF)
Statement of Cash Flows
Year Ended December 31, 20X9

Cash flows from operating activities
 Net income
  Adjustments to reconcile net income to net cash provided by operating activities:
  + Depreciation/depletion/amortization expense
  + Loss on sale of long-term assets
  − Gain on sale of long-term assets
  − Increases in current assets other than cash
  + Decreases in current assets other than cash
  + Increases in current liabilities
  − Decreases in current liabilities
    Net cash provided by (used for) operating activities
Cash flows from investing activities:
 Sales of long-term assets (investments, land, building, equipment, and so on)
  − Purchases of long-term assets
  + Collections of notes receivable
  − Loans to others
    Net cash provided by (used for) investing activities
Cash flows from financing activities:
 Issuance of stock
  + Sale of treasury stock
  − Purchase of treasury stock
  + Borrowing (issuance of notes or bonds payable)
  − Payment of notes or bonds payable
  − Payment of dividends
    Net cash provided by (used for) financing activities
Net increase (decrease) in cash during the year
 + Cash at December 31, 20X8
 = Cash at December 31, 20X9

Go to "Cash Flows from Operating Activities" on page 628.

EXHIBIT 12-3 Part 2: Positive and Negative Items on the
Statement of Cash Flows: Indirect Method

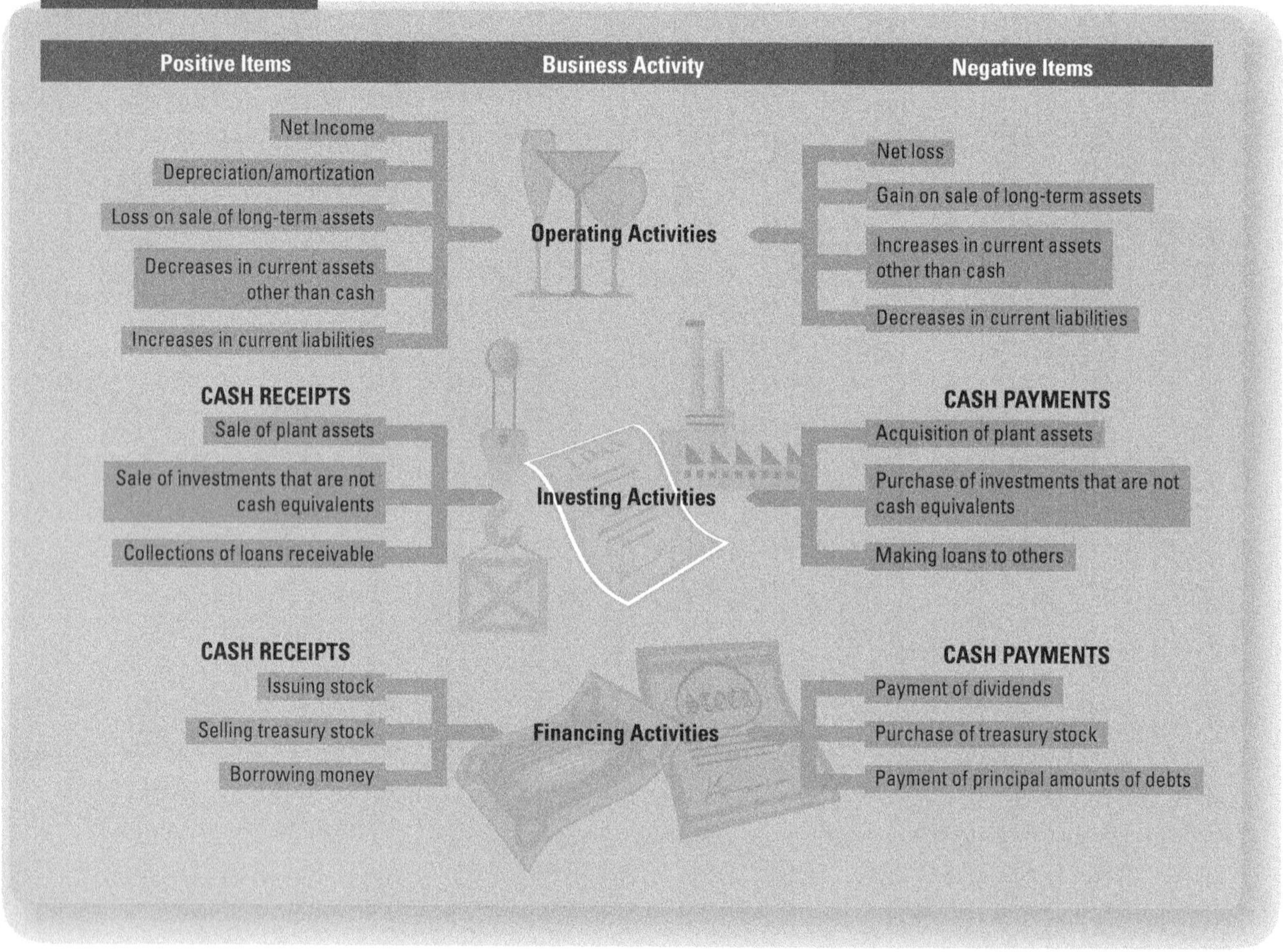

Positive Items	Business Activity	Negative Items
Net Income		Net loss
Depreciation/amortization		Gain on sale of long-term assets
Loss on sale of long-term assets	**Operating Activities**	Increases in current assets other than cash
Decreases in current assets other than cash		Decreases in current liabilities
Increases in current liabilities		

CASH RECEIPTS		**CASH PAYMENTS**
Sale of plant assets		Acquisition of plant assets
Sale of investments that are not cash equivalents	**Investing Activities**	Purchase of investments that are not cash equivalents
Collections of loans receivable		Making loans to others

CASH RECEIPTS		**CASH PAYMENTS**
Issuing stock		Payment of dividends
Selling treasury stock	**Financing Activities**	Purchase of treasury stock
Borrowing money		Payment of principal amounts of debts

EXHIBIT 12-4 Comparative Balance Sheet

The Roadster Factory, Inc. (TRF)
Comparative Balance Sheet
December 31, 20X9 and 20X8

(In thousands)	20X9	20X8	Increase (Decrease)	
Assets				
Current:				
Cash	$ 34	$ 42	$ (8)	⎫
Accounts receivable	96	81	15	⎬ Changes in current assets—*Operating*
Inventory	35	38	(3)	
Prepaid expenses	8	7	1	⎭
Notes receivable	21	—	21	⎫ Changes in noncurrent assets—*Investing*
Plant assets, net of depreciation	343	219	124	⎬
Total	$537	$387	$150	
Liabilities				
Current:				
Accounts payable	$ 91	$ 57	$ 34	⎫
Salary and wage payable	4	6	(2)	⎬ Changes in current liabilities—*Operating*
Accrued liabilities	1	3	(2)	⎭
Long-term debt	160	77	83	⎫ Changes in long-term liabilities and paid-in capital accounts—*Financing*
Stockholders' Equity				
Common stock	162	158	4	⎭
Retained earnings	119	86	33	⎫ Changes due to net income—*Operating* Change due to dividends—*Financing*
Total	$537	$387	$150	

EXHIBIT 12-5 Income Statement

The Roadster Factory, Inc. (TRF)
Income Statement
Year Ended December 31, 20X9

	(In thousands)
Revenues and gains:	
Sales revenue	$303
Interest revenue	2
Gain on sale of plant assets	8
Total revenues and gains	$313
Expenses:	
Cost of goods sold	$150
Salary and wage expense	56
Depreciation expense	18
Other operating expense	17
Income tax expense	15
Interest expense	7
Total expenses	263
Net income	$ 50

EXHIBIT 12-6	Statement of Cash Flows—Operating Activities by the Indirect Method

The Roadster Factory, Inc. (TRF)
Statement of Cash Flows (Indirect Method)
For the Year Ended December 31, 20X9

		(In thousands)
Cash flows from operating activities:		
Net income		$50
Adjustments to reconcile net income to net cash provided by operating activities:		
Ⓐ Depreciation	$ 18	
Ⓑ Gain on sale of plant assets	(8)	
Increase in accounts receivable..................................	(15)	
Decrease in inventory..	3	
Ⓒ Increase in prepaid expenses	(1)	
Increase in accounts payable	34	
Decrease in salary and wage payable.........................	(2)	
Decrease in accrued liabilities....................................	(2)	27
Net cash provided by operating activities.............		$77

Cash Flows from Operating Activities

> **Operating activities are related to the transactions that make up net income.[1]**

The operating section begins with the net income, taken from the income statement, (Exhibit 12-5) and is followed by "Adjustments to reconcile net income to net cash provided by operating activities." Let's discuss these adjustments.

Ⓐ **Depreciation, Depletion, and Amortization Expenses.** These expenses are added back to net income to convert net income to cash flow. Let's see why. Depreciation is recorded as follows:

Depreciation Expense	18,000	
Accumulated Depreciation		18,000

Depreciation has no effect on cash. But depreciation, like all other expenses, decreases net income. Therefore, to convert net income to cash flows, we add depreciation back to net income. The add-back cancels the earlier deduction.

---
[1]The authors thank Professor Alfonso Oddo for suggesting this summary.

Example: Suppose you had only 2 transactions, a $1,000 cash sale and depreciation expense of $300. Cash flow from operations is $1,000, and net income is $700 ($1,000 − $300). To go from net income ($700) to cash flow ($1,000), we add back the depreciation ($300). Depletion and amortization are treated like depreciation.

Gains and Losses on the Sale of Assets. Sales of long-term assets are *investing* Ⓑ activities and there's often a gain or loss on the sale. On the statement of cash flows, the gain or loss is an adjustment to net income. Exhibit 12-6 includes an adjustment for a gain. During 20X9, The Roadster Factory sold equipment for $62,000. The book value was $54,000, so there was a gain of $8,000.

The $62,000 cash received from the sale is an investing activity, and the $62,000 includes the $8,000 gain. Net income also includes the gain, so we must subtract the gain from net cash provided by operations, as shown in the statement of cash flows (Exhibit 12-7). (We explain investing activities in the next section.)

A loss on the sale of plant assets also creates an adjustment in the operating section. Losses are *added back* to net income to compute cash flow from operations.

Changes in the Current Asset and Current Liability Accounts. Most current assets and current liabilities result from operating activities. For example, accounts receivable result from sales, inventory relates to cost of goods sold, and so on. Changes in the current accounts are adjustments to net income on the cash-flow statement. The reasoning follows:

1. **An increase in another current asset decreases cash.** It takes cash to acquire assets. Suppose you make a sale on account. Accounts receivable are increased, but cash isn't affected yet. Exhibit 12-4 (p. 627) reports that during 20X9, The Roadster Factory's Accounts Receivable increased by $15,000. To compute cash flow from operations, we must subtract the $15,000 increase in Accounts Receivable, as shown in Exhibit 12-6. The reason is this: We have *not* collected this $15,000 in cash. The same logic applies to all the other current assets. If they increase, cash decreases.

2. **A decrease in another current asset increases cash.** Suppose TRF's Accounts Receivable balance decreased by $4,000. Cash receipts caused Accounts Receivable to decrease, so we add decreases in Accounts Receivable and the other current assets to net income.

3. **A decrease in a current liability decreases cash.** Payment of a current liability decreases both cash and the liability, so we subtract decreases in current liabilities from net income. In Exhibit 12-6, the $2,000 decrease in Accrued Liabilities is *subtracted* to compute net cash provided by operations.

4. **An increase in a current liability increases cash.** The Roadster Factory's Accounts Payable increased. That can occur only if cash was not spent to pay this debt. Cash payments are therefore less than expenses and TRF has more cash on hand. Thus, increases in current liabilities increase cash.

EXHIBIT 12-7 Statement of Cash Flows—
Indirect Method

The Roadster Factory, Inc. (TRF)
Statement of Cash Flows (Indirect Method)
For the Year Ended December 31, 20X9

		(In thousands)
Cash flows from operating activities:		
Net income		$ 50
Adjustments to reconcile net income to net cash		
provided by operating activities:		
Ⓐ Depreciation	18	
Ⓑ Gain on sale of plant assets	(8)	
Increase in accounts receivable	(15)	
Decrease in inventory	3	
Increase in prepaid expenses	(1)	
Ⓒ Increase in accounts payable	34	
Decrease in salary and wage payable	(2)	
Decrease in accrued liabilities	(2)	27
Net cash provided by operating activities		77
Cash flows from investing activities:		
Acquisition of plant assets	$(196)	
Loan to another company	(21)	
Proceeds from sale of plant assets	62	
Net cash used for investing activities		(155)
Cash flows from financing activities:		
Proceeds from issuance of long-term debt	$ 94	
Proceeds from issuance of common stock	4	
Payment of long-term debt	(11)	
Payment of dividends	(17)	
Net cash provided by financing avctivities		70
Net (decrease) in cash		$ (8)
Cash balance, December 31, 20X8		42
Cash balance, December 31, 20X9		$ 34

Evaluating Cash Flows from Operating Activities. Let's step back and evaluate The Roadster Factory's operating cash flows during 20X9. TRF's operations provided net cash flow of $77,000. This amount exceeds net income, and it should because of the add-back of depreciation. Now let's examine TRF's investing and financing activities, as reported in Exhibit 12-7.

Cash Flows from Investing Activities

Investing activities affect long-term assets, such as Plant Assets, Investments, and Notes Receivable.

Most of the data come from the balance sheet.

Computing Purchases and Sales of Plant Assets. Companies keep a separate account for each plant asset. But for computing cash flows, it is helpful to combine all the plant assets into a single summary account. Also, we subtract accumulated depreciation and use the net figure. It's easier to work with a single plant asset account.

To illustrate, observe that The Roadster Factory's

- balance sheet reports beginning plant assets, net of accumulated depreciation, of $219,000. The ending balance is $343,000 (Exhibit 12-4).
- income statement shows depreciation expense of $18,000 and an $8,000 gain on sale of plant assets (Exhibit 12-5).

TRF's purchases of plant assets total $196,000 (take this amount as given; see Exhibit 12-7). How much, then, are the proceeds from the sale of plant assets? First, we must determine the book value of the plant assets sold, as follows:

Plant Assets, Net

Beginning balance	+	Acquisitions	−	Depreciation	−	Book value of assets sold	=	Ending balance
$219,000	+	$196,000	−	$18,000		−X	=	$343,000
						−X	=	$343,000 − $219,000 − $196,000 + $18,000
						X	=	$54,000

The sale proceeds are $62,000, determined as follows:

Sale proceeds	=	Book value of assets sold	+	Gain	−	Loss
X	=	$54,000	+	$8,000	−	$0
X	=	$62,000				

Trace the sale proceeds of $62,000 to the statement of cash flows in Exhibit 12-7. The Plant Assets T-account provides another look at the computation of the book value of the assets sold.

Plant Assets, Net

Beginning balance	219,000	Depreciation	18,000
Acquisitions	196,000	Book value of assets sold	54,000
Ending balance	343,000		

If the sale resulted in a loss of $3,000, the sale proceeds would be $51,000 ($54,000 − $3,000), and the statement of cash flows would report $51,000 as a cash receipt from this investing activity.

Computing Purchases and Sales of Investments, and Loans and Collections. The cash amounts of investment transactions can be computed in the manner illustrated for plant assets. Investments are easier because there is no depreciation, as shown in the following equation:

Investments (amounts assumed for illustration only)

Beginning balance	+	Purchases	−	Book value of investments sold	=	Ending balance
$100,000	+	$50,000		−X	=	$140,000
				−X	=	$140,000 − $100,000 − $50,000
				X	=	$10,000

HH CHAPTER 12

The investments T-account provides another look (amounts assumed).

Investments			
Beginning balance	100		
Purchases	50	Book value of investments sold	10
Ending balance	140		

The Roadster Factory has a long-term receivable, and the cash flows from loan transactions on notes receivable can be determined as follows (data from Exhibit 12-4):

Notes Receivable							
Beginning balance	+	New loans made	–	Collections	=	Ending balance	
$0	+	X		–0	=	$21,000	
		X			=	$21,000	

Notes Receivable			
Beginning balance	0		
New loans made	21	Collections	0
Ending balance	21		

Exhibit 12-8 summarizes the cash flows from investing activities, highlighted in color.

EXHIBIT 12-8   Computing Cash Flows from Investing Activities

Receipts

From sale of plant assets	Beginning plant assets, net	+	Acquisition cost	–	Depreciation	–	Book value of assets sold	=	Ending plant assets, net
	Cash received	=	Book value of assets sold	+ or –	Gain on sale Loss on sale				
From sale of investments	Beginning investments	+	Purchase cost of investments	–	Cost of investments sold	=	Ending investments		
	Cash received	=	Cost of investments sold	+ or –	Gain on sale Loss on sale				
From collection of notes receivable	Beginning notes receivable	+	New loans made	–	Collections	=	Ending notes receivable		

Payments

For acquisition of plant assets	Beginning plant assets, net	+	Acquisition cost	–	Depreciation	–	Book value of assets sold	=	Ending plant assets, net
For purchase of investments	Beginning investments	+	Purchase cost of investments	–	Cost of investments sold	=	Ending investments		
For new loans made	Beginning notes receivable	+	New loans made	–	Collections	=	Ending notes receivable		

Cash Flows from Financing Activities

> **Financing activities affect liabilities and stockholders' equity, such as Notes Payable, Bonds Payable, Long-Term Debt, Common Stock, Paid-in Capital in Excess of Par, and Retained Earnings. Most of the data come from the balance sheet.**

Computing Issuances and Payments of Long-Term Debt. The beginning and ending balances of Long-Term Debt, Notes Payable, or Bonds Payable come from the balance sheet. If either new issuances or payments are known, the other amount can be computed. The Roadster Factory's new debt issuances total $94,000 (take this amount as given; Exhibit 12-7). Debt payments are computed from the Long-Term Debt account (see Exhibit 12-4).

Long-Term Debt (Notes Payable, Bonds Payable)

Beginning balance	+	Issuance of new debt	−	Payments of debt	=	Ending balance
$77,000	+	$94,000		−X	=	$160,000
				−X	=	$160,000 − $77,000 − $94,000
				X	=	$11,000

Long-Term Debt

		Beginning balance	77,000
Payments	11,000	Issuance of new debt	94,000
		Ending balance	160,000

Computing Issuances of Stock and Purchases of Treasury Stock. These cash flows can be determined from the stock accounts. For example, cash received from issuing common stock is computed from Common Stock and Capital in Excess of Par. We use a single summary Common Stock account as we do for plant assets. The Roadster Factory data are

Common Stock

Beginning balance	+	Issuance of new stock	=	Ending balance
$158,000	+	$4,000	=	$162,000

Common Stock

	Beginning balance	158,000
	Issuance of new stock	4,000
	Ending balance	162,000

The Roadster Factory has no treasury stock, but cash flows from purchasing treasury stock can be computed as follows (using assumed amounts):

Treasury Stock (amounts assumed for illustration only)					
Beginning balance	+	Purchase of treasury stock	=	Ending balance
$16,000	+	$3,000	=	$19,000

Treasury Stock		
Beginning balance	16,000	
Purchase of treasury stock	3,000	
Ending balance	19,000	

Computing Dividend Payments. If dividend payments are not given elsewhere, they can be computed. The Roadster Factory's dividend payments are

Retained Earnings						
Beginning balance	+	Net income	−	Dividend declarations and payments	=	Ending balance
$86,000	+	$50,000		−X	=	$119,000
				−X	=	$119,000 − $86,000 − $50,000
				X	=	$17,000

The T-accounts also show the dividend computation.

Retained Earnings			
Dividend declarations and payments	17,000	Beginning balance	86,000
		Net income	50,000
		Ending balance	119,000

Exhibit 12-9 summarizes the cash flows from financing activities, highlighted in color.

EXHIBIT 12-9 Computing Cash Flows from Financing Activities

Receipts

From borrowing—issuance of long-term debt (notes payable)	Beginning long-term debt (notes payable)	+	Cash received from issuance of long-term debt	−	Payment of debt	=	Ending long-term debt (notes payable)
From issuance of stock	Beginning stock	+	Cash received from issuance of new stock			=	Ending stock

Payments

Of long-term debt	Beginning long-term debt (notes payable)	+	Cash received from issuance of long-term debt	−	Payment of debt	=	Ending long-term debt (notes payable)
To purchase treasury stock	Beginning treasury stock + Purchase cost of treasury stock = Ending treasury stock						
Of dividends	Beginning retained earnings + Net income − Dividend declarations and payments = Ending retained earnings						

STOP & think. . .

Classify each of the following as an operating activity, an investing activity, or a financing activity as reported on the statement of cash flows prepared by the *indirect* method.

a. Issuance of stock
b. Borrowing
c. Sales revenue
d. Payment of dividends
e. Purchase of land
f. Purchase of treasury stock

g. Paying bonds payable
h. Interest expense
i. Sale of equipment
j. Cost of goods sold
k. Purchase of another company
l. Making a loan

Answer:

a. Financing
b. Financing
c. Operating
d. Financing

e. Investing
f. Financing
g. Financing
h. Operating

i. Investing
j. Operating
k. Investing
l. Investing

Noncash Investing and Financing Activities

Companies make investments that do not require cash. They also obtain financing other than cash. Our examples have included none of these transactions. Now suppose The Roadster Factory issued common stock valued at $300,000 to acquire a warehouse. TRF would journalize this transaction as follows:

Warehouse Building	300,000	
Common Stock		300,000

This transaction would not be reported as a cash payment because TRF paid no cash. But the investment in the warehouse and the issuance of stock are important. These noncash investing and financing activities can be reported in a separate schedule under the statement of cash flows. Exhibit 12-10 illustrates noncash investing and financing activities (all amounts are assumed).

EXHIBIT 12-10   Noncash Investing and Financing Activities (All Amounts Assumed)

	Thousands
Noncash Investing and Financing Activities:	
Acquisition of building by issuing common stock	$300
Acquisition of land by issuing note payable	70
Payment of long-term debt by issuing common stock	100
Total noncash investing and financing activities	$470

Now let's apply what you've learned about the statement of cash flows prepared by the indirect method.

MID-CHAPTER SUMMARY PROBLEM

Lucas Corporation reported the following income statement and comparative balance sheet, along with transaction data for 20X5:

Lucas Corporation
Income Statement
Year Ended December 31, 20X5

Sales revenue		$662,000
Cost of goods sold		560,000
Gross profit		102,000
Operating expenses		
Salary expenses	$46,000	
Depreciation expense—		
equipment	7,000	
Amortization expense—		
patent	3,000	
Rent expense	2,000	
Total operating expenses		58,000
Income from operations		44,000
Other items:		
Loss on sale of equipment		(2,000)
Income before income tax		42,000
Income tax expense		16,000
Net income		$ 26,000

Lucas Corporation
Balance Sheet
December 31, 20X5 and 20X4

Assets	20X5	20X4	Liabilities	20X5	20X4
Current:			Current:		
Cash and equivalents	$ 19,000	$ 3,000	Accounts payable	$ 35,000	$ 26,000
Accounts receivable	22,000	23,000	Accrued liabilities	7,000	9,000
Inventories	34,000	31,000	Income tax payable	10,000	10,000
Prepaid expenses	1,000	3,000	Total current liabilities	52,000	45,000
Total current assets	76,000	60,000	Long-term note payable	44,000	—
Long-term investments	18,000	10,000	Bonds payable	40,000	53,000
Equipment, net	67,000	52,000	**Owners' Equity**		
Patent, net	44,000	10,000	Common stock	52,000	20,000
			Retained earnings	27,000	19,000
			Less: Treasury stock	(10,000)	(5,000)
Total assets	$205,000	$132,000	Total liabilities and equity	$205,000	$132,000

Transaction Data for 20X5:

Purchase of equipment	$ 98,000	Issuance of long-term note payable	
Payment of cash dividends	18,000	to purchase patent	$ 37,000
Issuance of common stock to		Issuance of long-term note payable to	
retire bonds payable	13,000	borrow cash	7,000
Purchase of long-term investment	8,000	Issuance of common stock for cash	19,000
Purchase of treasury stock	5,000	Sale of equipment (book value, 76,000)	74,000

❚ Required

Prepare Lucas Corporation's statement of cash flows (indirect method) for the year ended December 31, 20X5. Follow the 4 steps outlined below. For Step 4, prepare a T-account to show the transaction activity in each long-term balance sheet account. For each plant asset, use a single account, net of accumulated depreciation (for example: Equipment, Net).

❚ Requirement 1

Step 1 Lay out the template of the statement of cash flows.

Step 2 From the comparative balance sheet, determine the increase in cash during the year, $16,000.

Step 3 From the income statement, take net income, depreciation, amortization, and the loss on sale of equipment, to the statement of cash flows.

Step 4 Complete the statement of cash flows. Account for the year-to-year change in each balance sheet account.

Answer

<table>
<tr><td colspan="3" align="center">Lucas Corporation
Statement of Cash Flows
Year Ended December 31, 20X5</td></tr>
<tr><td colspan="3">**Cash flows from operating activities:**</td></tr>
<tr><td>Net income ....</td><td></td><td>$ 26,000</td></tr>
<tr><td>Adjustments to reconcile net income to</td><td></td><td></td></tr>
<tr><td>net cash provided by operating activities:</td><td></td><td></td></tr>
<tr><td>Depreciation ....</td><td>$ 7,000</td><td></td></tr>
<tr><td>Amortization...</td><td>3,000</td><td></td></tr>
<tr><td>Loss on sale of equipment ....</td><td>2,000</td><td></td></tr>
<tr><td>Decrease in accounts receivable....................</td><td>1,000</td><td></td></tr>
<tr><td>Increase in inventories.................................</td><td>(3,000)</td><td></td></tr>
<tr><td>Decrease in prepaid expenses ....</td><td>2,000</td><td></td></tr>
<tr><td>Increase in accounts payable ....</td><td>9,000</td><td></td></tr>
<tr><td>Decrease in accrued liabilities......................</td><td>(2,000)</td><td>19,000</td></tr>
<tr><td>Net cash provided by operating activities.............</td><td></td><td>45,000</td></tr>
<tr><td colspan="3">**Cash flows from investing activities:**</td></tr>
<tr><td>Purchase of equipment.................................</td><td>$(98,000)</td><td></td></tr>
<tr><td>Sale of equipment...</td><td>74,000</td><td></td></tr>
<tr><td>Purchase of long-term investment ....</td><td>(8,000)</td><td></td></tr>
<tr><td>Net cash used for investing activities...................</td><td></td><td>(32,000)</td></tr>
<tr><td colspan="3">**Cash flows from financing activities:**</td></tr>
<tr><td>Issuance of common stock ....</td><td>$ 19,000</td><td></td></tr>
<tr><td>Payment of cash dividends ....</td><td>(18,000)</td><td></td></tr>
<tr><td>Issuance of long-term note payable ....</td><td>7,000</td><td></td></tr>
<tr><td>Purchase of treasury stock.............................</td><td>(5,000)</td><td></td></tr>
<tr><td>Net cash provided by financing activities.............</td><td></td><td>3,000</td></tr>
<tr><td>**Net increase in cash**...</td><td></td><td>$ 16,000</td></tr>
<tr><td>Cash balance, December 31, 20X4 ....</td><td></td><td>3,000</td></tr>
<tr><td>Cash balance, December 31, 20X5 ....</td><td></td><td>$ 19,000</td></tr>
<tr><td colspan="3">**Noncash investing and financing activities:**</td></tr>
<tr><td>Issuance of long-term note payable to purchase patent...</td><td></td><td>$ 37,000</td></tr>
<tr><td>Issuance of common stock to retire bonds payable.........</td><td></td><td>13,000</td></tr>
<tr><td>Total noncash investing and financing activities.........</td><td></td><td>$ 50,000</td></tr>
</table>

HH   CHAPTER 12

Long-Term Investments	
Bal. 10,000	
8,000	
Bal. 18,000	

Equipment, Net	
Bal. 52,000	
98,000	76,000
	7,000
Bal. 67,000	

Patent, Net	
Bal. 10,000	
37,000	3,000
Bal. 44,000	

Long-term Note Payable	
	Bal. 0
	37,000
	7,000
	Bal. 44,000

Bonds Payable	
	Bal. 53,000
13,000	
	Bal. 40,000

Common Stock	
	Bal. 20,000
	13,000
	19,000
	Bal. 52,000

Retained Earnings	
	Bal. 19,000
18,000	26,000
	Bal. 27,000

Treasury Stock	
Bal. 5,000	
5,000	
Bal. 10,000	

PREPARING THE STATEMENT OF CASH FLOWS: DIRECT METHOD

OBJECTIVE

4 Prepare a statement of cash flows by the direct method

The Financial Accounting Standards Board (FASB) prefers the direct method of reporting operating cash flows because it provides clearer information about the sources and uses of cash. But only about 1% of companies use this method because it takes more computations than the indirect method. Investing and financing cash flows are unaffected by the operating cash flows.

To illustrate the statement of cash flows, we use The Roadster Factory, Inc. (TRF), a dealer in auto parts for sports cars. To prepare the statement of cash flows by the direct method, proceed as follows:

Step 1 Lay out the template of the statement of cash flows by the direct method, as shown in Part 1 of Exhibit 12-11. Part 2 (p. 640) gives a visual picture of the statement.

Step 2 Use the balance sheet to determine the increase or decrease in cash during the period. The change in cash is the "check figure" for the statement of cash flows. The Roadster Factory's comparative balance sheet shows that cash decreased by $8,000 during 20X9 (Exhibit 12-4, p. 627). *Why* did cash fall during 20X9? The statement of cash flows explains.

EXHIBIT 12-11	Part 1: Template of the Statement of Cash Flows—Direct Method

The Roadster Factory, Inc. (TRF)
Statement of Cash Flows
Year Ended December 31, 20X9

Cash flows from operating activities:
Receipts:
    Collections from customers
    Interest received on notes receivable
    Dividends received on investments in stock
        Total cash receipts
Payments:
    To suppliers
    To employees
    For interest
    For income tax
        Total cash payments
Net cash provided by (used for) operating activities
Cash flows from investing activities:
    Sales of long-term assets (investments, land, building, equipment, and so on)
  – Purchases of long-term assets
  + Collections of notes receivable
  – Loans to others
Net cash provided by (used for) investing activities
Cash flows from financing activities:
    Issuance of stock
  + Sale of treasury stock
  – Purchase of treasury stock
  + Borrowing (issuance of notes or bonds payable)
  – Payment of notes or bonds payable
  – Payment of dividends
Net cash provided by (used for) financing activities
Net increase (decrease) in cash during the year
  + Cash at December 31, 20X8
  = Cash at December 31, 20X9

HH CHAPTER 12

EXHIBIT 12-11   Part 2: Cash Receipts and Cash Payments on the Statement of Cash Flows—Direct Method

CASH RECEIPTS	Business Activity	CASH PAYMENTS

Operating Activities

CASH RECEIPTS
- Collections from customers
- Receipts of interest and dividends on investments
- Other operating receipts

CASH PAYMENTS
- Payments to suppliers
- Payments to employees
- Payments of interest and income tax
- Other operating payments

Investing Activities

CASH RECEIPTS
- Sale of plant assets
- Sale of investments that are not cash equivalents
- Collections of loans receivable

CASH PAYMENTS
- Acquisition of plant assets
- Purchase of investments that are not cash equivalents
- Making loans to others

Financing Activities

CASH RECEIPTS
- Issuing stock
- Selling treasury stock
- Borrowing money

CASH PAYMENTS
- Payment of dividends
- Purchase of treasury stock
- Payment of principal amounts of debts

Step 3 Use the available data to prepare the statement of cash flows. The Roadster Factory's transaction data appear in Exhibit 12-12. These transactions affected both the income statement (Exhibit 12-5, p. 627) and the statement of cash flows. Some transactions affect one statement and some affect the other. For example, sales (item 1) are reported on the income statement. Cash collections (item 2) go on the statement of cash flows. Other transactions, such as interest expense and payments (item 11) affect both statements. *The statement of cash flows reports only those transactions with cash effects* (those with an asterisk in Exhibit 12-12). Exhibit 12-13 gives The Roadster Factory's statement of cash flows for 20X9.

Cash Flows from Operating Activities. Operating cash flows are listed first because they are most important. Exhibit 12-13 shows that The Roadster Factory is sound; operating activities were the largest source of cash.

Cash Collections from Customers. Both cash sales and collections of accounts receivable are reported on the statement of cash flows as "Collections from customers . . . $288,000" in Exhibit 12-13.

Cash Receipts of Interest and Dividends. The income statement reports interest revenue and dividend revenue. Only the cash receipts of interest and dividends appear on the statement of cash flows—$2,000 of interest received in Exhibit 12-13.

EXHIBIT 12-12	Summary of The Roadster Factory's 20X9 Transactions

Operating Activities
1. Sales on credit, $303,000
*2. Collections from customers, $288,000
*3. Interest revenue and receipts, $2,000
4. Cost of goods sold, $150,000
5. Purchases of inventory on credit, $147,000
*6. Payments to suppliers, $133,000
7. Salary and wage expense, $56,000
*8. Payments of salary and wages, $58,000
9. Depreciation expense, $18,000
10. Other operating expense, $17,000
*11. Income tax expense and payments, $15,000
*12. Interest expense and payments, $7,000

Investing Activities
*13. Cash payments to acquire plant assets, $196,000
*14. Loan to another company, $21,000
*15. Proceeds from sale of plant assets, $62,000, including $8,000 gain

Financing Activities
*16. Proceeds from issuance of long-term debt, $94,000
*17. Proceeds from issuance of common stock, $4,000
*18. Payment of long-term debt, $11,000
*19. Declaration and payment of cash dividends, $17,000

*Indicates a cash flow to be reported on the statement of cash flows.
Note: Income statement data are taken from Exhibit 12-16, page 645.

Payments to Suppliers. Payments to suppliers include all expenditures for inventory and operating expenses except employee pay, interest, and income taxes. *Suppliers* are those entities that provide inventory and essential services. For example, a clothing store's suppliers may include **Tommy Hilfiger, Adidas,** and **Ralph Lauren.** Other suppliers provide advertising, utilities, and office supplies. Exhibit 12-13 shows that The Roadster Factory paid suppliers $133,000.

Payments to Employees. This category includes salaries, wages, and other forms of employee pay. Accrued amounts are excluded because they have not yet been paid. The statement of cash flows reports only the cash payments ($58,000).

Payments for Interest Expense and Income Tax Expense. Interest and income tax payments are reported separately. The Roadster Factory paid cash for all its interest and income taxes. Therefore, the same amount goes on the income statement and the statement of cash flows. These payments are operating cash flows because the interest and income tax are expenses.

EXHIBIT 12-13	Statement of Cash Flows— Direct Method

The Roadster Factory, Inc. (TRF)
Statement of Cash Flows (Direct Method)
For Year Ended December 31, 20X9

	(In thousands)	
Cash flows from operating activities:		
Receipts:		
Collections from customers	$ 288	
Interest received	2	
Total cash receipts		$ 290
Payments:		
To suppliers	$(133)	
To employees	(58)	
For income tax	(15)	
For interest	(7)	
Total cash payments		(213)
Net cash provided by operating activities		77
Cash flows from investing activities:		
Acquisition of plant assets	$(196)	
Loans to another company	(21)	
Proceeds from sale of plant assets	62	
Net cash used for investing activities		(155)
Cash flows from financing activities:		
Proceeds from issuance of long-term debt	$ 94	
Proceeds from issuance of common stock	4	
Payment of long-term debt	(11)	
Payment of dividends	(17)	
Net cash provided by financing activities		70
Net (decrease) in cash		$ (8)
Cash balance, December 31, 20X8		42
Cash balance, December 31, 20X9		$ 34

Depreciation, Depletion, and Amortization Expense. These expenses are *not* listed on the direct-method statement of cash flows because they do not affect cash.

Cash Flows from Investing Activities

Investing is critical because a company's investments affect the future. Large purchases of plant assets signal expansion. Meager investing activity means the business is not growing.

Purchasing Plant Assets and Investments and Making Loans to Other Companies. These cash payments acquire long-term assets. The Roadster Factory's first investing activity in Exhibit 12-13 is the purchase of plant assets ($196,000). TRF also made a $21,000 loan and thus got a note receivable.

Proceeds from Selling Plant Assets and Investments and from Collecting Notes Receivable. These cash receipts are also investing activities. The sale of the plant assets needs explanation. The Roadster Factory received $62,000 cash from the sale of plant assets, and there was an $8,000 gain on this transaction. What is the appropriate amount to show on the cash-flow statement? It is $62,000, the cash received from the sale, not the $8,000 gain.

Investors are often critical of a company that sells large amounts of its plant assets. That may signal an emergency. For example, problems in the airline industry have caused some companies to sell airplanes to generate cash.

Cash Flows from Financing Activities

Cash flows from financing activities include the following:

Proceeds from Issuance of Stock and Debt (Notes and Bonds Payable). Issuing stock and borrowing money are 2 ways to finance a company. In Exhibit 12-13, The Roadster Factory received $4,000 when it issued common stock. TRF also received $94,000 cash when it issued long-term debt (such as a note payable) to borrow money.

Payment of Debt and Purchasing the Company's Own Stock. Paying debt (notes payable) is the opposite of borrowing. TRF reports long-term debt payments of $11,000. The purchase of treasury stock is another example of a use of cash.

Payment of Cash Dividends. Paying cash dividends is a financing activity, as shown by The Roadster Factory's $17,000 payment in Exhibit 12-13. A *stock* dividend has no effect on Cash and is *not* reported on the cash-flow statement.

Noncash Investing and Financing Activities

Companies make investments that do not require cash. They also obtain financing other than cash. Our examples thus far have included none of these transactions. Now suppose that The Roadster Factory issued common stock valued at $300,000 to acquire a warehouse. TRF would journalize this transaction as follows:

Warehouse Building	300,000	
Common Stock		300,000

This transaction would not be reported as a cash payment because TRF paid no cash. But the investment in the warehouse and the issuance of stock are important. These noncash investing and financing activities can be reported in a separate schedule under the statement of cash flows. Exhibit 12-14 illustrates noncash investing and financing activities (all amounts are assumed).

EXHIBIT 12-14 Noncash Investing and Financing Activities (All Amounts Assumed)

	Thousands
Noncash Investing and Financing Activities:	
Acquisition of building by issuing common stock	$300
Acquisition of land by issuing note payable	70
Payment of long-term debt by issuing common stock	100
Total noncash investing and financing activities	$470

HH CHAPTER 12

STOP & think...

Classify each of the following as an operating activity, an investing activity, or a financing activity. Also identify those items that are not reported on the statement of cash flows prepared by the *direct* method.

a. Net income	i. Issuance of stock
b. Payment of dividends	j. Purchase of another company
c. Borrowing	k. Payment of a note payable
d. Payment of cash to suppliers	l. Payment of income taxes
e. Making a loan	m. Collections from customers
f. Sale of treasury stock	n. Accrual of interest revenue
g. Depreciation expense	o. Expiration of prepaid expense
h. Purchase of equipment	p. Receipt of cash dividends

Answer:

a. Not reported	e. Investing	i. Financing	m. Operating
b. Financing	f. Financing	j. Investing	n. Not reported
c. Financing	g. Not reported	k. Financing	o. Not reported
d. Operating	h. Investing	l. Operating	p. Operating

Now let's see how to compute the operating cash flows by the direct method.

Computing Operating Cash Flows by the Direct Method

To compute operating cash flows by the direct method, we use the income statement and the *changes* in the balance sheet accounts. Exhibit 12-15 diagrams the process. Exhibit 12-16 is The Roadster Factory's income statement, and Exhibit 12-17 is the comparative balance sheet.

EXHIBIT 12-15   Direct Method of Computing Cash Flows from Operating Activities

RECEIPTS / PAYMENTS	Income Statement Account	Change in Related Balance Sheet Account	
RECEIPTS:			
From customers	Sales Revenue	+ Decrease in Accounts Receivable − Increase in Accounts Receivable	
Of interest	Interest Revenue	+ Decrease in Interest Receivable − Increase in Interest Receivable	
PAYMENTS:			
To suppliers	Cost of Goods Sold	+ Increase in Inventory − Decrease in Inventory	+ Decrease in Accounts Payable − Increase in Accounts Payable
	Operating Expense	+ Increase in Prepaids − Decrease in Prepaids	+ Decrease in Accrued Liabilities − Increase in Accrued Liabilities
To employees	Salary (Wage) Expense	+ Decrease in Salary (Wage) Payable − Increase in Salary (Wage) Payable	
For interest	Interest Expense	+ Decrease in Interest Payable − Increase in Interest Payable	
For income tax	Income Tax Expense	+ Decrease in Income Tax Payable − Increase in Income Tax Payable	

*We thank Professor Barbara Gerrity for suggesting this exhibit.

EXHIBIT 12-16 Income Statement

The Roadster Factory, Inc. (TRF)
Income Statement
Year Ended December 31, 20X9

	(In thousands)	
Revenues and gains:		
Sales revenue..................................	$303	
Interest revenue.............................	2	
Gain on sale of plant assets............	8	
Total revenues and gains............		$313
Expenses:		
Cost of goods sold	$150	
Salary and wage expense................	56	
Depreciation expense	18	
Other operating expense	17	
Income tax expense........................	15	
Interest expense..............................	7	
Total expenses............................		263
Net income..		$ 50

EXHIBIT 12-17 Comparative Balance Sheet

The Roadster Factory, Inc. (TRF)
Comparative Balance Sheet
December 31, 20X9 and 20X8

(In thousands)	20X9	20X8	Increase (Decrease)	
Assets				
Current:				
Cash..	$ 34	$ 42	$ (8)	⎫
Accounts receivable..................	96	81	15	⎬ Changes in current assets—*Operating*
Inventory....................................	35	38	(3)	
Prepaid expenses.......................	8	7	1	⎭
Notes receivable.........................	21	—	21	⎫ Changes in noncurrent assets—*Investing*
Plant assets, net of depreciation...	343	219	124	⎬
Total	$537	$387	$150	
Liabilities				
Current:				
Accounts payable	$ 91	$ 57	$ 34	⎫
Salary and wage payable.........	4	6	(2)	⎬ Changes in current liabilities—*Operating*
Accrued liabilities....................	1	3	(2)	⎭
Long-term debt	160	77	83	⎫ Changes in long-term liabilities and paid-in capital accounts—*Financing*
Stockholders' Equity				
Common stock...........................	162	158	4	⎭
Retained earnings......................	119	86	33	⎬ Changes due to net income—*Operating* Change due to dividends—*Financing*
Total	$537	$387	$150	

Computing Cash Collections from Customers. Collections start with sales revenue (an accrual-basis amount). The Roadster Factory's income statement (Exhibit 12-16) reports sales of $303,000. Accounts receivable increased from $81,000 at the beginning of the year to $96,000 at year end, a $15,000 increase (Exhibit 12-17). Based on those amounts, Cash Collections equal $288,000, as follows. We must solve for cash collections (X):

Accounts Receivable					
Beginning balance	+	Sales	− Collections	=	Ending balance
$81,000	+	$303,000	−X	=	$96,000
			−X	=	$96,000 − $81,000 − $303,000
			X	=	$288,000

The T-account for Accounts Receivable provides another view of the same computation.

Accounts Receivable			
Beginning balance	81,000		
Sales	303,000	Collections	288,000
Ending balance	96,000		

Accounts Receivable increased, so collections must be less than sales.

All collections of receivables are computed this way. Let's turn now to cash receipts of interest revenue. In our example, The Roadster Factory earned interest revenue and collected cash of $2,000. The amounts of interest revenue and cash receipts of interest often differ and exhibit 12-15 shows how to make this computation.

Computing Payments to Suppliers. This computation includes 2 parts:

■ Payments for inventory
■ Payments for operating expenses (other than interest and income tax)

Payments for inventory are computed by converting cost of goods sold to the cash basis. We use Cost of Goods Sold, Inventory, and Accounts Payable. First, we must solve for purchases. All the amounts come from Exhibits 12-16 and 12-17.

Cost of Goods Sold					
Beginning inventory	+	Purchases	− Ending inventory	=	Cost of goods sold
$38,000	+	X	− $35,000	=	$150,000
		X		=	$150,000 − $38,000 + $35,000
		X		=	$147,000

Now we can compute cash payments for inventory (Y), as follows:

Accounts Payable					
Beginning balance	+	Purchases	− Payments for inventory	=	Ending balance
$57,000	+	$147,000	−Y	=	$91,000
			−Y	=	$91,000 − $57,000 − $147,000
			Y	=	$113,000

The T-accounts show where the data come from. Start with Cost of Goods Sold.

Cost of Goods Sold			
Beg. inventory	38,000	End. inventory	35,000
Purchases	147,000		
Cost of goods sold	150,000		

Accounts Payable			
Payments for inventory	113,000	Beg. bal.	57,000
		Purchases	147,000
		End. bal.	91,000

Accounts Payable increased, so payments for inventory are less than purchases.

Computing Payments for Operating Expenses. Payments for operating expenses other than interest and income tax are computed from three accounts: Prepaid Expenses, Accrued Liabilities, and Other Operating Expenses. All The Roadster Factory data come from Exhibits 12-16 and 12-17.

Prepaid Expenses

Beginning balance	+	Payments	−	Expiration of prepaid expense (assumed)	=	Ending balance
$7,000	+	X	−	$7,000	=	$8,000
		X			=	$8,000 − $7,000 + $7,000
		X			=	$8,000

Accrued Liabilities

Beginning balance	+	Accrual of expense at year end (assumed)	−	Payments	=	Ending balance
$3,000	+	$1,000	−	−X	=	$1,000
				−X	=	$1,000 − $3,000 − $1,000
				X	=	$3,000

Other Operating Expenses

Accrual of expense at year end	+	Expiration of prepaid expense	−	Payments	=	Ending balance
$1,000	+	$7,000	−	X	=	$17,000
				X	=	$17,000 − $1,000 − $7,000
				X	=	$9,000

Total payments for operating expenses = $8,000 + $3,000 + $9,000
= $20,000

The T-accounts give another picture of the same data.

Prepaid Expenses				Accrued Liabilities				Other Operating Expenses		
Beg. bal.	7,000	Expiration of		Payment	3,000	Beg. bal.	3,000	Accrual of	1,000	
Payments	8,000	prepaid				Accrual of		expense at		
		expense	7,000			expense at		year end		
End. bal.	8,000					year end	1,000	Expiration of		
						End. bal.	1,000	prepaid		
								expense	7,000	
								Payments	9,000	
Total payments for operating expenses = $20,000($8,000 + $3,000 + $9,000)								End. bal.	17,000	

Now we can compute Payments to Suppliers as follows:

Payments to Suppliers		Payments for Inventory		Payments for Operating Expenses
$133,000	=	$113,000	+	$20,000

Computing Payments to Employees. It is convenient to combine all payments to employees into 1 account, Salary and Wage Expense. We then adjust the expense for the change in Salary and Wage Payable, as shown here:

Salary and Wage Payable

Beginning balance		Salary and wage expense		Payments		Ending balance
$6,000	+	$56,000	−	−X	=	$4,000
				−X	=	$4,000 − $6,000 − $56,000
				X	=	$58,000

		Salary and Wage Payable	
		Beginning balance	6,000
Payments to employees	58,000	Salary and wage expense	56,000
		Ending balance	4,000

Computing Payments of Interest and Income Taxes. The Roadster Factory's expense and payment amounts are the same for interest and income tax, so no analysis is required. If the expense and the payment differ, the payment can be computed as shown in Exhibit 12-15.

Computing Investing and Financing Cash Flows

Investing and financing activities are explained on pages 630–634. These computations are the same for both the direct and the indirect methods.

STOP & think...

Fidelity Company reported the following for 2006 and 2005 (in millions):

At December 31,	2006	2005
Receivables, net	$3,500	$3,900
Inventory	5,200	5,000
Accounts payable	900	1,200
Income taxes payable	600	700

Year Ended December 31,	2006
Revenues...	$23,000
Cost of goods sold.........................	14,100
Income tax expense......................	900

Based on these figures, how much cash did
- Fidelity collect from customers during 2006?
- Fidelity pay for inventory during 2006?
- Fidelity pay for income taxes during 2006?

		Beginning Receivables	+	Revenues	−	Collections	=	Ending Receivables
Collections from customers	= $23,400:	$3,900	+	$23,000	−	$23,400	=	$3,500

		Cost of Goods Sold	+	Increase in Inventory	+	Decrease in Accounts Payable	=	Payments
Payments for inventory	= $14,600:	$14,100	+	($5,200 − $5,000)	+	($1,200 − $900)	=	$14,600

		Beginning Income Taxes Payable	+	Income Tax Expense	−	Payment	=	Ending Income Taxes Payable
Payment of income taxes	= $1,000:	$700	+	$900	−	$1,000	=	$600

HH CHAPTER 12

MEASURING CASH ADEQUACY: FREE CASH FLOW

Throughout this chapter, we have focused on cash flows from operating, investing, and financing activities. Some investors want to know how much cash a company can "free up" for new opportunities. **Free cash flow** is the amount of cash available from operations after paying for planned investments in plant assets. Free cash flow can be computed as follows:

$$\text{Free cash flow} = \frac{\text{Net cash provided}}{\text{by operating activities}} - \frac{\text{Cash payments earmarked for}}{\text{investments in plant assets}}$$

PepsiCo, Inc., uses free cash flow to manage its operations. Suppose PepsiCo expects net cash inflow of $2.3 billion from operations. Assume PepsiCo plans to spend $1.9 billion to modernize its bottling plants. In this case, PepsiCo's free cash flow would be $0.4 billion ($2.3 billion - $1.9 billion). If a good investment opportunity comes along, PepsiCo should have $0.4 billion to invest in the other company. **Shell Oil Company** also uses free-cash-flow analysis. A large amount of free cash flow is preferable because it means that a lot of cash is available for new investments. The Decision Guidelines that follow shows some ways to use cash-flow and income data for investment and credit analysis.

DECISION GUIDELINES

INVESTORS' AND CREDITORS' USE OF CASH-FLOW AND RELATED INFORMATION

Jan Childres is a private investor. Through years of experience she has devised some guidelines for evaluating both stock investments and bond investments. Childres uses a combination of accrual-accounting data and cash-flow information. Here are her decision guidelines for both investors and creditors.

INVESTORS

Questions	Factors to Consider*	Financial Statement Predictor/Decision Model*
1. How much in dividends can I expect to receive from an investment in stock?	Expected future net income	Income from continuing operations**
	Expected future cash balance	Net cash flows from (in order): • Operating activities • Investing activities • Financing activities
	Future dividend policy	Current and past dividend policy
2. Is the stock price likely to increase or decrease?	Expected future net income	Income from continuing operations**
	Expected future cash flows from operating activities	Income from continuing operations** Net cash flow from operating activities
3. What is the future stock price likely to be?	Expected future income from • continuing operations, and • net cash flow from operating activities	$$\text{Expected future price of a share of stock} = \frac{\text{Expected future earnings per share**}}{\text{Investment capitalization rate**}}$$ $$\text{Expected future price of a share of stock} = \frac{\text{Net cash flow from operations per share}}{\text{Investment capitalization rate**}}$$

CREDITORS

Questions	Factors to Consider	Financial Statement Predictor
Can the company pay the interest and principal at the maturity of a loan?	Expected future net cash flow from operating activities	Income from continuing operations** Net cash flow from operating activities

*There are many other factors to consider in making these decisions. These are some of the more common.
**See Chapter 11.

END-OF-CHAPTER SUMMARY PROBLEM

Adeva Health Foods, Inc., reported the following comparative balance sheet and income statement for 20X6.

Adeva Health Foods, Inc.
Comparative Balance Sheet
December 31, 20X6 and 20X5

	20X6	20X5
Cash..	$ 19,000	$ 3,000
Accounts receivable................	22,000	23,000
Inventories	34,000	31,000
Prepaid expenses....................	1,000	3,000
Equipment, net........................	90,000	79,000
Intangible assets	9,000	9,000
	$175,000	$148,000
Accounts payable...................	$ 14,000	$ 9,000
Accrued liabilities...................	16,000	19,000
Income tax payable................	14,000	12,000
Notes payable	45,000	50,000
Common stock........................	31,000	20,000
Retained earnings...................	64,000	40,000
Treasury stock........................	(9,000)	(2,000)
	$175,000	$148,000

Adeva Health Foods, Inc.
Income Statement
Year Ended December 31, 20X6

Sales revenue...	$190,000
Gain on sale of equipment.................	6,000
Total revenue and gains	$196,000
Cost of goods sold.............................	$ 85,000
Depreciation expense	19,000
Other operating expenses..................	36,000
Total expenses	140,000
Income before income tax	56,000
Income tax expense............................	18,000
Net income..	$ 38,000

Assume that **Berkshire Hathaway** is considering buying Adeva. Berkshire Hathaway requests the following cash-flow data for 20X6. There were no noncash investing and financing activities.

a. Collections from customers
b. Cash payments for inventory
c. Cash payments for operating expenses

d. Cash payment for income tax

e. Cash received from the sale of equipment. Adeva paid $40,000 for new equipment during the year.

f. Issuance of common stock

g. Issuance of notes payable. Adeva paid off $20,000 during the year.

h. Cash dividends. There were no stock dividends.

Provide the requested data. Show your work.

Answer

a. Analyze Accounts Receivable (let X = Collections from customers):

Beginning	+	Sales	−	Collections	=	Ending
+ 23,000	+	190,000	−	X	=	$22,000
				X	=	$191,000

b. Analyze Inventory and Accounts Payable (let X = Purchases, and let Y = Payments for inventory):

Beginning Inventory	+	Purchases	−	Ending inventory	=	Cost of Goods Sold
$31,000	+	X	−	$34,000	=	$85,000
		X			=	$88,000

Beginning Accounts Payable	+	Purchases	−	Payments	=	Ending Accounts Payable
$9,000	+	$88,000	−	Y	=	$14,000
				Y	=	$83,000

c. Start with Other Operating Expenses, and adjust for the changes in Prepaid Expenses and Accrued Liabilities:

Other Operating Expenses	− Decrease in Prepaid Expenses	+ Decrease in Accrued Liabilities	=	Payments for Operating Expenses
$36,000	− $2,000	+ $3,000	=	$37,000

d. Analyze Income Tax Payable (let X = Payment of income tax):

Beginning	+	Income Tax Expense	−	Payments	=	Ending
$12,000	+	$18,000	−	X	=	$14,000
				X	=	$16,000

e. Analyze Equipment, Net (let X = Book value of equipment sold. Then combine with the gain or loss to compute cash received from the sale.)

Beginning	+	Aquisitions	–	Depreciation	–	Book Value Sold	=	Ending
$79,000	+	$40,000	–	$19,000	–	X	=	$90,000
						X	=	$10,000

Cash Received from Sale	=	Book Value Sold	+	Gain on Sale
$16,000	=	$10,000	+	$6,000

f. Analyze Common Stock (let X = issuance)

Beginning	+	Issuance	=	Ending
$20,000	+	X	=	$31,000
		X	=	$11,000

g. Analyze Notes Payable (let X = issuance):

Beginning	+	Issuance	–	Payment	=	Ending
$50,000	+	X	–	$20,000	=	$45,000
		X			=	$15,000

h. Analyze Retained Earnings (let X = dividends)

Beginning	+	Net Income	–	Dividends	=	Ending
$40,000	+	$38,000	–	X	=	$64,000
				X	=	$14,000

REVIEW STATEMENT OF CASH FLOWS

Quick Check (Answers are given on page 684.)

1. All of the following activities are reported on the statement of cash flows except:
   a. operating activities.
   b. investing activities.
   c. financing activities.
   d. marketing activities.
2. Activities that create long-term liabilities are usually
   a. operating activities.
   b. investing activities.
   c. financing activities.
   d. noncash investing and financing activities.

3. Activities affecting long-term assets are
   a. operating activities.
   b. investing activities.
   c. financing activities.
   d. marketing activities.

4. In 20X9, IMC Corporation borrowed $50,000, paid dividends of $12,000, issued 2,000 shares of stock for $30 per share, purchased land for $24,000, and received dividends of $6,000. Net income was $80,000, and depreciation for the year totaled $5,000. How much should be reported as net cash provided by operating activities by the indirect method?
   a. $85,000
   b. $98,000
   c. $110,000
   d. $104,000

5. Activities that obtain the cash needed to launch and sustain a company are
   a. income activities
   b. investing activities.
   c. financing activities.
   d. marketing activities.

6. The exchange of stock for land would be reported as
   a. Exchanges are not reported on the statement of cash flows.
   b. noncash investing and financing activities.
   c. investing activities.
   d. financing activities.

Use the following Carolina Company information for questions 7–10.

Net income.....................................	$47,000	Increase in accounts payable	$ 7,000
Depreciation expense	8,000	Acquisition of equipment	24,000
Payment of dividends	2,000	Sale of treasury stock	3,000
Increase in accounts receivable.........	4,000	Payment of long-term debt.........	9,000
Collection of notes receivable...........	6,000	Proceeds from sale of land.........	36,000
Loss on sale of land.........................	12,000	Decrease in inventories..............	2,000

7. Under the indirect method, net cash provided by operating activities would be:
   a. $72,000
   b. $76,000
   c. $83,000
   d. $84,000

8. Net cash provided by (used for) investing activities would be:
   a. $18,000
   b. $(12,000)
   c. $(6,000)
   d. $24,000

9. Net cash provided by (used for) financing activities would be:
   a. $4,000
   b. $2,000
   c. $(8,000)
   d. $(11,000)

10. The cost of land must have been
    a. $30,000.
    b. $48,000.
    c. $54,000.
    d. Cannot be determined from the data given.

11. Blue Bunny Ice Cream began the year with $45,000 in accounts receivable and ended the year with $31,000 in accounts receivable. If sales for the year were $650,000, the cash collected from customers during the year amounted to:
    a. $664,000
    b. $672,000
    c. $733,000
    d. $655,000

12. Hampshire Farms, Ltd., made sales of $690,000 and had cost of goods sold of $390,000. Inventory decreased by $15,000 and accounts payable decreased by $9,000. Operating expenses were $175,000. How much was Hampshire Farms' net income for the year?
    a. $110,000
    b. $116,000
    c. $125,000
    d. $300,000

13. Use the Hampshire Farms data from question 12. How much cash did Hampshire Farms pay for inventory during the year?
    a. $374,000
    b. $390,000
    c. $396,000
    d. (Some other amount_____).

Accounting Vocabulary

cash equivalents (p. 622) Highly liquid short-term investments that can be converted into cash immediately.

cash flows (p. 621) Cash receipts and cash payments (disbursements).

direct method (p. 624) Format of the operating activities section of the statement of cash flows; lists the major categories of operating cash receipts (collections from customers and receipts of interest and dividends) and cash disbursements (payments to suppliers, to employees, for interest and income taxes).

financing activities (p. 623) Activities that obtain from investors and creditors the cash needed to launch and sustain the business; a section of the statement of cash flows.

free cash flow (p. 649) The amount of cash available from operations after paying for planned investments in plant assets.

indirect method (p. 624) Format of the operating activities section of the statement of cash flows; starts with net income and reconciles to cash flows from operating activities.

investing activities (p. 623) Activities that increase or decrease the long-term assets available to the business; a section of the statement of cash flows.

operating activities (p. 623) Activities that create revenue or expense in the entity's major line of business; a section of the statement of cash flows. Operating activities affect the income statement.

statement of cash flows (p. 621) Reports cash receipts and cash payments classified according to the entity's major activities: operating, investing, and financing.

ASSESS YOUR PROGRESS

Short Exercises

S12-1 (*Learning Objective 1: Purposes of the statement of cash flows*) State how the statement of cash flows helps investors and creditors perform each of the following functions. (pp. 620–621)

  a. Predict future cash flows.
  b. Evaluate management decisions.

S12-2 (*Learning Objective 2: Evaluating operating cash flows—indirect method*) Examine the **Google** cash-flow statement on page 620. Suppose Google's operating activities *used*, rather than *provided*, cash. Identify 3 things under the indirect method that could cause operating cash flows to be negative. (pp. 620, 624–625)

S12-3 (*Learning Objective 3: Reporting cash flows from operating activities—indirect method*) Majestic America Transportation (MAT) began 20X6 with accounts receivable, inventory, and prepaid expenses totaling $65,000. At the end of the year MAT had a total of $78,000 for these current assets. At the beginning of 20X6, MAT owed current liabilities of $42,000, and at year end current liabilities totaled $40,000.

  Net income for the year was $80,000. Included in net income were a $4,000 gain on the sale of land and depreciation expense of $9,000.

  Show how MAT should report cash flows from operating activities for 20X6. MAT uses the *indirect* method. Use Exhibit 12-6 (p. 628) as a guide.

S12-4 (*Learning Objective 2: Identifying items for reporting cash flows from operations—indirect method*) Cooper Clinic, Inc., is preparing its statement of cash flows (indirect method) for the year ended September 30, 20X7. Consider the following items in preparing the company's statement of cash flows. Identify each item as an operating activity—addition to net income (O+), or subtraction from net income (O-); an investing activity (I); a financing activity (F); or an activity that is not used to prepare the cash-flow statement by the indirect method (N). Place the appropriate symbol in the blank space. (pp. 624–635).

(*continued*)

a.	Loss on sale of land	h.	Increase in accounts payable
b.	Depreciation expense	i.	Net income
c.	Increase in inventory	j.	Payment of dividends
d.	Decrease in prepaid expense	k.	Decrease in accrued liabilities
e.	Decrease in accounts receivable	l.	Issuance of common stock
f.	Purchase of equipment	m.	Gain on sale of building
g.	Collection of cash from customers	n.	Retained earnings

S12-5 (*Learning Objective 3: Computing operating cash flows—indirect method*) (Short Exercise S12-6 is an alternate exercise.) Edwards Corporation accountants have assembled the following data for the year ended June 30, 20X8.

Net income..............................	$?	Cost of goods sold....................	$100,000
Payment of dividends..............	6,000	Other operating expenses.........	35,000
Proceeds from issuance		Purchase of equipment.............	40,000
of common stock............	20,000	Decrease in current liabilities....	5,000
Sales revenue..........................	224,000	Payment of note payable..........	30,000
Increase in current		Proceeds from sale of land........	60,000
assets other than cash	30,000	Depreciation expense	8,000
Purchase of treasury stock........	5,000		

Prepare the *operating activities section* of Edwards' statement of cash flows for the year ended June 30, 20X8. Edwards uses the *indirect* method for operating cash flows. (pp. 627–628)

S12-6 (*Learning Objective 3: Preparing a statement of cash flows—indirect method*) Use the data in Short Exercise S12-5 to prepare Edwards Corporations' statement of cash flows for the year ended June 30, 20X8. Edwards uses the *indirect* method for operating activities. Use Exhibit 12-7, page 630, as a guide, but you may stop after determining the net increase (or decrease) in cash.

S12-7 (*Learning Objective 3: Computing investing cash flows*) Motorcars of Phoenix, Inc., reported the following financial statements for 20X6:

Motorcars of Phoenix, Inc.
Income Statement
Year Ended December 31, 20X6

(In thousands)	
Sales revenue.............................	$710
Cost of goods sold....................	$340
Salary expense..........................	70
Depreciation expense	20
Other expenses.........................	130
Total expenses.........................	560
Net income	$150

Motorcars of Phoenix, Inc.
Comparative Balance Sheet
December 31, 20X6 and 20X5

(In thousands)

Assets	20X6	20X5	Liabilities	20X6	20X5
Current:			Current:		
Cash	$ 19	$ 16	Accounts payable..........	$ 47	$ 42
Accounts receivable	59	48	Salary payable	23	21
Inventory.....................	75	84	Accrued liabilities	8	11
Prepaid expenses...........	3	2	Long-term notes payable........	68	58
Long-term investments...........	55	75			
Plant assets, net.....................	225	185	**Stockholders' Equity**		
			Common stock......................	40	32
			Retained earnings..................	250	246
Total	$436	$410	Total	$436	$410

Compute the following investing cash flows. (p. 632):

a. Acquisitions of plant assets (all were for cash). Motorcars of Phoenix sold no plant assets.

b. Proceeds from the sale of investments. Motorcars of Phoenix purchased no investments.

S12-8 (*Learning Objective 3: Computing financing cash flows*) Use the Motorcars of Phoenix data in Short Exercise S12-7 to compute. (pp. 634–635)

a. New borrowing or payment of long-term notes payable. Motorcars of Phoenix had only 1 long-term note payable transaction during the year.

b. Issuance of common stock or retirement of common stock. Motorcars of Phoenix had only 1 common stock transaction during the year.

c. Payment of cash dividends (same as dividends declared).

S12-9 (*Learning Objective 4: Preparing a statement of cash flows—direct method*) Tally-Ho Horse Farm, Inc., began 20X6 with cash of $44,000. During the year, Tally-Ho earned service revenue of $500,000 and collected $510,000 from customers. Expenses for the year totaled $420,000, with $400,000 paid in cash to suppliers and employees. Tally-Ho also paid $100,000 to purchase equipment and a cash dividend of $50,000 to stockholders. During 20X6 Tally-Ho borrowed $20,000 by issuing a note payable.

Prepare the company's statement of cash flows for the year. Format operating activities by the direct method. (pp. 641–642)

S12-10 (*Learning Objective 4: Computing operating cash flows—direct method*) Short Exercise S12-11 is an alternate. Millbrook Golf Club, Inc., provides the following data for the year ended June 30, 20X9.

Cost of goods sold............................	$100,000	Payment of dividends...........................	$	6,000
Payments to suppliers......................	87,000	Proceeds from issuance		
Purchase of equipment	40,000	of common stock		20,000
Payments to employees.....................	70,000	Sales revenue.......................................		210,000
Payment of note payable.................	30,000	Collections from customers...............		180,000
Proceeds from sale of land...............	60,000	Payment of income tax......................		10,000
Depreciation expense	8,000	Purchase of treasury stock.................		5,000

(*continued*)

Prepare the *operating activities section* of Millbrook Golf Club, Inc.'s, statement of cash flows for the year ended June 30, 20X9. Millbrook uses the *direct* method for operating cash flows. (pp. 641–642)

S12-11 (*Learning Objective 4: Preparing a statement of cash flows—direct method*) Use the data in Short Exercise S12-10 to prepare Millbrook Golf Club, Inc.'s, statement of cash flows for the year ended June 30, 20X9. Millbrook uses the *direct* method for operating activities. Use Exhibit 12-13, page 642, as a guide, but you may stop after determining the net increase (or decrease) in cash.

S12-12 (*Learning Objective 4: Computing operating cash flows—direct method*) Use the Motorcars of Phoenix data in Short Exercise S12-7 to compute the following:

  a. Collections from customers (pp. 644–645) **b.** Payments for inventory (pp. 646–647)

S12-13 (*Learning Objective 4: Computing operating cash flows—direct method*) Use the Motorcars of Phoenix data in Short Exercise S12-7 to compute the following:

  a. Payments to employees (pp. 647–648)   **b.** Payments of other expenses (pp. 647–648)

Exercises

writing assignment ■

E12-14 (*Learning Objective 1: Identifying the purposes of the statement of cash flows*) U.S. Plating, Inc., has experienced an unbroken string of 10 years of growth in net income. Nevertheless, the company is facing bankruptcy. Creditors are calling all of U.S. Plating's loans for immediate payment, and the cash is simply not available. It is clear that the company's top managers overemphasized profits and gave too little attention to cash flows.

I Required

Write a brief memo, in your own words, to explain to the managers of U.S. Plating, Inc., the purposes of the statement of cash flows. (pp. 620–621)

E12-15 (*Learning Objective 2: Identifying activities for the statement of cash flows—indirect method*) Tyler-Bolton Investments specializes in low-risk government bonds. Identify each of Tyler-Bolton's transactions as operating (O), investing (I), financing (F), noncash investing and financing (NIF), or a transaction that is not reported on the statement of cash flows (N). Indicate whether each item increases (+) or decreases (−) cash. The indirect method is used for operating activities. (pp. 624–635)

__	a. Net income		__	k. Acquisition of equipment by issuance of note payable
__	b. Payment of cash dividend			
__	c. Sale of long-term investment		__	l. Payment of long-term debt
__	d. Loss on sale of equipment		__	m. Acquisition of building by cash payment
__	e. Amortization of intangible assets		__	n. Accrual of salary expense
__	f. Issuance of long-term note payable to borrow cash		__	o. Purchase of long-term investment
__	g. Depreciation of equipment		__	p. Decrease in merchandise inventory
__	h. Purchase of treasury stock			
__	i. Issuance of common stock for cash		__	q. Increase in prepaid expenses
			__	r. Cash sale of land
__	j. Increase in accounts payable		__	s. Decrease in accrued liabilities

E12-16 (*Learning Objective 2: Classifying transactions for the statement of cash flows—indirect method*) Indicate whether each of the following transactions records an operating activity, an investing activity, a financing activity, or a noncash investing and financing activity. The statement of cash flows is prepared by the *indirect* method. (pp. 624–635)

a.	Equipment	18,000		h.	Cash	81,000	
	Cash		18,000		Common Stock		12,000
b.	Cash	7,200			Capital in Excess of Par		69,000
	Long-Term Investment		7,200	i.	Treasury Stock	13,000	
c.	Bonds Payable	45,000			Cash		13,000
	Cash		45,000	j.	Cash	60,000	
d.	Building	164,000			Accounts Receivable	10,000	
	Note Payable, Long-Term		164,000		Service Revenue		70,000
e.	Loss on Disposal of Equipment	1,400		k.	Salary Expense	22,000	
	Equipment, Net		1,400		Cash		22,000
f.	Dividends Payable	16,500		l.	Land	87,000	
	Cash		16,500		Cash		87,000
g.	Furniture and Fixtures	22,100		m.	Depreciation Expense	9,000	
	Cash		22,100		Accumulated Depreciation		9,000

E12-17 (*Learning Objective 3: Computing cash flows from operating activities—indirect method*) The accounting records of North Central Distributors, Inc., reveal the following: **writing assignment ■**

Net income	$35,000	Depreciation	$18,000
Collection of dividend		Decrease in current	
revenue	7,000	liabilities	20,000
Payment of interest	16,000	Increase in current assets	
Sales revenue	9,000	other than cash	27,000
Loss on sale of land	5,000	Payment of dividends	7,000
Acquisition of land	37,000	Payment of income tax	13,000

Required

Compute cash flows from operating activities by the indirect method. Use the format of the operating activities section of Exhibit 12-6 (p. 628). Also evaluate the operating cash flow of North Central Distributors. Give the reason for your evaluation.

E12-18 (*Learning Objective 3: Computing cash flows from operating activities—indirect method*) The accounting records of Saskatoon Fur Traders include these accounts:

Cash

Mar. 1	5,000		
Receipts	447,000	Payments	448,000
Mar. 31	4,000		

Accounts Receivable

Mar. 1	18,000		
Receipts	443,000	Collections	447,000
Mar. 31	14,000		

Inventory

Mar. 1	19,000		
Purchases	337,000	Cost of sales	335,000
Mar. 31	21,000		

Equipment

Mar. 1	93,000		
Acquisition	6,000		
Mar. 31	99,000		

Accumulated Depreciation—Equipment

		Mar. 1	52,000
		Depreciation	3,000
		Mar. 31	55,000

Accounts Payable

		Mar. 1	14,000
Payments	332,000	Purchases	337,000
		Mar. 31	19,000

Accrued Liabilities

		Mar. 1	9,000
Payments	14,000	Receipts	11,000
		Mar. 31	6,000

Retained Earnings

Quarterly		Mar. 1	64,000
dividend	18,000	Net income	41,000
		Mar. 31	87,000

(continued)

Compute Saskatoon's net cash provided by (used for) operating activities during March. Use the indirect method. Does Saskatoon have trouble collecting receivables or selling inventory? How can you tell? (pp. 627–628)

writing assignment ■ **E12-19** (*Learning Objective 3: Preparing the statement of cash flows—indirect method*) The income statement and additional data of Noel Travel Products, Inc., follow:

Noel Travel Products, Inc.
Income Statement
Years Ended December 31, 20X6

Revenues:		
Sales revenue..........................	$229,000	
Dividend revenue.....................	8,000	$237,000
Expenses:		
Cost of goods sold	$ 91,000	
Salary expense	45,000	
Depreciation expense...............	29,000	
Advertising expense	4,000	
Interest expense	2,000	
Income tax expense.................	9,000	180,000
Net income		$ 57,000

Additional data:

a. Acquisition of plant assets was $150,000. Of this amount, $100,000 was paid in cash and $50,000 by signing a note payable.
b. Proceeds from sale of land totaled $24,000.
c. Proceeds from issuance of common stock totaled $30,000.
d. Payment of long-term note payable was $15,000.
e. Payment of dividends was $11,000.
f. From the balance sheet:

	December 31,	
	20X6	**20X5**
Current Assets:		
Cash	$47,000	$20,000
Accounts receivable	43,000	58,000
Inventory...............................	83,000	77,000
Prepaid expenses....................	9,000	8,000
Current Liabilities:		
Accounts payable...................	$35,000	$22,000
Accrued liabilities	13,000	21,000

❙ Required

1. Prepare Noel's statement of cash flows for the year ended December 31, 20X6, using the indirect method. (p. 630)

2. Evaluate Noel's cash flows for the year. In your evaluation, mention all 3 categories of cash flows and give the reason for your evaluation. (pp. 622–623)

E12-20 (*Learning Objective 3: Interpreting a cash-flow statement—indirect method*)
Consider 3 independent cases for the cash flows of 827 Boulevard Shoes. For each case, identify from the cash-flow statement how 827 Boulevard Shoes generated the cash to acquire new plant assets. Rank the 3 cases from the most healthy financially to the least healthy. (p. 630)

	Case A	Case B	Case C
Cash flows from operating activities:			
Net income	$ 30,000	$ 30,000	$ 30,000
Depreciation and amortization	11,000	11,000	11,000
Increase in current assets	(1,000)	(19,000)	(7,000)
Decrease in current liabilities	0	(6,000)	(8,000)
	$ 40,000	$ 16,000	$ 26,000
Cash flows from investing activities:			
Acquisition of plant assets	$(91,000)	$(91,000)	$ (91,000)
Sales of plant assets	8,000	97,000	4,000
	$(83,000)	$ 6,000	$ (87,000)
Cash flows from financing activities:			
Issuance of stock	$ 50,000	$ 16,000	$104,000
Payment of debt	(9,000)	(21,000)	(29,000)
	$ 41,000	$ (5,000)	$ 75,000
Net increase (decrease) in cash	$ (2,000)	$ 17,000	$ 14,000

E12-21 (*Learning Objective 3: Computing investing and financing amounts for the statement of cash flows*) Compute the following items for the statement of cash flows:

  a. Beginning and ending Plant Assets, Net, are $103,000 and $107,000, respectively. Depreciation for the period was $21,500, and purchases of new plant assets were $27,000. Plant assets were sold at a $1,000 loss. What were the cash proceeds of the sale? (pp. 630–632)
  b. Beginning and ending Retained Earnings are $45,000 and $73,000, respectively. Net income for the period was $47,000, and stock dividends were $8,000. How much were cash dividends? (pp. 634–635)

E12-22 (*Learning Objective 4: Identifying activities for the statement of cash flows—direct method*) Identify each of the following transactions as operating (O), investing (I), financing (F), noncash investing and financing (NIF), or not reported on the statement of cash flows (N). Indicate whether each transaction increases (+) or decreases (−) cash. The *direct* method is used for operating activities. (pp. 638–644)

  ___ a. Purchase of treasury stock
  ___ b. Issuance of common stock for cash
  ___ c. Payment of accounts payable
  ___ d. Issuance of preferred stock for cash
  ___ e. Payment of cash dividend
  ___ f. Sale of long-term investment
  ___ g. Amortization of patent
  ___ h. Collection of accounts receivable
  ___ i. Issuance of long-term note payable to borrow cash
  ___ j. Depreciation of equipment
  ___ k. Acquisition of equipment by issuance of note payable
  ___ l. Payment of long-term debt
  ___ m. Acquisition of building by payment of cash
  ___ n. Accrual of salary expense
  ___ o. Purchase of long-term investment
  ___ p. Payment of wages to employees
  ___ q. Collection of cash interest
  ___ r. Cash sale of land
  ___ s. Distribution of stock dividend

E12-23 (*Learning Objective 4: Classifying transactions for the statement of cash flows—direct method*) Indicate where, if at all, each of the following transactions would be reported on a statement of cash flows prepared by the *direct* method and the accompanying schedule of noncash investing and financing activities. (pp. 638–644)

a.	Equipment	18,000		h.	Retained Earnings	36,000	
	Cash		18,000		Common Stock		36,000
b.	Cash	7,200		i.	Cash	2,000	
	Long-Term Investment		7,200		Interest Revenue		2,000
c.	Bonds Payable	45,000		j.	Land	87,700	
	Cash		45,000		Cash		87,700
d.	Building	164,000		k.	Accounts Payable	8,300	
	Cash		164,000		Cash		8,300
e.	Cash	1,400		l.	Salary Expense	4,300	
	Accounts Receivable		1,400		Cash		4,300
f.	Dividends Payable	16,500		m.	Cash	81,000	
	Cash		16,500		Common Stock		12,000
g.	Furniture and Fixtures	22,100			Capital in Excess of Par		69,000
	Note Payable, Short-Term		22,100	n.	Treasury Stock	13,000	
					Cash		13,000

writing assignment ■

E12-24 (*Learning Objective 4: Computing cash flows from operating activities—direct method*) The accounting records of Jasmine Pharmaceuticals, Inc., reveal the following:

Payment of salaries and			Net income.................................	$34,000
wages.................................	$34,000		Payment of income tax...............	13,000
Depreciation...............................	22,000		Collection of dividend	
Decrease in current			revenue............................	7,000
liabilities...........................	20,000		Payment of interest....................	16,000
Increase in current assets			Cash sales..................................	38,000
other than cash................	27,000		Loss on sale of land	5,000
Payment of dividends...............	12,000		Acquisition of land	37,000
Collection of accounts			Payment of accounts	
receivable........................	93,000		payable	54,000

▌ *Required*

Compute cash flows from operating activities by the *direct* method. Use the format of the operating activities section of Exhibit 12-13 (pp. 641–642). Also evaluate Jasmine's operating cash flow. Give the reason for your evaluation. (pp. 622–623, 641–642)

E12-25 (*Learning Objective 4: Identifying items for the statement of cash flows—direct method*) Selected accounts of Fishbowl Antiques show the following:

Salary Payable

		Beginning balance	9,000
Payments	40,000	Salary expense	38,000
		Ending balance	7,000

Buildings

Beginning balance	90,000	Depreciation	18,000
Acquisitions	145,000	Book value of building sold	109,000*
Ending balance	108,000		

*Sale price was 140,000.

Notes Payable

		Beginning balance	273,000
Payments	69,000	Issuance of note payable for cash	83,000
		Ending balance	287,000

❙ Required

For each account, identify the item or items that should appear on a statement of cash flows prepared by the *direct* method. State where to report the item. (pp. 639–644)

E12-26 (*Learning Objective 4: Preparing the statement of cash flows—direct method*) The income statement and additional data of Floral World, Inc., follow:

writing assignment ■

Floral World, Inc.
Income Statement
Year Ended June 30, 20X6

Revenues:		
Sales revenue	$229,000	
Dividend revenue	15,000	$244,000
Expenses:		
Cost of goods sold	$103,000	
Salary expense	45,000	
Depreciation expense	29,000	
Advertising expense	11,000	
Interest expense	2,000	
Income tax expense	9,000	199,000
Net income		$ 45,000

Additional data:

a. Collections from customers are $30,000 more than sales.

b. Payments to suppliers are $1,000 more than the sum of cost of goods sold plus advertising expense.

(*continued*)

c. Payments to employees are $1,000 more than salary expense.

d. Dividend revenue, interest expense, and income tax expense equal their cash amounts.

e. Acquisition of plant assets is $150,000. Of this amount, $101,000 is paid in cash and $49,000 by signing a note payable.

f. Proceeds from sale of land total $24,000.

g. Proceeds from issuance of common stock total $30,000.

h. Payment of long-term note payable is $15,000.

i. Payment of dividends is $11,000.

j. Cash balance, June 30, 20X5, was $20,000.

❙ Required

1. Prepare Floral World, Inc.'s, statement of cash flows and accompanying schedule of noncash investing and financing activities. Report operating activities by the *direct* method. (pp. 641–644)

2. Evaluate Floral World's cash flows for the year. In your evaluation, mention all 3 categories of cash flows and give the reason for your evaluation. (pp. 622–623)

E12-27 (*Learning Objective 4: Computing amounts for the statement of cash flows—direct method*) Compute the following items for the statement of cash flows:

a. Beginning and ending Accounts Receivable are $22,000 and $32,000, respectively. Credit sales for the period total $60,000. How much are cash collections from customers? (pp. 644–645)

b. Cost of goods sold is $111,000. Beginning Inventory was $25,000, and ending Inventory is $21,000. Beginning and ending Accounts Payable are $14,000 and $8,000, respectively. How much are cash payments for inventory? (pp. 646–647)

Challenge Exercises

E12-28 (*Learning Objective 3, 4: Computing cash-flow amounts*) 500 Broad Street, Inc., reported the following in its financial statements for the year ended August 31, 20X9 (in thousands):

	20X9	20X8
Income Statement		
Net sales	$24,623	$21,207
Cost of sales	18,048	15,466
Depreciation	269	230
Other operating expenses	3,883	4,248
Income tax expense	537	486
Net income	$ 1,886	$ 777
Balance Sheet		
Cash and equivalents	$ 17	$ 13
Accounts receivable	601	615
Inventory	3,100	2,831
Property and equipment, net	4,345	3,428
Accounts payable	1,547	1,364
Accrued liabilities	938	631
Income tax payable	201	194
Long-term liabilities	478	464
Common stock	519	446
Retained earnings	4,380	3,788

Determine the following cash receipts and payments for 500 Broad Street, Inc., during 20X9:

a. Collections from customers (pp. 644–645)

b. Payments for inventory (pp. 646–647)

c. Payments for other operating expenses (pp. 646–647)

d. Payment of income tax (pp. 647–648)

e. Proceeds from issuance of common stock (p. 633)

f. Payment of cash dividends (pp. 634–635)

E12-29 (*Learning Objective 3: Using the balance sheet and the cash-flow statement together*) Crown Specialties reported the following at December 31, 20X8 (in thousands):

	20X8	20X7
From the comparative balance sheet:		
Property and equipment, net..	$11,150	$9,590
Long-term notes payable...	4,400	3,080
From the statement of cash flows:		
Depreciation	$ 1,920	
Capital expenditures..	(4,130)	
Proceeds from sale of		
property and equipment	770	
Proceeds from issuance of long-term note payable........	1,190	
Payment of long-term note payable............................	(110)	
Issuance of common stock	383	

Determine the following items for Crown Specialties during 20X8:

1. Gain or loss on the sale of property and equipment (p. 631)

2. Amount of long-term debt issued for something other than cash (pp. 633, 635–636)

Quiz

Test your understanding of the statement of cash flows by answering the following questions. Select the best choice from among the possible answers given.

Q12-30 Paying off bonds payable is reported on the statement of cash flows under (pp. 624–625)

a. operating activities.

b. investing activities.

c. financing activities.

d. noncash investing and financing activities.

Q12-31 The sale of inventory for cash is reported on the statement of cash flows under (pp. 624–625, 630)

a. operating activities.

b. investing activities.

c. financing activities.

d. noncash investing and financing activities.

Q12-32 Selling equipment is reported on the statement of cash flows under (pp. 624–625)

a. operating activities.

b. investing activities.

c. financing activities.

d. noncash investing and financing activities.

Q12-33 Which of the following terms appears on a statement of cash flows—indirect method? (pp. 624–625)

a. Payments to suppliers

b. Depreciation expense

c. Collections from customers

d. Cash receipt of interest revenue

Q12-34 On an indirect method statement of cash flows, an increase in a prepaid insurance would be: (pp. 624–625)

a. included in payments to suppliers.

b. added to net income.

c. added to increases in current assets.

d. deducted from net income.

Q12-35 On an indirect method statement of cash flows, an increase in accounts payable would be: (pp. 624–625)

a. reported in the investing activities section.
b. reported in the financing activities section.
c. added to net income in the operating activities section.
d. deducted from net income in the operating activities section.

Q12-36 On an indirect method statement of cash flows, a gain on the sale of plant assets would be (pp. 624–625)

a. ignored, since the gain did not generate any cash.
b. reported in the investing activities section.
c. deducted from net income in the operating activities section.
d. added to net income in the operating activities section.

Q12-37 Paying cash dividends is a/an _____ activity. (pp. 624–625)

Receiving cash dividends is a/an _____ activity. (pp. 641–642)

Q12-38 Matlock Camera Co. sold equipment with a cost of $20,000 and accumulated depreciation of $8,000 for an amount that resulted in a gain of $3,000. What amount should Matlock report on the statement of cash flows as "proceeds from sale of plant assets"? (p. 631)

a. $9,000
c. $15,000
b. $17,000
d. Some other amount (<u>fill in the blank</u>)

Questions 39–47 use the following data. Taft Corporation formats operating cash flows by the *indirect* method.

Taft's Income Statement for 20X3

Sales revenue	$180,000	
Gain on sale of equipment	8,000*	$188,000
Cost of goods sold	$110,000	
Depreciation	6,000	
Other operating expenses	25,000	141,000
Net income		$ 47,000

*The book value of equipment sold during 20X3 was $20,000.

Taft's Comparative Balance Sheet at the end of 20X3

	20X3	20X2		20X3	20X2
Cash	$ 4,000	$ 1,000	Accounts payable	$ 6,000	$ 7,000
Accounts receivable	7,000	11,000	Accrued liabilities	7,000	3,000
Inventory	10,000	9,000	Common stock	20,000	10,000
Plant and equipment, net	93,000	69,000	Retained earnings	81,000	70,000
	$114,000	$90,000		$114,000	$90,000

Q12-39 How many items enter the computation of Taft's net cash provided by operating activities? (pp. 624–625)

a. 2

b. 3

c. 5

d. 7

Q12-40 How do Taft's accrued liabilities affect the company's statement of cash flows for 20X3? (pp. 624–625)

a. They don't because the accrued liabilities are not yet paid.

b. Increase in cash provided by operating activities.

c. Increase in cash used by investing activities.

d. Increase in cash used by financing activities

Q12-41 How do accounts receivable affect Taft's cash flows from operating activities for 20X3? (pp. 624–625)

a. Increase in cash provided by operating activities.

b. Decrease in cash provided by operating activities

c. They don't because accounts receivable result from investing activities.

d. Decrease in cash used by investing activities.

Q12-42 Taft's net cash provided by operating activities during 20X3 was: (pp. 627–628)

a. $3,000

b. $47,000

c. $51,000

d. $58,000

Q12-43 How many items enter the computation of Taft's net cash flow from investing activities for 20X3? (pp. 624–625)

a. 2

b. 3

c. 5

d. 7

Q12-44 The book value of equipment sold during 20X3 was $20,000. Taft's net cash flow from investing activities for 20X3 was: (pp. 631)

a. net cash used of $22,000.

b. net cash used of $28,000.

c. net cash used of $50,000.

d. net cash used of $28,000.

Q12-45 How many items enter the computation of Taft's net cash flow from financing activities for 20X3? (pp. 624–625)

a. 2

b. 3

c. 5

d. 7

Q12-46 Taft's largest financing cash flow for 20X3 resulted from: (p. 630)

a. sale of equipment.

b. purchase of equipment.

c. issuance of common stock.

d. payment of dividends.

Q12-47 Taft's net cash flow from financing activities for 20X3 was: (p. 630)

a. net cash used of $25,000.

b. net cash used of $20,000.

c. net cash provided of $10,000.

d. net cash used of $26,000.

Q12-48 Sales totaled $800,000, accounts receivable increased by $40,000, and accounts payable decreased by $35,000. How much cash did the company collect from customers? (pp. 644–645)

a. $760,000

b. $795,000

c. $800,000

d. $840,000

Q12-49 Income Tax Payable was $5,000 at the end of the year and $2,800 at the beginning. Income tax expense for the year totaled $59,100. What amount of cash did the company pay for income tax during the year? (pp. 647–648)

a. $56,900

b. $59,100

c. $61,300

d. $61,900

HH CHAPTER 12

Problems
(Group A)

MyAccountingLab

Some of these A problems can be found within My Accounting Lab (MAL), an online homework and practice environment. Your instructor may ask you to complete these exercises using PHGA.

writing assignment ■

P12-50A (*Learning Objective 1, 2: Using cash-flow data to evaluate performance*) Top managers of Relax Inns are reviewing company performance for 20X9. The income statement reports a 20% increase in net income over 20X8. However, most of the increase resulted from an extraordinary gain on insurance proceeds from storm damage to a building. The balance sheet shows a large increase in receivables. The cash-flow statement, in summarized form, reports the following:

Net cash used for operating activities....................	$(80,000)
Net cash provided by investing activities...............	40,000
Net cash provided by financing activities..............	50,000
Increase in cash during 20X9.............................	$ 10,000

❙ Required

Write a memo giving Relax Inns' managers your assessment of 20X9 operations and your outlook for the future. Focus on the information content of the cash-flow data. (pp. 622–623)

P12-51A (*Learning Objective 2, 3: Preparing an income statement, balance sheet, and statement of cash flows—indirect method*) Vintage Automobiles of Philadelphia, Inc., was formed on January 1, 20X8, when Vintage issued its common stock for $300,000. Early in January, Vintage made the following cash payments:

    a. $150,000 for equipment
    b. $120,000 for inventory (4 cars at $30,000 each)
    c. $20,000 for 20X8 rent on a store building

In February, Vintage purchased 6 cars for inventory on account. Cost of this inventory was $260,000 ($43,333.33 each). Before year end, Vintage paid $208,000 of this debt. Vintage uses the FIFO method to account for inventory.

During 20X8, Vintage sold 8 vintage autos for a total of $500,000. Before year end, Vintage collected 80% of this amount.

The business employs 3 people. The combined annual payroll is $95,000, of which Vintage owes $4,000 at year end. At the end of the year, Vintage paid income tax of $10,000.

Late in 20X8, Vintage declared and paid cash dividends of $11,000.

For equipment, Vintage uses the straight-line depreciation method, over 5 years, with zero residual value.

❙ Required

1. Prepare Vintage Automobiles of Philadelphia, Inc.'s, income statement for the year ended December 31, 20X8. Use the single-step format, with all revenues listed together and all expenses together. (pp. 627–628)
2. Prepare Vintage's balance sheet at December 31, 20X8. (pp. 625–626)
3. Prepare Vintage's statement of cash flows for the year ended December 31, 20X8. Format cash flows from operating activities by using the *indirect* method. (p. 630)

P12-52A (*Learning Objective 2, 3: Preparing the statement of cash flows—indirect method*) Primrose Software Corp. has assembled the following data for the year ended December 31, 20X7.

	December 31,	
	20X7	20X6
Current Accounts:		
Current assets:		
Cash and cash equivalents	$38,700	$22,700
Accounts receivable	69,700	64,200
Inventories.......................................	88,600	83,000
Prepaid expenses..............................	5,300	4,100
Current liabilities:		
Accounts payable..............................	$57,200	$55,800
Income tax payable..........................	18,600	16,700
Accrued liabilities	15,500	27,200

Transaction Data for 20X7:

Acquisition of land by issuing		Purchase of treasury stock	$14,300
long-term note payable	$95,000	Loss on sale of equipment	11,700
Stock dividends	31,800	Payment of cash dividends	18,300
Collection of loan..................	8,700	Issuance of long-term note	
Depreciation expense	21,800	payable to borrow cash.....	34,400
Purchase of building..............	125,300	Net income..........................	45,100
Retirement of bonds payable		Issuance of common stock	
by issuing common stock	65,000	for cash	41,200
Purchase of long-term		Procedes from sale of	
investment..........................	31,600	equipment	58,000
		Amortization expense..........	5,300

▌ Required

Prepare Primrose Software Corp.'s statement of cash flows using the *indirect* method to report operating activities. Include an accompanying schedule of noncash investing and financing activities. (pp. 630, 635–636)

P12-53A (*Learning Objective 2, 3: Preparing the statement of cash flows—indirect method*) The comparative balance sheet of Northern Movie Theater Company at March 31, 20X9, reported the following:

writing assignment ■

■ **spreadsheet**

	March 31,	
	20X9	20X8
Current assets:		
Cash and cash equivalents	$ 9,900	$14,000
Accounts receivable	14,900	21,700
Inventories.......................................	63,200	60,600
Prepaid expenses..............................	1,900	1,700
Current liabilities:		
Accounts payable..............................	$30,300	$27,600
Accrued liabilities	10,700	11,100
Income tax payable..........................	8,000	4,700

Northern's transactions during the year ended March 31, 20X9, included the following:

Acquisition of land		Sale of long-term investment.	$13,700
by issuing note payable	$101,000	Depreciation expense	15,300
Amortization expense............	2,000	Cash purchase of building.....	47,000
Payment of cash dividend......	30,000	Net income............................	50,000
Cash purchase of		Issuance of common	
equipment........................	78,700	stock for cash..................	11,000
Issuance of long-term note		Stock dividend......................	18,000
payable to borrow cash.....	50,000		

I Required

1. Prepare Northern Movie Theater Company's statement of cash flows for the year ended March 31, 20X9, using the *indirect* method to report cash flows from operating activities. Report non-cash investing and financing activities in an accompanying schedule. (pp. 630, 635–636)
2. Evaluate Northern's cash flows for the year. Mention all 3 categories of cash flows and give the reason for your evaluation. (pp. 622–623)

P12-54A (*Learning Objective 2, 3: Preparing the statement of cash flows—indirect method*) The 20X8 comparative balance sheet and income statement of 4 Seasons Supply Corp. follow. 4 Seasons had no noncash investing and financing transactions during 20X8. During the year, there were no sales of land or equipment, no issuance of notes payable, no retirements of stock, and no treasury stock transactions.

I Required

1. Prepare the 20X8 statement of cash flows, formatting operating activities by using the *indirect* method. (p. 630)
2. How will what you learned in this problem help you evaluate an investment? (Challenge)

4 Season Supply Corp.
Comparative Balance Sheet

	December 31, 20X8	December 31, 20X7	Increase (Decrease)
Current assets:			
Cash and cash equivalents	$ 17,600	$ 5,300	$ 12,300
Accounts receivable	27,200	27,600	(400)
Inventories...................................	83,600	87,200	(3,600)
Prepaid expenses...........................	2,500	1,900	600
Plant assets:			
Land...	89,000	60,000	29,000
Equipment,net	53,500	49,400	4,100
Total assets...................................	$273,400	$231,400	$ 42,000
Current liabilities:			
Accounts payable..........................	$ 35,800	$ 33,700	$ 2,100
Salary payable	3,100	6,600	(3,500)
Other accrued liabilities.................	22,600	23,700	(1,100)
Long-term liabilities:			
Notes payable..............................	75,000	100,000	(25,000)
Stockholders' equity:			
Common stock, no-par.................	88,300	64,700	23,600
Retained earnings	48,600	2,700	45,900
Total liabilities and stockholders' equity.....	$273,400	$231,400	$ 42,000

4 Season Supply Corp.
Income Statement for 20X8

Revenues:

Sales revenue $228,700

Expenses:

Cost of goods sold	$70,600	
Salary expense	27,800	
Depreciation expense	4,000	
Other operating expense	10,500	
Interest expense	11,600	
Income tax expense	29,100	
Total expenses		153,600
Net income		$ 75,100

P12-55A *(Learning Objective 2, 4: Preparing the statement of cash flows—direct method)* **writing assignment ■**
Ethan Allen Furniture Gallery, Inc., provided the following data from the company's records for the year ended April 30, 20X7:

a. Credit sales, $583,900
b. Loan to another company, $12,500
c. Cash payments to purchase plant assets, $59,400
d. Cost of goods sold, $382,600
e. Proceeds from issuance of common stock, $8,000
f. Payment of cash dividends, $48,400
g. Collection of interest, $4,400
h. Acquisition of equipment by issuing short-term note payable, $16,400
i. Payments of salaries, $93,600
j. Proceeds from sale of plant assets, $22,400, including $6,800 loss
k. Collections on accounts receivable, $428,600
l. Interest revenue, $3,800
m. Cash receipt of dividend revenue, $4,100
n. Payments to suppliers, $368,500
o. Cash sales, $171,900
p. Depreciation expense, $59,900
q. Proceeds from issuance of note payable, $19,600
r. Payments of long-term notes payable, $50,000
s. Interest expense and payments, $13,300
t. Salary expense, $95,300
u. Loan collections, $12,800
v. Proceeds from sale of investments, $9,100, including $2,000 gain
w. Payment of short-term note payable by issuing long-term note payable, $63,000
x. Amortization expense, $2,900
y. Income tax expense and payments, $37,900
z. Cash balance: April 30, 20X6, $39,300; April 30, 20X7, $36,600

I Required

1. Prepare Ethan Allen Furniture Gallery, Inc.'s, statement of cash flows for the year ended April 30, 20X7. Use the *direct* method for cash flows from operating activities. Follow the format of Exhibit 12-13 (p. 642), but do *not* show amounts in thousands. Include an accompanying schedule of noncash investing and financing activities. (pp. 641–642, 643–644)
2. Evaluate 20X7 from a cash-flow standpoint. Give your reasons. (pp. 622–623)

P12-56A *(Learning Objective 2, 4: Preparing an income statement, balance sheet, and statement of cash flows—direct method)* Use the Vintage Automobiles of Philadelphia, Inc., data from Problem P12-51A.

(continued)

I *Required*

1. Prepare Vintage's income statement for the year ended December 31, 20X8. Use the single-step format, with all revenues listed together and all expenses together. (pp. 645–646)
2. Prepare Vintage's balance sheet at December 31, 20X8. (pp. 645–646)
3. Prepare Vintage's statement of cash flows for the year ended December 31, 20X8. Format cash flows from operating activities by using the *direct* method. (pp. 641–642)

P12-57A (*Learning Objective 2, 4: Preparing the statement of cash flows—direct method*) Use the 4 Seasons Supply Corp. data from Problem P12-54A.

I *Required*

writing assignment ■

1. Prepare the 20X8 statement of cash flows by using the *direct* method. (pp. 641–642)
2. How will what you learned in this problem help you evaluate an investment? (Challenge)

■ spreadsheet

P12-58A (*Learning Objective 3, 4: Preparing the statement of cash flows—direct and indirect methods*) To prepare the statement of cash flows, accountants for Franklin Electric Company have summarized 20X8 activity in 2 accounts as follows:

Cash			
Beginning balance	53,600	Payments on accounts payable	399,100
Sale of long-term investment	21,200	Payments of dividends	27,200
Collections from customers	661,700	Payments of salaries and wages	143,800
Issuance of common stock	47,300	Payments of interest	26,900
Receipts of dividends	17,100	Purchase of equipment	31,400
		Payments of operating expenses	34,300
		Payment of long-term note payable	41,300
		Purchase of treasury stock	26,400
		Payment of income tax	18,900
Ending balance	51,600		

Common Stock		
	Beginning balance	84,400
	Issuance for cash	47,300
	Issuance to acquire land	80,100
	Issuance to retire note payable	19,000
	Ending balance	230,800

I *Required*

1. Prepare the statement of cash flows of Franklin Electric Company for the year ended December 31, 20X8, using the *direct* method to report operating activities. Also prepare the accompanying schedule of noncash investing and financing activities. (pp. 641–644)
2. Use the following data from Franklin's 20X8 income statement and balance sheet to prepare a supplementary schedule of cash flows from operating activities by using the *indirect* method. (pp. 627–628)

Franklin Electric Company
Income Statement
Year Ended December 31, 20X8

Revenues:		
Sales revenue		$689,300
Dividend revenue		17,100
Total revenue		706,400
Expenses and losses:		
Cost of goods sold	$402,600	
Salary and wage expense	150,800	
Depreciation expense	19,300	
Other operating expense	44,100	
Interest expense	28,800	
Income tax expense	16,200	
Loss on sale of investments	1,100	
Total expenses and losses		662,900
Net income		$ 43,500

Franklin Electric Company
Selected Balance Sheet Data

	20X8 Increase (Decrease)
Current assets:	
Cash and cash equivalents	$ (2,000)
Accounts receivable	27,600
Inventories	(11,800)
Prepaid expenses	600
Long-term investments	(22,300)
Equipment, net	12,100
Land	80,100
Current liabilities:	
Accounts payable	$ (8,300)
Interest payable	1,900
Salary payable	7,000
Other accrued liabilities	10,400
Income tax payable	(2,700)
Long-term note payable	(60,300)
Common stock	146,400
Retained earnings	16,300
Treasury stock	(26,400)

HH **CHAPTER 12**

P12-59A (*Learning Objective 3, 4: Preparing the statement of cash flows—indirect and direct methods*) The comparative balance sheet of Graphic Design Studio, Inc., at June 30, 20X9, included these amounts.

Graphic Design Studio
Balance Sheet
June 30, 20X9 and 20X8

	20X9	20X8	Increase (Decrease)
Current assets:			
Cash	$ 28,600	$ 8,600	$ 20,000
Accounts receivable	48,800	51,900	(3,100)
Inventories..................................	68,600	60,200	8,400
Prepaid expenses...........................	3,700	2,800	900
Long-term investment	10,100	5,200	4,900
Equipment, net..	74,500	73,600	900
Land	42,400	96,000	(53,600)
	$276,700	$298,300	$(21,600)
Current liabilities:			
Notes payable, short-term	$ 13,400	$18,100	$(4,700)
Accounts payable...........................	42,400	40,300	2,100
Income tax payable........................	13,800	14,500	(700)
Accrued liabilities	8,200	9,700	(1,500)
Interest payable	3,700	2,900	800
Salary payable	900	2,600	(1,700)
Long-term note payable	47,400	94,100	(46,700)
Common stock...	59,800	51,200	8,600
Retained earnings....................................	87,100	64,900	22,200
	$276,700	$298,300	$(21,600)

Transaction data for the year ended June 30, 20X9:

a. Net income, $60,300
b. Depreciation expense on equipment, $13,400
c. Purchased long-term investment, $4,900
d. Sold land for $46,900, including $6,700 loss
e. Acquired equipment by issuing long-term note payable, $14,300
f. Paid long-term note payable, $61,000
g. Received cash for issuance of common stock, $3,900
h. Paid cash dividends, $38,100
i. Paid short-term note payable by issuing common stock, $4,700

❙ *Required*

1. Prepare the statement of cash flows of Graphic Design Studio, Inc., for the year ended June 30, 20X9, using the *indirect* method to report operating activities. Also prepare the accompanying schedule of noncash investing and financing activities. All current accounts except short-term notes payable result from operating transactions. (pp. 630, 635–636)
2. Prepare a supplementary schedule showing cash flows from operations by the *direct* method. The accounting records provide the following: collections from customers

$261,800; interest received, $1,300; payments to suppliers, $133,500; payments to employees, $40,500; payments for income tax, $10,600; and payment of interest, $5,300. (pp. 641–642)

(Group B)

writing assignment ■

P12-60B (*Learning Objective 1, 2: Using cash-flow information to evaluate performance*) Top managers of Culinary Imports are reviewing company performance for 20X7. The income statement reports a 15% increase in net income, the fifth consecutive year showing an income increase above 10%. The income statement includes a nonrecurring loss without which net income would have increased by 16%. The balance sheet shows modest increases in assets, liabilities, and stockholders' equity. The assets posting the largest increases are plant and equipment because the company is halfway through a 5-year expansion program. No other asset and no liabilities are increasing dramatically. A summarized version of the cash-flow statement reports the following:

Net cash provided by operating activities............	$ 310,000
Net cash used for investing activities..................	(290,000)
Net cash provided by financing activities	50,000
Increase in cash during 20X7	$ 70,000

I Required

Write a memo giving top managers of Culinary Imports your assessment of 20X7 operations and your outlook for the future. Focus on the net income and the cash-flow data. (pp. 622–623)

P12-61B (*Learning Objective 2, 3: Preparing an income statement, balance sheet, and statement of cash flows—indirect method*) Cruise America Motorhomes, Inc. (CAM), was formed on January 1, 20X8, when the company issued its common stock for $200,000. Early in January, CAM made the following cash payments:

- **a.** For store fixtures, $50,000
- **b.** For inventory 2 motorhomes at $60,000 each, a total of $120,000
- **c.** For rent on a store building, $12,000

In February, CAM purchased 3 motorhomes on account. Cost of this inventory was $160,000 ($53,333.33 each). Before year end, CAM paid $140,000 of this debt. CAM uses the FIFO method to account for inventory.

During 20X8, CAM sold 4 motorhomes for a total of $560,000. Before year end, CAM collected 90% of this amount.

The store employs 3 people. The combined annual payroll is $90,000, of which CAM owes $3,000 at year end. At the end of the year, CAM paid income tax of $64,000.

Late in 20X8, CAM declared and paid cash dividends of $40,000.

For store fixtures, CAM uses the straight-line depreciation method, over 5 years, with zero residual value.

I Required

1. Prepare Cruise America Motorhomes, Inc.'s, income statement for the year ended December 31, 20X8. Use the single-step format, with all revenues listed together and all expenses together. (pp. 627–628)
2. Prepare CAM's balance sheet at December 31, 20X8. (p. 626)
3. Prepare CAM's statement of cash flows for the year ended December 31, 20X8. Format cash flows from operating activities by the indirect method. (p. 630)

P12-62B (*Learning Objective 2, 3: Preparing the statement of cash flows—indirect method*) Accountants for Crowne Plaza Products, Inc., have assembled the following data for the year ended December 31, 20X4:

	December 31,	
	20X4	**20X3**
Current Accounts:		
Current assets:		
Cash and cash equivalents	$29,100	$34,800
Accounts receivable	70,100	73,700
Inventories	90,600	96,500
Prepaid expenses	3,200	2,100
Current liabilities:		
Accounts payable	$71,600	$67,500
Income tax payable	5,900	6,800
Accrued liabilities	28,300	23,200

Transaction Data for 20X4:

Payment of cash dividends	$48,300	Stock dividends	$ 12,600
Issuance of long-term note		Collection of loan	10,300
payable to borrow cash	71,000	Depreciation expense	29,200
Net income	31,000	Purchase of equipment	69,000
Issuance of preferred stock		Payment of note payable	
for cash	36,200	by issuing common stock	89,400
Sale of long-term investment ...	12,200	Purchase of long-term	
Amortization expense	1,100	investment	44,800
Payment of long-term		Acquisition of building by	
note payable	47,800	issuing long-term note	
Gain on sale of investment	3,500	payable	201,000

❙ Required

Prepare Crowne Plaza Products' statement of cash flows using the *indirect* method to report operating activities. Include an accompanying schedule of noncash investing and financing activities. (pp. 630, 635–636)

P12-63B (*Learning Objective 2, 3: Preparing the statement of cash flows—indirect method*) The comparative balance sheet of Crossbow Novelties Corp. at December 31, 20X5, reported the following:

	December 31,	
	20X5	**20X4**
Current Assets:		
Cash and cash equivalents	$28,800	$12,500
Accounts receivable	28,600	29,300
Inventories	51,600	53,000
Prepaid expenses	4,200	3,700
Current Liabilities:		
Accounts payable	$31,100	$28,000
Accrued liabilities	14,300	16,800
Income tax payable	11,000	14,300

Crossbow's transactions during 20X5 included the following:

Cash purchase of		Amortization expense................	5,000
building...............	$124,000	Payment of cash dividends.........	17,000
Net income...................	52,000	Cash purchase of equipment......	55,000
Issuance of common		Issuance of long-term note	
stock for cash......	105,600	payable to borrow cash....	32,000
Stock dividend..............	13,000	Retirement of note payable	
Sale of long-term		by issuing common stock....	30,000
investment...........	6,000	Depreciation expense................	12,800

❚ Required

1. Prepare the statement of cash flows of Crossbow Novelties Corp. for the year ended December 31, 20X5. Use the *indirect* method to report cash flows from operating activities. Report noncash investing and financing activities in an accompanying schedule. (pp. 630, 635–636)
2. Evaluate Crossbow's cash flows for the year. Mention all 3 categories of cash flows and give the reason for your evaluation.

P12-64B (*Learning Objective 2, 3: Preparing the statement of cash flows—indirect method*) The 20X8 comparative balance sheet and income statement of Riverbend Pools, Inc., follows. Riverbend had no noncash investing and financing transactions during 20X8. During the year, there were no sales of land or equipment, no issuances of notes payable, no retirements of stock, and no treasury stock transactions.

writing assignment ■

■ spreadsheet

❚ Required

1. Prepare the statement of cash flows of Riverbend Pools, Inc., for the year ended December 31, 20X8. Format operating activities by the indirect method. (p. 630)
2. How will what you learned in this problem help you evaluate an investment? (Challenge)

HH CHAPTER 12

Riverbend Pools, Inc.
Comparative Balance Sheet
December 31, 20X8 and 20X7

	20X8	20X7	Increase (Decrease)
Current assets:			
Cash and cash equivalents...........................	$ 28,700	$ 15,600	$13,100
Accounts receivable.....................................	47,100	44,000	3,100
Inventories...	94,300	89,900	4,400
Prepaid expenses..	1,700	2,200	(500)
Plant assets:			
Land..	35,100	10,000	25,100
Equipment, net..	100,900	93,700	7,200
Total assets...	$307,800	$255,400	$52,400
Current liabilities:			
Accounts payable..	$ 22,700	$ 24,600	$ (1,900)
Salary payable..	2,100	1,400	700
Other accrued liabilities..............................	24,400	22,500	1,900
Long-term liabilities:			
Notes payable..	55,000	65,000	(10,000)
Stockholders' equity:			
Common stock, no-par..............................	131,100	122,300	8,800
Retained earnings......................................	72,500	19,600	52,900
Total liabilities and stockholders' equity..............	$307,800	$255,400	$52,400

(continued)

Riverbend Pools, Inc.
Income Statement for 20X8

Revenues:

Sales revenue		$438,000
Interest revenue		11,700
Total revenues		449,700

Expenses:

Cost of goods sold	$185,200	
Salary expense	76,400	
Depreciation expense	15,300	
Other operating expense	49,700	
Interest expense	24,600	
Income tax expense	16,900	
Total expenses		368,100
Net income		$ 81,600

writing assignment ■

P12-65B (*Learning Objective 2, 4: Preparing the statement of cash flows—direct method*)
Rocco's Gourmet Foods, Inc., provides the following data from the company's records for the year ended July 31, 20X5:

a. Salary expense, $105,300

b. Cash payments to purchase plant assets, $181,000

c. Proceeds from issuance of note payable, $44,100

d. Payments of long-term note payable, $18,800

e. Proceeds from sale of plant assets, $59,700, including $10,600 gain

f. Interest revenue, $12,100

g. Cash receipt of dividend revenue on stock investments, $2,700

h. Payments to suppliers, $673,300

i. Interest expense and payments, $37,800

j. Cost of goods sold, $481,100

k. Collection of interest revenue, $11,700

l. Acquisition of equipment by issuing short-term note payable, $35,500

m. Payments of salaries, $104,000

n. Credit sales, $768,100

o. Loan to another company, $35,000

p. Income tax expense and payments, $56,400

q. Depreciation expense, $27,700

r. Collections on accounts receivable, $741,100

s. Loan collections, $74,400

t. Proceeds from sale of investments, $34,700, including $3,800 loss

u. Payment of long-term note payable by issuing preferred stock, $107,300

v. Amortization expense, $23,900

w. Cash sales, $146,000

x. Proceeds from issuance of common stock, $50,000

y. Payment of cash dividends, $50,500

z. Cash balance: July 31, 20X4—$23,800; July 31, 20X5—$31,400

I *Required*

1. Prepare Rocco's Gourmet Foods, Inc.'s, statement of cash flows for the year ended July 31, 20X5. Use the *direct* method for cash flows from operating activities. Follow the format of Exhibit 12-13, but do *not* show amounts in thousands. Include an accompanying schedule of noncash investing and financing activities. (pp. 641–644)

2. Evaluate 20X5 in terms of cash flow. Give your reasons. (pp. 622–623)

P12-66B (*Learning Objective 2, 4: Preparing an income statement, balance sheet, and statement of cash flows—direct method*) Use the Cruise America Motorhomes, Inc. (CAM), data from Problem P12-61B.

I Required

1. Prepare CAM's income statement for the year ended December 31, 20X8. Use the single-step format, with all the revenues listed together and all expenses together. (pp. 645–646)
2. Prepare CAM's balance sheet at December 31, 20X8. (pp. 645–646)
3. Prepare CAM's statement of cash flows for the year ended December 31, 20X8. Format cash flows from operating activities by using the *direct* method. (pp. 641–642)

P12-67B (*Learning Objective 2, 4: Preparing the statement of cash flows—direct method*) Use the Riverbend Pools, Inc., data from Problem P12-64B.

writing assignment ■

■ spreadsheet

I Required

1. Prepare the 20X8 statement of cash flows by using the *direct* method. (pp. 641–642)
2. How will what you learned in this problem help you evaluate an investment? (Challenge)

P12-68B (*Learning Objective 3, 4: Preparing the statement of cash flows—direct and indirect methods*) To prepare the statement of cash flows, accountants for Powers Art Gallery, Inc., have summarized 20X6 activity in 2 accounts as follows:

Cash

Beginning balance	87,100	Payments of operating expenses	46,100
Issuance of common stock	34,600	Payment of long-term note payable	78,900
Receipts of dividends	1,900	Purchase of treasury stock	10,400
Collection of loan	18,500	Payment of income tax	8,000
Sale of long-term investments	9,900	Payments on accounts payable	101,600
Receipts of interest	12,200	Payments of dividends	1,800
Collections from customers	308,100	Payments of salaries and wages	67,500
Sale of treasury stock	26,200	Payments of interest	21,800
		Purchase of equipment	79,900
Ending balance	82,500		

Common Stock

		Beginning balance	103,500
		Issuance for cash ·	34,600
		Issuance to acquire land	62,100
		Issuance to retire long-term note payable	21,100
		Ending balance	221,300

I Required

1. Prepare Powers' statement of cash flows for the year ended December 31, 20X6, using the *direct* method to report operating activities. Also prepare the accompanying schedule of noncash investing and financing activities. Powers' 20X6 income statement and selected balance sheet data follow. (pp. 641–644)
2. Prepare a supplementary schedule showing cash flows from operating activities by the *indirect* method. (pp. 627–628)

(continued)

Powers Art Gallery, Inc.
Income Statement
Year Ended December 31, 20X6

Revenues and gains:		
Sales revenue		$291,800
Interest revenue		12,200
Dividend revenue		1,900
Gain on sale of investments		700
Total revenues and gains		306,600
Expenses:		
Cost of goods sold	$103,600	
Salary and wage expense	66,800	
Depreciation expense	20,900	
Other operating expense	44,700	
Interest expense	24,100	
Income tax expense	2,600	
Total expenses		262,700
Net income		$ 43,900

Power Art Gallery, Inc.
Selected Balance Sheet Data

	20X6 Increase (Decrease)
Current assets:	
Cash and cash equivalents	$ (4,600)
Accounts receivable	(16,300)
Inventories	5,700
Prepaid expenses	(1,900)
Loan receivable	(18,500)
Long-term investments	(9,200)
Equipment, net	59,000
Land	62,100
Current liabilities:	
Accounts payable	$ 7,700
Interest payable	2,300
Salary payable	(700)
Other accrued liabilities	(3,300)
Income tax payable	(5,400)
Long-term note payable	(100,000)
Common stock	117,800
Retained earnings	42,100
Treasury stock	15,800

P12-69B (*Learning Objective 3, 4: Preparing the statement of cash flows—indirect and direct method*) Artes de Mexico, Inc.'s, comparative balance sheet at September 30, 20X9 included the following balances:

Artes de Mexico, Inc.
Balance Sheet
September 30, 20X9 and 20X8

	20X9	20X8	Increase (Decrease)
Current assets:			
Cash	$ 21,700	$ 17,600	$ 4,100
Accounts receivable	46,000	46,800	(800)
Inventories	121,700	116,900	4,800
Prepaid expenses	8,600	9,300	(700)
Long-term investments	51,100	13,800	37,300
Equipment, net	131,900	92,100	39,800
Land	47,100	74,300	(27,200)
	$428,100	$370,800	$ 57,300
Current liabilities:			
Notes payable, short-term	$ 22,000	$ 0	$ 22,000
Accounts payable	88,100	98,100	(10,000)
Accrued liabilities	17,900	29,100	(11,200)
Salary payable	1,500	1,100	400
Long-term note payable	123,000	121,400	1,600
Common stock	113,900	62,000	51,900
Retained earnings	61,700	59,100	2,600
	$428,100	$370,800	$ 57,300

Transaction data for the year ended September 30, 20X9:

a. Net income, $66,900
b. Depreciation expense on equipment, $8,500
c. Purchased long-term investments, $37,300
d. Sold land for $38,100, including $10,900 gain
e. Acquired equipment by issuing long-term note payable, $26,300
f. Paid long-term note payable, $24,700
g. Received cash of $51,900 for issuance of common stock
h. Paid cash dividends, $64,300
i. Acquired equipment by issuing short-term note payable, $22,000

❙ Required

1. Prepare Artes de Mexico's statement of cash flows for the year ended September 30, 20X9, using the *indirect* method to report operating activities. Also prepare the accompanying schedule of noncash investing and financing activities. All current accounts except short-term notes payable result from operating transactions. (pp. 630, 635–636)
2. Prepare a supplementary schedule showing cash flows from operations by using the *direct* method. The accounting records provide the following: collections from customers, $343,100; interest received, $8,600; payments to suppliers, $216,400; payments to employees, $63,000; payment of income tax, $21,200; payment of interest, $10,700. (pp. 641–642)

APPLY YOUR KNOWLEDGE

Decision Cases

Case 1. (*Learning Objective 3: Preparing and using the statement of cash flows to evaluate operations*) The 20X8 income statement and the 20X8 comparative balance sheet of T-Bar-M Camp, Inc., have just been distributed at a meeting of the camp's board of directors. The

writing assignment ■

directors raise a fundamental question: Why is the cash balance so low? This question is especially troublesome since 20X8 showed record profits. As the controller of the company, you must answer the question.

T–Bar–M Camp, Inc.
Comparative Income Statement
Year Ended December 31, 20X8

(In thousands)	
Revenues:	
Sales revenue	$436
Expenses:	
Cost of goods sold	$221
Salary expense	48
Depreciation expense	46
Interest expense	13
Amortization expense	11
Total expenses	339
Net income	$ 97

T–Bar–M Camp, Inc.
Comparative Balance Statement
December 31, 20X8 and 20X7

(In thousands)	20X8	20X7
Assets		
Cash	$ 17	$ 63
Accounts receivable, net	72	61
Inventories	194	181
Long-term investments	31	0
Property, plant and equipment	369	259
Accumulated depreciation	(244)	(198)
Patents	177	188
Totals	$ 616	$ 554
Liabilities and Owners' Equity		
Accounts payable	$ 63	$ 56
Accrued liabilities	12	17
Notes payable, long-term	179	264
Common stock, no par	149	61
Retained earnings	213	156
Totals	$ 616	$ 554

I Required

1. Prepare a statement of cash flows for 20X8 in the format that best shows the relationship between net income and operating cash flow. The company sold no plant assets or long-term investments and issued no notes payable during 20X8. There were *no* noncash investing and financing transactions during the year. Show all amounts in thousands. (pp. 630, 635–636)

2. Answer the board members' question: Why is the cash balance so low? Point out the 2 largest cash payments during 20X8. (Challenge)

3. Considering net income and the company's cash flows during 20X8, was it a good year or a bad year? Give your reasons. (pp. 622–623)

Case 2. *(Learning Objective 1, 2: Using cash-flow data to evaluate an investment)* Applied Technology, Inc., and Four-Star Catering are asking you to recommend their stock to your clients. Because Applied and Four-Star earn about the same net income and have similar financial positions, your decision depends on their cash-flow statements, summarized as follows:

writing assignment ■

	Applied		Four–Star	
Net cash provided by operating activities:...............		$ 30,000		$ 70,000
Cash provided by (used for) investing activities:				
Purchase of plant assets............................	$(20,000)		$(100,000)	
Sale of plant assets.................................	40,000	20,000	10,000	(90,000)
Cash provided by (used for) financing activities:				
Issuance of common stock		—		30,000
Paying off long-term debt		(40,000)		—
Net increase in cash................................		$ 10,000		$10,000

Based on their cash flows, which company looks better? Give your reasons. (Challenge)

Ethical Issue

Columbia Motors is having a bad year. Net income is only $37,000. Also, 2 important overseas customers are falling behind in their payments to Columbia, and Columbia's accounts receivable are ballooning. The company desperately needs a loan. The Columbia board of directors is considering ways to put the best face on the company's financial statements. Columbia's bank closely examines cash flow from operations. Daniel Peavey, Columbia's controller, suggests reclassifying as long-term the receivables from the slow-paying clients. He explains to the board that removing the $80,000 rise in accounts receivable from current assets will increase net cash provided by operations. This approach may help Columbia get the loan.

writing assignment ■

I *Required*

1. Using only the amounts given, compute net cash provided by operations, both without and with the reclassification of the receivables. Which reporting makes Columbia look better?
2. Under what condition would the reclassification of the receivables be ethical? Unethical?

Focus on Financials: ■ YUM! Brands

(Learning Objective 1, 2, 3, 4: Using the statement of cash flows) Use **YUM! Brands, Inc.'s**, statement of cash flows along with the company's other financial statements, all in Appendix A at the end of the book, to answer the following questions.

I *Required*

1. By which method does YUM report cash flows from *operating* activities? How can you tell (pp. 623–625)?
writing assignment ■
2. Suppose YUM reported net cash flows from operating activities by using the direct method. Compute these amounts for the year ended December 30, 2006 (ignore the statement of cash flows, and use only YUM's income statement and balance sheet).
   a. Collections from customers, franchises, and licenses. (p. 633)
   b. Payments for inventory. YUM calls its Cost of Goods Sold "Food and Paper Expense." Note 11 gives the Accounts Payable balance. (pp. 646–647)
3. Prepare a T-account for Property, Plant, and Equipment, Net and show all activity in this account for 2006. Use the depreciation amount in note 9 and assume that YUM (a) sold property, plant, and equipment with book value of $53 million and (b) acquired $180 million of property, plant, and equipment as part of YUM's acquisitions of other companies. (p. 631)
4. Evaluate 2006 in terms of net income, total assets, stockholders' equity, cash flows from operating activities, and overall results. Be specific. (Challenge)

HH CHAPTER 12

Focus on Analysis: ■ Pier 1 Imports

(*Learning Objective 1, 2, 3, 4: Analyzing cash flows*) Refer to the **Pier 1 Imports** financial statements in Appendix B at the end of this book. Focus on 2006.

1. What is Pier 1's main source of cash? Is this good news or bad news to Pier 1 managers, stockholders, and creditors? What is Pier 1's main use of cash? Good news or bad news? Explain all answers in detail. (pp. 622–623)

2. Explain in detail the 3 main reasons why net cash provided by operations differs from net income. (pp. 624–625)

3. Did Pier 1 buy more fixed assets or sell more fixed assets during 2006? How can you tell? (pp. 624–625)

4. Identify the sale price, the book value, and the gain or loss from selling fixed assets during 2006. *Fixed assets* is another name of property, plant, and equipment. (p. 631)

5. How much cash in total did Pier 1 return to stockholders during 2006? (pp. 633–635)

Group Projects

Project 1. Each member of the group should obtain the annual report of a different company. Select companies in different industries. Evaluate each company's trend of cash flows for the most recent 2 years. In your evaluation of the companies' cash flows, you may use any other information that is publicly available—for example, the other financial statements (income statement, balance sheet, statement of stockholders' equity, and the related notes) and news stories from magazines and newspapers. Rank the companies' cash flows from best to worst and write a 2-page report on your findings.

Project 2. Select a company and obtain its annual report, including all the financial statements. Focus on the statement of cash flows and, in particular, the cash flows from operating activities. Specify whether the company uses the direct method or the indirect method to report operating cash flows. As necessary, use the other financial statements (income statement, balance sheet, and statement of stockholders' equity) and the notes to prepare the company's cash flows from operating activities by using the *other* method.

For Internet Exercises go to the Web site www.prenhall.com/harrison.

Quick Check Answers

1. *d*
2. *c*
3. *b*
4. *a* ($80,000 + $5,000 = $85,000)
5. *c*
6. *b*
7. *a* ($47,000 + $8,000 – $4,000 + $12,000 + $7,000 + $2,000 = $72,000)
8. *a* ($6,000 – $24,000 + $36,000 = $18,000)
9. *c* (–$2,000 + $3,000 – $9,000 = –$8,000)
10. *b* ($12,000 + $36,000 = $48,000)
11. *a* [$650,000 + ($45,000 – $31,000) = $664,000]
12. *c* ($690,000 – $390,000 – $175,000 = $125,000)
13. *d* ($390,000 –$15,000 + $9,000 = $384,000)

13 Financial Statement Analysis

SPOTLIGHT

HOW WELL IS YUM! BRANDS DOING?

This book began with the financial statements of **YUM! Brands, Inc.**, the company that owns **Pizza Hut**, **Taco Bell**, **A&W**, **KFC**, and **Long John Silver** restaurants. Throughout the book we have shown how to account for companies such as **YUM! Brands**, **Pier 1 Imports**, and **Google**. Only one aspect of the course remains: the overall analysis of financial statements.

We begin with the analysis of YUM! Brands' income statement. In 2006 YUM had revenues of $9,561 million, and the company earned net income of $824 million. These numbers look pretty good, but *how* good are they? We need to compare 2006 with prior years to see if YUM made progress during 2006. It could turn out that 2006 was worse than 2005. We also need to compare YUM to its competitors.

YUM! Brands, Inc.
Statements of Income (Adapted)
Years Ended December 31, 2006 and 2005

In millions	2006	2005
Revenues	$9,561	$9,349
Expenses:		
Food and paper (Cost of goods sold)	2,549	2,584
Payroll and employee benefits	2,142	2,171
Occupancy and other operating expenses	2,403	2,315
General and administrative expenses	1,187	1,158
Interest expense	154	127
Other expense (income), net	18	(32)
Income before income taxes	1,108	1,026
Income tax expense	284	264
Net income	$ 824	$ 762

This chapter covers the basic tools of financial analysis. The first part of the chapter shows how to evaluate YUM! Brands from year to year and how to compare YUM! Brands to other companies. For this comparison we use 2 leading fast-food chains, **YUM! Brands** and **McDonald's**. The second part of the chapter discusses the most widely used financial ratios. You have seen many of these ratios in earlier chapters—the current ratio, days' sales in receivables, and inventory turnover, return on assets, and return on equity.

By studying all these ratios together,

- You will learn the basic tools of financial analysis.
- You will enhance your business education.

Regardless of your chosen field—marketing, management, finance, entrepreneurship, or accounting—you will find these analytical tools useful as you move through your career.

LEARNING OBJECTIVES

1 **Perform** a horizontal analysis of financial statements

2 **Perform** a vertical analysis of financial statements

3 **Prepare** common-size financial statements

4 **Use** the statement of cash flows for decisions

5 **Compute** the standard financial ratios

6 **Use** ratios in decision making

7 **Measure** the economic value added by operations

HOW DOES AN INVESTOR EVALUATE A COMPANY?

Investors and creditors cannot evaluate a company by examining only 1 year's data. This is why most financial statements cover at least 2 periods, like the **YUM! Brands** income statement that begins this chapter. In fact, most financial analysis covers trends of 3 to 5 years. The goal of financial analysis is to predict the future.

The graphs in Exhibit 13-1 show YUM! Brands' 3-year trend of revenues and net income.

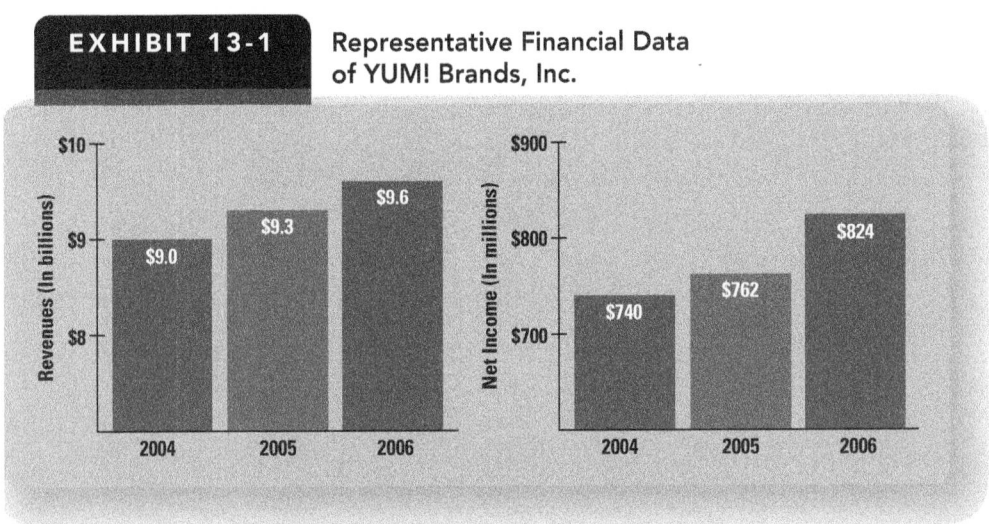

EXHIBIT 13-1 Representative Financial Data of YUM! Brands, Inc.

Both YUM's revenues and net income increased during 2005 and 2006. These are good signs. How would you predict YUM's revenues and net income for 2007 and beyond? Based on the recent past, you would probably extend the revenue line and the net income line upward. Let's examine some financial analysis tools. We begin with horizontal analysis.

HORIZONTAL ANALYSIS

Many decisions hinge on the trend of revenues, expenses, net income, and so on. Have revenues increased from last year? By how much? Suppose sales have increased by $50,000. Considered alone this fact is not very helpful, but the *percentage change* in sales helps a lot. It's better to know that sales have increased by 20% than to know that the increase is $50,000.

The study of percentage changes from year to year is called **horizontal analysis**. Computing a percentage change takes 2 steps:

1. Compute the dollar amount of the change from one period (the base period) to the next.

2. Divide the dollar amount of change by the base-period amount.

OBJECTIVE

1 **Perform** a horizontal analysis of financial statements

HH CHAPTER 13

Illustration: YUM! Brands

Horizontal analysis is illustrated for YUM! Brands as follows (dollars in millions):

			Increase (Decrease)	
	2006	2005	Amount	Percentage
Revenue	$9,561	$9,349	$212	2.3%

YUM's revenues increased by 2.3% during 2006, computed as follows:

STEP 1 Compute the dollar amount of change from 2005 to 2006:

2006		2005		Increase
$9,561	–	$9,349	=	$212

STEP 2 Divide the dollar amount of change by the base-period amount. This computes the percentage change for the period:

$$\text{Percentage change} = \frac{\text{Dollar amount of change}}{\text{Base-year amount}}$$

$$= \frac{\$212}{\$9,349} = 2.3\%$$

Exhibits 13-2 and 13-3 are detailed horizontal analysis for YUM! Brands. The income statements show that revenues increased by 2.3% during 2006. But net income on the bottom line grew by 8.1%. Why the difference? YUM's revenues grew faster than expenses.

EXHIBIT 13-2   Comparative Income Statement—Horizontal Analysis

YUM! Brands, Inc.
Statement of Income (Adapted)
Years Ended December 31, 2006 and 2005

			Increase (Decrease)	
Dollars in millions	2006	2005	Amount	Percentage
Revenues...	$9,561	$9,349	$212	2.3 %
Expenses:				
Food and paper (Cost of goods sold).....................	2,549	2,584	(35)	(1.4)
Payroll and employee benefits............................	2,142	2,171	(29)	(1.3)
Occupancy and other operating expenses	2,403	2,315	88	3.8
General and administrative expenses	1,187	1,158	29	2.5
Interest expense	154	127	27	21.3
Other expense, net..	18	(32)	50	156.3
Income before income taxes	1,108	1,026	82	8.0
Income tax expense...	284	264	20	7.6
Net income..	$ 824	$ 762	$ 62	8.1 %

| EXHIBIT 13-3 | Comparative Balance Sheet—Horizontal Analysis |

YUM! Brands, Inc.
Balance Sheet (Adapted)
December 31, 2006 and 2005

(Dollars in millions)	2006	2005	Increase (Decrease) Amount	Percentage
Assets				
Current Assets:				
Cash and cash equivalents	$ 319	$ 158	$161	101.9 %
Short-term investments	6	43	(37)	(86.0)
Receivables, net	220	236	(16)	(6.8)
Inventories	93	85	8	9.4
Prepaid expenses and other	263	333	(70)	(21.0)
Total current assets	901	855	46	5.4
Property, plant, and equipment, net	3,631	3,356	275	8.2
Intangible assets	1,009	868	141	16.2
Other assets	812	718	94	13.1
Total assets	$6,353	$5,797	$556	9.6 %
Liabilities and Shareholders' Equity				
Current Liabilities:				
Accounts payable	$1,386	$1,256	$130	10.4 %
Income tax payable	37	79	(42)	(53.2)
Short-term debt	227	211	16	7.6
Other	74	77	(3)	(3.9)
Total current liabilities	1,724	1,623	101	6.2
Long-term debt	2,045	1,649	396	24.0
Other liabilities	1,147	1,076	71	6.6
Total liabilities	4,916	4,348	568	13.1
Shareholders' Equity				
Common stock	—*	—*	—	
Retained earnings	1,593	1,619	(26)	(1.6)
Accumulated other comprehensive (loss)	(156)	(170)	14	8.2
Total shareholders' equity	1,437	1,449	(12)	(0.8)
Total liabilities and shareholders' equity	$6,353	$5,797	$556	9.6 %

*Amount rounds to 0.

STOP & think. . .

Examine Exhibit 13-2. Which item had the largest percentage increase during 2006? Should this increase cause alarm? Explain your reasoning.

Answer:
Other expense had the largest percentage increase (156.3%). This increase would *not* cause alarm because the dollar amount of the expense is low. This illustrates the materiality concept, which says to give major consideration to big items and less attention to small (immaterial) items. In this case, other expense is immaterial to the analysis of YUM! Brands.

The comparative balance sheets in Exhibit 13-3 show that total assets grew by 9.6% and total liabilities increased by 13.1%. Shareholders' equity therefore decreased by 0.8%. YUM! Brands' growth during 2006 is modest.

Trend Percentages

Trend percentages are a form of horizontal analysis. Trends indicate the direction a business is taking. How have revenues changed over a 5-year period? What trend does net income show? These questions can be answered by trend percentages over a representative period, such as the most recent 5 years.

Trend percentages are computed by selecting a base year whose amounts are set equal to 100%. The amount for each following year is stated as a percentage of the base amount. To compute a trend percentage, divide an item for a later year by the base-year amount.

$$\text{Trend \%} = \frac{\text{Any year \$}}{\text{Base year \$}}$$

YUM! Brands showed net income for the past 6 years as follows:

(In millions)	2006	2005	2004	2003	2002	Base 2001
Net income...............	$824	$762	$740	$617	$583	$492

We want trend percentages for the 5-year period 2002 to 2006. The base year is 2001. Trend percentages are computed by dividing each year's amount by the 2001 amount. The resulting trend percentages follow (2001 = 100%):

	2006	2005	2004	2003	2002	Base 2001
Net income...............	167	155	150	125	118	100

Net income rose sharply in 2002 and in 2004, and grew steadily in the other years.

You can perform a trend analysis on any item you consider important. Trend analysis is widely used for predicting the future.

Horizontal analysis highlights changes over time. However, no single technique gives a complete picture of a business.

VERTICAL ANALYSIS

OBJECTIVE

2 **Perform** a vertical analysis of financial statements

Vertical analysis shows the relationship of a financial-statement item to its base, which is the 100% figure. All items on the statement are reported as a percentage of the base. For the income statement, total revenue is usually the base. Suppose under normal conditions a company's net income is 8% of revenue. A drop to 6% may cause the company's stock price to fall.

Illustration: YUM! Brands

Exhibit 13-4 shows the vertical analysis of YUM! Brands' income statement as a percentage of revenue. In this case,

$$\text{Vertical analysis \%} = \frac{\text{Each income statement item}}{\text{Total revenue}}$$

EXHIBIT 13-4	Comparative Income Statement—Vertical Analysis

YUM! Brands, Inc.
Statements of Income (Adapted)
Years Ended December 31, 2006 and 2005

	2006		2005	
(Dollars in millions)	Amount	Percentage of Total	Amount	Percentage of Total
Revenues..	$9,561	100.0%	$9,349	100.0 %
Expenses:				
Food and paper (Cost of goods sold)......................	2,549	26.7	2,584	27.6
Payroll and employee benefits................................	2,142	22.4	2,171	23.2
Occupancy and other operating expenses	2,403	25.1	2,315	24.8
General and administrative expenses	1,187	12.4	1,158	12.4
Interest expense	154	1.6	127	1.3
Other expense (income), net	18	0.2	(32)	(0.3)
Income before income taxes....................................	1,108	11.6	1,026	11.0
Income tax expense...	284	3.0	264	2.8
Net income..	$ 824	8.6%	$ 762	8.2 %

For YUM! Brands in 2006, the vertical-analysis percentage for cost of goods sold is 26.7% ($2,549/$9,561 = .267). YUM's major expenses decreased in 2006. Net income's percentage of revenue (8.6%) is a little higher than the year earlier.

Exhibit 13-5 shows the vertical analysis of YUM's balance sheet. The base amount (100%) is total assets. The vertical analysis of YUM! Brands' balance sheet reveals several things about YUM's financial position at December 31, 2006:

■ Cash increased nicely in 2006.

■ Current assets make up a small percentage of total assets (only 14.2%), and prepaid expenses are the second largest current asset. It makes sense that inventory is a small percentage because food spoils quickly.

■ Total liabilities make up 77.4% of YUM's total assets. This is a heavy debt load. YUM's financial position improved modestly during 2006.

How Do We Compare One Company to Another?

OBJECTIVE

3 **Prepare** common-size financial statements

Exhibits 13-4 and 13-5 can be modified to report only percentages (no dollar amounts). Such a statement is called a **common-size statement**. Envision these statements with only the percentages.

EXHIBIT 13-5 Comparative Balance Sheet—Vertical Analysis

YUM! Brands, Inc.
Balance Sheet (Adapted)
December 31, 2006 and 2005

	2006		2005	
(Dollars in millions)	Amount	Percentage of Total	Amount	Percentage of Total
Assets				
Current Assets:				
Cash and cash equivalents	$ 319	5.0 %	$ 158	2.7 %
Short-term investments	6	0.1	43	0.7
Receivables, net	220	3.5	236	4.1
Inventories	93	1.5	85	1.5
Prepaid expenses and other	263	4.1	333	5.7
Total current assets	901	14.2	855	14.7
Property, plant, and equipment, net	3,631	57.1	3,356	57.9
Intangible assets	1,009	15.9	868	15.0
Other assets	812	12.8	718	12.4
Total assets	$6,353	100.0 %	$5,797	100.0 %
Liabilities and Shareholders' Equity				
Current Liabilities:				
Accounts payable	$1,386	21.8 %	$1,256	21.7 %
Income tax payable	37	0.6	79	1.4
Short-term debt	227	3.5	211	3.6
Other	74	1.2	77	1.3
Total current liabilities	1,724	27.1	1,623	28.0
Long-term debt	2,045	32.2	1,649	28.4
Other liabilities	1,147	18.1	1,076	18.6
Total liabilities	4,916	77.4	4,348	75.0
Shareholders' Equity				
Common stock	—*		—*	
Retained earnings	1,593	25.1	1,619	27.9
Accumulated other comprehensive (loss)	(156)	(2.5)	(170)	(2.9)
Total shareholders' equity	1,437	22.6	1,449	25.0
Total liabilities and shareholders' equity	$6,353	100.0 %	$5,797	100.0 %

*Amount rounds to zero.

On a common-size income statement, each item is expressed as a percentage of the revenue amount. Total revenue is therefore the *common size*. In the balance sheet, the common size is total assets. A common-size statement aids the comparison of different companies because all amounts are stated in percentages.

STOP & think. . .

Calculate the common-size percentages for the following income statement:

Net sales..................................	$150,000
Cost of goods sold.................	60,000
Gross profit............................	90,000
Operating expense.................	40,000
Operating income..................	50,000
Income tax expense..............	15,000
Net income............................	$ 35,000

Answer:

Net sales................................	100%	(= $150,000 ÷ $150,000)
Cost of goods sold.................	40	(= $ 60,000 ÷ $150,000)
Gross profit............................	60	(= $ 90,000 ÷ $150,000)
Operating expense.................	27	(= $ 40,000 ÷ $150,000)
Operating income..................	33	(= $ 50,000 ÷ $150,000)
Income tax expense..............	10	(= $ 15,000 ÷ $150,000)
Net income............................	23%	(= $ 35,000 ÷ $150,000)

Benchmarking

Benchmarking compares a company to some standard set by others. The goal of benchmarking is improvement. Suppose you are a financial analyst for **Edward Jones Company**. You are considering investing in a fast-food company, say, YUM! Brands or McDonald's. A direct comparison of their financial statements is not meaningful because McDonald's is larger. But you can convert both companies' income statements to common size and compare the percentages. This comparison is meaningful, as we shall see.

HH CHAPTER 13

Benchmarking Against a Key Competitor

Exhibit 13-6 presents the common-size income statements of YUM! Brands and McDonald's. McDonald's is the fast-food market leader. In this comparison, McDonald's comes out the winner. McDonald's seems to control expenses better than YUM! Brands. Net income is a higher percentage of revenue at The Golden Arches.

EXHIBIT 13-6 Common-Size Income Statement Compared with a Key Competitor

YUM! Brands, Inc.
Common-Size Income Statement for Comparison with Key Competitor
Year Ended During 2006

	YUM! Brands	McDonald's
Revenues	100.0%	100.0%
Cost of goods sold	26.7	24.8
Payroll expenses	22.4	19.4
Occupancy and other operating expenses	25.1	18.6
General and administrative expenses	12.4	10.8
Other expenses (income), net	4.8	10.0
Net income	8.6%	16.4%

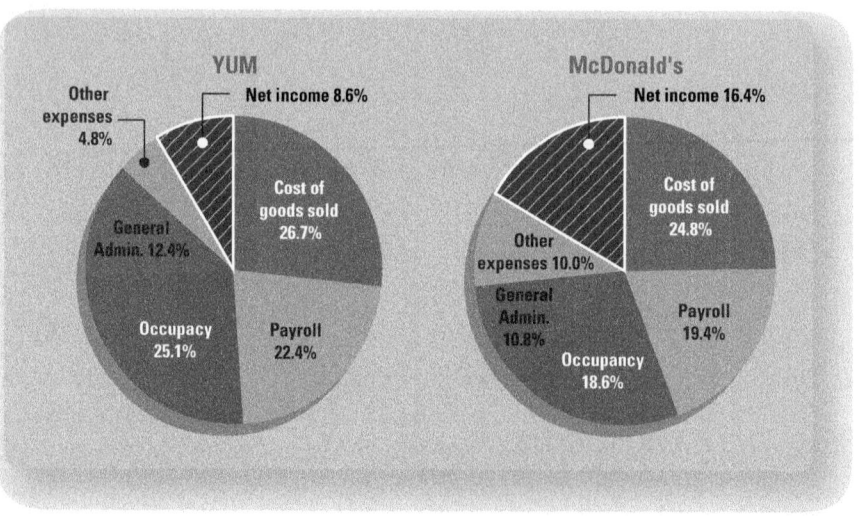

Using the Statement of Cash Flows

OBJECTIVE

4 Use the statement of cash flows for decisions

This chapter has focused on the income statement and balance sheet. We may also perform horizontal and vertical analyses on the statement of cash flows. To continue our discussion of its role in decision making, let's use Exhibit 13-7, the statement of cash flows of Unix Corporation.

EXHIBIT 13-7   Statement of Cash Flows

Unix Corporation
Statement of Cash Flows
Year Ended June 30, 2006

	Millions	
Operating activities:		
Net income		$ 35,000
Adjustments for noncash items:		
Depreciation	$ 14,000	
Net increase in current assets other than cash	(24,000)	
Net increase in current liabilities........................	8,000	(2,000)
Net cash provided by operating activities................		33,000
Investing activities:		
Sale of property, plant, and equipment	$ 91,000	
Net cash provided by investing activities.................		91,000
Financing activities:		
Borrowing...	$ 22,000	
Payment of long-term debt...	(90,000)	
Purchase of treasury stock	(9,000)	
Payment of dividends..	(23,000)	
Net cash used for financing activities		(100,000)
Increase (decrease) in cash..		$ 24,000

Analysts find the statement of cash flows more helpful for spotting weakness than for gauging success. Why? Because a *shortage* of cash can throw a company into bankruptcy, but lots of cash doesn't ensure success. The statement of cash flows in Exhibit 13-7 reveals the following:

- Unix's operations provide less cash than net income. That's strange. Ordinarily, cash provided by operations exceeds net income because of the add-back of depreciation. The increases in current assets and current liabilities should cancel out over time. For Unix Corporation, current assets increased far more than current liabilities during the year. This may be harmless. But it may signal difficulty in collecting receivables or selling inventory. Either event will cause trouble.
- The sale of plant assets is Unix's major source of cash. This is okay if this is a one-time situation. Unix may be shifting from one line of business to another, and it may be selling off old assets. But if the sale of plant assets is the major source of cash for several periods, Unix will face a cash shortage. A company can't sell off its plant assets forever. Soon it will go out of business.
- The only strength shown by the statement of cash flows is that Unix paid off more long-term debt than it did new borrowing. This will improve the debt ratio and Unix's credit standing.

Here are some cash-flow signs of a healthy company:

- Operations are the major *source* of cash (not a *use* of cash).
- Investing activities include more purchases than sales of long-term assets.
- Financing activities are not dominated by borrowing.

MID-CHAPTER SUMMARY PROBLEM

Perform a horizontal analysis and a vertical analysis of the comparative income statement of Hard Rock Products, Inc., which makes metal detectors. State whether 20X6 was a good year or a bad year, and give your reasons.

Hard Rock Products, Inc.
Comparative Income Statement
Years Ended December 31, 20X6 and 20X5

	20X6	20X5
Total revenues	$275,000	$225,000
Expenses:		
Cost of goods sold	194,000	165,000
Engineering, selling, and administrative expenses	54,000	48,000
Interest expense	5,000	5,000
Income tax expense	9,000	3,000
Other expense (income)	1,000	(1,000)
Total expenses	263,000	220,000
Net income	$ 12,000	$ 5,000

Answer

The horizontal analysis shows that total revenues increased 22.2%. This was greater than the 19.5% increase in total expenses, resulting in a 140% increase in net income.

Hard Rock Products, Inc.
Horizontal Analysis of Comparative Income Statement
Years Ended December 31, 20X6 and 20X5

	20X6	20X5	Increase (Decrease) Amount	Increase (Decrease) Percent
Total revenues	$275,000	$225,000	$50,000	22.2%
Expenses:				
Cost of goods sold	194,000	165,000	29,000	17.6
Engineering, selling, and administrative expenses	54,000	48,000	6,000	12.5
Interest expense	5,000	5,000	—	—
Income tax expense	9,000	3,000	6,000	200.0
Other expense (income)	1,000	(1,000)	2,000	—*
Total expenses	263,000	220,000	43,000	19.5
Net income	$ 12,000	$ 5,000	$ 7,000	140.0%

*Percentage changes are typically not computed for shifts from a negative to a positive amount and vice versa.

The vertical analysis on the next page shows decreases in the percentages of net sales consumed by the cost of goods sold (from 73.3% to 70.5%) and by the engineering, selling, and administrative expenses (from 21.3% to 19.6%). Because these 2 items are Hard Rock's largest dollar expenses, their percentage decreases are quite important. The relative reduction in expenses raised 20X6 net income to 4.4% of sales, compared with 2.2% the preceding year. The overall analysis indicates that 20X6 was significantly better than 20X5.

Hard Rock Products, Inc.
Vertical Analysis of Comparative Income Statement
Years Ended December 31, 20X6 and 20X5

	20X6		20X5	
	Amount	Percent	Amount	Percent
Total revenues.............................	$275,000	100.0 %	$225,000	100.0 %
Expenses:				
Cost of goods sold..................	194,000	70.5	165,000	73.3
Engineering, selling, and				
administrative expenses........	54,000	19.6	48,000	21.3
Interest expense	5,000	1.8	5,000	2.2
Income tax expense.................	9,000	3.3	3,000	1.4**
Other expense (income)	1,000	0.4	(1,000)	(0.4)
Total expenses.....................	263,000	95.6	220,000	97.8
Net income.................................	$ 12,000	4.4 %	$ 5,000	2.2 %

**Number rounded up.

USING RATIOS TO MAKE BUSINESS DECISIONS

Ratios are a major tool of financial analysis. A ratio expresses the relationship of one number to another. Suppose your balance sheet shows current assets of $100,000 and current liabilities of $50,000. The ratio of current assets to current liabilities is $100,000 to $50,000. We can express this ratio as 2 to 1, or 2:1. The current ratio is 2.0.

Many companies include ratios in a special section of their annual reports. RubberMate Corporation displays ratio data in the Summary section. Exhibit 13-8 shows data from that summary section. Investment services—**Moody's, Standard & Poor's, Risk Management Association**, and others—report these ratios.

OBJECTIVE

5 **Compute** the standard financial ratios

EXHIBIT 13-8 Financial Summary of RubberMate Corporation (Dollar Amounts in Millions Except per-share Amounts)

Year Ended December 31	20X6	20X5	20X4
Operating Results			
Net income...	$ 218	$ 164	$ 163
Per common share..	$1.32	$1.02	$1.02
Percent of sales..	10.8%	9.1%	9.8%
Return on average shareholders' equity...............	20.0%	17.5%	19.7%
Financial Position			
Current assets..	$ 570	$ 477	$ 419
Current liabilities	$ 359	$ 323	$ 345
Working capital..	$ 211	$ 154	$ 74
Current ratio...	1.59	1.48	1.21

The ratios we discuss in this chapter are classified as follows:

1. Ability to pay current liabilities

2. Ability to sell inventory and collect receivables

3. Ability to pay long-term debt

4. Profitability

5. Analyze stock as an investment

How much can a computer help in analyzing financial statements for investment purposes? Time yourself as you complete the problems in this chapter. Multiply your efforts by 10 as though you were comparing 10 companies. Now rank these 10 companies on the basis of 4 or 5 ratios.

Measuring Ability to Pay Current Liabilities

Working capital is defined as follows:

$$\text{Working capital} = \text{Current assets} - \text{Current liabilities}$$

Working capital measures the ability to pay current liabilities with current assets. In general, the larger the working capital, the better the ability to pay debts. Recall that capital is total assets minus total liabilities. Working capital is like a "current" version of total capital. Consider 2 companies with equal working capital:

	Company	
	Jones	Smith
Current assets......................	$100,000	$200,000
Current liabilities	50,000	150,000
Working capital	$ 50,000	$ 50,000

Both companies have working capital of $50,000, but Jones's working capital is as large as its current liabilities. Smith's working capital is only one-third as large as current liabilities. Jones is in a better position because its working capital is a higher percentage of current liabilities. Two decision-making tools based on working-capital data are the *current ratio* and the *acid-test ratio*.

Current Ratio. The most common ratio evaluating current assets and current liabilities is the **current ratio**, which is current assets divided by current liabilities. The current ratio measures the ability to pay current liabilities with current assets. Exhibit 13-9, page 699, gives the income statement and balance sheet data of Palisades Furniture.

The current ratios of Palisades Furniture, Inc., at December 31, 20X8 and 20X7, follow, along with the average for the retail furniture industry:

	Formula	Palisades' Current Ratio		Industry Average
		20X8	20X7	
Current ratio =	$\dfrac{\text{Current assets}}{\text{Current liabilities}}$	$\dfrac{\$262,000}{\$142,000} = 1.85$	$\dfrac{\$236,000}{\$126,000} = 1.87$	1.50

EXHIBIT 13-9 Comparative Financial Statements

Palisades Furniture, Inc.
Comparative Income Statement
Years Ended December 31, 20X8 and 20X7

	20X8	20X7
Net sales	$858,000	$803,000
Cost of goods sold	513,000	509,000
Gross profit	345,000	294,000
Operating expenses:		
Selling expenses	126,000	114,000
General expenses	118,000	123,000
Total operating expenses	244,000	237,000
Income from operations	101,000	57,000
Interest revenue	4,000	—
Interest (expense)	(24,000)	(14,000)
Income before income taxes	81,000	43,000
Income tax expense	33,000	17,000
Net income	$ 48,000	$ 26,000

Palisades Furniture, Inc.
Comparative Balance Sheet
December 31, 20X8 and 20X7

	20X8	20X7
Assets		
Current Assets:		
Cash	$ 29,000	$ 32,000
Accounts receivable, net	114,000	85,000
Inventories	113,000	111,000
Prepaid expenses	6,000	8,000
Total current assets	262,000	236,000
Long-term investments	18,000	9,000
Property, plant, and equipment, net	507,000	399,000
Total assets	$787,000	$644,000
Liabilities		
Current Liabilities:		
Notes payable	$ 42,000	$ 27,000
Accounts payable	73,000	68,000
Accrued liabilities	27,000	31,000
Total current liabilities	142,000	126,000
Long-term debt	289,000	198,000
Total liabilities	431,000	324,000
Stockholders' Equity		
Common stock, no par	186,000	186,000
Retained earnings	170,000	134,000
Total stockholders' equity	356,000	320,000
Total liabilities and stockholders' equity	$787,000	$644,000

HH CHAPTER 13

The current ratio was virtually unchanged during 20X8. In general, a higher current ratio indicates a stronger financial position. The business has sufficient current assets to maintain its operations. Palisades Furniture's current ratio of 1.85 compares favorably with the current ratios of some well-known companies:

Company	Current Ratio
YUM! Brands	0.52
Hewlett-Packard Company	1.35
eBay	2.14

Note: These figures show that ratio values vary widely from one industry to another.

What is an acceptable current ratio? The answer depends on the industry. The norm for companies in most industries is around 1.50, as reported by the Risk Management Association. Palisades Furniture's current ratio of 1.85 is better than average.

The Limitations of Ratio Analysis

Business decisions are made in a world of uncertainty. As useful as ratios are, they aren't a cure-all. Consider a physician's use of a thermometer. A reading of 102.0° Fahrenheit tells a doctor something is wrong with the patient, but that doesn't indicate what the problem is or how to cure it.

In financial analysis, a sudden drop in the current ratio signals that *something* is wrong, but that doesn't identify the problem. A manager must analyze the figures to learn what caused the ratio to fall. A drop in current assets may mean a cash shortage or that sales are slow. The manager must evaluate all the ratios in the light of factors such as increased competition or a slowdown in the economy.

Legislation, international affairs, scandals, and other factors can turn profits into losses. To be useful, ratios should be analyzed over a period of years to consider all relevant factors. Any 1 year, or even any 2 years, may not represent the company's performance over the long term.

Acid-Test Ratio. The **acid-test** (or *quick*) **ratio** tells us whether the entity could pass the acid test of paying all its current liabilities if they came due immediately. The acid-test ratio uses a narrower base to measure liquidity than the current ratio does.

To compute the acid-test ratio, we add cash, short-term investments, and net current receivables (accounts and notes receivable, net of allowances) and divide by current liabilities. Inventory and prepaid expenses are excluded because they are less liquid. A business may be unable to convert inventory to cash immediately.

Palisades Furniture's acid-test ratios for 20X8 and 20X7 follow.

Formula	Palisades' Acid-Test Ratio		Industry Average
	20X8	20X7	
Acid-test ratio = $\dfrac{\text{Cash + Short-term investments} + \text{Net current receivables}}{\text{Current liabilities}}$	$\dfrac{\$29,000 + \$0 + \$114,000}{\$142,000} = 1.01$	$\dfrac{\$32,000 + \$0 + \$85,000}{\$126,000} = 0.93$	0.40

The company's acid-test ratio improved during 20X8 and is significantly better than the industry average. Compare Palisades' acid test ratio with the values of some leading companies.

Company	Acid-Test Ratio
Best Buy........................	0.70
IHOP............................	1.02
Pier 1 Imports...............	1.08

An acid-test ratio of 0.90 to 1.00 is acceptable in most industries. How can a company such as Best Buy function with such a low acid-test ratio? Best Buy prices its inventory to turn it over quickly. And most of Best Buy's sales are for cash or credit cards, so the company collects cash quickly. This points us to the next two ratios.

Measuring Ability to Sell Inventory and Collect Receivables

The ability to sell inventory and collect receivables is critical. In this section, we discuss 3 ratios that measure this ability.

Inventory Turnover. Companies generally strive to sell their inventory as quickly as possible. The faster inventory sells, the sooner cash comes in.

Inventory turnover measures the number of times a company sells its average level of inventory during a year. A fast turnover indicates ease in selling inventory; a low turnover indicates difficulty. A value of 6 means that the company's average level of inventory has been sold 6 times during the year, and that's usually better than a turnover of 3 times. But too high a value can mean that the business is not keeping enough inventory on hand, which can lead to lost sales if the company can't fill orders. Therefore, a business strives for the most *profitable* rate of turnover, not necessarily the *highest* rate.

To compute inventory turnover, divide cost of goods sold by the average inventory for the period. We use the cost of goods sold—*not sales*—in the computation because both cost of goods sold and inventory are stated *at cost*. Palisades Furniture's inventory turnover for 20X8 is

Formula	Palisades' Inventory Turnover	Industry Average
Inventory turnover = $\dfrac{\text{Cost of goods sold}}{\text{Average inventory}}$	$\dfrac{\$513,000}{\$112,000} = 4.6$	1.50

Cost of goods sold comes from the income statement (Exhibit 13-9). Average inventory is the average of beginning ($111,000) and ending inventory ($113,000). (See the balance sheet, Exhibit 13-9.) If inventory levels vary greatly from month to month, you should compute the average by adding the 12 monthly balances and dividing the sum by 12.

Inventory turnover varies widely with the nature of the business. For example, YUM! Brands has an inventory turnover ratio of 29 times per year because food spoils so quickly. **Pier 1 Imports**, on the other hand, turns over its furniture only around 3 times per year. Pier 1 keeps enough inventory on hand for customers to make their selections.

To evaluate inventory turnover, compare the ratio over time. A sharp decline suggests the need for corrective action.

Accounts Receivable Turnover. **Accounts receivable turnover** measures the ability to collect cash from customers. In general, the higher the ratio, the better. However, a receivable turnover that is too high may indicate that credit is too tight, and that may cause you to lose sales to good customers.

To compute accounts receivable turnover, divide net sales by average net accounts receivable. The ratio tells how many times during the year average receivables were turned into cash. Palisades Furniture's accounts receivable turnover ratio for 20X8 is

Formula	Palisades' Accounts Receivable Turnover	Industry Average
$\text{Accounts receivable turnover} = \dfrac{\text{Net sales}}{\text{Average net accounts receivable}}$	$\dfrac{\$858,000}{\$99,500} = 8.6$	51.0

Average net accounts receivable is figured by adding beginning ($85,000) and ending receivables ($114,000), then dividing by 2. If accounts receivable vary widely during the year, compute the average by using the 12 monthly balances.

Palisades' receivable turnover of 8.6 times per year is much slower than the industry average. Why the slow collection? Palisades is a hometown store that sells to local people who pay bills over a period of time. Many larger furniture stores sell their receivables to other companies called *factors*. This practice keeps receivables low and receivable turnover high. But companies that factor (sell) their receivables receive less than face value of the receivables. Palisades Furniture follows a different strategy.

Days' Sales in Receivables. Businesses must convert accounts receivable to cash. All else being equal, the lower the receivable balance, the better the cash flow.

The **days'-sales-in-receivables** ratio shows how many days' sales remain in Accounts Receivable. Compute the ratio by a 2-step process:

1. Divide net sales by 365 days to figure average sales per day.
2. Divide average net receivables by average sales per day.

The data to compute this ratio for Palisades Furniture, Inc., are taken from the 20X8 income statement and the balance sheet (Exhibit 13-9):

Formula	Palisades' Days' Sales in Accounts Receivable	Industry Average
Days' Sales in Average Accounts Receivable:		
1. One day's sales $= \dfrac{\text{Net sales}}{365 \text{ days}}$	$\dfrac{\$858,000}{365 \text{ days}} = \$2,351$	
2. Days' sales in average accounts receivable $= \dfrac{\text{Average net accounts receivable}}{\text{One day's sales}}$	$\dfrac{\$99,500}{\$2,351} = 42 \text{ days}$	7 days

Days' sales in average receivables can also be computed in a single step: $99,500/($858,000/365 days) = 42 days.

Measuring Ability to Pay Debts

The ratios discussed so far relate to current assets and current liabilities. They measure the ability to sell inventory, collect receivables, and pay current bills. Two indicators of the ability to pay total liabilities are the *debt ratio* and the *times-interest-earned ratio*.

Debt Ratio. Suppose you are a bank loan officer and you have received $500,000 loan applications from 2 similar companies. The first firm already owes $600,000, and the second owes only $250,000. Which company gets the loan? Company 2, because it owes less.

This relationship between total liabilities and total assets is called the **debt ratio**. It tells us the proportion of assets financed with debt. A debt ratio of 1 reveals that debt has financed all the assets. A debt ratio of 0.50 means that debt finances half the assets. The higher the debt ratio, the greater the pressure to pay interest and principal. The lower the ratio, the lower the risk.

The debt ratios for Palisades Furniture in 20X8 and 20X7 follow.

| | | Palisades' Debt Ratio | | Industry |
	Formula	20X8	20X7	Average
Debt ratio =	$\dfrac{\text{Total liabilities}}{\text{Total assets}}$	$\dfrac{\$431,000}{\$787,000} = 0.55$	$\dfrac{\$324,000}{\$644,000} = 0.50$	0.64

Risk Management Association reports that the average debt ratio for most companies ranges around 0.62, with relatively little variation from company to company. Palisades' 0.55 debt ratio indicates a fairly low-risk debt position compared with the retail furniture industry average of 0.64.

Times-Interest-Earned Ratio. Analysts use a second ratio—the **times-interest-earned ratio**—to relate income to interest expense. To compute the times-interest-earned ratio, divide income from operations (operating income) by interest expense. This ratio measures the number of times operating income can *cover* interest expense and is also called the *interest-coverage ratio*. A high ratio indicates ease in paying interest; a low value suggests difficulty.

Palisades' times-interest-earned ratios are

| | | Palisades' Times-Interest-Earned Ratio | | Industry |
	Formula	20X8	20X7	Average
Times-interest-earned ratio =	$\dfrac{\text{Income from operations}}{\text{Interest expense}}$	$\dfrac{\$101,000}{\$24,000} = 4.21$	$\dfrac{\$57,000}{\$14,000} = 4.07$	2.80

The company's times-interest-earned ratio increased in 20X8. This is a favorable sign.

Measuring Profitability

The fundamental goal of business is to earn a profit, and so the ratios that measure profitability are reported widely.

Rate of Return on Sales. In business, *return* refers to profitability. Consider the **rate of return on net sales**, or simply *return on sales*. (The word *net* is usually omitted for convenience.) This ratio shows the percentage of each sales dollar earned as net income. The return-on-sales ratios for Palisades Furniture are

		Palisades' Rate of Return on Sales		Industry
	Formula	20X8	20X7	Average
Rate of return on sales	$= \dfrac{\text{Net income}}{\text{Net sales}}$	$\dfrac{\$48,000}{\$858,000} = 0.056$	$\dfrac{\$26,000}{\$803,000} = 0.032$	0.008

Companies strive for a high rate of return. The higher the percentage, the more profit is being generated by sales dollars. Palisades Furniture's return on sales is higher than the average furniture store. Compare Palisades' rate of return on sales to the rates of some leading companies:

Company	Rate of Return on Sales
FedEx....................	0.056
PepsiCo................	0.125
Intel......................	0.143

Rate of Return on Total Assets. The **rate of return on total assets**, or simply *return on assets*, measures a company's success in using assets to earn a profit. Creditors have loaned money, and the interest they receive is their return on investment. Shareholders have bought the company's stock, and net income is their return. The sum of interest expense and net income is the return to the 2 groups that have financed the company. This sum is the numerator of the ratio. Average total assets is the denominator. The return-on-assets ratio for Palisades Furniture is

	Formula	Palisades' 20X8 Rate of Return on Total Assets	Industry Average
Rate of return on assets	$= \dfrac{\text{Net income} + \text{Interest expense}}{\text{Average total assets}}$	$\dfrac{\$48,000 + \$24,000}{\$715,500} = 0.101$	0.078

To compute average total assets, add the beginning and ending balances and divide by 2. Compare Palisades Furniture's rate of return on assets to the rates of these leading companies:

Company	Rate of Return on Assets
General Electric................	0.059
Starbucks	0.145
Google	0.214

Rate of Return on Common Stockholders' Equity. A popular measure of profitability is **rate of return on common stockholders' equity**, often shortened to *return on equity*. This ratio shows the relationship between net income and common stockholders' investment in the company—how much income is earned for every $1 invested.

To compute this ratio, first subtract preferred dividends from net income to measure income available to the common stockholders. Then divide income available to common by average common equity during the year. Common equity is total equity minus preferred equity. The 20X8 return on common equity for Palisades Furniture is

Formula		Palisades' 20X8 Rate of Return on Common Stockholders' Equity	Industry Average
Rate of return on common stockholders' equity $=$	$\dfrac{\text{Net income} - \text{Preferred dividends}}{\text{Average common stockholders' equity}}$	$\dfrac{\$48,000 - \$0}{\$338,000} = 0.142$	0.121

Average equity uses the beginning and ending balances [($320,000 + $356,000)/2 = $338,000].

Observe that Palisades' return on equity (0.142) is higher than its return on assets (0.101). This is a good sign. The difference results from borrowing at one rate—say, 8%—and investing the funds to earn a higher rate, such as the firm's 14.2% return on equity. This practice is called using **leverage**, or **trading on the equity**. The higher the debt ratio, the higher the leverage. Companies that finance operations with debt are said to *leverage* their positions.

For Palisades Furniture, leverage increases profitability. This is not always the case, because leverage can hurt profits. If revenues drop, debts still must be paid. Therefore, leverage is a double-edged sword. It increases profits during good times but compounds losses during bad times.

Palisades Furniture's rate of return on equity lags behind those of GE, Google, and Starbucks.

Company	Rate of Return on Common Equity
General Electric...............	0.188
Google	0.233
Starbucks	0.261

Earnings per Share of Common Stock. *Earnings per share of common stock*, or simply **earnings per share (EPS)**, is the amount of net income earned for each share of outstanding *common* stock. EPS is the most widely quoted of all financial statistics. It's the only ratio that appears on the income statement.

Earnings per share is computed by dividing net income available to common stockholders by the average number of common shares outstanding during the year. Preferred dividends are subtracted from net income because the preferred stockholders have a prior claim to their dividends. Palisades Furniture has no preferred stock and thus has no preferred dividends. The firm's EPS for 20X8 and 20X7 follows (Palisades has 10,000 shares of common stock outstanding).

Formula	Palisades' Earnings per Share	
	20X8	20X7
Earnings per share of common stock $= \dfrac{\text{Net income} - \text{Preferred dividends}}{\text{Average number of shares of common stock outstanding}}$	$\dfrac{\$48,000 - \$0}{10,000} = \$4.80$	$\dfrac{\$26,000 - \$0}{10,000} = \$2.60$

Palisades Furniture's EPS increased 85% during 20X8, and that's good news. The Palisades stockholders should not expect such a significant boost every year. Most companies strive to increase EPS by 10% to 15% annually.

Analyzing Stock Investments

OBJECTIVE

6 **Use** ratios in decision making

Investors buy stock to earn a return on their investment. This return consists of 2 parts: (1) gains (or losses) from selling the stock and (2) dividends.

Price/Earnings Ratio. The **price/earnings ratio** is the ratio of common stock price to earnings per share. This ratio, abbreviated P/E, appears in *The Wall Street Journal* stock listings and online. It shows the market price of $1 of earnings.

Calculations for the P/E ratios of Palisades Furniture, Inc., follow. The market price of Palisades' common stock was $60 at the end of 20X8 and $35 at the end of 20X7. Stock prices can be obtained from a company's Web site, a financial publication, or a stockbroker.

Formula	Palisades' Price/Earnings Ratio	
	20X8	20X7
P/E ratio $= \dfrac{\text{Market price per share of common stock}}{\text{Earnings per share}}$	$\dfrac{\$60.00}{\$4.80} = 12.5$	$\dfrac{\$35.00}{\$2.60} = 13.5$

Given Palisades Furniture's 20X8 P/E ratio of 12.5, we would say that the company's stock is selling at 12.5 times earnings. Each $1 of Palisades' earnings is worth $12.50 to the stock market.

Dividend Yield. **Dividend yield** is the ratio of dividends per share of stock to the stock's market price. This ratio measures the percentage of a stock's market value returned annually to the stockholders as dividends. *Preferred* stockholders pay special attention to this ratio because they invest primarily to receive dividends.

Palisades Furniture paid annual cash dividends of $1.20 per share in 20X8 and $1.00 in 20X7. The market prices of the company's common stock were $60 in 20X8 and $35 in 20X7. The firm's dividend yields on common stock are

Formula	Dividend Yield on Palisades' Common Stock	
	20X8	20X7
Dividend yield on common stock* $= \dfrac{\text{Dividend per share of common stock}}{\text{Market price per share of common stock}}$	$\dfrac{\$1.20}{\$60.00} = 0.020$	$\dfrac{\$1.00}{\$35.00} = 0.029$

*Dividend yields may also be calculated for preferred stock.

An investor who buys Palisades Furniture common stock for $60 can expect to receive around 2% of the investment annually in the form of cash dividends. Dividend yields vary widely, from 5% to 8% for older, established firms (such as **Procter & Gamble** and **General Motors**) down to the range of 0% to 3% for young, growth-oriented companies. **Google**, **Starbucks**, and **eBay** pay no cash dividends.

Book Value per Share of Common Stock. **Book value per share of common stock** is simply common stockholders' equity divided by the number of shares of common stock outstanding. Common equity equals total equity less preferred equity. Palisades Furniture has no preferred stock outstanding. Calculations of its book value per share of common follow. Recall that 10,000 shares of common stock were outstanding.

	Formula	*Book Value per Share of Palisades' Common Stock*	
		20X8	**20X7**
Book value per share of common stock =	$\dfrac{\text{Total stockholders' equity} - \text{Preferred equity}}{\text{Number of shares of common stock outstanding}}$	$\dfrac{\$356{,}000 - \$0}{10{,}000} = \$35.60$	$\dfrac{\$320{,}000 - \$0}{10{,}000} = \$32.00$

Book value indicates the recorded accounting amount for each share of common stock outstanding. Many experts believe book value is not useful for investment analysis because it bears no relationship to market value and provides little information beyond what's reported on the balance sheet. But some investors base their investment decisions on book value. For example, some investors rank stocks by the ratio of market price to book value. The lower the ratio, the more attractive the stock. These investors are called "value" investors, as contrasted with "growth" investors, who focus more on trends in net income.

OTHER MEASURES

Economic Value Added (EVA®)

The top managers of **Coca-Cola, Quaker Oats**, and other leading companies use **economic value added (EVA®)** to evaluate operating performance. EVA® combines accounting and finance to measure whether operations have increased stockholder wealth. EVA® can be computed as follows:

OBJECTIVE

7 **Measure** the economic value added by operations

$$\text{EVA}^{®} = \text{Net income} + \text{Interest expense} - \text{Capital charge}$$

$$\text{Capital charge} = \left(\begin{array}{c} \text{(Beginning balances)} \\ \text{Notes} + \text{Current maturities of long-term debt} + \text{Long-term debt} + \text{Stockholders' equity} \end{array} \right) \times \text{Cost of capital}$$

All amounts for the EVA® computation, except the cost of capital, come from the financial statements. The **cost of capital** is a weighted average of the returns demanded by the company's stockholders and lenders. Cost of capital varies with the company's level of risk. For example, stockholders would demand a higher return from a start-up company than from YUM! Brands because the new company is untested and therefore more risky. Lenders would also charge the new company a higher interest rate because of its greater risk. Thus, the new company has a higher cost of capital than YUM! Brands.

The cost of capital is a major topic in finance classes. In the following discussions we assume a value for the cost of capital (such as 10%, 12%, or 15%) to illustrate the computation of EVA®.

The idea behind EVA® is that the returns to the company's stockholders (net income) and to its creditors (interest expense) should exceed the company's capital charge. The **capital charge** is the amount that stockholders and lenders *charge* a company for the use of their money. A positive EVA® amount suggests an increase in stockholder wealth, and so the company's stock should remain attractive to investors. If EVA® is negative, stockholders will probably be unhappy with the company and sell its stock, resulting in a decrease in the stock's price. Different companies tailor the EVA® computation to meet their own needs.

Let's apply EVA® to YUM! Brands. The company's EVA® for 2006 can be computed as follows, assuming a 10% cost of capital (dollars in millions):

				(Beginning balances)			
YUM! Brand's EVA® =	Net income	+ Interest expense	−	Short-term borrowings +	Long-term debt +	Stockholders' equity	× Cost of capital
=	$824	+ $154	−	[($74 +	$2,045 +	$1,437)	× 0.10]
=	$978		−		$3,556		× 0.10
=	$978		−			$356	
=				$622			

By this measure, YUM! Brands' operations added $622 million of value to its stockholders' wealth after meeting the company's capital charge. This performance is very strong.

Red Flags in Financial Statement Analysis

Recent accounting scandals have highlighted the importance of *red flags* in financial analysis. The following conditions may mean a company is very risky.

- **Earnings Problems.** Have income from continuing operations and net income decreased for several years in a row? Has income turned into a loss? This may be okay for a company in a cyclical industry, such as an airline or a home builder, but a company such as YUM! Brands may be unable to survive consecutive loss years.
- **Decreased Cash Flow.** Cash flow validates earnings. Is cash flow from operations consistently lower than net income? Are the sales of plant assets a major source of cash? If so, the company may be facing a cash shortage.

- **Too Much Debt.** How does the company's debt ratio compare to that of major competitors and to the industry average? If the debt ratio is much higher than average, the company may be unable to pay debts during tough times. As we saw earlier, YUM! Brands' debt ratio of 77% is quite high.[1]
- **Inability to Collect Receivables.** Are days' sales in receivables growing faster than for other companies in the industry? A cash shortage may be looming. YUM's cash collections are very strong.
- **Buildup of Inventories.** Is inventory turnover slowing down? If so, the company may be unable to move products, or it may be overstating inventory as reported on the balance sheet. Recall from the cost-of-goods-sold model that one of the easiest ways to overstate net income is to overstate ending inventory. YUM! Brands has no problem here.
- **Trends of Sales, Inventory, and Receivables.** Sales, receivables, and inventory generally move together. Increased sales lead to higher receivables and require more inventory in order to meet demand. Strange movements among these items may spell trouble. YUM's relationships look normal.

Efficient Markets

An **efficient capital market** is one in which market prices fully reflect all information available to the public. Because stock prices reflect all publicly accessible data, it can be argued that the stock market is efficient. Market efficiency has implications for management action and for investor decisions. It means that managers cannot fool the market with accounting gimmicks. If the information is available, the market as a whole can set a "fair" price for the company's stock.

Suppose you are the president of Anacomp Corporation. Reported earnings per share are $4, and the stock price is $40—so the P/E ratio is 10. You believe Anacomp's stock is underpriced. To correct this situation, you are considering changing your depreciation method from accelerated to straight-line. The accounting change will increase earnings per share to $5. Will the stock price then rise to $50? Probably not; the company's stock price will probably remain at $40 because the market can understand the accounting change. After all, the company merely changed its method of computing depreciation. There is no effect on Anacomp's cash flows, and the company's economic position is unchanged: An efficient market interprets data in light of their true underlying meaning.

In an efficient market, the search for "underpriced" stock is fruitless unless the investor has relevant *private* information. But it is unlawful to invest on the basis of *inside* information. An appropriate strategy seeks to manage risk, diversify investments, and minimize transaction costs. Financial analysis helps mainly to identify the risks of various stocks and then to manage the risk.

The Decision Guidelines feature summarizes the most widely used ratios.

---

[1] In 2003, YUM's debt ratio was 89%, and we stated, "YUM's debt ratio needs to shrink over the next several years." The company has made significant progress—with a 77% debt ratio at the end of 2006.

DECISION GUIDELINES

USING RATIOS IN FINANCIAL STATEMENT ANALYSIS

Lane and Kay Collins operate a financial services firm. They manage other people's money and do most of their own financial-statement analysis. How do they measure companies' ability to pay bills, sell inventory, collect receivables, and so on? They use the standard ratios we have covered throughout this book.

Ratio	Computation	Information Provided
Measuring ability to pay current liabilities:		
1. Current ratio	$\dfrac{\text{Current assets}}{\text{Current liabilities}}$	Measures ability to pay current liabilities with current assets
2. Acid-test (quick) ratio	$\dfrac{\text{Cash} + \text{Short-term investments} + \text{Net current receivables}}{\text{Current liabilities}}$	Shows ability to pay all current liabilities if they come due immediately
Measuring ability to sell inventory and collect receivables:		
3. Inventory turnover	$\dfrac{\text{Cost of goods sold}}{\text{Average inventory}}$	Indicates saleability of inventory— the number of times a company sells its average level of inventory during a year.
4. Accounts receivable turnover	$\dfrac{\text{Net credit sales}}{\text{Average net accounts receivable}}$	Measures ability to collect cash from credit customers
5. Days' sales in receivables	$\dfrac{\text{Average net accounts receivable}}{\text{One day's sales}}$	Shows how many days' sales remain in Accounts Receivable— how many days it takes to collect the average level of receivables.
Measuring ability to pay long-term debt:		
6. Debt ratio	$\dfrac{\text{Total liabilities}}{\text{Total assets}}$	Indicates percentage of assets financed with debt
7. Times-interest-earned ratio	$\dfrac{\text{Income from operations}}{\text{Interest expense}}$	Measures the number of times operating income can cover interest expense
Measuring profitability:		
8. Rate of return on net sales	$\dfrac{\text{Net income}}{\text{Net sales}}$	Shows the percentage of each sales dollar earned as net income
9. Rate of return on total assets	$\dfrac{\text{Net income} + \text{Interest expense}}{\text{Average total assets}}$	Measures how profitably a company uses its assets
10. Rate of return on common stockholders' equity	$\dfrac{\text{Net income} - \text{Preferred dividends}}{\text{Average common stockholders' equity}}$	Gauges how much income is earned with the money invested by the common shareholders

Ratio	Computation	Information Provided
11. Earnings per share of common stock	$$\frac{\text{Net income} - \text{Preferred dividends}}{\text{Average number of shares of common stock outstanding}}$$	Gives the amount of net income earned for each share of the company's common stock outstanding

Analyzing stock as an investment:

Ratio	Computation	Information Provided
12. Price/earnings ratio	$$\frac{\text{Market price per share of common stock}}{\text{Earnings per share}}$$	Indicates the market price of $1 of earnings
13. Dividend yield	$$\frac{\text{Dividend per share of common (or preferred) stock}}{\text{Market price per share of common (or preferred) stock}}$$	Shows the percentage of a stock's market value returned as dividends to stockholders each period
14. Book value per share of common stock	$$\frac{\text{Total stockholders' equity} - \text{Preferred equity}}{\text{Number of shares of common stock outstanding}}$$	Indicates the recorded accounting amount for each share of common stock outstanding

HH CHAPTER 13

END-OF-CHAPTER SUMMARY PROBLEM

The following financial data are adapted from the annual reports of Lampeer Corporation.

Lampeer Corporation
Four-Year Selected Financial Data
Years Ended January 31, 2008, 2007, 2006 and 2005

Operating Results*	2008	2007	2006	2005
Net Sales	$13,848	$13,673	$11,635	$9,054
Cost of goods sold and occupancy expenses excluding depreciation and amortization......................	9,704	8,599	6,775	5,318
Interest expense	109	75	45	46
Income from operations...............	338	1,445	1,817	1,333
Net earnings (net loss)	(8)	877	1,127	824
Cash dividends............................	76	75	76	77
Financial Position				
Merchandise inventory................	1,677	1,904	1,462	1,056
Total assets	7,591	7,012	5,189	3,963
Current ratio................................	1.48:1	0.95:1	1.25:1	1.20:1
Stockholders' equity.....................	3,010	2,928	2,630	1,574
Average number of shares of common stock outstanding (in thousands)	860	879	895	576

*Dollar amounts are in thousands.

I *Required*

Compute the following ratios for 2006 through 2008, and evaluate Lampeer's operating results. Are operating results strong or weak? Did they improve or deteriorate during the 3-year period? Your analysis will reveal a clear trend.

1. Gross profit percentage*
2. Net income as a percentage of sales
3. Earnings per share
4. Inventory turnover
5. Times-interest-earned ratio
6. Rate of return on stockholders' equity

*Refer to Chapter 6 if necessary.

Answer

	2008	2007	2006
1. Gross profit percentage	$\dfrac{\$13,848 - \$9,704}{\$13,848} = 29.9\%$	$\dfrac{\$13,673 - \$8,599}{\$13,673} = 37.1\%$	$\dfrac{\$11,635 - \$6,775}{\$11,635} = 41.8\%$
2. Net income as a percentage of sales	$\dfrac{\$(8)}{\$13,848} = (0.06)\%$	$\dfrac{\$877}{\$13,673} = 6.4\%$	$\dfrac{\$1,127}{\$11,635} = 9.7\%$
3. Earnings per share	$\dfrac{\$(8)}{860} = \$(0.01)$	$\dfrac{\$877}{879} = \$1.00$	$\dfrac{\$1,127}{895} = \$1.26$
4. Inventory turnover	$\dfrac{\$9,704}{(\$1,677 + \$1,904)/2} = 5.4 \text{ times}$	$\dfrac{\$8,599}{(\$1,904 + \$1,462)/2} = 5.1 \text{ times}$	$\dfrac{\$6,775}{(\$1,462 + \$1,056)/2} = 5.4 \text{ times}$
5. Times-interest-earned ratio	$\dfrac{\$338}{\$109} = 3.1 \text{ times}$	$\dfrac{\$1,445}{\$75} = 19.3 \text{ times}$	$\dfrac{\$1,817}{\$45} = 40.4 \text{ times}$
6. Rate of return on stockholders' equity	$\dfrac{\$(8)}{(\$3,010 + \$2,928)/2} = (0.3\%)$	$\dfrac{\$877}{(\$2,928 + \$2,630)/2} = 31.6\%$	$\dfrac{\$1,127}{(\$2,630 + \$1,574)/2} = 53.6\%$

Evaluation: During this period, Lampeer's operating results deteriorated on all these measures except inventory turnover. The gross profit percentage is down sharply, as are the times-interest-earned ratio and all the return measures. From these data it is clear that Lampeer could sell its merchandise, but not at the markups the company enjoyed in the past. The final result, in 2008, was a net loss for the year.

REVIEW FINANCIAL STATEMENT ANALYSIS

Quick Check (Answers are given on page 744.)

Analyze the Donaldson Company financial statements by answering the questions that follow. Donaldson owns a chain of restaurants.

Donaldson Company
Consolidated Statement of Income (Adapted)
Years Ended December 31, 2008, 2007, and 2006

In Millions, Except per Share Data	2008	2007	2006
Revenues			
Sales by Company-operated restaurants	$12,795.4	$11,499.6	$11,040.7
Revenues from franchised and affiliated restaurants	4,345.1	3,906.1	3,829.3
Total revenues	17,140.5	15,405.7	14,870.0
Operating Expenses			
Company-operated restaurant expenses			
Food & paper (Cost of goods sold)	4,314.8	3,917.4	3,802.1
Payroll & employee benefits	3,411.4	3,078.2	2,901.2
Occupancy & other operating expenses	3,279.8	2,911.0	2,750.4
Franchised restaurants—occupancy expenses	937.7	840.1	800.2
Selling, general & administrative expenses	1,833.0	1,712.8	1,661.7
Other operating expense, net	531.6	833.3	257.4
Total operating expenses	14,308.3	13,292.8	12,173.0
Operating income	2,832.2	2,112.9	2,697.0
Interest expense	388.0	374.1	452.4
Gain on sale of subsidiary			(137.1)
Nonoperating expense, net	97.8	76.7	52.0
Income before income taxes and cumulative effect of accounting changes	2,346.4	1,662.1	2,329.7
Income tax expense	838.2	670.0	693.1
Income before cumulative effect of accounting changes	1,508.2	992.1	1,636.6
Cumulative effect of accounting changes, net of tax benefits of $9.4 and $17.6	(36.8)	(98.6)	
Net income	$ 1,471.4	$ 893.5	$ 1,636.6
Per common share–basic:			
Income before cumulative effect of accounting changes	$ 1.19	$ 0.78	$ 1.27
Cumulative effect of accounting changes	(0.03)	(0.08)	
Net income	$ 1.16	$ 0.70	$ 1.27
Dividends per common share	$ 0.40	$ 0.24	$ 0.23

Donaldson Company
Consolidated Balance Sheet
Years Ended December 31, 2008 and 2007

In Millions, Except per Share Data	2008	2007
Assets		
Current assets		
Cash and equivalents	$ 492.8	$ 330.4
Accounts and notes receivable	734.5	855.3
Inventories, at cost, not in excess of market	129.4	111.7
Prepaid expenses and other current assets	528.7	418.0
Total current assets	1,885.4	1,715.4
Other assets		
Investments in affiliates	1,089.6	1,037.7
Goodwill, net	1,665.1	1,558.5
Miscellaneous	960.3	1,075.5
Total other assets	3,715.0	3,671.7
Property and equipment		
Property and equipment, at cost	28,740.2	26,218.6
Accumulated depreciation and amortization	(8,815.5)	(7,635.2)
Net property and equipment	19,924.7	18,583.4
Total assets	$25,525.1	$23,970.5
Liabilities and Shareholders' Equity		
Current liabilities		
Accounts payable	$ 577.4	$ 635.8
Income taxes	71.5	16.3
Other taxes	222.0	191.8
Accrued interest	193.1	199.4
Accrued restructuring and restaurant closing costs	115.7	328.5
Accrued payroll and other liabilities	918.1	774.7
Current maturities of long-term debt	388.0	275.8
Total current liabilities	2,485.8	2,422.3
Long-term debt	9,342.5	9,703.6
Other long-term liabilities and minority interests	699.8	560.0
Deferred income taxes	1,015.1	1,003.7
Shareholders' equity		
Preferred stock, no par value; authorized—165.0 million shares; issued—none		
Common stock, $.01 par value; authorized—3.5 billion shares; issued—1,660.6 million shares	16.6	16.6
Additional paid-in capital	1,837.5	1,747.3
Unearned ESOP compensation	(90.5)	(98.4)
Retained earnings	20,172.3	19,204.4
Accumulated other comprehensive income (loss)	(635.5)	(1,601.3)
Common stock in treasury, at cost; 398.7 and 392.4 million shares	(9,318.5)	(8,987.7)
Total shareholders' equity	11,981.9	10,280.9
Total liabilities and shareholders' equity	$25,525.1	$23,970.5

1. Horizontal analysis of Donaldson's income statement for 2008 would show which of the following for Selling, general, & administrative expenses? (pp. 687–688)
   a. 1.14
   b. 1.10
   c. 1.07
   d. None of the above (<u>fill in the blank</u>).

2. Vertical analysis of Donaldson's income statement for 2008 would show which of the following for Selling, general, & administrative expenses? (pp. 691–692)
   a. 1.144
   b. 0.143
   c. 0.107
   d. None of the above (<u>fill in the blank</u>).

3. Which item on Donaldson's income statement has the most favorable trend during 2007–2008? (pp. 690–691)
   a. Total revenues
   b. Net income
   c. Food and paper costs
   d. Payroll & employee benefits

4. On Donaldson's common-size balance sheet, Goodwill would appear as (pp. 693–694)
   a. 0.065.
   b. up by 6.8%.
   c. $1,665.1 million.
   d. 9.7% of total revenues.

5. A good benchmark for Donaldson Company would be (pp. 693–694)
   a. Whataburger.
   b. Boeing.
   c. Intel.
   d. All of the above.

6. Donaldson's inventory turnover for 2008 was (pp. 701–702)
   a. 91 times.
   b. 62 times.
   c. 21 times.
   d. 36 times.

7. Donaldson's acid-test ratio at the end of 2008 was (pp. 701–702)
   a. 1.49.
   b. 0.49.
   c. 0.30.
   d. 0.20.

8. Donaldson's average collection period for accounts and notes receivables is (pp. 701–703)
   a. 1 day.
   b. 2 days.
   c. 30 days.
   d. 17 days.

9. Donaldson's total debt position looks (p. 703)
   a. safe.
   b. middle-ground.
   c. risky.
   d. Cannot tell from the financials.

10. Donaldson's return on total revenues for 2008 was (p. 704)
    a. 13.2%.
    b. $1.16.
    c. 5.9%.
    d. 8.6%.

11. Donaldson's return on stockholders' equity for 2008 was (pp. 705–706)
    a. 13.2%.
    b. 8.6%.
    c. 5.9%.
    d. $1,471.4 million.

12. On June 30, 2009, Donaldson's common stock sold for $26 per share. At that price, how much did investors say $1 of the company's net income was worth? (pp. 706–707)
    a. $1.00
    b. $22.41
    c. $21.85
    d. $26.00

13. Use Donaldson's financial statements and the data in question 12 to compute Donaldson's dividend yield during 2008. (pp. 706–707)
    a. 3.1%
    b. 2.4%
    c. 2.2%
    d. 1.5%

14. How much EVA® did Donaldson generate for investors during 2008? Assume the cost of capital was 8%. (pp. 707–708)
    a. $973 million
    b. $1,471 million
    c. $239 million
    d. $1,859 million

Accounting Vocabulary

accounts receivable turnover (p. 702) Measures a company's ability to collect cash from credit customers. To compute accounts receivable turnover, divide net credit sales by average net accounts receivable.

acid-test ratio (p. 700) Ratio of the sum of cash plus short-term investments plus net current receivables to total current liabilities. Tells whether the entity can pay all its current liabilities if they come due immediately. Also called the *quick ratio*.

benchmarking (p. 693) The comparison of a company to a standard set by other companies, with a view toward improvement.

book value per share of common stock (p. 707) Common stockholders' equity divided by the number of shares of common stock outstanding. The recorded amount for each share of common stock outstanding.

capital charge (p. 708) The amount that stockholders and lenders charge a company for the use of their money. Calculated as (Notes payable + Loans payable + Long-term debt + Stockholders' equity) × Cost of capital.

common-size statement (p. 692) A financial statement that reports only percentages (no dollar amounts).

cost of capital (p. 707) A weighted average of the returns demanded by the company's stockholders and lenders.

current ratio (p. 698) Current assets divided by current liabilities. Measures a company's ability to pay current liabilities with current assets.

days' sales in receivables (p. 702) Ratio of average net accounts receivable to 1 day's sales. Indicates how many days' sales remain in Accounts Receivable awaiting collection. Also called the *collection period*.

debt ratio (p. 703) Ratio of total liabilities to total assets. States the proportion of a company's assets that is financed with debt.

dividend yield (p. 706) Ratio of dividends per share of stock to the stock's market price per share. Tells the percentage of a stock's market value that the company returns to stockholders as dividends.

earnings per share (EPS) (p. 705) Amount of a company's net income earned for each share of its outstanding common stock.

economic value added (EVA®) (p. 707) Used to evaluate a company's operating performance. EVA combines the concepts of accounting income and corporate finance to measure whether the company's operations have increased stockholder wealth. EVA = Net income + Interest expense – Capital charge.

efficient capital market (p. 709) A capital market in which market prices fully reflect all information available to the public.

horizontal analysis (p. 688) Study of percentage changes in comparative financial statements.

inventory turnover (p. 701) Ratio of cost of goods sold to average inventory. Indicates how rapidly inventory is sold.

leverage (p. 705) Earning more income on borrowed money than the related interest expense, thereby increasing the earnings for the owners of the business. Also called *trading on the equity*.

price/earnings ratio (p. 706) Ratio of the market price of a share of common stock to the company's earnings per share. Measures the value that the stock market places on $1 of a company's earnings.

quick ratio (pg. 700) Another name for the *acid-text ratio*.

rate of return on common stockholders' equity (p. 705) Net income minus preferred dividends, divided by average common stockholders' equity. A measure of profitability. Also called *return on equity*.

rate of return on net sales (p. 704) Ratio of net income to net sales. A measure of profitability. Also called *return on sales*.

rate of return on total assets (p. 704) Net income plus interest expense, divided by average total assets. This ratio measures a company's success in using its assets to earn income for the persons who finance the business. Also called *return on assets*.

return on equity (p. 705) Another name for *rate of return on common stockholders' equity*.

times-interest-earned ratio (p. 703) Ratio of income from operations to interest expense. Measures the number of times that operating income can cover interest expense. Also called the *interest-coverage ratio*.

trading on the equity (p. 705) Another name for *leverage*.

trend percentages (p. 690) A form of horizontal analysis that indicates the direction a business is taking.

vertical analysis (p. 698) Analysis of a financial statement that reveals the relationship of each statement item to a specified base, which is the 100% figure.

working capital (p. 698) Current assets minus current liabilities; measures a business's ability to meet its short-term obligations with its current assets.

ASSESS YOUR PROGRESS

Short Exercises

S13-1 (*Learning Objective 1: Horizontal analysis of revenues and net income*) Cannes Corporation, reported the following amounts on its 2008 comparative income statement.

writing assignment ■

(In thousands)	2008	2007	2006
Revenues......................	$10,889	$10,095	$9,777
Total expenses...............	5,985	5,604	5,194

Perform a horizontal analysis of revenues and net income—both in dollar amounts and in percentages—for 2008 and 2007. (pp. 687–688)

S13-2 (*Learning Objective 1: Trend analysis of sales and net income*) Zoobilee, Inc., reported the following sales and net income amounts:

(In thousands)	2009	2008	2007	2006
Sales..........................	$9,180	$8,990	$8,770	$8,550
Net income..................	520	500	460	400

Show Zoobilee's trend percentages for sales and net income. Use 2006 as the base year. (pp. 690–691)

S13-3 (*Learning Objective 2: Vertical analysis to correct a cash shortage*) Vision Software reported the following amounts on its balance sheets at December 31, 20X4, 20X3, and 20X2.

writing assignment ■

	20X4	20X3	20X2
Cash.....................................	$ 6,000	$ 6,000	$ 5,000
Receivables, net..................	30,000	22,000	19,000
Inventory.............................	148,000	106,000	74,000
Prepaid expenses	2,000	2,000	1,000
Property, plant, and			
equipment, net	96,000	88,000	87,000
Total assets	$282,000	$224,000	$186,000

Sales and profits are high. Nevertheless, Vision is experiencing a cash shortage. Perform a vertical analysis of Vision Software's assets at the end of years 20X4, 20X3, 20X2. Use the analysis to explain the reason for the cash shortage. (pp. 692–693)

S13-4 (*Learning Objective 3: Common-size income statements of 2 companies*) (pp. 691–692) Porterfield, Inc., and Beasley Corporation are competitors. Compare the 2 companies by converting their condensed income statements to common size.

(In millions)	Porterfield	Beasley
Net sales..	$9,489	$19,536
Cost of goods sold.......................................	5,785	14,101
Selling and administrative expenses...............	2,690	3,846
Interest expense...	59	16
Other expense	34	38
Income tax expense......................................	331	597
Net income...	$ 590	$ 938

(continued)

Which company earned more net income? Which company's net income was a higher percentage of its net sales? Which company is more profitable? Explain your answer. (p. 704)

S13-5 *(Learning Objective 5, 6: Evaluating the trend in a company's current ratio)* Examine the financial data of RubberMate Corporation in Exhibit 13-8 (p. 697). Show how to compute RubberMate's current ratio for each year 20X4 through 20X6. Is the company's ability to pay its current liabilities improving or deteriorating? (p. 700)

S13-6 *(Learning Objective 5, 6: Evaluating a company's acid-test ratio)* Use the **YUM! Brands** balance sheet data in Exhibit 13-3, page 698.

1. Compute YUM's acid-test ratio at December 31, 2006 and 2005. (pp. 701–702)
2. Compare YUM's ratio values to those of **Best Buy**, **IHOP**, and **Pier 1 Imports** on page 701. Is YUM's acid-test ratio strong or weak? Explain. (pp. 701–702)

S13-7 *(Learning Objective 5: Computing inventory turnover and days' sales in receivables)* Use the YUM! Brands 2006 income statement (p. 686) and balance sheet (p. 689) to compute the following:

   a. YUM's rate of inventory turnover for 2006. (pp. 701–702)
   b. Days' sales in average receivables during 2006. (Round dollar amounts to 1 decimal place.) (pp. 702–703)

Do these measures look strong or weak? Give the reason for your answer. (pp. 701–703)

S13-8 *(Learning Objective 5, 6: Measuring ability to pay long-term debt)* Use the financial statements of YUM! Brands (pp. 686, 689).

1. Compute the company's debt ratio at December 31, 2006. In which text exhibit does this ratio value appear? (p. 703)
2. Compute the company's times-interest-earned ratio for 2006. For operating income, use income before both interest expense and income taxes. You can simply add interest expense back to income before taxes. (p. 703)
3. Is YUM's ability to pay liabilities and interest expense strong or weak? Comment on the value of each ratio computed for requirements 1 and 2. (p. 703)

S13-9 *(Learning Objective 5, 6: Measuring profitability)* Use the financial statements of YUM! Brands (p. 686, 689) to locate or, if necessary, to compute these profitability measures for 2006. Show each computation.

   a. Rate of return on sales. (p. 704)
   b. Rate of return on total assets. (p. 704)
   c. Rate of return on common stockholders' equity. (pp. 705–706)

Are these rates of return strong or weak? Explain. (pp. 705–706)

S13-10 *(Learning Objective 5: Computing EPS and the price/earnings ratio)* The annual report of Classic Cars, Inc., for the year ended December 31, 2007, included the following items (in millions):

Preferred stock outstanding, 4%	$500
Net income	$990
Number of shares of common stock outstanding	200

1. Compute earnings per share (EPS) and the price/earnings ratio for Classic Cars' stock. Round to the nearest cent. The price of a share of Classic Car stock is $77.60. (pp. 705–708)
2. How much does the stock market say $1 of Classic Cars' net income is worth? (pp. 706–707)

S13-11 (*Learning Objective 5: Using ratio data to reconstruct an income statement*) A skeleton of Hill Country Florist's income statement appears as follows (amounts in thousands):

Income Statement

Net sales	$7,278
Cost of goods sold.........................	(a)
Selling expenses.............................	1,510
Administrative expenses................	326
Interest expense.............................	(b)
Other expenses...............................	151
Income before taxes	1,042
Income tax expense.......................	(c)
Net income.....................................	$ (d)

Use the following ratio data to complete Hill Country Florist's income statement:
- **a.** Inventory turnover was 5 (beginning inventory was $787; ending inventory was $755). (pp. 701–702)
- **b.** Rate of return on sales is 0.12. (p. 704)

S13-12 (*Learning Objective 5: Using ratio data to reconstruct a balance sheet*) A skeleton of Hill Country Florist's balance sheet appears as follows (amounts in thousands):

Balance Sheet

Cash..	$ 253		Total current liabilities	$1,164
Receivables.............................	(a)		Long-term debt	(e)
Inventories	555		Other long-term liabilities..........	826
Prepaid expenses	(b)			
Total current assets...........	(c)			
Plant assets, net.....................	(d)		Common stock...........................	185
Other assets...........................	1,150		Retained earnings.......................	2,846
Total assets...........................	$6,315		Total liabilities and equity..........	$ (f)

Use the following ratio data to complete Hill Country Florist's balance sheet: (pp. 700–703)
a. Debt ratio is 0.52.   **b.** Current ratio is 1.20.   **c.** Acid-test ratio is 0.70.

S13-13 (*Learning Objective 7: Measuring economic value added*) Compute economic value added (EVA®) for Mainstream Software. The company's cost of capital is 12%. Net income was $695 thousand, interest expense $394 thousand, beginning long-term debt $1,294 thousand, and beginning stockholders' equity was $3,031 thousand. Round all amounts to the nearest thousand dollars. (pp. 707–708)

Should the company's stockholders be happy with the EVA®? (pp. 707–708)

Exercises

E13-14 *(Learning Objective 1: Computing year-to-year changes in working capital)* What were the dollar amount of change and the percentage of each change in Rocky Mountain Lodge's working capital during 2008 and 2007? Is this trend favorable or unfavorable? (pp. 690–691)

	2008	2007	2006
Total current assets	$326,000	$290,000	$280,000
Total current liabilities	170,000	167,000	150,000

▪ spreadsheet

E13-15 *(Learning Objective 1: Horizontal analysis of an income statement)* Prepare a horizontal analysis of the comparative income statement of Stamps Music Co. Round percentage changes to the nearest one-tenth percent (3 decimal places). (pp. 687–688)

Stamps Music Co.
Comparative Income Statement
Years Ended December 31, 2007 and 2006

	2007	2006
Total revenue	$403,000	$430,000
Expenses:		
Cost of goods sold	$188,000	$202,000
Selling and general expenses	93,000	90,000
Interest expense	4,000	10,000
Income tax expense	37,000	42,000
Total expenses	322,000	344,000
Net income	$ 81,000	$ 86,000

E13-16 *(Learning Objective 1: Computing trend percentages)* Compute trend percentages for Carmel Valley Sales & Service's total revenue, and net income for the following 5-year period, using year 0 as the base year. Round to the nearest full percent (pp. 690–691).

(In thousands)	Year 4	Year 3	Year 2	Year 1	Year 0
Total revenue	$1,418	$1,287	$1,106	$1,009	$1,043
Net income	125	104	93	81	85

Which grew faster during the period, total revenue or net income?

E13-17 *(Learning Objective 2: Vertical analysis of a balance sheet)* Cobra Golf Company has requested that you perform a vertical analysis of its balance sheet to determine the component percentages of its assets, liabilities, and stockholders' equity. (pp. 692–693)

Cobra Golf Company
Balance Sheet
December 31, 20X8

Assets

Total current assets	$ 92,000
Property, plant, and equipment, net	247,000
Other assets	35,000
Total assets	$374,000

Liabilities

Total current liabilities	$ 48,000
Long-term debt	108,000
Total liabilities	156,000

Stockholders' Equity

Total stockholders' equity	218,000
Total liabilities and stockholders' equity	$374,000

E13-18 (*Learning Objective 3: Preparing a common-size income statement*) Prepare a comparative common-size income statement for Stamps Music Co., using the 2007 and 2006 data of Exercise 13-15 and rounding percentages to one-tenth percent (3 decimal places). (pp. 691–692)

■ spreadsheet

E13-19 (*Learning Objective 4: Analyzing the statement of cash flows*) Identify any weaknesses revealed by the statement of cash flows of Florida Citrus Growers, Inc. (pp. 623–635, 643)

writing assignment ■

Florida Citrus Growers, Inc.
Statement of Cash Flows
For the Current Year

Operating activities:		
Income from operations		$ 42,000
Add (subtract) noncash items:		
Depreciation	$ 23,000	
Net increase in current assets other than cash	(45,000)	
Net decrease in current liabilities exclusive of short-term debt	(7,000)	(29,000)
Net cash provided by operating activities		13,000
Investing activities:		
Sale of property, plant, and equipment		101,000
Financing activities:		
Issuance of bonds payable	$ 102,000	
Payment of short-term debt	(159,000)	
Payment of long-term debt	(79,000)	
Payment of dividends	(42,000)	
Net cash used for financing activities		(178,000)
Increase (decrease) in cash		$ (64,000)

■ **spreadsheet**

E13-20 (*Learning Objective 5: Computing 5 ratios*) The financial statements of National News, Inc., include the following items:

	Current Year	Preceding Year
Balance Sheet:		
Cash	$ 17,000	$ 22,000
Short-term investments	11,000	26,000
Net receivables	64,000	73,000
Inventory	77,000	71,000
Prepaid expenses	16,000	8,000
Total current assets	185,000	200,000
Total current liabilities	111,000	91,000
Income Statement:		
Net credit sales	$654,000	
Cost of goods sold	327,000	

❚ *Required*

Compute the following ratios for the current year: (pp. 700–703)

a. Current ratio
b. Acid-test ratio
c. Inventory turnover
d. Accounts receivable turnover
e. Days' sales in average receivables

writing assignment ■

■ **spreadsheet**

E13-21 (*Learning Objective 5, 6: Analyzing the ability to pay current liabilities*) Patio Furniture Company has asked you to determine whether the company's ability to pay its current liabilities and long-term debts improved or deteriorated during 20X9. To answer this question, compute the following ratios for 20X9 and 20X8. (pp. 700–703)

a. Current ratio
b. Acid-test ratio
c. Debt ratio
d. Times-interest-earned ratio

Summarize the results of your analysis in a written report.

	20X9	20X8
Cash	$ 61,000	$ 47,000
Short-term investments	28,000	—
Net receivables	142,000	116,000
Inventory	286,000	263,000
Prepaid expenses	11,000	9,000
Total assets	643,000	489,000
Total current liabilities	255,000	221,000
Long-term debt	46,000	52,000
Income from operations	165,000	158,000
Interest expense	40,000	39,000

E13-22 (*Learning Objective 5, 6: Analyzing profitability*) Compute 4 ratios that measure ability to earn profits for PGI Decor, Inc., whose comparative income statement follows: (pp. 704–706)

PGI Decor, Inc.
Comparative Income Statement
Years Ended December 31, 20X8 and 20X7

Dollars in thousands	20X8	20X7
Net sales..	$174,000	$158,000
Cost of goods sold..............................	93,000	86,000
Gross profit......................................	81,000	72,000
Selling and general expenses................	46,000	41,000
Income from operations	35,000	31,000
Interest expense.................................	9,000	10,000
Income before income tax	26,000	21,000
Income tax expense	9,000	8,000
Net income	$ 17,000	$ 13,000

Additional data:

	20X8	20X7	20X6
Total assets..	$204,000	$191,000	$171,000
Common stockholders' equity.................	$ 96,000	$ 89,000	$ 79,000
Preferred dividends..................................	$ 3,000	$ 3,000	$ 0
Common shares outstanding during the year	21,000	20,000	18,000

Did the company's operating performance improve or deteriorate during 20X8?

E13-23 (*Learning Objective 5, 6: Evaluating a stock as an investment*) Evaluate the common stock of Phillips Distributing Company as an investment. Specifically, use the 3 common stock ratios to determine whether the common stock increased or decreased in attractiveness during the past year. (pp. 705–707)

writing assignment ■

	20X7	20X6
Net income...	$112,000	$ 96,000
Dividends to common	25,000	20,000
Total stockholders' equity at year end..............	580,000	500,000
(includes 80,000 shares of common stock)		
Preferred stock, 8%................................	100,000	100,000
Market price per share of common stock at year end..............................	$ 22.50	$ 16.75

E13-24 (*Learning Objective 7: Using economic value added to measure corporate performance*) Two companies with different economic-value-added (EVA®) profiles are **Amazon.com** and **eBay**. Adapted versions of the 2 companies' financial statements are presented here (in millions):

	Amazon.com	eBay
Balance sheet data:		
Total assets	$ 4,363	$13,494
Interest-bearing debt	$ 1,247	$ 0
All other liabilities.............................	2,685	2,589
Stockholders' equity..........................	431	10,905
Total liabilities and equity................	$ 4,363	$13,494
Income statement data:		
Total revenue	$10,711	$ 3,271
Interest expense..................................	78	9
Net income..	$ 190	$ 778

I *Required*

1. Before performing any calculations, which company do you think represents the better investment? Give your reason. (Challenge)

2. Compute the EVA® for each company and then decide which company's stock you would rather hold as an investment. Assume both companies' cost of capital is 10%. (pp. 707–708)

Challenge Exercises

E13-25 (*Learning Objective 2, 3, 5: Using ratio data to reconstruct a company's balance sheet*) The following data (dollar amounts in millions) are taken from the financial statements of Phase 1 Industries, Inc.

Total liabilities	$11,800
Preferred stock	$ 0
Total current assets	$10,200
Accumulated depreciation................	$ 1,400
Debt ratio...	59%
Current ratio....................................	1.50

I *Required*

Complete the following condensed balance sheet. Report amounts to the nearest million dollars. (pp. 700, 703)

Current assets..		$?
Property, plant, and equipment.............................	$?	
Less Accumulated depreciation....................	(?)	?
Total assets		$?
Current liabilities		$?
Long-term liabilities		?
Stockholders' equity..		?
Total liabilities and stockholders' equity		$?

E13-26 *(Learning Objective 2, 3, 5: Using ratio data to reconstruct a company's income statement)* The following data (dollar amounts in millions) are from the financial statements of Federal Corporation:

Average stockholders' equity...............................	$3,600
Interest expense...	$ 400
Preferred stock	$ 0
Operating income as a percent of sales...............	25%
Rate of return on stockholders' equity	20%
Income tax rate	40%

❚ Required

Complete the following condensed income statement. Report amounts to the nearest million dollars. (pp. 704–706)

Sales..	$?
Operating expense..................	?
Operating income...................	?
Interest expense.....................	?
Pretax income	?
Income tax expense...............	?
Net income...........................	$?

Practice Quiz

Use the Miami Bell Corporation *financial statements to answer the questions that follow.*

(continued)

Miami Bell Corporation
Consolidated Statements of Financial Position
(In millions)

	December 31,	
	20X4	20X3
Assets		
Current assets:		
Cash and cash equivalents	$ 4,317	$ 4,232
Short-term investments	835	406
Accounts receivable, net	3,635	2,586
Inventories	327	306
Other	1,519	1,394
Total current assets	10,633	8,924
Property, plant, and equipment, net	1,517	913
Investments	6,770	5,267
Other noncurrent assets	391	366
Total assets	$19,311	$15,470
Liabilities and Stockholders' Equity		
Current liabilities:		
Accounts payable	$ 7,316	$ 5,989
Accrued and other	3,580	2,944
Total current liabilities	10,896	8,933
Long-term debt	505	506
Other noncurrent liabilities	1,630	1,158
Commitments and contingent liabilities (Note 7)	—	—
Total liabilities	13,031	10,597
Stockholders' equity:		
Preferred stock and capital in excess of $0.01 par value; shares issued and outstanding: none	—	—
Common stock and capital in excess of $0.01 par value; shares authorized: 7,000; shares issued: 2,721 and 2,681, respectively	6,823	6,018
Treasury stock, at cost; 165 and 102 shares, respectively	(6,539)	(4,539)
Retained earnings	6,131	3,486
Other comprehensive loss	(83)	(33)
Other	(52)	(59)
Total stockholders' equity	6,280	4,873
Total liabilities and stockholders' equity	$19,311	$15,470

Miami Bell Corporation
Consolidated Statements of Income
(In millions, except per share amounts)

	Year ended December 31,		
	20X4	20X3	20X2
Net revenue..	$41,444	$35,404	$31,168
Cost of goods sold....................................	33,892	29,055	25,661
Gross profit	7,552	6,349	5,507
Operating expenses:			
Selling, general, and administrative......	3,544	3,050	2,784
Research, development, and			
engineering	464	455	452
Special charges....................................	—	—	482
Total operating expenses	4,008	3,505	3,718
Operating income..........................	3,544	2,844	1,789
Investment and other income (loss), net	180	183	(58)
Income before income taxes.................	3,724	3,027	1,731
Income tax expense.....................................	1,079	905	485
Net income...	$ 2,645	$ 2,122	$ 1,246
Earnings per common share:			
Basic..	$ 1.03	$ 0.82	$ 0.48

Q13-27 During 20X4, Miami Bell's total assets (pp. 687–688)
a. increased by $8,341 million.
b. increased by 24.8%.
c. Both a and b.
d. increased by 19.9%.

Q13-28 Miami Bell's current ratio at year end 20X4 is closest to (p. 700)
a. 1.2.
b. 1.1.
c. 1.0.
d. 0.80.

Q13-29 Miami Bell's acid-test ratio at year end 20X4 is closest to (pp. 701–702)
a. $0.80.
b. $0.65.
c. 0.47.
d. $8,787 million.

Q13-30 What is the largest single item included in Miami Bell's debt ratio at December 31, 20X4? (p. 703)
a. Cash and cash equivalents
b. Accounts payable
c. Investments
d. Common stock

Q13-31 Using the earliest year available as the base year, the trend percentage for Miami Bell's net revenue during 20X4 was (pp. 690–691)
a. 117%.
b. up by $10,276 million.
c. up by 17.1%.
d. 133%.

Q13-32 Miami Bell's common-size income statement for 20X4 would report cost of goods sold as (pp. 691–692)
a. $33,892 million.
b. Up by 16.6%.
c. 81.8%.
d. 132.1%.

Q13-33 Miami Bell's days' sales in average receivables during 20X4 was (pp. 702–703)
a. 22 days.
b. 27 days.
c. 32 days.
d. 114 days.

Q13-34 Miami Bell's inventory turnover during fiscal year 20X4 was (pp. 701–702)

a. very slow.
b. 54 times.

c. 107 times.
d. 129 times.

Q13-35 Miami Bell's long-term debt bears interest at 6%. During the year ended December 31, 20X4, Bell's times-interest-earned ratio was (p. 703)

a. 117 times.
b. 110 times.

c. 100 times.
d. 125 times.

Q13-36 Miami Bell's trend of return on sales is (p. 704)

a. improving.
b. declining.

c. stuck at 6%.
d. worrisome.

Q13-37 How many shares of common stock did Miami Bell have outstanding, on average, during 20X4? Hint: Compute earnings per share. (pp. 705–706)

a. 2,721 million
b. 2,701 million

c. 2,645 million
d. 2,568 million

Q13-38 Book value per share of Miami Bell's common stock outstanding at December 31, 20X4, was (pp. 707–708)

a. $2.72.
b. $4.37.

c. $6,280.
d. $2.46.

Problems
(Group A)

MyAccountingLab

> Some of these A problems can be found within My Accounting Lab (MAL), an online homework and practice environment. Your instructor may ask you to complete these exercises using MAL.

P13-39A *(Learning Objective 1, 5, 6: Trend percentages, return on sales, and comparison with the industry)* Net sales, net income, and total assets for Container Shipping, Inc., for a 5-year period follow:

(In thousands)	20X8	20X7	20X6	20X5	20X4
Net sales...............	$367	$313	$266	$281	$197
Net income............	27	11	11	18	16
Total assets	286	254	209	197	185

❚ Required

1. Compute trend percentages for each item for 20X5 through 20X8. Use 20X4 as the base year and round to the nearest percent. (pp. 690–691)
2. Compute the rate of return on net sales for 20X6 through 20X8, rounding to 3 decimal places. (p. 704)
3. How does Container Shipping's return on net sales compare with that of the industry? (p. 704) In the shipping industry, rates above 5% are considered good, and rates above 7% are outstanding. (p. 704)

P13-40A *(Learning Objective 2, 3, 5, 6: Common-size statements, analysis of profitability, and comparison with the industry)* Top managers of Medical Products, Inc., have asked for your help in comparing the company's profit performance and financial position with the average for the industry. The accountant has given you the company's income statement and balance sheet and also the following data for the industry:

Medical Products, Inc.
Income Statement Compared with Industry Average
Year Ended December 31, 20X5

	Medical Products	Industry Average
Net sales..................................	$957,000	100.0%
Cost of goods sold.................	652,000	55.9
Gross profit...........................	305,000	44.1
Operating expenses................	200,000	28.1
Operating income..................	105,000	16.0
Other expenses......................	3,000	2.4
Net income	$102,000	13.6%

Medical Products, Inc.
Balance Sheet Compared with Industry Average
December 31, 20X5

	Medical Products	Industry Average
Current assets...........................	$486,000	74.4%
Fixed assets, net	117,000	20.0
Intangible assets, net	24,000	0.6
Other assets.............................	3,000	5.0
Total	$630,000	100.0%
Current liabilities	$245,000	45.6%
Long-term liabilities.................	114,000	19.0
Stockholders' equity.................	271,000	35.4
Total	$630,000	100.0%

❙ Required

writing assignment ■

1. Prepare a common-size income statement and balance sheet for Medical Products. The first column of each statement should present Medical Products' common-size statement, and the second column should show the industry averages. (pp. 691–693)

2. For the profitability analysis, compute Medical Products' (a) ratio of gross profit to net sales (b) ratio of operating income to net sales, and (c) ratio of net income to net sales. Compare these figures with the industry averages. Is Medical Products' profit performance better or worse than the average for the industry? (p. 704)

3. For the analysis of financial position, compute Medical Products' (a) ratios of current assets and current liabilities to total assets and (b) ratio of stockholders' equity to total assets. Compare these ratios with the industry averages. Is Medical Products' financial position better or worse than the average for the industry? (pp. 692–693)

P13-41A (*Learning Objective 4: Using the statement of cash flows for decision making*) You are evaluating 2 companies as possible investments. The 2 companies, similar in size, are commuter airlines that fly passengers up and down the East Coast. All other available information has been analyzed and your investment decision depends on the cash-flow statement.

writing assignment ■

(continued)

Commonwealth Airlines (Comair)
Statement of Cash Flows
Years Ended November 30, 20X9 and 20X8

	20X9	20X8
Operating activities:		
Net income (net loss)	$ (67,000)	$154,000
Adjustments for noncash items:		
Total	84,000	(23,000)
Net cash provided by operating activities	17,000	131,000
Investing activities:		
Purchase of property, plant, and		
equipment..	$ (50,000)	$ (91,000)
Sale of long-term investments	52,000	4,000
Net cash provided by (used for)		
investing activities................................	2,000	(87,000)
Financing activities:		
Issuance of short-term notes payable	$ 122,000	$143,000
Payment of short-term notes payable........	(179,000)	(134,000)
Payment of cash dividends........................	(45,000)	(64,000)
Net cash used for financing activities........	(102,000)	(55,000)
Increase (decrease) in cash......................	$ (83,000)	$ (11,000)
Cash balance at beginning of year......................	92,000	103,000
Cash balance at the end of year..........................	$ 9,000	$ 92,000

Jetway, Inc.
Statement of Cash Flows
Years Ended November 30, 20X9 and 20X8

	20X9	20X8
Operating activities:		
Net income	$ 184,000	$ 131,000
Adjustments for noncash items:		
Total	64,000	62,000
Net cash provided by operating activities	248,000	193,000
Investing activities:		
Purchase of property, plant,		
and equipment......................................	$(303,000)	$(453,000)
Sale of property, plant, and equipment	46,000	72,000
Net cash used for investing activities	(257,000)	(381,000)
Financing activities:		
Issuance of long-term notes payable..........	$ 174,000	$ 118,000
Payment of short-term notes payable........	(66,000)	(18,000)
Net cash provided by financing activities......	108,000	100,000
Increase (decrease) in cash................................	$ 99,000	$ (88,000)
Cash balance at beginning of year......................	116,000	204,000
Cash balance at end of year...............................	$ 215,000	$ 116,000

I *Required*

Discuss the relative strengths and weaknesses of Comair and Jetway. Conclude your discussion by recommending 1 of the companies' stocks as an investment. (pp. 694–695)

P13-42A (*Learning Objective 5, 6: Effects of business transactions on selected ratios*)
Financial statement data of Metroplex Engineering include the following items:

Cash	$ 47,000	Accounts payable	$142,000
Short-term investments	21,000	Accrued liabilities	50,000
Accounts receivable, net	102,000	Long-term notes payable	146,000
Inventories	274,000	Other long-term liabilities	78,000
Prepaid expenses	15,000	Net income	104,000
Total assets	933,000	Number of common	
Short-term notes payable	72,000	shares outstanding	22,000

I *Required*

1. Compute Metroplex's current ratio, debt ratio, and earnings per share. Use the following format for your answer: (pp. 700, 703, 705–706)

Requirement 1
Current ratio   Debt ratio   Earnings per share

2. Compute the 3 ratios after evaluating the effect of each transaction that follows. Consider each transaction *separately*.
   a. Borrowed $27,000 on a long-term note payable.
   b. Issued 10,000 shares of common stock, receiving cash of $108,000.
   c. Paid short-term notes payable, $51,000.
   d. Purchased merchandise of $48,000 on account, debiting Inventory.
   e. Received cash on account, $6,000.

Format your answer as follows:

Requirement 2
Transaction (letter)   Current ratio   Debt ratio   Earnings per share

P13-43A (*Learning Objective 5, 6: Using ratios to evaluate a stock investment*) Comparative financial statement data of Crest Optical Mart follow:

Crest Optical Mart
Comparative Income Statement
Years Ended December 31, 20X6 and 20X5

	20X6	20X5
Net sales	$667,000	$599,000
Cost of goods sold	378,000	313,000
Gross profit	289,000	286,000
Operating expenses	129,000	147,000
Income from operations	160,000	139,000
Interest expense	37,000	41,000
Income before income tax	123,000	98,000
Income tax expense	44,000	43,000
Net income	$ 79,000	$ 55,000

(continued)

HH CHAPTER 13

Crest Optical Mart
Comparative Balance Sheet
December 31, 20X6 and 20X5

	20X6	20X5	20X4*
Current assets:			
Cash	$ 37,000	$ 40,000	
Current receivables, net	208,000	151,000	$138,000
Inventories	152,000	186,000	144,000
Prepaid expenses	5,000	20,000	
Total current assets	402,000	397,000	
Property, plant, and equipment, net	287,000	256,000	
Total assets	$689,000	$653,000	607,000
Total current liabilities	$286,000	$217,000	
Long-term liabilities	145,000	185,000	
Total liabilities	431,000	402,000	
Preferred stockholders' equity, 4%, $20 par	50,000	50,000	
Common stockholders' equity, no par	208,000	201,000	198,000
Total liabilities and stockholders' equity	$689,000	$653,000	

*Selected 20X4 amounts.

Other information:

1. Market price of Crest common stock: $61 at December 31, 20X6, and $45.50 at December 31, 20X5.
2. Common shares outstanding: 15,000 during 20X6 and 14,000 during 20X5.
3. All sales on credit.

❙ Required

1. Compute the following ratios for 20X6 and 20X5:
   a. Current ratio (p. 700)
   b. Inventory turnover (pp. 701–702)
   c. Times-interest-earned ratio (p. 703)
   d. Return on assets (p. 704)
   e. Return on common stockholders' equity (pp. 705–706)
   f. Earnings per share of common stock (pp. 705–706)
   g. Price/earnings ratio (pp. 706–707)
2. Decide whether (a) Crest's financial position improved or deteriorated during 20X6 and (b) the investment attractiveness of Crest's common stock appears to have increased or decreased. (Challenge)
3. How will what you learned in this problem help you evaluate an investment? (Challenge)

writing assignment ■

P13-44A *(Learning Objective 5, 6, 7: Using ratios to decide between 2 stock investments; measuring economic value added)* Assume that you are considering purchasing stock as an investment. You have narrowed the choice to Video.com and On-Line Express and have assembled the following data:

Selected income statement data for current year:

	Video	Express
Net sales (all on credit)..................	$603,000	$519,000
Cost of goods sold.........................	454,000	387,000
Income from operations................	93,000	72,000
Interest expense.............................	—	12,000
Net income..................................	56,000	38,000

Selected balance sheet and market price data at *end* of current year:

	Video	Express
Current assets:		
Cash	$ 25,000	$ 39,000
Short-term investments	6,000	13,000
Current receivables, net	189,000	164,000
Inventories..	211,000	183,000
Prepaid expenses..	19,000	15,000
Total current assets	450,000	414,000
Total assets..	974,000	938,000
Total current liabilities	366,000	338,000
Total liabilities	667,000*	691,000*
Preferred stock, 4%, $100 par...............................		25,000
Common stock, $1 par (150,000 shares)................	150,000	
$5 par (20,000 shares)...................		100,000
Total stockholders' equity	307,000	247,000
Market price per share of common stock	$ 9	$ 47.50

*Includes Long-term debt: Video $-0-, and Express $350,000

Selected balance sheet data at *beginning* of current year:

	Video	Express
Current receivables, net...	$142,000	$193,000
Inventories	209,000	197,000
Total assets..	842,000	909,000
Long-term debt	—	303,000
Preferred stock, 4%, $100 par...............................		25,000
Common stock, $1 par (150,000 shares)................	150,000	
$5 par (20,000 shares).................		100,000
Total stockholders' equity	263,000	215,000

Your strategy is to invest in companies that have low price/earnings ratios but appear to be in good shape financially. Assume that you have analyzed all other factors and that your decision depends on the results of ratio analysis.

(continued)

❚ Required

1. Compute the following ratios for both companies for the current year and decide which company's stock better fits your investment strategy.
   a. Acid-test ratio (pp. 701–702)
   b. Inventory turnover (pp. 701–702)
   c. Days' sales in average receivables (pp. 702–703)
   d. Debt ratio (p. 703)
   e. Times-interest-earned ratio (p. 703)
   f. Return on common stockholders' equity (pp. 705–706)
   g. Earnings per share of common stock (pp. 705–706)
   h. Price/earnings ratio (pp. 706–707)

2. Compute each company's economic-value-added (EVA®) measure and determine whether the companies' EVA®s confirm or alter your investment decision. Each company's cost of capital is 10%. (pp. 707–708)

writing assignment ■

P13-45A *(Learning Objective 6: Analyzing a company based on its ratios)* Take the role of an investment analyst at **Merrill Lynch**. It is your job to recommend investments for your client. The only information you have is the following ratio values for 2 companies in the graphics software industry.

Ratio	Omicron.net	Data Miners
Days' sales in receivables............................	51	43
Inventory turnover....................................	9	7
Gross profit percentage.............................	62%	71%
Net income as a percent of sales................	16%	14%
Times interest earned	12	18
Return on equity.......................................	29%	36%
Return on assets.......................................	19%	14%

Write a report to the Merrill Lynch investment committee. Recommend 1 company's stock over the other. State the reasons for your recommendation. (pp. 701–706)

(Group B)

P13-46B *(Learning Objective 1, 5, 6: Trend percentages, return on common equity, and comparison with the industry)* Net revenues, net income, and common stockholders' equity for Accenté Corporation for a 5-year period follow.

(In thousands)	2008	2007	2006	2005	2004
Net revenues	$781	$714	$681	$662	$581
Net income..	41	35	32	28	20
Ending common stockholders' equity..............	386	354	330	296	263

❚ Required

1. Compute trend percentages for each item for 2005 through 2008. Use 2004 as the base year. Round to the nearest percent. (pp. 690–691)
2. Compute the rate of return on common stockholders' equity for 2006 through 2008, rounding to 3 decimal places. (pp. 705–706)

3. In this industry, rates of return on common stockholders' equity of 13% are average, rates above 16% are good, and rates above 20% are outstanding. Accenté has no preferred stock outstanding. How does Accenté's return on common stockholders' equity compare with the industry? (pp. 705–706)

P13-47B (*Learning Objective 2, 3, 5, 6: Common-size statements, analysis of profitability, and comparison with the industry*) Pathfinder, Inc., has asked you to compare the company's profit performance and financial position with the industry average. The proprietor has given you the company's income statement and balance sheet as well as the industry average data for retailers.

writing assignment ■

HH CHAPTER 13

Pathfinder, Inc.
Income Statement Compared with Industry Average
Year Ended December 31, 20X6

	Pathfinder	Industry Average
Net sales...........................	$700,000	100.0%
Cost of goods sold.................	497,000	65.8
Gross profit...........................	203,000	34.2
Operating expenses................	163,000	19.7
Operating income..................	40,000	14.5
Other expenses......................	3,000	0.4
Net income	$ 37,000	14.1%

Pathfinder, Inc.
Balance Sheet Compared with Industry Average
December 31, 20X6

	Pathfinder	Industry Average
Current assets...........................	$300,000	70.9%
Fixed assets, net	74,000	23.6
Intangible assets, net	4,000	0.8
Other assets.............................	22,000	4.7
Total	$400,000	100.0%
Current liabilities	$206,000	48.1%
Long-term liabilities.................	64,000	16.6
Stockholders' equity................	130,000	35.3
Total	$400,000	100.0%

▌Required

1. Prepare a common-size income statement and balance sheet for Pathfinder. The first column of each statement should present Pathfinder's common-size statement, and the second column, the industry averages. (pp. 691–693)

(continued)

2. For the profitability analysis, compute Pathfinder's (a) ratio of gross profit to net sales, (b) ratio of operating income to net sales, and (c) ratio of net income to net sales. Compare these figures with the industry averages. Is Pathfinder's profit performance better or worse than the industry average? (p. 704)

3. For the analysis of financial position, compute Pathfinder's (a) ratio of current assets to total assets, and (b) ratio of stockholders' equity to total assets. Compare these ratios with the industry averages. Is Pathfinder's financial position better or worse than the industry averages? (pp. 692–693)

writing assignment ■

P13-48B (*Learning Objective 4: Using the statement of cash flows for decision making*) You have been asked to evaluate 2 companies as possible investments. The 2 companies, Norfolk Southern Corp. and Stafford Crystal Company, are similar in size. Assume that all other available information has been analyzed, and the decision concerning which company's stock to purchase depends on their cash-flow data.

I Required

Discuss the relative strengths and weaknesses of each company. Conclude your discussion by recommending 1 company's stock as an investment. (pp. 694–695)

Norfolk Southern Corp.
Statement of Cash Flows
Years Ended September 30, 20X7 and 20X6

	20X7	20X6
Operating activities:		
Net income	$ 17,000	$44,000
Adjustments for noncash items:		
Total	(14,000)	(4,000)
Net cash provided by operating activities	3,000	40,000
Investing activities:		
Purchase of property, plant, and equipment	$ (13,000)	$ (3,000)
Sale of property, plant, and equipment	86,000	79,000
Net cash provided by investing activities	73,000	76,000
Financing activities:		
Issuance of short-term notes payable	$ 43,000	$ 19,000
Payment of short-term notes payable	(101,000)	(108,000)
Net cash used for financing activities	(58,000)	(89,000)
Increase in cash	$ 18,000	$ 27,000
Cash balance at beginning of year	31,000	4,000
Cash balance at end of year	$ 49,000	$ 31,000

Strafford Crystal Company
Statement of Cash Flows
Years Ended September 30, 20X7 and 20X6

	20X7	20X6
Operating activities:		
Net income	$ 89,000	$ 71,000
Adjustments for noncash items:		
Total	19,000	—
Net cash provided by operating activities.	108,000	71,000
Investing activities:		
Purchase of property, plant, and equipment	$(121,000)	$(91,000)
Net cash used for investing activities	(121,000)	(91,000)
Financing activities:		
Issuance of long-term notes payable	$ 46,000	$ 43,000
Payment of short-term notes payable	(15,000)	(40,000)
Payment of cash dividends	(12,000)	(9,000)
Net cash provided by (used for) financing activities	19,000	(6,000)
Increase (decrease) in cash	6,000	$(26,000)
Cash balance at beginning of year	54,000	80,000
Cash balance at end of year	$ 60,000	$ 54,000

P13-49B (*Learning Objective 5, 6: Effects of business transactions on selected ratios*) Financial statement data of HiFlite Electronics include the following items (dollars in thousands):

Cash	$ 22,000
Short-term investments	39,000
Accounts receivable, net	83,000
Inventories	141,000
Prepaid expenses	8,000
Total assets	677,000
Short-term notes payable	49,000
Accounts payable	103,000
Accrued liabilities	38,000
Long-term notes payable	160,000
Other long-term liabilities	31,000
Net income	91,000
Number of common shares outstanding	40,000

❙ Required

1. Compute HiFlite's current ratio, debt ratio, and earnings per share. Use the following format for your answer: (pp. 700, 703, 705–706)

Requirement 1
Current ratio   Debt ratio   Earnings per share

(continued)

2. Compute the 3 ratios after evaluating the effect of each transaction that follows. Consider each transaction *separately*.
   a. Purchased store supplies of $46,000 on account.
   b. Borrowed $125,000 on a long-term note payable.
   c. Issued 5,000 shares of common stock, receiving cash of $120,000.
   d. Paid short-term notes payable, $32,000.
   e. Received cash on account, $19,000.

Format your answer as follows:

Requirement 2 Transaction (letter)	Current ratio	Debt ratio	Earnings per share

writing assignment ■

P13-50B (*Learning Objective 5, 6: Using ratios to evaluate a stock investment*) Comparative financial statement data of Mira TV Sales follow.

Mira TV Sales
Comparative Income Statement
Years Ended December 31, 20X9 and 20X8

	20X9	20X8
Net sales	$662,000	$527,000
Cost of goods sold	429,000	318,000
Gross profit	233,000	209,000
Operating expenses	136,000	134,000
Income from operations	97,000	75,000
Interest expense	9,000	8,000
Income before income tax	88,000	67,000
Income tax expense	30,000	27,000
Net income	$ 58,000	$ 40,000

Mira TV Sales
Comparative Balance Sheet
December 31, 20X9 and 20X8

	20X9	20X8	20X7*
Current assets:			
Cash	$ 96,000	$ 97,000	
Current receivables, net	162,000	116,000	$103,000
Inventories	147,000	162,000	207,000
Prepaid expenses	16,000	7,000	
Total current assets	421,000	382,000	
Property, plant, and equipment, net	214,000	178,000	
Total assets	$635,000	$560,000	598,000
Total current liabilities	$206,000	$223,000	
Long-term liabilities	119,000	117,000	
Total liabilities	325,000	340,000	
Preferred stockholders' equity, 6%, $100 par	100,000	100,000	
Common stockholders' equity, no par	210,000	120,000	90,000
Total liabilities and stockholders' equity	$635,000	$560,000	

*Selected 20X7 amounts.

Other information:

1. Market price of Mira's common stock: $83 at December 31, 20X9, and $62.50 at December 31, 20X8.
2. Common shares outstanding: 10,000 during 20X9 and 9,000 during 20X8.
3. All sales on credit.

I Required

1. Compute the following ratios for 20X9 and 20X8:
   a. Current ratio (p. 700)
   b. Inventory turnover (pp. 701–702)
   c. Times-interest-earned ratio (p. 703)
   d. Return on common stockholders' equity (pp. 705–706)
   e. Earnings per share of common stock (pp. 705–706)
   f. Price/earnings ratio (pp. 706–707)
2. Decide (a) whether Mira's financial position improved or deteriorated during 20X9 and (b) whether the investment attractiveness of Mira's common stock appears to have increased or decreased. (Challenge)
3. How will what you learned in this problem help you evaluate an investment? (Challenge)

P13-51B (*Learning Objective 5, 6, 7: Using ratios to decide between 2 stock investments; measuring economic value added*) Assume that you are purchasing an investment and have decided to invest in a company in the publishing business. You have narrowed the choice to Thrifty Nickel Corp. and The Village Cryer and have assembled the following data:

Selected income statement data for the current year:

	Thrifty Nickel	Village Cryer
Net sales (all on credit).................	$371,000	$497,000
Cost of goods sold.........................	209,000	258,000
Income from operations................	79,000	138,000
Interest expense............................	—	19,000
Net income	48,000	72,000

Selected balance sheet data at *beginning* of the current year:

	Thrifty Nickel	Village Cryer
Current receivables, net..	$ 40,000	$ 48,000
Inventories	93,000	88,000
Total assets..	259,000	270,000
Long-term debt	—	86,000
Preferred stock, 5%, $100 par.............................	—	20,000
Common stock, $1 par (10,000 shares)................	10,000	
$2.50 par (5,000 shares)..............		12,500
Total stockholders' equity.....................................	118,000	126,000

(continued)

writing assignment ■

HH CHAPTER 13

Selected balance sheet and market price data at *end* of the current year:

	Thrifty Nickel	Village Cryer
Current assets:		
Cash	$ 22,000	$ 19,000
Short-term investments	20,000	18,000
Current receivables, net	42,000	46,000
Inventories	87,000	100,000
Prepaid expenses	2,000	3,000
Total current assets	173,000	186,000
Total assets	265,000	328,000
Total current liabilities	108,000	98,000
Total liabilities	108,000*	131,000*
Preferred stock: 5%, $100 par		20,000
Common stock, $1 par (10,000 shares)	10,000	
$2.50 par (5,000 shares)		12,500
Total stockholders' equity	157,000	197,000
Market price per share of common stock	$ 51	$ 112

* Includes Long-term debt: Thrifty Nickel $-0- and Village Cryer $86,000

Your strategy is to invest in companies that have low price/earnings ratios but appear to be in good shape financially. Assume that you have analyzed all other factors and your decision depends on the results of ratio analysis.

▌ Required

1. Compute the following ratios for both companies for the current year, and decide which company's stock better fits your investment strategy.
   a. Acid-test ratio (pp. 701–702)
   b. Inventory turnover (pp. 701–702)
   c. Days' sales in average receivables (pp. 702–703)
   d. Debt ratio (p. 703)
   e. Times-interest-earned ratio (p. 703)
   f. Return on common stockholders' equity (pp. 705–706)
   g. Earnings per share of common stock (pp. 705–706)
   h. Price/earnings ratio (pp. 706–707)
2. Compute each company's economic-value-added (EVA®) measure and determine whether the companies' EVA®s confirm or alter your investment decision. Each company's cost of capital is 12%. (pp. 707–708)

P13-52B (*Learning Objective 6: Analyzing a company based on its ratios*) Take the role of an investment analyst at **Solomon Brothers**. It is your job to recommend investments for your clients. The only information you have is the following ratio values for 2 companies in the pharmaceuticals industry.

Ratio	MONY Group	Pegasus, Inc.
Days' sales in receivables............................	36	42
Inventory turnover......................................	6	8
Gross profit percentage.............................	49%	51%
Net income as a percent of sales................	7.2%	8.3%
Times interest earned	16	9
Return on equity..	32.3%	21.5%
Return on assets..	12.1%	16.4%

Write a report to Solomon Brothers investment committee. Recommend 1 company's stock over the others'. State the reasons for your recommendation. (pp. 701–706)

APPLY YOUR KNOWLEDGE

Decision Cases

Case 1. *(Learning Objective 5, 6: Assessing the effects of transactions on a company)* **AOL Time Warner Inc.** had a bad year in 20X1; the company suffered a $4.9 billion net loss. The loss pushed most of the return measures into the negative column and the current ratio dropped below 1.0. The company's debt ratio is still only 0.27. Assume top management of AOL Time Warner is pondering ways to improve the company's ratios. In particular, management is considering the following transactions:

1. Sell off the cable television segment of the business for $30 million (receiving half in cash and half in the form of a long-term note receivable). Book value of the cable television business is $27 million.

2. Borrow $100 million on long-term debt.

3. Purchase treasury stock for $500 million cash.

4. Write off one-fourth of goodwill carried on the books at $128 million.

5. Sell advertising at the normal gross profit of 60%. The advertisements run immediately.

6. Purchase trademarks from **NBC**, paying $20 million cash and signing a 1-year note payable for $80 million.

❙ Required

1. Top management wants to know the effects of these transactions (increase, decrease, or no effect) on the following ratios of AOL Time Warner:
   a. Current ratio (p. 700)
   b. Debt ratio (p. 703)
   c. Times-interest-earned ratio (measured as [net income + interest expense]/interest expense) (p. 703)
   d. Return on equity (pp. 705–706)
   e. Book value per share of common stock (pp. 707–708)

2. Some of these transactions have an immediately positive effect on the company's financial condition. Some are definitely negative. Others have an effect that cannot be judged as clearly positive or negative. Evaluate each transaction's effect as positive, negative, or unclear. (Challenge)

writing assignment ■

Case 2. (*Learning Objective 5, 6: Analyzing the effects of an accounting difference on the ratios*) **Gap Inc.** uses the first-in, first-out (FIFO) method to account for its inventory, and **Lands' End** uses last-in, first-out (LIFO). Analyze the effect of this difference in accounting method on the 2 companies' ratio values. For each ratio discussed in this chapter, indicate which company will have the higher (and the lower) ratio value. Also identify those ratios that are unaffected by the FIFO/LIFO difference. Ignore the effects of income taxes, and assume inventory costs are increasing. Then, based on your analysis of the ratios, summarize your conclusions as to which company looks better overall. (pp. 319, 323, 700–708).

writing assignment ■

Case 3. (*Learning Objective 2, 5, 6: Identifying action to cut losses and establish profitability*) Suppose you manage Outward Bound, Inc., a Vermont sporting goods store that lost money during the past year. To turn the business around, you must analyze the company and industry data for the current year to learn what is wrong. The company's data follow:

Outward Bound, Inc.
Common-Size Balance Sheet Data

	Outward Bound	Industry Average
Cash and short-term investments	3.0%	6.8%
Trade receivables, net	15.2	11.0
Inventory	64.2	60.5
Prepaid expenses	1.0	0.0
Total current assets	83.4%	78.3%
Fixed assets, net	12.6	15.2
Other assets	4.0	6.5
Total assets	100.0%	100.0%
Notes payable, short-term, 12%	17.1%	14.0%
Accounts payable	21.1	25.1
Accrued liabilities	7.8	7.9
Total current liabilities	46.0	47.0
Long-term debt, 11%	19.7	16.4
Total liabilities	65.7	63.4
Common stockholders' equity	34.3	36.6
Total liabilities and stockholders' equity	100.0%	100.0%

Outward Bound, Inc.
Common-Size Income Statement Data

	Outward Bound	Industry Average
Net sales	100.0%	100.0%
Cost of sales	(68.2)	(64.8)
Gross profit	31.8	35.2
Operating expense	(37.1)	(32.3)
Operating income (loss)	(5.3)	2.9
Interest expense	(5.8)	(1.3)
Other revenue	1.1	0.3
Income (loss) before income tax	(10.0)	1.9
Income tax (expense) saving	4.4	(0.8)
Net income (loss)	(5.6)%	1.1%

❚ *Required*

On the basis of your analysis of these figures, suggest 4 courses of action Outward Bound might take to reduce its losses and establish profitable operations. Give your reason for each suggestion. (Challenge)

Ethical Issue

Turnberry Golf Corporation's long-term debt agreements make certain demands on the business. For example, Turnberry may not purchase treasury stock in excess of the balance of retained earnings. Also, long-term debt may not exceed stockholders' equity, and the current ratio may not fall below 1.50. If Turnberry fails to meet any of these requirements, the company's lenders have the authority to take over management of the company.

Changes in consumer demand have made it hard for Turnberry to attract customers. Current liabilities have mounted faster than current assets, causing the current ratio to fall to 1.47. Before releasing financial statements, Turnberry management is scrambling to improve the current ratio. The controller points out that an investment can be classified as either long-term or short-term, depending on management's intention. By deciding to convert an investment to cash within 1 year, Turnberry can classify the investment as short-term—a current asset. On the controller's recommendation, Turnberry's board of directors votes to reclassify long-term investments as short-term.

❚ *Required*

1. What effect will reclassifying the investments have on the current ratio? Is Turnberry's financial position stronger as a result of reclassifying the investments?

writing assignment ■

2. Shortly after the financial statements are released, sales improve; so, too, does the current ratio. As a result, Turnberry management decides not to sell the investments it had reclassified as short term. Accordingly, the company reclassifies the investments as long term. Has management behaved unethically? Give the reasoning underlying your answer.

Focus on Financials: ■ YUM! Brands

writing assignment ■

(*Learning Objective 1, 6: Measuring profitability and analyzing stock as an investment*) Use the financial statements and the data in **YUM! Brands'** 5-year summary of selected financial data (Appendix A at the end of the book) to answer the following questions.

❚ *Required*

1. Using 2003 as the base year, perform a trend analysis of YUM's selected Financial Data for total revenue, operating profit, net income, and net cash provided by operating activities for each year 2004 through 2006. (pp. 690–691)

2. Evaluate YUM's operating performance during 2004 through 2006. Comment on each item computed. (Challenge)

Focus on Analysis: ■ Pier 1 Imports

writing assignment ■

(*Learning Objective 1, 6: Analyzing trend data*) Use the **Pier 1 Imports** financial statements in Appendix B at the end of this book to address the following questions. Study the Financial Summary that precedes the financial statements.

1. During 2006, Pier 1's sales decreased and the company suffered a net loss. Perform a trend analysis of Pier 1's Financial Summary data for net sales, gross profit, operating income, and net income. Use 2002 as the base year, and compute trend figures for 2003, 2004, 2005, and 2006. (pp. 690–691)

2. Discuss the results of Pier 1's operations based on your trend analysis during 2003–2006. (Challenge)

3. What in your opinion is the company's outlook for the future? (Challenge)

Group Projects

writing assignment ■

Project 1. Select an industry you are interested in, and use the leading company in that industry as the benchmark. Then select 2 other companies in the same industry. For each category of ratios in the Decision Guidelines feature on pages 710 and 711, compute at least 2 ratios for all 3 companies. Write a 2-page report that compares the 2 companies with the benchmark company.

Project 2. Select a company and obtain its financial statements. Convert the income statement and the balance sheet to common size and compare the company you selected to the industry average. **Risk Management Association's** *Annual Statement Studies*, **Dun & Bradstreet's** *Industry Norms & Key Business Ratios*, and **Prentice Hall's** *Almanac of Business and Industrial Financial Ratios* by Leo Troy, publish common-size statements for most industries.

For Internet Exercises go to the Web site www.prenhall.com/harrison.

Quick Check Answers

1. *c* ($1,833/$1,712.8 = 1.070)
2. *c* ($1,833/$17,140.5 = 0.107)
3. *b* (Net income: $1,471.4 − $893.5 = $577.9; $577.9/$893.5 = Increase of 64.7%)
4. *a* ($1,665.1/$25,525.1 = 0.065)
5. *a*
6. *d* $\left[\dfrac{\$4,314.8}{(\$129.4 + \$111.7)/2}\right] = 35.8 \approx 36$ times
7. *b* [($492.8 + $734.5)/ $2,485.8 = 0.49]
8. *d* $\left[\dfrac{\$734.5 + \$855.3/2}{\$17,140.5/365}\right] = 16.9 \approx 17$ days
9. *a* (Debt ratio is ($25,525.1 − $11,981.9)/$25,525.1 = 0.53. This debt ratio is lower than the average for most companies, given in the chapter as 0.62.)
10. *d* ($1,471.4/$17,140.5 = 0.086)
11. *a* $\left[\dfrac{\$1,471.4}{(\$11,981.9 + \$10,280.9)/2}\right] = 0.132$
12. *b* ($26/$1.16 = 22.41)
13. *d* ($0.40/$26.00 = 0.015)
14. *c* ($1,471.4 + $388 − ($275.8 + $9,703.6 + $10,280.9) × 0.08 = $238.6 ≈ $239

Appendix A

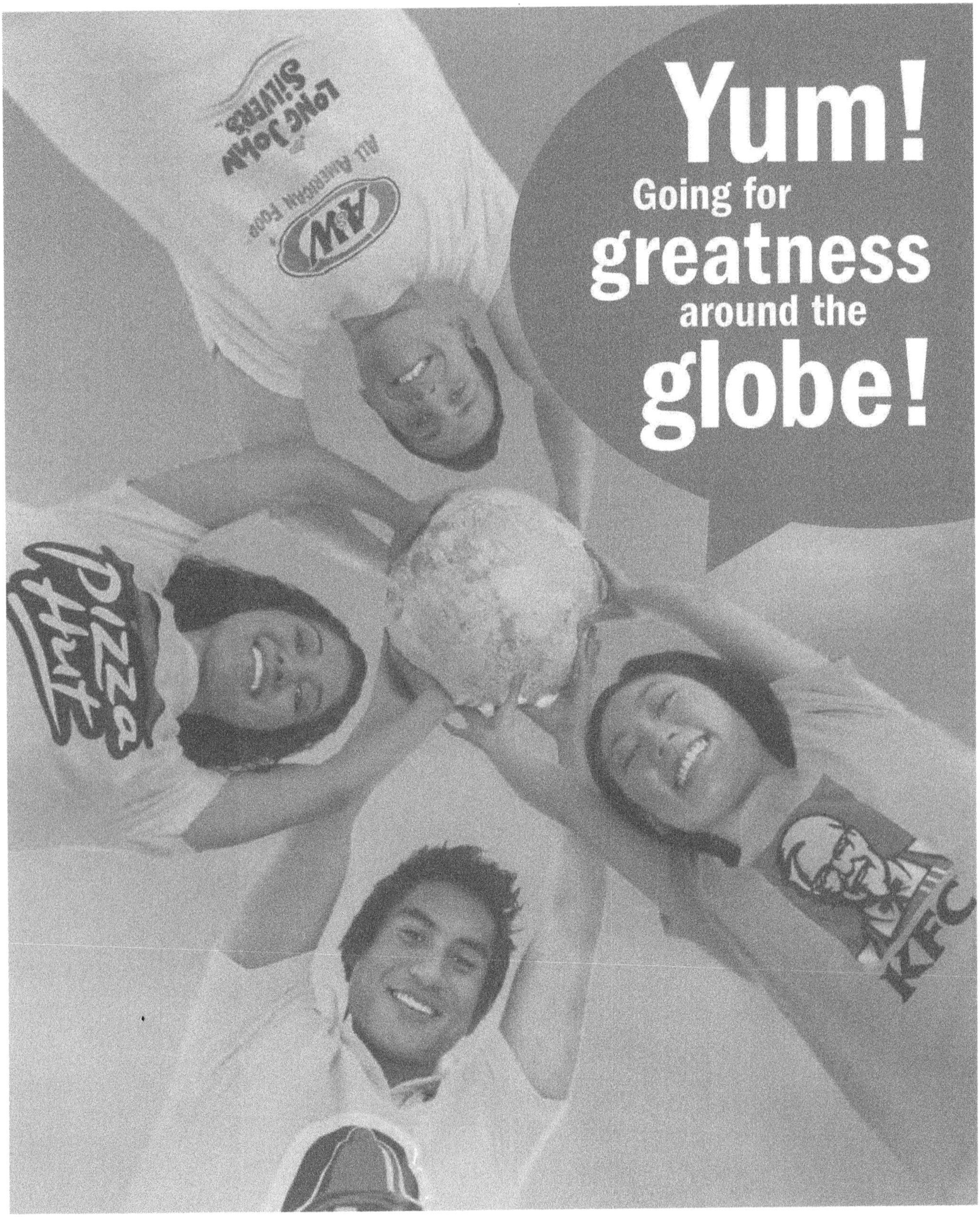

Report of Independent Registered Public Accounting Firm

The Board of Directors and Shareholders
YUM! Brands, Inc.:

We have audited the accompanying consolidated balance sheets of YUM! Brands, Inc. and Subsidiaries ("YUM") as of December 30, 2006 and December 31, 2005, and the related consolidated statements of income, cash flows and shareholders' equity and comprehensive income for each of the years in the three-year period ended December 30, 2006. These consolidated financial statements are the responsibility of YUM's management. Our responsibility is to express an opinion on these consolidated financial statements based on our audits.

We conducted our audits in accordance with the standards of the Public Company Accounting Oversight Board (United States). Those standards require that we plan and perform the audit to obtain reasonable assurance about whether the financial statements are free of material misstatement. An audit includes examining, on a test basis, evidence supporting the amounts and disclosures in the financial statements. An audit also includes assessing the accounting principles used and significant estimates made by management, as well as evaluating the overall financial statement presentation. We believe that our audits provide a reasonable basis for our opinion.

In our opinion, the consolidated financial statements referred to above present fairly, in all material respects, the financial position of YUM as of December 30, 2006 and December 31, 2005, and the results of its operations and its cash flows for each of the years in the three-year period ended December 30, 2006, in conformity with U.S. generally accepted accounting principles.

We also have audited, in accordance with the standards of the Public Company Accounting Oversight Board (United States), the effectiveness of YUM's internal control over financial reporting as of December 30, 2006, based on criteria established in *Internal Control—Integrated Framework* issued by the Committee of Sponsoring Organizations of the Treadway Commission (COSO), and our report dated February 28, 2007 expressed an unqualified opinion on management's assessment of, and the effective operation of, internal control over financial reporting.

As discussed in Notes 2 and 16 to the consolidated financial statements, YUM adopted the provisions of the Financial Accounting Standards Board's Statement of Financial Accounting Standards No. 123R (Revised 2004), "Share-Based Payment," and changed its method for accounting for share-based payments in 2005.

As discussed in Note 2 to the consolidated financial statements, YUM changed its method of quantifying errors in 2006. Also, as discussed in Notes 2 and 15 to the consolidated financial statements, YUM adopted the provisions of the Financial Accounting Standards Board's Statement of Financial Accounting Standards No. 158, "Employers' Accounting for Defined Benefit Pension and Other Postretirement Plans—an amendment of FASB Statements No. 87, 88, 106 and 132 (R)," in 2006.

KPMG LLP

KPMG LLP
Louisville, Kentucky
February 28, 2007

Management's Report on Internal Control Over Financial Reporting

Our management is responsible for establishing and maintaining adequate internal control over financial reporting, as such term is defined in Rule 13a-15(f) under the Securities Exchange Act of 1934. Under the supervision and with the participation of our management, including our principal executive officer and principal financial officer, we conducted an evaluation of the effectiveness of our internal control over financial reporting based on the framework in *Internal Control — Integrated Framework* issued by the Committee of Sponsoring Organizations of the Treadway Commission. Based on our evaluation under the framework in *Internal Control — Integrated Framework*, our management concluded that our internal control over financial reporting was effective as of December 30, 2006. Our management's assessment of the effectiveness of our internal control over financial reporting as of December 30, 2006 has been audited by KPMG LLP, an independent registered public accounting firm, as stated in their report which is included herein.

Supplement to Yum! Brands, Inc. Annual Report to Shareholders

On June 12, 2006, David Novak, Yum Brands, Inc. Chairman and Chief Executive Officer submitted a certification to the New York Stock Exchange (the NYSE) as required by Section 303A.12(a) of the NYSE Listed Company Manual. This certification indicated that Mr. Novak was not aware of any violations by the Company of NYSE Corporate Governance listing standards.

In connection with the filing of the Company's Form 10-K for the year ended December 30, 2006, the Company has included as exhibits certifications signed by Mr. Novak and Mr. Richard Carucci, Chief Financial Officer, pursuant to Rule 13a-14(a) of Securities Exchange Act of 1934, as adopted pursuant to Section 302 of the Sarbanes-Oxley Act of 2002.

These statements are required by the NYSE as part of the Company's Annual Report to Shareholders.

HH APPENDIX A

Consolidated Statements of Income
YUM! Brands, Inc. and Subsidiaries

Fiscal years ended December 30, 2006,
December 31, 2005 and December 25, 2004
(in millions, except per share data)

	2006	2005	2004
Revenues			
Company sales	$ 8,365	$ 8,225	$ 7,992
Franchise and license fees	1,196	1,124	1,019
Total revenues	9,561	9,349	9,011
Costs and Expenses, Net			
Company restaurants			
Food and paper	2,549	2,584	2,538
Payroll and employee benefits	2,142	2,171	2,112
Occupancy and other operating expenses	2,403	2,315	2,183
	7,094	7,070	6,833
General and administrative expenses	1,187	1,158	1,056
Franchise and license expenses	35	33	26
Closures and impairment expenses	59	62	38
Refranchising (gain) loss	(24)	(43)	(12)
Other (income) expense	(51)	(80)	(55)
Wrench litigation (income) expense	—	(2)	(14)
AmeriServe and other charges (credits)	(1)	(2)	(16)
Total costs and expenses, net	8,299	8,196	7,856
Operating Profit	1,262	1,153	1,155
Interest expense, net	154	127	129
Income before Income Taxes	1,108	1,026	1,026
Income tax provision	284	264	286
Net Income	$ 824	$ 762	$ 740
Basic Earnings Per Common Share	$ 3.02	$ 2.66	$ 2.54
Diluted Earnings Per Common Share	$ 2.92	$ 2.55	$ 2.42
Dividends Declared Per Common Share	$ 0.865	$ 0.445	$ 0.30

See accompanying Notes to Consolidated Financial Statements.

HH APPENDIX A

Consolidated Statements of Cash Flows

YUM! Brands, Inc. and Subsidiaries

Fiscal years ended December 30, 2006,
December 31, 2005 and December 25, 2004
(in millions)

	2006	2005	2004
Cash Flows—Operating Activities			
Net income	$ 824	$ 762	$ 740
Adjustments to reconcile net income to net cash provided by operating activities:			
Depreciation and amortization	479	469	448
Closures and impairment expenses	59	62	38
Refranchising (gain) loss	(24)	(43)	(12)
Contributions to defined benefit pension plans	(43)	(74)	(55)
Deferred income taxes	(30)	(101)	142
Equity income from investments in unconsolidated affiliates	(51)	(51)	(54)
Distributions of income received from unconsolidated affiliates	32	44	55
Excess tax benefits from share-based compensation	(62)	(87)	—
Share-based compensation expense	65	62	3
Other non-cash charges and credits, net	101	78	83
Changes in operating working capital, excluding effects of acquisitions and dispositions:			
Accounts and notes receivable	24	(1)	(39)
Inventories	(3)	(4)	(7)
Prepaid expenses and other current assets	(33)	78	(5)
Accounts payable and other current liabilities	(46)	(10)	(20)
Income taxes payable	10	54	(131)
Net change in operating working capital	(48)	117	(202)
Net Cash Provided by Operating Activities	1,302	1,238	1,186
Cash Flows—Investing Activities			
Capital spending	(614)	(609)	(645)
Proceeds from refranchising of restaurants	257	145	140
Acquisition of remaining interest in unconsolidated affiliate, net of cash assumed	(178)	—	—
Acquisition of restaurants from franchisees	(7)	(2)	(38)
Short-term investments	39	12	(36)
Sales of property, plant and equipment	57	81	52
Other, net	(30)	28	(14)
Net Cash Used in Investing Activities	(476)	(345)	(541)
Cash Flows—Financing Activities			
Proceeds from issuance of long-term debt	300	—	—
Repayments of long-term debt	(211)	(14)	(371)
Short-term borrowings by original maturity			
More than three months—proceeds	236	—	—
More than three months—payments	(54)	—	—
Three months or less, net	4	(34)	—
Revolving credit facilities, three months or less, net	(23)	160	19
Repurchase shares of common stock	(983)	(1,056)	(569)
Excess tax benefit from share-based compensation	62	87	—
Employee stock option proceeds	142	148	200
Dividends paid on common shares	(144)	(123)	(58)
Other, net	(2)	—	—
Net Cash Used in Financing Activities	(673)	(832)	(779)
Effect of Exchange Rate on Cash and Cash Equivalents	8	1	4
Net (Decrease) Increase in Cash and Cash Equivalents	161	62	(130)
Net Increase in Cash and Cash Equivalents of Mainland China for December 2004	—	34	—
Cash and Cash Equivalents—Beginning of Year	158	62	192
Cash and Cash Equivalents—End of Year	$ 319	$ 158	$ 62

See accompanying Notes to Consolidated Financial Statements.

HH APPENDIX A

Consolidated Balance Sheets
YUM! Brands, Inc. and Subsidiaries

December 30, 2006 and December 31, 2005
(in millions)

	2006	2005
ASSETS		
Current Assets		
Cash and cash equivalents	$ 319	$ 158
Short-term investments	6	43
Accounts and notes receivable, less allowance: $18 in 2006 and $23 in 2005	220	236
Inventories	93	85
Prepaid expenses and other current assets	132	75
Deferred income taxes	57	181
Advertising cooperative assets, restricted	74	77
Total Current Assets	901	855
Property, plant and equipment, net	3,631	3,356
Goodwill	662	538
Intangible assets, net	347	330
Investments in unconsolidated affiliates	138	173
Other assets	369	320
Deferred income taxes	305	225
Total Assets	$ 6,353	$ 5,797
LIABILITIES AND SHAREHOLDERS' EQUITY		
Current Liabilities		
Accounts payable and other current liabilities	$ 1,386	$ 1,256
Income taxes payable	37	79
Short-term borrowings	227	211
Advertising cooperative liabilities	74	77
Total Current Liabilities	1,724	1,623
Long-term debt	2,045	1,649
Other liabilities and deferred credits	1,147	1,076
Total Liabilities	4,916	4,348
Shareholders' Equity		
Preferred stock, no par value, 250 shares authorized; no shares issued	—	—
Common stock, no par value, 750 shares authorized; 265 shares and 278 shares issued in 2006 and 2005, respectively	—	—
Retained earnings	1,593	1,619
Accumulated other comprehensive loss	(156)	(170)
Total Shareholders' Equity	1,437	1,449
Total Liabilities and Shareholders' Equity	$ 6,353	$ 5,797

See accompanying Notes to Consolidated Financial Statements.

Consolidated Statements of Shareholders' Equity and Comprehensive Income

YUM! Brands, Inc. and Subsidiaries

Fiscal years ended December 30, 2006, December 31, 2005 and December 25, 2004 (in millions, except per share data)	Issued Common Stock		Retained Earnings	Accumulated Other Comprehensive Income (Loss)	Total
	Shares	Amount			
Balance at December 27, 2003	292	$ 916	$ 414	$ (210)	$ 1,120
Net income			740		740
Foreign currency translation adjustment arising during the period				73	73
Minimum pension liability adjustment (net of tax impact of $3 million)				6	6
Comprehensive Income					819
Dividends declared on common shares ($0.30 per common share)			(87)		(87)
Repurchase of shares of common stock	(14)	(569)			(569)
Employee stock option exercises (includes tax impact of $102 million)	12	302			302
Compensation-related events		10			10
Balance at December 25, 2004	290	$ 659	$ 1,067	$ (131)	$ 1,595
Net income			762		762
Foreign currency translation adjustment arising during the period				(31)	(31)
Foreign currency translation adjustment included in net income				6	6
Minimum pension liability adjustment (net of tax impact of $8 million)				(15)	(15)
Net unrealized gain on derivative instruments (net of tax impact of $1 million)				1	1
Comprehensive Income					723
Dividends declared on common shares ($0.445 per common share)			(129)		(129)
China December 2004 net income			6		6
Repurchase of shares of common stock	(21)	(969)	(87)		(1,056)
Employee stock option exercises (includes tax impact of $94 million)	9	242			242
Compensation-related events		68			68
Balance at December 31, 2005	278	$ —	$ 1,619	$ (170)	$ 1,449
Adjustment to initially apply SAB No. 108			100		100
Net income			824		824
Foreign currency translation adjustment arising during the period (includes tax impact of $13 million)				59	59
Minimum pension liability adjustment (net of tax impact of $11 million)				17	17
Net unrealized gain on derivative instruments (net of tax impact of $3 million)				5	5
Comprehensive Income					905
Adjustment to initially apply SFAS No. 158 (net of tax impact of $37 million)				(67)	(67)
Dividends declared on common shares ($0.865 per common share)			(234)		(234)
Repurchase of shares of common stock	(20)	(284)	(716)		(1,000)
Employee stock option exercises (includes tax impact of $68 million)	7	210			210
Compensation-related events		74			74
Balance at December 30, 2006	**265**	**$ —**	**$ 1,593**	**$ (156)**	**$ 1,437**

See accompanying Notes to Consolidated Financial Statements.

Notes to Consolidated Financial Statements
(Tabular amounts in millions, except share data)

Description of Business

YUM! Brands, Inc. and Subsidiaries (collectively referred to as "YUM" or the "Company") comprises the worldwide operations of KFC, Pizza Hut, Taco Bell and since May 7, 2002, Long John Silver's ("LJS") and A&W All-American Food Restaurants ("A&W") (collectively the "Concepts"), which were added when we acquired Yorkshire Global Restaurants, Inc. ("YGR"). YUM is the world's largest quick service restaurant company based on the number of system units, with more than 34,000 units of which approximately 42% are located outside the U.S. in more than 100 countries and territories. YUM was created as an independent, publicly-owned company on October 6, 1997 (the "Spin-off Date") via a tax-free distribution by our former parent, PepsiCo, Inc. ("PepsiCo"), of our Common Stock (the "Spin-off") to its shareholders. References to YUM throughout these Consolidated Financial Statements are made using the first person notations of "we," "us" or "our."

Through our widely-recognized Concepts, we develop, operate, franchise and license a system of both traditional and non-traditional quick service restaurants. Each Concept has proprietary menu items and emphasizes the preparation of food with high quality ingredients as well as unique recipes and special seasonings to provide appealing, tasty and attractive food at competitive prices. Our traditional restaurants feature dine-in, carryout and, in some instances, drive-thru or delivery service. Non-traditional units, which are principally licensed outlets, include express units and kiosks which have a more limited menu and operate in non-traditional locations like airports, gasoline service stations, convenience stores, stadiums, amusement parks and colleges, where a full-scale traditional outlet would not be practical or efficient. We also operate multibrand units, where two or more of our Concepts are operated in a single unit. In addition, we continue to pursue the multibrand combination of Pizza Hut and WingStreet, a flavored chicken wings concept we have developed.

In 2005, we began reporting information for our international business in two separate operating segments as a result of changes to our management reporting structure. The China Division includes mainland China ("China"), Thailand and KFC Taiwan, and the International Division includes the remainder of our international operations. While this reporting change did not impact our consolidated results, segment information for 2004 was restated to be consistent with the current period presentation.

Beginning in 2005, we also changed the China business reporting calendar to more closely align the timing of the reporting of its results of operations with our U.S. business. Previously our China business, like the rest of our international businesses, closed one month (or one period for certain of our international businesses) earlier than YUM's period end date to facilitate consolidated reporting. To maintain comparability of our consolidated results of operations, amounts related to our China business for December 2004 have not been reflected in our Consolidated Statements of Income and net income for the China business for the one month period ended December 31, 2004 was recognized as an adjustment directly to consolidated retained earnings in the year ended December 31, 2005. Our consolidated results of operations for the years ended December 30, 2006 and December 31, 2005 both include the results of operations of the China business for the months of January through December. Our consolidated results of operations for the year ended December 25, 2004 continue to include the results of operations of the China business for the months of December 2003 through November 2004 as previously reported.

For the month of December 2004 the China business had revenues of $79 million and net income of $6 million. As mentioned previously, neither of these amounts is included in our Consolidated Statement of Income for the year ended December 31, 2005 and the net income figure was credited directly to retained earnings in the first quarter of 2005. Net income for the month of December 2004 was negatively impacted by costs incurred in preparation of opening a significant number of new stores in early 2005 as well as increased advertising expense, all of which was recorded in December's results of operations. Additionally, the net increase in cash for the China business in December 2004 has been presented as a single line item on our Consolidated Statement of Cash Flows for the year ended December 31, 2005. The $34 million net increase in cash was primarily attributable to short-term borrowings for working capital purposes, a majority of which were repaid prior to the end of the China business' first quarter of 2006.

Summary of Significant Accounting Policies

Our preparation of the accompanying Consolidated Financial Statements in conformity with accounting principles generally accepted in the United States of America requires us to make estimates and assumptions that affect reported amounts of assets and liabilities, disclosure of contingent assets and liabilities at the date of the financial statements, and the reported amounts of revenues and expenses during the reporting period. Actual results could differ from these estimates.

PRINCIPLES OF CONSOLIDATION AND BASIS OF PREPARATION Intercompany accounts and transactions have been eliminated. Certain investments in businesses that operate our Concepts are accounted for by the equity method. Our lack of majority voting rights precludes us from controlling these affiliates, and thus we do not consolidate these affiliates. Our share of the net income or loss of those unconsolidated affiliates is included in other (income) expense.

We participate in various advertising cooperatives with our franchisees and licensees established to collect and administer funds contributed for use in advertising and promotional programs designed to increase sales and enhance the reputation of the Company and its franchise owners. Contributions to the advertising cooperatives are required for both company operated and franchise restaurants and are generally based on a percent of restaurant sales. In certain of these cooperatives we possess majority voting rights, and thus control and consolidate the cooperatives. We report all assets and liabilities of these advertising cooperatives that we consolidate as advertising cooperative assets, restricted and advertising cooperative liabilities in the Consolidated Balance Sheet. The advertising cooperatives assets, consisting primarily of cash received from franchisees and accounts receivable from franchisees, can only be used for selected purposes and are considered restricted. The advertising cooperative liabilities represent the corresponding obligation arising from the receipt of the contributions to purchase advertising and promotional programs. As the contributions to these cooperatives are designated and segregated for advertising, we act as an agent for the franchisees and licensees with regard to these contributions. Thus, in accordance with Statement of Financial Accounting Standards ("SFAS") No. 45, "Accounting for Franchise Fee Revenue," we do not reflect franchisee and licensee contributions to these cooperatives in our Consolidated Statements of Income or Consolidated Statements of Cash Flows.

In 2004, we adopted Financial Accounting Standards Board ("FASB") Interpretation No. 46 (revised December 2003), "Consolidation of Variable Interest Entities, an interpretation of ARB No. 51" ("FIN 46R"). FIN 46R addresses the consolidation of an entity whose equity holders either (a) have not provided sufficient equity at risk to allow the entity to finance its own activities or (b) do not possess certain characteristics of a controlling financial interest. FIN 46R requires the consolidation of such an entity, known as a variable interest entity ("VIE"), by the primary beneficiary of the entity. The primary beneficiary is the entity, if any, that is obligated to absorb a majority of the risk of loss from the VIE's activities, entitled to receive a majority of the VIE's residual returns, or both. FIN 46R excludes from its scope businesses (as defined by FIN 46R) unless certain conditions exist.

The principal entities in which we possess a variable interest include franchise entities, including our unconsolidated affiliates described above. We do not possess any ownership interests in franchise entities except for our investments in various unconsolidated affiliates accounted for under the equity method. Additionally, we generally do not provide financial support to franchise entities in a typical franchise relationship.

We also possess variable interests in certain purchasing cooperatives we have formed along with representatives of the franchisee groups of each of our Concepts. These purchasing cooperatives were formed for the purpose of purchasing certain restaurant products and equipment in the U.S. Our equity ownership in each cooperative is generally proportional to our percentage ownership of the U.S. system units for the Concept. We account for our investments in these purchasing cooperatives using the cost method, under which our recorded balances were not significant at December 30, 2006 or December 31, 2005.

As a result of the adoption of FIN 46R, we have not consolidated any franchise entities, purchasing cooperatives or other entities.

FISCAL YEAR   Our fiscal year ends on the last Saturday in December and, as a result, a 53rd week is added every five or six years. Fiscal year 2005 included 53 weeks. The first three quarters of each fiscal year consist of 12 weeks and the fourth quarter consists of 16 weeks in fiscal years with 52 weeks and 17 weeks in fiscal years with 53 weeks. In fiscal year 2005, the 53rd week added $96 million to total revenues and $23 million to total operating profit in our Consolidated Statement of Income. Our subsidiaries operate on similar fiscal calendars with period or month end dates suited to their businesses. The subsidiaries' period end dates are within one week of YUM's period end date with the exception of all of our international businesses except China. The international businesses except China close one period or one month earlier to facilitate consolidated reporting.

RECLASSIFICATIONS   We have reclassified certain items in the accompanying Consolidated Financial Statements and Notes thereto for prior periods to be comparable with the classification for the fiscal year ended December 30, 2006. These reclassifications had no effect on previously reported net income.

The most significant reclassification we made was related to the presentation of deferred taxes on our Consolidated Balance Sheet at December 31, 2005. Previously, deferred tax assets and liabilities were netted for all tax jurisdictions outside of the U.S. Due to the implementation of new tax accounting software, we netted our deferred tax assets and liabilities at the individual tax jurisdiction level outside the U.S. at December 30, 2006. We reclassified certain amounts on our Consolidated Balance Sheet at December 31, 2005 to be consistent with this presentation which resulted in an increase to both current deferred income tax assets and liabilities of $18 million and an increase to both long term deferred income tax assets and liabilities of $87 million.

FRANCHISE AND LICENSE OPERATIONS   We execute franchise or license agreements for each unit which set out the terms of our arrangement with the franchisee or licensee. Our franchise and license agreements typically require the franchisee or licensee to pay an initial, non-refundable fee and continuing fees based upon a percentage of sales. Subject to our approval and their payment of a renewal fee, a franchisee may generally renew the franchise agreement upon its expiration.

We incur expenses that benefit both our franchise and license communities and their representative organizations and our Company operated restaurants. These expenses, along with other costs of servicing of franchise and license agreements are charged to general and administrative ("G&A") expenses as incurred. Certain direct costs of our franchise and license operations are charged to franchise and license expenses. These costs include provisions for estimated uncollectible fees, franchise and license marketing funding, amortization expense for franchise related intangible assets and certain other direct incremental franchise and license support costs.

We monitor the financial condition of our franchisees and licensees and record provisions for estimated losses on receivables when we believe that our franchisees or licensees are unable to make their required payments. While we use the best information available in making our determination, the ultimate recovery of recorded receivables is also dependent upon future economic events and other conditions that may be beyond our control. Net provisions for uncollectible franchise and license receivables of $2 million, $3 million and $1 million were included in franchise and license expense in 2006, 2005 and 2004, respectively.

REVENUE RECOGNITION   Our revenues consist of sales by Company operated restaurants and fees from our franchisees and licensees. Revenues from Company operated restaurants are recognized when payment is tendered at the time of sale. We recognize initial fees received from a franchisee or licensee as revenue when we have performed substantially all initial services required by the franchise or license agreement, which is generally upon the opening of a store. We recognize continuing fees based upon a percentage of franchisee and licensee sales as earned. We recognize renewal fees when a renewal agreement with a franchisee or licensee becomes effective. We include initial fees collected upon the sale of a restaurant to a franchisee in refranchising (gain) loss.

DIRECT MARKETING COSTS We charge direct marketing costs to expense ratably in relation to revenues over the year in which incurred and, in the case of advertising production costs, in the year the advertisement is first shown. Deferred direct marketing costs, which are classified as prepaid expenses, consist of media and related advertising production costs which will generally be used for the first time in the next fiscal year and have historically not been significant. To the extent we participate in advertising cooperatives, we expense our contributions as incurred. Our advertising expenses were $492 million, $497 million and $458 million in 2006, 2005 and 2004, respectively. We report substantially all of our direct marketing costs in occupancy and other operating expenses.

RESEARCH AND DEVELOPMENT EXPENSES Research and development expenses, which we expense as incurred, are reported in G&A expenses. Research and development expenses were $33 million, $33 million and $26 million in 2006, 2005 and 2004, respectively.

IMPAIRMENT OR DISPOSAL OF LONG-LIVED ASSETS In accordance with SFAS No. 144, "Accounting for the Impairment or Disposal of Long-Lived Assets" ("SFAS 144"), we review our long-lived assets related to each restaurant to be held and used in the business, including any allocated intangible assets subject to amortization, semi-annually for impairment, or whenever events or changes in circumstances indicate that the carrying amount of a restaurant may not be recoverable. We evaluate restaurants using a "two-year history of operating losses" as our primary indicator of potential impairment. Based on the best information available, we write down an impaired restaurant to its estimated fair market value, which becomes its new cost basis. We generally measure estimated fair market value by discounting estimated future cash flows. In addition, when we decide to close a restaurant it is reviewed for impairment and depreciable lives are adjusted based on the expected disposal date. The impairment evaluation is based on the estimated cash flows from continuing use through the expected disposal date plus the expected terminal value.

We account for exit or disposal activities, including store closures, in accordance with SFAS No. 146, "Accounting for Costs Associated with Exit or Disposal Activities" ("SFAS 146"). Store closure costs include costs of disposing of the assets as well as other facility-related expenses from previously closed stores. These store closure costs are generally expensed as incurred. Additionally, at the date we cease using a property under an operating lease, we record a liability for the net present value of any remaining lease obligations, net of estimated sublease income, if any. Any subsequent adjustments to that liability as a result of lease termination or changes in estimates of sublease income are recorded in store closure costs. To the extent we sell assets, primarily land, associated with a closed store, any gain or loss upon that sale is also recorded in store closure costs (income).

Refranchising (gain) loss includes the gains or losses from the sales of our restaurants to new and existing franchisees and the related initial franchise fees, reduced by transaction costs. In executing our refranchising initiatives, we most often offer groups of restaurants. We classify restaurants as held for sale and suspend depreciation and amortization when (a) we make a decision to refranchise; (b) the stores can be immediately removed from operations; (c) we have begun an active program to locate a buyer; (d) significant changes to the plan of sale are not likely; and (e) the sale is probable within one year. We recognize estimated losses on refranchisings when the restaurants are classified as held for sale. We also recognize as refranchising loss impairment associated with stores we have offered to refranchise for a price less than their carrying value, but do not believe have met the criteria to be classified as held for sale. We recognize gains on restaurant refranchisings when the sale transaction closes, the franchisee has a minimum amount of the purchase price in at-risk equity, and we are satisfied that the franchisee can meet its financial obligations. If the criteria for gain recognition are not met, we defer the gain to the extent we have a remaining financial exposure in connection with the sales transaction. Deferred gains are recognized when the gain recognition criteria are met or as our financial exposure is reduced. When we make a decision to retain a store, or group of stores, previously held for sale, we revalue the store at the lower of its (a) net book value at our original sale decision date less normal depreciation and amortization that would have been recorded during the period held for sale or (b) its current fair market value. This value becomes the store's new cost basis. We record any difference between the store's carrying amount and its new cost basis to refranchising gain (loss).

Considerable management judgment is necessary to estimate future cash flows, including cash flows from continuing use, terminal value, sublease income and refranchising proceeds. Accordingly, actual results could vary significantly from our estimates.

IMPAIRMENT OF INVESTMENTS IN UNCONSOLIDATED AFFILIATES
We record impairment charges related to an investment in an unconsolidated affiliate whenever events or circumstances indicate that a decrease in the fair value of an investment has occurred which is other than temporary. In addition, we evaluate our investments in unconsolidated affiliates for impairment when they have experienced two consecutive years of operating losses. We recorded no impairment associated with our investments in unconsolidated affiliates during the years ended December 30, 2006, December 31, 2005 and December 25, 2004.

Considerable management judgment is necessary to estimate future cash flows. Accordingly, actual results could vary significantly from our estimates.

GUARANTEES We account for certain guarantees in accordance with FASB Interpretation No. 45, "Guarantor's Accounting and Disclosure Requirements for Guarantees, Including Indirect Guarantees of Indebtedness to Others, an interpretation of FASB Statements No. 5, 57 and 107 and a rescission of FASB Interpretation No. 34" ("FIN 45"). FIN 45 elaborates on the disclosures to be made by a guarantor in its interim and annual financial statements about its obligations under guarantees issued. FIN 45 also clarifies that a guarantor is required to recognize, at inception of a guarantee, a liability for the fair value of certain obligations undertaken.

We have also issued guarantees as a result of assigning our interest in obligations under operating leases as a condition to the refranchising of certain Company restaurants. Such guarantees are subject to the requirements of SFAS No. 145, "Rescission of FASB Statements No. 4, 44, and 64, Amendment of FASB Statement No. 13, and Technical Corrections" ("SFAS 145"). We recognize a liability for the fair value of such lease guarantees under SFAS 145 upon refranchising and upon any subsequent renewals of such leases when we remain contingently liable. The related expense in both instances is included in refranchising gain (loss).

HH APPENDIX A

CASH AND CASH EQUIVALENTS   Cash equivalents represent funds we have temporarily invested (with original maturities not exceeding three months) as part of managing our day-to-day operating cash receipts and disbursements.

INVENTORIES   We value our inventories at the lower of cost (computed on the first-in, first-out method) or net realizable value.

PROPERTY, PLANT AND EQUIPMENT   We state property, plant and equipment at cost less accumulated depreciation and amortization and valuation allowances. We calculate depreciation and amortization on a straight-line basis over the estimated useful lives of the assets as follows: 5 to 25 years for buildings and improvements, 3 to 20 years for machinery and equipment and 3 to 7 years for capitalized software costs. As discussed above, we suspend depreciation and amortization on assets related to restaurants that are held for sale.

LEASES AND LEASEHOLD IMPROVEMENTS   We account for our leases in accordance with SFAS No. 13, "Accounting for Leases" and other related authoritative guidance. When determining the lease term, we often include option periods for which failure to renew the lease imposes a penalty on the Company in such an amount that a renewal appears, at the inception of the lease, to be reasonably assured. The primary penalty to which we are subject is the economic detriment associated with the existence of leasehold improvements which might be impaired if we choose not to continue the use of the leased property.

In 2004, we recorded an adjustment to correct instances where our leasehold improvements were not being depreciated over the shorter of their useful lives or the term of the lease, including options in some instances, over which we were recording rent expense, including escalations, on a straight line basis. The cumulative adjustment, primarily through increased U.S. depreciation expense, totaled $11.5 million ($7 million after tax). The portion of this adjustment that related to 2004 was approximately $3 million. As the portion of the adjustment recorded that was a correction of errors of amounts reported in our prior period financial statements was not material to any of those prior period financial statements, the entire adjustment was recorded in the 2004 Consolidated Financial Statements and no adjustment was made to any prior period financial statements.

We record rent expense for leases that contain scheduled rent increases on a straight-line basis over the lease term, including any option periods considered in the determination of that lease term. Contingent rentals are generally based on sales levels in excess of stipulated amounts, and thus are not considered minimum lease payments and are included in rent expense as they accrue. We generally do not receive leasehold improvement incentives upon opening a store that is subject to a lease.

Prior to fiscal year 2006, we capitalized rent while we were constructing a restaurant even if such construction period was subject to a rent holiday. Such capitalized rent was then expensed on a straight-line basis over the remaining term of the lease upon opening of the restaurant. Effective January 1, 2006 as required by FASB Staff Position No. 13-1, "Accounting for Rental Costs Incurred during a Construction Period" ("FSP 13-1"), we began expensing rent associated with leased land or buildings for construction periods whether rent was paid or we were subject to a rent holiday. The adoption of FSP 13-1 did not significantly impact our results of operations in 2006 and we do not anticipate significant future impact.

INTERNAL DEVELOPMENT COSTS AND ABANDONED SITE COSTS
We capitalize direct costs associated with the site acquisition and construction of a Company unit on that site, including direct internal payroll and payroll-related costs. Only those site-specific costs incurred subsequent to the time that the site acquisition is considered probable are capitalized. If we subsequently make a determination that a site for which internal development costs have been capitalized will not be acquired or developed, any previously capitalized internal development costs are expensed and included in G&A expenses.

GOODWILL AND INTANGIBLE ASSETS   The Company accounts for acquisitions of restaurants from franchisees and other acquisitions of businesses that may occur from time to time in accordance with SFAS No. 141, "Business Combinations" ("SFAS 141"). Goodwill in such acquisitions represents the excess of the cost of a business acquired over the net of the amounts assigned to assets acquired, including identifiable intangible assets, and liabilities assumed. SFAS 141 specifies criteria to be used in determining whether intangible assets acquired in a business combination must be recognized and reported separately from goodwill. We base amounts assigned to goodwill and other identifiable intangible assets on independent appraisals or internal estimates.

The Company accounts for recorded goodwill and other intangible assets in accordance with SFAS No. 142, "Goodwill and Other Intangible Assets" ("SFAS 142"). In accordance with SFAS 142, we do not amortize goodwill and indefinite-lived intangible assets. We evaluate the remaining useful life of an intangible asset that is not being amortized each reporting period to determine whether events and circumstances continue to support an indefinite useful life. If an intangible asset that is not being amortized is subsequently determined to have a finite useful life, we amortize the intangible asset prospectively over its estimated remaining useful life. Amortizable intangible assets are amortized on a straight-line basis.

In accordance with the requirements of SFAS 142, goodwill has been assigned to reporting units for purposes of impairment testing. Our reporting units are our operating segments in the U.S. (see Note 21) and our business management units internationally (typically individual countries). We evaluate goodwill and indefinite-lived assets for impairment on an annual basis or more often if an event occurs or circumstances change that indicate impairments might exist. Goodwill impairment tests consist of a comparison of each reporting unit's fair value with its carrying value. The fair value of a reporting unit is an estimate of the amount for which the unit as a whole could be sold in a current transaction between willing parties. We generally estimate fair value based on discounted cash flows. If the carrying value of a reporting unit exceeds its fair value, goodwill is written down to its implied fair value. We have selected the beginning of our fourth quarter as the date on which to perform our ongoing annual impairment test for goodwill. For 2006, 2005 and 2004, there was no impairment of goodwill identified during our annual impairment testing.

For indefinite-lived intangible assets, our impairment test consists of a comparison of the fair value of an intangible asset with its carrying amount. Fair value is an estimate of the price a willing buyer would pay for the intangible asset and is generally estimated by discounting the expected future cash flows associated with the intangible asset. We also perform our annual test for impairment of our indefinite-lived intangible assets at the beginning of our fourth quarter. No impairment of indefinite-lived intangible assets was recorded in 2006, 2005 or 2004.

HH APPENDIX A

Our amortizable intangible assets are evaluated for impairment whenever events or changes in circumstances indicate that the carrying amount of the intangible asset may not be recoverable. An intangible asset that is deemed impaired is written down to its estimated fair value, which is based on discounted cash flows. For purposes of our impairment analysis, we update the cash flows that were initially used to value the amortizable intangible asset to reflect our current estimates and assumptions over the asset's future remaining life.

SHARE-BASED EMPLOYEE COMPENSATION In the fourth quarter 2005, the Company adopted SFAS No. 123 (Revised 2004), "Share-Based Payment" ("SFAS 123R"), which replaced SFAS No. 123 "Accounting for Stock-Based Compensation" ("SFAS 123"), superseded APB 25, "Accounting for Stock Issued to Employees" and related interpretations and amended SFAS No. 95, "Statement of Cash Flows." The provisions of SFAS 123R are similar to those of SFAS 123, however, SFAS 123R requires all new, modified and unvested share-based payments to employees, including grants of employee stock options and stock appreciation rights ("SARs"), be recognized in the financial statements as compensation cost over the service period based on their fair value on the date of grant. Compensation cost is recognized over the service period on a straight-line basis for the fair value of awards that actually vest.

We adopted SFAS 123R using the modified retrospective application transition method effective September 4, 2005, the beginning of our 2005 fourth quarter. As permitted by SFAS 123R, we applied the modified retrospective application transition method to the beginning of the fiscal year of adoption (our fiscal year 2005). As such, the results for the first three fiscal quarters of 2005 were required to be adjusted to recognize the compensation cost previously reported in the pro forma footnote disclosures under the provisions of SFAS 123. However, years prior to 2005 were not restated.

The adoption of SFAS 123R resulted in a decrease in operating profit, the associated income tax benefits and a decrease in net income as shown below. Additionally, cash flows from operating activities decreased $62 million and $87 million in 2006 and 2005, respectively, and cash flows from financing activities increased $62 million and $87 million in 2006 and 2005, respectively.

	2006	2005
Payroll and employee benefits	$ 9	$ 10
General and administrative expense	51	48
Operating profit	60	58
Income tax benefit	(21)	(20)
Net income impact	$ 39	$ 38

Prior to 2005, all share-based payments were accounted for under the recognition and measurement principles of APB 25 and its related interpretations. Accordingly, no expense was reflected in the Consolidated Statements of Income for stock options, as all stock options granted had an exercise price equal to the market value of our underlying common stock on the date of grant. The following table illustrates the pro forma effect on net income and earnings per share if the Company had applied the fair value recognition provisions of SFAS 123 to all share-based payments for 2004.

	2004
Net Income, as reported	$ 740
Add: Compensation expense included in reported net income, net of related tax	3
Deduct: Total stock-based employee compensation expense determined under fair value based method for all awards, net of related tax effects	(40)
Net Income, pro forma	703
Basic Earnings per Common Share	
As reported	$ 2.54
Pro forma	2.42
Diluted Earnings per Common Share	
As reported	$ 2.42
Pro forma	2.30

DERIVATIVE FINANCIAL INSTRUMENTS We do not use derivative instruments for trading purposes and we have procedures in place to monitor and control their use. Our use of derivative instruments has included interest rate swaps and collars, treasury locks and foreign currency forward contracts. These derivative contracts are entered into with financial institutions.

We account for these derivative financial instruments in accordance with SFAS No. 133, "Accounting for Derivative Instruments and Hedging Activities" ("SFAS 133") as amended by SFAS No. 149, "Amendment of Statement 133 on Derivative Instruments and Hedging Activities" ("SFAS 149"). SFAS 133 requires that all derivative instruments be recorded on the Consolidated Balance Sheet at fair value. The accounting for changes in the fair value (i.e., gains or losses) of a derivative instrument is dependent upon whether the derivative has been designated and qualifies as part of a hedging relationship and further, on the type of hedging relationship. For derivative instruments that are designated and qualify as a fair value hedge, the gain or loss on the derivative instrument as well as the offsetting gain or loss on the hedged item attributable to the hedged risk are recognized in the results of operations. For derivative instruments that are designated and qualify as a cash flow hedge, the effective portion of the gain or loss on the derivative instrument is reported as a component of other comprehensive income (loss) and reclassified into earnings in the same period or periods during which the hedged transaction affects earnings. Any ineffective portion of the gain or loss on the derivative instrument is recorded in the results of operations immediately. For derivative instruments not designated as hedging instruments, the gain or loss is recognized in the results of operations immediately. See Note 14 for a discussion of our use of derivative instruments, management of credit risk inherent in derivative instruments and fair value information.

COMMON STOCK SHARE REPURCHASES From time to time, we repurchase shares of our Common Stock under share repurchase programs authorized by our Board of Directors. Shares repurchased constitute authorized, but unissued shares under the North Carolina laws under which we are incorporated. Additionally, our Common Stock has no par or stated value. Accordingly, we record the full value of share repurchases against Common Stock except when to do so would result in a negative balance in our Common Stock account. In such instances, on a period basis, we record the cost of any further share repurchases as a reduction in retained earnings. Due to the large number of share repurchases and the increase in our Common Stock market value over the past several years, our Common Stock balance is frequently zero at the end of any period. Accordingly, $716 million and $87 million in share repurchases were recorded as a reduction in retained earnings in 2006 and 2005, respectively. We have no legal restrictions on the payment of dividends. See Note 19 for additional information.

PENSION AND POSTRETIREMENT MEDICAL BENEFITS In the fourth quarter of 2006, we adopted the recognition and disclosure provisions of SFAS No. 158, "Employers' Accounting for Defined Benefit Pension and Other Postretirement Plans—an amendment of FASB Statements No. 87, 88, 106 and 132(R)" ("SFAS 158"). SFAS 158 amends SFAS No. 87, "Employers' Accounting for Pensions" ("SFAS 87"), SFAS No. 88, "Employers' Accounting for Settlements and Curtailments of Defined Benefit Plans and for Termination Benefits" ("SFAS 88"), SFAS No. 106, "Employers' Accounting for Postretirement Benefits Other Than Pensions" ("SFAS 106") and SFAS No. 132(R), "Employers' Disclosures about Pensions and Other Postretirement Benefits."

SFAS 158 required the Company to recognize the funded status of its pension and postretirement plans in the December 30, 2006 Consolidated Balance Sheet, with a corresponding adjustment to accumulated other comprehensive income, net of tax. Gains or losses and prior service costs or credits that arise in future years will be recognized as a component of other comprehensive income to the extent they have not been recognized as a component of net periodic benefit cost pursuant to SFAS 87 or SFAS 106.

The incremental effects of adopting the provisions of SFAS 158 on the Company's Consolidated Balance Sheet at December 30, 2006 are presented as follows. The adoption of SFAS 158 had no impact on the Consolidated Statement of Income.

	Before Application of SFAS 158	Adjustments	After Application of SFAS 158
Intangible assets, net	$ 350	$ (3)	$ 347
Deferred income taxes	268	37	305
Total assets	6,319	34	6,353
Accounts payable and other current liabilities	1,384	2	1,386
Other liabilities and deferred credits	1,048	99	1,147
Total liabilities	4,815	101	4,916
Accumulated other comprehensive loss	(89)	(67)	(156)
Total stockholders' equity	1,504	(67)	1,437

SFAS 158 also requires measurement of the funded status of pension and postretirement plans as of the date of a Company's fiscal year end effective in the year ended 2008. Certain of our plans currently have measurement dates that do not coincide with our fiscal year end and thus we will be required to change their measurement dates in 2008.

QUANTIFICATION OF MISSTATEMENTS In September 2006, the Securities and Exchange Commission (the "SEC") issued Staff Accounting Bulletin No. 108, "Considering the Effects of Prior Year Misstatements when Quantifying Misstatements in Current Year Financial Statements" ("SAB 108"). SAB 108 provides interpretive guidance on how the effects of the carryover or reversal of prior year misstatements should be considered in quantifying a current year misstatement for the purpose of a materiality assessment. SAB 108 requires that registrants quantify a current year misstatement using an approach that considers both the impact of prior year misstatements that remain on the balance sheet and those that were recorded in the current year income statement. Historically, we quantified misstatements and assessed materiality based on a current year income statement approach. We were required to adopt SAB 108 in the fourth quarter of 2006.

The transition provisions of SAB 108 permit uncorrected prior year misstatements that were not material to any prior periods under our historical income statement approach but that would have been material under the dual approach of SAB 108 to be corrected in the carrying amounts of assets and liabilities at the beginning of 2006 with the offsetting adjustment to retained earnings for the cumulative effect of misstatements. We have adjusted certain balances in the accompanying Consolidated Financial Statements at the beginning of 2006 to correct the misstatements discussed below which we considered to be immaterial in prior periods under our historical approach. The impact of the January 1, 2006 cumulative effect adjustment, net of any income tax effect, was an increase to retained earnings as follows:

Deferred tax liabilities adjustments	$ 79
Reversal of unallocated reserve	6
Non-GAAP conventions	15
Net increase to January 1, 2006 retained earnings	$ 100

DEFERRED TAXES Our opening Consolidated Balance Sheet at Spin-off included significant deferred tax assets and liabilities. Over time we have determined that deferred tax liability amounts were recorded in excess of those necessary to reflect our temporary differences.

UNALLOCATED RESERVES A reserve was established in 1999 equal to certain out of year corrections recorded during that year such that there was no misstatement under our historical approach. No adjustments have been recorded to this reserve since its establishment and we do not believe the reserve is required.

NON-GAAP ACCOUNTING CONVENTIONS Prior to 2006, we used certain non-GAAP conventions to account for capitalized interest on restaurant construction projects, the leases of our Pizza Hut United Kingdom unconsolidated affiliate and certain state tax benefits. The net income statement impact on any given year from the use of these non-GAAP conventions was immaterial both individually and in the aggregate under our historical approach. Below is a summary of the accounting policies we adopted effective the beginning of 2006 and the impact of the cumulative effect adjustment under SAB 108, net of any income tax effect. The impact of these accounting policy changes was not significant to our results of operations in 2006.

INTEREST CAPITALIZATION SFAS No. 34, "Capitalization of Interest Cost" requires that interest be capitalized as part of an asset's acquisition cost. We traditionally have not capitalized interest on individual restaurant construction projects. We increased our 2006 beginning retained earnings balance by approximately $12 million for the estimated capitalized interest on existing restaurants, net of accumulated depreciation.

LEASE ACCOUNTING BY OUR PIZZA HUT UNITED KINGDOM UNCONSOLIDATED AFFILIATE   Prior to our fourth quarter acquisition of the remaining fifty percent interest in our Pizza Hut United Kingdom unconsolidated affiliate, we accounted for our ownership under the equity method. The unconsolidated affiliate historically accounted for all of its leases as operating and we made no adjustments in recording equity income. We decreased our 2006 beginning retained earnings balance by approximately $4 million to reflect our fifty percent share of the cumulative equity income impact of properly recording certain leases as capital.

RECOGNITION OF CERTAIN STATE TAX BENEFITS   We have historically recognized certain state tax benefits on a cash basis as they were recognized on the respective state tax returns instead of in the year the benefit originated. We increased our 2006 beginning retained earnings by approximately $7 million to recognize these state tax benefits as deferred tax assets.

NEW ACCOUNTING PRONOUNCEMENTS NOT YET ADOPTED
In July 2006, the FASB issued FASB Interpretation No. 48, "Accounting for Uncertainty in Income Taxes" ("FIN 48"), an interpretation of FASB Statement No. 109, "Accounting for Income Taxes." FIN 48 is effective for fiscal years beginning after December 15, 2006, the year beginning December 31, 2006 for the Company. FIN 48 requires that a position taken or expected to be taken in a tax return be recognized in the financial statements when it is more likely than not (i.e., a likelihood of more than fifty percent) that the position would be sustained upon examination by tax authorities. A recognized tax position is then measured at the largest amount of benefit that is greater than fifty percent likely of being realized upon ultimate settlement. Upon adoption, the cumulative effect of applying the recognition and measurement provisions of FIN 48, if any, shall be reflected as an adjustment to the opening balance of retained earnings. We do not currently anticipate that the adjustment to the opening balance of retained earnings we will record upon adoption of FIN 48 will materially impact our financial condition.

FIN 48 requires that subsequent to initial adoption a change in judgment that results in subsequent recognition, derecognition or change in a measurement of a tax position taken in a prior annual period (including any related interest and penalties) be recognized as a discrete item in the period in which the change occurs. Currently, we record such changes in judgment, including audit settlements, as a component of our annual effective rate. Thus, our reported quarterly income tax rate may become more volatile upon adoption of FIN 48. This change will not impact the manner in which we record income tax expense on an annual basis.

FIN 48 also requires expanded disclosures including identification of tax positions for which it is reasonably possible that total amounts of unrecognized tax benefits will significantly change in the next twelve months, a description of tax years that remain subject to examination by major tax jurisdiction, a tabular reconciliation of the total amount of unrecognized tax benefits at the beginning and end of each annual reporting period, the total amount of unrecognized tax benefits that, if recognized, would affect the effective tax rate and the total amounts of interest and penalties recognized in the statements of operations and financial position.

In September 2006, the FASB issued SFAS No. 157, "Fair Value Measures" ("SFAS 157"). SFAS 157 defines fair value, establishes a framework for measuring fair value and enhances disclosures about fair value measures required under other accounting pronouncements, but does not change existing guidance as to whether or not an instrument is carried at fair value. SFAS 157 is effective for fiscal years beginning after November 15, 2007, the year beginning December 30, 2007 for the Company. We are currently reviewing the provisions of SFAS 157 to determine any impact for the Company.

In February 2007, the FASB issued SFAS No. 159 "The Fair Value Option for Financial Assets and Financial Liabilities," ("SFAS 159"). SFAS 159 provides companies with an option to report selected financial assets and financial liabilities at fair value. Unrealized gains and losses on items for which the fair value option has been elected are reported in earnings at each subsequent reporting date. SFAS 159 is effective for fiscal years beginning after November 15, 2007, the year beginning December 30, 2007 for the Company. We are currently reviewing the provisions of SFAS 159 to determine any impact for the Company.

Earnings Per Common Share ("EPS")

	2006	2005	2004
Net income	$ 824	$ 762	$ 740
Weighted-average common shares outstanding (for basic calculation)	273	286	291
Effect of dilutive share-based employee compensation	9	12	14
Weighted-average common and dilutive potential common shares outstanding (for diluted calculation)	282	298	305
Basic EPS	$ 3.02	$ 2.66	$ 2.54
Diluted EPS	$ 2.92	$ 2.55	$ 2.42
Unexercised employee stock options and stock appreciation rights (in millions) excluded from the diluted EPS computation(a)	0.1	0.5	0.4

(a) These unexercised employee stock options and stock appreciation rights were not included in the computation of diluted EPS because their exercise prices were greater than the average market price of our Common Stock during the year.

4.

Items Affecting Comparability of Net Income

FACILITY ACTIONS Refranchising (gain) loss, store closure (income) costs and store impairment charges by reportable segment are as follows:

	2006	2005	2004
U.S.			
Refranchising net (gain) loss[a][b]	$ (20)	$ (40)	$ (14)
Store closure costs (income)	(1)	2	(3)
Store impairment charges	38	44	17
Closure and impairment expenses	$ 37	$ 46	$ 14
International Division			
Refranchising net (gain) loss[a][b]	$ (4)	$ (3)	$ 3
Store closure costs (income)	1	(1)	1
Store impairment charges	15	10	19
Closure and impairment expenses	$ 16	$ 9	$ 20
China Division			
Refranchising net (gain) loss[a]	$ —	$ —	$ (1)
Store closure costs (income)	(1)	(1)	(1)
Store impairment charges	7	8	5
Closure and impairment expenses	$ 6	$ 7	$ 4
Worldwide			
Refranchising net (gain) loss[a][b]	$ (24)	$ (43)	$ (12)
Store closure costs (income)	(1)	—	(3)
Store impairment charges	60	62	41
Closure and impairment expenses	$ 59	$ 62	$ 38

(a) Refranchising (gain) loss is not allocated to segments for performance reporting purposes.
(b) Includes initial franchise fees in the U.S. of $11 million in 2006, $7 million in 2005 and $2 million in 2004, and in the International Division of $6 million in 2006, $3 million in 2005 and $8 million in 2004. See Note 7.

The following table summarizes the 2006 and 2005 activity related to reserves for remaining lease obligations for closed stores.

	Beginning Balance	Amounts Used	New Decisions	Estimate/ Decision Changes	Other	Ending Balance
2005 Activity	$ 43	(13)	14	—	—	$ 44
2006 Activity	**$ 44**	**(17)**	**8**	**1**	**—**	**$ 36**

Assets held for sale at December 30, 2006 and December 31, 2005 total $13 million and $11 million, respectively, of U.S. property, plant and equipment, primarily land, on which we previously operated restaurants and are included in prepaid expenses and other current assets on our Consolidated Balance Sheets.

WRENCH LITIGATION In fiscal year 2003, we recorded a charge of $42 million related to a lawsuit filed against Taco Bell Corp. (the "Wrench litigation"). Income of $14 million was recorded for 2004 reflecting settlements associated with the Wrench litigation for amounts less than previously accrued as well as related insurance recoveries. We recorded income of $2 million in 2005 from a settlement with an insurance carrier related to the Wrench litigation. We continue to pursue additional recoveries which, if any, will be recorded as realized.

AMERISERVE AND OTHER CHARGES (CREDITS) AmeriServe Food Distribution Inc. ("AmeriServe") was the primary distributor of food and paper supplies to our U.S. stores when it filed for protection under Chapter 11 of the U.S. Bankruptcy Code on January 31, 2000. A plan of reorganization for AmeriServe (the "POR") was approved on November 28, 2000, which resulted in, among other things, the assumption of our distribution agreement, subject to certain amendments, by McLane Company, Inc. During the AmeriServe bankruptcy reorganization process, we took a number of actions to ensure continued supply to our system. Those actions resulted in significant expense for the Company, primarily recorded in 2000. Under the POR, we are entitled to proceeds from certain residual assets, preference claims and other legal recoveries of the estate.

Income of $1 million, $2 million and $16 million was recorded as AmeriServe and other charges (credits) for 2006, 2005 and 2004, respectively. These amounts primarily resulted from cash recoveries related to the AmeriServe bankruptcy reorganization process.

 5.

Supplemental Cash Flow Data

	2006	2005	2004
Cash Paid For:			
Interest	$ 185	$ 132	$ 146
Income taxes	304	232	276
Significant Non-Cash Investing and Financing Activities:			
Assumption of capital leases related to the acquisition of restaurants from franchisees	$ —	$ —	$ 8
Capital lease obligations incurred to acquire assets	9	7	13

Additionally, we assumed the full liability associated with capital leases of $95 million and short-term borrowings of $23 million when we acquired the remaining fifty percent ownership interest of our Pizza Hut United Kingdom unconsolidated affiliate (See Note 6). Previously, our fifty percent share of these liabilities were reflected in our Investment in unconsolidated affiliate balance under the equity method of accounting and were not presented as liabilities on our Consolidated Balance Sheet.

 6.

Pizza Hut United Kingdom Acquisition

On September 12, 2006, we completed the acquisition of the remaining fifty percent ownership interest of our Pizza Hut United Kingdom ("U.K.") unconsolidated affiliate for $187 million in cash, including transaction costs and prior to $9 million of cash assumed. This unconsolidated affiliate owned more than 500 restaurants in the U.K. The acquisition was driven by growth opportunities we see in the market and the desire of our former partner in the unconsolidated affiliate to refocus its business to other industry sectors. Prior to this acquisition, we accounted for our ownership interest under the equity method of accounting. Our Investment in unconsolidated affiliate balance for the Pizza Hut U.K. unconsolidated affiliate was $58 million at the date of this acquisition.

HH APPENDIX A

Subsequent to the acquisition we consolidated all of the assets and liabilities of Pizza Hut U.K. These assets and liabilities were valued at fifty percent of their historical carrying value and fifty percent of their fair value upon acquisition. We have preliminarily assigned fair values such that assets and liabilities recorded for Pizza Hut U.K. at the acquisition date were as follows:

Current assets, including cash of $9	$ 27
Property, plant and equipment	340
Intangible assets	19
Goodwill	117
Total assets acquired	503
Current liabilities, other than capital lease obligations and short-term borrowings	102
Capital lease obligation, including current portion	95
Short-term borrowings	23
Other long-term liabilities	38
Total liabilities assumed	258
Net assets acquired (cash paid and investment allocated)	$ 245

All of the $19 million in intangible assets (primarily reacquired franchise rights) are subject to amortization with a weighted average life of approximately 18 years. The $117 million in goodwill is not expected to be deductible for income tax purposes and will be allocated to the International Division in its entirety.

Under the equity method of accounting, we reported our fifty percent share of the net income of the unconsolidated affiliate (after interest expense and income taxes) as Other (income) expense in the Consolidated Statements of Income. We also recorded a franchise fee for the royalty received from the stores owned by the unconsolidated affiliate. From the date of the acquisition through December 4, 2006 (the end of our fiscal year for Pizza Hut U.K.), we reported Company sales and the associated restaurant costs, general and administrative expense, interest expense and income taxes associated with the restaurants previously owned by the unconsolidated affiliate in the appropriate line items of our Consolidated Statements of Income. We no longer recorded franchise fee income for the restaurants previously owned by the unconsolidated affiliate nor did we report other income under the equity method of accounting. As a result of this acquisition, company sales and restaurant profit increased $164 million and $16 million, respectively, franchise fees decreased $7 million and G&A expenses increased $8 million compared to the year ended December 31, 2005. The impacts on operating profit and net income were not significant.

If the acquisition had been completed as of the beginning of the years ended December 30, 2006 and December 31, 2005, pro forma Company sales and franchise and license fees would have been as follows:

	2006	2005
Company sales	$ 8,886	$ 8,944
Franchise and license fees	$ 1,176	$ 1,095

The pro forma impact of the acquisition on net income and diluted earnings per share would not have been significant in 2006 and 2005. The pro forma information is not necessarily indicative of the results of operations had the acquisition actually occurred at the beginning of each of these periods nor is it necessarily indicative of future results.

7. Franchise and License Fees

	2006	2005	2004
Initial fees, including renewal fees	$ 57	$ 51	$ 43
Initial franchise fees included in refranchising gains	(17)	(10)	(10)
	40	41	33
Continuing fees	1,156	1,083	986
	$ 1,196	$ 1,124	$ 1,019

8. Other (Income) Expense

	2006	2005	2004
Equity income from investments in unconsolidated affiliates	$ (51)	$ (51)	$ (54)
Gain upon sale of investment in unconsolidated affiliate[a]	(2)	(11)	—
Recovery from supplier[b]	—	(20)	—
Contract termination charge[c]	8	—	—
Foreign exchange net (gain) loss and other	(6)	2	(1)
Other (income) expense	$ (51)	$ (80)	$ (55)

(a) Reflects net gains related to the 2005 sale of our fifty percent interest in the entity that operated almost all KFCs and Pizza Huts in Poland and the Czech Republic to our then partner in the entity, principally for cash. This transaction has generated net gains of approximately $13 million for YUM as cumulative cash proceeds (net of expenses) of approximately $27 million from the sale of our interest in the entity exceeded our recorded investment in this unconsolidated affiliate.

(b) Relates to a financial recovery from a supplier ingredient issue in mainland China totaling $24 million, $4 million of which was recognized through equity income from investments in unconsolidated affiliates. Our KFC business in mainland China was negatively impacted by the interruption of product offerings and negative publicity associated with a supplier ingredient issue experienced in late March 2005. During 2005, we entered into agreements with the supplier for a partial recovery of our losses.

(c) Reflects an $8 million charge associated with the termination of a beverage agreement in the United States segment.

9. Property, Plant and Equipment, net

	2006	2005
Land	$ 541	$ 567
Buildings and improvements	3,449	3,094
Capital leases, primarily buildings	221	126
Machinery and equipment	2,566	2,399
	6,777	6,186
Accumulated depreciation and amortization	(3,146)	(2,830)
	$ 3,631	$ 3,356

Depreciation and amortization expense related to property, plant and equipment was $466 million, $459 million and $434 million in 2006, 2005 and 2004, respectively.

Goodwill and Intangible Assets

The changes in the carrying amount of goodwill are as follows:

	U.S.	International Division	China Division	Worldwide
Balance as of December 25, 2004	$ 395	$ 100	$ 58	$ 553
Acquisitions	—	1	—	1
Disposals and other, net[a]	(11)	(5)	—	(16)
Balance as of December 31, 2005	$ 384	$ 96	$ 58	$ 538
Acquisitions	—	123	—	123
Disposals and other, net[a]	(17)	18	—	1
Balance as of December 30, 2006	**$ 367**	**$ 237**	**$ 58**	**$ 662**

(a) Disposals and other, net for the International Division primarily reflects the impact of foreign currency translation on existing balances. Disposals and other, net for the U.S. Division, primarily reflects goodwill write-offs associated with refranchising.

Intangible assets, net for the years ended 2006 and 2005 are as follows:

	2006		2005	
	Gross Carrying Amount	Accumulated Amortization	Gross Carrying Amount	Accumulated Amortization
Amortized intangible assets				
Franchise contract rights	$ 153	$ (66)	$ 144	$ (59)
Trademarks/brands	220	(18)	208	(9)
Favorable operating leases	15	(10)	18	(14)
Reacquired franchise rights[a]	18	—	—	—
Pension-related intangible[b]	—	—	7	—
Other	5	(1)	5	(1)
	$ 411	$ (95)	$ 382	$ (83)
Unamortized intangible assets				
Trademarks/brands	$ 31		$ 31	

(a) Increase is primarily due to the acquisition of the remaining fifty percent interest in our former Pizza Hut U.K. unconsolidated affiliate.
(b) Subsequent to the adoption of SFAS 158 a pension-related intangible asset is no longer recorded. See Note 2 for further discussion.

We have recorded intangible assets through past acquisitions representing the value of our KFC, LJS and A&W trademarks/brands. The value of a trademark/brand is determined based upon the value derived from the royalty we avoid, in the case of Company stores, or receive, in the case of franchise and licensee stores, for the use of the trademark/brand. We have determined that our KFC trademark/brand intangible asset has an indefinite life and therefore is not amortized. We have determined that our LJS and A&W trademarks/brands are subject to amortization and are being amortized over their expected useful lives which are currently thirty years.

On March 24, 2006, we finalized an agreement with Rostik's Restaurant Ltd. ("RRL"), a franchisor and operator of a chicken chain in Russia known as Rostik's, under which we acquired the Rostik's brand and associated intellectual property for $15 million. We will also provide financial support, including loans and guarantees, up to $30 million to support future development by RRL in Russia, an insignificant amount of which has been incurred as of December 30, 2006. This agreement also includes a put/call option that may be exercised, subject to certain conditions, between the fifth and seventh year whereby ownership of then existing restaurants would be transferred to YRI. The majority of the purchase price of $15 million was allocated to the trademarks acquired for the International Division and will be amortized over a period of seven years.

Amortization expense for all definite-lived intangible assets was $15 million in 2006, $13 million in 2005 and $8 million in 2004. Amortization expense for definite-lived intangible assets will approximate $17 million annually in 2007 through 2011.

Accounts Payable and Other Current Liabilities

	2006	2005
Accounts payable	$ 554	$ 473
Accrued compensation and benefits	302	274
Dividends payable	119	32
Other current liabilities	411	477
	$ 1,386	$ 1,256

Short-term Borrowings and Long-term Debt

	2006	2005
Short-term Borrowings		
Unsecured Term Loans, expire January 2007	$ 183	$ —
Current maturities of long-term debt	16	211
Other	28	—
	$ 227	$ 211
Long-term Debt		
Unsecured International Revolving Credit Facility, expires November 2010	$ 174	$ 180
Unsecured Revolving Credit Facility, expires September 2009	—	—
Senior, Unsecured Notes, due April 2006	—	200
Senior, Unsecured Notes, due May 2008	251	251
Senior, Unsecured Notes, due April 2011	646	646
Senior, Unsecured Notes, due July 2012	399	398
Senior, Unsecured Notes, due April 2016	300	—
Capital lease obligations (See Note 13)	228	114
Other, due through 2019 (11%)	76	77
	2,074	1,866
Less current maturities of long-term debt	(16)	(211)
Long-term debt excluding SFAS 133 adjustment	2,058	1,655
Derivative instrument adjustment under SFAS 133 (See Note 14)	(13)	(6)
Long-term debt including SFAS 133 adjustment	$ 2,045	$ 1,649

HH APPENDIX A

Selected Financial Data
YUM! Brands, Inc. and Subsidiaries

(in millions, except per share and unit amounts)

	2006	2005	2004	2003	2002
Summary of Operations					
Revenues					
Company sales	$ 8,365	$ 8,225	$ 7,992	$ 7,441	$ 6,891
Franchise and license fees	1,196	1,124	1,019	939	866
Total	9,561	9,349	9,011	8,380	7,757
Closures and impairment expenses[a]	(59)	(62)	(38)	(40)	(51)
Refranchising gain (loss)[a]	24	43	12	4	19
Wrench litigation income (expense)[b]	—	2	14	(42)	—
AmeriServe and other (charges) credits[c]	1	2	16	26	27
Operating profit	1,262	1,153	1,155	1,059	1,030
Interest expense, net	154	127	129	173	172
Income before income taxes and cumulative effect of accounting change	1,108	1,026	1,026	886	858
Income before cumulative effect of accounting change	824	762	740	618	583
Cumulative effect of accounting change, net of tax[d]	—	—	—	(1)	—
Net income	824	762	740	617	583
Basic earnings per common share	3.02	2.66	2.54	2.10	1.97
Diluted earnings per common share	2.92	2.55	2.42	2.02	1.88
Cash Flow Data					
Provided by operating activities	$ 1,302	$ 1,238	$ 1,186	$ 1,099	$ 1,112
Capital spending, excluding acquisitions	614	609	645	663	760
Proceeds from refranchising of restaurants	257	145	140	92	81
Repurchase shares of common stock	983	1,056	569	278	228
Dividends paid on common shares	144	123	58	—	—
Balance Sheet					
Total assets	$ 6,353	$ 5,797	$ 5,696	$ 5,620	$ 5,400
Long-term debt	2,045	1,649	1,731	2,056	2,299
Total debt	2,272	1,860	1,742	2,066	2,445
Other Data					
Number of stores at year end					
Company	7,736	7,587	7,743	7,854	7,526
Unconsolidated Affiliates	1,206	1,648	1,662	1,512	2,148
Franchisees	23,516	22,666	21,858	21,471	20,724
Licensees	2,137	2,376	2,345	2,362	2,526
System	34,595	34,277	33,608	33,199	32,924
U.S. Company blended same store sales growth[e]	—	4%	3%	—	2%
International Division system sales growth[f]					
Reported	7%	9%	14%	13%	6%
Local currency[g]	7%	6%	6%	5%	7%
China Division system sales growth[f]					
Reported	26%	13%	23%	23%	25%
Local currency[g]	23%	11%	23%	23%	25%
Shares outstanding at year end	265	278	290	292	294
Cash dividends declared per common share	$ 0.865	$ 0.445	$ 0.30	—	—
Market price per share at year end	$ 58.80	$ 46.88	$ 46.27	$ 33.64	$ 24.12

Fiscal years 2006, 2004, 2003 and 2002 include 52 weeks and fiscal year 2005 includes 53 weeks.

Fiscal years 2006 and 2005 include the impact of the adoption of Statement of Financial Accounting Standards ("SFAS") No. 123R (Revised 2004). "Share Based Payment" ("SFAS 123R"). This resulted in a $39 million and $38 million decrease in net income, or a decrease of $0.14 and $0.13 to both basic and diluted earnings per share for 2006 and 2005, respectively. If SFAS 123R had been effective for prior years presented, reported basic and diluted earnings per share would have decreased $0.12 and $0.12, $0.12 and $0.12, and $0.14 and $0.13 per share for 2004, 2003 and 2002, respectively, consistent with previously disclosed pro-forma information. See Note 2 to the Consolidated Financial Statements.

From May 7, 2002, results include Long John Silver's ("LJS") and A&W All-American Food Restaurants ("A&W"), which were added when we acquired Yorkshire Global Restaurants, Inc.

The selected financial data should be read in conjunction with the Consolidated Financial Statements and the Notes thereto.

(a) See Note 4 to the Consolidated Financial Statements for a description of Closures and Impairment Expenses and Refranchising Gain (Loss) in 2006, 2005 and 2004.

(b) See Note 4 to the Consolidated Financial Statements for a description of Wrench litigation in 2006, 2005 and 2004.

(c) See Note 4 to the Consolidated Financial Statements for a description of AmeriServe and other (charges) credits in 2006, 2005 and 2004.

(d) Fiscal year 2003 includes the impact of the adoption of SFAS No. 143, "Accounting for Asset Retirement Obligations," which addresses the financial accounting and reporting for legal obligations associated with the retirement of long-lived assets and the associated asset retirement costs.

(e) U.S. Company blended same-store sales growth includes the results of Company owned KFC, Pizza Hut and Taco Bell restaurants that have been open one year or more. LJS and A&W are not included.

(f) International Division and China Division system sales growth includes the results of all restaurants regardless of ownership, including Company owned, franchise, unconsolidated affiliate and license restaurants. Sales of franchise, unconsolidated affiliate and license restaurants generate franchise and license fees for the Company (typically at a rate of 4% to 6% of sales). Franchise, unconsolidated affiliate and license restaurant sales are not included in Company sales we present on the Consolidated Statements of Income; however, the fees are included in the Company's revenues. We believe system sales growth is useful to investors as a significant indicator of the overall strength of our business as it incorporates all our revenue drivers, Company and franchise same store sales as well as net unit development. Additionally, as previously noted, we began reporting information for our international business in two separate operating segments (the International Division and the China Division) in 2005 as a result of changes in our management structure. Segment information for periods prior to 2005 has been restated to reflect this reporting.

(g) Local currency represents the percentage change excluding the impact of foreign currency translation. These amounts are derived by translating current year results at prior year average exchange rates. We believe the elimination of the foreign currency translation impact provides better year-to-year comparability without the distortion of foreign currency fluctuations.

Pier1 imports®

2006 Annual Report

Item 6. *Selected Financial Data.*

FINANCIAL SUMMARY

	2006	2005	2004	2003	2002
			Year Ended		
			($ in millions except per share amounts)		
SUMMARY OF OPERATIONS*:					
Net sales	$1,776.7	1,825.3	1,806.1	1,703.4	1,505.1
Gross profit	$ 601.7	703.6	760.9	736.4	636.9
Selling, general and administrative expenses	$ 588.3	549.6	526.1	487.0	435.7
Depreciation and amortization	$ 56.2	55.8	48.9	44.7	41.2
Operating income (loss)	$ (42.8)	98.2	186.0	204.8	160.0
Nonoperating (income) and expenses, net	$ (0.9)	(0.9)	(1.0)	(0.6)	(0.1)
Income (loss) from continuing operations before income taxes	$ (41.9)	99.1	187.0	205.6	160.1
Income (loss) from continuing operations, net of tax	$ (27.5)	62.8	117.7	129.6	101.3
Income (loss) from discontinued operations, net of tax	$ (12.3)	(2.3)	0.3	(0.3)	(1.1)
Net income (loss)	$ (39.8)	60.5	118.0	129.4	100.2
PER SHARE AMOUNTS:					
Basic earnings (loss) from continuing operations	$ (.32)	.72	1.32	1.40	1.07
Diluted earnings (loss) from continuing operations	$ (.32)	.71	1.29	1.36	1.05
Basic earnings (loss) from discontinued operations	$ (.14)	(.03)	.00	(.00)	(.01)
Diluted earnings (loss) from discontinued operations	$ (.14)	(.03)	.00	(.00)	(.01)
Basic earnings (loss) consolidated	$ (.46)	.69	1.32	1.39	1.06
Diluted earnings (loss) consolidated	$ (.46)	.68	1.29	1.36	1.04
Cash dividends declared	$ .40	.40	.30	.21	.16
Shareholders' equity	$ 6.81	7.63	7.66	6.93	6.20
OTHER FINANCIAL DATA:					
Working capital	$ 486.1	387.4	433.0	432.3	408.6
Current ratio	2.7	2.3	2.5	2.8	3.0
Total assets	$1,169.9	1,075.7	1,052.2	972.7	867.3
Long-term debt	$ 184.0	19.0	19.0	25.0	25.4
Shareholders' equity	$ 590.0	664.4	683.6	643.9	585.7
Weighted average diluted shares outstanding (millions)	86.6	88.8	91.6	95.3	96.2
Effective tax rate	34.5%	36.7	37.1	37.0	36.7
Return on average shareholders' equity	(4.4%)	9.3	17.7	21.1	18.1
Return on average total assets	(2.4%)	5.9	11.6	14.1	12.6
Pre-tax return on sales	(2.4%)	5.4	10.4	12.1	10.6

* Amounts are from continuing operations unless otherwise specified.

Item 8. *Financial Statements and Supplementary Data.*

REPORT OF INDEPENDENT REGISTERED PUBLIC ACCOUNTING FIRM

To the Board of Directors of Pier 1 Imports, Inc.

We have audited the accompanying consolidated balance sheets of Pier 1 Imports, Inc. as of February 25, 2006 and February 26, 2005, and the related consolidated statements of operations, shareholders' equity, and cash flows for each of the three years in the period ended February 25, 2006. These financial statements are the responsibility of the Company's management. Our responsibility is to express an opinion on these financial statements based on our audits.

We conducted our audits in accordance with the standards of the Public Company Accounting Oversight Board (United States). Those standards require that we plan and perform the audit to obtain reasonable assurance about whether the financial statements are free of material misstatement. An audit includes examining, on a test basis, evidence supporting the amounts and disclosures in the financial statements. An audit also includes assessing the accounting principles used and significant estimates made by management, as well as evaluating the overall financial statement presentation. We believe that our audits provide a reasonable basis for our opinion.

In our opinion, the financial statements referred to above present fairly, in all material respects, the consolidated financial position of Pier 1 Imports, Inc. at February 25, 2006 and February 26, 2005, and the consolidated results of its operations and its cash flows for each of the three years in the period ended February 25, 2006, in conformity with U.S. generally accepted accounting principles.

As discussed in Note 2 of the Notes to Consolidated Financial Statements, the Company corrected its classification of non-monetary transactions related to its beneficial interest in securitized receivables on the consolidated statements of cash flows. The prior periods presented have been restated for this correction.

We also have audited, in accordance with the standards of the Public Company Accounting Oversight Board (United States), the effectiveness of Pier 1 Imports, Inc.'s internal control over financial reporting as of February 25, 2006, based on criteria established in Internal Control — Integrated Framework issued by the Committee of Sponsoring Organizations of the Treadway Commission and our report dated April 25, 2006 expressed an unqualified opinion thereon.

/s/   Ernst & Young LLP

Fort Worth, Texas
April 25, 2006

Pier 1 Imports, Inc.

CONSOLIDATED STATEMENTS OF OPERATIONS
(In thousands except per share amounts)

	Year Ended		
	2006	2005	2004
Net sales	$1,776,701	$1,825,343	$1,806,092
Operating costs and expenses:			
Cost of sales (including buying and store occupancy costs)	1,175,011	1,121,697	1,045,180
Selling, general and administrative expenses	588,273	549,635	526,060
Depreciation and amortization	56,229	55,762	48,869
	1,819,513	1,727,094	1,620,109
Operating income (loss)	(42,812)	98,249	185,983
Nonoperating (income) and expenses:			
Interest and investment income	(3,510)	(2,635)	(2,724)
Interest expense	2,610	1,735	1,688
	(900)	(900)	(1,036)
Income (loss) from continuing operations before income taxes	(41,912)	99,149	187,019
Provision (benefit) for income taxes	(14,441)	36,384	69,315
Income (loss) from continuing operations	(27,471)	62,765	117,704
Discontinued operations:			
Income (loss) from discontinued operations (including write down of assets held for sale of $7,441 in 2006)	(17,583)	(2,308)	297
Income tax benefit	(5,250)	—	—
Income (loss) from discontinued operations	(12,333)	(2,308)	297
Net income (loss)	$ (39,804)	$ 60,457	$ 118,001
Earnings (loss) per share from continuing operations:			
Basic	$ (.32)	$ .72	$ 1.32
Diluted	$ (.32)	$ .71	$ 1.29
Earnings (loss) per share from discontinued operations:			
Basic	$ (.14)	$ (.03)	$ .00
Diluted	$ (.14)	$ (.03)	$ .00
Earnings (loss) per share:			
Basic	$ (.46)	$ .69	$ 1.32
Diluted	$ (.46)	$ .68	$ 1.29
Dividends declared per share:	$ .40	$ .40	$ .30
Average shares outstanding during period:			
Basic	86,629	87,037	89,294
Diluted	86,629	88,838	91,624

The accompanying notes are an integral part of these financial statements.

Pier 1 Imports, Inc.

CONSOLIDATED BALANCE SHEETS
(In thousands except share amounts)

	2006	2005
ASSETS		
Current assets:		
Cash and cash equivalents, including temporary investments of $238,463 and $178,289, respectively	$ 246,115	$ 185,722
Beneficial interest in securitized receivables	50,000	35,690
Other accounts receivable, net of allowance for doubtful accounts of $1,119 and $82, respectively	13,916	11,089
Inventories	368,978	365,767
Income tax receivable	18,011	—
Assets held for sale	32,359	39,815
Prepaid expenses and other current assets	45,544	40,864
Total current assets	774,923	678,947
Properties, net	298,922	320,138
Other noncurrent assets	96,016	76,664
	$1,169,861	$1,075,749
LIABILITIES AND SHAREHOLDERS' EQUITY		
Current liabilities:		
Accounts payable	$ 105,916	$ 108,132
Gift cards and other deferred revenue	63,835	60,844
Accrued income taxes payable	4,763	11,716
Liabilities related to assets held for sale	16,841	15,163
Other accrued liabilities	97,493	95,723
Total current liabilities	288,848	291,578
Long-term debt	184,000	19,000
Other noncurrent liabilities	107,031	100,802
Shareholders' equity:		
Common stock, $1.00 par, 500,000,000 shares authorized, 100,779,000 issued	100,779	100,779
Paid-in capital	132,075	141,850
Retained earnings	582,221	656,692
Cumulative other comprehensive loss	(583)	(1,426)
Less — 13,761,000 and 14,459,000 common shares in treasury, at cost, respectively	(222,254)	(233,526)
Less — unearned compensation	(2,256)	—
	589,982	664,369
Commitments and contingencies	—	—
	$1,169,861	$1,075,749

The accompanying notes are an integral part of these financial statements.

38

Pier 1 Imports, Inc.

CONSOLIDATED STATEMENTS OF CASH FLOWS

(In thousands)

	Year Ended		
	2006	**2005**	**2004**
		(As restated, See Note 2)	(As restated, See Note 2)
Cash flow from operating activities:			
Net income (loss)	$(39,804)	$ 60,457	$118,001
Adjustments to reconcile to net cash (used in) provided by operating activities:			
Depreciation and amortization	78,781	75,624	64,606
Loss (gain) on disposal of fixed assets	1,781	315	(316)
Loss on impairment of fixed assets	6,024	741	459
Write-down of assets held for sale	7,441	—	—
Deferred compensation	11,402	7,710	6,573
Lease termination expense	4,176	2,243	3,258
Deferred income taxes	(14,496)	2,035	184
Sale of receivables in exchange for beneficial interest in securitized receivables	(74,550)	(91,071)	(83,931)
Tax benefit from options exercised by employees	760	3,668	4,897
Other	(524)	(222)	4,894
Change in cash from:			
Inventories	882	(6,860)	(40,520)
Other accounts receivable, prepaid expenses and other current assets	(22,778)	(11,302)	(16,927)
Income tax receivable	(18,011)	—	—
Accounts payable and accrued expenses	7,369	21,572	34,410
Income taxes payable	(6,966)	(14,116)	184
Other noncurrent assets	(2,558)	336	(2,027)
Other noncurrent liabilities	(3,226)	—	—
Net cash (used in) provided by operating activities	(64,297)	51,130	93,745
Cash flow from investing activities:			
Capital expenditures	(50,979)	(99,239)	(121,190)
Proceeds from disposition of properties	1,401	3,852	34,450
Proceeds from sale of restricted investments	3,226	—	—
Purchase of restricted investments	(3,500)	(10,807)	(8,752)
Collections of principal on beneficial interest in securitized receivables	60,240	99,712	78,788
Net cash provided by (used in) investing activities	10,388	(6,482)	(16,704)
Cash flow from financing activities:			
Cash dividends	(34,667)	(34,762)	(26,780)
Purchases of treasury stock	(4,047)	(58,210)	(76,009)
Proceeds from stock options exercised, stock purchase plan and other, net	7,641	12,473	15,709
Issuance of long-term debt	165,000	—	—
Notes payable borrowings	86,500	—	—
Repayment of notes payable	(86,500)	—	(6,390)
Debt issuance costs	(6,739)	(169)	(584)
Purchase of call option	(9,145)	—	—
Net cash provided by (used in) financing activities	118,043	(80,668)	(94,054)
Change in cash and cash equivalents	64,134	(36,020)	(17,013)
Cash and cash equivalents at beginning period (including cash held for sale of $3,359, $6,148 and $6,506, respectively)	189,081	225,101	242,114
Cash and cash equivalents at end of period (including cash held for sale of $7,100, $3,359 and $6,148, respectively)	$253,215	$189,081	$225,101
Supplemental cash flow information:			
Interest paid	$ 8,136	$ 868	$ 1,791
Income taxes paid	$ 21,342	$ 45,655	$ 63,788

The accompanying notes are an integral part of these financial statements.

Pier 1 Imports, Inc.

CONSOLIDATED STATEMENTS OF SHAREHOLDERS' EQUITY
(In thousands except per share amounts)

	Common Stock Outstanding Shares	Amount	Paid-in Capital	Retained Earnings	Cumulative Other Comprehensive Income (Loss)	Treasury Stock	Unearned Compensation	Total Shareholders' Equity
Balance March 1, 2003	90,685	$100,779	$144,247	$539,776	$(2,210)	$(138,656)	$ —	$643,936
Comprehensive income:								
Net income	—	—	—	118,001	—	—	—	118,001
Other comprehensive income:								
Minimum pension liability adjustments, net of tax	—	—	—	—	(1,033)	—	—	(1,033)
Currency translation adjustments	—	—	—	—	4,910	—	—	4,910
Comprehensive income								121,878
Purchases of treasury stock	(3,758)	—	—	—	—	(76,009)	—	(76,009)
Exercise of stock options, stock purchase plan and other	1,300	—	1,137	—	—	19,469	—	20,606
Cash dividends ($.30 per share)	—	—	—	(26,780)	—	—	—	(26,780)
Balance February 28, 2004	88,227	100,779	145,384	630,997	1,667	(195,196)	—	683,631
Comprehensive income:								
Net income	—	—	—	60,457	—	—	—	60,457
Other comprehensive income (loss), net of tax:								
Minimum pension liability adjustments	—	—	—	—	(4,780)	—	—	(4,780)
Currency translation adjustments	—	—	—	—	1,687	—	—	1,687
Comprehensive income								57,364
Purchases of treasury stock	(3,225)	—	—	—	—	(58,210)	—	(58,210)
Exercise of stock options, stock purchase plan and other	1,238	—	(3,534)	—	—	19,880	—	16,346
Cash dividends ($.40 per share)	—	—	—	(34,762)	—	—	—	(34,762)
Balance February 26, 2005	86,240	100,779	141,850	656,692	(1,426)	(233,526)	—	664,369
Comprehensive income (loss):								
Net loss	—	—	—	(39,804)	—	—	—	(39,804)
Other comprehensive income (loss), net of tax:								
Minimum pension liability adjustments	—	—	—	—	1,149	—	—	1,149
Currency translation adjustments	—	—	—	—	(306)	—	—	(306)
Comprehensive loss								(38,961)
Purchases of treasury stock	(250)	—	—	—	—	(4,047)	—	(4,047)
Restricted stock grant and amortization	203	—	(386)	—	—	3,278	(2,256)	636
Exercise of stock options, stock purchase plan and other	746	—	(3,640)	—	—	12,041	—	8,401
Cash dividends ($.40 per share)	—	—	—	(34,667)	—	—	—	(34,667)
Purchase of call option, net of tax	—	—	(5,749)	—	—	—	—	(5,749)
Balance February 25, 2006	86,939	$100,779	$132,075	$582,221	$ (583)	$(222,254)	$(2,256)	$589,982

The accompanying notes are an integral part of these financial statements.

NOTES TO CONSOLIDATED FINANCIAL STATEMENTS

NOTE 1 — SUMMARY OF SIGNIFICANT ACCOUNTING POLICIES

Organization — Pier 1 Imports, Inc. and its consolidated subsidiaries (the "Company") is one of North America's largest specialty retailers of imported decorative home furnishings, gifts and related items, with retail stores located primarily in the United States, Canada, Puerto Rico and Mexico. On March 20, 2006, the Company sold its subsidiary based in the United Kingdom, The Pier Retail Group Limited ("The Pier"). At fiscal 2006 year end, The Pier was classified as held for sale and included in discontinued operations for all years presented. In the fourth quarter of fiscal 2006, the Company recorded an impairment charge of $7,441,000 to write goodwill and long-lived assets related to The Pier down by $918,000 and $6,523,000, respectively, to fair value less selling costs. *See Note 3 of the Notes to Consolidated Financial Statements for further discussion.*

Basis of consolidation — The consolidated financial statements of the Company include the accounts of all subsidiary companies except Pier 1 Funding, LLC, which is a non-consolidated, bankruptcy remote, securitization subsidiary. *See Note 4 of the Notes to Consolidated Financial Statements.* Material intercompany transactions and balances have been eliminated.

Segment information — The Company is a specialty retailer that offers a broad range of products in its stores and conducts business as one operating segment. The Company's domestic operations provided 93.0%, 93.7% and 94.1% of its net sales, with 6.7%, 6.0% and 5.7% provided by stores in Canada, and the remainder from royalties received from Sears Roebuck de Mexico S.A. de C.V. during fiscal 2006, 2005 and 2004, respectively. As of February 25, 2006 and February 26, 2005, $8,765,000 and $8,888,000, respectively, of the Company's long-lived assets were located in Canada. There were no long-lived assets in Mexico during either period.

Use of estimates — Preparation of the financial statements in conformity with U.S. generally accepted accounting principles requires management to make estimates and assumptions that affect the amounts reported in the financial statements and accompanying notes. Actual results could differ from those estimates.

Reclassifications — Certain reclassifications have been made in the prior years' consolidated financial statements to conform to the fiscal 2006 presentation. These reclassifications had no effect on net income and shareholders' equity with minimal effects on total assets and total liabilities. During the fourth quarter of fiscal 2006, the Company determined that a reclassification within its consolidated statements of cash flows was required to properly reflect the exchanges of securitized receivables as non-monetary transactions in the operating activities section of the Company's consolidated statements of cash flows. This reclass required a restatement for fiscal years 2005 and 2004. *See Note 2 of the Notes to Consolidated Financial Statements for further discussion.*

Fiscal periods — The Company utilizes 5-4-4 (week) quarterly accounting periods with the fiscal year ending on the Saturday nearest the last day of February. Fiscal 2006 ended February 25, 2006, fiscal 2005 ended February 26, 2005 and fiscal 2004 ended February 28, 2004, all of which contained 52 weeks.

Cash and cash equivalents — The Company considers all highly liquid investments with an original maturity date of three months or less to be cash equivalents, except for those investments that are restricted and have been set aside in a trust to satisfy pension obligations. As of February 25, 2006 and February 26, 2005, the Company's short-term investments classified as cash equivalents included investments in money market mutual funds totaling $238,463,000 and $178,289,000, respectively. The effect of foreign currency exchange rate fluctuations on cash is not material.

Translation of foreign currencies — Assets and liabilities of foreign operations are translated into United States dollars at fiscal year-end exchange rates. Income and expense items are translated at average exchange rates prevailing during the year. Translation adjustments arising from differences in exchange rates from period to period are included as a separate component of shareholders' equity and are included in other comprehensive income (loss). As of February 25, 2006, February 26, 2005 and

NOTES TO CONSOLIDATED FINANCIAL STATEMENTS — (Continued)

February 28, 2004, the Company had cumulative other comprehensive income balances of $4,990,000, $5,296,000, and $3,609,000, respectively, related to cumulative translation adjustments. The adjustments for currency translation during fiscal 2006, 2005 and 2004 resulted in other comprehensive income (loss) of ($306,000), $1,687,000, and $4,910,000, respectively. During fiscal 2006 and 2005, the Company provided deferred taxes of $531,000 and $703,000, respectively, on the portion of its cumulative currency translation adjustment considered not to be permanently reinvested abroad. Taxes on this portion of cumulative currency translation adjustments were insignificant in fiscal 2004.

Concentrations of risk — The Company has some degree of risk concentration with respect to sourcing the Company's inventory purchases. However, the Company believes alternative sources of products could be procured over a relatively short period of time. Pier 1 sells merchandise imported from over 40 different countries, with 35% of its sales derived from merchandise produced in China, 14% derived from merchandise produced in India, 13% derived from merchandise produced in the United States and 33% derived from merchandise produced in Indonesia, Brazil, Italy, Thailand, the Philippines, Vietnam and Mexico. The remaining 5% of sales was from merchandise produced in various Asian, European, Central American, South American and African countries.

Financial instruments — The fair value of financial instruments is determined by reference to various market data and other valuation techniques as appropriate. There were no assets or liabilities with a fair value significantly different from the recorded value as of February 25, 2006 and February 26, 2005.

From time to time, the Company purchases auction rate securities with the intention to hold them for short periods of time and considers them to be trading securities. The cash flows from the purchases and sales of these securities are reported in cash provided by operating activities. The Company had no auction rate securities outstanding at either February 25, 2006 or February 26, 2005.

Risk management instruments: The Company may utilize various financial instruments to manage interest rate and market risk associated with its on- and off-balance sheet commitments.

The Company hedges certain commitments denominated in foreign currencies through the purchase of forward contracts. The forward contracts are purchased only to cover specific commitments to buy merchandise for resale. The Company also uses contracts to hedge its exposure associated with the repatriation of funds from its Canadian operations. At February 25, 2006, there were no outstanding contracts to hedge exposure associated with the Company's merchandise purchases denominated in foreign currencies or the repatriation of Canadian funds. For financial accounting purposes, the Company does not designate such contracts as hedges. Thus, changes in the fair value of both types of forward contracts would be included in the Company's consolidated statements of operations. Both the changes in fair value and settlement of these contracts are included in cost of sales for forwards related to merchandise purchases and in selling, general and administrative expense for the contracts associated with the repatriation of Canadian funds.

The Company enters into forward foreign currency exchange contracts with major financial institutions and continually monitors its positions with, and the credit quality of, these counterparties to such financial instruments. The Company does not expect non-performance by any of the counterparties, and any losses incurred in the event of non-performance would not be material.

Beneficial interest in securitized receivables — The Company securitizes its entire portfolio of proprietary credit card receivables. During fiscal 2006, 2005 and 2004, the Company sold all of its proprietary credit card receivables, except those that failed certain eligibility requirements, to a special-purpose wholly owned subsidiary, Pier 1 Funding, LLC ("Funding"), which transferred the receivables to the Pier 1 Imports Credit Card Master Trust (the "Master Trust"). Neither Funding nor the Master Trust is consolidated by the Company and the Master Trust meets the requirements of a qualifying special-purpose entity under Statement of Financial Accounting Standards ("SFAS") No. 140. The Master Trust issues beneficial interests that represent undivided interests in the assets of the Master Trust consisting of

NOTES TO CONSOLIDATED FINANCIAL STATEMENTS — (Continued)

the transferred receivables and all cash flows from collections of such receivables. The beneficial interests include certain interests retained by Funding, which are represented by Class B Certificates, and the residual interest in the Master Trust (the excess of the principal amount of receivables held in the Master Trust over the portion represented by the certificates sold to a third-party investor and the Class B Certificates). Gain or loss on the sale of receivables depends in part on the previous carrying amount of the financial assets involved in the transfer, allocated between the assets sold and the retained interests based on their relative fair value at the date of transfer.

The beneficial interest in the Master Trust is accounted for as an available-for-sale security and is recorded at fair value. The Company estimates fair value of its beneficial interest in the Master Trust, both upon initial securitization and thereafter, based on the present value of future expected cash flows using management's best estimates of key assumptions including credit losses and payment rates. As of February 25, 2006 and February 26, 2005, the Company's assumptions used to calculate the present value of the future cash flows included estimated credit losses of 4.75% and 5%, respectively, of the outstanding balance, expected payment within a six-month period and a discount rate representing the average market rate the Company would expect to pay if it sold securities representing ownership in the excess receivables not required to collateralize the Class A Certificates. A sensitivity analysis performed assuming a hypothetical 20% adverse change in both interest rates and credit losses resulted in an immaterial impact on the fair value of the Company's beneficial interest. Although not anticipated by the Company, a significant deterioration in the financial condition of the Company's credit card holders, interest rates, or other economic conditions could result in other than temporary losses on the beneficial interest in future periods. *See Note 4 of the Notes to Consolidated Financial Statements for further discussion.*

Inventories — Inventories are comprised of finished merchandise and are stated at the lower of average cost or market, cost being determined on a weighted average inventory method. Cost is calculated based upon the actual landed cost of an item at the time it is received in the Company's warehouse using actual vendor invoices, the cost of warehousing and transporting product to the stores and other direct costs associated with purchasing products.

The Company recognizes known inventory losses, shortages and damages when incurred and maintains a reserve for estimated shrinkage since the last physical count, when actual shrink was recorded. The reserves for estimated shrink at the end of fiscal years 2006 and 2005 were $8,218,000 and $4,711,000, respectively. The increase was a result of timing of physical counts and not of an increase in rates of shrink.

Properties, maintenance and repairs — Buildings, equipment, furniture and fixtures, and leasehold improvements are carried at cost less accumulated depreciation. Depreciation is computed using the straight-line method over estimated remaining useful lives of the assets, generally thirty years for buildings and three to ten years for equipment, furniture and fixtures. Depreciation of improvements to leased properties is based upon the shorter of the remaining primary lease term or the estimated useful lives of such assets. Depreciation related to the Company's distribution centers is included in cost of sales. All other depreciation costs are included in depreciation and amortization. Depreciation costs were $54,870,000, $54,404,000 and $47,514,000 in fiscal 2006, 2005 and 2004, respectively.

Expenditures for maintenance, repairs and renewals that do not materially prolong the original useful lives of the assets are charged to expense as incurred. In the case of disposals, assets and the related depreciation are removed from the accounts and the net amount, less proceeds from disposal, is credited or charged to income.

Long-lived assets are reviewed at the store level for impairment at least annually and whenever an event or change in circumstances indicates that its carrying value may not be recoverable. If the carrying value exceeds the sum of the expected undiscounted cash flows, the asset is impaired. Expected cash flows are estimated based on management's estimate of changes in sales, merchandise margins, and expenses over the remaining expected terms of the leases. Impairment is measured as the amount by which the

43

NOTES TO CONSOLIDATED FINANCIAL STATEMENTS — (Continued)

carrying value of the asset exceeds the fair value of the asset. Fair value is determined by discounting expected cash flows. Impairment, if any, is recorded in the period in which the impairment occurred. Impairment charges were $5,601,000, $370,000 and $459,000 in fiscal 2006, 2005 and 2004, respectively, and included in selling, general and administrative expenses.

Goodwill and intangible assets — The Company applies the provisions of SFAS No. 142, "Goodwill and Intangible Assets." Under SFAS No. 142, goodwill and intangible assets with indefinite useful lives are not amortized, but instead are tested for impairment at least annually. In accordance with SFAS No. 142, the Company's reporting units were identified as components, and the goodwill assigned to each represents the excess of the original purchase price over the fair value of the net identifiable assets acquired for that component. The Company completed the annual impairment tests as of February 25, 2006 and February 26, 2005 for fiscal 2006 and 2005, respectively. The impairment tests were conducted by performing analyses of discounted future cash flows for the applicable reporting units. The analysis resulted in a write-down of intangible assets of $239,000, included in selling, general and administrative expenses, in fiscal 2006. No impairment loss was recognized in fiscal 2005 or fiscal 2004. *See Note 6 of the Notes to Consolidated Financial Statements for additional discussion of goodwill and intangible assets.*

Revenue recognition — Revenue is recognized upon customer receipt or delivery for retail sales, net of sales tax, including sales under deferred payment promotions on the Company's proprietary credit card. A reserve has been established for estimated merchandise returns based upon historical experience and other known factors. The reserves for estimated merchandise returns at the end of fiscal years 2006 and 2005 were $3,060,000 and $3,330,000, respectively. The Company's revenues are reported net of discounts and returns, and include wholesale sales and royalties received from franchise stores and Sears Roebuck de Mexico S.A. de C.V. Amounts billed to customers for shipping and handling are included in net sales and the costs incurred by the Company for these items are recorded in cost of sales.

Gift cards — Revenue associated with gift cards is recognized upon redemption of the gift card. Gift card breakage is estimated and recorded as income based upon an analysis of the Company's historical redemption patterns and represents the remaining unused portion of the gift card liability for which the likelihood of redemption is remote.

Leases — The Company leases certain property consisting principally of retail stores, warehouses, and material handling and office equipment under leases expiring through fiscal 2021. Most retail store locations are leased for primary terms of 10 to 15 years with varying renewal options and rent escalation clauses. Escalations occurring during the primary terms of the leases are included in the calculation of the minimum lease payments, and the rent expense related to these leases is recognized on a straight-line basis over this lease term. Prior to fiscal 2005, the Company recognized straight-line rent expense for store leases beginning on the earlier of the rent commencement date or the store opening date, which had the effect of excluding the build-out period of its stores from the calculation of the period over which it expenses rent. During the fourth quarter of fiscal 2005, the Company revised its accounting practices to extend the lease term to include this free rent period prior to the opening of its stores. This revision in practice resulted in a cumulative pre-tax charge of $6,264,000 for leases entered into prior to fiscal 2005, which was not material to any previously reported fiscal year. This cumulative adjustment had no effect on historical or future cash flows from operations or the timing of payments under the related leases. The portion of rent expense applicable to a store before opening is included in selling, general and administrative expenses. Once opened for business, rent expense is included in cost of sales. Certain leases provide for additional rental payments based on a percentage of sales in excess of a specified base. This additional rent is accrued when it appears that the sales will exceed the specified base. Construction allowances received from landlords are initially recorded as lease liabilities and amortized as a reduction of rental expense over the primary lease term. The Company's lease obligations are considered operating leases under SFAS No. 13.

NOTES TO CONSOLIDATED FINANCIAL STATEMENTS — (Continued)

NOTE 5 — PROPERTIES

Properties are summarized as follows at February 25, 2006 and February 26, 2005 (in thousands):

	2006	2005
Land	$ 18,778	$ 19,627
Buildings	95,056	98,184
Equipment, furniture and fixtures	271,702	297,034
Leasehold improvements	217,795	218,006
Computer software	60,208	63,515
Projects in progress	5,673	6,394
	669,212	702,760
Less accumulated depreciation and amortization	370,290	382,622
Properties, net	$298,922	$320,138

NOTE 6 — GOODWILL AND OTHER INTANGIBLE ASSETS

The Company's intangible assets at February 25, 2006 and February 26, 2005 included the right to do business within certain geographical markets where franchise stores were previously granted exclusive rights to operate, favorable operating leases acquired from a third party and goodwill related primarily to the acquisition of Pier 1 Kids. These intangible assets were included in other noncurrent assets in the Company's consolidated balance sheets. Amortization expense for fiscal 2006, 2005 and 2004 was $1,654,000, $1,656,000 and $1,493,000, respectively. The following is a summary of the Company's intangible assets at February 25, 2006 and February 26, 2005 (in thousands):

	2006	2005
Geographic market rights, gross	$ 14,926	$ 15,023
Accumulated amortization	(13,088)	(11,639)
Geographic market rights, net	$ 1,838	$ 3,384
Acquired operating leases, gross	$ 1,615	$ 1,975
Accumulated amortization	(463)	(257)
Acquired operating leases, net	$ 1,152	$ 1,718
Goodwill, not amortized	$ 4,088	$ 4,088

Estimated future amortization expense related to intangible assets at February 25, 2006 is as follows (in thousands):

Fiscal Year	Amortization Expense
2007	$1,530
2008	617
2009	155
2010	153
2011	129
Thereafter	406
Total future amortization expense	$2,990

53

Item 9. *Changes in and Disagreements with Accountants on Accounting and Financial Disclosure.*

None.

Item 9A. *Controls and Procedures.*

REPORT OF MANAGEMENT ON INTERNAL CONTROL OVER FINANCIAL REPORTING

Management is responsible for establishing and maintaining a system of internal control over financial reporting designed to provide reasonable assurance that transactions are executed in accordance with management authorization and that such transactions are properly recorded and reported in the financial statements, and that records are maintained so as to permit preparation of the financial statements in accordance with U.S. generally accepted accounting principles. Because of its inherent limitations, internal control over financial reporting may not prevent or detect misstatements. Management has assessed the effectiveness of the Company's internal control over financial reporting utilizing the criteria set forth by the Committee of Sponsoring Organizations of the Treadway Commission in *Internal Control — Integrated Framework*. Management concluded that based on its assessment, Pier 1 Imports, Inc.'s internal control over financial reporting was effective as of February 25, 2006. Management's assessment of the effectiveness of the Company's internal control over financial reporting as of February 25, 2006 has been audited by Ernst & Young LLP, an independent registered public accounting firm, as stated in their report which is included in this Annual Report on Form 10-K.

/s/   Marvin J. Girouard
_____
Marvin J. Girouard
Chairman of the Board and
Chief Executive Officer

/s/   Charles H. Turner
_____
Charles H. Turner
Executive Vice President, Finance,
Chief Financial Officer and Treasurer

This page intentionally left blank

Appendix C

Time Value of Money: Future Value and Present Value

The following discussion of future value lays the foundation for our explanation of present value in Chapter 8 but is not essential. For the valuation of long-term liabilities, some instructors may wish to begin on page 781 of this appendix.

The term *time value of money* refers to the fact that money earns interest over time. *Interest* is the cost of using money. To borrowers, interest is the expense of renting money. To lenders, interest is the revenue earned from lending. We must always recognize the interest we receive or pay. Otherwise, we overlook an important part of the transaction. Suppose you invest $4,545 in corporate bonds that pay 10% interest each year. After 1 year, the value of your investment has grown to $5,000. The difference between your original investment ($4,545) and the future value of the investment ($5,000) is the amount of interest revenue you will earn during the year ($455). If you ignored the interest, you would fail to account for the interest revenue you have earned. Interest becomes more important as the time period lengthens because the amount of interest depends on the span of time the money is invested.

Let's consider a second example, this time from the borrower's perspective. Suppose you purchase a machine for your business. The cash price of the machine is $8,000, but you cannot pay cash now. To finance the purchase, you sign an $8,000 note payable. The note requires you to pay the $8,000 plus 10% interest 1 year from the date of purchase. Is your cost of the machine $8,000, or is it $8,800 [$8,000 plus interest of $800 ($8,000 × .10)]? The cost is $8,000. The additional $800 is interest expense and not part of the cost of the machine.

Future Value

The main application of future value is the accumulated balance of an investment at a future date. In our first example above, the investment earned 10% per year. After 1 year, $4,545 grew to $5,000, as shown in Exhibit C-1.

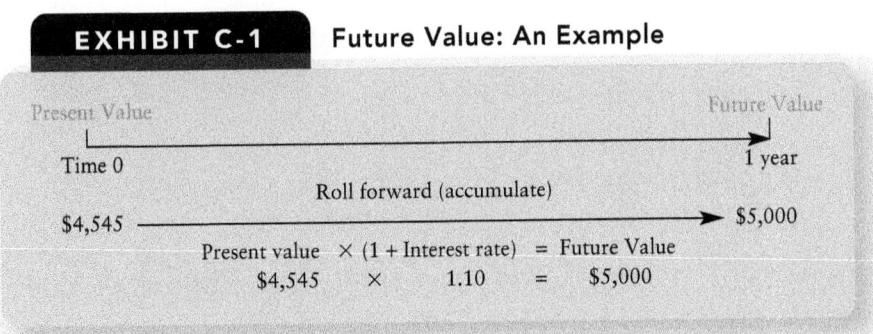

EXHIBIT C-1   Future Value: An Example

Present Value   Future Value
Time 0   1 year
              Roll forward (accumulate)
$4,545 ————————————————————————————→ $5,000
       Present value × (1 + Interest rate) = Future Value
          $4,545   ×   1.10   = $5,000

If the money were invested for 5 years, you would have to perform 5 such calculations. You would also have to consider the compound interest that your investment is earning. *Compound interest* is not only the interest you earn on your principal amount, but also the interest you receive on the interest you have already earned. Most business applications include compound interest. The following table shows the interest revenue earned on the original $4,545 investment each year for 5 years at 10%:

End of Year	Interest	Future Value
0	—	$4,545
1	$4,545 × 0.10 = $455	5,000
2	5,000 × 0.10 = 500	5,500
3	5,500 × 0.10 = 550	6,050
4	6,050 × 0.10 = 605	6,655
5	6,655 × 0.10 = 666	7,321

Earning 10%, a $4,545 investment grows to $5,000 at the end of 1 year, to $5,500 at the end of 2 years, and $7,321 at the end of 5 years. Throughout this appendix we round off to the nearest dollar.

Future-Value Tables

The process of computing a future value is called *accumulating* because the future value is *more* than the present value. Mathematical tables ease the computational burden. Exhibit C-2, Future Value of $1, gives the future value for a single sum (a present value), $1, invested to earn a particular interest rate for a specific number of periods. Future value depends on 3 factors: (1) the amount of the investment, (2) the length of time between investment and future accumulation, and (3) the interest rate. Future-value and present-value tables are based on $1 because unity (the value 1) is so easy to work with.

EXHIBIT C-2 Future Value of $1

Future Value of $1

Periods	4%	5%	6%	7%	8%	9%	10%	12%	14%	16%
1	1.040	1.050	1.060	1.070	1.080	1.090	1.100	1.120	1.140	1.160
2	1.082	1.103	1.124	1.145	1.166	1.188	1.210	1.254	1.300	1.346
3	1.125	1.158	1.191	1.225	1.260	1.295	1.331	1.405	1.482	1.561
4	1.170	1.216	1.262	1.311	1.360	1.412	1.464	1.574	1.689	1.811
5	1.217	1.276	1.338	1.403	1.469	1.539	1.611	1.762	1.925	2.100
6	1.265	1.340	1.419	1.501	1.587	1.677	1.772	1.974	2.195	2.436
7	1.316	1.407	1.504	1.606	1.714	1.828	1.949	2.211	2.502	2.826
8	1.369	1.477	1.594	1.718	1.851	1.993	2.144	2.476	2.853	3.278
9	1.423	1.551	1.689	1.838	1.999	2.172	2.358	2.773	3.252	3.803
10	1.480	1.629	1.791	1.967	2.159	2.367	2.594	3.106	3.707	4.411
11	1.539	1.710	1.898	2.105	2.332	2.580	2.853	3.479	4.226	5.117
12	1.601	1.796	2.012	2.252	2.518	2.813	3.138	3.896	4.818	5.936
13	1.665	1.886	2.133	2.410	2.720	3.066	3.452	4.363	5.492	6.886
14	1.732	1.980	2.261	2.579	2.937	3.342	3.798	4.887	6.261	7.988
15	1.801	2.079	2.397	2.759	3.172	3.642	4.177	5.474	7.138	9.266
16	1.873	2.183	2.540	2.952	3.426	3.970	4.595	6.130	8.137	10.748
17	1.948	2.292	2.693	3.159	3.700	4.328	5.054	6.866	9.276	12.468
18	2.026	2.407	2.854	3.380	3.996	4.717	5.560	7.690	10.575	14.463
19	2.107	2.527	3.026	3.617	4.316	5.142	6.116	8.613	12.056	16.777
20	2.191	2.653	3.207	3.870	4.661	5.604	6.728	9.646	13.743	19.461

In business applications, interest rates are always stated for the annual period of 1 year unless specified otherwise. In fact, an interest rate can be stated for any period, such as 3% per quarter or 5% for a 6-month period. The length of the period is arbitrary. For example, an investment may promise a return (income) of 3% per quarter for 6 months (2 quarters). In that case, you would be working with 3% interest for 2 periods. It would be incorrect to use 6% for 1 period because the interest is 3% compounded quarterly, and that amount differs from 6% compounded semiannually. *Take care in studying future-value and present-value problems to align the interest rate with the appropriate number of periods.*

Let's see how a future-value table like the one in Exhibit C-2 is used. The future value of $1.00 invested at 8% for 1 year is $1.08 ($1.00 × 1.080, which appears at the junction of the 8% column and row 1 in the Periods column). The figure 1.080 includes both the principal (1.000) and the compound interest for 1 period (0.080).

Suppose you deposit $5,000 in a savings account that pays annual interest of 8%. The account balance at the end of 1 year will be $5,400. To compute the future value of $5,000 at 8% for 1 year, multiply $5,000 by 1.080 to get $5,400. Now suppose you invest in a 10-year, 8% certificate of deposit (CD). What will be the future value of the CD at maturity? To compute the future value of $5,000 at 8% for 10 periods, multiply $5,000 by 2.159 (from Exhibit C-2) to get $10,795. This future value of $10,795 indicates that $5,000, earning 8% interest compounded annually, grows to $10,795 at the end of 10 years. Using Exhibit C-2, you can find any present amount's future value at a particular future date. Future value is especially helpful for computing the amount of cash you will have on hand for some purpose in the future.

Future Value of an Annuity

In the preceding example, we made an investment of a single amount. Other investments, called *annuities*, include multiple investments of an equal periodic amount at fixed intervals over the duration of the investment. Consider a family investing for a child's education. The Dietrichs can invest $4,000 annually to accumulate a college fund for 15-year-old Helen. The investment can earn 7% annually until Helen turns 18—a 3-year investment. How much will be available for Helen on the date of the last investment? Exhibit C-3 shows the accumulation—a total future value of $12,860.

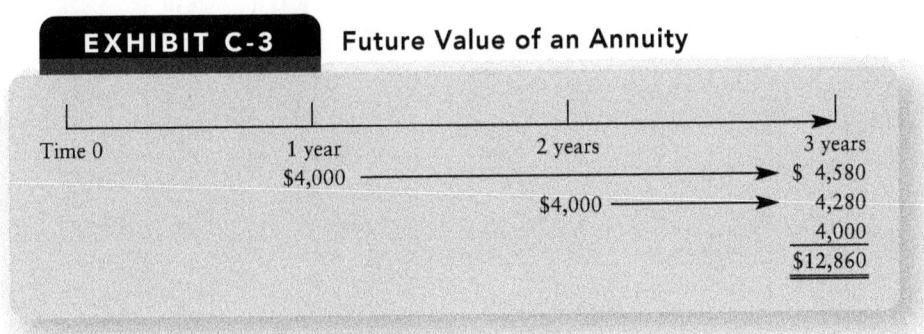

EXHIBIT C-3 **Future Value of an Annuity**

Time 0	1 year	2 years	3 years
	$4,000 ⟶		$ 4,580
		$4,000 ⟶	4,280
			4,000
			$12,860

The first $4,000 invested by the Dietrichs grows to $4,580 over the investment period. The second amount grows to $4,280, and the third amount stays at $4,000 because it has no time to earn interest. The sum of the 3 future values

($4,580 + $4,280 + $4,000) is the future value of the annuity ($12,860), which can also be computed as follows:

End of Year	Annual Investment	Interest	Increase for the Year	Future Value of Annuity
0	—	—	—	0
1	$4,000	—	$4,000	$ 4,000
2	4,000	+ ($4,000 × 0.07 = $280) =	4,280	8,280
3	4,000	+ ($8,280 × 0.07 = $580) =	4,580	12,860

These computations are laborious. As with the Future Value of $1 (a lump sum), mathematical tables ease the strain of calculating annuities. Exhibit C-4, Future Value of Annuity of $1, gives the future value of a series of investments, each of equal amount, at regular intervals.

What is the future value of an annuity of 3 investments of $1 each that earn 7%? The answer, 3.215, can be found at the junction of the 7% column and row 3 in Exhibit C-4. This amount can be used to compute the future value of the investment for Helen's education, as follows:

Amount of each periodic investment	×	Future value of annuity of $1 (Exhibit C-4)	×	Future value of investment
$4,000	×	3.215	×	$12,860

EXHIBIT C-4   Future Value of Annuity of $1

Future Value of Annuity of $1

Periods	4%	5%	6%	7%	8%	9%	10%	12%	14%	16%
1	1.000	1.000	1.000	1.000	1.000	1.000	1.000	1.000	1.000	1.000
2	2.040	2.050	2.060	2.070	2.080	2.090	2.100	2.120	2.140	2.160
3	3.122	3.153	3.184	3.215	3.246	3.278	3.310	3.374	3.440	3.506
4	4.246	4.310	4.375	4.440	4.506	4.573	4.641	4.779	4.921	5.066
5	5.416	5.526	5.637	5.751	5.867	5.985	6.105	6.353	6.610	6.877
6	6.633	6.802	6.975	7.153	7.336	7.523	7.716	8.115	8.536	8.977
7	7.898	8.142	8.394	8.654	8.923	9.200	9.487	10.089	10.730	11.414
8	9.214	9.549	9.897	10.260	10.637	11.028	11.436	12.300	13.233	14.240
9	10.583	11.027	11.491	11.978	12.488	13.021	13.579	14.776	16.085	17.519
10	12.006	12.578	13.181	13.816	14.487	15.193	15.937	17.549	19.337	21.321
11	13.486	14.207	14.972	15.784	16.645	17.560	18.531	20.655	23.045	25.733
12	15.026	15.917	16.870	17.888	18.977	20.141	21.384	24.133	27.271	30.850
13	16.627	17.713	18.882	20.141	21.495	22.953	24.523	28.029	32.089	36.786
14	18.292	19.599	21.015	22.550	24.215	26.019	27.975	32.393	37.581	43.672
15	20.024	21.579	23.276	25.129	27.152	29.361	31.772	37.280	43.842	51.660
16	21.825	23.657	25.673	27.888	30.324	33.003	35.950	42.753	50.980	60.925
17	23.698	25.840	28.213	30.840	33.750	36.974	40.545	48.884	59.118	71.673
18	25.645	28.132	30.906	33.999	37.450	41.301	45.599	55.750	68.394	84.141
19	27.671	30.539	33.760	37.379	41.446	46.018	51.159	63.440	78.969	98.603
20	29.778	33.066	36.786	40.995	45.762	51.160	57.275	72.052	91.025	115.380

This one-step calculation is much easier than computing the future value of each annual investment and then summing the individual future values. In this way, you can compute the future value of any investment consisting of equal periodic amounts at regular intervals. Businesses make periodic investments to accumulate funds for equipment replacement and other uses—an application of the future value of an annuity.

Present Value

Often a person knows a future amount and needs to know the related present value. Recall Exhibit C-1, in which present value and future value are on opposite ends of the same time line. Suppose an investment promises to pay you $5,000 at the *end* of 1 year. How much would you pay *now* to acquire this investment? You would be willing to pay the present value of the $5,000 future amount.

Like future value, present value depends on 3 factors: (1) the *amount of payment* (*or receipt*), (2) the length of *time* between investment and future receipt (or *payment*), and (3) the *interest rate*. The process of computing a present value is called *discounting* because the present value is *less* than the future value.

In our investment example, the future receipt is $5,000. The investment period is 1 year. Assume that you demand an annual interest rate of 10% on your investment. With all 3 factors specified, you can compute the present value of $5,000 at 10% for 1 year:

$$\text{Present value} = \frac{\text{Future value}}{1 + \text{Interest rate}} = \frac{\$5,000}{1.10} = \$4,545$$

By turning the data around into a future-value problem, we can verify the present-value computation:

Amount invested (present value)	$4,545
Expected earnings ($4,545 × 0.10)	455
Amount to be received one year from now (future value)	$5,000

This example illustrates that present value and future value are based on the same equation:

$$\text{Future value} = \text{Present value} \times (1 + \text{Interest rate})$$
$$\text{Present value} = \frac{\text{Future value}}{1 + \text{Interest rate}}$$

If the $5,000 is to be received 2 years from now, you will pay only $4,132 for the investment, as shown in Exhibit C-5. By turning the data around, we verify that $4,132 accumulates to $5,000 at 10% for 2 years:

Amount invested (present value)	$4,132
Expected earnings for first year ($4,132 × 0.10)	413
Value of investment after 1 year	4,545
Expected earnings for second year ($4,545 × 0.10)	455
Amount to be received 2 years from now (future value)	$5,000

You would pay $4,132—the present value of $5,000—to receive the $5,000 future amount at the end of 2 years at 10% per year. The $868 difference between the amount invested ($4,132) and the amount to be received ($5,000) is the return on the investment, the sum of the 2 interest receipts: $413 + $455 = $868.

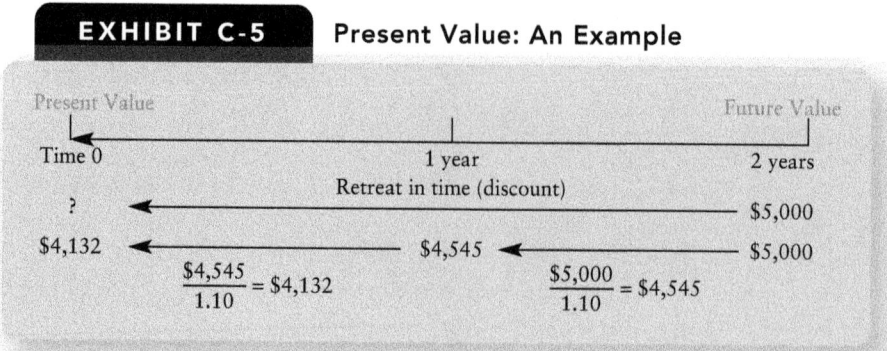

EXHIBIT C-5   Present Value: An Example

Present-Value Tables

We have shown the simple formula for computing present value. However, figuring present value "by hand" for investments spanning many years is time-consuming and presents too many opportunities for arithmetic errors. Present-value tables ease our work. Let's reexamine our examples of present value by using Exhibit C-6, Present Value of $1, given below.

EXHIBIT C-6   Present Value of $1

Present Value of $1

Periods	4%	5%	6%	7%	8%	10%	12%	14%	16%
1	0.962	0.952	0.943	0.935	0.926	0.909	0.893	0.877	0.862
2	0.925	0.907	0.890	0.873	0.857	0.826	0.797	0.769	0.743
3	0.889	0.864	0.840	0.816	0.794	0.751	0.712	0.675	0.641
4	0.855	0.823	0.792	0.763	0.735	0.683	0.636	0.592	0.552
5	0.822	0.784	0.747	0.713	0.681	0.621	0.567	0.519	0.476
6	0.790	0.746	0.705	0.666	0.630	0.564	0.507	0.456	0.410
7	0.760	0.711	0.665	0.623	0.583	0.513	0.452	0.400	0.354
8	0.731	0.677	0.627	0.582	0.540	0.467	0.404	0.351	0.305
9	0.703	0.645	0.592	0.544	0.500	0.424	0.361	0.308	0.263
10	0.676	0.614	0.558	0.508	0.463	0.386	0.322	0.270	0.227
11	0.650	0.585	0.527	0.475	0.429	0.350	0.287	0.237	0.195
12	0.625	0.557	0.497	0.444	0.397	0.319	0.257	0.208	0.168
13	0.601	0.530	0.469	0.415	0.368	0.290	0.229	0.182	0.145
14	0.577	0.505	0.442	0.388	0.340	0.263	0.205	0.160	0.125
15	0.555	0.481	0.417	0.362	0.315	0.239	0.183	0.140	0.108
16	0.534	0.458	0.394	0.339	0.292	0.218	0.163	0.123	0.093
17	0.513	0.436	0.371	0.317	0.270	0.198	0.146	0.108	0.080
18	0.494	0.416	0.350	0.296	0.250	0.180	0.130	0.095	0.069
19	0.475	0.396	0.331	0.277	0.232	0.164	0.116	0.083	0.060
20	0.456	0.377	0.312	0.258	0.215	0.149	0.104	0.073	0.051

For the 10% investment for 1 year, we find the junction of the 10% column and row 1 in Exhibit C-6. The figure 0.909 is computed as follows: 1/1.10 = 0.909. This work has been done for us, and only the present values are given in the table. To figure the present value for $5,000, we multiply 0.909 by $5,000. The result is $4,545, which matches the result we obtained by hand.

For the 2-year investment, we read down the 10% column and across row 2. We multiply 0.826 (computed as 0.909/1.10 = 0.826) by $5,000 and get $4,130, which confirms our earlier computation of $4,132 (the difference is due to rounding in the present-value table). Using the table, we can compute the present value of any single future amount.

Present Value of an Annuity

Return to the investment example near the bottom of page 781 of this appendix. That investment provided the investor with only a single future receipt ($5,000 at the end of 2 years). *Annuity investments* provide multiple receipts of an equal amount at fixed intervals over the investment's duration.

Consider an investment that promises *annual* cash receipts of $10,000 to be received at the end of 3 years. Assume that you demand a 12% return on your investment. What is the investment's present value? That is, what would you pay today to acquire the investment? The investment spans 3 periods, and you would pay the sum of 3 present values. The computation follows.

Year	Annual Cash Receipt	Present Value of $1 at 12% (Exhibit C-6)	Present Value of Annual Cash Receipt
1	$10,000	0.893	$ 8,930
2	10,000	0.797	7,970
3	10,000	0.712	7,120
Total present value of investment...............			$24,020

The present value of this annuity is $24,020. By paying this amount today, you will receive $10,000 at the end of each of the 3 years while earning 12% on your investment.

This example illustrates repetitive computations of the 3 future amounts, a time-consuming process. One way to ease the computational burden is to add the 3 present values of $1 (0.893 + 0.797 + 0.712) and multiply their sum (2.402) by the annual cash receipt ($10,000) to obtain the present value of the annuity ($10,000 × 2.402 = $24,020).

An easier approach is to use a present-value-of-an-annuity table. Exhibit C-7 shows the present value of $1 to be received periodically for a given number of periods. The present value of a 3-period annuity at 12% is 2.402 (the junction of row 3 and the 12% column). Thus, $10,000 received annually at the end of each of 3 years, discounted at 12%, is $24,020 ($10,000 × 2.402), which is the present value.

EXHIBIT C-7   Present Value of Annuity of $1

Present Value of Annuity of $1

Periods	4%	5%	6%	7%	8%	10%	12%	14%	16%
1	0.962	0.952	0.943	0.935	0.926	0.909	0.893	0.877	0.862
2	1.886	1.859	1.833	1.808	1.783	1.736	1.690	1.647	1.605
3	2.775	2.723	2.673	2.624	2.577	2.487	2.402	2.322	2.246
4	3.630	3.546	3.465	3.387	3.312	3.170	3.037	2.914	2.798
5	4.452	4.329	4.212	4.100	3.993	3.791	3.605	3.433	3.274
6	5.242	5.076	4.917	4.767	4.623	4.355	4.111	3.889	3.685
7	6.002	5.786	5.582	5.389	5.206	4.868	4.564	4.288	4.039
8	6.733	6.463	6.210	5.971	5.747	5.335	4.968	4.639	4.344
9	7.435	7.108	6.802	6.515	6.247	5.759	5.328	4.946	4.608
10	8.111	7.722	7.360	7.024	6.710	6.145	5.650	5.216	4.833
11	8.760	8.306	7.887	7.499	7.139	6.495	5.938	5.453	5.029
12	9.385	8.863	8.384	7.943	7.536	6.814	6.194	5.660	5.197
13	9.986	9.394	8.853	8.358	7.904	7.103	6.424	5.842	5.342
14	10.563	9.899	9.295	8.745	8.244	7.367	6.628	6.002	5.468
15	11.118	10.380	9.712	9.108	8.559	7.606	6.811	6.142	5.575
16	11.652	10.838	10.106	9.447	8.851	7.824	6.974	6.265	5.669
17	12.166	11.274	10.477	9.763	9.122	8.022	7.120	6.373	5.749
18	12.659	11.690	10.828	10.059	9.372	8.201	7.250	6.467	5.818
19	13.134	12.085	11.158	10.336	9.604	8.365	7.366	6.550	5.877
20	13.590	12.462	11.470	10.594	9.818	8.514	7.469	6.623	5.929

Present Value of Bonds Payable

The present value of a bond—its market price—is the present value of the future principal amount at maturity plus the present value of the future stated interest payments. The principal is a *single amount* to be paid at maturity. The interest is an *annuity* because it occurs periodically.

Let's compute the present value of the assumed 9% 5-year bonds of **Southwest Airlines** (discussed on pages 432–433). The face value of the bonds is $100,000, and they pay 4½% stated (cash) interest semiannually (that is, twice a year).[1] At issuance, the market interest rate is expressed as 10% annually, but it is computed at 5% semiannually. Therefore, the effective interest rate for each of the 10 semiannual periods is 5%. We thus use 5% in computing the present value (PV) of the maturity and of the interest. The market price of these bonds is $96,149, as follows:

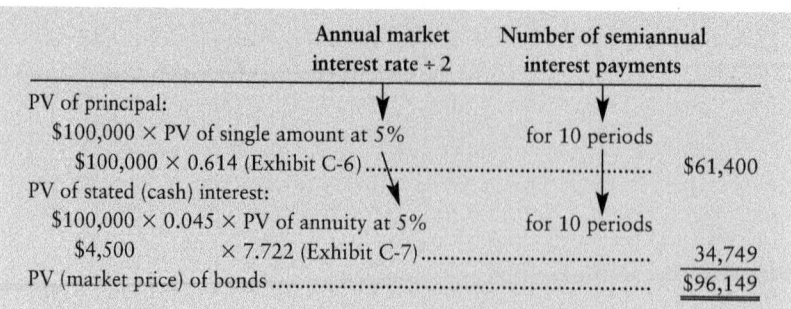

The market price of the Southwest bonds shows a discount because the contract interest rate on the bonds (9%) is less than the market interest rate (10%). We discuss these bonds in more detail on pages 428–439.

Let's consider a premium price for the 9% Southwest bonds. Assume that the market interest rate is 8% (rather than 10%) at issuance. The effective interest rate is thus 4% for each of the 10 semiannual periods:

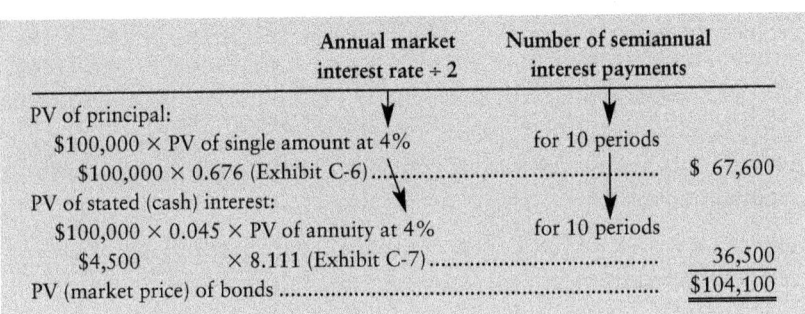

	Annual market interest rate ÷ 2	Number of semiannual interest payments	
PV of principal:			
$100,000 × PV of single amount at 4%		for 10 periods	
$100,000 × 0.676 (Exhibit C-6)			$ 67,600
PV of stated (cash) interest:			
$100,000 × 0.045 × PV of annuity at 4%		for 10 periods	
$4,500 × 8.111 (Exhibit C-7)			36,500
PV (market price) of bonds			$104,100

We discuss accounting for these bonds on pages 436–439. It may be helpful for you to reread this section ("Present Value of Bonds Payable") after you've studied those pages.

Capital Leases

How does a lessee compute the cost of an asset acquired through a capital lease? (See page 446 for the definition of *capital leases*.) Consider that the lessee gets the use of the asset but does *not* pay for the leased asset in full at the beginning of the lease. A capital lease is therefore similar to an installment purchase of the leased asset. The lessee must record the leased asset at the present value of the lease liability. The time value of money must be weighed.

The cost of the asset to the lessee is the sum of any payment made at the beginning of the lease period plus the present value of the future lease payments. The lease payments are equal amounts occurring at regular intervals—that is, they are annuity payments.

Consider a 20-year building lease that requires 20 annual payments of $10,000 each, with the first payment due immediately. The interest rate in the lease is 10%, and the present value of the 19 future payments is $83,650 ($10,000 × PV of annuity at 10% for 19 periods, or 8.365 from Exhibit C-7). The lessee's cost of the building is $93,650 (the sum of the initial payment, $10,000, plus the present value of the future payments, $83,650). The lessee would base its accounting for the leased asset (and the related depreciation) and for the lease liability (and the related interest expense) on the cost of the building that we have just computed.

Appendix Problems

PC-1. For each situation, compute the required amount.
a. **Kellogg Corporation** is budgeting for the acquisition of land over the next several years. Kellogg can invest $100,000 today at 9%. How much cash will Kellogg have for land acquisitions at the end of 5 years? At the end of 6 years?
b. Davidson, Inc., is planning to invest $50,000 each year for 5 years. The company's investment adviser believes that Davidson can earn 6% interest without taking on too much risk. What will be the value of Davidson's investment on the date of the last deposit if Davidson can earn 6%? If Davidson can earn 8%?

PC-2. For each situation, compute the required amount.
a. **Intel Corporation** operations are generating excess cash that will be invested in a special fund. During 20X2, Intel invests $5,643,341 in the fund for a planned advertising campaign on a new product to be released 6 years later, in 20X8. If

Intel's investments can earn 10% each year, how much cash will the company have for the advertising campaign in 20X8?

b. Intel will need $10 million to advertise a new type of chip in 20X8. How much must Intel invest in 20X2 to have the cash available for the advertising campaign? Intel's investments can earn 10% annually.

c. Explain the relationship between your answers to *a* and *b*.

PC-3. Determine the present value of the following notes and bonds:

1. Ten-year bonds payable with maturity value of $500,000 and stated interest rate of 12%, paid semiannually. The market rate of interest is 12% at issuance.
2. Same bonds payable as in number 1, but the market interest rate is 14%.
3. Same bonds payable as in number 1, but the market interest rate is 10%.

PC-4. On December 31, 20X1, when the market interest rate is 8%. Libby, Libby, & Short, a partnership, issues $400,000 of 10-year, 7.25% bonds payable. The bonds pay interest semiannually.

❙ Required

1. Determine the present value of the bonds at issuance.
2. Assume that the bonds are issued at the price computed in Requirement 1. Prepare an effective-interest-method amortization table for the first 2 semiannual interest periods. (p. 433)
3. Using the amortization table prepared in Requirement 2, journalize issuance of the bonds and the first 2 interest payments and amortization of the bonds. (p. 431–436)

PC-5. St. Mere Eglise Children's Home needs a fleet of vans to transport the children to singing engagements throughout Normandy. **Renault** offers the vehicles for a single payment of 630,000 euros due at the end of 4 years. **Peugeot** prices a similar fleet of vans for 4 annual payments of 150,000 euros at the end of each year. The children's home could borrow the funds at 6%, so this is the appropriate interest rate. Which company should get the business, Renault or Peugeot? Base your decision on present value, and give your reason.

PC-6. American Family Association acquired equipment under a capital lease that requires 6 annual lease payments of $40,000. The first payment is due when the lease begins, on January 1, 20X6. Future payments are due on January 1 of each year of the lease term. The interest rate in the lease is 16%.

❙ Required

Compute the association's cost of the equipment. (p. 446)

Answers

PC-1	a. 5 yrs. $153,900		
	6 yrs. $167,700		
	b. 6% $281,850		
	8% $293,350		
PC-2	a. $10,000,000		
	b. $5,640,000		
PC-3	1. $500,100	2. $446,820	3. $562,360
PC-4	1. $379,455	2. Bond	
	carry. amt. at 12-31-X2 $380,838		
PC-5	Renault PV €498,960		
	Peugeot PV €519,750		
PC-6	Cost $170,960		

Pages 787–788 intentionally omitted

Appendix E

Summary of Generally Accepted Accounting Principles (GAAP)

Every technical area has professional associations and regulatory bodies that govern the practice of the profession. Accounting is no exception. In the United States, generally accepted accounting principles (GAAP) are influenced most by the Financial Accounting Standards Board (FASB). The FASB has 7 full-time members and a large staff. Its financial support comes from professional associations such as the American Institute of Certified Public Accountants (AICPA).

The FASB is an independent organization with no government or professional affiliation. The FASB's pronouncements, called *Statements of Financial Accounting Standards*, specify how to account for certain business transactions. Each new *Standard* becomes part of GAAP, the "accounting law of the land." In the same way that our laws draw authority from their acceptance by the people, GAAP depends on general acceptance by the business community. Throughout this book, we refer to GAAP as the proper way to do financial accounting.

The U.S. Congress has given the Securities and Exchange Commission (SEC), a government organization that regulates the trading of investments, ultimate responsibility for establishing accounting rules for companies that are owned by the general investing public. However, the SEC has delegated much of its rule-making power to the FASB. Exhibit E-1 outlines the flow of authority for developing GAAP.

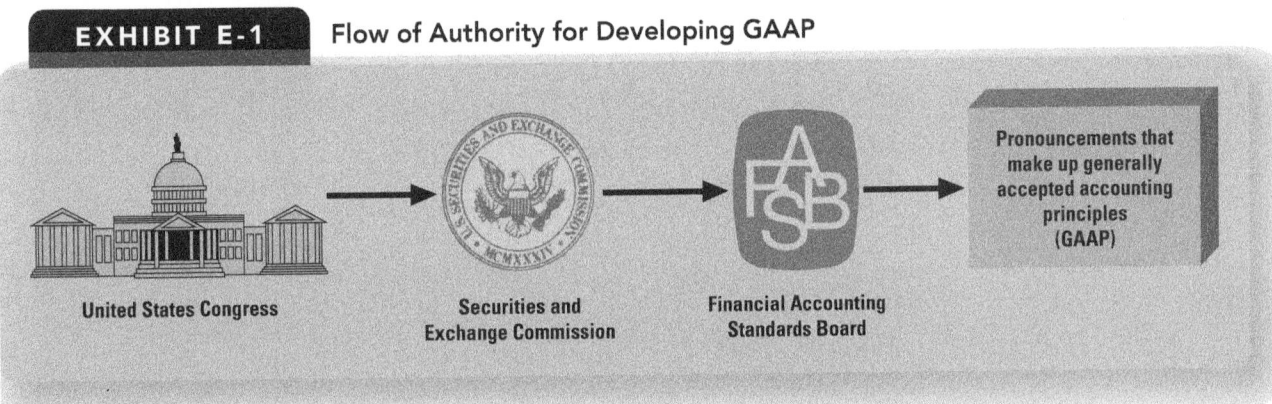

EXHIBIT E-1 Flow of Authority for Developing GAAP

United States Congress

Securities and Exchange Commission

Financial Accounting Standards Board

Pronouncements that make up generally accepted accounting principles (GAAP)

The Objective of Financial Reporting

The basic objective of financial reporting is to provide information that is useful in making investment and lending decisions. The FASB believes that accounting information can be useful in decision making only if it is *relevant, reliable, comparable*, and *consistent*.

Relevant information is useful in making predictions and for evaluating past performance—that is, the information has feedback value. For example, PepsiCo's disclosure of the profitability of each of its lines of business is relevant for investor evaluations of the company. To be relevant, information must be timely. *Reliable* information is free from significant error—that is, it has validity. Also, it is free from the bias of a particular viewpoint—that is, it is verifiable and neutral. *Comparable* and *consistent* information can be compared from period to period to help investors and creditors track the entity's progress through time. These characteristics combine to shape the concepts and principles that make up GAAP. Exhibit E-2 summarizes the concepts and principles that accounting has developed to provide useful information for decision making.

EXHIBIT E-2 Summary of Important Accounting Concepts, Principles, and Financial Statements

Concepts, Principles, and Financial Statements	Quick Summary	Text Reference
Concepts		
Entity concept	Accounting draws a boundary around each organization to be accounted for.	Chapter 1, page 8
Going-concern concept	Accountants assume the business will continue operating for the foreseeable future.	Chapter 1, page 9
Stable-monetary-unit concept	Accounting information is expressed primarily in monetary terms that ignore the effects of inflation.	Chapter 1, page 9
Time-period concept	Ensures that accounting information is reported at regular intervals.	Chapter 3, page 128
Conservatism concept	Accountants report items in the financial statements in a way that avoids overstating assets, owners' equity, and revenues and avoids understating liabilities and expenses.	
Materiality concept	Accountants perform strictly proper accounting only for items that are significant to the company's financial statements.	
Principles		
Reliability (objective) principle	Accounting records and statements are based on the most reliable data available.	Chapter 1, page 8
Cost principle	Assets and services, revenues and expenses are recorded at their actual historical cost.	Chapter 1, page 9
Revenue principle	Tells accountants when to record revenue (only after it has been earned) and the amount of revenue to record (the cash value of what has been received).	Chapter 3, page 128
Matching principle	Directs accountants to (1) identify and measure all expenses incurred during the period and (2) match the expenses against the revenues earned during the period. The goal is to measure net income.	Chapter 3, page 129
Consistency principle	Businesses should use the same accounting methods from period to period.	
Disclosure principle	A company's financial statements should report enough information for outsiders to make informed decisions about the company.	
Financial Statements		
Balance sheet	Assets = Liabilities + Owners' Equity at a point in time.	Chapter 1
Income statement	Revenues and gains − Expenses and losses = Net income or net loss for the period.	Chapter 1
Statement of cash flows	Cash receipts − Cash payments = Increase or decrease in cash during the period, grouped under operating, investing, and financing activities.	Chapters 1 and 12
Statement of retained earnings	Beginning retained earnings + Net income (or − Net loss) − Dividends = Ending retained earnings.	Chapter 1
Statement of stockholders' equity	Shows the reason for the change in each stockholders' equity account, including retained earnings.	
Financial statement notes	Provide information that cannot be reported conveniently on the face of the financial statements. The notes are an integral part of the statements.	

HH APPENDIX E

This page intentionally left blank

Taken from *Managerial Accounting*, First Edition, by Linda Smith Bamber, Karen Wilken Braun, and Walter T. Harrison, Jr.

1 Introduction to Managerial Accounting

In 1988, Outback Steakhouse's cofounders decided to create a chain of four or five restaurants that would generate enough income to let them have a nice lifestyle, stay in the Tampa Bay area, and play golf. That was then; this is now. Outback Steakhouse Inc., currently owns over 900 steakhouses that operate in all 50 states and in 20 different countries. Outback also owns six other restaurant brands, including Carrabba's Italian Grill. Annual sales have topped $3.2 billion, and operating income is over $252 million. How did Outback become so successful? Part of the answer is managerial accounting. Outback won't invest in a new restaurant location unless the projected annual sales are at least double the initial cost of the

location's property, improvements, and equipment. Outback motivates restaurant managers by requiring them to buy into the property for $25,000 and sign a five-year contract. In exchange, the manager receives an annual base salary of $45,000 plus 10% of the location's cash flow, resulting in an average pay of $118,000. Outback's founders also decided that the cost of replacing overworked managers and employees would exceed profits from lunchtime business. So, they bucked the industry trend and open only for dinner. As a result, managers have incentives to ensure their restaurant is profitable and employee turnover is far lower than industry standards.

Sources: "Bounce of the Kangaroo," *Maddux Business Report,* September 2004, pp. 18–23; www.outbacksteakhouse.com; "Inside Outback," *Nation's Restaurant News,* March 27, 1995, pp. 51–69. ▪

Learning Objectives

1 Identify managers' four primary responsibilities

2 Distinguish financial accounting from managerial accounting

3 Describe organizational structure and the roles and skills required of management accountants within the organization

4 Describe the role of the Institute of Management Accountants (IMA) and use its ethical standards to make reasonable ethical judgments

5 Discuss trends in the business environment

6 Use cost-benefit analysis to make business decisions

As the Outback story shows, managers use accounting information for much more than preparing annual financial statements. They use managerial accounting (or management accounting) information to guide their actions and decisions, such as building a new restaurant. In this chapter, we'll introduce managerial accounting and discuss how managers use it to fulfill their duties. We will also explore how managerial accounting differs from financial accounting. Finally, we will discuss the business environment in which today's managers and management accountants operate.

Managerial Accounting: Information for Managers

1 Identify managers' four primary responsibilities

As you will see throughout the book, managerial accounting is very different from financial accounting. Financial accounting focuses on providing stockholders and creditors with the information they need to make investment and lending decisions. This information takes the form of financial statements: the balance sheet, income

BBH CHAPTER 1

statement, statement of shareholders' equity, and statement of cash flows. Managerial accounting focuses on providing internal management with the information it needs to run the company efficiently and effectively. This information takes many forms depending on management's needs.

To understand the kind of information managers need, let's first look at their primary responsibilities.

Managers' Four Primary Responsibilities

Managerial accounting helps managers fulfill their four primary responsibilities, as shown in Exhibit 1-1: planning, directing, controlling, and decision making.

- **Planning** involves setting goals and objectives for the company and determining how to achieve them. For example, one of Outback's goals is to generate more sales. One strategy to achieve this goal is to open more restaurants, so management may plan to build and begin operating 25 new steakhouses next year. Managerial accounting translates these plans into **budgets**—the quantitative expression of a plan. Management analyzes the budgets before proceeding to determine whether its expansion plans make financial sense.

- **Directing** means overseeing the company's day-to-day operations. Management uses product cost reports, product sales information, and other managerial accounting reports to run daily business operations. Outback uses product sales data to determine which menu items are generating the most sales and then uses that information to adjust menus and marketing strategies.

- **Controlling** means evaluating the results of business operations against the plan and making adjustments to keep the company pressing toward its goals. Outback uses performance reports to compare each restaurant's actual performance against budget and then uses that *feedback* to take corrective actions if needed. If actual costs are higher than planned or actual sales are lower than planned, management may revise its plans or adjust operations. Perhaps the newly opened steakhouses are not generating as much income as budgeted. As a result, management may decide to increase local advertising to increase sales.

EXHIBIT 1-1   **Managers' Four Primary Responsibilities**

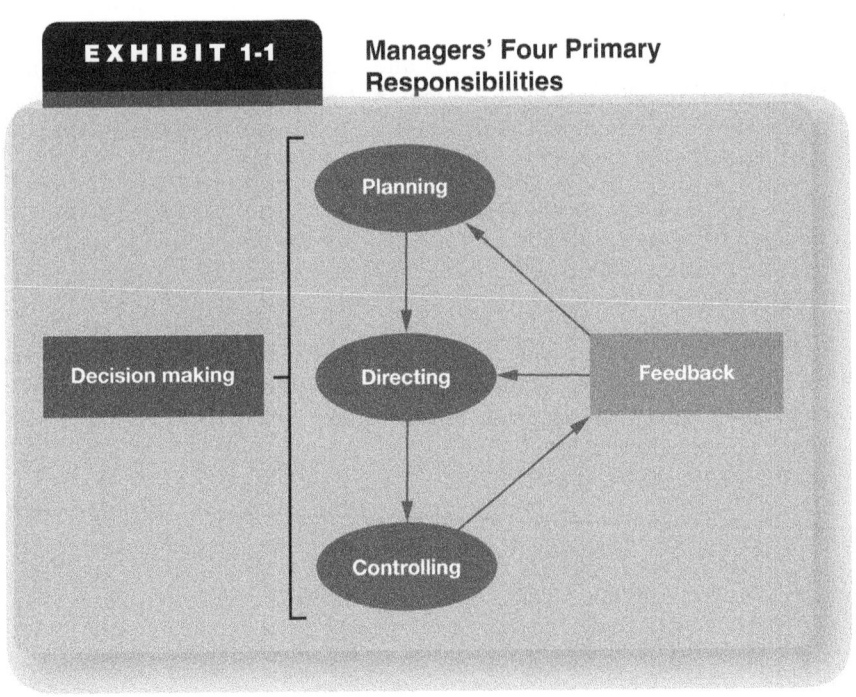

- Management is continually **making decisions** while it plans, directs, and controls operations. Outback must decide where to open new restaurants, which restaurants to refurnish, what prices to set for meals, what entrees to offer, and so forth. Because Outback is in business to generate profits for its stockholders, management must consider the financial impact of each of these decisions. Managerial accounting gathers, summarizes, and reports cost and revenue data relevant to each of these decisions.

A Road Map: How Does Managerial Accounting Fit In?

This book will show you how managerial accounting information helps managers fulfill their responsibilities. The rest of the text is organized around the following themes:

1. **Managerial Accounting Building Blocks**   Chapter 1 helps you understand more about the management accounting profession and today's business environment. Chapter 2 teaches you some of the language that is commonly used in managerial accounting. Just as musicians must know the notes to the musical scale, management accountants *and* managers must understand managerial accounting terms to effectively use managerial accounting information to run the business.

2. **Determining Unit Cost (Product Costing)**   How does a company decide how high to set its prices? It must first figure out how much it costs to make its product or deliver its service. Outback must calculate the cost of each item on the menu to set prices high enough to cover costs and generate a profit. This is tougher than it sounds. Outback's cost to prepare each meal includes more than just the cost of the ingredients. Outback's cost also includes the chefs' and servers' wages and benefits, restaurant lease payments, property taxes, utilities, business and alcohol licenses, and so forth. Chapter 5 discusses how businesses determine their product costs. Once management knows its product costs, it uses that information for decision making, planning, directing, and controlling.

3. **Making Decisions**   Before Outback opened any restaurants, management determined how many meals it would have to serve just to break even—that is, just to cover costs. Management had to understand how costs behave before it could calculate a *breakeven* point. Chapters 6 and 7 discuss how costs behave, how to determine a breakeven point, and how managers use cost behavior knowledge to make good decisions and accurate forecasts. Then, Chapter 8 walks you through some very common business decisions, such as *outsourcing* and pricing. For example, should Outback outsource its desserts—that is, have another company make them? Many restaurants do.

4. **Planning**   Budgets are management's primary tool for expressing its plans. Chapter 10 discusses all of the components of the *master budget* and the way a large company like Outback rolls its 900-plus steakhouse budgets into one corporate budget.

5. **Controlling and Evaluating**   Management uses *budget variances*—the difference between actual costs and the budget—to control operations. Chapters 10 and 11 show how management uses variance analysis to determine how and where to adjust operations.

Managerial Accounting Versus Financial Accounting

Managerial accounting information differs from financial accounting information in many respects. Exhibit 1-2 summarizes these differences. Take a few minutes to study the exhibit, and then we'll apply it to Outback.

EXHIBIT 1-2   **Managerial Accounting Versus Financial Accounting**

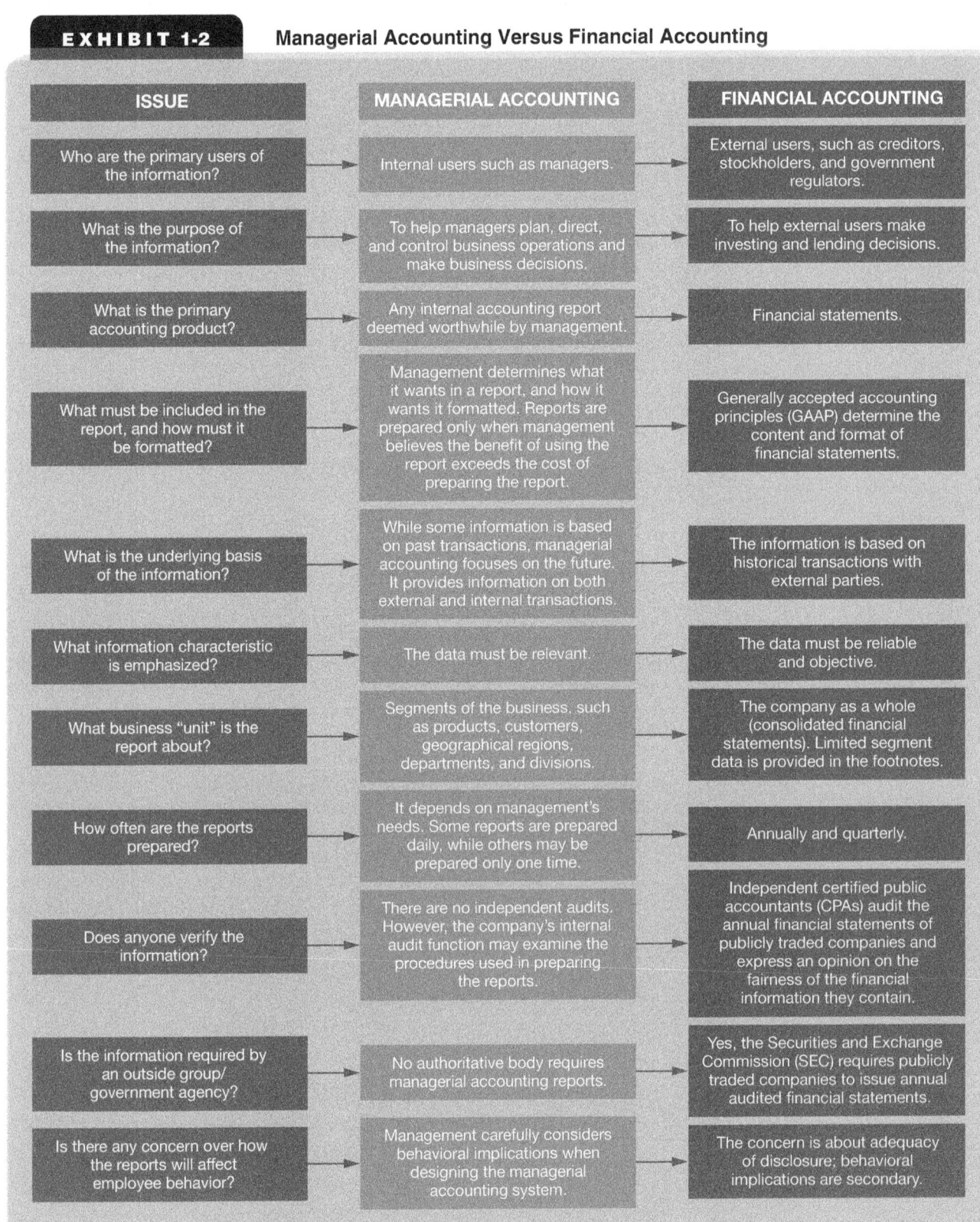

ISSUE	MANAGERIAL ACCOUNTING	FINANCIAL ACCOUNTING
Who are the primary users of the information?	Internal users such as managers.	External users, such as creditors, stockholders, and government regulators.
What is the purpose of the information?	To help managers plan, direct, and control business operations and make business decisions.	To help external users make investing and lending decisions.
What is the primary accounting product?	Any internal accounting report deemed worthwhile by management.	Financial statements.
What must be included in the report, and how must it be formatted?	Management determines what it wants in a report, and how it wants it formatted. Reports are prepared only when management believes the benefit of using the report exceeds the cost of preparing the report.	Generally accepted accounting principles (GAAP) determine the content and format of financial statements.
What is the underlying basis of the information?	While some information is based on past transactions, managerial accounting focuses on the future. It provides information on both external and internal transactions.	The information is based on historical transactions with external parties.
What information characteristic is emphasized?	The data must be relevant.	The data must be reliable and objective.
What business "unit" is the report about?	Segments of the business, such as products, customers, geographical regions, departments, and divisions.	The company as a whole (consolidated financial statements). Limited segment data is provided in the footnotes.
How often are the reports prepared?	It depends on management's needs. Some reports are prepared daily, while others may be prepared only one time.	Annually and quarterly.
Does anyone verify the information?	There are no independent audits. However, the company's internal audit function may examine the procedures used in preparing the reports.	Independent certified public accountants (CPAs) audit the annual financial statements of publicly traded companies and express an opinion on the fairness of the financial information they contain.
Is the information required by an outside group/government agency?	No authoritative body requires managerial accounting reports.	Yes, the Securities and Exchange Commission (SEC) requires publicly traded companies to issue annual audited financial statements.
Is there any concern over how the reports will affect employee behavior?	Management carefully considers behavioral implications when designing the managerial accounting system.	The concern is about adequacy of disclosure; behavioral implications are secondary.

Outback is a publicly traded company, so its financial accounting system must generate consolidated financial statements, in accordance with generally accepted accounting principles (GAAP), on an annual and quarterly basis. The annual financial statements, which are audited by independent certified public accountants (CPAs), objectively summarize the transactions that occurred between Outback and external parties during the previous year. Outback's financial statements are useful to its investors and creditors, but they do not provide management with enough information to run the company effectively.

Outback's managerial accounting system is designed to provide its managers with the accounting information they need to plan, direct, control and make decisions. There are no GAAP-type standards, or audits required, for managerial accounting. Outback's managers tailor the company's managerial accounting system to provide the information they need to help them make better decisions. Outback must weigh the benefits of the system (information that helps the company make decisions that increase profits) against the costs to develop and run the system. The costs and benefits of any particular managerial accounting system differ from one company to another. Different companies create different systems, so Outback's system will differ from Nissan's system.

In contrast to financial statements, most managerial accounting reports focus on the *future*, providing *relevant* information that helps managers make profitable business decisions. For example, before putting their plans into action, Outback's managers determine if their plans make sense by quantitatively expressing them in the form of budgets. Outback's managerial accounting reports may also plan for and reflect *internal* transactions, such as the daily movement of beverages and dry ingredients from central warehouses to individual restaurant locations.

To make good decisions, Outback's managers need information about smaller units of the company, not just the company as a whole. For example, management uses revenue and cost data on individual restaurants, geographical regions, and individual menu items to increase the company's profitability. Regional data helps Outback's management decide where to open more restaurants. Sales and profit reports on individual menu items help management choose menu items and decide what items to offer on a seasonal basis. Rather than preparing these reports just once a year, companies prepare and revise managerial accounting reports as often as needed. For example, Outback revises its budget when new menu items and additional restaurant locations are added.

When designing the managerial accounting system, management must carefully consider how the system will affect employees' behavior. Employees try to perform well on the parts of their jobs that the accounting system measures. If an Outback restaurant manager were evaluated only on her ability to control costs, she may use cheaper ingredients or hire less experienced servers. Although these actions cut costs, they can hurt profits if the quality of the meals or service declines as a result. As another example, Outback wants to focus each restaurant manager's attention on cash flow. As a result, Outback pays its restaurant managers a percentage of the restaurant's cash flows in addition to a base salary.

The Management Accountant Within the Organization

Let's look at how management accountants fit into the company's organizational structure, how their roles are changing, what skills they need to successfully fill their roles, and what their professional association is. We'll also discuss ethical standards.

3 Describe organizational structure and the roles and skills required of management accountants within the organization

Organizational Structure

Most corporations are too large to be governed directly by their stockholders. Therefore, stockholders elect a **board of directors** to oversee the company. Exhibit 1-3 shows a typical organizational structure, with the green boxes representing employees of the firm and the orange and blue boxes representing nonemployees.

The board meets only periodically, so they hire a **chief executive officer (CEO)** to manage the company on a daily basis. The CEO hires other executives to run various aspects of the organization, including the **chief operating officer (COO)** and the **chief financial officer (CFO)**. The COO is responsible for the company's operations, such as research and development (R&D), production, and distribution. The CFO is responsible for all of the company's financial concerns. The **treasurer** and the **controller** report directly to the CFO. The treasurer is primarily responsible for raising capital (through issuing stocks and bonds) and investing funds. The controller is usually responsible for general financial accounting, managerial accounting, and tax reporting.

The New York Stock Exchange requires that listed companies have an **internal audit function**. The role of the internal audit function is to ensure that the company's internal controls and risk management policies are functioning properly. The internal audit department reports directly to a subcommittee of the board of directors called the **audit committee**. The audit committee oversees the internal audit function as well as the annual audit of the financial statements by independent CPAs. Both the internal audit

EXHIBIT 1-3   **Typical Organizational Structure**

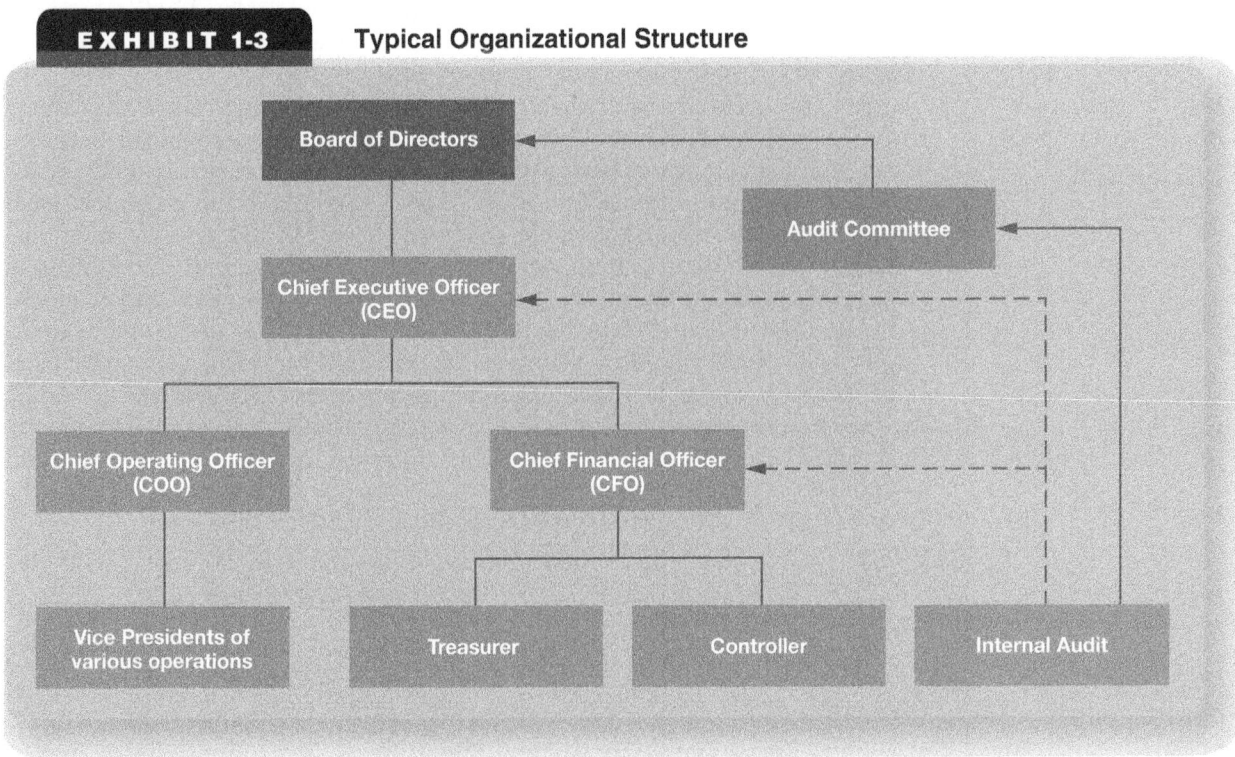

BBH CHAPTER 1

department and the independent CPAs report directly to the audit committee for one very important reason: to ensure that management will not intimidate them or bias their work. However, since the audit committee meets only periodically, it isn't practical for the audit committee to manage the internal audit function on a day-to-day basis. Therefore, the internal audit function also reports to a senior executive, such as the CFO or CEO, for administrative matters.

When you look at the organizational chart pictured in Exhibit 1-3, where do you think management accountants work? It depends on the company. Management accountants used to work in accounting departments and reported directly to the controller. Now, over half of management accountants are located throughout the company and work on cross-functional teams. **Cross-functional teams** consist of employees representing various functions of the company, such as R&D, design, production, marketing, distribution, and customer service. Cross-functional teams are effective because each member can address business decisions from a different viewpoint. These teams often report to various vice presidents of operations. Management accountants often take the leadership role in the teams. Here is what two managers had to say in a study about management accountants:[1]

> Finance (the management accountant) has a unique ability and responsibility to see across all the functions and try and make sense of them. They have the neat ability to be a member of all of the different groups (functions) and yet not be a member of any of them at the same time. (U.S. West)

> Basically the role of the financial person on the team is analyzing the financial impact of the business decision and providing advice. Does this make sense financially or not? (Abbott Laboratories)

The Changing Roles of Management Accountants

Technology has changed the roles of management accountants. Management accountants no longer perform routine mechanical accounting tasks. Computer programs perform those tasks. Yet, management accountants are in more demand than ever before. Company managers used to view management accountants as "scorekeepers" or "bean counters" because they spent most of their time recording historical transactions. Now, they view management accountants as internal consultants or business advisors.

Does this mean that management accountants are no longer involved with the traditional task of recording transactions? No. Management accountants must still ensure that the company's financial records adequately capture economic events. They help design the information systems that capture and record transactions and make sure that the information system generates accurate data. They use professional judgment to record nonroutine transactions and make adjustments to the financial records as needed. Management accountants still need to know what transactions to record and how to record them, but they let technology do most of the routine work.

Freed from the routine mechanical work, management accountants spend more of their time planning, analyzing, and interpreting accounting data and providing decision support. Because their role is changing, management accountants rarely bear the job title "management accountant" any more; managers often refer to them as business management support, financial advisors, business partners, or analysts. Here is what two management accountants have said about their jobs:[2]

> We are looked upon as more business advisors than just accountants, which has a lot to do with the additional analysis and forward-looking goals that we are setting. We spend more of our time analyzing and understanding our margins, our

---

[1,2]*Counting More, Counting Less: The 1999 Practice Analysis of Management Accounting*, Institute of Management Accountants, Montvale, NJ, 1999.

prices, and the markets in which we do business. People have a sense of purpose; they have a real sense of "I'm adding value to the company." (Caterpillar, Inc.)

Accounting is changing. You're no longer sitting behind a desk just working on a computer, just crunching the numbers. You're actually getting to be a part of the day-to-day functions of the business. (Abbott Laboratories)

The Skills Required of Management Accountants

Because computers now do the routine "number crunching," do management accountants need to know as much as they did 20 years ago? The fact is, management accountants now need to know *more*! They have to understand what information management needs and how to generate that information accurately. Therefore, management accountants must be able to communicate with the computer/IT system programmers to create an effective information system. Once the information system generates the data, management accountants interpret and analyze the raw data and turn it into *useful* information management can use.[3]

Twenty years ago we would say, "Here are the costs and you guys need to figure out what you want to do with them." Now we are expected to say, "Here are the costs and this is why the costs are what they are, and this is how they compare to other things, and here are some suggestions where we could possibly improve." (Caterpillar, Inc.)

Today's management accountants need the following skills:[4]

- Solid knowledge of both financial and managerial accounting
- Analytical skills
- Knowledge of how a business functions
- Ability to work on a team
- Oral *and* written communication skills

The skills shown in Exhibit 1-4 are critical to these management accountants:

We're making more presentations that are seen across the division. So you have to summarize the numbers . . . you have to have people in sales understand what those numbers mean. If you can't communicate information to the individuals, then the information is never out there; it's lost. So, your communication skills are very important. (Abbott Laboratories)

Usually when a nonfinancial person comes to you with financial questions, they don't really ask the right things so that you can give them the correct answer. If they ask you for cost, well, you have to work with them and say, "Well, do you want total plant cost, a variable cost, or an accountable cost?" Then, "What is the reason for those costs?" Whatever they're using this cost for determines what type of cost you will provide them with. (Caterpillar, Inc.)

Chapter 2 explains these cost terms. The point here is that management accountants need to have a solid understanding of managerial accounting, including how different types of costs are relevant to different situations. Additionally, they must be able to communicate that information to employees from different business functions.

---

[3]*Counting More, Counting Less: The 1999 Practice Analysis of Management Accounting*, Institute of Management Accountants, Montvale, NJ, 1999.
[4]Gary Siegel and James Sorenson, *What Corporate America Wants in Entry-Level Accountants*, Institute of Management Accountants, Montvale, NJ, 1994.

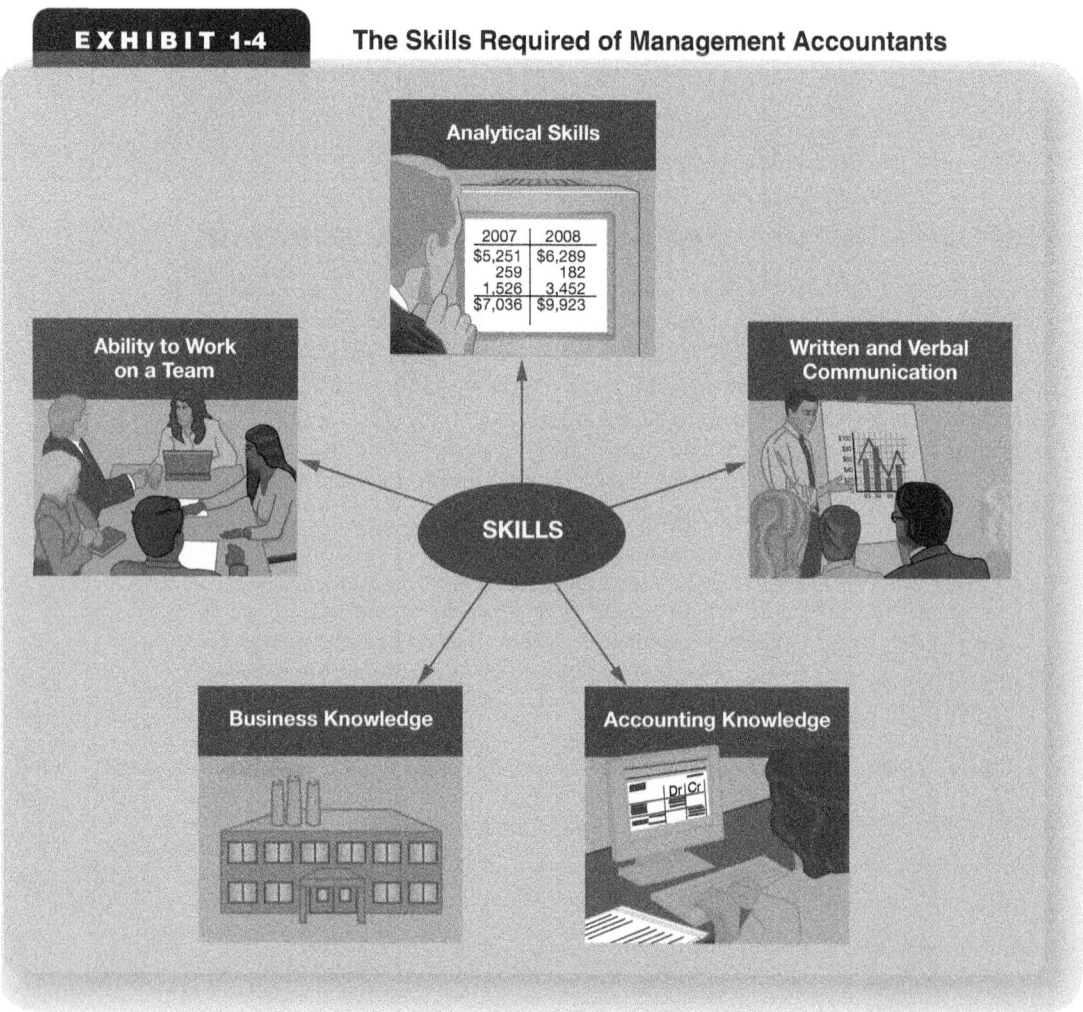

EXHIBIT 1-4 The Skills Required of Management Accountants

Average Salaries of Management Accountants

The average salaries of management accountants reflect their large skill set. Naturally, salaries will vary with the accountant's level of experience, his or her specific job responsibilities, and the size and geographical location of the company.[5] However, to give you a general idea, in 2007, a cost analyst with less than one year of experience could expect to earn between $35,250 and $42,250 at a medium-size company. With one to three years of experience, the average salary increased to $41,750–$52,250. With more experience, salaries ranged upward to approximately $80,500.[6] Accountants in leadership positions command even greater pay. For example, the CFO, controller, treasurer, and internal audit manager of a medium-size company can expect to earn annual salaries exceeding well over $100,000.

You can obtain more specific accounting and finance salary information in a yearly guide published by Robert Half International Inc. The guide also provides information on current hiring trends for accounting and finance professionals. To obtain a free copy of the *Salary Guide*, go to www.roberthalf.com.

---

[5] A medium-size company is defined as a company with annual sales ranging from $25 million to $250 million.

[6] *2007 Salary Guide, Accounting and Finance Salaries*, Robert Half International Inc., Menlo Park, CA.

Professional Association

The **Institute of Management Accountants (IMA)** is the professional association for management accountants. The goal of the IMA is to advance the managerial accounting profession primarily through certification, practice development, education, and networking. They also want to educate society about the role management accountants play in organizations. According to the IMA, about 85% of accountants work in organizations, performing the roles discussed earlier. The IMA publishes a monthly journal called *Strategic Finance*. (Prior to 1999, the journal was called *Management Accounting*; but as the role of management accountants changed, so did the journal's title.) The journal addresses current topics of interest to management accountants and helps them keep abreast of recent techniques and trends.

The IMA also issues two professional certifications: the **Certified Management Accountant (CMA)** and the **Certified Financial Manager (CFM)**. To become a CMA or CFM, you must pass a rigorous examination and maintain continuing professional education. The CMA exam focuses on managerial accounting topics similar to those discussed in this book, as well as economics and business finance. The CFM exam focuses on financial statement analysis, working capital policy, capital structure, business valuation, and risk management. While most employers do not require the CMA or CFM designation, management accountants bearing the CMA or CFM designation usually command higher salaries and obtain higher-level positions within the company. You can find out more about the IMA and the certifications it offers at its Web site: www.imanet.org.

 Describe the role of the Institute of Management Accountants (IMA) and use its ethical standards to make reasonable ethical judgments

Ethics

Management accountants continually face ethical challenges. The IMA has developed principles and standards to help management accountants deal with these challenges. The principles and standards remind us that society expects professional accountants to exhibit the highest level of ethical behavior. The IMA adopted a new *Statement on Ethical Professional Practice* in 2005, which requires management accountants to:

- Maintain their professional competence.
- Preserve the confidentiality of the information they handle.
- Uphold their integrity.
- Perform their duties with credibility.

These ethical standards are summarized in Exhibit 1-5, while the full *Statement of Ethical Professional Practice* appears in Exhibit 1-6.

To resolve ethical dilemmas, the IMA suggests that management accountants first follow their company's established policies for reporting unethical behavior. If the conflict is not resolved through the company's procedures, the management accountant should consider the following steps:

- Discuss the unethical situation with the immediate supervisor unless the supervisor is involved in the unethical situation. If so, notify the supervisor at the next higher managerial level. If the immediate supervisor involved is the CEO, notify the audit committee or board of directors.
- Discuss the unethical situation with an objective advisor, such as an IMA ethics counselor. The IMA offers a confidential "Ethics Hotline" to its members. Members may call the hotline and discuss their ethical dilemma. The ethics counselor will not provide a specific resolution but will clarify how the dilemma relates to the IMA's *Statement of Ethical Professional Practice* shown in Exhibit 1-6.
- Consult an attorney regarding legal obligations and rights.

BBH CHAPTER 1

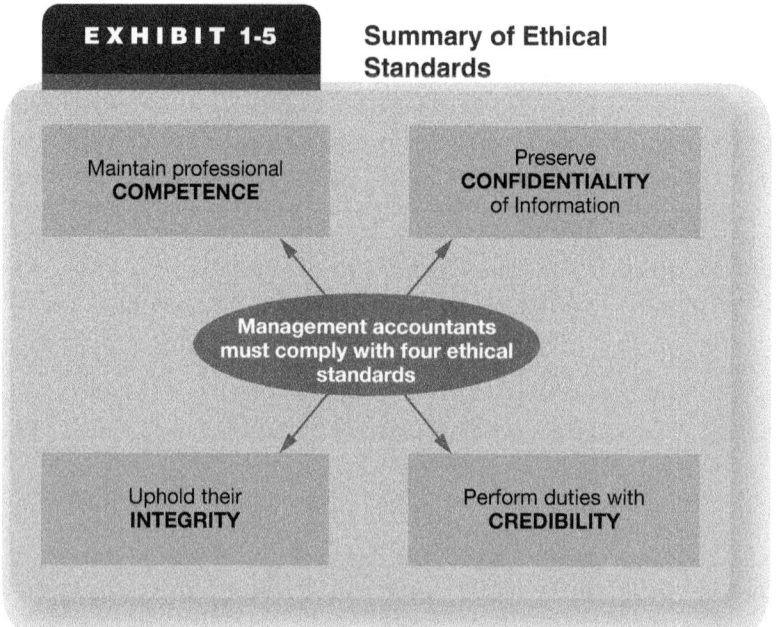

EXHIBIT 1-5   Summary of Ethical Standards

Maintain professional **COMPETENCE**

Preserve **CONFIDENTIALITY** of Information

Management accountants must comply with four ethical standards

Uphold their **INTEGRITY**

Perform duties with **CREDIBILITY**

Examples of Ethical Dilemmas

Unfortunately, the ethical path is not always clear. You may want to act ethically and do the right thing, but the consequences can make it difficult to decide what to do. Let's consider several ethical dilemmas in light of the *Statement of Ethical Professional Practice*:

Dilemma #1

Sarah Baker is examining the expense reports of her staff, who counted inventory at Top-Flight's warehouses in Arizona. She discovers that Mike Flinders has claimed but not included hotel receipts for over $1,000 of accommodation expenses. Other staff, who also claimed $1,000, did attach hotel receipts. When asked about the receipts, Mike admits that he stayed with an old friend, not in the hotel, but he believes that he deserves the money he saved. After all, the company would have paid his hotel bill.

By asking to be reimbursed for hotel expenses he did not incur, Flinders violated the IMA's integrity standards (conflict of interest in which he tried to enrich himself at the company's expense). Because Baker discovered the inflated expense report, she would not be fulfilling her ethical responsibilities of integrity and credibility if she allowed the reimbursement.

Dilemma #2

As the accountant of Entreé Computer, you are aware of your company's weak financial condition. Entreé is close to signing a lucrative contract that should ensure its future. To do so, the controller states that the company must report a profit this year (ending December 31). He suggests: "Two customers have placed orders that are really not supposed to be shipped until early January. Ask production to fill and ship those orders on December 31 so we can record them in this year's sales."

EXHIBIT 1-6	IMA Statement of Ethical Professional Practice

Members of IMA shall behave ethically. A commitment to ethical professional practice includes: overarching principles that express our values, and standards that guide our conduct.

Principles
IMA's overarching ethical principles include: Honesty, Fairness, Objectivity, and Responsibility. Members shall act in accordance with these principles and shall encourage others within their organizations to adhere to them.

Standards
A member's failure to comply with the following standards may result in disciplinary action.

I. Competence
Each member has a responsibility to:
1. Maintain an appropriate level of professional expertise by continually developing knowledge and skills.
2. Perform professional duties in accordance with relevant laws, regulations, and technical standards.
3. Provide decision support information and recommendations that are accurate, clear, concise, and timely.
4. Recognize and communicate professional limitations or other constraints that would preclude responsible judgment or successful performance of an activity.

II. Confidentiality
Each member has a responsibility to:
1. Keep information confidential except when disclosure is authorized or legally required.
2. Inform all relevant parties regarding appropriate use of confidential information. Monitor subordinates' activities to ensure compliance.
3. Refrain from using confidential information for unethical or illegal advantage.

III. Integrity
Each member has a responsibility to:
1. Mitigate actual conflicts of interest. Regularly communicate with business associates to avoid apparent conflicts of interest. Advise all parties of any potential conflicts.
2. Refrain from engaging in any conduct that would prejudice carrying out duties ethically.
3. Abstain from engaging in or supporting any activity that might discredit the profession.

IV. Credibility
Each member has a responsibility to:
1. Communicate information fairly and objectively.
2. Disclose all relevant information that could reasonably be expected to influence an intended user's understanding of the reports, analyses, or recommendations.
3. Disclose delays or deficiencies in information, timeliness, processing, or internal controls in conformance with organization policy and/or applicable law.

Institute of Management Accountants. Adapted with permission (2006).

The resolution of this dilemma is less clear-cut. Many people believe that following the controller's suggestion to manipulate the company's income would violate the standards of competence, integrity, and credibility. Others would argue that because Entreé Computer already has the customer orders, shipping the goods and recording the sale in December is still ethical behavior. You might discuss the available alternatives with the next managerial level or the IMA ethics hotline counselor.

Dilemma #3

As a new accounting staff member at Central City Hospital, your supervisor has asked you to prepare the yearly *Medicare Cost Report*, which the government uses to determine its reimbursement to the hospital for serving Medicare patients. The report requires specialized knowledge that you don't believe you possess. The supervisor is busy planning for the coming year and cannot offer much guidance while you prepare the report.

This situation is not as rare as you might think. You may be asked to perform tasks that you don't feel qualified to perform. The competence standard requires you to perform professional duties in accordance with laws, regulations, and technical standards; but laws and regulations are always changing. For this reason, the competence standard also requires you to continually develop knowledge and skills. CPAs and CMAs are required to complete annual continuing professional education (about 40 hours per year) to fulfill this responsibility. However, even continuing professional education courses will not cover every situation you may encounter.

In the Medicare cost report situation, advise your supervisor that you currently lack the knowledge required to complete the Medicare cost report. By doing so, you are complying with the competence standard that requires you to recognize and communicate any limitations that would preclude you from fulfilling an activity. You should ask for training on the report preparation and supervision by someone experienced in preparing the report. If the supervisor denies your requests, you should ask him to reassign the Medicare report to a qualified staff member.

Dilemma #4

> Your company is negotiating a large multiyear sales contract that, if won, would substantially increase the company's future earnings. At a dinner party over the weekend, your friends ask you how you like your job and the company you work for. In your enthusiasm, you tell them not only about your responsibilities at work but also about the contract negotiations. As soon as the words pop out of your mouth, you worry that you've said too much.

This situation is difficult to avoid. You may be so excited about your job and the company you work for that information unintentionally "slips out" during casual conversation with friends and family. The confidentiality standard requires you to refrain from disclosing information or using confidential information for unethical or illegal advantage. Was the contract negotiation confidential? If so, would your friends invest in company stock in hopes that the negotiations increase stock prices? Or were the negotiations public knowledge in the financial community? If so, your friends would gain no illegal advantage from the information. Recent cases, such as those involving Martha Stewart, remind us that insider trading (use of inside knowledge for illegal gain) has serious consequences. Even seemingly mundane information about company operations could give competitors an advantage. Therefore, it's best to disclose only information that is meant for public consumption.

Unethical Versus Illegal Behavior

Finally, is there a difference between unethical and illegal behavior? Not all unethical behavior is illegal, but all illegal behavior is unethical. For example, consider the competence standard. The competence standard states that management accountants have a responsibility to provide decision support information that is accurate, clear, concise, and timely. Failure to follow this standard is unethical but in most cases not illegal. Now, consider the integrity standard. It states that management accountants must abstain from any activity that might discredit the profession. A management accountant who commits an illegal act is violating this ethical standard. In other words, ethical behavior encompasses more than simply following the law. The IMA's ethical principles include honesty, fairness, objectivity, and responsibility—principles that are much broader than what is codified in the law.

Decision Guidelines

Outback made the following decisions in designing its managerial accounting system to provide managers with the information they need to run operations efficiently and effectively.

Decision	Guidelines
What information should management accountants provide? What is the primary focus of managerial accounting?	Managerial accounting provides information that helps managers plan, direct, and control operations and make better decisions; it has a: • *Future* orientation. • Focus on *relevance* to business decisions.
How do managers design a company's managerial accounting system that is not regulated by GAAP?	Managers design the managerial accounting system so that the benefits (from helping managers make wiser decisions) outweigh the costs of the system.
How should managers decide if their plans make financial sense? How do they decide if the company is operating according to plans?	Managers quantitatively express their plans in the form of budgets. They can analyze the budgets to determine whether the plans will be profitable. Once the plans have been put into place, managers compare actual results to plans and make adjustments where needed.
In designing the organizational structure, where should managers place management accountants?	In the past, most management accountants worked in isolated departments. Now, over 50% of management accountants are deployed throughout the company and work on cross-functional teams. Management must decide which structure best suits its needs.
What skills do management accountants need to possess?	Because of their expanding role within the organization, most management accountants need financial and managerial accounting knowledge, analytical skills, knowledge of how a business functions, ability to work on teams, and written and oral communication skills.
How should a management accountant resolve an ethical dilemma?	Consult the IMA's *Statement of Ethical Professional Practice* and the company's policies. The Statement offers guidance through overarching ethical principles (honesty, fairness, objectivity, and responsibility) and standards (competence, confidentiality, integrity, and credibility).

BBH CHAPTER 1

Summary Problem 1

Requirements

1. Each of the following statements describes a responsibility of management. Match each statement to the management responsibility being fulfilled.

Statement	Management Responsibility
1. Identifying alternative courses of action and choosing among them	a. Planning
2. Running the company on a day-to-day basis	b. Decision making
3. Determining whether the company's units are operating according to plan	c. Directing
4. Setting goals and objectives for the company and determining strategies to achieve them	d. Controlling

2. Are the following statements more descriptive of managerial accounting or financial accounting information?
    a. Describes historical transactions with external parties
    b. Is not required by any authoritative body, such as the SEC
    c. Reports on the company's subunits, such as products, geographical areas, and departments
    d. Is intended to be used by creditors and investors
    e. Is formatted in accordance with GAAP

3. Each of the following statements paraphrases an ethical responsibility. Match each statement to the standard of ethical professional practice being fulfilled. Each standard may be used more than once or not at all.

Responsibility	Standard of Ethical Professional Practice
1. Don't disclose company information unless authorized to do so.	a. Competence
2. Continue to develop skills and knowledge.	b. Confidentiality
3. Don't bias the information and reports presented to management.	c. Integrity
4. If you don't have the skills to complete a task correctly, don't pretend you do.	d. Credibility
5. Avoid actual *and* apparent conflicts of interest.	

Solutions

Requirement 1

1. (b) Decision making
2. (c) Directing
3. (d) Controlling
4. (a) Planning

Requirement 2

a. financial accounting
b. managerial accounting
c. managerial accounting
d. financial accounting
e. financial accounting

Requirement 3

1. (b) Confidentiality
2. (a) Competence
3. (d) Credibility
4. (a) Competence
5. (c) Integrity

Today's Business Environment

5 Discuss trends in the business environment

The following chapters describe managerial accounting tools that managers use to plan, direct, and control operations and make business decisions. Before we turn to these tools, let's first consider recent trends that affect managers' decisions and the managerial accounting systems that support them. These trends include the Sarbanes-Oxley Act; the shifting economy; the rise of the global marketplace; time-based competition (including changes in information systems, electronic commerce, and just-in-time management); and total quality management.

Sarbanes-Oxley Act of 2002

As a result of recent corporate accounting scandals, such as those at Enron and WorldCom, the U.S. Congress enacted the **Sarbanes-Oxley Act of 2002 (SOX)**. The purpose of SOX is to restore trust in publicly traded corporations, their management, their financial statements, and their auditors. SOX enhances internal control and financial reporting requirements and establishes new regulatory requirements for publicly traded companies and their independent auditors. Publicly traded companies have spent millions of dollars upgrading their internal controls and accounting systems to comply with SOX regulations.

As shown in Exhibit 1-7, SOX requires the company's CEO and CFO to assume responsibility for the financial statements and disclosures. The CEO and CFO must certify that the financial statements and disclosures fairly present, in all material respects, the operations and financial condition of the company. Additionally, they must accept responsibility for establishing and maintaining an adequate internal control structure and procedures for financial reporting. The company must have its internal controls and financial reporting procedures assessed annually.

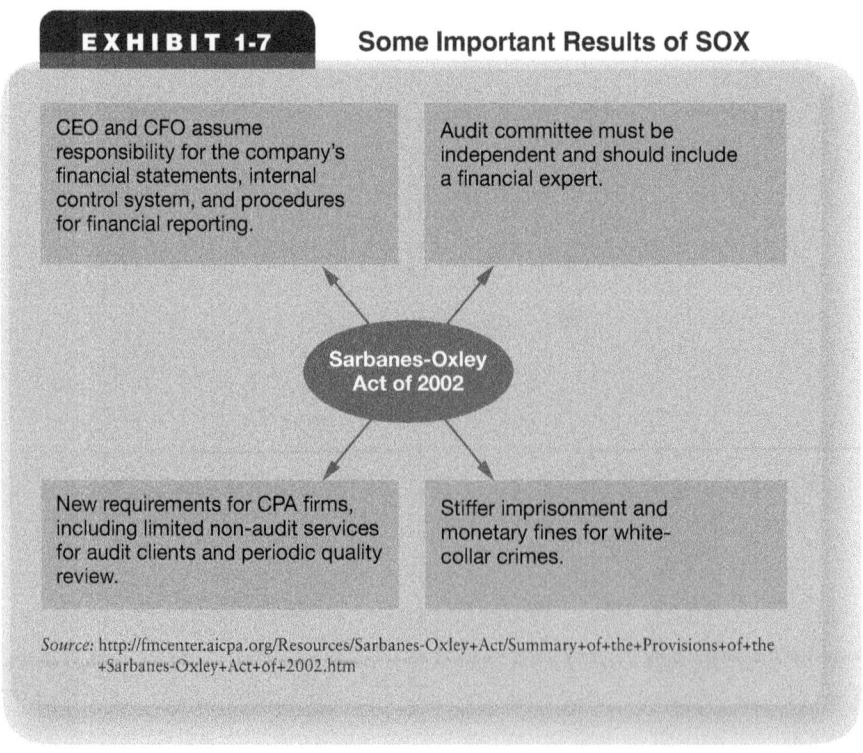

EXHIBIT 1-7   **Some Important Results of SOX**

CEO and CFO assume responsibility for the company's financial statements, internal control system, and procedures for financial reporting.

Audit committee must be independent and should include a financial expert.

Sarbanes-Oxley Act of 2002

New requirements for CPA firms, including limited non-audit services for audit clients and periodic quality review.

Stiffer imprisonment and monetary fines for white-collar crimes.

Source: http://fmcenter.aicpa.org/Resources/Sarbanes-Oxley+Act/Summary+of+the+Provisions+of+the+Sarbanes-Oxley+Act+of+2002.htm

SOX also requires audit committee members to be independent, meaning that they may not receive any consulting or advisory fees from the company other than for their service on the board of directors. In addition, at least one of the members should be a financial expert. The audit committee oversees not only the internal audit function but also the company's audit by independent CPAs.

To ensure that CPA firms maintain independence from their client company, SOX does not allow CPA firms to provide certain non-audit services (such as book-keeping and financial information systems design) to companies during the same period of time in which they are providing audit services. If a company wants to obtain such services from a CPA firm, it must hire a different firm to do the non-audit work. Tax services may be provided by the same CPA firm if preapproved by the audit committee. The audit partner must rotate off the audit engagement every five years, and the audit firm must undergo quality reviews every one to three years.

SOX also increases the penalties for white-collar crimes such as corporate fraud. These penalties include both monetary fines and substantial imprisonment. For example, knowingly destroying or creating documents to "impede, obstruct, or influence" any federal investigation can result in up to 20 years of imprisonment.[7] Since its enactment in 2002, SOX has significantly affected the internal operations of publicly traded corporations and their auditors. SOX will continue to play a major role in corporate management and the audit profession.

Shifting Economy

In the last century, North American economies have shifted away from manufacturing toward service. Service companies provide health care, communication, transportation, banking, and other important benefits to society. Service companies now make up the largest sector of the U.S. economy and employ 55% of the workforce. The U.S. Census Bureau expects services, especially technology and health care services, to be among the fastest-growing industries over the next decade. Even companies that traditionally carried out manufacturing, such as General Electric (GE), are shifting toward selling more services. It's easy to see why. In GE's jet engine business, services contribute only 30% of the revenues but generate two-thirds of the profit.

Managerial accounting has its roots in the industrial age of manufacturing. Most traditional managerial accounting practices were developed to fill the needs of manufacturing firms. However, since the U.S. economy has shifted away from manufacturing, managerial accounting has shifted, too. The field of managerial accounting has *expanded* to meet the needs of service and merchandising firms as well as manufacturers. For example:

1. Manufacturers still need to know how much each unit of their product costs to manufacture. In addition to using this information for inventory valuation and pricing decisions, manufacturers now use cost information to determine whether they should outsource production to another company or to an overseas location.

2. Service companies also need cost information to make decisions. They need to know the cost of providing a service rather than manufacturing a product. For example, banks must include the cost of servicing checking and savings accounts in the fees they charge customers. And hospitals need to know the cost of performing appendectomies to justify reimbursement from insurance companies and from Medicare.

---

[7]If you want to learn more about SOX, the AICPA provides a summary at http://fmcenter.aicpa.org/Resources/Sarbanes-Oxley+Act/Summary+of+the+Provisions+of+the+Sarbanes-Oxley+Act+of+2002.htm.

BBH CHAPTER 1

3. Retailers need to consider importing costs when determining the cost of their merchandise. Because many goods are now produced overseas rather than domestically, determining the cost of a product is often more difficult than it was in the past. Management accountants need to consider foreign currency translation, shipping costs, and import tariffs when determining the cost of imported products.

Competing in the Global Marketplace

The barriers to international trade have fallen over the past decades, allowing foreign companies to compete with domestic firms. Firms that are not world-class competitors will vanish from the global market. However, global markets provide competitive companies with great potential: Foreign operations account for over 35% of GE's revenues, over 40% of Amazon.com's revenues, and over 65% of Coca-Cola's and McDonald's revenues.

Manufacturers often move operations to other countries to be closer to new markets and less expensive labor. For example, Thomson SA, maker of GE's television sets, closed the world's largest TV factory in Bloomington, Indiana, and moved the work to Mexico to save an estimated $75 million a year in labor costs. Ford, General Motors, and DaimlerChrysler all built plants in Brazil to feed Brazil's car-hungry middle class. The same week Alcoa announced it was closing two plants in the United States, it spelled out plans to build a $1 billion plant in Iceland.

Globalization has several implications for managerial accounting:

1. Stiffer competition means managers need more accurate information to make wise decisions. For example, if Nokia overestimates the cost of its new cell phone, it may set prices too high and lose business to competitors.

2. Companies must decide whether to expand sales and/or production into foreign countries. Managers need estimates of the costs and benefits of international expansion.

3. Globalization fosters the transfer of management philosophy across international borders. Many U.S. companies now follow the just-in-time philosophy developed in Japan.

Time-Based Competition

The Internet, electronic commerce (e-commerce), and other new technologies speed the pace of business. Think about your last trip to the grocery store or Wal-Mart. Did you use the self-scanning checkout? Retailers install expensive self-scanning technology to give shoppers an alternative to standing in longer checkout lines. Some studies have shown that, on average, the self-scanning checkout process is really not faster. However, shoppers *perceive* the checkout time to be faster because they are actively engaged rather than passively standing in line. Businesses are doing whatever they can to shorten the time a customer has to wait for their order. Why? Because *time* is the latest competitive weapon in business.

Dell Computer commits to delivering your desktop computer within a week of receiving your order. Toyota says that it can make a car within five days of receiving a custom order. Sweden's Ericsson Radio Systems has increased on-time delivery from 20% to 99.98%—nearly perfect. How do they do it? By using advanced information systems, e-commerce, and just-in-time management.

Advanced Information Systems

Many small businesses use QuickBooks or Peachtree software to track their costs and to develop the information that owners and managers need to run the business. But large companies such as Fujitsu and Allstate Insurance are turning to **enterprise resource planning (ERP) systems** that can integrate all of a company's worldwide functions, departments, and data. ERP systems such as SAP, Oracle, and PeopleSoft gather company data into a centralized data warehouse. The system feeds the data into software for all of the company's business activities, from budgeting and purchasing to production and customer service.

Advantages of ERP systems include the following:

- Companies streamline their operations before mapping them into ERP software. Streamlining operations saves money.
- ERP helps companies respond quickly to changes. A change in sales instantly ripples through the ERP's purchases, production, shipping, and accounting systems.
- An ERP system can replace hundreds of separate software systems, such as different software in different regions, or different payroll, shipping, and production software.

ERP is expensive. Major installations cost Fujitsu and Allstate over $40 million. ERP also requires a large commitment of time and people. For example, Hershey Foods tried to shrink a four-year ERP project into two and one-half years. The result? The software did not map into Hershey Foods' operations, and it disrupted deliveries and hurt profits during the critical Halloween season.

E-commerce

To survive in a competitive, globally wired economy, companies use the Internet in everyday operations such as budgeting, planning, selling, and customer service. Imagine a salesclerk who can sell to thousands of customers at once. This clerk instantly provides every product, option, and price the company offers. It works 24 hours a day, 365 days a year, and never takes a break or vacation. This salesclerk is an e-commerce Web site!

Business-to-business e-commerce takes speed and efficiency to new levels. Imagine sitting in your office anywhere in the world. You enter Dell's Web site and customize the new computer you're buying. After you fill your virtual shopping cart, business-to-business software automates ordering, approval, and delivery.

Electronic purchases below specified dollar limits are often untouched by human hands, generate little if any paper, and avoid the time and cost of processing paperwork. Even the federal government is on the e-bandwagon. An electronic marketplace, E-Mall, allows buyers in the Department of Defense and other federal agencies access to 17 million items online. An order on E-Mall costs about $11 to process, while one placed by hand costs around $150.

Stop & Think...

Electronically billing customers is also becoming more popular. Analysts estimate that:

1. Companies save $7 per invoice by billing customers electronically.
2. The average large company issues 800,000 invoices a year.
3. The average cost of installing an e-billing system is $500,000. Should companies that issue 800,000 invoices a year consider e-billing?

Answer: Yes, these companies should consider e-billing. Comparing expected benefits to costs reveals significant expected net benefits from e-billing:

Expected benefits:	
800,000 invoices × $7 savings per invoice	$5,600,000
Expected costs:	
Installation of e-billing system	(500,000)
Net expected benefits	$5,100,000

Managers of Krispy Kreme's stores use the company's customized Web portal to plan production and order supplies. Weather news appears on the opening screen. Why? Because Krispy Kreme found that people buy more coffee and doughnuts when the weather is bad. This simple innovation helps managers forecast how many doughnuts to make. "I've seen a good 2 to 3 percent increase in profitability just from the portal," says the manager of a Miami-based store.[8]

Firms also use the Internet to tap into other companies' business processes. Companies that supply component parts to Dell use the Internet to look into Dell's production process through a customized virtual window. Each supplier sees the current demand for and inventory levels of the parts it supplies Dell. Access to real-time information that lets suppliers automate the size of the next day's order helps Dell cut order-to-delivery times and control costs.

E-commerce is an important means of **supply-chain management**, where companies exchange information with suppliers to reduce costs, improve quality, and speed delivery of goods and services from suppliers to the company itself and on to the customer. E-commerce also increases a firm's ability (and need) to use just-in-time management.

Just-in-Time Management

The costs of holding inventory can add up to 25% or more of the inventory's value. Money tied up in inventory cannot be used for other purposes. Inventory held too long becomes obsolete. Storing inventory costs money and takes up space that could be used to increase production. The just-in-time philosophy helps managers cut holding costs by speeding the transformation of raw materials into new, finished products. Let's see how it works.

Toyota generally gets credit for pioneering the **just-in-time (JIT)** philosophy, which means producing *just in time* to satisfy needs. Exhibit 1-8 shows that ideally, suppliers deliver materials for today's production in exactly the right quantities *just in time* to begin production and finished units are completed *just in time* for delivery to customers. This means that raw materials are not stored before production and that finished units are shipped directly to the customer when they are completed, rather than first being stored in a finished goods warehouse. By reducing the amount of inventory stored, JIT reduces storage costs (warehousing and associated security, utilities, and shrinkage costs) and handling costs (labor costs associated with storing and unstoring inventory). Firms adopting JIT report sharp reductions in inventory and related carrying costs.

JIT also cuts **throughput time,** the time between buying raw materials and selling finished products. For example, Dell Computer recently cut its throughput time from 17 days to fewer than 5 days. Why is this important? An article in *The Wall Street Journal* estimates that new technologies reduce the value of a completed PC by 1% *per week*.[9] Moving inventory quickly means that Dell can cut prices immediately when costs of component parts decline. Less inventory means that Dell can quickly incorporate new technologies and that more plant space is available for production.

Manufacturers adopting JIT have a limited safety stock of raw materials, so they depend on their suppliers to make on-time deliveries of perfect-quality materials. As noted earlier, Dell designed special Web pages for its major suppliers that give them a "virtual window" into Dell's operations. Suppliers use these windows to decide when and how much raw material to deliver to Dell.

Companies that adopt JIT strive for perfect quality because defects stop production lines. Firms that adopt JIT also commit to total quality management.

---

[8]Catherine Skip, "Hot Bytes, by the Dozen," *Newsweek,* April 28, 2003, p. 42.
[9]"Compaq Stumbles as PCs Weather New Blow," *Wall Street Journal,* March 9, 1998, p. B1.

BBH CHAPTER 1

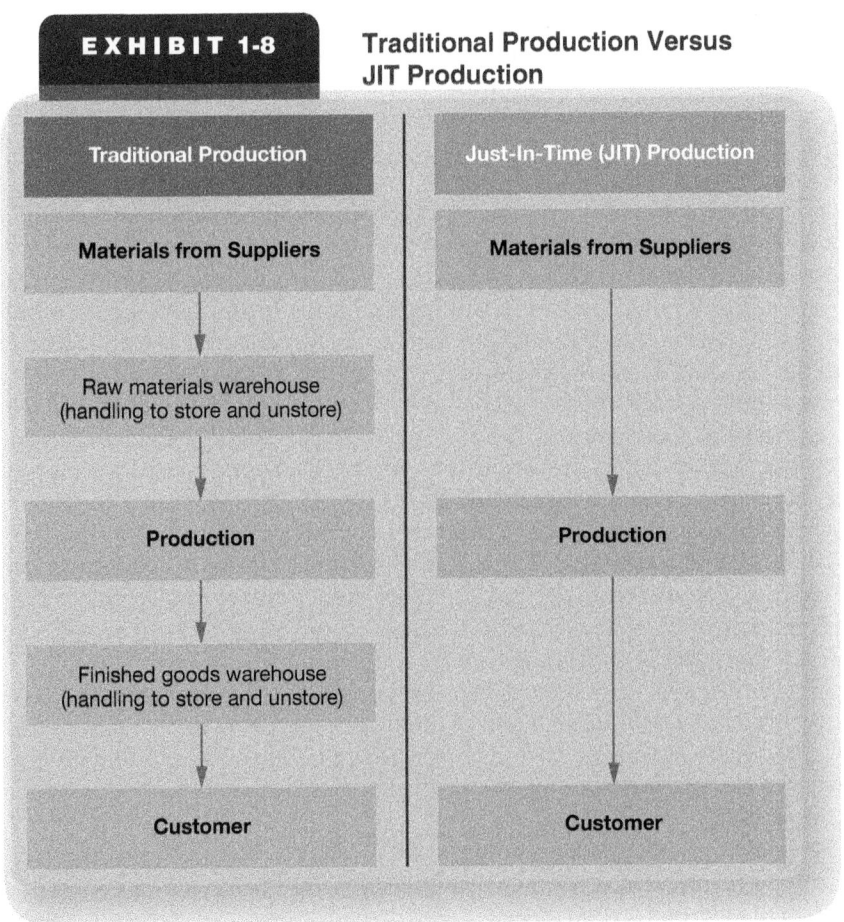

EXHIBIT 1-8 — Traditional Production Versus JIT Production

Total Quality Management

Companies must deliver high-quality goods and services to remain competitive. Hewlett-Packard and Ford in the United States, British Telecom in the United Kingdom, and Toyota in Japan view **total quality management (TQM)** as a key to succeeding in the global economy. The goal of TQM is to delight customers by providing them with superior products and services. Companies achieve this goal by improving quality and eliminating defects and waste.

In TQM, each business function examines its own activities and works to improve performance by continually setting higher goals. For example, Motorola wanted to reduce the time required to issue a purchase order. The TQM team of Motorola's purchasing department reduced the number of steps in handling a purchase order from 17 to 6, slashing average processing time from 30 minutes to 3.

ISO 9001:2000

Many firms want to demonstrate their commitment to continuous quality improvement. The International Organization for Standardization (ISO), made up of 146 member countries, has developed international quality management standards and guidelines. Firms may become ISO 9001:2000-certified by complying with the quality management standards set forth by the ISO and undergoing extensive audits of their quality management processes. The prestigious certification gives firms a competitive advantage in the global marketplace. Many companies will purchase supplies only from firms bearing the ISO 9001:2000 certification. To better understand the ISO's global impact, consider the following: by 2005, over 650,000 certificates had been issued to firms in 154 countries! The certification does not only apply

BBH CHAPTER 1

to manufacturing firms. Service firms account for over 31% of all certificates issued. The American Institute of Certified Public Accountants was the first professional membership organization in the United States to earn the ISO 9001 certification.

Cost-Benefit Analysis

6 | Use cost-benefit analysis to make business decisions

How do managers decide which quality improvement initiatives to undertake? They use **cost-benefit analysis**—weighing costs against benefits. Most decisions involve comparing the estimated costs of the project with the estimated benefits. Quality improvement programs cost money up front, but the benefits accrue over time. In deciding whether to undertake such projects, managers compare the project's present cost to the present value of the project's future benefits. (This is called *discounting* the future amounts to their *present values*. You may already be familiar with present value concepts and calculations from previous accounting and finance classes. For now, the present value of the benefits is given.) Because no one can foresee the future, the exact amount of the future benefits is not known. Let's see how managers adjust for this uncertainty in performing cost-benefit analysis.

GE recently started nearly 3,000 quality-related projects at a cost of more than $200 million. The first-year cost savings from these projects totaled only $170 million. Does this mean that GE made a bad decision? Not necessarily. GE expects these projects to continue yielding benefits in the future.

Suppose GE managers predict that these projects will be moderately successful or extremely successful. Assume that if the projects are moderately successful, they will yield additional benefits (cost savings) with a present value of $20 million. If the projects are extremely successful, they will yield extra benefits with a present value of $100 million.

Suppose the managers estimate a 60% chance that the projects will be extremely successful and a 40% chance that they will be moderately successful. In an uncertain environment, managers make decisions based on expected values. We compute expected values by multiplying the dollar value of each possible outcome by the probability of that outcome and then adding the results:

Outcome	Benefit	×	Probability	=	Expected Value
Extremely successful	$100 million	×	60% chance	=	$60 million
Moderately successful	20 million	×	40% chance	=	8 million
					$68 million

What does this $68 million mean? If GE faced this exact situation ten times, it would expect to get $100 million in extra benefits six times and only $20 million of additional benefits four times. The *average* extra benefits across the ten situations is $68 million.

Thus, the total benefits expected from GE's quality projects ($238 million, calculated as $170 million initial benefits + $68 million additional expected benefits) exceed the $200 million cost of the projects. This analysis suggests that GE's quality initiative was worthwhile.

Even after adopting quality programs, companies cannot "rest on their laurels." TQM requires that companies (and individual employees) continually look for ways to improve performance. This is the **continuous improvement** philosophy.

How do companies improve? Many businesses find that they can save money in the long run by spending more up front on *preventing* defects from occurring in the first place. Successful companies design and build quality into their products and services rather than depending on finding and fixing defects later. For example, by increasing the proportion of vehicles built right the first time from 50% to 70%, General Motors cut average warranty costs from roughly $1,600 to $1,000 per vehicle, in addition to reducing costs of rework and inspections.

Decision Guidelines

THE CHANGING BUSINESS ENVIRONMENT

Successful companies have to respond to changes in the business environment. Here are some of the key decisions managers consider to ensure that the company thrives in the future.

Decision	Guidelines
What companies need to comply with SOX?	Publicly traded companies must comply with SOX. Many of the law's specific requirements focus on implementing adequate internal controls and financial reporting procedures and maintaining independence from the company's auditors.
How do companies compete in a global economy?	They use advanced information systems; embrace e-commerce; and use supply-chain management, JIT, and TQM to compete more effectively. They consider becoming ISO 9001:2000-certified.
How do companies decide whether to undertake new projects such as international expansion, ERP, JIT, and TQM?	They use cost-benefit analysis. They compute the benefits of the project and compare them with the costs. They undertake the project if benefits exceed costs. They abandon the project if costs exceed benefits.
How do companies adjust the cost-benefit analysis if they do not know the exact amount of the benefit (or cost)?	They compute the expected value of the benefits (or costs) of each outcome as follows:

$$\begin{array}{ccc} \text{Estimated} & \text{Probability} & \text{Expected} \\ \text{amount of} \ \times & \text{of} & = \ \text{value of} \\ \text{outcome} & \text{outcome} & \text{outcome} \end{array}$$

Then, they add the expected values across all possible outcomes.

BBH CHAPTER 1

Summary Problem 2

This summary review problem shows how you can apply cost-benefit analysis to a decision about international expansion.

EZ-Rider Motorcycles is considering whether to expand into Germany. If gas prices increase, EZ-Rider Motorcycles expects more interest in fuel-efficient transportation such as motorcycles. EZ-Rider Motorcycles is considering setting up a motorcycle assembly plant on the outskirts of Berlin.

EZ-Rider Motorcycles estimates it will cost €850,000 (850,000 euros) to convert an existing building to motorcycle production. Workers will need training, at a total cost of €65,000. The CEO of EZ-Rider Motorcycles, Dennis Popper, would have to spend a month in Berlin to organize the business and to establish relationships. He estimates the cost of this travel at €43,000.

Popper sees a 60% chance that the price of gasoline in Germany will increase significantly. If this increase occurs, he believes EZ-Rider Motorcycles can earn profits (before considering the costs in the preceding paragraph) with a present value of €1,624,000. However, if gas prices remain stable, Popper expects to earn profits with a present value of only about €812,000. He believes there is a 40% chance that gas prices will remain stable.

Requirements

1. What are the total costs of EZ-Rider Motorcycles' proposed expansion into Germany?

2. Compute the *expected value* of the benefits if EZ-Rider Motorcycles expands into Germany.

3. Do the benefits outweigh the costs of expanding into Germany? Explain.

Solution

Requirement 1
The total costs are as follows:

Conversion of building to manufacturing plant...........	€850,000
Workforce training	65,000
Popper's trip to Berlin	43,000
Total costs..	€958,000

Requirement 2
Expected value of the benefits is computed as follows:

Benefit	× Probability	=	Expected Value
€1,624,000	× 0.60	=	€ 974, 400
812,000	× 0.40	=	324,800
			€ 1,299,200

The *expected value* of the benefits, or profits, is €1,299,200. This means that should EZ-Rider Motorcycles find itself in this exact situation many times, its average profits across all of the situations would be €1,299,200.

Requirement 3

Yes, the total expected benefits outweigh the costs of the expansion:

Total expected value of benefits of expansion (from requirement 2)...	€1,299,200
Total costs of expansion (from requirement 1).................................	958,000
Net benefits of expansion...	€ 341,200

BBH CHAPTER 1

Review Introduction to Managerial Accounting

Accounting Vocabulary

Audit Committee. (p. 7)
A subcommittee of the board of directors that is responsible for overseeing both the internal audit function and the annual financial statement audit by independent CPAs.

Board of Directors. (p. 7)
The body elected by shareholders to oversee the company.

Budget. (p. 3)
Quantitative expression of a plan that helps managers coordinate and implement the plan.

Certified Financial Manager (CFM). (p. 11)
A professional certification issued by the IMA to designate expertise in the areas of financial statement analysis, working capital policy, capital structure, business valuation, and risk management.

Certified Management Accountant (CMA). (p. 11)
A professional certification issued by the IMA to designate expertise in the areas of managerial accounting, economics, and business finance.

Chief Executive Officer (CEO). (p. 7)
The position hired by the board of directors to oversee the company on a daily basis.

Chief Financial Officer (CFO). (p. 7)
The position responsible for all of the company's financial concerns.

Chief Operating Officer (COO). (p. 7)
The position responsible for overseeing the company's operations.

Continuous Improvement. (p. 24)
A philosophy requiring employees to continually look for ways to improve performance.

Controller. (p. 7)
The position responsible for general financial accounting, managerial accounting, and tax reporting.

Controlling. (p. 3)
One of management's primary responsibilities; evaluating the results of business operations against the plan and making adjustments to keep the company pressing toward its goals.

Cost-Benefit Analysis. (p. 24)
Weighing costs against benefits to help make decisions.

Cross-Functional Teams. (p. 8)
Corporate teams whose members represent various functions of the organization, such as R&D, design, production, marketing, distribution, and customer service.

Decision Making. (p. 4)
One of management's primary responsibilities; identifying possible courses of action and choosing among them.

Directing. (p. 3)
One of management's primary responsibilities; running the company on a day-to-day basis.

Enterprise Resource Planning (ERP). (p. 20)
Software systems that can integrate all of a company's worldwide functions, departments, and data into a single system.

Institute of Management Accountants (IMA). (p. 11)
The professional organization that promotes the advancement of the management accounting profession.

Internal Audit Function. (p. 7)
The corporate function charged with assessing the effectiveness of the company's internal controls and risk management policies.

Just-In-Time (JIT). (p. 22)
A system in which a company produces just in time to satisfy needs. Suppliers deliver materials just in time to begin production, and finished units are completed just in time for delivery to customers.

Planning. (p. 3)
One of management's primary responsibilities; setting goals and objectives for the company and deciding how to achieve them.

Sarbanes-Oxley Act of 2002 (SOX). (p. 18)
A congressional act that enhances internal control and financial reporting requirements and establishes new regulatory requirements for publicly traded companies and their independent auditors.

Supply-Chain Management. (p. 22)
Exchange of information with suppliers to reduce costs, improve quality, and speed delivery of goods and services from suppliers to the company itself and on to customers.

Throughput Time. (p. 22)
The time between buying raw materials and selling finished products.

Treasurer. (p. 7)
The position responsible for raising the firm's capital and investing funds.

Total Quality Management (TQM). (p. 23)
A philosophy of delighting customers by providing them with superior products and services. Requires improving quality and eliminating defects and waste throughout the value chain.

■ Quick Check

1. Which of the following is *not* one of the four primary responsibilities of management?
   a. controlling
   b. costing
   c. directing
   d. planning

2. Which of the following about managerial accounting is *true*?
   a. GAAP requires managerial accounting.
   b. Internal decision makers use managerial accounting.
   c. CPAs audit managerial accounting reports.
   d. Managerial accounting reports are usually prepared on an annual basis.

3. Which of the following is *not* a characteristic of managerial accounting information?
   a. emphasizes relevance
   b. focuses on the future more than the past
   c. provides detailed information about parts of the company, not just the company as a whole
   d. emphasizes reliability

4. What company position is in charge of raising the firm's capital?
   a. director of internal audit
   b. controller
   c. COO
   d. treasurer

5. Which of the following statements is *true*?
   a. The COO reports to the CFO.
   b. The treasurer reports to the CEO.
   c. The internal audit department reports to the audit committee.
   d. The controller reports to the internal auditor.

6. To get a job as a management accountant in most companies, you must:
   a. join the IMA
   b. be certified as a CMA
   c. be certified as a CFM
   d. none of the above

7. In addition to accounting knowledge, management accountants must possess all of the following skills *except*:

   a. written communication skills

   b. knowledge of how a business functions

   c. computer programming skills

   d. analytical skills

8. A management accountant who refuses an expensive gift from a software salesperson meets the ethical standard of:

   a. credibility

   b. confidentiality

   c. integrity

   d. competence

9. Which of the following is not one of the provisions of the Sarbanes-Oxley Act of 2002?

   a. The company's auditors assume responsibility for the financial statements.

   b. The penalties (i.e., prison time and fines) for corporate fraud were increased.

   c. At least one audit committee member should be a financial expert.

   d. The CEO and CFO must certify that the financial statements fairly present the company's operations and financial condition.

10. All of the following tools help companies compete in today's market *except*:

   a. JIT

   b. KJD

   c. ERP

   d. TQM

Quick Check Answers

1. b 2. b 3. d 4. d 5. d 6. c 7. c 8. c 9. a 10. b

For Internet Exercises, Excel in Practice, and additional online activities, go to this book's Web site at www.prenhall.com/bamber.

Assess Your Progress

■ Learning Objectives

1 Identify managers' four primary responsibilities

2 Distinguish financial accounting from managerial accounting

3 Describe organizational structure and the roles and skills required of management accountants within the organization

4 Describe the role of the Institute of Management Accountants (IMA) and use its ethical standards to make reasonable ethical judgments

5 Discuss trends in the business environment

6 Use cost-benefit analysis to make business decisions

■ Short Exercises

S1-1 **Roles of managers** *(Learning Objective 1)*
Describe the four primary roles of managers and the way they relate to one another.

S1-2 **Contrast managerial and financial accounting** *(Learning Objective 2)*
Your roommate, who plans to specialize in international business, is considering whether to enroll in the second principles of accounting course. She says, "I don't want to be an accountant, so why do I need a second accounting course? I just spent a whole term on financial accounting. Most of this second course focuses on managerial accounting, but how can that be so different from what I already learned in financial accounting?" Respond.

S1-3 **Roles and skills of management accountants** *(Learning Objective 3)*
Your friends call you a "bean counter" because you are taking an accounting class. Explain to them why they are wrong.

S1-4 **Role of internal audit function** *(Learning Objective 3)*
Explain what the role of the internal audit function is and why the internal audit function usually reports to the CEO or CFO and the audit committee.

S1-5 **Importance of ethical standards** *(Learning Objective 4)*
Explain why each of the four broad ethical standards in the IMA's *Statement of Ethical Professional Practice* is necessary.

S1-6 **Violations of ethical standards** *(Learning Objective 4)*
The IMA's *Statement of Ethical Professional Practice* (Exhibit 1-6) requires management accountants to meet standards regarding:

- Competence.
- Confidentiality.
- Integrity.
- Credibility.

continued . . .

Consider the following situations. Which guidelines are violated in each situation?

a. You tell your brother that your company will report earnings significantly above financial analysts' estimates.

b. You see that other employees take home office supplies for personal use. As an intern, you do the same thing, assuming that this is a "perk."

c. At a conference on e-commerce, you skip the afternoon session and go sightseeing.

d. You failed to read the detailed specifications of a new general ledger package that you asked your company to purchase. After it is installed, you are surprised that it is incompatible with some of your company's older accounting software.

e. You do not provide top management with the detailed job descriptions they requested because you fear they may use this information to cut a position from your department.

S1-7 **Just-in-time management** *(Learning Objective 5)*
Is JIT more appropriate for Amazon.com, a book, music, and electronics e-tailer, or Mouton-Rothschild, a French winemaker specializing in fine red wines? Explain.

S1-8 **Cost-benefit analysis** *(Learning Objective 6)*
Consider the cost-benefit analysis for GE's quality program discussed on page 24. Suppose GE's managers now estimate an 85% chance that the projects will yield an extra $20 million in benefits and a 15% chance that the projects will yield an extra $80 million. What is the expected value of the additional benefits *now*? Assuming that total costs remain at $200 million, and cost savings in the first year already amounted to $170 million, does this change your mind about whether the quality program was a worthwhile investment?

■Exercises

E1-9 **Managers' responsibilities** *(Learning Objective 1)*
Categorize each of the following activities as to which management responsibility it fulfills: planning, directing, controlling, or decision making. Some activities may fulfill more than one responsibility.

a. Management conducts variance analysis by comparing budget to actual.

b. Management reviews hourly sales reports to determine the level of staffing needed to service customers.

c. Management decides to increase sales growth by 10% next year.

d. Management uses information on product costs to determine sales prices.

e. To lower product costs, management moves production to Mexico.

E1-10 **Define key terms** *(Learning Objectives 1, 2)*
Complete the following statements with one of the terms listed here. You may use a term more than once, and some terms may not be used at all.

Budget	Creditors	Managerial accounting	Planning
Controlling	Financial accounting	Managers	Shareholders

a. Companies must follow GAAP in their _____ systems.

b. Financial accounting develops reports for external parties such as _____ and _____.

c. When managers evaluate the company's performance compared to the plan, they are performing the _____ role of management.

d. _____ are decision makers inside a company.

e. _____ provides information on a company's past performance to external parties.

f. _____ systems are not restricted by GAAP but are chosen by comparing the costs versus the benefits of the system.

g. Choosing goals and the means to achieve them is the _____ function of management.

h. _____ systems report on various segments or business units of the company.

i. _____ statements of public companies are audited annually by CPAs.

E1-11   Classify roles within the organization *(Learning Objective 3)*
Complete the following statements with one of the terms listed here. You may use a term more than once, and some terms may not be used at all.

Audit committee	Board of directors	CEO	CFO
Treasurer	Controller	Cross-functional teams	COO

a. The _____ and the _____ report to the CEO.

b. The internal audit function reports to the CFO or _____ and the _____.

c. The _____ is directly responsible for financial accounting, managerial accounting, and tax reporting.

d. The CEO is hired by the _____.

e. The _____ is directly responsible for raising capital and investing funds.

f. The _____ is directly responsible for the company's operations.

g. Management accountants often work with _____.

h. A subcommittee of the board of directors is called the _____.

E1-12   Describe needed skills and knowledge *(Learning Objective 3)*
A study by the IMA found that management accountants need skills and knowledge above and beyond pure accounting knowledge. Describe the set of skills and knowledge identified in the study and explain why they are important to the new role of management accountants.

E1-13   Professional organization and certification *(Learning Objective 4)*
Complete the following sentences:

a. The _____ is the professional association for management accountants.

b. The institute offers two types of certification: the _____ and _____.

c. The _____ exam focuses on managerial accounting topics, economics, and business finance.

d. The _____ exam focuses on financial statement analysis, business valuation, risk management, working capital policy, and capital structure.

e. The institute's monthly publication, called _____, addresses current topics of interest to management accountants.

f. The institute says that approximately _____ percent of accountants work in organizations rather than at CPA firms.

E1-14 Ethical dilemma *(Learning Objective 4)*

Mary Gonzales is the controller at Automax, a car dealership. She recently hired Cory Loftus as a bookkeeper. Loftus wanted to attend a class on Excel spreadsheets, so Gonzales temporarily took over Loftus's duties, including overseeing a fund for topping off a car's gas tank before a test drive. Gonzales found a shortage in this fund and confronted Loftus when he returned to work. Loftus admitted that he occasionally uses this fund to pay for his own gas. Gonzales estimated that the amount involved is close to $300.

Requirements

1. What should Gonzales do?
2. Would you change your answer to the previous question if Gonzales was the one recently hired as controller and Loftus was a well-liked, longtime employee who indicated that he always eventually repaid the fund?

E1-15 Classify ethical responsibilities *(Learning Objective 4)*

According to the IMA's *Statement of Ethical Professional Practice* (Exhibit 1-6), management accountants should follow four standards: competence, confidentiality, integrity, and credibility. Each of these standards contains specific responsibilities. Classify each of the following responsibilities according to the standard it addresses.

Responsibility:

1. Refrain from using confidential information for unethical or illegal advantage.
2. Maintain an appropriate level of professional expertise by continually developing knowledge and skills.
3. Communicate information fairly and objectively.
4. Recognize and communicate professional limitations that would preclude responsible judgment or successful performance of an activity.
5. Mitigate actual conflicts of interest. Regularly communicate with business associates to avoid apparent conflicts of interest. Advise all parties of any potential conflicts.
6. Provide decision support information and recommendations that are accurate, clear, concise, and timely.
7. Abstain from engaging in or supporting any activity that might discredit the profession.
8. Disclose all relevant information that could reasonably be expected to influence an intended user's understanding of the reports, analyses, or recommendations.
9. Inform all relevant parties regarding the appropriate use of confidential information. Monitor subordinates' activities to ensure compliance.
10. Perform professional duties in accordance with relevant laws, regulations, and technical standards.
11. Refrain from engaging in any conduct that would prejudice carrying out duties ethically.
12. Keep information confidential except when disclosure is authorized or legally required.
13. Disclose delays or deficiencies in information, timeliness, processing, or internal controls in conformance with organization policy and/or applicable law.

E1-16 **Define key terms** *(Learning Objectives 5, 6)*

Complete the following statements with one of the terms listed here. You may use a term more than once, and some terms may not be used at all.

E-commerce	Future value	Shift to service economy
ERP	JIT	Throughput time
Expected value	Present	TQM
Future	Present value	ISO 9001:2000

a. To account for uncertainty in the amounts of future costs and benefits, we compute the _____ by multiplying the probability of each outcome by the dollar value of that outcome.

b. To make a cost-benefit decision today, we must find the _____ of the costs and benefits that are incurred in the future.

c. The goal of _____ is to meet customers' expectations by providing them with superior products and services by eliminating defects and waste throughout the value chain.

d. Most of the costs of adopting ERP and JIT, expanding into a foreign market, or improving quality are incurred in the _____; but most of the benefits occur in the _____.

e. _____ is the time between buying raw materials and selling the finished products.

f. _____ serves the information needs of people in accounting as well as people in marketing and in the warehouse.

g. Firms adopt _____ to conduct business on the Internet.

h. Firms acquire the _____ certification to demonstrate their commitment to quality.

E1-17 **Summarize the Sarbanes-Oxley Act** *(Learning Objective 5)*

You just obtained an entry-level job as a management accountant. Other newly hired accountants have heard of the Sarbanes-Oxley Act of 2002 (SOX), but don't know much about it (they attended a different university). Write a short memo to your colleagues discussing the reason for SOX, the goal of SOX, and some of the specific requirements of SOX that will affect your company.

E1-18 **JIT cost-benefit analysis** *(Learning Objective 6)*

Wild Rides manufactures snowboards. Shawn Mobbs, the CEO, is trying to decide whether to adopt JIT. He expects that in present-value terms, adopting JIT would save $97,000 in warehousing expenses and $46,000 in spoilage costs. Adopting JIT will require several one-time up-front expenditures: (1) $13,500 for an employee training program, (2) $37,000 to streamline the plant's production process, and (3) $8,000 to identify suppliers that will guarantee zero defects and on-time delivery.

Requirements

1. What are the total costs of adopting JIT?
2. What are the total benefits of adopting JIT?
3. Should Wild Rides adopt JIT? Why or why not?

P1-19A **Summarize managerial accounting and recent business trends** *(Learning Objectives 1, 2, 3, 5)*

Your roommate is an engineering student who has developed a new marketable technology as part of her graduate studies. As soon as she finishes her degree, she intends to start her own company to manufacture and sell the technology. She has not taken any business classes but has begun to read business periodicals to develop some business savvy. She has several issues on which she would like your input. Discuss what you know about the following:

1. Your roommate feels confident about her abilities as the company's chief product engineer but questions whether she should manage the company herself. She wonders what her role as company manager would be.

2. She's heard of financial and managerial accounting and wonders if they are the same thing.

3. Because you are taking an accounting class, she asks you to explain how to structure the financial arm of a large organization.

4. Your roommate has high hopes for her company. She's already anticipating it to be publicly traded some day in the near future. She wants to know how SOX will affect her business.

5. The business magazines often mention TQM and the ISO. She wants to know more about TQM and the ISO 9001:2000 certification.

6. Your roommate also sees frequent references to JIT production. She would like to know what JIT is about and if she should consider adopting it.

7. Because she will sell the new technology to other companies rather than consumers, your roommate doesn't see the need to set up an electronic purchasing Web site. Explain to her why e-commerce is helpful even if she isn't selling directly to individual consumers.

P1-20A **Ethical dilemmas** *(Learning Objective 4)*

Kate Royer is the new controller for ED Software, which develops and sells educational software. Shortly before the December 31 fiscal year-end, Matt Adams, the company president, asks Royer how things look for the year-end numbers. He is not happy to learn that earnings growth may be below 15% for the first time in the company's five-year history. Adams explains that financial analysts have again predicted a 15% earnings growth for the company and that he does not intend to disappoint them. He suggests that Royer talk to the assistant controller, who can explain how the previous controller dealt with this situation. The assistant controller suggests the following strategies:

a. Persuade suppliers to postpone billing until January 1.

b. Record as sales certain software awaiting sale that is held in a public warehouse.

c. Delay the year-end closing a few days into January of the next year so that some of next year's sales are included as this year's sales.

d. Reduce the allowance for bad debts (and bad debts expense).

e. Postpone routine monthly maintenance expenditures from December to January.

Which of these suggested strategies are inconsistent with IMA standards? What should Royer do if Adams insists that she follow all of these suggestions?

P1-21A ERP cost-benefit analysis *(Learning Objectives 5, 6)*

As CEO of SeaSpray Marine, Ron Greenwood knows it is important to control costs and to respond quickly to changes in the highly competitive boat-building industry. When IDG Consulting proposes that SeaSpray Marine invest in an ERP system, he forms a team to evaluate the proposal: the plant engineer, the plant foreman, the systems specialist, the human resources director, the marketing director, and the management accountant.

A month later, management accountant Mike Cobalt reports that the team and IDG estimate that if SeaSpray Marine implements the ERP system, it will incur the following costs:

a. $350,000 in software costs

b. $80,000 to customize the ERP software and load SeaSpray's data into the new ERP system

c. $125,000 for employee training

The team estimates that the ERP system should provide several benefits:

a. More efficient order processing should lead to savings with a present value of $185,000.

b. Streamlining the manufacturing process so that it maps into the ERP system will create savings with a present value of $275,000.

c. Integrating purchasing, production, marketing, and distribution into a single system will allow SeaSpray Marine to reduce inventories, saving $220,000.

d. Higher customer satisfaction should increase sales, which, in turn, should increase the present value of profits by $150,000.

The team knows that because of complexity, some ERP installations are not successful. If SeaSpray Marine's system fails, there will be no cost savings and no additional sales. The team predicts that there is an 80% chance that the ERP installation will succeed and a 20% chance that it will fail.

Requirements

1. If the ERP installation succeeds, what is the dollar amount of the benefits?

2. Should SeaSpray Marine install the ERP system? Why or why not? Show your calculations.

P1-22A Continuation of P1-21A: revised probabilities *(Learning Objectives 5, 6)*

P1-21A asked you to perform a quantitative analysis to help SeaSpray Marine's managers decide whether to embark on the project. Now consider some qualitative factors in SeaSpray Marine's ERP project.

1. Why did Greenwood create a team to evaluate IDG's proposal? Consider each piece of cost-benefit information that management accountant Cobalt reported. Which person on the team is most likely to have contributed each item? *(Hint: Which team member is likely to have the most information about each cost or benefit?)*

2. Quantifying ERP benefits can be difficult. After further discussion, the team predicts that there is a 60% chance that the ERP installation will succeed and a 40% chance that it will fail. Should SeaSpray Marine still install the new ERP system?

P1-23A E-commerce cost-benefit analysis *(Learning Objectives 5, 6)*

Sun Gas wants to move its sales order system to the Web. Under the proposed system, gas stations and other merchants will use a Web browser and, after typing in a password for the Sun Gas Web page, will be able to check the availability and current price of various products and place an order. Currently, customer service representatives take dealers' orders over the phone; they record the information on a paper form, then manually enter it into the firm's computer system.

CFO Carrie Smith believes that dealers will not adopt the new Web system unless Sun Gas provides financial assistance to help them purchase or upgrade their PCs. Smith estimates this one-time cost at $750,000. Sun Gas will also have to invest $150,000 in upgrading its own computer hardware. The cost of the software and the consulting fee for installing the system will be $230,000. The Web system will enable Sun Gas to eliminate 25 clerical positions. Smith estimates that the benefits of the new system's lower labor costs will have a present value of $1,357,000.

Requirements

Use a cost-benefit analysis to recommend to Smith whether Sun Gas should proceed with the Web-based ordering system. Give your reasons, showing supporting calculations.

P1-24A Continuation of P1-23A: revised probabilities *(Learning Objectives 5, 6)*

Consider the Sun Gas proposed entry into e-commerce in P1-23A. Smith revises her estimates of the benefits from the new system's lower labor costs. She now thinks there is a 40% chance of receiving the $1,357,000 in benefits and a 60% chance the benefits will be only $933,000.

Requirements

1. Compute the expected benefits of the Web-based ordering system.
2. Would you recommend that Sun Gas accept the proposal?
3. Before Smith makes a final decision, what other factors should she consider?

Problems (Problem Set B)

P1-25B Summarize managerial accounting and recent business trends *(Learning Objectives 1, 2, 3, 5)*

One of your friends has taken a great interest in Australia and wants to import home décor items from Australia after college. He has not taken any business classes but has begun to read business newspapers and magazines to develop some business knowledge. He has several issues on which he would like your input. Discuss with him what you know about the following:

1. Your friend feels confident about his abilities to select marketable Australian home décor, but questions whether he should manage the company himself or hire someone to manage the company while he takes on the role of the chief buyer. He wonders what his role would be if he were the company manager as well.

2. He's heard of financial and managerial accounting and wonders if they are the same thing.

3. Because you are taking an accounting class, he asks you to explain how to structure the financial arm of a large organization.

4. Your friend has high hopes for his company. He foresees his business growing into a chain of home décor stores, similar to Pier 1 Imports or Cost Plus World Market. To grow the business to this level, he will have to take the company public. He wants to know how SOX will affect a publicly traded company.

5. The business magazines often mention TQM and the ISO. He wants to know if TQM and the ISO 9001:2000 certification apply only to manufacturers.

6. Your friend also sees frequent references to JIT production. First, he would like to know what JIT is. Second, he wonders if it would apply to his business.

7. Your friend wonders if he should invest in e-commerce or depend solely on sales generated by foot traffic into his "brick-and-mortar" retail stores.

P1-26B Ethical dilemmas *(Learning Objective 4)*

Kara Williams is the new controller for Colors, a designer and manufacturer of sportswear. Shortly before the December 31 fiscal year-end, Lashea Lucas (the company president) asks Williams how things look for the year-end numbers. Lucas is not happy to learn that earnings growth may be below 10% for the first time in the company's five-year history. Lucas explains that financial analysts have again predicted a 12% earnings growth for the company and that she does not intend to disappoint them. She suggests that Williams talk to the assistant controller, who can explain how the previous controller dealt with this situation. The assistant controller suggests the following strategies:

a. Postpone planned advertising expenditures from December to January.

b. Do not record sales returns and allowances on the basis that they are individually immaterial.

c. Persuade retail customers to accelerate January orders to December.

d. Reduce the allowance for bad debts (and bad debts expense).

e. Colors ships finished goods to public warehouses across the country for temporary storage until it receives firm orders from customers. As Colors receives orders, it directs the warehouse to ship the goods to nearby customers. The assistant controller suggests recording goods sent to the public warehouses as sales.

Which of these suggested strategies are inconsistent with IMA standards? What should Williams do if Lucas insists that she follow all of these suggestions?

P1-27B TQM cost-benefit analysis *(Learning Objectives 5, 6)*

CRM manufactures computer disk drives. It sells these disk drives to other manufacturers, which use them in assembling computers. CRM is having trouble with its new DVD drive. About half the time, CRM employees find defects while the disk drive is still on the production line. These drives are immediately reworked in the plant. Otherwise, CRM's customers do not identify the problem until they install the disk drives they've purchased. Customers return defective drives for replacement under warranty. They have also complained that after they install the disk drive, the drive's connector (which plugs into the computer system board) often shakes loose while the computer is being assembled. The customers must then reassemble the computer after fixing the loose connection.

CRM's CEO Jay Rich has just returned from a seminar on TQM. He forms a team to address these quality problems. The team includes the plant engineer, the production supervisor, a customer service representative, the marketing director, and the management accountant.

continued . . .

Three months later, the team proposes a major project to *prevent* these quality problems. CRM's accountant Anna Crowe reports that implementing the team's proposal will require CRM to incur the following costs over the next three months:

- $180,500 for CRM's scientists to develop a completely new disk drive.
- $70,000 for the company's engineers to redesign the connector so that it better tolerates rough treatment.

The project team is unsure whether this investment will pay off. If the effort fixes the problem, Crowe expects that:

- A reputation for higher quality will increase sales, which, in turn, will increase the present value of profits by $200,000.
- Fewer disk drives will fail. The present value of the savings from fewer warranty repairs is $170,300.
- The plant will have fewer defective disk drives to rework. The present value of this savings is $100,200.

However, if this project is not successful, there will be no cost savings and no additional sales. The team predicts a 70% chance that the project will succeed and a 30% chance that it will fail.

Requirements

1. If the quality improvement project succeeds, what is the dollar amount of the benefits?
2. Should CRM undertake this project? Why or why not? Show supporting calculations.

P1-28B Continuation of P1-27B: revised probabilities *(Learning Objectives 5, 6)*

P1-27B asked you to perform a quantitative analysis to help CRM's managers decide whether to embark on the project. Now consider some qualitative factors in CRM's quality improvement project.

1. Why did Rich create a team to address this quality problem rather than assigning the task to one person? Consider each piece of cost/benefit information reported by management accountant Crowe. Which person on the team is most likely to have contributed each item? (*Hint:* Which team member is likely to have the most information about each cost or benefit?)
2. Quantifying TQM benefits can be difficult. After further discussion, the team predicts that there is only a 50% chance that the proposal will succeed, and a 50% chance that it will fail. Should CRM still implement the project?

P1-29B Information system cost-benefit analysis *(Learning Objectives 5, 6)*

Smart Bank processes checks for smaller banks and insurance companies. When a customer complains that a check was not deposited to its account, a Smart Bank clerk takes the complaint over the phone and fills out a paper form. The complaint form triggers a long search through piles of canceled checks in a warehouse to find the check in question. Smart Bank then compares this check to its computer and paper records.

Smart Bank is considering moving this process to the Web. When a customer has a question, an employee simply uses a Web browser and a password to access Smart Bank's databases. The customer's employee pulls up a computerized image of the check in question to verify the amount and then queries Smart Bank's databases to locate the mistake. If required, a credit to the customer's account can be issued immediately.

The Web-based system will require the bank to invest $83,000 in a new server and check-scanning equipment. eNow! Consultants will charge $110,000 for the software and consulting fees to get the system running. The system will also require increasing the bank's Internet capacity. The present value of this cost is $20,000.

Smart Bank has identified two benefits of this project. First, several bank clerks freed from searching through stacks of canceled checks will be reassigned, which will lead to cost savings with a present value of $173,000. Second, the new system's additional capacity will enable Smart Bank to accept more check-processing business, which should lead to additional profits with a present value of $43,200.

Requirements
Does a cost-benefit analysis justify the Web-based system? Explain why, showing supporting calculations.

P1-30B **Continuation of P1-29B: revised probabilities** *(Learning Objectives 5, 6)*

Consider the Smart Bank project described in P1-29B. Smart Bank has revised its estimates of additional profits the bank is likely to earn. There is an 80% chance that the bank will earn $43,200 in extra profits, but also a 20% chance the bank will earn $75,000.

Requirements
1. Compute the expected value of the benefits from the additional business.
2. Would you recommend that Smart Bank accept the proposal? Give your reason, showing supporting calculations.
3. Are there other potential benefits not listed in P1-29B or P1-30B that may make the proposal more attractive to Smart Bank?

Apply Your Knowledge

▪ Decision Case

Case 1-31. Ethical standards *(Learning Objective 4)*
The IMA's *Statement of Ethical Professional Practice* (Exhibit 1-6) can be applied to more than just managerial accounting. It is also relevant to college students. Explain at least one situation that shows how each IMA standard is relevant to your experiences as a student. For example, the ethical standard of competence would suggest not cutting classes.

▪ Ethical Issue

Issue 1-32. Ethical dilemma *(Learning Objective 4)*
Ricardo Valencia recently resigned his position as controller for Tom White Automotive, a small, struggling foreign car dealer in Austin, Texas. Valencia has just started a new job as controller for Mueller Imports, a much larger dealer for the same car manufacturer. Demand for this particular make of car is exploding, and the manufacturer cannot produce enough cars to satisfy demand. Each manufacturer's regional sales managers is given a certain number of cars. Each regional sales manager then decides how to divide the cars among the independently owned dealerships in the region. Because most dealerships can sell every car they receive, the key is getting a large number of cars from the manufacturer's regional sales manager.

Valencia's former employer, Tom White Automotive, received only about 25 cars a month. Consequently, the dealership was not very profitable.

Valencia is surprised to learn that his new employer, Mueller Imports, receives over 200 cars a month. Valencia soon gets another surprise. Every couple of months, a local jeweler bills the dealer $5,000 for "miscellaneous services." Franz Mueller, the owner of the dealership, personally approves the payment of these invoices, noting that each invoice is a "selling expense." From casual conversations with a salesperson, Valencia learns that Mueller frequently gives Rolex watches to the manufacturer's regional sales manager and other sales executives. Before talking to anyone about this, Valencia decides to work through his ethical dilemma by answering the following questions:

1. What is the ethical issue?
2. What are my options?
3. What are the possible consequences?
4. What should I do?

■ Team Project

Project 1-33. Interviewing a local company about e-commerce *(Learning Objective 5)*

Search the Internet for a nearby company that also has a Web page. Arrange an interview with a management accountant, a controller, or another accounting/finance officer of the company. Before you conduct the interview, answer the following questions:

1. What is the company's primary product or service?

2. Is the primary purpose of the company's Web site to provide information about the company and its products, to sell online, or to provide financial information for investors?

3. Are parts of the company's Web site restricted so that you need password authorization to enter? What appears to be the purpose of limiting access?

4. Does the Web site provide an e-mail link for contacting the company?

   At the interview, begin by clarifying your answers to questions 1 through 4 and ask the following additional questions:

5. If the company sells over the Web, what benefits has the company derived? Did the company perform a cost-benefit analysis before deciding to begin Web sales?

   Or

   If the company does not sell over the Web, why not? Has the company performed a cost-benefit analysis and decided not to sell over the Web?

6. What is the biggest cost of operating the Web site?

7. Does the company make any purchases over the Internet? What percentage?

8. How has e-commerce affected the company's managerial accounting system? Have the management accountant's responsibilities become more or less complex? more or less interesting?

9. Does the company use Web-based accounting applications such as accounts receivable or accounts payable?

10. Does the company use an ERP system? If so, does it view the system as a success? What have been the benefits? the costs?

    Prepare a report describing the results of your interview.

This page intentionally left blank

2 Building Blocks of Managerial Accounting

n 1999, Nissan Motor Company had a problem. With no cash dividends and a net *loss* of over ¥684 billion yen (approximately $4.1 billion), CEO Carlos Ghosn knew he had to do something. In his words: "The *lack* of profit is like a fever. When your business is not profitable, that's a serious signal that something is wrong. Either the products are not right, or marketing is inefficient, or the cost base is too high—something is wrong. If you ignore a fever, you can get very sick. If you ignore unprofitability, the situation can only worsen." Ghosn launched the *Nissan Revival Plan* that turned the company around by designing and marketing new models, investing in new plant technologies, slashing supply costs, and emphasizing the company's most profitable products. Five years later, Nissan's annual operating income tops ¥861 billion yen (approximately $7.6 billion).

Nissan's operating margin is now the highest in the automotive industry, and it is paying its shareholders cash dividends at record levels.

Before Nissan could attack its problems, it had to know where its costs were incurred and whether it could control those costs by making different decisions. Was the company spending too much in production, using outdated equipment and technologies? Was it spending enough on designing new products that better met customers' needs and desires? Was it targeting the right audiences in its television advertising? In this chapter, we talk about many costs: costs that both managers and management accountants must understand to successfully run a business.

Sources: NissanUSA.com; Nissan-Global.com; and Nissan Motor Co., Ltd., Annual Reports 2002, 2003, 2004. ■

Learning Objectives

1 Distinguish among service, merchandising, and manufacturing companies

2 Describe the value chain and its elements

3 Distinguish between direct and indirect costs

4 Identify the inventoriable product costs and period costs of merchandising and manufacturing firms

5 Prepare the financial statements for service, merchandising, and manufacturing companies

6 Describe costs that are relevant and irrelevant for decision making

7 Classify costs as fixed or variable and calculate total and average costs at different volumes

So far, we have seen how managerial accounting provides information that managers use to run their businesses more efficiently. Managers must understand basic managerial accounting terms and concepts before they can use the information to make good decisions. This terminology provides the "common ground" through which managers and accountants communicate. Without a common understanding of these concepts, managers may ask for (and accountants may provide) the wrong information for making decisions. As you will see, different types of costs are useful for different purposes. Both managers and accountants must have a clear understanding of the situation and the types of costs that are relevant to the decision at hand.

Three Business Sectors and the Value Chain

Before we talk about specific types of costs, let's consider the three most common types of companies and the business activities in which they incur costs.

Service, Merchandising, and Manufacturing Companies

 Distinguish among service, merchandising, and manufacturing companies

Organizations other than not-for-profits and governmental agencies are in business to generate profits for their owners. The primary means of generating that profit generally fall into one of three categories:

Service Companies

Service companies are in business to sell intangible services—such as health care, insurance, and consulting—rather than tangible products. Recall from the last chapter that service firms now make up the largest sector of the U.S. economy, providing jobs to over 55% of the workforce. For service companies such as eBay (online auction), H&R Block (tax return preparation), and Accountemps (temporary personnel services), salaries and wages often make up over 70% of their costs. Because service companies sell services, they generally don't have Inventory or Cost of Goods Sold accounts. Some service providers carry a minimal amount of supplies inventory; however, this inventory is used for internal operations—not sold for profit. In addition to labor costs, service companies incur costs to develop new services, advertise, and provide customer service.

Merchandising Companies

Merchandising companies such as Amazon.com, Wal-Mart, and Foot Locker resell tangible products they buy from suppliers. Amazon.com, for example, buys books, CDs, and DVDs and resells them to customers at higher prices than what it pays its own suppliers for these goods. Merchandising companies include retailers (such as Home Depot) and wholesalers. **Retailers** sell to consumers such as you. **Wholesalers**, often referred to as "middlemen," buy products in bulk from manufacturers, mark up the prices, and then sell those products to retailers. Because merchandising companies sell tangible products, they have inventory. Even merchandising companies that use just-in-time (JIT) systems have inventory; they just have *less* inventory than their non-JIT competitors. The cost of merchandise inventory is the cost merchandisers pay for the goods *plus* all costs necessary to get the merchandise in place and ready to sell, including freight-in costs and any import duties or tariffs. Because the entire inventory is ready for sale, a merchandiser's balance sheet usually reports just one inventory account called Inventory or Merchandise Inventory. Merchandisers also incur other costs to identify new products and locations for new stores, to advertise and sell their products, and to provide customer service.

Manufacturing Companies

Manufacturing companies use labor, plant, and equipment to convert raw materials into new finished products. For example, Nissan's production workers use the company's factories (plant and equipment) to transform raw materials such as steel and tires into high-performance automobiles. Manufacturers sell their products to retailers or wholesalers at a price that is high enough to cover their costs and generate a profit.

Because of their broader range of activities, manufacturers have three types of inventory (pictured in Exhibit 2-1):

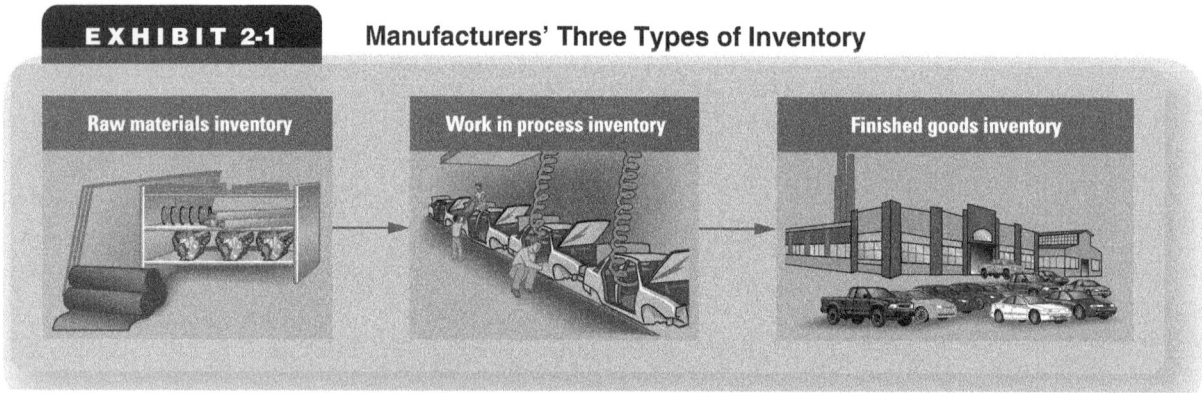

EXHIBIT 2-1   **Manufacturers' Three Types of Inventory**

| Raw materials inventory | Work in process inventory | Finished goods inventory |

1. **Raw materials inventory:** *All raw materials used in manufacturing.* Nissan's raw materials include steel, glass, carpeting, tires, upholstery fabric, engines, and other automobile components. It also includes other physical materials used in the plant, such as machine lubricants and janitorial supplies.

2. **Work in process inventory:** *Goods that are partway through the manufacturing process but not yet complete.* At Nissan, the work in process inventory consists of partially completed vehicles.

3. **Finished goods inventory:** *Completed goods that have not yet been sold.* Nissan is in business to sell completed cars, not work in process. Manufacturers sell their finished goods inventory to merchandisers. Nissan, for example, sells its completed automobiles to retail dealerships. Some manufacturers, such as The Original Mattress Factory, sell their products directly to consumers.

Exhibit 2-2 summarizes the differences among service, merchandising, and manufacturing companies.

EXHIBIT 2-2   **Service, Merchandising, and Manufacturing Companies**

	Service Companies	Merchandising Companies	Manufacturing Companies
Examples	Advertising agencies Banks Law firms Insurance companies	Amazon.com Kroger Wal-Mart Wholesalers	Procter & Gamble DaimlerChrysler Dell Computer Nissan
Primary Output	Intangible services	Tangible products purchased from suppliers	New tangible products made as workers and equipment convert raw materials into new finished products
Type(s) of Inventory	None	Inventory (or Merchandise Inventory)	Raw materials inventory Work in process inventory Finished goods inventory

BBH CHAPTER 2

Stop & Think...

What type of company is Outback Steakhouse, Inc.?

Answer: Some companies don't fit nicely into one of the three categories discussed previously. Outback has some elements of a service company (it serves hungry patrons), some elements of a manufacturing company (its chefs convert raw ingredients into finished meals), and some elements of a merchandising company (it sells ready-to-serve bottles of wine and beer). Outback is really a hybrid of the three types of companies we just discussed.

As the "Stop & Think" shows, not all companies are strictly service, merchandising, or manufacturing firms. Recall from Chapter 1 that the U.S. economy is shifting more toward service. Many traditional manufacturers, such as General Electric (GE), have developed profitable service segments that provide much of their company's profits. General Motors now earns more from its financing and insurance operations than it does from car sales. Even merchandising firms are getting into the "service game" by selling extended warranty contracts on merchandise sold. Retailers offer extended warranties on products ranging from furniture and major appliances to sporting equipment and consumer electronics. While the merchandiser recognizes a liability for these warranties, the price charged to customers for the warranties greatly exceeds the company's cost of fulfilling its warranty obligations.

Which Business Activities Make Up the Value Chain?

2 Describe the value chain and its elements

Many people describe Nissan, Dell Computer, and Coca-Cola as manufacturing companies. But it would be more accurate to say that these are companies that *do* manufacturing. Why? Because companies that do manufacturing also do many other things. Nissan also conducts research to determine what type of new technology to integrate into next year's models. Nissan designs the new models based on its research and then produces, markets, distributes, and services the cars. These activities form Nissan's **value chain**—the activities that add value to products and services.

To set a selling price or to determine how profitable the Xterra model is, Nissan must know how much it costs to research, design, produce, market, distribute, and service the product. In other words, Nissan can't set selling prices high enough to *just* cover the costs of production. Pricing decisions require Nissan to calculate the *full cost* of the Xterra, including costs incurred across all six elements of the value chain pictured in Exhibit 2-3.

EXHIBIT 2-3   **The Value Chain**

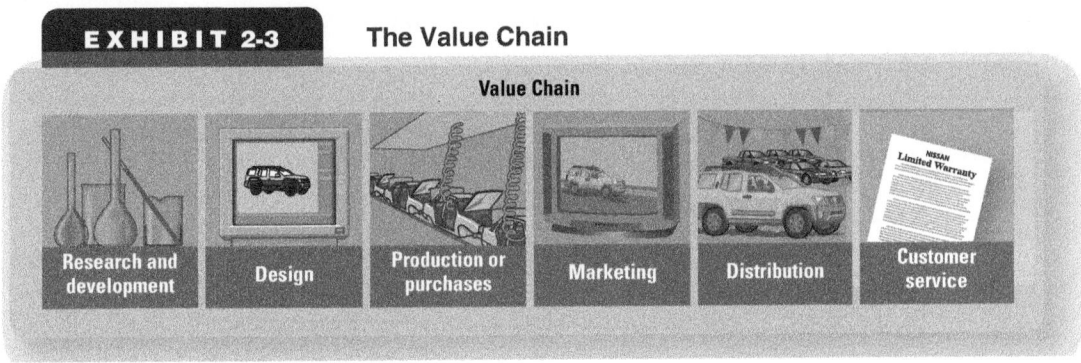

Value Chain

Research and development | Design | Production or purchases | Marketing | Distribution | Customer service

Research and Development (R&D): *Researching and developing new or improved products or services and the processes for producing them.* Nissan continually engages in researching and developing new technologies to incorporate in its vehicles (such as GPS systems, "smart keys," and automatic headlamps) and in its manufacturing plants (such as manufacturing robotics). Nissan's GREEN program aims at developing fuel cells for vehicles, new ultra-low emission vehicles, new hybrid vehicles, and better fuel economy on existing models. Nissan currently spends over ¥300 billion (approximately $2.6 billion) a year in R&D.

Design: *Detailed engineering of products and services and the processes for producing them.* Nissan's CEO describes design as the "interface between customers and the brand." Nissan's designers need to fulfill customers' desires for vehicle style, features, safety, and quality. Nissan's goal is to engineer its products to create "total customer satisfaction." (Nissan has embraced total quality management.) As a result, Nissan employs over 500 designers in North America and introduced 12 new models as part of its revival plan. Designers consider not only what the customers want but also how to mass-produce the vehicles. Because Nissan produces over 3 million vehicles per year, engineers must design production processes to be flexible (to allow for new features and models) and efficient. These initiatives cost a lot of money. Nissan's new technical center alone cost over $118 million to build. Despite these costs, new models and production designs were critical to Nissan's turnaround.

Production or Purchases: *Resources used to produce a product or service or to purchase finished merchandise intended for resale.* For a manufacturer such as Nissan, the production activity in the value chain includes the costs incurred to *make* the vehicles. These costs include raw materials (such as steel), plant labor (such as machine operators' wages and benefits), and manufacturing overhead (such as plant utilities and equipment depreciation). For a merchandiser such as Best Buy, this value-chain activity includes the cost of inventory, such as CDs, TVs, and PCs that the company buys to resell to customers. It also includes all costs associated with getting the inventory to the store ready for sale, including freight-in costs and any import duties and tariffs.

As part of Nissan's revival plan, it opened new manufacturing facilities, including a state-of-the-art facility in Canton, Mississippi. Nissan's new investments in plant and equipment cost over ¥377 billion (approximately $3.3 billion). These costs are part of the production stage of the value chain. Nissan was also able to cut some production costs. Nissan slashed purchasing costs over 20% by working with suppliers of major components, such as tires, engines, and steel. To cut costs through JIT production, some of Nissan's suppliers have moved their own manufacturing facilities right next door to Nissan's!

Marketing: *Promotion and advertising of products or services.* The goal of marketing is to create consumer demand for products and services. Nissan uses print advertisements in magazines and newspapers, billboards, and television advertising to market its vehicles. But Nissan's revival plan includes much more than simply advertising their new models. Part of its marketing effort was directed at the dealerships that sold its vehicles. Nissan worked with dealerships to make them more effective and attractive to consumers shopping for cars so that customers would "sense quality" when walking into a Nissan dealership's showroom. As a result, most dealerships improved their cosmetic appearance and interior layout.

Distribution: *Delivery of products or services to customers.* Nissan sells most of its vehicles through traditional dealerships. However, more customers are ordering "build-your-own" vehicles through Nissan's Web site. People who are willing to wait a short time can have the features they want rather than settle for one of the vehicles in stock at the local dealership. Forrester Research, an independent research firm specializing in the impact of technology on business and consumers, expects build-to-order car sales to account for 21% of all new car sales by 2010, up from 5% in 2001.[1] Nissan's distribution costs include the costs of shipping the vehicles to retailers and customers and the costs of setting up and administering Web-based sales portals. Other industries use different distribution mechanisms. Tupperware primarily sells its products through home-based parties. Amazon.com sells only through the Internet. Until recently, Lands' End sold only through catalogs and the Web. Now, it also distributes its products through Sears' retail outlets. WebVan tried, but failed, to create an online delivery-only grocery store.

Distribution

Customer Service: *Support provided for customers after the sale.* Nissan incurs substantial customer service costs, especially in connection with warranties on new car sales. Nissan generally warranties its vehicles for the first three years and/or 36,000 miles, whichever comes first. Nissan cut warranty costs by ¥41 million in 2004. How? Through total quality management (TQM). Nissan tests *every* vehicle rolling off the Canton plant production line before shipping it out. Nissan also emphasizes quality right from the start, beginning with R&D.

Customer service

Coordinating Activities Across the Value Chain

Many of the value-chain activities occur in the order discussed here. However, managers cannot simply work on R&D and not think about customer service until after selling the car. Rather, cross-functional teams work on R&D, design, production, marketing, distribution, and customer service simultaneously. As the teams develop new model features, they also plan how to produce, market, and distribute the redesigned vehicles. They also consider how the new design will affect warranty costs. Recall from the last chapter that management accountants typically participate in these cross-functional teams. Even at the highest level of global operations, Nissan used cross-functional teams to implement its revival plans.

The value chain in Exhibit 2-3 also reminds managers to control costs over the value chain as a whole. For example, Nissan spends more in R&D and product design to increase the quality of its vehicles, which, in turn, reduces customer service costs. Even though R&D and design costs are higher, the total cost of the vehicle— as measured throughout the entire value chain—is lower as a result of this tradeoff. Enhancing its reputation for high-quality products may also enable Nissan to increase sales or to charge higher selling prices.

The value chain applies to service and merchandising firms as well as manufacturing firms. For example, an advertising agency such as Saatchi & Saatchi incurs:

- *Design* costs to develop each client's ad campaign.
- *Marketing* costs to obtain new clients.
- *Distribution* costs to get the ads to the media.
- *Customer service* costs to address each client's concerns.

[1]Dave Hirshchman, *"Coming soon: built-to-order cars delivered in 10–15 days," The Atlanta Journal Constitution,* March 25, 2001, p. Q1.

Determining the Costs to Serve a Customer or to Make a Product

How do companies such as eBay, Amazon.com, and Nissan determine how much it costs to serve a customer, fill an order, or produce an Xterra? Before we can answer this question, let's first consider some of the specialized language that accountants use when referring to costs.

3 Distinguish between direct and indirect costs

Cost Objects, Direct Costs, and Indirect Costs

A **cost object** is anything for which managers want a separate measurement of cost. Nissan's cost objects may include the following:

- Individual products (the Xterra, Pathfinder, and Altima)
- Alternative marketing strategies (sales through dealers versus built-to-order Web sales)
- Geographic segments of the business (United States, Europe, Japan)
- Departments (human resources, payroll, legal)

Costs are classified as either direct or indirect with respect to the cost object. A **direct cost** is a cost that can be traced to the cost object. For example, say the cost object is one Xterra. Nissan can trace the cost of tires to a specific Xterra; therefore, the tires are a direct cost of the vehicle. An **indirect cost** is a cost that relates to the cost object but cannot be traced to it. For example, Nissan incurs substantial cost to run the Xterra manufacturing plant, including utilities, property taxes, and depreciation on the plant and equipment. Nissan cannot build an Xterra without incurring these costs, so the costs are related to the Xterra. However, it's impossible to trace a specific amount of these costs to one Xterra. Therefore, these costs are indirect costs of an Xterra.

As shown in Exhibit 2-4, the same costs can be indirect with respect to one cost object yet direct with respect to another cost object. For example, plant and equipment

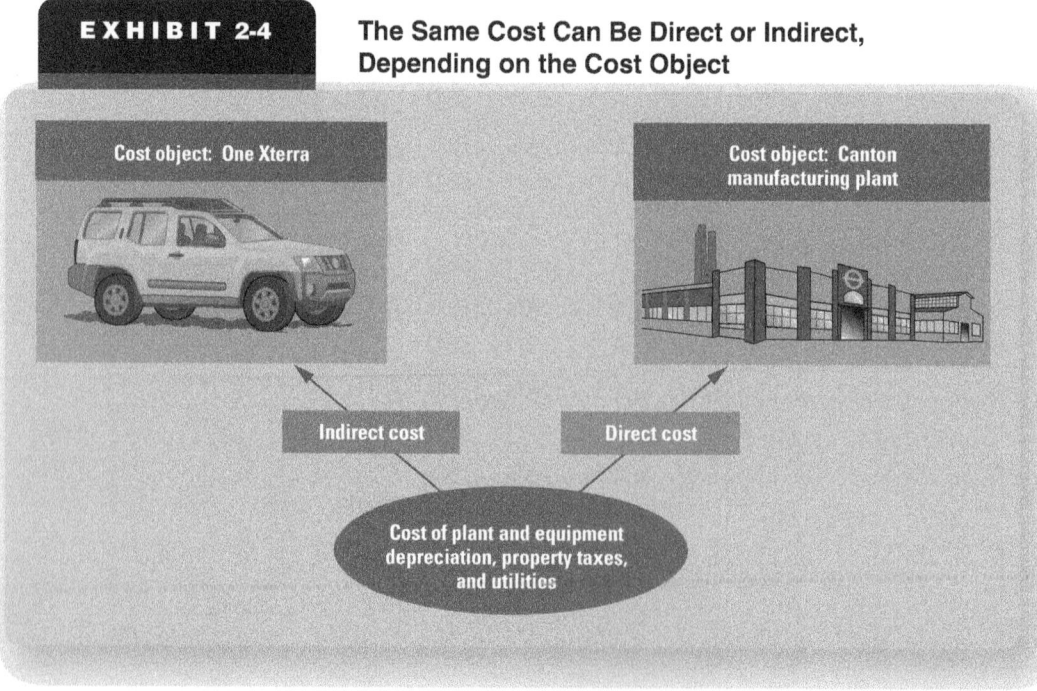

EXHIBIT 2-4   **The Same Cost Can Be Direct or Indirect, Depending on the Cost Object**

Cost object: One Xterra

Cost object: Canton manufacturing plant

Indirect cost

Direct cost

Cost of plant and equipment depreciation, property taxes, and utilities

BBH CHAPTER 2

depreciation, property taxes, and utilities are indirect costs of an Xterra. However, if management wants to know how much it costs to run the Canton manufacturing plant, the plant becomes the cost object; so the same depreciation, tax, and utility costs are direct costs of the manufacturing facility. Whether a cost is direct or indirect depends on the specified cost object. In most cases, we'll be talking about a unit of product (such as one Xterra) as the cost object.

If a company wants to know the *total* cost attributable to a cost object, it must **assign** all direct *and* indirect costs to the cost object. Assigning a cost simply means that you are "attaching" a cost to the cost object. Why? Because the cost object caused the company to incur that cost. In determining the cost of an Xterra, Nissan assigns both the cost of the tires *and* the cost of running the manufacturing plant to the Xterras built at the plant. Nissan assigns direct costs to each Xterra by **tracing** those costs to specific units, or batches. However, because Nissan cannot trace indirect costs to specific units or batches, it must **allocate** these costs to the vehicles produced at the plant. We will discuss the allocation process in more detail in the next chapter; but for now, think of allocation as dividing up the indirect costs over all of the units produced, just as you might divide a pizza among friends. Exhibit 2-5 illustrates these concepts.

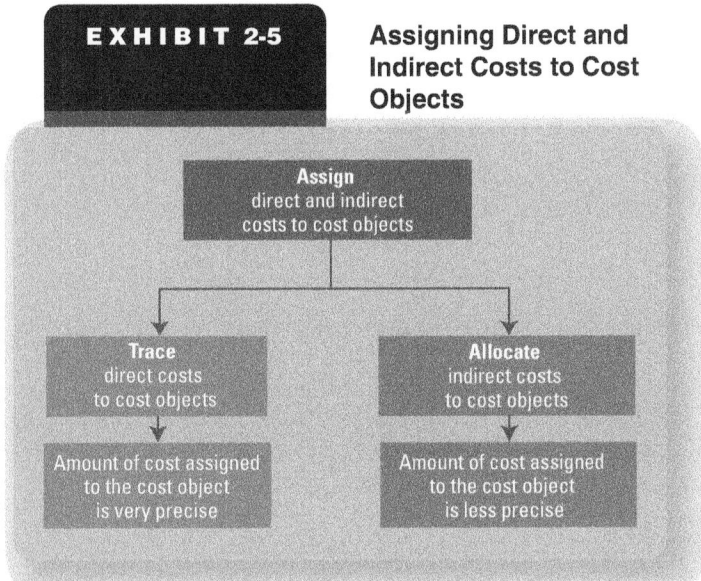

EXHIBIT 2-5   **Assigning Direct and Indirect Costs to Cost Objects**

Why is this terminology important? Because it helps managers understand how accountants arrive at cost figures. Direct costs are traced to cost objects so that managers and accountants are confident that the amount of direct cost assigned to a cost object is very accurate. For example, managers are confident in the tire cost assigned to one Xterra because they can *trace* a particular Xterra's four tires (plus a spare tire) back to a specific invoice. In contrast, indirect costs are *allocated* rather than traced; so the amount of indirect cost assigned to a cost object is more of an estimate. As a result, managers and accountants are less confident in the amount of indirect cost assigned each Xterra. Managers know the total amount of indirect costs from paying utility and tax bills and recording depreciation expense. However, the *division* of the total amount of indirect costs among the vehicles is less precise. Therefore, managers are less confident in the amount of indirect cost that should be assigned to the cost object (for example, the amount of utilities cost that should be assigned to a particular Xterra).

Product Costs for Internal Decision Making and External Reporting

Let's look more carefully at how companies determine the costs of one of the most common cost objects: products. As a manager, you'll want to focus on the products that are most profitable. But which products are these? To determine a product's profitability, you subtract the cost of the product from its selling price. But how do you calculate the cost of the product? Most companies use two different definitions of product costs: (1) full product costs for internal decision making and (2) inventoriable product costs for external reporting. Let's see what they are and how managers use each type of cost.

Full Product Costs for Internal Decision Making

Full product costs include the costs of *all resources used throughout the value chain*. For Nissan, the full product cost of a particular model is the total cost to research, design, manufacture, market, and distribute the model, as well as to service the customers who buy it. Before launching a new model, managers predict the full product costs of the vehicle to set a selling price that will cover *all costs* plus return a profit. Nissan also compares each model's sale price to its full cost to determine which models are most profitable. Perhaps Xterras are more profitable than Pathfinders. Marketing can then focus on advertising and promoting the most profitable models. We'll talk more about full costs in Chapter 8, where we discuss business decisions. For the next few chapters, we'll concentrate primarily on inventoriable product costs.

Inventoriable Product Costs for External Reporting

GAAP does not allow companies to use full product costs when reporting the cost of their inventories in the financial statements. For external reporting, GAAP allows only a *portion* of the full product cost to be treated as an inventoriable product cost. GAAP specifies which costs are inventoriable product costs and which costs are not. **Inventoriable product costs** include *only* the costs incurred during the "production or purchases" stage of the value chain (see Exhibit 2-6). Inventoriable product costs are treated as an asset (inventory) until the product is sold. When the product is sold, these costs are removed from inventory and expensed as cost of goods sold. Since inventoriable product costs include only costs incurred during the production or purchases stage of the value chain, all cost incurred in the *other* stages of the value chain must be expensed in the period in which they are incurred. Hence, we refer to R&D, design, marketing, distribution, and customer service costs as **period costs**. Period costs are often called "operating costs" or "selling, general, and administrative costs" (SG&A). Period costs are *never* part of an inventory asset account. Period costs are expensed in the period in which they are incurred.

Exhibit 2-6 shows that a company's full product cost has two components: inventoriable product costs (those costs treated as part of inventory until the product is sold) and period costs (those costs expensed in the current period regardless of when inventory is sold). GAAP requires this distinction for external financial reporting. Study the exhibit carefully to make sure you understand how the two components of full product costs—inventoriable product costs and period costs—affect the income statement and balance sheet.

Now that you understand the difference between inventoriable product costs and period costs, let's take a closer look at the costs that are inventoriable in merchandising and manufacturing companies. Inventoriable costs include only those costs incurred at the purchase stage in merchandising companies and at the production stage in manufacturing companies.

BBH CHAPTER 2

EXHIBIT 2-6 Full Product Costs, Inventoriable Product Costs, and Period Costs

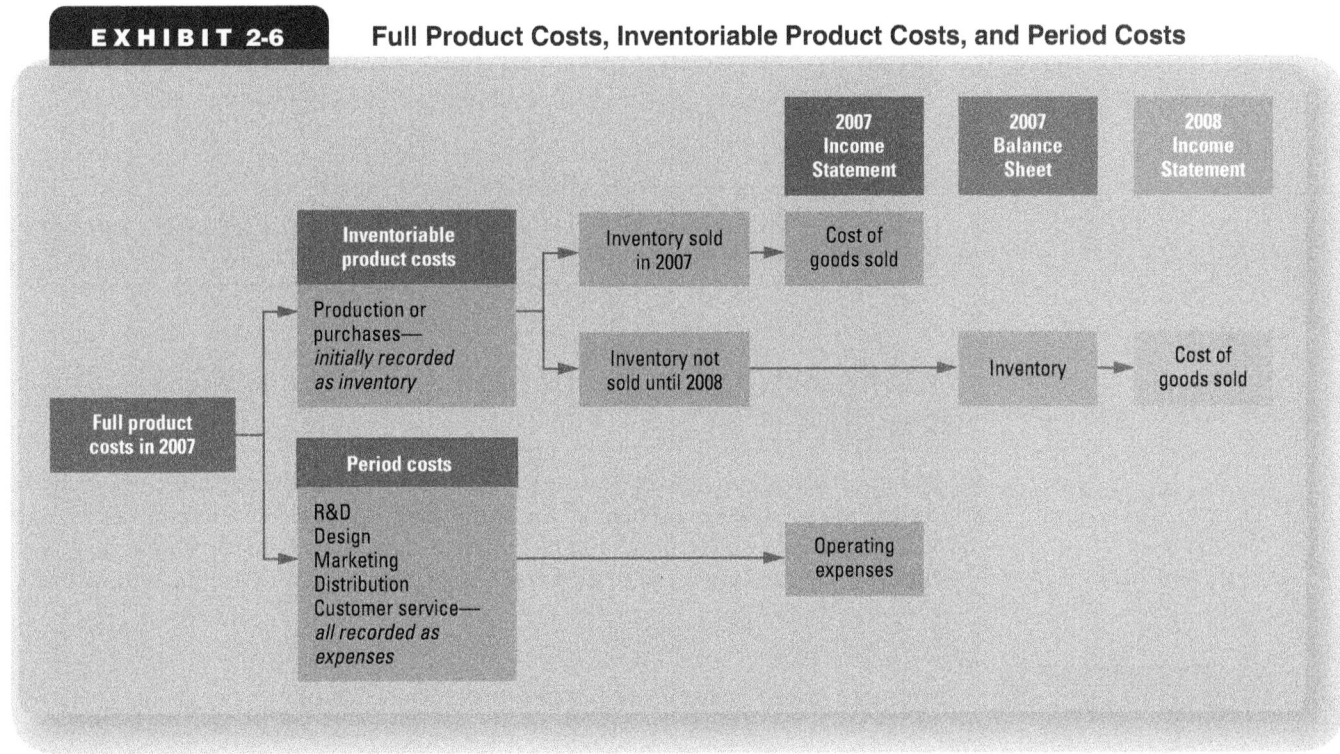

Merchandising Companies' Inventoriable Product Cost

Merchandising companies' inventoriable costs include *only* the cost of purchasing the inventory from suppliers plus any costs incurred to get the merchandise to the merchandiser's place of business and ready for sale. Typically, these additional costs include freight-in costs and import duties or tariffs, if any. Why does their inventory include freight-in charges? Think of the last time you purchased a shirt from a catalog such as J.Crew. The catalog may have shown the shirt's price as $30, but by the time you paid the shipping and handling charges, the shirt really cost you around $35. Likewise, merchandising companies pay freight charges to get the goods to their place of business (plus import duties if the goods were manufactured overseas). These charges become part of the cost of their inventory.

For instance, Home Depot's inventoriable costs include what the company paid for its store merchandise plus freight-in and import duty charges. Home Depot records these costs in an asset account—Inventory—until it *sells* the merchandise. Once the merchandise sells, it belongs to the customer, not Home Depot. Therefore, Home Depot takes the cost out of the inventory account and records it as an expense—the *cost of goods sold*. Home Depot expenses costs incurred in other elements of the value chain as period costs, such as employee salaries, advertising expenses, and store operating costs (for example, utilities and depreciation).

Some companies, such as Pier 1 Imports, refer to their cost of goods sold as "cost of sales." However, we use the more specific term *cost of goods sold* throughout the text because it more aptly describes the actual cost being expensed in the account—the inventoriable product cost of the goods themselves, not the total cost of making the sale (which would include selling and marketing costs).

BBH CHAPTER 2

BBH CHAPTER 2

Stop & Think...

What are the inventoriable costs for a service firm such as H&R Block?

Answer: Service firms such as H&R Block have no inventory of products for sale. Services cannot be produced today and stored up to sell later. Because service firms have no inventory, they have no inventoriable costs. Instead, they have only period costs that are expensed as incurred.

Manufacturing Companies' Inventoriable Product Cost

Manufacturing companies' inventoriable costs include *only* those costs incurred during the production element of the value chain. As shown in Exhibit 2-7, manufacturers such as Nissan incur three types of manufacturing costs when making a product (the product is the cost object): direct materials, direct labor, and manufacturing overhead.

EXHIBIT 2-7   **Summary of the Three Types of Manufacturing Costs**

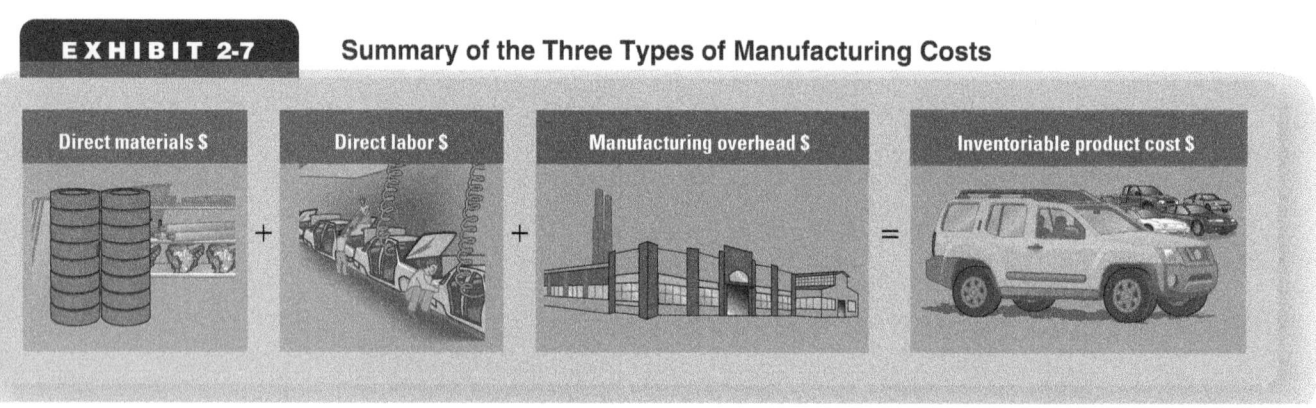

Direct Materials (DM)

Manufacturers convert raw materials into finished products. **Direct materials** are the *primary* raw materials that become a physical part of the finished product. Xterra's direct materials include steel, tires, engines, upholstery, carpet, and dashboard instruments such as the speedometer and odometer. Nissan can trace the cost of these materials (including freight-in and any other charges, such as import duties, necessary to obtain the materials) to specific units or batches of vehicles; thus, they are direct costs of the vehicles.

Direct Labor (DL)

Although many manufacturing facilities are highly automated, most still require some direct labor to convert raw materials into a finished product. **Direct labor** is the cost of compensating employees who physically convert raw materials into the company's products. At Nissan, direct labor includes the wages and benefits of assembly workers, machine operators, and technicians who assemble the parts and wire the electronics to build the completed vehicle. These costs are *direct* with respect to the cost object (the vehicle) because Nissan can *trace* the time each of these employees spends working on specific units or batches of vehicles.

Manufacturing Overhead (MOH)

The third production cost is manufacturing overhead. **Manufacturing overhead** includes all manufacturing costs other than direct materials and direct labor. Manufacturing overhead includes all *indirect* costs of production. Manufacturing overhead is also referred to as factory overhead because all of these costs relate to the factory. Manufacturers must incur these costs to produce their products; but because these costs are indirect, they can't be traced to individual units or batches. As a result, the amount of manufacturing overhead that should be assigned to each completed unit is more uncertain. The allocation process (discussed in Chapter 3) estimates the amount of manufacturing overhead to assign to each completed unit. As shown in Exhibit 2-8, manufacturing overhead includes indirect materials, indirect labor, and other indirect manufacturing costs.

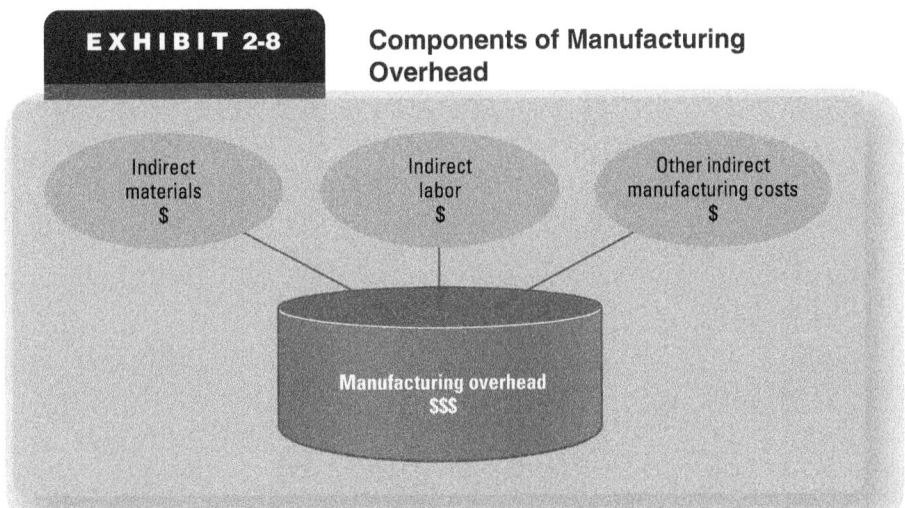

EXHIBIT 2-8   **Components of Manufacturing Overhead**

- **Indirect material** includes materials used in the plant that are not easily traced to individual units. For example, indirect materials often include janitorial supplies, oil and lubricants for the machines, and any physical components of the finished product that are inexpensive. For example, Nissan might treat the invoice sticker placed on each vehicle's window as an indirect material. Even though the cost of the sticker (about $0.10) *could* be traced to the vehicle, it wouldn't make much sense to do so. Why? Because the cost of tracing the sticker to the vehicle outweighs the benefit management receives from the increased accuracy of the information. Therefore, Nissan treats the cost of the sticker as indirect material, which becomes part of manufacturing overhead.

- **Indirect labor** includes the cost of all employees *in the plant* other than those employees directly converting the raw materials into the finished product. For example, at Nissan, indirect labor includes the salaries, wages, and benefits of plant forklift operators, plant security officers, plant janitors, and plant supervisors.

- **Other indirect manufacturing costs** include insurance and depreciation on the plant, plant equipment depreciation, plant property taxes, plant repairs and maintenance, and plant utilities. Indirect manufacturing costs have grown in recent years as manufacturers automate their plants. These costs continue to increase as manufacturers install the latest technology.

In summary, *manufacturing overhead includes only those indirect costs that are related to the manufacturing plant*. Insurance and depreciation on the *plant's* building and equipment are indirect manufacturing costs, so they are part of manufacturing overhead. In contrast, depreciation on *delivery trucks* is not a manufacturing cost. Delivery is part of the distribution element of the value chain, so its cost is a distribution expense (a period expense). Similarly, auto insurance for the sales force's vehicles is part of the marketing element of the value chain, so its cost is a marketing expense (a period expense). These two expenses are *not* part of *manufacturing* overhead because they do not relate to production at the plant.

Prime and Conversion Costs

Managers and accountants sometimes talk about certain combinations of manufacturing costs. As shown in Exhibit 2-9, **prime costs** refer to the combination of direct materials and direct labor. Prime costs used to be the primary costs of production. However, as companies have automated production with expensive machinery, manufacturing overhead has become a greater cost of production. **Conversion costs** refer to the combination of direct labor and manufacturing overhead. These are the costs of *converting* direct materials into finished goods.

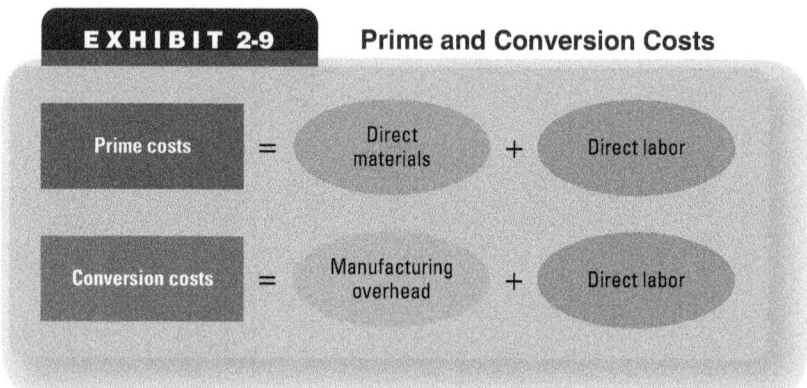

EXHIBIT 2-9   Prime and Conversion Costs

Prime costs = Direct materials + Direct labor

Conversion costs = Manufacturing overhead + Direct labor

Direct and Indirect Labor Compensation

The cost of direct and indirect labor includes more than the salaries and wages paid to the plant employees. The cost also includes company-paid fringe benefits such as health insurance, retirement plan contributions, payroll taxes, and paid vacations. These costs are very expensive. Health insurance premiums, which have seen double-digit increases for many years, often amount to $500 to $1,000 per month for *each* employee electing family coverage. Many companies also contribute an amount equal to 3% to 6% of their employees' salaries to company-sponsored retirement 401(k) plans. Employers must pay Federal Insurance Contributions Act (FICA) payroll taxes to the federal government for Social Security and Medicare, amounting to 7.65% of each employee's gross pay. In addition, most companies offer paid vacation and other benefits. Together, these fringe benefits usually cost the company an *additional* 35% beyond gross salaries and wages. Thus, an assembly-line worker who makes a $40,000 salary costs Nissan another $14,000 (= $40,000 × 35%) in fringe benefits. Believe it or not,

BBH CHAPTER 2

for automobiles manufactured in the United States, the cost of health care assigned to the vehicle is greater than the cost of the steel in the vehicle! Throughout the remainder of this book, any references to wages or salaries also include the cost of fringe benefits.

Review: Inventoriable Product Costs or Period Costs?

Exhibit 2-10 summarizes the differences between inventoriable product costs and period costs for service, merchandising, and manufacturing companies. Study this exhibit carefully. When are such costs as depreciation, insurance, utilities, and property taxes inventoriable product costs? *Only* when those costs are related to the manufacturing plant. When those costs are related to nonmanufacturing activities such as R&D or marketing, they are treated as period costs. Service companies and merchandisers do no manufacturing, so they always treat depreciation, insurance, utilities, and property taxes as period costs. When you studied financial accounting, you studied nonmanufacturing firms. Therefore, salaries, depreciation, insurance, and taxes were always expensed.

EXHIBIT 2-10   Inventoriable Product Costs and Period Costs for Service, Merchandising, and Manufacturing Companies

	Inventoriable Product Costs	Period Costs
Accounting Treatment	• Initially recorded as inventory • Expensed only when inventory is sold	• Always recorded as an expense • Never considered part of inventory
Type of Company:		
Service company	• None	• All costs along the value chain • For example, salaries, depreciation expense, utilities, insurance, property taxes, and advertising
Merchandising company	• Purchases of merchandise • Freight-in; customs and duties	• All costs along the value chain *except* for the purchases element • For example, salaries, depreciation expense, utilities, insurance, property taxes, advertising, and freight-out
Manufacturing company	• Direct materials • Direct labor • Manufacturing overhead (including indirect materials, indirect labor, and other indirect manufacturing costs)	• All costs along the value chain *except* for the production element • For example, R&D; freight-out; all expenses for executive headquarters (separate from plant), including depreciation, utilities, insurance, and property taxes; advertising; and CEO's salary

Decision Guidelines

BUILDING BLOCKS OF MANAGERIAL ACCOUNTING

Dell engages in *manufacturing* when it assembles its computers, *merchandising* when it sells them on its Web site, and support *services* such as start-up and implementation services. Dell had to make the following types of decisions as it developed its accounting systems.

Decision	Guidelines

How do you distinguish among service, merchandising, and manufacturing companies? How do their balance sheets differ?	*Service companies:*
	• Provide customers with intangible services
	• Have no inventories on the balance sheet
	
	Merchandising companies:
	• Resell tangible products purchased ready-made from suppliers
	• Have only one category of inventory
	
	Manufacturing companies:
	• Use labor, plant, and equipment to transform raw materials into new finished products
	• Have three categories of inventory:
	
	  1. Raw materials inventory
	  2. Work in process inventory
	  3. Finished goods inventory

What business activities add value to companies?	All of the elements of the value chain, including: • R&D • Design • Production or Purchases • Marketing • Distribution • Customer Service
What costs should be assigned to cost objects such as products, departments, and geographic segments?	Both direct and indirect costs are assigned to cost objects. Direct costs are traced to cost objects, whereas indirect costs are allocated to cost objects.
Which product costs are useful for internal decision making, and which product costs are used for external reporting?	Managers use *full product costs* for product pricing and profitability decisions. However, GAAP requires companies to use only *inventoriable product costs* for external financial reporting.
What costs are inventoriable under GAAP?	• *Service companies:* No inventoriable product costs • *Merchandising companies:* Purchases and all costs of getting the merchandise to its place of business (for example, freight-in and import duties) • *Manufacturing companies:* Direct materials, direct labor, and manufacturing overhead
How are inventoriable product costs treated on the financial statements?	Inventoriable product costs are initially treated as assets (Inventory) on the balance sheet. These costs are expensed (as cost of goods sold) on the income statements when the products are sold.

Summary Problem1

1. Classify each of the following business costs into one of the six value chain elements:
   a. Costs associated with warranties and recalls
   b. Cost of shipping finished goods to overseas customers
   c. Costs a pharmaceutical company incurs to develop new drugs
   d. Cost of a 30-second commercial during the Super Bowl
   e. Cost of making a new product prototype
   f. Cost of assembly labor used in the plant

2. For a manufacturing company, identify the following as either an inventoriable product cost or a period cost. If it is an inventoriable product cost, classify it as direct materials, direct labor, or manufacturing overhead.
   a. Depreciation on plant equipment
   b. Depreciation on salespeople's automobiles
   c. Insurance on plant building
   d. Marketing manager's salary
   e. Cost of major components of the finished product
   f. Assembly-line workers' wages
   g. Costs of shipping finished products to customers
   h. Forklift operator's salary

Solutions

Requirement 1

a. Customer service

b. Distribution

c. Research and Development

d. Marketing

e. Design

f. Production

Requirement 2

a. Inventoriable product cost; manufacturing overhead

b. Period cost

c. Inventoriable product cost; manufacturing overhead

d. Period cost

e. Inventoriable product cost; direct materials

f. Inventoriable product cost; direct labor

g. Period cost

h. Inventoriable product cost; manufacturing overhead

BBH CHAPTER 2

Inventoriable Product Costs and Period Costs in Financial Statements

5 Prepare the financial statements for service, merchandising, and manufacturing companies

The difference between inventoriable product costs and period costs is important because they are treated differently in the financial statements. All costs incurred in the production or purchases stage of the value chain are inventoriable product costs that remain in inventory accounts until the merchandise is sold—then, these costs become the cost of goods sold. However, costs incurred in all other areas of the value chain (R&D, design, marketing, distribution, and customer service) are period costs, which are expensed on the income statement in the period in which they are incurred. Keep these differences in mind as we review the financial statements of service firms (which have no inventory), merchandising companies (which purchase their inventory), and manufacturers (which make their inventory).

Service Companies

Service companies have the simplest accounting. Exhibit 2-11 shows the income statement of eNow!, a group of e-commerce consultants. The firm has no inventory and, thus, no inventoriable costs, so eNow!'s income statement has no Cost of Goods Sold. Rather, all of the company's costs are period costs, so they are shown grouped together under operating expenses.

EXHIBIT 2-11 Service Company Income Statement

eNOW!
Income Statement
Year Ended December 31, 2007

Revenues		$160,000
Operating expenses:		
Salary expense	$106,000	
Office rent expense	18,000	
Depreciation expense—furniture and equipment	3,500	
Marketing expense	2,500	
Total operating expenses		(130,000)
Operating income		$ 30,000

In this textbook, we always use "operating income" rather than "net income" as the bottom line on the income statement since internal managers are particularly concerned with the income generated through operations. To determine "net income," we would have to deduct interest expense and income taxes from "operating income" and add back interest income. In general, "operating income" is simply the company's income before interest and income taxes.

Merchandising Companies

In contrast with service companies, merchandisers' income statements feature Cost of Goods Sold as the major expense. Consider Apex Showrooms, a merchandiser of lighting fixtures. Apex's *only* inventoriable costs are for the purchase of chandeliers

BBH CHAPTER 2

and track lights that it buys to resell, plus freight-in. Merchandisers such as Apex compute the Cost of Goods Sold as follows:[2]

Beginning inventory	$ 9,500	What Apex had at the beginning of the period
+ Purchases and freight-in	110,000	What Apex bought during the period
= Cost of goods available for sale	119,500	Total available for sale during the period
− Ending inventory.................	(13,000)	What Apex had left at the end of the period
= Cost of goods sold...............	$106,500	What Apex sold during the period

Exhibit 2-12 shows Apex's complete income statement, where we have highlighted the Cost of Goods sold computation. Notice that the Cost of Goods Sold is deducted from Sales Revenue to determine the company's gross profit. All operating expenses (period costs) are then deducted from gross profit to arrive at operating income.

EXHIBIT 2-12   **Merchandiser's Income Statement**

APEX SHOWROOMS
Income Statement
Year Ended December 31, 2007

Sales revenue		$150,000
Cost of goods sold:		
Beginning inventory................................	$ 9,500	
Purchases and freight-in	110,000	
Cost of goods available for sale.................	119,500	
Ending inventory....................................	(13,000)	
Cost of goods sold		106,500
Gross profit		43,500
Operating expenses:		
Showroom rent expense............................	5,000	
Sales salary expense	4,000	9,000
Operating income.......................................		$ 34,500

Manufacturing Companies

Exhibit 2-13 shows the income statement of Top-Flight, a manufacturer of golf equipment and athletic shoes. Compare its income statement with the merchandiser's income statement in Exhibit 2-12. The only difference is that the merchandiser (Apex) uses *purchases and freight-in* in computing Cost of Goods Sold, whereas the manufacturer (Top-Flight) uses the *cost of goods manufactured* (we've highlighted both in blue). Notice that the term **cost of goods manufactured** is in the past tense. It is the cost of manufacturing the goods that Top-Flight *finished producing during*

---

[2]To highlight the roles of beginning inventory, purchases, and ending inventory, we assume that Apex uses a periodic inventory system. However, even companies that use perpetual inventory systems during the year recalculate Cost of Goods Sold this way before preparing their annual financial statements.

2007. This is the manufacturer's cost to obtain new finished goods that are ready to sell. Thus, it is the counterpart to the merchandiser's *purchases.*

EXHIBIT 2-13   **Manufacturer's Income Statement**

TOP-FLIGHT
Income Statement
Year Ended December 31, 2007

Sales revenue		$65,000
Cost of goods sold:		
Beginning finished goods inventory	$ 6,000	
Cost of goods manufactured*	42,000	
Cost of goods available for sale	48,000	
Ending finished goods inventory	(8,000)	
Cost of goods sold		40,000
Gross profit		25,000
Operating expenses:		
Sales salary expense	3,000	
Delivery expense	7,000	10,000
Operating income		$15,000

*From the Schedule of Cost of Goods Manufactured in Exhibit 2-15.

Calculating the Cost of Goods Manufactured

The cost of goods manufactured summarizes the cost of activities that take place in a manufacturing plant over the period. Let's begin by reviewing these activities. Exhibit 2-14 reminds us that the manufacturer starts by buying direct materials, which are stored in Raw Materials Inventory until they are needed for production. During production, the company uses direct labor and manufacturing overhead to convert direct materials into a finished product.

These are all inventoriable product costs because they are related to manufacturing. All units being worked on are in Work in Process Inventory. When the units are completed, they move out of Work in Process Inventory into Finished Goods Inventory.

Finished goods are the only inventory that is ready to sell. The cost of the finished goods that the manufacturer sells becomes its Cost of Goods Sold on the income statement. Costs the manufacturer incurs in other (nonmanufacturing) elements of the value chain are operating expenses, or period costs, that are expensed in the period incurred. Exhibit 2-14 shows that these operating expenses are deducted from gross profit to obtain operating income.

Exhibit 2-15 shows how Top-Flight computes its cost of goods manufactured—the cost of the goods the plant *finished* during 2007. The computation of the cost of goods manufactured summarizes the activities and related costs incurred on Top-Flight's plant floor throughout 2007. For simplicity, we'll assume that Top-Flight's raw materials inventory contains only direct materials.[3]

---

[3]We assume that Top-Flight uses its indirect materials as soon as they are purchased rather than storing them in Raw Materials Inventory. In Chapter 3, we expand the discussion to include manufacturers who store indirect materials in the Raw Materials Inventory account until they are used in production.

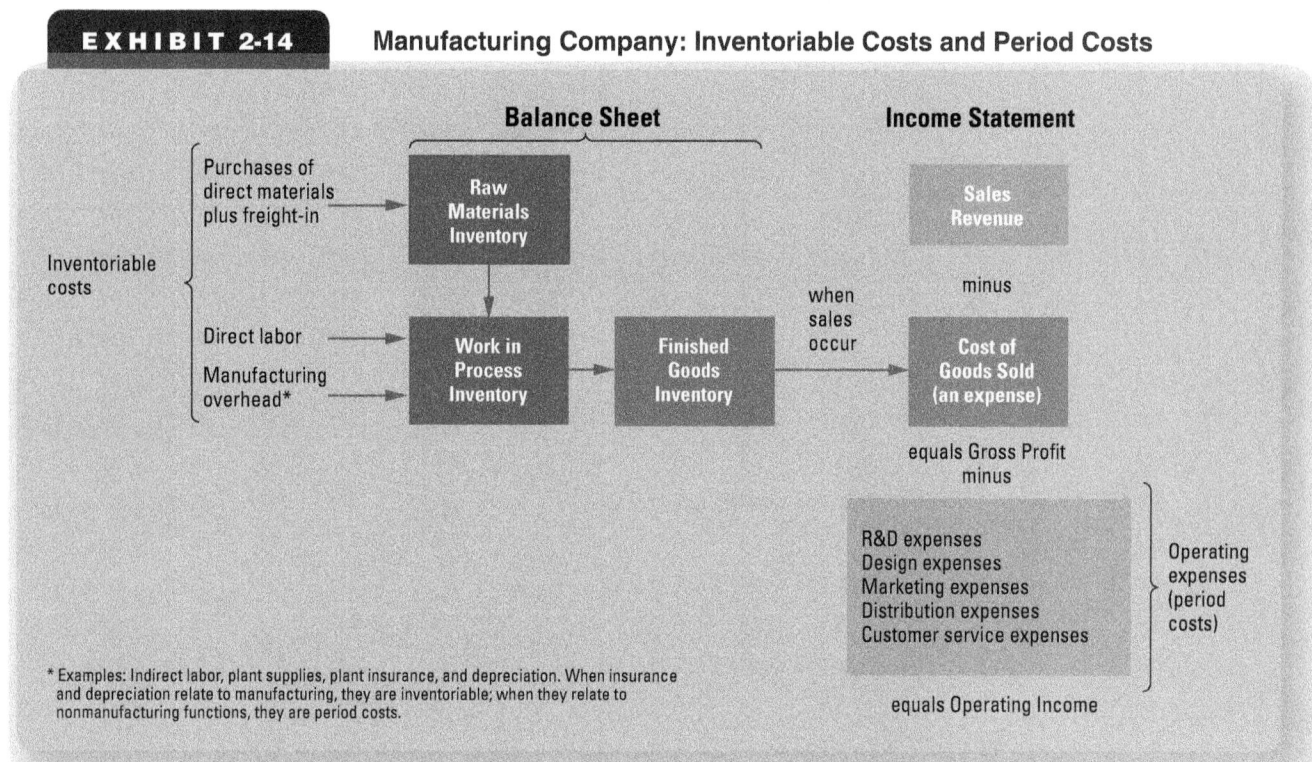

EXHIBIT 2-14   Manufacturing Company: Inventoriable Costs and Period Costs

BBH CHAPTER 2

Exhibit 2-15 shows that Top-Flight begins 2007 with $2,000 of partially completed golf clubs and shoes that remained on the plant floor at the close of business on December 31, 2006.

During 2007, Top-Flight's production plant used $14,000 of direct materials, $19,000 of direct labor, and $12,000 of manufacturing overhead. The sum of these three costs ($45,000) represents the total manufacturing costs incurred during the year. Adding the total manufacturing costs incurred *during* the year ($45,000) to the *beginning* Work in Process Inventory balance ($2,000) gives the total manufacturing costs to account for ($47,000). This figure represents the total manufacturing cost assigned to *all* goods the plant worked on during the year. The plant finished most of these goods and sent them to Finished Goods Inventory, but some were not finished. By the close of business on December 31, 2007, Top-Flight had spent $5,000 on ending work in process inventory that lay partially complete on the plant floor.

The final step is to figure out the *cost of goods manufactured during 2007—* that is, the cost of the goods that Top-Flight *finished* during 2007. Of the $47,000 total manufacturing costs to account for during the year, $5,000 has been assigned to unfinished units in ending work in process inventory. That means the rest of the cost ($42,000) is assigned to units that were finished. Top-Flight's cost of goods manufactured for 2007 is $42,000 ($47,000 – $5,000).

EXHIBIT 2-15   Schedule of Cost of Goods Manufactured

TOP-FLIGHT
Schedule of Cost of Goods Manufactured
Year Ended December 31, 2007

Beginning work in progress inventory...............................			$ 2,000
Add: Direct materials used			
Beginning raw materials inventory*..........................	$ 9,000		
Purchases of direct materials including freight-in			
and any import duties.......................................	27,000		
Available for use...	36,000		
Ending raw materials inventory..............................	(22,000)		
Direct materials used...		$14,000	
Direct labor..		19,000	
Manufacturing overhead:			
Indirect materials	$ 1,500		
Indirect labor...	3,500		
Depreciation—plant and equipment........................	3,000		
Plant utilities, insurance, and property taxes............	4,000		
Manufacturing overhead....................................		12,000	
Total manufacturing costs incurred during year...............			45,000
Total manufacturing costs to account for........................			47,000
Less: Ending work in process inventory............................			(5,000)
Costs of goods manufactured..			$42,000

*For simplicity, we assume that Top-Flight's Raw Materials Inventory account contains only direct materials because the company uses indirect materials as soon as they are purchased. In Chapter 3, we expand the discussion to include manufacturers who store both direct and indirect materials in the Raw Materials Inventory account until they are used in production.

Flow of Costs Through Inventory Accounts

Exhibit 2-16 diagrams the flow of costs through Top-Flight's three inventory accounts. Notice how the final amount at each stage flows into the next stage. The format is the same for all three inventory accounts:

- Each inventory account starts with a beginning inventory balance.
- Top-Flight adds costs to each inventory account (it adds direct materials *purchased* to Raw Materials Inventory; it adds direct materials *used*, direct labor, and manufacturing overhead to Work in Process Inventory; and it adds the cost of goods manufactured to Finished Goods Inventory).
- Top-Flight subtracts the ending inventory balance to find out how much inventory passed through the account during the period *and on to the next stage*. At all stages, the flow of costs follows the flow of physical goods.

Take time to see how the Schedule of Cost of Goods Manufactured (Exhibit 2-15) captures the flow of costs through the Raw Materials and Work in Process Inventory accounts. The Income Statement (Exhibit 2-13) captures the flow of costs through the Finished Goods Inventory account. Some manufacturers combine the flow of costs through *all three* inventory accounts into one combined Schedule of Cost of Goods Manufactured and Cost of Goods Sold, and then show only the resulting Cost of Goods Sold figure on the income statement.

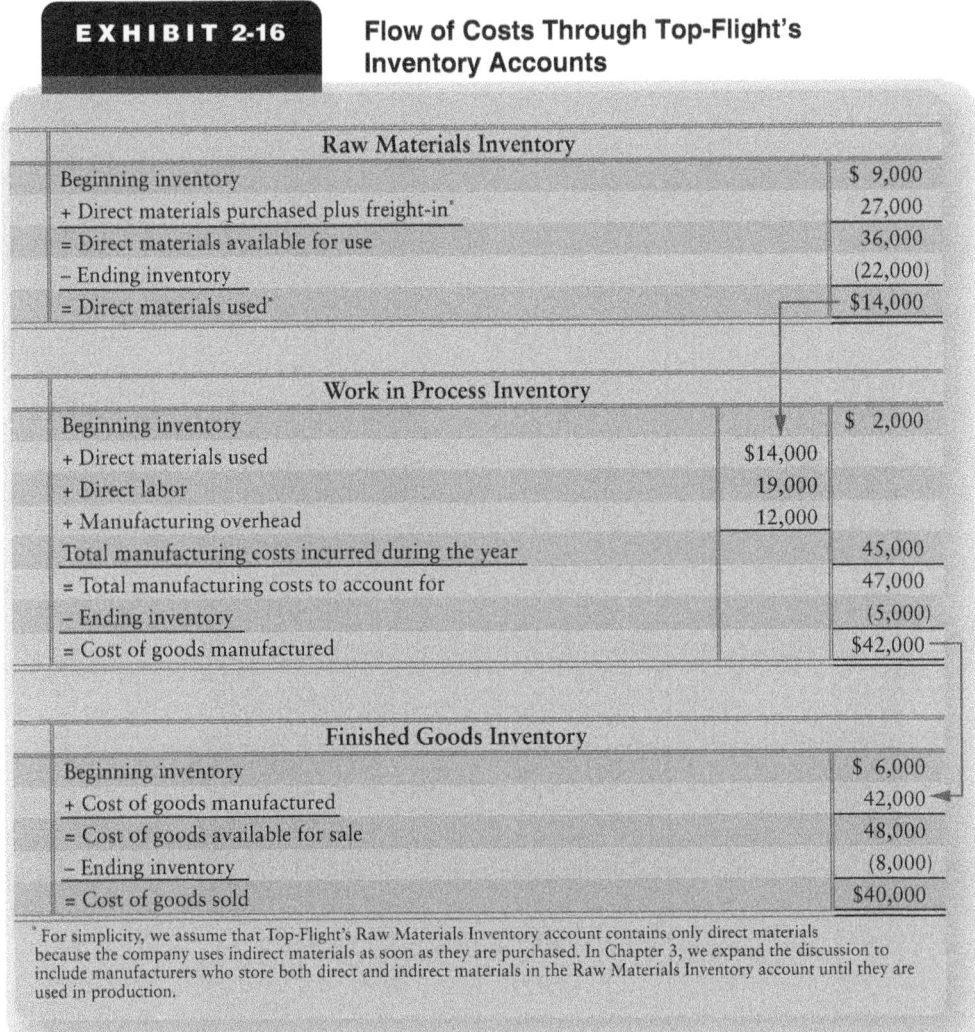

EXHIBIT 2-16   **Flow of Costs Through Top-Flight's Inventory Accounts**

Raw Materials Inventory

Beginning inventory	$ 9,000
+ Direct materials purchased plus freight-in*	27,000
= Direct materials available for use	36,000
– Ending inventory	(22,000)
= Direct materials used*	$14,000

Work in Process Inventory

Beginning inventory		$ 2,000
+ Direct materials used	$14,000	
+ Direct labor	19,000	
+ Manufacturing overhead	12,000	
Total manufacturing costs incurred during the year		45,000
= Total manufacturing costs to account for		47,000
– Ending inventory		(5,000)
= Cost of goods manufactured		$42,000

Finished Goods Inventory

Beginning inventory	$ 6,000
+ Cost of goods manufactured	42,000
= Cost of goods available for sale	48,000
– Ending inventory	(8,000)
= Cost of goods sold	$40,000

* For simplicity, we assume that Top-Flight's Raw Materials Inventory account contains only direct materials because the company uses indirect materials as soon as they are purchased. In Chapter 3, we expand the discussion to include manufacturers who store both direct and indirect materials in the Raw Materials Inventory account until they are used in production.

Effects on the Balance Sheet

Now that we've looked at the income statement, let's turn our attention to the balance sheet. The only difference in the balance sheets of service, merchandising, and manufacturing companies relates to inventories. Exhibit 2-17 shows how the current asset sections of eNOW! (service company), Apex Showrooms (merchandising company), and Top-Flight (manufacturing company) might differ at the end of 2007. eNOW! has no inventory at all, Apex Showrooms has a single category of inventory, and Top-Flight has three categories of inventory (raw materials, work in process, and finished goods).

EXHIBIT 2-17 **Current Asset Sections of Balance Sheets**

eNOW! (SERVICE COMPANY)

Cash	$ 4,000
Accounts receivable	5,000
Prepaid expenses	1,000
Total current assets	$10,000

APEX SHOWROOMS (MERCHANDISING COMPANY)

Cash	$ 4,000
Accounts receivable	5,000
Inventory (Exhibit 2-12)	13,000
Prepaid expenses	1,000
Total current assets	$23,000

TOP-FLIGHT (MANUFACTURING COMPANY)

Cash		$ 4,000
Accounts receivable		5,000
Inventories:		
Raw materials inventory (Exhibit 2-15)	22,000	
Work in process inventory (Exhibit 2-15)	5,000	
Finished goods inventory (Exhibit 2-13)	8,000	
Total inventories		35,000
Prepaid expenses		1,000
Total current assets		$45,000

Other Cost Terms for Planning and Decision Making

So far in this chapter, we have discussed direct versus indirect costs and inventoriable product costs versus period costs. Now let's turn our attention to other cost terms that managers and accountants use when planning and making decisions.

 Describe costs that are relevant and irrelevant for decision making

Controllable Versus Uncontrollable Costs

As discussed in the chapter opening story, Nissan knew that it had to make changes if it was to stay in business. But what changes to make? Management had to distinguish controllable costs from uncontrollable costs. In the long run, most costs are **controllable**, meaning management is able to influence or change them. However, in the short run, companies are often "locked in" to certain costs arising from previous decisions. These are called **uncontrollable costs**. For example, Nissan had little or no control over the property tax and insurance costs of their existing plants. These costs were "locked in" when Nissan built its plants. Nissan could replace existing production facilities with different-sized plants in different areas of the world that might cost less to operate, but that would take time. To see immediate benefits, management had to change those costs that were controllable at present. For example, management could control costs of research and development, design, and advertising. Recall that Nissan's management chose to *increase* rather than decrease these costs! Management knew it would have to design and market new models to successfully compete. However, Nissan was able to *decrease* other controllable costs, such as the price paid for raw materials, by working with its suppliers. In short, management's plans to revitalize the company focused first on costs that were controllable in the short run.

Relevant and Irrelevant Costs

Decision making involves identifying various courses of action and then choosing among them. When managers make decisions, they focus on those costs and revenues that are relevant to the decision. For example, Nissan wanted to build a new state-of-the-art production facility. After considering alternative locations, management decided to build the facility in Canton, Mississippi. The decision was based on relevant information such as the **differential cost** of building and operating the facility in Canton versus building and operating the facility in other potential locations. Differential cost refers to the difference in cost between two alternatives.

Say you want to buy a new car. You narrow your decision to two choices: the Nissan Sentra or the Toyota Corolla. As shown in Exhibit 2-18, the Sentra you like costs $14,480, whereas the Corolla costs $15,345. Because sales tax is based on the sales price, the Corolla's sales tax is higher. However, your insurance agent quotes you a higher price to insure the Sentra ($365 per month versus $319 per month for the Corolla). All of these costs are relevant to your decision because they differ between the two cars. Other costs are not relevant to your decision. For example, both cars run on regular unleaded gasoline and have the same fuel economy ratings, so the cost of operating the vehicles is about the same. Likewise, you don't expect cost differences in servicing the vehicles because they both carry the same warranty and have received excellent quality ratings in *Consumer Reports*. Because you project operating and maintenance costs to be the *same* for both cars, these costs are irrelevant to your decision. In other words, they won't influence your decision either way. Based on your analysis, the differential cost is $1,825 in favor of the Corolla. Does this mean that you will choose the Corolla? Not necessarily. The Sentra may have some characteristics you like better, such as a particular paint color, more comfortable seating, or more trunk space. When making decisions, management must also consider qualitative factors (such as effect on employee morale) in addition to differential costs.

EXHIBIT 2-18   **Comparison of Relevant Information**

	Sentra	Corolla	Differential Cost
Car's price	$14,480	$15,345	($865)
Sales tax (8%) (rounded to the nearest dollar)	1,158	1,228	(70)
Insurance*	21,900	19,140	2,760
Total relevant costs	$37,538	$35,713	$1,825

*Over the five years (60 months) you plan to keep the car.

Another cost that is irrelevant to your decision is the cost you paid for the vehicle you currently own. Say you just bought a Ford F-150 pickup truck two months ago, but you've decided you need a small sedan rather than a pickup truck. The cost of the truck is a **sunk cost**. Sunk costs are costs that have already been incurred. Nothing you do now can change the fact that you already bought the truck. Thus, the cost of the truck is not relevant to your decision of whether to buy the Sentra versus the Corolla. The only thing you can do now is (1) keep your truck or (2) sell it for the best price you can get. Management often has trouble ignoring sunk costs when making decisions, even though they should. Perhaps they invested in a factory or a computer system that no longer serves the company's needs. Many times, new technology makes management's past investments in older technology look like bad decisions, even though they weren't at the time. Management should ignore sunk costs because its decisions about the future cannot alter decisions made in the past.

Fixed and Variable Costs

7 Classify costs as fixed or variable and calculate total and average costs at different volumns

Managers cannot make good plans and decisions without first knowing how their costs behave. Costs generally behave as fixed costs or variable costs. We will spend all of Chapter 6 discussing cost behavior. For now, let's look just at the basics. **Fixed costs** stay constant in total over a wide range of activity levels. For example, let's say you decide to buy the Corolla, so your insurance cost for the year is $3,828 ($319 per month × 12 months). As shown in Exhibit 2-19, your insurance cost stays fixed whether you drive your car 0 miles, 1,000 miles, or 10,000 miles during the year.

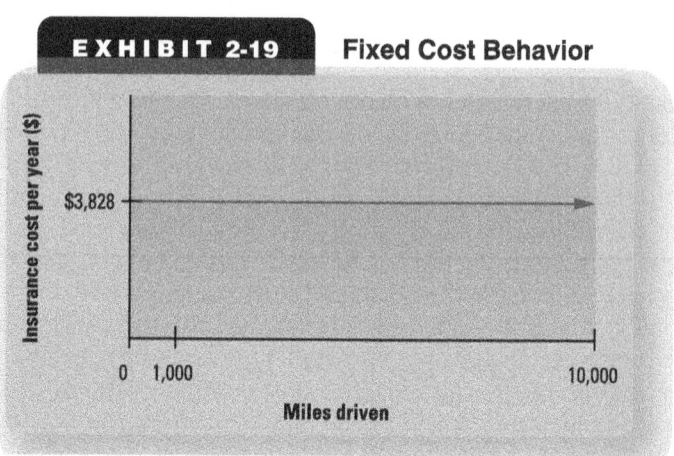

EXHIBIT 2-19   **Fixed Cost Behavior**

However, the total cost of gasoline to operate your car varies depending on whether you drive 0 miles, 1,000 miles, or 10,000 miles. The more miles you drive, the higher your total gasoline cost for the year. If you don't drive your car at all, you won't incur any costs for gasoline. Your gasoline costs are **variable costs**, as shown in Exhibit 2-20. Variable costs change in total in direct proportion to changes in volume. To accurately forecast the total cost of operating your Corolla during the year, you need to know which operating costs are fixed and which are variable.

BBH CHAPTER 2

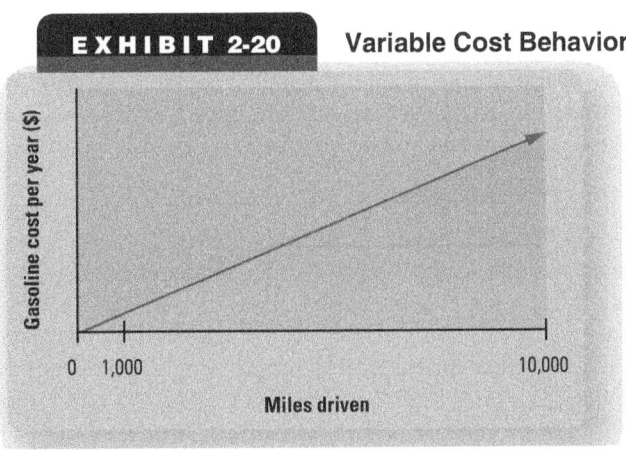

EXHIBIT 2-20 Variable Cost Behavior

How Manufacturing Costs Behave

Most companies have both fixed and variable costs. Manufacturing companies such as Nissan know that their direct materials are variable costs. The more cars Nissan makes, the higher its total cost for tires, steel, and parts. The behavior of direct labor is harder to characterize. Salaried employees are paid a fixed amount per year. Hourly wage earners are paid only when they work. The more hours they work, the more they are paid. Nonetheless, direct labor is generally treated as a variable cost because the more cars Nissan produces, the more assembly-line workers and machine operators it must employ. Manufacturing overhead includes both variable and fixed costs. For example, the cost of indirect materials is variable, while the cost of property tax, insurance, and straight-line depreciation on the plant and equipment is fixed. The cost of utilities is partially fixed and partially variable. Factories incur a certain level of utility costs just to keep the lights on. However, when more cars are produced, more electricity is used to run the production equipment. Exhibit 2-21 summarizes the behavior of manufacturing costs.

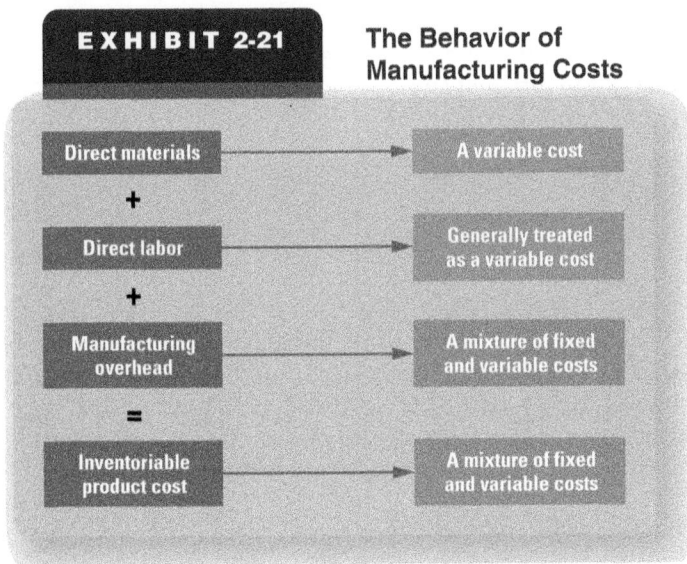

EXHIBIT 2-21 The Behavior of Manufacturing Costs

Calculating Total and Average Costs

Why is cost behavior important? Managers need to understand how costs behave to predict total costs and calculate average costs. In our example, we'll look at Nissan's total and average *manufacturing* costs; but the same principles apply to nonmanufacturing costs.

Let's say Nissan wants to predict the total cost of manufacturing 10,000 Xterras next year. To do so, Nissan must know its total fixed manufacturing costs and the variable cost of manufacturing each vehicle (direct material + direct labor + variable manufacturing overhead). Let's say total fixed manufacturing costs for the year at the Xterra plant are $20,000,000 and the variable cost of manufacturing each Xterra is $5,000. How much total manufacturing cost should Nissan budget for the year? Nissan calculates it as follows:

> Total fixed cost + (Variable cost per unit × Number of units) = Total cost
>
> $20,000,000 + ($5,000 per vehicle × 10,000 vehicles) = $70,000,000

What is the **average cost** of manufacturing each Xterra next year? It's the total cost divided by the number of units:

$$\frac{\text{Total cost}}{\text{Number of units}} = \text{Average cost per unit}$$

$$\frac{\$70,000,000}{10,000 \text{ vehicles}} = \$7,000 \text{ per vehicle}$$

If Nissan's managers decide they need to produce 12,000 Xterras instead, can they simply predict total costs as follows?

> Average cost per unit × Number of units = Total cost???
>
> $7,000 × 12,000 = $84,000,000???

No! They cannot! Why? *Because the average cost per unit is NOT appropriate for predicting total costs at different levels of output.* Nissan's managers should forecast total cost based on cost behavior:

> Total fixed cost + (Variable cost per unit × Number of units) = Total cost
>
> $20,000,000 + ($5,000 per vehicle × 12,000 vehicles) = $80,000,000

Why is the *correct* forecasted cost of $80 million less than the *faulty* prediction of $84 million? The difference stems from fixed costs. Remember, Nissan incurs $20 million of fixed manufacturing costs whether it makes 10,000 vehicles or 12,000 vehicles. As Nissan makes more Xterras, the fixed manufacturing costs are spread over more vehicles, so the average cost per vehicle declines. If Nissan ends up making 12,000 vehicles, the new average manufacturing cost per Xterra decreases as follows:

$$\frac{\text{Total cost}}{\text{Number of units}} = \text{Average cost per unit}$$

$$\frac{\$80,000,000}{12,000 \text{ vehicles}} = \$6,667 \text{ per vehicle (rounded)}$$

The average cost per unit is lower when Nissan produces more vehicles because it is using the fixed manufacturing costs more efficiently—taking the same $20 million of resources and making more vehicles with it.

> *The moral of the story: The average cost per unit is valid only at ONE level of output—the level used to compute the average cost per unit. Thus, NEVER use average costs to forecast costs at different output levels; if you do, you will miss the mark!*

Finally, a **marginal cost** is the cost of making *one more unit*. Fixed costs will not change when Nissan makes one more Xterra unless the plant is operating at 100% capacity (24 hours a day, 7 days a week, 365 days a year) and simply cannot make one more unit. (If that's the case, Nissan will need to incur additional costs to expand the plant.) So, the marginal cost of a unit is simply its variable cost.

As you have seen, management accountants and managers use specialized terms for discussing costs. They use different costs for different purposes. Without a solid understanding of these terms, managers are likely to make serious judgment errors.

Decision Guidelines

BUILDING BLOCKS OF MANAGERIAL ACCOUNTING

As a manufacturer, Dell needs to know how to calculate its inventoriable product costs for external reporting. Dell also needs to know many characteristics about its costs (that is, which are controllable, which are relevant to different decisions, which are fixed, and so forth) in order to plan and make decisions.

Decision	Guidelines
How do you compute cost of goods sold?	• *Service companies:* No cost of goods sold because they don't sell tangible goods • *Merchandising companies:* Beginning inventory + Purchases plus freight-in and import duties, if any = Cost of goods available for sale − Ending inventory = Cost of goods sold • *Manufacturing companies:* Beginning finished goods inventory + Cost of goods manufactured = Cost of goods available for sale − Ending finished goods inventory = Cost of goods sold
How do you compute the cost of goods manufactured for a manufacturer?	Beginning work in process inventory + Total manufacturing costs incurred during year (direct materials used + direct labor + manufacturing overhead) = Total manufacturing costs to account for − Ending work in process inventory = Cost of goods manufactured
How do managers decide which costs are relevant to their decisions?	Costs are relevant to a decision when they differ between alternatives and affect the future. Thus, *differential costs* are relevant, whereas *sunk costs* and costs that don't differ are not relevant.
How should managers forecast total costs for different production volumes?	To forecast total costs, managers should compute: $$\text{Total cost} = \text{Total fixed costs} + (\text{Variable cost per unit} \times \text{Number of units})$$ Managers should *not* use a product's *average cost* to forecast total costs because it will change as production volume changes. As production increases, the average cost per unit declines (because fixed costs are spread over more units).

Summary Problem 2

Requirements

1. Show how to compute cost of goods manufactured. Use the following amounts: direct materials used ($24,000), direct labor ($9,000), manufacturing overhead ($17,000), beginning work in process inventory ($5,000), and ending work in process inventory ($4,000).

2. Auto-USA spent $300 million in total to produce 50,000 cars this year. The $300 million breaks down as follows: The company spent $50 million on fixed costs to run its manufacturing plants and $5,000 of variable costs to produce each car. Next year, it plans to produce 60,000 cars using the existing production facilities.
   a. What is the current *average cost* per car this year?
   b. Assuming there is no change in fixed costs or variable costs per unit, what is the *total forecasted cost* to produce 60,000 cars next year?
   c. What is the *forecasted average cost* per car next year?
   d. Why does the average cost per car vary between years?

Solutions

Requirement 1
Cost of goods manufactured:

Beginning work in process inventory		$ 5,000
Add: Direct materials used	24,000	
Direct labor	9,000	
Manufacturing overhead	17,000	
Total manufacturing costs incurred during the period		50,000
Total manufacturing costs to account for		55,000
Less: Ending work in process inventory		(4,000)
Cost of goods manufactured		$51,000

Requirement 2

a. Total cost ÷ Number of units = Current average cost

   $300 million ÷ 50,000 cars = $6,000 per car

b. Total fixed costs + Total variable costs = Total projected costs

   $50 million + (60,000 cars × $5,000 per car) = $350 million

c. Total cost ÷ Number of units = Projected average cost

   $350 million ÷ 60,000 cars = $5,833 per car

d. The average cost per car decreases because Auto-USA will use the same fixed costs ($50 million) to produce more cars next year. Auto-USA will be using its resources more efficiently, so the average cost per unit will decrease.

Review *Building Blocks of Managerial Accounting*

■ Accounting Vocabulary

Allocate. (p. 53)
To assign an *indirect* cost to a cost object.

Assign. (p. 53)
To attach a cost to a cost object.

Average cost. (p. 72)
The total cost divided by the number of units.

Controllable Costs. (p. 69)
Costs that can be influenced or changed by management.

Conversion Costs. (p. 58)
The combination of direct labor and manufacturing overhead costs.

Cost Object. (p. 52)
Anything for which managers want a separate measurement of costs.

Cost of Goods Manufactured. (p. 63)
The manufacturing (or plant-related) cost of the goods that finished the production process this period.

Customer Service. (p. 51)
Support provided for customers after the sale.

Design. (p. 50)
Detailed engineering of products and services and the processes for producing them.

Differential Cost. (p. 69)
The difference in cost between two alternative courses of action.

Direct Cost. (p. 52)
A cost that can be traced to a cost object.

Direct Labor. (p. 56)
The cost of compensating employees who physically convert raw materials into the company's products; labor costs that are directly traceable to the finished product.

Direct Materials. (p. 56)
Primary raw materials that become a physical part of a finished product and whose costs are traceable to the finished product.

Distribution. (p. 51)
Delivery of products or services to customers.

Finished Goods Inventory. (p. 48)
Completed goods that have not yet been sold.

Fixed Costs. (p. 70)
Costs that stay constant in total despite wide changes in volume.

Full Product Costs. (p. 54)
The costs of all resources used throughout the value chain for a product.

Indirect Cost. (p. 52)
A cost that relates to the cost object but cannot be traced to it.

Indirect Labor. (p. 57)
Labor costs that are difficult to trace to specific products.

Indirect Materials. (p. 57)
Materials whose costs are difficult to trace to specific products.

Inventoriable Product Costs. (p. 54)
All costs of a product that GAAP requires companies to treat as an asset (inventory) for external financial reporting. These costs are not expensed until the product is sold.

Manufacturing Company. (p. 47)
A company that uses labor, plant, and equipment to convert raw materials into new finished products.

Manufacturing Overhead. (p. 57)
All manufacturing costs other than direct materials and direct labor. Also called factory overhead and indirect manufacturing cost.

Marginal Cost. (p. 73)
The cost of producing one more unit.

Marketing. (p. 50)
Promotion and advertising of products or services.

Merchandising Company. (p. 47)
A company that resells tangible products previously bought from suppliers.

Period Costs. (p. 54)
Operating costs that are expensed in the period in which they are incurred.

Prime Costs. (p. 58)
The combination of direct material and direct labor costs.

Production or Purchases. (p. 50)
Resources used to produce a product or service or to purchase finished merchandise intended for resale.

Raw Materials Inventory. (p. 48)
All raw materials (direct materials and indirect materials) not yet used in manufacturing.

Research and Development (R&D). (p. 50)
Researching and developing new or improved products or services or the processes for producing them.

Retailer. (p. 47)
Merchandising company that sells to consumers.

Service Company. (p. 47)
A company that sells intangible services rather than tangible products.

Sunk Cost. (p. 70)
A cost that has already been incurred.

Trace. (p. 53)
To assign a *direct* cost to a cost object.

Uncontrollable Costs. (p. 69)
Costs that cannot be changed or influenced in the short run by management.

Value Chain. (p. 49)
The activities that add value to a firm's products and services. Includes R&D, design, production or purchases, marketing, distribution, and customer service.

Variable Costs. (p. 70)
Costs that change in total in direct proportion to changes in volume.

Wholesaler. (p. 47)
Merchandising companies that buy in bulk from manufacturers, mark up the prices, and then sell those products to retailers.

Work in Process Inventory. (p. 48)
Goods that are partway through the manufacturing process but not yet complete.

▪ Quick Check

1. Wal-Mart is a:
   a. service company
   b. retailer
   c. wholesaler
   d. manufacturer

2. Which is *not* an element of Nissan's value chain?
   a. administrative costs
   b. cost of shipping cars to dealers
   c. salaries of engineers who update car design
   d. cost of print ads and television commercials

3. For Nissan, which is a direct cost with respect to the Xterra?
   a. depreciation on plant and equipment
   b. cost of vehicle engine
   c. salary of engineer who rearranges plant layout
   d. cost of customer hotline

4. Which of the following is *not* part of Nissan's manufacturing overhead?
   a. insurance on plant and equipment
   b. depreciation on its North American corporate headquarters in Nashville
   c. plant property taxes
   d. plant utilities

5. In computing cost of goods sold, which of the following is the manufacturer's counterpart to the merchandiser's purchases?
   a. direct materials used
   b. total manufacturing costs incurred during the period
   c. total manufacturing costs to account for
   d. cost of goods manufactured

Questions 6, 7, and 8 refer to the following list. Suppose Nissan reports (in millions of dollars):

Beginning raw materials inventory	$ 6
Ending raw materials inventory	5
Beginning work in process inventory	2
Ending work in process inventory	1
Beginning finished goods inventory	3
Ending finished goods inventory	5
Direct labor	30
Purchases of materials	100
Manufacturing overhead	20

6. What is the cost of the materials that Nissan used (in millions)?
   a. 99
   b. 100
   c. 101
   d. 106

7. What is the cost of goods manufactured (in millions)?
   a. 149
   b. 150
   c. 151
   d. 152

8. What is the cost of goods sold (in millions)?
   a. 150
   b. 152
   c. 153
   d. 154

9. Which of the following is irrelevant to most business decisions?
   a. differential costs
   b. sunk costs
   c. variable costs
   d. qualitative factors

10. Which of the following is true?
   a. Total fixed costs increase as production volume increases.
   b. Total fixed costs decrease as production volume decreases.
   c. Total variable costs increase as production volume increases.
   d. Total variable costs stay constant as production volume increases.

Quick Check Answers

1. b 2. a 3. b 4. b 5. b 6. d 7. c 8. d 9. a 10. c

For Internet Exercises, Excel in Practice, and additional online activities, go to this book's Web site at www.prenhall.com/bamber.

Assess Your Progress

■ Learning Objectives

1 Distinguish among service, merchandising, and manufacturing companies

2 Describe the value chain and its elements

3 Distinguish between direct and indirect costs

4 Identify the inventoriable product costs and period costs of merchandising and manufacturing firms

5 Prepare the financial statements for service, merchandising, and manufacturing companies

6 Describe costs that are relevant and irrelevant for decision making

7 Classify costs as fixed or variable and calculate total and average costs at different volumes

■ Short Exercises

S2-1 **Indentify type of company from balance sheets** *(Learning Objective 1)*
The current asset sections of the balance sheets of three companies follow. Which company is a service company? Which is a merchandiser? Which is a manufacturer? How can you tell?

X-Treme		Y-Not?		Zesto	
Cash.............	$ 2,500	Cash.................	$3,000	Cash.............	$ 2,000
Accounts receivable....	5,500	Accounts receivable........	6,000	Accounts receivable....	5,000
Inventory.......	8,000	Prepaid expenses..........	500	Raw materials inventory.....	1,000
Prepaid expenses......	300	Total................	$9,500	Work in process inventory.....	800
Total.............	$16,300			Finished goods inventory.....	4,000
				Total.............	$12,800

S2-2 **Identify types of companies and inventories** *(Learning Objective 1)*
Fill in the blanks with one of the following terms: *manufacturing, service, merchandising, retailer(s), wholesaler(s), raw materials inventory, merchandise inventory, work in process inventory, finished goods inventory, freight-in, the cost of merchandise.*

a. _____ companies generally have no inventory.

b. Boeing is a _____ company.

c. Merchandisers' inventory consists of _____ and _____.

d. _____ companies carry three types of inventories: _____, _____, and _____.

e. Prudential Insurance Company is a _____ company.

f. Two types of _____ companies include _____ and _____.

g. Direct materials are stored in _____.

h. Sears is a _____ company.

i. Manufacturers sell from their stock of _____.

j. Labor costs usually account for the highest percentage of _____ companies' costs.

k. Partially completed units are kept in the _____.

S2-3 **Give examples of value chain functions** *(Learning Objective 2)*
Give an example of costs that E*TRADE (an online brokerage firm) might incur in each of the six business functions in the value chain. Provide another example that shows how E*TRADE might deliberately decide to spend more money on one of the six business functions to reduce the costs in other business functions.

S2-4 **Label value chain functions** *(Learning Objective 2)*
List the correct value chain element for each of the six business functions described below.

a. Delivery of products and services

b. Detailed engineering of products and services and the processes for producing them

c. Promotion and advertising of product or services

d. Investigating new or improved products or services and the processes for producing them

e. Support provided to customers after the sale

f. Resources used to make a product or obtain finished merchandise

S2-5 **Classify costs by value chain function** *(Learning Objective 2)*
Classify each of Hewlett-Packard's (HP's) costs as one of the six business functions in the value chain.

a. Depreciation on Roseville, California, plant

b. Costs of a customer support center Web site

c. Transportation costs to deliver laser printers to retailers such as Best Buy

d. Depreciation on research lab

e. Cost of a prime-time TV ad featuring the new HP logo

f. Salary of scientists at HP laboratories who are developing new printer technologies

g. Purchase of plastic used in printer casings

h. Salary of engineers who are redesigning the printer's on-off switch

i. Depreciation on delivery vehicles

j. Plant manager's salary

S2-6 **Classify costs as direct or indirect** *(Learning Objective 3)*

Classify the following as direct or indirect costs with respect to a local Blockbuster store (the store is the cost object). In addition, state whether Blockbuster would trace or allocate these costs to the store.

a. Store utilities

b. The CEO's salary

c. The cost of the DVDs

d. The cost of national advertising

e. The wages of store employees

f. The cost of operating the corporate payroll department

g. The cost of Xbox, PlayStation, and Nintendo games

h. The cost of popcorn and candy sold at the store

S2-7 **Give examples of manufacturing costs** *(Learning Objective 4)*

Consider Marvin Windows' manufacturing plant. Give two examples of each of the following:

a. Direct materials

b. Direct labor

c. Indirect materials

d. Indirect labor

e. Other manufacturing overhead

S2-8 **Classify inventoriable and period costs** *(Learning Objective 4)*

Classify each of Georgia-Pacific's costs as either inventoriable product costs or period costs. Georgia-Pacific is a manufacturer of paper, lumber, and building material products.

a. Depreciation on the gypsum board plant

b. Purchase of lumber to be cut into boards

c. Life insurance on CEO

d. Salaries of scientists studying ways to speed forest growth

e. Cost of new software to track inventory during production

f. Cost of electricity at one of Georgia-Pacific's paper mills

g. Salaries of Georgia-Pacific's top executives

h. Cost of chemical applied to lumber to inhibit mold from developing

i. Cost of TV ads promoting environmental awareness

S2-9 **Classify a manufacturer's costs** *(Learning Objective 4)*

Classify each of the following costs as a period cost or an inventoriable product cost. If you classify the cost as an inventoriable product cost, further classify it as direct material (DM), direct labor (DL), or manufacturing overhead (MOH).

a. Depreciation on automated production equipment

b. Telephone bills relating to customer service call center

c. Wages and benefits paid to assembly-line workers in the manufacturing plant

d. Repairs and maintenance on factory equipment

e. Lease payment on administrative headquarters

f. Salaries paid to quality control inspectors in the plant

g. Property insurance—40% of building is used for sales and administration; 60% of building is used for manufacturing

h. Standard packaging materials used to package individual units of product for sale (for example, cereal boxes in which cereal is packaged)

S2-10   Classify costs incurred by a dairy processing company *(Learning Objective 4)*

Each of the following costs pertains to DairyPlains, a dairy processing company. Classify each of the company's costs as a period cost or an inventoriable product cost. Further classify inventoriable product costs as direct material (DM), direct labor (DL), or manufacturing overhead (MOH).

Cost	Period Cost or Inventoriable Product Cost?	DM, DL, or MOH?
1. Cost of milk purchased from local dairy farmers		
2. Lubricants used in running bottling machines		
3. Depreciation on refrigerated trucks used to collect raw milk from local dairy farmers		
4. Property tax on dairy processing plant		
5. Television advertisements for DairyPlains' products		
6. Gasoline used to operate refrigerated trucks delivering finished dairy products to grocery stores		
7. Company president's annual bonus		
8. Plastic gallon containers in which milk is packaged		
9. Depreciation on marketing department's computers		
10. Wages and salaries paid to machine operators at dairy processing plant		
11. Research and development on improving milk pasteurization process		

S2-11   Determine total manufacturing overhead *(Learning Objective 4)*

Snap's manufactures disposable cameras. Suppose the company's March records include the items described below. What is Snap's total manufacturing overhead cost in March?

Glue for camera frames	$ 250
Depreciation expense on company cars used by sales force	3,000
Plant depreciation expense	10,000
Interest expense	2,000
Company president's salary	25,000
Plant supervisor's salary	4,000
Plant janitor's salary	1,000
Oil for manufacturing equipment	25
Flashbulbs	50,000

S2-12 Compute Cost of Goods Sold for a merchandiser *(Learning Objective 5)*

Given the following information for Circuits Plus, an electronics e-tailer, compute the cost of goods sold.

Web site maintenance	$ 7,000
Delivery expenses	1,000
Freight-in	3,000
Import duties	1,000
Purchases	40,000
Ending inventory	5,500
Revenues	60,000
Marketing expenses	10,000
Beginning inventory	3,500

S2-13 Prepare a retailer's income statement *(Learning Objective 5)*

Salon Secrets is a retail chain specializing in salon-quality hair care products. During the year, Salon Secrets had sales of $38,230,000. The company began the year with $3,270,000 of merchandise inventory and ended the year with $3,920,000 of inventory. During the year, Salon Secrets purchased $23,450,000 of merchandise inventory. The company's selling, general, and administrative expenses totaled $6,115,000 for the year. Prepare Salon Secrets' income statement for the year.

S2-14 Recalculate Cost of Goods Manufactured *(Learning Objective 5)*

Turn to Exhibit 2-15. If direct material purchases and freight-in were $20,000 rather than $27,000, what would be the cost of direct materials used and the cost of goods manufactured? (Other costs remain the same as in Exhibit 2-15.)

S2-15 Calculate direct materials used *(Learning Objective 5)*

You are a new accounting intern at Sunny's Bikes. Your boss gives you the following information and asks you to compute the cost of direct materials used (assume that the company's raw materials inventory contains only direct materials).

Purchases of direct materials	$16,000
Import duties	1,000
Freight-in	200
Freight-out	1,000
Ending raw materials inventory	1,500
Beginning raw materials inventory	4,000

S2-16 Compute Cost of Goods Manufactured *(Learning Objective 5)*

Smith Manufacturing found the following information in their accounting records: $524,000 of direct materials used, $223,000 of direct labor, and $742,000 of manufacturing overhead. The Work in Process Inventory account had a beginning balance of $76,000 and an ending balance of $85,000. Compute the company's Cost of Goods Manufactured.

S2-17 Consider relevant information *(Learning Objective 6)*

You've been offered an entry-level marketing position at two highly respectable firms: one in Los Angeles, California, and one in Sioux Falls, South Dakota. What quantitative and qualitative information might be relevant to your decision? What characteristics about this information make it relevant?

S2-18 Classify costs as fixed or variable *(Learning Objective 7)*

Classify each of the following personal expenses as either fixed or variable. In some cases, your answer may depend on specific circumstances. If so, briefly explain your answer.

a. Apartment rental

b. Television cable service

c. Cost of groceries

d. Water and sewer bill

e. Cell phone bill

f. Health club dues

g. Bus fare

▪ Exercises

E2-19 Identify types of companies and their inventories *(Learning Objective 1)*

Complete the following statements with one of the terms listed here. You may use a term more than once, and some terms may not be used at all.

Finished goods inventory	Inventory (merchandise)	Service companies
Manufacturing companies	Merchandising companies	Work in process inventory
Raw materials inventory	Wholesalers	Retailers

a. _____ produce their own inventory.

b. _____ typically have a single category of inventory.

c. _____ do not have tangible products intended for sale.

d. _____ resell products they previously purchased ready-made from suppliers.

e. _____ use their workforce and equipment to transform raw materials into new finished products.

f. _____ sell to consumers.

g. Swaim, a company based in North Carolina, makes furniture. Partially completed sofas are _____. Completed sofas that remain unsold in the warehouse are _____. Fabric and wood are _____.

h. For Kellogg's, corn, cardboard boxes, and waxed paper liners are classified as _____.

i. _____ buy in bulk from manufacturers and sell to retailers

E2-20 Classify costs along the value chain for a retailer *(Learning Objective 2)*

Suppose Radio Shack incurred the following costs at its Charleston, South Carolina, store:

Research on whether store should sell satellite radio service	$ 400	Payment to consultant for advise on location of new store	$2,500
Purchases of merchandise	30,000	Freight-in	3,000
Rearranging store layout	750	Salespeople's salaries	4,000
Newspaper advertisements	5,000	Customer complaint department	800
Depreciation expense on delivery trucks	1,000		

Requirements

1. Use the following format to classify each cost according to its place in the value chain.

R&D	Design	Purchases	Marketing	Distribution	Customer Service

2. Compute the total costs for each value-chain category.
3. How much are the total inventoriable product costs?

E2-21 Classify costs along the value chain for a manufacturer *(Learning Objectives 2, 3)*

Suppose the cell phone manufacturer Samsung Electronics provides the following information for its costs last month (in hundreds of thousands):

Salaries of telephone salespeople	$ 5	Transmitters	$61
Depreciation on plant and equipment	65	Rearrange production process to accommodate new robot	2
Exterior case for phone	6	Assembly-line workers' wages	10
Salaries of scientists who developed new model	12	Technical customer support hotline	3
Delivery expense to customers via UPS	7	1-800 (toll-free) line for customer orders	1

Requirements

1. Use the following format to classify each cost according to its place in the value chain. (*Hint:* You should have at least one cost in each value-chain function.)

		Production					
R&D	Design of Products or Processes	Direct Materials	Direct Labor	Manufacturing Overhead	Marketing	Distribution	Customer Service

2. Compute the total costs for each value-chain category.
3. How much are the total inventoriable product costs?
4. How much are the total prime costs?
5. How much are the total conversion costs?

E2-22 **Classify costs as direct or indirect** *(Learning Objective 3)*
Classify each of the following costs as a *direct cost* or an *indirect cost* assuming the cost object is the produce department (fruit and vegetable department) of a local grocery store.

a. Produce manager's salary

b. Cost of the produce

c. Store utilities

d. Bags and twist ties provided to customers in the produce department for packaging fruits and vegetables

e. Depreciation expense on refrigerated produce display shelves

f. Cost of shopping carts and baskets

g. Wages of checkout clerks

h. Cost of grocery store's advertisement flyer placed in the weekly newspaper

i. Store manager's salary

j. Cost of equipment used to peel and core pineapples at the store

k. Free grocery delivery service provided to senior citizens

l. Depreciation on self-checkout machines

E2-23 **Define cost terms** *(Learning Objectives 3, 4)*
Complete the following statements with one of the terms listed here. You may use a term more than once, and some terms may not be used at all.

Prime costs	Cost objects	Inventoriable product costs
Assigned	Direct costs	Fringe benefits
Period costs	Assets	Cost of goods sold
Indirect costs	Conversion costs	Full product costs

a. _____ can be traced to cost objects.

b. _____ are expensed when incurred.

c. _____ are the combination of direct materials and direct labor.

d. Compensation includes wages, salaries, and _____.

e. _____ are treated as _____ until sold.

f. _____ include costs from only the production or purchases element of the value chain.

g. _____ are allocated to cost objects.

h. Both direct and indirect costs are _____ to _____.

i. _____ include costs from every element of the value chain.

j. _____ are the combination of direct labor and manufacturing overhead.

k. _____ are expensed as _____ when sold.

l. Manufacturing overhead includes all _____ of production.

E2-24 Classify and calculate a manufacturer's costs *(Learning Objectives 3, 4)*

An airline manufacturer incurred the following costs last month (in thousands of dollars):

a.	Airplane seats	$ 250
b.	Depreciation on administrative offices	60
c.	Assembly workers' wages	600
d.	Plant utilities	120
e.	Production supervisors' salaries	100
f.	Jet engines	1,000
g.	Machine lubricants	15
h.	Depreciation on forklifts	50
i.	Property tax on corporate marketing office	25
j.	Cost of warranty repairs	225
k.	Factory janitors' wages	30
l.	Cost of designing new plant layout	175
m.	Machine operators' health insurance	40
	TOTAL	$2,690

Requirements

1. If the cost object is an airplane, classify each cost as one of the following: direct material (DM), direct labor (DL), indirect labor (IL), indirect materials (IM), other manufacturing overhead (other MOH), or period cost. (*Hint:* Set up a column for each type of cost.) What is the total for each type of cost?

2. Calculate total manufacturing overhead costs.

3. Calculate total inventoriable product costs.

4. Calculate total prime costs.

5. Calculate total conversion costs.

6. Total period costs.

E2-25 Prepare the current assest section of the balance sheet *(Learning Objective 5)*

Consider the following selected amounts and account balances of Lords:

Cost of goods sold	$104,000	Prepaid expenses	$ 6,000
Direct labor	47,000	Marketing expense	30,000
Direct materials used	20,000	Work in process inventory	40,000
Accounts receivable	80,000	Manufacturing overhead	26,000
Cash	15,000	Finished goods inventory	63,000
Cost of goods manufactured	94,000	Raw materials inventory	10,000

Show how Lords reports current assets on the balance sheet. Not all data are used. Is Lords a service company, a merchandiser, or a manufacturer? How do you know?

E2-26 **Prepare a retailer's income statement** *(Learning Objective 5)*

Robbie Roberts is the sole proprietor of Precious Pets, an e-tail business specializing in the sale of high-end pet gifts and accessories. Precious Pets' sales totaled $987,000 during 2007. During the year, the company spent $56,000 on expenses relating to Web site maintenance; $22,000 on marketing; and $25,000 on wrapping, boxing, and shipping the goods to customers. Precious Pets also spent $642,000 on inventory purchases and an additional $21,000 on freight-in charges. The company started the year with $17,000 of inventory on hand and ended the year with $15,000 of inventory. Prepare Precious Pets' 2007 income statement.

E2-27 **Compute direct materials used and cost of goods manufactured** *(Learning Objective 5)*

Danielle's Die-cuts is preparing its Cost of Goods Manufactured Schedule at year-end. Danielle's accounting records show the following: The Raw Materials Inventory account had a beginning balance of $13,000 and an ending balance of $17,000. During the year, Danielle purchased $58,000 of direct materials. Direct labor for the year totaled $123,000, while manufacturing overhead amounted to $152,000. The Work in Process Inventory account had a beginning balance of $21,000 and an ending balance of $15,000. Compute the Cost of Goods Manufactured for the year. (*Hint:* The first step is to calculate the direct materials used during the year. Model your answer after Exhibit 2-15.)

E2-28 **Compute cost of goods manufactured and cost of goods sold** *(Learning Objective 5)*

Compute the 2007 cost of goods manufactured and cost of goods sold for Strike Marine Company using the amounts described below. Assume that raw materials inventory contains only direct materials.

	Beginning of Year	End of Year		End of Year
Raw materials inventory	$25,000	$28,000	Insurance on plant	$ 9,000
Work in process inventory	50,000	35,000	Depreciation—plant building and equipment	13,000
Finished goods inventory	18,000	25,000	Repairs and maintenance—plant	4,000
Purchases of direct materials		78,000	Marketing expenses	77,000
Direct labor		82,000	General and administrative expenses	29,000
Indirect labor		15,000		

E2-29 **Continues E2-28: Prepare income statement** *(Learning Objective 5)*

Prepare the 2007 income statement for Strike Marine Company in E2-28. Assume that the company sold 32,000 units of its product at a price of $12 each during 2007.

E2-30 **Work backwards to find missing amounts** *(Learning Objective 5)*

Smooth Sounds manufactures and sells a new line of MP3 players. Unfortunately, Smooth Sounds suffered serious fire damage at its home office. As a result, the accounting records for October were partially destroyed—and completely jumbled. Smooth Sounds has hired you to help figure out the missing pieces of the accounting puzzle. Assume that Smooth Sounds' raw materials inventory contains only direct materials.

continued . . .

Work in process inventory, October 31	$ 1,500
Finished goods inventory, October 1	4,300
Direct labor in October	3,000
Purchases of direct materials in October	9,000
Work in process inventory, October 1	0
Revenues in October	27,000
Gross profit in October	12,000
Direct materials used in October	8,000
Raw materials inventory, October 31	3,000
Manufacturing overhead in October	6,300

Requirement

Find the following amounts:

a. Cost of goods sold in October

b. Beginning raw materials inventory

c. Ending finished goods inventory
(*Hint:* You may find Exhibits 2-15 and 2-16 helpful.)

E2-31 **Determine whether information is relevant** (*Learning Objective 6*)
Classify each of the following costs as relevant or irrelevant to the decision at hand and briefly explain your reason.

a. Cost of operating automated production machinery versus the cost of direct labor when deciding whether to automate production

b. Cost of computers purchased six months ago when deciding whether to upgrade to computers with a faster processing speed

c. Cost of purchasing packaging materials from an outside vendor when deciding whether to continue manufacturing the packaging materials in-house

d. The property tax rates in different locales when deciding where to locate the company's headquarters

e. The type of gas (regular or premium) used by delivery vans when deciding which make and model of van to purchase for the company's delivery van fleet

f. Depreciation expense on old manufacturing equipment when deciding whether to replace it with newer equipment

g. The fair market value of old manufacturing equipment when deciding whether to replace it with new equipment

h. The interest rate paid on invested funds when deciding how much inventory to keep on hand

i. The cost of land purchased three years ago when deciding whether to build on the land now or wait two more years

j. The total amount of the restaurant's fixed costs when deciding whether to add additional items to the menu

E2-32 **Describe other cost terms** *(Learning Objectives 6, 7)*
Complete the following statements with one of the terms listed here. You may use a term more than once, and some terms may not be used at all.

Differential costs	Irrelevant costs	Controllable costs
Marginal costs	Sunk costs	Average cost
Uncontrollable costs	Fixed costs	Variable costs

a. Managers cannot influence _____ in the short run.

b. Total _____ decrease when production volume decreases.

c. For decision-making purposes, costs that do not differ between alternatives are _____.

d. Costs that have already been incurred are called _____.

e. Total _____ stay constant over a wide range of production volumes.

f. The _____ is the difference in cost between two alternative courses of action.

g. The product's _____ is the cost of making one more unit.

h. A product's _____ and _____, not the product's _____, should be used to forecast total costs at different production volumes.

E2-33 **Classify costs as fixed or variable** *(Learning Objective 7)*
Classify each of the following costs as fixed or variable:

a. Thread used by a garment manufacturer

b. Property tax on a manufacturing facility

c. Yearly salaries paid to sales staff

d. Gasoline used to operate delivery vans

e. Annual contract for pest (insect) control

f. Boxes used to package breakfast cereal at Kellogg's

g. Straight-line depreciation on production equipment

h. Cell phone bills for sales staff—contract billed at $.03 cents per minute

i. Wages paid to hourly assembly-line workers in the manufacturing plant

j. Monthly lease payment on administrative headquarters

k. Commissions paid to the sales staff—5% of sales revenue

l. Credit card transaction fee paid by retailer—$0.20 per transaction plus 2% of the sales amount

m. Annual business license fee from city

n. Cost of ice cream sold at Baskin-Robbins

o. Cost of shampoo used at a hair salon

E2-34 **Compute total and average costs** *(Learning Objective 7)*
Fizzy-Cola spends $1 on direct materials, direct labor, and variable manufacturing overhead for every unit (12-pack of soda) it produces. Fixed manufacturing overhead costs $5 million per year. The plant, which is currently operating at only 75% of capacity, produced 20 million units this year. Management plans to operate closer to full capacity next year, producing 25 million units. Management doesn't anticipate any changes in the prices it pays for materials, labor, and overhead.

continued . . .

Requirements

a. What is the current total product cost (for the 20 million units), including fixed and variable costs?

b. What is the current average product cost per unit?

c. What is the current fixed cost per unit?

d. What is the forecasted total product cost next year (for the 25 million units)?

e. What is the forecasted average product cost next year?

f. What is the forecasted fixed cost per unit?

g. Why does the average product cost decrease as production increases?

■ Problems (Problem Set A)

P2-35A Classify costs along the value chain (*Learning Objectives 2, 4*)

ShaZam Cola produces a lemon-lime soda. The production process starts with workers mixing the lemon syrup and lime flavors in a secret recipe. The company enhances the combined syrup with caffeine. Finally, ShaZam dilutes the mixture with carbonated water. ShaZam Cola incurs the following costs (in thousands):

Plant utilities	$ 750
Depreciation on plant and equipment	3,000
Payment for new recipe	1,000
Salt	25
Replace products with expired dates upon customer complaint	50
Rearranging plant layout	1,100
Lemon syrup	18,000
Lime flavoring	1,000
Production costs of "cents-off" store coupons for customers	600
Delivery truck drivers' wages	250
Bottles	1,300
Sales commissions	400
Plant janitors' wages	1,000
Wages of workers who mix syrup	8,000
Customer hotline	200
Depreciation on delivery trucks	150
Freight-in on materials	1,500
Total	$38,325

Requirements

1. Use the following format to classify each of these costs according to its place in the value chain. (*Hint:* You should have at least one cost in each value-chain function.)

	Design of Products or	Production					
R&D	Processes	Direct Materials	Direct Labor	Manufacturing Overhead	Marketing	Distribution	Customer Service

2. Compute the total costs for each value-chain category.

3. How much are the total inventoriable product costs?

4. Suppose the managers of the R&D and design functions receive year-end bonuses based on meeting their unit's target cost reductions. What are they likely to do? How might this affect costs incurred in other elements of the value chain?

P2-36A Prepare income statements *(Learning Objective 5)*

Part One: In 2007, Hannah Summit opened Hannah's Pets, a small retail shop selling pet supplies. On December 31, 2007, her accounting records show the following:

Inventory on December 31, 2007	$10,250
Inventory on January 1, 2007	15,000
Sales revenue	54,000
Utilities for shop	2,450
Rent for shop	4,000
Sales commissions	2,300
Purchases of merchandise	27,000

Requirement

Prepare an income statement for Hannah's Pets, a merchandiser, for the year ended December 31, 2007.

Part Two: Hannah's Pets succeeded so well that Hannah decided to manufacture her own brand of pet toys—Best Friends Manufacturing. At the end of December 2008, her accounting records show the following:

Work in process inventory, December 31, 2008	$ 720
Finished goods inventory, December 31, 2007	0
Finished goods inventory, December 31, 2008	5,700
Sales revenue	105,000
Customer service hotline expense	1,000
Utilities for plant	4,600
Delivery expense	1,500
Sales salaries expense	5,000
Plant janitorial services	1,250
Direct labor	18,300
Direct material purchases	31,000
Rent on manufacturing plant	9,000
Raw materials inventory, December 31, 2007	13,500
Raw materials inventory, December 31, 2008	9,275
Work in process inventory, December 31, 2007	0

Requirements

1. Prepare a schedule of cost of goods manufactured for Best Friends Manufacturing for the year ended December 31, 2008.

2. Prepare an income statement for Best Friends Manufacturing for the year ended December 31, 2008.

continued . . .

3. How does the format of the income statement for Best Friends Manufacturing differ from the income statement of Hannah's Pets?

Part Three: Show the ending inventories that would appear on these balance sheets:

1. Hannah's Pets at December 31, 2007
2. Best Friends Manufacturing at December 31, 2008

P2-37A Fill in missing amounts *(Learning Objective 5)*

Certain item descriptions and amounts are missing from the monthly schedule of cost of goods manufactured below and the income statement of Tretinik Manufacturing. Fill in the missing items.

TRETINIK MANUFACTURING COMPANY

_____ June 30, 2007

Beginning _____				$ 21,000
Add: Direct _____ :				
Beginning raw materials inventory	$ X			
Purchases of direct materials	51,000			
_____	78,000			
Ending raw materials inventory	(23,000)			
Direct _____		$ X		
Direct _____		X		
Manufacturing overhead		40,000		
Total _____ costs _____				166,000
Total _____ costs _____				X
Less: Ending _____				(25,000)
_____				$ X

TRETINIK MANUFACTURING COMPANY

_____ June 30, 2007

Sales revenue			$ X
Cost of goods sold:			
Beginning _____	$115,000		
_____	X		
Cost of goods _____	X		
Ending _____	X		
Cost of goods sold			209,000
Gross profit			254,000
_____ expenses:			
Marketing expense	99,000		
Administrative expense	X		154,000
_____ income			$ X

P2-38A **Identify relevant information** *(Learning Objective 6)*

You receive two job offers in the same big city. The first job is close to your parents' house, and they have offered to let you live at home for a year so you won't have to incur expenses for housing, food, or cable TV. This job pays $30,000 per year. The second job is far from your parents' house, so you'll have to rent an apartment with parking ($6,000 per year), buy your own food ($2,400 per year), and pay for your own cable TV ($600 per year). This job pays $35,000 per year. You still plan to do laundry at your parents' house once a week if you live in the city, and you plan to go into the city once a week to visit with friends if you live at home. Thus, the cost of operating your car will be about the same either way. In addition, your parents refuse to pay for your cell phone service ($720 per year), and you can't function without it.

Requirements

a. Based on this information alone, what is the net difference between the two alternatives (salary, net of relevant costs)?

b. What information is irrelevant? Why?

c. What qualitative information is relevant to your decision?

d. Assume that you really want to take Job #2, but you also want to live at home to cut costs. What new quantitative and qualitative information will you need to incorporate into your decision?

P2-39A **Calculate the total and average costs** *(Learning Objective 7)*

The owner of Pizza-House Restaurant is disappointed because the restaurant has been averaging 3,000 pizza sales per month, but the restaurant and wait staff can make and serve 5,000 pizzas per month. The variable cost (for example, ingredients) of each pizza is $2.00. Monthly fixed costs (for example, depreciation, property taxes, business license, and manager's salary) are $6,000 per month. The owner wants cost information about different volumes so that he can make some operating decisions.

Requirements

1. Fill in the chart below to provide the owner with the cost information he wants. Then use the completed chart to help you answer the remaining questions.

Monthly pizza volume	2,500	3,000	5,000
Total fixed costs	$	$	$
Total variable costs	___	___	___
Total costs	___	___	___
Fixed cost per pizza	$	$	$
Variable cost per pizza	___	___	___
Average cost per pizza	___	___	___
Sales price per pizza	$10.00	$10.00	$10.00
Average profit per pizza	___	___	___

2. From a cost standpoint, why do companies such as Pizza-House Restaurant want to operate near or at full capacity?

continued . . .

3. The owner has been considering ways to increase the sales volume. He believes he could sell 5,000 pizzas a month by cutting the sales price from $10 a pizza to $9.50. How much extra profit (above the current level) would he generate if he decreased the sales price? (*Hint:* Find the restaurant's current monthly profit and compare it to the restaurant's projected monthly profit at the new sales price and volume.)

4. The owner's other idea is to advertise his restaurant on the local radio stations. If he keeps the sales price at $10 per pizza, the advertising agency says he'll have to spend $10,000 in advertising each month to increase monthly sales to 5,000 pizzas. How much extra profit (above the current level) would he generate if he kept the sales price at $10 per pizza but spent $10,000 per month on advertising? Which of the owner's ideas is most profitable?

5. The owner is surprised by your calculations. Because the current average profit per pizza is $6.00, he thought the restaurant would make $30,000 of income per month (before advertising costs) if it sold 5,000 pizzas at the normal $10 sales price. How did the owner arrive at this figure, and why is it wrong?

■ Problems (Problem Set B)

P2-40B Classify costs along the value chain *(Learning Objectives 2, 4)*

Suppose Apple Computer reported the following costs last month (all costs are in millions):

Payment to UPS for delivering PCs to customers	$ 300
Cost of hard drives used	4,700
Cost of Internet banner ads	650
Plant janitors' wages	10
Wages of workers who assemble the PCs	1,500
Cost of customer hotline for troubleshooting problems	40
Wages of forklift drivers on the plant floor	25
Plant utilities	35
Cost of software loaded on computers	30
Depreciation on plant and equipment	300
Salaries of scientists working on next-generation laptops	45
Insurance and taxes on plant property	40
Cost of oil used for conveyor belts and other plant equipment	5
Payment to engineers redesigning the exterior case	20
Wages of sales associates taking phone orders	50
Cost of circuit boards used	5,500
Total	$13,250

Requirements

1. Use the following format to classify each of these costs according to its place in the value chain. (*Hint:* You should have at least one cost in each value-chain function.)

R&D	Design of Products or Processes	Production			Marketing	Distribution	Customer Service
		Direct Materials	Direct Labor	Manufacturing Overhead			

2. Compute the total costs for each category.
3. How much are the total inventoriable product costs?
4. Suppose the managers of the R&D and design departments receive year-end bonuses based on meeting their department's target cost reductions. What are they likely to do? How might this affect costs incurred in other elements of the value chain?

P2-41B **Prepare income statements** (*Learning Objective 5*)

Part One: On January 1, 2007, Terri Shaw opened Precious Memories, a small retail store dedicated to selling picture frames, crafts, and art. On December 31, 2007, her accounting records show the following:

Store rent	$ 7,000
Sales salaries...	4,500
Freight-in	550
Inventory on December 31, 2007...........	8,750
Sales revenue..	90,000
Store utilities	1,950
Purchases of merchandise.......................	36,000
Inventory on January 1, 2007	12,700
Advertising expense................................	2,300

Requirement

Prepare an income statement for Precious Memories, a merchandiser, for the year ended December 31, 2007.

continued . . .

Part Two: Precious Memories succeeded so well that Shaw decided to manufacture her own special brand of picture frames, to be called Forever Manufacturing. At the end of December 2009, her accounting records show the following:

Finished goods inventory, December 31, 2009	$ 2,000
Work in process inventory, December 31, 2009	1,750
Raw materials inventory, December 31, 2009	7,750
R&D for graphic designs	3,700
Sales commissions	4,000
Utilities for plant	2,000
Plant janitorial services	750
Direct labor	20,000
Direct material purchases	32,000
Rent on plant	11,000
Finished goods inventory, December 31, 2008	0
Depreciation expense on delivery truck	2,500
Depreciation expense on plant equipment	3,500
Work in process inventory December 31, 2008	0
Sales revenue	126,450
Customer warranty refunds	1,500
Raw materials inventory, December 31, 2008	13,000

Requirements

1. Prepare a schedule of cost of goods manufactured for Forever Manufacturing for the year ended December 31, 2009.

2. Prepare an income statement for Forever Manufacturing for the year ended December 31, 2009.

3. How does the format of the income statement for Forever Manufacturing differ from the income statement of Precious Memories?

Part Three: Show the ending inventories that would appear on these balance sheets:

1. Precious Memories at December 31, 2007

2. Forever Manufacturing at December 31, 2009

P2-42B Fill in missing amounts *(Learning Objective 5)*

Certain item descriptions and amounts are missing from the monthly schedule of cost of goods manufactured and income statement of Pacific Manufacturing Company. Fill in the missing items.

PACIFIC MANUFACTURING COMPANY

_____ April 30, 2007

			$ 15,000
_____ work in process inventory			
Add: Direct materials used:			
_____ materials _____	$ X		
_____ of direct materials	65,000		
_____	75,000		
_____ materials _____	(23,000)		
Direct _____		$ X	
Direct _____		68,000	
Manufacturing overhead		X	
Total _____ costs _____			X
Total _____ costs _____			175,000
Less: _____ work in process inventory			X
_____			$150,000

PACIFIC MANUFACTURING COMPANY

_____ April 30, 2007

_____ revenue			$450,000
_____:			
Beginning _____	$ X		
_____	X		
Cost of goods _____	X		
Ending _____	(67,000)		
Cost of goods sold			X
_____			243,000
_____ expenses:			
Marketing expenses		X	
Administrative expenses		$64,000	X
_____			$ 76,000

P2-43B **Identify relevant information** (_Learning Objective 6_)

You receive two job offers in the same big city. The first job is close to your parents' house, and they have offered to let you live at home for a year so you won't have to incur expenses for housing, food, or cable TV. This job pays $45,000 per year. The second job is far away from your parents' house, so you'll have to rent an apartment with parking ($10,000 per year), buy your own food ($3,000 per year), and pay for your own cable TV ($700 per year). This job pays $50,000 per year. You still plan to do laundry at your parents' house once a week if you live in the city, and you plan to go into the city once a week to visit with friends if you live at home. Thus, the cost of operating your car will be about the same either way. In addition, your parents refuse to pay for your cell phone service ($720 per year), and you can't function without it.

continued . . .

Requirements

a. Based on this information alone, what is the net difference between the two alternatives (salary, net of relevant costs)?

b. What information is irrelevant? Why?

c. What qualitative information is relevant to your decision?

d. Assume that you really want to take Job #2, but you also want to live at home to cut costs. What new quantitative and qualitative information will you need to incorporate into your decision?

P2-44B **Calculate total and average costs** *(Learning Objective 7)*

The owner of New York Deli restaurant is disappointed because the restaurant has been averaging 4,000 sandwich sales per month, but the restaurant can make and serve 6,000 sandwiches per month. The variable cost (for example, ingredients) of each sandwich is $1.25. Monthly fixed costs (for example, depreciation, property taxes, business license, manager's salary) are $6,000 per month. The owner wants cost information about different volumes so that he can make some operating decisions.

Requirements

1. Fill in the chart below to provide the owner with the cost information he wants. Then use the completed chart to help you answer the remaining questions.

Monthly sandwich volume	3,000	4,000	6,000
Total fixed costs	$	$	$
Total variable costs			
Total costs			
Fixed cost per sandwich	$	$	$
Variable cost per sandwich			
Average cost per sandwich			
Sales price per sandwich	$6.00	$6.00	$6.00
Average profit per sandwich			

2. From a cost standpoint, why do companies such as New York Deli want to operate near or at full capacity?

3. The owner has been considering ways to increase the sales volume. He believes he could sell 6,000 sandwiches a month by cutting the sales price from $6.00 a sandwich to $5.50. How much extra profit (above the current level) would he generate if he decreased the sales price? (*Hint:* Find the deli's current monthly profit and compare it to the deli's projected monthly profit at the new sales price and volume.)

4. The owner's other idea is to advertise his restaurant on the local radio stations. If he keeps the sales price at $6 per sandwich, the advertising agency says he'll have to spend $4,000 in advertising each month to increase monthly sales to 6,000 sandwiches. How much extra profit (above the current level) would he generate if he kept the sales price at $6 per sandwich but spent $4,000 per month on advertising? Which of the owner's two ideas is most profitable?

5. The owner is surprised by your calculations. Because the current average profit per sandwich is $3.25, he thought the restaurant would make $19,500 of income per month (before advertising costs) if it sold 6,000 sandwiches at the normal $6.00 sales price. How did the owner arrive at this figure, and why is it wrong?

Apply Your Knowledge

■ Decision Case

Case 2-45. Determine ending inventory balances *(Learning Objective 5)*

PowerBox designs and manufactures switches used in telecommunications. Serious flooding throughout North Carolina affected PowerBox's facilities. Inventory was completely ruined, and the company's computer system, including all accounting records, was destroyed.

Before the disaster recovery specialists clean the buildings, Annette Plum, the company controller, is anxious to salvage whatever records she can to support an insurance claim for the destroyed inventory. She is standing in what is left of the accounting department with Paul Lopez, the cost accountant.

"I didn't know mud could smell so bad," Paul says. "What should I be looking for?"

"Don't worry about beginning inventory numbers," responds Annette. "We'll get them from last year's annual report. We need first-quarter cost data."

"I was working on the first-quarter results just before the storm hit," Paul says. "Look, my report's still in my desk drawer. But all I can make out is that for the first quarter, material purchases were $476,000 and that direct labor, manufacturing overhead (other than indirect materials), and total manufacturing costs to account for were $505,000, $245,000, and $1,425,000, respectively. Wait, and cost of goods available for sale was $1,340,000."

"Great," says Annette. "I remember that sales for the period were approximately $1.7 million. Given our gross profit of 30%, that's all you should need."

Paul is not sure about that, but decides to see what he can do with this information. The beginning inventory numbers are as follows:

- Raw materials, $113,000
- Work in process, $229,000
- Finished goods, $154,000

He remembers a schedule he learned in college that may help him get started.

Requirements

1. Exhibit 2-16 resembles the schedule Paul has in mind. Use it to determine the ending inventories of raw materials, work in process, and finished goods.

2. Draft an insurance claim letter for the controller, seeking reimbursement for the flood damage to inventory. PowerBox's insurance representative is Gary Streer, at Industrial Insurance, 1122 Main Street, Hartford, CT 06268. The policy number is #3454340-23. PowerBox's address is 5 Research Triangle Way, Raleigh, NC 27698.

5 Activity-Based Costing and Other Cost Management Tools

After Dell reported its first-ever quarterly loss several years ago, CEO Michael Dell knew he had to focus on the company's most profitable products. But which products were they? The accounting system traced direct materials and direct labor to individual product lines, but it did not do a good job matching indirect costs throughout the value chain with the specific products that caused those costs (Dell wanted to find the full product cost of each product, not just the inventoriable product cost).

Dell needed a more finely tuned cost accounting system: *activity-based costing (ABC)*. Employee teams identified the ten most important indirect activities—for example, purchases of raw materials, indirect assembly labor, and warranty service. *For each activity*, the teams

developed a separate indirect cost allocation rate. The goal was to assign the cost of each activity to the product lines that caused that activity's cost. For example:

- Purchasing costs are assigned based on the number of different parts in a product.
- Indirect assembly labor is assigned based on the number of times the product is "touched."
- Warranty costs are assigned based on the number of service calls for the product line.

ABC assigns costs more accurately than simpler systems that combine the indirect costs of many activities into a single cost pool and then allocate those costs using a single allocation base.

Has ABC worked for Dell? By 2003, Dell was the leader in worldwide PC sales. Given the rapidly changing costs in the computer industry, Dell uses ABC costs for pricing its computers every day. ABC also helps Dell's managers cut costs, especially by highlighting nonvalue-added activities such as inventory storage. As the controller of Dell's American operations says, "Activity-based costing has really allowed Dell to go to the next level of understanding of its profitability for each of the products it sells." ▪

Learning Objectives

1 Develop and use departmental overhead rates in place of a traditional plantwide rate

2 Develop activity-based costs (ABC) and use activity-based management (ABM) to make business decisions

3 Explain when ABC is most likely to pass the cost-benefit test

4 Describe a just-in-time (JIT) production system

5 Describe the four costs of quality and use them to make decisions

6 (Appendix) Use JIT costing to record costs in a JIT production environment

To thrive in a globally competitive market, Dell must deliver value to the customer by providing goods or services at an attractive price, while managing costs so the company still earns a profit. This chapter will show you several methods that today's managers use to deliver value to the customer at a profit:

- Refined costing systems such as ABC
- Just-in-time systems
- Costs of quality

Refined Cost Systems

Organizations from Dell to Carolina Power and Light to the U.S. Marine Corps use refined costing systems. Why? Because simple systems that do not match costs with the consumption of resources can assign costs inequitably. The following example shows why.

Why Managers Need More Accurate Cost Systems

David, Matt, and Marc are three college friends who share an apartment. They agree to split the following monthly costs equally:

Rent and utilities	$570
Cable TV	50
High-speed Internet access	40
Groceries	240
Total monthly costs	$900

Each roommate's share is $300 ($900/3).

Things go smoothly for the first few months. But then David calls a meeting. "Since I started having dinner at Amy's each night, I shouldn't have to chip in for the groceries." Matt then pipes in: "I'm so busy studying and using the Internet that I never have time to watch TV. I don't want to pay for the cable TV anymore. And Marc, since your friend Jennifer eats here most evenings, you should pay a double share of the grocery bill." Marc replies, "If that's the way you feel, Matt, then you should pay for the Internet access since you're the only one around here who uses it!"

What happened? The friends originally agreed to share the costs equally. But they are not participating equally in watching cable TV, using the Internet, and using the groceries. Splitting these costs equally is not equitable.

The roommates could use a cost allocation approach that better matches costs with the people who participate in each activity. This means splitting the cable TV costs between David and Marc, assigning the Internet access cost to Matt, and allocating the grocery bill one-third to Matt and two-thirds to Marc. Exhibit 5-1 compares the results of this refined cost allocation system with the original cost allocation system.

EXHIBIT 5-1	**More-Refined Versus Less-Refined Cost Allocation System**			
	David	Matt	Marc	Total
More-refined cost allocation system:				
Rent and utilities	$190	$190	$190	$570
Cable TV	25	0	25	50
High-speed Internet access	0	40	0	40
Groceries	0	80	160	240
Total costs allocated	$215	$310	$375	$900
Less-refined original cost allocation system	$300	$300	$300	$900
Difference	$ (85)	$ 10	$ 75	$ 0

No wonder David called a meeting! The original cost allocation system charged him $300 a month, but the refined system shows that a more equitable share would be only $215. The new system allocates Marc $375 a month instead of $300. David was paying for resources he did not use (Internet and groceries), while Marc was not paying for all of the resources (groceries) he and his guest consumed. David was "overcosted" and Marc was "undercosted" by the old system.

Total monthly costs are the same ($900) under both systems. The only difference is how that $900 is allocated among the three roommates. The amount by which David was "overcosted" ($85) exactly equals the amounts by which Matt and Marc were "undercosted" ($10 + $75).

As we'll see in the following sections, companies often refine their cost allocation systems to minimize the amount of overcosting and undercosting caused by the simpler traditional cost allocation systems. Overcosting some products while undercosting other products is known as **cost distortion.** By refining their costing systems, companies can more equitably assign indirect costs to their individual products or services, thereby reducing cost distortion.

Sharpening the Focus: From Business Functions to Departments to Activities

1   Develop and use departmental overhead rates in place of a traditional plantwide rate

As the chapter-opening story explained, Dell decided that it needed to refine its costing system so it could better understand which of its products were most profitable. There is little error in assigning direct costs, direct materials and direct labor to computers and servers. So, Dell focused on refining the way it allocated *indirect costs.* The goal was to more accurately reflect the cost of the resources that each product uses. How? By drilling down from the indirect costs incurred in each of the six functions in the value chain to the indirect costs incurred in each individual *department* within each value-chain function and, finally, to the indirect costs of the specific *activities* in each department. Let's look at each step.

The first column of Exhibit 5-2 lists the six value-chain functions: R&D, design, production, marketing, distribution, and customer service. We'll focus on how Dell refined costs in the *production* element of the value chain because that is where most companies, like Dell, begin refining their costing systems.

| EXHIBIT 5-2 | Sharpening the Focus from Business Functions to Departments to Activities |

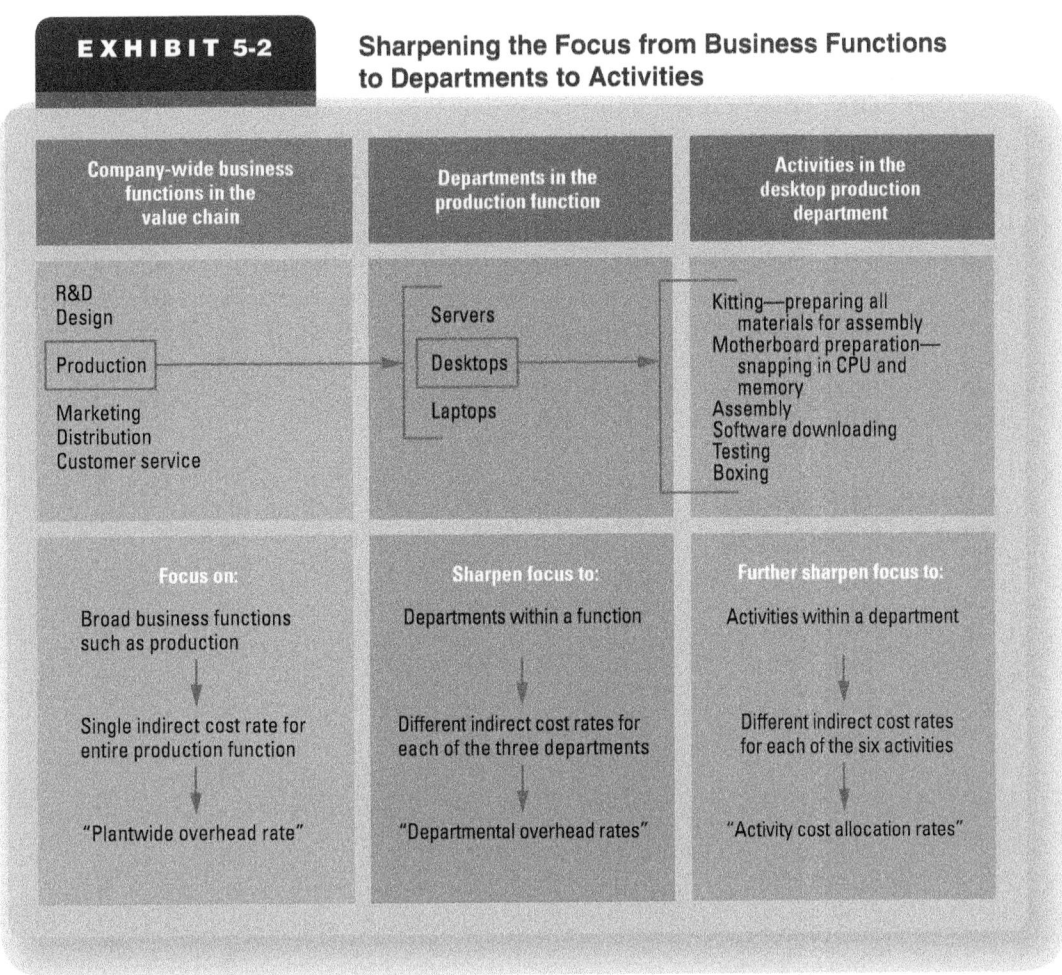

Company-wide business functions in the value chain	Departments in the production function	Activities in the desktop production department
R&D Design Production Marketing Distribution Customer service	Servers Desktops Laptops	Kitting—preparing all materials for assembly Motherboard preparation— snapping in CPU and memory Assembly Software downloading Testing Boxing
Focus on: Broad business functions such as production ↓ Single indirect cost rate for entire production function ↓ "Plantwide overhead rate"	**Sharpen focus to:** Departments within a function ↓ Different indirect cost rates for each of the three departments ↓ "Departmental overhead rates"	**Further sharpen focus to:** Activities within a department ↓ Different indirect cost rates for each of the six activities ↓ "Activity cost allocation rates"

BBH CHAPTER 5

Plantwide Overhead Rate

In the past, simple costing systems were often good enough. Many companies used a single plantwide manufacturing overhead rate, as we did in Chapter 3, to allocate indirect costs within the production function. For example, assume that Dell originally allocated manufacturing overhead costs based on direct labor (DL) hours. If Dell planned to incur $10 million of manufacturing overhead costs and 500,000 direct labor hours in a year, its manufacturing overhead rate was:

$$\$10 \text{ million} \div 500{,}000 \text{ DL hours} = \$20/\text{DL hour}$$

This is called a **plantwide overhead rate** because Dell allocated manufacturing overhead to every product produced in the plant (whether server, desktop, or laptop) using this *same* manufacturing overhead rate. This is also often referred to as a *traditional system* because most manufacturers have traditionally used a plantwide overhead rate for allocating manufacturing overhead costs to their products.

Departmental Overhead Rates

Companies today face incredible competition from all over the globe. As a result, they need more accurate cost information to help them set their prices more competitively and identify their most profitable products. Traditional plantwide overhead rates may no longer provide good enough cost information. If this is the case, managers drill down to focus on the indirect costs incurred by each *department* within the function. Exhibit 5-2 shows that Dell's production function includes separate departments (or production lines) for its three main products: servers, desktops, and laptops. One step in refining a costing system is to establish separate manufacturing overhead rates, known as **departmental overhead rates,** for each department—one rate for the Server Department, another for the Desktop Department, and a third for the Laptop Department, as shown in Exhibit 5-3.

EXHIBIT 5-3   **Example of Departmental Overhead Rates**

Department	Total Departmental Manufacturing Overhead Costs		Total Departmental Direct Labor Hours		Departmental Overhead Rate
Servers	$2 million	÷	50,000 hours	=	$40/DL hour
Desktops	$5 million	÷	250,000 hours	=	$20/DL hour
Laptops	$3 million	÷	200,000 hours	=	$15/DL hour
TOTAL	$10 million		500,000 hours		

Notice that the *total* manufacturing overhead costs ($10 million) and *total* DL hours (500,000 DL hours) are the same as before. However, the costs and DL hours are now identified with the production department in which they occur. As a result, each production department has its own unique overhead rate. We see that the plantwide overhead rate of $20/DL hour was right for desktops but *too high* for laptops and *too low* for servers. The plantwide overhead rate was causing cost distortion: Laptops were overcosted while servers were undercosted. Just as we saw with the roommate example, the plantwide overhead rate did not fairly distribute indirect costs among products. Departmental overhead rates do a better job matching manufacturing overhead to the products using that overhead.

Our Dell example assumes that all three departments used direct labor hours as the allocation base. However, many firms use different allocation bases for different departments. For example, direct labor hours may be the best allocation base for an "assembly" department, but machine hours may be a better allocation base for a "machining" department. Ideally, companies should identify each department's main cost driver and use that cost driver as the allocation base. Recall from Chapter 3 that a cost driver is the primary factor that causes a cost.

If a product passes through more than one department, the product is allocated overhead in *each* department using each department's unique departmental overhead rate. For example, let's say that a company's Assembly Department overhead rate is based on direct labor hours and its Machining Department overhead rate is based on machine hours. A job passing through *both* the Assembly and Machining Departments is allocated overhead based on the number of direct labor hours it uses in the Assembly Department *and* the number of machine hours it uses in the Machining Department.

Stop & Think...

Wilken Industries produces custom furniture in two production departments: Machining and Assembly. The departmental overhead rates are $150 per machine hour (MH) in the Machining Department and $40 per direct labor (DL) hour in the Assembly Department. Job 101 incurs 2 MH and 1 DL hour in the Machining Department and 10 DL hours in the Assembly Department.

a. How much manufacturing overhead should Wilken Industries allocate to Job 101?

b. If wages and benefits in both departments cost $20/DL hour and Job 101 uses $1,000 of direct material, what is the total cost of the job?

Answer:

a. The company should allocate manufacturing overhead to Job #101 as follows:

Machining department: $150/MH × 2 MH.................. =		$300
Assembly department: $40/DL hour × 10 DL hours...... =		+ $400
Total manufacturing overhead allocated to Job 101.... =		$700

Notice that Wilken Industries does *not* use the 1 DL hour incurred by Job 101 in the Machining Department for allocating overhead. Why? Because Machining Department overhead is allocated based *only* on machine hours used *in the Machining Department*, while Assembly Department overhead is allocated based *only* on DL hours incurred *in the Assembly Department*.

b. The total cost of Job 101 equals:

Direct labor (11 DL hours in *total* × $20/DL hour) ..... =		$ 220
Direct materials.. =		1,000
Manufacturing overhead .... =		700
Total job cost... =		$1,920

Activity Cost Allocation Rates

To obtain an even *more* accurate estimate of the resources that each product uses, managers drill down deeper yet to analyze the indirect costs of each *activity* in a department. Exhibit 5-2 shows the six activities in the Desktop Production Department. Rather than using a single departmental overhead rate for the entire Desktop Department, Dell develops separate cost allocation rates for each of these six activities, from kitting to boxing. This is called activity-based costing (ABC).

Think about the three roommates for a moment. The most equitable and accurate cost allocation system for the roommates was one in which the roommates were charged only for the *activities* in which they participated. As shown in Exhibit 5-1, David was not charged for groceries because he no longer ate at the apartment. Furthermore, the roommates were charged for the *extent* to which they used those activities. Marc was charged *twice* as much for groceries as Matt because Marc always had Jennifer over for dinner. Likewise, activity-based costing systems generally cause the *least* amount of cost distortion among products because indirect costs are allocated to the products based on the (1) *type* of activities used by the product and (2) the *extent* to which the activity is used. We'll spend the rest of this half of the chapter discussing activity-based costing in more detail.

BBH   CHAPTER 5

Activity-Based Costing

2 Develop activity-based costs (ABC) and use activity-based management (ABM) to make business decisions

Activity-based costing (ABC) focuses on *activities* as the fundamental cost objects. The costs of those activities become building blocks for compiling the indirect costs of products, services, and customers. Companies such as Allied Signal, Coca-Cola, and American Express use ABC to more accurately estimate the cost of resources required to produce different products, to render different services, and to serve different customers.

Companies that use ABC trace direct costs (such as direct materials and direct labor) to cost objects, as described in Chapter 3. The only difference is that ABC systems make more of an effort to allocate *indirect costs*—such as manufacturing overhead—to the products, services, or customers that caused those costs. How? By separately estimating the indirect costs of each activity and then allocating those indirect costs based on what caused them.

Each activity's indirect cost has its own (usually unique) cost driver. For example, Dell allocates indirect assembly costs (such as depreciation on the equipment used in the assembly process) based on the number of times workers touch a computer as it moves through assembly. Computers that require more touches are allocated more costs. Exhibit 5-4 illustrates other common activities and related cost drivers.

EXHIBIT 5-4   **Activities and Cost Drivers**

Activity costs	Purchasing department costs	Quality inspection costs	Warranty services costs	Shipping costs
Cost drivers	Number of purchase orders	Number of inspections	Number of service calls	Number of pounds

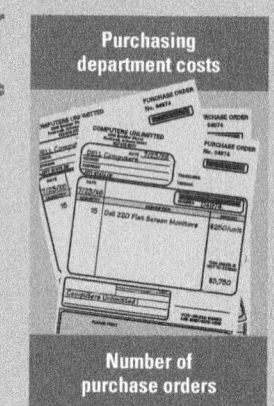

Data warehouses and other information technology have made detailed ABC systems easier to use. Optical scanning and bar coding reduce the cost of collecting cost-driver information. ERP systems such as SAP, Oracle, and PeopleSoft have ABC modules. Managers can also buy specialized ABC software. But Dell began its ABC system simply using Excel spreadsheets!

Developing an ABC System

The main difference between ABC and traditional systems is that ABC systems have separate indirect cost allocation rates for *each activity*. ABC requires seven steps:

1. Identify the activities.

2. Estimate the total indirect costs associated with each activity.

3. Identify the allocation base for each activity's indirect costs—this is the primary cost driver.

4. Estimate the total quantity of each allocation base.

5. Compute the cost allocation rate for each activity:

$$\text{Activity cost allocation rate} = \frac{\text{Estimated total indirect costs of activity}}{\text{Estimated total quantity of cost allocation base}}$$

6. Obtain the actual quantity of each allocation base used by the cost object (for example, the quantity used by a particular job).

7. Allocate the costs to the cost object:

$$\text{Allocated activity cost} = \text{Activity cost allocation rate} \times \frac{\text{Actual quantity of cost allocation}}{\text{base used by the cost object}}$$

The first step in developing an ABC system is to identify the activities. Analyzing all of the activities required to make a product forces managers to think about how each activity might be improved—or whether the activity is necessary at all. Steps 2 through 7 are the same approach used to allocate manufacturing overhead, as explained in Chapter 3. The only difference is that ABC systems repeat Steps 2 through 7 for *each activity.*

Using ABC for Job Costing

Let's see how Dell would develop an ABC system and use it for job costing. Recall that six key activities occur in Dell's Desktop Production Department (Exhibit 5-2) and the department incurs $5 million of manufacturing overhead (Exhibit 5-3). After identifying the activities, Dell estimates how much of the total $5 million of indirect manufacturing cost is associated with *each* activity. Dell also identifies a cost allocation base, or cost driver, for each activity. Next, Dell computes a unique activity cost allocation rate for each of the activities using the formula shown in Step 5 above. Let's say this process results in the activity cost allocation rates shown in Exhibit 5-5.

EXHIBIT 5-5   **Activity Cost Allocation Rates for Dell's Desktop Production Department**

Activity	Cost Allocation Base	Activity Cost Allocation Rate
Kitting	Number of parts	$0.50 per part
Motherboard preparation	Number of preparations	$1.15 per preparation
Assembly	Number of touches	$0.20 per touch
Software downloading	Number of minutes spent downloading software	$0.25 per minute
Testing	Number of tests performed	$2.50 per test
Boxing	Cubic feet boxed	$0.60 per cubic foot

Just as with a traditional system, these rates are predetermined for the whole year using budgeted information. Once Dell has computed these activity cost allocation rates, it simply allocates manufacturing overhead to each job worked on during the year by multiplying these rates by each job's actual usage of the cost allocation bases (Step 7 above). If a job doesn't use a particular activity, the job isn't charged any indirect cost related to that activity.

Let's use Dell's Job 2690 (an order for one desktop computer) as an example. The amount of manufacturing overhead allocated to Job 2690 is calculated as follows:

Activity	Activity Cost Allocation Rate (from Exhibit 5-5)		Job 2690: Actual Usage of Cost Allocation Base*		Allocated Activity Cost
Kitting	$0.50 per part	×	12 parts	=	$ 6.00
Motherboard preparation	$1.15 per preparation	×	1 preparation	=	1.15
Assembly	$0.20 per touch	×	10 touches	=	2.00
Software downloading	$0.25 per minute	×	12 minutes	=	3.00
Testing	$2.50 per test	×	1 test	=	2.50
Boxing	$0.60 per cubic foot	×	4 cubic feet	=	2.40
Total manufacturing overhead allocated to job					$17.05

*Information would be reported on Job 2690's job cost record.

To find the total inventoriable product cost of Job 2690, Dell adds $17.05 of manufacturing overhead (calculated above) to the direct materials and direct labor traced to the job, just as we did in Chapter 3.[1]

As you can see, the procedure for costing a job using ABC is almost identical to the procedure we used in Chapter 3. The main difference is that the manufacturing overhead allocated to a job involves several activity cost allocation rates rather than one plantwide rate. In addition to using ABC to allocate manufacturing overhead costs in the production function, Dell can extend its use of ABC to the other five functions of the value chain. By doing so, Dell can determine the full cost of each of its products. This helps Dell's managers set prices and determine its most profitable products and customers.

Using ABC to Assess Product Profitability: Chemtech

We just looked at how Dell uses ABC to allocate manufacturing overhead to individual jobs it produces throughout the year. Now, let's see how another company, Chemtech, used ABC to reassess the profitability of its entire product lines. By implementing ABC, Chemtech discovered that its traditional plantwide overhead rate had been causing significant cost distortion between its products.

Keep in mind that our example simplifies the process that would occur in a real company that might identify more than 50 different activities and have hundreds of products.

Chemtech is a chemical development and manufacturing firm. Most of the chemicals the company develops are licensed and sold to other manufacturers. However, Chemtech's Chemical Manufacturing Department continues to produce two types of chemicals: a common chemical (Aldehyde) used for producing plastics and a specialty chemical (Phenylephrine Hydrochloride) used in a blood-pressure medication. Chemtech produces mass quantities of the common chemical for large customers. It produces small batches of the specialty chemical for only one customer (a pharmaceutical company).

Last updated several years ago, the Chemical Manufacturing Department's cost system uses a single plantwide overhead rate that allocates manufacturing overhead ($5 million for the year) at 200% of direct labor cost. Based on this traditional costing system, Chemtech analyzes its products' profitability as shown in Exhibit 5-6.

Explain when ABC is most likely to pass the cost-benefit test

EXHIBIT 5-6	Chemtech's Traditional Costing System: Product Cost and Gross Profit

	Common Chemical	Specialty Chemical
Sales price per pound	$10.00	$70.00
Less: Manufacturing cost per pound:		
Direct materials	5.00	20.00
Direct labor	1.00	10.00
Manufacturing overhead (at 200% of direct labor cost)	2.00	20.00
Total manufacturing cost per pound	8.00	50.00
Gross profit per pound	$2.00	$20.00
Number of pounds produced and sold	2,000,000	50,000

The gross profit per pound for the specialty chemical ($20) is ten times as high as the gross profit for the common chemical ($2), which surprised Chemtech's CEO. He had expected that the department would be more efficient at producing large batches of the common chemical than producing small batches of the specialty chemical. However, the production supervisor says that it takes no more time to mix a large batch of the common chemical than it does to mix a small batch of the specialty chemical. The CEO is also puzzled because Chemtech's competitors seem to be earning good profits even though they sometimes undercut Chemtech's prices on the common chemical.

Because of the profitability of the specialty chemical, the CEO wonders whether Chemtech should switch its focus to specialty chemicals. Before making such a major shift in operations, the CEO wants to make sure the financial information is correct. Because the cost of direct labor and direct materials is accurate (the company has traced these costs to the products), the only questionable part of the manufacturing cost is the allocation of manufacturing overhead.

Exhibit 5-7 shows how Chemtech's *total* manufacturing overhead ($5 million) is currently allocated between the two products. Since Chemtech allocates overhead at 200% of direct labor cost, it first finds the *total* direct labor cost traced to each product (number of pounds produced × direct labor cost per pound). Then, Chemtech multiplies the total direct labor cost by the 200% plantwide overhead rate.

EXHIBIT 5-7	Current Allocation of Total Manufacturing Overhead

	Common Chemical	Specialty Chemical
Number of pounds (from Exhibit 5-6)	2,000,000	50,000
× Direct labor cost per pound (from Exhibit 5-6)	× $1.00	× $10.00
Total Direct labor cost	$2,000,000	$500,000
× Manufacturing overhead rate	× 200% of DL cost	× 200% of DL cost
Total Manufacturing overhead allocated	$4,000,000	$1,000,000
		$5,000,000

Because Chemtech allocates overhead based on direct labor cost, it currently assigns four times as much overhead to the common chemical ($4 million) as it does to the specialty chemical ($1 million). This method of allocation makes sense only if direct labor really is the primary cost driver of manufacturing overhead costs. Does the common chemical really use four times as much overhead as the specialty chemical? If not, Chemtech should allocate the $5 million of manufacturing overhead differently.

The CEO wants to better understand manufacturing overhead—what drives it and how it should be allocated. The CEO asks managers to create a cross-functional team (including members from accounting, engineering, and production) to develop a pilot ABC system. A cross-functional team will ensure that the new ABC system incorporates a wide variety of perspectives. In addition, these managers are more likely to believe costs from a costing system they helped build.

Exhibit 5-8 presents a bird's-eye overview that compares Chemtech's traditional manufacturing overhead allocation system based on direct labor (Panel A) to the new ABC system the team developed (Panel B).

EXHIBIT 5-8   **Chemtech's Traditional and ABC Systems**

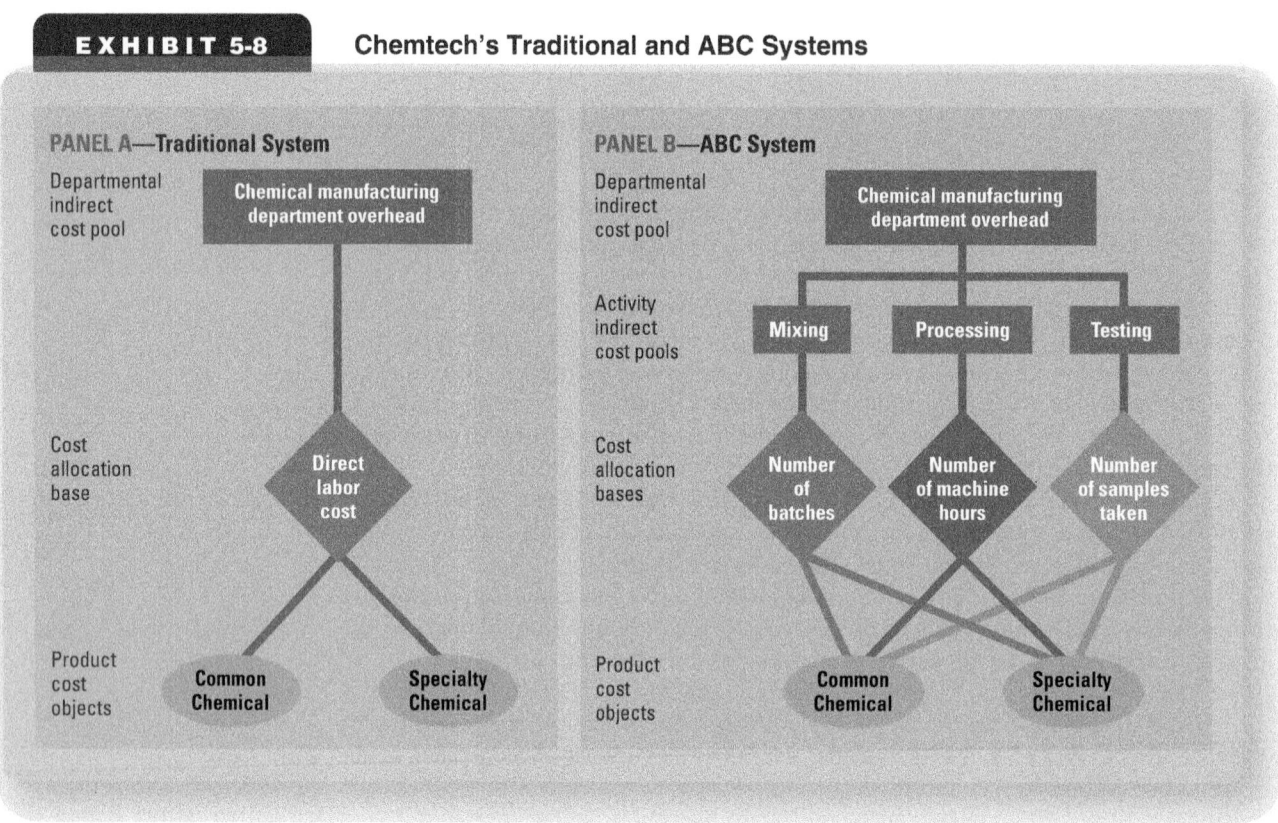

Panel B of Exhibit 5-8 shows that Chemtech's ABC team identifies three manufacturing activities: mixing, processing, and testing. Each activity has its own indirect cost pool and cost driver. But exactly how does this work? The ABC team develops the new system by following the seven steps described earlier. Let's walk through each step.

Step 1: Identify activities

The team identifies three primary activities in the Chemical Manufacturing Department:

- **mixing**
- **processing**
- **testing**

Step 2: Estimate total indirect costs of each activity

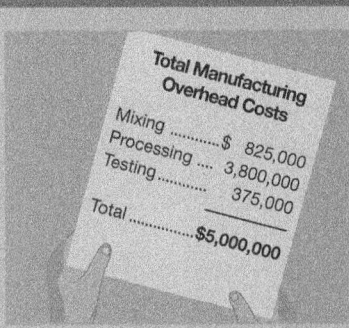

The team identifies (or estimates) the total manufacturing overhead costs associated with each activity for the year:

Mixing	$ 825,000
Processing	3,800,000
Testing	375,000
Total manufacturing overhead	$5,000,000

Notice how the total manufacturing overhead is the same as before ($5 million), but now it is divided between the activities according to how much overhead each activity incurs.

Step 3: Identify allocation base for each activity

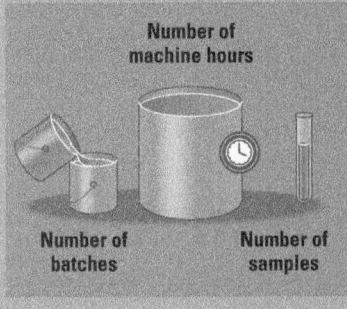

The team determines the most appropriate allocation base for each activity. The allocation base should be the activity's cost driver.

Mixing: Workers mix ingredients separately for each batch of chemicals, so the number of batches drives mixing costs.

Processing: Machine depreciation, repairs and maintenance, and utilities make up most of the processing costs; so machine hours (MH) is selected as the cost driver.

Testing: Testing costs are driven by the number of samples collected and tested for quality.

Step 4: Estimate total quantity of each allocation base

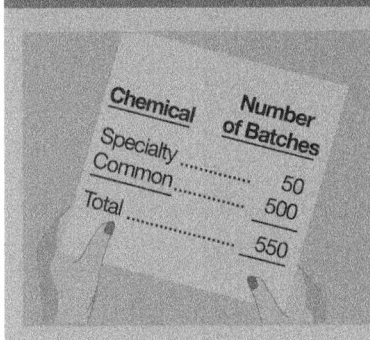

The team estimates the total quantity of each cost allocation base Chemtech will use during the year. For example, the team estimates the total number of batches of each chemical it plans to produce and adds them together. The team estimates the total quantities (for both chemicals combined) to be:

Mixing: 550 batches   **Processing:** 15,200 MH   **Testing:** 750 samples

Step 5: Compute cost allocation rates for each activity

$$\frac{\$825,000}{550 \text{ batches}}$$

$$= \$1,500/\text{batch}$$

The team calculates a cost allocation rate for *each* activity as follows:

$$\text{Activity cost allocation rate} = \frac{\text{Estimated total indirect costs of activity}}{\text{Estimated total quantity of cost allocation base}}$$

Mixing: $\dfrac{\$825,000}{550 \text{ batches}} = \$1,500$ per batch

Processing: $\dfrac{\$3,800,000}{15,200 \text{ MH}} = \$250$ per MH

Testing: $\dfrac{\$375,000}{750 \text{ samples}} = \$500$ per sample

Step 6: Obtain actual quantity of each allocation base used by each product

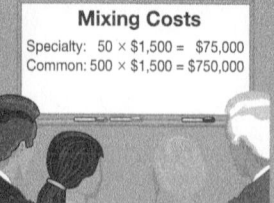

Number of Batches Produced
Common 500
Specialty 50

During the year, Chemtech collects data on the *actual* number of batches, machine hours, and samples that each product uses:

	Common	Specialty
Mixing: (number of batches)	500	50
Processing: (number of machine hours)	8,000	7,200
Testing: (number of samples)	500	250

Mixing: Chemtech makes about two large batches of the common chemical each work day, but only one small batch of the specialty chemical each week.

Processing: Due to the nature of the chemical, each batch of the specialty chemical requires a far longer processing time than each batch of the common chemical. Over the course of the year, the *total* processing time is only slightly higher for the common chemical than for the specialty chemical.

Testing: One sample per batch of the common chemical is sufficient. However, since the specialty chemical must process for several days, Chemtech must take several samples throughout the processing period.

Step 7: Allocate costs to each cost object

Mixing Costs
Specialty: 50 × $1,500 = $75,000
Common: 500 × $1,500 = $750,000

Chemtech allocates costs to each product as follows:
   For each activity, the team allocates manufacturing overhead to the products as follows:

Actual quantity of allocation base used × Activity cost allocation rate = Allocated cost

	Common Chemical			Specialty Chemical	
Mixing:	500 batches × $1,500 per batch	= $ 750,000		50 batches × $1,500 per batch	= $ 75,000
Processing:	8,000 MH × $ 250 per MH	= 2,000,000		7,200 MH × $ 250 per MH	= 1,800,000
Testing:	500 samples × $ 500 per sample =	250,000		250 samples × $ 500 per sample =	125,000
Total manufacturing overhead allocated:		$3,000,000			$2,000,000

BBH CHAPTER 5

Exhibit 5-9 summarizes the seven steps. Study Exhibit 5-9 carefully, following each of the seven steps to make sure you understand how the activity costs are allocated.

| **EXHIBIT 5-9** | | | **Summary of Chemtech's ABC System** | | | | | | |

Step 1	Step 2	Step 3	Step 4	Step 5	Step 6		Step 7	
					Actual Quantity of Cost Allocation Base Used By		Allocated Activity Cost	
		Cost	Estimated Total Quantity					
	Estimated	Allocation	of Cost	Compute Activity	Common	Specialty	Common	Specialty
Activity	Costs	Base	Allocation Base	Cost Allocation Rate	Chemical	Chemical	Chemical	Chemical
Mixing	$825,000	# batches	550 Batches	$\frac{\$825,000}{550} = \$1,500/\text{batch}$	500 batches	50 batches	$1,500 × 500 = $750,000	$1,500 × 50 = $75,000
Processing	$3,800,000	# machine hours (MH)	15,200 MH	$\frac{\$3,800,000}{15,200} = \$250/\text{MH}$	8,000 MH	7,200 MH	$250 × 8,000 = $2,000,000	$250 × 7,200 = $1,800,000
Testing	$375,000	# samples	750 Samples	$\frac{\$375,000}{750} = \$500/\text{sample}$	500 samples	250 samples	$500 × 500 = $250,000	$500 × 250 = $125,000
	$5,000,000						$3,000,000	$2,000,000

Notice in Step 7 how the *total* manufacturing overhead is the *same* as before ($3 million + $2 million = $5 million). However, the amount of manufacturing overhead allocated to *each* product is *different* from before:

- The ABC system allocates $3 million of manufacturing overhead to the common chemical rather than $4 million (as calculated under the traditional system in Exhibit 5-7). The traditional system had *overcosted* the common chemical by $1 million.

- The ABC system allocates $2 million of manufacturing overhead to the specialty chemical rather than $1 million (as calculated under the traditional system in Exhibit 5-7). The traditional system had *undercosted* the specialty chemical by $1 million.

The ABC system shows that the traditional costing system had resulted in a $1 million cost distortion between Chemtech's two product lines. Just as with the roommates sharing the apartment, the overcosting and the undercosting even out. The *overcosting* of the common chemical exactly equals the *undercosting* of the specialty chemical.

How do we know that the ABC costs are more accurate than the costs assigned by the traditional system? *ABC costs are more accurate because ABC takes into account the resources (mixing costs, processing costs, and testing costs) each product actually uses, and the extent to which they use these resources.* Recall that Chemtech's traditional plantwide overhead rate (based on direct labor) allocated *four times as much* overhead to the common chemical as to the specialty chemical. With more precise allocations, ABC shifts manufacturing overhead costs away from the common chemical to the specialty chemical, where the costs belong. Why? Exhibit 5-9 shows that the common chemical uses more of each activity's resources than the specialty chemical, but *not always four* times as much. Step 6 shows that the common chemical requires ten times as many batches (mixing costs), but only about 11% more machine hours (processing costs) and only twice as many samples (testing costs) as the specialty chemical. ABC captures the differences in resource consumption by each product more accurately than the traditional costing system.

Now that we know that Chemtech should allocate $3 million of overhead to the common chemical and $2 million of overhead to the specialty chemical, let's see how this affects the overhead cost per pound. To determine the manufacturing overhead cost per pound, Chemtech simply divides the total manufacturing overhead allocated to each product by the number of pounds produced (from Exhibit 5-6). Exhibit 5-10 compares the overhead cost per pound under the traditional system and the ABC system.

EXHIBIT 5-10   Comparison of the Manufacturing Overhead Cost per Pound Under the Traditional and ABC Systems

	Manufacturing Overhead Cost per Pound (Total manufacturing overhead allocated to product ÷ number of pounds produced)		
	Traditional System	ABC System	Overallocation or (Underallocation)
Common Chemical	$2.00 ($4,000,000 ÷ 2 million pounds)	$1.50 ($3,000,000 ÷ 2 million pounds)	$0.50 overallocation per pound
Specialty Chemical	$20.00 ($1,000,000 ÷ 50,000 pounds)	$40.00 ($2,000,000 ÷ 50,000 pounds)	($20.00) (underallocation per pound)

Exhibit 5-10 shows that the traditional system had *undercosted* the specialty chemical by $20 per pound. Allocating overhead based on the actual resources used by individual products generally *increases* the unit costs of *low-volume* products such as the specialty chemical that are produced in small batches. Why? Because costs such as mixing and testing are spread over the small number of units (pounds) in that batch, which can dramatically increase unit product costs.

The traditional system had *overcosted* the common chemical by $0.50 per pound. For *high-volume* products produced in large batches, such as the common chemical, mixing and testing costs are spread over the larger number of units (pounds) in the batch. So, ABC often assigns *fewer* costs to each unit of high-volume products than do plantwide overhead rates.

After implementing ABC, companies often realize they were overcosting high-volume products (such as the common chemical) and undercosting low-volume products (such as the specialty chemical), as shown in Exhibit 5-11.

EXHIBIT 5-11   Typical Result of ABC Costing

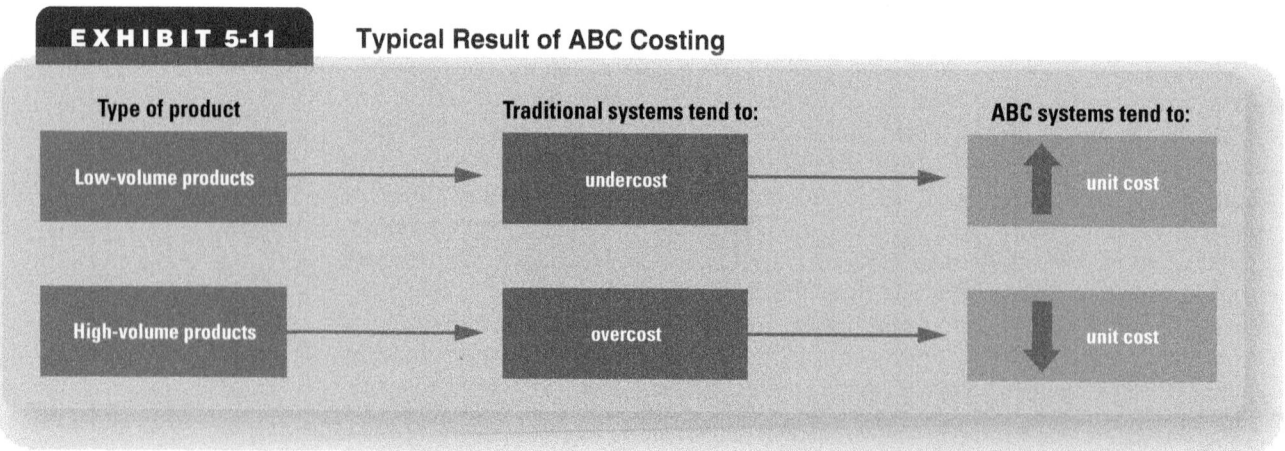

Now that we've seen how ABC revealed cost distortion, let's see how Chemtech's managers *use* this new cost information to reassess the profitability of its two products.

Pages 247–269 intentionally omitted

Review *Activity-Based Costing and Other Cost Management Tools*

Accounting Vocabulary

Activity-Based Costing (ABC) (p. 237)
Focuses on *activities* as the fundamental cost objects. The costs of those activities become building blocks for compiling the indirect costs of products, services, and customers.

Activity-Based Management (ABM) (p. 247)
Using activity-based cost information to make decisions that increase profits while satisfying customers' needs.

Appraisal Costs (p. 259)
Costs incurred to *detect* poor-quality goods or services.

Cost Distortion (p. 234)
Overcosting some products while undercosting other products.

Cost of Quality Report (p 258)
A report that lists the costs incurred by the company related to quality. The costs are categorized as prevention costs, appraised costs, internal failure costs, and external failure costs.

Departmental Overhead Rates (p. 236)
Separate manufacturing overhead rates established for each department.

External Failure Costs (p. 259)
Costs incurred when the company does not detect poor-quality goods or services until *after* delivery is made to customers.

Internal Failure Costs (p. 259)
Costs incurred when the company detects and corrects poor-quality goods or services *before* making delivery to customers.

Just-in-Time (JIT) Costing (p. 266)
A standard costing system that starts with output completed and then assigns manufacturing costs to units sold and to inventories. Also called backflush costing.

Plantwide Overhead Rate (p. 235)
When overhead is allocated to every product using the same manufacturing overhead rate.

Prevention Costs (p. 258)
Costs incurred to *avoid* poor-quality goods or services.

Value Engineering (p. 248)
Reevaluating activities to reduce costs while satisfying customer needs.

Quick Check

1. Which of the following is *false*?
   a. The distinguishing feature of ABC is that it focuses on allocating indirect costs.
   b. Advances in information technology have made it feasible for more companies to adopt ABC.
   c. ABC is only for manufacturing firms.
   d. A system that uses ABC is more refined than one that uses departmental overhead rates.

   The following data apply to Questions 2 through 4. Two of Dell's primary production activities are *kitting* (assembling raw materials needed for a particular computer or server in one kit) and *boxing* the completed products for shipment to customers. Assume that Dell spends $5 million a month on the kitting activity and $10 million a month on boxing. It allocates kitting activity costs based on the number of parts used in the product and boxing activity costs based on the cubic feet of space the product requires. Suppose Dell estimates it will use 800 million parts a month and ship products with a total volume of 20 million cubic feet.

Assume that each desktop computer requires 100 parts and has a volume of 5 cubic feet. Assume that each server requires 150 parts and has a volume of 7 cubic feet.

2. What is the activity cost allocation rate for kitting and boxing?
   a. $0.00625/part, $0.50/cubic foot
   b. $0.0125/part, $0.25/cubic foot
   c. $0.50/part, $40/cubic foot
   d. $160/part, $2/cubic foot

3. What are the kitting and boxing costs assigned to one desktop computer?
   a. $0.625, $2.50
   b. $0.9375, $3.50
   c. $1.25, $1.25
   d. $50.00, $200.00

4. Dell contracts with its suppliers to pre-kit certain component parts before delivering them to Dell. Assume that this saves $1.5 million of the kitting activity cost and that it reduces the total number of parts by 400 million (because Dell considers each pre-kit as one part). If a server now uses 80 parts, what is the new kitting cost assigned to one server?
   a. $0.35
   b. $0.70
   c. $0.9375
   d. $1.00

5. Dell can use ABC information for what decisions?
   a. pricing
   b. cost cutting
   c. evaluating managers' performance
   d. all of the above

6. Which of the following is *not* a good reason for Dell to use ABC?
   a. The computer industry is highly competitive.
   b. Dell produces many more desktops than servers, and servers are more difficult to assemble.
   c. Most costs are direct; indirect costs are a small proportion of total costs.
   d. Dell has advanced information technology, including bar-coded materials and labor.

7. Dell enjoys many benefits from committing to JIT. Which is *not* a benefit of adopting JIT?

 a. lower inventory carrying costs

 b. more space available for production

 c. ability to respond more quickly to changes in customer demand

 d. ability to continue production despite disruptions in deliveries of raw materials

8. (Appendix:) The following account is not used in JIT costing:

 a. Raw and In Process Inventory

 b. Conversion Costs

 c. Work In Process Inventory

 d. Finished Goods Inventory

9. The cost of lost future sales after a customer finds flaws in a product or service is which of the following quality costs?

 a. external failure cost

 b. internal failure cost

 c. appraisal cost

 d. prevention cost

10. Dell's spending on testing its computers before shipping them to customers helps *reduce* which of the following costs?

 a. prevention cost

 b. appraisal cost

 c. external failure cost

 d. none of the above

Quick Check Answers

1. c   2. a   3. a   4. b   5. d   6. c   7. d   8. c   9. a   10. c

For Internet Exercises, Excel in Practice, and additional online activities, go to this book's Web site at www.prenhall.com/bamber.

Assess Your Progress

■ Learning Objectives

1 Develop and use departmental overhead rates in place of a traditional plantwide rate

2 Develop activity-based costs (ABC) and use activity-based management (ABM) to make business decisions

3 Explain when ABC is most likely to pass the cost-benefit test

4 Describe a just-in-time (JIT) production system

5 Describe the four costs of quality and use them to make decisions

6 (Appendix) Use JIT costing to record costs in a JIT production environment

■ Short Exercises

S5-2 Compute departmental overhead rates *(Learning Objective 1)*

Uncle Bruce's Snacks makes potato chips, corn chips, and cheese puffs using three different production lines within the same manufacturing plant. Currently, Uncle Bruce uses a single plantwide overhead rate to allocate its $3,500,000 of annual manufacturing overhead. Of this amount, $1,800,000 is associated with the potato chip line, $1,000,000 is associated with the corn chip line, and $700,000 is associated with the cheese puff line. Uncle Bruce's plant is currently running a total of 17,500 machine

continued . . .

hours: 11,250 in the potato chip line, 3,450 in the corn chip line, and 2,800 in the cheese puff line. Uncle Bruce considers machine hours to be the cost driver of manufacturing overhead costs.

1. What is Uncle Bruce's plantwide overhead rate?

2. Calculate the departmental overhead rates for Uncle Bruce's three production lines. Round all answers to the nearest cent.

3. Which products had been overcosted by the plantwide rate? Which products had been undercosted by the plantwide rate?

S5-3   **Compute activity cost allocation rates** *(Learning Objective 2)*
Uncle Bruce produces different styles of potato chips (ruffled, flat, thick-cut, gourmet) for different corporate customers. Each style of potato chip requires different preparation time, different cooking and draining times (depending on desired fat content), and different packaging (single serving versus bulk). Therefore, Uncle Bruce has decided to try ABC costing to better capture the manufacturing overhead costs incurred by each style of chip. Uncle Bruce has identified the following activities related to yearly manufacturing overhead costs and cost drivers associated with producing potato chips:

Activity	Manufacturing Overhead	Cost Driver
Preparation	$600,000	Preparation time
Cooking and draining	$900,000	Cooking and draining time
Packaging	$300,000	Units packaged

Compute the activity cost allocation rates for each activity assuming the following total estimated activity for the year: 12,000 preparation hours, 30,000 cooking and draining hours, and 6 million packages.

S5-4   **Continuation of S5-3: Use ABC to allocate overhead** *(Learning Objective 2)*
Uncle Bruce just received an order to produce 12,000 single-serving bags of gourmet, fancy-cut, low-fat potato chips. The order will require 16 preparation hours and 32 cooking and draining hours. Use the activity rates you calculated in S5-3 to compute the following:

1. What is the total amount of manufacturing overhead that should be allocated to this order?

2. How much manufacturing overhead should be assigned to each bag?

3. What other costs will Uncle Bruce need to consider to determine the total manufacturing costs of this order?

Pages 275–282 intentionally omitted

E5-24 **Using ABC to bill clients at a service firm** *(Learning Objective 2)*

Curtis & Company is an architectural firm specializing in home remodeling for private clients and new office buildings for corporate clients.

Curtis & Company charges customers at a billing rate equal to 135% of the client's total job cost. A client's total job cost is a combination of (1) professional time spent on the client ($65 per hour cost of employing each professional) and (2) operating overhead allocated to the client's job. Curtis allocates operating overhead to jobs based on professional hours spent on the job. Curtis estimates its five professionals will incur a total of 10,000 professional hours working on client jobs during the year.

All operating costs other than professional salaries (travel reimbursements, copy costs, secretarial salaries, office lease, and so forth) can be assigned to the three activities. Total activity costs, cost drivers, and total usage of those cost drivers are estimated as follows:

Activity	Total Activity Cost	Cost Driver	Total Usage by Corporate Clients	Total Usage by Private Clients
Transportation to clients	$ 9,000	Round-trip mileage to clients	3,000 miles	12,000 miles
Blueprint copying	35,000	Number of copies	300 copies	700 copies
Office support	190,000	Secretarial time	2,200 secretarial hours	2,800 secretarial hours
Total operating overhead	$234,000			

Amy Lee hired Curtis & Company to design her kitchen remodeling. A total of 24 professional hours were incurred on this job. In addition, Amy's remodeling job required one of the professionals to travel back and forth to her house for a total of 125 miles. The blueprints had to be copied four times because Amy changed the

continued . . .

plans several times. In addition, 18 hours of secretarial time were used lining up the subcontractors for the job.

1. Calculate the current operating overhead allocation rate per professional hour.
2. Calculate the amount that would be billed to Amy Lee given the current costing structure.
3. Calculate the activity cost allocation rates that could be used to allocate operating overhead costs to client jobs.
4. Calculate the amount that would be billed to Amy Lee using ABC costing.
5. Which type of billing system is fairer to clients? Explain.

E5-26 **Use ABC to allocate manufacturing overhead** *(Learning Objective 2)*

Several years after reengineering its production process, Enke Corp. hired a new controller, Natalie Babin. She developed an ABC system very similar to the one used by Enke's chief rival, Northstar. Part of the reason Babin developed the ABC system was because Enke's profits had been declining even though the company had shifted its product mix toward the product that had appeared most profitable under the old system. Before adopting the new ABC system, Enke had used a plantwide overhead rate based on direct labor hours that was developed years ago.

For 2007, Enke's budgeted ABC manufacturing overhead allocation rates are:

Activity	Allocation Base	Activity Cost Allocation Rate
Materials handling	Number of parts	$ 3.75 per part
Machine setup	Number of setups	300.00 per setup
Insertion of parts	Number of parts	24.00 per part
Finishing	Finishing direct labor hours	50.00 per hour

The number of parts is now a feasible allocation base because Enke recently purchased bar-coding technology. Enke produces two wheel models: standard and deluxe. Budgeted data for 2007 are as follows:

	Standard	Deluxe
Parts per wheel	4.0	6.0
Setups per 1,000 wheels	15.0	15.0
Finishing direct labor hours per wheel	1.0	2.5
Total direct labor hours per wheel	2.0	3.0

The company's managers expect to produce 1,000 units of each model during the year.

Requirements

1. Compute the total budgeted manufacturing overhead cost for 2007.
2. Compute the manufacturing overhead cost per wheel of each model using ABC.
3. Compute Enke's traditional plantwide overhead rate. Use this rate to determine the manufacturing overhead cost per wheel under the traditional system.

E5-27 **Continuation of E5-26: Determine product profitability** *(Learning Objective 2)*
Refer to your answers in E5-26. In addition to the manufacturing overhead costs, the
following data are budgeted for the company's standard and deluxe models for 2008:

	Standard	Deluxe
Sales price per wheel	$300.00	$440.00
Direct materials per wheel....................................	30.00	46.00
Direct labor per wheel...	45.00	50.00

Requirements

1. Compute the gross profit per wheel if managers rely on the ABC unit cost data
   computed in E5-26.

2. Compute the gross profit per wheel if the managers rely on the plantwide
   allocation cost data.

3. Which product line is more profitable for Enke?

Pages 287–290 intentionally omitted

P5-38A **Comprehensive ABC implementation** *(Learning Objectives 2, 3)*

Xnet develops software for Internet applications. The market is very competitive, and Xnet's competitors continue to introduce new products at low prices. Xnet offers a wide variety of software—from simple programs that enable new users to create personal Web pages to complex commercial search engines. Like most software companies, Xnet's raw material costs are insignificant.

Xnet has just hired Tom Merrell, a recent graduate of State University's accounting program. Merrell asks Software Department Manager Jeff Gire to join him in a pilot activity-based costing study. Merrell and Gire identify the following activities, related costs, and cost-allocation bases:

Activity	Estimated Indirect Activity Costs	Allocation Base	Estimated Quantity of Allocation Base
Applications development	$1,600,000	New applications	4 new applications
Content production.................	2,400,000	Lines of code	12 million lines
Testing	288,000	Testing hours	1,800 testing hours
Total indirect costs.................	$4,288,000		

Xnet is planning to develop the following new applications:

- X-Page—software for developing personal Web pages
- X-Secure—commercial security and firewall software

continued . . .

X-Page requires 500,000 lines of code and 100 hours of testing, while X-Secure requires 7.5 million lines of code and 600 hours of testing. Xnet expects to produce and sell 30,000 units of X-Page and 10 units of X-Secure.

Requirements

1. Compute the cost allocation rate for each activity.

2. Use the activity-based cost allocation rates to compute the indirect cost of each unit of X-Page and X-Secure. (*Hint:* Compute the total activity costs allocated to each product line and then compute the cost per unit.)

3. Xnet's original single-allocation-based cost system allocated indirect costs to products at $100 per programmer hour. X-Page requires 10,000 programmer hours, while X-Secure requires 15,000 programmer hours. Compute the total indirect costs allocated to X-Page and X-Secure under the original system. Then, compute the indirect cost per unit for each product.

4. Compare the activity-based costs per unit to the costs from the simpler original system. How have the unit costs changed? Explain why the costs changed as they did.

5. What are the clues that Xnet's ABC system is likely to pass the cost-benefit test?

Pages 293–297 intentionally omitted

Apply Your Knowledge

▪ Decision Cases

Case 5-46. Comprehensive ABC *(Learning Objectives 2, 3)*

Axis Systems specializes in servers for work-group, e-commerce, and ERP applications. The company's original job cost system has two direct cost categories: direct materials and direct labor. Overhead is allocated to jobs at the single rate of $22 per direct labor hour.

A task force headed by Axis's CFO recently designed an ABC system with four activities. The ABC system retains the current system's two direct cost categories. Thus, it budgets only overhead costs for each activity. Pertinent data follow.

Activity	Allocation Base	Cost Allocation Rate
Materials handling	Number of parts	$ 0.85
Machine setup	Number of setups	500.00
Assembling	Assembling hours	80.00
Shipping	Number of shipments	1,500.00

Axis Systems has been awarded two new contracts, which will be produced as Job A and Job B. Budget data relating to the contracts follow.

	Job A	Job B
Number of parts....................................	15,000	2,000
Number of setups...................................	6	4
Number of assembling hours..................	1,500	200
Number of shipments............................	1	1
Total direct labor hours	8,000	600
Number of output units	100	10
Direct materials cost.............................	$210,000	$30,000
Direct labor cost...................................	$160,000	$12,000

Requirements

1. Compute the product cost per unit for each job using the original costing system (with two direct cost categories and a single overhead allocation rate).

2. Suppose Axis Systems adopts the ABC system. Compute the product cost per unit for each job using ABC.

3. Which costing system more accurately assigns to jobs the costs of the resources consumed to produce them? Explain.

4. A dependable company has offered to produce both jobs for Axis for $5,400 per output unit. Axis may outsource (buy from the outside company) Job A only, Job B only, or both jobs. Which course of action will Axis's managers take if they base their decision on (a) the original system? (b) ABC system costs? Which course of action will yield more income? Explain.

Case 5-47. Continues Case 5-46: meeting target costs

To remain competitive, Axis Systems' management believes the company must produce Job B–type servers (from Decision Case 5-46) at a target cost of $5,400. Axis Systems has just joined a B2B e-market site that management believes will enable the firm to cut direct material costs by 10%. Axis's management also believes that a value-engineering team can reduce assembly time.

Requirement

Compute the assembly cost savings per Job B–type server required to meet the $5,400 target cost. (*Hint:* Begin by calculating the direct material, direct labor, and allocated activity cost per server.)

▪ Ethical Issue

Issue 5-48. ABC and ethical dilemma *(Learning Objective 2, 3)*

Mary Lipe is assistant controller at Stone Packaging, a manufacturer of cardboard boxes and other packaging materials. Lipe has just returned from a packaging industry conference on ABC. She realizes that ABC may help Stone meet its goal of reducing costs by 5% over each of the next three years.

Stone Packaging's Order Department is a likely candidate for ABC. While orders are entered into a computer that updates the accounting records, clerks manually check customers' credit history and hand-deliver orders to shipping. This process occurs whether the sales order is for a dozen specialty boxes worth $80 or 10,000 basic boxes worth $8,000.

Lipe believes that identifying the cost of processing a sales order would justify (1) further computerizing the order process and (2) changing the way the company processes small orders. However, the significant cost savings would arise from elimination of two positions in the Order Department. The company's sales order clerks have been with the company many years. Lipe is uncomfortable with the prospect of proposing a change that will likely result in terminating these employees.

Requirement

Use the IMA *Statement of Ethical Professional Practice* (Exhibit 1-6) to consider Lipe's responsibility when cost comes at the expense of employees' jobs.

This page intentionally left blank

6 Cost Behavior

High above the rushing waters and mist of Niagara Falls, hundreds of tourists from around the world return to the 512-room Embassy Suites to enjoy a complimentary afternoon refreshment hour, relax in the hotel's pool and spa, and rest in luxurious suites overlooking the Falls. A similar scene occurs across the street at the Sheraton, Marriott, and DoubleTree hotels, as well as at thousands of other travel destinations around the world.

How do hotel managers set prices high enough to cover costs and earn a profit, but low enough to fill most rooms each night? How do they plan for higher occupancy during the busy summer months and lower occupancy during the off-season? They know how their costs behave. Some of the hotel's costs, such as the complimentary morning breakfast and afternoon refreshment hour, vary with the number of

guests staying each night. These *variable* costs rise and fall with the number of guests. But most of the hotel's costs, such as depreciation on the building and furniture, stay the same whether 50 or 2,000 guests stay each night. These costs are *fixed*. Most hotel costs are fixed, so the extra costs to serve each additional guest are low. Once these costs are covered, the revenue from extra guests goes toward profits. ■

Learning Objectives

1 Describe key characteristics and graphs of various cost behaviors

2 Use cost equations to express and predict costs

3 Use account analysis and scatter plots to analyze cost behavior

4 Use the high-low method to analyze cost behavior

5 Use regression analysis to analyze cost behavior

6 Prepare contribution margin income statements for service firms and merchandising firms

7 Use variable costing to prepare contribution margin income statements for manufacturers (Appendix)

Up to this point, we have focused our attention on product costing. We have discussed how managers use job costing, process costing, and ABC to figure out the cost of making a product or providing a service. Product costs are useful for valuing inventory and calculating cost of goods sold. Product costs are also used as a starting place for setting sales prices. However, product costs are not very helpful for planning and some decision making because they contain a mixture of fixed and variable costs. Some of these costs change as volume changes, but other costs do not. To make good decisions and accurate projections, managers must understand **cost behavior**—that is, how costs change as volume changes. In this chapter, we discuss typical cost behaviors and explain methods managers use to determine how their costs behave. The Appendix discusses an alternative product costing system based on cost behavior that manufacturers can use for internal decision making. In the following chapters, we show how managers use cost behavior for planning and decision making.

Cost Behavior: How Do Changes in Volume Affect Costs?

1 Describe key characteristics and graphs of various cost behaviors

The Embassy Suites at Niagara Falls has 512 guest suites that can accommodate between 512 and 2,048 people (four to a room) per night. This means that if every hotel room is booked (100% occupancy rate), the hotel can accommodate between 3,584 and 14,336 guests per week. How do managers plan for such a wide range of volume? They use historic occupancy patterns to determine the most likely range of volume. The room occupancy rate (percentage of rooms booked) varies depending on the season and day of the week. In addition to understanding occupancy patterns, managers must know how changes in volume (number of guests) affect their costs. We first consider three of the most common cost behaviors:

1. **Variable costs** are costs that change in total in direct proportion to changes in volume. For Embassy Suites, complimentary morning breakfast, afternoon refreshments, and in-room toiletries (soap, shampoo, and lotion) are variable costs because these costs increase in total with the number of guests.

2. **Fixed costs** are costs that do not change in total despite wide changes in volume. For Embassy Suites, property taxes, insurance, and depreciation on the hotel building and furnishings are fixed costs that will be the same regardless of the number of hotel guests.

3. **Mixed costs** are costs that change in total, but *not* in direct proportion to changes in volume. Mixed costs have both variable and fixed components. For Embassy Suites, utilities (electricity, gas, water) are mixed costs. Some utility costs will be incurred no matter how many guests stay the night. However, utility costs will also rise as the number of guests turning up the heat or air conditioning, taking showers, and using freshly laundered linens rises.

Variable Costs

Every guest at Embassy Suites is entitled to a complimentary morning breakfast and afternoon refreshment hour (drinks and snacks). In addition, guests receive complimentary toiletries, including shampoo, soap, lotion, and mouthwash, that they typically use or take with them. Let's assume that these toiletries cost the hotel $3 per guest and that the breakfast and refreshment hour costs the hotel $10 per guest. Exhibit 6-1 graphs Embassy Suite's $3-per-guest toiletry cost and the $10-per-guest breakfast and refreshment hour cost. The vertical axis (y-axis) shows total variable costs, while the horizontal axis (x-axis) shows total volume of activity (thousands of guests, in this case).

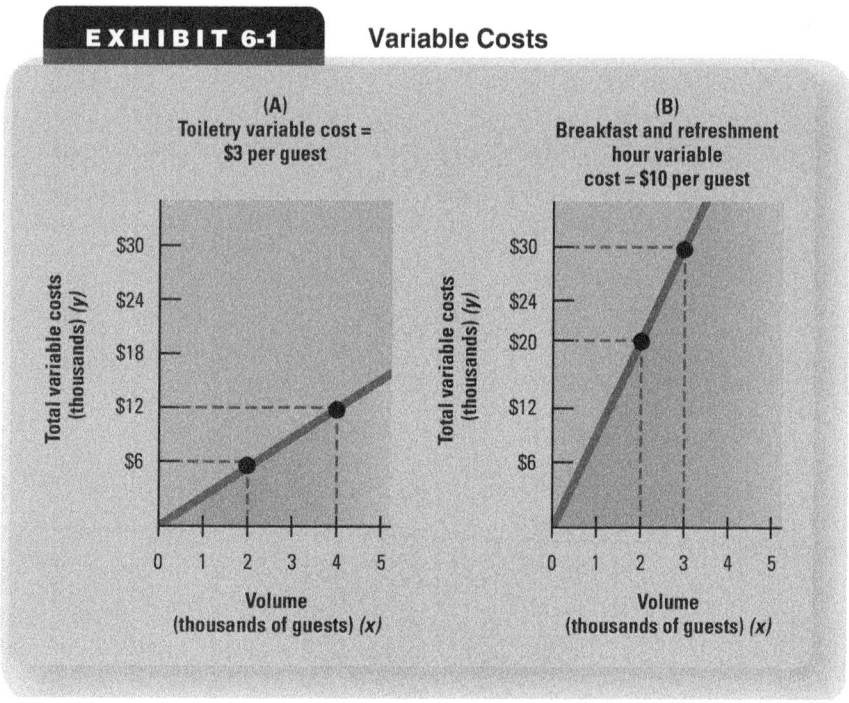

EXHIBIT 6-1   **Variable Costs**

(A)
Toiletry variable cost = $3 per guest

(B)
Breakfast and refreshment hour variable cost = $10 per guest

Look at the total variable toiletry costs in Exhibit 6-1(a). If there are no guests, Embassy Suites doesn't incur any costs for the toiletries, so the total variable cost line begins at the bottom left corner. This point is called the *origin*, and it represents zero volume and zero cost. Total variable cost graphs always begin at the origin. The *slope* of the total variable cost line is the *variable cost per unit of activity*. In Exhibit 6-1(a), the slope of the toiletry variable cost line is $3 because the hotel spends an additional $3 on toiletries for each additional guest. If the hotel serves 2,000 guests, it will spend a total of $6,000 on complimentary toiletries. Doubling the number of guests to 4,000 likewise doubles the total variable cost to $12,000. This example illustrates several important points about variable costs—total variable costs change in *direct proportion* to changes in volume. If volume of activity doubles, total variable costs double. If volume triples, total variable costs triple.

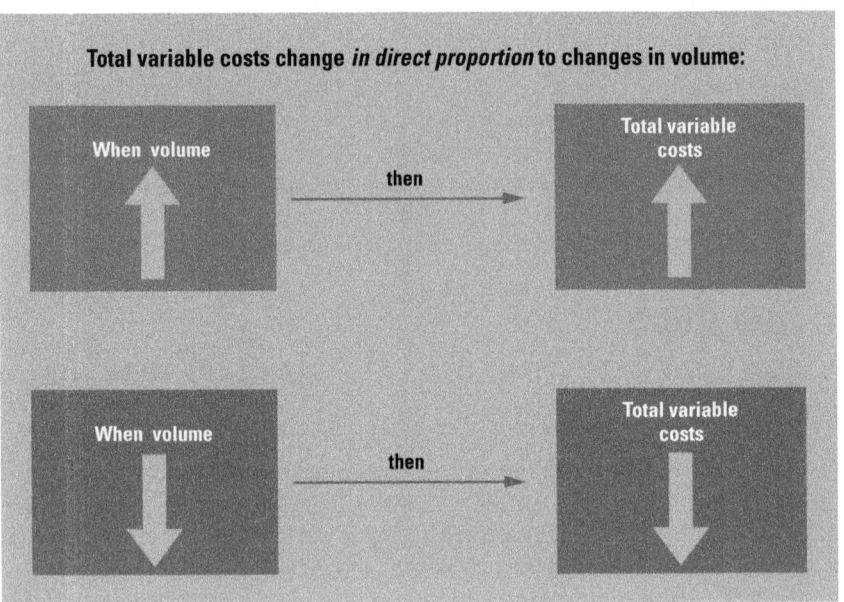

Managers do not need to rely on graphs to predict total variable costs at different volumes of activity. They can use a **cost equation**, a mathematical equation for a straight line, to express how a cost behaves. On cost graphs like the ones pictured in Exhibit 6-1, the vertical (y-axis) always shows total costs while the horizontal axis (x-axis) shows volume of activity. Therefore, any variable cost line can be mathematically expressed as:

2   Use cost equations to express and predict costs

Total variable cost (y) = variable cost per unit of activity (v) × volume of activity (x)

Or simply:

$$y = vx$$

The hotel's total toiletry cost is:

$$y = \$3x$$

where:

y = total toiletry cost
$3 = variable cost per guest
x = number of guests

We can confirm the observations made in Exhibit 6-1(a) using the cost equation. If the hotel has no guests ($x = 0$), total toiletry costs are zero, as shown in the graph. If the hotel has 2,000 guests, total toiletry costs will be:

$$y = \$3 \text{ per guest} \times 2,000 \text{ guests}$$
$$= \$6,000$$

If the hotel has 4,000 guests, managers will expect total toiletry costs to be:

$$y = \$3 \text{ per guest} \times 4,000 \text{ guests}$$
$$= \$12,000$$

Stop & Think...

If the hotel serves 3,467 guests next week, how much will the hotel spend on complimentary toiletries?

Answer: *You would have a hard time answering this question by simply looking at the graph in Exhibit 6-1(a), but cost equations can be used for any volume. We "plug in" the expected volume to our variable cost equation as follows:*

$$y = \$3 \text{ per guest} \times 3,467 \text{ guests}$$
$$= \$10,401$$

Management expects complimentary toiletries next week to cost about $10,401.

Now, look at Exhibit 6-1(b), the total variable costs for the complimentary breakfast and refreshment hour. The slope of the line is $10, representing the cost of providing each guest with the complimentary breakfast and refreshments. We can express the total breakfast and refreshment hour cost as:

$$y = \$10x$$

where:

$$y = \text{total breakfast and refreshment hour cost}$$
$$\$10 = \text{variable cost per guest}$$
$$x = \text{number of guests}$$

The total cost of the breakfast and refreshment hour for 2,000 guests is:

$$y = \$10 \text{ per guest} \times 2,000 \text{ guests}$$
$$= \$20,000$$

This is much higher than the $6,000 toiletry cost for 2,000 guests, so the slope of the line is much steeper than it was for the toiletries. *The higher the variable cost per unit of activity (v), the steeper the slope of the total variable cost line.*

BBH CHAPTER 6

Both graphs in Exhibit 6-1 show how *total* variable costs vary with the number of guests. *But note that the variable cost per guest (v) remains constant in each of the graphs.* That is, Embassy Suites incurs $3 in toiletry costs and $10 in breakfast and refreshment hour costs for each guest no matter how many guests the hotel serves. Some key points to remember about variable costs are shown in Exhibit 6-2.

EXHIBIT 6-2 **Key Characteristics of Variable Costs**

- *Total* variable costs change in *direct proportion* to changes in volume
- The *variable cost per unit of activity (v)* remains constant and is the slope of the variable cost line
- Total variable cost graphs always begin at the origin (if volume is zero, total variable costs are zero)
- Total variable costs can be expressed as:

$$y = vx,$$

where:

y = total variable cost

v = variable cost per unit of activity

x = volume of activity

Fixed Costs

In contrast to total variable costs, total fixed costs do *not* change over wide ranges of volume. Many of Embassy Suites' costs are fixed because the hotel continues to operate daily regardless of the number of guests. Some of the hotel's fixed costs include:

- Property taxes and insurance.
- Depreciation and maintenance on parking ramp, hotel, and room furnishings.
- Pool, fitness room, and spa upkeep.
- Cable TV and wireless Internet access for all rooms.
- Salaries of hotel department managers (housekeeping, food service, special events, etc.).

Most of these costs are **committed fixed costs**, meaning that the hotel is locked in to these costs because of previous management decisions. For example, as soon as the hotel was built, management became locked in to a certain level of property taxes and depreciation, simply because of the location and size of the hotel, and management's choice of furnishings and amenities (pool, fitness room, restaurant, and so forth). Management has little or no control over these committed fixed costs in the short run.

However, the hotel also incurs **discretionary fixed costs**, such as advertising expenses, that are a result of annual management decisions. Companies have more control over discretionary fixed costs because the companies can adjust the costs as necessary in the short run.

Suppose Embassy Suites incurs $100,000 of fixed costs each week. In Exhibit 6-3, the vertical axis (y-axis) shows total fixed costs while the horizontal axis (x-axis) plots volume of activity (thousands of guests). The graph shows total fixed costs as a *flat line* that intersects the y-axis at $100,000 (this is known as the vertical intercept) because the hotel will incur the same $100,000 of fixed costs regardless of the number of guests that stay during the week.

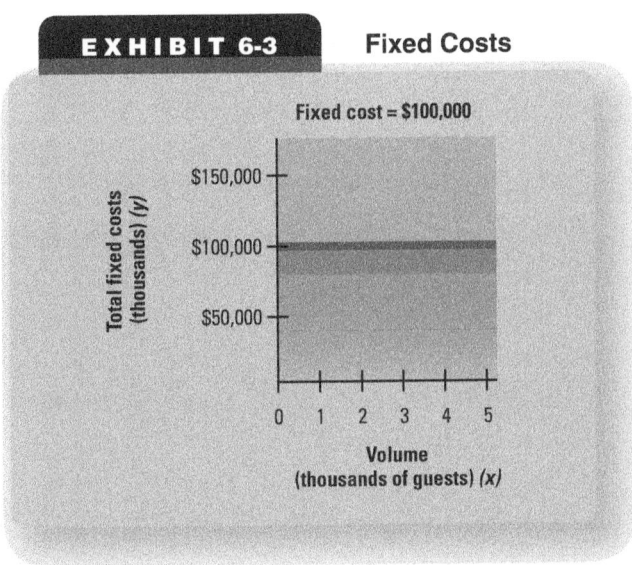

EXHIBIT 6-3   **Fixed Costs**

The cost equation for a fixed cost is simply:

Total fixed costs (y) = fixed amount over a period of time (f)

Or simply:

$$y = f$$

Embassy Suites' *weekly* fixed cost equation is:

$$y = \$100,000$$

where:

y = total fixed cost per week

In contrast to the *total fixed costs* shown in Exhibit 6-3, the *fixed cost per guest* depends on the number of guests. If the hotel serves 2,000 guests during the week, the fixed cost per guest is:

$100,000 ÷ 2,000 guests = $50/guest

If the number of guests *doubles* to 4,000, the fixed cost per guest is *cut in half*:

$100,000 ÷ 4,000 guests = $25/guest

The fixed cost per guest is *inversely proportional* to the number of guests. When volume *increases*, the fixed cost per guest *decreases*. When volume *decreases*, the fixed cost per guest *increases*.

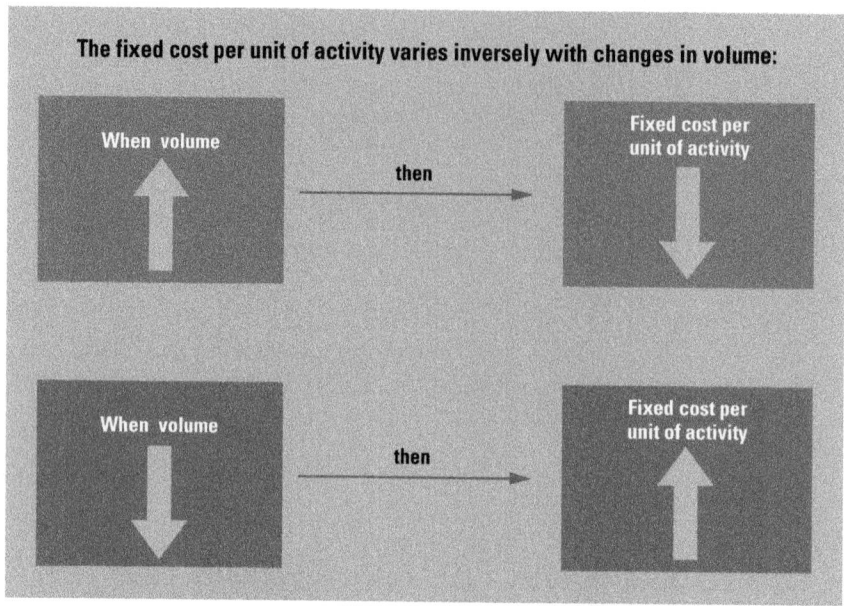

Key points to remember about fixed costs appear in Exhibit 6-4.

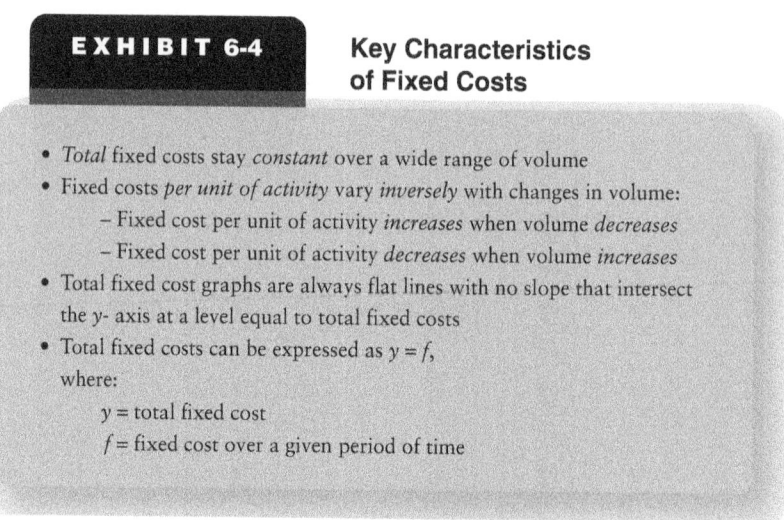

EXHIBIT 6-4   **Key Characteristics of Fixed Costs**

- *Total* fixed costs stay *constant* over a wide range of volume
- Fixed costs *per unit of activity* vary *inversely* with changes in volume:
  - Fixed cost per unit of activity *increases* when volume *decreases*
  - Fixed cost per unit of activity *decreases* when volume *increases*
- Total fixed cost graphs are always flat lines with no slope that intersect the y- axis at a level equal to total fixed costs
- Total fixed costs can be expressed as $y = f$,
  where:
    y = total fixed cost
    f = fixed cost over a given period of time

Stop & Think...

Compute the (a) total fixed cost and (b) fixed cost per guest if the hotel reaches full occupancy of 14,336 guests next week (512 rooms booked with four people per room). Compare the fixed cost per guest at full occupancy to the fixed cost per guest when only 2,000 guests stay during the week. Explain why hotels and other businesses like to operate near 100% capacity.

Answer:

a. *Total fixed costs do not react to wide changes in volume; therefore, total fixed costs will still be $100,000.*

b. *Fixed costs per unit decrease as volume increases. At full occupancy, the fixed cost per guest is:*

$$\$100,000 \div 14,336 \text{ guests} = \$6.98 \text{ (rounded) per guest}$$

When only 2,000 guests stay, the fixed cost per guest is much higher ($50 = $100,000 ÷ 2,000 guests). Businesses like to operate near full capacity because it lowers their fixed cost per unit. A lower cost per unit gives businesses the flexibility to lower their prices to compete more effectively.

Mixed Costs

Mixed costs contain both variable and fixed cost components. Embassy Suites' utilities are mixed costs because the hotel requires a certain amount of utilities just to operate. However, the more guests at the hotel, the more water, electricity, and gas required. Exhibit 6-5 illustrates mixed costs.

For example, let's assume that utilities for the common areas of the hotel and unoccupied rooms cost $2,000 per week. In addition, these costs increase by $8 per guest as they cool or heat their rooms, take showers, turn on the TV and lights, and use freshly laundered sheets and towels.

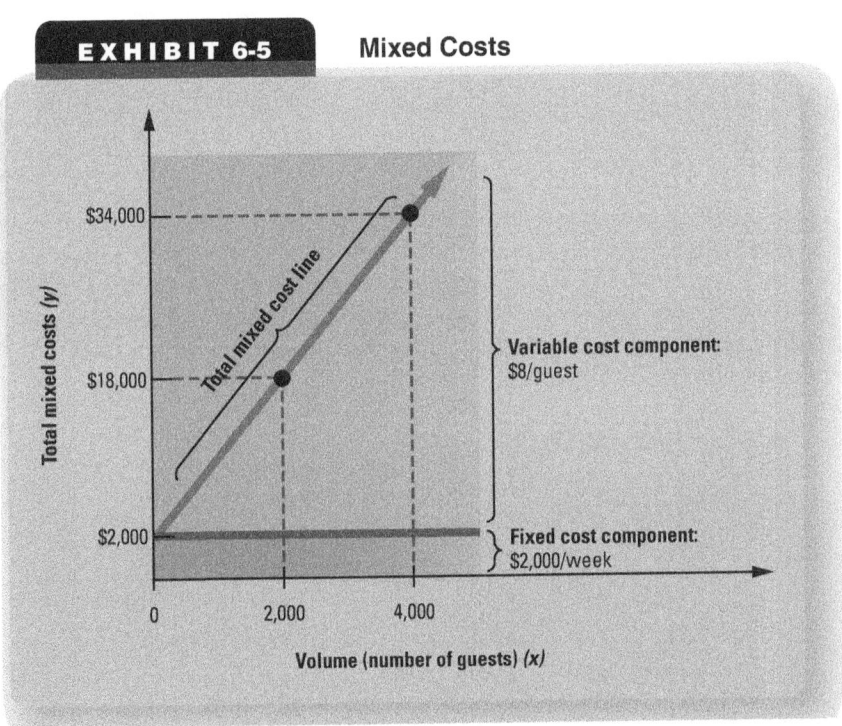

EXHIBIT 6-5   **Mixed Costs**

Variable cost component: $8/guest

Fixed cost component: $2,000/week

Total mixed cost line

Total mixed costs (y): $34,000 / $18,000 / $2,000

Volume (number of guests) (x): 0 / 2,000 / 4,000

Notice the two components—variable and fixed—of the mixed cost in Exhibit 6-5. Similar to a variable cost, the total mixed cost line increases as the volume of activity increases. However, *the line does **not** begin at the origin*. Rather, it intersects the y-axis at a level equal to the fixed cost component. Even if no guests stay this week, the hotel will still incur $2,000 of utilities cost.

Managers can once again use a cost equation to express the mixed cost line so that they can predict total mixed costs at different volumes. The mixed cost equation simply *combines* the variable cost and fixed cost equations:

Total mixed costs = Variable cost component + Fixed cost component
$$y \quad = \quad vx \quad + \quad f$$

Embassy Suites' weekly utilities cost equation is:

$$y = \$8x + \$2,000$$

where:

$$y = \text{total utilities cost per week}$$
$$x = \text{number of guests}$$

If the hotel serves 2,000 guests this week, they expect utilities to cost:

$$y = (\$8 \text{ per guest} \times 2,000 \text{ guests}) + \$2,000$$
$$= \$18,000$$

If the hotel serves 4,000 guests this week, they expect utilities to cost:

$$y = (\$8 \text{ per guest} \times 4,000 \text{ guests}) + \$2,000$$
$$= \$34,000$$

Total mixed costs increase as volume increases, *but **not** in direct proportion to changes in volume*. The total mixed cost did *not* double when volume doubled. This is because of the fixed cost component. Additionally, consider the mixed cost *per guest*:

If the hotel serves 2,000 guests: $18,000 total cost ÷ 2,000 guests = $9.00 per guest
If the hotel serves 4,000 guests: $34,000 total cost ÷ 4,000 guests = $8.50 per guest

The mixed cost per guest did *not* decrease by half when the hotel served twice as many guests. This is because of the variable cost component. Mixed costs per unit decrease as volume increases, but ***not** in direct proportion* to changes in volume. Because mixed costs contain both fixed cost and variable cost components, they behave differently than purely variable costs and purely fixed costs. Key points to remember about mixed costs appear in Exhibit 6-6.

EXHIBIT 6-6 **Key Characteristics of Mixed Costs**

- *Total* mixed costs increase as volume increases because of the variable cost component
- Mixed costs *per unit* decrease as volume increases because of the fixed cost component
- Total mixed cost graphs slope upward but do *not* begin at the origin—they intersect the y-axis at the level of fixed costs
- Total mixed costs can be expressed as a *combination* of the variable and fixed cost equations:

Total mixed costs = variable cost component + fixed cost component
$$y = vx + f$$

where:

$y = $ total mixed cost
$v = $ variable cost per unit of activity (slope)
$x = $ volume of activity
$f = $ fixed cost over a given period of time (vertical intercept)

Stop & Think...

If your cell phone plan charges $10 per month plus $0.15 for each minute you talk, how could you express the monthly cell phone bill as a cost equation? How much will your cell phone bill be if you (a) talk 100 minutes this month or (b) talk 200 minutes this month? If you double your talk time from 100 to 200 minutes, does your total cell phone bill double? Explain.

Answer: *The cost equation for the monthly cell phone bill is:*

$$y = \$0.15x + \$10$$

where:

> y = total cell phone bill for the month
> x = number of minutes talked

a. At 100 minutes, the total cost is $25 [= ($0.15 per minute × 100 minutes) + $10]

b. At 200 minutes, the total cost is $40 [= ($0.15 per minute × 200 minutes) + $10]

The cell phone bill does not double when talk time doubles. The variable portion of the bill doubles from $15 ($0.15 × 100 minutes) to $30 ($0.15 × 200 minutes), but the fixed portion of the bill stays constant ($10).

Relevant Range

Managers always need to keep their **relevant range** in mind when predicting total costs. The relevant range is the band of volume where the following remain constant:

- *Total fixed costs*
- The *variable cost per unit*

A change in cost behavior means a change to a different relevant range.

Let's consider how the concept of relevant range applies to Embassy Suites. As shown in Exhibit 6-3, the hotel's current fixed costs are $100,000 per week. However, since the hotel's popularity continues to grow, room occupancy rates continue to increase. As a result, guests are becoming dissatisfied with the amount of time they have to wait for breakfast tables and elevators. To increase customer satisfaction, management is deciding whether to expand the breakfast facilities and add a 30-passenger elevator to its existing bank of elevators. This expansion, if carried out, will increase the hotel's fixed costs to a new level. Exhibit 6-7 illustrates the hotel's current relevant range and future potential relevant range for fixed costs.

BBH CHAPTER 6

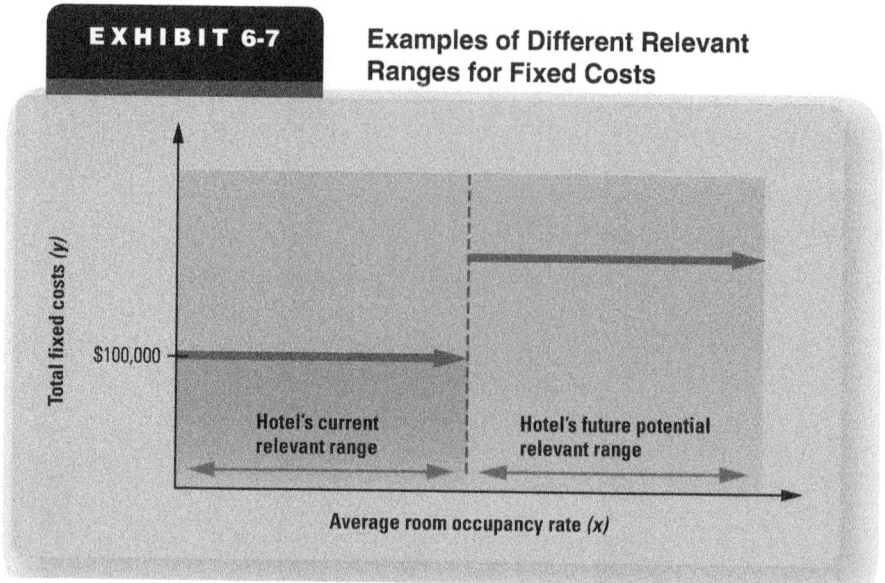

EXHIBIT 6-7 Examples of Different Relevant Ranges for Fixed Costs

Does the concept of relevant range apply only to fixed costs? No, it also applies to variable costs. As shown in Exhibit 6-1, the hotel's current variable cost for toiletries is $3 per guest. However, as room occupancy rates continue to grow, management hopes to negotiate greater volume discounts on the toiletries from its suppliers. These volume discounts will decrease the variable toiletries cost per guest (for example, down to $2.75 per guest). Exhibit 6-8 illustrates the hotel's current relevant range and future potential relevant range for variable toiletries costs.

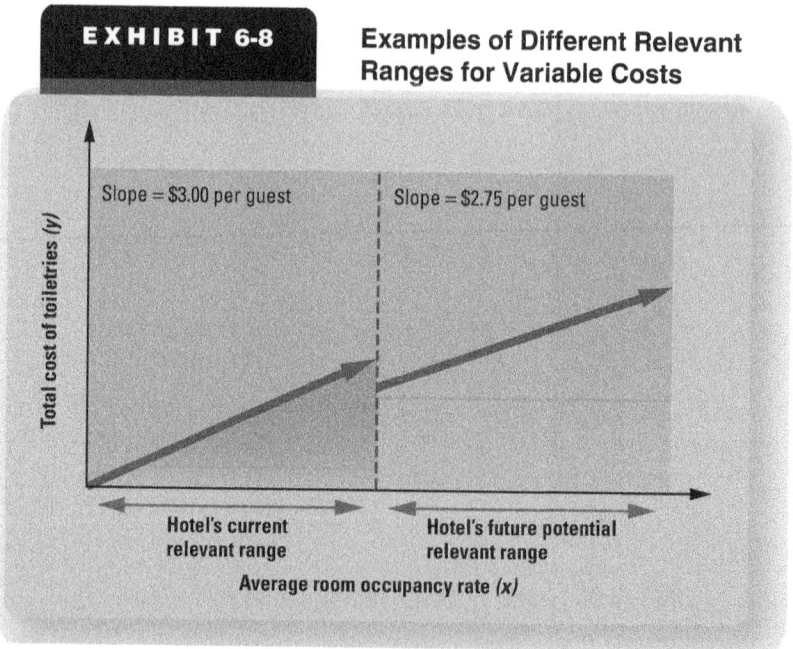

EXHIBIT 6-8 Examples of Different Relevant Ranges for Variable Costs

Why is the concept of relevant range important? Managers can predict costs accurately only if they use cost information for the appropriate relevant range. For example, think about your cell phone plan. Many cell phone plans offer a large block of "free" minutes for a set fee each month. If the user exceeds the allotted minutes, the cell phone company charges an additional per-minute fee. Exhibit 6-9 shows a cell phone plan in which the first 1,000 minutes of call time each month cost $50. After the 1,000 minutes are used, the user must pay an additional $0.30 per minute for every minute of call time. This cell phone plan has two relevant ranges. The first relevant range extends from 0 to 1,000 minutes. In this range, the $50 fee behaves strictly as a

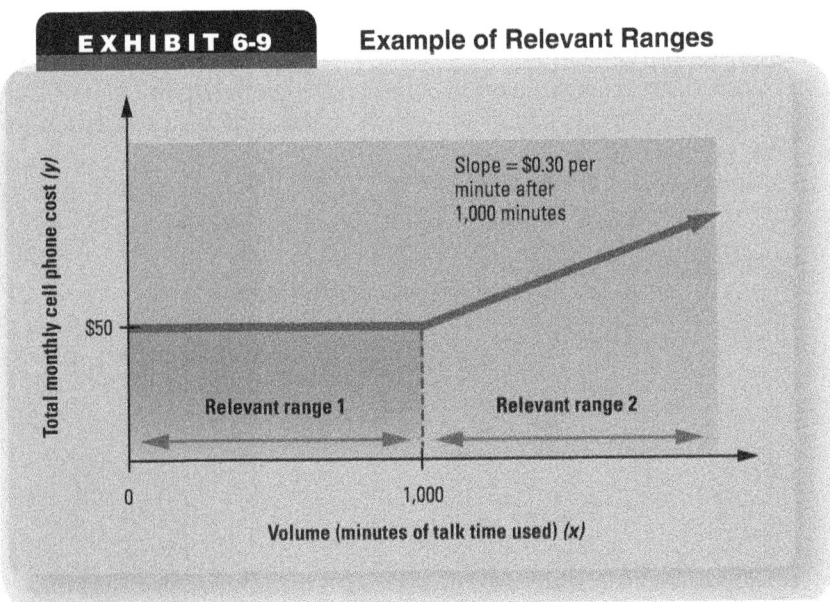

EXHIBIT 6-9   **Example of Relevant Ranges**

fixed cost. You could use 0, 100, or 975 minutes and you would still pay a flat $50 fee that month. The second relevant range starts at 1,001 minutes and extends indefinitely. In this relevant range, the cost is mixed: $50 plus $0.30 per minute. To forecast your cell phone bill each month, you need to know in which relevant range you plan to operate. The same holds true for businesses: To accurately predict costs, they need to know the relevant range in which they plan to operate.

Other Cost Behaviors

While many business costs behave as variable, fixed, or mixed costs, some costs do not neatly fit these patterns. We'll briefly describe other cost behaviors you may encounter.

Step costs resemble stair steps: They are fixed over a small range of activity and then jump up to a new fixed level with moderate changes in volume. Hotels, restaurants, hospitals, and educational institutions typically experience step costs. For example, states usually require day care centers to limit the caregiver-to-child ratio to 1:7—that is, there must be one caregiver for every seven children. As shown in Exhibit 6-10, a day care center that takes on an eighth child must incur the cost of employing another caregiver. The new caregiver can watch the eighth through fourteenth child enrolled at the day care center. If the day care center takes on a fifteenth child, management will once again need to hire another caregiver, costing another $15,000 in salary. The same step cost patterns occur with hotels

EXHIBIT 6-10   **Step Costs**

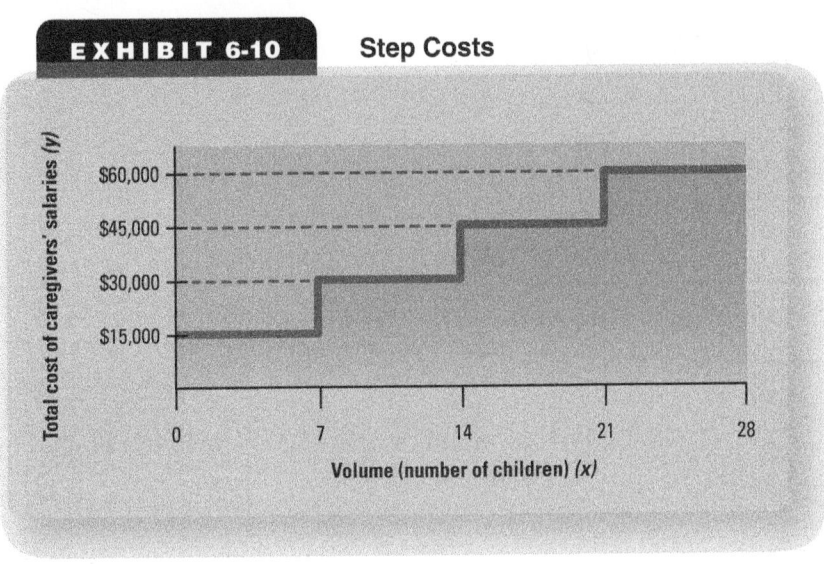

(maid-to-room ratio), restaurants (server-to-table ratio), hospitals (nurse-to-bed ratio), and schools (teacher-to-student ratio).

Step costs differ from fixed costs only in that they "step up" to a new relevant range with relatively small changes in volume. Fixed costs hold constant over much larger ranges of volume.

As shown by the red lines in Exhibit 6-11, **curvilinear costs** are not linear (not a straight line) and, therefore, do not fit into any neat pattern.

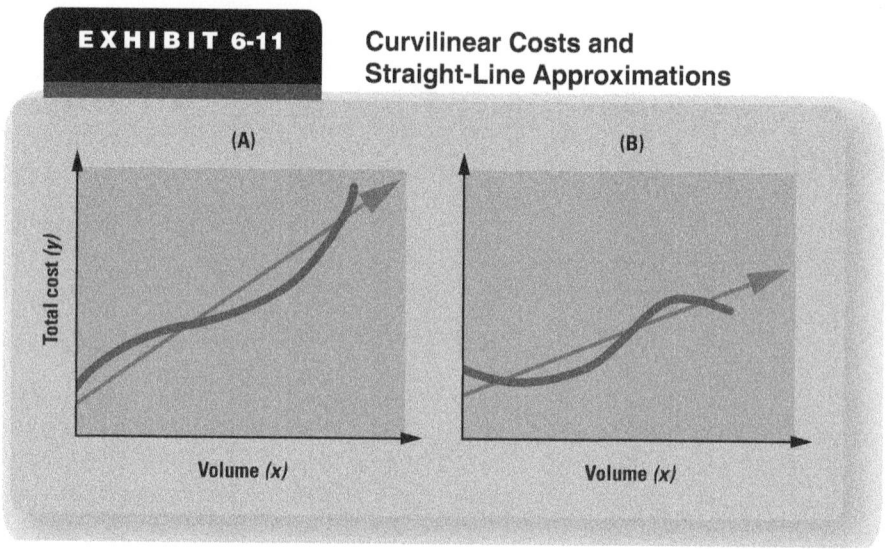

EXHIBIT 6-11   Curvilinear Costs and Straight-Line Approximations

As shown by the straight green arrows in Exhibit 6-11, businesses usually *approximate* these types of costs as mixed costs. Sometimes managers also approximate step costs the same way: They simply draw a straight mixed cost line through the steps. If managers need more accurate predictions, they can simply break these types of costs into smaller relevant ranges and make their predictions based on the particular relevant range. For example, the day care center may want to predict total caregiver salaries if it enrolls 26 children. The manager knows this enrollment falls into the relevant range of 21 to 28 children, where she needs to employ four caregivers. She can then predict total caregiver salaries to be $60,000 (4 caregivers × $15,000 salary per caregiver).

We have just described the most typical cost behaviors. In the next part of the chapter, we will discuss methods managers use for determining how their costs behave.

Decision Guidelines

COST BEHAVIOR

Suppose you manage a local fitness club. To be an effective manager, you need to know how the club's costs behave. Here are some decisions you will need to make.

Decision	Guideline
How can you tell if a *total* cost is variable, fixed, or mixed?	• Total variable costs rise in *direct proportion* to increases in volume. • Total fixed costs stay *constant* over a wide range of volumes. • Total mixed costs rise, but *not* in direct proportion to increases in volume.

Decision	Guideline
How can you tell if a *per-unit* cost is variable, fixed, or mixed?	• On a per-unit basis, variable costs stay constant. • On a per-unit basis, fixed costs decrease in proportion to increases in volume (that is to say they are inversely proportional). • On a per-unit basis, mixed costs decrease, but not in direct proportion to increases in volume.
How can you tell by looking at a graph if a cost is variable, fixed, or mixed?	• Variable cost lines slope upward and begin at the origin. • Fixed cost lines are flat (no slope) and intersect the y-axis at a level equal to total fixed costs (this is known as the vertical intercept). • Mixed cost lines slope upward but do *not* begin at the origin. They intersect the y-axis at a level equal to their fixed cost component.
How can you mathematically express different cost behaviors?	• Cost equations mathematically express cost behavior using the equation for a straight line: $$y = vx + f$$ where: y = total cost v = variable cost per unit of activity (slope) x = volume of activity f = fixed cost (the vertical intercept) • For a variable cost, f is zero, leaving: $$y = vx$$ • For a fixed cost, v is zero, leaving: $$y = f$$ • Because a mixed cost has both a fixed cost component and a variable cost component, its cost equation is f: $$y = vx + f$$

BBH CHAPTER 6

Summary Problem 1

The previous manager of Fitness-for-Life started the following schedule, but left before completing it. He wasn't sure but thought the club's fixed operating costs were $10,000 per month and the variable operating costs were $1 per member. The club's existing facilities could serve up to 750 members per month.

Requirements

1. Complete the following schedule for different levels of monthly membership assuming the previous manager's cost behavior estimates are accurate:

Monthly Operating Costs	100 Members	500 Members	750 Members
Total variable costs			
Total fixed costs			
Total operating costs			
Variable cost per member			
Fixed cost per member			
Average cost per member			

2. As the manager of the fitness club, why shouldn't you use the average cost per member to predict total costs at different levels of membership?

Solution

Requirement 1

As volume increases, fixed costs stay constant in total but decrease on a per-unit basis. As volume increases, variable costs stay constant on a per-unit basis but increase in total in direct proportion to increases in volume:

	100 Members	500 Members	750 Members
Total variable costs	$ 100	$ 500	$ 750
Total fixed costs	$10,000	$10,000	$10,000
Total operating costs	$10,100	$10,500	$10,750
Variable cost per member	$ 1.00	$ 1.00	$ 1.00
Fixed cost per member	$100.00	$ 20.00	$ 13.33
Average cost per member	$101.00	$ 21.00	$ 14.33

Requirement 2

The average cost per member should not be used to predict total costs at different volumes of membership because it changes as volume changes. The average cost per member decreases as volume increases due to the fixed component of the club's operating costs. Managers should base cost predictions on cost behavior patterns, not on the average cost per member.

Pages 317–325 intentionally omitted

The Contribution Margin Income Statement: A Summary of Cost Behavior

6 Prepare contribution margin income statements for service firms and merchandising firms

Almost all businesses, including Embassy Suites, have some fixed costs, some variable costs, and some mixed costs. Companies use account analysis, the high-low method, or regression analysis (or a combination of the three methods) to determine how their costs behave. They may analyze cost behavior on an account-by-account basis, as we did in the previous examples (they prepare separate cost equations for toiletry costs, complimentary breakfast and refreshment costs, utilities costs, and so forth). Or if they do not need so much detail, companies may develop *one* mixed cost equation for *all* operating costs lumped together. Once they have cost behavior information, how do companies communicate it to their managers so that the managers can use it for planning and decision making?

Unfortunately, traditional income statements do not provide managers with any cost behavior information. Traditional income statements are organized by *function*, not by cost behavior. Costs related to the production or purchases function of the value chain appear as cost of goods sold, above the gross profit line, when the manufactured products or merchandise is sold. All other costs (related to all other value-chain functions) appear as operating expenses (period costs), below the gross profit line.

Exhibit 6-17 illustrates this *functional* separation of costs for a retailer specializing in fitness equipment. Notice how the traditional format does not provide managers with much information, if any, on cost behavior. The cost of goods sold is a variable cost for a retailer, but contains a mixture of variable and fixed production costs for manufacturers. Recall from Chapter 2 that manufacturers classify direct materials and direct labor as variable costs, but treat manufacturing overhead as a mixed cost. Likewise, traditional income statements do not distinguish fixed operating costs from variable operating costs. While external users such as investors and creditors find traditional income statements useful, these statements are not very useful for internal managers who need cost behavior information for planning and decision making.

EXHIBIT 6-17	Traditional Income Statement of a Retailer

AAA FITNESS EQUIPMENT
Income Statement
Month Ended July 31

Sales revenue..	$ 52,500
Less: Cost of goods sold...	(27,300)
Gross profit	25,200
Less: Operating expenses	(14,600)
Operating income	$ 10,600

To provide managers with cost behavior information, companies often prepare **contribution margin income statements**. Contribution margin income statements can only be used internally. GAAP does not allow companies to use the contribution margin format for external reporting purposes. Contribution margin income statements organize costs by *behavior* rather than by *function*. Therefore, managers find contribution margin income statements more helpful than traditional income statements for planning and decision making. The contribution margin income statement (shown in Exhibit 6-18) presents *all variable costs*—whether relating to the merchandise sold or selling and administrative activities—*above* the contribution margin line. The contribution margin income statement shows *all fixed costs*—whether relating to the merchandise sold or selling and administrative activities—*below* the contribution margin line. The contribution margin, not the gross profit, is the dividing line. The **contribution margin** is equal to sales revenue minus variable expenses.

EXHIBIT 6-18	Contribution Margin Income Statement

AAA FITNESS EQUIPMENT
Contribution Margin Income Statement
Month Ended July 31

Sales revenue...	$ 52,500
Less: Variable expenses	(30,900)
Contribution margin..	21,600
Less: Fixed expenses	(11,000)
Operating income	$ 10,600

Managers can use contribution margin income statements to predict how changes in volume will affect operating income. Changes in volume will affect total sales revenue and total variable costs (and, therefore, the contribution margin). However, changes in volume will *not* affect fixed costs within the same relevant range. Therefore, the contribution margin income statement distinguishes the financial figures that *will* change from those that *will not* change in response to fluctuations in volume. Traditional income statements do not make this distinction.

In the next chapter, we will discuss many ways managers use the contribution margin to answer business questions, including how changes in volume and costs affect the firm's profits.

The appendix in this chapter is devoted to variable costing. Variable costing is an optional product costing system that *manufacturers* can use for internal purposes. Variable costing results in contribution margin income statements for manufacturers.

Decision Guidelines

Cost Behavior

As the manager of a local fitness club, Fitness-for-Life, you'll want to plan for operating costs at various levels of membership. Before you can make forecasts, you'll need to make some of the following decisions.

Decision	Guidelines
How can I sort out the fixed and the variable components of mixed costs?	• Managers typically use the high-low method or regression analysis. • The high-low method is fast and easy but uses only two data points to form the cost equation and, therefore, may not be very indicative of the costs' true behavior. • Regression analysis uses every data point provided to determine the cost equation that best fits the data. It is simple to do with Excel, but tedious to do by hand.
I've used the high-low method to formulate a cost equation. Can I tell how well the cost equation fits the data?	The only way to determine how well the high-low cost equation fits the data is by (1) plotting the data, (2) drawing a line through the data points associated with the highest and lowest volume, and (3) "visually inspecting" the resulting graph to see if the line is representative of the other plotted data points.
I've used regression analysis to formulate a cost equation. Can I tell how well the cost equation fits the data?	The R-square is a "goodness-of-fit" statistic that tells how well the regression analysis cost equation fits the data. The R-square ranges from 0 to 1, with 1 being a perfect fit. When the R-square is high, the cost equation should render fairly accurate predictions.
Do I need to be concerned about anything before using the high-low method or regression analysis?	Cost equations are only as good as the data on which they are based. Managers should plot the historical data to see if a relationship between cost and volume exists. In addition, scatter plots help managers identify outliers. Managers should remove outliers before further analysis. Managers should also adjust cost equations for seasonal data, inflation, and price changes.
Can I present the club's financial statements in a manner that will help with planning and decision making?	Managers often use contribution margin income statements for internal planning and decision making. Contribution margin income statements organize costs by *behavior* (fixed versus variable) rather than by *function* (product versus period).

Summary Problem 2

As the new manager of a local fitness club, Fitness-for-Life, you have been studying the club's financial data. You would like to determine how the club's costs behave in order to make accurate predictions for next year. Here is information from the last six months:

Month	Club Membership (number of members)	Total Operating Costs	Operating Costs per Member
July	450	$ 8,900	$19.78
August	480	$ 9,800	$20.42
September	500	$10,100	$20.20
October	550	$10,150	$18.45
November	560	$10,500	$18.75
December	525	$10,200	$19.43

Requirements

1. By looking at the "Total Operating Costs" and the "Operating Costs per Member," can you tell whether the club's operating costs are variable, fixed, or mixed? Explain your answer.

2. Use the high-low method to determine the club's monthly operating cost equation.

3. Using your answer from Requirement 2, predict total monthly operating costs if the club has 600 members.

4. Can you predict total monthly operating costs if the club has 3,000 members? Explain your answer.

5. Prepare the club's traditional income statement and its contribution margin income statement for the month of July. Assume that your cost equation from Requirement 2 accurately describes the club's cost behavior. The club charges members $30 per month for unlimited access to its facilities.

6. *Optional:* Perform regression analysis using Microsoft Excel. What is the monthly operating cost equation? What is the R-square? Why is the cost equation different from that in Requirement 2?

Solution

Requirement 1
By looking at "Total Operating Costs," we can see that the club's operating costs are not purely fixed; otherwise, total costs would remain constant. Operating costs appear to be either variable or mixed because they increase in total as the number of members increases. By looking at the "Operating Costs per Member," we can see that the operating costs aren't purely variable; otherwise, the "per-member" cost would remain constant. Therefore, the club's operating costs are mixed.

Requirement 2
Use the high-low method to determine the club's operating cost equation:

continued . . .

Step 1: The highest volume month is November, and the lowest volume month is July. Therefore, we use *only these two months* to determine the cost equation. The first step is to find the variable cost per unit of activity, which is the slope of the line connecting the November and July data points:

$$\frac{\text{Rise}}{\text{Run}} = \frac{\text{Change in } y}{\text{Change in } x} = \frac{y \text{ (high)} - y \text{ (low)}}{x \text{ (high)} - x \text{ (low)}} = \frac{(\$10,500 - \$8,900)}{(560 - 450 \text{ members})} = \$14.55 \text{ per member (rounded)}$$

Step 2: The second step is to find the fixed cost component (vertical intercept) by plugging in the slope and either July or November data to a mixed cost equation:

$$y = vx + f$$

Using November data:

$$\$10,500 = (\$14.55/\text{member} \times 560 \text{ guests}) + f$$

Solving for f:

$$f = \$2,352$$

Or we can use July data to reach the same conclusion:

$$\$8,900 = (\$14.55/\text{members} \times 450 \text{ guests}) + f$$

Solving for f:

$$f = \$2,352 \text{ (rounded)}$$

Step 3: Write the monthly operating cost equation:

$$y = \$14.55x + \$2,352$$

where:

$$x = \text{number of members}$$
$$y = \text{total monthly operating costs}$$

Requirement 3

Predict total monthly operating costs when volume reaches 600 members:

$$y = (\$14.55 \times 600) + \$2,352$$
$$y = \$11,082$$

Requirement 4

Our current data and cost equation are based on 450 to 560 members. If membership reaches 3,000, operating costs could behave much differently. That volume falls outside our current relevant range.

Requirement 5

The club had 450 members in July and total operating costs of $8,900. Thus, its traditional income statement is:

FITNESS-FOR-LIFE
Income Statement
Month Ended July 31

Club membership revenue (450 × $30)	$13,500
Less: Operating expenses (given)	(8,900)
Operating income	$ 4,600

To prepare the club's contribution margin income statement, we need to know how much of the total $8,900 operating costs is fixed and how much is variable. If the cost equation from Requirement 2 accurately reflects the club's cost behavior, fixed costs will be $2,352 and variable costs will be $6,548 (= $14.55 × 450). The 3 contribution margin income statement would look like this:

FITNESS-FOR-LIFE
Contribution Margin Income Statement
Month Ended July 31

Club membership revenue (450 × $30)	$13,500
Less: Variable expenses (450 × $14.55)	(6,548)
Contribution margin	6,952
Less: Fixed expenses	(2,352)
Operating income	$ 4,600

Requirement 6

Regression analysis using Microsoft Excel results in the following cost equation and R-square:

$$y = \$11.80x + \$3,912$$

where:

$$x = \text{number of members}$$
$$y = \text{total monthly operating costs}$$

R-square = .8007

The regression analysis cost equation uses all of the data points, not just the data from November and July. Therefore, it better represents all of the data. The high R-square means that the regression line fits the data well and predictions based on this cost equation should be quite accurate.

Pages 332–340 intentionally omitted

Review *Cost Behavior*

Accounting Vocabulary

Absorption Costing (p. 332)
The costing method where products "absorb" both fixed and variable manufacturing costs.

Account Analysis (p. 317)
A method for determining cost behavior that is based on a manager's judgment in classifying each general ledger account as a variable, fixed, or mixed cost.

Committed Fixed Costs (p. 306)
Fixed costs that are locked in because of previous management decisions; management has little or no control over these costs in the short run.

Contribution Margin (p. 327)
Sales revenue minus variable expenses.

Contribution Margin Income Statement (p. 327)
Income statement that organizes costs by *behavior* (variable costs or fixed costs) rather than by *function*.

Cost Behavior (p. 302)
Describes how costs change as volume changes.

Cost Equation (p. 304)
A mathematical equation for a straight line that expresses how a cost behaves.

Curvilinear Costs (p. 314)
A cost behavior that is not linear (not a straight line).

Discretionary Fixed Costs (p. 306)
Fixed costs that are a result of annual management decisions; fixed costs that are controllable in the short run.

Fixed Costs (p. 303)
Costs that do not change in total despite wide changes in volume.

High-Low Method (p. 320)
A method for determining cost behavior that is based on two historical data points: the highest and lowest volume of activity.

Mixed Cost (p. 303)
Costs that change, but *not* in direct proportion to changes in volume. Mixed costs have both variable cost and fixed cost components.

Regression Analysis (p. 322)
A statistical procedure for determining the line that best fits the data by using *all of the historical data points, not just the high and low data points*.

Relevant Range (p. 311)
The band of volume where total fixed costs remain constant at a certain level and where the variable cost *per unit* remains constant at a certain level.

Step Costs (p. 313)
A cost behavior that is fixed over a small range of activity and then jumps to a different fixed level with moderate changes in volume.

Outliers (p. 319)
Abnormal data points; data points that do not fall in the same general pattern as the other data points.

Variable Costs (p. 303)
Costs that change in total in direct proportion to changes in volume.

Variable Costing (p. 332)
The costing method that assigns only *variable* manufacturing costs to products.

Quick Check

1. For most businesses, straight-line depreciation on the company's buildings is a
   a. variable cost
   b. fixed cost
   c. mixed cost
   d. step cost

2. If a *per-unit* cost remains constant over a wide range of volume, the cost is most likely a
   a. variable cost
   b. fixed cost
   c. mixed cost
   d. step cost

3. The following graph indicates which type of cost behavior?

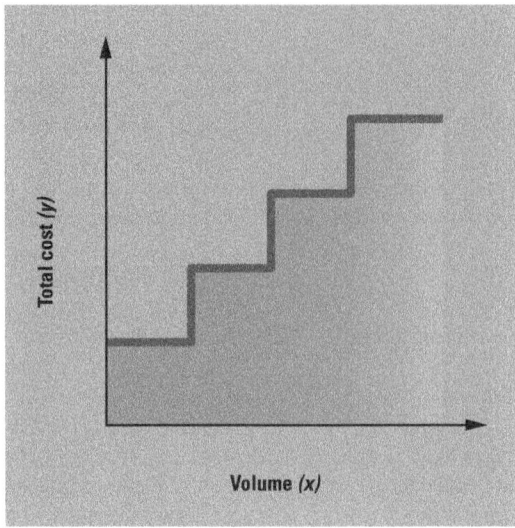

   a. variable cost
   b. fixed cost
   c. mixed cost
   d. step cost

4. In the following mixed cost equation, what amount represents the **total variable cost component**: $y = vx + f$?
   a. y
   b. v
   c. f
   d. vx

5. The cost per unit decreases as volume increases for which of the following cost behaviors?
   a. variable costs and fixed costs
   b. variable costs and mixed costs
   c. fixed costs and mixed costs
   d. only fixed costs

6. Which of the following cost behaviors best explains why companies like to operate at or near full capacity?
   a. variable cost
   b. fixed cost
   c. mixed cost
   d. step cost

7. Each month, a fitness club incurs $7,000 of fixed operating costs plus $6 of operating costs for every club member. If x represents the number of club members, which of the following best describes the club's total monthly operating costs?

a. $y = \$7,000x$

b. $y = \$6$

c. $y = \$6x$

d. $y = \$7,000 + \$6x$

8. Manufacturing overhead is usually a

a. variable cost

b. fixed cost

c. mixed cost

d. step cost

9. (Appendix) The only difference between variable costing and absorption costing lies in the treatment of

a. fixed manufacturing overhead costs

b. variable manufacturing overhead costs

c. direct materials and direct labor costs

d. variable nonmanufacturing costs

10. (Appendix) When inventories decline, operating income under variable costing is

a. lower than operating income under absorption costing

b. the same as operating income under absorption costing

c. higher than operating income under absorption costing

Quick Check Answers

1. b 2. a 3. d 4. d 5. c 6. b 7. d 8. c 9. a 10. c

For Internet Exercises, Excel in Practice, and additional online activities, go to this book's Web site at www.prenhall.com/bamber.

Assess Your Progress

▪ Learning Objectives

1 Describe key characteristics and graphs of various cost behaviors

2 Use cost equations to express and predict costs

3 Use account analysis and scatter plots to analyze cost behavior

4 Use the high-low method to analyze cost behavior

5 Use regression analysis to analyze cost behavior

6 Prepare contribution margin income statements for service firms and merchandising firms

7 Use variable costing to prepare contribution margin income statements for manufacturers (Appendix)

▪ Short Exercises

S6-1 **Identify cost behavior** (*Learning Objective 1*)
The chart below shows three different costs: Cost A, Cost B, and Cost C. For each cost, the chart shows the total cost and cost per unit at two different volumes within the same relevant range. Based on this information, identify each cost as fixed, varable, or mixed. Explain your answers.

	At 5,000 units		At 6,000 units	
	Total Cost	Cost per Unit	Total Cost	Cost per Unit
Cost A	$30,000	$6.00	$36,000	$6.00
Cost B	$30,000	$6.00	$30,000	$5.00
Cost C	$30,000	$6.00	$33,000	$5.50

S6-2 **Sketch cost behavior graphs** (*Learning Objective 1*)
Sketch graphs of the following cost behaviors. In each graph, the y-axis should be "total costs" and the x-axis should be "volume of activity."

a. Step

b. Fixed

c. Curvilinear

d. Mixed

e. Variable

S6-5   **Predict total mixed costs** *(Learning Objective 2)*

Ritter Razors produces deluxe razors that compete with Gillette's Mach line of razors. Total manufacturing costs are $100,000 when 20,000 packages are produced. Of this amount, total variable costs are $40,000. What are the total production costs when 25,000 packages of razors are produced? Assume the same relevant range.

Page 346 intentionally omitted

S6-13 **Prepare a contribution margin income statement** *(Learning Objective 6)*

Pam's Quilt Shoppe sells homemade Amish quilts. Pam buys the quilts from local Amish artisans for $250 each, and her shop sells them for $350 each. Pam also pays a sales commission of 5% of sales revenue to her sales staff. Pam leases her country-style shop for $1,000 per month and pays $1,200 per month in payroll costs in addition to the sales commissions. Pam sold 80 quilts in February. Prepare Pam's traditional income statement and contribution margin income statement for the month.

▪ Exercises

E6-16 **Graph specific costs** *(Learning Objective 1)*

Graph these cost behavior patterns over a relevant range of 0 to 10,000 units:

a. Variable expenses of $8 per unit

b. Mixed expenses made up of fixed costs of $20,000 and variable costs of $3 per unit

c. Fixed expenses of $15,000

E6-18 Forecast costs at different volumes *(Learning Objectives 1, 2)*
Perreth Drycleaners has capacity to clean up to 5,000 garments per month.

Requirements

1. Complete the following schedule for the three volumes shown:

	2,000 Garments	3,500 Garments	5,000 Garments
Total variable costs		$2,625	
Total fixed costs			
Total operating costs			
Variable cost per garment			
Fixed cost per garment		$ 2.00	
Average cost per garment			

2. Why does the average cost per garment change?

3. Suppose the owner, Dan Perreth, erroneously uses the average cost per unit *at full capacity* to predict total costs at a volume of 2,000 garments. Would he overestimate or underestimate his total costs? By how much?

E6-19 Prepare income statement in two formats *(Learning Objective 6)*
Refer to the Perreth Drycleaners in E6-18. Assume that Perreth charges customers $7 per garment for dry cleaning. Prepare Perreth's *projected* income statement if 4,252 garments are cleaned in March. First, prepare the income statement using the traditional format; then, prepare Perreth's contribution margin income statement.

Pages 349–355 intentionally omitted

P6-40B **Contribution margin income statement** (*Learning Objective 6*)

Rachel's Rock Shop is a full-service music store. Rachel rents and sells instruments, sells sheet music, and hires musicians on an "as-needed" hourly basis to give student lessons. She also has one full-time employee who helps her run the shop. Her general ledger accounts indicate the following for the year:

Instrument rental revenue...	$22,000
Cost of sheet music sold..	$ 2,000
Instrument sales	$27,000
Straight-line depreciation expense on owned rental equipment...	$ 4,000
Sheet music sales	$ 7,000
Music lesson revenue...	$40,000
Cost of instruments sold..	$ 7,500
Store lease payments	$12,000
Payments to musicians	$25,000
Full-time employee salary...	$30,000

Based on this information, prepare Rachel's income statement using two formats: traditional format and contribution margin format. When preparing the income statements, you may combine the sales revenue accounts, but show all other detail. Which income statement will be more useful to Rachel as she plans for next year? Why?

Pages 357 and 358 intentionally omitted

7 Cost-Volume-Profit Analysis

The Internet boom of the 1990s led many entrepreneurs to believe that they could earn profits well above those of traditional retail stores by avoiding the high fixed costs of brick-and-mortar retail outlets. Online business flourished for a while, but when the dot.com bubble burst, many of these Internet dreams died. Many, but not all. Consider art.com, an e-tail business that offers over 100,000 different prints, photos, and posters to customers ranging from budget-minded college students to professional decorators searching for high-end art. Founded in 1995, art.com has enjoyed positive cash flows and double-digit revenue growth since 2000. In 2003, Deloitte & Touche named art.com one of the fastest-growing tech companies in America. It attracts more than a million people to its award-winning Web site each month.

Even though art.com doesn't face the fixed costs of traditional retail outlets, it still incurs fixed costs tied to its Web site and its custom-framing facilities. It also incurs variable costs for each piece of art. The bottom line: e-tail or retail, every business faces fixed and variable costs, and

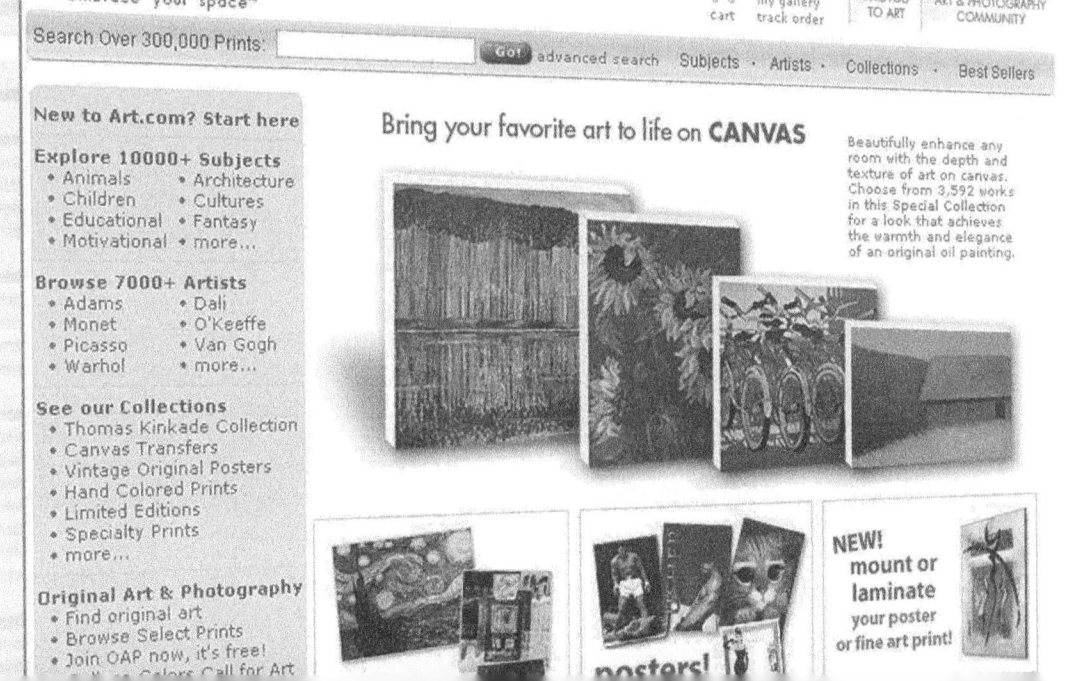

art.com is no exception. Before they launched the company, how did art.com managers figure out what sales volume they had to reach to break even? How did they forecast the volume needed to achieve their target profit levels? And as the company continues to operate, how do managers respond to fluctuating business conditions, changing variable and fixed costs, and pricing pressure from new competitors? Cost-volume-profit (CVP) analysis helps managers answer such questions. ■

Learning Objectives

1 Calculate the unit contribution margin and the contribution margin ratio

2 Use CVP analysis to find breakeven points and target profit volumes

3 Perform sensitivity analysis in response to changing business conditions

4 Find breakeven and target profit volumes for multiproduct companies

5 Determine a firm's margin of safety and operating leverage

In the last chapter, we discussed cost behavior patterns and methods managers use to determine how their costs behave. We showed how managers use the contribution margin income statement to separately display the firm's variable and fixed costs. In this chapter, we show how managers identify the volume of sales necessary to achieve breakeven and target profit levels. We also look at how changes in costs, sales price, and volume affect the firm's profit. Finally, we discuss ways to identify the firm's risk level, including ways to gauge how easily a firm's profits could turn to loss if sales volume declines.

How Does Cost-Volume-Profit Analysis Help Managers?

Cost-volume-profit, or CVP, analysis is a powerful tool that helps managers make important business decisions. **Cost-volume-profit analysis** expresses the relationships among costs, volume, and profit or loss. For example, at art.com, managers need to determine how many pieces of art the company must sell each month just to cover costs or to break even. CVP can provide the answer. CVP also helps art.com's managers determine how many pieces of art the company must sell to earn a target profit, such as $1,000,000 per month. And if costs or sales prices change, CVP can help managers decide how sales volume would need to change to achieve the same profit level.

However, to use CVP, managers need certain data. They must also make sure the data are consistent with the assumptions underlying CVP analysis. In addition, managers need a solid understanding of the contribution margin concept introduced in the last chapter. In this section, we'll take a look at the data requirements, assumptions, and contribution margin in more detail.

BBH CHAPTER 7

Data Required for Effective CVP Analysis

CVP analysis relies on the interdependency of five components, or pieces of information, shown in Exhibit 7-1.

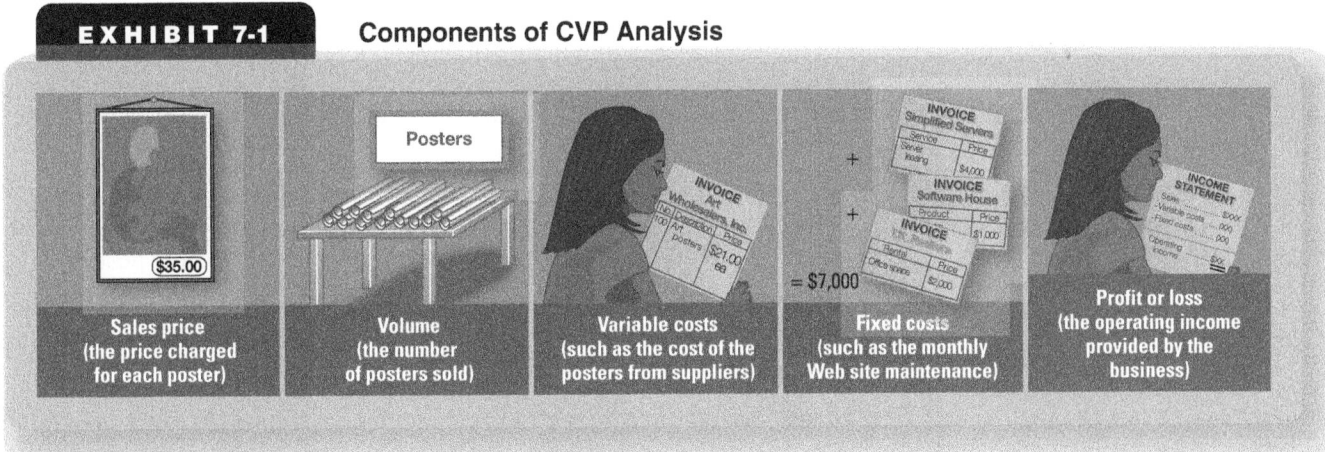

EXHIBIT 7-1	Components of CVP Analysis

If you know or can estimate four of these five components, you can use CVP analysis to compute the remaining unknown amount. Therefore, CVP helps managers discover how changes in any of these components will affect their business. Because business conditions are always changing, CVP helps managers prepare for and respond to economic changes. Now, let's review the assumptions required for CVP analysis.

CVP Assumptions

CVP analysis assumes that:

1. A change in volume is the only factor that affects costs.

2. Managers can classify each cost (or the components of mixed costs) as either variable or fixed. These costs are linear throughout the relevant range of volume.

3. Revenues are linear throughout the relevant range of volume.

4. Inventory levels will not change.

5. The sales mix of products will not change. **Sales mix** is the combination of products that make up total sales. For example, art.com may sell 15% posters, 25% unframed photographs, and 60% framed prints. If profits differ across products, changes in sales mix will affect CVP analysis.

Let's start by looking at a simple firm that has only one product. Later, we'll expand the firm to include a wider selection of products. Kay Pak, an entrepreneur, has just started an e-tail business selling art posters on the Internet. Kay is a "virtual retailer" and carries no inventory. Kay's software tabulates all customer orders each day and then automatically places the order to buy posters from a wholesaler. Kay buys only what she needs to fill the prior day's sales orders. The posters cost $21 each, and Kay sells them for $35 each. Customers pay the shipping costs, so there are no other variable selling costs. Monthly fixed costs for server leasing and maintenance, software, and office rental total $7,000. Kay's relevant range extends from 0 to 2,000 posters a month. Beyond this volume, Kay will need to hire an employee and upgrade her Web site software in order to handle the increased volume.

Let's see if Kay's business meets the CVP assumptions:

1. Sales volume is the only factor that affects her costs.

2. The $21 purchase cost for each poster is a variable cost. Thus, Kay's *total variable cost* increases in direct proportion to the number of posters she sells (an extra $21 in cost for each extra poster she sells). The $7,000 monthly server leasing and maintenance, software, and office rental costs are fixed and do not change no matter how many posters she sells within the relevant range. We could graph each of these costs as a straight line, so they are linear within the relevant range.

3. Kay's revenue is also linear. She sells each poster for $35, so a graph of her revenues is a straight line beginning at the origin (if she doesn't sell any posters, she won't have any revenue) that slopes upward at a rate of $35 per poster.

4. Kay has no inventory. If she did carry inventory, she wouldn't need to worry about this assumption as long as she didn't allow her inventory levels to fluctuate too much.

5. Kay sells just one size poster, so her sales mix is constant at 100% art posters. Later, we'll expand her product line to include two different size posters—each with a different sales price and variable cost. The resulting CVP modification works for any firm that offers two or more products as long as it assumes that sales mix will remain constant.

Kay's business meets all five assumptions, so her CVP analysis will be accurate. Because most business conditions do not meet these assumptions *perfectly*, managers regard CVP analysis as approximate, not exact.

The Unit Contribution Margin

Calculate the unit contribution margin and the contribution margin ratio

The last chapter introduced the **contribution margin income statement**, which separates costs by behavior rather than function. Many managers prefer the contribution margin income statement because it gives them the information for CVP analysis in a "ready-to-use" format. On these income statements, the contribution margin is the "dividing line"—all variable expenses go above the line, and all fixed expenses go below the line. The results of Kay's first month of operations is shown in Exhibit 7-2.

EXHIBIT 7-2	**Contribution Margin Income Statement**

KAY PAK POSTERS
Contribution Margin Income Statement
Month Ended August 31

Sales revenue (550 posters)	$ 19,250
Less: Variable expenses	(11,550)
Contribution margin	7,700
Less: Fixed expenses	(7,000)
Operating income	$ 700

Notice that the **contribution margin** is the excess of sales revenue over variable expenses. The contribution margin tells managers how much revenue is left—after paying variable expenses—for *contributing* toward covering fixed costs and then generating a profit. Hence the name contribution margin.

The contribution margin is stated as a *total* amount on the contribution margin income statement. However, managers often state the contribution margin on a *per unit* basis and as a *percentage,* or *ratio.* A product's **contribution margin per unit**— or **unit contribution margin**—is the excess of the selling price per unit over the variable cost of obtaining *and* selling each unit. Some businesses pay a sales commission on each unit or have other variable costs, such as shipping costs, for each unit sold. However, Kay's variable cost per unit is simply the price she pays for each poster. Therefore, her unit contribution margin is:

Sales price per poster	$35
Less: Variable cost per poster	(21)
Contribution margin per poster	$14

The unit contribution margin indicates how much profit each unit provides *before* fixed costs are considered. Each unit *first* contributes this profit toward covering the firm's fixed costs. Once the company sells enough units to cover its fixed costs, the unit contribution margin contributes *directly* to profit. For example, every poster Kay sells generates $14 of contribution margin that can be used to pay for the monthly $7,000 of fixed costs. After Kay sells enough posters to cover fixed costs, each additional poster she sells will generate $14 of operating income.

Managers can use the unit contribution margin to quickly forecast income at any volume within their relevant range. First, they project the total contribution margin by multiplying the unit contribution margin by the number of units sold. Then, they simply subtract fixed costs. For example, let's assume that Kay hopes to sell 650 posters next month. She can project her operating income as follows:

Contribution margin (650 posters × $14 per poster)	$9,100
Less: Fixed expenses	(7,000)
Operating income	$2,100

If Kay sells 650 posters next month, her operating income should be $2,100.

The Contribution Margin Ratio

In addition to computing the unit contribution margin, managers often compute the **contribution margin ratio,** which is the ratio of contribution margin to sales revenue. Kay can compute her contribution margin ratio at the unit level as follows:

$$\text{Contribution margin ratio} = \frac{\text{Unit contribution margin}}{\text{Sales price per unit}} = \frac{\$14}{\$35} = 40\%$$

Kay could also compute the contribution margin ratio using any volume of sales. Let's use her current sales volume, pictured in Exhibit 7-2:

$$\text{Contribution margin ratio} = \frac{\text{Contribution margin}}{\text{Sales revenue}} = \frac{\$7,700}{\$19,250} = 40\%$$

The 40% contribution margin ratio means that each *$1.00* of sales revenue contributes $0.40 toward fixed expenses and profit, as shown in Exhibit 7-3. The remaining $0.60 of each sales dollar is used to pay for variable costs. *The contribution margin ratio is the percentage of each sales dollar that is available for covering fixed expenses and generating a profit.*

BBH CHAPTER 7

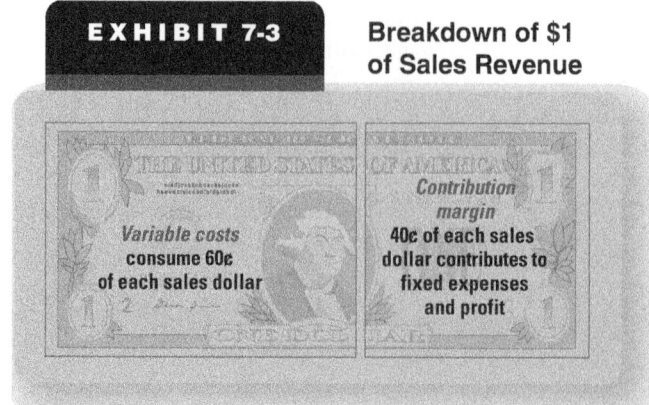

EXHIBIT 7-3 Breakdown of $1 of Sales Revenue

Variable costs consume 60¢ of each sales dollar

Contribution margin 40¢ of each sales dollar contributes to fixed expenses and profit

Managers can also use the contribution margin ratio to quickly forecast operating income within their relevant range. When using the contribution margin ratio, managers project income based on sales *dollars* rather than sales *units*. For example, what will Kay's income be if sales revenue reaches $70,000 one month? To find out, simply multiply projected sales revenue by the contribution margin ratio to get the total contribution margin. Then, subtract fixed expenses:

Contribution margin ($70,000 sales × 40%) =....................	$28,000
Less: Fixed expenses..	(7,000)
Operating income...	$21,000

Let's verify. If Kay has $70,000 of sales revenue, she has sold 2,000 posters ($70,000 ÷ $35 price per poster). Her complete contribution margin income statement would be calculated as follows:

Sales revenue (2,000 posters × $35/poster)...........................	$70,000
Less: Variable expenses (2,000 posters × $21/poster)...........	(42,000)
Contribution margin (2,000 posters × $14/poster)...............	$28,000
Less: Fixed expenses...	(7,000)
Operating income..	$21,000

The contribution margin per unit and contribution margin ratio help managers quickly and easily project income at different sales volumes. However, when projecting profits, managers must keep in mind the relevant range. For instance, if Kay wants to project income at a volume of 5,000 posters, she shouldn't use the existing contribution margin and fixed costs. Her current relevant range extends to only 2,000 posters per month. At a higher volume of sales, her variable cost per unit may be lower than $21 (due to volume discounts from her suppliers) and her monthly fixed costs may be higher than $7,000 (due to upgrading her system and hiring an employee to handle the extra sales volume).

Rather than use individual unit contribution margins on each of their products, large companies that offer hundreds or thousands of products (like art.com) use their contribution margin *ratio* to predict profits. As long as the sales mix remains constant (one of our CVP assumptions), the contribution margin ratio will remain constant.

We've seen how managers use the contribution margin to project income; but managers use the contribution margin for other purposes too, such as motivating the sales force. Salespeople who know the contribution margin of each product can generate more profit by emphasizing high-margin products. This is why many companies base sales commissions on the contribution margins produced by sales rather than on sales revenue alone.

In the next section, we'll see how managers use the contribution margin in CVP analysis to determine their breakeven point and to determine how many units they need to sell to reach target profits.

Using CVP Analysis to Find the Breakeven Point

A company's **breakeven point** is the sales level at which *operating income is zero.* Sales below the breakeven point result in a loss. Sales above the breakeven point provide a profit. Before Kay started her business, she wanted to figure out how many posters she would have to sell just to break even.

There are three ways to calculate the breakeven point. All of the approaches are based on the income statement, so they all reach the same conclusion. The first two methods find breakeven in terms of sales *units.* The last approach finds breakeven in terms of sales *dollars.*

1. The income statement approach

2. The shortcut approach using the *unit* contribution margin

3. The shortcut approach using the contribution margin *ratio*

Let's examine these three approaches in detail.

2 Use CVP analysis to find breakeven points and target profit volumes

The Income Statement Approach

The income statement approach simply breaks the income statement equation into smaller components:

SALES REVENUE	−	VARIABLE EXPENSES	− FIXED EXPENSES	= OPERATING INCOME
$\left(\dfrac{\text{Sales price}}{\text{per unit}} \times \text{Units sold}\right)$ −		$\left(\dfrac{\text{Variable cost}}{\text{per unit}} \times \text{Units sold}\right)$ −	Fixed expenses	= Operating income

Let's use this approach to find Kay's breakeven point. Recall that Kay sells her posters for $35 each and that her variable cost is $21 per poster. Kay's fixed expenses total $7,000. At the breakeven point, operating income is zero. We use this information to solve the income statement equation for the number of posters Kay must sell to break even.

SALES REVENUE	−	VARIABLE EXPENSES	− FIXED EXPENSES	= OPERATING INCOME
$\left(\dfrac{\text{Sales price}}{\text{per unit}} \times \text{Units sold}\right)$ −		$\left(\dfrac{\text{Variable cost}}{\text{per unit}} \times \text{Units sold}\right)$ −	Fixed expenses	= Operating income
($35 × Units sold) −		($21 × Units sold) −	$7,000	= $0
($35	−	$21) × Units sold −	$7,000	= $0
		$14 × Units sold		= $7,000
		Units sold		= $7,000/$14
		Sales in units		= 500 posters

Kay must sell 500 posters to break even. Her breakeven point in sales dollars is $17,500 (500 posters × $35).

You can check your answer by substituting the breakeven number of units into the income statement and checking that this level of sales results in zero profit:

Sales revenue (500 posters × $35)...	$17,500
Less: Variable expenses (500 posters × $21).........................	(10,500)
Contribution margin	$ 7,000
Less: Fixed expenses...	(7,000)
Operating income..	$ 0

Notice that at breakeven, a firm's fixed expenses equal its contribution margin. In other words, the firm has generated just enough contribution margin to cover its fixed expenses (but *not* enough to generate a profit).

The Shortcut Approach Using the Unit Contribution Margin

The shortcut method simply rearranges the income statement equation and isolates "Units sold" on the left:

$$\text{Sales revenue} - \text{Variable expenses} - \text{Fixed expenses} = \text{Operating income}$$

$$\underbrace{\text{Contribution margin}} - \text{Fixed expenses} = \text{Operating income}$$

$$(\text{Contribution margin per unit} \times \text{Units sold}) = \text{Fixed expenses} + \text{Operating income}$$

Dividing both sides of the equation by contribution margin per unit yields the shortcut method:

$$\text{Sales in units} = \frac{\text{Fixed expenses} + \text{Operating income}}{\text{Contribution margin per unit}}$$

Kay can use this shortcut method to find her breakeven point in units. Kay's fixed expenses total $7,000, and her unit contribution margin is $14. At the breakeven point, operating income is zero. Thus, Kay's breakeven point in units is:

$$\text{Sales in units} = \frac{\$7,000 + \$0}{\$14}$$
$$= 500 \text{ posters}$$

Why does this shortcut method work? Recall that each poster provides $14 of contribution margin. To break even, Kay must generate enough contribution margin to cover $7,000 of fixed expenses. At the rate of $14 per poster, Kay must sell 500 posters ($7,000/$14) to cover her $7,000 of fixed expenses. Because the shortcut method simply rearranges the income statement equation, the breakeven point is the same under both methods (500 posters).

Stop & Think...

What would Kay's operating income be if she sold 501 posters? What would it be if she sold 600 posters?

Answer: Every poster sold provides $14 of contribution margin, which first contributes toward covering fixed costs, then profit. Once Kay reaches her breakeven point (500 posters), she has covered all fixed costs. Therefore, each additional poster sold after the breakeven point contributes $14 *directly to profit*. If Kay sells 501 posters, she has sold one more poster than breakeven. Her operating income is $14. If she sells 600 posters, she has sold 100 more posters than breakeven. Her operating income is $1,400 ($14 per poster × 100 posters). We can verify as follows:

Contribution margin (600 posters × $14 per poster)	$8,400
Less: Fixed expenses	(7,000)
Operating income	$1,400

Once a company achieves breakeven, each additional unit sold contributes its unique unit contribution margin directly to profit.

The Shortcut Approach Using the Contribution Margin Ratio

It's easy to compute the breakeven point in *units* for a simple business like Kay's that has only one product. But what about companies that have thousands of products such as art.com, Home Depot, and Amazon.com? It doesn't make sense for these companies to determine the number of each various product they need to sell to break even. Can you imagine a Home Depot manager describing breakeven as 100,000 wood screws, 2 million nails, 3,000 lawn mowers, 10,000 gallons of paint, and so forth? It simply doesn't make sense. Therefore, multiproduct companies usually compute breakeven in terms of *sales dollars*.

This shortcut approach differs from the other shortcut we've just seen in only one way: Fixed expenses plus operating income are divided by the contribution margin *ratio* (not by contribution margin *per unit*) to yield sales in *dollars* (not *units*):

$$\text{Sales in dollars} = \frac{\text{Fixed expenses} + \text{Operating income}}{\text{Contribution margin ratio}}$$

Recall that Kay's contribution margin ratio is 40%. At the breakeven point, operating income is $0, so Kay's breakeven point in sales dollars is:

$$\text{Sales in units} = \frac{\$7,000 + \$0}{0.40}$$
$$= \$17,500$$

This is the same breakeven sales revenue we calculated earlier (500 posters × $35 sales price = $17,500).

Why does the contribution margin ratio formula work? Each dollar of Kay's sales contributes $0.40 to fixed expenses and profit. To break even, she must generate enough contribution margin at the rate of $0.40 per sales dollar to cover the $7,000 fixed expenses ($7,000 ÷ 0.40 = $17,500).

> *To recall which shortcut formula gives which result, remember this: Dividing fixed costs by the **unit** contribution margin provides breakeven in sales **units**. Dividing fixed costs by the contribution margin **ratio** provides breakeven in sales **dollars**.*

Stop & Think...

Suppose Amazon.com's total revenues are $4.5 billion, its variable expenses are $3.15 billion, and its fixed expenses are $1.1 billion. What is the breakeven point in sales dollars?

Answer: We can use the shortcut approach that uses the contribution margin ratio to determine the breakeven point. First, we compute the contribution margin ratio: The contribution margin ratio is 30% [($4.5 − $3.15) ÷ $4.5]. Then, we use the ratio in the shortcut formula:

$$
\begin{aligned}
\text{Sales in dollars} &= \frac{\text{Fixed expenses} + \text{Operating income}}{\text{Contribution margin ratio}} \\[6pt]
&= \frac{\$1.1 \text{ billion} + \$0}{0.30} \\[6pt]
&= \$3.667 \text{ billion (rounded)}
\end{aligned}
$$

Amazon.com must achieve sales revenue of $3.667 billion just to break even.

Using CVP to Plan Profits

For established products and services, managers are more interested in the sales level needed to earn a target profit than in the breakeven point. Managers of new business ventures are also interested in the profits they can expect to earn. For example, Kay doesn't want to just break even—she wants her business to be her sole source of income. She would like the business to earn $4,900 of profit each month. How many posters must Kay sell each month to reach her target profit?

How Much Must We Sell to Earn a Target Profit?

The only difference from our prior analysis is that instead of determining the sales level needed for *zero profit* (breakeven), Kay now wants to know how many posters she must sell to earn a $4,900 profit. We can use the income statement approach or the shortcut approach to find the answer. Because Kay wants to know the number of *units*, we'll use the shortcut approach based on the *unit* contribution margin. This time, instead of an operating income of zero (breakeven), we'll insert Kay's target operating income of $4,900:

$$\text{Sales in } units = \frac{\text{Fixed expenses + Operating income}}{\text{Contribution margin } per\ unit}$$

$$= \frac{\$7,000 + \$4,900}{\$14}$$

$$= \frac{\$11,900}{\$14}$$

$$= 850 \text{ posters}$$

This analysis shows that Kay must sell 850 posters each month to earn profits of $4,900 a month. Notice that this level of sales falls within Kay's current relevant range (0–2,000 posters per month), so the conclusion that she would earn $4,900 of income at this sales volume is valid. If the calculation resulted in a sales volume outside the current relevant range (greater than 2,000 units), we would need to reassess our cost assumptions.

Assume that Kay also wants to know how much sales revenue she needs to earn $4,900 of monthly profit. Because she already knows the number of units needed (850), she can easily translate this volume into sales revenue:

$$850 \text{ posters} \times \$35 \text{ sales price/poster} = \$29,750 \text{ sales revenue}$$

If Kay only wanted to know the sales revenue needed to achieve her target profit rather than the number of units needed, she could have found the answer directly by using the shortcut approach based on the contribution margin *ratio*:

$$\text{Sales in } dollars = \frac{\text{Fixed expenses + Operating income}}{\text{Contribution margin } ratio}$$

$$= \frac{\$7,000 + \$4,900}{0.40}$$

$$= \frac{\$11,900}{0.40}$$

$$= \$29,750$$

Finally, Kay could have used the income statement approach to find the same answers:

SALES REVENUE	–	VARIABLE EXPENSES	–	FIXED EXPENSES	=	OPERATING INCOME
($35 × Units sold)	–	($21 × Units sold)	–	$7,000	=	$4,900
($35	–	$21) × Units sold	–	$7,000	=	$4,900
		$14 × Units sold			=	$11,900
				Units sold	=	$11,900/$14
				Units sold	=	850 posters

We can prove that our answers (from any of the three approaches) are correct by preparing Kay's income statment for a sales volume of 850 units:

Sales revenue (850 posters × \$35).....................................	\$29,750
Less: Variable expenses (850 posters × \$21).............................	(17,850)
Contribution margin	11,900
Less: Fixed expenses...	(7,000)
Operating income...	\$ 4,900

Graphing CVP Relationships

By graphing the CVP relationships for her business, Kay can see at a glance how changes in the levels of sales will affect profits. As in the last chapter, the volume of units (posters) is placed on the horizontal *x*-axis; dollars, on the vertical *y*-axis. Then, she follows five steps to graph the CVP relations for her business, as illustrated in Exhibit 7-4.

EXHIBIT 7-4   **Cost-Volume-Profit Graph**

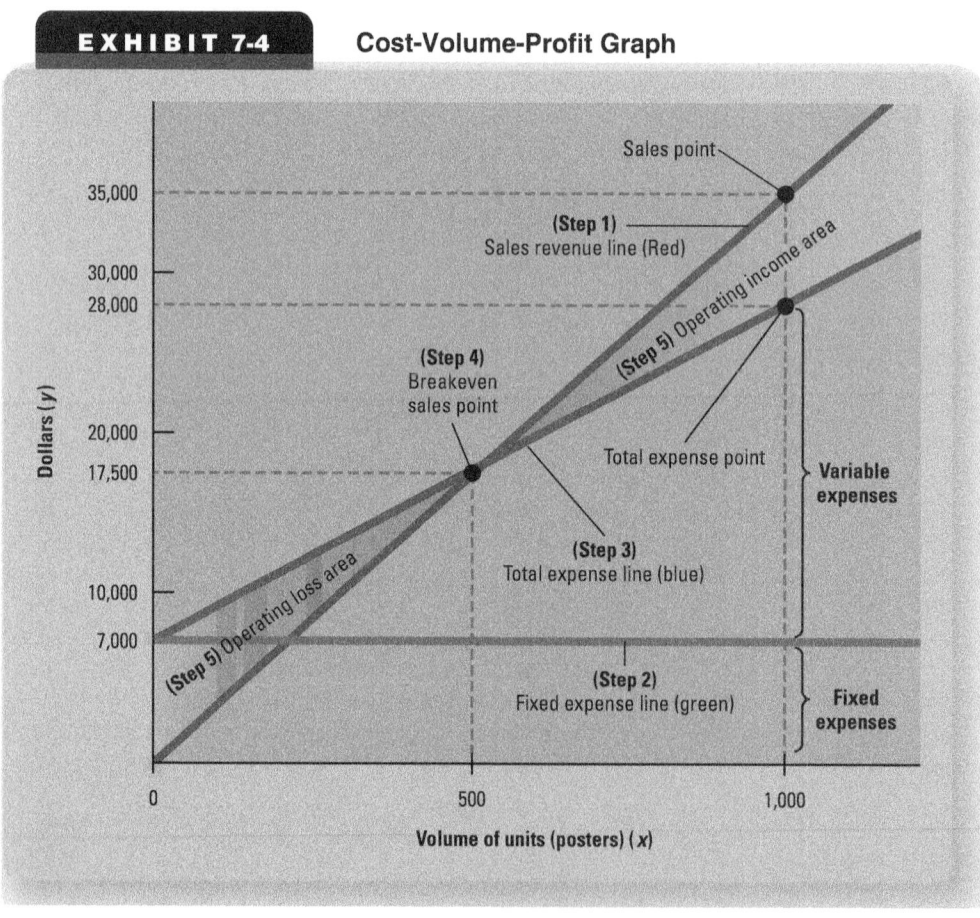

STEP 1: Choose a sales volume, such as 1,000 posters. Plot the point for total sales revenue at that volume: 1,000 posters × \$35 per poster = sales of \$35,000. Draw the *sales revenue line* from the origin (0) through the \$35,000 point. Why does the sales revenue line start at the origin? If Kay does not sell any posters, there is no sales revenue.

STEP 2: Draw the *fixed expense line*, a horizontal line that intersects the *y*-axis at \$7,000. Recall that the fixed expense line is flat because fixed

BBH CHAPTER 7

expenses are the same ($7,000) no matter how many posters Kay sells within her relevant range (up to 2,000 posters per month).

STEP 3: Draw the *total expense line*. Total expense is the sum of variable expense plus fixed expense. Thus, total expense is a *mixed* cost. So, the total expense line follows the form of the mixed cost line. Begin by computing variable expense at the chosen sales volume: 1,000 posters × $21 per poster = variable expense of $21,000. Add variable expense to fixed expense: $21,000 + $7,000 = $28,000. Plot the total expense point ($28,000) for 1,000 units. Then, draw a line through this point from the $7,000 fixed expense intercept on the dollars axis. This is the *total expense line*. Why does the total expense line start at the fixed expense line? If Kay sells no posters, she still incurs the $7,000 fixed cost for the server leasing, software, and office rental, but she incurs no variable costs.

STEP 4: Identify the *breakeven point*. The breakeven point is the point where the sales revenue line intersects the total expense line. This is the point where sales revenue equals total expenses. Our previous analyses told us that Kay's breakeven point is 500 posters, or $17,500 in sales. The graph shows this information visually.

STEP 5: Mark the *operating income* and the *operating loss* areas on the graph. To the left of the breakeven point, the total expense line lies above the sales revenue line. Expenses exceed sales revenue, leading to an operating loss. If Kay sells only 300 posters, she incurs an operating loss. The amount of the loss is the vertical distance between the total expense line and the sales revenue line:

Sales revenue – Variable expenses – Fixed expenses = Operating income (Loss)
(300 × $35) –   (300 × $21)   – $7,000   = $(2,800)

To the right of the breakeven point, the business earns a profit. The vertical distance between the sales revenue line and the total expense line equals income. Exhibit 7-4 shows that if Kay sells 1,000 posters, she earns operating income of $7,000 ($35,000 sales revenue − $28,000 total expenses).

Why bother with a graph? Why not just use the income statement approach or the shortcut contribution margin approach? Graphs like Exhibit 7-4 help managers quickly estimate the profit or loss earned at different levels of sales. The income statement and contribution margin approaches indicate income or loss for only a single sales amount.

Decision Guidelines

CVP ANALYSIS

Your friend wants to open her own ice cream parlor after college. She needs help making the following decisions:

Decision	Guidelines
How much will I earn on every ice cream cone I sell?	The unit contribution margin shows managers how much they earn on each unit sold after paying for variable costs *but before considering fixed expenses*. The unit

continued . . .

Decision	**Guidelines**
	contribution margin is the amount each unit earns that contributes toward covering fixed expenses and generating a profit. It is computed as: Sales price per unit Less: Variable cost per unit Contribution margin per unit The contribution margin ratio shows managers how much contribution margin is earned on every $1 of sales. It is computed as: $$\frac{\text{Contribution margin}}{\text{Sales revenue}} = \text{Contribution margin ratio}$$
Can I quickly forecast my income without creating a full income statement?	The contribution margin concept allows managers to forecast income quickly at different sales volumes. First, find the total contribution margin (by multiplying the forecasted number of units by the unit contribution margin *or* by multiplying the forecasted sales revenue by the contribution margin ratio) and then subtract all fixed expenses.
• How can I compute the *number of ice cream cones* I'll have to sell to break even or earn a target profit?	*Income Statement Approach:* 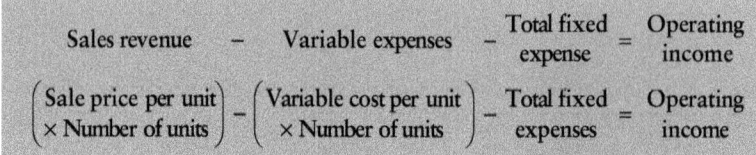 *Shortcut Unit Contribution Margin Approach:* $$\text{Sales in } \textit{units} = \frac{\text{Fixed expenses} + \text{Operating income}}{\text{Contribution margin } \textit{per unit}}$$
• How can I compute the *dollars of sales revenue* I'll have to generate to break even or earn a target profit?	*Shortcut Contribution Margin Ratio Approach:* $$\text{Sales in } \textit{dollars} = \frac{\text{Fixed expenses} + \text{Operating income}}{\text{Contribution margin } \textit{ratio}}$$
What will my profits look like over a range of volumes?	CVP graphs show managers, at a glance, how different sales volumes will affect profits.

Summary Problem 1

Fleet Foot buys hiking socks for $6 a pair and sells them for $10. Management budgets monthly fixed expenses of $10,000 for sales volumes between 0 and 12,000 pairs.

Requirements

1. Use the income statement approach and the shortcut unit contribution margin approach to compute monthly breakeven sales in units.

2. Use the shortcut contribution margin ratio approach to compute the breakeven point in sales dollars.

3. Compute the monthly sales level (in units) required to earn a target operating income of $14,000. Use either the income statement approach or the shortcut contribution margin approach.

4. Prepare a graph of Fleet Foot's CVP relationships, similar to Exhibit 7-4. Draw the sales revenue line, the fixed expense line, and the total expense line. Label the axes, the breakeven point, the operating income area, and the operating loss area.

Solution

Requirement 1
Income statement approach:

Sales revenue	−	Variable expenses	−	Fixed expenses	=	Operating income
$\left(\dfrac{\text{Sale price}}{\text{per unit}} \times \dfrac{\text{Units}}{\text{sold}}\right)$	−	$\left(\dfrac{\text{Variable}}{\text{cost per unit}} \times \dfrac{\text{Units}}{\text{sold}}\right)$	−	Fixed expenses	=	Operating income
($10 × Units sold)	−	($6 × Units sold)	−	$10,000	=	$0
($10	−	$6) × Units sold			=	$10,000
		$4 × Units sold			=	$10,000
		Units sold			=	$10,000 ÷ $4
		Breakeven sales in units			=	2,500 units

Shortcut unit contribution margin approach:

$$\text{Sales in units} = \frac{\text{Fixed expenses} + \text{Operating income}}{\text{Contribution margin per unit}}$$

$$= \frac{\$10,000 + \$0}{\$10 - \$6}$$

$$= \frac{\$10,000}{\$4}$$

$$= 2,500 \text{ units}$$

Requirement 2

$$\text{Sales in dollars} = \frac{\text{Fixed expenses} + \text{Operating income}}{\text{Contribution margin ratio}}$$

$$= \frac{\$10,000 + \$0}{0.40^*}$$

$$= \$25,000$$

$$^*\text{Contribution margin ratio} = \frac{\text{Contribution margin per unit}}{\text{Sale price per unit}} = \frac{\$4}{\$10} = 0.40$$

Requirement 3

Income statement equation approach:

Sales revenue	−	Variable expenses	−	Fixed expenses	=	Operating income
$\left(\begin{array}{c}\text{Sale price}\\ \text{per unit}\end{array} \times \begin{array}{c}\text{Units}\\ \text{sold}\end{array}\right)$	−	$\left(\begin{array}{c}\text{Variable}\\ \text{cost per unit}\end{array} \times \begin{array}{c}\text{Units}\\ \text{sold}\end{array}\right)$	−	Fixed expenses	=	Operating income
($10 × Units sold)	−	($6 × Units sold)	−	$10,000	=	$14,000
($10	−	$6) × Units sold			=	$10,000 + $14,000
		$4 × Units sold			=	$24,000
		Units sold			=	$24,000 ÷ $4
		Units sold			=	6,000 units

Shortcut unit contribution margin approach:

$$\text{Sales in units} = \frac{\text{Fixed expenses} + \text{Operating income}}{\text{Contribution margin per unit}}$$

$$= \frac{\$10,000 + \$14,000}{\left(\$10 - \$6\right)}$$

$$= \frac{\$24,000}{\$4}$$

$$= 6000 \text{ units}$$

Requirement 4

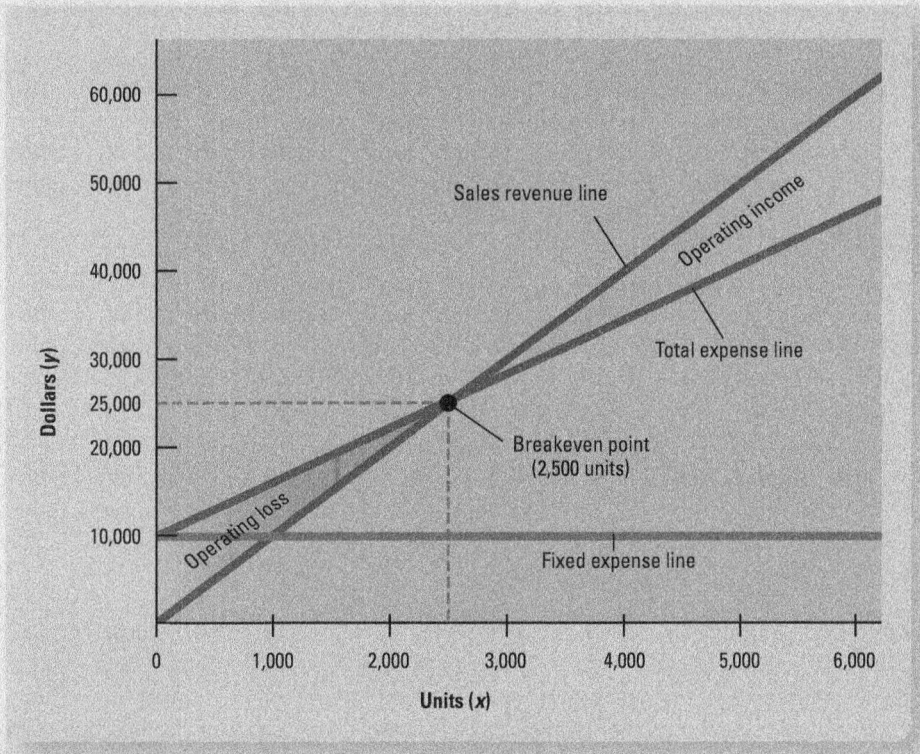

Using CVP When Business Conditions Change

3 Perform sensitivity analysis in response to changing business conditions

In today's fast-changing business world, managers need to quickly estimate how changes in sales price, costs, or volume affect profits. In a recent drive to increase profitability, Starbucks analyzed the profitability of each product at the store level. Then, it realigned prices. For example, coffee mugs and CDs had been money losers, so it raised the prices of these items.

To predict how raising or lowering prices will affect profits, managers use CVP to conduct **sensitivity analysis**. Sensitivity analysis is a "what-if" technique that asks what results will be if actual prices or costs change or if an underlying assumption such as sales mix changes. For example, increased competition may force Kay to lower her sales price, while at the same time her suppliers increase poster costs. How will these changes affect Kay's breakeven and target profit volumes? What will happen if Kay changes her sales mix by offering posters in two different sizes? How will she modify her CVP analysis? We'll tackle these issues next.

Changing the Sales Price

Let's assume that Kay has now been in business for several months. Because of competition, Kay is considering cutting her sales price to $31 per poster. If her variable expenses remain $21 per poster and her fixed expenses stay at $7,000, how many posters will she need to sell to break even? To answer this question, Kay calculates a new unit contribution margin using the new sales price:

New sales price per poster..	$31
Less: Variable cost per poster..	(21)
New contribution margin per poster	$10

She then uses the new unit contribution margin to compute breakeven sales in units:

$$\text{Sales in units} = \frac{\text{Fixed expenses} + \text{Operating income}}{\text{Contribution margin per unit}}$$

$$= \frac{\$7,000 + \$0}{\$10}$$

$$= 700 \text{ posters}$$

With the original $35 sale price, Kay's breakeven point was 500 posters. If Kay lowers the sales price to $31 per poster, her breakeven point increases to 700 posters. The lower sales price means that each poster contributes *less* toward fixed expenses ($10 versus $14 before the price change), so Kay must sell 200 *more* posters to break even. Each dollar of sales revenue would contribute $0.32 ($10/$31) rather than $0.40 toward covering fixed expenses and generating a profit.

If Kay reduces her sales price to $31, how many posters must she sell to achieve her $4,900 monthly target profit? Kay again uses the new unit contribution margin to determine how many posters she will need to sell to reach her profit goals:

$$\text{Sales in units} = \frac{\$7{,}000 + \$4{,}900}{\$10}$$
$$= 1{,}190 \text{ posters}$$

With the original sales price, Kay needed to sell only 850 posters per month to achieve her target profit level. If Kay cuts her sales price (and, therefore, her contribution margin), she must sell more posters to achieve her financial goals. Kay could have found these same results using the income statement approach. Exhibit 7-5 shows the effect of changes in sales price on breakeven and target profit volumes.

EXHIBIT 7-5   **The Effect of Changes in Sales Price on Breakeven and Target Profit Volumes**

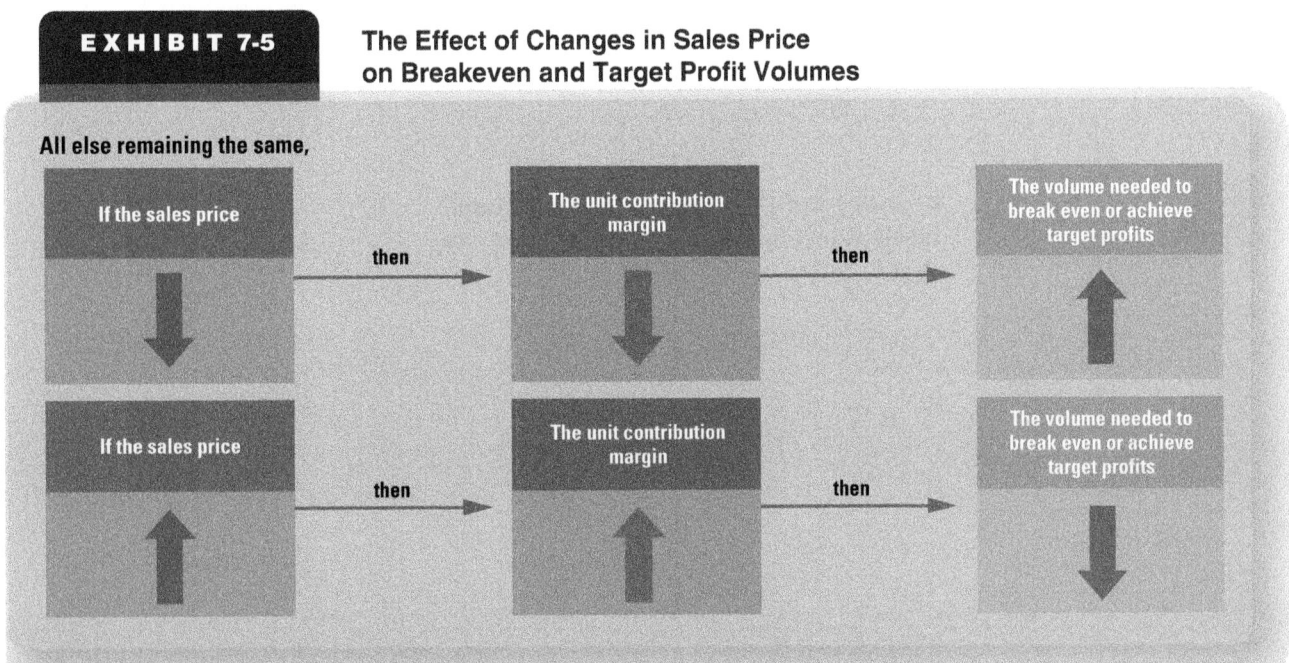

Stop & Think...

Kay believes she could dominate the e-commerce art poster business if she cut the sales price to $20. Is this a good idea?

Answer: No. The variable cost per poster is $21. If Kay sells posters for $20 each, she loses $1 on each poster. Kay will incur a loss if the sales price is less than the variable cost.

Changing Variable Costs

Let's assume that Kay does *not* lower her sales price. However, Kay's supplier raises his price for each poster to $23.80 (instead of the original $21). Kay does not want to pass this increase on to her customers, so she holds her sales price at the original

$35 per poster. Her fixed costs remain $7,000. How many posters must she sell to break even after her supplier raises his prices? Kay's new contribution margin per unit drops to $11.20 ($35 sales price per poster − $23.80 variable cost per poster). So, her new breakeven point is:

$$\text{Sales in units} = \frac{\text{Fixed expenses} + \text{Operating income}}{\text{Contribution margin per unit}}$$
$$= \frac{\$7,000 + \$0}{\$11.20}$$
$$= 625 \text{ posters}$$

Higher variable costs per unit have the same effect as lower selling prices per unit—they both reduce the product's unit contribution margin. As a result, Kay will have to sell *more* units to break even and achieve target profits. As shown in Exhibit 7-6, a *decrease* in variable costs would have just the opposite effect. Lower variable costs increase the contribution margin each poster provides and, therefore, lowers the breakeven point.

EXHIBIT 7-6 **The Effect of Changes in Variable Costs on Breakeven and Target Profit Volumes**

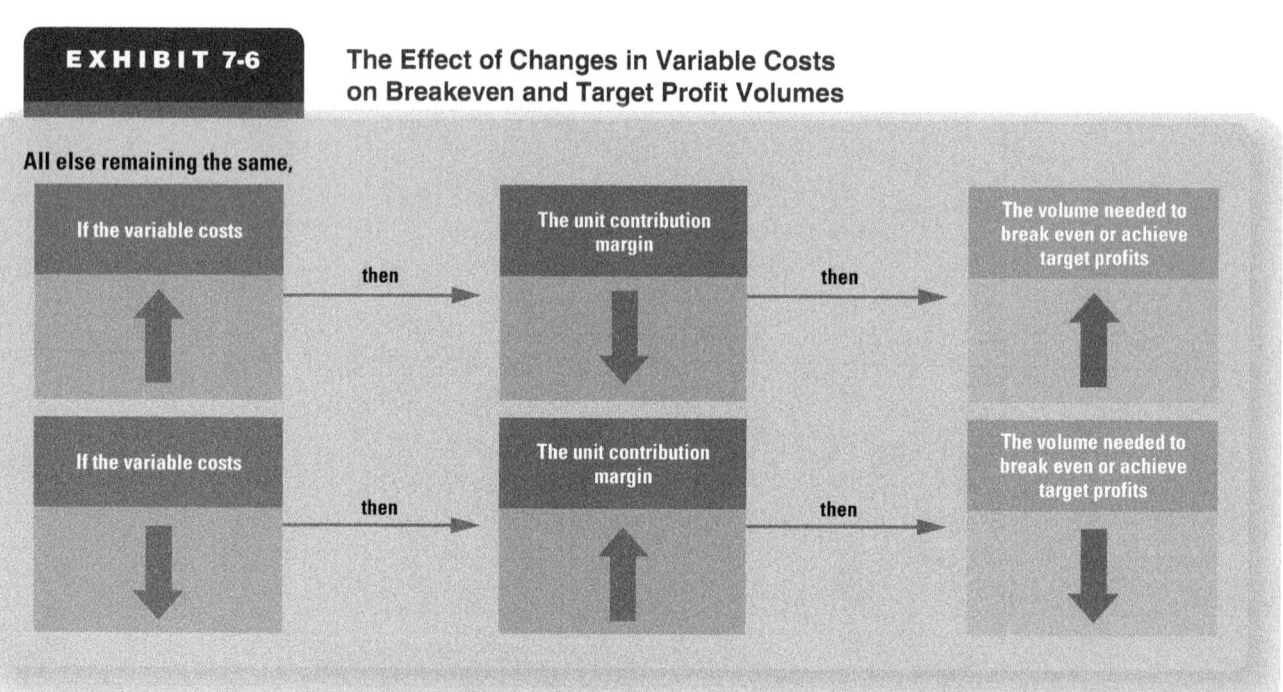

Stop & Think...

Suppose Kay is squeezed from both sides: Her supply costs have increased to $23.80 per poster, yet she must lower her price to $31 in order to compete. Under these conditions, how many posters will Kay need to sell to achieve her monthly target profit of $4,900? If Kay doesn't think she can sell that many posters, how else might she attempt to achieve her profit goals?

Answer: Kay is now in a position faced by many companies—her unit contribution margin is squeezed by both higher supply costs and lower sales prices:

New sales price per poster..	$31.00
Less: New variable cost per poster	(23.80)
New contribution margin per poster	$ 7.20

Kay's new contribution margin is about half of what it was when she started her business ($14). To achieve her target profit, her volume will have to increase dramatically (yet, it would still fall within her current relevant range for fixed costs—which extends to 2,000 posters per month):

$$\text{Sales in units} = \frac{\text{Fixed expenses} + \text{Operating income}}{\text{Contribution margin per unit}}$$

$$= \frac{\$7,000 + \$4,900}{\$7.20}$$

$$= 1,653 \text{ posters (rounded)}$$

Based on her current volume, Kay may not believe she can sell so many posters. To maintain a reasonable profit level, Kay may need to take other measures. For example, she may try to find a different supplier with lower poster costs. She may also attempt to lower her fixed costs. For example, perhaps she could negotiate a cheaper lease on her office space or move her business to a less expensive location. She could also try to increase her volume by spending *more* on fixed costs, such as advertising. Kay could also investigate selling other products, in addition to her regular-size posters, that would have higher unit contribution margins. We'll discuss these measures next.

Changing Fixed Costs

Let's return to Kay's original data ($35 selling price and $21 variable cost). Kay has decided she really doesn't need a storefront office at the retail strip mall because she doesn't have many walk-in customers. She could decrease her monthly fixed costs from $7,000 to $4,200 by moving her office to an industrial park.

How will this decrease in fixed costs affect Kay's breakeven point? *Changes in fixed costs do not affect the contribution margin.* Therefore, Kay's unit contribution margin is still $14 per poster. However, her breakeven point changes because her fixed costs change:

$$\text{Sales in units} = \frac{\text{Fixed expenses} + \text{Operating income}}{\text{Contribution margin per unit}}$$

$$= \frac{\$4,200 + \$0}{\$14.00}$$

$$= 300 \text{ posters}$$

Because of the decrease in fixed costs, Kay will need to sell only 300 posters, rather than 500 posters, to break even. The volume needed to achieve her monthly $4,900 target profit will also decline. However, if Kay's fixed costs *increase*, she will have to sell *more* units to break even. Exhibit 7-7 shows the effect of changes in fixed costs on breakeven and target profit volumes.

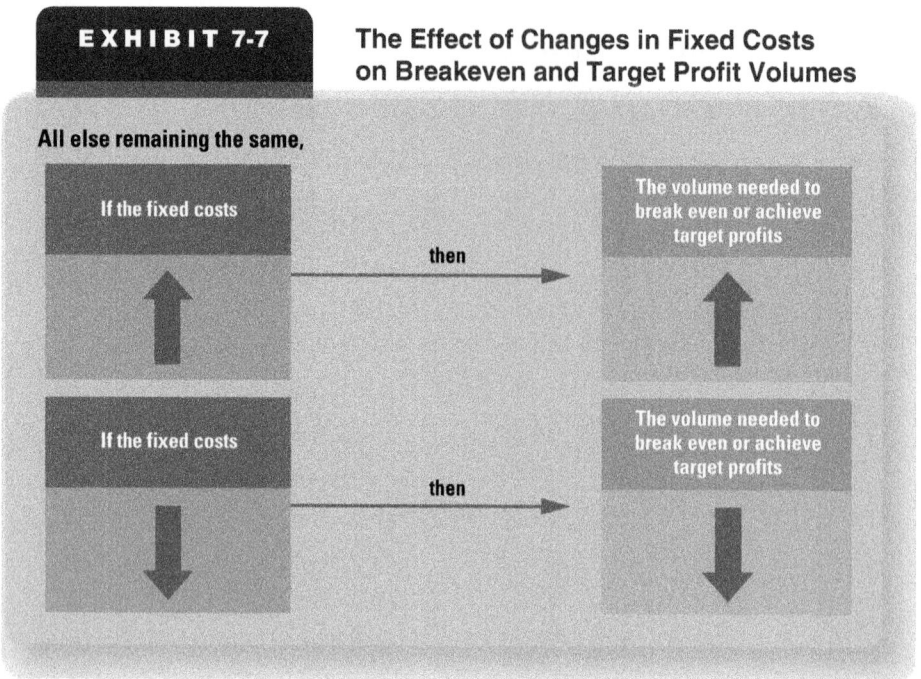

EXHIBIT 7-7 The Effect of Changes in Fixed Costs on Breakeven and Target Profit Volumes

We have seen that changes in sales prices, variable costs, and fixed costs can have dramatic effects on the volume of product that companies must sell to achieve breakeven and target profits. Companies often turn to automation to decrease variable costs (direct labor); but this, in turn, increases their fixed costs (equipment depreciation). Companies often move production overseas to decrease variable and fixed production costs, feeling forced to take these measures to keep their prices as low as their competitors. For example, Charbroil, the maker of gas grills, said that if it didn't move production overseas, profits would decline, or worse yet, the company would go out of business.

Pages 381–384 intentionally omitted

BBH CHAPTER 7

Risk Indicators

A firm's level of risk depends on many factors, including the general health of the economy and the specific industry in which the company operates. In addition, a firm's risk depends on its current volume of sales and the relative amount of fixed and variable costs that make up its total costs. Next, we discuss how a firm can gauge its level of risk, to some extent, by its margin of safety and its operating leverage.

5 Determine a firm's margin of safety and operating leverage

Margin of Safety

The **margin of safety** is the excess of expected sales over breakeven sales. This is the "cushion," or drop in sales, the company can absorb without incurring a loss. The higher the margin of safety, the greater the cushion against loss and the less risky the business plan. Managers use the margin of safety to evaluate the risk of current operations as well as the risk of new plans.

Let's continue to assume that Kay has been in business for several months and that she generally sells 950 posters a month. Kay's breakeven point in our original data is 500 posters. Kay can express her margin of safety in units or in sales dollars:

$$\text{Margin of safety in units} = \text{Expected sales in units} - \text{Breakeven sales in units}$$
$$= \quad 950 \text{ posters} \quad - \quad 500 \text{ posters}$$
$$= \quad 450 \text{ posters}$$

$$\text{Margin of safety in dollars} = \text{Margin of safety in units} \times \text{Sale price per unit}$$
$$= \quad 450 \text{ posters} \quad \times \quad \$35$$
$$= \quad \$15{,}750$$

Sales can drop by 450 posters, or \$15,750 a month, before Kay incurs a loss. This is a comfortable margin.

Managers can also compute the margin of safety as a percentage of sales. Simply divide the margin of safety by sales. We obtain the same percentage whether we use units or dollars.

In units:

$$\text{Margin of safety as a percentage} = \frac{\text{Margin of safety in units}}{\text{Expected sales in units}}$$
$$= \frac{450 \text{ posters}}{950 \text{ posters}}$$
$$= 47.4\% \text{ (rounded)}$$

In dollars:

$$\text{Margin of safety as a percentage} = \frac{\text{Margin of safety in dollars}}{\text{Expected sales in dollars}}$$
$$= \frac{450 \text{ units} \times \$35}{950 \text{ units} \times \$35}$$
$$= \frac{\$15{,}750}{\$33{,}250}$$
$$= 47.4\% \text{ (rounded)}$$

BBH   CHAPTER 7

The margin of safety percentage tells Kay that sales would have to drop by more than 47.4% before she would incur a loss. If sales fall by less than 47.4%, she would still earn a profit. If sales fall exactly 47.4%, she would break even. This ratio tells Kay that her business plan is not unduly risky.

Operating Leverage

A company's **operating leverage** refers to the relative amount of fixed and variable costs that make up its total costs. Most companies have both fixed and variable costs. However, companies with *high* operating leverage have *relatively more fixed costs* and relatively fewer variable costs. Companies with high operating leverage include golf courses, airlines, and hotels. Because they have fewer variable costs, their contribution margin ratio is relatively high. Recall from the last chapter that Embassy Suites' variable cost of servicing each guest is low, which means that the hotel has a high contribution margin and high operating leverage.

What does high operating leverage have to do with risk? If sales volume decreases, the total contribution margin will drop significantly because each sales dollar contains a high percentage of contribution margin. Yet, the high fixed costs of running the company remain. Therefore, the operating income of these companies can easily turn from profit to loss if sales volume declines. For example, airlines were financially devastated after September 11, 2001, because the number of people flying suddenly dropped, creating large reductions in contribution margin. Yet, the airlines had to continue paying their high fixed costs. High operating leverage companies are at *more* risk because their income declines drastically when sales volume declines.

What if the economy is growing and sales volume *increases*? High operating leverage companies will reap high rewards. Remember that after breakeven, each unit sold contributes its unit contribution margin directly to profit. Because high operating leverage companies have high contribution margin ratios, each additional dollar of sale will contribute more to the firm's operating income. Exhibit 7-8 summarizes these characteristics.

EXHIBIT 7-8   **Characteristics of High Operating Leverage Firms**

- High operating leverage companies have:
  —*Higher* levels of fixed costs and *lower* levels of variable costs
  —*Higher* contribution margin ratios
- For high operating leverage companies, changes in volume significantly affect operating income, so they face:
  —*Higher* risk
  —*Higher* potential for reward
Examples include golf courses, hotels, rental car agencies, theme parks, airlines, cruise lines

---

However, companies with low operating leverage have relatively *fewer* fixed costs and relatively *more* variable costs. For example, retailers incur significant levels of fixed costs, but more of every sales dollar is used to pay for the merchandise (a variable cost), so less ends up as contribution margin. If sales volume declines, these companies have relatively fewer fixed costs to cover, so they are at *less* risk of incurring a loss. If sales volume increases, their relatively small contribution margins ratios add to the bottom line, but in smaller increments. Therefore, they reap less reward than high operating leverage companies experiencing the same volume increases. *In other words, at low operating leverage companies, changes in sales volume do not have as much impact on operating income as they do at high operating leverage companies.* Exhibit 7-9 summarizes these characteristics.

EXHIBIT 7-9 **Characteristics of Low Operating Leverage Companies**

- Low operating leverage companies have:
    - —*Higher* levels of variable costs and *lower* levels of fixed costs
    - —*Lower* contribution margin ratios
- For low operating leverage companies, changes in volume do NOT have as significant an effect on operating income, so they face:
    - —*Lower* risk
    - —*Lower* potential for reward

Examples include merchandising companies.

A company's **operating leverage factor** tells us how responsive a company's operating income is to changes in volume. The greater the operating leverage factors, the greater the impact a change in sales volume has on operating income.

The operating leverage factor, at a given level of sales, is calculated as:

$$\text{Operating leverage factor} = \frac{\text{Contribution margin}}{\text{Operating income}}$$

Why do we say, "at a given level of sales"? A company's operating leverage factor will depend, to some extent, on the sales level used to calculate the contribution margin and operating income. Most companies compute the operating leverage factor at their current or expected volume of sales, which is what we'll do in our examples.

What does the operating leverage factor tell us?

The operating leverage factor, at a given level of sales, indicates the percentage change in operating income that will occur from a 1% change in volume. In other words, it tells us how responsive a company's operating income is to changes in volume.

The *lowest* possible value for this factor is 1, which occurs only if the company has *no* fixed costs (an extremely *low* operating leverage company). *For a minute, let's assume that Kay has no fixed costs.* Given this scenario, her unit contribution margin ($14 per poster) contributes directly to profit because she has no fixed costs to cover. In addition, she has *no* risk. The worst she can do is break even, and that will occur only if she doesn't sell any posters. Let's continue to assume that she generally sells 950 posters a month, so this will be the level of sales at which we calculate the operating leverage factor:

Sales revenue (950 posters × $35/poster)	$ 33,250
Less: Variable expenses (950 posters × $21/poster)	(19,950)
Contribution margin (950 posters × $14/poster)	$ 13,300
Less: Fixed expenses	(0)
Operating income	$ 13,300

Her operating leverage factor is:

$$\text{Operating leverage factor} = \frac{\$13,300}{\$13,300}$$
$$= 1$$

What does this tell us? If Kay's volume changes by 1%, her operating income will change by 1% (her operating leverage factor of 1 multiplied by a 1% change in volume). What would happen to Kay's operating income if her volume changed by 15% rather than 1%? Her operating income would then change by 15% (her operating leverage factor of 1 multiplied by a 15% change in volume).

Let's now see what happens if we assume, as usual, that Kay's fixed expenses are $7,000. We'll once again calculate the operating leverage factor given Kay's current level of sales (950 posters per month):

Contribution margin (950 posters × $14/poster)	$13,300
Less: Fixed expenses	(7,000)
Operating income	$ 6,300

Now that we have once again assumed that Kay's fixed expenses are $7,000, her operating leverage factor is:

$$\text{Operating leverage factor} = \frac{\$13,300}{\$6,300}$$
$$= 2.11 \text{ (rounded)}$$

Notice that her operating leverage factor is *larger* (2.11 versus 1) when she has *more* fixed costs ($7,000 versus $0). If Kay's sales volume changes by 1%, her operating income will change by 2.11% (her operating leverage factor of 2.11 multiplied by a 1% change in volume). Again, what would happen to Kay's operating income if her volume changed by 15% rather than 1%? Her operating income would then change by 31.65% (her operating leverage factor of 2.11 multiplied by a 15% change in volume).

Managers use the firm's operating leverage factor to determine how vulnerable their operating income is to changes in sales volume—both positive and negative. The larger the operating leverage factor is, the greater the impact a change in sales volume has on operating income. This is true for both increases *and* decreases in volume. Therefore, companies with higher operating leverage factors are particularly vulnerable to changes in volume. In other words, they have *both* higher risk of incurring losses if volume declines *and* higher potential reward if volume increases. Hoping to capitalize on the reward side, many companies have intentionally increased their operating leverage by lowering their variable costs while at the same time increasing their fixed costs. This strategy works well during periods of economic growth but can be detrimental when sales volume slides.

Stop & Think...

Assume Kay's original data ($14 unit contribution margin, $7,000 fixed costs, and 950 posters per month sales volume). Use Kay's operating leverage factor to determine the percentage impact of a 10% *decrease* in sales volume on Kay's operating income. Prove your results.

continued . . .

Answer: If sales volume decreases by 10%, Kay's operating income will decrease by 21.1% (her operating leverage factor of 2.11 multiplied by a 10% decrease in volume).

Proof:		
Current volume of posters		950
Less: Decrease in volume (10% × 950) of posters		(95)
New volume of posters		855
Multiplied by: Unit contribution margin		× $14
New total contribution margin		$11,970
Less: Fixed expenses		(7,000)
New operating income		$ 4,970
versus operating income before change in volume		$ 6,300*
Decrease in operating income		$ (1,330)
Percentage change ($1,330/$6,300)		21.1% (rounded)

*(950 posters × $14/unit contribution margin) − $7,000 fixed expenses

In this chapter, we have discussed how managers use the contribution margin and CVP analysis to predict profits, determine breakeven points and target profit levels, and assess how changes in the business environment affect their profits. In the next chapter, we look at several types of short-term decisions managers must make. Cost behavior and the contribution margin will continue to play an important role in these decisions.

Decision Guidelines

CVP Analysis

Your friend did open the ice cream parlor. But now she's facing changing business conditions. She needs help making the following decisions:

Decision	Guidelines
The cost of ice cream is rising, yet my competitors have lowered their prices. How will these factors affect my breakeven and target profit levels?	Increases in variable costs (such as ice cream) and decreases in sales prices both decrease the unit contribution margin and contribution margin ratio. You will have to sell more units in order to achieve breakeven and target profit levels. You can use sensitivity analysis to better pinpoint the actual volume you'll need to sell. Simply compute your new unit contribution margin and use it in the shortcut unit contribution margin formula.
Would it help if I could renegotiate my lease with the landlord?	Decreases in fixed costs do not affect the firm's contribution margin. However, a decrease in fixed costs means that the company will have to sell fewer units to achieve breakeven and target profit levels. Increases in fixed costs have the opposite effect.

continued . . .

BBH CHAPTER 7

Decision	Guidelines
I've been thinking about selling other products in addition to ice cream. Will this affect my target profit levels?	Your contribution margin ratio will change depending on your sales mix. A company earns more income by selling higher-margin products than by selling an equal number of lower-margin products. If you can shift sales toward higher contribution margin products, you will have to sell fewer units to reach breakeven and target profit levels.
If the economy takes a downturn, how much risk do I face of incurring a loss?	The margin of safety indicates how far sales volume can decline before you would incur a loss:

$$\text{Margin of safety} = \text{Expected sales} - \text{Breakeven sales}$$

The operating leverage factor indicates the percentage change in operating income that will occur from a 1% change in volume. It tells you how sensitive your company's operating income is to changes in volume. At a given level of sales, the operating leverage factor is:

$$\text{Operating leverage factor} = \frac{\text{Contribution margin}}{\text{Operating income}}$$

Summary Problem 2

Recall from Summary Problem 1 that Fleet Foot buys hiking socks for $6 a pair and sells them for $10. Monthly fixed costs are $10,000 (for sales volumes between 0 and 12,000 pairs), resulting in a breakeven point of 2,500 units. Assume that Fleet Foot has been selling 8,000 pairs of socks per month.

Requirements

1. What is Fleet Foot's current margin of safety in units, in sales dollars, and as a percentage? Explain the results.

2. At this level of sales, what is Fleet Foot's operating leverage factor? If volume declines by 25% due to increasing competition, by what percentage will the company's operating income decline?

3. Competition has forced Fleet Foot to lower its sales price to $9 a pair. How will this affect Fleet's breakeven point?

4. To compensate for the lower sales price, Fleet Foot wants to expand its product line to include men's dress socks. Each pair will sell for $7.00 and cost $2.75 from the supplier. Fixed costs will not change. Fleet expects to sell four pairs of dress socks for every one pair of hiking socks (at its new $9 sales price). What is Fleet's weighted-average contribution margin? Given the 4:1 sales mix, how many of each type of sock will it need to sell to break even?

Solution

Requirement 1

$$\text{Margin of safety in units} = \text{Expected sales in units} - \text{Breakeven sales in units}$$
$$= 8,000 - 2,500$$
$$= 5,500 \text{ units}$$

$$\text{Margin of safety in sales dollars} = \text{Margin of safety in units} \times \text{sales price per unit}$$
$$= 5,500 \text{ units} \times \$10/\text{unit}$$
$$= \$55,000$$

$$\text{Margin of safety as a percentage} = \frac{\text{Margin of safety in units}}{\text{Expected sales in units}}$$
$$= \frac{5,500 \text{ pairs}}{8,000 \text{ pairs}}$$
$$= 68.75\%$$

Fleet Foot's margin of safety is quite high. Sales have to fall by more than 5,500 units (or $55,000) before Fleet incurs a loss. Fleet will continue to earn a profit unless sales drop by more than 68.75%.

Requirement 2

At its current level of volume, Fleet's operating income is:

Contribution margin (8,000 pairs × $4/pair).................................	$ 32,000
Less: Fixed expenses..	(10,000)
Operating income..	$ 22,000

Fleet's operating leverage factor at this level of sales is computed as:

$$\text{Operating leverage factor} = \frac{\text{Contribution margin}}{\text{Operating income}}$$

$$= \frac{\$32,000}{\$22,000}$$

$$= 1.45 \text{ (rounded)}$$

If sales volume declines by 25%, operating income will decline by 36.25% (Fleet's operating leverage factor of 1.45 multiplied by 25%).

Requirement 3

If Fleet drops its sales price to $9 per pair, its contribution margin per pair declines to $3 (sales price of $9 − variable cost of $6). Each sale contributes less toward covering fixed costs. Fleet's new breakeven point *increases* to 3,334 pairs of socks ($10,000 fixed costs ÷ $3 unit contribution margin).

Requirement 4

	Hiking Socks	Dress Socks	Total
Sales price per unit	$ 9.00	$ 7.00	
Deduct: Variable expense per unit	(6.00)	(2.75)	
Contribution margin per unit	$ 3.00	$ 4.25	
Sales mix	× 1	× 4	5
Contribution margin	$ 3.00	$17.00	$20.00
Weighted-average contribution margin per unit ($20/5)			$ 4.00

$$\text{Sales in total units} = \frac{\text{Fixed expenses} + \text{Operating income}}{\text{Weighted-average contribution margin per unit}}$$

$$= \frac{\$10,000 + 0}{\$4}$$

$$= 2,500 \text{ pairs of socks}$$

Breakeven sales of dress socks (2,500 × 4/5).........	2,000 pairs dress socks
Breakeven sales of hiking socks (2,500 × 1/5).......	500 pairs hiking socks

By expanding its product line to include higher-margin dress socks, Fleet is able to decrease its breakeven point back to its original level (2,500 pairs). However, to achieve this breakeven point, Fleet must sell the planned ratio of four pairs of dress socks to every one pair of hiking socks.

Review *Cost-Volume-Profit Analysis*

■ Accounting Vocabulary

Breakeven Point (p. 365)
The sales level at which operating income is zero: Total revenues equal total expenses.

Contribution Margin Per Unit (p. 363)
The excess of the unit sales price over the variable cost per unit. Also called unit contribution margin.

Contribution Margin Income Statement (p. 362)
An income statement that groups costs by behavior rather than function; can be used only by internal management.

Contribution Margin Ratio (p. 363)
Ratio of contribution margin to sales revenue.

Cost-Volume-Profit (CVP) Analysis (p. 360)
Expresses the relationships among costs, volume, and profit or loss.

Margin of Safety (p. 385)
Excess of expected sales over breakeven sales. The drop in sales a company can absorb without incurring an operating loss.

Operating Leverage (p. 386)
The relative amount of fixed and variable costs that make up a firm's total costs.

Operating Leverage Factor (p. 387)
At a given level of sales, the contribution margin divided by operating income. The operating leverage factor indicates the percentage change in operating income that will occur from a 1% change in sales volume.

Sales Mix (p. 361)
The combination of products that make up total sales.

Sensitivity Analysis (p. 376)
A "what-if" technique that asks what results will be if actual prices or costs change or if an underlying assumption changes.

■ Quick Check

Use the following information for Questions 1 through 10. Grand Canyon Railway operates a turn-of-the-century train that transports passengers from Williams, Arizona, to the Grand Canyon and back every day. Assume that the train tickets sell for $60 per passenger, the railway's variable costs are $10 per passenger, and its fixed expenses are $50,000 each month.

1. What is the contribution margin ratio (rounded)?
    a. 16.67%
    b. 100%
    c. 83.33%
    d. need sales volume to calculate

2. Compute the breakeven point in sales dollars.
    a. $300,000
    b. $60,000
    c. $50,000
    d. $100,000

3. What will the Railway's operating income be if they sell 1,001 tickets in one month?

   a. $50
   b. $10
   c. $60
   d. $60,060

4. If the Grand Canyon Railway wants to earn $100,000 in profit per month, how many tickets must it sell?

   a. 1,000
   b. 31,000
   c. 30,000
   d. 3,000

5. On the Grand Canyon Railway's CVP graph, the total cost line intersects the total revenue line at which of the following points?

   a. the level of the fixed costs
   b. the level of the variable costs
   c. the breakeven point
   d. the origin

6. If the Grand Canyon Railway expects to serve 1,200 passengers next month, what is the margin of safety?

   a. 200 passengers
   b. 1,000 passengers
   c. 1,200 passengers
   d. 2,200 passengers

7. If the Grand Canyon Railway serves 1,200 passengers, what is its operating leverage factor?

   a. 1
   b. 6
   c. 3.27
   d. 0.16

8. If the Grand Canyon Railway's volume decreases by 8%, by what percentage will its operating income decrease?

   a. 48%
   b. 1%
   c. 26.16%
   d. 8%

9. If the Grand Canyon Railway cuts its ticket price to $50 per passenger, what is the new breakeven point?

   a. 100 more passengers than with the original $60 ticket price
   b. 250 more passengers than with the original $60 ticket price
   c. 100 fewer passengers than with the original $60 ticket price
   d. 250 fewer passengers than with the original $60 ticket price

10. The Grand Canyon Railway is thinking about selling souvenirs on the train. The souvenirs will sell for $10 each and have a variable cost of $4 each. The Grand Canyon Railway managers think that they will sell an average of one souvenir to each passenger. Assuming that fixed expenses remain at $50,000, how will the sale of souvenirs affect the number of passengers needed to break even?

   a. It will have no effect.

   b. It will increase the number needed.

   c. It will decrease the number needed.

   d. Not enough information is provided.

Quick Check Answers

1. c 2. b 3. a 4. d 5. d 6. c 7. b 8. a 9. b 10. c

For Internet Exercises, Excel in Practice, and additional online activities, go to this book's Web site at www.prenhall.com/bamber.

Assess Your Progress

■ Learning Objectives

1. Calculate the unit contribution margin and the contribution margin ratio

2. Use CVP analysis to find breakeven points and target profit volumes

3. Perform sensitivity analysis in response to changing business conditions

4. Find breakeven and target profit volumes for multiproduct companies

5. Determine a firm's margin of safety and operating leverage

■ Short Exercises

Bay Cruiseline Data Set used for S7-1 through S7-12

Bay Cruiseline offers nightly dinner cruises off the coast of Miami, San Francisco, and Seattle. Dinner cruise tickets sell for $60 per passenger. Bay Cruiseline's variable cost of providing the dinner is $20 per passenger, and the fixed cost of operating the vessels (depreciation, salaries, docking fees, and so forth) is $275,000 per month. The company's relevant range extends to 10,000 monthly passengers.

S7-1 **Compute unit contribution margin and contribution margin ratio** *(Learning Objective 1)*
Use the information from the Bay Cruiseline Data Set to compute the following:

a. What is the contribution margin per passenger?

b. What is the contribution margin ratio (round to five digits)?

c. Use the unit contribution margin to project operating income if monthly sales total 10,000 passengers.

d. Use the contribution margin ratio to project operating income if monthly sales revenue totals $500,000.

S7-2 **Project change in income** *(Learning Objective 1)*
Use the information from the Bay Cruiseline Data Set. If Bay Cruiseline sells an additional 500 tickets, by what amount will its operating income increase (or operating loss decrease)?

S7-3 **Find breakeven** *(Learning Objective 2)*
Use the information from the Bay Cruiseline Data Set to compute the number of dinner cruise tickets it must sell to break even.

a. Use the income statement equation approach.

b. Using the shortcut *unit* contribution margin approach, perform a numerical proof to ensure that your answer is correct.

c. Use your answers from a and b to determine the sales revenue needed to break even.

d. Use the shortcut contribution margin *ratio* approach to verify the sales revenue needed to break even.

S7-4 **Find target profit volume** *(Learning Objective 2)*
Use the information from the Bay Cruiseline Data Set. If Bay Cruiseline has a target operating income of $40,000 per month, how many dinner cruise tickets must the company sell?

S7-5 **Prepare a CVP graph** *(Learning Objective 2)*
Use the information from the Bay Cruiseline Data Set. Draw a graph of Bay Cruiseline's CVP relationships. Include the sales revenue line, the fixed expense line, and the total expense line. Label the axes, the breakeven point, the income area, and the loss area.

S7-6 **Interpret a CVP graph** *(Learning Objective 2)*
Describe what each letter stands for in the CVP graph.

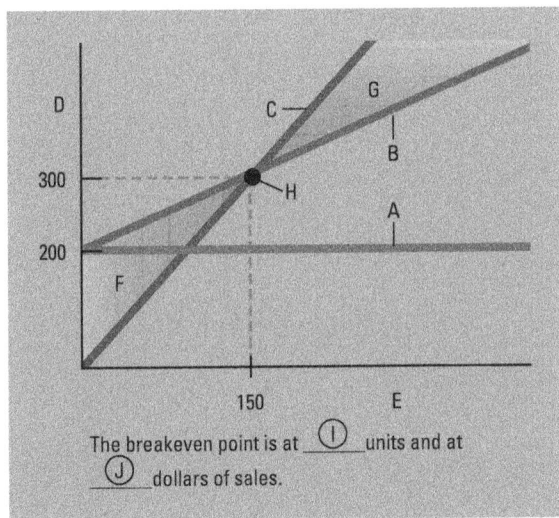

S7-7 **Changes in sales price and variable costs** *(Learning Objective 3)*
Use the information from the Bay Cruiseline Data Set.

1. Suppose Bay Cruiseline cuts its dinner cruise ticket price from $60 to $50 to increase the number of passengers. Compute the new breakeven point in units and in sales dollars. Explain how changes in sales price generally affect the breakeven point.

2. Assume that Bay Cruiseline does *not* cut the price. Bay Cruiseline could reduce its variable costs by no longer serving an appetizer before dinner. Suppose this operating change reduces the variable expense from $20 to $15 per passenger. Compute the new breakeven point in units and in dollars. Explain how changes in variable costs generally affect the breakeven point.

S7-8 **Changes in fixed costs** *(Learning Objective 3)*
Use the information from the Bay Cruiseline Data Set. Suppose Bay Cruiseline embarks on a cost-reduction drive and slashes fixed expenses from $275,000 per month to $200,000 per month.

1. Compute the new breakeven point in units and in sales dollars.

2. Is the breakeven point higher or lower than in S7-3? Explain how changes in fixed costs generally affect the breakeven point.

S7-11   **Compute margin of safety** *(Learning Objective 5)*

Use the information from the Bay Cruiseline Data Set. If Bay Cruiseline sells 7,000 dinner cruises, compute the margin of safety:

a. In units (dinner cruise tickets).

b. In sales dollars.

c. As a percentage of sales.

S7-12   **Compute and use operating leverage factor** *(Learning Objective 5)*

Use the information from the Bay Cruiseline Data Set.

a. Compute the operating leverage factor when Bay Cruiseline sells 10,000 dinner cruises.

b. If volume increases by 10%, by what percentage will operating income increase?

c. If volume decreases by 5%, by what percentage will operating income decrease?

BBH CHAPTER 7

Pages 399–403 intentionally omitted

E7-35 Comprehensive CVP analysis *(Learning Objectives 1, 2, 3, 4, 5)*

FlashCo. manufactures 1 GB flash drives (jump drives). Price and cost data for a relevant range extending to 200,000 units per month are as follows:

Sales price per unit (current monthly sales volume is 120,000 units)...	$ 20.00
Variable costs per unit:	
Direct materials...	6.40
Direct labor..	5.00
Variable manufacturing overhead	2.20
Variable selling and administrative expenses...........................	1.40
Monthly fixed expenses:	
Fixed manufacturing overhead...	$191,400
Fixed selling and administrative expenses................................	276,600

Requirements

1. What is the company's contribution margin per unit? Contribution margin percentage? Total contribution margin?

2. What would the company's monthly operating income be if the company sold 150,000 units?

3. What would the company's monthly operating income be if the company had sales of $4,000,000?

4. What is the breakeven point in units? In sales dollars?

5. How many units would the company have to sell to earn a target monthly profit of $260,000?

6. Management is currently in contract negotiations with the labor union. If the negotiations fail, direct labor costs will increase by 10% and fixed costs will increase by $22,500 per month. If these costs increase, how many units will the company have each month to break even?

7. Return to the original data for this question and the rest of the questions. What is the company's current operating leverage factor (round to two decimals)?

8. If sales volume increases by 8%, by what percentage will operating income increase?

9. What is the firm's current margin of safety in sales dollars? What is its margin of safety as a percentage of sales?

10. Say FlashCo. adds a second line of flash drives (2 GB rather than 1 GB). A package of the 2 GB flash drives will sell for $45 and have variable cost per unit of $20 per unit. The expected sales mix is three of the small flash drives (1 GB) for every one large flash drive (2 GB). Given this sales mix, how many of each type of flash drive will FlashCo. need to sell to reach its target monthly profit of $260,000? Is this volume higher or lower than previously needed (in Question 5) to achieve the same target profit? Why?

P7-38A Comprehensive CVP problem *(Learning Objectives 1, 2, 5)*

Team Spirit imprints calendars with college names. The company has fixed expenses of $1,035,000 each month plus variable expenses of $3.60 per carton of calendars. Of the variable expense, 70% is Cost of Goods Sold, while the remaining 30% relates to variable operating expenses. Team Spirit sells each carton of calendars for $10.50.

Requirements

1. Use the income statement equation approach to compute the number of cartons of calendars that Team Spirit must sell each month to break even.

continued . . .

2. Use the contribution margin ratio shortcut formula to compute the dollar amount of monthly sales Team Spirit needs in order to earn $285,000 in operating income (round the contribution margin ratio to two decimal places).

3. Prepare Team Spirit's contribution margin income statement for June for sales of 450,000 cartons of calendars.

4. What is June's margin of safety (in dollars)? What is the operating leverage factor at this level of sales?

5. By what percentage will operating income change if July's sales volume is 13% higher? Prove your answer.

Pages 407–409 intentionally omitted

Apply Your Knowledge

■ Decision Cases

Case 7-46. Determine feasibility of business plan *(Learning Objective 2)*

Brian and Nui Soon live in Macon, Georgia. Two years ago, they visited Thailand. Nui, a professional chef, was impressed with the cooking methods and the spices used in the Thai food. Macon does not have a Thai restaurant, and the Soons are contemplating opening one. Nui would supervise the cooking, and Brian would leave his current job to be the maitre d'. The restaurant would serve dinner Tuesday through Saturday.

Brian has noticed a restaurant for lease. The restaurant has seven tables, each of which can seat four. Tables can be moved together for a large party. Nui is planning two seatings per evening, and the restaurant will be open 50 weeks per year.

The Soons have drawn up the following estimates:

Average revenue, including beverages and dessert.......	$ 40 per meal
Average cost of the food...	$ 12 per meal
Chef's and dishwasher's salaries.................................	$50,400 per *year*
Rent (premises, equipment)..	$ 4,000 per month
Cleaning (linen and premises).....................................	$ 800 per month
Replacement of dishes, cutlery, glasses.......................	$ 300 per month
Utilities, advertising, telephone..................................	$ 1,900 per month

Requirements

Compute *annual* breakeven number of meals and sales revenue for the restaurant. Also, compute the number of meals and the amount of sales revenue needed to earn operating income of $75,600 for the year. How many meals must the Soons serve each night to earn their target income of $75,600? Should the couple open the restaurant? Support your answer.

■ Ethical Issue

Issue 7-47. Ethical dilemma with CVP analysis error *(Learning Objective 2)*

You have just begun your summer internship at Tmedic. The company supplies sterilized surgical instruments for physicians. To expand sales, Tmedic is considering paying a commission to its sales force. The controller, Jane Hewitt, asks you to compute (1) the new breakeven sales figure and (2) the operating profit if sales increase 15% under the new sales commission plan. She thinks you can handle this task because you learned CVP analysis in your accounting class.

You spend the next day collecting information from the accounting records, performing the analysis, and writing a memo to explain the results. The company president is pleased with your memo. You report that the new sales commission plan will lead to a significant increase in operating income and only a small increase in breakeven sales.

The following week, you realize that you made an error in the CVP analysis. You overlooked the sales personnel's $2,500 monthly salaries, and you did not include this fixed marketing expense in your computations. You are not sure what to do. If you tell Hewitt of your mistake, she will have to tell the president. In this case, you are afraid Tmedic might not offer you permanent employment after your internship.

Requirements

1. How would your error affect breakeven sales and operating income under the proposed sales commission plan? Could this cause the president to reject the sales commission proposal?

2. Consider your ethical responsibilities. Is there a difference between (a) initially making an error and (b) subsequently failing to inform the controller?

3. Suppose you tell Hewitt of the error in your analysis. Why might the consequences not be as bad as you fear? Should Hewitt take any responsibility for your error? What could Hewitt have done differently?

4. After considering all of the factors, should you inform Hewitt or simply keep quiet?

■ Team Project

Project 7-48. Advertising campaign and production level decisions
(Learning Objectives 1, 3)

EZPAK Manufacturing produces filament packaging tape. In 2008, EZPAK Manufacturing produced and sold 15 million rolls of tape. The company has recently expanded its capacity, so it can now produce up to 30 million rolls per year. EZPAK Manufacturing's accounting records show the following results from 2008:

Sale price per roll	$ 3.00
Variable manufacturing expenses per roll	$ 2.00
Variable marketing and administrative expenses per roll	$ 0.50
Total fixed manufacturing overhead costs	$8,400,000
Total fixed marketing and administrative expenses	$ 600,000
Sales	15 million rolls
Production	15 million rolls

There were no beginning or ending inventories in 2008.

In January 2009, EZPAK Manufacturing hired a new president, Kevin McDaniel. McDaniel has a one-year contract specifying that he will be paid 10% of EZPAK Manufacturing's 2009 operating income (based on traditional absorption costing) instead of a salary. In 2009, McDaniel must make two major decisions:

1. Should EZPAK Manufacturing undertake a major advertising campaign? This campaign would raise sales to 25 million rolls. This is the maximum level of sales that EZPAK Manufacturing can expect to make in the near future. The ad campaign would add an additional $3.5 million in marketing and administrative costs. Without the campaign, sales will be 15 million rolls.

2. How many rolls of tape will EZPAK Manufacturing produce?

At the end of the year, EZPAK Manufacturing's board of directors will evaluate McDaniel's performance and decide whether to offer him a contract for the following year.

continued . . .

Requirements

Within your group, form two subgroups. The first subgroup assumes the role of Kevin McDaniel, EZPAK Manufacturing's new president. The second subgroup assumes the role of EZPAK Manufacturing's board of directors. McDaniel will meet with the board of directors shortly after the end of 2009 to decide whether he will remain at EZPAK Manufacturing. Most of your effort should be devoted to advance preparation for this meeting. Each subgroup should meet separately to prepare for the meeting between the board and McDaniel. [*Hint:* Keep computations (other than per-unit amounts) in millions.]

Kevin McDaniel should:

1. Compute EZPAK Manufacturing's 2008 operating income.

2. Decide whether to adopt the advertising campaign by calculating the projected increase in operating income from the advertising campaign. Do not include the executive bonus in this calculation. Prepare a memo to the board of directors explaining this decision. Use the memo format outlined in Case 6-43. Give this memo to the board of directors as soon as possible (before the joint meeting).

3. Assume that EZPAK Manufacturing adopts the advertising campaign. Decide how many rolls of tape to produce in 2009. Assume that no safety stock is considered necessary to EZPAK's business.

4. Given your response to Question 3, prepare an absorption costing income statement for the year ended December 31, 2009, ending with operating income before bonus. Then, compute your bonus separately. The variable cost per unit and the total fixed expenses (with the exception of the advertising campaign) remain the same as in 2008. Give this income statement and your bonus computation to the board of directors as soon as possible (before your meeting with the board).

5. Decide whether you want to remain at EZPAK Manufacturing for another year. You currently have an offer from another company. The contract with the other company is identical to the one you currently have with EZPAK Manufacturing—you will be paid 10% of absorption costing operating income instead of a salary.

The board of directors should:

1. Compute EZPAK Manufacturing's 2008 operating income.

2. Determine whether EZPAK Manufacturing should adopt the advertising campaign by calculating the projected increase in operating income from the advertising campaign. Do not include the executive bonus in this calculation.

3. Determine how many rolls of tape EZPAK Manufacturing should produce in 2009. Assume that no safety stock is considered necessary to EZPAK's business.

4. Evaluate McDaniel's performance based on his decisions and the information he provided to the board. (*Hint:* You may want to prepare a variable costing income statement.)

5. Evaluate the contract's bonus provision. Are you satisfied with this provision? If so, explain why. If not, recommend how it should be changed.

After McDaniel has given the board his memo and income statement and after the board has had a chance to evaluate McDaniel's performance, McDaniel and the board should meet. The purpose of the meeting is to decide whether it is in their mutual interest for McDaniel to remain with EZPAK Manufacturing and, if so, the terms of the contract EZPAK Manufacturing will offer McDaniel.

Chapter 7: Demo Doc 1

■ Using CVP for Sensitivity Analysis

Learning Objectives 2, 3, 4

Hacker Golf has developed a unique swing trainer golf club. The company currently pays a production company to produce the golf club at a cost of $22 each. Other variable costs total $6 per golf club, and monthly fixed expenses are $16,000. Hacker Golf currently sells the trainer golf club for $48.

NOTE: Solve each requirement as a separate situation.

Requirements

1. Calculate Hacker Golf's breakeven point in units.

2. Hacker Golf is considering raising the club's selling price to $49.95. Calculate the new breakeven in units.

3. Hacker Golf has found a new company to produce the golf club at a lower cost of $19. Calculate the new breakeven in units.

4. Because many customers have requested a golf glove to go along with the trainer club, Hacker Golf is considering selling gloves. They expect to sell only one glove for every four trainer clubs they sell. Hacker Golf can purchase the gloves for $5 a pair and sell them for $9 a pair. Total fixed costs should remain the same at $16,000 per month. Calculate the breakeven point in units for trainer clubs and golf gloves.

5. Use a contribution margin income statement to prove the breakeven point calculated in Requirement 4.

Demo Doc 1 Solutions

Requirement 1

Calculate Hacker's breakeven point in units.

To determine how changes in sales prices, costs, or volume affect profits, let's first start by calculating the current breakeven point.

To determine the breakeven point, we first must calculate the contribution margin per unit. The contribution margin is calculated by subtracting variable costs from the sales revenue. Therefore:

> Contribution margin per unit = Sales price per unit − Variable cost per unit

Hacker Golf's variable cost per club (unit) is the price it pays for each club ($22) plus its additional variable costs per golf club ($6). Therefore, its unit contribution margin is:

Selling price per club	$48
Variable cost per club ($22 + $6)	(28)
Contribution margin per club	$20

The contribution margin represents the amount from each unit sold that is available to cover fixed expenses. That means Hacker Golf earns $20 per club, which contributes toward fixed expenses until fixed expenses are covered. After fixed expenses are covered, each club sold contributes $20 directly to the company's operating income.

Breakeven is the level of sales at which income is zero. The breakeven point can be calculated as follows:

$$\text{Breakeven in units} = \frac{\text{Fixed expenses} + \text{Operating income}}{\text{Contribution margin per unit}}$$

$$\text{Breakeven in units} = \frac{\$16,000 + \$0}{\$20}$$

$$= 800 \text{ trainer clubs}$$

Requirement 2

Hacker Golf is considering raising the club's selling price to $49.95. Calculate the new breakeven in units.

Even if Hacker Golf raises its sales price per club to $49.95, its variable costs ($28 per unit) and fixed expenses ($16,000) will stay the same. As a result of increasing the sales price, the company will now have a higher contribution margin per unit:

Selling price per club	$49.95
Variable cost per club ($22 + $6)	(28.00)
Contribution margin per club	$21.95

Once again, you can use the breakeven formula to find the new breakeven point:

$$\text{Breakeven in units} = \frac{\text{Fixed expenses} + \text{Operating income}}{\text{Contribution margin per unit}}$$

$$\text{Breakeven in units} = \frac{\$16,000 + \$0}{\$21.95}$$

$$= 728.93 \text{ rounded to } 729 \text{ trainer clubs}$$

With the increased selling price, breakeven has been reduced from 800 clubs to 729 clubs. The higher price means that each club contributes more to fixed expenses.

You can prove the answer by preparing an income statement for a sales volume of 729 units:

Sales revenue (729 × $49.95)...............................	$ 36,412 (rounded)
Less: Variable expenses (729 × $28)..........................	(20,412)
Total contribution margin...	16,000
Less: Fixed expenses..	(16,000)
Operating income..	0

If the selling price increases, the volume required to break even or achieve target profit goals decreases (provided costs do not change). Conversely, if the selling price decreases, the volume required to break even or achieve target profit goals increases.

Requirement 3

Hacker Golf has found a new company to produce the golf club at a lower cost of $19. Calculate the new breakeven in units.

Let's return to Hacker Golf's original sales price ($48). Assuming that Hacker Golf has found a new company to produce the golf club for $19 each, the company's variable costs per club will decrease. However, fixed expenses remain the same ($16,000). Once again, Hacker Golf's contribution margin per unit will increase as a result of this change in business conditions:

Selling price per club	$48
Variable cost per club ($19 + $6)	(25)
Contribution margin per club...	$23

The new breakeven point is found as follows:

$$\text{Breakeven in units} = \frac{\text{Fixed expenses} + \text{Operating income}}{\text{Contribution margin per unit}}$$

$$\text{Breakeven in units} = \frac{\$16,000 + \$0}{\$23}$$

$$= 695.65 \text{ rounded to } 696 \text{ clubs}$$

With the reduced variable cost, Hacker Golf's breakeven in units decreases from 800 clubs to 696 clubs. Using this information, Hacker Golf's management must decide if it is worth the risk to switch to a new producer.

You can also prove this result by preparing an income statement:

Sales revenue (696 × $48)...	$ 33,400 (rounded)
Less: Variable expenses (696 × $25)...........................	(17,400)
Total contribution margin..	16,000
Less: Fixed expenses..	(16,000)
Operating income..	$ 0

As variable or fixed expenses increase, so does the volume needed to break even or achieve target profits. Conversely, as these expenses decrease, the volume needed to break even or achieve target profits also decreases.

Requirement 4

Because many customers have requested a golf glove to go along with the trainer club, Hacker Golf is considering selling gloves. They expect to sell only one glove for every four trainer clubs they sell. Hacker Golf can purchase the gloves for $5 a pair and sell them for $9 a pair. Total fixed expenses should remain the same at $16,000 per month. Calculate the breakeven point in units for trainer clubs and golf gloves.

Calculating the breakeven point is fairly straightforward when a company is selling only one product. But Hacker Golf is now considering selling two products. Now, breakeven becomes more complicated. Different products will have different effects on the contribution margins because of different costs and selling prices. So, the company needs to consider the sales mix (a combination of products that make up total sales) in determining CVP relationships.

Finding the breakeven point for multiproduct firms involves a simple three-step process. The first step is to calculate a combined weighted-average contribution margin for all of the products that the company sells.

Step 1: Calculate the weighted-average contribution margin.

Hacker Golf believes that it can sell one glove for every four clubs that it sells. This would give the company a 4:1 sales mix. So, Hacker expects that 1/5 (or 20%) of sales will be gloves and 4/5 (or 80%) of sales will be trainer clubs.

Let's return to Hacker's original selling price and variable costs for the trainer club. Recall that Hacker Golf earns a $20 contribution margin on each golf club that it sells. Hacker will also earn a $4 contribution margin on each golf glove that it sells:

	Clubs	Gloves
Sales price per unit.....................................	$ 48	$ 9
Less: Variable cost per unit	(28)	(5)
Contribution margin per unit....................	$ 20	$ 4

The weighted-average contribution margin is calculated by multiplying the contribution margin per unit by the sales mix expected for each product. Once we have a total contribution margin for the bundle of products ($80 + $4 = $84, in this case), we divide it by the total number of units (5) in the sales mix, as follows:

	Clubs	Gloves	Total
Sales price per unit	$ 48	$ 9	
Less: Variable cost per unit	(28)	(5)	
Contribution margin per unit	$ 20	$ 4	
Sales mix in units	× 4	× 1	5
Contribution margin	$ 80	$ 4	$ 84
Weighted-average contribution margin per unit ($84/5)			$16.80

The $16.80 represents a weighted-average contribution margin for all of the products that Hacker Golf sells. The golf clubs are weighted more heavily because Hacker Golf expects to sell four times as many clubs as golf gloves.

The next step is to calculate the breakeven in units for the bundle of products.

Step 2: Calculate the breakeven point in units for the total of both products combined.

This is calculated using the breakeven formula modified for the weighted-average contribution margin in the denominator:

$$\text{Sales in total units} = \frac{\text{Fixed expenses} + \text{Operating income}}{\text{Weighted-average contribution margin per unit}}$$

We know from the question that fixed expenses will not be affected, so they should remain at $16,000. The weighted-average contribution margin, as we just calculated, is $16.80 per unit. So, we compute total sales as follows:

$$\text{Sales in total units} = \frac{\$16,000 + \$0}{\$16.80}$$

$$= 952.38 \text{ rounded to } 953$$

Hacker Golf must sell 953 clubs and gloves combined to break even. We round up because Hacker Golf cannot sell a partial unit. Management needs to know how many units of *each* product must be sold to break even. Therefore, the next step is to determine how many of the total sales units (953) need to be clubs and how many need to be gloves in order to break even.

Step 3: Calculate the breakeven in units for each product line.

Because Hacker Golf believes that it will sell four trainer clubs for every one pair of gloves, the total number of units, 953, is multiplied by each product's sales mix percentage:

Breakeven sales of clubs: [953 × (4/5)] = 762.4 rounded to 763

Breakeven sales of gloves: [953 × (1/5)] = 190.6 rounded to 191

From this analysis, we know that Hacker Golf needs to sell 763 trainer clubs and 191 pairs of gloves to break even.

Requirement 5

Use a contribution margin income statement to prove the breakeven point calculated in Requirement 4.

To test the calculation of the breakeven point, you would add the revenue generated from all sales, subtract the variable costs associated with all sales, and subtract the total fixed expenses. The result should balance to zero (or close to zero in cases in which rounding occurs).

	Clubs	Gloves	Total
Sales revenue:			
Trainer clubs (763 × $48)..................	$ 36,624		
Gloves (191 × $9)..............................		$1,719	$ 38,343
Variable expenses:			
Trainer clubs (763 × $28)..................	(21,364)		
Gloves (191 × $5)..............................		(955)	(22,319)
Contribution margin	$ 15,260	$ 764	$ 16,024
Fixed expenses			(16,000)
Operating income.....................................			$ 24

There is a slight $24 profit because of a rounding error.

8 Short-Term Business Decisions

Most major airlines, including Delta, outsource work. In 2002, Delta announced plans to save over $15 million a year by outsourcing its reservation work to call centers in the Philippines and India. In 2005, Delta revealed plans to cut maintenance costs 34% a year by outsourcing much of its airplane maintenance to Miami- and Canadian-based firms. But why would Delta outsource so much of its work? Primarily to cut costs. Most of the major airlines are experiencing financial difficulties due to rising fuel costs and tight competition, so they need to find ways to cut costs. One way is through outsourcing. Companies can save 20% or more by outsourcing call center work to English-speaking workers in developing countries.

Outsourcing also enables companies to concentrate on their core competencies—the operating activities in which they are experts. When

BBH CHAPTER 8

companies focus on just their core competencies, they often outsource the activities that do not give them a competitive advantage. For example, heavy maintenance of aircraft, which can take two to three weeks per plane, requires specialized expertise. This expertise is provided by members of the outside airline maintenance industry, which performs over half of all airline maintenance. Delta's strategy is to focus on its core competency—flying passengers—and outsource other operating activities, such as reservations and airplane maintenance, to companies who excel at those activities. ■

Learning Objectives

1 Describe and identify information relevant to short-term business decisions

2 Make special order decisions

3 Make pricing decisions

4 Make dropping a product, department, or territory decisions

5 Make product mix decisions

6 Make outsourcing (make-or-buy) decisions

7 Make sell as is or process further decisions

In the last chapter, we saw how managers use cost behavior to determine the company's breakeven point and to estimate the sales volume needed to achieve target profits. In this chapter, we'll see how managers use their knowledge of cost behavior to make six special business decisions, such as whether to outsource operating activities. The decisions we'll discuss in this chapter pertain to short periods of time, so managers do not need to worry about the time value of money. In other words, they do not need to compute the present value of the revenues and expenses relating to the decision. In Chapter 9, we will discuss longer-term decisions (such as buying equipment and undertaking plant expansions) in which the time value of money becomes important. Before we look at the six business decisions in detail, let's consider a manager's decision-making process and the information managers need to evaluate their options.

How Managers Make Decisions

Exhibit 8-1 illustrates how managers decide among alternative courses of action. Management accountants help gather and analyze *relevant information* to compare alternatives. Management accountants also help with the follow-up: comparing the actual results of a decision to those originally anticipated. This feedback helps management as it faces similar types of decisions in the future. It also helps management adjust current operations if actual results of its decision are markedly different from those anticipated.

| EXHIBIT 8-1 | How Managers Make Decisions |

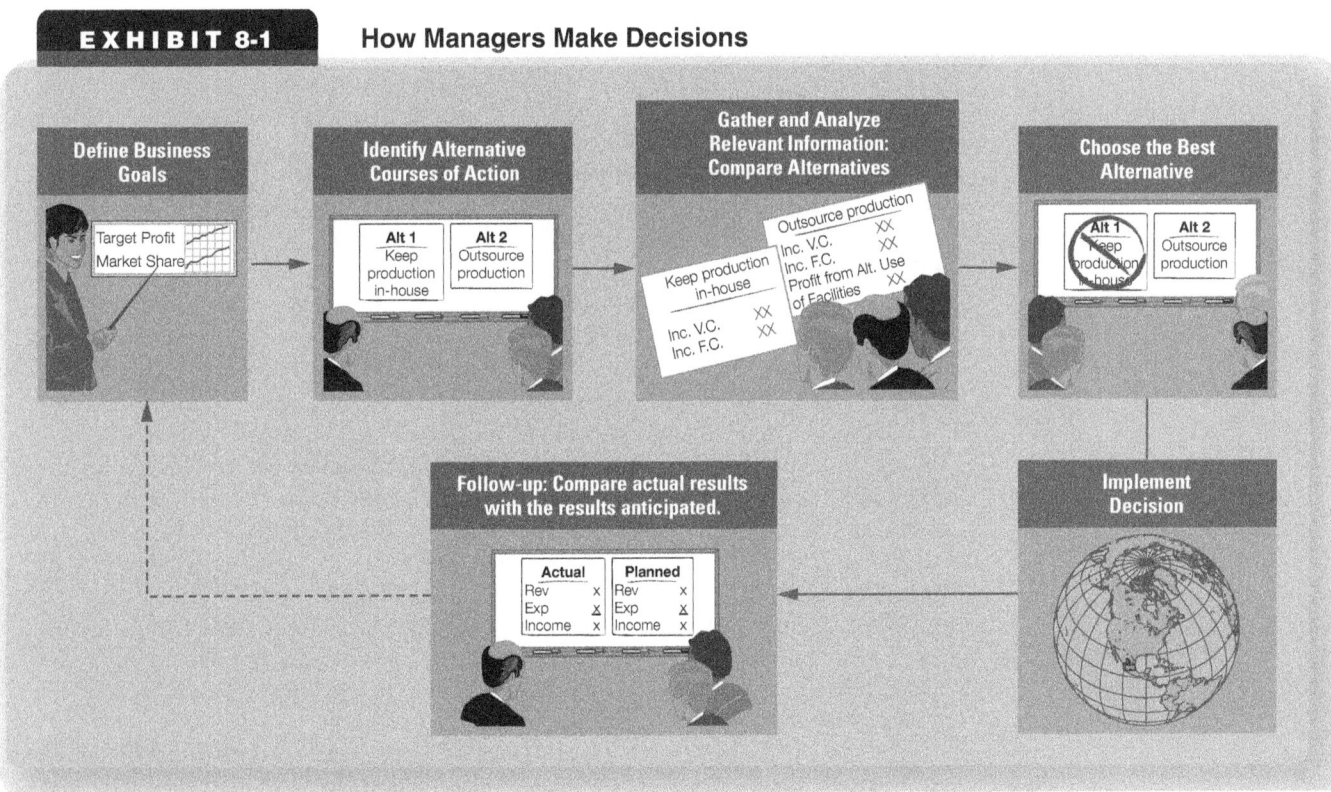

Relevant Information

When managers make decisions, they focus on costs and revenues that are relevant to the decisions. Exhibit 8-2 shows that **relevant information:**

1. Is expected *future* data.

2. *Differs* among alternatives.

1 Describe and identify information relevant to short-term business decisions

BBH CHAPTER 8

| EXHIBIT 8-2 | Relevant Information |

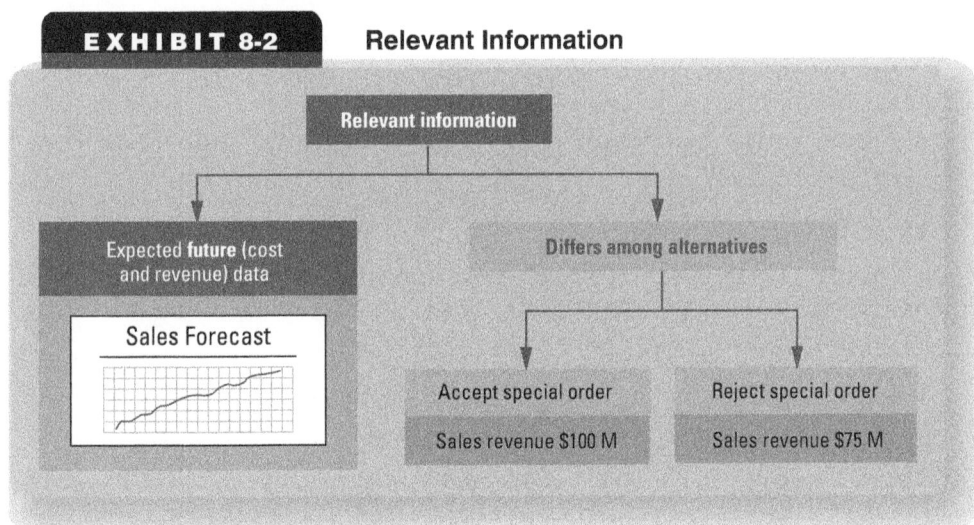

Recall our discussion of relevant costs in Chapter 2. In deciding whether to purchase a Toyota Corolla or Nissan Sentra, the cost of the car, the sales tax, and the insurance premium are relevant because these costs:

• Are incurred in the *future* (after you decide to buy the car).

• *Differ between alternatives* (each car has a different invoice price, sales tax, and insurance premium).

These costs are *relevant* because they affect your decision of which car to purchase.

Irrelevant costs are costs that *do not* affect your decision. For example, because the Corolla and Sentra both have similar fuel efficiency and maintenance ratings, we do not expect the car operating costs to differ between alternatives. Because these costs do not differ, they do not affect your decision. In other words, they are *irrelevant* to the decision. Similarly, the cost of a campus parking sticker is also irrelevant because the sticker costs the same whether you buy the Sentra or the Corolla.

Sunk costs are also irrelevant to your decision. Sunk costs are costs that were incurred in the *past* and cannot be changed regardless of which future action is taken. Perhaps you want to trade in your current truck when you buy your new car. The amount you paid for the truck—which you bought for $15,000 a year ago—is a sunk cost. In fact, it doesn't matter whether you paid $15,000 or $50,000—it's still a sunk cost. No decision made *now* can alter the past. You already bought the truck, so *the price you paid for it is a sunk cost.* All you can do *now* is keep the truck, trade it in, or sell it for the best price you can get, even if that price is substantially less than what you originally paid for the truck.

What *is* relevant is what you can get for your truck in the future. Suppose the Nissan dealership offers you $8,000 for your truck. The Toyota dealership offers you $10,000. Because the amounts differ and the transaction will take place in the future, the trade-in value is relevant to your decision.

The same principle applies to all situations—*only relevant data affect decisions.* Let's consider another application of this general principle.

Suppose Pendleton Woolen Mills is deciding whether to use pure wool or a wool blend in a new line of sweaters. Assume that Pendleton Woolen Mills predicts the following costs under the two alternatives:

| | Expected Materials and Labor Cost per Sweater | | |
	Wool	Wool Blend	Cost Difference
Direct materials...........................	$10	$6	$4
Direct labor.................................	2	2	0
Total cost of direct materials and direct labor.....................	$12	$8	$4

The cost of direct materials is relevant because this cost differs between alternatives (the wool costs $4 more than the wool blend). The labor cost is irrelevant because that cost is the same for both kinds of wool.

Stop & Think...

You are considering replacing your Pentium IV computer with the latest model. Is the $1,200 you spent (in 2005) on the Pentium relevant to your decision about buying the new model?

Answer: The $1,200 cost of your Pentium is irrelevant. The $1,200 is a *sunk* cost that you incurred in the past, so it is the same whether or not you buy the new computer.

Relevant Nonfinancial Information

Nonfinancial, or qualitative factors, also play a role in managers' decisions. For example, closing manufacturing plants and laying off employees can seriously hurt employee morale. Outsourcing can reduce control over delivery time and product quality. Offering discounted prices to select customers can upset regular customers and tempt them to take their business elsewhere. Managers must think through the likely quantitative *and* qualitative effects of their decisions.

Managers who ignore qualitative factors can make serious mistakes. For example, the City of Nottingham, England, spent $1.6 million on 215 solar-powered parking meters after seeing how well the parking meters worked in countries along the Mediterranean Sea. However, the city did not consider that British skies are typically overcast. The result? The meters didn't always work because of the lack of sunlight. The city *lost* money because people ended up parking for free! Relevant qualitative information has the same characteristics as relevant financial information: The qualitative factor occurs in the *future,* and it *differs* between alternatives. The amount of *future* sunshine required *differed* between alternatives: The mechanical meters didn't require any sunshine, but the solar-powered meters needed a great deal of sunshine.

Likewise, in deciding between the Corolla and Sentra, you will likely consider qualitative factors that differ between the cars (legroom, trunk capacity, dashboard design, and so forth) before making your final decision. Since you must live with these factors in the future, they become relevant to your decision.

Keys to Making Short-Term Special Decisions

Our approach to making short-term special decisions is called the *relevant information approach* or the *incremental analysis approach.* Instead of looking at the company's *entire* income statement under each decision alternative, we'll just look at how operating income would *change or differ* under each alternative. Using this approach, we'll leave out irrelevant information—the costs and revenues that won't differ between alternatives.

We'll consider six kinds of decisions in this chapter:

1. Special sales orders

2. Pricing

3. Dropping products, departments, and territories

4. Product mix

5. Outsourcing (make or buy)

6. Selling as is or processing further

As you study these decisions, keep in mind the two keys in analyzing short-term special business decisions shown in Exhibit 8-3:

1. **Focus on relevant revenues, costs, and profits.** Irrelevant information only clouds the picture and creates information overload. That's why we'll use the incremental analysis approach.

2. **Use a contribution margin approach that separates variable costs from fixed costs.** Because fixed costs and variable costs behave differently, they must be analyzed separately. Traditional (absorption costing) income statements, which blend fixed and variable costs, can mislead managers. Contribution margin income statements, which isolate costs by behavior (variable or fixed), help managers gather the cost-behavior information they need. Keep in mind that unit manufacturing costs are mixed costs, too, so they can also mislead managers. If you use unit manufacturing costs in your analysis, make sure you separate the cost's fixed and variable components first.

We'll use these two keys in each decision.

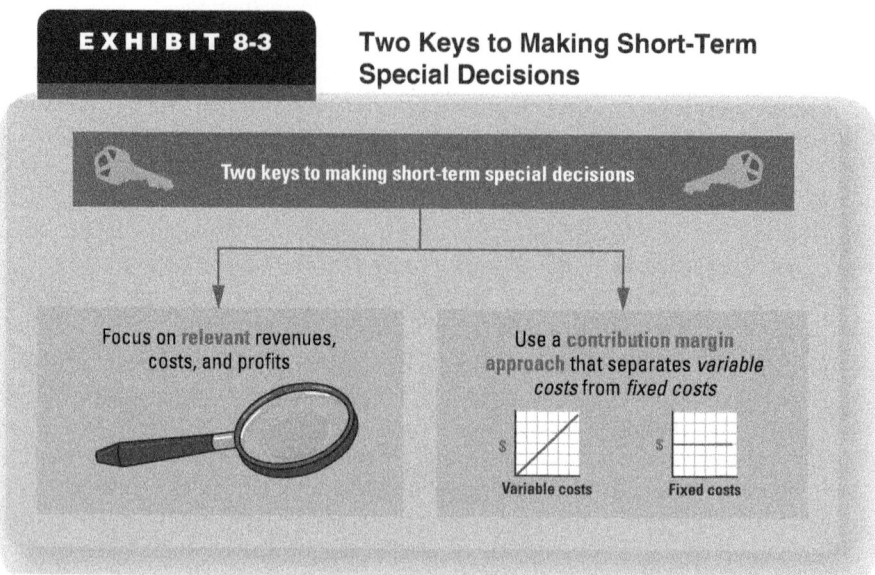

EXHIBIT 8-3   Two Keys to Making Short-Term Special Decisions

Special Sales Order and Regular Pricing Decisions

We'll start our discussion on the six business decisions by looking at special sales order decisions and regular pricing decisions. In the past, managers did not consider pricing to be a short-term decision. However, product life cycles are shrinking in most industries. Companies often sell products for only a few months before replacing them with an updated model. The clothing and technology industries have always had short life cycles. Even auto and housing styles change frequently. Pricing has become a shorter-term decision than it was in the past.

Let's examine a special sales order in detail; then we will discuss regular pricing decisions.

Special Sales Order Decisions

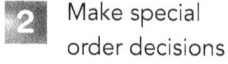
Make special order decisions

A special order occurs when a customer requests a one time order at a *reduced* sales price. Often, these special orders are for large quantities. Before agreeing to the special deal, management must consider the questions shown in Exhibit 8-4.

EXHIBIT 8-4   Special Order Considerations

- Do we have excess capacity available to fill this order?

- Will the reduced sales price be high enough to cover the *incremental* costs of filling the order (the variable costs and any additional fixed costs)?

- Will the special order affect regular sales in the long run?

First, managers must consider available capacity. If the company is already making as many units as possible and selling them all at its *regular* sales price, it wouldn't make sense to fill a special order at a *reduced* sales price. Why sell for *less* than the current sales price? Therefore, available excess capacity is a necessity for accepting a special order. This is true for service firms (law firms, caterers, and so forth) as well as manufacturers.

Second, managers need to consider whether the special reduced sales price is high enough to cover the incremental costs of filling the order. The special price *must* exceed the variable costs of filling the order, or the company will lose money on the deal. In other words, the special order must provide a positive contribution margin. Next, the company must consider fixed costs. If the company has excess capacity, fixed costs probably won't be affected by producing more units (or delivering more service). However, in some cases, management may need to hire a consultant or incur some other fixed cost to fill the special order. If so, management will need to consider whether the special sales price is high enough to generate a positive contribution margin *and* cover the additional fixed costs.

Finally, managers need to consider whether the special order will affect regular sales in the long run. Will regular customers find out about the special order and demand a lower price or take their business elsewhere? Will the special order customer come back *again and again*, asking for the same reduced price? Will the special order price start a price war with competitors? Managers must gamble that the answers to these questions are no or consider how customers will respond. Managers may decide that any profit from the special sales order is not worth these risks.

Let's consider a special sales order example. Suppose ACDelco sells oil filters for $3.20 each. Assume that a mail-order company has offered ACDelco $35,000 for 20,000 oil filters, or $1.75 per filter ($35,000 ÷ 20,000 = $1.75). This sale will:

- Use manufacturing capacity that would otherwise be idle.
- Not change fixed costs.
- Not require any variable *nonmanufacturing* expenses (because no extra marketing costs are incurred with this special order).
- Not affect regular sales.

We have addressed every consideration except one: Is the special sales price high enough to cover the variable *manufacturing* costs associated with the order? Let's take a look at the *wrong* way and then the *right* way to figure out the answer to that question.

Suppose ACDelco made and sold 250,000 oil filters before considering the special order. Using the traditional (absorption costing) income statement on the left-hand side of Exhibit 8-5, the manufacturing cost per unit is $2 ($500,000 ÷ 250,000). A manager who does not examine these numbers carefully may believe that ACDelco should *not* accept the special order at a sale price of $1.75 because each oil filter costs $2.00 to manufacture. But appearances can be deceiving! Remember that the unit manufacturing cost of a product ($2) is a *mixed* cost containing both fixed and variable cost components. To correctly answer our question, we need to find only the variable portion of the manufacturing unit cost.

EXHIBIT 8-5	Traditional (Absorption Costing) Format and Contribution Margin Format Income Statements

INCOME STATEMENT
(at a production and sales level of 250,000 units)
Year Ended December 31, 2007

Traditional (Absorption Costing) Format		Contribution Margin Format		
Sales revenue	$800,000	Sales revenue		$800,000
Less cost of goods sold	(500,000)	Less variable expenses:		
Gross profit	300,000	Manufacturing	$(300,000)	
Less marketing and administrative expenses	(200,000)	Marketing and administrative	(75,000)	(375,000)
		Contribution margin		425,000
		Less fixed expenses:		
		Manufacturing	$(200,000)	
		Marketing and administrative	(125,000)	(325,000)
Operating income	$100,000	Operating income		$100,000

The right-hand side of Exhibit 8-5 shows the contribution margin income statement that separates variable expenses from fixed expenses. The contribution margin income statement shows that the *variable* manufacturing cost per unit is only $1.20 ($300,000 ÷ 250,000). The special sales price of $1.75 is *higher* than the variable manufacturing cost of $1.20. Therefore, the special order will provide a positive contribution margin of $0.55 per unit ($1.75 − $1.20). Since the special order is for 20,000 units, ACDelco's total contribution margin should increase by $11,000 (20,000 units × $0.55 per unit) if it accepts this order.

Remember that in this example, ACDelco's variable marketing expenses are irrelevant because the company will not incur the usual variable marketing expenses on this special order. However, this won't always be the case. Many times, companies will also incur variable operating expenses (such as freight-out) on special orders.

Using an incremental analysis approach, ACDelco compares the additional revenues from the special order with the incremental expenses to see if the special order will contribute to profits. Exhibit 8-6 shows that the special sales order will increase revenue by $35,000 (20,000 × $1.75), but it will also increase variable manufacturing cost by $24,000 (20,000 × $1.20). As a result, ACDelco's contribution margin will increase by $11,000, as previously anticipated.

EXHIBIT 8-6	Incremental Analysis of Special Sales Order

Expected increase in revenues—sale of 20,000 oil filters × $1.75 each	$ 35,000
Expected increase in expenses—variable manufacturing costs:	
20,000 oil filters × $1.20 each	(24,000)
Expected increase in operating income	$ 11,000

The other costs shown in Exhibit 8-5 are irrelevant. Variable marketing and administrative expenses will be the same whether or not ACDelco accepts the special order because ACDelco made no marketing efforts to get this sale. Fixed manufacturing expenses won't change because ACDelco has enough idle capacity to produce 20,000 extra oil filters without requiring additional facilities. Fixed marketing and administrative expenses won't be affected by this special order either.

Because there are no additional fixed costs, the total increase in contribution margin flows directly to operating income. As a result, the special sales order will increase operating income by $11,000.

Notice that the analysis follows the two keys to making short-term special business decisions discussed earlier: (1) focus on relevant data (revenues and costs that *will change* if ACDelco accepts the special order) and (2) use a contribution margin approach that separates variable costs from fixed costs.

To summarize, for special sales orders, the decision rule is:

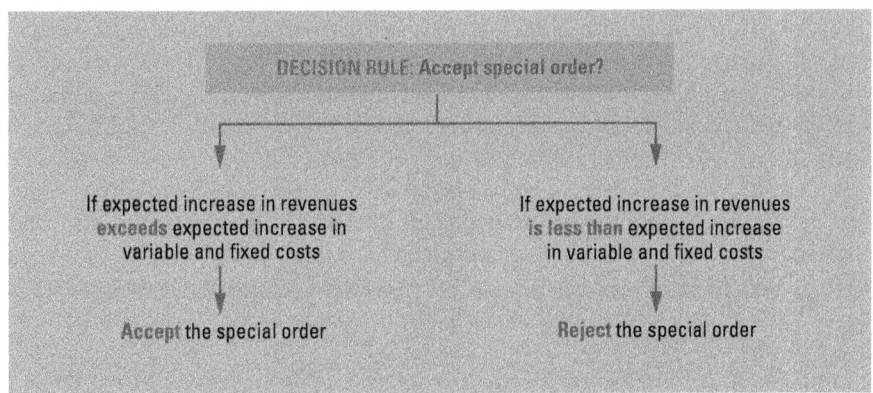

DECISION RULE: Accept special order?

| If expected increase in revenues exceeds expected increase in variable and fixed costs | If expected increase in revenues is less than expected increase in variable and fixed costs |

Accept the special order   Reject the special order

Stop & Think...

The absorption costing income statement on the left-hand side of Exhibit 8-5 shows that the total cost of manufacturing 250,000 filters is $500,000. What is the flaw in reasoning that ACDelco should accept special orders only if the sale price exceeds $2 each?

Answer: The flaw in this analysis arises from treating a mixed cost as though it were variable. Manufacturing one extra oil filter will cost only $1.20—the variable manufacturing cost. Fixed expenses are irrelevant because ACDelco will incur $200,000 of fixed manufacturing overhead expenses whether or not the company accepts the special order. Producing 20,000 more oil filters will not increase *total* fixed expenses, so manufacturing costs increase at the rate of $1.20 per unit, not $2.00 per unit.

Regular Pricing Decisions

In the special order decision, ACDelco decided to sell a limited quantity of oil filters for $1.75 each even though the normal price was $3.20 per unit. But how did ACDelco decide to set its regular price at $3.20 per filter? Exhibit 8-7 shows that managers start with three basic questions when setting regular prices for their products or services.

3 Make pricing decisions

| **EXHIBIT 8-7** | **Regular Pricing Considerations** |

- What is our target profit?
- How much will customers pay?
- Are we a price-taker or a price-setter for this product?

The answers to these questions are often complex and ever-changing. Stockholders expect the company to achieve certain profits. Economic conditions, historical company earnings, industry risk, competition, and new business developments all affect the level of profit that stockholders expect. Stockholders usually tie their profit expectations to the amount of assets invested in the company. For example, stockholders may expect a 10% annual return on their investment. A company's stock price tends to decline if the company does not meet target profits, so managers must keep costs low while generating enough revenue to meet target profits.

This leads to the second question: How much will customers pay? Managers cannot set prices above what customers are willing to pay, or sales will decline. The amount customers will pay depends on the competition, the product's uniqueness, the effectiveness of marketing campaigns, general economic conditions, and so forth.

To address the third pricing question, imagine a continuum with price-takers at one end and price-setters at the other end. A company's products and services fall somewhere along this continuum, shown in Exhibit 8-8. Companies are price-takers when they have little or no control over the prices of their products or services. This occurs when their products and services are *not* unique or when competition is heavy. Examples include food commodities (milk and corn), natural resources (oil and lumber), and generic consumer products and services (paper towels, dry cleaning, and banking).

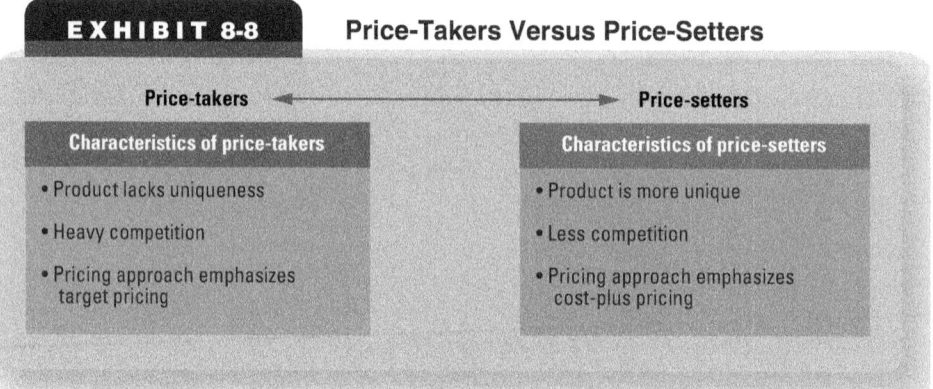

EXHIBIT 8-8   **Price-Takers Versus Price-Setters**

Price-takers ←——————→ Price-setters

Characteristics of price-takers	Characteristics of price-setters
• Product lacks uniqueness	• Product is more unique
• Heavy competition	• Less competition
• Pricing approach emphasizes target pricing	• Pricing approach emphasizes cost-plus pricing

Companies are price-setters when they have more control over pricing—in other words, they can "set" the price to some extent. Companies are price-setters when their products are unique, which results in less competition. Unique products such as original art and jewelry, specially manufactured machinery, patented perfume scents, and custom-made furniture can command higher prices.

Obviously, managers would rather be price-setters than price-takers. To gain more control over pricing, companies try to differentiate their products. They want to make their products unique in terms of features, service, or quality—or at least make you *think* their product is unique or somehow better even if it isn't. How do they do this? Primarily through advertising. Consider Nike's tennis shoes, Starbucks' coffee, Hallmark's wrapping paper, Nexus' shampoo, Tylenol's acetaminophen, General Mills' cereal, Capital One's credit cards, Shell's gas, Abercrombie and Fitch's jeans—the list goes on and on. Are these products really better or significantly different from their lower-priced competitors? Possibly. If these companies can make you think so, they've gained more control over their pricing because you are willing to pay *more* for their products or services. The downside? These companies must charge higher prices or sell more just to cover their advertising costs.

A company's approach to pricing depends on whether its product or service is on the price-taking or price-setting side of the spectrum. Price-takers emphasize a target-pricing approach. Price-setters emphasize a cost-plus pricing approach. Keep in mind that many products fall somewhere along the continuum. Therefore, managers tend to use both approaches to some extent. We'll now discuss each approach in turn.

Target Pricing

When a company is a price-taker, it emphasizes a target pricing approach to pricing. Target pricing starts with the market price of the product (the price customers are willing to pay) and subtracts the company's desired profit to determine the product's **target full cost**—the *full* cost to develop, design, produce, market, deliver, and service the product. In other words, the full cost includes every cost incurred throughout the value chain.

> Revenue at market price
> Less: Desired profit
> Target full cost

In this relationship, the market price is "taken." If the product's current cost is higher than the target cost, the company must find ways to reduce costs; otherwise it will not meet its profit goals. Managers often use ABC costing along with value engineering (as discussed in Chapter 5) to find ways to cut costs. Let's look at an example of target pricing.

Let's assume that oil filters are a commodity and that the current market price is $3.00 per filter (not the $3.20 sales price assumed in the earlier ACDelco example). Because the oil filters are a commodity, ACDelco will emphasize a target-pricing approach. Let's assume that ACDelco's stockholders expect a 10% annual return on the company's assets. If the company has $1,000,000 of assets, the desired profit is $100,000 ($1,000,000 × 10%). Exhibit 8-9 calculates the target full cost at the current sales volume (250,000 units). Once we know the target full cost, we can analyze the fixed and variable cost components separately.

EXHIBIT 8-9   **Calculating Target Full Cost**

	Calculations	Total
Revenue at market price	250,000 units × $3.00 price =	$750,000
Less: Desired profit	10% × $1,000,000 of assets	(100,000)
Target full cost		$650,000

Can ACDelco make and sell 250,000 oil filters at a full cost of $650,000? We know from ACDelco's contribution margin income statement (Exhibit 8-5) that the company's variable costs are $1.50 per unit ($375,000 ÷ 250,000 units). This variable cost per unit includes both manufacturing costs ($1.20 per unit) and marketing and administrative costs ($0.30 per unit). We also know that the company incurs $325,000 in fixed costs in its current relevant range. Again, some fixed cost stems from manufacturing and some from marketing and administrative activities. *In setting regular sales prices, companies must cover **all** of their costs— whether inventoriable or period, fixed or variable.*

Making and selling 250,000 filters currently costs the company $700,000 [(250,000 units × $1.50 variable cost per unit) + $325,000 of fixed costs], which is more than the target full cost ($650,000). So, what are ACDelco's options?

1. Accept a lower profit (an operating income of $50,000, which is a 5% return, not the 10% target return)

2. Cut fixed costs

3. Cut variable costs

4. Use other strategies. For example, ACDelco could attempt to increase sales volume. Recall that the company has excess capacity, so making and selling more units would affect only variable costs. The company could also consider changing or adding to its product mix. Finally, it could attempt to differentiate its oil filters (or strengthen its name brand) to gain more control over sales prices.

Let's look at some of these options. ACDelco may first try to cut fixed costs. As shown in Exhibit 8-10, the company would have to reduce fixed costs to $275,000 to meet its target profit level.

EXHIBIT 8-10   **Calculating Target Fixed Cost**

	Calculations	Total
Target full cost		$650,000
Less: Current variable costs	250,000 units × $1.50	(375,000)
Target fixed cost		$275,000

The company would start by considering whether any discretionary fixed costs could be eliminated without harming the company. Since committed fixed costs are nearly impossible to change in the short run, ACDelco will probably not be able to reduce this type of fixed cost.

If the company can't reduce its fixed costs by $50,000 ($325,000 current fixed costs − $275,000 target fixed costs), it would have to lower its variable cost to $1.30 per unit, as shown in Exhibit 8-11.

EXHIBIT 8-11   **Calculating Target Unit Variable Cost**

	Total
Target full cost	$650,000
Less: Current fixed costs	(325,000)
Target total variable costs	$325,000
Divided by number of units	÷ 250,000
Target variable cost per unit	$ 1.30

Perhaps the company could renegotiate raw materials costs with its suppliers or find a less costly way of packaging or shipping the air filters.

However, if ACDelco can't reduce variable costs to $1.30 per unit, could it meet its target profit through a combination of lowering both fixed costs and variable costs?

Stop & Think...

Suppose ACDelco can reduce its current fixed costs but only by $25,000. If it wants to meet its target profit, by how much will it have to reduce the variable cost of each unit? Assume that sales volume remains at 250,000 units.

Answer: Companies typically try to cut both fixed and variable costs. Because ACDelco can cut its fixed costs only by $25,000, to meet its target profit, it would have to cut its variable costs as well:

Target full cost...	$ 650,000
Less: Reduced fixed costs ($325,000 – $25,000)......................	(300,000)
Target total variable costs...	$ 350,000
Divided by number of units..	÷ 250,000
Target variable cost per unit..	$ 1.40

In addition to cutting its fixed costs by $25,000, the company must reduce its variable costs by $0.10 per unit ($1.50 — $1.40) to meet its target profit at the existing volume of sales.

Another strategy would be to increase sales. ACDelco's managers can use CVP analysis, as you learned in Chapter 7, to figure out how many oil filters the company would have to sell to achieve its target profit. How could the company increase demand for the oil filters? Perhaps it could reach new markets or advertise. How much would advertising cost—and how many extra oil filters would the company have to sell to cover the cost of advertising? These are only some of the questions managers must ask. As you can see, managers don't have an easy task when the current cost exceeds the target full cost. Sometimes, companies just can't compete given the current market price. If that's the case, they may have no other choice than to exit the market for that product.

Cost-Plus Pricing

When a company is a price-setter, it emphasizes a cost-plus approach to pricing. This pricing approach is essentially the *opposite* of the target-pricing approach. **Cost-plus pricing** starts with the product's full costs (as a given) and *adds* its desired profit to determine a cost-plus price.

> Full cost
> Plus: Desired profit
> Cost-plus price

When the product is unique, the company has more control over pricing. However, the company still needs to make sure that the cost-plus price is not higher than what customers are willing to pay. Let's go back to our original ACDelco example. This time, let's assume that the oil filters benefit from brand recognition, so the company has some control over the price it charges for its filters. Exhibit 8-12 takes a cost-plus pricing approach assuming the current level of sales:

EXHIBIT 8-12   **Calculating Cost-Plus Price**

	Calculations	Total
Current variable costs	250,000 units × $1.50 per unit =	$375,000
Plus: Current fixed costs		+ 325,000
Full product cost		$700,000
Plus: Desired profit	10% × $1,000,000 of assets	+ 100,000
Target revenue		$800,000
Divided by number of units		÷ 250,000
Cost-plus price per unit		$ 3.20

If the current market price for generic oil filters is $3.00, as we assumed earlier, can ACDelco sell its brand-name filters for $3.20 apiece? The answer depends on how well the company has been able to differentiate its product or brand name. The company may use focus groups or marketing surveys to find out how customers would respond to its cost-plus price. The company may find out that its cost-plus price is too high, or it may find that it could set the price even higher without jeopardizing sales.

Stop & Think...

Which costing system (job costing or process costing) do you think price-setters and price-takers typically use?

Answer: Companies tend to be price-setters when their products are unique. Unique products are produced as single items or in small batches. Therefore, these companies use job costing to determine the product's cost. However, companies are price-takers when their products are high-volume commodities. Process costing better suits this type of product.

Notice how pricing decisions used our two keys to decision making: (1) focus on relevant information and (2) use a contribution margin approach that separates variable costs from fixed costs. In pricing decisions, all cost information is relevant because the company must cover *all* costs along the value chain before it can generate a profit. However, we still needed to consider variable costs and fixed costs separately because they behave differently at different volumes.

Our pricing decision rule is:

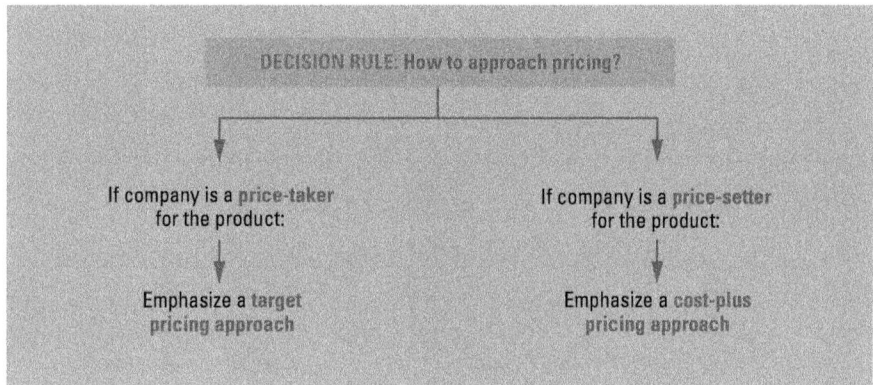

Decision Guidelines

RELEVANT INFORMATION FOR BUSINESS DECISIONS

Nike makes special order and regular pricing decisions. Even though it sells mass-produced tennis shoes and sports clothing, Nike has differentiated its products with advertising. Nike's managers consider both quantitative and qualitative factors as they make pricing decisions. Here are key guidelines that Nike's managers follow in making their decisions.

Decision	Guideline
What information is relevant to a short-term special business decision?	Relevant information: 1. Pertains to the *future* 2. *Differs* between alternatives
What are two key guidelines in making short-term special business decisions?	1. Focus on *relevant* data. 2. Use a *contribution margin* approach that separates variable costs from fixed costs.
Should Nike accept a lower sales price than the regular price for a large order from a customer in São Paulo, Brazil?	If the revenue from the order exceeds the extra variable and fixed costs incurred to fill the order, then accepting the order will increase operating income.
What should Nike consider in setting its regular product prices?	Nike considers: 1. What profit stockholders expect 2. What price customers will pay 3. Whether it is a price-setter or a price-taker
What approach should Nike take to pricing?	Nike has differentiated its products through advertising its brand name. Thus, Nike tends to be a price-setter. Nike's managers can emphasize a cost-plus approach to pricing.
What approach should discount shoe stores such as Payless ShoeSource take to pricing?	Payless ShoeSource sells generic shoes (no-name brands) at low prices. Payless is a price-taker, so managers use a target-pricing approach to pricing.

Summary Problem 1

Szigety Industries makes tennis balls. Szigety's only plant can produce up to 2.5 million cans of balls per year. Current production is 2 million cans. Annual manufacturing, selling, and administrative fixed costs total $700,000. The variable cost of making and selling each can of balls is $1. Stockholders expect a 12% annual return on the company's $3 million of assets.

Requirements

1. What is Szigety's current full cost of making and selling 2 million cans of tennis balls? What is the current full *unit* cost of each can of tennis balls?

2. Assume that Szigety Industries is a price-taker and the current market price is $1.45 per can of balls (this is the price at which manufacturers sell to retailers). What is the *target* full cost of producing and selling 2 million cans of balls? Given Szigety Industries' current costs, will the company reach stockholders' profit goals?

3. If Szigety Industries cannot change its fixed costs, what is the target variable cost per can of balls?

4. Suppose Szigety Industries could spend an extra $100,000 on advertising to differentiate its product so that it could be a price-setter. Assuming the original volume and costs plus the $100,000 of new advertising costs, what cost-plus price will Szigety Industries want to charge for a can of balls?

5. Nike has just asked Szigety Industries to supply 400,000 cans of balls at a special order price of $1.20 per can. Nike wants Szigety Industries to package the balls under the Nike label (Szigety will imprint the Nike logo on each ball and can). Szigety Industries will have to spend $10,000 to change the packaging machinery. Assuming the original volume and costs, should Szigety Industries accept this special order? (Unlike the chapter problem, assume that Szigety will incur variable selling costs as well as variable manufacturing costs related to this order.)

Solution

Requirement 1
The full unit cost is:

Fixed costs	$ 700,000
Plus: Total variable costs (2 million cans × $1 per unit)	+ 2,000,000
Total full costs	$2,700,000
Divided by number of cans...	÷ 2,000,000
Full cost per can..	$ 1.35

Requirement 2
The target full cost is:

Revenue at market price (2,000,000 units × $1.45 price)	$2,900,000
Less: Desired profit (12% × $3,000,000 of assets)	(360,000)
Target *full* cost...	$2,540,000

Szigety Industries' current total full costs ($2,700,000 from Requirement 1) are $160,000 higher than the target full cost ($2,540,000). If Szigety Industries can't cut costs, it won't be able to meet stockholders' profit expectations.

Requirement 3

Assuming that Szigety Industries cannot reduce its fixed costs, the target variable cost per can is:

Target *full* cost (from Requirement 2)	$ 2,540,000
Less: Fixed costs	(700,000)
Target total variable costs	$ 1,840,000
Divided by number of units	÷ 2,000,000
Target variable cost per unit	$ 0.92

Since Szigety Industries cannot reduce its fixed costs, it needs to reduce variable costs by $0.08 per can ($1.00 − $0.92) to meet its profit goals. This would require an 8% cost reduction in variable costs, which may not be possible.

Requirement 4

If Szigety Industries can differentiate its tennis balls, it will gain more control over pricing. The company's new cost-plus price would be:

Current total costs (from Requirement 1)	$2,700,000
Plus: Additional cost of advertising	+ 100,000
Plus: Desired profit (from Requirement 2)	+ 360,000
Target revenue	$3,160,000
Divided by number of units	÷ 2,000,000
Cost-plus price per unit	$ 1.58

Szigety Industries must study the market to determine whether retailers would pay $1.58 per can of balls.

Requirement 5

Nike's special order price ($1.20) is less than the current full cost of each can of balls ($1.35 from Requirement 1). However, this should not influence management's decision. Szigety Industries could fill Nike's special order using existing excess capacity. Szigety Industries takes an incremental analysis approach to its decision: comparing the extra revenue with the incremental costs of accepting the order. Variable costs will increase if Szigety Industries accepts the order, so the variable costs are relevant. Only the *additional* fixed costs of changing the packaging machine ($10,000) are relevant since all other fixed costs will remain unchanged.

Revenue from special order (400,000 × $1.20 per unit)	$480,000
Less: Variable cost of special order (400,000 × $1.00)	(400,000)
Contribution margin from special order	$ 80,000
Less: Additional fixed costs of special order	(10,000)
Operating income provided by special order	$ 70,000

Szigety Industries should accept the special order because it will increase operating income by $70,000. However, Szigety Industries also needs to consider whether its regular customers will find out about the special price and demand lower prices, too.

Other Short-Term Special Business Decisions

In the second part of the chapter, we'll look at other short-term business decisions that managers face, including:

- When to drop a product, department, or territory.
- Which products to emphasize in product mix decisions.
- When to outsource.
- When to sell as is or process further.

Decisions to Drop Products, Departments, or Territories

 4 Make dropping a product, department, or territory decisions

Managers often must decide whether to drop products, departments, or territories that are not as profitable as desired. Newell Rubbermaid—maker of Sharpie markers, Graco strollers, and Rubbermaid plastics—recently dropped some of its European products lines. Home Depot closed some of its Expo stores. Kroger food stores replaced some in-store movie rental departments with health food departments. How do managers make these decisions? Exhibit 8-13 shows some questions managers must consider when deciding whether to drop a product line, department, or territory.

EXHIBIT 8-13 **Considerations for Dropping Products, Departments, or Territories**

- Does the product provide a positive contribution margin?
- Will fixed costs continue to exist even if we drop the product?
- Are there any direct fixed costs that can be avoided if we drop the product?
- Will dropping the product affect sales of the company's other products?
- What could we do with the freed capacity?

Once again, we follow the two key guidelines for special business decisions: (1) focus on relevant data and (2) use a contribution margin approach. The relevant financial data are still the changes in revenues and expenses, but now we are considering a *decrease* in volume rather than an *increase*, as we did in the special sales order decision. In the following example, we will consider how managers decide to drop a product. Managers use the same process in deciding whether to drop a department or territory.

Earlier, we assumed that ACDelco offered only one product—oil filters. Now, let's assume that it makes and sells air cleaners, too. Exhibit 8-14 shows the company's contribution margin income statement by product line. Because the air cleaner product line has an operating loss of $19,074, management is considering dropping it.

The first question management should ask is, does the product provide a positive contribution margin? If the product line has a negative contribution margin, the product is not even covering its variable costs. Therefore, the company should drop the product line. However, if the product line has a positive contribution margin, it is

EXHIBIT 8-14	**Contribution Margin Income Statements by Product Line**

	Total (270,000 units)	Product Line	
		Oil Filters (250,000 units)	Air Cleaners (20,000 units)
Sales revenue	$835,000	$800,000	$ 35,000
Less: Variable expenses	(405,000)	(375,000)	(30,000)
Contribution margin	430,000	425,000	5,000
Less: Fixed expenses:			
Manufacturing	(200,000)	(185,185)*	(14,815)*
Marketing and administrative	(125,000)	(115,741)†	(9,259)†
Total fixed expenses	(325,000)	(300,926)	(24,074)
Operating income (loss)	$105,000	$124,074	$(19,074)

* $200,000 ÷ 270,000 units = $0.74074 per unit; 250,000 units × $0.74074 = $185,185; 20,000 units × $0.74074 = $14,815
† $125,000 ÷ 270,000 units = $0.462963 per unit; 250,000 units × $0.462963 = $115,741; 20,000 units × $0.462963 = $9,259

helping to cover at least some of the company's fixed costs. In ACDelco's case, the air cleaners provide a $5,000 positive contribution margin. ACDelco's managers now need to consider fixed costs.

Suppose ACDelco allocates fixed expenses between product lines in proportion to the number of units sold. Dividing the fixed manufacturing expense of $200,000 by 270,000 total units (oil filters, 250,000; air cleaners, 20,000) yields a fixed manufacturing cost of $0.74074 per unit. Allocating this unit cost to the 250,000 oil filters assigns fixed manufacturing cost of $185,185 to this product, as shown in Exhibit 8-14. The same procedure allocates $14,815 to the 20,000 air cleaners. Fixed marketing and administrative expenses are allocated in the same manner.

It is important to note that this allocation method is arbitrary. ACDelco could allocate fixed costs in many different ways, and each way would have allocated a different amount of fixed costs to each product line. Since the amount of fixed costs allocated to each product line will differ depending on the allocation method used, we need to look at fixed costs in a different light. What matters is this:

1. Will the total fixed costs continue to exist *even if* the product line is dropped?

2. Can any *direct* fixed costs of the air cleaners be avoided if the product line is dropped?

Fixed Costs Continue to Exist (Unavoidable Fixed Costs)

Fixed costs that will continue to exist even after a product is dropped are often called unavoidable fixed costs. Unavoidable fixed costs are irrelevant to the decision because they *will not* differ between alternatives — they will be incurred regardless of whether the product line is dropped. Let's assume that all of ACDelco's fixed costs ($325,000) will continue to exist even if the company drops the air cleaners. Perhaps ACDelco makes the air cleaners in the same manufacturing facilities as the oil filters and uses the same administrative overhead. If that is the case, only the contribution margin the air cleaners provide is relevant. If ACDelco drops the air cleaners, it will lose the $5,000 contribution margin that they provide.

The incremental analysis shown in Exhibit 8-15 verifies the loss. If ACDelco drops the air cleaners, revenue will decrease by $35,000; but variable expenses will decrease by only $30,000, resulting in a net $5,000 decrease in operating income. Because the company's total fixed costs are unaffected, they aren't included in the analysis. This analysis suggests that management should *not* drop the air cleaners.

EXHIBIT 8-15	Incremental Analysis for Dropping a Product When Fixed Costs Continue to Exist	

Expected decrease in revenues:		
Sale of air cleaners (20,000 × $1.75)		$35,000
Expected decrease in expenses:		
Variable manufacturing expenses (20,000 × $1.50)		30,000
Expected *decrease* in operating income		$ (5,000)

We could also verify that our analysis is correct by looking at what would *remain* if the air cleaners were dropped:

Contribution margin from oil filters	$ 425,000
Less: Company's fixed expenses (all unavoidable)	(325,000)
Remaining operating income	$ 100,000

The company's operating income after dropping the air cleaners ($100,000) would be $5,000 less than before ($105,000). This verifies our earlier conclusion: ACDelco's income would decrease by $5,000 if it dropped the air cleaners. Keep in mind that most companies have many product lines. Therefore, analyzing the decision to drop a particular product line is accomplished more easily by performing an incremental analysis (as we did in Exhibit 8-15) rather than adding up all of the revenues and expenses that would remain after dropping one product line. We simply show this second analysis as a means of proving our original result.

Direct Fixed Costs That Can Be Avoided

Even though ACDelco allocates its fixed costs between product lines, some of the fixed costs might *belong* strictly to the air cleaner product line. These would be direct fixed costs of the air cleaners.[1] For example, suppose ACDelco employs a part-time supervisor to oversee *just* the air cleaner product line. The supervisor's $13,000 salary is a direct fixed cost that ACDelco can *avoid* if it stops producing air cleaners. Avoidable fixed costs, such as the supervisor's salary, *are relevant* to the decision because they differ between alternatives (they will be incurred if the company keeps the product line; they will *not* be incurred if the company drops the product line).

Exhibit 8-16 shows that in this situation, operating income will *increase* by $8,000 if ACDelco drops air cleaners. Why? Because revenues will decline by $35,000 but expenses will decline even more—by $43,000. The result is a net increase to operating income of $8,000. This analysis suggests that management should drop the air cleaners.

Other Considerations

Management must also consider whether dropping the product line, department, or territory would hurt other sales. In the examples given so far, we assumed that dropping the air cleaners would not affect oil filter sales. However, think about a

---

[1]To aid in decision making, companies should separate direct fixed costs from indirect fixed costs on their contribution margin income statements. Companies should *trace direct fixed costs* to the appropriate product line and *allocate only indirect fixed costs* among product lines. As in the ACDelco example, companies do not always make this distinction on the income statement.

EXHIBIT 8-16	Incremental Analysis for Dropping a Product When Direct Fixed Costs Can Be Avoided

Expected decrease in revenues:		
Sale of air cleaners (20,000 × $1.75)		$35,000
Expected decrease in expenses:		
Variable manufacturing expenses (20,000 × $1.50)	$30,000	
Direct fixed expenses—supervisor's salary	13,000	
Expected decrease in total expenses		43,000
Expected *increase* in operating income		$ 8,000

grocery store. Even if the produce department is not profitable, would managers drop it? Probably not, because if they did, they would lose customers who want one-stop shopping. In such situations, managers must also include the loss of contribution margin from *other* departments affected by the change when performing the financial analysis shown previously.

Management should also consider what they could do with freed capacity. In the ACDelco example, we assumed that the company produces oil filters and air cleaners using the same manufacturing facilities. If ACDelco drops the air cleaners, could it make and sell another product using the freed capacity? Managers should consider whether using the facilities to produce a different product would be more profitable than using the facilities to produce air cleaners.

Stop & Think...

Assume that all of ACDelco's fixed costs are unavoidable. If the company drops air cleaners, they could make spark plugs with the freed capacity. The company expects spark plugs would provide $50,000 of sales, incur $30,000 of variable costs, and incur $10,000 of new direct fixed costs. Should ACDelco drop the air cleaners and use the freed capacity to make spark plugs?

Answer: If all fixed costs are unavoidable, ACDelco would lose $5,000 of contribution margin if it dropped air cleaners. ACDelco should compare this loss with the expected gain from producing and selling spark plugs with the freed capacity:

Sales of spark plugs	$ 50,000
Less: Variable costs of spark plugs	(30,000)
Less: Direct fixed costs of spark plugs	(10,000)
Operating income gained from spark plugs	$ 10,000

The gain from producing spark plugs ($10,000) outweighs the loss from dropping air cleaners ($5,000). This suggests that management should replace air cleaner production with spark plug production.

Special decisions should take into account all costs affected by the choice of action. Managers must ask what total costs—variable and fixed—will change. As Exhibits 8-15 and 8-16 show, the key to deciding whether to drop products, departments, or territories is to compare the lost revenue against the costs that can be saved and to consider what would be done with the freed capacity. The decision rule is:

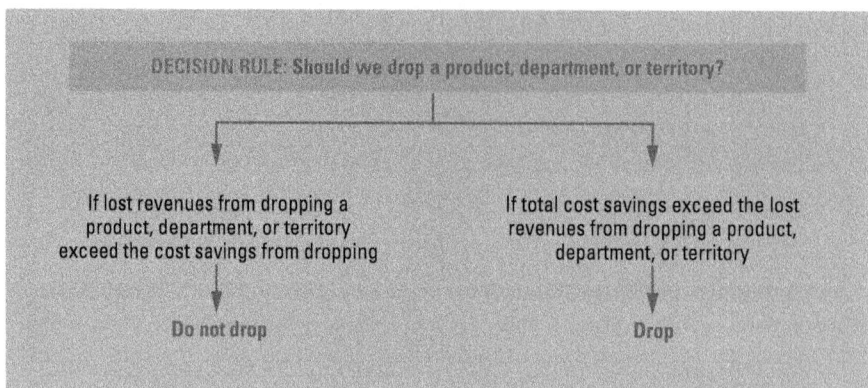

Product Mix Decisions

5 Make product mix decisions

Companies do not have unlimited resources. **Constraints** that restrict production or sale of a product vary from company to company. For a manufacturer such as Dell, the production constraint is often (because it's not always the case) labor hours, machine hours, or available materials. For a merchandiser such as Wal-Mart, the primary constraint is cubic feet of display space. Other companies are constrained by sales demand. Competition may be stiff, so the company may be able to sell only a limited number of units. In such cases, the company produces only as much as it can sell. However, if a company can sell all of the units it produces, which products should it emphasize, or make more of? Companies facing constraints consider the questions in Exhibit 8-17.

EXHIBIT 8-17   **Product Mix Considerations**

- What constraint(s) stops us from making (or displaying) all of the units we can sell?
- Which products offer the highest contribution margin per unit of the constraint?
- Would emphasizing one product over another affect fixed costs?

Consider Chazz, a manufacturer of shirts and jeans. The company can sell all of the shirts and jeans it produces, but it has only 2,000 machine hours of capacity. The company uses the same machines to produce both jeans and shirts. In this case, machine hours is the constraint. Note that this is a short-term decision, because in the long run, Chazz could expand its production facilities to meet sales demand if it

BBH CHAPTER 8

made financial sense to do so. The following data suggest that shirts are more profitable than jeans:

	Per Unit	
	Shirts	**Jeans**
Sale price	$30	$60
Less: Variable expenses	(12)	(48)
Contribution margin	$18	$12
Contribution margin ratio:		
Shirts—$18 ÷ $30	60%	
Jeans—$12 ÷ $60		20%

However, an important piece of information is missing—the time it takes to make each product. Let's assume that Chazz can produce either 20 pairs of jeans *or* 10 shirts per machine hour. *The company will incur the same fixed costs either way, so fixed costs are irrelevant.* Which product should it emphasize?

To maximize profits when fixed costs are irrelevant, follow the decision rule:

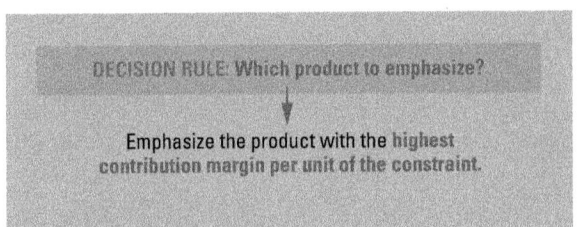

DECISION RULE: Which product to emphasize?

Emphasize the product with the highest contribution margin per unit of the constraint.

Because *machine hours* is the constraint, Chazz needs to figure out which product has the *highest contribution margin per machine hour*. Exhibit 8-18 shows the contribution margin per machine hour for each product.

EXHIBIT 8-18   **Product Mix—Which Product to Emphasize**

	Shirts	Jeans
(1) Units that can be produced each machine hour	10	20
(2) Contribution margin per unit	× $18	× $12
Contribution margin per machine hour (1) × (2)	$180	$240
Available capacity—number of machine hours	× 2,000	× 2,000
Total contribution margin at full capacity	$360,000	$480,000

Jeans have a higher contribution margin per machine hour ($240) than shirts ($180). Therefore Chazz will earn more profit by producing jeans. Why? Because even though jeans have a lower contribution margin *per unit*, Chazz can make

BBH CHAPTER 8

twice as many jeans as shirts in the available machine hours. Exhibit 8-18 also proves that Chazz earns more total profit by making jeans. Multiplying the contribution margin per machine hour by the available number of machine hours shows that Chazz can earn $480,000 of contribution margin by producing jeans but only $360,000 by producing shirts.

To maximize profit, Chazz should make 40,000 jeans (2,000 machine hours × 20 jeans per hour) and zero shirts. Why zero shirts? Because for every machine hour spent making shirts, Chazz would *give up* $60 of contribution margin ($240 per hour for jeans versus $180 per hour for shirts).

Changing Assumptions: Product Mix When Demand Is Limited

We made two assumptions about Chazz: (1) Chazz's sales of other products, if any, won't be hurt by this decision and (2) Chazz can sell as many jeans and shirts as it can produce. Let's challenge these assumptions. First, how could making only jeans (and not shirts) hurt sales of the company's other products? Using other production equipment, Chazz also makes ties and knit sweaters that coordinate with their shirts. Tie and sweater sales might fall if Chazz no longer offers coordinating shirts.

Let's challenge our second assumption. A new competitor has decreased the demand for Chazz's jeans. Now, the company can sell only 30,000 pairs of jeans. Chazz should make only as many jeans as it can sell and use the remaining machine hours to produce shirts. Let's see how this constraint in sales demand changes profitability.

Recall from Exhibit 8-18 that Chazz will earn $480,000 of contribution margin from using all 2,000 machine hours to produce jeans. However, if Chazz makes only 30,000 jeans, it will use only 1,500 machine hours (30,000 jeans ÷ 20 jeans per machine hour). That leaves 500 machine hours available for making shirts. Chazz's new contribution margin will be:

	Shirts	Jeans	Total
Contribution margin per machine hour (from Exhibit 8-18)...............	$ 180	$ 240	
Machine hours devoted to product......	× 500	× 1,500	2,000
Total contribution margin at full capacity.................................	$90,000	$360,000	$450,000

Because of the change in product mix, Chazz's total contribution margin will fall from $480,000 to $450,000, a $30,000 decline. Chazz had to give up $60 of contribution margin per machine hour ($240 − $180) on the 500 hours it spent producing shirts rather than jeans. However, Chazz had no choice—the company would have incurred an *actual loss* from producing jeans that it could not sell. If Chazz had produced 40,000 jeans but sold only 30,000, the company would have spent $480,000 to make the unsold jeans (10,000 jeans × $48 variable cost per pair of jeans) yet would have received no sales revenue from them.

What about fixed costs? In most cases, changing the product mix emphasis in the short run will not affect fixed costs, so fixed costs are irrelevant. However, fixed costs could differ when a different product mix is emphasized. What if Chazz had a month-to-month lease on a zipper machine used only for making jeans? If Chazz made only shirts, it could *avoid* the lease cost. However, if Chazz makes any jeans, it needs the machine. In this case, the fixed costs become relevant because they differ between alternative product mixes (shirts only *versus* jeans only or jeans and shirts).

Stop & Think...

Would Chazz's product mix decision change if it had a $20,000 cancelable lease on a zipper machine needed only for jean production? Assume that Chazz can sell as many units as it makes.

Answer: We would compare the profitability as follows:

	Shirts	Jeans
Total contribution margin at full capacity (from Exhibit 8-18)	$360,000	$480,000
Less: Avoidable fixed costs	-0-	(20,000)
Net benefit	$360,000	$460,000

Even considering the zipper machine lease, producing jeans is more profitable than producing shirts. Chazz would prefer producing jeans over shirts unless demand for jeans drops so low that the net benefit from jeans is less than $360,000 (the benefit gained from solely producing shirts).

Notice that the analysis again follows the two guidelines for special business decisions: (1) focus on relevant data (only those revenues and costs that differ) and (2) use a contribution margin approach, which separates variable from fixed costs.

Outsourcing Decisions (Make-or-Buy)

Recall from the chapter's opening story that Delta outsources much of its reservation work and airplane maintenance. **Outsourcing** decisions are sometimes called **make-or-buy** decisions because managers must decide whether to buy a component product or service or produce it in-house. The heart of these decisions is *how best to use available resources.*

Let's see how managers make outsourcing decisions. DefTone, a manufacturer of music CDs, is deciding whether to make paper liners for CD jewel boxes (the plastic cases in which CDs are sold) in-house or whether to outsource them to Mūz-Art, a company that specializes in producing paper liners. DefTone's cost to produce 250,000 liners is:

6 Make outsourcing (make-or-buy) decisions

	Total Cost (250,000 liners)
Direct materials	$ 40,000
Direct labor	20,000
Variable manufacturing overhead	15,000
Fixed manufacturing overhead	50,000
Total manufacturing cost	$125,000
Number of liners	÷ 250,000
Cost per liner	$ 0.50

BBH CHAPTER 8

Mūz-Art offers to sell DefTone the liners for $0.37 each. Should DefTone make the liners or buy them from Mūz-Art? DefTone's $0.50 cost per unit to make the liner is $0.13 higher than the cost of buying it from Mūz-Art. It first appears that DefTone should outsource the liners. But the correct answer is not so simple. Why? Because manufacturing unit costs contain both fixed and variable components. In deciding whether to outsource, managers must consider fixed and variable costs separately. Exhibit 8-19 shows some of the questions management must consider when deciding whether to outsource.

EXHIBIT 8-19	**Outsourcing Considerations**

- How do our variable costs compare to the outsourcing cost?
- Are any fixed costs avoidable if we outsource?
- What could we do with the freed capacity?

Let's see how these considerations apply to DefTone. By purchasing the liners, DefTone can avoid all variable manufacturing costs—$40,000 of direct materials, $20,000 of direct labor, and $15,000 of variable manufacturing overhead. In total, the company will save $75,000 in variable manufacturing costs, or $0.30 per liner ($75,000 ÷ 250,000 liners). However, DefTone will have to pay the variable outsourcing cost of $0.37 per unit, or $92,500 for the 250,000 liners. Based only on variable costs, the lower cost alternative is to manufacture the liners in-house. However, managers must still consider fixed costs.

Assume that DefTone cannot avoid any of the fixed costs by outsourcing. In this case, the company's fixed costs are irrelevant to the decision because DefTone would continue to incur $50,000 of fixed costs regardless of whether the company outsources the liners. The fixed costs are irrelevant because they do not differ between alternatives. DefTone should continue to make its own liners because the variable cost of outsourcing the liners ($92,500) exceeds the variable cost of making the liners ($75,000).

However, what if DefTone can avoid some fixed costs by outsourcing the liners? Let's assume that management can reduce fixed overhead cost by $10,000 by outsourcing the liners. DefTone will still incur $40,000 of fixed overhead ($50,000 − $10,000) even if they outsource the liners. In this case, fixed costs become relevant to the decision because they differ between alternatives. Exhibit 8-20 shows the differences in costs between the make and buy alternatives under this scenario.

EXHIBIT 8-20	**Incremental Analysis for Outsourcing Decision**

Liner Costs	Make Liners	Buy Liners	Difference
Variable costs:			
Direct materials	$ 40,000	—	$40,000
Direct labor	20,000	—	20,000
Variable overhead	15,000	—	15,000
Purchase cost from Mūz-Art			
(250,000 × $0.37)	—	$ 92,500	(92,500)
Fixed overhead	50,000	40,000	10,000
Total cost of liners	$125,000	$132,500	$ (7,500)

Exhibit 8-20 shows that it would still cost DefTone less to make the liners than to buy them from Mūz-Art, even with the $10,000 reduction in fixed costs. The net savings from making 250,000 liners is $7,500.

Exhibit 8-20 also shows that outsourcing decisions follow our two key guidelines for special business decisions: (1) focus on relevant data (differences in costs in this case) and (2) use a contribution margin approach that separates variable costs from fixed costs.

Note how the unit cost—which does not separate costs according to behavior—can be deceiving. If DefTone's managers made their decision by comparing the total manufacturing cost per liner ($0.50) to the outsourcing unit cost per liner ($0.37), they would have incorrectly decided to outsource. Recall that the manufacturing unit cost ($0.50) contains both fixed and variable components whereas the outsourcing cost ($0.37) is strictly variable. To make the correct decision, DefTone had to separate the two cost components and analyze them separately.

Our decision rule for outsourcing is:

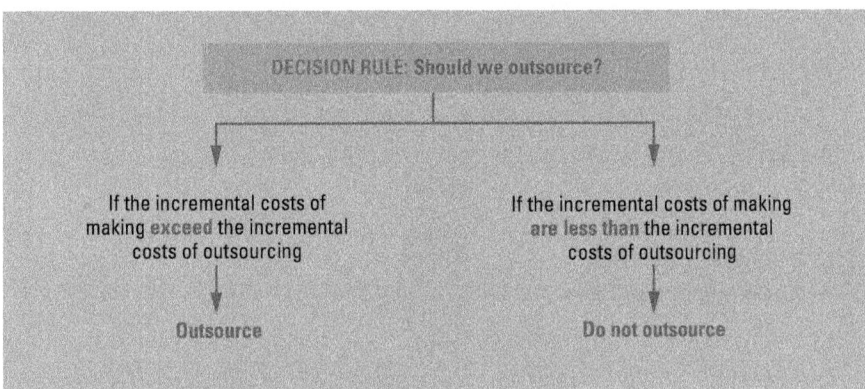

Stop & Think...

Assuming that DefTone could save $10,000 in fixed costs by outsourcing, what is the most the company would be willing to pay per liner to outsource production of 250,000 liners?

Answer: To answer that question, we must find the outsourcing price at which DefTone would be *indifferent* about making the liners or outsourcing the liners. DefTone would be indifferent if the total costs were the *same* either way:

$$\text{Costs if making liners} = \text{Costs if outsourcing liners}$$
$$\text{Variable manufacturing costs} + \text{Fixed costs} = \text{Variable outsourcing costs} + \text{Fixed costs}$$
$$(250,000 \text{ units} \times \$0.30 \text{ per unit}) + \$50,000 = (250,000 \times \text{outsourcing cost per unit}) + \$40,000$$
$$\$75,000 + \$50,000 - \$40,000 = (250,000 \times \text{outsourcing cost per unit})$$
$$\$85,000 = (250,000 \times \text{outsourcing cost per unit})$$
$$\$85,000 \div 250,000 = \text{outsourcing cost per unit}$$
$$\$0.34 = \text{outsourcing cost per unit}$$

DefTone would be indifferent about making or outsourcing the liners if the outsourcing cost price was $0.34 per unit. At that price, DefTone would incur the same cost to manufacture or outsource the liners. DefTone would save money only if the outsourcing price was less than $0.34 per unit. Therefore, the most DefTone would pay to outsource is $0.33 per liner. As shown below, at $0.33 per liner, DefTone would save $2,500 from outsourcing:

Liner Costs	Make Liners	Buy Liners	Difference
Variable costs	$ 75,000 (250,000 units × $0.30 per unit)	$ 82,500 (250,000 × $0.33 per unit)	($7,500)
Plus: Fixed costs	50,000	40,000	10,000
Total costs	$125,000	$122,500	$2,500

BBH CHAPTER 8

We haven't considered what DefTone could do with the freed capacity it would have if it decided to outsource the liners. The analysis in Exhibit 8-20 assumes no other use for the production facilities if DefTone buys the liners from Mūz-Art. But suppose DefTone has an opportunity to use its freed capacity to make more CDs for an additional profit of $18,000. Now, DefTone must consider its **opportunity cost**—the benefit forgone by not choosing an alternative course of action. In this case, DefTone's opportunity cost of making the liners is the $18,000 profit it forgoes if it does not free its production facilities to make the additional CDs.

Let's see how DefTone's managers decide among three alternatives:

1. Use the facilities to make the liners

2. Buy the liners and leave facilities idle (continue to assume $10,000 of avoidable fixed costs from outsourcing liners)

3. Buy the liners and use facilities to make more CDs (continue to assume $10,000 of avoidable fixed costs from outsourcing liners)

The alternative with the lowest *net* cost is the best use of DefTone's facilities. Exhibit 8-21 compares the three alternatives.

EXHIBIT 8-21   Best Use of Facilities Given Opportunity Costs

	Make Liners	Buy Liners	
		Facilities Idle	Make Additional CDs
Expected cost of 250,000 liners (from Exhibit 8-20)	$125,000	$132,500	$132,500
Expected *profit* from additional CDs	—	—	(18,000)
Expected net cost of obtaining 250,000 liners	$125,000	$132,500	$114,500

DefTone should buy the liners from Mūz-Art and use the vacated facilities to make more CDs. If DefTone makes the liners or buys the liners from Mūz-Art but leaves its production facilities idle, it will forgo the opportunity to earn $18,000.

Stop & Think...

How will the $18,000 opportunity cost change the *maximum* amount DefTone is willing to pay to outsource each liner?

Answer: DefTone will now be willing to pay *more* to outsource its liners. In essence, the company is willing to pay for the opportunity to make more CDs.

DefTone's managers should consider qualitative factors as well as revenue and cost differences in making their final decision. For example, DefTone managers may believe they can better control quality or delivery schedules by making the liners themselves. This argues for making the liners.

Outsourcing decisions are increasingly important in today's globally wired economy. In the past, make-or-buy decisions often ended up as "make" because coordination, information exchange, and paperwork problems made buying from suppliers too inconvenient. Now, companies can use the Internet to tap into information systems of suppliers and customers located around the world.

Paperwork vanishes, and information required to satisfy the strictest JIT delivery schedule is available in real time. As a result, companies are focusing on their core competencies and outsourcing more functions.

Sell As Is or Process Further Decisions

At what point in processing should a company sell its product? Many companies, especially in the food processing and natural resource industries, face this business decision. Companies in these industries process a raw material (milk, corn, livestock, crude oil, lumber, and so forth) to a point before it is saleable. For example, Kraft pasteurizes raw milk before it is saleable. Kraft must then decide whether it should sell the pasteurized milk as is or process it further into other dairy products (reduced-fat milk, butter, sour cream, cottage cheese, yogurt, blocks of cheese, shredded cheese, and so forth). Managers consider the questions shown in Exhibit 8-22 when deciding whether to sell as is or process further.

 Make sell as is or process further decisions

EXHIBIT 8-22 **Sell As Is or Process Further Considerations**

- How much revenue will we receive if we sell the product as is?
- How much revenue will we receive if we sell the product *after* processing it further?
- How much will it cost to process the product further?

Let's look at one of Chevron's sell or process further decisions. Suppose Chevron spent $125,000 to process crude oil into 50,000 gallons of regular gasoline, as shown in Exhibit 8-23. After processing crude oil into regular gasoline, should Chevron sell the regular gas as is or should it spend more to process the gasoline into premium grade? In making the decision, Chevron's managers consider the following relevant information:

EXHIBIT 8-23 **Sell As Is or Process Further Decision**

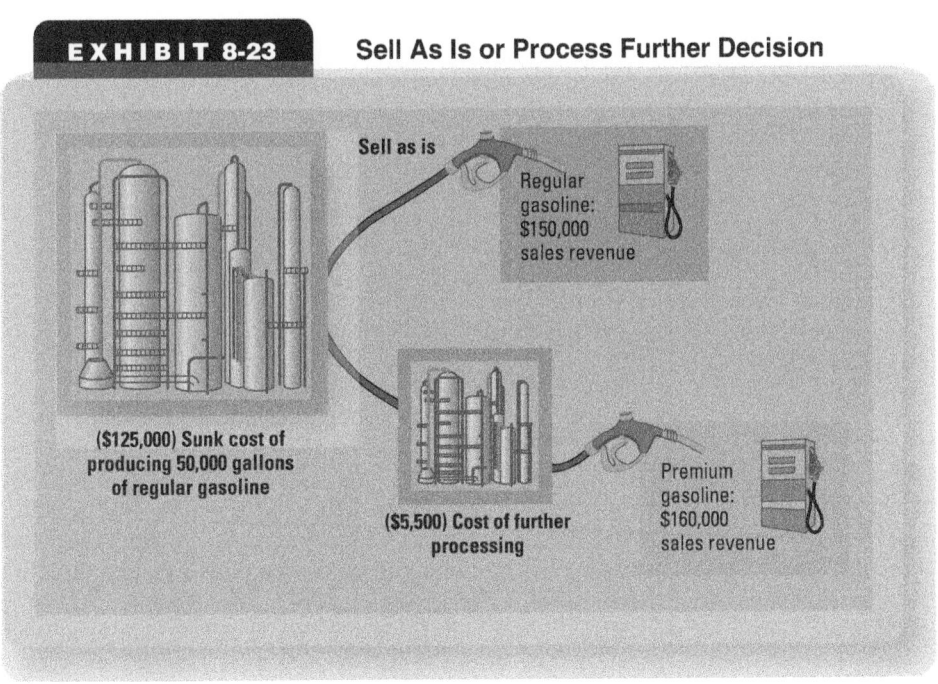

Sell as is

Regular gasoline: $150,000 sales revenue

($125,000) Sunk cost of producing 50,000 gallons of regular gasoline

($5,500) Cost of further processing

Premium gasoline: $160,000 sales revenue

BBH CHAPTER 8

- Chevron could sell regular gasoline for $3 per gallon, for a total of $150,000 (50,000 × $3.00).

- Chevron could sell premium gasoline for $3.20 per gallon, for a total of $160,000 (50,000 × $3.20).

- Chevron would have to spend $0.11 per gallon, or $5,500 (50,000 gallons × $0.11), to further process regular gasoline into premium-grade gas.

Notice that Chevron's managers do *not* consider the $125,000 spent on processing crude oil into regular gasoline. Why? It is a sunk cost. Recall from our previous discussion that a sunk cost is a past cost that cannot be changed regardless of which future action the company takes. Chevron has incurred $125,000 regardless of whether it sells the regular gasoline as is or processes it further into premium gasoline. Therefore, the cost is *not* relevant to the decision.

EXHIBIT 8-24   **Incremental Analysis for Sell As Is or Process Further Decision**

	Sell As Is	Process Further	Difference
Expected revenue from selling 50,000 gallons of regular gasoline at $3.00 per gallon	$150,000		
Expected revenue from selling 50,000 gallons of premium gasoline at $3.20 per gallon		$160,000	$10,000
Additional costs of $0.11 per gallon to convert 50,000 gallons of regular gasoline into premium gasoline		(5,500)	(5,500)
Total net revenue	$150,000	$154,500	$ 4,500

By analyzing only the relevant costs in Exhibit 8-24, managers see that they can increase profit by $4,500 if they convert the regular gasoline into premium gasoline. The $10,000 extra revenue ($160,000 − $150,000) outweighs the incremental $5,500 cost of the extra processing.

Thus, the decision rule is:

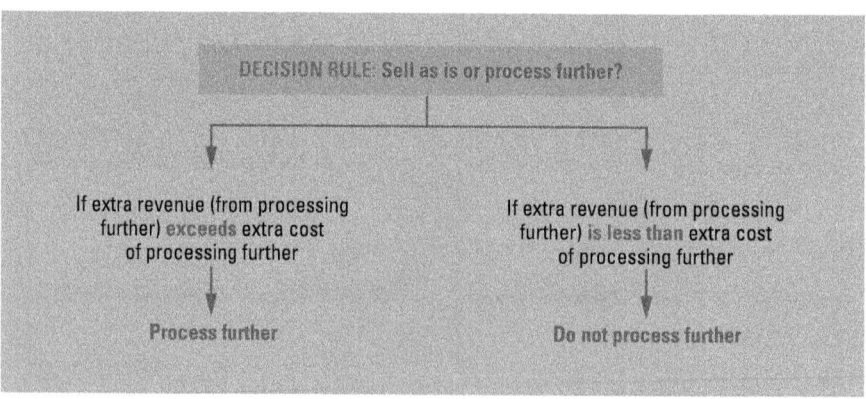

Recall that our keys to decision making include (1) focusing on relevant information and (2) using a contribution margin approach that separates variable costs from fixed costs. The analysis in Exhibit 8-24 includes only those *future* costs and revenues that *differ* between alternatives. We assumed that Chevron already has the equipment and labor necessary to convert regular gasoline into premium-grade gasoline. Because fixed costs would not differ between alternatives, they were irrelevant. However, if

Chevron has to acquire equipment or hire employees to convert the gasoline into premium-grade gasoline, the extra fixed costs would be relevant. Once again, we see that fixed costs are relevant only if they *differ* between alternatives.

Stop & Think...

Suppose one of Chevron's customers wants to buy the 50,000 gallons, but in the form of regular gasoline, not premium gasoline. The customer is willing to pay more than $3 a gallon for the regular gasoline. What is the minimum price Chevron should charge?

Answer: Exhibit 8-24 shows that if Chevron does not process the gasoline into premium grade, it will give up $154,500 of net revenue ($160,000 revenues given up − $5,500 further processing cost not incurred). To obtain at least the same income from selling the gasoline as regular grade, Chevron must sell the regular gasoline for at least $3.09 per gallon ($154,500 ÷ 50,000 gallons of regular gasoline). At $3.09 per gallon, Chevron would be indifferent about the two alternatives. If the customer offers to pay more than $3.09 per gallon, Chevron will be better off selling regular gasoline to this customer. If the customer offers less than $3.09, Chevron will be better off further processing the gasoline into premium-grade gasoline.

Decision Guidelines

SHORT-TERM SPECIAL BUSINESS DECISIONS

Amazon.com has confronted most of the special business decisions we've covered. Here are the key guidelines Amazon.com's managers follow in making their decisions.

Decision	Guideline
Should Amazon.com drop its electronics product line?	If the cost savings exceed the lost revenues from dropping the electronics product line, then dropping will increase operating income.
Given limited warehouse space, which products should Amazon.com focus on selling?	Amazon.com should focus on selling the products with the highest contribution margin per unit of the constraint, which is cubic feet of warehouse space.
Should Amazon.com outsource its warehousing operations?	If the incremental costs of operating its own warehouses exceed the costs of outsourcing, then outsourcing will increase operating income.
How should a company decide whether to sell a product as is or process further?	Process further only if the extra sales revenue (from processing further) exceeds the extra costs of additional processing.

Summary Problem 2

BBH CHAPTER 8

Requirements

1. Aziz produces standard and deluxe sunglasses:

	Per Pair	
	Standard	Deluxe
Sale price	$20	$30
Variable expenses	16	21

The company has 15,000 machine hours available. In one machine hour, Aziz can produce 70 pairs of the standard model or 30 pairs of the deluxe model. Assuming machine hours is a constraint, which model should Aziz emphasize?

2. Just Do It! incurs the following costs for 20,000 pairs of its high-tech hiking socks:

Direct materials	$ 20,000
Direct labor	80,000
Variable manufacturing overhead	40,000
Fixed manufacturing overhead	80,000
Total manufacturing cost	$220,000
Cost per pair ($220,000 ÷ 20,000)	$ 11

Another manufacturer has offered to sell Just Do It! similar socks for $10 a pair, a total purchase cost of $200,000. If Just Do It! outsources *and* leaves its plant idle, it can save $50,000 of fixed overhead cost. Or the company can use the released facilities to make other products that will contribute $70,000 to profits. In this case, the company will not be able to avoid any fixed costs. Identify and analyze the alternatives. What is the best course of action?

Solution

Requirement 1

	Style of Sunglasses	
	Standard	Deluxe
Sale price per pair	$ 20	$ 30
Variable expense per pair	(16)	(21)
Contribution margin per pair	$ 4	$ 9
Units produced each machine hour	× 70	× 30
Contribution margin per machine hour	$ 280	$ 270
Capacity—number of machine hours	× 15,000	× 15,000
Total contribution margin at full capacity	$4,200,000	$4,050,000

Decision: Emphasize the standard model because it has the higher contribution margin per unit of the constraint—machine hours—resulting in a higher contribution margin for the company.

Requirement 2

| | Make Socks | Buy Socks | |
		Facilities Idle	Make Other Products
Relevant costs:			
Direct materials............................	$ 20,000	—	—
Direct labor.................................	80,000	—	—
Variable overhead	40,000	—	—
Fixed overhead.............................	80,000	$ 30,000	$ 80,000
Purchase cost from outsider (20,000 × $10)	—	200,000	200,000
Total cost of obtaining socks......	220,000	230,000	280,000
Profit from other products	—	—	(70,000)
Net cost of obtaining 20,000 pairs of socks	$220,000	$230,000	$210,000

Decision: Just Do It! should buy the socks from the outside supplier and use the released facilities to make other products.

Review *Short-Term Business Decisions*

■ Accounting Vocabulary

Constraint. (p. 434)
A factor that restricts production or sale of a product.

Cost-Plus Pricing. (p. 425)
An approach to pricing that begins with the product's full costs and adds a desired profit to determine a cost-plus price.

Opportunity Cost. (p. 440)
The benefit forgone by not choosing an alternative course of action.

Outsourcing. (p. 437)
A make-or-buy decision: Managers decide whether to buy a component product or service or produce it in-house.

Relevant Information. (p. 415)
Expected *future* data that *differs* among alternatives.

Sunk Cost. (p. 416)
A past cost that cannot be changed regardless of which future action is taken.

Target Full Cost. (p. 423)
The total cost to develop, design, produce, market, deliver, and service a product.

■ Quick Check

1. In making short-term special decisions, you should
   a. focus on total costs
   b. separate variable from fixed costs
   c. use a traditional absorption costing approach
   d. focus only on quantitative factors

2. Which of the following is relevant to Amazon.com's decision to accept a special order at a lower sale price from a large customer in China?
   a. the cost of Amazon.com's warehouses in the United States
   b. Amazon.com's investment in its Web site
   c. the cost of shipping the order to the customer
   d. founder Jeff Bezos's salary

3. In deciding whether to drop its electronics product line, Amazon.com would consider
   a. the costs it could save by dropping the product line
   b. the revenues it would lose from dropping the product line
   c. how dropping the electronics product line would affect sales of its other products, such as CDs
   d. all of the above

4. In deciding which product lines to emphasize, Amazon.com should focus on the product line that has the highest
   a. contribution margin per unit of the constraining factor
   b. contribution margin per unit of product
   c. contribution margin ratio
   d. profit per unit of product

5. When making outsourcing decisions
   a. the manufacturing full unit cost of making the product in-house is relevant
   b. the variable cost of producing the product in-house is relevant
   c. avoidable fixed costs are irrelevant
   d. expected use of the freed capacity is irrelevant

6. When companies are price-setters, their products and services
   a. are priced by managers using a target-pricing emphasis
   b. tend to be unique
   c. tend to have a great many competitors
   d. tend to be commodities

7. When pricing a product or service, managers must consider which of the following?
   a. only variable costs
   b. only period costs
   c. only manufacturing costs
   d. all costs

8. Which of the following costs are irrelevant to business decisions?
   a. sunk costs
   b. costs that differ between alternatives
   c. variable costs
   d. avoidable costs

9. When deciding whether to sell as is or process a product further, managers should ignore which of the following?
   a. the revenue if the product is processed further
   b. the cost of processing further
   c. the costs of processing the product thus far
   d. the revenue if the product is sold as is

10. When making decisions, managers should
    a. consider sunk costs
    b. consider costs that do not differ between alternatives
    c. consider only variable costs
    d. consider revenues that differ between alternatives

Quick Check Answers

1. b 2. c 3. d 4. a 5. b 6. b 7. d 8. a 9. c 10. d

For Internet Exercises, Excel in Practice, and additional online activities, go to this book's Web site at www.prenhall.com/bamber.

Assess Your Progress

▣ Learning Objectives

1 Describe and identify information relevant to short-term business decisions

2 Make special order decisions

3 Make pricing decisions

4 Make dropping a product, department, or territory decisions

5 Make product mix decisions

6 Make outsourcing (make-or-buy) decisions

7 Make sell as is or process further decisions

▣ Short Exercises

S8-1 **Determine relevance of information** *(Learning Objective 1)*

You are trying to decide whether to trade in your ink-jet printer for a more recent model. Your usage pattern will remain unchanged, but the old and new printers use different ink cartridges. Are the following items relevant or irrelevant to your decision?

a. The price of the new printer

b. The price you paid for the old printer

c. The trade-in value of the old printer

d. Paper costs

e. The difference between the cost of ink cartridges

S8-2 **Special order decision given revised data** *(Learning Objective 2)*

Consider the ACDelco special sales order example on pages 419–421. Suppose ACDelco's variable manufacturing cost is $1.35 per oil filter (instead of $1.20). In addition, ACDelco would have to buy a special stamping machine that costs $9,000 to mark the customer's logo on the special-order oil filters. The machine would be scrapped when the special order is complete.

Would you recommend that ACDelco accept the special order under these conditions? Show your analysis.

S8-3 **Determine pricing approach and target price** *(Learning Objective 3)*

SnowDreams operates a Rocky Mountain ski resort. The company is planning its lift ticket pricing for the coming ski season. Investors would like to earn a 15% return on the company's $100 million of assets. The company incurs primarily fixed costs to groom the runs and operate the lifts. SnowDreams projects fixed costs to be $33,750,000 for the ski season. The resort serves about 750,000 skiers and snowboarders each season. Variable costs are about $10 per guest. Currently, the resort has such a favorable reputation among skiers and snowboarders that it has some control over the lift ticket prices.

1. Would SnowDreams emphasize target pricing or cost-plus pricing. Why?

2. If other resorts in the area charge $70 per day, what price should SnowDreams charge?

S8-4 **Use target pricing to analyze data** *(Learning Objective 3)*
Consider SnowDreams from S8-3. Assume that SnowDreams' reputation has diminished and other resorts in the vicinity are charging only $65 per lift ticket. SnowDreams has become a price-taker and won't be able to charge more than its competitors. At the market price, SnowDreams managers believe they will still serve 750,000 skiers and snowboarders each season.

1. If SnowDreams can't reduce its costs, what profit will it earn? State your answer in dollars and as a percent of assets. Will investors be happy with the profit level? Show your analysis.

2. Assume that SnowDreams has found ways to cut its fixed costs to $30 million. What is its new target variable cost per skier/snowboarder? Compare this to the current variable cost per skier/snowboarder. Comment.

S8-5 **Decide whether to drop a department** *(Learning Objective 4)*
Knight Fashion in New York operates three departments: Men's, Women's, and Accessories. Knight Fashion allocates all fixed expenses (unavoidable building depreciation and utilities) based on each department's square footage. Departmental operating income data for the third quarter of 2007 are as follows:

	Department			
	Men's	Women's	Accessories	Total
Sales revenue	$105,000	$54,000	$100,000	$259,000
Variable expenses	60,000	30,000	80,000	170,000
Fixed expenses	25,000	20,000	25,000	70,000
Total expenses	85,000	50,000	105,000	240,000
Operating income (loss)	$20,000	$4,000	$(5,000)	$19,000

The store will remain in the same building regardless of whether any of the departments are dropped. Should Knight Fashion drop any of the departments? Give your reason.

S8-6 **Drop a department: revised information** *(Learning Objective 4)*
Consider Knight Fashion from S8-5. Assume that the fixed expenses assigned to each department include only direct fixed costs of the department (rather than unavoidable fixed costs as given in S8-5):

• Salary of the department's manager

• Cost of advertising directly related to that department

If Knight Fashion drops a department, it will not incur these fixed expenses. Under these circumstances, should Knight Fashion drop any of the departments? Give your reason.

S8-7 **Replace a department** *(Learning Objective 4)*
Consider Knight Fashion from S8-5. Assume once again that all fixed costs are unavoidable. If Knight Fashion drops one of the current departments, it plans to replace the dropped department with a shoe department. The company expects the shoe department to produce $80,000 in sales and have $50,000 of variable costs. Because the shoe business would be new to Knight Fashion, the company would have to incur an additional $7,000 of fixed costs (advertising, new shoe display racks, and so forth) per quarter related to the department. What should Knight Fashion do now?

S8-8   **Product mix decision: unlimited demand** *(Learning Objective 5)*
StoreAll produces plastic storage bins for household storage needs. The company makes two sizes of bins: large (50 gallon) and regular (35 gallon). Demand for the product is so high that StoreAll can sell as many of each size as it can produce. The company uses the same machinery to produce both sizes. The machinery can be run for only 3,000 hours per period. StoreAll can produce 10 large bins every hour compared to 15 regular bins in the same amount of time. Fixed expenses amount to $100,000 per period. Sales prices and variable costs are as follows:

	Regular	Large
Sales price per unit...	$8.00	$10.00
Variable cost per unit..	$3.00	$ 4.00

1. Which product should StoreAll emphasize? Why?
2. To maximize profits, how many of each size bin should StoreAll produce?
3. Given this product mix, what will the company's operating income be?

S8-9   **Product mix decision: limited demand** *(Learning Objective 5)*
Consider StoreAll in S8-8. Assume that demand for regular bins is limited to 30,000 units and demand for large bins is limited to 25,000 units.

1. How many of each size bin should StoreAll make now?
2. Given this product mix, what will be the company's operating income?
3. Explain why the operating income is less than it was when StoreAll was producing its optimal product mix.

S8-10   **Outsourcing production decision** *(Learning Objectives 1, 6)*
Suppose an Olive Garden restaurant is considering whether to (1) bake bread for its restaurant in-house or (2) buy the bread from a local bakery. The chef estimates that variable costs of making each loaf include $0.50 of ingredients, $0.25 of variable overhead (electricity to run the oven), and $0.75 of direct labor for kneading and forming the loaves. Allocating fixed overhead (depreciation on the kitchen equipment and building) based on direct labor assigns $1.00 of fixed overhead per loaf. None of the fixed costs are avoidable. The local bakery would charge Olive Garden $1.75 per loaf.

1. What is the unit cost of making the bread in-house (use absorption costing)?
2. Should Olive Garden bake the bread in-house or buy from the local bakery? Why?
3. In addition to the financial analysis, what else should Olive Garden consider when making this decision?

S8-11   **Relevant information for outsourcing delivery function** *(Learning Objectives 1, 6)*
U.S. Food in Lexington, Kentucky, manufactures and markets snack foods. Betsy Gonzalez manages the company's fleet of 200 delivery trucks. Gonzalez has been charged with "reengineering" the fleet-management function. She has an important decision to make.

- Should she continue to manage the fleet in-house with the five employees reporting to her? To do so, she will have to acquire new fleet-management software to streamline U.S. Food's fleet-management process.

- Should she outsource the fleet-management function to Fleet Management Services, a company that specializes in managing fleets of trucks for other companies? Fleet Management Services would take over the maintenance, repair, and scheduling of U.S. Food's fleet (but U.S. Food would retain ownership). This alternative would require Gonzalez to lay off her five employees. However, her own job would be secure, as she would be U.S. Food's liaison with Fleet Management Services.

  Assume that Gonzalez's records show the following data concerning U.S. Food's fleet:

Book value of U.S. Food's trucks, with an estimated five-year life...	$3,500,000
Annual leasing fee for new fleet-management software	8,000
Annual maintenance of trucks..	145,500
Fleet Supervisor Gonzalez's annual salary	60,000
Total annual salaries of U.S. Food's five other fleet-management employees...............................	150,000

Suppose that Fleet Management Services offers to manage U.S. Food's fleet for an annual fee of $290,000.

Which alternative will maximize U.S. Food's short-term operating income?

S8-12 Outsourcing qualitative considerations *(Learning Objectives 1, 6)*
Refer to U.S. Food in S8-11. What qualitative factors should Gonzalez consider before making a final decision?

S8-13 Scrap or process further decision *(Learning Objective 7)*
Auto Components has an inventory of 500 obsolete remote entry keys that are carried in inventory at a manufacturing cost of $80,000. Production Supervisor Terri Smith must decide to do one of the following:

- Process the inventory further at a cost of $20,000, with the expectation of selling it for $28,000
- Scrap the inventory for a sale price of $6,000

  What should Smith do? Present figures to support your decision.

S8-14 Determine most profitable final product *(Learning Objective 7)*
Chocolite processes cocoa beans into cocoa powder at a processing cost of $10,000 per batch. Chocolite can sell the cocoa powder as is, or it can process the cocoa powder further into chocolate syrup or boxed assorted chocolates. Once processed, each batch of cocoa beans would result in the following sales revenue:

Cocoa powder...	$15,000
Chocolate syrup	$100,000
Boxed assorted chocolates...	$200,000

The cost of transforming the cocoa powder into chocolate syrup would be $70,000. Likewise, the company would incur $180,000 to transform the cocoa powder into boxed assorted chocolates. The company president has decided to make boxed assorted chocolates owing to its high sales value and to the fact that the $10,000 cost of processing cocoa beans "eats up" most of the cocoa powder profits. Has the president made the right or wrong decision? Explain your answer. Be sure to include the correct financial analysis in your response.

E8-15 **Determine relevant and irrelevant information** (*Learning Objective 1*)

Joe Roberts, production manager for Fabricut, invested in computer-controlled production machinery last year. He purchased the machinery from Advanced Design at a cost of $2 million. A representative from Advanced Design recently contacted Joe because the company has designed an even more efficient piece of machinery. The new design would double the production output of the year-old machinery but cost Fabricut another $3 million. Roberts is afraid to bring this new equipment to the company president's attention because he persuaded the president to invest $2 million in the machinery last year.

Requirement

Explain what is relevant and irrelevant to Roberts's dilemma. What should he do?

E8-16 **Special order decisions given two scenarios** (*Learning Objective 2*)

Suppose the Baseball Hall of Fame in Cooperstown, New York, has approached Sports-Cardz with a special order. The Hall of Fame wants to purchase 50,000 baseball card packs for a special promotional campaign and offers $0.40 per pack, a total of $20,000. Sports-Cardz's total production cost is $0.60 per pack, as follows:

Variable costs:	
Direct materials...	$0.14
Direct labor..	0.08
Variable overhead	0.13
Fixed overhead..	0.25
Total cost..	$0.60

Sports-Cardz has enough excess capacity to handle the special order.

Requirements

1. Prepare an incremental analysis to determine whether Sports-Cardz should accept the special sales order assuming fixed costs would not be affected by the special order.

2. Now, assume that the Hall of Fame wants special hologram baseball cards. Sports-Cardz must spend $5,000 to develop this hologram, which will be useless after the special order is completed. Should Sports-Cardz accept the special order under these circumstances? Show your analysis.

E8-17 Special order decision and considerations *(Learning Objective 2)*

Maui Jane Sunglasses sell for about $150 per pair. Suppose the company incurs the following average costs per pair:

Direct materials..	$40
Direct labor...	12
Variable manufacturing overhead	8
Variable marketing expenses..	4
Fixed manufacturing overhead...	20*
Total costs...	$84

$$* \frac{\$2,000,000 \text{ total fixed manufacturing overhead}}{100,000 \text{ pairs of sunglasses}}$$

Maui Jane has enough idle capacity to accept a one-time-only special order from LensCrafters for 20,000 pairs of sunglasses at $76 per pair. Maui Jane will not incur any variable marketing expenses for the order.

Requirements

1. How would accepting the order affect Maui Jane's operating income? In addition to the special order's effect on profits, what other (longer-term qualitative) factors should Maui Jane's managers consider in deciding whether to accept the order?

2. Maui Jane's marketing manager, Jim Revo, argues against accepting the special order because the offer price of $76 is less than Maui Jane's $84 cost to make the sunglasses. Revo asks you, as one of Maui Jane's staff accountants, to write a memo explaining whether his analysis is correct.

E8-18 Pricing decisions given two scenarios *(Learning Objective 3)*

Bennett Builders builds 1,500-square-foot starter tract homes in the fast-growing suburbs of Atlanta. Land and labor are cheap, and competition among developers is fierce. The homes are "cookie-cutter," with any upgrades added by the buyer after the sale. Bennett Builders' cost per developed sublot are as follows:

Land..	$50,000
Construction	$125,000
Landscaping..	$5,000
Variable marketing costs...	$2,000

Bennett Builders would like to earn a profit of 15% of the variable cost of each home sale. Similar homes offered by competing builders sell for $200,000 each.

Requirements

1. Which approach to pricing should Bennett Builders emphasize? Why?

2. Will Bennett Builders be able to achieve its target profit levels? Show your computations.

continued ...

3. Bathrooms and kitchens are typically the most important selling features of a home. Bennett Builders could differentiate the homes by upgrading bathrooms and kitchens. The upgrades would cost $20,000 per home but would enable Bennett Builders to increase the selling prices by $35,000 per home (in general, kitchen and bathroom upgrades typically add at least 150% of their cost to the value of any home). If Bennett Builders upgrades, what will the new cost-plus price per home be? Should the company differentiate its product in this manner? Show your analysis.

E8-19   **Decide whether to drop a product line** (*Learning Objective 4*)

Top managers of Video Avenue are alarmed by their operating losses. They are considering dropping the VCR-tape product line. Company accountants have prepared the following analysis to help make this decision:

	Total	DVD Discs	VCR Tapes
Sales revenue	$420,000	$300,000	$120,000
Variable expenses	230,000	150,000	80,000
Contribution margin	190,000	150,000	40,000
Fixed expenses:			
Manufacturing	125,000	70,000	55,000
Marketing and administrative	70,000	55,000	15,000
Total fixed expenses	195,000	125,000	70,000
Operating income (loss)	$ (5,000)	$ 25,000	$ (30,000)

Total fixed costs will not change if the company stops selling VCR tapes.

Requirements

1. Prepare an incremental analysis to show whether Video Avenue should drop the VCR-tape product line. Will dropping VCR tapes add $30,000 to operating income? Explain.

2. Assume that Video Avenue can avoid $30,000 of fixed expenses by dropping the VCR-tape product line (these costs are direct fixed costs of the VCR product line). Prepare an incremental analysis to show whether Video Avenue should stop selling VCR tapes.

3. Now, assume that all $70,000 of fixed costs assigned to VCR tapes are direct fixed costs and can be avoided if the company stops selling VCR tapes. However, marketing has concluded that DVD sales would be adversely affected by discontinuing the VCR line (retailers want to buy both from the same supplier). DVD production and sales would decline 10%. What should the company do?

E8-20 **Dropping a product line** *(Learning Objective 4)*

Suppose Kellogg's is considering dropping its Special-K product line. Assume that during the past year, Special-K's product line income statement showed the following:

Sales...	$7,600,000
Cost of goods sold...	6,400,000
Gross profit...	1,200,000
Operating expenses..	1,400,000
Operating loss...	$ (200,000)

Fixed manufacturing overhead costs account for 40% of the cost of goods, while only 30% of the operating expenses are fixed. Since the Special-K line is only one of Kellogg's breakfast cereals, only $750,000 of direct fixed costs (the majority of which is advertising) will be eliminated if the product line is discontinued. The remainder of the fixed costs will still be incurred by Kellogg's. If the company decides to drop the product line, what will happen to the company's operating income? Should Kellogg's drop the product line?

E8-21 **Identify constraint, then determine product mix** *(Learning Objective 5)*

Lifemaster produces two types of exercise treadmills: Regular and Deluxe. The exercise craze is such that Lifemaster could use all of its available machine hours producing either model. The two models are processed through the same production department.

	Per Unit	
	Deluxe	Regular
Sale price..	$1,000	$ 550
Costs:		
Direct materials....................................	$ 290	$ 100
Direct labor...	80	180
Variable manufacturing overhead..........	240	80
Fixed manufacturing overhead*.............	120	40
Variable operating expenses.................	115	65
Total cost...	845	465
Operating income.......................................	$ 155	$ 85

Allocated on the basis of machine hours.

What product mix will maximize operating income? (*Hint:* Use the allocation of fixed manufacturing overhead to determine the proportion of machine hours used by each product.)

E8-22   **Determine product mix for retailer** *(Learning Objective 5)*
Vivace sells both designer and moderately priced fashion accessories. Top management is deciding which product line to emphasize. Accountants have provided the following data:

	Per Item	
	Designer	Moderately Priced
Average sale price....................................	$200	$84
Average variable expenses........................	85	24
Average fixed expenses (allocated)............	20	10
Average operating income........................	$95	$50

The Vivace store in Reno, Nevada, has 10,000 square feet of floor space. If Vivace emphasizes moderately priced goods, it can display 650 items in the store. If Vivace emphasizes designer wear, it can display only 300 designer items to create more of a boutique-like atmosphere. These numbers are also the average monthly sales in units.

Prepare an analysis to show which product to emphasize.

E8-23   **Determine product mix for retailer—two stocking scenarios** *(Learning Objective 5)*
Each morning, Max Imery stocks the drink case at Max's Beach Hut in Myrtle Beach, South Carolina. Max's Beach Hut has 100 linear feet of refrigerated display space for cold drinks. Each linear foot can hold either six 12-ounce cans or four 20-ounce plastic or glass bottles. Max's Beach Hut sells three types of cold drinks:

1. Coca-Cola in 12-oz. cans for $1.50 per can
2. A&W Root Beer in 20-oz. plastic bottles for $1.75 per bottle
3. Mountian Dew in 20-oz. glass bottles for $2.20 per bottle

Max's Beach Hut pays its suppliers:

1. $0.25 per 12-oz. can of Coca-Cola
2. $0.40 per 20-oz. bottle of A&W Root Beer
3. $0.75 per 20-oz. bottle of Mountain Dew

Max's Beach Hut's monthly fixed expenses include:

Hut rental	$ 375
Refrigerator rental..	75
Max's salary...	1,550
Total fixed expenses	$2,000

Max's Beach Hut can sell all drinks stocked in the display case each morning.

Requirements

1. What is Max's Beach Hut's constraining factor? What should Max stock to maximize profits? What is the maximum contribution margin he could generate from refrigerated drinks each day?

2. To provide variety to customers, suppose Max refuses to devote more than 60 linear feet and no less than 10 linear feet to any individual product. Under this condition, how many linear feet of each drink should Max stock? How many units of each product will be available for sale each day?

3. Assuming the product mix calculated in Requirement 2, what contribution margin will Max generate from refrigerated drinks each day?

E8-24   Make-or-buy product component *(Learning Objective 6)*
Fiber Systems manufactures an optical switch that it uses in its final product. Fiber Systems incurred the following manufacturing costs when it produced 70,000 units last year:

Direct materials	$ 630,000
Direct labor	105,000
Variable overhead	140,000
Fixed overhead	455,000
Total manufacturing cost for 70,000 units	$1,330,000

Fiber Systems does not yet know how many switches it will need this year; however, another company has offered to sell Fiber Systems the switch for $14 per unit. If Fiber Systems buys the switch from the outside supplier, the manufacturing facilities that will be idle cannot be used for any other purpose, yet none of the fixed costs are avoidable.

Requirements
1. Given the same cost structure, should Fiber Systems make or buy the switch? Show your analysis.

2. Now, assume that Fiber Systems can avoid $100,000 of fixed costs a year by outsourcing production. In addition, because sales are increasing, Fiber Systems needs 75,000 switches a year rather than 70,000. What should Fiber Systems do now?

3. Given the last scenario, what is the most Fiber Systems would be willing to pay to outsource the switches?

E8-25   Make-or-buy with alternative use of facilities *(Learning Objective 6)*
Refer to E8-24. Fiber Systems needs 80,000 optical switches next year (assume same relevant range). By outsourcing them, Fiber Systems can use its idle facilities to manufacture another product that will contribute $220,000 to operating income, but none of the fixed costs will be avoidable. Should Fiber Systems make or buy the switches? Show your analysis.

E8-26   Determine maximum outsourcing price *(Learning Objective 6)*
DefTone's sales have increased; as a result, the company needs 400,000 jewel-case liners rather than 250,000. DefTone has enough existing capacity to make all of the liners it needs. In addition, due to volume discounts, its variable costs of making each liner will decline to $0.28 per liner. Assume that by outsourcing, DefTone can reduce its current fixed costs ($50,000) by $10,000. There is no alternative use for the factory space freed through outsourcing, so it will just remain idle. What is the maximum DefTone will pay to outsource production of its CD liners?

E8-27 Sell as is or process further *(Learning Objective 7)*

Dairymaid processes organic milk into plain yogurt. Dairymaid sells plain yogurt to hospitals, nursing homes, and restaurants in bulk, one-gallon containers. Each batch, processed at a cost of $800, yields 500 gallons of plain yogurt. Dairymaid sells the one-gallon tubs for $6.00 each and spends $0.10 for each plastic tub. Dairymaid has recently begun to reconsider its strategy. Dairymaid wonders if it would be more profitable to sell individual-size portions of fruited organic yogurt at local food stores. Dairymaid could further process each batch of plain yogurt into 10,667 individual portions (3/4 cup each) of fruited yogurt. A recent market analysis indicates that demand for the product exists. Dairymaid would sell each individual portion for $0.50. Packaging would cost $0.08 per portion, and fruit would cost $0.10 per portion. Fixed costs would not change. Should Dairymaid continue to sell only the gallon-size plain yogurt (sell as is) or convert the plain yogurt into individual-size portions of fruited yogurt (process further)? Why?

■ Problems (Problem Set A)

P8-28A Special order decision and considerations *(Learning Objective 2)*

Buoy manufactures flotation vests in Tampa, Florida. Buoy's contribution margin income statement for the most recent month contains the following data:

Sales in units	31,000
Sales revenue	$434,000
Variable expenses:	
Manufacturing	$ 93,000
Marketing and administrative	107,000
Total variable expenses	200,000
Contribution margin	234,000
Fixed expenses:	
Manufacturing	126,000
Marketing and administrative	90,000
Total fixed expenses	216,000
Operating income	$ 18,000

Suppose Overton's wants to buy 5,000 vests from Buoy. Acceptance of the order will not increase Buoy's variable marketing and administrative expenses or any of its fixed expenses. The Buoy plant has enough unused capacity to manufacture the additional vests. Overton's has offered $10 per vest, which is below the normal sale price of $14.

Requirements

1. Prepare an incremental analysis to determine whether Buoy should accept this special sales order.
2. Identify long-term factors Buoy should consider in deciding whether to accept the special sales order.

P8-29A **Pricing of nursery plants** *(Learning Objective 3)*

GreenThumb operates a commercial plant nursery where it propagates plants for garden centers throughout the region. GreenThumb has $5 million in assets. Its yearly fixed costs are $600,000, and the variable costs for the potting soil, container, label, seedling, and labor for each gallon-size plant total $1.25. GreenThumb's volume is currently 500,000 units. Competitors offer the same quality plants to garden centers for $3.50 each. Garden centers then mark them up to sell to the public for $8 to $10, depending on the type of plant.

Requirements

1. GreenThumb's owners want to earn a 12% return on the company's assets. What is GreenThumb's target full cost?

2. Given that GreenThumb's current costs, will its owners be able to achieve their target profit? Show your analysis.

3. Assume that GreenThumb has identified ways to cut its variable costs to $1.10 per unit. What is its new target fixed cost? Will this decrease in variable costs allow the company to achieve its target profit? Show your analysis.

4. GreenThumb started an aggressive advertising campaign strategy to differentiate its plants from those grown by other nurseries. Monrovia Plants made this strategy work, so GreenThumb has decided to try it, too. GreenThumb doesn't expect volume to be affected, but it hopes to gain more control over pricing. If GreenThumb has to spend $100,000 this year to advertise and its variable costs continue to be $1.10 per unit, what will its cost-plus price be? Do you think GreenThumb will be able to sell its plants to garden centers at the cost-plus price? Why or why not?

P8-30A **Prepare and use contribution margin statements for dropping a line decision** *(Learning Objective 4)*

Members of the board of directors of Security Systems have received the following operating income data for the year just ended:

	Product Line		
	Industrial Systems	Household Systems	Total
Sales revenue..........................	$300,000	$310,000	$610,000
Cost of goods sold:			
Variable	$ 38,000	$ 42,000	$ 80,000
Fixed..................................	210,000	69,000	279,000
Total cost of goods sold	248,000	111,000	359,000
Gross profit............................	52,000	199,000	251,000
Marketing and administrative expenses:			
Variable	66,000	71,000	137,000
Fixed.............................	40,000	22,000	62,000
Total marketing and administrative expenses..	106,000	93,000	199,000
Operating income (loss)	$ (54,000)	$106,000	$ 52,000

continued . . .

Members of the board are surprised that the industrial systems product line is losing money. They commission a study to determine whether the company should drop the line. Company accountants estimate that dropping industrial systems will decrease fixed cost of goods sold by $80,000 and decrease fixed marketing and administrative expenses by $12,000.

Requirements

1. Prepare an incremental analysis to show whether Security Systems should drop the industrial systems product line.

2. Prepare contribution margin income statements to show Security Systems' total operating income under the two alternatives: (a) with the industrial systems line and (b) without the line. Compare the *difference* between the two alternatives' income numbers to your answer to Requirement 1. What have you learned from this comparison?

P8-31A **Product mix decision under constraint** (*Learning Objective 5*)
Brun, located in St. Cloud, Minnesota, produces two lines of electric toothbrushes: deluxe and standard. Because Brun can sell all of the toothbrushes it produces, the owners are expanding the plant. They are deciding which product line to emphasize. To make this decision, they assemble the following data:

	Per Unit	
	Deluxe Toothbrush	Standard Toothbrush
Sale price................................	$80	$48
Variable expenses........................	20	18
Contribution margin	$60	$30
Contribution margin ratio..............	75%	62.5%

After expansion, the factory will have a production capacity of 4,500 machine hours per month. The plant can manufacture either 60 standard electric toothbrushes or 24 deluxe electric toothbrushes per machine hour.

Requirements

1. Identify the constraining factor for Brun.

2. Prepare an analysis to show which product line to emphasize.

P8-32A **Outsourcing decision given alternative use of capacity** (*Learning Objective 6*)
X-Perience manufactures snowboards. Its cost of making 1,800 bindings is:

Direct materials..	$ 20,000
Direct labor...	80,000
Variable manufacturing overhead	40,000
Fixed manufacturing overhead.......................................	80,000
Total manufacturing cost	$220,000
Cost per pair ($220,000 ÷ 20,000)..................................	$ 11

Suppose O'Brien will sell bindings to X-Perience for $14 each. X-Perience will pay $1.00 per unit to transport the bindings to its manufacturing plant, where it will add its own logo at a cost of $0.20 per binding.

Requirements

1. X-Perience's accountants predict that purchasing the bindings from O'Brien will enable the company to avoid $2,200 of fixed overhead. Prepare an analysis to show whether X-Perience should make or buy the bindings.

2. The facilities freed by purchasing bindings from O'Brien can be used to manufacture another product that will contribute $3,100 to profit. Total fixed costs will be the same as if X-Perience had produced the bindings. Show which alternative makes the best use of X-Perience's facilities: (a) make bindings, (b) buy bindings and leave facilities idle, or (c) buy bindings and make another product.

P8-33A **Sell or process further decisions** (*Learning Objective 7*)

Vision Chemical has spent $240,000 to refine 72,000 gallons of acetone, which can be sold for $2.16 a gallon. Alternatively, Vision Chemical can process the acetone further. This processing will yield a total of 60,000 gallons of lacquer thinner that can be sold for $3.20 a gallon. The additional processing will cost $0.62 per gallon of lacquer thinner. To sell the lacquer thinner, Vision Chemical must pay shipping of $0.22 a gallon and administrative expenses of $0.10 a gallon on the thinner.

Requirements

1. Diagram Vision's decision, using Exhibit 8-23 as a guide.

2. Identify the sunk cost. Is the sunk cost relevant to Vision's decision? Why or why not?

3. Should Vision sell the acetone or process it into lacquer thinner? Show the expected net revenue difference between the two alternatives.

▪ Problems (Problem Set B)

P8-34B **Special order decision and considerations** (*Learning Objective 2*)

United Packaging's contribution margin income statement follows:

Sales in units	360,000
Sales revenue	$432,000
Variable expenses:	
Manufacturing	$108,000
Marketing and administrative	53,000
Total variable expenses	161,000
Contribution margin	271,000
Fixed expenses:	
Manufacturing	156,000
Marketing and administrative	40,000
Total fixed expenses	196,000
Operating income	$ 75,000

continued . . .

Wallace Farms wants to buy 5,000 produce boxes from United Packaging. Acceptance of the order will not increase any of United Packaging's variable marketing and administrative expenses or any of its fixed expenses. United Packaging's plant has enough unused capacity to manufacture the additional boxes. Wallace Farms has offered $0.80 per box, which is considerably below the normal sale price of $1.20.

Requirements

1. Prepare an incremental analysis to determine whether United Packaging should accept this special sales order.

2. Identify long-term factors that United Packaging should consider in deciding whether to accept the special sales order.

P8-35B Pricing of facial tissues *(Learning Objective 3)*
Softies produces facial tissues. Softies has $50 million in assets. Its yearly fixed costs are $12 million, and the variable cost of producing and selling each box of tissues is $0.25. Softies currently sells 30 million boxes of tissues. Generic facial tissues such as Softies' product generally sell to retailers for $0.75 per box, while name brands such as Kleenex and Puffs sell to retailers for $1.00 per box.

Requirements

1. Softies' stockholders expect a 10% return on the company's assets. What is Softies' target full cost?

2. Given Softies' current costs, will its owners achieve their target profit? Show your analysis.

3. Softies has identified ways to cut its fixed costs by $500,000. What is its new target variable cost per unit? Will Softies be able to reach its target profit?

4. Softies started an aggressive advertising campaign to transform its product into a name brand able to compete with Kleenex and Puffs. Softies doesn't think volume will be affected, but it hopes to gain more control over pricing. If Softies spends $3 million a year to advertise, what will its cost-plus price be? (Continue to assume that fixed costs have declined by $500,000 but that Softies was unable to reduce its variable cost per unit below $0.25). Do you think Softies will be able to sell its facial tissues to retailers at the cost-plus price? Why or why not?

P8-36B Prepare and use contribution margin statements for dropping a line decision *(Learning Objective 4)*
The following operating income data of Abalone Seafood highlight the losses of the fresh seafood product line:

| | | Product Line | |
	Total	Fresh Seafood	Frozen Seafood
Sales revenue............................	$730,500	$190,500	$540,000
Cost of goods sold:			
Variable	$138,000	$ 44,000	$ 94,000
Fixed..................................	61,000	20,000	41,000
Total cost of goods sold	199,000	64,000	135,000
Gross profit............................	531,500	126,500	405,000
Marketing and administrative expenses:			
Variable	223,000	98,000	125,000
Fixed..................................	93,000	38,000	55,000
Total marketing and administrative expenses...	316,000	136,000	180,000
Operating income (loss)	$215,500	$ (9,500)	$225,000

Abalone Seafood is considering discontinuing the fresh seafood product line. The company's accountants estimate that dropping the fresh seafood line will decrease fixed cost of goods sold by $16,000 and decrease fixed marketing and administrative expenses by $10,000.

Requirements

1. Prepare an incremental analysis to show whether Abalone Seafood should drop the fresh seafood product line.

2. Prepare contribution margin income statements to compare Abalone Seafood's total operating income (a) with the fresh seafood product line and (b) without it. Compare the *difference* between the two alternatives' income numbers to your answer to Requirement 1. What have you learned from this comparison?

P8-37B Product mix under constraint (*Learning Objective 5*)
Easy Living of Charlotte, North Carolina, specializes in outdoor furniture and spas. Owner Linda Spring is expanding the store. She is deciding which product line to emphasize. To make this decision, she assembles the following data:

| | Per Unit | |
	Spas	Patio Sets
Sale price..................................	$1,000	$800
Variable expenses.......................	480	440
Contribution margin	$ 520	$360
Contribution margin ratio...............	52%	45%

continued . . .

After renovation, the store will have 8,000 square feet of floor space. By devoting the new floor space to patio sets, Easy Living can display 60 patio sets. Alternatively, Easy Living could display 30 spas. Spring expects monthly sales to equal the maximum number of units displayed.

Requirements

1. Identify the constraining factor for Easy Living.
2. Prepare an analysis to show which product line to emphasize.

P8-38B Outsourcing: alternative use of capacity *(Learning Objective 6)*

Morning Grain makes organic cereal. Costs of producing 140,000 boxes of cereal each year follow:

Direct materials	$220,000
Direct labor	140,000
Variable overhead	60,000
Fixed overhead	440,000
Total manufacturing costs	$860,000

Suppose Kellogg's will sell Morning Grain the cereal for $4 a box. Morning Grain would also pay $0.19 a box to transport the cereal to its warehouse.

Requirements

1. Morning Grain's accountants predict that purchasing the cereal from Kellogg's will enable the company to avoid $140,000 of fixed overhead. Prepare an analysis to show whether Morning Grain should make or buy the cereal.
2. Assume that the Morning Grain facilities freed up by purchasing the cereal from Kellogg's can be used to manufacture snack bars that will contribute $180,000 to profit. Total fixed costs will be the same as if Morning Grain used the plant to make cereal. Prepare an analysis to show which alternative makes the best use of Morning Grain's facilities: (a) make cereal, (b) buy cereal and leave facilities idle, or (c) buy cereal and make snack bars.

P8-39B Sell or process further decision *(Learning Objective 7)*

Acme Petroleum has spent $200,000 to refine 60,000 gallons of petroleum distillate. Suppose Acme Petroleum can sell the distillate for $6 a gallon. Alternatively, it can process the distillate further and produce 60,000 gallons of cleaner fluid. The additional processing will cost another $1.75 a gallon, and the cleaner can be sold for $8.50 a gallon. To sell cleaner fluid, Acme Petroleum must pay a sales commission of $0.10 a gallon and a transportation charge of $0.15 a gallon.

Requirements

1. Diagram Acme Petroleum's alternatives, using Exhibit 8-23 (sell as is or process further) as a guide.
2. Identify the sunk cost. Is the sunk cost relevant to Acme Petroleum's decision? Why or why not?
3. Prepare an analysis to indicate whether Acme Petroleum should sell the distillate or process it into cleaner fluid. Show the expected net revenue difference between the two alternatives.

Apply Your Knowledge

▪ Decision Case

Case 8-40. Outsourcing e-mail (*Learning Objective 6*)

BKFin.com provides banks access to sophisticated financial information and analysis systems via the Web. The company combines these tools with benchmarking data access, including e-mail and wireless communications, so that banks can instantly evaluate individual loan applications and entire loan portfolios.

BKFin.com's CEO, Jon Wise, is happy with the company's growth. To better focus on client service, Wise is considering outsourcing some functions. CFO Jenny Lee suggests that the company's e-mail may be the place to start. She recently attended a conference and learned that companies such as Continental Airlines, DellNet, GTE, and NBC were outsourcing their e-mail function. Wise asks Lee to identify costs related to BKFin.com's in-house Microsoft Exchange mail application, which has 2,300 mailboxes. This information follows:

Variable costs:	
E-mail license	$7 per mailbox per month
Virus protection license	$1 per mailbox per month
Other variable costs	$8 per mailbox per month
Fixed costs:	
Computer hardware costs	$94,300 per month
$8,050 monthly salary for two information technology staff members who work only on e-mail	$16,100 per month

Requirements

1. Compute the *total cost* per mailbox per month of BKFin.com's current e-mail function.

2. Suppose Mail.com, a leading provider of Internet messaging outsourcing services, offers to host BKFin.com's e-mail function for $9 per mailbox per month. If BKFin.com outsources its e-mail to Mail.com, BKFin.com will still need the virus protection software; its computer hardware; and one information technology staff member who would be responsible for maintaining virus protection, quarantining suspicious e-mail, and managing content (e.g., screening e-mail for objectionable content). Should CEO Wise accept Mail.com's offer? Why or why not?

3. Suppose for an additional $5 per mailbox per month, Mail.com will also provide virus protection, quarantine, and content-management services. Outsourcing these additional functions would mean that BKFin.com would not need an e-mail information technology staff member or the separate virus protection license. Should CEO Wise outsource these extra services to Mail.com? Why or why not?

Ethical Issue

Issue 8-41. Outsourcing and ethics *(Learning Objective 6)*

Mary Tan is the controller for Duck Associates, a property management company in Portland, Oregon. Each year, Tan and payroll clerk Toby Stock meet with the external auditors about payroll accounting. This year, the auditors suggest that Tan consider outsourcing Duck Associates' payroll accounting to a company specializing in payroll processing services. This would allow Tan and her staff to focus on their primary responsibility: accounting for the properties under management. At present, payroll requires 1.5 employee positions—payroll clerk Toby Stock and a bookkeeper who spends half her time entering payroll data in the system.

Tan considers this suggestion, and she lists the following items relating to outsourcing payroll accounting:

a. The current payroll software that was purchased for $4,000 three years ago would not be needed if payroll processing were outsourced.

b. Duck Associates' bookkeeper would spend half her time preparing the weekly payroll input form that is given to the payroll processing service. She is paid $450 a week.

c. Duck Associates would no longer need payroll clerk Toby Stock, whose annual salary is $42,000.

d. The payroll processing service would charge $2,000 a month.

Requirements

1. Would outsourcing the payroll function increase or decrease Duck Associates' operating income?

2. Tan believes that outsourcing payroll would simplify her job, but she does not like the prospect of having to lay off Stock, who has become a close personal friend. She does not believe there is another position available for Stock at his current salary. Can you think of other factors that might support keeping Stock rather than outsourcing payroll processing? How should each of the factors affect Tan's decision if she wants to do what is best for Duck Associates and act ethically?

Team Project

Project 8-42. Relevant information to outsourcing decision *(Learning Objective 6)*

John Menard is the founder and sole owner of Menards. Analysts have estimated that his chain of home improvement stores scattered around nine midwestern states generate about $3 billion in annual sales. But how can Menards compete with giant Home Depot?

Suppose Menard is trying to decide whether to invest $45 million in a state-of-the-art manufacturing plant in Eau Claire, Wisconsin. Menard expects the plant would operate for 15 years, after which it would have no residual value. The plant would produce Menards' own line of Formica countertops, cabinets, and picnic tables.

Suppose Menards would incur the following unit costs in producing its own product lines:

	Per Unit		
	Countertops	Cabinets	Picnic Tables
Direct materials...	$15	$10	$25
Direct labor...	10	5	15
Variable manufacturing overhead	5	2	6

Rather than Menard making these products, assume that he can buy them from outside suppliers. Suppliers would charge Menards $40 per countertop, $25 per cabinet, and $65 per picnic table.

Whether Menard makes or buys these products, assume that he expects the following annual sales:

- Countertops—487,200 at $130 each
- Picnic tables—100,000 at $225 each
- Cabinets—150,000 at $75 each

If "making" is sufficiently more profitable than outsourcing, Menard will build the new plant. John Menard has asked your consulting group for a recommendation. Menard uses the straight-line depreciation method.

Requirements

1. Are the following items relevant or irrelevant in Menard's decision to build a new plant that will manufacture his own products?

   a. The unit sale prices of the countertops, cabinets, and picnic tables (the sale prices that Menards charges its customers)

   b. The prices that outside suppliers would charge Menards for the three products if Menards decides to outsource the products rather than make them

   c. The $45 million to build the new plant

   d. The direct materials, direct labor, and variable overhead that Menards would incur to manufacture the three product lines

   e. Menard's salary

2. Determine whether Menards should make or outsource the countertops, cabinets, and picnic tables *assuming that the company has already built the plant and, therefore, has the manufacturing capacity to produce these products.* In other words, what is the annual difference in cash flows if Menards decides to make rather than outsource each of these three products?

3. Write a memo giving your recommendation to Menard. The memo should clearly state your recommendation and briefly summarize the reasons for your recommendation.

This page intentionally left blank

10 The Master Budget and Responsibility Accounting

ver 20% of sales of books, music, and electronics occur online. If you're one of the millions of customers worldwide who points and clicks to buy your books and CDs on Amazon.com, then you're part of Amazon.com's strategy to "get big fast." This strategy increased Amazon.com's sales, but at a cost. Spending was out of control. There was no budget, and managers spared no expense to help the company grow. As a result, Amazon.com lost more than $860 *million* in 2000.

Founder and CEO Jeff Bezos had to turn this sea of red ink into income. Bezos set up a *budget* for Amazon.com's plan of action. Now, each division budgets both sales and expenses. In weekly meetings, managers compare actual results to the budget, which helps them correct problems quickly.

The result? Between 2000 and 2002, Amazon.com's sales increased 42%. With such an increase in sales, you'd expect expenses also to increase. But Amazon.com's new budget helped managers *cut* operating expenses. How did the company decrease expenses when sales were increasing so dramatically? The budget helped Amazon.com reduce order-filling and distribution costs by 5%. Switching to lower-cost computer systems reduced "technical and content" operating costs by 20%. The result? Amazon.com reported its first-ever income from operations in 2002. By 2004, income from operations had risen to over $588 million.

Sources: Katrina Brooker, "Beautiful Dreamer," *Fortune*, December 18, 2000, pp. 234–239; Fred Vogelstein, "Bezos," *Fortune*, September 2, 2002, pp. 186–187; Fred Vogelstein, "What Went Right 2002," *Fortune*, December 30, 2002, p. 166; Nick Wingfield, "Survival Strategy: Amazon Takes Page from Wal-Mart to Prosper on Web," *Wall Street Journal*, November 22, 2002, p. A1; Fred Vogelstein, "Mighty Amazon," *Fortune*, May 26, 2003, pp. 60–74. ■

Learning Objectives

1 Learn why managers use budgets

2 Prepare an operating budget

3 Prepare a financial budget

4 Use sensitivity analysis in budgeting

5 Prepare performance reports for responsibility centers

Perhaps, like Amazon.com, you've prepared a budget to ensure that you have enough cash to pay your expenses. The budget forces you to plan. If your budgeted cash inflow falls short of expenses, you can do one or both of the following:

- Increase your cash inflow (by taking on a job or a student loan).
- Cut your expenses.

In addition to planning, your personal budget can help you control expenses. To stay within your grocery budget, you may buy macaroni and cheese instead of shrimp. At the end of the month, if your bank balance is less than expected, you can compare your actual cash inflows and expenses to your budget to see why. You need to know whether cash inflows are lower than expected or expenses are higher than expected to know what corrective action to take.

As Amazon.com learned, it's easy for spending to get out of control if you don't have a budget. That's why everyone, from individuals like you to complex international organizations like Amazon.com, uses budgets. Careful budgeting helps both individuals and businesses stay out of trouble by reducing the risk that they will spend more than they earn.

As you'll see throughout this chapter, knowing how costs behave continues to be important in forming budgets. Total fixed costs will not change as volume changes within the relevant range. However, total variable costs must be adjusted when sales volume is expected to fluctuate.

Why Managers Use Budgets

Let's continue our study of budgets by moving from your personal budget to see how a small service business develops a simple budget. Assume that you begin an online service that provides travel itineraries for leisure travelers. You want to earn $550 a month to help with your college expenses. You expect to sell 20 itineraries per month at a price of $30 each. Over the past six months, you paid your Internet service provider an average of $18 a month and you spent an additional $20 per month on reference materials. You expect these monthly costs to remain about the same. These are your monthly fixed costs. Finally, you spend 5% of your sales revenues for banner ads on other travel Web sites. Because advertising costs fluctuate with sales revenue, these costs are variable.

> **1** Learn why managers use budgets

Exhibit 10-1 shows how to compute budgeted revenues and then subtract budgeted expenses to arrive at budgeted operating income.

EXHIBIT 10-1	Service Company Budget

CUSTOM TRAVEL ITINERARIES
Budget for May 2009

Budgeted sales revenue (20 × $30)		$600
Less budgeted expenses:		
Internet access expense	$18	
Reference materials expense	20	
Advertising expense (5% × $600)	30	
Total expenses		68
Budgeted operating income		$532

If business goes according to plan, you will not meet your $550 per month operating income goal. You will have to increase revenue (perhaps through word-of-mouth advertising) or cut expenses (perhaps by finding a less-expensive Internet access provider).

Using Budgets to Plan and Control

Large international for-profit companies such as Amazon.com and nonprofit organizations such as Habitat for Humanity use budgets for the same reasons you do in your personal life or in your small business—to plan and control actions and the related revenues and expenses. Exhibit 10-2 shows how managers use budgets in fulfilling their major responsibilities. First, they develop strategies—overall business goals like Amazon.com's goal to expand its international operations or Gateway's goal to be a value leader in the personal computer market while diversifying into other markets. Then, companies plan and budget for specific actions to achieve those goals. The next step is to act. For example, Amazon.com recently planned for and then added the Marketplace auction feature to its Web sites for the United Kingdom, Germany, and Japan. And Gateway is leaning on its suppliers to cut costs, while at the same time it is pumping out new products such as plasma TVs and audio and video gear.

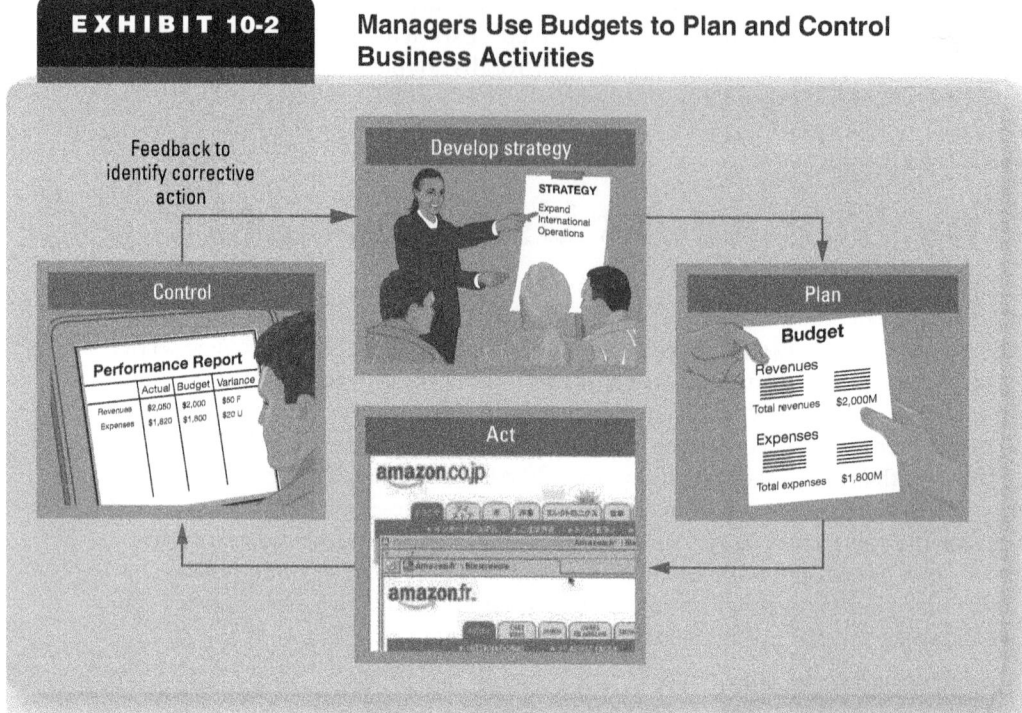

EXHIBIT 10-2 Managers Use Budgets to Plan and Control Business Activities

After acting, managers compare actual results to the budget. This feedback allows them to determine what, if any, corrective action to take. If Amazon.com spent more than expected to add the Marketplace to its international Web sites, managers must cut other costs or increase revenues. These decisions affect the company's future strategies and plans.

Amazon.com has a number of budgets. Each manager develops a budget for his or her division. Software then "rolls up" the division budgets to create an organization-wide budget for the company as a whole. Managers also prepare long-term and short-term budgets. Boeing's long-term budget forecasts demand for planes for the next 20 years.

However, most companies (including Boeing) budget their cash flows monthly, weekly, and even daily to ensure that they have enough cash. They also budget revenues and expenses—and operating income—for months, quarters, and years. This chapter focuses on short-term budgets of one year or less.

Benefits of Budgeting

Exhibit 10-3 summarizes three key benefits of budgeting. Budgeting forces managers to plan, promotes coordination and communication, and provides a benchmark for evaluating actual performance.

Planning

Exhibit 10-1 shows that your expected income from the online travel itinerary business falls short of the target. The sooner you learn of the expected shortfall, the more time you have to plan how to increase revenues or cut expenses. The better your plan and the more time you have to act on the plan, the more likely you will find a way to meet your target. Amazon.com's budget required that managers plan the expansion of the Web sites tailored for customers in Germany, France, and Japan.

EXHIBIT 10-3   **Benefits of Budgeting**

Budgets force managers to plan.

Budgets promote coordination and communication.

Budgets provide a benchmark that motivates employees and helps managers evaluate performance.

Coordination and Communication

The master budget coordinates a company's activities. It forces managers to consider relations among operations across the entire value chain. For example, Amazon.com stimulates sales by offering free shipping on orders over a specified dollar amount. The budget encourages managers to ensure that the extra profits from increased sales outweigh the revenue lost from not charging for shipping.

Budgets also communicate a consistent set of plans throughout the company. For example, the initial Amazon.com budget communicated the message that all employees should help control costs.

Benchmarking

Budgets provide a benchmark that motivates employees and helps managers evaluate performance. In most companies, part of the manager's performance evaluation depends on how actual results compare to the budget. So, for example, the budgeted expenses for international expansion encourage Amazon.com's employees to increase the efficiency of international warehousing operations and to find less-expensive technology to support the Web sites.

Let's return to your online travel business. Suppose that comparing actual results to the budget in Exhibit 10-1 leads to the performance report in Exhibit 10-4.

EXHIBIT 10-4   **Summary Performance Report**

	Actual	Budget	Variance (Actual – Budget)
Sales revenue	$550	$600	$(50)
Less: Total expenses	90	68	(22)
Net income	$460	$532	$(72)

This report should prompt you to investigate why actual sales are $50 less than budgeted ($550 − $600). There are three possibilities:

1. The budget was unrealistic.

2. You did a poor selling job.

3. Uncontrollable factors (such as a sluggish economy) reduced sales.

BBH CHAPTER 10

All three may have contributed to the poor results.

You also want to know why expenses are $22 higher than expected ($90 − $68). Did your Internet service provider increase rates? Did you have to buy more reference materials than planned? Did you spend more than 5% of your revenue on Web banner ads? You need to know the answers to these kinds of questions to decide how to get your business back on track.

Preparing the Master Budget

Now that you know *why* managers go to the trouble of developing budgets, let's consider the steps they take to prepare a budget.

Components of the Master Budget

The **master budget** is the set of budgeted financial statements and supporting schedules for the entire organization. Appendix 10A briefly discusses the similarities and differences between the master budgets for merchandising companies, service companies, and manufacturers. Exhibit 10-5 shows the order in which managers prepare the components of the master budget for a merchandiser such as Amazon.com.

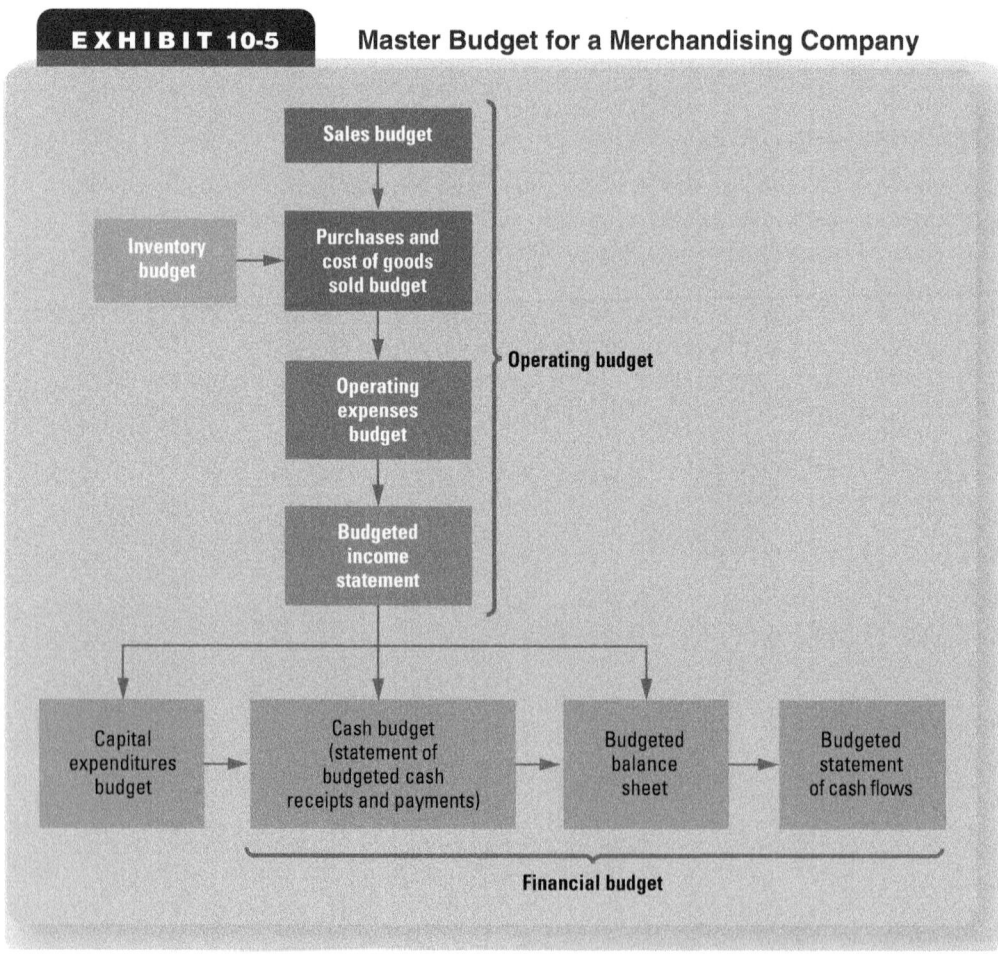

EXHIBIT 10-5   **Master Budget for a Merchandising Company**

The exhibit shows that the master budget includes three types of budgets:

1. The operating budget

2. The capital expenditures budget

3. The financial budget

Let's consider each in turn.

The first component of the **operating budget** is the sales budget, the cornerstone of the master budget. Why? Because sales affect most other components of the master budget. After projecting sales revenue, cost of goods sold, and operating expenses, management prepares the end result of the operating budget: the budgeted income statement that projects operating income for the period.

The second type of budget is the **capital expenditures budget**. This budget presents the company's plan for purchasing property, plant, equipment, and other long-term assets.

The third type of budget is the **financial budget**. The financial budget has three components:

- Cash budget
- Budgeted balance sheet
- Budgeted statement of cash flows

The cash budget, which projects cash inflows and outflows, feeds into the budgeted period-end balance sheet, which, in turn, feeds into the budgeted statement of cash flows. These budgeted financial statements look like ordinary statements. The only difference is that they list budgeted (projected) rather than actual amounts.

Data Set for Whitewater Sporting Goods' Master Budget

We'll use Whitewater Sporting Goods Store No. 18 to see how managers prepare operating and financial budgets. These budgets are normally prepared for a full 12-month period. However, to simplify, we'll present the budgets over a four-month period. We'll refer to this Data Set by item number as we create the operating and financial budgets, so you may want to bookmark this page.

1. **You manage Whitewater Sporting Goods Store No. 18, which carries a complete line of outdoor recreation gear.** You are to prepare the store's master budget for April, May, June, and July, the main selling season. The division manager and the head of the accounting department will arrive from headquarters next week to review the budget with you.

2. **Your store's budgeted balance sheet at March 31, 2009, appears in Exhibit 10-6.**

3. **Sales in March were budgeted at $40,000.** The sales force predicts these future monthly sales:

April	$50,000
May	80,000
June	60,000
July	50,000

EXHIBIT 10-6 **Balance Sheet**

WHITEWATER SPORTING GOODS STORE NO. 18
Budgeted Balance Sheet
March 31, 2009

Assets		Liabilities	
Current assets:		Current liabilities:	
Cash	$ 15,000	Accounts payable	$ 16,800
Accounts receivable	16,000	Salary and commissions	
Inventory	48,000	payable	4,250
Prepaid insurance	1,800	Total liabilities	21,050
Total current assets	80,800		
Plant assets:		**Owners' Equity**	
Equipment and fixtures	32,000	Owners' equity	78,950
Accumulated depreciation	(12,800)		
Total plant assets	19,200	Total liabilities and owners'	
Total assets	$100,000	equity	$100,000

4. **Cash collections follow sales because some sales are made on account.** Sales are 60% cash and 40% credit. Whitewater collects all credit sales the month *after* the sale. The $16,000 of budgeted accounts receivable at March 31 arose from credit sales in March (40% of $40,000). Uncollectible accounts are immaterial.

5. **Whitewater wants to maintain inventory at a level equal to $20,000 plus 80% of the budgeted cost of goods sold for the following month.** Whitewater prices its product to earn a 30% gross profit on sales revenue. This means that cost of goods sold averages 70% of sales revenue. Therefore, we compute inventory on March 31 as follows:

$$\text{March 31 inventory} = \$20,000 + 0.80 \text{ (cost of goods sold for next month)}$$
$$= \$20,000 + 0.80 \times (0.70 \times \text{April sales of } \$50,000)$$
$$= \$20,000 + (0.80 \times \$35,000)$$
$$= \$20,000 + \$28,000$$
$$= \$48,000$$

See how this agrees with the March 31 inventory shown in Exhibit 10-6. The same procedure is used to calculate budgeted ending inventory every month. Budgeted ending inventory on July 31 is $42,400 (calculated from data not given).

Whitewater *pays* for inventory as follows: 50% during the month of purchase and 50% during the next month. Accounts payable consists of inventory purchases only. Budgeted March purchases were $33,600, so budgeted accounts payable at the end of March totals $16,800 ($33,600 × 0.50).

6. **Monthly payroll has two parts: a salary of $2,500 plus sales commissions equal to 15% of sales.** This is a mixed cost, with both a fixed and variable component. The company pays half this amount during the month and half early the following month. Therefore, at the end of each month, Whitewater reports salary and commissions payable equal to half the month's payroll. The $4,250 liability on the March 31 budgeted balance sheet is half the March payroll of $8,500:

$$\text{March payroll} = \text{Salary of } \$2,500 + \text{Sales commissions of } \$6,000 \ (0.15 \times \$40,000)$$
$$= \$8,500$$

$$\text{March 31 salary and commissions payable} = 0.50 \times \$8,500 = \$4,250$$

7. Other monthly expenses are as follows:

Rent expense (fixed cost)........................	$2,000, paid as incurred
Depreciation expense, including truck (fixed cost)................................	500
Insurance expense (fixed cost)..............	200 expiration of prepaid amount
Miscellaneous expenses (variable cost)...	5% of sales, paid as incurred

8. **Whitewater plans to purchase a used delivery truck in April for $3,000 cash.** This information will be recorded on the capital expenditures budget.

9. **Whitewater requires each store to maintain a minimum cash balance of $10,000 at the end of each month.** The store can borrow money on six-month notes payable of $1,000 each at an annual interest rate of 12%. Management borrows no more than the amount needed to maintain the $10,000 minimum. Total interest expense will vary as the amount of borrowing varies from month to month. Notes payable require six equal monthly payments of principal plus monthly interest on the entire unpaid principal. Borrowing and all principal and interest payments occur at the end of the month.

10. **Income taxes are the responsibility of corporate headquarters, so you can ignore tax.**

As you prepare the master budget, remember that you are developing the store's operating and financial plan for the next four months. Normally, managers prepare the budgets for a full 12-month period. However, to simplify, we consider the next four months here. The steps in this process may seem mechanical; but you must think carefully about pricing, product lines, job assignments, needs for additional equipment, and negotiations with banks. Successful managers use this opportunity to make decisions that affect the future course of business.

Preparing the Operating Budget

The first three components of the operating budget, as shown in Exhibit 10-5, are:

2 │ Prepare an operating budget

1. Sales budget (Exhibit 10-7).

2. Inventory, purchases, and cost of goods sold budget (Exhibit 10-8).

3. Operating expenses budget (Exhibit 10-9).

The results of these three budgets feed into the fourth element of the operating budget: the budgeted income statement (Exhibit 10-10). We consider each in turn.

The Sales Budget

The forecast of sales revenue is the cornerstone of the master budget because the level of sales affects expenses and almost all other elements of the master budget. Budgeted total sales for each product is the sales price multiplied by the expected number of units sold. The overall sales budget in Exhibit 10-7 is the sum of the budgets for the individual products.

EXHIBIT 10-7 **Sales Budget**

WHITEWATER SPORTING GOODS STORE NO. 18
Sales Budget

	April	May	June	July	April–July Total
Cash sales, 60%	$30,000	$48,000	$36,000	$30,000	
Credit sales, 40%	20,000	32,000	24,000	20,000	
Total sales, 100%	$50,000	$80,000	$60,000	$50,000	$240,000

NOTE: From Data Set items 3 and 4, pages 543–544.

The total sales shown is from Data Set item 3. The breakdown between cash and credit sales is based on Data Set item 4. Trace the April through July total sales ($240,000) to the budgeted income statement in Exhibit 10-10.

The Inventory, Purchases, and Cost of Goods Sold Budget

This budget determines cost of goods sold for the budgeted income statement, ending inventory for the budgeted balance sheet, and purchases for the cash budget. The familiar cost of goods sold computation specifies the relations among these items:

$$\text{Beginning inventory} + \text{Purchases} - \text{Ending inventory} = \text{Cost of goods sold}$$

Beginning inventory is known from last month's budgeted balance sheet, budgeted cost of goods sold is 70% of sales (from Data Set item 5), and budgeted ending inventory is computed as $20,000 + 80% of the cost of goods sold for the next month (from Data Set item 5). You must solve for the budgeted purchases figure. To do this, rearrange the previous equation to isolate purchases on the left side:

$$\text{Purchases} = \text{Cost of goods sold} + \text{Ending inventory} - \text{Beginning inventory}$$

This equation makes sense. How much does Whitewater Sporting Goods have to purchase? Enough to cover its current month's sales and desired ending inventory less the amount of beginning inventory already on hand at the start of the period. Exhibit 10-8 shows Whitewater Sporting Goods' inventory, purchases, and cost of goods sold budget. Remember: Inventory, purchases, and cost of goods sold are all stated at Whitewater's *cost*, not at its sales prices.

Trace the total budgeted cost of goods sold from Exhibit 10-8 ($168,000) to the budgeted income statement in Exhibit 10-10. We will use the budgeted inventory

EXHIBIT 10-8 Inventory, Purchases, and Cost of Goods Sold Budget

WHITEWATER SPORTING GOODS STORE NO. 18
Inventory, Purchases, and Cost of Goods Sold Budget

	April	May	June	July	April–July Total
Cost of goods sold					
(0.70 × sales, from Sales budget in Exhibit 10-7)	$35,000	$56,000	$42,000	$35,000	$168,000
+ Desired ending inventory					
[($20,000 + (0.80 × cost of goods sold for the next month)]	64,800*	53,600	48,000	42,400‡	
= Total inventory required	99,800	109,600	90,000	77,400	
− Beginning inventory	(48,000)†	(64,800)	(53,600)	(48,000)	
= Purchases	$51,800	$44,800	$36,400	$29,400	

*$20,000 + (0.80 × $56,000) = $64,800.
†Balance at March 31 (Exhibit 10-6).
‡Given in Data Set item 5 on page 544.

and purchases amounts later, when we create the budgeted balance sheet and the budgeted cash payments for these four months.

The Operating Expenses Budget

Exhibit 10-9 shows the operating expenses budget. The information used to create the budget is from Data Set items 6 and 7. Study each expense to make sure you know how it is computed. For example, sales commissions fluctuate with sales. Other expenses, such as rent and insurance, are the same each month (fixed).

EXHIBIT 10-9 Operating Expenses Budget

WHITEWATER SPORTING GOODS STORE NO. 18
Operating Expenses Budget

	April	May	June	July	April–July Total
Salary, fixed amount (Data Set item 6)	$ 2,500	$ 2,500	$ 2,500	$ 2,500	
Commission, 15% of sales (Data Set item 6 and Exhibit 10-7)	7,500	12,000	9,000	7,500	
Total salary and commissions	10,000	14,500	11,500	10,000	$46,000
Rent expense, fixed amount (Data Set item 7)	2,000	2,000	2,000	2,000	8,000
Depreciation expense, fixed amount (Data Set item 7)	500	500	500	500	2,000
Insurance expense, fixed amount (Data Set item 7)	200	200	200	200	800
Miscellaneous expenses, 5% of sales (Data Set item 7,					
and Exhibit 10-7)	2,500	4,000	3,000	2,500	12,000
Total operating expenses	$15,200	$21,200	$17,200	$15,200	$68,800

From Data Set items on page 544–545.

Trace the April through July totals from the operating expenses budget in Exhibit 10-9 (salary and commissions of $46,000, rent expense of $8,000, and so forth) to the budgeted income statement in Exhibit 10-10.

The Budgeted Income Statement

We use the sales budget (Exhibit 10-7); the inventory, purchases, and cost of goods sold budget (Exhibit 10-8); and the operating expenses budget (Exhibit 10-9) to prepare the budgeted income statement in Exhibit 10-10. (We explain the computation of interest expense as part of the cash budget in the next section.)

EXHIBIT 10-10   **Budgeted Income Statement**

WHITEWATER SPORTING GOODS STORE NO. 18
Budgeted Income Statement
Four Months Ending July 31, 2009

		Amount	Source
Sales revenue		$240,000	Sales budget (Exhibit 10-7)
Cost of goods sold		168,000	Inventory, purchases, and cost of goods
Gross profit		72,000	sold budget (Exhibit 10-8)
Operating expenses:			
Salary and commissions	$ 46,000		Operating expenses budget (Exhibit 10-9)
Rent expense	8,000		Operating expenses budget (Exhibit 10-9)
Depreciation expense	2,000		Operating expenses budget (Exhibit 10-9)
Insurance expense	800		Operating expenses budget (Exhibit 10-9)
Miscellaneous expenses	12,000	68,800	Operating expenses budget (Exhibit 10-9)
Operating income		3,200	
Interest expense		225*	Cash budget (Exhibit 10-14)
Net income		$ 2,975	

*$90 + $75 + $60

Take this opportunity to solidify your understanding of operating budgets by carefully working out Summary Problem 1.

Summary Problem 1

Review the Whitewater Sporting Goods example. Suppose you now think July sales will be $40,000 instead of the projected $50,000 in Exhibit 10-7. You want to see how this change in sales affects the budget.

Requirement

Revise the sales budget (Exhibit 10-7); the inventory, purchases, and cost of goods sold budget (Exhibit 10-8); and the operating expenses budget (Exhibit 10-9). Prepare a revised budgeted income statement for the four months ended July 31, 2009.

Note: You need not repeat the parts of the revised schedules that do not change. Assume that interest does not change.

Solution

Although not required, this solution repeats the budgeted amounts for April, May, and June. Revised figures appear in color for emphasis.

WHITEWATER SPORTING GOODS STORE NO. 18
Revised—Sales Budget

	April	May	June	July	Total
Cash sales, 60%	$30,000	$48,000	$36,000	$24,000	
Credit sales, 40%	20,000	32,000	24,000	16,000	
Total sales, 100%	$50,000	$80,000	$60,000	$40,000	$230,000

WHITEWATER SPORTING GOODS STORE NO. 18
Revised—Inventory, Purchases, and Cost of Goods Sold Budget

	April	May	June	July	Total
Cost of goods sold (0.70 × sales, from revised sales budget)	$35,000	$56,000	$42,000	$28,000	$161,000
+ Desired ending inventory					
($20,000 + 0.80 × cost of goods sold for next month)	64,800	53,600	42,400	42,400†	
= Total inventory required	99,800	109,600	84,400	70,400	
− Beginning inventory	(48,000)*	(64,800)	(53,600)	(42,400)	
= Purchases	$51,800	$44,800	$30,800	$28,000	

*Balance at March 31 (Exhibit 10-6).
†Given in Data Set item 5 on page 544.

WHITEWATER SPORTING GOODS STORE NO. 18
Revised—Operating Expenses Budget

	April	May	June	July	Total
Salary, fixed amount	$ 2,500	$ 2,500	$ 2,500	$ 2,500	
Commission, 15% of sales from revised sales budget	7,500	12,000	9,000	6,000	
Total salary and commissions	10,000	14,500	11,500	8,500	$ 44,500
Rent expense, fixed amount	2,000	2,000	2,000	2,000	8,000
Depreciation expense, fixed amount	500	500	500	500	2,000
Insurance expense, fixed amount	200	200	200	200	800
Miscellaneous expenses, 5% of sales from revised sales budget	2,500	4,000	3,000	2,000	11,500
Total operating expenses	$15,200	$21,200	$17,200	$13,200	$66,800

WHITEWATER SPORTING GOODS STORE NO. 18
Revised Budgeted Income Statement
Four Months Ending July 31, 2009

		Amount	Source
Sales revenue		$230,000	Revised sales budget
Cost of goods sold		161,000	Revised inventory, purchases, and cost of goods sold budget
Gross profit		69,000	
Operating expenses:			
Salary and commissions	$44,500		Revised operating expenses budget
Rent expense	8,000		Revised operating expenses budget
Depreciation expense	2,000		Revised operating expenses budget
Insurance expense	800		Revised operating expenses budget
Miscellaneous expenses	11,500	66,800	Revised operating expenses budget
Operating income		2,200	
Interest expense		225	Given, Exhibit 10-10
Net income		$ 1,975	

Preparing the Financial Budget

Now that we have prepared the operating budget, we're ready to move on to the financial budget. Recall from Exhibit 10-5 that the financial budget includes the cash budget, the budgeted balance sheet, and the budgeted statement of cash flows. We'll start with the cash budget.

3 Prepare a financial budget

Preparing the Cash Budget

The **cash budget**, or **statement of budgeted cash receipts and payments**, details how the business expects to go from the beginning cash balance to the desired ending balance. The cash budget has five major parts:

- Cash collections from customers (Exhibit 10-11)
- Cash payments for purchases (Exhibit 10-12)
- Cash payments for operating expenses (Exhibit 10-13)
- Cash payments for capital expenditures (for example, the $3,000 capital expenditure to acquire the delivery truck would be shown on the company's capital expenditures budget) less any proceeds from the sale of capital assets
- Cash financing (borrowings, repayments, and interest)

Cash collections and payments depend heavily on revenues and expenses, which appear in the operating budget. This is why you cannot prepare the cash budget until you have finished the operating budget.

Budgeted Cash Collections from Customers

The cash collections budget is all about timing: *When* does Whitewater expect to receive cash from its sales? Of course, Whitewater will receive cash immediately on its cash sales. Whitewater also expects to collect cash for all of its credit sales in the month *after* the sales are made (Data Set item 4). Therefore, Exhibit 10-11 shows two components to each month's cash collections: (1) collections from cash sales and (2) collection of the previous month's credit sales. These components are found on the sales budget shown in Exhibit 10-7.

EXHIBIT 10-11 **Budgeted Cash Collections**

WHITEWATER SPORTING GOODS STORE NO. 18
Budgeted Cash Collections from Customers

	April	May	June	July	April—July Total
Cash sales, from Sales budget (Exhibit 10-7)	$30,000	$48,000	$36,000	$30,000	
Collections of last month's credit sales, from Sales budget (Exhibit 10-7)	16,000*	20,000	32,000	24,000	
Total collections	$46,000	$68,000	$68,000	$54,000	$236,000

*March 31 accounts receivable (Exhibit 10-6).

Take a moment and trace each month's total cash collections in Exhibit 10-11 to the cash budget shown in Exhibit 10-14.

Budgeted Cash Payments for Purchases

The cash payments budget is also about timing: *When* will Whitewater pay for its purchases? Whitewater pays for half of its inventory purchases in the month of purchase and pays for the other half in the month *after* purchase (Data Set item 5). Therefore, Exhibit 10-12 shows two components to each month's cash payments for purchases: (1) 50% of last month's purchases and (2) 50% of this month's purchases. These components are calculated from the purchases shown on the inventory, purchases, and cost of goods sold budget (Exhibit 10-8). For example, May's cash payments for purchases consists of (1) 50% of April's purchases (50% × $51,800 = $25,900) and (2) 50% of May's purchases (50% × $44,800 = $22,400).

EXHIBIT 10-12   **Budgeted Cash Payments for Purchases**

WHITEWATER SPORTING GOODS STORE NO. 18 Budgeted Cash Payments for Purchases					
	April	May	June	July	April–July Total
50% of last month's purchases, from Inventory, purchases, and cost of goods sold budget (Exhibit 10-8)	$16,800*	$25,900	$22,400	$18,200	
50% of this month's purchases, from Inventory, purchases, and cost of goods sold budget (Exhibit 10-8)	25,900	22,400	18,200	14,700	
Total payments for purchases	$42,700	$48,300	$40,600	$32,900	$164,500

*March 31 accounts payable (Exhibit 10-6).

Take a moment and trace each month's total cash payments for purchases in Exhibit 10-12 to the cash budget shown in Exhibit 10-14.

Budgeted Cash Payments for Operating Expenses

To budget cash payments for operating expenses, Whitewater must consider the *timing* of when it pays for payroll expenses (Data Set item 6) and other operating expenses (Data Set item 7).

EXHIBIT 10-13   **Budgeted Cash Payments for Operating Expenses**

WHITEWATER SPORTING GOODS STORE NO. 18 Budgeted Cash Payments for Operating Expenses					
	April	May	June	July	April–July Total
Salary and commissions:					
50% of last month's expenses, from Operating expenses budget (Exhibit 10-9)	$ 4,250*	$ 5,000	$ 7,250	$ 5,750	
50% of this month's expenses, from Operating expenses budget (Exhibit 10-9)	5,000	7,250	5,750	5,000	
Total salary and commissions	9,250	12,250	13,000	10,750	
Rent expense, from Operating expenses budget (Exhibit 10-9)	2,000	2,000	2,000	2,000	
Miscellaneous expenses, from Operating expenses budget (Exhibit 10-9)	2,500	4,000	3,000	2,500	
Total payments for operating expenses	$13,750	$18,250	$18,000	$15,250	$65,250

*March 31 salary and commissions payable (Exhibit 10-6).

BBH CHAPTER 10

Notice that depreciation and insurance expenses are *not* included in this cash payments budget (See the next Stop & Think).

Take a moment and trace each month's total cash payments for operating expenses in Exhibit 10-13 to the cash budget in Exhibit 10-14.

Stop & Think...

Why are depreciation expense and insurance expense from the operating expenses budget (Exhibit 10-9) *excluded* from the budgeted cash payments for operating expenses in Exhibit 10-13?

Answer: These expenses do not require cash outlays in the current period. Depreciation is the periodic write-off of the cost of the equipment and fixtures that Whitewater Sporting Goods acquired previously. Insurance expense is the expiration of insurance that was prepaid at an earlier date.

The Cash Budget

The top portion of the cash budget shown in Exhibit 10-14 shows all cash collections and payments. We start with the beginning cash balance, then *add* cash collections to determine the cash available. Next, we *subtract* cash payments for purchases (Exhibit 10-12), cash payments for operating expenses (Exhibit 10-13), and cash payments for capital expenditures (from the company's capital expenditures budget). This yields the ending cash balance before financing, shown in blue.

EXHIBIT 10-14   Cash Budget

WHITEWATER SPORTING GOODS STORE NO. 18
Cash Budget
Four Months Ending July 31, 2009

	April	May	June	July
Beginning cash balance	$15,000*	$10,550	$10,410	$18,235
Cash collections (Exhibit 10-11)	46,000	68,000	68,000	54,000
Cash available	$61,000	$78,550	$78,410	$72,235
Cash payments:				
Purchases of inventory (Exhibit 10-12)	$42,700	$48,300	$40,600	$32,900
Operating expenses (Exhibit 10-13)	13,750	18,250	18,000	15,250
Purchase of delivery truck (Data Set item 8)	3,000	—	—	—
Total cash payments	59,450	66,550	58,600	48,150
(1) Ending cash balance before financing	1,550	12,000	19,810	24,085
Less: Minimum cash balance desired	(10,000)	(10,000)	(10,000)	(10,000)
Cash excess (deficiency)	$ (8,450)	$ 2,000	$ 9,810	$14,085
Financing of cash deficiency (see notes *a–c*):				
Borrowing (at end of month)	$ 9,000			
Principal payments (at end of month)		$ (1,500)	$ (1,500)	$ (1,500)
Interest expense (at 12% annually)		(90)	(75)	(60)
(2) Total effects of financing	9,000	(1,590)	(1,575)	(1,560)
Ending cash balance (1) + (2)	$10,550	$10,410	$18,235	$22,525

*March 31 budgeted cash balance (Exhibit 10-6).
Notes
^{a}Borrowing occurs in multiples of $1,000 and only for the amount needed to maintain a minimum cash balance of $10,000.
^{b}Monthly principal payments: $9,000 ÷ 6 = $1,500.
^{c}Interest expense:
  May: $9,000 × (0.12 × 1/12) = $90
  June: ($9,000 − $1,500) × (0.12 × 1/12) = $75
  July: ($9,000 − $1,500 − $1,500) × (0.12 × 1/12) = $60

BBH CHAPTER 10

The lower portion of the cash budget is the financing section. Recall that Whitewater wants to maintain a minimum cash balance of $10,000 at each store (Data Set item 9). April's cash balance before financing ($1,550) falls $8,450 short of this goal, so Whitewater will have to borrow cash. Since Whitewater borrows in increments of $1,000 notes, it will have to borrow a full $9,000 to bring its cash balance above the minimum $10,000 required. After financing, the ending cash balance for April is $10,550.

April's ending cash balance becomes May's beginning cash balance ($10,550). Whitewater follows the same process in May: adding cash collections and subtracting cash payments. In May, Whitewater's ending cash balance before financing ($12,000) is $2,000 greater than the minimum required cash balance. Therefore, Whitewater can start repaying its notes payable.

Data Set item 9 states that Whitewater must repay the notes in six equal installments. Thus, May through July shows principal repayments of $1,500 ($9,000 ÷ 6) per month. Whitewater also pays interest expense on the outstanding notes payable at 12% per year. Interest expense is paid monthly. The June interest expense is $75 [($9,000 principal − $1,500 repayment at the end of May) × 12% × $\frac{1}{12}$]. Interest expense for the four months totals $225 ($90 + $75 + $60). This interest expense appears on the budgeted income statement in Exhibit 10-10.

The cash balance at the end of July ($22,525) is the cash balance in the July 31 budgeted balance sheet in Exhibit 10-15.

The Budgeted Balance Sheet

To prepare the budgeted balance sheet, project each asset, liability, and owners' equity account based on the plans outlined in the previous exhibits.

Study the budgeted balance sheet in Exhibit 10-15 to make certain you understand the computation of each figure. For example, on the budgeted balance sheet as of July 31, 2009, budgeted cash equals the ending cash balance from the cash budget in Exhibit 10-14 ($22,525). Accounts receivable as of July 31 equal July's credit sales of $20,000, shown in the sales budget (Exhibit 10-7). July 31 inventory of $42,400 is July's desired ending inventory in the inventory, purchases, and cost of goods sold budget in Exhibit 10-8. Detailed computations for each of the other accounts appear in Exhibit 10-15.

The Budgeted Statement of Cash Flows

The final step is preparing the budgeted statement of cash flows. Use the information from the schedules of cash collections and payments, the cash budget, and the beginning balance of cash to project cash flows from operating, investing, and financing activities. Take time to study Exhibit 10-16 on page 556 and make sure you understand the origin of each figure.

Getting Employees to Accept the Budget

What is the most important part of Whitewater Sporting Goods' budgeting system? Despite all of the numbers we have crunched, it is not the mechanics. It is getting managers and employees to accept the budget so Whitewater Sporting Goods can reap the planning, coordination, and control benefits illustrated in Exhibit 10-3.

EXHIBIT 10-15   Budgeted Balance Sheet

WHITEWATER SPORTING GOODS STORE NO. 18		
Budgeted Balance Sheet		
July 31, 2009		
Assets		
Current assets:		
Cash (Exhibit 10-14)	$22,525	
Accounts receivable (Sales budget, Exhibit 10-7)	20,000	
Inventory (Inventory, purchases, and cost of goods sold budget, Exhibit 10-8)	42,400	
Prepaid insurance (beginning balance of $1,800 − $800* for four months' expiration; Operating expenses budget, Exhibit 10-9)	1,000	
Total current assets		$ 85,925
Plant assets:		
Equipment and fixtures (beginning balance of $32,000* + $3,000 truck acquisition; Data Set item 8)	$35,000	
Accumulated depreciation (beginning balance of $12,800* + $2,000 for four months' depreciation; Operating expenses budget, Exhibit 10-9)	(14,800)	
Total plant assets		20,200
Total assets		$106,125
Liabilities		
Current liabilities:		
Account payable (0.50 × July purchases of $29,400; Inventory, purchases, and cost of goods sold budget, Exhibit 10-8)	$14,700	
Short-term note payable ($9,000 − $4,500 paid back; Exhibit 10-14)	4,500	
Salary and commissions payable (0.50 × July expenses of $10,000; Operating expenses budget, Exhibit 10-9)	5,000	
Total liabilities		$ 24,200
Owners' Equity		
Owners' equity (beginning balance of $78,950* + $2,975 net income; Exhibit 10-10)		81,925
Total liabilities and owners' equity		$106,125

*March 31, 2009, Balance Sheet (Exhibit 10-6).

Few people enjoy having their work monitored and evaluated. So, if managers use the budget as a benchmark to evaluate employees' performance, managers must motivate employees to accept the budget's goals. Here's how managers can do it:

- Support the budget themselves, or no one else will.
- Show employees how budgets can help them achieve better results.
- Have employees participate in developing the budget.

But these principles alone are not enough. As the manager of Store No. 18, your performance is evaluated by comparing actual results to the budget. When you develop your store's budget, you may be tempted to build in *slack*. For example, you might want to budget fewer sales and higher purchases than you expect. This increases the chance that actual performance will be better than the budget and that you will receive a good evaluation. But adding slack into the budget makes it less accurate—and less useful for planning and control. When the division manager and the head of the accounting department arrive from headquarters next week, they will scour your budget to find any slack that you may have inserted.

EXHIBIT 10-16   Budgeted Statement of Cash Flows

WHITEWATER SPORTING GOODS STORE NO. 18
Budgeted Statement of Cash Flows
Four Months Ending July 31, 2009

Cash flows from operating activities:		
Receipts:		
Collections from customers (Exhibit 10-11)	$ 236,000	
Total cash receipts		$236,000
Payments:		
Purchases of inventory (Exhibit 10-12)	$(164,500)	
Operating expenses (Exhibit 10-13)	(65,250)	
Payment of interest expense (Exhibits 10-14 and 10-10)	(225)	
Total cash payments		(229,975)
Net cash inflow from operating activities		6,025
Cash flows from investing activities:		
Acquisition of delivery truck (Data Set item 8)	$ (3,000)	
Net cash outflow from investing activities		(3,000)
Cash flows from financing activities:		
Proceeds from issuance of notes payable (Exhibit 10-14)	$ 9,000	
Payment of notes payable (Exhibit 10-14)	(4,500)	
Net cash inflow from financing activities		4,500
Net increase in cash		$ 7,525
Cash balance, April 1, 2009 (Exhibits 10-6 and 10-14)		15,000
Cash balance, July 31, 2009 (Exhibits 10-14 and 10-15)		$ 22,525

Using Information Technology for Sensitivity Analysis and Rolling Up Unit Budgets

Exhibits 10-7 through 10-16 show that the manager must prepare many calculations to develop the master budget for just one of the retail stores in the Whitewater Sporting Goods merchandising chain. No wonder managers embrace information technology to help prepare budgets! Let's see how advances in information technology make it more cost-effective for managers to:

- Conduct sensitivity analysis on their own unit's budget.
- Roll up individual unit budgets to create the company-wide budget.

Sensitivity Analysis

The master budget models the company's *planned* activities. Top management pays special attention to ensure that the results of the budgeted income statement (Exhibit 10-10), the cash budget (Exhibit 10-14), and the budgeted balance sheet (Exhibit 10-15) support key strategies.

4 Use sensitivity analysis in budgeting

But actual results often differ from plans, so management wants to know how budgeted income and cash flows would change if key assumptions turned out to be incorrect. Chapter 7 defined *sensitivity analysis* as a *what-if* technique that asks *what* a result will be *if* a predicted amount is not achieved or *if* an underlying assumption changes. *What if* the stock market crashes? How will this affect Amazon.com's sales? Will it have to postpone the planned expansion in Asia and Europe? *What* will be Whitewater Sporting Goods Store No. 18's cash balance on July 31 *if* the period's sales are 45% cash, not 60% cash? Will Whitewater Sporting Goods have to borrow more cash?

Most companies use computer spreadsheet programs (or special budget software) to prepare master budget schedules and statements. One of the earliest spreadsheet programs was developed by graduate business students who realized that computers could take the drudgery out of hand-computed master budget sensitivity analyses. Today, managers answer what-if questions simply by changing a number. At the press of a key, the computer screen flashes a revised budget that includes all of the effects of the change.

Technology makes it cost effective to perform more comprehensive sensitivity analyses. Armed with a better understanding of how changes in sales and costs are likely to affect the company's bottom line, today's managers can react quickly if key assumptions underlying the master budget (such as sales price or quantity) turn out to be wrong.

Stop & Think...

Consider two budget situations: (1) Whitewater Sporting Goods' marketing analysts produce a near-certain forecast for four-month sales of $4,500,000 for the company's 20 stores. (2) Much uncertainty exists about the period's sales. The most likely amount is $4,500,000, but marketing considers any amount between $3,900,000 and $5,100,000 to be possible. How will the budgeting process differ in these two circumstances?

Answer: Whitewater Sporting Goods will prepare a master budget for the expected sales level of $4,500,000 in either case. Because of the uncertainty in the second situation, executives will want a set of budgets covering the entire range of volume rather than a single level. Whitewater's managers may prepare budgets based on sales of, for example, $3,900,000, $4,200,000, $4,500,000, $4,800,000, and $5,100,000. These budgets will help managers plan for sales levels throughout the forecasted range.

Rolling Up Individual Unit Budgets into the Company-Wide Budget

Whitewater Sporting Goods Store No. 18 is just one of the company's many retail stores. As Exhibit 10-17 shows, Whitewater Sporting Goods' headquarters must roll up the budget data from Store No. 18, along with budgets for each of the other stores, to prepare the company-wide master budget. This roll-up can be difficult for companies whose units use different spreadsheets to prepare the budgets.

| EXHIBIT 10-17 | Rolling Up Individual Unit Budgets into the Company-Wide Budget |

Whitewater Sporting Goods, Inc.

Companywide Budgeted Income Statement
Budgeted sales $1,125
Budgeted expenses (992)
Budgeted income $ 133

Budgeted Income Statement
Budgeted sales $ 315
Budgeted expenses (275)
Budgeted income $ 40

Store No. 1

Budgeted Income Statement
Budgeted sales $ 570
Budgeted expenses (480)
Budgeted income $ 90

Store No. 9

Budgeted Income Statement
Budgeted sales $ 240
Budgeted expenses (237)
Budgeted income $ 3

Store No. 18

Companies such as Sunoco turn to budget management software to solve this problem. Often designed as a component of the company's Enterprise Resource Planning (ERP) system (or data warehouse), this software helps managers develop and analyze budgets.

Across the globe, managers sit at their desks, log in to the company's budget system, and enter their numbers. The software allows them to conduct sensitivity analyses on their unit's data. When the manager is satisfied with the budget, he or she can enter it in the company-wide budget with the click of a mouse. The unit's budget automatically rolls up with budgets from all of the other units around the world.

Before the store's budget is officially accepted, it will most likely go through a corporate review process involving division managers and corporate accountants. This review process helps to ensure that the budget is realistic.

Whether at headquarters or on the road, top executives can log in to the budget system and conduct their own sensitivity analyses on individual units' budgets or on the company-wide budget. Managers can spend less time compiling and summarizing data and more time analyzing the information to ensure that the budget leads the company to achieve its key strategic goals.

Responsibility Accounting

5 Prepare performance reports for responsibility centers

You've seen how managers set strategic goals and develop plans and budget resources for activities that help reach those goals. Let's look more closely at how managers *use* budgets to control operations.

Each manager is responsible for planning and controlling some part of the firm's activities. A **responsibility center** is a part or subunit of an organization whose manager is accountable for specific activities. Lower-level managers are often responsible for budgeting and controlling costs of a single value-chain function. For example, one manager is responsible for planning and controlling the *production* of Pace picante sauce at the plant, while another is responsible for planning and controlling the *distribution* of the product to customers. Lower-level managers report to higher-level managers, who have broader responsibilities. Managers in charge of production and distribution report to senior managers responsible for profits (revenues minus costs) earned by an entire product line.

Four Types of Responsibility Centers

Responsibility accounting is a system for evaluating the performance of each responsibility center and its manager. Responsibility accounting performance reports compare plans (budgets) with actions (actual results) for each center. Superiors then evaluate how well each manager (1) used the budgeted resources to achieve the responsibility center's goals and thereby (2) controlled the operations for which he or she was responsible.

Exhibit 10-18 illustrates four types of responsibility centers.

1. **In a cost center, managers are accountable for costs (expenses) only.** Manufacturing operations, such as the Pace picante sauce production lines, are cost centers. The line supervisor controls costs by ensuring that employees work efficiently. The supervisor is *not* responsible for generating revenues because he or she is not involved in selling the product. The plant manager evaluates the supervisor on his or her ability to control *costs* by comparing actual costs to budgeted costs. All else being equal (for example, holding quality constant), the supervisor is likely to receive a more favorable evaluation when actual costs are less than budgeted costs.

2. **In a revenue center, managers are accountable primarily for revenues.** Examples include the Midwest and Southeast sales regions of businesses such as Pace Foods. These managers of revenue centers may also be responsible for the costs of their own sales operations. Revenue center performance reports compare actual with budgeted revenues and may include the costs incurred by the revenue center itself. All else being equal, the manager is likely to receive a more favorable evaluation when actual revenues exceed the budget.

EXHIBIT 10-18   **Four Types of Responsibility Centers**

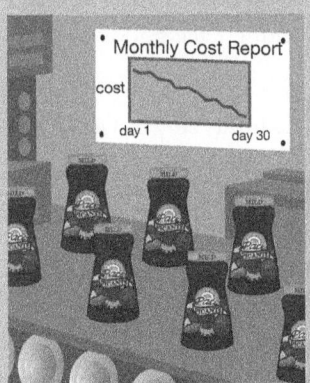
In a **cost center**, such as a production line for Pace picante sauce, managers are responsible for costs.

In a **revenue center**, such as the Midwest sales region, managers are responsible for generating sales revenue.

In a **profit center**, such as a line of products, managers are responsible for generating income.

In an **investment center**, such as Campbell Soups and Sauces division, managers are responsible for income and invested capital.

3. **In a profit center, managers are accountable for both revenues and costs (expenses) and, therefore, profits.** The (higher-level) manager responsible for the entire Pace product line is accountable for increasing sales revenue *and* controlling costs to achieve the profit goals. Profit center reports include both revenues and expenses to show the profit center's income. Superiors evaluate the manager's performance by comparing actual revenues, expenses, and profits to the budget. All else being equal, the manager is likely to receive a more favorable evaluation when actual profits exceed the budget.

4. **In an investment center, managers are accountable for investments, revenues, and costs (expenses).** Investment centers are generally large divisions of a corporation. For example, the North American Sauces and Beverages Division (which includes Pace Foods) of Campbell Soup is considered an investment center. Managers of investment centers are responsible for (1) generating sales, (2) controlling expenses, and (3) managing the amount of investment (assets) required to earn the income. Investment centers are treated almost as if they were stand-alone companies. Managers have decision-making authority over how all of the division's assets are used. As a result, managers are held responsible for generating as much income as they can with those assets.

   Top management often evaluates investment center managers based on performance measures such as return on investment (ROI), residual income, and economic value added (EVA). All else being equal, the manager will receive a more favorable evaluation if the division's actual ROI, residual income, or EVA exceeds the amount budgeted.

Responsibility Accounting Performance Reports

Exhibit 10-19 shows how an organization such as Campbell Soup Company assigns responsibility.

At the top level, the CEO oversees each of the four divisions. Division managers generally have broad responsibility, including deciding how to use assets to maximize ROI. Most companies consider divisions as *investment centers*.

Each division manager supervises all of the product lines in that division. Exhibit 10-19 shows that the VP of North American Sauces and Beverages oversees the Prego Italian sauces, Pace Mexican sauces, V8 juice, and Franco-American canned pasta product lines. Product lines are generally considered *profit centers*. Thus, the manager of the Pace Foods product line is responsible for evaluating lower-level managers of both of the following:

- *Cost centers* (such as plants that make Pace Foods products)
- *Revenue centers* (such as managers responsible for selling Pace Foods products)

Exhibit 10-20 illustrates responsibility accounting performance reports for each level of management shown in Exhibit 10-19. Exhibit 10-20 uses assumed numbers to illustrate reports like those:

- The CEO may use to evaluate divisions.
- The divisional VPs may use to evaluate individual product lines.
- The product line managers may use to evaluate the development, production, marketing, and distribution of their products.

At each level, the reports compare actual results with the budget.

Start with the lowest level and move to the top. Follow the $25 million budgeted operating income from the Mexican sauces product line report to the report of the VP—North American Sauces and Beverages. The VP's report summarizes the budgeted and actual operating incomes for each of the four product lines he or she supervises.

BBH CHAPTER 10

EXHIBIT 10-19   Partial Organization Chart

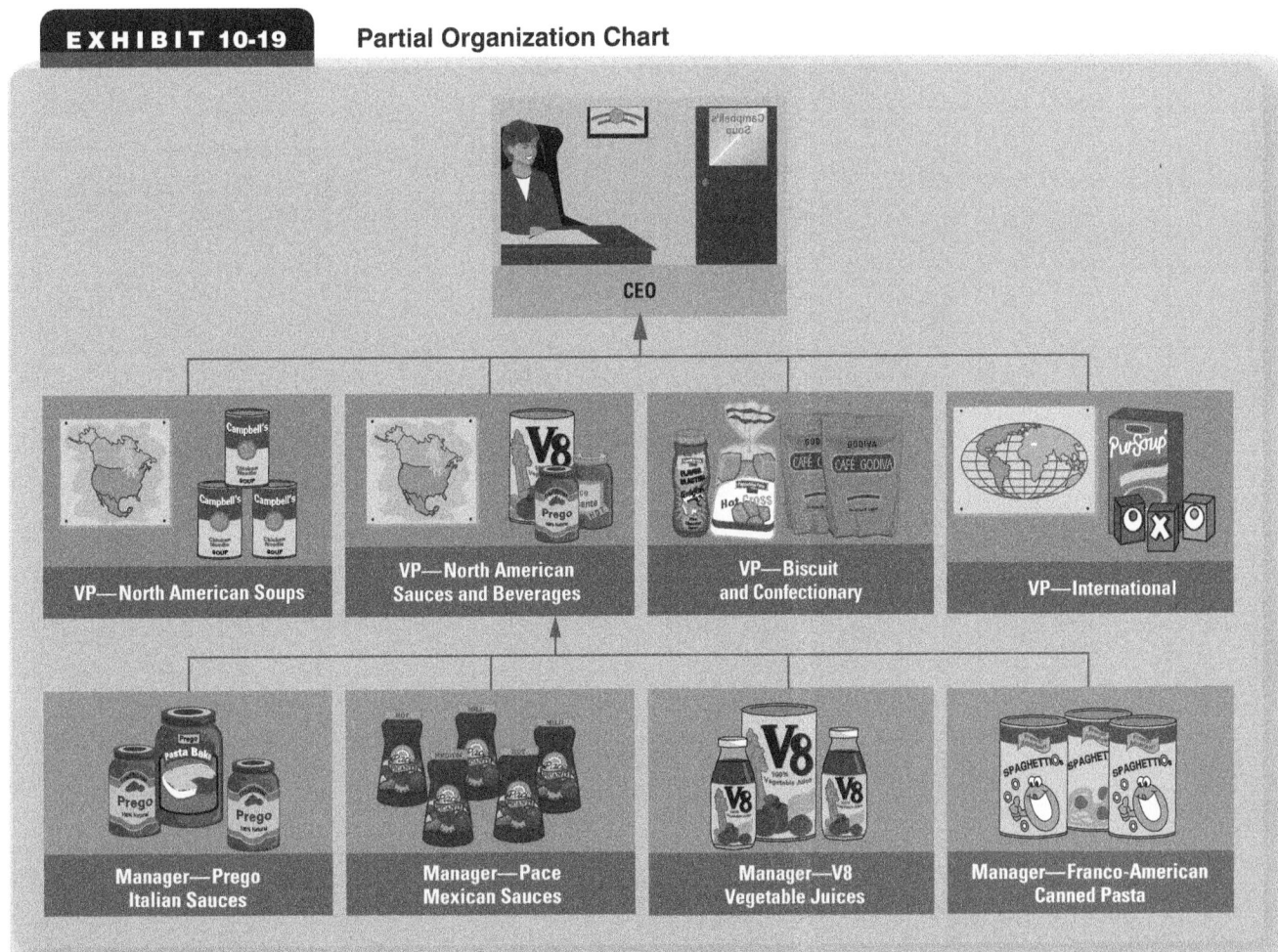

Now, trace the $70 million budgeted operating income from the VP's report to the CEO's report. The CEO's report includes a summary of each division's actual and budgeted profits, as well as the costs incurred by corporate headquarters, which are not assigned to any of the divisions.

Management by Exception

The variances reported in Exhibit 10-20 aid **management by exception,** which directs executives' attention to important differences between actual and budgeted amounts. Look at the CEO's report. The International Soups and Sauces Division's actual operating income of $34 million is very close to the budgeted $35 million. Unless there are other signs of trouble, the CEO will not waste time investigating such a small variance.

In contrast, the North American Sauces and Beverages Division earned a great deal more profit than budgeted. The CEO will want to know why. Suppose the VP of the division believes that a national sales promotion was especially effective. That promotion may be repeated or adapted by other divisions. One reason managers investigate large, favorable variances (not just large, unfavorable ones) is to identify the reason for exceptional results so that other parts of the organization may benefit. Another is to ensure that employees are not skimping on ingredients, marketing, or R&D, which could hurt the company's long-term success. Also, it's possible that large variances are the result of unrealistic budgets.

A CEO who received the report at the top of Exhibit 10-20 would likely concentrate on improving the North American Soups Division because its actual income fell $9 million below budget. The CEO would want to see which product lines

EXHIBIT 10-20   **Responsibility Accounting Performance Reports at Various Levels**

CEO'S QUARTERLY RESPONSIBILITY REPORT
(in millions of dollars)

Operating Income of Divisions and Corporate Headquarters Expense	Actual	Budget	Variance Favorable/ (Unfavorable)
North American Soups	$209	$218	$ (9)
North American Sauces and Beverages	84	70	14
Biscuits and Confectionary	87	79	8
International Soups and Sauces	34	35	(1)
Corporate Headquarters Expense	(29)	(33)	4
Operating Income	$385	$369	$16

VP—NORTH AMERICAN SAUCES AND BEVERAGES QUARTERLY RESPONSIBILITY REPORT
(in millions of dollars)

Operating Income of Product Lines	Actual	Budget	Variance Favorable/ (Unfavorable)
Italian Sauces	$18	$20	$ (2)
Mexican Sauces	38	25	13
Vegetable Juices	15	10	5
Canned Pastas	13	15	(2)
Operating Income	$84	$70	$14

MANAGER—MEXICAN SAUCES QUARTERLY RESPONSIBILITY REPORT
(in millions of dollars)

Revenue and Expenses	Actual	Budget	Variance Favorable/ (Unfavorable)
Sales revenue	$ 84	$ 80	$ 4
Cost of goods sold	(30)	(36)	6
Gross profit	54	44	10
Marketing expenses	(9)	(12)	3
Research and development expenses	(3)	(2)	(1)
Other expenses	(4)	(5)	1
Operating income	$ 38	$ 25	$13

caused the shortfall so that he or she and the VP of the division could work together to correct any problems.

Exhibit 10-20 also shows how summarized data can hide problems. Although as a whole, the North American Sauces and Beverages Division performed well, the Italian sauces and canned pasta lines did not. If the CEO received only the condensed report at the top of the exhibit, he or she would rely on division managers to spot and correct problems in individual product lines.

Not a Question of Blame

Responsibility accounting assigns managers responsibility for their unit's actions and provides a way to evaluate both the managers and their unit's performance. But superiors should not misuse responsibility accounting to find fault or place blame. The question is not who is to blame for an unfavorable variance. Instead, the question is who can best explain why a specific variance occurred. Consider the North American Soups Division in Exhibit 10-20. Suppose a tornado devastated the primary production plant. The remaining plants may have operated very efficiently, and this efficiency kept the income variance down to $9 million. If so, the North American Soups Division and its VP actually did a good job.

Other Performance Measures

Top management uses responsibility accounting performance reports to assess each responsibility center's *financial* performance. Top management also often assesses each responsibility center's nonfinancial *operating* performance. Typical nonfinancial performance measures include customer satisfaction ratings, delivery time, product quality, and employee expertise.

The following Decision Guidelines review budgets and the way managers use them in responsibility accounting. Study these guidelines before working on Summary Problem 2.

BBH CHAPTER 10

Decision Guidelines

THE MASTER BUDGET AND RESPONSIBILITY ACCOUNTING

Amazon.com's initial strategy was to "get big fast." But without a budget, spending got out of control. So, founder and CEO Jeff Bezos added a second strategic goal—to become the world's most cost-efficient, high-quality e-tailer. Today, Amazon.com's managers use budgets to help reach growth and cost-efficiency goals. Let's consider some of the decisions Amazon.com made as it set up its budgeting process.

Decision	Guidelines
What benefits should Amazon.com expect to obtain from developing a budget?	Requires managers to *plan* how to increase sales and how to cut costs.
	Promotes *coordination and communication*, such as communicating the importance of the cost-efficiency goal.
	Provides a *benchmark* that motivates employees and helps managers evaluate how well employees contributed to the sales growth and cost-efficiency goals.
In what order should Amazon.com's managers prepare the components of the master budget?	1. Begin with the *operating budget*: • Start with the *sales budget*, which feeds into all other budgets.

continued . . .

Decision	Guidelines
	• Then, determine the inventory, purchases, and cost of goods sold budget. • Next, prepare the operating expenses budget. • From these three budgets, create the *budgeted income statement*. 2. Next, prepare the *capital expenditures budget*. 3. Finally, prepare the *financial budget*. • Start with the *cash budget*. • The cash budget provides the ending cash balance for the *budgeted balance sheet* and the details for the *budgeted statement of cash flows*.
What extra steps should Amazon.com take given the uncertainty of Internet-based sales forecasts?	Prepare a *sensitivity analysis* by projecting budgeted results at different sales levels.
How does Amazon.com compute budgeted purchases?	$$\text{Beginning inventory} + \text{Purchases} - \text{Ending inventory} = \text{Cost of goods sold}$$ so $$\text{Purchases} = \text{Cost of goods sold} + \text{Ending inventory} - \text{Beginning inventory}$$
What kind of a responsibility center does each manager supervise?	**Cost center:** Manager is responsible for costs. **Revenue center:** Manager is responsible for revenues. **Profit center:** Manager is responsible for both revenues and costs and, therefore, profits. **Investment center:** Manager is responsible for revenues, costs, and the amount of the investment required to earn the income.
How should Amazon.com evaluate managers?	Compare actual performance with the budget for the manager's responsibility center. *Management by exception* focuses on large differences between budgeted and actual results. The emphasis should be on information, not blame.

Summary Problem 2

Continue the revised Whitewater Sporting Goods illustration from Summary Problem 1. Now that you think July sales will be $40,000 instead of $50,000, as projected in Exhibit 10-7, how will this affect the financial budget?

Requirements

Revise the schedule of budgeted cash collections (Exhibit 10-11), the schedule of budgeted cash payments for purchases (Exhibit 10-12), and the schedule of budgeted cash payments for operating expenses (Exhibit 10-13). Prepare a revised cash budget; a revised budgeted balance sheet at July 31, 2009; and a revised budgeted statement of cash flows for the four months ended July 31, 2009. *Note:* You need not repeat the parts of the revised schedule that do not change.

    Hint: You will need to refer to the revised budgets created in Summary Problem 1.

Solution

Although not required, this solution repeats the budgeted amounts for April, May, and June. Revised figures appear in color for emphasis.

WHITEWATER SPORTING GOODS STORE NO. 18 Revised—Budgeted Cash Collections from Customers	April	May	June	July	Total
Cash sales, from revised sales budget	$30,000	$48,000	$36,000	$24,000	
Collections of last month's credit sales, from revised sales budget	16,000*	20,000	32,000	24,000	
Total collections	$46,000	$68,000	$68,000	$48,000	$230,000

*March 31 accounts receivable (Exhibit 10-6)

WHITEWATER SPORTING GOODS STORE NO. 18 Revised—Budgeted Cash Payments for Purchases	April	May	June	July	Total
50% of last month's purchases, from revised inventory, purchases, and cost of goods sold budget	$16,800*	$25,900	$22,400	$15,400	
50% of this month's purchases, from revised inventory, purchases, and cost of goods sold budget	25,900	22,400	15,400	14,000	
Total payments for purchases	$42,700	$48,300	$37,800	$29,400	$158,200

*March 31 accounts payable (Exhibit 10-6).

WHITEWATER SPORTING GOODS STORE NO. 18
Revised—Budgeted Cash Payments for Operating Expenses

	April	May	June	July	Total
Salary and commissions:					
50% of last month's expenses, from revised operating expenses budget	$ 4,250*	$ 5,000	$ 7,250	$ 5,750	
50% of this month's expenses, from revised operating expenses budget	5,000	7,250	5,750	4,250	
Total salary and commissions	9,250	12,250	13,000	10,000	
Rent expense, from revised operating expenses budget	2,000	2,000	2,000	2,000	
Miscellaneous expenses, from revised operating expenses budget	2,500	4,000	3,000	2,000	
Total payments for operating expenses	$13,750	$18,250	$18,000	$14,000	$64,000

*March 31 salary and commissions payable (Exhibit 10-6).

WHITEWATER SPORTING GOODS STORE NO. 18
Revised Cash Budget
Four Months Ending July 31, 2009

	April	May	June	July
Beginning cash balance	$15,000*	$10,550	$10,410	$21,035
Cash collections (revised budgeted cash collections)	46,000	68,000	68,000	48,000
Cash available	$61,000	$78,550	$78,410	$69,035
Cash payments:				
Purchases of inventory (revised budgeted cash payments for purchases)	$42,700	$48,300	$37,800	$29,400
Operating expenses (revised budgeted cash payments for operating expenses)	13,750	18,250	18,000	14,000
Purchase of delivery truck (Data Set item 8)	3,000	—	—	—
Total cash payments	59,450	66,550	55,800	43,400
(1) Ending cash balance before financing	1,550	12,000	22,610	25,635
Less: Minimum cash balance desired	(10,000)	(10,000)	(10,000)	(10,000)
Cash excess (deficiency)	$ (8,450)	$ 2,000	$12,610	$15,635
Financing of cash deficiency (see notes a–c):				
Borrowing (at end of month)	$ 9,000			
Principal payments (at end of month)		$ (1,500)	$ (1,500)	$ (1,500)
Interest expense (at 12% annually)		(90)	(75)	(60)
(2) Total effects of financing	9,000	(1,590)	(1,575)	(1,560)
Ending cash balance (1) + (2)	$10,550	$10,410	$21,035	$24,075

*March 31 cash balance (Exhibit 10-6).
Notes
aBorrowing occurs in multiples of $1,000 and only for the amount needed to maintain a minimum cash balance of $10,000.
bMonthly principal payments: $9,000 ÷ 6 = $1,500.
cInterest expense:
May: $9,000 × (0.12 × 1/12) = $90
June: ($9,000 − $1,500) × (0.12 × 1/12) = $75
July: ($9,000 − $1,500 − $1,500) × (0.12 × 1/12) = $60

WHITEWATER SPORTING GOODS STORE NO. 18
Revised Budgeted Balance Sheet
July 31, 2009

Assets		
Current assets:		
Cash (revised cash budget)	$24,075	
Accounts receivable (revised sales budget)	16,000	
Inventory	42,400	
Prepaid insurance	1,000	
Total current assets		$ 83,475
Plant assets:		
Equipment and fixtures	$35,000	
Accumulated depreciation	(14,800)	
Total plant assets		20,200
Total assets		$103,675
Liabilities		
Current liabilities:		
Accounts payable (0.50 × July purchases of $28,000; revised		
inventory, purchases, and cost of goods sold budget)	$14,000	
Short-term note payable	4,500	
Salary and commissions payable (0.50 × July expenses of $8,500;		
revised operating expenses budget)	4,250	
Total liabilities		$ 22,750
Owners' Equity		
Owners' equity (beginning balance of $78,950* + $1,975 net income,		
revised budgeted income statement)		80,925
Total liabilities and owners' equity		$103,675

*March 31, 2009, balance sheet (Exhibit 10-6).

WHITEWATER SPORTING GOODS STORE NO. 18
Revised Budgeted Statement of Cash Flows
Four Months Ending July 31, 2009

Cash flows from operating activities:		
Receipts:		
Collections (revised budgeted cash collections)	$ 230,000	
Total cash receipts		$230,000
Payments:		
Purchases of inventory (revised budgeted cash payments for purchases)	$(158,200)	
Operating expenses (revised budgeted cash payments for operating expenses)	(64,000)	
Payment of interest expense	(225)	
Total cash payments		(222,425)
Net cash inflow from operating activities		7,575
Cash flows from investing activities:		
Acquisition of delivery truck	$ (3,000)	
Net cash outflow from investing activities		(3,000)
Cash flows from financing activities:		
Proceeds from issuance of notes payable	$ 9,000	
Payment of notes payable	(4,500)	
Net cash inflow from financing activities		4,500
Net increase in cash		$ 9,075
Cash balance, April 1, 2009 (Exhibit 10-6)		15,000
Cash balance, July 31, 2009 (revised cash budget)		$ 24,075

Page 569 intentionally omitted

Review *The Master Budget and Responsibility Accounting*

Accounting Vocabulary

Capital Expenditures Budget. (p. 543)
A company's plan for purchases of property, plant, equipment, and other long-term assets.

Cash Budget. (p. 551)
Details how the business expects to go from the beginning cash balance to the desired ending balance. Also called the statement of budgeted cash receipts and payments.

Financial Budget. (p. 543)
The cash budget (cash inflows and outflows), the budgeted period-end balance sheet, and the budgeted statement of cash flows.

Management by Exception. (p. 561)
Directs management's attention to important differences between actual and budgeted amounts.

Master Budget. (p. 542)
The set of budgeted financial statements and supporting schedules for an entire organization. Includes the operating budget, the capital expenditures budget, and the financial budget.

Operating Budget. (p. 543)
Projects sales revenue, cost of goods sold, and operating expenses, leading to the budgeted income statement that projects operating income for the period.

Responsibility Accounting. (p. 559)
A system for evaluating the performance of each responsibility center and its manager.

Responsibility Center. (p. 558)
A part or subunit of an organization whose manager is accountable for specific activities.

Quick Check

1. Amazon.com expected to receive which of the following benefits when it started its budgeting process?
   a. The planning required to develop the budget helps managers foresee and avoid potential problems before they occur.
   b. The budget helps motivate employees to achieve Amazon.com's sales growth and cost reduction goals.
   c. The budget provides Amazon.com's managers with a benchmark against which to compare actual results for performance evaluation.
   d. All of the above.

2. Which of the following is the cornerstone (or most critical element) of the master budget?
   a. the sales budget
   b. the inventory budget
   c. the purchases and cost of goods sold budget
   d. the operating expenses budget

3. The income statement is part of which element of Amazon.com's master budget?
   a. the operating budget
   b. the capital expenditures budget
   c. the financial budget
   d. none of the above

Use the following information to answer Questions 4 through 6. Suppose Amazon.com sells 1 million hardcover books a day at an average price of $30 and 1.5 million paperback books a day at an average price of $15. Assume that Amazon.com's purchase price for the books is 60% of the selling price it charges retail customers. Amazon.com has no beginning inventory, but it wants to have a three-day supply of ending inventory. Assume that operating expenses are $0.5 million per day.

4. Compute Amazon.com's budgeted sales for the next (seven-day) week.
   a. $52.5 million
   b. $210 million
   c. $220.5 million
   d. $367.5 million

5. Determine Amazon.com's budgeted purchases for the next (seven-day) week.
   a. $220.5 million
   b. $315 million
   c. $367.5 million
   d. $525 million

6. What is Amazon.com's budgeted operating income for a (seven-day) week?
   a. $52.5 million
   b. $56 million
   c. $143.5 million
   d. $147 million

7. Which of the following expenses would *not* appear in Amazon.com's cash budget?
   a. depreciation expense
   b. wages expense
   c. interest expense
   d. marketing expense

8. IT has made it easier for Amazon.com's managers to perform all of the following tasks *except*
   a. sensitivity analyses
   b. rolling up individual units' budgets into the company-wide budget
   c. removing slack from the budget
   d. preparing responsibility center performance reports that identify variances between actual and budgeted revenues and costs

9. Which of the following managers is at the highest level of the organization?
   a. cost center manager
   b. revenue center manager
   c. profit center manager
   d. investment center manager

10. Suppose Amazon.com budgets $5 million for customer service costs but actually spends $4 million. Which of the following is true?

a. Because this $1 million variance is favorable, management does not need to investigate further.

b. Management will investigate this $1 million favorable variance to ensure that the cost savings do not reflect skimping on customer service.

c. Management will investigate this $1 million unfavorable variance to try to identify and then correct the problem that led to the unfavorable variance.

d. Management should investigate every variance, especially unfavorable ones.

Quick Check Answers

1. d 2. a 3. a 4. d 5. b 6. c 7. a 8. c 9. d 10. b

For Internet Exercises, Excel in Practice, and additional online activities, go to this book's Web site at www.prenhall.com/bamber.

Assess Your Progress

■ Learning Objectives

1 Learn why managers use budgets

2 Prepare an operating budget

3 Prepare a financial budget

4 Use sensitivity analysis in budgeting

5 Prepare performance reports for responsibility centers

■ Short Exercises

S10-1 **Explain benefits of budgeting** *(Learning Objective 1)*
Consider the budget for your travel itinerary business (page 539). Explain how you benefit from preparing the budget.

S10-2 **Order of preparation and components of master budget** *(Learning Objectives 2, 3)*
In what order should you prepare the following components of the master budget?

Budgeted income statement	Operating expense budget	Cash budget
Budgeted statement of cash flows	Purchases and cost of goods sold budget	Capital expenditures budget
Budgeted balance sheet	Sales budget	Inventory budget

Which are components of the operating budget? Which are components of the financial budget?

S10-3 **Sales Budget** *(Learning Objective 2)*
In a series of Short Exercises, you will prepare parts of the master budget for Grippers, which sells its rock-climbing shoes worldwide. We will concentrate on Grippers' budget for January and February.

Grippers expects to sell 4,000 pairs of shoes for $185 each in January and 3,500 pairs of shoes for $220 each in February. All sales are cash only. Prepare the sales budget for January and February.

S10-4 **Continuation of S10-3: inventory, purchases, and cost of goods sold** *(Learning Objective 2)*
In S10-3, Grippers expects cost of goods sold to average 65% of sales revenue and the company expects to sell 4,300 pairs of shoes in March for $240 each. Grippers' target ending inventory is $10,000 plus 50% of the next month's cost of goods sold. Use this information and the sales budget from S10-3 to prepare Grippers' inventory, purchases, and cost of goods sold budget for January and February.

S10-5 **Continuation of S10-3: cash collections** *(Learning Objective 3)*
You prepared Grippers' sales budget in S10-3. Now, assume that Grippers' sales are 25% cash and 75% credit. Grippers' collection history indicates that credit sales are collected as follows:

> 30% in the month of the sale
>
> 60% in the month after the sale
>
> 6% two months after the sale
>
> 4% are never collected

November sales totaled $391,500, and December sales were $398,250. Prepare a schedule for the budgeted cash collections for January and February.

S10-6 **Continuation of S10-5: cash budget** *(Learning Objective 3)*
Refer to S10-5. Grippers has $8,300 cash on hand on January 1. The company requires a minimum cash balance of $7,500. January cash collections are $548,330 (as you calculated in S10-5). Total cash payments for January are $583,200. Prepare a cash budget for January. Will Grippers need to borrow cash by the end of January?

S10-7 **Revise sales budget** *(Learning Objective 4)*
Turn to the original Whitewater Sporting Goods Data Set item 3. Suppose June sales are expected to be $40,000 rather than $60,000. Revise Whitewater Sporting Goods' sales budget. What other components of Whitewater Sporting Goods' master budget would be affected by this change in the sales budget?

S10-8 **Revise inventory, purchases, and cost of goods sold budget** *(Learning Objective 4)*
Refer to the original Whitewater Sporting Goods Data Set item 5. Suppose cost of goods sold averages 75% of sales rather than 70%. Revise Whitewater Sporting Goods' inventory, purchases, and cost of goods sold budget for April and May. What other components of Whitewater Sporting Goods' master budget would be affected by the change in the budgeted cost of goods sold?

S10-9 **Revise cash collections budget** *(Learning Objective 4)*
Turn to the original Whitewater Sporting Goods Data Set item 4. Suppose 70% of sales are cash and 30% are credit. Revise Whitewater's sales budget and budgeted cash collections from customers for April and May.

S10-10 **Revise cash payments for purchases** *(Learning Objective 4)*
Refer to the original Whitewater Sporting Goods Data Set item 5. Suppose Whitewater Sporting Goods pays for 60% of inventory purchases in the month of the purchase and 40% during the next month. Revise Whitewater Sporting Goods' budgeted cash payments for purchases of inventory for April and May. (*Hint*: Assume that these new percentages also apply to March purchases of $33,600 given in Data Set item 5.)

S10-11 **Identify responsibility centers** *(Learning Objective 5)*

Fill in the blanks with the phrase that best completes the sentence.

A cost center	A responsibility center	Lower
An investment center	A revenue center	Higher
A profit center		

a. The maintenance department at the San Diego Zoo is _____.

b. The concession stand at the San Diego Zoo is _____.

c. The menswear department at Bloomingdale's, which is responsible for buying and selling merchandise, is _____.

d. A production line at a PalmPilot plant is _____.

e. _____ is any segment of the business whose manager is accountable for specific activities.

f. Gatorade, a division of Quaker Oats, is _____.

g. The sales manager in charge of Nike's northwest sales territory oversees _____.

h. Managers of cost and revenue centers are at _____ levels of the organization than are managers of profit and investment centers.

S10-12 **Corporate headquarters expenses** *(Learning Objective 5)*

In Exhibit 10-20, the next to last line of the CEO's report consists entirely of expenses. Describe the kinds of expenses that would be included in this category.

S10-13 **Management by exception** *(Learning Objective 5)*

Look at the performance report in Exhibit 10-20. According to the management by exception principle, on which variances should the manager of the Mexican sauces product line focus his or her efforts? For these variances, compute the variance as a percent of the budgeted amount and suggest some questions the manager may want to investigate.

S10-14 **Interpret favorable variance** *(Learning Objective 5)*

Exhibit 10-20 shows that the Mexican sauces product line had a favorable marketing expense variance. Does this favorable variance necessarily mean that the manager of the Mexican sauces line is doing a good job? Explain.

▪ Exercises

E10-15 **Prepare summary performance report** *(Learning Objective 1)*

Hanna White owns a chain of travel goods stores. Last year, her sales staff sold 10,000 suitcases at an average sales price of $150. Variable expenses were 80% of sales revenue, and the total fixed expense was $100,000. This year, the chain sold more expensive product lines. Sales were 8,000 suitcases at an average price of $200. The variable expense percentage and the total fixed expense were the same both years. White evaluates the chain manager by comparing this year's income with last year's income.

Prepare a performance report for this year, similar to Exhibit 10-4. How would you improve White's performance evaluation system to better analyze this year's results?

E10-16 **Prepare inventory, purchases, and cost of goods sold budget** *(Learning Objective 2)*

Leno sells tire rims. Its sales budget for the nine months ended September 30 follows:

	Quarter Ended			Nine-Month Total
	March 31	June 30	Sept. 30	
Cash sales, 30%	$ 30,000	$ 45,000	$ 37,500	$112,500
Credit sales, 70%	70,000	105,000	87,500	262,500
Total sales, 100%	$100,000	$150,000	$125,000	$375,000

In the past, cost of goods sold has been 60% of total sales. The director of marketing and the financial vice president agree that each quarter's ending inventory should not be below $20,000 plus 10% of cost of goods sold for the following quarter. The marketing director expects sales of $220,000 during the fourth quarter. The January 1 inventory was $19,000.

Prepare an inventory, purchases, and cost of goods sold budget for each of the first three quarters of the year. Compute cost of goods sold for the entire nine-month period (use Exhibit 10-8 as a model).

E10-17 **Prepare a cash collections budget** *(Learning Objective 3)*

Refer to the sales budget presented in E10-16. Credit sales are typically collected as follows: 60% in the quarter of the sale, 30% in the quarter after the sale, 7% in the second quarter after the sale, and 3% uncollectible. Prepare the cash collections budget for the third quarter (the quarter ended September 30).

E10-18 **Prepare a sales budget for a not-for-profit organization** *(Learning Objective 2)*

Great Start Preschool operates a not-for-profit morning preschool. Each family pays a nonrefundable registration fee of $120 per child per school year. Monthly tuition for the nine-month school year varies depending on the number of days per week that the child attends preschool. The monthly tuition is $115 for the two-day program, $130 for the three-day program, $145 for the four-day program, and $160 for the five-day program. The following enrollment has been projected for the coming year:

two-day program:	56 children
three-day program:	32 children
four-day program:	48 children
five-day program:	16 children

In addition to the morning preschool, Great Start Preschool offers a Lunch Bunch program where kids have the option of staying an extra hour for lunch and playtime. Great Start charges an additional $3 per child for every Lunch Bunch attended. Historically, half the children stay for Lunch Bunch an average of ten times a month.

Requirement

Calculate Great Start Preschool's budgeted revenue for the school year.

E10-19 **Continuation of E10-18: prepare an operating expenses budget** *(Learning Objectives 1, 2)*

Refer to Great Start Preschool's data in E10-18. Great Start's primary expense is payroll. The state allows a student-to-teacher ratio of no more than eight children to each teacher. Teachers are paid a flat salary each month as follows:

Teachers of two-day program:	$432 per month
Teachers of three-day program:	$648 per month
Teachers of four-day program:	$864 per month
Teachers of five-day program:	$1,080 per month
Preschool director's salary:	$1,500 per month

In addition to the salary expense, Great Start must pay federal payroll taxes (FICA taxes) in the amount of 7.65% of salary expense. Great Start leases its facilities from a local church, paying $2,000 per month plus 10% of monthly tuition revenue. Fixed operating expenses (telephone, Internet access, bookkeeping services, and so forth) amount to $850 per month over the nine-month school year. Variable monthly expenses (over the nine-month school year) for art supplies and other miscellaneous supplies are $12 per child.

Requirements

1. Prepare Great Start Preschool's monthly operating budget. Round all amounts to the nearest dollar.

2. Using your answer from E10-18 and Requirement 1, create Great Start Preschool's budgeted income statement for the entire nine-month school year. You may group all revenues together and all operating expenses together.

3. Great Start is a not-for-profit preschool. What might Great Start do with their projected income for the year?

E10-20 **Prepare an inventory, purchases, and cost of goods sold budget** *(Learning Objective 2)*

University Logos buys logo-imprinted merchandise and then sells it to university bookstores. Sales are expected to be $2,000,000 in September, $2,160,000 in October, $2,376,000 in November, and $2,500,000 in December. University Logos sets its prices to earn an average 30% gross profit on sales revenue. The company does not want inventory to fall below $400,000 plus 15% of the next month's cost of goods sold.

Prepare an inventory, purchases, and cost of goods sold budget for the months of October and November.

E10-21 **Prepare budgeted income statement** *(Learning Objective 2)*

Wheels is an exotic car dealership. Suppose its Miami office projects that 2009 quarterly sales will increase by 3% in Quarter 1, by another 4% in Quarter 2, by another 6% in Quarter 3, and by another 5% in Quarter 4. Management expects operating expenses to be 80% of revenues during each of the first two quarters, 79% of revenues during the third quarter, and 81% during the fourth quarter. The office manager expects to borrow $100,000 on July 1, with quarterly principal payments of $10,000 beginning on September 30 and interest paid at an annual rate of 13%. Assume that fourth-quarter 2008 sales were $4,000,000.

continued . . .

Prepare a budgeted income statement for each of the four quarters of 2009 and for the entire year. Present the 2009 budget as follows:

Quarter 1	Quarter 2	Quarter 3	Quarter 4	Full Year

E10-22 Compute cash receipts and payments *(Learning Objective 3)*

Aqua Pure is a distributor of bottled water. For each of the items a through c, compute the amount of cash receipts or payments Aqua Pure will budget for September. The solution to one item may depend on the answer to an earlier item.

a. Management expects to sell equipment that costs $14,000 at a gain of $2,000. Accumulated depreciation on this equipment is $7,000.

b. Management expects to sell 7,500 cases of water in August and 9,200 in September. Each case sells for $12. Cash sales average 30% of total sales, and credit sales make up the rest. On average, three-fourths of credit sales are collected in the month of sale, with the balance collected the following month.

c. The company pays rent and property taxes of $4,200 each month. Commissions and other selling expenses average 25% of sales. Aqua Pure pays two-thirds of commissions and other selling expenses in the month incurred, with the balance paid the following month.

E10-23 Prepare sales and cash collections budgets *(Learning Objectives 2, 3)*

Rovniak Reeds, a manufacturer of saxophone, oboe, and clarinet reeds, has projected sales to be $890,000 in October, $950,000 in November, $1,025,000 in December, and $920,000 in January. Rovniak's sales are 25% cash and 75% credit. Rovniak's collection history indicates that credit sales are collected as follows:

25% in the month of the sale
65% in the month after the sale
8% two months after the sale
2% are never collected

Requirements

1. Prepare a sales budget for all four months, showing the breakdown between cash and credit sales.

2. Prepare a cash collections budget for December and January. Round all answers up to the nearest dollar.

E10-24 Prepare cash budget, then revise *(Learning Objectives 3, 4)*

Battery Power, a family-owned battery store, began October with $10,500 cash. Management forecasts that collections from credit customers will be $11,000 in October and $15,000 in November. The store is scheduled to receive $6,000 cash on a business note receivable in October. Projected cash payments include inventory purchases ($13,000 in October and $13,900 in November) and operating expenses ($3,000 each month).

Battery Power's bank requires a $10,000 minimum balance in the store's checking account. At the end of any month when the account balance dips below $10,000, the bank automatically extends credit to the store in multiples of $1,000. Battery Power borrows as little as possible and pays back loans in quarterly installments of $2,000 plus 4% interest on the entire unpaid principal. The first payment occurs three months after the loan.

Requirements

1. Prepare Battery Power's cash budget for October and November.

2. How much cash will Battery Power borrow in November if collections from customers that month total $12,000 instead of $15,000?

E10-25 **Finish an incomplete cash budget** *(Learning Objective 3)*

You recently began a job as an accounting intern at Outdoor Adventures. Your first task was to help prepare the cash budget for February and March. Unfortunately, the computer with the budget file crashed, and you did not have a backup or even a hard copy. You ran a program to salvage bits of data from the budget file. After entering the following data in the budget, you may have just enough information to reconstruct the budget.

Outdoor Adventures eliminates any cash deficiency by borrowing the exact amount needed from State Street Bank, where the current interest rate is 8%. Outdoor Adventures pays interest on its outstanding debt at the end of each month. The company also repays all borrowed amounts at the end of the month as cash becomes available.

Complete the following cash budget:

OUTDOOR ADVENTURES LTD.
Cash Budget
February and March

	February	March
Beginning cash balance	$ 16,900	$?
Cash collections	?	79,600
Cash from sale of plant assets	0	1,800
Cash available	106,900	?
Cash payments:		
Purchase of inventory	$?	$41,000
Operating expenses	47,200	?
Total payments	98,000	?
(1) Ending cash balance before financing	?	25,100
Minimum cash balance desired	20,000	20,000
Cash excess (deficiency)	$?	$?
Financing of cash deficiency:		
Borrowing (at end of month)	$?	$?
Principal repayments (at end of month)	?	?
Interest expense	?	?
(2) Total effects of financing	?	?
Ending cash balance (1) + (2)	$?	$?

E10-26 **Prepare budgeted balance sheet** *(Learning Objective 3)*

Use the following information to prepare a budgeted balance sheet for Marine.com at March 31, 2009. Show computations for the cash and owners' equity amounts.

a. March 31 inventory balance, $15,000

b. March payments for inventory, $4,600

c. March payments of accounts payable and accrued liabilities, $8,200

d. March 31 accounts payable balance, $4,300

continued . . .

e. February 28 furniture and fixtures balance, $34,800; accumulated depreciation balance, $29,870

f. February 28 owners' equity, $26,700

g. March depreciation expense, $600

h. Cost of goods sold, 60% of sales

i. Other March expenses, including income tax, total $5,000; paid in cash

j. February 28 cash balance, $11,400

k. March budgeted sales, $12,200

l. March 31 accounts receivable balance, one-fourth of March sales

m. March cash receipts, $14,300

E10-27 **Identify types of responsibility centers** *(Learning Objective 5)*

Identify each responsibility center as a cost center, a revenue center, a profit center, or an investment center.

a. The bakery department of a Publix supermarket reports income for the current year.

b. Pace Foods is a subsidiary of Campbell Soup Company.

c. The personnel department of State Farm Insurance Companies prepares its budget and subsequent performance report on the basis of its expected expenses for the year.

d. The shopping section of Burpee.com reports both revenues and expenses.

e. Burpee.com's investor relations Web site provides operating and financial information to investors and other interested parties.

f. The manager of a BP service station is evaluated based on the station's revenues and expenses.

g. A charter airline records revenues and expenses for each airplane each month. Each airplane's performance report shows its ratio of operating income to average book value.

h. The manager of the southwest sales territory is evaluated based on a comparison of current period sales against budgeted sales.

E10-28 **Prepare performance reports at different organizational levels**
(Learning Objective 5)

InTouch is a Seattle company that sells cell phones and PDAs on the Web. InTouch has assistant managers for its digital and video cell phone operations. These assistant managers report to the manager of the total cell phone product line, who, with the manager of PDAs, reports to the manager for all sales of handheld devices, Beth Beverly. Beverly received the following data for November operations:

	Cell Phones		
	Digital	Video	PDAs
Revenues, budget	$204,000	$800,000	$300,000
Expenses, budget...........	140,000	390,000	225,000
Revenues, actual............	214,000	840,000	290,000
Expenses, actual............	135,000	400,000	230,000

Arrange the data in a performance report similar to Exhibit 10-20. Show November results, in thousands of dollars, for digital cell phones, for the total cell phone product line, and for all devices. Should Beverly investigate the performance of digital cell phone operations? Why or why not?

■ Problems (Problem Set A)

P10-29A Prepare budgeted income statement *(Learning Objective 2)*

The budget committee of Vinning Office Supply has assembled the following data. As the business manager, you must prepare the budgeted income statements for May and June 2009.

a. Sales in April were $42,100. You forecast that monthly sales will increase 2.0% in May and 2.4% in June.

b. Vinning Office Supply maintains inventory of $9,000 plus 25% of sales budgeted for the following month. Monthly purchases average 50% of sales revenues in that same month. Actual inventory on April 30 is $14,000. Sales budgeted for July are $42,400.

c. Monthly salaries amount to $4,000. Sales commissions equal 4% of sales for that month. Combine salaries and commissions into a single figure.

d. Other monthly expenses are:

Rent expense.............................	$3,000, paid as incurred
Depreciation expense	$600
Insurance expense	$200, expiration of prepaid amount
Income tax	20% of operating income

Prepare Vinning Office Supply's budgeted income statements for May and June. Show cost of goods sold computations. Round *all* amounts to the nearest $100. (Round amounts ending in $50 or more upward and amounts ending in less than $50 downward.) For example, budgeted May sales are $42,900 ($42,100 × 1.02) and June sales are $43,900 ($42,900 × 1.024).

P10-30A Continuation of P10-29A: cash budgets

Refer to P10-29A. Vinning Office Supply's sales are 70% cash and 30% credit (use the rounded sales on the last line of P10-29A). Credit sales are collected in the month after sale. Inventory purchases are paid 50% in the month of purchase and 50% the following month. Salaries and sales commissions are also paid half in the month earned and half the next month. Income tax is paid at the end of the year.

The April 30, 2009, balance sheet showed the following balances:

Cash..	$11,000
Accounts payable	7,400
Salary and commissions payable	2,850

continued . . .

Requirements

1. Prepare schedules of (a) budgeted cash collections, (b) budgeted cash payments for purchases, and (c) budgeted cash payments for operating expenses. Show amounts for each month and totals for May and June. Round your computations to the nearest dollar.

2. Prepare a cash budget similar to Exhibit 10-14. If no financing activity took place, what is the budgeted cash balance on June 30, 2009?

P10-31A Prepare budgeted balance sheet and statement of cash flows *(Learning Objective 3)*

Alliance Printing of Baltimore has applied for a loan. Bank of America has requested a budgeted balance sheet at April 30, 2009, and a budgeted statement of cash flows for April. As Alliance Printing's controller, you have assembled the following information:

a. March 31 equipment balance, $52,400; accumulated depreciation, $41,300.

b. April capital expenditures of $42,800 budgeted for cash purchase of equipment.

c. April depreciation expense, $900.

d. Cost of goods sold, 60% of sales.

e. Other April operating expenses, including income tax, total $13,200, 25% of which will be paid in cash and the remainder accrued at April 30.

f. March 31 owners' equity, $93,700.

g. March 31 cash balance, $40,600.

h. April budgeted sales, $90,000, 70% of which is for cash. Of the remaining 30%, half will be collected in April and half in May.

i. April cash collections on March sales, $29,700.

j. April cash payments of March 31 liabilities incurred for March purchases of inventory, $17,300.

k. March 31 inventory balance, $29,600.

l. April purchases of inventory, $10,000 for cash and $36,800 on credit. Half of the credit purchases will be paid in April and half in May.

Requirements

1. Prepare the budgeted balance sheet for Alliance Printing at April 30, 2009. Show separate computations for cash, inventory, and owners' equity balances.

2. Prepare the budgeted statement of cash flows for April.

3. Suppose Alliance Printing has become aware of more efficient (and more expensive) equipment than it budgeted for purchase in April. What is the total amount of cash available for equipment purchases in April, before financing, if the minimum desired ending cash balance is $21,000? (For this requirement, disregard the $42,800 initially budgeted for equipment purchases.)

P10-32A Continuation of P10-31A: revised sales *(Learning Objective 4)*

Refer to P10-31A. Before granting a loan to Alliance Printing, Bank of America asks for a sensitivity analysis assuming that April sales are only $60,000 rather than the $90,000 originally budgeted. (While the cost of goods sold will change, assume that purchases, depreciation, and the other operating expenses will remain the same as in P10-31A.)

Requirements

1. Prepare a revised budgeted balance sheet for Alliance Printing, showing separate computations for cash, inventory, and owners' equity balances.
2. Suppose Alliance Printing has a minimum desired cash balance of $23,000. Will the company need to borrow cash in April?
3. In this sensitivity analysis, sales declined by 33⅓% ($30,000 ÷ $90,000). Is the decline in expenses and income more or less than 33⅓%? Explain.

P10-33A **Identify responsibility centers** *(Learning Objective 5)*

Is each of the following most likely a cost center, a revenue center, a profit center, or an investment center?

a. Shipping department of Amazon.com
b. Eastern district of a salesperson's territory
c. Child care department of a church or synagogue
d. Catering operation of Sonny's BBQ restaurant
e. Executive headquarters of the United Way
f. Accounts payable section of the accounting department at Home Depot
g. Proposed new office of Coldwell Banker, a real estate firm
h. Disneyland
i. The Empire State Building in New York City
j. Branch warehouse of Dalton Carpets
k. Information systems department of Habitat for Humanity
l. Service department of Audio Forest stereo shop
m. Investments department of Citibank
n. Assembly-line supervisors at Dell Computer
o. American subsidiary of a Japanese manufacturer
p. Surgery unit of a privately owned hospital
q. Research and development department of Cisco Systems
r. Childrenswear department at a Target store
s. Typesetting department of Northend Press, a printing company
t. Prescription-filling department of Drugstore.com
u. Order-taking department at L.L.Bean
v. Personnel department of Goodyear Tire and Rubber Company
w. Grounds maintenance department at Augusta National Golf Club

P10-34A **Prepare performance reports for various organizational levels** (*Learning Objectives 1, 5*)

Winnie's World operates a chain of pet stores in the Midwest. The manager of each store reports to the region manager, who, in turn, reports to the headquarters in Milwaukee, Wisconsin. The *actual* income statements for the Dayton store, the Ohio region (including the Dayton store), and the company as a whole (including the Ohio region) for July 2009 are:

	Dayton	Ohio	Company-Wide
Revenue	$148,900	$1,647,000	$4,200,000
Expenses:			
Region manager/			
headquarters office	$ —	$ 60,000	$ 116,000
Cost of materials	81,100	871,900	1,807,000
Salary expense..............	38,300	415,100	1,119,000
Depreciation expense	7,200	91,000	435,000
Utilities expense	4,000	46,200	260,000
Rent expense.................	2,400	34,700	178,000
Total expenses................	133,000	1,518,900	3,915,000
Operating income............	$ 15,900	$ 128,100	$ 285,000

Budgeted amounts for July were as follows:

	Dayton	Ohio	Company-Wide
Revenue	$162,400	$1,769,700	$4,450,000
Expenses:			
Region manager/			
headquarters office	$ —	$ 65,600	$ 118,000
Cost of materials	86,400	963,400	1,972,000
Salary expense..............	38,800	442,000	1,095,000
Depreciation expense	7,200	87,800	449,000
Utilities expense	4,400	54,400	271,000
Rent expense.................	3,600	32,300	174,000
Total expenses................	140,400	1,645,500	4,079,000
Operating income	$ 22,000	$ 124,200	$ 371,000

Requirements

1. Prepare a report for July 2009 that shows the performance of the Dayton store, the Ohio region, and the company as a whole. Follow the format of Exhibit 10-20.

2. As the Ohio region manager, would you investigate the Dayton store on the basis of this report? Why or why not?

3. Briefly discuss the benefits of budgeting. Base your discussion on Winnie's World's performance report.

Problems (Problem Set B)

P10-35B Prepare budgeted income statement *(Learning Objective 2)*

Representatives of the various departments of Go Sports have assembled the following data. As the business manager, you must prepare the budgeted income statements for August and September 2009.

a. Sales in July were $196,000. You forecast that monthly sales will increase 3% in August and 2% in September.

b. Go Sports tries to maintain inventory of $50,000 plus 20% of sales budgeted for the following month. Monthly purchases average 60% of sales revenue in that same month. Actual inventory on July 31 is $90,000. Sales budgeted for October are $220,000.

c. Monthly salaries amount to $15,000. Sales commissions equal 6% of sales for that month. Combine salaries and commissions into a single figure.

d. Other monthly expenses are:

Rent expense.............................	$3,000, paid as incurred
Depreciation expense	$600
Insurance expense	$200, expiration of prepaid amount
Income tax.................................	20% of operating income

Prepare Go Sports' budgeted income statements for August and September. Show cost of goods sold computations. Round *all* amounts to the nearest $1,000. For example, budgeted August sales are $202,000 ($196,000 × 1.03) and September sales are $206,000 ($202,000 × 1.02).

P10-36B Continuation of P10-35B: cash budgets *(Learning Objective 3)*

Refer to P10-35B. Go Sports' sales are 50% cash and 50% credit (use sales on the last two lines of P10-35B). Credit sales are collected in the month after the sale. Inventory purchases are paid 60% in the month of purchase and 40% the following month. Salaries and sales commissions are paid three-fourths in the month earned and one-fourth the next month. Income tax is paid at the end of the year.

The July 31, 2009, balance sheet showed the following balances:

Cash..	$22,000
Accounts payable...	52,000
Salaries and commissions payable...	6,750

Requirements

1. Prepare schedules of (a) budgeted cash collections from customers, (b) budgeted cash payments for purchases, and (c) budgeted cash payments for operating expenses. Show amounts for each month and totals for August and September. Round your computations to the nearest dollar.

2. Prepare a cash budget similar to Exhibit 10-14. If no financing activity took place, what is the budgeted cash balance on September 30, 2009?

P10-37B **Prepare budgeted balance sheet and statement of cash flows** *(Learning Objective 3)*

The Music Box has applied for a loan. First Central Bank has requested a budgeted balance sheet at June 30, 2009, and a budgeted statement of cash flows for June. As the controller (chief accounting officer) of The Music Box, you have assembled the following information:

a. May 31 equipment balance, $80,800; accumulated depreciation, $12,400.

b. June capital expenditures of $16,400 budgeted for cash purchase of equipment.

c. June depreciation expense, $400.

d. Cost of goods sold, 50% of sales.

e. Other June operating expenses, including income tax, total $34,000, 75% of which will be paid in cash and the remainder accrued at June 30.

f. May 31 owners' equity, $137,500.

g. May 31 cash balance, $50,200.

h. June budgeted sales, $85,000, 40% of which is for cash. Of the remaining 60%, half will be collected in June and half in July.

i. June cash collections on May sales, $15,300.

j. June cash payments of liabilities for May inventory purchases on credit, $8,300.

k. May 31 inventory balance, $11,900.

l. June purchases of inventory, $11,000 for cash and $37,200 on credit. Half the credit purchases will be paid in June and half in July.

Requirements

1. Prepare the budgeted balance sheet for The Music Box at June 30, 2009. Show separate computations for cash, inventory, and owners' equity balances.

2. Prepare the budgeted statement of cash flows for June.

3. On the basis of this data, if you were a First Central Bank loan officer, would you grant The Music Box a loan? Give your reason.

P10-38B **Continuation of P10-37B: revised sales** *(Learning Objective 4)*

Refer to P10-37B. Before granting a loan to The Music Box, First Central Bank asks for a sensitivity analysis, assuming that June sales are only $65,000 rather than the $85,000 originally budgeted. (While cost of goods sold will change, assume that purchases, depreciation, and the other operating expenses will remain the same as in P10-37B.)

Requirements

1. Prepare a revised budgeted balance sheet for The Music Box, showing separate computations for cash, inventory, and owners' equity balances.

2. Suppose The Music Box has a minimum desired cash balance of $35,000. Will the company borrow cash in June?

3. How would this sensitivity analysis affect First Central's loan decision?

P10-39B **Identify responsibility centers** *(Learning Objective 5)*

Is each of the following most likely a cost center, a revenue center, a profit center, or an investment center?

a. Purchasing department of Milliken, a textile manufacturer

b. Quality control department of Mayfield Dairies

c. European subsidiary of Coca-Cola

d. Payroll department at the University of Wisconsin

e. Lighting department in a Sears store

f. Children's nursery in a church or synagogue

g. Personnel department of E*TRADE, the online broker

h. igourmet.com, an e-tailer of gourmet cheeses

i. Service department of an automobile dealership

j. Customer service department of Procter & Gamble

k. Proposed new office of Deutsche Bank

l. Southwest region of Pizza Inns

m. Delta Airlines

n. Order-taking department at Lands' End

o. Editorial department of *The Wall Street Journal*

p. A Ford Motor Company production plant

q. Police department of Boston

r. Century 21 Real Estate

s. A small pet-grooming business

t. Northeast sales territory for Boise-Cascade

u. Different product lines of Broyhill, a furniture manufacturer

v. McDonald's restaurants under the supervision of a regional manager

w. Job superintendents of a home builder

P10-40B **Prepare performance reports for various organizational levels** *(Learning Objectives 1, 5)*

Etown is a chain of home electronics stores. Each store has a manager who answers to a city manager, who, in turn, reports to a statewide manager. The actual income statements of Store No. 23, all stores in the Dallas area (including Store No. 23), and all stores in the state of Texas (including all Dallas stores) are summarized as follows for April:

	Store No. 23	Dallas	State of Texas
Sales revenue	$43,300	$486,000	$3,228,500
Expenses:			
City/state manager's office expenses	$ —	$ 18,000	$ 44,000
Cost of goods sold	15,000	171,300	1,256,800
Salary expense	4,000	37,500	409,700
Depreciation expense	3,700	13,100	320,000
Utilities expense	1,900	19,300	245,600
Rent expense	700	16,600	186,000
Total expenses	25,300	275,800	2,462,100
Operating income	$18,000	$210,200	$ 766,400

Budgeted amounts for April were as follows:

	Store No. 23	Dallas	State of Texas
Sales revenue......................	$39,000	$470,000	$3,129,000
Expenses:			
City/state manager's office expenses	$ —	$ 19,000	$ 45,000
Cost of goods sold.........	12,100	160,800	1,209,000
Salary expense...............	6,000	37,900	412,000
Depreciation expense	3,200	23,400	320,000
Utilities expense	1,000	15,000	240,000
Rent expense.................	700	15,700	181,000
Total expenses...................	23,000	271,800	2,407,000
Operating income..............	$16,000	$198,200	$ 722,000

Requirements

1. Prepare a report for April that shows the performance of Store No. 23, all of the stores in the Dallas area, and all of the stores in Texas. Follow the format of Exhibit 10-20.

2. As the city manager of Dallas, would you investigate Store No. 23 on the basis of this report? Why or why not?

3. Briefly discuss the benefits of budgeting. Base your discussion on Etown's performance report.

Apply Your Knowledge

▪ Decision Cases

Case 10-41. Suggest performance improvements *(Learning Objective 1)*

Donna Tse recently joined Cycle World, a bicycle store in St. Louis, as an assistant manager. She recently finished her accounting courses. Cycle World's manager and owner, Jeff Towry, asks Tse to prepare a budgeted income statement for 2009 based on the information he has collected. Tse's budget follows:

CYCLE WORLD Budgeted Income Statement For the Year Ending July 31, 2009		
Sales revenue		$244,000
Cost of goods sold		177,000
Gross profit		67,000
Operating expenses:		
Salary and commission expense	$46,000	
Rent expense	8,000	
Depreciation expense	2,000	
Insurance expense	800	
Miscellaneous expenses	12,000	68,800
Operating loss		(1,800)
Interest expense		225
Net loss		$ (2,025)

Requirements

Tse does not want to give Towry this budget without making constructive suggestions for steps Towry could take to improve expected performance. Write a memo to Towry outlining your suggestions. Your memo should take the following form:

> Date: _____
>
>   To: Mr. Jeff Towry, Manager
>   Cycle World
>
> From: Donna Tse
>
> Subject: Cycle World's 2009 budgeted income statement

Case 10-42. Prepare cash budgets under two alternatives *(Learning Objectives 2, 3)*

Each autumn, as a hobby, Suzanne De Angelo weaves cotton place mats to sell at a local crafts shop. The mats sell for $20 per set of four. The shop charges a 10% commission and remits the net proceeds to De Angelo at the end of December.

continued . . .

De Angelo has woven and sold 25 sets each of the last two years. She has enough cotton in inventory to make another 25 sets. She paid $7 per set for the cotton. De Angelo uses a four-harness loom that she purchased for cash exactly two years ago. It is depreciated at the rate of $10 per month. The accounts payable relate to the cotton inventory and are payable by September 30.

De Angelo is considering buying an eight-harness loom so that she can weave more intricate patterns in linen. The new loom costs $1,000; it would be depreciated at $20 per month. Her bank has agreed to lend her $1,000 at 18% interest, with $200 principal plus accrued interest payable each December 31. De Angelo believes she can weave 15 linen place mat sets in time for the Christmas rush if she does not weave any cotton mats. She predicts that each linen set will sell for $50. Linen costs $18 per set. De Angelo's supplier will sell her linen on credit, payable December 31.

De Angelo plans to keep her old loom whether or not she buys the new loom. The balance sheet for her weaving business at August 31, 2009, is as follows:

SUZANNE DE ANGELO, WEAVER
Balance Sheet
August 31, 2009

Current assets:			Current liabilities:	
Cash	$ 25		Accounts payable	$ 74
Inventory of cotton	175			
	200			
Fixed assets:				
Loom	500		Owner's equity	386
Accumulated depreciation	(240)			
	260			
Total assets	$460		Total liabilities and owner's equity	$460

Requirements

1. Prepare a cash budget for the four months ending December 31, 2009, for two alternatives: weaving the place mats in cotton using the existing loom and weaving the place mats in linen using the new loom. For each alternative, prepare a budgeted income statement for the four months ending December 31, 2009, and a budgeted balance sheet at December 31, 2009.

2. On the basis of financial considerations only, what should De Angelo do? Give your reason.

3. What nonfinancial factors might De Angelo consider in her decision?

▪ Ethical Issue

Issue 10-43. Ethical considerations for padded budgets *(Learning Objectives 1, 5)*
Residence Suites operates a regional hotel chain. Each hotel is operated by a manager and an assistant manager/controller. Many of the staff who run the front desk, clean the rooms, and prepare the breakfast buffet work part-time or have a second job, so turnover is high.

Assistant manager/controller Terry Dunn asked the new bookkeeper to help prepare the hotel's master budget. The master budget is prepared once a year and submitted to company headquarters for approval. Once approved, the master budget is used to evaluate the hotel's performance. These performance evaluations affect hotel managers' bonuses; they also affect company decisions about which hotels deserve extra funds for capital improvements.

When the budget was almost complete, Dunn asked the bookkeeper to increase amounts budgeted for labor and supplies by 15%. When asked why, Dunn responded that hotel manager Clay Murry told her to do this when she began working at the hotel. Murry explained that this budgetary cushion gave him flexibility in running the hotel. For example, because company headquarters tightly controls capital improvement funds, Murry can use the extra money budgeted for labor and supplies to replace broken televisions or to pay "bonuses" to keep valued employees. Dunn initially accepted this explanation because she had observed similar behavior at her previous place of employment.

Put yourself in Dunn's position. In deciding how to deal with the situation, answer the following questions:

1. What is the ethical issue?
2. What are my options?
3. What are the possible consequences?
4. What should I do?

■ Team Project

Project 10-44. Analyzing and discussing budget concerns *(Learning Objectives 1, 2, 5)*

Xellnet provides e-commerce software for the pharmaceuticals industry. Xellnet is organized into several divisions. A company-wide planning committee sets general strategy and goals for the company and its divisions, but each division develops its own budget.

Rick Watson is the new division manager of wireless communications software. His division has two departments: development and sales. Carrie Pronai manages the 20 or so programmers and systems specialists typically employed in the development department to create and update the division's software applications. Liz Smith manages the sales department.

Xellnet considers the divisions to be investment centers. To earn his bonus next year, Watson must achieve a 30% return on the $3 million invested in his division. This amounts to $900,000 of income (30% × $3 million). Within the wireless division, development is a cost center, while sales is a revenue center.

Budgeting is in progress. Pronai met with her staff and is now struggling with two sets of numbers. Alternative A is her best estimate of next year's costs. However, unexpected problems can arise in the writing of software, and finding competent programmers is an ongoing challenge. She knows that Watson was a programmer before he earned an MBA, so he should be sensitive to this uncertainty. Consequently, she is thinking of increasing her budgeted costs (Alternative B). Her department's bonuses largely depend on whether the department meets its budgeted costs.

continued . . .

XELLNET
Wireless Division
Development Budget 2009

	Alternative A	Alternative B
Salaries expense (including overtime and part-time)	$ 2,400,000	$2,640,000
Software expense	120,000	132,000
Travel expense	65,000	71,500
Depreciation expense	255,000	255,000
Miscellaneous expense	100,000	110,000
Total expense	$ 2,940,000	$3,208,500

Liz Smith is also struggling with her sales budget. Companies have made their initial investments in communications software, so it is harder to win new customers. If things go well, she believes her sales team can maintain the level of growth achieved over the last few years. This is Alternative A in the sales budget. However, if Smith is too optimistic, sales may fall short of the budget. If this happens, her team will not receive bonuses. Therefore, Smith is considering reducing the sales numbers and submitting Alternative B.

XELLNET
Wireless Division
Sales Budget 2009

	Alternative A	Alternative B
Sales revenue	$ 5,000,000	$4,500,000
Salaries expense	360,000	360,000
Travel expense	240,000	210,500

Split your team into three groups. Each group should meet separately before the entire team meets.

Requirements

1. The first group plays the role of Development Manager Carrie Pronai. Before meeting with the entire team, determine which set of budget numbers you are going to present to Rick Watson. Write a memo supporting your decision. Use the format shown in Case 10-41. Give this memo to the third group before the team meeting.

2. The second group plays the role of Sales Manager Liz Smith. Before meeting with the entire team, determine which set of budget numbers you are going to present to Rick Watson. Write a memo supporting your decision. Use the format shown in Case 10-41. Give this memo to the third group before the team meeting.

3. The third group plays the role of Division Manager Rick Watson. Before meeting with the entire team, use the memos that Pronai and Smith provided to prepare a division budget based on the sales and development budgets. Your divisional overhead costs (additional costs beyond those incurred by the development and sales departments) are approximately $390,000. Determine whether the wireless division can meet its targeted 30% return on assets given the budgeted alternatives submitted by your department managers.

During the meeting of the entire team, the group playing Watson presents the division budget and considers its implications. Each group should take turns discussing its concerns with the proposed budget. The team as a whole should consider whether the division budget must be revised. The team should prepare a report that includes the division budget and a summary of the issues covered in the team meeting.

This page intentionally left blank

Chapter 10: Demo Doc 1

■ Master Budget

Learning Objective 2

Joe University sells college sweatshirts. Actual sales for the month ended September 30 were $20,000. Joe expects sales to increase 8% in October and another 4% in November. Cash sales are expected to be 60% of total sales and credit sales about 40% of sales.

Cost of goods sold should be 60% of total sales. Joe doesn't want inventory to fall below $4,000 plus 10% of cost of goods sold for the next month. Sales of $25,000 are expected for December. Inventory on September 30 is $6,000.

Operating expenses include sales commission, 10% of sales; rent expense of $1,000; depreciation expense of $1,200; utility expense of $800; and insurance expense of $400.

Round all figures to the nearest dollar.

Requirement

Prepare the following budgets for October and November:

a. Sales budget

b. Inventory, purchases, and cost of goods sold budget

c. Operating expense budget

d. Budgeted income statement

Demo Doc 1 Solutions

Requirement

Prepare the following budgets for October and November:

a. **Sales budget**

We prepare the sales budget first because sales impact most elements of the other budgets we will be preparing for this period.

To complete the sales budget, we start by calculating the total sales for each month. We then compute the split between cash sales and credit sales for each month based on Joe's estimation that cash sales will be 60% of the total sales for each month and credit sales will be 40% of total sales for each month.

Let's begin by calculating Joe's total sales for October and November. We know that actual sales for the month ended September 30 were $20,000 and that Joe expects sales to increase by 8% over that amount in October and another 4% over October's sales in November:

October total sales   = September sales × 108%

October total sales   = $20,000 × 108% = $21,600

November total sales = October sales × 104%

November total sales = $21,600 × 104% = $22,464

So, we begin to build our sales budget with this data:

JOE UNIVERSITY
Sales Budget

	October	November	Total
Cash sales, 60%			
Credit sales, 40%			
Total sales	$21,600	$22,464	$44,064

Now, we work backward to calculate the split between cash and credit sales for each month. In this case, cash sales are 60% of total sales and credit sales are 40% of total sales for the current months:

Cash sales   = Total sales × 60%

October cash sales   = $21,600 × 60% = $12,960

November cash sales   = $22,464 × 60% = $13,478.40 (rounded to $13,478)

Credit sales   = Total sales × 40%

October credit sales   = $21,600 × 40% = $8,640

November credit sales = $22,464 × 40% = $8,985.60 (rounded to $8,986)

The following is the completed sales budget:

JOE UNIVERSITY
Sales Budget

	October	November	Total
Cash sales, 60%	$12,960	$13,478	$26,438
Credit sales, 40%	8,640	8,986	17,626
Total sales	$21,600	$22,464	$44,064

This gives us a total sales budget for October and November of $44,064, with 60% of that ($26,438) from cash and 40% ($17,626) from credit.

Because the sales budget calculates values you will use when preparing other budgets, it's always a good idea to check your work.

b. **Inventory, purchases, and cost of goods sold budget**

The inventory, purchases, and cost of goods sold budget takes the following format:

Cost of goods sold	(what we need for current month sales)
+ Desired ending inventory	(what we need to have on hand at month-end)
= Total inventory required	(what we need)
– Beginning inventory	(what we have)
= Purchases	(what we need to buy)

First, we calculate the cost of goods sold. We know from the question that cost of goods sold is expected to be 60% of total sales for the period. From the sales budget, we know that total sales for October are expected to be $21,600 and total sales for November are expected to be $22,464. We can calculate cost of goods sold as follows:

Cost of goods sold = 60% of budgeted sales from the sales budget

October = $21,600 × 60% = $12,960

November = $22,464 × 60% = $13,478

Here's our budget so far:

JOE UNIVERSITY
Inventory, Purchases, and Cost of Goods Sold Budget

	October	November	
Cost of goods sold	$12,960	$13,478	
+ Desired ending inventory			
= Total inventory required			
− Beginning inventory			
= Purchases			

Next, we need to add the desired ending inventory for each month. The information states that Joe doesn't want inventory to fall below $4,000 plus 10% of cost of goods sold for the next month. To calculate the desired ending inventory for November, we need to know the cost of goods sold for December. December's sales are expected to be $25,000. Returning to our calculation for cost of goods sold:

Cost of goods sold = 60% of budgeted sales from the sales budget
December = $25,000 × 60% = $15,000

Desired ending inventory is calculated as follows:

Desired ending inventory = [$4,000 + (10% of cost of goods sold for the next month)]
October = $4,000 + (10% × $13,478) = $5,348
November = $4,000 + (10% × $15,000) = $5,500

We can now calculate the total inventory required:

JOE UNIVERSITY
Inventory, Purchases, and Cost of Goods Sold Budget

	October	November	
Cost of goods sold	$12,960	$13,478	
+ Desired ending inventory	5,348	5,500	
= Total inventory required	$18,308	$18,978	
− Beginning inventory			
= Purchases			

Beginning inventory is equal to the previous month's desired ending inventory. We know that the inventory on September 30 is $6,000, so this becomes October's beginning inventory. Once we determine beginning inventory, we subtract it from the total inventory required to determine purchases for the period:

JOE UNIVERSITY
Inventory, Purchases, and Cost of Goods Sold Budget

	October	November	
Cost of goods sold	$12,960	$13,478	
+ Desired ending inventory	5,348	5,500	
= Total inventory required	$18,308	$18,978	
− Beginning inventory	6,000	5,348	
= Purchases	$12,308	$13,630	

c. Operating expense budget

With the exception of the sales commission, which we know to be 10% of sales, all expenses remain constant between October and November, as follows:

JOE UNIVERSITY
Operating Expense Budget

	October	November	Total
Sales commission			
Rent expense	1,000	1,000	2,000
Insurance expense	400	400	800
Depreciation expense	1,200	1,200	2,400
Utility expense	800	800	1,600

The only calculation to perform here is sales commission. We can compute sales commissions for October and November using the respective sales computations ($21,600 and $22,464) from the sales budget:

Sales commission = Expected sales × 10%

October sales commission = $21,600 × 10% = $2,160

November sales commission = $22,464 × 10% = $2,246.40 (rounded to $2,246)

Here's our completed operating expense budget for October and November:

JOE UNIVERSITY
Operating Expense Budget

	October	November	Total
Sales commission	$2,160	$2,246	$4,406
Rent expense	1,000	1,000	2,000
Insurance expense	400	400	800
Depreciation expense	1,200	1,200	2,400
Utility expense	800	800	1,600
Total operating expenses	$5,560	$5,646	$11,206

d. Budgeted income statement

The results of the budgets you've created so far are carried over into the fourth element: the budgeted income statement.

Sales revenue is traced from the sales budget in part a.

Cost of goods sold is traced from the inventory, purchases, and cost of goods sold budget in part b.

We compute gross profit by subtracting the cost of goods sold from sales revenue:

JOE UNIVERSITY
Budgeted Income Statement

	October	November	Total
Sales revenue	$21,600	$22,464	$44,064
Cost of goods sold	12,960	13,478	26,438
Gross profit	8,640	8,986	17,626
Operating expenses			
Operating income			

Operating expenses are traced from the operating expenses budget.

We compute operating income (loss) by subtracting operating expenses from gross profit. Our completed budgeted income statement looks like this:

JOE UNIVERSITY
Budgeted Income Statement

	October	November	Total
Sales revenue	$21,600	$22,464	$44,064
Cost of goods sold	12,960	13,478	26,438
Gross profit	8,640	8,986	17,626
Operating expenses	5,560	5,646	11,206
Operating income	$ 3,080	$ 3,340	$ 6,420

Page 594 intentionally omitted

11 Flexible Budgets and Standard Costs

How does McDonald's make sure that its 30,000 restaurants deliver quality, service, cleanliness, and value to over 46 million customers worldwide each day? By using budgets, standards, and variances. Managers budget sales for each hour and schedule just enough workers to handle the budgeted level of sales. During the day, the manager computes variances for sales (for example, actual sales minus budgeted sales) and for direct labor. If actual sales fall short of the budget, the manager can send employees home early. This helps control direct labor cost.

McDonald's also sets budgets and standards for direct materials. From Beijing to Miami, the standards for a regular McDonald's hamburger are the same: 1 bun, 1 hamburger patty, 1 pickle slice, 1/8 teaspoon of onion, 1/4 teaspoon of mustard, and 1/2 ounce of ketchup. To control direct materials costs, for example, the manager compares the

number of hamburger patties actually used with the number of patties that should have been used, given the store's actual sales.

McDonald's uses budgets, standards, and variances to control costs so prices remain low enough that customers believe McDonald's provides good *value*. McDonald's also uses standards and variances to motivate employees to focus on:

- Quality—sandwiches unsold within ten minutes are thrown away.
- Service—customers should receive food within 90 seconds of ordering.
- Cleanliness—mystery shoppers score restaurants' cleanliness. ▪

Learning Objectives

1 Prepare a flexible budget for planning purposes

2 Use the sales volume variance and flexible budget variance to explain why actual results differ from the master budget

3 Identify the benefits of standard costs and learn how to set standards

4 Compute standard cost variances for direct materials and direct labor

5 Compute manufacturing overhead variances

6 (Appendix) Record transactions at standard cost and prepare a standard cost income statement

This chapter builds on your knowledge of budgeting (from Chapter 10) to show how managers use variances to learn *why* actual results differ from budgets. Why is this important? Because you must know *why* actual costs differ from the budget to identify problems and to decide what, if any, action to take.

In this chapter, you'll learn how you—like managers of companies from McDonald's to Dell—can use flexible budgets, standards, and variances to pinpoint *why* actual results differ from the budget. This is the first step in determining how to correct problems.

How Managers Use Flexible Budgets

In this chapter we'll see how Kool-Time Pools, an installer of in-ground swimming pools, uses flexible budgets and standard costs to help control its operations. Kool-Time uses direct materials, direct labor, and manufacturing overhead (such as the monthly lease on the earth moving equipment) to manufacture the swimming pools directly on the customer's site. In addition to manufacturing costs, the company incurs selling and administrative expenses in conjunction with its marketing and sales efforts. As with most companies, some of these costs are variable, while others are fixed.

What Is a Static Budget?

At the beginning of the year, Kool-Time's managers prepared a master budget like the one in Chapter 10. The master budget is a **static budget**, which means that it is prepared for *one* level of sales volume. Once the master budget is developed, it does not change.

Exhibit 11-1 compares June's actual results with the static (master) budget for June. The difference between actual results and the budget is called a **variance**. In this case, because we are comparing actual results against the static budget, this particular variance is called the static budget variance. Variances are considered favorable (F) when a higher actual amount increases operating income and unfavorable (U) when a higher actual amount decreases operating income. Favorable variances should not necessarily be interpreted as "good." Likewise, unfavorable variances should not be interpreted as "bad." Rather, they simply indicate the variance's effect on operating income. Exhibit 11-1 shows that Kool-Time's revenues were $25,000 higher than expected and its expenses were $21,000 higher than expected. Together, these variances resulted in a $4,000 favorable static budget variance for operating income. However, Kool-Time's managers are still concerned about the $21,000 unfavorable expense variance.

EXHIBIT 11-1   **Actual Results Versus Static Budget**

KOOL-TIME POOLS
Comparison of Actual Results with Static Budget
Month Ended June 30, 2007

	Actual Results	Static (Master) Budget	Static Budget Variance
Output units (pools installed)	10	8	2 F
Sales revenue	$121,000	$96,000	$25,000 F
Expenses	(105,000)	(84,000)	(21,000) U
Operating income	$ 16,000	$12,000	$ 4,000 F

What Is a Flexible Budget?

The static budget variance in Exhibit 11-1 is hard to analyze because the static budget is based on eight pools, but actual results are for ten pools. Trying to compare actual results against a budget prepared for a different volume is like comparing apples to oranges. Why did the $21,000 unfavorable expense variance occur? Were materials wasted? Did the cost of materials suddenly increase? How much of the additional expense arose because Kool-Time installed ten pools rather than eight? The simple comparison presented in Exhibit 11-1 does not give managers enough information to answer these questions.

However, flexible budgets can help managers answer such questions. Exhibit 11-2 shows that in contrast to the static budget developed for a single level of sales volume, **flexible budgets** are summarized budgets prepared for different levels of volume. Flexible budgets can be used to help managers plan for future periods *and* to evaluate performance after the period has ended. We'll consider both uses and then get back to the question of why the $21,000 unfavorable expense variance occurred.

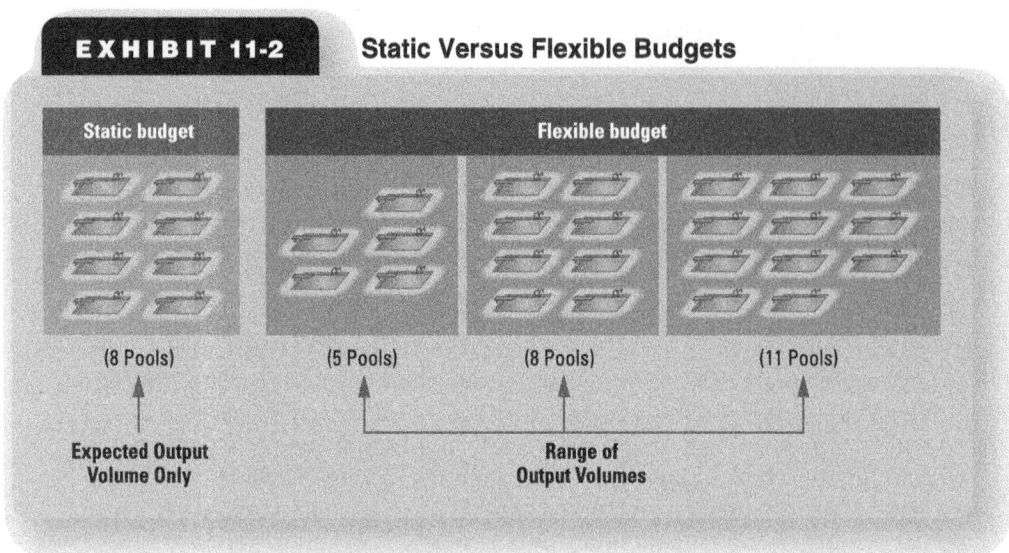

EXHIBIT 11-2   Static Versus Flexible Budgets

Using Flexible Budgets for Planning

1 Prepare a flexible budget for planning purposes

Managers can use flexible budgets for planning revenues and expenses at different sales volumes. Even though Kool-Time's managers believe the company will install eight pools in June, company managers know that they might not be correct about this estimate. Pool sales could be higher or lower during the month, and managers need to be prepared for both possibilities. Flexible budgets show how Kool-Time's revenues and expenses *should* vary as the number of pools installed varies.

Let's prepare flexible budgets for Kool-Time, assuming pool sales for the month could be as low as 5 or as high as 11. We'll start with revenues: The budgeted sales price per pool is $12,000, so each additional pool sale should yield another $12,000 of revenue. Exhibit 11-3 shows projected revenues at three possible volumes: 5 pools, 8 pools, and 11 pools.

EXHIBIT 11-3   Flexible Budget

KOOL-TIME POOLS
Flexible Budget
Month Ended June 30, 2007

	Flexible Budget per Output Unit	Output Units (Pools Installed)		
		5	8	11
Sales revenue	$12,000	$60,000	$96,000	$132,000
Variable expenses	8,000	40,000	64,000	88,000
Fixed expenses		20,000	20,000	20,000
Total expenses		60,000	84,000	108,000
Operating income		$ 0	$12,000	$ 24,000

To project expenses at different volumes, managers must know how the company's costs behave. Total fixed costs will be the same regardless of volume as long as the volume is within the same relevant range. However, total variable costs will change as volume changes. Managers use a mixed cost equation, such as the one we discussed in Chapter 6, to budget expenses at different volumes. This is sometimes referred to as a flexible budget formula:

$$\text{Flexible budget total cost} = \left(\begin{array}{c} \text{Number of} \\ \text{output units} \end{array} \times \begin{array}{c} \text{Variable cost} \\ \text{per output unit} \end{array} \right) + \text{Total fixed cost}$$

Kool-Time's variable costs are $8,000 per pool. Of this amount, $7,000 is for variable manufacturing costs (direct materials, direct labor, and variable manufacturing overhead such as gasoline to operate the earth moving equipment), while $1,000 is for variable selling and administrative expenses (such as the commission paid to sales staff on every pool sold). It is these variable expenses that put the "flex" in the flexible budget because budgeted total monthly fixed costs remain constant. Kool-Time's monthly fixed costs are $20,000. This includes $12,000 of fixed monthly manufacturing overhead (such as the the monthly lease of earth-moving equipment), while $8,000 relates to fixed selling and administrative expenses (sales and administrative salaries, lease of sales office, telephone and Internet service, and so forth).

Using this information on cost behavior, managers can predict costs at different volumes, just as we did in Chapter 6. For example, the total budgeted cost for five pools is:

$60,000 = (5 pools × $8,000 variable cost per pool) + $20,000 fixed cost

Likewise, the total budgeted cost for 11 pools is:

$108,000 = (11 pools × $8,000 variable cost per pool) + $20,000 fixed cost

Exhibit 11-3 shows the revenues and expenses anticipated if Kool-Time sells 5, 8, or 11 pools during the month. Kool-Time's best estimate is 8 pools, but by acknowledging that sales could be as low as 5 or as high as 11, Kool-Time's managers will be better prepared for any differences in volume that may arise.

Managers develop flexible budgets like Exhibit 11-3 for any number of volumes using a simple Excel spreadsheet or more sophisticated Web-based budget management software. However, managers must be careful: *They must consider the company's relevant range.* Why? Because total monthly fixed costs and the variable cost per pool change outside this range. Kool-Time's relevant range is 0 to 11 pools. If the company installs 12 pools, it will have to lease additional equipment, so fixed monthly costs will exceed $20,000. Kool-Time also will have to pay workers an overtime premium, so the variable cost per pool will be more than $8,000.

Graphing Flexible Budget Costs

Sometimes, it's helpful for managers to see a graph of the flexible budget costs. Exhibit 11-4 shows budgeted total costs for the entire relevant range of 0 to 11 pools. Because Kool-Time has both fixed and variable costs, its total costs are mixed. Kool-Time's flexible budget graph has the same characteristics as the mixed cost graphs we discussed in Chapter 6. The total cost line intersects the vertical axis at the level of total fixed cost ($20,000) that Kool-Time will incur whether it installs 0 pools or 11 pools. The total cost line also slopes upward at the rate of $8,000 per pool, which is Kool-Time's variable cost per pool. Each additional pool, up to 11 pools, should cost Kool-Time an extra $8,000.

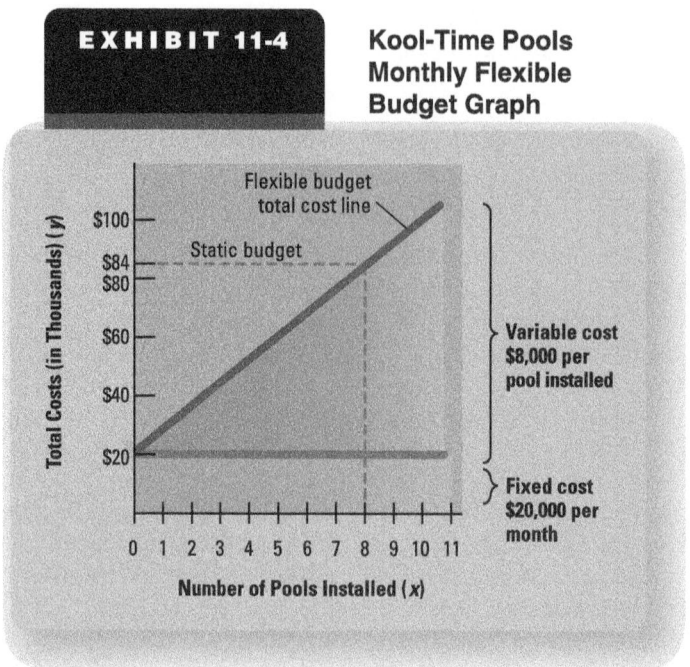

EXHIBIT 11-4 Kool-Time Pools Monthly Flexible Budget Graph

As shown by the dotted line in Exhibit 11-4, Kool-Time expects to install eight pools in June (at a total cost of $84,000). But managers also can use this graph to *plan* costs for anywhere from 0 to 11 pools.

Using Flexible Budgets for Evaluating Performance

We just saw how managers can use flexible budgets for planning purposes. But managers can also use flexible budgets *at the end of the period* to evaluate the company's financial performance and help control costs. Rather than comparing actual revenues and expenses against the static budget (as shown in Exhibit 11-1), managers can compare the actual results against the flexible budget *for the actual volume of output* that occurred during the period.

Consider June, when Kool-Time *actually* installed ten pools. The flexible budget graph in Exhibit 11-5 show that *flexible budgeted* total costs for ten pools are:

Variable costs (10 × $8,000)	$ 80,000
Fixed costs	20,000
Total costs	$100,000

June's *actual* costs were $105,000 (Exhibit 11-1). Consequently, June's actual costs for ten pools ($105,000) slightly exceed the budget for ten pools ($100,000). Managers can use graphs such as Exhibit 11-5 to see at a glance whether actual costs are either of the following:

- Higher than budgeted for the actual volume of output (as in April, June, and August)
- Lower than budgeted for the actual volume of output (as in May and July)

Kool-Time Pools Graph of Actual and Budgeted Monthly Costs

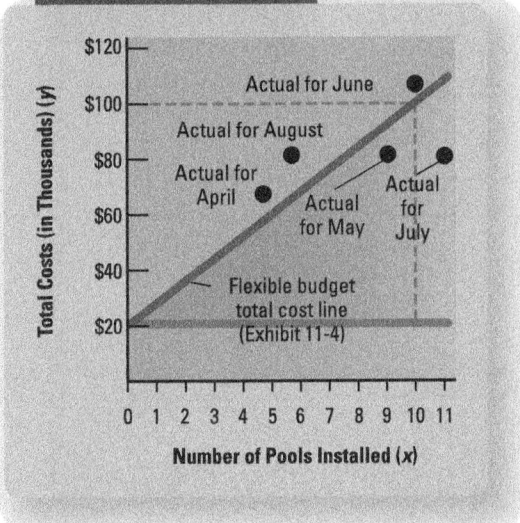

We used a simple graph to illustrate how Kool-Time's managers can compare actual costs against flexible budgeted costs. Unlike the apples-to-oranges comparison in Exhibit 11-1, comparing actual costs against flexible budgeted costs allows managers to make an apples-to-apples comparison. Why? Because both the actual costs and the flexible budgeted costs are based on the *same actual volume of activity (ten pools)*. In other words, if management would have had a crystal ball before the month began, they would have budgeted for ten pools rather than eight. By comparing the actual costs with the flexible budgeted costs for ten pools, Kool-Time's managers see that their expenses were only $5,000 higher than anticipated *for this volume*. This explains a portion of the $21,000 unfavorable expense variance shown in Exhibit 11-1. In the next section, we'll see how managers can perform a more in-depth analysis to find out more about why the $21,000 unfavorable expense variance shown in Exhibit 11-1 occurred.

Stop & Think...

Use the graph in Exhibit 11-5 and Kool-Time's flexible budget mixed cost equation to answer the following questions:

1. How many pools did Kool-Time install in July?
2. What were Kool-Time's actual costs in July?
3. Using Kool-Time's flexible budget mixed cost equation, what is the flexible budget total cost for the month of July?
4. Is Kool-Time's variance for total costs favorable or unfavorable in July?

Answer:

1. Exhibit 11-5 shows that Kool-Time installed 11 pools in July.
2. Exhibit 11-5 shows that Kool-Time's actual costs in July were about $80,000.

continued . . .

3. Using Kool-Time's flexible budget mixed cost equation:

Variable costs (11 × $8,000)..	$ 88,000
Fixed costs...	20,000
Total costs...	$108,000

4. Kool-Time's July variance for total costs is $28,000 ($108,000 − $80,000) favorable because actual costs are less than the budget.

Computing the Sales Volume Variance and Flexible Budget Variance

BBH CHAPTER 11

2 Use the sales volume variance and flexible budget variance to explain why actual results differ from the master budget

Managers must know *why* a variance occurred to pinpoint problems and to identify corrective action. Recall that Kool-Time's managers had a hard time understanding why the static budget variances in Exhibit 11-1 occurred because comparing the figures in that exhibit was like comparing apples to oranges: The actual results were based on the ten pools installed, yet the budget was for eight pools. To get more answers as to why the static budget variance occurred, managers often separate the static budget variance into two different parts: (1) the sales volume variance and (2) the flexible budget variance. Exhibit 11-6 shows how the static budget variance can be separated into these two variances. To obtain these variances managers first need to prepare a flexible budget for the actual level of output for the period (ten pools).

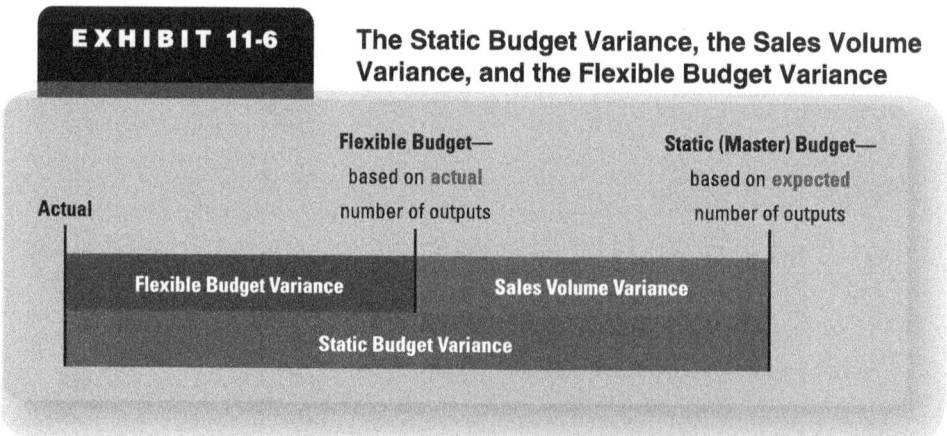

EXHIBIT 11-6   The Static Budget Variance, the Sales Volume Variance, and the Flexible Budget Variance

Exhibit 11-6 shows that:

- The **sales volume variance** is the difference between the *static* (master) budget and the *flexible* budget (for the actual number of outputs). As the name suggests, this variance arises *only* because the number of units actually sold differs from the volume originally planned for in the static master budget.
- The **flexible budget variance** is the difference between the *flexible* budget and the *actual* results. This variance arises because the company actually earned more or less revenue or incurred more or less expense than expected *for the actual level of output (ten pools)*. In other words, this variance is due to factors *other than* volume.

Let's see how Kool-Time's managers calculate and interpret these two different variances. Exhibit 11-7 shows Kool-Time's performance report for June. Column 1 shows Kool-Time's actual results for the period. This information is gathered from the general ledger. Now, consider the static master budget amounts presented in column 5. Recall that at the *beginning* of the period, Kool-Time *expected* to sell eight pools. For these eight pools, Kool-Time's:

- Budgeted sales revenue is $96,000 (8 × $12,000).
- Budgeted variable expenses are $64,000 (8 × $8,000).
- Budgeted fixed expenses are $20,000.

Notice that the amounts shown in columns 1 and 5 are the same as those shown in Exhibit 11-1. The only difference is that here we show a little more detail: Variable and fixed costs are shown separately; they are not lumped together.

EXHIBIT 11-7 **Income Statement Performance Report**

KOOL-TIME POOLS
Income Statement Performance Report
Month Ended June 30, 2007

	(1) Actual Results at Actual Prices	(2) (1)–(3) Flexible Budget Variance	(3) Flexible Budget for Actual Number of Output Units*	(4) (3)–(5) Sales Volume Variance	(5) Static (Master) Budget*
Output units (pools installed)	10	–0–	10	2 F	8
Sales revenue	$121,000	$1,000 F	$120,000	$24,000 F	$96,000
Variable expenses	83,000	3,000 U	80,000	16,000 U	64,000
Fixed expenses	22,000	2,000 U	20,000	–0–	20,000
Total expenses	105,000	5,000 U	100,000	16,000 U	84,000
Operating income	$ 16,000	$4,000 U	$ 20,000	$ 8,000 F	$12,000

Flexible budget variance, $4,000 U   Sales volume variance, $8,000 F

Static budget variance, $4,000 F

*Budgeted sales price is $12,000 per pool, budgeted variable expense is $8,000 per pool, and budgeted total monthly fixed expenses are $20,000.

Finally, consider column 3. In contrast to the static budget, which is developed *before* the period, the flexible budget used in the performance report is not developed until the *end* of the period. Why? Because *flexible budgets used in performance reports are based on the actual number of outputs, which is not known until the end of the period*. For Kool-Time, this flexible budget is based on the *ten pools actually installed*:

- Budgeted sales revenue is $120,000 (10 × $12,000).
- Budgeted variable expenses are $80,000 (10 × $8,000).
- Budgeted fixed expenses are $20,000.

Now that you know how this performance report was developed, let's take a look at the variances in more detail.

Sales Volume Variance

The sales volume variance (shown in column 4 of Exhibit 11-7) is the difference between the static master budget (column 5) and the flexible budget (column 3). The *only difference* between the static and flexible budgets in the performance report is the *number of outputs on which the budget is based* (eight pools versus ten pools). Both budgets use the same

- Budgeted sales price per unit ($12,000 per pool).
- Budgeted variable cost per unit ($8,000 per pool).
- Budgeted total fixed costs ($20,000 per month).

Holding selling price per unit, variable cost per unit, and total fixed costs constant highlights the effects of differences in sales volume—the variance shown in column 4. Exhibit 11-7 shows that by installing two more pools than initially expected, Kool-Time's:

- Sales revenue *should* increase from $96,000 (8 × $12,000) to $120,000 (10 × $12,000)—a $24,000 favorable sales volume variance.
- Variable costs *should* increase from $64,000 (8 × $8,000) to $80,000 (10 × $8,000)—a $16,000 unfavorable sales volume variance.

Budgeted total fixed expenses are unaffected because eight pools and ten pools are within the relevant range where fixed expenses total $20,000. Consequently, installing two more pools should increase operating income by $8,000 ($24,000 F − $16,000 U). So, Kool-Time's June sales volume variance is $8,000 F.

Since the sales volume variance arises *only* because the number of units actually sold differs from the volume originally planned for in the master budget, this variance is typically marketing's responsibility.

Stop & Think...

When is there a sales volume variance for fixed expenses?

Answer: Only when the number of units actually sold falls within a different relevant range than the static budget sales volume. When actual and expected number of units sold fall in the same relevant range, there is no sales volume variance for fixed expenses.

Flexible Budget Variance

As the name suggests, the flexible budget variance (shown in column 2 of Exhibit 11-7) is the difference between the *flexible* budget (column 3) and the *actual* results (column 1). Recall that the flexible budget is based on the actual level of output (ten pools), so it shows the revenues and expenses that Kool-Time's managers expect for a volume of ten pools. Therefore, the flexible budget *variance* highlights *unexpected* revenues and expenses.

Exhibit 11-7 shows a $1,000 favorable flexible budget variance for sales revenue. Kool-Time actually received $121,000 for installing ten pools rather than the $120,000 expected for ten pools (10 pools × $12,000). This variance means that the average sales price was $12,100 per pool ($121,000 ÷ 10 pools), which is $100 higher than the budgeted sales price of $12,000 per pool. This variance is typically marketing's responsibility.

Answer: Marketing

Exhibit 11-7 also shows a $3,000 unfavorable flexible budget variance for variable expenses. Kool-Time actually incurred $83,000 of variable expenses rather than the $80,000 expected for ten pools (ten pools × $8,000 per pool). The company also spent $2,000 more on fixed expenses than was budgeted ($22,000 − $20,000). Consequently, the flexible budget variance for total expenses is $5,000 unfavorable ($3,000 U + $2,000 U). In other words, Kool-Time spent $5,000 more than it would expect to spend for installing ten pools. This is the same $5,000 flexible budget expense variance we saw graphed in Exhibit 11-5. This variance is typically the responsibility of the purchasing, production, and human resources managers.

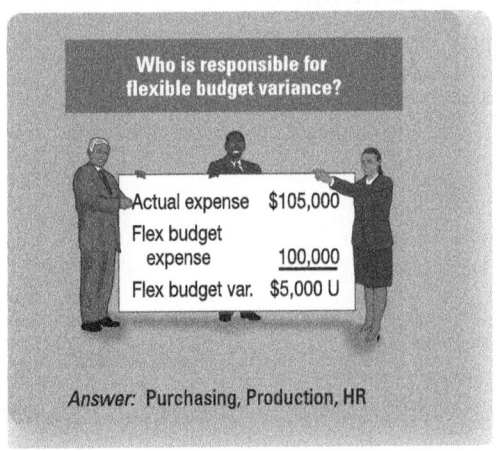

Answer: Purchasing, Production, HR

Interpreting the Variances

How would Kool-Time's managers use these variances? The favorable sales volume variance reveals that strong sales should have increased Kool-Time's income by $8,000. In addition, the sales staff increased sales without discounting prices: The favorable $1,000 flexible budget variance for sales revenue shows that the sales price was, on average, *higher* than budgeted. These favorable variances due to the quantity of pools sold (the $8,000 favorable sales volume variance) and the sales price per pool (the $1,000 favorable sales revenue price variance) suggest that Kool-Time's marketing staff did a better-than-expected job in selling pools and maintaining sales prices. Perhaps the high sales commissions paid on each pool sale is doing a good job of motivating the sales staff.

However, higher-than-expected expenses offset much of the favorable sales volume variance. Exhibit 11-7 shows a $5,000 unfavorable flexible budget variance for expenses. Management will want to find out why. The reason might be an uncontrollable increase in the cost of materials. Or higher costs might have resulted from more-controllable factors, such as employees wasting materials or working inefficiently. If so, managers can take action to reduce waste or inefficiency. Although Kool-Time does not have any favorable expense variances, in general, managers can benefit from examining favorable as well as unfavorable expense variances. Favorable variances may be the result of some type of efficiency that could be used in other areas of the company, too.

Let's get back to Kool-Time's original question from Exhibit 11-1: Why did the company have an unfavorable static budget variance of $21,000 for expenses? The *sales volume variance* shows that $16,000 of this amount is due to the fact that Kool-Time installed two more pools than it originally planned to install. The *flexible budget variance* shows that the remaining $5,000 (of the $21,000 variance) is due to cost overruns caused by other factors. In the second part of this chapter, we will see how managers drill down deeper to find the root cause(s) for this $5,000 flexible budget expense variance. Once managers identify the reason for the cost overruns, they can decide what action to take to avoid similar overruns in the future.

Decision Guidelines

FLEXIBLE BUDGETS

You and your roommate have started a business printing T-shirts for special customer requests (for example, including school or student organization logos). How can you use flexible budgets to plan and control your costs?

Decision	Guidelines
How should we estimate sales revenues, costs, and profits over the range of likely sales (output) levels?	Prepare a set of flexible budgets for different sales levels.
How should we prepare a flexible budget for total costs?	Use a mixed cost equation to predict costs at different volumes within the relevant range: $$\text{Flexible budget total cost} = \left(\text{Number of T-shirts} \times \text{Variable cost per T-shirts} \right) + \text{Fixed cost}$$
How should we use budgets to help control costs?	• Graph actual costs versus flexible budget costs, as in Exhibit 11-5. • Prepare an income statement performance report, as in Exhibit 11-7.

Decision	**Guidelines**
On which output level is the budget based?	Static (master) budget—*expected* number of T-shirts, estimated before the period. Flexible budget—*actual* number of T-shirts, not known until the end of the period.
Why does your actual income differ from budgeted income?	Prepare an income statement performance report comparing actual results, flexible budget for actual number of T-shirts sold, and static (master) budget, as in Exhibit 11-7.
How do we interpret favorable and unfavorable variances?	• Favorable variances increase operating income. • Unfavorable variances decrease operating income.
How much of the difference is because the actual number of T-shirts sold does not equal budgeted sales?	Compute the sales volume variance (SVV) by comparing the flexible budget with the static budget. • Favorable SVV— Actual number of T-shirts sold > Expected number of T-shirts sold • Unfavorable SVV— Actual number of T-shirts sold < Expected number of T-shirts sold
How much of the difference occurs because actual revenues and costs are not what they should have been for the actual number of T-shirts sold?	Compute the flexible budget variance (FBV) by comparing actual results with the flexible budget. • Favorable FBV— Actual sales revenue > Flexible budget sales revenue OR Actual expenses < Flexible budget expenses • Unfavorable FBV— Actual sales revenue < Flexible budget sales revenue OR Actual expenses > Flexible budget expenses
What actions can we take to avoid an unfavorable sales volume variance?	• Design more-attractive T-shirts to increase demand. • Provide marketing incentives to increase number of T-shirts sold.
What actions can we take to avoid an unfavorable flexible budget variance?	• Maintain (do not discount) sales prices. • Control variable expenses, such as the cost of the plain T-shirts, dye, and labor. • Control fixed expenses.

BBH CHAPTER 11

Summary Problem 1

Exhibit 11-7 indicates that Kool-Time installed ten swimming pools during June. Now, assume that Kool-Time installed seven pools (instead of ten) and that the actual sales price averaged $12,500 per pool. Actual variable expenses were $57,400, and actual fixed expenses were $19,000.

Requirements

1. Prepare a revised income statement performance report using Exhibit 11-7 as a guide.

2. Show that the sum of the flexible budget variance and the sales volume variance for operating income equals the static budget variance for operating income.

3. As the company owner, which employees would you praise and which employees would you criticize after you analyze this performance report?

Solution

Requirements 1 and 2

KOOL-TIME POOLS
Income Statement Performance Report—Revised
Month Ended June 30, 2007

	(1) Actual Results at Actual Prices	(2) (1)–(3) Flexible Budget Variance	(3) Flexible Budget for Actual Number of Output Units	(4) (3)–(5) Sales Volume Variance	(5) Static (Master) Budget
Output units	7	–0–	7	1 U	8
Sales revenue	$ 87,500	$ 3,500 F	$ 84,000	$ 12,000 U	$ 96,000
Variable expenses	57,400	1,400 U	56,000	8,000 F	64,000
Fixed expenses	19,000	1,000 F	20,000	—	20,000
Total expenses	76,400	400 U	76,000	8,000 F	84,000
Operating income	$ 11,100	$ 3,100 F	$ 8,000	$ 4,000 U	$ 12,000

Flexible budget variance, $3,100 F

Sales volume variance, $4,000 U

Static budget variance, $900 U

Requirement 3

As the company owner, you should determine the *causes* of the variances before deciding who deserves praise or criticism. It is especially important to determine who is responsible for the variance and whether the variance is due to factors the manager can control. For example, the unfavorable sales volume variance could be due to an ineffective sales staff. Or it could be due to an uncontrollable long period of heavy rain that brought work to a standstill. Similarly, the $1,000 favorable flexible budget variance for fixed expenses could be due to an employee finding a lower-cost source of rented equipment. Or the savings might have come from delaying a needed overhaul of equipment that would increase the company's costs in the long run. Smart managers use variances to raise questions and direct attention, not to fix blame.

Standard Costs

Think of a **standard cost** as a budget for a single unit. In Kool-Time's case, a single unit would be one swimming pool. Most companies use standard costs to develop their flexible budgets. Recall that Kool-Time developed its flexible budget using a *standard variable cost per pool* of $8,000 (see Exhibit 11-3). Of the total standard variable cost per pool, $7,000 relates to the cost of variable manufacturing inputs: the direct materials, direct labor, and variable manufacturing overhead costs necessary to install one pool. The other $1,000 relates to selling and administrative costs associated with *selling* each pool (sales commission, for example). For the rest of this chapter, we are going to concentrate on *standard manufacturing costs*, although the same concepts apply to selling, general, and administrative costs.

In a standard cost system, each manufacturing input (such as direct materials) has a quantity standard and a price standard. For example, McDonald's has a standard for the amount of beef used per hamburger and a standard for the price paid per pound of beef. Likewise, Kool-Time has a standard for the amount of gunite (a concrete-like material) used per pool and a standard for the price it pays per cubic foot of gunite. Let's see how managers set these quantity and price standards.

3 Identify the benefits of standard costs and learn how to set standards

Quantity Standards

Engineers and production managers set direct material and direct labor quantity standards, usually allowing for unavoidable waste and spoilage. For example, each pool that Kool-Time installs requires 975 cubic feet of gunite. As part of the normal installation process, an additional 25 cubic feet of gunite is typically wasted due to unavoidable spoilage from hardened, unusable gunite. Kool-Time calculates the standard quantity of gunite per pool as follows:

Gunite required	975	cubic feet per pool
Unavoidable waste and spoilage	25	cubic feet per pool
Standard quantity of gunite	1,000	cubic feet per pool

Kool-Time also develops quantity standards for direct labor based on time records from past pool installations and current installation requirements. In setting labor standards, managers usually allow for unavoidable work interruptions and normal downtime for which the employee would still be paid. Considering these factors, Kool-Time has set its direct labor quantity standard at 400 direct labor hours per pool.

Price Standards

Now, let's turn our attention to price standards. Accountants help managers set direct material price standards after considering the base purchase price of materials, early-payment discounts, receiving costs, and freight-in. For example, the manager in charge of purchasing gunite for Kool-Time indicates that the purchase price, net of discounts, is $1.90 per cubic foot and that freight-in costs $0.10 per cubic foot. Kool-Time calculates its price standard for gunite as follows:

Purchase price, net of discounts..	$1.90	per cubic foot
Freight-in	0.10	per cubic foot
Standard cost of gunite...	$2.00	per cubic foot

For direct labor, accountants work with personnel or human resources managers to determine standard labor rates, taking into account payroll taxes and fringe benefits as well as the hourly wage rate. Kool-Time's Human Resources Department indicates that the hourly wage rate for production workers is $8.00 and that payroll taxes and fringe benefits total $2.50 per direct labor hour. Kool-Time's direct labor price (or rate) standard is:

Hourly wage rate	$ 8.00	per direct labor hour
Payroll taxes and fringe benefits.............................	2.50	per direct labor hour
Standard direct labor rate..	$10.50	per direct labor hour

Standard Manufacturing Overhead Rates

In addition to direct materials and direct labor price and quantity standards, companies also set standard manufacturing overhead rates. The standard predetermined manufacturing overhead rates are calculated as usual except that *two* rates are calculated: one for fixed overhead and one for variable overhead. Why? Because isolating the variable overhead component helps managers create flexible budgets for different volumes. For setting standard overhead rates, accountants work with production managers to estimate variable and fixed manufacturing overhead expenses. Managers then identify an appropriate allocation base for computing the standard manufacturing overhead rates.

For example, recall that Kool-Time's fixed manufacturing overhead costs are expected to be $12,000 per month (the other $8,000 of fixed costs related to selling and administrative expenses). Production managers also estimate variable manufacturing overhead costs to be $800 per pool, or a total of $6,400 for the eight pools they plan to produce during the month ($800 × 8 = $6,400). Kool-Time has decided to use direct labor hours as its overhead allocation base, so they estimate the total number of direct labor hours they expect to incur during the month:

8 pools × 400 standard direct labor hours per pool = 3,200 direct labor hours

Kool-Time computes the standard variable overhead rate as follows:

$$\text{Standard } variable \text{ overhead rate} = \frac{\text{Estimated total } variable \text{ overhead cost}}{\text{Estimated total quality of allocation base}}$$

$$= \frac{\$6,400}{3,200 \text{ direct labor hours}}$$

$$= \underline{\$2.00} \text{ per direct labor hour}$$

Kool-Time computes the standard fixed overhead rate in a similar way:

$$\text{Standard } \textit{fixed} \text{ overhead rate} = \frac{\text{Estimated total } \textit{fixed} \text{ overhead cost}}{\text{Estimated total quality of allocation base}}$$

$$= \frac{\$12,000}{3,200 \text{ direct labor hours}}$$

$$= \underline{\$3.75} \text{ per direct labor hour}$$

The standard total overhead rate is the *sum* of the standard *variable* overhead and the standard *fixed* overhead rates:

Variable overhead rate	+ Fixed overhead rate	= Standard overhead rate
$2.00 per direct labor hour	+ $3.75 per direct labor hour	= $5.75 per direct labor hour

Notice that the standard manufacturing overhead rate ($5.75 per direct labor hour) is the rate we would have computed based on all anticipated manufacturing overhead costs, regardless of cost behavior ($5.75 = $18,400 total estimated manufacturing overhead costs ÷ 3,200 total estimated direct labor hours).

Standard Cost of Inputs

Once managers have developed quantity and price standards, they calculate the standard cost of *each input* (such as direct materials, direct labor, and manufacturing overhead) by multiplying the quantity standard by the price standard:

Quantity standard × Price standard = Standard cost of input

For example, Kool-Time's standard direct materials cost per pool is:

1,000 cubic feet of gunite × $2.00 per cubic foot = $2,000 of direct materials per pool

Likewise, Kool-Time's standard direct labor cost per pool is:

400 direct labor hours × $10.50 per direct labor hour = $4,200 of direct labor per pool

Exhibit 11-8 shows Kool-Time's standard costs for variable and fixed overhead. The exhibit also shows that by adding the standard cost of all of the inputs Kool-Time can find the standard cost of *manufacturing* one pool ($8,500). However, this cost can be misleading to managers because it contains a fixed overhead component. It's really only valid when Kool-Time installs exactly eight pools in a month.

Rather than run the risk of misleading managers, it is often more helpful to highlight just the standard *variable* manufacturing cost per pool. Exhibit 11-8 shows that Kool-Time's standard costs for direct materials ($2,000) and direct labor ($4,200) and variable overhead ($800) amount to $7,000 variable manufacturing cost per pool. How does this correspond with variable cost per pool used for flexible budgeting? In addition to variable *manufacturing* costs, recall that Kool-Time expects to incur $1,000 of variable *selling and administrative* expenses per pool (for sales commissions, for example). Added together, these two costs

BBH CHAPTER 11

EXHIBIT 11-8   Kool-Time's Standard Manufacturing Costs per Pool

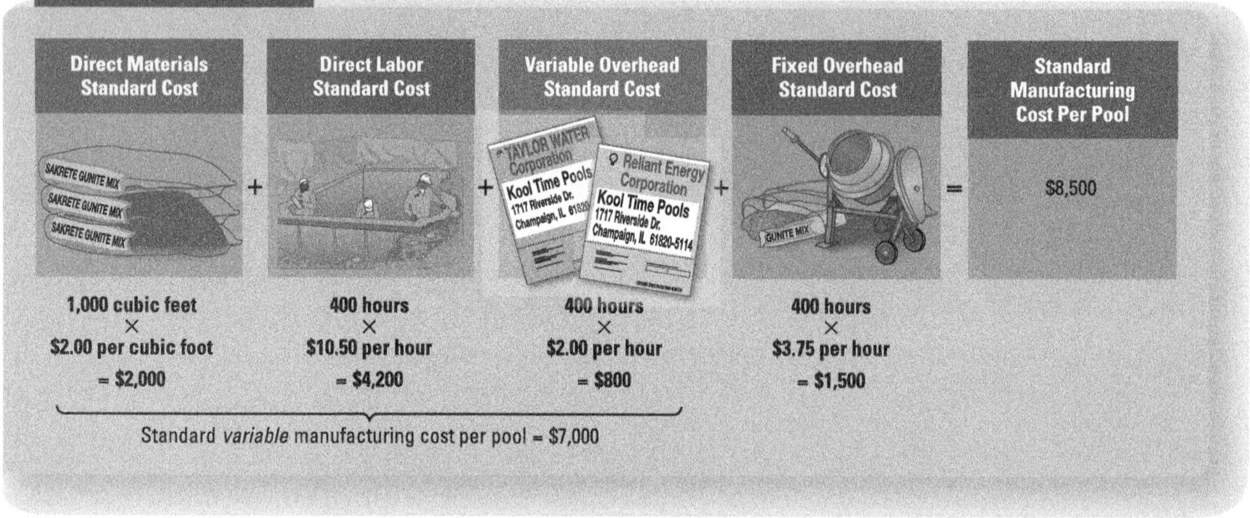

total the $8,000 variable cost per pool that Kool-Time used for flexible budgeting in Exhibit 11-3.

Kool-Time is not alone in its use of standards. U.S. surveys have shown that more than 80% of responding companies use standard costs. International surveys show that over half of responding companies in the United Kingdom, Ireland, Sweden, and Japan use standard costs. Why? Most companies believe that the benefits from using standard costs outweigh the costs of developing the standards and periodically revising them as business conditions change.

For example, companies should reassess their price standards when input prices such as the price of raw materials or labor rates change due to nontemporary market conditions. They should also reassess quantity standards when the product or production process is modified and, as a result, different quantities of materials or labor are required.

Exhibit 11-9 shows five benefits that companies, such as McDonald's, obtain from using standard costs.

EXHIBIT 11-9   The Benefits of Standard Costs

Now, let's take a look at how Kool-Time uses its standard costs to analyze flexible budget variances.

Using Standard Costs to Analyze Direct Material and Direct Labor Variances

Let's return to our Kool-Time example. Exhibit 11-7 showed that the main cause for concern at Kool-Time is the $5,000 unfavorable flexible budget variance for expenses. The first step in identifying the causes of this variance is to take a more detailed look at what is included in the *expenses*. See Panel A of Exhibit 11-10. Note that this exhibit is different from Exhibit 11-7 in three ways: (1) It shows only expenses (it leaves out all revenue data), (2) it contains only actual and flexible budget data (it leaves out the static master budget and sales volume variance), and (3) it shows the *components* of Kool-Time's variable and fixed expenses (detailed production costs are shown separately from marketing and administrative expenses). Take a moment to see that the total variable expenses ($83,000 actual versus $80,000 budgeted), total fixed expenses ($22,000 actual versus $20,000 budgeted), and total expenses ($105,000 actual versus $100,000 budgeted) agree with Exhibit 11-7. The total $5,000 unfavorable flexible budget variance for expenses also agrees with Exhibit 11-7.

Study Exhibit 11-10 carefully because we will continue to refer to it throughout the rest of the chapter. Panel B (shown on page 614) shows how we used Kool-Time's price and quantity standards to compute the flexible budget amounts shown in Panel A. Panel C (also shown on page 614) shows how we computed the actual direct materials and direct labor costs shown in Panel A.

4 Compute standard cost variances for direct materials and direct labor

EXHIBIT 11-10	Data for Standard Costing Example

KOOL-TIME POOLS
Data for Standard Costing Example
Month of June 2007

PANEL A—Comparison of Actual Results with Flexible Budget for 10 Swimming Pools

	(1) Actual Results at Actual Prices	(2) Flexible Budget for 10 Pools	(1) – (2) Flexible Budget Variance
Variable expenses:			
Direct materials	$ 23,100*	$ 20,000†	$3,100 U
Direct labor	41,800*	42,000†	200 F
Variable overhead	9,000	8,000†	1,000 U
Marketing and administrative expenses	9,100	10,000	900 F
Total variable expenses	83,000	80,000	3,000 U
Fixed expenses:			
Fixed overhead	12,300	12,000‡	300 U
Marketing and administrative expenses	9,700	8,000	1,700 U
Total fixed expenses	22,000	20,000	2,000 U
Total expenses	$105,000	$100,000	$5,000 U

*See Panel C.
†See Panel B.
‡Fixed overhead was budgeted at $12,000 per month.

continued...

BBH CHAPTER 11

EXHIBIT 11-10	Data for Standard Costing Example

KOOL-TIME POOLS
Data for Standard Costing Example
Month of June 2007

PANEL B—Computation of Flexible Budget for Direct Materials, Direct Labor, and Variable Overhead for 10 Swimming Pools

	(1) Standard Quantity of Inputs Allowed for 10 Pools	(2) Standard Price per Unit of Input	(1) × (2) Flexible Budget for 10 Pools
Direct materials	1,000 cubic feet per pool × 10 pools = 10,000 cubic feet	× $ 2.00	= $20,000
Direct labor	400 hours per pool × 10 pools = 4,000 hours	× 10.50	= 42,000
Variable overhead	400 hours per pool × 10 pools = 4,000 hours	× 2.00	= 8,000

PANEL C—Computation of Actual Costs for Direct Materials and Direct Labor for 10 Swimming Pools

	(1) Actual Quantity of Inputs Used for 10 Pools	(2) Actual Price per Unit of Input	(1) × (2) Actual Cost for 10 Pools
Direct materials	11,969 cubic feet actually used × $1.93 actual cost/cubic foot		= $23,100
Direct labor	3,800 hours actually used × $11.00 actual cost/hour		= 41,800

Direct Material Variances

The largest single component of the flexible budget variance in Panel A of Exhibit 11-10 is the $3,100 unfavorable variance in direct materials. Recall that the flexible budget variance is the difference between the actual cost incurred and the flexible budget (as shown in Exhibits 11-6 and 11-7). Exhibit 11-11 shows that Kool-Time computes the direct materials flexible budget variance as the difference between (1) the actual amount paid for gunite and (2) the flexible budget amount (*not the static budget amount!*) that Kool-Time should have spent on gunite for the ten pools that it actually installed.

EXHIBIT 11-11   **Kool-Time Pools Direct Materials Flexible Budget Variance**

The actual amount paid for the direct materials (Panel C of Exhibit 11-10)	The flexible budget for the amount of gunite that *should have been used to install 10 pools* (Panel B of Exhibit 11-10)
Actual quantity of gunite × Actual price per cubic foot of gunite	Standard quantity of gunite for actual number of pools × Standard price per cubic foot of gunite
11,969 cubic feet of gunite used × $1.93 actual price paid per cubic foot of gunite = $23,100	(1,000 cubic feet of gunite per pool × 10 pools) × $2.00 standard price per cubic foot of gunite = $20,000

$3,100 unfavorable direct materials flexible budget variance

Now that Kool-Time knows that it spent $3,100 more than it should have on gunite, the next question is why. Did the $3,100 unfavorable variance arise because Kool-Time:

- Did not meet the price standard because it paid too much for each cubic foot of gunite?
- Did not meet the quantity standard because workers used more gunite than they should have used to install ten pools?

To answer those questions, Kool-Time's managers separate the flexible budget variance for direct materials into price and efficiency components, as shown in Exhibit 11-12.

EXHIBIT 11-12   **The Relations Among Price, Efficiency, Flexible Budget, Sales Volume, and Static Budget Variances**

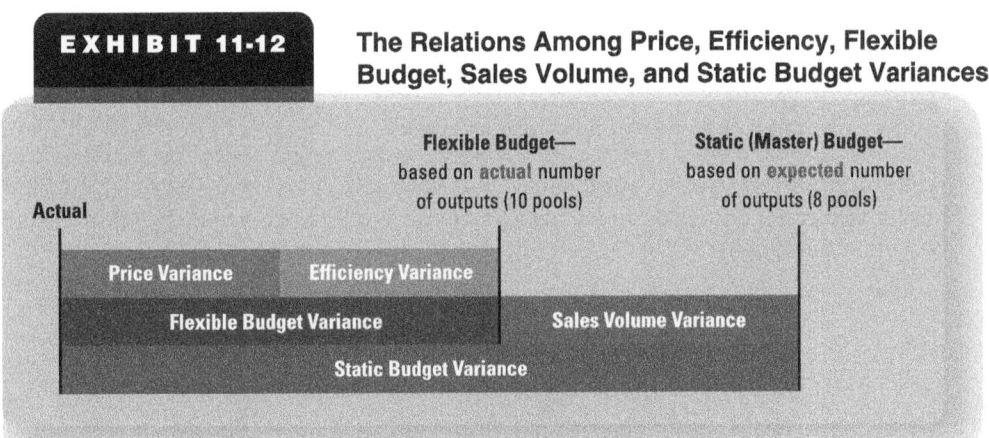

Exhibit 11-12 emphasizes two points. First, the price and efficiency variances sum to the flexible budget variance. Second, *static budgets (like column 5 of Exhibit 11-7) play no role in computing the flexible budget variance or in determining how it is split into price and efficiency variances.* The static budget is used *only* in computing the sales volume variance—never in computing the flexible budget variance or its component price and efficiency variances.

Direct Materials Price Variance

A **price variance** measures how well the business keeps unit prices of material and labor inputs within standards. As the name suggests, the price variance is the *difference in prices* (actual price per unit – standard price per unit) of an input, multiplied by the *actual quantity* of the input:

$$\text{Price variance} = \left(\begin{array}{c}\text{Actual}\\\text{price per}\\\text{input unit}\end{array} - \begin{array}{c}\text{Standard}\\\text{price per}\\\text{input unit}\end{array}\right) \times \left(\begin{array}{c}\text{Actual quantity}\\\text{of input}\end{array}\right)$$

For Kool-Time, the direct materials price variance for gunite is:

$$\begin{array}{l}\text{Direct materials}\\\text{price variance}\end{array} = \left(\begin{array}{c}\$1.93\text{ per}\\\text{cubic foot}\end{array} - \begin{array}{c}\$2.00\text{ per}\\\text{cubic foot}\end{array}\right) \times 11{,}969 \text{ cubic feet}$$

$$= (\$0.07 \text{ per cubic foot}) \times 11{,}969 \text{ cubic feet}$$
$$= \$838 \text{ F (rounded)}$$

The $838 direct materials price variance is *favorable* because the purchasing manager spent $0.07 *less* per cubic foot of gunite than budgeted ($1.93 actual price – $2.00 standard price).

The purchasing manager is responsible for the price variance on the *actual quantity* of materials he buys, so we multiply the $0.07 favorable price variance per cubic foot by the 11,969 cubic feet of gunite he *actually purchased*. Thus, Kool-Time's June operating income is $838 higher [($1.93 – $2.00) × 11,969] than the flexible budget because the purchasing manager paid less than the standard price for gunite. (If the purchasing manager had paid *more* than the $2.00 per cubic foot standard price, the direct materials price variance would have been *unfavorable*.)

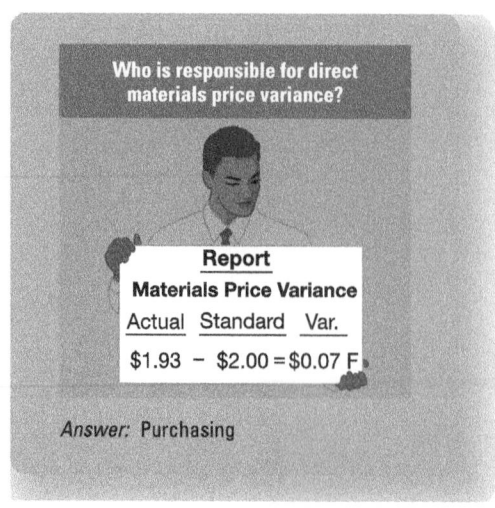

Answer: Purchasing

Direct Materials Efficiency Variance

An **efficiency variance** measures whether the firm meets its quantity standards. In other words, it measures whether the quantity of materials actually used to make the *actual number of outputs* is within the standard allowed for that number of outputs. The efficiency variance is the *difference in quantities* (actual quantity of input used − standard quantity of input allowed for the actual number of outputs) multiplied by the *standard price per unit* of the input.

$$\text{Efficiency variance} = \left(\begin{array}{c} \text{Actual} \\ \text{quantity} \\ \text{of input} \end{array} - \begin{array}{c} \text{Standard quantity of input} \\ \text{allowed for the actual} \\ \text{number of outputs} \end{array} \right) \times \left(\begin{array}{c} \text{Standard price} \\ \text{per input unit} \end{array} \right)$$

The standard quantity of inputs is the *quantity that should have been used*, or the standard quantity of inputs *allowed*, for the actual output. For Kool-Time, the *standard quantity of inputs (gunite) that workers should have used for the actual number of outputs* (ten pools) is:

1,000 cubic feet of gunite per pool × 10 pools installed = 10,000 cubic feet of gunite

Thus, the direct materials efficiency variance is:

$$\begin{aligned} \text{Direct materials efficiency variance} &= \left(\begin{array}{c} 11,969 \\ \text{cubic feet} \end{array} - \begin{array}{c} 10,000 \\ \text{cubic feet} \end{array} \right) \times \begin{array}{c} \$2 \text{ per} \\ \text{cubic foot} \end{array} \\ &= (1,969 \text{ cubic feet}) \times \$2 \text{ per cubic foot} \\ &= \$3,938 \text{ U} \end{aligned}$$

The $3,938 direct materials efficiency variance is *unfavorable* because workers actually used 1,969 *more* cubic feet of gunite than they should have used to install ten pools (11,969 actual cubic feet − 10,000 standard cubic feet).

The manager in charge of installing the pools is responsible for the variance in the quantity of the materials (gunite) used—in this case, the extra 1,969 cubic feet of gunite. However, this manager generally is *not* the person who purchases the gunite. The manager who installs the pools often has no control over the actual price paid for the gunite. Thus, we multiply the extra 1,969 cubic feet of gunite his workers used by the *standard price* of $2 per cubic foot to obtain the direct materials efficiency variance. Kool-Time's operating income is $3,938 lower [(11,969 − 10,000) × $2] than the flexible budget because workers used more gunite than they should have to install the ten pools in June. (If workers had used *less* than the standard 10,000 cubic feet to install the ten pools, the direct materials efficiency variance would have been *favorable*.)

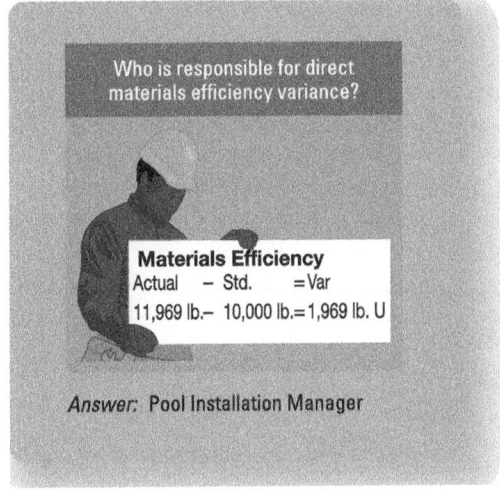

Who is responsible for direct materials efficiency variance?

Materials Efficiency
Actual − Std. = Var
11,969 lb.− 10,000 lb.=1,969 lb. U

Answer: Pool Installation Manager

Summary of Direct Material Variances

Exhibit 11-13 summarizes how Kool-Time splits the $3,100 unfavorable direct materials flexible budget variance first identified in Panel A of Exhibit 11-10 into price and efficiency variances.

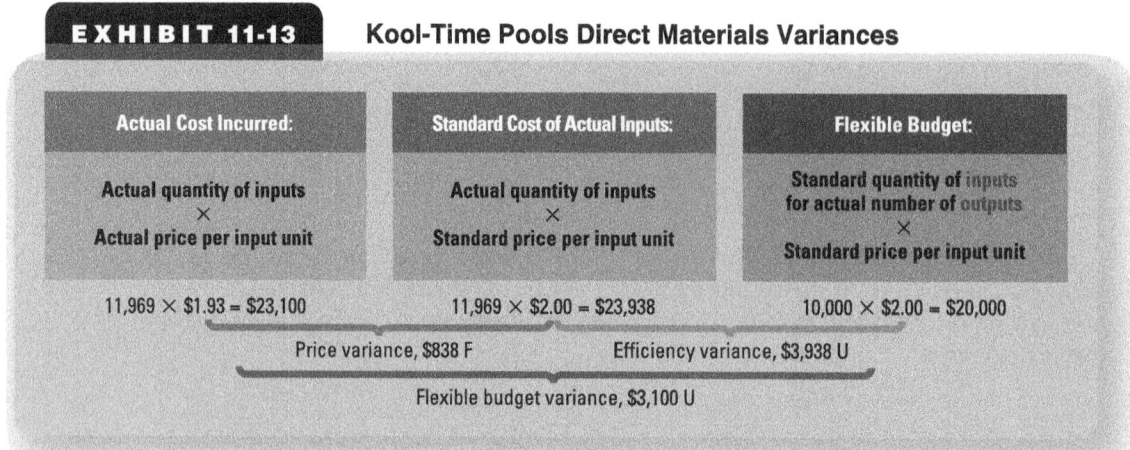

EXHIBIT 11-13   **Kool-Time Pools Direct Materials Variances**

Actual Cost Incurred:	Standard Cost of Actual Inputs:	Flexible Budget:
Actual quantity of inputs × Actual price per input unit	Actual quantity of inputs × Standard price per input unit	Standard quantity of inputs for actual number of outputs × Standard price per input unit
11,969 × $1.93 = $23,100	11,969 × $2.00 = $23,938	10,000 × $2.00 = $20,000

Price variance, $838 F   Efficiency variance, $3,938 U

Flexible budget variance, $3,100 U

Kool-Time actually spent $3,100 more than it should have for gunite because a good price for the gunite increased profits by $838 but inefficient use of the gunite reduced profits by $3,938.

Let's review who is responsible for each of these variances and consider why each variance may have occurred.

1. *Purchasing managers typically are responsible for direct materials price variances* because they should know why the actual price differs from the standard price. Kool-Time's purchasing manager may have negotiated a good price for gunite, or perhaps the supplier did not increase the price of gunite as much as expected when Kool-Time developed its standard cost. In either case, the purchasing manager is in the best position to explain the favorable price variance.

2. *Production managers typically are responsible for direct materials efficiency variances* because they are responsible for ensuring that workers use materials efficiently and effectively. The manager in charge of installing pools should be able to explain why workers used more gunite than they should have to install the ten pools. Was the gunite of lower quality? Did workers waste materials? Did their equipment malfunction? Kool-Time's top management needs answers to those questions to decide what corrective action to take. Should they require purchasing to buy higher-quality gunite, train and supervise workers more closely to reduce waste, or improve maintenance of equipment?

Smart managers know that these variances raise questions that can help pinpoint problems. But be careful! A favorable variance does not necessarily mean that a manager did a good job, nor does an unfavorable variance mean that a manager did a bad job. Perhaps Kool-Time's purchasing manager obtained a lower price by purchasing inferior-quality gunite, which, in turn, led to waste and spoilage. If so, the purchasing manager's decision hurt the company because the $838 favorable price variance is more than offset by the $3,938 unfavorable efficiency variance. This illustrates why good managers (1) use variances as a guide for investigation rather than as a simple tool to assign blame and (2) investigate favorable as well as unfavorable variances.

Direct Labor Variances

Kool-Time uses a similar approach to analyze the direct labor flexible budget variance. Using the information from Panels B and C of Exhibit 11-10, Exhibit 11-14 shows how Kool-Time computes this variance as the difference between the actual amount paid for direct labor and the flexible budget amount that Kool-Time should have spent on direct labor for ten pools.

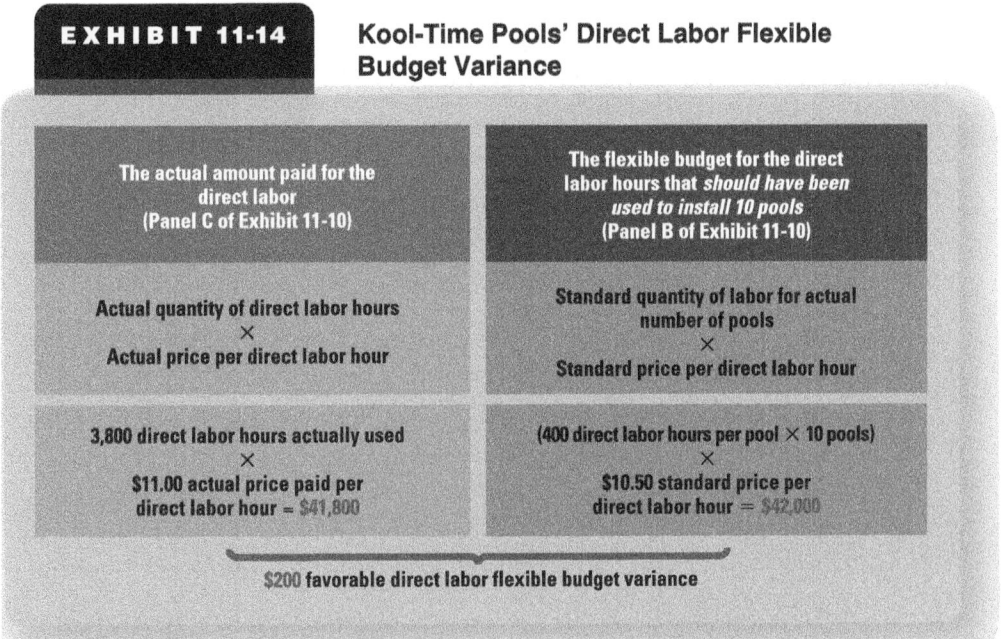

EXHIBIT 11-14   Kool-Time Pools' Direct Labor Flexible Budget Variance

Why did Kool-Time spend $200 less on labor than it should have to install ten pools? To answer that question, Kool-Time splits the direct labor flexible budget variance into price and efficiency variances the same way it did for direct materials.

Direct Labor Price Variance

The direct labor price variance is computed the same way as the direct materials price variance, so we use the same formula for price variance shown earlier:

$$\text{Price variance} = \left(\begin{array}{c} \text{Actual} \\ \text{price per} \\ \text{input unit} \end{array} - \begin{array}{c} \text{Standard} \\ \text{price per} \\ \text{input unit} \end{array} \right) \times \begin{array}{c} \text{Actual quantity} \\ \text{of input} \end{array}$$

$$\begin{aligned} \text{Direct labor} \atop \text{price variance} &= \left(\$11.00 \text{ per hour} - \$10.50 \text{ per hour} \right) \times 3{,}800 \text{ hours} \\ &= (\$0.50 \text{ per hour}) \times 3{,}800 \text{ hours} \\ &= \$1{,}900 \text{ U} \end{aligned}$$

The $1,900 direct labor price variance is *unfavorable* because the human resources (or personnel) department hired workers at $0.50 *more* per direct labor hour than budgeted ($11.00 actual price − $10.50 standard price).

The human resources manager is responsible for the price variance on the *actual quantity* of labor she hires, so we multiply the $0.50 unfavorable price variance per direct labor hour by the 3,800 hours of labor she *actually purchased*.

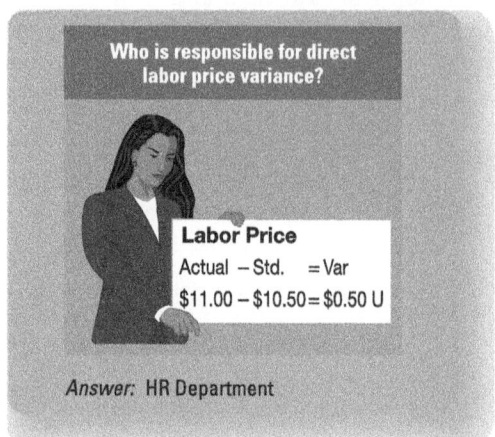

Direct Labor Efficiency Variance

The direct labor efficiency variance is computed the same way as the direct materials efficiency variance, so once again, we use the same formula for efficiency variance shown earlier:

$$\text{Efficiency variance} = \left(\begin{array}{c} \text{Actual} \\ \text{quantity} \\ \text{of input} \end{array} - \begin{array}{c} \text{Standard quantity of} \\ \text{input allowed for the} \\ \text{actual number of outputs} \end{array} \right) \times \begin{array}{c} \text{Standard} \\ \text{price per} \\ \text{input unit} \end{array}$$

For Kool-Time, the *standard quantity of direct labor hours that workers should have used for the actual number of outputs* (ten pools) is:

400 direct labor hours per pool × 10 pools installed = 4,000 direct labor hours

Thus, the direct labor efficiency variance is:

$$
\begin{aligned}
\text{Direct labor efficiency variance} &= (3{,}800 \text{ hours} - 4{,}000 \text{ hours}) \times \$10.50 \text{ per hour} \\
&= (200 \text{ hours}) \times \$10.50 \text{ per hour} \\
&= \$2{,}100 \text{ F}
\end{aligned}
$$

The $2,100 direct labor efficiency variance is *favorable* because installers actually worked 200 *fewer* hours than they should have to install ten pools (3,800 actual hours − 4,000 standard hours).

The manager in charge of installing the pools is responsible for the variance in the quantity of direct labor hours used—in this case, the 200 fewer hours used. Assuming that this manager is not also responsible for setting employees' pay rates (which is usually the responsibility of the human resources or personnel department), the manager in charge of installing the pools has little control over the actual price paid per labor hour. Thus, we multiply the 200 fewer direct labor hours by the *standard price* of $10.50 per direct labor hour to obtain the direct labor efficiency variance.

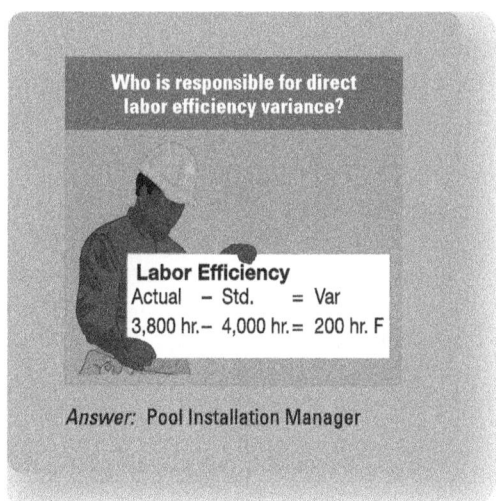

Answer: Pool Installation Manager

Summary of Direct Labor Variances

Exhibit 11-15 summarizes how Kool-Time splits the $200 favorable direct labor flexible budget variance into price and efficiency variances.

Had they looked only at the $200 favorable direct labor flexible budget variance, Kool-Time's managers might have thought direct labor costs were close to expectations. But this illustrates the danger in ending the analysis after computing only the flexible budget variance. "Peeling the onion" to examine the price and efficiency variances yields more insight:

- The unfavorable direct labor price variance means that Kool-Time's operating income is $1,900 lower than expected because the company paid its employees an average of $11.00 per hour in June instead of the standard rate of $10.50. But this unfavorable variance was more than offset by the favorable direct labor efficiency variance.

EXHIBIT 11-15   **Kool-Time Pools Direct Labor Variances**

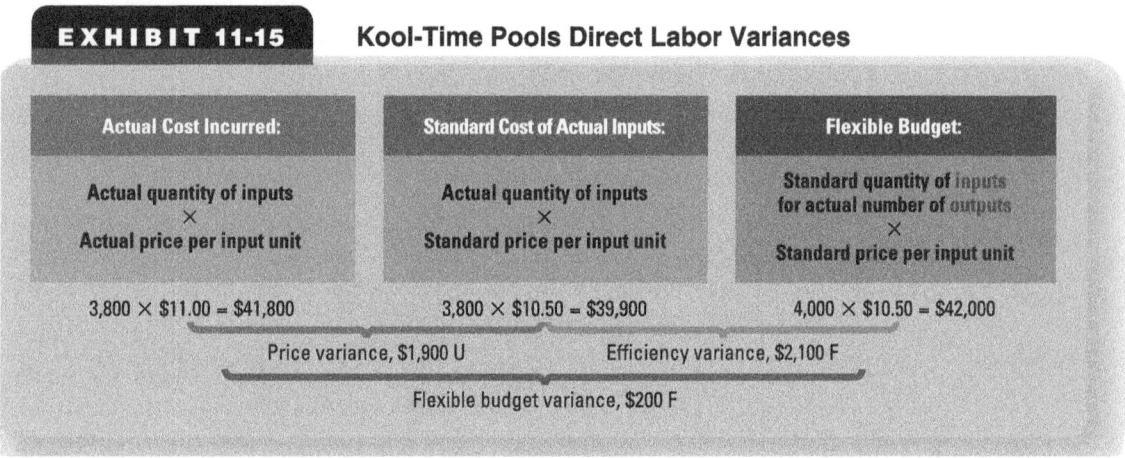

- The favorable direct labor efficiency variance means that Kool-Time's operating income is $2,100 higher than expected because workers installed ten pools in 3,800 hours instead of the budgeted 4,000 hours.

Kool-Time's top management will ask the human resources department to explain the unfavorable labor price variance, and it will ask the manager in charge of installing the pools to explain the favorable labor efficiency variance. Once again, there might have been a trade-off. Kool-Time might have hired more-experienced (and thus more highly paid) workers and traded off an unfavorable price variance for a favorable efficiency variance. If so, the strategy was successful—the overall effect on profits was favorable. This possibility reminds us that managers should be careful in using variances to evaluate performance.

You have now seen how Kool-Time analyzes flexible budget variances for direct materials and direct labor. Variances for variable marketing and administrative expenses could be calculated the same way, but for simplicity, we limit our detailed analysis to the variances in the production element of the value chain. Before leaving this topic, we need to examine three common pitfalls in computing price and efficiency variances.

Price and Efficiency Variances: Three Common Pitfalls

Here are three common pitfalls to avoid in computing price and efficiency variances for direct materials and direct labor:

1. *Static budgets like column 5 of Exhibit 11-7 play no role in computing the flexible budget variance or in determining how it is split into the price and efficiency variances.* Exhibit 11-12 shows that the static budget is used *only* in computing the sales volume variance—never in computing the flexible budget variance or its component price and efficiency variances.

2. In the efficiency variance, the standard quantity is the *standard quantity of inputs allowed for the actual number of outputs*—the basis for the flexible budget. To compute the standard quantity of inputs allowed, determine the actual number of outputs. For Kool-Time, the actual number of outputs is ten pools. Next, compute how many inputs should have been used to produce the actual number of outputs (ten pools). For example, each pool should use 400 direct labor hours, so the standard quantity of direct labor hours allowed for ten pools is 10 × 400 hours = 4,000 hours.

    Notice that the standard quantity of inputs is *not* based on the budgeted number of outputs (eight pools). That number is the basis for the static budget, which is not used to compute price and efficiency variances.

3. In the direct materials price variance, the difference in prices is multiplied by the *actual quantity* of materials. In the direct materials efficiency variance, the difference in quantities is multiplied by the *standard price* of the materials. The following explanation can help you remember this difference:

    - The materials price variance is usually the responsibility of purchasing personnel; they purchase the actual quantity used, not just the amount of materials that should have been used (the standard quantity). So, the price variance is the difference in prices multiplied by the *actual quantity* of materials purchased.

    - The materials efficiency variance is usually the responsibility of production personnel; they have no influence over the actual price paid. So, the efficiency variance is computed as the difference in quantities multiplied by the *standard* price (the price that should have been paid).

Similar logic applies to the direct labor price and efficiency variances.

Using Variances

Let's look at some practical tips for using variances.

How Often to Compute Variances?

Many firms monitor sales volume, direct materials efficiency, and direct labor efficiency variances day to day or even hour to hour. McDonald's restaurants compute variances for sales and direct labor each hour. Material efficiencies are computed for each shift. The Brass Products Division of Parker Hannifin computes efficiency variances for each job the day after workers finish the job. This allows managers to ask questions about any large variances while the job is still fresh in workers' minds.

Technology such as bar coding of materials and even labor and computerized data entry allows McDonald's and Parker Hannifin to compute efficiency variances quickly. In contrast to efficiency variances, monthly computations of material and labor price variances may be sufficient if long-term contracts with suppliers or labor unions make large price variances unlikely.

Using Variances to Evaluate Employees' Performance

Good managers use variances as a way to raise questions, not as simple indicators of whether employees performed well or poorly. Why should you take care in using variances to evaluate performance?

- Some variances are caused by factors that managers cannot control. For example, perhaps Kool-Time used more gunite than budgeted because workers had to repair cracked foundations resulting from an earthquake.

- Sometimes, variances are the result of inaccurate or outdated standards. Management must take care to review and update standards on a regular basis. If the production process changes or if supply prices change, the standards will need to be updated to reflect current operating conditions.

- Managers often make trade-offs among variances. Chrysler intentionally accepted a large order for customized Dodge vans because it expected the favorable sales volume variance to more than offset the unfavorable direct labor price variance from the overtime premium and the unfavorable sales revenue price variance from extra rebates offered to the customer. Similarly, managers often trade off price variances against efficiency variances. Purchasing personnel may decide to buy higher-quality (but more expensive) direct materials to reduce waste and spoilage. The unfavorable price variance may be more than offset by a favorable efficiency variance.

- Evaluations based primarily on one variance can encourage managers to take actions that make the variance look good but hurt the company in the long run. For example, Kool-Time's managers could:

  - Purchase low-quality gunite or hire less-experienced labor to get favorable price variances.

  - Use less gunite or less labor (resulting in lower-quality installed pools) to get favorable efficiency variances.

How can upper management discourage such actions? One approach is to base performance evaluation on *nonfinancial* measures as well, such as quality indicators (for example, variances in the grade of gunite or labor used) or customer satisfaction measures. For instance, McDonald's discourages skimping on labor by evaluating nonfinancial measures, such as the difference between actual and standard time to serve drive-through customers. If the McDonald's shift manager does not have enough workers, drive-through customers may have to wait to get their french fries. They may take their business to Wendy's or Burger King.

Stop & Think...

Why might an auto assembly plant experience a favorable direct labor efficiency variance? Should managers investigate favorable as well as unfavorable efficiency variances? Why or why not?

Answer:

1. The plant may have redesigned the manufacturing process to avoid wasted motion. For example, a Dodge van plant in Canada significantly reduced direct labor by reorganizing production so employees reach for raw materials as needed rather than carry armloads of materials across the plant floor.
2. Employees may have worked harder or more intensely than budgeted.
3. Employees may have rushed through the work and skimped on quality.

There are two reasons why managers should investigate favorable efficiency variances. First, managers want to maximize improvements that increase profits. For example, can managers capitalize on 1 and 2 to further improve labor efficiency at this or other plants? Second, managers want to prevent employees from achieving favorable variances at the expense of long-run profits through strategies like 3.

Using Standard Costs to Analyze Manufacturing Overhead Variances

5 Compute manufacturing overhead variances

In the last section, we looked at how managers analyze direct materials and direct labor variances. In this section, we look at manufacturing overhead variances. A company's total manufacturing overhead variance *is the difference between the actual overhead incurred and the standard overhead allocated to production.* In other words, this is the amount by which manufacturing overhead has been overallocated or underallocated to production. The total manufacturing overhead variance can be broken into two components: (1) overhead flexible budget variance and (2) production volume variance.

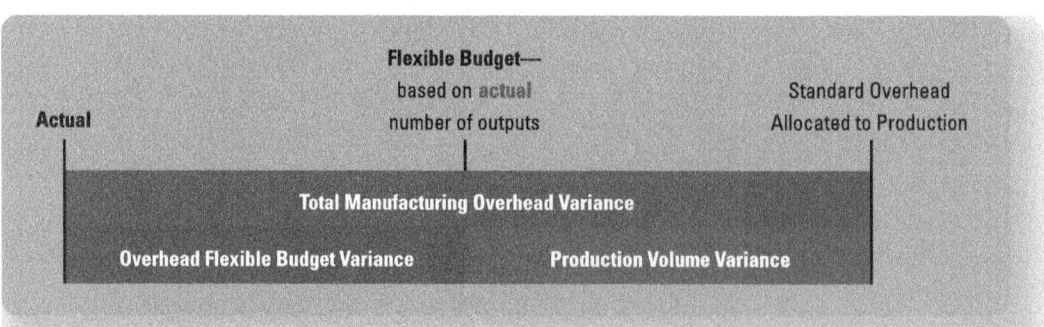

Overhead Flexible Budget Variance

The **overhead flexible budget variance** shows how well management has controlled overhead costs. Therefore, this variance is often referred to as the overhead controllable variance. It is computed *the same way* as the flexible budget variances for direct materials and direct labor. It is the *difference between actual overhead costs and the flexible budget overhead for the actual number of outputs (ten pools).*

The following information about Kool-Time's overhead is taken directly from Exhibit 11-10.

	(1)	(2)	(1) – (2)
	Actual Results	Flexible Budget for 10 Pools	Flexible Budget Variance
Variable overhead ($800 per pool)	$ 9,000	$ 8,000	$1,000 U
Fixed overhead	12,300	12,000	300 U
Total overhead	$21,300	$20,000	$1,300 U

Before continuing, let's quickly review how we arrived at the flexible budget numbers shown above.

The amount of *variable* overhead budgeted for the actual output is calculated as follows:

(400 direct labor hours allowed per pool × $2.00 per direct labor hour variable overhead rate) × 10 pools = $8,000

Since ten pools falls within the relevant range of 0 to 11 pools, *fixed* production overhead for the month is budgeted at $12,000. Therefore, the total flexible budget for overhead is $20,000. Actual overhead for the month is $21,300. Therefore, Kool-Time's calculates the overhead flexible budget variance as follows:

Overhead flexible budget variance = Actual overhead – Flexible budget overhead for actual output

= $21,300 – $20,000

= $1,300 U

Why did Kool-Time spend $1,300 more on overhead items than it should have to install the ten pools in June? You can see that $1,000 ($9,000 − $8,000) of the variance is due to higher-than-expected spending on variable overhead items and that the remaining $300 ($12,300 − $12,000) is due to higher spending on fixed overhead items. Kool-Time will investigate the reason for each of these variances.

Most companies compile actual and budget cost information for the individual component items that make up overhead, such as indirect materials, indirect labor, utilities, and depreciation on plant and equipment. Managers "drill down" by comparing actual costs to budgeted costs for each of these items. For example, Kool-Time's drill-down analysis might reveal that variable overhead costs were higher than expected because the price of gasoline for the earth moving equipment increased. Perhaps spending on fixed overhead increased because Kool-Time's monthly lease on its earth moving equipment expired and it had to negotiate a new lease. Advanced books on cost accounting explain this drill-down variance analysis in more detail.

Production Volume Variance

The second component of the total manufacturing overhead variance is the **production volume variance**. *The production volume variance is the difference between the flexible budget overhead and the standard overhead allocated to production.* As the name suggests, this variance arises when actual production volume differs from expected production volume. The production volume variance arises because companies treat fixed overhead as if it were variable in order to allocate it.

Recall from our discussion on standard costs that Kool-Time allocates overhead at a rate of $5.75 per direct labor hour. The total standard overhead rate consists of $2.00 per direct labor hour for variable overhead and $3.75 per direct labor hour for fixed overhead. Kool-Time computed these standard overhead rates based on the assumption that they would sell eight pools. Because Kool-Time actually installed ten pools, the amount of standard overhead *allocated* to production was:

Standard overhead rate per direct labor hour...............................	$ 5.75
Standard direct labor hours (400 DL hours per pool × 10 pools)	× 4,000
Standard overhead allocated to production....................................	$23,000

Notice that when companies use standard costing, they allocate manufacturing overhead to the units produced using the standard overhead rate multiplied by the *standard quantity of the allocation base allowed* (400 DL hours per pool × 10 pools), *not by the actual quantity* of the allocation base used (3,800 hours for the ten pools). The production volume variance is calculated as follows:

Production volume variance = Flexible budget overhead for actual output − Standard overhead allocated to production

= $20,000 − $23,000

= $3,000 F

The production volume variance is favorable whenever actual output (ten pools for Kool-Time) exceeds expected output (eight pools). By installing ten pools instead of eight, Kool-Time used its production capacity more fully than originally planned. In other words, it used its capacity more efficiently, resulting in a favorable variance. If Kool-Time had installed seven or fewer pools, the production volume variance would have been unfavorable because the company would have used less production capacity than expected.

The production volume variance is due only to *fixed* overhead. Why? Because the amount of *variable* overhead in the flexible budget ($8,000) is the *same* as the variable overhead allocated to production ($8,000 = 10 pools × 400 DL hours/pool × $2/DL hour). *In essence, the production volume variance arises because companies treat fixed overhead ($12,000) as if it were variable ($3.75 per DL hour) to allocate it.* The $3,000 favorable production volume variance arises because Kool-Time budgeted fixed overhead of $12,000 (Exhibit 11-10) but allocated $15,000 of fixed overhead to the ten pools it installed (10 pools × 400 DL hours/pool × $3.75 *fixed* overhead per DL hour).

Another way to see this is by examining the hours used to determine the overhead allocation rate versus the hours used to actually allocate overhead. Since the variance is due *strictly* to the fixed overhead, we multiply the difference in hours by the fixed overhead rate:

Total hours used to determine allocation rate (*8 pools* × 400 direct labor hours)	= 3,200
Total hours used to allocate overhead (*10 pools* × 400 direct labor hours)	= 4,000
Difference in hours (additional hours of overhead allocated)	800
Fixed overhead rate per hour	× $3.75
Production volume variance	$3,000

As you can see, the production volume variance is due to the fact that Kool-Time allocated more fixed overhead than it had budgeted.

Overview of Kool-Time's Manufacturing Overhead Variances

Kool-Time's overhead variances are summarized as follows:

Total overhead variance:	
Actual overhead cost ($9,000 variable + $12,300 fixed)	$21,300
Standard overhead allocated to production (10 pools × 400 standard direct labor hours per pool × $5.75)	23,000
Total overhead variance	$ 1,700 F
Overhead flexible budget variance:	
Actual overhead cost (from above)	$21,300
Flexible budget overhead for actual outputs ($8,000 variable + $12,000 fixed)	20,000
Overhead flexible budget variance	$ 1,300 U
Production volume variance:	
Flexible budget overhead for actual outputs (from above)	$20,000
Standard overhead allocated to production (from above)	23,000
Production volume variance	$ 3,000 F

As we have just seen, many companies use standard costs independent of the general ledger accounting system to develop flexible budgets and evaluate performance through variance analysis. Once managers know the causes of the variances, they can use that information to improve operations.

Other companies integrate standards directly into their general ledger accounting. This method of accounting, called standard costing, is discussed in the Appendix to this chapter.

Decision Guidelines

STANDARD COSTS AND VARIANCE ANALYSIS

You've seen how managers use standard costs and variances in actual and budgeted costs to identify potential problems. Variances help managers see *why* actual costs differ from the budget. This is the first step in determining how to correct problems.

Let's review how Kool-Time made some of the key decisions in setting up and using its standard cost system.

Decision	Guidelines
How does Kool-Time set standards?	Historical performance data
	Engineering analysis/time-and-motion studies

How does Kool-Time compute a price variance for materials or labor?	$\text{Price variance} = \left(\begin{array}{c} \text{Actual price} \\ \text{per input unit} \end{array} - \begin{array}{c} \text{Standard price} \\ \text{per input unit} \end{array} \right) \times \begin{array}{c} \text{Actual} \\ \text{quantity of} \\ \text{input} \end{array}$

How does Kool-Time compute an efficiency variance for materials or labor?	$\text{Efficiency variance} = \left(\begin{array}{c} \text{Actual} \\ \text{quantity of} \\ \text{input} \end{array} - \begin{array}{c} \text{Standard quantity} \\ \text{of input for actual} \\ \text{number of outputs} \end{array} \right) \times \begin{array}{c} \text{Standard} \\ \text{price per} \\ \text{input unit} \end{array}$

Who is most likely responsible for:	
Sales volume variance?	Marketing department
Sales revenue flexible budget variance?	Marketing department
Direct materials price variance?	Purchasing department
Direct materials efficiency variance?	Production department
Direct labor price variance?	Human resources or personnel department
Direct labor efficiency variance?	Production department

How does Kool-Time allocate manufacturing overhead in a standard costing system?	$\begin{array}{c} \text{Manufacturing} \\ \text{overhead} \\ \text{allocated} \end{array} = \left(\begin{array}{c} \text{Standard} \\ \text{predetermined} \\ \text{manufacturing} \\ \text{overhead rate} \end{array} \right) \times \left(\begin{array}{c} \text{Standard quantity of} \\ \text{allocation base allowed} \\ \text{for actual outputs} \end{array} \right)$

How does Kool-Time analyze overallocated or underallocated manufacturing overhead?	Split overallocated or underallocated overhead as follows:
	$\text{Flexible budget variance} = \begin{array}{c} \text{Actual} \\ \text{overhead} \end{array} - \begin{array}{c} \text{Flexible budget} \\ \text{overhead} \\ \text{for actual outputs} \end{array}$
	$\begin{array}{c} \text{Production volume} \\ \text{variance} \end{array} = \begin{array}{c} \text{Flexible budget} \\ \text{overhead} \\ \text{for actual outputs} \end{array} - \begin{array}{c} \text{Standard overhead} \\ \text{allocated to} \\ \text{actual outputs} \end{array}$

Summary Problem 2

Exhibit 11-10 indicates that Kool-Time installed ten swimming pools in June. Suppose Kool-Time had installed seven pools instead of ten and that actual expenses were:

Direct materials (gunite)............................	7,400 cubic feet @ $2 per cubic foot
Direct labor...	2,740 hours @ $10 per hour
Variable overhead	$5,400
Fixed overhead..	$11,900

Requirements

1. Given these new data, prepare an exhibit similar to Exhibit 11-10. Ignore marketing and administrative expenses.

2. Compute price and efficiency variances for direct materials and direct labor.

3. Compute the total overhead variance, the overhead flexible budget variance, and the production volume variance. Prepare a summary similar to the one on page 627.

Solution

Requirement 1

KOOL-TIME POOLS
Revised Data for Standard Costing Example
Month of June 2007

PANEL A—Comparison of Actual Results with Flexible Budget for 7 Swimming Pools

	Actual Results at Actual Prices	Flexible Budget for 7 Pools	Flexible Budget Variance
Variable expenses:			
Direct materials	$14,800*	$14,000‡	$ 800 U
Direct labor	27,400*	29,400†	2,000 F
Variable overhead	5,400	5,600†	200 F
Total variable expenses	47,600	49,000	1,400 F
Fixed expenses:			
Fixed overhead	11,900	12,000‡	100 F
Total expenses	$59,500	$61,000	$1,500 F

*See Panel C.
†See Panel B.
‡Fixed overhead was budgeted at $12,000 per month.

PANEL B—Computation of Flexible Budget for Direct Materials, Direct Labor, and Variable Overhead for 7 Swimming Pools

	(1) Standard Quantity of Inputs Allowed for 7 Pools	(2) Standard Price per Unit of Input	(1) × (2) Flexible Budget for 7 Pools
Direct materials	1,000 cubic feet per pool × 7 pools = 7,000 cubic feet	× $2.00	= $14,000
Direct labor	400 hours per pool × 7 pools = 2,800 hours	× 10.50	= 29,400
Variable overhead	400 hours per pool × 7 pools = 2,800 hours	× 2.00	= 5,600

PANEL C—Computation of Actual Costs for Direct Materials and Direct Labor for 7 Swimming Pools

	(1) Actual Quantity of Inputs Used for 7 Pools	(2) Actual Price per Unit of Input	(1) × (2) Actual Cost for 7 Pools
Direct materials	7,400 cubic feet actually used ×	$2.00 actual cost/cubic foot	$14,800
Direct labor	2,740 hours actually used ×	$10.00 actual cost/hour	27,400

Requirement 2

$$\text{Price variance} = \left(\begin{array}{c}\text{Actual price} \\ \text{per input unit}\end{array} - \begin{array}{c}\text{Standard price} \\ \text{per input unit}\end{array}\right) \times \begin{array}{c}\text{Actual} \\ \text{quantity of} \\ \text{input}\end{array}$$

Direct materials:

$$\text{Price variance} = (\$2.00 - \$2.00) \times 7{,}400 \text{ cubic feet} = \$0$$

Direct labor:

$$\text{Price variance} = (\$10.00 - \$10.50) \times 2{,}740 \text{ hours} = \$1{,}370 \text{ F}$$

$$\text{Efficiency variance} = \left(\begin{array}{c}\text{Actual} \\ \text{quantity} \\ \text{of input}\end{array} - \begin{array}{c}\text{Standard} \\ \text{quantity of} \\ \text{input}\end{array}\right) \times \begin{array}{c}\text{Standard} \\ \text{price per} \\ \text{input unit}\end{array}$$

Direct materials:

$$\text{Efficiency variance} = \left(\begin{array}{c}7{,}400 \\ \text{cubic feet}\end{array} - \begin{array}{c}7{,}000 \\ \text{cubic feet}\end{array}\right) \times \begin{array}{c}\$2.00 \text{ per} \\ \text{cubic foot}\end{array} = \$800 \text{ U}$$

Direct labor:

$$\text{Efficiency variance} = \left(\begin{array}{c}2{,}740 \\ \text{hours}\end{array} - \begin{array}{c}2{,}800 \\ \text{hours}\end{array}\right) \times \begin{array}{c}\$10.50 \text{ per} \\ \text{hours}\end{array} = \$630 \text{ F}$$

Requirement 3

Total overhead variance:	
Actual overhead cost ($5,400 variable + $11,900 fixed)...............	$17,300
Standard overhead allocated to production (2,800 standard direct labor hours × $5.75)	16,100
Total overhead variance...	$ 1,200 U
Overhead flexible budget variance:	
Actual overhead cost ($5,400 + $11,900)	$17,300
Flexible budget overhead for actual outputs ($5,600 + $12,000)	17,600
Overhead flexible budget variance	$ 300 F
Production volume variance:	
Flexible budget overhead for actual outputs ($5,600 + $12,000)	$17,600
Standard overhead allocated to (actual) production (2,800 standard direct labor hours × $5.75)	16,100
Production volume variance...	$ 1,500 U

Review *Flexible Budgets and Standard Costs*

■ Accounting Vocabulary

Efficiency Variance. (p. 617)
Measures whether the quantity of materials or labor used to make the actual number of outputs is within the standard allowed for that number of outputs.

Flexible Budget. (p. 597)
A summarized budget prepared for different levels of volume.

Flexible Budget Variance. (p. 602)
The difference arising because the company actually earned more or less revenue or incurred more or less cost than expected for the actual level of output.

Overhead Flexible Budget Variance. (p. 624)
The difference between the actual overhead cost and the flexible budget overhead for the actual number of outputs.

Price Variance. (p. 616)
The difference in prices (actual price per unit minus standard price per unit) of an input multiplied by the actual quantity of the input.

Production Volume Variance. (p. 625)
The difference between the manufacturing overhead cost in the flexible budget for actual outputs and the standard overhead allocated to production.

Sales Volume Variance. (p. 602)
The difference between a static budget amount and a flexible budget amount arising only because the number of units actually sold differs from the static budget units.

Standard Cost. (p. 609)
A budget for a single unit.

Static Budget. (p. 597)
The budget prepared for only one level of sales volume. Also called the master budget.

Variance. (p. 597)
The difference between an actual amount and the budget.

■ Quick Check

Use the following data for Questions 1 through 4. Digital Systems is a start-up company that makes connectors for high-speed Internet connections. The company has budgeted variable costs of $130 for each connector and fixed costs of $8,000 per month.

Digital's static budget predicted production and sales of 100 connectors in January, but the company actually produced and sold only 75 connectors at a total cost of $23,000.

1. Digital Systems' total flexible budget cost for 75 connectors per month is
   a. $17,750
   b. $9,750
   c. $13,000
   d. $8,130

2. Digital Systems' sales volume variance for total costs is
   a. $3,250 F
   b. $5,250 F
   c. $3,250 U
   d. $5,250 U

3. Digital Systems' flexible budget variance for total costs is
   a. $3,250 F
   b. $5,250 F
   c. $3,250 U
   d. $5,250 U

4. Digital Systems' managers could set direct labor standards based on
   a. past actual performance
   b. continuous improvement
   c. benchmarking
   d. time-and-motion studies
   e. any of the above

Use the following data for Questions 5 through 7. Digital Systems has budgeted three hours of direct labor per connector at a standard cost of $15 per hour. During January, technicians actually worked 210 hours completing the 75 connectors. Digital Systems paid the technicians $15.50 per hour.

5. What is Digital Systems' direct labor price variance for January?
   a. $37.50 U
   b. $105.00 U
   c. $112.50 U
   d. $120.00 U

6. What is Digital Systems' direct labor efficiency variance for January?
   a. $75.00 F
   b. $225.00 F
   c. $232.50 F
   d. $1,350.00 F

7. (Appendix) The journal entry to record Digital Systems' *assignment* of direct labor to jobs is
   a. Manufacturing Wages
          Direct Labor Price Variance
          Work in Process Inventory
   b. Manufacturing Wages
          Direct Labor Efficiency Variance
          Work in Process Inventory
   c. Work in Process Inventory
          Direct Labor Price Variance
          Manufacturing Wages
   d. Work in Process Inventory
          Direct Labor Efficiency Variance
          Manufacturing Wages

8. Digital Systems allocates manufacturing overhead based on machine hours. Each connector should require ten machine hours. According to the static budget, Digital Systems is expected to incur:

> 1,000 machine hours per month (100 connectors × 10 machine hours per connector)
>
> $5,250 in variable manufacturing overhead costs
>
> $8,000 in fixed manufacturing overhead costs

During January, Digital Systems actually used 825 machine hours to make the 75 connectors. Digital Systems' predetermined standard total manufacturing overhead rate is

a. $5.25 per machine hour

b. $8.00 per machine hour

c. $13.25 per machine hour

d. $16.06 per machine hour

9. The total manufacturing overhead variance is composed of

a. price variance and efficiency variance

b. price variance and production volume variance

c. efficiency variance and production volume variance

d. flexible budget variance and production volume variance

10. (Appendix) When Digital Systems *uses* direct materials, the amount of the debit to Work in Process Inventory is based on

a. actual quantity of the materials used × actual price per unit of the materials

b. standard quantity of the materials allowed for the actual production of 75 connectors × actual price per unit of the materials

c. standard quantity of the materials allowed for the actual production of 75 connectors × standard price per unit of the materials

d. actual quantity of the materials used × standard price per unit of the materials

Quick Check Answers

1. *a* 2. *a* 3. *d* 4. *e* 5. *b* 6. *b* 7. *d* 8. *c* 9. *d* 10. *c*

For Internet Exercises, Excel in Practice, and additional online activities, go to this book's Web site at www.prenhall.com/bamber.

Assess Your Progress

▪ Learning Objectives

1 Prepare a flexible budget for planning purposes

2 Use the sales volume variance and flexible budget variance to explain why actual results differ from the master budget

3 Identify the benefits of standard costs and learn how to set standards

4 Compute standard cost variances for direct materials and direct labor

5 Compute manufacturing overhead variances

6 (Appendix) Record transactions at standard cost and prepare a standard cost income statement

▪ Short Exercises

S11-1 **Prepare a flexible budget** *(Learning Objective 1)*
Turn to Kool-Time's flexible budget in Exhibit 11-3.

Requirements
1. Using the data from Exhibit 11-3, develop flexible budgets for four- and nine-pool levels of output.
2. Would Kool-Time's managers use the flexible budgets you developed in Requirement 1 for planning or for controlling? What specific insights can Kool-Time's managers gain from the flexible budgets you prepared in Requirement 1?

S11-2 **Interpret a flexible budget graph** *(Learning Objective 1)*
Look at Kool-Time's graph of actual and budgeted monthly costs in Exhibit 11-5.
1. How many pools did Kool-Time install in May?
2. How much were Kool-Time's actual expenses in May?
3. Using Kool-Time's flexible budget formula, what is the flexible budget total cost for May?
4. What is Kool-Time's flexible budget variance for total costs? Is the variance favorable or unfavorable in May?

S11-3 **Interpret a performance report** *(Learning Objective 2)*
The following is a partially completed performance report for Surf-Side Pools, one of Kool-Time's competitors:

	Actual Results at Actual Prices	Flexible Budget Variance	Flexible Budget for Actual Number of Output Units	Sales Volume Variance	Static (Master) Budget
SURF-SIDE POOLS Income Statement Performance Report Year Ended April 30					
Output units (pools installed)	6	?	?	?	5
Sales revenue	$102,000	?	$108,000	?	$90,000
Variable expenses	57,000	?	60,000	?	50,000
Fixed expenses	21,000	?	25,000	?	25,000
Total expenses	78,000	?	85,000	?	75,000
Operating income	$ 24,000	?	$ 23,000	?	$15,000

Requirements

1. How many pools did Surf-Side originally think it would install in April?
2. How many pools did Surf-Side actually install in April?
3. How many pools is the flexible budget based on? Why?
4. What was the budgeted sales price per pool?
5. What was the budgeted variable cost per pool?
6. Define the sales volume variance. What causes it?
7. Define the flexible budget variance. What causes it?

S11-4 **Complete a performance report** *(Learning Objective 2)*
Complete the performance report shown in S11-3 by filling in all missing values. Be sure to label each variance as favorable (F) or unfavorable (U). Then, answer the following questions:

1. What was the *total* static budget variance?
2. What was the *total* sales volume variance.
3. What was the *total* flexible budget variance?
4. Show that the total sales volume variance and total flexible budget variance sum to the total static budget variance.
5. Interpret the variances and then give one plausible explanation for the variances shown in this performance report.

S11-5 **Interpret the sales volume variance** *(Learning Objective 2)*
Recall that Kool-Time's relevant range is 0 to 11 pools per month.
Explain whether Kool-Time would have a sales volume variance for fixed expenses in Exhibit 11-7 if:
   a. Kool-Time installs 14 pools per month.
   b. Kool-Time installs 7 pools per month.

S11-6 **Understand key terms** *(Learning Objectives 1, 2)*
Fill in the blank with the phrase that best completes the sentence.

Actual number of outputs	Beginning of the period	Static budget variance
Expected number of outputs	End of the period	
Sales volume variance	Flexible budget variance	

    a. The static budget is developed at the _____.

    b. The flexible budget used in an income statement performance report is based on the _____.

    c. The master budget is based on the _____.

    d. The flexible budget used in an income statement performance report is developed at the _____.

    e. The difference between actual costs and the costs that should have been incurred for the actual number of outputs is the _____.

S11-7 **Explain the benefits of standard costs** *(Learning Objective 3)*
Lladró is a Spanish manufacturer of porcelain art objects. Raw materials are mixed to form clay, which is shaped into figurines. The pieces are then glazed and fired at high temperatures.

    Explain how the five benefits of standard costs (Exhibit 11-9) apply to Lladró. Be as specific as possible.

McDonald's Data Set: Used for S11-8 through S11-12

As explained in the chapter opening story, the standard direct materials for a regular McDonald's hamburger are:

1 bun	1 pickle slice	1/4 teaspoon of mustard
1 hamburger patty	1/8 teaspoon of onion	1/2 ounce of ketchup

Assume that the company has set the following standard materials prices:

Buns..................................	$0.10 each	Onion................	$0.08 per teaspoon
Hamburger patties	$0.20 each	Mustard	$0.04 per teaspoon
Pickle slices	$0.03 per slice	Ketchup............	$0.10 per ounce

In addition to the direct materials standards, the company sets standards for direct labor. The standard labor wage rate is $6 per hour. Since the griddles are so large, the restaurants cook the hamburgers in batches of 20. The standard time allotted to cook, apply condiments, and wrap each batch of 20 hamburgers is 4 minutes.

Assume that a San Diego, California, McDonald's sold 5,000 hamburgers yesterday and actually used the following materials:

5,150 buns	4,800 pickle slices	1,400 teaspoons of mustard
5,100 hamburger patties	800 teaspoons of onion	2,750 ounces of ketchup

S11-8 **Compute standard cost of direct materials** *(Learning Objective 3)*
Refer to the McDonald's Data Set on page 643. Compute the standard direct materials cost per hamburger.

S11-9 **Compute standard cost of direct labor** *(Learning Objective 3)*
Refer to the McDonald's Data Set on page 643. Compute the standard direct labor cost per hamburger. (*Hint:* Find the quantity and price standards in minutes.)

S11-10 **Compute direct materials efficiency variances** *(Learning Objective 4)*
Refer to the McDonald's Data Set on page 643.

1. Compute the direct materials efficiency variance for buns, hamburger patties, and pickle slices.

2. As a manager, what would you learn from the variances and supporting data?

S11-11 **Compute more direct materials efficiency variances** *(Learning Objective 4)*
Refer to the McDonald's Data Set on page 643.

1. Compute the direct materials efficiency variance for onion, mustard, and ketchup.

2. As a manager, what would you learn from the variances and supporting data?

S11-12 **Compute direct materials price variances** *(Learning Objective 4)*
Refer to the McDonald's Data Set on page 643.
Actual prices paid for ingredients purchased during the week were:

Buns...............................	$0.12 each	Onion.............................	$0.07 per teaspoon
Hamburger patties	$0.25 each	Mustard	$0.01 per teaspoon
Pickle slices	$0.02 per slice	Ketchup.........................	$0.12 per ounce

1. Compute the direct materials price variance for each ingredient.

2. As a manager, what would you learn from the variances and supporting data?

S11-13 **Compute standard overhead allocation rates** *(Learning Objective 3)*
McDonald's supplies its restaurants with many premanufactured ingredients (such as bags of frozen french fries), while other ingredients (such as lettuce and tomatoes) are obtained from local suppliers. Assume that the manufacturing plant processing the fries anticipated incurring a total of $3,080,000 of manufacturing overhead during the year. Of this amount, $1,320,000 is fixed. Manufacturing overhead is allocated based on machine hours. The plant anticipates running the machines 220,000 hours next year.

1. Compute the standard *variable* overhead rate.

2. Compute the *fixed* overhead rate.

3. Compute the standard *total* overhead rate.

S11-14 **Compute manufacturing overhead variances** *(Learning Objective 5)*
Assume that the McDonald's french fries manufacturing facility actually incurred $2,975,000 of manufacturing overhead for the year. Based on the actual output of french fries, the flexible budget indicated that total manufacturing overhead should have been $3,000,000. Using a standard costing system, the company allocated $2,940,000 of manufacturing overhead to production.

1. Calculate the total manufacturing overhead variance. What does this tell managers?
2. Determine the overhead flexible budget variance. What does this tell managers?
3. Determine the production volume variance. What does this tell managers?
4. Double-check: Do the two variances (computed in Requirements 2 and 3) sum to the total overhead variance computed in Requirement 1?

S11-15 **Compute manufacturing overhead variances** *(Learning Objective 5)*
Rovnovsky Industries produces high-end flutes for professional musicians across the globe. Actual manufacturing overhead for the year was $1,240,000. The flexible budget indicated that fixed overhead should have been $800,000 and variable overhead should have been $400,000 for the number of flutes actually produced. Using a standard costing system, the company allocated $1,300,000 of overhead to production.

1. Calculate the total overhead variance. What does this tell managers?
2. Determine the overhead flexible budget variance. What does this tell managers?
3. Determine the production volume variance. What does this tell managers?

S11-16 **(Appendix) Record direct materials purchase and use** *(Learning Objective 6)*
During the week, McDonald's french fry manufacturing facility purchased 10,000 pounds of potatoes at a price of $1.10 per pound. The standard price per pound is $1.05. During the week, 9,760 pounds of potatoes were used. The standard quantity of potatoes that should have been used for the actual volume of output was 9,700 pounds. Record the following transactions using a standard cost accounting system:

1. The purchase of potatoes
2. The use of potatoes

Are the variances favorable, or unfavorable? Explain.

S11-17 **(Appendix) Record direct labor purchase and use** *(Learning Objective 6)*
During the week, McDonald's french fry manufacturing facility incurred 2,000 hours of direct labor. Direct laborers were paid $12.25 per hour. The standard hourly labor rate is $12. Standards indicate that for the volume of output actually achieved, the factory should have used 2,100 hours. Record the following transactions using a standard cost accounting system:

1. The accumulation of labor costs
2. The assignment of direct labor to production

Are the variances favorable, or unfavorable? Explain.

▪ Exercises

E11-18 **Prepare flexible budgets for planning** *(Learning Objective 1)*
Logiclik sells its main product, ergonomic mouse pads, for $11 each. Its variable cost is $5 per pad. Fixed expenses are $200,000 per month for volumes up to 60,000 pads. Above 60,000 pads, monthly fixed expenses are $250,000.

Prepare a monthly flexible budget for the product, showing sales, variable expenses, fixed expenses, and operating income or loss for volume levels of 40,000, 50,000, and 70,000 pads.

E11-19　Graph flexible budget costs *(Learning Objective 1)*

Graph the flexible budget total cost line for Logiclik in Exercise 11-18. Show total costs for volume levels of 40,000, 50,000, and 70,000 pads.

E11-20　Complete and interpret a performance report *(Learning Objective 2)*

Joe Boxer Company's managers received the following incomplete performance report:

JOE BOXER COMPANY
Income Statement Performance Report
Year Ended July 31, 2007

	Actual Results at Actual Prices	Flexible Budget Variance	Flexible Budget for Actual Number of Output Units	Sales Volume Variance	Static (Master) Budget
Output units	36,000	?	36,000	4,000 F	?
Sales revenue	$216,000	?	$216,000	$24,000 F	?
Variable expenses	84,000	?	81,000	9,000 U	?
Fixed expenses	106,000	?	100,000	–0–	?
Total expenses	190,000	?	181,000	9,000 U	?
Operating income	$ 26,000	?	$ 35,000	$15,000 F	?

Complete the performance report. Identify the employee group that may deserve praise and the group that may be subject to criticism. Give your reasons.

E11-21　Prepare an income statement performance report *(Learning Objective 2)*

Kool-Times installed nine pools during May. Prepare an income statement performance report for Kool-Time for May, using Exhibit 11-7 as a guide. Assume that the actual sales price per pool is $12,000, actual variable expenses total $61,000, and actual fixed expenses are $19,000 in May. The master budget was prepared with the following assumptions: variable cost of $8,000 per pool; fixed expenses of $20,000 per month; anticipated sales volume of eight pools at $12,000 per pool.

Compute the sales volume variance and flexible budget variance. Use these variances to explain to Kool-Time's management why May's operating income differs from operating income shown in the static budget.

E11-22　Compute sales volume and flexible budget variances *(Learning Objective 2)*

Top managers of Manion Industries predicted 2008 sales of 145,000 units of its product at a unit price of $8. Actual sales for the year were 140,000 units at $9.50 each. Variable expenses were budgeted at $2.20 per unit, and actual variable expenses were $2.30 per unit. Actual fixed expenses of $420,000 exceeded budgeted fixed expenses by $20,000. Prepare Manion Industries' income statement performance report in a format similar to E11-20. What variance contributed most to the year's favorable results? What caused this variance?

E11-23　Work backward to find missing values *(Learning Objective 2)*

Hanco has a relative range extending to 30,000 units each month. The following performance report provides information about Hanco's budget and actual performance for April.

HANCO
Income Statement Performance Report
Month Ended April 30, 2007

	Actual Results at Actual Prices	(A)	Flexible Budget for Actual Number of Output Units	(B)	Static (Master) Budget
Output units	25,000		(C)		30,000
Sales revenue	$240,000	$ 5,000 (F)	(D)		
Variable cost			(E)		$187,000
Fixed cost	$ 15,000	(F)			$ 20,000
Operating income					(G)

Requirement
Find the missing data for letters A through F. Be sure to label any variances as favorable or unfavorable. (*Hint:* A and B are titles.)

E11-24 **Calculate standard costs** *(Learning Objective 3)*

Rachel's Bakery makes desserts for local restaurants. Each pan of gourmet brownies requires 2 cups flour, ½ cup chopped pecans, ¼ cup cocoa, 1 cup sugar, ½ cup chocolate chips, 2 eggs, and ⅓ cup oil. Each pan requires 10 minutes of direct labor for mixing, cutting, and packaging. Each pan must bake for 30 minutes. Restaurants purchase the gourmet brownies by the pan, not by the individual serving. Each pan is currently sold for $12. Standard costs are $1.92 per bag of flour (16 cups in a bag), $6.00 per bag of pecans (3 cups per bag), $2.40 per tin of cocoa (2 cups per tin), $2.40 per 5-pound bag of sugar (16 cups in a bag), $1.80 per bag of chocolate chips (2 cups per bag), $1.08 per dozen eggs, $1.26 per bottle of oil (6 cups per bottle), and $0.50 for packaging materials. The standard wage rate is $12 per hour. Rachel allocates bakery overhead at $7.00 per oven hour.

1. What is the standard cost per pan of gourmet brownies?
2. What is the standard gross profit per pan of gourmet brownies?
3. How often should Rachel reassess her standard quantities and standard prices for inputs?

E11-25 **Calculate materials and labor variances** *(Learning Objective 4)*

McDonald's manufactures the bags of frozen french fries used at its franchised restaurants. Last week, McDonald's purchased and used 100,000 pounds of potatoes at a price of $0.75 per pound. During the week, 2,000 direct labor hours were incurred in the plant at a rate of $12.25 per hour. The standard price per pound of potatoes is $0.85, and the standard direct labor rate is $12.00 per hour. Standards indicate that for the number of bags of frozen fries produced, the factory should have used 97,000 pounds of potatoes and 1,900 hours of direct labor.

Requirements
1. Determine the direct materials price and efficiency variances. Be sure to label each variance as favorable or unfavorable.
2. Think of a plausible explanation for the variances found in Requirement 1.
3. Determine the direct labor price and efficiency variances. Be sure to label each variance as favorable or unfavorable.
4. Could the explanation for the labor variances be tied to the material variances? Explain.

E11-26 **Compute direct materials variance** *(Learning Objective 4)*
The following direct materials variance computations are incomplete:

> Price variance = ($? − $10) × 9,600 pounds = $4,800
> Efficiency variance = (? − 10,400 pounds) × $10 = ? F
> Flexible budget variance = $?

Fill in the missing values and identify the flexible budget variance as favorable or unfavorable.

E11-27 **Calculate materials and labor variances** *(Learning Objective 4)*
Dock Guard, which uses a standard cost accounting system, manufactured 200,000 boat fenders during the year, using 1,450,000 feet of extruded vinyl purchased at $1.05 per foot. Production required 4,500 direct labor hours that cost $14 per hour. The materials standard was 7 feet of vinyl per fender at a standard cost of $1.10 per foot. The labor standard was 0.025 direct labor hour per fender at a standard cost of $13 per hour. Compute the price and efficiency variances for direct materials and direct labor. Does the pattern of variances suggest that Dock Guard's managers have been making trade-offs? Explain.

E11-28 **Compute standard manufacturing overhead rates** *(Learning Objective 3)*
Fresh-Cut processes bags of organic frozen vegetables sold at specialty grocery stores. Fresh-Cut allocates manufacturing overhead based on direct labor hours. Fresh-Cut has projected total overhead for the year to be $800,000. Of this amount, $600,000 relates to fixed overhead expenses. Fresh-Cut expects to process 160,000 cases of frozen organic vegetables this year. The direct labor standard for each case is one-quarter of an hour.

1. Compute the standard *variable* overhead rate.
2. Compute the *fixed* overhead rate.
3. Compute the standard *total* overhead rate.

E11-29 **Continuation of E11-28: compute overhead variances** *(Learning Objective 5)*
Fresh-Cut actually processed 180,000 cases of frozen organic vegetables during the year and incurred $840,000 of manufacturing overhead. Of this amount, $610,000 was fixed.

Requirements

1. What is the flexible budget (for the actual output) for variable overhead? for fixed overhead? for total overhead?
2. How much overhead would have been allocated to production?
3. Use your answer from Requirement 1 to determine the overhead flexible budget variance. What does this tell managers?
4. Use your answer from Requirements 1 and 2 to determine the production volume variance. What does this tell managers?
5. What is the total overhead variance?

E11-30 **Compute manufacturing overhead variances** *(Learning Objective 5)*

Deelux manufactures paint. The company charges the following standard unit costs to production on the basis of static budget volume of 30,000 gallons of paint per month:

Direct materials...	$2.50
Direct labor...	2.00
Manufacturing overhead..	1.50
Standard unit cost	$6.00

Deelux allocates overhead based on standard machine hours, and it uses the following monthly flexible budget for overhead:

	Number of Outputs (gallons)		
	27,000	30,000	33,000
Standard machine hours.......................	2,700	3,000	3,300
Budgeted manufacturing overhead cost:			
Variable	$13,500	$15,000	$16,500
Fixed...	30,000	30,000	30,000

Deelux actually produced 33,000 gallons of paint using 3,100 machine hours. Actual variable overhead was $16,200, and fixed overhead was $32,500. Compute the total overhead variance, the overhead flexible budget variance, and the production volume variance.

Watermate Data Set: Used for E11-31 through E11-36

Watermate is a manufacturer of ceramic bottles. The company has these standards:

Direct materials (clay)	1 pound per bottle, at a cost of $0.40 per pound
Direct labor..	1/5 hour per bottle, at a cost of $14 per hour
Static budget variable overhead....................	$70,000
Static budget fixed overhead	$30,000
Static budget direct labor hours....................	10,000 hours
Static budget number of bottles....................	50,000

Watermate allocates manufacturing overhead to production based on standard direct labor hours. Last month, Watermate reported the following actual results for the production of 70,000 bottles:

Direct materials...	1.1 pound per bottle, at a cost of $0.50 per pound
Direct labor..	1/4 hour per bottle, at a cost of $13 per hour
Actual variable overhead...............................	$104,000
Actual fixed overhead	$28,000

E11-31 Compute the standard cost of one unit *(Learning Objective 3)*
Refer to the Watermate Data Set on page 649.

1. Compute the standard predetermined variable manufacturing overhead rate, the standard predetermined fixed manufacturing overhead rate, and the total standard predetermined overhead rate.

2. Compute the standard cost of each of the following inputs: direct materials, direct labor, variable manufacturing overhead, and fixed manufacturing overhead.

3. Determine the standard cost of one ceramic bottle.

E11-32 Compute and interpret direct materials variances *(Learning Objective 4)*
Refer to the Watermate Data Set on page 649.

1. Compute the direct materials price variance and the direct materials efficiency variance.

2. What is the total flexible budget variance for direct materials?

3. Who is generally responsible for each variance?

4. Interpret the variances.

E11-33 Compute and interpret direct labor variances *(Learning Objective 4)*
Refer to the Watermate Data Set on page 649.

1. Compute the direct labor price variance and the direct labor efficiency variance.

2. What is the total flexible budget variance for direct labor?

3. Who is generally responsible for each variance?

4. Interpret the variances.

E11-34 Compute and interpret manufacturing overhead variances *(Learning Objective 5)*
Refer to the Watermate Data Set on page 649.

1. Compute the total manufacturing overhead variance. What does this tell management?

2. Compute the overhead flexible budget variance. What does this tell management?

3. Compute the production volume variance. What does this tell management?

E11-35 Record journal entries in a standard costing system *(Learning Objective 6)*
Refer to the Watermate Data Set on page 649. Use a standard cost accounting system to:

1. Record Watermate's direct materials and direct labor journal entries.

2. Record Watermate's journal entries for manufacturing overhead, including the entry that records the overhead variances and closes the Manufacturing Overhead account.

3. Record the journal entries for the completion and sale of the 70,000 bottles, assuming Watermate sold (on account) all of the 70,000 bottles at a sales price of $8 each (there were no beginning or ending inventories).

E11-36 **Prepare a standard cost income statement** *(Learning Objective 6)*

Refer to the Watermate Data Set on page 649. Prepare a standard cost income statement for Watermate's management, using Exhibit 11-17 as a guide. Assume that sales were $560,000 and actual marketing and administrative expenses were $76,500.

E11-37 **(Appendix) Record materials and labor transactions** *(Learning Objective 6)*

Make the journal entries to record the purchase and use of direct materials and direct labor made by Dock Guard in E11-27.

E11-38 **(Appendix) Interpret a standard cost income statement** *(Learning Objective 6)*

The managers of Viewx, a contract manufacturer of DVD drives, are seeking explanations for the variances in the following report. Explain the meaning of each of Viewx's materials, labor, and overhead variances.

<table>
<tr><td colspan="3" align="center">**VIEWX CO.**
Standard Cost Income Statement
Year Ended December 31, 2007</td></tr>
<tr><td>Sales revenue</td><td></td><td>$1,200,000</td></tr>
<tr><td>Cost of goods sold at standard cost</td><td></td><td>700,000</td></tr>
<tr><td>Manufacturing cost variances:</td><td></td><td></td></tr>
<tr><td>   Direct materials price variance</td><td>$ 8,000 F</td><td></td></tr>
<tr><td>   Direct materials efficiency variance</td><td>32,000 U</td><td></td></tr>
<tr><td>   Direct labor price variance</td><td>24,000 F</td><td></td></tr>
<tr><td>   Direct labor efficiency variance</td><td>10,000 U</td><td></td></tr>
<tr><td>   Manufacturing overhead flexible budget variance</td><td>28,000 U</td><td></td></tr>
<tr><td>   Production volume variance</td><td>8,000 F</td><td></td></tr>
<tr><td>   Total manufacturing variances</td><td></td><td>30,000</td></tr>
<tr><td>Cost of goods sold at actual cost</td><td></td><td>730,000</td></tr>
<tr><td>Gross profit</td><td></td><td>470,000</td></tr>
<tr><td>Marketing and administrative expenses</td><td></td><td>418,000</td></tr>
<tr><td>Operating income</td><td></td><td>$ 52,000</td></tr>
</table>

E11-39 **(Appendix) Prepare a standard cost income statement** *(Learning Objective 6)*

Western Outfitters' revenue and expense information for April follows:

Sales revenue...	$560,000
Cost of good sold (standard)...	342,000
Direct materials price variance......................................	2,000 F
Direct materials efficiency variance.................................	6,000 F
Direct labor price variance..	4,000 U
Direct labor efficiency variance.....................................	2,000 F
Overhead flexible budget variance....................................	3,500 U
Production volume variance...	8,000 F

Prepare a standard cost income statement for management through gross profit. Report all standard cost variances for management's use. Has management done a good or poor job of controlling costs? Explain.

■ Problems (Problem Set A)

P11-40A **Prepare a flexible budget for planning** *(Learning Objective 1)*

Lasting Bubbles produces multicolored bubble solution used for weddings and other events. The company's static budget income statement for August 2007 follows. It is based on expected sales volume of 55,000 bubble kits.

LASTING BUBBLES, INC.
Static Budget Income Statement
Month Ended August 31, 2007

Sales revenue	$165,000
Variable expenses:	
Cost of goods sold	63,250
Sales commissions	13,750
Utilities expense	6,050
Fixed expenses:	
Salary expense	32,500
Depreciation expense	20,000
Rent expense	11,000
Utilities expense	5,200
Total expenses	151,750
Operating income	$ 13,250

Lasting Bubbles' plant capacity is 62,500 kits. If actual volume exceeds 62,500 kits, the company must expand the plant. In that case, salaries will increase by 10%, depreciation by 15%, and rent by $6,000. Fixed utilities will be unchanged by any volume increase.

Requirements

1. Prepare flexible budget income statements for the company, showing output levels of 55,000, 60,000, and 65,000 kits.

2. Graph the behavior of the company's total costs.

3. Why might Lasting Bubbles' managers want to see the graph you prepared in Requirement 2 as well as the columnar format analysis in Requirement 1? What is the disadvantage of the graphic approach?

P11-41A Prepare and interpret a performance report *(Learning Objective 2)*

Refer to the Lasting Bubbles data in P11-40A. The company sold 60,000 bubble kits during August 2007, and its actual operating income was as follows:

LASTING BUBBLES, INC.
Income Statement
Month Ended August 31, 2007

Sales revenue	$185,000
Variable expenses:	
Cost of goods sold	$ 69,500
Sales commissions	18,000
Utilities expense	6,600
Fixed expenses:	
Salary expense	34,000
Depreciation expense	20,000
Rent expense	10,000
Utilities expense	5,200
Total expenses	163,300
Operating income	$ 21,700

Requirements

1. Prepare an income statement performance report for August 2007 in a format similar to Exhibit 11-7.

2. What accounts for most of the difference between actual operating income and static budget operating income?

3. What is Lasting Bubbles' static budget variance? Explain why the income statement performance report provides Lasting Bubbles' managers with more useful information than the simple static budget variance. What insights can Lasting Bubbles' managers draw from this performance report?

P11-42A Comprehensive flexible budget, standards, and variances problem *(Learning Objectives 2, 3, 4, 5)*

One System assembles PCs and uses flexible budgeting and a standard cost system. One System allocates overhead based on the number of direct materials parts. The company's performance report includes the following selected data:

	Static Budget (20,000 PCs)	Actual Results (22,000 PCs)
Sales (20,000 PCs × $400)	$8,000,000	
(22,000 PCs × $420)		$9,240,000
Variable manufacturing expenses:		
Direct materials (200,000 parts × $10.00)	2,000,000	
(214,200 parts × $9.80)		2,099,160
Direct labor (40,000 hr × $14.00)	560,000	
(42,500 hr × $14.60)		620,500
Variable overhead (200,000 parts × $4.00)	800,000	
(214,200 parts × $4.10)		878,220
Fixed manufacturing expenses:		
Fixed overhead	900,000	930,000
Total cost of goods sold	4,260,000	4,527,880
Gross profit	$3,740,000	$4,712,120

Requirements

1. Determine the company's standard cost for one unit.
2. Prepare a flexible budget based on the actual number of PCs sold.
3. Compute the price variance for direct materials and for direct labor.
4. Compute the efficiency variances for direct materials and direct labor.
5. For manufacturing overhead, compute the total variance, the flexible budget variance, and the production volume variance.
6. What is the total flexible budget variance for One System's manufacturing costs? Show how the total flexible budget variance is divided into materials, labor, and overhead variances.
7. Have One System's managers done a good job or a poor job controlling material and labor costs? Why?
8. Describe how One System's managers can benefit from the standard costing system.

P11-43A Work backward through labor variances *(Learning Objective 4)*

Amanda's Music manufactures harmonicas. Amanda uses standard costs to judge performance. Recently, a clerk mistakenly threw away some of the records, and Amanda has only partial data for October. She knows that the direct labor flexible budget variance for the month was $330 F and that the standard labor price was $10 per hour. A recent pay cut caused a favorable labor price variance of $0.50 per hour. The standard direct labor hours for actual October output were 5,600.

Requirements

1. Find the actual number of direct labor hours worked during October. First, find the actual direct labor price per hour. Then, determine the actual number of direct labor hours worked by setting up the compuation of the direct labor flexible budget variance of $330 F.

2. Compute the direct labor price and efficiency variances. Do these variances suggest that the manager may have made trade-offs? Explain.

P11-44A Determine all variances *(Learning Objectives 4, 5)*

Avanti manufactures embroidered jackets. The company prepares flexible budgets and uses a standard cost system to control manufacturing costs. The following standard unit cost of a jacket is based on the static budget volume of 14,000 jackets per month:

Direct materials (3.0 sq. ft × $4.00 per sq. ft)...........		$ 12.00
Direct labor (2 hours × $9.40 per hour)..................		18.80
Manufacturing overhead:		
Variable (2 hours × $0.65 per hour)....................	$1.30	
Fixed (2 hours × $2.20 per hour)........................	4.40	5.70
Total cost per jacket...		$36.50

Data for November of the current year include the following:

a. Actual production was 13,600 jackets.

b. Actual direct materials usage was 2.70 square feet per jacket at an actual cost of $4.15 per square foot.

c. Actual direct labor usage of 24,480 hours cost $235,008.

d. Total actual overhead cost was $79,000.

Requirements

1. Compute the price and efficiency variances for direct materials and direct labor.

2. For manufacturing overhead, compute the total variance, the flexible budget variance, and the production volume variance.

3. Avanti's management intentionally purchased superior materials for November production. How did this decision affect the other cost variances? Overall, was the decision wise? Explain.

P11-45A (Appendix) Journalize standard cost transactions *(Learning Objective 6)*

Refer to the data in P11-44A. Journalize the usage of direct materials and the assignment of direct labor, including the related variances.

P11-46A **Compute variances and prepare standard cost income statement** *(Learning Objectives 4, 5, 6)*

Happ and Sons makes ground covers to prevent weed growth. During May, the company produced and sold 44,000 rolls and recorded the following cost data:

	Standard Unit Cost	Actual Total Cost
Direct materials:		
Standard (3 lb × $1.10 per pound)	$3.30	
Actual (136,600 lb × $1.05 per pound)		$143,430
Direct labor:		
Standard (0.1 hr × $9.00 per hr)....................	0.90	
Actual (4,600 hr × $8.80 per hr)....................		40,480
Manufacturing overhead:		
Standard:		
Variable (0.2 machine hr × $9.00 per hr)........... $1.80		
Fixed ($96,000 for static budget volume of 40,000 units and 8,000 machine hours)................................. 2.40		
	4.20	
Actual		168,800
Total manufacturing costs....................................	$8.40	$352,710

Requirements

1. Compute the price and efficiency variances for direct materials and direct labor.

2. For manufacturing overhead, compute the total variance, the flexible budget variance, and the production volume variance.

3. Prepare a standard cost income statement through gross profit to report all variances to management. Sales price was $10.60 per roll.

4. Happ and Sons intentionally purchased cheaper materials during May. Was the decision wise? Discuss the trade-off between the two materials variances.

■ Problems (Problem Set B)

P11-47B **Prepare a flexible budget for planning** *(Learning Objective 1)*

Digital Technologies manufactures capacitors for cellular base stations and other communications applications. The company's static budget income statement for October 2007 follows. It is based on expected sales volume of 9,000 units.

Digital Technologies' plant capacity is 9,500 units. If actual volume exceeds 9,500 units, Digital Technologies must rent additional space. In that case, salaries will increase by 15%, rent will double, and insurance expense will increase by $1,000. Depreciation will be unaffected.

DIGITAL TECHNOLOGIES
Static Budget Income Statement
Month Ended October 31, 2007

Sales revenue	$207,000
Variable expenses:	
Cost of goods sold	90,000
Sales commissions	9,900
Shipping expense	6,300
Fixed expenses:	
Salary expense	30,500
Depreciation expense	12,750
Rent expense	11,500
Insurance expense	3,750
Total expenses	164,700
Operating income	$ 42,300

Requirements

1. Prepare flexible budget income statements for 7,500, 9,000, and 11,000 units.
2. Graph the behavior of the company's total costs.
3. Why might Digital Technologies' managers want to see the graph you prepared in Requirement 2 as well as the columnar format analysis in Requirement 1? What is the disadvantage of the graphic approach in Requirement 2?

P11-48B **Prepare and interpret a performance report** *(Learning Objective 2)*
Refer to the Digital Technologies data in P11-47B. The company sold 11,000 units during October 2007, and its actual operating income was as follows:

DIGITAL TECHNOLOGIES
Income Statement
Month Ended October 31, 2007

Sales revenue	$257,000
Variable expenses:	
Cost of goods sold	112,250
Sales commissions	11,800
Shipping expense	8,950
Fixed expenses:	
Salary expense	36,650
Depreciation expense	12,750
Rent expense	22,500
Insurance expense	4,700
Total expenses	209,600
Operating income	$ 47,400

continued . . .

Requirements

1. Prepare an income statement performance report for October in a format similar to Exhibit 11-7.

2. What was the effect on Digital Technologies' operating income of selling 2,000 units more than the static budget level of sales?

3. What is Digital Technologies' static budget variance? Explain why the income statement performance report provides more useful information to Digital Technologies' managers than the simple static budget variance. What insights can Digital Technologies' managers draw from this performance report?

P11-49B **Comprehensive flexible budget, standards, and variances problem** *(Learning Objectives 2, 3, 4, 5)*

Relax-the-Back manufactures leather recliners and uses flexible budgeting and a standard cost system. Relax-the-Back allocates overhead based on yards of direct materials. The company's performance report includes the following selected data:

	Static Budget (1,000 recliners)	Actual Results (980 recliners)
Sales (1,000 recliners × $500)	$500,000	
(980 recliners × $490)		$480,200
Variable manufacturing expenses:		
Direct materials (6,000 yd × $8.90)	53,400	
(6,150 yd × $8.70)		53,505
Direct labor (10,000 hr × $9.00)................	90,000	
(9,600 hr × $9.15)		87,840
Variable overhead (6,000 yd × $5.00)........	30,000	
(6,150 yd × $6.40)		39,360
Fixed manufacturing expenses:		
Fixed overhead..	60,000	66,000
Total cost of goods sold	233,400	246,705
Gross profit...	$266,600	$233,495

Requirements

1. Determine the company's standard cost for one unit.
2. Prepare a flexible budget based on the actual number of recliners sold.
3. Compute the price variance for direct materials and for direct labor.
4. Compute the efficiency variances for direct materials and direct labor.
5. For manufacturing overhead, compute the total variance, the flexible budget variance, and the production volume variance.
6. What is the total flexible budget variance for Relax-the-Back's manufacturing costs? Show how the total flexible budget variance is divided into materials, labor, and overhead variances.
7. Have Relax-the-Back's managers done a good job or a poor job controlling material and labor costs? Why?
8. Describe how Relax-the-Back's managers can benefit from the standard costing system.

P11-50B **Work backward through labor variances** *(Learning Objective 4)*

Adam's Shades manufactures lamp shades. The manager uses standard costs to judge performance. Recently, a clerk mistakenly threw away some of the records, and the manager has only partial data for March. The manager knows that the direct labor flexible budget variance for the month was $1,050 U and that the standard labor price was $9 per hour. The shop experienced an unfavorable labor price variance of $0.50 per hour. The standard direct labor hours for actual March output were 4,000.

Requirements

1. Find the actual number of direct labor hours worked during March. First, find the actual direct labor price per hour. Then, determine the actual direct labor hours by setting up the computation of the direct labor flexible budget variance of $1,050 U.

2. Compute the direct labor price and efficiency variances. Do these variances suggest the manager may have made trade-offs? Explain.

P11-51B **Determine all variances** *(Learning Objectives 4, 5)*

Alon manufactures paperweights that it sells to other companies for customizing with their own logos. Alon prepares flexible budgets and uses a standard cost system to control manufacturing costs. The standard unit cost of a paperweight is based on static budget volume of 60,000 paperweights per month. The unit cost is computed as follows:

Direct materials (0.2 pounds × $0.25 per pound)		$0.05
Direct labor (3 minutes × $0.12 per minute)............		0.36
Manufacturing overhead:		
Variable (3 minutes × $0.06 per minute).............	$0.18	
Fixed (3 minutes × $0.14 per minute).................	0.42	0.60
Total cost per paperweight........................		$1.01

Transactions during May of the current year included the following:

a. Actual production and sales were 62,700 paperweights.

b. Actual direct materials usage was 0.18 pound per paperweight at an actual cost of $0.20 per pound.

c. Actual direct labor usage of 210,000 minutes cost $29,400.

d. Actual overhead cost was $40,800.

Requirements

1. Compute the price and efficiency variances for direct materials and direct labor.

2. For manufacturing overhead, compute the total variance, the flexible budget variance, and the production volume variance. (*Hint:* Remember that the total fixed overhead in the flexible budget equals the total fixed overhead in the static budget.)

3. Alon intentionally hired more skilled workers during May. How did this decision affect the cost variances? Overall, was the decision wise? Explain.

P11-52B **(Appendix) Journalize standard cost transactions** *(Learning Objective 6)*

Refer to the data in P11-51B. Journalize the usage of direct materials and the assignment of direct labor, including the related variances.

P11-53B Compute variances and prepare standard cost income statement (*Learning Objectives 4, 5, 6*)

Protex Industries manufactures sunglass cases. During August, the company produced and sold 106,000 cases and recorded the following cost data:

	Standard Unit Cost	Actual Total Cost
Direct materials:		
Standard (2 parts × $0.16 per part)..............	$0.32	
Actual (218,000 parts × $0.20 per part)..........		$43,600
Direct labor:		
Standard (0.02 hr × $8.00 per hr)................	0.16	
Actual (1,650 hr × $8.20 per hr)		13,530
Manufacturing overhead:		
Standard:		
Variable		
(0.02 machine hr × $8.00 per hr) $0.16		
Fixed ($32,000 for static budget volume of 100,000 units and 2,000 machine hours) 0.32		
	0.48	
Actual		60,500
Total manufacturing costs	$0.96	$117,630

Requirements

1. Compute the price and efficiency variances for direct materials and direct labor.

2. For manufacturing overhead, compute the total variance, the flexible budget variance, and the production volume variance.

3. Prepare a standard cost income statement through gross profit to report all variances to management. Sales price of the sunglass cases was $1.50 each.

4. Protex Industries' management used more experienced workers during August. Discuss the trade-off between the two direct labor variances.

Apply Your Knowledge

■ Decision Cases

Case 11-54. Compute flexible budget and sales volume variances *(Learning Objective 2)*

ReelTime distributes DVDs to movie retailers, including dot-coms. ReelTime's top management meets monthly to evaluate the company's performance. Controller Terri Lon prepared the following performance report for the meeting.

REELTIME, INC.
Income Statement Performance Report
Month Ended July 31, 2007

	Actual Results	Static Budget	Variance
Sales revenue	$1,640,000	$1,960,000	$320,000 U
Variable expenses:			
Cost of goods sold	773,750	980,000	206,250 F
Sales commissions	77,375	107,800	30,425 F
Shipping expense	42,850	53,900	11,050 F
Fixed expenses:			
Salary expense	311,450	300,500	10,950 U
Depreciation expense	208,750	214,000	5,250 F
Rent expense	128,250	108,250	20,000 U
Advertising expense	81,100	68,500	12,600 U
Total expenses	1,623,525	1,832,950	209,425 F
Operating income	$ 16,475	$ 127,050	$110,575 U

Lon also revealed that the actual sales price of $20 per movie was equal to the budgeted sales price and that there were no changes in inventories for the month.

Management is disappointed by the operating income results. CEO Lyle Nesbitt exclaims, "How can actual operating income be roughly 13% of the static budget amount when there are so many favorable variances?"

Requirements

1. Prepare a more informative performance report. Be sure to include a flexible budget for the actual number of DVDs bought and sold.

2. As a member of ReelTime's management team, which variances would you want investigated? Why?

3. Nesbitt believes that many consumers are postponing purchases of new movies until after the introduction of a new format for recordable DVD players. In light of this information, how would you rate the company's performance?

Case 11-55. Calculate efficiency variances *(Learning Objective 4)*

Assume that you manage your local Marble Slab Creamery ice cream parlor. In addition to selling ice cream cones, you make large batches of a few flavors of milk shakes to sell throughout the day. Your parlor is chosen to test the company's "Made-for-You" system. The system allows patrons to customize their milk shakes by choosing different flavors.

continued . . .

Customers like the new system, and your staff appears to be adapting, but you wonder whether this new made-to-order system is as efficient as the old system where you made just a few large batches. Efficiency is a special concern because your performance is evaluated in part on the restaurant's efficient use of materials and labor. Assume that your superiors consider efficiency variances greater than 5% unacceptable.

You decide to look at your sales for a typical day. You find that the parlor used 390 pounds of ice cream and 72 hours of direct labor to produce and sell 2,000 shakes. Assume that the standard quantity allowed for a shake is 0.2 pound of ice cream and 0.03 hours (1.8 minutes) of direct labor. Further, assume that standard costs are $1.50 per pound for ice cream and $8.00 an hour for labor.

Requirements

1. Compute the efficiency variances for direct labor and direct materials.

2. Provide likely explanations for the variances. Do you have reason to be concerned about your performance evaluation? Explain.

3. Write a memo to Marble Slab Creamery's national office explaining your concern and suggesting a remedy. Use the following format for your memo:

Date: _____

    To: Marble Slab Creamery's National Office

From: _____

Subject: "Made-for-You" System

▪ Ethical Issues

Case 11-56. Ethical dilemmas relating to standards *(Learning Objective 3)*

Austin Landers is the accountant for Sun Coast, a manufacturer of outdoor furniture that is sold through specialty stores and Internet companies. Annually, Landers is responsible for reviewing the standard costs for the following year. While reviewing the standard costs for the coming year, two ethical issues arise. Use the IMA's *Statement of Ethical Professional Practice* (in Chapter 1) to identify the ethical dilemma in each situation. Identify the relevant factors in each situation and suggest what Landers should recommend to the controller.

Issue 1

Landers has been approached by Kara Willis, a former colleague who worked with Landers when they were both employed by a public accounting firm. Willis recently started her own firm, Willis Benchmarking Associates, which collects and sells data on industry benchmarks. She offers to provide Landers with benchmarks for the outdoor furniture industry free of charge if he will provide her with the last three years of Sun Coast's standard and actual costs. Willis explains that this is how she obtains most of her firm's benchmarking data. Landers always has a difficult time with the standard-setting process and believes that the benchmark data would be very useful.

Issue 2

Sun Coast's management is starting a continuous improvement policy that requires a 10% reduction in standard costs each year for the next three years. Dan Jones, manufacturing supervisor of the Teak furniture line, asks Landers to set loose standard costs this year before the continuous improvement policy is implemented. Jones argues that there is no other way to meet the tightening standards while maintaining the high quality of the Teak line.

■ Team Project

Project 11-57. Evaluate standard setting approaches *(Learning Objective 3)*

Pella is the world's second-largest manufacturer of wood windows and doors. In 1992, Pella entered the national retail market with its ProLine windows and doors, manufactured in Carroll, Iowa. Since then, Pella has introduced many new product lines with manufacturing facilities in several states.

Suppose Pella has been using a standard cost system that bases price and quantity standards on Pella's historical long-run average performance. Assume Pella's controller has engaged your team of management consultants to recommend whether Pella should use some basis other than historical performance for setting standards.

1. List the types of variances you recommend that Pella compute (for example, direct materials price variance for glass). For each variance, what specific standards would Pella need to develop? In addition to cost standards, do you recommend that Pella develop any nonfinancial standards? Explain.

2. There are many approaches to setting standards other than simply using long-run average historical prices and quantities.

   a. List three alternative approaches that Pella could use to set standards and explain how Pella could implement each alternative.

   b. Evaluate each alternative method of setting standards, including the pros and cons of each method.

   c. Write a memo to Pella's controller detailing your recommendations. First, should Pella retain its historical data-based standard cost approach? If not, which alternative approach should it adopt? Use the following format for your memo:

Date: _____

   To: Controller, Pella Corporation

From: _____, Management Consultants

Subject: Standard Costs

This page intentionally left blank

Taken from *Auditing After Sarbanes-Oxley: Illustrative Cases,* Second Edition, by Dr. Jay C. Thibodeau and Deborah Freier

This page intentionally left blank

Fraud Cases: Violations of Generally Accepted Accounting Principles (GAAP)

In July 2002 the Sarbanes-Oxley Act was passed by the U.S. Senate by a vote of 98 to 0. The bipartisan support for the legislation emanated directly from the investing public's lack of tolerance for financial statement fraud. Not surprisingly, when formulating its post-Sarbanes technical audit guidance, the Public Company Accounting Oversight Board (PCAOB) made it clear that detecting fraud must be the focus of the audit process. Consider that in the board's first internal control standard (Auditing Standard No. 2), *fraud* was mentioned 76 times. The PCAOB has continued its emphasis on detecting fraud in its revised internal control standard, Auditing Standard No. 5.

As their fundamental responsibility, financial statement auditors must determine whether economic transaction activity has been accounted for by the audit client in accordance with Generally Accepted Accounting Principles (GAAP). In this spirit, the cases in this section are designed to illustrate different types of recent GAAP violations.

The case readings have been developed solely as a basis for class discussion. The case readings are not intended to serve as a source of primary data or as an illustration of effective or ineffective auditing.

Reprinted by permission from Jay C. Thibodeau and Deborah Freier.
Copyright © Jay C. Thibodeau and Deborah Freier; all rights reserved.

Case 1.1

Waste Management: The Matching Principle

Synopsis

In February 1998 Waste Management announced that it was restating the financial statements it had issued for the years 1993 through 1996. In its restatement, Waste Management said that it had materially overstated its reported pretax earnings by $1.43 billion. After the announcement, the company's stock dropped by more than 33 percent and shareholders lost over $6 billion.

The SEC brought charges against the company's founder, Dean Buntrock, and five other former top officers. The charges alleged that management had made repeated changes to depreciation-related estimates to reduce expenses and had employed several improper accounting practices related to capitalization policies, also designed to reduce expenses.[1] In its final judgment, the SEC permanently barred Buntrock and three other executives from acting as officers or directors of public companies and required payment from them of $30.8 million in penalties.[2]

Waste Management's Major Fixed Assets

The major fixed assets of Waste Management's North American business consisted of garbage trucks, containers, and equipment, which amounted to approximately $6 billion in assets. The second largest asset of the company (after vehicles, containers, and equipment) was land, in the form of the more than 100 fully operational landfills that the company both owned and operated. Under GAAP, depreciation expense is determined by allocating the historical cost of tangible capital assets (less the salvage value) over the estimated useful life of the assets.

Unsupported Changes to the Estimated Useful Lives of Assets

From 1988 through 1996, management allegedly made numerous unsupported changes to the estimated useful lives and/or salvage values of one or more categories of vehicles, containers, and equipment.[3] Such changes reduced the amount of depreciation expense recorded in a particular period. In addition, such changes were recorded as top-side adjustments at the corporate level (detached from the operating unit level). Most often the entries were made during the fourth quarter, and then improperly applied cumulatively from the beginning of the year. Management did not appear to disclose the changes or their impact on profitability to their investors.

In a letter to the management team dated May 29, 1992, Arthur Andersen's team wrote, "[i]n each of the past five years the Company added a new consolidating entry in the fourth quarter to increase salvage value and/or useful life of its trucks, machinery, equipment, or containers." Andersen recommended that the company conduct a "comprehensive, one-time study to evaluate the proper level of WMNA's salvage value and useful lives," and then send these adjustments to the respective WMNA groups. However, top management allegedly continued to change depreciation estimates at headquarters.

---

[1] SEC, Accounting and Auditing Enforcement Release No. 1532, March 26, 2002.

[2] SEC, Accounting and Auditing Enforcement Release No. 2298, August 29, 2005.

[3] SEC, Accounting and Auditing Enforcement Release No. 1532, March 26, 2002.

Carrying Impaired Land at Cost

Because of the nature of landfills, GAAP also requires that a company compare a landfill's cost to its anticipated salvage value, with the difference depreciated over the estimated useful life of the landfill.[4] Waste Management disclosed in the footnotes to the financial statements in its annual reports that "[d]isposal sites are carried at cost and to the extent this exceeds end use realizable value, such excess is amortized over the estimated life of the disposal site." However, in reality, the SEC found evidence that Waste Management allegedly carried almost all of its landfills on the balance sheet at cost.

In response to this treatment of landfills on the balance sheet, after its 1988 audit, Andersen issued a management letter to the board of directors recommending that the company conduct a "site by site analysis of its landfills to compare recorded land values with its anticipated net realizable value based on end use." Andersen further instructed that any excess needed to be amortized over the "active site life" of the landfill. Andersen made similar demands after its audit in 1994. Management never conducted such a study; they also failed to reduce the carrying values of overvalued land, despite their commitment to do so after Andersen's audit in 1994.

[4] SEC, Accounting and Auditing Enforcement Release No. 1532, March 26, 2002.

Case Questions

1. Consider the principles, assumptions, and constraints of Generally Accepted Accounting Principles (GAAP). Define the *matching principle* and explain why it is important to users of financial statements.

2. Based on the case information provided, describe specifically how Waste Management violated the matching principle.

3. Consult Paragraph 2 and Paragraph A5 (in Appendix A) of PCAOB Auditing Standard No. 5. Do you believe that Waste Management had established an effective system of internal control over financial reporting related to the depreciation expense recorded in its financial statements? Why or why not?

4. Under what circumstances is a company allowed to change the useful life and salvage value of its fixed assets under GAAP? As an auditor, what type of evidence would you want to examine to determine whether Waste Management's decision to change the useful life and salvage value of its assets was appropriate under GAAP?

TF CASE 1.1

Case
1.3

Qwest: The Full Disclosure Principle

Synopsis

When Joseph Nacchio became Qwest's CEO in January 1997, its existing strategy to construct a fiber optic network across major cities in the United States began to shift toward communications services as well. By the time it released earnings in 1998, Nacchio proclaimed Qwest's successful transition from a network construction company to a communications services provider. "We successfully transitioned Qwest ... into a leading Internet protocol-based multimedia company focused on the convergence of data, video, and voice services."[1]

During 1999 and 2000, Qwest consistently met its aggressive revenue targets and became a darling to its investors. Yet when the company announced its intention to restate revenues, its stock price plunged to a low of $1.11 per share in August 2002, from a high of $55 per share in July 2000. During this period, its market capitalization declined by 98 percent, from a high of $91 billion to a low of $1.9 billion.[2] Civil and criminal charges related to fraudulent activity were brought against several Qwest executives, including CFO Robin Szeliga and CEO Joseph Nacchio. Szeliga pleaded guilty in a federal court in Denver to a single count of insider trading and was sentenced to two years of probation, six months of house arrest, and a $250,000 fine. Nacchio was convicted on 19 counts of illegal insider trading and was sentenced to six years in prison in July 2007. He was also ordered to pay a $19 million fine and forfeit $52 million that he gained in illegal stock sales.[3]

Background

To facilitate its growth in communications services revenue, Qwest unveiled an aggressive acquisition strategy in the late 1990s. Indeed, after a slew of other acquisitions, Qwest entered into a merger agreement with telecommunications company US West on July 18, 1999. The merger agreement gave US West the option to terminate the agreement if the average price of Qwest stock was below $22 per share or the closing price was below $22 per share for 20 consecutive trading days. Less than a month after the merger announcement, Qwest's stock price had dropped from $34 to $26 per share. So to prevent any further drops in its stock price, executives and managers were allegedly pressured by CEO Nacchio to meet earnings targets to ensure that the price per share did not fall below the level specified in the agreement. Although Qwest's stock price had dropped from $34 to $26 per share less than a month after the merger announcement, Qwest stock was trading above $50 per share by June 2000; Qwest was, therefore, able to acquire US West by using Qwest's common stock.

Following the merger, Qwest's senior management set ambitious targets for revenue and earnings of the merged company.[4] These targets were especially ambitious in the face of difficult industry conditions. For example, in Qwest's earnings release for the second quarter of 2000, on July 19, 2000, Nacchio said that Qwest would "generate compound annual growth rates of 15-17 percent revenue ... through 2005." At a January 2001 all-employee meeting, Nacchio states his philosophy on the importance of meeting targeted revenues:

> [T]he most important thing we do is meet our numbers. It's more important than any individual product, it's more important than any individual philosophy, it's more important than any individual cultural change we're making. We stop everything else when we don't make the numbers.

---

[1] *SEC v. Joseph P. Nacchio, Robert S. Woodruff, Robin R. Szeliga, Afshin Mohebbi, Gregory M. Casey, James J. Kozlowski, Frank T. Noyes,* Defendants, Civil Action No. 05-MK-480 (OES), pp. 11–14.

[2] *SEC v. Qwest,* pp.1–2.

[3] Dionne Searcey, "Qwest Ex-Chief Gets 6 Years in Prison for Insider Trading," *The Wall Street Journal,* July 28, 2007, p. A3.

[4] *SEC v. Qwest,* pp. 6–7.

Challenges

By 1999 Qwest encountered several obstacles that challenged its ability to meet its aggressive revenue and earnings targets. It faced increased competition from long distance providers, steep declines in the demand for Internet services, an overcapacity in the market resulting from the formation of other major fiber optic networks, and a decline in the price at which Qwest could sell its excess fiber optic capacity.[5]

Despite these significant industry challenges, Qwest's senior management publicly claimed that the company would continue its pattern of dramatic revenue increases because of a "flight to quality" that customers would enjoy when they left competitors to use Qwest's services. Within the company, Qwest senior management exerted extraordinary pressure on subordinate managers and employees to meet or exceed the publicly announced revenue targets. In addition, they paid bonuses to management and employees only for periods when they achieved targeted revenue.[6]

Sale of Network Assets Initially Held for Use and Capital Equipment

To help meet revenue targets, senior management also began to sell portions of its own domestic fiber optic network. Originally this network was to be held for Qwest's own use and had previously been identified as the "principal asset" of Qwest. Specifically, Qwest sold indefeasible rights of use (IRUs) for specific fiber capacity that it had constructed and used in its own communications services business. In addition, Qwest sold pieces of the network it had acquired from other third parties. Finally, Qwest sold used capital equipment to generate additional revenue.

Unlike recurring service revenue from its communication services business that produced a predictable amount of revenue in future quarters, revenue from IRUs and other equipment sales had no guarantee of recurrence in future quarters. In fact, both IRUs and equipment sales were referred to internally as "one hit wonders."[7]

In its earnings releases during 1999 through 2001, Qwest executives would often fail to disclose the impact of nonrecurring revenues. (See Table 1.3.1.) In its earnings releases and the management's discussion and analysis portion of its SEC filings, Qwest improperly characterized nonrecurring revenue as service revenue, often within the "data and Internet service revenues" line item on the financial statements. Qwest's nonrecurring revenue was included primarily in the wholesale services segment and, to a lesser extent, the retail services segment.[8]

---

[5] *SEC v. Qwest*, pp. 7–8.
[6] *SEC v. Qwest*, p. 8.
[7] *SEC v. Qwest*, pp. 9–10.
[8] *SEC v. Qwest*, pp. 12–13.

TABLE 1.3.1 Management's Failure to Disclose Impact of Nonrecurring Revenue[9]

2Q 1999	Qwest failed to disclose that nonrecurring revenue made up 96 percent of data and Internet services revenue, 192 percent of the growth in data and Internet services, and 19 percent of total revenue. Excluding nonrecurring revenue, data and Internet services revenue actually declined 92 percent from the same quarter of the previous year.
3Q 1999	Qwest failed to disclose that nonrecurring revenue made up 140 percent of Qwest's reported data and Internet services revenue, and 32 percent of total revenue. Excluding nonrecurring revenue, total revenue actually declined 13 percent from the same quarter of the previous year.
4Q 1999	By the end of 1999, nonrecurring revenue comprised 33 percent of total revenue for the fourth quarter, and 26 percent of Qwest's total revenue for the year. Without inclusion of the nonrecurring revenue, Qwest's fourth quarter total revenue declined 9 percent from the same quarter of the previous year. Qwest's corporate accounting department drafted proposed disclosure language for the company's 1999 Form 10-K detailing the amount of IRU revenue, but Qwest's CFO and CEO rejected the language and refused to disclose any material information about nonrecurring revenue in the 1999 Form 10-K filed on March 7, 2000.
1Q 2000	By the end of the quarter, nonrecurring revenue comprised 97 percent of data and Internet services revenue, and 29 percent of total revenue. Without nonrecurring revenue, data and Internet services declined 92 percent from the same quarter of the prior year, and total revenue grew only 17 percent over the same quarter of the previous year. (This information was not disclosed.)
2Q 2000	Qwest did not disclose that nonrecurring revenue made up 86 percent of data and Internet services revenue, and 29 percent of total revenue. Excluding nonrecurring revenue, total revenue grew only 23 percent.
3Q 2000	Even after acquiring US West, which resulted in a fivefold increase in revenue, nonrecurring revenue made up 35 percent of data and Internet service revenue, and 8 percent of total revenue. The company continued not to disclose this information to the public.
1Q 2001	Contrary to Qwest's statements, during the first quarter 2001, nonrecurring revenue was 36 percent of data and Internet services revenue, 11 percent of total revenue, and 35 percent of Qwest's total revenue growth. Excluding nonrecurring revenue, Qwest's total revenue grew only 8 percent over the same period of the previous year.
2Q 2001	Qwest did not disclose that nonrecurring revenue had grown to 13 percent of total revenue, and 39 percent of data and Internet services revenue. Without including the nonrecurring revenue, Qwest's total revenue grew only 6 percent over the same period of the previous year.

[9] *SEC v. Qwest,* pp. 13–18. Data for 4Q 2000 unavailable.

Case Questions

1. Consider the principles, assumptions, and constraints of Generally Accepted Accounting Principles (GAAP). Define the *full disclosure principle* and explain why it is important to users of financial statements.

2. Explain specifically why Qwest's failure to disclose the extent of nonrecurring revenue violated the full disclosure principle in this situation.

3. Consult Paragraph 2 and Paragraph A5 (in Appendix A) of PCAOB Auditing Standard No. 5. Do you believe that Qwest had established an effective system of internal control over financial reporting related to the presentation and disclosure of its nonrecurring revenue? Why or why not?

4. Consult Paragraph 25 of PCAOB Auditing Standard No. 5. Define what is meant by *control environment.* Why does the "tone at the top" have such an important effect on internal control over financial reporting? Based on the case information, do you believe that the proper "tone at the top" was established at Qwest? Why or why not?

5. Consult Paragraph A4 (in the appendix) of PCAOB Auditing Standard No. 5. What is the auditor's responsibility related to information disclosed by management at the time of an earnings release, if any? What is the auditor's responsibility related to the information disclosed by management in the management's discussion and analysis section, if any? Do you agree with these responsibilities? Why or why not?

This page intentionally left blank

Case 1.4

Sunbeam: The Revenue Recognition Principle

Synopsis

In April 1996 Sunbeam named Albert J. Dunlap as its CEO and chairman. Formerly with Scott Paper Co., Dunlap was known as a turnaround specialist and was even nicknamed "Chainsaw Al" because of the cost-cutting measures he typically employed. Almost immediately, Dunlap began replacing nearly all of the upper management team and led the company into an aggressive corporate restructuring that included the elimination of half of its 12,000 employees and the elimination of 87 percent of Sunbeam's products.

Unfortunately, in May 1998 Sunbeam disappointed investors with its announcement that it had earned a worse-than-expected loss of $44.6 million in the first quarter of 1998.[1] CEO and Chairman Dunlap was fired in June 1998. In October Sunbeam announced that it would need to restate its financial statements for 1996, 1997, and 1998.[2]

Sunbeam's Customer Discounts and Other Incentives and Sales to Distributors

Under GAAP, sales revenue can be recognized only if the buyer assumes the risks and rewards of ownership of merchandise—for example, the risk of damage or physical loss. A sale with a right of return can be recognized as revenue only if the seller takes a reserve against possible future returns. The size of this reserve must be based on the company's history with returns; the sales revenue may not be recorded if no such history exists.

Beginning with the first quarter of 1997, Sunbeam began offering its customers discounts and other incentives if they placed their orders in the current period rather than holding off until the next period. Sunbeam did not disclose this practice of accelerating expected sales from later periods in its financial statements, however. In the other quarters of 1997, Sunbeam also allegedly relied on additional price discounting and other incentives in an attempt to accelerate recognition of revenue from future periods.[3]

One example of a special arrangement with a customer took place at the end of March 1997, just before the first quarter closed. Sunbeam recognized $1.5 million in revenue and contributed $400,000 toward net income from the sale of barbecue grills to a wholesaler. The contract with the wholesaler provided that the wholesaler could return all of the merchandise, with Sunbeam paying all costs of shipment and storage, if it was unable to sell it. In fact, the wholesaler wound up returning all of the grills to Sunbeam during the third quarter of 1997, and the wholesaler incurred no expenses in the transaction.[4]

Sales to Distributors

In December 1997 Sunbeam devised a "distributor program" that would help improve the company's sales. The program was designed to help Sunbeam accelerate the recognition of sales revenue for merchandise it placed with distributors in advance of actual retail demand. Sunbeam allegedly used favorable payment terms, discounts, guaranteed markups, and, consistently, the right to return unsold product as incentives for distributors to participate in the program.

[1] Robert Frank and Joann S. Lublin. "Dunlap's Ax Falls—6,000 Times—at Sunbeam." *The Wall Street Journal,* November 13, 1996, p. B1.

[2] GAO-03-138, Appendix XVII, "Sunbeam Corporation," p. 201.

[3] SEC Accounting and Auditing Enforcement Release No. 1393, May 15, 2001.

[4] SEC Accounting and Auditing Enforcement Release No. 1393, May 15, 2001.

The sales under the distributor program represented a new distribution channel for the company. Therefore Sunbeam was unable to set an appropriate level of reserves for any returns.[5]

Bill and Hold Sales

In the second quarter of 1997 Sunbeam recognized $14 million in sales revenue from bill and hold sales. By the fourth quarter Sunbeam had recognized $29 million in revenues and contributed an additional $4.5 million toward net income in bill and hold sales after it began promoting its bill and hold program. In all, bill and hold sales contributed to 10 percent of the fourth quarter's revenue.[6]

At year-end 1997, Sunbeam disclosed in its annual filing to the SEC that "the amount of [the] bill and hold sales at December 29, 1997, was approximately 3 percent of consolidated revenues." It did not disclose the extent to which the bill and hold sales had been booked in the final quarter.[7]

Revenue Recognition Criteria for Bill and Hold Sales

The SEC had stipulated that the following criteria must be met for revenue to be recognized in bill and hold transactions:[8]

- The risks of ownership must have passed to the buyer.
- The buyer must have made a fixed commitment to purchase the goods.
- The buyer must request that the transaction be on a bill and hold basis and must have a substantial business purpose for this request.
- There must be a fixed schedule for delivery of the goods.
- The seller must not have retained any specific performance obligations such that the earning process is not complete.
- The ordered goods must be segregated from the seller's inventory.
- The goods must be complete and ready for shipment.

Characteristics of Sunbeam's Bill and Hold Sales

The SEC found that Sunbeam's bill and hold sales were not requested by Sunbeam's customers and served no business purpose other than to accelerate revenue recognition by Sunbeam. Sunbeam's bill and hold sales were typically accompanied by financial incentives being offered to customers, such as discounted pricing, to encourage the sale to occur long before the customer actually needed the goods. Sunbeam would then typically hold the product until delivery was requested by the customer. Sunbeam also paid the costs of storage, shipment, and insurance related to the products. In addition, Sunbeam's customers had the right to return the unsold product.[9]

Restatement of Revenues

In 1998 Sunbeam restated its revenues for 1997 from $1,168,182 to $1,073,090. In an amended filing of its 10-K to the SEC, management wrote, "Upon examination, it was determined that certain revenue was improperly recognized (principally "bill and hold" and guaranteed sales transactions)."[10] The company had reversed all bill and hold sales, which amounted to $29 million in 1997, and about $36 million in guaranteed or consignment sales, whose liberal return policies made the recognition of their revenue improper.[11]

---

[5] SEC Accounting and Auditing Enforcement Release No. 1706, January 27, 2003.

[6] SEC Accounting and Auditing Enforcement Release No. 1394, May 15, 2001.

[7] SEC Accounting and Auditing Enforcement Release No. 1394, May 15, 2001.

[8] Staff Accounting Bulletin No. 101.

[9] SEC Accounting and Auditing Enforcement Release No. 1393, May 15, 2001.

[10] Amended 1997 10K filing to SEC.

[11] Martha Brannigan, "Sunbeam Slashes Its 1997 Earnings in Restatement," *The Wall Street Journal,* October 21, 1998.

Case Questions

1. Consider the principles, assumptions, and constraints of Generally Accepted Accounting Principles (GAAP). Define the *revenue recognition principle* and explain why it is important to users of financial statements.

2. Provide one specific example of how Sunbeam violated the revenue recognition principle in this situation.

3. As an auditor, what type of evidence would you want to examine to determine whether Sunbeam was inappropriately recording revenue from special discount sales?

4. Consult Paragraph 69 of PCAOB Auditing Standard No. 5 and Sections 301 and 204 of SARBOX. Identify one action that the audit committee of Sunbeam could have taken to help ensure that revenue recognition fraud would not have occurred.

This page intentionally left blank

Case 1.5

Waste Management: The Definition of an Asset

Synopsis

In February 1998 Waste Management announced that it was restating the financial statements it had issued for the years 1993 through 1996. In its restatement, Waste Management said that it had materially overstated its reported pretax earnings by $1.43 billion. After the announcement, the company's stock dropped by more than 33 percent, and shareholders lost over $6 billion.

The SEC brought charges against the company's founder, Dean Buntrock, and five other former top officers. The charges alleged that management had made repeated changes to depreciation-related estimates to reduce expenses and had employed several improper accounting practices related to capitalization policies, also designed to reduce expenses.[1] In its final judgment, the SEC permanently barred Buntrock and three other executives from acting as officers or directors of public companies and required payment from them of $30.8 million in penalties.[2]

Capitalization of Landfill Costs and Other Expenses

Under Generally Accepted Accounting Principles (GAAP), a cost can be capitalized if it provides economic benefits to be used or consumed in future operations. A company is required to write off, as a current period expense, any deferred costs at the time the company learns that the underlying assets have been either impaired or abandoned. Any costs to repair or return property to its original condition are required to be expensed when incurred. Finally, interest can be capitalized as part of the cost of acquiring assets for the period of time that it takes to put the asset in the condition required for its intended use. However, GAAP requires that the capitalization of interest must cease once the asset is substantially ready for its intended user.

Capitalization of Landfill Permitting Costs[3]

Waste Management capitalized the costs related to obtaining the required permits to develop and expand its many landfills. It also capitalized interest on landfill construction costs, as well as costs related to systems development at its landfills.

As part of its normal business operations, Waste Management allocated substantial resources toward the development of new landfills and the expansion of existing landfills. A significant part of the landfill development and expansion costs related to the process of obtaining required permits from government authorities. Over the years, the company faced increasing difficulty in obtaining the required landfill permits, and had already invested significantly in many projects that had to be abandoned or were materially impaired when the required permits could not be obtained.

The company routinely capitalized the costs related to obtaining the required permits, so it could defer recording expenses related to those landfills until they were put into productive use. However, instead of writing off the costs related to impaired and/or abandoned landfill projects and disclosing the impact of such write-offs, management only disclosed in its Form 10-K filed with the SEC the *risk* of future write-offs related to such projects.

---

[1] SEC, Accounting and Auditing Enforcement Release No. 1532, March 26, 3002.

[2] SEC, Accounting and Auditing Enforcement Release No. 2298, August 29, 2005.

[3] Ibid.

The management team of Waste Management also allegedly transferred the costs of unsuccessful efforts to obtain permits to other sites that had received permits or sites for which the company was still seeking permits. In effect, it was commingling impaired or abandoned landfill project costs with the costs of a permitted site (a practice known as "basketing," which did not comply with GAAP). In addition to basketing, the company also allegedly transferred unamortized costs from landfill facilities that had closed earlier than expected to other facilities that were still in operation (a practice known as "bundling," which also did not comply with GAAP). Management never disclosed the use of bundling or basketing in its Form 10-Ks.

In 1994, after its auditor Arthur Andersen discovered these practices, management allegedly agreed to write off $40 million related to dead projects over a span of 10 years, and also promised to write off future impairments and abandonments in a prompt manner. However, during 1994, 1995, 1996, and 1997, management effectively buried the write-offs related to abandoned and impaired projects by netting them against other gains, as opposed to identifying the costs separately as it had promised Andersen.

Capitalization of Interest on Landfill Construction Costs[4]

In accordance with GAAP, Waste Management was able to capitalize interest related to landfill development because of the relatively long time required to obtain permits, construct landfills, and prepare them to receive waste. However, Waste Management utilized the "net book value (NBV) method," which essentially enabled it to avoid GAAP's requirement that interest capitalization cease once the asset became substantially ready for its intended use. Waste Management's auditor, Arthur Andersen, advised the company from its first use of the NBV method (in 1989) that this method did not conform to GAAP.

Corporate controller Thomas Hau admitted that the method was "technically inconsistent with FAS Statement No. 34 [the controlling GAAP pronouncement] because it included interest [capitalization] related to cells of landfills that were receiving waste." Yet the company wrote in the footnotes to its financial statements that "[i]nterest has been capitalized on significant landfills, trash-to-energy plants and other projects under development in accordance with FAS No. 34."

Ultimately the company agreed to utilize a new method that conformed to GAAP, beginning January 1, 1994. Corporate controller Thomas Hau and CFO James Koenig allegedly determined that the new GAAP method would result in an increased annual interest expense of about $25 million; therefore they chose to phase in the new method over three years, beginning in 1995. However, the company was still utilizing the NBV method for interest capitalization as of 1997.

Capitalization of Other Costs[5]

The company also chose to capitalize other costs, such as systems development costs, rather than record them as expenses in the periods in which they were incurred. In fact, they used excessive amortization periods (10- and 20-year periods for the two largest systems) that did not recognize the impact of technological obsolescence on the useful lives of the underlying systems.

The SEC found evidence that the company's auditor Arthur Andersen proposed several adjusting journal entries to write off the improperly deferred systems development costs. Andersen also repeatedly advised management to shorten the amortization periods. In 1994 management finally agreed to shorten the amortization periods and to write off financial statement misstatements resulting from improperly capitalized systems costs over a period of five years. During 1995 the company changed the amortization periods and wrote off improperly capitalized systems costs by netting them against other gains.

[4] Ibid.
[5] Ibid.

Case Questions

1. Consider the principles, assumptions, and constraints of Generally Accepted Accounting Principles (GAAP). What is the specific definition of an asset?

2. Consider the practices of basketing and bundling. Briefly explain why each practice is not appropriate under GAAP.

3. Describe why netting write-offs against other gains would be effective for Waste Management's management team in trying to cover up their fraudulent behavior.

4. As an auditor, what type of evidence would allow you to detect whether your client was engaging in behaviors that are designed to mask fraudulent behavior (such as basketing, bundling, or netting)?

This page intentionally left blank

Case 1.7

WorldCom: The Matching Principle

Synopsis

On June 25, 2002, WorldCom announced that it would be restating its financial statements for 2001 and the first quarter of 2002. On July 21, 2002, WorldCom announced that it had filed for bankruptcy. It was later revealed that WorldCom had likely engaged in improper accounting that took two major forms: the overstatement of revenue by at least $958 million and the understatement of line costs, its largest category of expenses, by over $7 billion. Several executives pled guilty to charges of fraud and were sentenced to prison terms, including CFO Scott Sullivan (five years) and Controller David Myers (one year and one day). Convicted of fraud in 2005, CEO Bernie Ebbers was the first to receive his prison sentence: 25 years.

Line Cost Expenses

WorldCom generally maintained its own lines for local service in heavily populated urban areas. However, it relied on non-WorldCom networks to complete most residential and commercial calls outside of these urban areas and paid the owners of these networks to use their services. For example, a call from a WorldCom customer in Boston to Rome might start on a local (Boston) phone company's line, flow to WorldCom's own network, and then get passed to an Italian phone company to be completed. In this example, WorldCom would have to pay both the local Boston phone company and the Italian provider for the use of their services.[1] The costs associated with carrying a voice call or data transmission from its starting point to its ending point were called *line cost expenses.*

Line cost expenses were WorldCom's largest single expense. They accounted for approximately half of the company's total expenses from 1999 to 2001. WorldCom regularly discussed its line cost expenses in public disclosures, emphasizing, in particular, its *line cost E/R ratio*—the ratio of line cost expense to revenue.[2]

GAAP for Line Costs

Under Generally Accepted Accounting Principles (GAAP), WorldCom was required to estimate its line costs each month and to expense the estimated cost immediately, even though many of these costs would be paid later. To reflect an estimate of amounts that had not yet been paid, WorldCom would set up a liability account, known as an *accrual,* on its balance sheet. As the bills arrived from its outside parties, sometimes many months later, WorldCom would pay them and reduce the previously established accruals accordingly.[3]

Because accruals are estimates, a company is required under GAAP to reevaluate them periodically to see if they have been stated at appropriate levels. If charges from service providers were lower than estimated, an accrual is "released." The amount of the release is set off against the reported line cost expenses in the period when the release occurred. For example, if an accrual of $500 million was established in the first quarter and $25 million of that amount was deemed excess or unnecessary in the second quarter, then $25 million should be released in that second quarter, thus reducing reported line cost expenses by $25 million.[4]

---

[1] Board of Directors' Special Investigative Committee Report, June 9, 2003, p. 58.

[2] Ibid., pp. 58–59.

[3] Ibid., pp. 62–63.

[4] Ibid., pp. 63–64.

WorldCom's Line Cost Releases

Beginning in the second quarter of 1999, management allegedly started ordering several releases of line cost accruals, often without any underlying analysis to support the releases. When requests were met with resistance, management allegedly made the adjustments themselves. For example, in the second quarter of 2000, David Myers, a CPA who served as senior vice president and controller of WorldCom, requested that UUNET (a largely autonomous WorldCom subsidiary at the time) release $50 million in line cost accruals. UUNET's acting CFO David Schneeman asked that Myers explain the reasoning for the requested release, but Myers insisted that Schneeman book the entry without an explanation. When Schneeman refused, Myers wrote to him in an e-mail, "I guess the only way I am going to get this booked is to fly to DC and book it myself. Book it right now, I can't wait another minute." After Schneeman refused again, Betty Vinson in general accounting allegedly completed Myers's request by making a "top-side" corporate-level adjusting journal entry releasing $50 million in UUNET accruals.[5]

In 2000 senior members of WorldCom's corporate finance organization allegedly directed a number of similar releases from accruals established for other reasons to offset domestic line cost expenses. For example, in the second quarter of 2000, Senior Vice President and Controller David Myers asked Charles Wasserott, Director of Domestic Telco Accounting, to release $255 million in domestic line cost accruals to reduce domestic line cost expenses. Wasserott refused to release such a large amount. It later emerged that the entire $255 million used to reduce line cost expenses came instead from a release of a Mass Markets accrual related to WorldCom's Selling General & Administrative expenses.[6]

The largest release of accruals from other areas to reduce line of cost expenses occurred after the close of the third quarter of 2000. During this time, a number of entries were made to release various accruals that reduced domestic line cost expenses by $828 million.[7]

In addition to allegations that WorldCom's management released line cost accruals without proper support for doing so and released accruals that has been established for other purposes, there were also allegations that management often did not release certain line costs in the period in which they were identified. Rather, certain line cost accruals were kept as "rainy-day" funds that could be released when management needed to improve reported results.[8]

[5] Ibid., p. 83.
[6] Ibid., pp. 87–88.
[7] Ibid., pp. 88–89.
[8] Ibid., p. 10.

Case Questions

1. Consider the principles, assumptions, and constraints of Generally Accepted Accounting Principles (GAAP). Define the *matching principle* and explain why it is important to users of financial statements

2. Based on the case information provided, describe specifically how WorldCom violated the matching principle.

3. Consult Paragraph 2 and Paragraph A5 (in Appendix A) of PCAOB Auditing Standard No. 5. Do you believe that WorldCom had established an effective system of internal control over financial reporting related to the line cost expense recorded in its financial statements? Why or why not?

4. As an auditor at WorldCom, what type of evidence would you want to examine to determine whether the company was in appropriately releasing line costs? Please be specific.

TF CASE 1.7

Case 1.9

Qwest: The Revenue Recognition Principle[1]

Synopsis

When Joseph Nacchio became Qwest's CEO in January 1997, its existing strategy to construct a fiber optic network across major cities in the United States began to shift toward communications services as well. By the time it released earnings in 1998, Nacchio proclaimed Qwest's successful transition from a network construction company to a communications services provider. "We successfully transitioned Qwest ... into a leading Internet protocol-based multimedia company focused on the convergence of data, video, and voice services."[2]

During 1999 and 2000 Qwest consistently met its aggressive revenue targets and became a darling to its investors. Yet when the company announced its intention to restate revenues, its stock price plunged to a low of $1.11 per share in August 2002, from a high of $55 per share in July 2000. During this period, its market capitalization declined by 98 percent, from a high of $91 billion to a low of $1.9 billion.[3] Civil and criminal charges related to fraudulent activity were brought against several Qwest executives, including CFO Robin Szeliga and CEO Joseph Nacchio. Szeliga pleaded guilty in a federal court in Denver to a single count of insider trading and was sentenced to two years of probation, six months of house arrest, and a $250,000 fine. Nacchio was convicted on 19 counts of illegal insider trading and was sentenced to six years in prison in July 2007. He was also ordered to pay a $19 million fine and forfeit $52 million that he gained in illegal stock sales.[4]

Background

Qwest executives allegedly made false and misleading disclosures concerning revenues from its directory services unit, Qwest Dex Inc. (Dex). In addition, executives were charged with having manipulated revenue from Dex for 2000 and 2001 by secretly altering directory publication dates and the lives of directories.

Dex's Changes to Publication Dates and Lives of Directories

Dex published telephone directories year-round in approximately 300 markets in 14 states. It earned revenue by selling advertising space in its directories. Each of its directories typically had a life of 12 months, and Qwest traditionally recognized directory revenue over the life of the directory. However, in late 1999 Dex adopted a "point of publication" method of accounting and began to recognize all advertising revenue for a directory as soon as Dex began deliveries of that directory to the public.

In August 2000 Dex executives allegedly informed Qwest senior management that Dex would be unable to achieve the aggressive 2000 earnings' targets that management had set for it. As one option for making up for the shortfall, Dex suggested that it could publish Dex's Colorado Springs directory in December 2000 rather than January 2001 as scheduled, thereby allowing Qwest to recognize revenue from the directory in 2000 rather than 2001. One Dex executive expressed opposition, citing his concern that such a sched-

---

[1] Much of the information in this case is based on *SEC v. Qwest*, pp. 40–42.

[2] *SEC v. Joseph P. Nacchio, Robert S. Woodruff, Robin R. Szeliga, Afshin Mohebbi, Gregory M. Casey, James J. Kozlowski, Frank T. Noyes, Defendants*, Civil Action No. 05-MK-480 (OES), pp. 11–14.

[3] *SEC v. Qwest*, pp. 1–2.

[4] Dionne Searcey, "Qwest Ex-Chief Gets 6 Years in Prison for Insider Trading," *The Wall Street Journal*, July 28, 2007, p. A3.

ule change would merely reduce 2001 revenue and earnings. He also expressed his view that Qwest probably would be required to disclose the change in the regulatory filings with the SEC. Despite this executive's opposition, Qwest senior management allegedly instructed Dex to move forward with the proposed change.

By recognizing revenue from the Colorado Springs directory in 2000, Qwest generated $28 million in additional revenue and $18 million in additional earnings before interest and tax, depreciation, and amortization (EBITDA) for the year. The additional revenue generated in 2000 accounted for about 30 percent of Dex's 2000 year-over-year revenue increase. It further allowed Dex to show 6.6 percent year-over-year revenue growth versus 4.6 percent if the schedule change had not been made.

In Qwest's 2000 Form 10-K, Qwest informed investors that Dex's revenue for 2000 increased by almost $100 million. It wrote that the increase was due in part to "an increase in the number of directories published." At the same time, it failed to inform investors that Dex generated nearly one-third of that amount by publishing the Colorado Springs directory twice in 2000. It also did not inform investors that the schedule change would produce a corresponding decline in Dex revenue for the first quarter of 2001.

For 2001 Qwest senior management established revenue and EBITDA targets for Dex that were higher than what Dex management believed was possible to achieve. In fact, the EBITDA target was allegedly $80-100 million greater than the amount Dex management believed was achievable. The SEC found that Dex management complained to Qwest's senior management about the unrealistic targets. Yet Qwest's senior management not only allegedly refused to change the targets but also did not allow Dex a reduction in the targets to compensate for the revenue from the Colorado Springs directory that was recognized in 2000.

In March 2001 Dex management met with some of Qwest's senior management to discuss "gap-closing" ideas for the first two quarters of 2001 in an attempt to achieve its 2001 financial targets. One idea was to advance the publication dates of several directories, thus allowing Dex to recognize revenue in earlier quarters; another idea was to lengthen the lives of other directories from 12 to 13 months, thereby allowing Dex to bill each advertiser for one additional month of advertising fees in 2001. Senior managers at Qwest allegedly instructed the Dex managers to implement the changes, as well as other changes to allow it to meet its third and fourth quarter financial targets.

During 2001 Dex advanced the publication dates or extended the lives of 34 directories. Those schedule changes produced $42 million in additional revenue and $41 million in additional EBITDA. Qwest's Forms 10-Q for the first three quarters of 2001 stated that period-over-period improvements in Dex's revenue were due in part to changes in the "mix" and/or the "lengths" of directories published. Like the 2000 Form 10-K, these reports did not include any information about the directory schedule changes or the reasons for those changes.

Case Questions

1. Consider the principles, assumptions, and constraints of Generally Accepted Accounting Principles (GAAP). Define the *revenue recognition principle* and explain why it is important to users of financial statements.

2. Describe specifically why the revenue recognition practices of Dex were not appropriate under GAAP.

3. Consult Paragraph 2 and Paragraph A5 (in Appendix A) of PCAOB Auditing Standard No. 5. Do you believe that Qwest had established an effective system of internal control over financial reporting related to the revenue recorded by Dex in its financial statements? Why or why not?

4. Consult Paragraph 25 of PCAOB Auditing Standard No. 5. Next consider the impact of the pressure exerted by Qwest's senior management team to meet aggressive revenue and earnings targets. Comment about why such a "tone at the top" would have a pervasive effect on the reliability of financial reporting at a company like Qwest.

Case
1.10

The Baptist Foundation of Arizona: The Conservatism Constraint

Synopsis

The Baptist Foundation of Arizona (BFA) was organized as an Arizona non-profit organization primarily to help provide financial support for various Southern Baptist causes. Under William Crotts's leadership, the foundation engaged in a major strategic shift in its operations. BFA began to invest heavily in the Arizona real estate market and also accelerated its efforts to sell investment agreements and mortgage-backed securities to church members.

Two of BFA's most significant affiliates were ALO and New Church Ventures. It was later revealed that BFA had set up these affiliates to facilitate the "sale" of its real estate investments at prices significantly above fair market value. In so doing, BFA's management perpetrated a fraudulent scheme that cost at least 13,000 investors more than $590 million. In fact, Arizona Attorney General Janet Napolitano called the BFA collapse the largest bankruptcy of a religious nonprofit in the history of the United States.[1]

Background

A former BFA director incorporated both ALO and New Church Ventures. The entities had no employees of their own, and both organizations paid BFA substantial management fees to provide accounting, marketing, and administrative services. As a result, both ALO and New Church Ventures owed BFA significant amounts by the end of 1995. On an overall basis, BFA, New Church Ventures, and ALO had a combined negative net worth of $83.2 million at year-end 1995, $102.3 million at year-end 1996, and $124.0 million at year-end 1997.[2]

From 1984 to 1997, BFA's independent auditor, Arthur Andersen, issued unqualified audit opinions on BFA's combined financial statements. However, it was later revealed that BFA had sold real estate to ALO and New Church Ventures and other related entities at its cost (or at a profit), even though the fair market value of the assets was significantly lower than the amounts recorded on BFA's books.

Year-End Transactions

In December of each year, BFA engaged in significant year-end transactions with its related parties, ALO and New Church Ventures. These related party transactions primarily included real estate sales, gifts, pledges, and charitable contributions. Without these year-end transactions, BFA, on a stand-alone basis, would have been forced to report a significant decrease in net assets in each year from 1991 to 1994. Yet BFA did not disclose any information about these material related party transactions in its financial statements for the years 1991 to 1994.[3]

As an example, the significant real estate transactions that occurred in December 1995 with Harold Friend, Dwain Hoover, and subsidiaries of ALO enabled BFA to report an increase in net assets of $1.6 million for the year ended December 31, 1995, as opposed to a decrease in net assets that would have been reported. Importantly, for BFA to recognize a gain on these transactions in

[1] Terry Greene Sterling, "Arthur Andersen and the Baptists," *Salon.com Technology*, February 7, 2002.

[2] Notice of Public Hearing and Complaint No. 98.230-ACY, Before the Arizona State Board of Accountancy, pp. 3–4.

[3] Ibid., pp. 19–20.

accordance with GAAP, the down payment for the buyer's initial investment could not be "funds that have been or will be loaned, refunded, or directly or indirectly provided to the buyer by the seller, or loans guaranteed or collateralized by the seller for the buyer."[4] However, in reality, the cash for the initial down payments on many of these real estate sales could be traced back to BFA via transactions with affiliates of ALO and New Church Ventures.

Foundation Investments, Inc.'s Sale of Santa Fe Trails Ranch II, Inc., Stock

Santa Fe Trails Ranch II, Inc., was a subsidiary of Select Trading Group, Inc., which was a subsidiary of ALO. The only significant asset owned by Santa Fe Trails Ranch II was 1,357 acres of undeveloped land in San Miguel County, New Mexico.

On December 26, 1995, 100 percent of the issued and outstanding common stock of Santa Fe Trails Ranch II was transferred from Select Trading Group to ALO. ALO then sold the stock to New Church Ventures in exchange for a $1.6 million reduction in ALO's credit line that was already owed to New Church Ventures. On the same day, New Church Ventures sold the Santa Fe Trails Ranch II stock to Foundation Investments, Inc., a BFA subsidiary, in exchange for a $1.6 million reduction in the New Church Ventures's credit line that was already owed to Foundation Investments. Also on the same day, Foundation Investments sold the Santa Fe Trails Ranch II stock to Harold Friend for $3.2 million, resulting in Foundation Investments recognizing a gain of $1.6 million in its financial statements.

The terms of the sale of the Santa Fe Trails Ranch II stock by Foundation Investments to Friend for $3.2 million was a 25 percent cash down payment ($800,000) with the balance of $2.4 million in a carryback note receivable to Foundation Investments. To audit the transaction, Arthur Andersen's senior auditor John Bauerle vouched the payment received from Friend via wire transfer back to the December 31, 1995, bank statement. However, he did not complete any additional work to determine the source of the cash down payment.

To assess the true nature and purpose of this series of transactions, Arthur Andersen reviewed a feasibility study and a 1993 cash flow analysis for the proposed development of Cedar Hills. An independent appraisal was not obtained. Arthur Andersen prepared a net present value calculation using the 1993 cash flow analysis to support the $3.2 million value that Friend paid to Foundation Investments on December 26, 1995. Arthur Andersen accepted the $3.2 million value without questioning why that same property was valued at only $1.6 million when New Church Ventures sold it to Foundation Investments on the same day.

TFCI's Sale to Hoover[5]

TF

CASE 1.10

In December 1995 The Foundation Companies, Inc., a for-profit BFA subsidiary, sold certain joint venture interests in real estate developments to Dwain Hoover and recognized a gain on the transaction of approximately $4.4 million. In this particular transaction, the cash down payment from Hoover to The Foundation Companies of approximately $2.9 million was funded by a loan to Hoover from FMC Holdings, Inc., a subsidiary of ALO. Importantly, FMC received its own funding from BFA and New Church Ventures.

The details of this transaction were documented in Arthur Andersen's workpapers, primarily through a memorandum prepared by Arthur Andersen's senior auditor John Bauerle on April 13, 1996. According to his memo, Bauerle concluded that the transaction did meet the criteria for gain recognition pursuant to SFAS No. 66. However, Bauerle's memorandum did not include any documentation to support how Arthur Andersen tested the source of the cash down payment to help assure that the down payment was not directly or indirectly provided by BFA.

In early 1996 Arthur Andersen was auditing The Foundation Companies and prepared their annual management representation letter to be signed by the Foundation Company's Chief Financial Officer, Ron Estes. However, because of the previously described Hoover transaction, Estes refused to sign the management representation letter. CFO Estes protested against the Hoover transaction and ultimately resigned in June 1996. Arthur Andersen's audit workpapers related to the Foundation Companies 1995 audit did not address the absence of Estes's signature on the final management representation letter or indicate whether it asked Estes why he refused to sign the letter.

---

[4] Notice of Public Hearing and Complaint No. 98.230-ACY, Before the Arizona State Board of Accountancy, p. 25.

[5] Notice of Public Hearing and Complaint No. 98.230-ACY, Before the Arizona State Board of Accountancy, pp. 27–28.

Case Questions

1. Consider the principles, assumptions, and constraints of Generally Accepted Accounting Principles (GAAP). Define the *conservatism constraint* and explain why it is important to users of financial statements.

2. Consider the significant year-end transactions consummated by BFA. Do you believe that the accounting for these transactions violated the conservatism constraint? Why or why not? Please be specific when answering the question.

3. Consult Paragraph 2 and Paragraph A5 (in Appendix A) of PCAOB Auditing Standard No. 5. Do you believe that BFA had established an effective system of internal control over financial reporting related to its significant year-end transactions? Why or why not?

4. Consider the sale of the Santa Fe Trails Ranch II stock by Foundation Investments to Friend. Do you believe that the auditor should have completed any additional testing beyond vouching the payment received from Friend? Provide the rational for your decision.

This page intentionally left blank

2

Ethics and Professional Responsibility Case

It can be argued that the most dramatic change ushered in by the Sarbanes-Oxley Act of 2002 (SARBOX) is that the auditing profession is now regulated. The Public Company Accounting Oversight Board (PCAOB) is solely responsible for setting all auditing standards pertaining to audits of publicly traded companies. The PCAOB is also now required to perform detailed inspections of audit work completed and the quality control processes employed by audit firms. These changes have had a dramatic impact on audit quality and the auditing profession. The following case is designed to illustrate the ethical and professional responsibility of auditors in the post-Sarbanes auditing environment.

The case reading has been developed solely as a basis for class discussion. The case reading is not intended to serve as a source of primary data or as an illustration of effective or ineffective auditing.

Reprinted by permission from Jay C. Thibodeau and Deborah Freier.
Copyright © Jay C. Thibodeau and Deborah Freier; all rights reserved.

TF SECTION 2

Case 2.1

Enron: Independence

Synopsis

In its 2000 annual report, Enron prided itself on having "metamorphosed from an asset-based pipeline and power generating company to a marketing and logistics company whose biggest assets are its well-established business approach and its innovative people."[1] Enron's strategy seemed to pay off. In 2000 it was the seventh largest company on the *Fortune* 500, with assets of $65 billion and sales revenues of over $100 billion.[2] From 1996 to 2000 Enron's revenues had increased by more than 750 percent (over 65 percent per year), which was unprecedented in any industry.[3] Yet just a year later, Enron filed for bankruptcy, and billions of shareholder and retirement savings dollars were lost.

Arthur Andersen

Enron paid Arthur Andersen $46.8 million in fees for auditing, business consulting, and tax work for the fiscal year ended August 31, 1999; $58 million in 2000; and more than $50 million in 2001.[4] Andersen was collecting a million dollars a week from Enron in the year before its crash. Enron was one of Andersen's largest clients.

More than half of that amount was for fees that were charged for nonaudit services.[5] In 2000, for example, Enron paid Andersen $25 million for audit services and $27 million for consulting and other services, such as internal audit services.[6]

In fact, Andersen had performed Enron's internal audit function since 1993. That year Andersen had hired 40 Enron personnel, including the vice president of internal audit, to be part of Andersen's team providing internal audit services.[7] In 2000, as SEC chairman Arthur Levitt was trying to reform the industry practice of an audit firm also offering consulting services to their audit clients, Enron's Chairman and Chief Executive Officer Ken Lay sent a letter to Levitt (the letter was secretly coauthored by Andersen partner David Duncan), in which he wrote,

> While the agreement Enron has with its independent auditors displaces a significant portion of the activities previously performed by internal resources it is structured to ensure that Enron management maintains appropriate audit plan design, results assessment and overall monitoring and oversight responsibilities. . . . Enron has found its "integrated audit" arrangement to be more efficient and cost-effective than the more traditional roles of separate internal and external auditing functions.[8]

Interestingly, at Andersen, an audit partner's compensation depended in large part on his or her ability to sell other services (in addition to auditing) to clients.[9] Therefore, the nonaudit services provided to Enron had a big impact on the salary of the lead Andersen partner on the Enron engagement, David Duncan, who was earning around $1 million a year.[10]

---

[1] Enron 2000 annual report, p. 7.

[2] Joseph F. Berardino, remarks to U.S. House of Representatives committee on Financial Services, December 12, 2001.

[3] Bala G. Dharan and William R. Bufkins, "Red Flags in Enron's Reporting of Revenues and Key Financial Measures," March 2003, prepublication draft (www.ruf.rice.edu/~bala/files/dharan-bufkins_enron_red_flags_041003.pdf), p. 4.

[4] Anita Raghavan, "Accountable: How a Bright Star at Andersen Fell Along with Enron," *The Wall Street Journal,* May 15, 2002. Accessed from Factiva (February 25, 2005).

[5] Jane Mayer, "The Accountants' War," *New Yorker,* April 22, 2002. Accessed from LexisNexis Academic (February 25, 2005).

[6] Nanette Byrnes, "Accounting in Crisis," *BusinessWeek,* January 28, 2002. Accessed from LexisNexis Academic (February 25, 2005).

[7] Thaddeus Herrick and Alexei Barrionuevo, "Were Auditor and Client Too Close-Knit?" *The Wall Street Journal,* January 21, 2002. Accessed from ProQuest Research Library (February 26, 2005).

[8] "Letter from Kenneth Lay," Bigger Than Enron transcript, *Frontline,* aired on Public Broadcasting Service on June 20, 2002 (www.pbs.org/wghb/pages/frontline/shows/regulation/congress/lay.html).

Close Ties between Enron and Andersen

After graduating from Texas A&M University, Duncan joined Andersen in 1981, was made partner in 1995, and was named the lead partner for Enron two years later. Duncan developed a close personal relationship with Enron's Chief Accounting Officer Richard Causey, who himself had worked at Arthur Andersen for almost nine years. Duncan and Causey often went to lunch together, and heir families had even taken vacations together.[11]

Causey, who came to Enron in 1991, was appointed chief accounting officer in 1997. Causey was responsible for recruiting many Andersen alumni to work at Enron. Over the years, Enron hired at least 86 Andersen accountants.[12] Several were in senior executive positions, including Jeffrey McMahon, who had served as Enron's treasurer and president, and Vice President Sherron Watkins.

Although Andersen had separate offices in downtown Houston, Duncan and up to a hundred Andersen managers had a whole floor available to them within Enron's headquarters in Houston.[13] Duncan once remarked that he liked having the office space there because it "enhanced our ability to serve" and to "generate additional work."[14] Andersen boasted about the closeness of their relationship in a promotional video. "We basically do the same types of things. . . . We're trying to kinda cross lines and trying to, you know, become more of just a business person here at Enron," said one accountant. Another spoke about the advantage of being located in Enron's building: "Being here full-time, year-round, day-to-day gives us a chance to chase the deals with them and participate in the deal making process."[15]

In fact, Andersen and Enron employees went on ski trips and took annual golf vacations together. They played fantasy football against each other on their office computers and took turns buying each other margaritas at a local Mexican restaurant chain. One former senior audit manager at Andersen said that it was "like these very bright geeks at Andersen suddenly got invited to this really cool, macho frat party."[16]

---

[9] Jane Mayer, "The Accountants' War," *New Yorker,* April 22, 2002. Accessed from LexisNexis Academic (February 25, 2005).

[10] Bethany McLean and Peter Elkind, *The Smartest Guys in the Room: The Amazing Rise and Scandalous Fall of Enron* (New York: Penguin Group, 2003), pp. 146–147.

[11] Susan E. Squires, Cynthia J. Smith, Lorna McDougal, and William R. Yeack, *Inside Arthur Andersen* (Upper Saddle River, NJ: Prentice Hall, 2003), p. 2.

[12] Bethany McLean and Peter Elkind, *The Smartest Guys in the Room: The Amazing Rise and Scandalous Fall of Enron* (New York: Penguin Group, 2003), p. 145.

[13] Susan E. Squires, Cynthia J. Smith, Lorna McDougal, and William R. Yeack, *Inside Arthur Andersen* (Upper Saddle River, NJ: Prentice Hall, 2003), p. 126.

[14] Rebecca Smith and John R. Emshwiller, *24 Days: How Two Wall Street Journal Reporters Uncovered the Lies That Destroyed Faith in Corporate America* (New York: HarperBusiness, 2003), p. 289.

[15] Bethany McLean and Peter Elkind, *The Smartest Guys in the Room: The Amazing Rise and Scandalous Fall of Enron* (New York: Penguin Group, 2003), p. 146.

[16] Flynn McRoberts, "Ties to Enron Blinded Andersen," *Chicago Tribune,* September 3, 2002. Accessed from Factiva (February 3, 2004).

Case Questions

1. Refer to the second general standard of Generally Accepted Auditing Standards (GAAS). What is *auditor independence,* and what is its significance to the audit profession? What is the difference between independence in appearance and independence in fact?

2. Refer to Section 201 of SARBOX. Identify the services provided by Arthur Andersen that are no longer allowed to be performed. Do you believe that Section 201 was needed? Why or why not?

3. Refer to Sections 203 and 206 of SARBOX. How would these sections of the law have impacted the Enron audit? Do you believe that these sections were needed? Why or why not?

4. Refer to Section 301 of SARBOX. Do you believe that Section 301 is important to maintaining independence between the auditor and the client? Why or why not?

Section 4

Internal Control Systems: Entity-Level Control Case

Since 2004 audit firms have been required to express an opinion on the effectiveness of the internal control system over financial reporting for all publicly traded companies. In May 2007 the Public Company Accounting Oversight Board (PCAOB) issued Auditing Standard No. 5, "An Audit of Internal Control over Financial Reporting Performed in Conjunction with an Audit of Financial Statements," which supersedes AS 2 and all related staff questions and answers (e.g., May 16, 2005) and now provides the primary technical guidance to be followed by auditors in completing their internal control audits.

AS 5 makes it clear that the internal control audit process employed by CPA firms with auditing publicly traded companies must take a "top-down" approach. To execute a top-down approach, an auditor must first evaluate the entity-level controls, including all pervasive controls, before considering internal control activities at the business process, application, or transaction level. The case in this section is designed to illustrate the importance of entity-level controls and other pervasive controls to the effective design and operation of an internal control system.

The case reading has been developed solely as a basis for class discussion. The case reading is not intended to serve as a source of primary data or as an illustration of effective or ineffective auditing.

Reprinted by permission from Jay C. Thibodeau and Deborah Freier.
Copyright © Jay C. Thibodeau and Deborah Freier; all rights reserved.

Case 4.1

Enron: The Control Environment

Synopsis

In its 2000 annual report Enron prided itself on having "metamorphosed from an asset-based pipeline and power generating company to a marketing and logistics company whose biggest assets are its well-established business approach and its innovative people."[1] Enron's strategy seemed to pay off: In 2000 it was the seventh largest company on the Fortune 500, with assets of $65 billion and sales revenues of $100 billion.[2] From 1996 to 2000 Enron's revenues had increased by more than 750 percent and 65 percent per year, which was unprecedented in any industry.[3] Yet just a year later, Enron filed for bankruptcy, and billions of shareholder and retirement savings dollars were lost.

Executive Incentives

At Enron executives had incentives to achieve high-revenue growth because their salary increases and cash bonus amounts were linked to reported revenues. In the proxy statement filed in 1997, Enron wrote that "base salaries are targeted at the median of a competitor group that includes peer group companies. . . . and general industry companies similar in size to Enron."[4] In the proxy statement filed in 2001, Enron wrote, "The [Compensation] Committee determined the amount of the annual incentive award taking into consideration the competitive pay level for a CEO of a company with comparable revenue size and competitive bonus levels for CEO's in specific high performing companies."[5]

Employees also had incentives to achieve high revenues and earnings targets because of the shares of stock they held. Enron made significant use of stock options as a further means of providing incentives for its executives to achieve growth. For example, Enron noted in its 2001 proxy statement that the following stock option awards would become exercisable as of February 15, 2001: 5,285,542 shares for Chairman Kenneth Lay, 824,038 shares for President Jeffrey Skilling, and 12,611,385 shares for all officers and directors combines.[6] In fact, as of December 31, 2000, Enron had dedicated 96 million of its outstanding shares (almost 13 percent of its common shares outstanding) to stock option plans.[7]

Enron's Performance Review Committee

Enron's performance review committee (PRC) determined the salaries and bonuses of employees on a semiannual basis. The PRC was initially instituted in the gas services business during the early 1990s after the merger between Houston NaturalGas and InterNorth. One Enron employee said, "At the time, it was a great tool. . . . When we started the ranking process, we were trying to weed out the lower 5 or 6 percent of the company. We had some old dinosaurs, and we had some younger people who needed incentives."[8] The PRC was gradually instituted companywide when Jeffrey Skilling, a former McKinsey & Co. consultant who joined Enron in 1990 as the chief executive of the Enron finance division, was promoted to president and COO.

---

[1] Enron 2000 annual report, p. 7.

[2] Joseph F. Berardino, remarks to U.S. House of Representatives committee on Financial Services, December 12, 2001.

[3] Bala G. Dharan and William R. Bufkins, "Red Flags in Enron's Reporting of Revenues and Key Financial Measures," March 2003, prepublication draft (www.ruf.rice.edu/~bala/files/dharan-bufkins_enron_red_flags_041003.pdf), p. 4.

[4] Bala G. Dharan and William R. Bufkins, "Red Flags in Enron's Reporting of Revenues and Key Financial Measures," March 2003, prepublication draft (www.ruf.rice.edu/~bala/files/dharan-bufkins_enron_red_flags_041003.pdf), p. 6.

[5] Bala G. Dharan and William R. Bufkins, "Red Flags in Enron's Reporting of Revenues and Key Financial Measures," March 2003, prepublication draft (www.ruf.rice.edu/~bala/files/dharan-bufkins_enron_red_flags_041003.pdf), p. 6.

[6] Paul M. Healy and Krishna G. Palepu, "The Fall of Enron," *Journal of Economic Perspectives* 17, no. 2 (Spring 2003), p. 13.

[7] Paul M. Healy and Krishna G. Palepu, "The Fall of Enron," *Journal of Economic Perspectives* 17, no. 2 (Spring 2003), p. 13.

[8] Robert Bryce, *Pipe Dreams: Greed, Ego, and the Death of Enron* (New York: Perseus Book Group, 2002), p. 127.

The PRC made its determinations based on feedback reports that assessed the performance of employees on a scale from 1 to 5. Those who received ratings of 1 received large bonuses, and a rating of 2 or 3 could cost a vice president a six-figure sum.[9] Those who ranked in the bottom 10 percent of the review had until the next semiannual review to improve or they would be fired. Those in categories 2 and 3 were also given notice that they could be fired within the next year.[10]

Enron's Changes to Accounting Procedures

During the 1990s Enron made significant changes to several of its accounting procedures designed to improve reported earnings and financial position. For example, Enron began using mark-to-market (MTM) accounting for its trading business, which allowed the present value of a stream of *future* inflows and outflows under a contract to be recognized as revenues and expenses, respectively, once the contract was signed. Enron was the first company outside the financial services industry to use MTM accounting.[11] Enron also began establishing several special-purpose entities, which were formed to accomplish specific tasks such as building gas pipelines. If an SPE satisfied certain conditions, it did not have to be consolidated with the financial statements of the sponsoring company. Thus an SPE could be utilized by accompany hoping to achieve certain accounting purposes, such as hiding debt.

[9] Bethany McLean and Peter Elkind, *The Smartest Guys in the Room: The Amazing Rise and Scandalous Fall of Enron* (New York: Penguin Group, 2003), p. 63–64.

[10] Peter C. Fuasaro and Ross M. Miller, *What Went Wrong at Enron* (Hoboken, New Jersey: John Wiley & Sons, Inc., 2002), pp. 51–52.

[11] Bala G. Dharan and William R. Bufkins, "Red Flags in Enron's Reporting of Revenues and Key Financial Measures," March 2003, prepublication draft (www.ruf.rice.edu/~bala/files/dharan-bufkins_enron_red_flags_041003.pdf), pp. 7-11.

Case Questions

1. Based on your understanding of fraud risk assessment, what three conditions are likely to be present when a fraud occurs (the fraud triangle)? Based on the information provided in the case, which of these three conditions appears to have been the most prevalent an Enron, and why?

2. Consult paragraph 25 of PCAOB Auditing Standard No. 5. Define what is meant by control environment. Why is the *control environment* so important to effective internal control over financial reporting at an audit client like Enron?

3. Consult Paragraphs 21-22 of PCAOB Auditing Standard No. 5.Comment on how your understanding of Enron's control environment and other entity-level controls would help you implement a top-down approach for an internal control audit at Enron.

4. Consult Paragraph 69 of PCAOB Auditing Standard No. 5 and Sections 204 and 301 of SARBOX. What is the role of the audit committee in the financial reporting process? Do you believe that an audit committee can be effective providing oversight of a management team like Enron's?

5. Consult Sections 302 and 305and Title IX of SOX. Do you believe that these provisions could help deter fraudulent financial reporting by an upper management group? Why or why not?

TF CASE 4.1

Glossary/Index

Content from each source book is indicated as follows:

Business Essentials, Seventh Edition, by Ronald J. Ebert and Ricky W. Griffin: **(EG)**
Fundamentals of Corporate Finance, by Jonathan Berk, Peter DeMarzo, and Jarrad Harford: **(BDeH)**
Financial Accounting, Seventh Edition, by Walter T. Harrison Jr. and Charles T. Horngren: **(HH)**
Managerial Accounting, by Linda Smith Bamber, Karen Wilken Braun, and Walter T. Harrison, Jr.: **(BBH)**

INDEX

INDEX